KU-747-981

WISDEN

Anthology 1864-1900

WISDEN
Anthology 1864-1900

EDITED BY BENNY GREEN

Queen Anne Press
Macdonald and Jane's · London and Sydney

ISBN 0 354 08555 7

Printed in Great Britain by Spottiswoode Ballantyne Ltd.,
Colchester and London

Acknowledgements

I would like to thank John Arlott who stood aside, Haddon Whitaker for discussing the ground plan, Colin Webb for his invaluable assistance, and Clare Martin for coping so resourcefully with such a mass of material.

To Justin

CONTENTS

INTRODUCTION		1
MCC MATCHES		11
THE COUNTY MATCHES		181
	Derbyshire	185
	Essex	194
	Gloucestershire	204
	Hampshire	263
	Kent	288
	Lancashire	323
	Leicestershire	375
	Middlesex	386
	Nottinghamshire	424
	Somerset	455
	Surrey	472
	Sussex	547
	Formation of County Cricket Council	587
	Warwickshire	594
	Worcestershire	602
	The Development of Cricket, by Hon. R. H. Lyttelton	603
	Yorkshire	607
THE AUSTRALIANS AND OTHERS IN ENGLAND		653
	Australians	656
	"Throwing" by F. R. Spofforth	757
	South Africans	776
	Philadelphians	779
OTHER MATCHES		789
	Cambridge Matches	793
	"Cambridge Memories" by A. G. Steel	797
	Oxford Matches	805
	Public Schools Matches	812
ENGLAND IN AUSTRALIA		817
CRICKET IN AUSTRALIA		852
ENGLAND IN SOUTH AFRICA		866
GENTLEMEN v PLAYERS		873
PRINCE'S CLUB MATCHES		893
MISCELLANY –	Notable Feats	901
	Curious Contents	918
	Hints From the Press Box	949
	Obituaries	952
	E. M. Grace In the Cricket Field	956
	Personal Recollections of W. G. Grace, by Lord Harris	959
	W. G. Grace, by A. G. Steel	962
	John Wisden. R.I.P.	966
INDEX		967

FOREWORD

As a friend of mine – not wont to be demonstrative – assured me the other day that he had no pleasanter evenings in the whole year than when the appearance of *Wisden* enabled him to fight the battles of the cricket season over again, I am fortified in the belief that the Almanack fulfils its mission and preserves in a readable and attractive form a record of all that is essential in connection with our glorious game. Lest there should seem to be any suspicion of vanity or egotism in my saying this, I may point to the ever-increasing favour with which *Wisden* is received, and to a constantly-growing circulation.

Sydney H. Pardon 1893

Introduction

At the end of the 1863 season John Wisden, the great Sussex and United England cricketer, retired from the first-class game. His career had been a momentous one, and to this day the record books mark his achievement of taking ten wickets, all clean bowled, in an innings for North against South at Lord's in 1850. (This was only the second time in the history of the game that the feat had been performed. That Wisden, a native of Brighton, should have performed it for the North against the South is explained by the fact that he and George Parr had recently acquired a new ground at Leamington, Warwickshire, and were therefore Northerners, at least for the time being.) Although a competent enough batsman to have opened for the Players and made many useful scores, Wisden seems to have been undistinguished in this department. Indeed, one of the boys who played in the Harrow XI in the early 1850s, when Wisden was working at the school as a professional, later recalled that "as a batsman Wisden was a learner rather than a teacher, and greatly improved during the four years he was at Harrow," a verdict which must be seen in light of the fact that in 1850, two years before he arrived at the school, Wisden had scored exactly 100 for Sussex against Kent at Tunbridge Wells. But it was certainly his bowling on which his fame rested. Sadly, the details of many of his most spectacular performances are lost in the fogs of prehistory – performances achieved in matches against odds in which no bowling analyses have survived; even his great feat for North against South nods only curtly towards statistical exactitude by being claimed "for scarcely thirty runs". Of that immortal feat W. G. Grace says, "a very good authority who witnessed the performance told me that he kept up his break from the off from one to two feet right through the innings." Wisden also bowled unchanged through both completed innings twice in a match at Lord's, once took six wickets in six balls bowling underarm against Twenty Two of United States and Canada, and in all matches in 1851 took no fewer than 455 wickets.

Even more remarkable than his bowling prowess is the physique with which he had to contend to achieve success, for whatever else may happen in cricket, there is no question that John Wisden will remain the smallest, weakest, frailest successful fast bowler in its annals. Born in Brighton on 5 September, 1826, by the time he made his début for Sussex nineteen years later, he was no more than five feet four inches tall and weighed seven stone; although according to Altham he later found a little more weight, he remained throughout his playing days a strikingly small man who fully justified the soubriquet, "The Little Wonder". His delivery was described as "very straight, accurate in length, very fast and ripping," with a swift bowling action and a habit of swinging his bat "so that it looked like the pendulum of a grandfather clock". His style was conservative in that it remained true roundarm at a point in the evolution of bowling when the arm was tending to go higher with every season. By the time he retired in 1863, having once taken over 1,300 wickets in four consecutive seasons, and earned a reputation as an invincible single-wicket opponent, he must have guessed that his place in cricket history was secure.

But Wisden was very much more than an outstanding athlete, and it must have seemed unlikely to his contemporaries that his retirement would mark his disappearance from the game. Most of the professionals of Wisden's time were cricketers pure and simple, who, once they became too old, returned to the obscurity from which the game had raised them. But Wisden was utterly untypical, being by temperament an organiser and entrepreneur of formidable resource who had given evidence of his potential long before his retirement. When in the 1850s William Clarke's arrogance and parsimony had roused the democratic susceptibilities of his underlings in the All-England XI, it had been Wisden, with Jimmy Dean, who instigated the mutiny leading to the formation of the rival United England XI. And soon after this successful rebellion, Wisden had already begun to cast a shrewd eye on the commercial possibilities open to a man in his situation. Even more unusual, there were occasions when his perspicuity flowered into authentic wit, and he remains one of the very few Victorians who could claim justifiably to have outshone Oscar Wilde as a coiner of epigrams. When Wilde sailed for America in 1882 as a kind of animated sandwich-board on behalf of Gilbert and Sullivan, he is said to have responded to the spectacle of the Atlantic Ocean with the confession that he "found it disappointing"; when the same experience befell Wisden, on the 1859 tour with Parr's side, he glanced at the waters with the appraising eye of the athlete and observed, "what this pitch wants is ten minutes of the heavy roller." It was unlikely that so lively a man would fall out of the public eye simply because he had reached the age of sporting discretion. And for those who wondered which direction his future schemes might take, Wisden had already provided the broadest of hints.

In 1855 he had gone into business with his cricketing comrade Fred Lillywhite; the pair of them had opened what Altham describes as "a cricketing depot near Leicester Square"; a more explicit source defines the depot as "a cricketing and cigar business in New Coventry Street". Now by this time the name of Lillywhite was already famous in sporting circles for one particular reason, and it seems likely that Wisden, taking due note of his partner's success in another venture, decided to emulate it. The modern age tends to forget that Wisden's historic act of 1864 was by no means original. There had been cricket handbooks and annuals long before his retirement, the most successful of which, *Lillywhite's Guide to Cricketers*, had been established as early as 1845. Nor was Wisden's first attempt at a yearbook particularly distinguished, on either a commercial or a strictly functional level. That inspired curmudgeon of cricket writ, Rowland Bowen, has even suggested that the extreme rarity today of Wisden's first Almanack, for 1864, proves how small its sales were, and, although by the same reckoning Conan Doyle's *A Study in Scarlet* could hardly have gone through the presses at all, there is some truth in Bowen's surmise.

What is much more shocking about the 1864 edition is not that its circulation was poor, but that it deserved to be so. It is bad enough that the book should consist of a mere 112 pages, much worse that most of those pages are filled with material of the most wildly incongruous nature. Evidently Wisden was at a loss to know what to put into his book, and so, like most editors in that predicament, had decided to put in anything and everything. The sparse current cricket entries were padded out with match-cards of games already more than half a century old, including an exhaustive record of Gentlemen v Players matches. Even this had proved insufficient, and so Wisden had finally been pushed to the comically desperate extremity of appending a list of the winners of the Derby, Oaks and St Leger since 1779, the fact that China was first visited by a European in 1517, the rules of Bowls, Quoits and Knur, the date of foundation of the Antiquarian, Astronomical, Ethnological, Geological, Horticultural, Microscopical, Pharmaceutical and Philological Societies, the results of the University Boat Race, the length of the chief British canals, the dates of the principal battles of the Wars of the Roses, and a brief disquisition on the constitutional implications of the trial of Charles I.

But slowly, patiently, Wisden began to play himself in. Hastily dispensing with irrelevant material, by 1866 he was including full scores of the previous season's important matches. In 1867 there first appeared "Births and Deaths of Cricketers"; in the same year appeared the first advertisement, for "John Wisden and Co's Patent Catapulta, the principle of working which will be shown at 2, New Coventry Street, Leicester Square". In 1870 came the first match accounts; in 1872 an introductory essay to the records of each county. But it was not until 1887, three years after Wisden's death, that there came the great watershed, a full list of batting and bowling averages for the past season and a full fixture list for the next. In 1888 there appeared the first essay on a topical theme, and in the following edition readers were beguiled by two further innovations, photography and a Cricket Records section. In 1892 came the first Obituary notices, and from 1895 the practice was established of including amateurs and professionals together in the first-class averages. The final refinement for the period embraced by this volume came in 1899, when the averages were calculated in the modern style, to two places of decimals. By 1900 the almanack included for the first time over 500 pages of editorial text.

What did all this development represent in human terms? Clearly Wisden himself, who died before the almanack bearing his name began to take on an appearance familiar to the twentieth century reader, and whose idea of required reading for the lover of cricket included the fact that the Battle of Mortimer's Cross had been fought on 1 February, 1461, had contributed little more than a name, the germ of a great idea, and a considerable commercial flair. In a sense the story of Wisden constitutes the pageant of that small group of men who successively dictated its style. From 1870-9 much of the match reporting was done by W. H. Knight, the very archetype of the Victorian sporting journalist, whose fulsome orotundities betray that bias in favour of the Gentlemen which is so marked a feature of the almanack for at least the first fifty years of its existence. Less cramped for space than his modern successors, and unabashed by his own vocabulary, Knight was the first Wisden writer to realise that there was no reason why a mere almanack should not convey to its readers a visual impression of the events it was recording. Ironically the finest hour of Knight as a cricket writer is not to be found in Wisden; in describing a match in 1877 in which Dr E. M. Grace had carried his bat for 200, with Dr A. Grace 28 not out at the close, Knight achieved profundity with "a doctor at the beginning, and a doctor at the end. Such is life."

Knight's life ended at almost exactly the same time as the birth of the institution which assured the almanack of a healthy future. In 1880 there was formed an organisation called the Cricket Reporting Agency, synonymous ever since with Wisden itself. The Agency was started by Charles F. Pardon, with support from his brothers E. S. and S. H. and C. Stewart Caine. Some idea of the extent to which Wisden owes its survival to their dedication is conveyed by the fact that from this group of men was provided the almanack's editor from 1887 until 1933. Charles Pardon died in 1890, only four years after assuming the editorship, but even in that short period he was able to impose his mark on its style. Had he lived longer, he may well have proved himself one of the great editors in the history of sporting journalism; as it is his achievements have tended to be overshadowed by those of his younger brother Sydney, who reigned for thirty-five years, bringing to the task a general sophistication rarely to be found in the cricket pavilions of the day. Much of S.H.'s best work falls outside the scope of this volume, but the reader has only to balance the entries from the last decade of the Victorian age against those of the embryonic years of Knight and company to realise how much Pardon contributed in confidence of style and strength of personality. When he arrived, the almanack was a publication in disarray covering an area of parochial interest; by the time he left Wisden was one of the great almanacks of the world. S. H. Pardon was an examplar of the type who poses the rhetorical question, "What do they know of Cricket who only Cricket know?". For although the same paternalism which sometimes renders Knight comical also colours Pardon's editing, he was, in the context of the cricket writing of the period, a man of considerable urbanity whose outside interests not only embraced other sports like billiards, racing, athletics, rowing and boxing, but also extended into the arts, where his judgment in operatic and dramatic matters was considered subtle enough for him to be a contributor on them in *The Times*. He watched his first first-class match in 1863, the year of Wisden's retirement, and wrote his first match report in 1872; at least two aspects of his editorship will never be forgotten, his development of the Obituaries section into one of the pearls of sporting literature, and his uncompromising stand, over many years, against unfair bowling actions.

By the end of the century there had been 37 editions of the almanack, comprising more than 10,000 pages of closely printed cricketing data, a body of information whose amorphous mass was by now vast enough to have taken on a corporate personality subtly distinct from the component parts of which it was comprised. What Wisden by 1900 was beginning to represent, accidentally and yet perhaps inevitably, was a delightful social history of England. There is hardly an innovation offered by its editors, or a great event recorded by them during this period, which cannot now be seen as the analogue of some movement on the larger national stage. It may at first sight seem fanciful to suggest that the steadily growing importance of the Public Schools section reflected the work of the Clarendon Commission of 1861 which, by encouraging in public schools "the development of manly sports", formalised for the first time in English history the place of team games in education; or that in discarding the old idea of listing paid and unpaid in separate lists of averages Wisden was bowing before the wind of democratic change; or that the gradual eclipse of Knight's charming prolixities regarding the annual Canterbury Festival in favour of a technically better informed style of reporting was a harbinger of the new century; or that the melodramatic pace of London's urban sprawl, cunningly manipulated by the customary land speculators, drew from the game the ritual sacrifice of Prince's Ground. But none of these apparently purely sporting developments occurred in a social vacuum. Because the administrators and chroniclers of England's sporting life could not discern the forces impelling men and events, that did not mean that those forces did not exist. Both in the information it provided and in the attitudes it struck towards them, Wisden is thoroughly representative, and could not help being representative, of a certain type of professional man of the period who adhered to a specific code of behaviour, sporting and otherwise.

Nowhere is this function of cricket as a microcosm of the larger life more vividly exemplified than in the Church. It should not be forgotten that throughout the period represented by this volume, cricket was for millions of Englishmen synonymous with Christianity. A century later all that survives of this curious vanity is a handful of pietisms like "playing the game", "keeping one's end up", "keeping a straight bat", and of course, "it's not cricket". But when John Wisden launched his annual, the analogies were much more striking. Historians, being bookish men, have generally tended hopelessly to underestimate the significance of codified team games in the charter of the Pax Britannica, and it has been left to Sir Robert Ensor, in a standard work ironically bearing the imprint of the Clarendon Press (*The Oxford History of*

England; Volume 14) to remind posterity that "the development of organised games on any reckoning may stand among England's leading contributions to world-culture." On a more specific level, Professor L. C. B. Seamen, not a historian given to reckless romanticism, says of the England inhabited by John Wisden:

> Cricket was associated with religion: just as freemasons referred to God as the Great Architect of the Universe, young cricketers were taught to think of Him as the One Great Scorer, and almost to regard a Straight Bat as second in religious symbolism only to the cross of Jesus.

Whether in adhering to these beliefs the Victorian sportsman was elevating a game to the eminence of a religion, or merely debasing his religion to the level of a game it is difficult to know, but certainly no suspicion of any such conflict ever clouded the thought of the Victorian sportsman himself, who usually took his cricket so seriously as to perceive no hint of blasphemy in the drawing of religious parallels like the much-quoted one of Lord Harris, who likened the cricket field to God's classroom. And so it was that season after season the obituary columns of the sporting prints of the period bristled in a frenzy of sad devotion for the Venerables and Reverends who had delivered their last sermon and struck their last boundaries. There we find them, the sporting gentlemen of the cloth, happy diocesan butterflies who, throughout the emergent years of John Wisden's book, came fluttering out, white-flannelled and buckskin-booted, from vicarage and deanery, rectory and presbytery, glebe and oratory, to play their eager part in the bizarre and endearing ritual which posterity has since identified as Muscular Christianity. And, although it is true that this marriage between Holy Writ and the Laws of Cricket was solemnised at the Public Schools through whose gates so many great amateur cricketers emerged, it should not be forgotten that it was a professional, Albert Knight, who on arrival at the crease, would address a few well chosen words to the One Great Scorer before receiving his first ball; that it was a professional, Richard Tyldesley who once defined to Sir Neville Cardus his scrupulous probity as a fieldsman, "Westhaughton Sunday School, tha knows"; that it was a professional, Ted Wainwright, who once remarked of Ranjitsinhji, again to Cardus, "'E never made a Christian stroke in his life". (If, as dullards sometimes say, Cardus was making it all up, then the religious analogy is doubly confirmed, for Cardus was a creative artist probing tirelessly for the most truthful metaphor.)

Posterity would be most unwise to assume that cricket, to the players who feature in this volume, was only a game. But if it was not a game, and yet not quite a religion, what was it? It seems to have been a typically English compromise between a religious manifestation and an instrument of policy, a vaporous hinterland where ethics and biceps merged into a third entity, an exquisite refinement of that other Victorian concept, the White Man's Burden. A century later it remains a whimsical geo-political truth that all a schoolboy need do to name the component parts of the old Empire is to rattle off the names of the Test-playing nations. Where cricket is today, there was the Empire yesterday, although it is a cruel irony that John Wisden's own labours on behalf of the gospel met with failure. Today cricket in the United States and Canada remains what it has been for too long, a lost cause. "Sport", says James Morris of the British, "was their chief spiritual export, and was to prove among their more resilient memorials. They took cricket to Samoa and the Ionian Islands, and the Samoans and the Ionians took it up with enthusiasm." They took it also to Australia and South Africa, India and the West Indies, all of which colonial outposts figure in this volume. And they welcomed return visits, even permitting errant Americans to play out the blasphemous and barbaric melodrama of baseball on the sacred turf of Lord's.

The case for cricket as an instrument of imperial policy has been well proven, but the difficulty which still confronts a baffled posterity is to decide how far the deployment of games like cricket as a political expedient was calculated and how far fortuitous; the answer to that conundrum would tell us much about our great-grandfathers that we do not at present know. Perhaps no answer exists, but the received truth of the matter has been defined by another historian, Correlli Barnett:

> By the 1880s the playing-field had become what the parade ground is to an army – a powerful instrument for inculcating common responses, values, outlook. Games were now formal and compulsory rituals, governed by fixed and complicated rules . . . The purpose of this ritual elaboration of ball games was a debased version of Arnold's ideal of Christian moral education.

But which common responses, values and outlook? The observant reader of this volume cannot fail to be struck by the fact that whenever moral, as distinct from legal, breaches of the law are committed, the culprit is usually the gentleman-cricketer. (See the special pleading on behalf of W. G. Grace's shamateurism on page 753; also the tactics of the Oxford captain in the University match of 1893; page 164). Barnett goes on to build a half-truth into a solecism:

> Cricket tended to impress the importance of "good form" and "fair play" – of conforming to the "laws" and the accepted code of behaviour, the accepted notion of how things should be done. A "wrong stroke" that struck an off ball to the leg boundary was in its way less admirable than an elegant late cut which failed to connect. Cricket's influence on the upper middle-class British mind, with its sense of orthodoxy and respect for the rules and laws and the impartial authority of umpires, can hardly be exaggerated.

But the great hero of the period under discussion was William Gilbert Grace, whose life's work was a denial, couched in comic terms, of the very canons of good taste which so many non-cricketing historians appear to think was obligatory. If Grace's batting was a monument of classical orthodoxy, his etiquette was not, which is precisely why the British continue to celebrate him. But even in the strictest technical terms, the idea that "an elegant late cut which failed to connect" was more acceptable than a hoick to the boundary becomes nonsensical when seen in the lurid light of Dr Edward Mills Grace, whose international reputation as a perverse and eccentric improviser marks the beginning of this volume, and of Gilbert Laird Jessop, whose stupefying heresies signal its close. The careers of such originals are a derisive rejection of the idea that the iron law of technical sobriety was never relaxed on the cricket fields of Victorian England.

But both the religious and the empire-building elements of the cricket of the period, whether or not they might happen to be pillars of orthodoxy, certainly flourished, and it would be an unenterprising cricket-lover who could not, after studying the book now in the reader's hand, produce full elevens comprised of gentlemen of the cloth and of those holding the Queen's commission. Reality may have gone a little too far in providing a cricketing parson called Parsons (J. H.; of Warwickshire), but not even the wildest satirist would have dared to invent the idea of a team of army officers all from one county, even allowing for the extent to which

Hampshire County Club secretaries over the years have benefitted from the accident of the garrison at Aldershot; no profound conclusions should be drawn from the fact that in the amazing match between Somerset and Hampshire in 1899 (page 469), employees of the British Army scored between them 529 runs while employees of the Church of England were amassing exactly one. The reader will find in this volume the exemplar of both types, Charles Studd, of Cambridge University, the Gentlemen, Middlesex and England, who received the call from those ubiquitous evangelical vaudevillians, Moody and Sankey ending by dubbing his band of missionaries God's Etceteras in the style of a touring cricket club, and designing a church in the African bush measuring exactly twenty two yards; and Brigadier-General Robert Montagu Poore, of Hampshire, the Army, the Gentlemen and South Africa, who paused for long enough in his miraculous six-week assault on the journeymen bowlers of England in 1899 to win the prize for the best mounted man-at-arms at the Royal Tournament, and to play in the winning team in the Inter-Regimental Polo championships.

There is another, deeper sense in which the almanacks of this first period reflect the social climate which nurtured them, and that is their sense of unbounded confidence. It would simply never have occurred to either the players or the men who recorded their feats that the game they revered, the Empire they glorified, the planet they inhabited, might come to an end. To men like Tom Emmett and Arthur Shrewsbury as well as to their betters like milords Hawke and Harris, and to their chroniclers like Knight and the Pardons, the world was, so to speak, in a permanent state of permanence; indeed one of the cricketers, the extraordinary Midwinter, of Victoria, Gloucestershire, England and Australia, actually perfected, between the years 1878-82, a system of commuting between continents which literally staved off forever that most lugubrious of all sporting occasions, the last day of the season; summer's brief lease was extended indefinitely, for as long as the player wished it, which is why in a sense Midwinter is the most symbolic of all the cricketers who find their modest immortality in the pages of Wisden. Every one of them, safe inside the iridescent bubble of Victorian certitude, proceeded on the assumption that God was not only an Englishman, but a useful middle-order batsman. Men like Knight and the Pardons believed that the English had elevated the species to its present lofty eminence, morally and physically speaking, and it seemed doubtful to them if any other nation would ever catch up. And it followed that standards so proudly established must be zealously guarded, which possibly explains the glee with which Wisden so pitilessly poured its strictures down on to the heads of the poor Parsees who arrived in England so brimming with hope and good intentions in 1886 (page 135).

By the time the century ended, John Wisden had long since ceased to be a remembered cricketer and had undergone the flattering metamorphosis into one of the most august of English institutions. He had begun as a small boy earning sixpence an hour as long-stop on the Montpelier Ground at Brighton when Lillywhite was giving his patrons practice. His business partnership with Fred, launched in 1855, was dissolved three years later, Lillywhite being by all accounts a fractious and disagreeable commercial partner. By the end of the century, John Wisden's shop had become a mecca for cricket-lovers, the pivotal spot from which emanated the very spirit of the game. There is a passage of touching tenderness in the autobiography of the cricketing poet Siegfried Sassoon, who was recalling the sad fate of an uncle suffering from an obscure and incurable disease. One day in desperation, his adoring wife, Sassoon's aunt, made a pathetic attempt to force destiny's hand. By pretending to proceed on the assumption that her husband would soon recover,

Sassoon's aunt hoped to induce recovery, even though it was apparent to everyone else in the family that the cause was already lost:

> Auntie Rachel, however, refused to admit that he was becoming an invalid. Once, in 1897, when she was buying me a bat at Wisden's shop, she ordered a complete cricket outfit for Mr Beer, practice net, stumps and all. "The footmen can bowl to him down at Richmond," she remarked casually. They had a house at Richmond which they had ceased to use, for by that time poor Mr Beer was permanently upstairs, becoming paralysed and speechless, and we no longer saw him at all. Even then I was haunted by the pathetic futility of those cricket things which she had purchased for him. She must have loved him very much.

There are two points to be made about that passage, first that Sassoon saw no need to identify the shop in any more detail than simply "Wisden's", and second, that even formidably intellectual society ladies like Mrs Beer knew where the deepest delight of a dying man's heart might be located, as though she believed that in some magical way the proprietors of the shop just off Leicester Square had distilled the curative sunlight of the passing seasons. Mr Beer died soon afterwards, his net and his stumps a wordless epitaph, while his nephew grew up to be one of thousands of Englishmen in the habit of addressing to themselves the rhetorical question, "If Wisden comes, can spring be far behind?".

Today the almanack is so venerable as to be virtually beyond all assault, but the student of these early years should not forget that Wisden has never been short of its critics. The long-defunct weekly magazine *Cricket* once luxuriated in its "regret to see errors perpetuated in Wisden". Roy Webber once devoted six lines to Wisden, filling two of them with "unfortunately Wisden has never made a habit of including the full score of all first-class matches played outside England." This particular stricture is developed by Bowen, fulminating with wonderful relish in his favourite role of devil's advocate:

> It is always called Wisden, and its formal name does not really matter. It is part of cricket's mythology because claims are made for it and beliefs held about it which differ only in degree from those which the fanatical devotees of some religions make for their own revealed books. But it has never covered all first-class cricket, it does not and has not listed (let alone without error) the births and deaths of all first-class cricketers, it does not provide a comprehensive and accurate list of records even at the first-class level, and any reasonably well-informed enthusiast could prove Wisden wrong. Claims for its infallibility are after all rather ridiculous for a yearbook on any subject whatsoever, so that the phrase "It's not in Wisden" is scarcely one to be used in praise of a remarkable feat. Wisden is, in fact, at its weakest in its coverage of overseas cricket.

And then, having done his best, or rather his worst, Bowen closes, most incongruously with "when all is said and done, however, Wisden remains the most important annual in the cricket world and it has been that for most of the past seventy or eighty years." Or, to put it more succinctly, Wisden may not be an unblemished masterpiece, but it is the only masterpiece we have.

As for John Wisden himself, in the course of a lifetime's dedication to cricket in all its ramifications, he was not slow to perceive its central paradox, that it is a fusion of opposites, that a game of cricket is a unique compromise between open warfare and a social delight, that its presence transforms the vista into the subtlest compromise between battlefield and landscape, and that the conduct it requires is an indefinable balance between bellicosity and bonhomie. The Edwardian colonial administrator Arthur Grimble has preserved the observation of an old man of the Sun tribe in the Gilbert and Ellice Islands, who said, "we old men take joy in watching the *kirikiti* of our grandsons, because it is a fighting between factions which makes the fighters love each other." John Wisden echoed the identical sentiments when he said, "to be a good cricketer is to be wary, yet bold; self-possessed, yet cautious; strong, yet gentle; firm, yet manly." How far, one wonders, did he himself fulfil this ideal? In a tribute which the almanack once published, we learn that he was "quiet, modest, of unassuming character, with unfailing good temper and genial disposition," that he was "a respectable fellow in every way, liked and respected by everyone with whom he came into contact," that he was "modest and good-tempered, and never pushed himself forward," that he has left "a pleasant memory as a sportsman, a companion, a friend," and that "all spoke of him in the highest terms".

Ancient history perhaps, the conventional obsequies of long-dead men from an epoch which has been wiped out without trace. And yet not quite without trace, not yet. The casual wanderer through the desolation of central London in the fag-end of the twentieth century, may glance about him and, finding himself in a thoroughfare called Great Newport Street, suddenly notice, over the window of a tiny kiosk, some ancient russet tiles let into the brickwork; on the central tile there is a strange device, which on closer examination turns out to be three stumps leaning against a cricket bat. Under those tiles there once passed a patrician lady and her sporting nephew, each confident in the knowledge that from this building the buff tablets of the cricketing law had always been issued every spring. And always would be.

THE MARYLEBONE CRICKET CLUB

In arranging the material in a volume of this kind, an editor is bound to find himself in the predicament of a scoundrel of the period, standing at the hub of Seven Dials, at a loss to know which direction to choose. The most obvious plan would have been simply to adopt a strict chronological order, giving extracts first from the 1864 edition, then from 1865 and so on down to the end of the century. But paradoxically, such an arrangement shatters rather than preserves that sense of a continually unfolding saga which an accumulation of annual publications ought to convey. To require the reader to work his way through the April-to-September sequence of a cricket season thirty-seven times, seemed as impractical a tactic as it was unwise; moreover, the partisan student intent on studying the fortunes of, say, Surrey, or Cambridge University, or New South Wales, would find himself continually arriving at the start of a new season with his impressions of the previous one erased from his mind by so much intervening material relating to other themes.

There then followed a brief flirtation with the alphabetical method, beginning the volume with Abel, R; and ending it with Zingari, I. This plan engendered even more confusion than the first, being only marginally more acceptable than the plan to begin with the most prestigious games and arrange everything else in descending order of significance, so that the volume might come in like a Test match lion and go out like a Public Schools or Minor Counties lamb. A possible solution seemed to be to sub-divide the anthology into sections, perhaps using the decade as the unit of division. But the distiction between 1889 and 1890 was no greater in cricketing terms than that between 1890 and 1891, and the suggested sub-division would give a hopelessly misleading picture.

It then occurred to me that as the purpose of this anthology was to extol the virtues of one of the best-organised almanacks in the world, the obvious solution was to adhere to Wisden's methods as closely as possible. Although over the years there have been amendments to the arrangement of material in Wisden – for instance removing the Obituaries from the front and putting them at the back, and abandoning listing the counties in the order in which they last finished in the championship in favour of a simple alphabetical sequence – it is certainly true that a general line of succession has become familiar to the regular reader of Wisden over the last century, and that to respect this line might not be a bad idea. This course I have adopted, believing it to be the one which men like the Pardons might well have endorsed, and which Haddam Whitaker has in fact endorsed. If this ordering of so multifarious a mass of material requires any further justification, it is that such an ordering is the one which makes life as simple as possible for the reader.

In effect then, this anthology proceeds on the assumption that between 1864 and 1900 there was granted a divine dispensation which merged the seasons into a single season, its years compressed into weeks, its days into fleeting moments. Everything which happened to this or that team during the period is to be viewed as an Olympian might view it, from a perspective which renders thirty-seven independent campaigns homogeneous. In practical terms, this means that the reader turning to the section "Lancashire" will there find, in chronological order, every Lancashire home game between 1864 and 1900 which seemed worthy of inclusion. This is the traditional Wisden method, except that instead of proceeding on

Lancashire's behalf from April to September, the anthology proceeds from 1864 to 1900. Similarly, all the obituaries, regardless of the year in which they appeared, are placed here at the end of the anthology, as they would be in a modern Wisden, in alphabetical order, as though all the deaths had occurred in the span of a single year. For obvious reasons, the annual averages and analyses do not appear, and reference to the introductory summary of each club is made only when that summary contains material of unusual interest.

But what exactly constitutes "unusual interest"? On what basis has the material in this anthology been selected, and on what grounds have all the rest of the contents of Wisden through the years been omitted? It is a truism that if ten thousand cricket-lovers and students of its history were each invited to compile an anthology like this one, the result would be ten thousand publications whose contents would be strikingly similar and yet never quite identical. In letting instinct by my guide, I have discovered that there are three different ways in which the material has demanded inclusion.

Firstly the performing of some great individual or corporate feat; a mammoth innings perhaps, or the taking of a great number of the opposition's wickets; an opening batsman carrying his bat; a bowler performing the hat-trick; a team score so enormous that the opposition resorted to ten, or even on rare occasions, eleven bowlers, all these merit an entry. An amazing collapse, a sensational stand, some big hitting, a freakish quantity of extras, all ten wickets in an innings, a triple century, a game snatched out of the fire, or even more enjoyable, one where defeat was snatched out of the jaws of victory, these, too, have been included. The reader can add many instances of his own, but the criterion is obvious enough.

Secondly I have included events so unpredictable as to come under the heading of either historical evolution, for instance the juggling with the Follow-On law or a questionable bowling action; or whimsical freak, as in a match between MCC and a lesser side in which three MCC professionals were carried on, like the lady in Marie Lloyd's song, so far past their intended destination that they were unable to participate; or a match in which the same bowler delivered two consecutive overs, or where the pitch was found to be the wrong length, or where the match was played in Paris, or where the qualification to play was to be over sixty years of age. The history of cricket is rich in such affairs, and any history which neglected them would be guilty of a disservice to its readers.

Pure literary appeal, either intentional or otherwise, is the third category of material to be included. One of the most striking differences between the earlier and later Wisden is a tendency in the emergent years to indulge in literary embellishment. Each reader must take this rhapsodising as he finds it, but there is no question that there were times when the effusions of language were very much more fascinating than the games which served as the pretext for their composition. This is particularly so in the annual accounts of the Canterbury Festival which give glowing reports of haute couture, music and London drama; and in references to the Eton v Harrow match, where the issues arising out of the dispensation of facilities to the spectators often eclipse in dramatic importance those arising out the cricket itself. So far as accidental literary felicity is concerned, the reference to cads at Lord's during an MCC match in 1876 is quite wonderful, and the very heading "Huntsmen v Jockeys" has a Pooteresque ring about it, as indeed have "Married v Single", "Smokers v Non-Smokers", "Government v Opposition", and above all that extraordinary designation "One Arm v One Leg", to which Wisden at the time sadly appended no match report. I was moved by the storybook apotheosis of an unknown schoolboy in a match between MCC and Norfolk in 1873, just as moved in a different way by the death of a cricketer in the MCC match against Nottinghamshire two seasons earlier. It seemed appropriate to include the game in which four members of the Grace family appeared on the same side.

In the MCC section which follows, and in all others, the reader will find inserted at appropriate points, some of the essays and reports which in the annual Wisden appear either at the front of the almanack or preceding the club affairs which they summarise. In this anthology those essays and reports have been placed in immediate juxtaposition to the events to which they refer, as for instance the match report of the 1893 Oxford v Cambridge match, followed by the animated discussion which took place arising out of the events of that match. I have adopted the same strategy with the evolution of the County Championship, recurring crises concerning illegal bowling actions, fluctuating fortunes in the affairs of the clubs, and the occasional reflections of superannuated undergraduates, of which A. G. Steel's essay is a superlative example.

As to omissions, there are two which perhaps require a formal explanation. The reader will search in vain for either a Cricket Records section or the Births and Deaths of Cricketers. That these two features, both sacrosanct so far as Wisden is concerned, should be ignored might appear at first sight to constitute a most regrettable act of blasphemy, but a moment's thought will reveal why they make no appearance in this anthology. Where the content embraces nearly forty years, there is no such thing as a cricket record; almost none of the records which survived in 1870 were still surviving thirty years later, so that there is no criterion by which to measure a record-breaking performance. (Knight's analysis of all individual innings over 200 has been included not for its statistical interest but because while he was composing it Knight was clearly possessed by the divine literary afflatus.) The same logic rejected the practicability of a section listing Births and Deaths of Cricketers, for to have included one would have posed the impossible metaphorical question: When is a live cricketer dead and when is a dead one alive? Many of those performing their feats at the start of the period were dead before the end of it; how were they to be listed? As alive or dead? As both or as neither? The impossibility of compiling such a list, and the complications its compiling would demand, are so fundamental that the effect would have been to confuse rather than to elucidate.

As to the contents of this anthology, they have been selected with one very simple end in view, that the reader may pick up the volume and open it at random at any page knowing that he is certain to be confronted by something sensational, or comic, or profound, or revelatory, or outstanding, or socially significant, or technically extraordinary. At times the central reason for the inclusion of an item is less obvious than at others, but so far from being a shortcoming, such tantalising ambiguities contribute immeasurably to the pleasure the book should bring. For I hope most fervently that the subtlest delight of all conveyed by this volume and its two successors will arise out of the fact that the reader is constantly searching for reasons. And always finding them.

Benny Green

SOUTH WALES CLUB v I ZINGARI

At Lord's, July 28, 29, 1864

South Wales Club

First innings		Second innings	
E. M. Grace Esq. b Maitland	55	c Grimston b Maitland	18
W. G. Grace Esq. c and b Maitland	34	st Balfour b Maitland	47
J. Lloyd Esq. b Maitland	10	c Balfour b Burnett	1
H. Reade Esq. c Grimston b Milman	4	c Balfour b Maitland	17
W. G. Curgenven Esq. c Parnell b Maitland	7	b Burnett	16
F. R. Price Esq. c and b Milman	0	not out	23
J. J. Sewell Esq. st Balfour b Maitland	1	c Ponsonby b Maitland	0
J. H. Gibbs Esq. lbw b Milman	0	b Burnett	17
W. H. Wright Esq. b Buller	16	b Maitland	0
C. Bishop Esq. b Maitland	0	c Milman b Maitland	7
C. Hall Esq. not out	6	run out	1
B 1, l-b 1, w 5	7	B 6, l-b 2, w 4	12
	140		159

I Zingari

First innings		Second innings	
W. E. Grimston Esq. run out	12	run out	8
R. Balfour Esq. b E. M. Grace	32	b W. G. Grace	0
Captain Parnell b E. M. Grace	3	lbw b Reade	4
E. Buller Esq. b Curgenven	30	not out	58
R. A. Fitzgerald Esq. b Reade	9	c Wright b Gibbs	6
W. Maitland Esq. c and b Reade	16	b W. G. Grace	21
Hon. S. Ponsonby run out	3	b Reade	4
E. W. Burnett Esq. b Curgenven	5	not out	0
Major Milman lbw b Reade	18		
H. W. Fellows Esq. c Price b Reade	0		
Lord Garlies not out	2	c Price b E. M. Grace	31
B 4, w 9	13	B 8, l-b 2, w 16	26
	143		158

I Zingari won by three wickets.

THE PARIS CLUB v MARYLEBONE CLUB

At Paris, April 22, 23, 1867

The Paris Club

First innings		Second innings	
Sergeant W. McCanlis c Fellows b R. D. Walker	33	c Rose b R. D. Walker	16
Capt. Joy (7th Hussars) st Fellows b Wilkinson	12	lbw b R. D. Walker	7
G. T. Chinnery Esq. b Wilkinson	1	c Fellows b Wilkinson	5
W. Crawshay Esq. run out	10	c Fitzgerald b R. D. Walker	0
T. Arthur Esq. b Wilkinson	1	c Rose b R. D. Walker	2
C. P. Wilkes Esq. b Smith	1	not out	2
Colonel Ridley c Rose b Wilkinson	0	c Rose b Wilkinson	1
T. B. Mourilyan Esq. b Wilkinson	2	st Fellows b Wilkinson	1
S. Brunton Esq. b R. D. Walker	6	b R. D. Walker	2
C. Wylde Esq. c Fellows b R. D. Walker	5	c Rose b R. D. Walker	1
J. G. Pilter Esq. b R. D. Walker	5	run out	3
W. Arthur Esq. not out	1	c Fellows b Wilkinson	0
B 3, l-b 1	4		
	81		40

Marylebone Club

A. J. Wilkinson Esq. lbw b T. Arthur	4	H. W. Fellows Esq. c and b McCanlis	1
W. M. Rose Esq. b Joy	45	H. N. Tennent Esq. st Brunton b McCanlis	1
R. D. Walker Esq. c T. Arthur b Crawshay	19	R. Forster Esq. b Joy	2
A. Lubbock Esq. b McCanlis	102	C. Hall Esq. not out	4
R. A. Bayford Esq. c Brunton b McCanlis	18		
Earl Gosford c T. Arthur b McCanlis	0	B 4, l-b 1, w 24, n-b 1	30
A. L. Smith Esq. c Ridley b Joy	21		
R. A. Fitzgerald Esq. c McCanlis b Joy	9		256

MCC won by an innings and 135 runs.

Umpires: Colonel Hutchinson and James Grundy.

GENTLEMEN v PLAYERS

At Lord's, June 29, 30, 1868

Gentlemen

E. M. Grace Esq. run out	1	not out	22
B. B. Cooper Esq. b Willsher	28	not out	0
W. G. Grace Esq. not out	134		
C. F. Buller Esq. b Grundy	4	b Wootton	0
R. A. Mitchell Esq. b Willsher	1		
H. A. Richardson Esq. b Grundy	8		
W. F. Maitland Esq. b Lillywhite	2		
V. E. Walker Esq. c Pooley b Lillywhite	5		
C. A. Absolom Esq. b Lillywhite	3	c Grundy b Lillywhite	8
J. Round Esq. b Lillywhite	0		
R. Lipscombe Esq. thrown out by Willsher	7		
B 5, l-b 3	8	Extra	1
	201		31

Players

H. Jupp c Absolom b W. G. Grace	4	run out	14
G. Summers b Lipscombe	5	c and b Absolom	4
J. Ricketts c Mitchell b W. G. Grace	1	b Lipscombe	13
James Lillywhite c Maitland b W. G. Grace	0	b Absolom	0
W. Mortlock b W. G. Grace	9	lbw b E. M. Grace	19
E. Pooley b Lipscombe	21	c Buller b Lipscombe	4
F. Silcock run out	0	b W. G. Grace	26
T. Mantle c E. M. Grace b W. G. Grace	12	b W. G. Grace	4
G. Wootton b W. G. Grace	8	c Richardson b W. G. Grace	18
J. Grundy not out	29	c E. M. Grace b W. G. Grace	8
E. Willsher c Round b Absolom	22	not out	3
B 1, l-b 3	4	L-b 2, w 1	3
	115		116

The Gentlemen won by eight wickes.

Umpires: Hearne and Royston.

MCC AND GROUND v OXFORD UNIVERSITY

Played at Oxford, May 13, 14, 1869

In this match Mr W. G. Grace not only made a remarkable first appearance as a member of the MCC, but, with his 117 runs, he commenced the most wonderful series of large first-class innings ever played by one man in one season for the old club. The first day's cricket closed with MCC having scored 159 for six wickets, Mr W. Grace (in No. 1) then not out 86. Next day, Mr Grace was eighth man out, the score at 203; Mr G's 117 being made by two 6s, one 5, four 4s, eleven 3s, etc. This innings was the feature of the match; but there was a splendid catch made by Mr Fortescue, who ran twenty yards to the ball; an equally splendid throw out from cover-point by Capt. F. Watson (Mr Tylecote the victim), and an excellent catch at mid-on by Mr Case. The wickets were good, and the weather dry, but rough and cold. The match was over at five o'clock on the second day, MCC the winners in one innings by 30 runs. Wootton bowled 63 overs (36 maidens) for 67 runs, one wide, and twelve wickets – eight "bowled".

Oxford

A. T. Fortescue Esq. b Wootton	6	– hit wicket b Grace	9
E. Mathews Esq. c Wootton b Grace	5	– b Wootton	16
W. H. Hadow Esq. b Grace	0	– b Wootton	3
R. Digby Esq. c Sandford b Grace	8	– b Wootton	20
E. S. F. Tylecote Esq. b Grace	18	– run out	21
W. Evetts Esq. b Grace	21	– c Sutton b Wootton	31
B. Pauncefote Esq. b Wootton	9	– b Grace	9
W. E. Goschen Esq. c Stewart b Wootton	3	– b Wootton	0
W. R. Stewart Esq. b Wootton	0	– c Case b Wootton	0
T. H. Belcher Esq. b Wootton	4	– not out	0
E. Austin Esq. not out	0	– c Sutton b Wootton	10
W 1	1	B 1, l-b 3, w 1	5
	75		124

MCC and Ground

E. G. Sutton Esq. c Fortescue b Mathews	0	D. Sandford Esq. b Pauncefote	20
W. G. Grace Esq. c Austin b Pauncefote	117	L. Micklem Esq. b Pauncefote	9
T. Hearne c Tylecote b Pauncefote	37	Wootton not out	6
Capt. H. Stewart b Austin	1	West b Austin	0
Capt. F. Watson b Pauncefote	14	B 1, l-b 8, w 4, n-b 2	15
Walter Price st Stewart b Mathews	5		
T. Case Esq. st Stewart b Mathews	5		229

MCC Bowling

	Overs	Mdns	Runs	Wkts	Overs	Mdns	Runs	Wkts
Wootton	27.1	19	25	5	35.3	17	42	7
Mr Grace	27	7	49	5	26	10	61	2
West					9	4	16	—

Oxford Bowling

	Overs	Mdns	Runs	Wkts
Mr Belcher	39	18	39	—
Mr Mathews	33	8	57	3
Mr Pauncefote	29	9	43	5
Mr Austin	24	7	58	2
Mr Fortescue	8	3	17	—

MCC AND GROUND v THE COUNTY OF HERTFORDSHIRE

Played at Chorleywood, June 11, 12, 1869

For the score of this match the compiler is indebted to a report in *Bell's Life in London*, a most lucid, crisp, and compact cricket report, that commented on "King Charles the Second and Nell Gwynne; Macauley; The Evangelization of the Heathen; Mary-la-Bonne; War paint; A Straight Derby Tip; Knaves of Herts; Small Boys; A County Policeman and Stricken Herts." MCC and Ground won by 22 runs.

MCC and Ground

Capt. Tryon b Hughes	7	– c Sutton b Hughes	8
C. P. Coote Esq. b Hughes	1	– b Hughes	0
T. Hearne b Hughes	8	– c Hughes b Fisher	13
C. E. Boyle Esq. b Hughes	4	– c Sutton b Hughes	3
Walter Price c Lines b Hughes	19	– c Fitz-Gerald b Hughes	17
H. Perkins Esq. b Hughes	8	– run out	13
R. Forster Esq. b Hughes	8	– b Fisher	9
Lieut-Col Parnell b Hughes	13	– c Sandars b Fisher	2
J. Perkins Esq. b Fisher	5	– b Fisher	0
F. A. Eaton Esq. not out	3	– "given out"	1
A. Guest Esq. b Hughes	0	– not out	0
Extras	2	Extras	8
	78		74

Hertfordshire

E. G. Sutton Esq. b Hearne	0	– c Guest b Price	16
Hughes c Eaton b Hearne	0	– b Price	3
J. Lines c Boyle b Price	12	– c Tryon b Hearne	0
C. Reid Esq. c J. Perkins b Hearne	4	– c Price b Hearne	0
W. C. Sandars Esq. c J. Perkins b Price	11	– c J. Perkins b Hearne	1
Pearce b Price	1	– run out	0
R. A. Fitz-Gerald Esq. c Boyle b Price	1	– c Price b Hearne	4
H. W. Fellows Esq. c and b Hearne	37	– not out	2
H. M. Aitken Esq. c Hearne b Price	5	– c and b Hearne	0
Rev. F. Thackeray not out	19	– c Tryon b Price	1
Fisher b Parnell	1	– c Boyle b Hearne	5
Extras	6	Extra	1
	97		33

(The bowling figures of this match could not be obtained.)

MCC AND GROUND v CAMBRIDGE UNIVERSITY

Played at Lord's, June 14, 15, 1869

Showery weather and dead wickets. Mr Preston was fifty minutes at the wickets for his 9. To Mr Preston and Mr Money ten successive maiden overs were bowled by Mr Grace and Wootton, every ball of the forty being "there". Mr Thornton's 33 and 34 included a 6, a 5, and two 4s; they were innings as noteworthy – aye, and as praiseworthy – for good defence as for free fine hitting. Messrs Brune and Montgomery increased the score from 105 for eight wickets to 169 for nine. Mr Brune bowled well (58 overs for 56 runs and fourteen wickets). Mr Brune's last over in MCC's second innings took three wickets. Mr Money was "playing" well, when he fell and injured his arm. Mr W. Grace was the hitter on the MCC side; when MCC had scored 21, Mr Grace had made 20 of the 21 runs; when he was out for 32, MCC was 35 only; and when he was out (second innings) for 31, MCC was but 41. The Cantabs played good cricket and won by 116 runs.

Cambridge

J. W. Dale Esq. c Rutter b Grace	10	– c Green b Wootton	0
B. Preston Esq. b Wootton	9	– c Wilkinson b Grace	4
W. B. Money Esq. b Grace	6	– not out (hurt)	23
H. A. Richardson Esq. c Rutter b Grace	3	– run out	3
W. Yardley Esq. b Wootton	5	– b Grace	6
C. I. Thornton Esq. b Grace	33	– c Rutter b Grace	34
C. Absolom Esq. b Wootton	0	– b Grace	11
W. B. Weighell Esq. c Sutton b Grace	1	– b Grace	13
C. J. Brune Esq. b Grace	15	– b Wootton	31
H. H. Montgomery Esq. b Wootton	0	– not out	43
J. W. Wilson Esq. not out	0	– b Wootton	2
B 1, l-b 4	5	B 5, l-b 4, w 2	11
	87		181

MCC and Ground

W. G. Grace Esq. c Yardley b Absolom	32	– b Weighell	31
E. G. Sutton Esq. lbw b Brune	0	– b Brune	10
T. Hearne b Brune	0	– b Weighell	1
A. J. Wilkinson Esq. b Absolom	0	– b Brune	8
R. D. Balfour Esq. b Brune	10	– not out	3
C. E. Green Esq. not out	29	– b Brune	5
Capt. F. Watson c Yardley b Brune	2	– c Thornton b Weighell	1
Lieut-Col Milman c Preston b Brune	2	– c Weighell b Brune	0
E. Rutter Esq. b Brune	0	– b Weighell	4
Capt. H. Stewart lbw b Brune	3	– b Brune	0
Wootton b Brune	0	– b Brune	2
B 1, l-b 2, w 1	4	B 4, w 1	5
	82		70

Cambridge Bowling

	Overs	Mdns	Runs	Wkts	Overs	Mdns	Runs	Wkts
Mr Absolom	27	9	47	2	10	3	17	—
Mr Brune	26.1	12	31	8	32	20	25	6
Mr Weighell					22	8	23	4

MCC Bowling

	Overs	Mdns	Runs	Wkts	Overs	Mdns	Runs	Wkts
Wootton	43	22	48	4	64	36	65	3
Mr Grace	42.3	29	34	6	62	30	81	5
Hearne					11	6	8	—
Mr Rutter					9	5	10	—
Mr Green					7	3	6	—
Col Milman					1	1	—	—

Umpires: Grundy and Royston.

MCC AND GROUND v NOTTINGHAMSHIRE

Played at Lord's, July 5, 6, 7, 1869

This was the only match at Lord's in 1869 that took three days to play it out. The weather was dry and warm, the wickets and cricket good, and 746 runs were scored in the match.

At quarter past twelve on the Monday Nottinghamshire began the batting; at twenty minutes to four the Shire's innings was over for 129 runs. Wild hit his 13 runs in fifteen minutes. A drive for 5 and a 4 to leg formed the greater portion of Alfred Shaw's innings. So carefully – and so well – played was Mr Miles's 18, that a hearty cheer from the pavilion greeted that gentleman's return from the wicket. William Oscroft's 19 was good cricket all of it; and although the last Nottinghamshire wicket took a deal of getting, Marten's last fifteen overs were bowled for 4 runs and a wicket. At five minutes to four the Club's innings was commenced, and before the clock struck six, the MCC were all out for 112. Mr W. Grace and Hearne, by good hitting, increased the score from 31 to 86, when Mr Grace was run out for 48, an innings that included three splendid drives for 5 each. At one time "the two Shaws" bowled twelve consecutive maiden overs, the last three wickets being rapidly "bowled" down by J. C. Shaw. Mr Wilkinson's 15 not out was productive of much carefully played and excellent cricket. In the one hour then left for play Nottinghamshire lost two wickets (Bignall's and Oscroft's) of their second innings for 30 runs.

Tuesday was "Daft's day". He went in at twenty-five minutes past twelve, the score at 33 for three wickets, and he stayed in until eight minutes to seven, when the Nottinghamshire innings was over for 295 runs, and Daft had made 103 not out; so as many as 262 runs were made for the Shire whilst Daft was in. For cool, scientific, cautious, and successful defence, this innings of Daft's was a marvel; "slow" it certainly was, but then it was "sure". Whilst Daft was "defending", Alfred Shaw and Wild were "hitting" freely and well. 86 runs were put on whilst Wild was getting his 54, and although Daft went in at twenty-five past twelve and Alfred Shaw at ten past three, yet when Shaw left for 62, Daft had made 58 only. And there can be no doubt but to the steady, effective defence of Daft, and the free hitting of Wild and A. Shaw, the success of Nottinghamshire in this truly great match is due. The second day's cricket closed with the termination of Nottinghamshire's second innings.

Wednesday was Mr W. Grace's day. He and Mr Balfour commenced the Club's second innings at noon. At 2.30 the MCC score was at 119, four wickets down, and Mr Grace 75 not out (87 overs having then been bowled). Mr Richardson left with the score at 150 for five wickets, that gentleman's 34 having been made by really fine hitting. Mr Sutton and Mr Grace then hit the score to 186, when Mr Grace was bowled by Wild (in his third over) for 121. Mr Grace went to the wickets, first man in, at five minutes past twelve, he was sixth out at ten minutes past four, his 121 having been hit from the bowling of J. C. Shaw, Wootton, Alfred Shaw, Tinley, and others. After Mr Grace left the end quickly came, as J. C. Shaw, in two overs and two balls, obtained the last three wickets without a run having been obtained from those ten balls; and thus, at twenty minutes to five, Nottinghamshire had won by 102 runs. (The extras told four and a half to one in favour of Nottinghamshire.) The Nottinghamshire professionals fielded splendidly.

Nottinghamshire

Summers b Grace	12	– b Grace	9
Bignall run out	13	– run out	7
W. Oscroft c Sutton b Hearne	19	– c Grace b Marten	8
Richard Daft b Marten	1	– not out	103
Wild b Marten	13	– c Round b Wilkinson	54
Alfred Shaw b Hearne	14	– st Richardson b Money	62
P. W. H. Miles Esq. c Money b Hearne	18	– c Richardson b Hearne	17
Biddulph b Hearne	11	– c Wilkinson b Grace	6
R. C. Tinley c Sutton b Hearne	10	– b Hearne	4
Wootton not out	6	– c Balfour b Green	1
J. C. Shaw b Marten	2	– b Green	4
B 5, l-b 5	10	B 15, l-b 2, w 3	20
	129		295

MCC and Ground

W. G. Grace Esq. run out	48	– b Wild	121
E. G. Sutton Esq. b J. C. Shaw	3	– b Tinley	23
J. W. Dale Esq. st Biddulph b Wootton	6	– b J. C. Shaw	10
T. Hearne st Biddulph b J. C. Shaw	27	– b J. C. Shaw	7
W. B. Money Esq. b A. Shaw	0	– c and b J. C. Shaw	3
H. A. Richardson Esq. run out	5	– lbw b Tinley	34
C. E. Green Esq. b J. C. Shaw	0	– b J. C. Shaw	8
A. J. Wilkinson Esq. not out	15	– c Wild b Wootton	0
R. D. Balfour Esq. b J. C. Shaw	3	– b Wootton	1
J. Round Esq. b J. C. Shaw	0	– not out	0
Marten b J. C. Shaw	1	– c and b J. C. Shaw	0
B 3, l-b 1	4	B 1, l-b 2	3
	112		210

Nottinghamshire Bowling

	Overs	Mdns	Runs	Wkts	Overs	Mdns	Runs	Wkts
J. C. Shaw	34.2	16	48	6	60.2	26	99	5
A. Shaw	20	7	29	1	10	4	10	—
Wootton	15	5	31	1	39	18	50	2
Tinley					21	4	37	2
Wild					5	3	6	1
Mr Miles					5	1	5	—

MCC Bowling

	Overs	Mdns	Runs	Wkts	Overs	Mdns	Runs	Wkts
Marten	36.3	20	36	3	62	41	65	1
Hearne	26	16	27	5	77	27	50	2
Mr Grace	18	6	36	1	51	26	61	2
Mr Money	7	—	20	—	26	6	60	1
Mr Green					11.3	6	17	2
Mr Wilkinson					6	3	7	1
Mr Sutton					6	3	15	—

Umpires: Grundy and Royston.

ETON v HARROW

Played at Lord's, July 9, 10, 1869

That this, the most attractive match of the season, annually increases in popularity with the fair and fashionable portion of English society Lord's ground bore brilliant testimony on Friday, the 9th of last July, on which day £100 more was taken at the gates for admission than was ever before taken in one day at Lord's. The weather was fortunately fine; the attendance marvellous, both in numbers and quality; and the old ground, as it that day appeared, a fitting subject for a companion picture to Frith's "Derby Day". One writer described the Grand Stand as being "as gay as a bank of Summer Flowers", and so it was, for two-thirds of the occupants were "The Ladies of England", whose gay, varied, and brilliant hued attires pleasantly contrasted with the dark, sombre clad, dense mass of "he" humanity that thronged the seats and roof of the Pavilion, a majority of whom "had been" Public School Boys, many of whom "are" distinguished members of the highest and most honoured Institutions of the Country. As many of the Drags of "The Four-in-Hand Club" as could gain admission to the ground were grouped together at the NW end of the Pavilion. Around the ground flanking the ropes, closely clustered (at most parts six deep) were 600 carriages of the nobility and gentry, each vehicle fully, most of them "fairly" freighted. The tops of the wood-stacks had occupants, so had the window sills of the Racket Court, and the top of Mr Dark's garden wall; and how vast was the number of visitors each day may be estimated from the facts that on the Friday "about" £770, and on Saturday, "nearly" £500, was taken at the gates for admission money. In fact, the Eton and Harrow match at Lord's has now become one of the prominent events of the London Season; for years and years to come may it so continue to be, and thus materially aid in keeping alive the interest for the fine old game, at present so manifest and general, among its very best supporters, "The Gentlemen of England".

At eleven o'clock each day the cricket was commenced; at five minutes past one on the second day Eton had won in one innings. Their innings of 237 runs averaged 47 runs per hour. Mr Rhodes was one hour and a half at the wickets for his 11. Mr Higgins "played" well for his 32, and Mr Rodger "hit" freely for his 24; but the feature of the match was the steadily and truthfully played 108 of Mr Ottaway's, an innings that for correct "timing" and judicious "placing" of the ball, has rarely been excelled in a Public School match. Mr Ottaway went to the wickets at seventeen minutes past eleven, the score at 12 for one wicket; at three minutes to four he was seventh man out with the score at 214, his 108 being made by one 4, eleven 3s, twelve 2s, and 47 singles. Mr Baily kept wicket for Harrow in very promising form. Mr Crake's catch at square-leg that prevented Mr Harris scoring, and his one hand catch that settled Mr Rodger, were indeed fine ones; and equally excellent was the bit of fielding by Mr Gore and Mr Baily that ran out Lord Clifton. In fact, the general fielding of Harrow was of the very best Public School form. Harrow began batting well by Messrs Walker and Crake making 28 runs from the first nine Eton overs bowled, but then the wickets went down rapidly. A splendid throw out from long-field by Mr Harris run out Mr Gore. And although Mr Walker played steady cricket and scored 23, the innings ended at a quarter past six for 91 runs, Mr Apcar making the only hit over the ropes that day. In the second innings of Harrow, Mr Gore strove gallantly to save the one innings defeat; he hit in really fine form, one straight drive of his sent the ball bounding hard on to the Pavilion seat; but when he had made 41, a truly splendid left-hand "c and b" by Mr Maude (who leapt up, and with hand extended to its extreme height, "clutched" and held the hotly driven ball) ended Mr Gore's innings. Then in three overs Mr Maude had three wickets, and at five minutes past one, Eton had won the 1869 match by an innings and 19 runs.

Eton

G. H. Longman Esq. b Giles	15
A. S. Tabor Esq. b Giles	7
C. J. Ottaway Esq. b Gore	108
F. W. Rhodes Esq. c and b Law	11
Hon. G. Harris c Crake b Walker	0
F. Pickering Esq. c Gore b Walker	9
*W. C. Higgins Esq. c and b Walker	32
J. P. Rodger Esq. c Crake b Macan	24
S. E. Butler Esq. b Gore	13
Lord Clifton run out	3
J. Maude Esq. not out	1
B 10, l-b 1, w 3	14
	237

Harrow

C. W. Walker Esq. c Tabor b Butler	23	– b Butler	16
W. P. Crake Esq. run out	16	– b Maude	13
F. C. Baily Esq. c Rhodes b Butler	1	– b Maude	0
F. A. Currie Esq. b Higgins	4	– c Higgins b Maude	4
*S. W. Gore Esq. run out	4	– c and b Maude	41
A. A. Apcar Esq. c Longman b Clifton	13	– c Rhodes b Maude	12
W. Law Esq. b Clifton	0	– b Maude	1
A. J. Begbie Esq. c Harris b Butler	15	– c Rodger b Clifton	18
W. E. Openshaw Esq. b Butler	3	– b Maude	9
G. Macan Esq. c Higgins b Butler	1	– c Clifton b Butler	0
C. F. Giles Esq. not out	4	– not out	3
B 3, l-b 4	7	B 6, l-b 3, w 1	10
	91		127

* Captains.

Harrow Bowling

	Overs	Mdns	Runs	Wkts
Mr Walker	61	17	74	3
Mr Giles	60	32	69	2
Mr Law	25	12	31	1
Mr Macan	21.3	9	28	1
Mr Gore	19	9	21	2

(At one time Mr Giles bowled fifteen overs for 7 runs.)

Eton Bowling

	Overs	Mdns	Runs	Wkts	Overs	Mdns	Runs	Wkts
Mr Higgins	20	4	38	1	10	3	23	—
Mr Butler	16	9	25	5	29	10	50	2
Lord Clifton	9	4	13	2	12	6	8	1
Mr Maude	6	2	8	—	32	16	36	7

In Harrow's second innings Mr Maude finished his bowling with five overs for a hit for two and four wickets. Mr Butler at one time bowled five consecutive maiden overs, and Lord Clifton's first ten overs were bowled for a wicket and four singles.

Umpires: T. Hearne and Walter Price.

MCC AND GROUND v DEVONSHIRE

Played at Lord's, July 15, 1869

Another match played out in one day: this time the defeated team being MCC and Ground. All was over by a quarter to seven, Devon the winners by nine wickets. In MCC's first innings, the fourth, fifth, sixth, seventh and eights wickets all fell with the score at 25 – a cricket curiosity that, that amply deserves this special noting.

In Devon's first innings the first wicket fell for 2 runs; 60 were scored when the fifth and sixth wickets went down; 76 when the ninth fell, and 98 for the tenth.

In the second innings of MCC the first and second wickets went down before a run was scored; 51 runs were made when the fifth wicket fell, but the eighth, ninth and tenth, all three went with the score at 68. In all, there were 207 (only 180 "from the bat") runs made, and 155 overs bowled in this curious match.

MCC and Ground

C. R. Alexander Esq. b Smyth	7	– b Fellowes	13
Grundy b Mott	6	– c Seager b Fellowes	6
A. H. Hugh Esq. b Mott	7	– c Estridge b Mott	0
W. Parnell Esq. b Mott	1	– b Fellowes	11
Mumford b Smyth	0	– c and b Fellowes	16
R. Hall Esq. b Smyth	0	– b Fellowes	10
Captain Dyer run out	0	– b Mott	1
J. Sutton Esq. b Mott	2	– b Mott	0
Farrands b Smyth	0	– b Mott	0
R. J. Ward Esq. not out	0	– not out	3
Capt. Tryon run out	5	– b Smyth	0
B 5, l-b 1, w 1	7	B 4, l-b 4	8
	35		68

Devonshire

J. Bennett Esq. b Grundy	0		
T. Welman Esq. b Mumford	19		
H. W. Estridge Esq. c Tryon b Mumford	16	– lbw b Mumford	0
A. P. Handley Esq. b Grundy	5		
C. C. Mackarness Esq. hit wicket b Mumford	4	– not out	1
J. F. Scobell Esq. b Grundy	9		
M. B. Seager Esq. b Mumford	5		
E. A. Bennett Esq. c Hugh b Mumford	24	– not out	5
W. K. Mott Esq. b Grundy	0		
J. Fellowes Esq. b Grundy	0		
T. S. Smyth Esq. not out	4		
B 8, l-b 3, n-b 1	12		
	98		6

Devon Bowling

	Overs	Mdns	Runs	Wkts	Overs	Mdns	Runs	Wkts
Mr Mott	19	14	10	4	27	16	32	4
Mr Smyth	18.3	11	18	4	9	5	5	1
Mr Fellowes					18	10	23	4

MCC Bowling

	Overs	Mdns	Runs	Wkts	Overs	Mdns	Runs	Wkts
Grundy	29	17	28	5	2	—	2	—
Mumford	19	7	36	5	2	1	4	1
Farrands	11	3	22	—				

Umpires: T. Jordan sen. and T. Nixon jun.

MCC AND GROUND v NOTTINGHAMSHIRE

Played at Lord's, June 13, 14, 15, 1870

A lamentable celebrity will ever attach to this match, through the fatal accident to Summers, whose death resulted from a ball bowled by Platts in the second innings of Nottinghamshire. The wickets were excellent, and the sad mishap universally regretted.

As in 1869 so in 1870, the MCC v Nottinghamshire was the only match at Lord's that occupied three days in playing. In the 1869 match Mr W. G. Grace's 121 for MCC, and Daft's 103 not out for Nottinghamshire, were the two highest scores in the match. So in 1870 were Daft's 117 for Nottinghamshire and Mr Grace's 117 not out for MCC the highest scores in this contest. MCC lost their wicket-keeper and two crack bowlers, who played for their Shire; but the Club Eleven included several of the best amateur batsmen of the country, and yet in their first innings nine of the MCC Eleven were got out for 10 runs, seven of the nine being "bowled" out. That was indeed a remarkable innings; commenced at five minutes past six by Mr W. Grace and Mr I. D. Walker, the stumps were drawn at seven with the score 67, Mr Grace not out 49 and Mr Walker not out 17. At 12.15 next day play was resumed; at ten minutes to one the score was 102 no wicket down, but shortly after Mr Walker played the ball on, and MCC's first wicket went with the score 127. Then in such rapid contrast did the other wickets fall, that the second wicket went for 134 runs; the third for 138; the fourth for 145; the fifth for 148; the sixth for 149; the seventh for 154; the eighth for 168 (Mr Grace then 103); the ninth for 168; and tenth for 183, Mr Grace not out 117. When he had made about 60, Mr Grace played a ball from

J. C. Shaw hard on the wicket, but the bails remained fixed; and when he had made 90 he gave a (hot) chance to point; nevertheless, to go in No. 1, stay over four hours at wickets, and score 117 not out, is a great bit of batting to bring off at Lord's against Nottinghamshire's bowling. A minority of 84 necessitated MCC "following on". Mr Dale and Mr Grace began that innings; the third ball bowled by J. C. Shaw hit and broke and middle stump of Mr Grace's wicket, the great bat being this time out before a run was scored, his 0 and 117 not out forcibly illustrating "the glorious, etc.". Mr Green hit well for 33; Mr I. D. Walker (who went in two wickets down with the score 57) and Mr Dale then increased the score by 122 runs, as when Mr Walker was bowled for 63 the boards showed 179 for three wickets, and a prospect of a good match. From 179 Mr Yardley ably helped Mr Dale to move the score to 213, when McIntyre at cover-point ended Mr Dale's innings for 90. First man in (with Mr Grace) Mr Dale had played some of the best cricket seen last season, the fine form, the very fine form, he was down upon and stopped shooters eliciting hearty and general praise, especially from the professionals. The score was at 213 for four wickets when Mr Dale left. Very little good was done for MCC afterwards, as the other six wickets added but 27 runs to the score, J. C. Shaw having four wickets in the last eleven balls he bowled. Summers' last innings was a good one; at 12.48 he went in one wicket down with the score 29, at dinner call he had made 35 (the score 137), and at 3.30 his wicket fell to a shooter from the same hand that subsequently bowled the fatal ball. The score was 158 when Summers was out for 41 – a fact that tells how steadily and carefully he batted. This his final innings comprised eleven singles, eight 2s, three 3s, and one 5 – that 5 (a fine forward cut down to the tavern) being the last hit the poor fellow ever made, as he was then bowled by Platts; and the first ball bowled to him in the second innings was the fatal one. McIntyre with 27 and 34 (and four wickets and a catch) did well for the Shire. And with a 5, a 4, and four 3s (out of a total of 23), Wootton's hard hitting was also useful. But R. Daft's 117 and 53 were far away the most prominent items of Nottinghamshire cricket. In his first innings Daft, at one o'clock, went to the wickets two down with the score 39; at five minutes past four Mr Dale cleaned bowled him for 117, the score at 238 for eight wickets. Daft never scored so rapidly in a first-class match as he did in making that 117; and how very fine was his batting is attested by the fact of his being called up to the pavilion and there presented with a prize bat – a rare honour this at Lord's. In his second innings Daft went in one wicket down, the score 23; he was fifth out, with 103 on the boards. The sixth and seventh wickets both fell at 114. Biddulph and McIntyre then increased the score to 155, when McIntyre was had at leg. Biddulph made both the tie and the winning hits; and so, at twenty minutes past four on the third day, Nottinghamshire won this memorable match nominally by two wickets, really by one wicket.

Nottinghamshire

J. G. Beevor Esq. b Platts	3	– b Cobden	3
Bignall b Riddell	29	– b Platts	10
Summers b Platts	41	– hurt (not out)	0
Richard Daft b Dale	117	– c Riddell b Cobden	53
W. Oscroft lbw b Platts	0	– c Thornton b Cobden	12
Wyld c V. E. Walker b Cobden	0	– run out	15
Alfred Shaw run out	3	– c Hearne b Platts	9
W. McIntyre b Dale	27	– c Grace b Hearne	34
Wootton not out	23	– b Platts	0
Biddulph run out	0	– not out	15
J. C. Shaw b Hearne	6	– not out	0
B 14, l-b 4	18	B 4, l-b 1, w 1	6
	267		157

MCC and Ground

W. G. Grace Esq. not out	117 – b J. C. Shaw	0
I. D. Walker Esq. b J. C. Shaw	48 – b Alfred Shaw	63
C. E. Green Esq. c Beevor b McIntyre	1 – b Alfred Shaw	33
W. Yardley Esq. b McIntyre	4 – b Alfred Shaw	24
T. Hearne b J. C. Shaw	0 – c Biddulph b J. C. Shaw	1
C. I. Thornton Esq. b McIntyre	0 – b J. C. Shaw	8
J. W. Dale Esq. b J. C. Shaw	0 – c McIntyre b J. C. Shaw	90
H. A. Richardson Esq. b J. C. Shaw	4 – b Alfred Shaw	13
E. M. Riddell Esq. c Oscroft b J. C. Shaw	0 – not out	3
F. C. Cobden Esq. b J. C. Shaw	0 – b J. C. Shaw	0
Platts b McIntyre	1 – b J. C. Shaw	0
B 3, l-b 5	8 B 3, l-b 2	5
	183	240

MCC Bowling

	Overs	Mdns	Runs	Wkts	Overs	Mdns	Runs	Wkts
Platts	48	24	74	3	27.2	8	56	3
Mr Cobden	32	14	53	1	30	10	52	3
Mr Riddell	26	10	37	1	3	2	1	—
Hearne	18.3	8	24	1	16	6	24	1
Mr Grace	10	—	34	—	6	2	9	—
Mr Dale	9	3	16	2	8	4	9	—
Mr I. D. Walker	3	—	11	—				

Nottinghamshire Bowling

	Overs	Mdns	Runs	Wkts	Overs	Mdns	Runs	Wkts
J. C. Shaw	55	26	68	6	45	22	65	6
McIntyre	29.2	13	68	4	17	4	48	—
A. Shaw	9	2	12	—	40	17	52	4
Wootton	15	8	27	—	19	4	45	—
Daft					4	1	7	—
Wyld					3	—	18	—

(In this match Mr V. E. Walker was one of the MCC Eleven; he fielded at point in Nottinghamshire's first innings until an unfortunate injury to his hand, received when fielding, compelled him to retire. The question subsequently arose whether – Mr Walker having fielded – another could bat for him; however, Mr Richardson batted in both innings instead of Mr Walker.)

Umpires: Grundy and Royston.

CAMBRIDGE v OXFORD

Played at Lord's, June 27, 28, 1870

The large and brilliant attendances, the fine successful stand made for Cambridge at a critical phase of the match by Mr Yardley and Mr Dale, the truly great innings played by Mr Yardley and the extraordinary finish, stamps the University contest of 1870 as the most remarkable of the 36 yet played. In gloomy but dry weather the match was commenced by Cambridge batting. When Mr Dale had been bowled the ball split the top of one of the stumps; when Mr Money had hit the ball on; when Mr Francis had bowled Mr Tobin; and when Mr Yardley had been cleverly caught out at short leg, Cambridge had lost four of their most valuable wickets for 46 runs. Mr. Tobin was forty minutes at wickets for his 13 runs. Mr Scott went in four wickets down; 80 runs had been added to the score when he was seventh man out, his 45 being a promising display of hitting (all round) and good defence. Mr Thornton played steadily for his 17 and so did Mr Mackinnon, who witnessed four wickets fall and took his bat out. So good and true had been the bowling and fielding of Oxford, that it had taken the Cambridge men one hour and twenty minutes to score their first 50 runs. At ten past four the Oxford men commenced batting; at quarter to seven they had concluded their innings for 175 runs. They made 25 runs from the first eight overs bowled and 28 when their first wicket fell; 66 when the second wicket (Mr Fortescue's) went down; and 86 for three wickets when Mr Pauncefote was caught out at point. Mr Ottaway was one hour and twenty minutes scoring his 16; Mr Hill made 23 runs in twenty minutes; and, by four four 4s and two singles, Mr Butler made 18 runs in twelve minutes. A very fine catch by Mr Thornton ended Mr Tylecote's innings at 23; and (in a bad light for batting) Mr Cobden "bowled" down the eighth, the ninth and tenth wickets, thereby bringing the first day's play to an end at quarter to seven, each side having played an innings, Oxford having 23 runs in hand – a result deservedly due to their superior bowling and fielding. The attendance was one of high class and numerically estimated at 9,000. On the second day the weather was brilliant and the attendance (computed at 10,000) one of these rare assemblages of fashion, rank and eminent men of the country that meet on no other cricket ground but Lord's. Past and present University men mustered strongly; and as the day's extraordinary cricket frequently wavered in favour of Light or Dark Blue, so rang out the old cheering as zealously as ever. Mr Dale and Mr Tobin commenced the second innings of Cambridge. With the score at 6 only Mr Tobin was bowled; with it at 19 first Mr Money and then Mr Fryer "played the ball on;" and when a marvellously fine running catch by Mr Hadow had ended Mr Thornton's innings and Mr Scott had been caught out at point, there were five wickets down for 40 runs, Cambridge only 12 runs on. But then it was (at three minutes to one) Mr Yardley went to the wickets; and his brilliant – at times grand – hitting, aided by the careful, scientific play of Mr Dale, put quite another aspect on the match. So effectively did Mr Yardley hit, that at 1.30 the score was increased to 100; at ten minutes past two the 150 was up; but at 156 a magnificient right-hand catch (arm extended its full height) at deep leg by Mr Ottaway (close in front of the visitors) ended Mr Dale's display of first-class batting for 67 runs. At five minutes to twelve Mr Dale was first man in, at quarter past two he was sixth out, the score at 156. He was cheered and cheered again with a will. With the score at 189 Mr Mackinnon hit the ball on and at 195 Mr Francis ended Mr Yardley's innings for 100 exact – the highest individual score yet made in these matches and as fine a display of brilliant hitting as ever witnessed in them. The innings included fourteen 4s, the leg hitting being especially clean and fine. Earnest applause (in which the Oxford Eleven took part) justly complimented Mr Yardley on the completion of his great innings. During his stay the score had been increased by 155 runs, of which number Mr Yardley had made 100. At ten minutes to four the Cambridge innings was over for 200 runs, leaving the Oxford men 179 to win. It then became generally known that it had been previously arranged to play until 7.30, if necessary, to finish the match that day. It was necessary and the match was finished; how, none present will forget. At ten minutes past four Oxford began the innings and lost a wicket (Mr Hadow's) ere they had scored a run. Mr Ottaway then went to Mr Fortescue's aid, and, assisted by bad fielding, they increased the score to 72, when Mr Fortescue was bowled for 41. Mr Pauncefote was bowled at 86; then Mr Ottaway and Mr Tylecote (the fielding indifferent) swelled the score to 153, when Mr Tylecote was bowled; and at 160 a remarkably good catch at short-leg by Mr Fryer got rid of Mr Ottaway for 69, the highest Oxford score and one of the most finished exhibitions of artistic defence and correct cricket played in the match. When Mr Ottaway left the innings was at 160 for five wickets and the time ten past seven; so twenty minutes remained for five wickets to make the 19 runs then required to win. But a catch at slip and an "lbw" speedily got rid of Mr Townshend and Mr Francis, making seven wickets down for 175 runs, or 4 to win – an apparently easy task. But then (in an indifferent light for batting) Mr Cobden bowled his now famously effective last over:

From the first ball a single was made (3 to win with three wickets to fall).
From the 2nd ball Mr Butler was superbly caught out at mid off.
The third ball bowled Mr Belcher.
The fourth ball bowled Mr Stewart.

And so, accompanied by excitement unparalleled, did the eighth, ninth and tenth wickets fall with the score 176, Cambridge after all winning this "match of matches" by 2 runs. The sudden break up of "the ring;" the wild rush of thousands across the ground to the pavilion; the waving of hats, sunshades, handkerchiefs, fans, and sticks; the loud shouts for Cobden, Yardley, Dale, Ottaway, Fortescue, Francis and others, to come out and be tossed about by their partisans, formed a fitting climax to a match so excitingly contested and a result so astoundedly unexpected.

Cambridge

*J. W. Dale Esq. b Francis	15	– c Ottaway b Francis	67
E. Tobin Esq. b Francis	13	– b Belcher	2
*W. B. Money Esq. b Belcher	10	– b Francis	6
*W. Yardley Esq. c Butler b Francis	2	– c and b Francis	100
F. E. R. Fryer Esq. c Stewart b Hadow	8	– b Francis	0
A. T. Scott Esq. b Belcher	45	– c Tylecote b Francis	0
*C. I. Thornton Esq. b Belcher	17	– c Hadow b Butler	11
F. A. Mackinnon Esq. not out	17	– b Belcher	2
F. C. Cobden Esq. b Francis	7	– c Hadow b Francis	7
A. Bourne Esq. b Belcher	3	– b Francis	0
E. E. Ward Esq. st Stewart b Francis	2	– not out	3
B 3, l-b 4, w 1	8	B 4, l-b 3, w 1	8
	147		206

Oxford

*A. T. Fortescue Esq. b Money	35	– b Ward	44
W. H. Hadow Esq. b Cobden	17	– c Scott b Cobden	0
C. J. Ottaway Esq. b Bourne	16	– c Fryer b Ward	69
*B. Pauncefote Esq. c Dale b Ward	15	– b Ward	5
*E. F. S. Tylecote Esq. c Thornton b Ward	25	– b Ward	29
W. Townshend Esq. st Yardley b Money	0	– c Money b Ward	1
*F. H. Hill Esq. b Ward	23	– not out	13
C. K. Francis Esq. b Cobden	12	– lbw b Ward	1
S. E. Butler Esq. b Cobden	18	– c Bourne b Cobden	0
*W. A. Stewart Esq. b Cobden	0	– b Cobden	0
T. H. Belcher Esq. not out	0	– b Cobden	0
B 10, l-b 2, w 1, n-b 1	14	B 7, l-b 3, w 3, n-b 1	14
	175		176

* Were in the Elevens of 1869.

Oxford Bowling

	Overs	Mdns	Runs	Wkts	Overs	Mdns	Runs	Wkts
Mr Belcher	45	25	52	4	29	10	38	2
Mr Francis	42.2	16	59	5	42.3	12	102	7
Mr Butler	11	4	16	—	2	—	8	1
Mr Hadow	7	2	12	1	4	1	11	—
Mr Hill					13	6	27	—
Mr Pauncefote					4	2	5	—
Mr Fortescue					3	1	7	—

Cambridge Bowling

	Overs	Mdns	Runs	Wkts	Overs	Mdns	Runs	Wkts
Mr Bourne	21	11	36	1	30	15	41	—
Mr Cobden	19	6	41	4	27	10	35	4
Mr Money	17	4	37	2	7	—	24	—
Mr Ward	16	8	33	3	32	16	29	6
Mr Fryer	14	5	14	—	7	1	15	—
Mr Thornton					10	4	13	—
Mr Dale					3	1	5	—

Umpires: Grundy and T. Hearne.

MCC AND GROUND v THORNDON HALL

Played at Thorndon Hall, July 5, 1870

This match, the greater portion of which was played during a steady rainfall, is remarkable; for in the first instance one man (Baker) scoring 67 out of the gross total of 127 runs made for Thorndon Hall and in the next place for Alfred Shaw accomplishing the extraordinary bowling feat of having eighteen wickets (out of the twenty), nine in each innings, with his bowling – thirteen of the eighteen wickets being "bowled". The match was won by MCC by an innings and 17 runs.

Thorndon Hall

A. Baker b Alfred Shaw	52	– b Alfred Shaw	15
A. Nicholas c and b Alfred Shaw	2	– b Alfred Shaw	5
P. Colley hit wkt b Price	6	– st Jardine b Alfred Shaw	0
T. Nicholas b Alfred Shaw	4	– b Alfred Shaw	3
Hon. W. J. Petre b Alfred Shaw	1	– b Alfred Shaw	2
W. Boardman c Frost b Alfred Shaw	0	– not out	4
F. N. Evans lbw b Alfred Shaw	6	– b Alfred Shaw	3
G. Boardman b Alfred Shaw	0	– b Alfred Shaw	0
J. F. Lescher not out	6	– c Richards b Alfred Shaw	11
A. Crush b Alfred Shaw	0	– b Alfred Shaw	0
E. Boardman b Alfred Shaw	0	– run out	6
L-b 1	1		
	78		49

MCC and Ground

J. Jardine Esq. b Evans	20	H. Bass Esq. c Crush b Baker	22
C. P. Coote Esq. b Evans	15	J. McLaren Esq. not out	12
Walter Price c and b Evans	24	Alfred Shaw b Evans	33
Capt. Trevor lbw b Petre	1	R. J. Ward Esq. lbw b Petre	0
Rev. W. H. Richards c J. Boardman b Evans.	2	B 3, l-b 1, w 1	5
A. Frost Esq. b Evans	1		
C. S. Hope Esq. c and b Evans	9		144

MCC Bowling

	Overs	Mdns	Runs	Wkts	Overs	Mdns	Runs	Wkts
A. Shaw	24.3	11	33	9	22.3	12	19	9
Price	24	9	44	1	22	10	30	—

Thorndon Hall Bowling

	Overs	Mdns	Runs	Wkts
Evans	19	5	54	7
T. Nicholas	14	4	28	—
Hon. W. Petre	11	5	22	2
A. Nicholas	5	—	19	—
Baker	3	—	6	1
E. Boardman	1	—	10	—

Umpires: W. Marten and Harris.

(In the second innings of Thorndon Hall, the fifth, sixth, seventh, eighth and ninth wickets all fell with the score at 39.)

ETON v HARROW

Played at Lord's, July 8, 9, 1870

Their Royal Highnesses the Duchess of Cambridge and the Prince and Princess of Teck, with a host of the nobility, honoured this match with their presence at Lord's. The Grand Stand was thronged, a large majority of its occupants being ladies. The Pavilion seats and roof were crowded with members and their friends. "The Ring" was deeper and more densely packed and the outer ring of carriages more extensive than at any preceding match. Such an assemblage of rank, fashion and numbers had never before been seen even at Lord's. It was computed that quite 30,000 visitors attended the ground on those memorable two days; at all events so much as £790 was taken for admission on the Friday and £660 on the Saturday – this £1450 being nearly £200 in excess of any previous receipts for admission to the match. The weather was fortunately favourable and the attendance of ladies commensurately large. Down by Mr Dark's house, up by the NE corner, and fronting the whole row of well known dwarf chestnut trees, the accidental but graceful grouping of ladies elegantly attired, added a picturesque brilliancy to the old ground not seen at other matches. Two sights unusual on cricket grounds and curious by contrast, were witnessed at this match: the first occurred on the Friday, when on the "boys" retiring to luncheon the whole playing area of the ground was covered by a gay company promenading; the other on the Saturday, when on rain commencing falling at noon the youthful cricketers were suddenly surrounded by a dense ring of some thousands of opened umbrellas. Weather, attendances and exciting finish considered, there surely never was played a more successful Eton v Harrow match than this of 1870.

MCC AND GROUND v FIFTEEN WHO HAD NEVER PLAYED AT LORD'S

Played at Lord's, May 8, 9, 10, 1871

This was the opening match of the 85th season of The Marylebone Club and the weather at this opening match too truly foretold what was looming in the future for the Club's 85th season. On the first day there was a violent storm of lightning, thunder, wind and rain; on the second day frequent showers fell and a cold north wind blew; and on the third day it was so nippingly cold as to be more suggestive of February and football than May and maiden overs. The fifteen "who never," etc., were – with an exception or two – the best all-round lot of Freshmen that ever played as "Colts," and "on their merits" they conquered the Club by 34 runs. Richard Humphrey's two innings were displays of cricket so true and good as to win him the unanimous and hearty praise of all the old pro.'s who saw him play. Selby and Eastwood both batted up to County form (the young Nottinghamshire man "played" well), Clayton hit hard for his 20 and so did Coppinger for his 22. Humphrey fielded well at leg and cover-point, so did James Phillips at cover-slip and his brother

Henry at wicket. As bowlers "the strangers" shewed up well, Clayton taking first honours in that department. All told Clayton bowled as follows:

Overs	Mdns	Runs	Wkts	
85	39	82	6	(all bowled)

In his first innings Mr. Grace was missed at slip from Clayton's bowling when he had scored 3 runs only. Eastwood was not tried as bowler until close on the finish of the match; he commenced with seven successive maiden overs. But the most "effective" bit of bowling was that by young Grundy on the second day; he commenced and continued bowling maiden overs to Mr W. G. Grace, who the young Nottinghamshire man clean bowled in his fifth over; with the following ball he bowled Capt. Slaney and when rain shortly after sent all in, young Grundy had then bowled:

Overs	Mdns	Runs	Wkts	
9	8	1	3	(all bowled)

Grundy's bowling was subsequently hit a bit, and on the third day his bowling was severely thumped; but Grundy deserved Mr Grace's second wicket, as from the third ball he bowled that day Mr Grace was missed at short-leg; indeed, had the first chances given in each innings by Mr Grace been secured, the great batsman would have made only 3 runs in this match. This is the first match wherein John Smith was "bowled" both innings and it is also the first match wherein Alfred Shaw had "a pair of them;" in fact, so solicitous were "the Colts" of improving the sight of "the veterans," that they presented three of the eleven with sight improvers.

The Fifteen

Richard Humphrey (Surrey), c and b Alfred Shaw	34	– c Slaney b Wootton	18
J. Selby (Notts.) b Grace	11	– st Biddulph b Wilkinson	27
Eastwood (Yorks.) c Filgate b Alfred Shaw	16	– b Brune	16
Galpin (Hampshire) b Alfred Shaw	3	– b Brune	2
Berrington (Surrey) c and b Grace	3	– st Biddulph b Wootton	3
Henry Phillips (Sussex) c Filgate b Grace	10	– b Wootton	13
O. Shore, Esq. (Captain) not out	17	– b Brune	5
Howard (Kent) run out	0	– not out	1
W. Lambert (Herts.) lbw b Grace	4	– b Wootton	0
T. Hearne, jun. (Middlesex) c and b Grace	0	– b Brune	6
Jas. Phillips (Sussex) c Biddulph b Grace	3	– b Brune	2
James Grundy jun. (Notts.) b Alfred Shaw	8	– run out	1
W. Buttress (Cambs.) b Alfred Shaw	0	– c Smith b Brune	0
R. Clayton (Yorks.) b Grace	20	– b Brune	9
W. Coppinger (Kent) b Alfred Shaw	1	– b Wootton	22
B 6, w 1	7		
	137		125

MCC and Ground

W. G. Grace Esq. b Grundy	44	– b Buttress	31
John Smith b Galpin	17	– b Clayton	11
C. R. Filgrate Esq. b Galpin	0	– run out	4
A. J. Wilkinson Esq. b Clayton	4	– b Lambert	10
C. P. Coote Esq. b Grundy	10	– b Clayton	23
Capt. Kenyon Slaney b Grundy	0	– b Clayton	0
C. J. Brune Esq. b Grundy	4	– not out	28
J. Fellowes Esq. b Clayton	9	– b Clayton	17
Alfred Shaw run out	0	– c Shore b Coppinger	0
Biddulph b Grundy	0	– b Eastwood	0
Wootton not out	0	– b Eastwood	1
B 2, l-b 1, w 3, n-b 1	7	B 2, l-b 5, w 1	8
	95		133

MCC Bowling

	Overs	Mdns	Runs	Wkts	Overs	Mdns	Runs	Wkts
Mr. Grace	48	24	54	7	11	3	21	—
A. Shaw	48	23	52	6	20	12	13	—
Wooton	15	6	24	—	22	8	37	5
Mr Brune					28.3	14	33	7
Mr Wilkinson					15	5	21	1

The Fifteen's Bowling

	Overs	Mdns	Runs	Wkts	Overs	Mdns	Runs	Wkts
Clayton	42.2	16	49	2	43	23	33	4
Grundy	15	10	10	5	23	8	47	—
Galpin	13	7	13	2	8	4	8	—
Howard	9	3	11	—	6	4	4	—
Buttress	5	3	5	—	11	8	4	1
Eastwood					14.1	11	12	2
Coppinger					12	6	7	1
Lambert					6	2	10	1

Umpires: J. Grundy sen. and Royston.

(17 of "The Club" wickets were "bowled" down.)

GENTLEMEN OF MCC v ROYAL ENGINEERS

Played at Lord's, June 1, 2, 1871

The frightful number of 111 extras were scored in this unfinished match. Capt. Merriman's 38 included a drive for 6, a cut for 5 and three 4s; in scoring that 38, Capt. Merriman made 18 runs by four consecutive hits: to wit, a 6, a 4, a 4 and a 4. Lieut Maxwell's 33 included a drive for 6 and three 4s. Capt. Coningham's 40 included a cut for 5; and in Lieut Tailyour's 89 there were six 3s, eight 4s and one 5. Lieut Tailyour and Capt. Coningham increased the second innings of RE from 13 for two wickets to 134 for three wickets. For MCC Mr Pauncefote made 44, an innings that included a drive for 6 and two 4s. Mr Reid played well for his 27 and 49 not out; and Col Parnell commenced his innings of 41 in such telling form that the first six hits booked to him were – a 3, a 3, a 3, a 4, a 5 and a 3.

Royal Engineers

Lieut F. Maxwell c Blois b Coote	33	– c and b Blois	0
Capt. Jopp b Blois	0	– c Sutton b Blois	4
Lieut Renny-Tailyour b Blois	6	– c Wright b Blois	89
Capt. Conningham b Coote	0	– b Coote	40
Lieut L. K. Scott c Sutton b Rose	17	– b Blois	0
Lieut Edwardes c Rose	6	– b Coote	3
Lieut H. Mitchell b Rose	21	– b Coote	18
Capt. Merriman c Pauncefote b Blois	38	– b Ward	10
Capt. Maitland b Blois	2	– c and b Ward	16
Lieut F. B. D'Aguilar c Parnell b Blois	0	– not out	21
Lieut H. Clarke lbw b Blois	0	– st Reid b Ward	6
Lieut Addison not out	1	– run out	2
B 17, l-b 3, w 4	24	B 13, l-b 3, w 8	24
	148		233

MCC

J. Jardine Esq. c Scott b Tailyour	2	– b D'Aguilar	2
G. Wright Esq. b Tailyour	3		
C. P. Coote Esq. b D'Aguilar	1	– b Coningham	38
B. Pauncefote Esq. c and b Scott	44	– not out	2
E. G. Sutton Esq. run out	20		
C. H. Hamilton Esq. b Tailyour	17		
Lieut-Col Parnell b D'Aguilar	41		
R. T. Reid Esq. b D'Aguilar	27	– not out	49
Sir John Blois run out	4		
C. K. Rose Esq. b D'Aguilar	2		
R. J. Ward Esq. not out	0		
— Wadeson Esq. absent	—		
B 18, l-b 8, w 21	47	B 12, l-b 4	16
	208		107

Umpires: Wootton and Walter Price.

MCC AND GROUND v GLOUCESTERSHIRE

Played at Lord's, June 5, 6, 1871

In this match Mr W. Grace was (of course) opposed to the old Club. The Shire's eleven included "the four Grace's," this being the only London match wherein the Londoners' hard hitting old favourite, Dr E. M. Grace, played last season. Although no great score was knocked up by either side, some big hits were made. Mr Strachan made a drive for 7 from Farrands; Mr W. Grace in his two innings made four 5s and as many 4s; Dr Grace made a drive for 5 from Shaw; Mr Filgate made a 5, so did Mr Coote; and John Smith hit one 5 and five 4s in his two innings. The Club played seven professionals, but although MCC made so close a fight of it that the first innings ended in "a tie," the Shire eventually defeated the Club by five wickets. West's little bit of bowling reads well – a trifle more than one run per over and three good wickets, two "bowled".

MCC and Ground

D. R. Onslow Esq. b W. Grace	0	– b E. M. Grace	0
John Smith run out	21	– b Strachan	24
J. S. Martin Esq. b W. Grace	8	– st Bush b W. Grace	27
Alfred Shaw c W. Grace b Miles	1	– b E. M. Grace	9
C. P. Coote Esq. b E. M. Grace	35	– b Strachan	1
Walter Price c Filgate b Miles	4	– b W. Grace	24
— Ward Esq. b G. F. Grace	6	– b E. M. Grace	0
John West b E. M. Grace	12	– b Strachan	0
Biddulph run out	9	– c and b W. Grace	4
Wootton c Gordon b G. F. Grace	2	– c G. F. Grace b Strachan	0
Farrands not out	0	– not out	0
B 14, w 1	15	B 1	1
	113		90

Gloucestershire

Dr E. M. Grace b Alfred Shaw	16 – b West	11
W. G. Grace Esq. lbw b Farrands	49 – not out	34
C. Gordon Esq. st Biddulph b Alfred Shaw	1 – b Alfred Shaw	1
G. F. Grace Esq. c Price b Farrands	12 – b West	0
C. R. Filgate Esq. b Alfred Shaw	2 – c Alfred Shaw b West	33
G. Strachan Esq. not out	17 – run out	6
A. J. Bush Esq. ht wkt b Alfred Shaw	1 – not out	4
H. Grace Esq. b Farrands	0	
T. G. Matthews Esq. b Farrands	0	
R. F. Miles Esq. b Farrands	3	
D. Macpherson Esq. b Farrands	0	
B 5, l-b 7	12	B 2, l-b 1 3
	113	92

Gloucestershire Bowling

	Overs	Mdns	Runs	Wkts	Overs	Mdns	Runs	Wkts
Mr W. Grace	21	9	29	2	3.1	2	4	3
Mr Miles	21	5	38	2				
Dr Grace	15	9	11	2	19	1	43	3
Mr G. F. Grace	14.3	7	20	2	4	—	13	—
Mr Strachan					18	5	29	4

MCC Bowling

	Overs	Mdns	Runs	Wkts	Overs	Mdns	Runs	Wkts
Shaw	36	21	35	4	30	12	37	1
Farrands	31.3	13	50	6	10	4	18	—
Wootton	6	2	16	—	1.2	—	8	—
West					22	9	26	3

Umpires: J. Grundy sen. and Royston.

MCC AND GROUND v MIDDLESEX

Played at Lord's, June 12, 13, 14, 1871

This was the match of the MCC season 1871 and certainly it is the most extraordinary match ever played at Lord's ground, for in no preceding match on that world famed turf had so many runs been scored before a first wicket fell as the 161 scored by John Smith and Mr W. Grace for MCC's first wicket in this match. On no prior occasion at Lord's had 300 runs been hoisted on the score-boards with only 3 wickets down, as was the case in Middlesex's innings in this match. Never before were so many runs made in an innings at Lord's as Middlesex's 485. In no other match on the old ground has so many as 823 runs been made for two first innings and it is certain that neither on the old ground where Dorset Square now stands, or on the second Lord's ground where North Bank is now situate, nor on the present "Lord's ground," did an MCC eleven ever before make a first innings of 338 runs and then suffer defeat by one innings, as the MCC men did on this memorable occasion.

The match was commenced at 12.15 on the Monday and commenced in characteristic form for MCC by Mr W. Grace and John Smith, who, at twelve minutes past one, or three minutes under the hour, had made the score 100 – Smith 54, Mr Grace 45; at 123 the amateur was "neck and neck" with the professional, as then each batsman had made 61; but from thence the professional took up the running again, as at 150 he was two runs ahead and when at 161 the first MCC wicket fell, by Smith being "c and b" for 81, Mr Grace was 79; to these runs Mr Grace subsequently added a five to leg and four other runs and was then bowled, but none present will easily forget this fine close race in run-getting made by Mr Grace and John Smith. Dinner was called that day with four MCC wickets down, 184 runs scored and 66 overs bowled. After dinner Mr Thornton "hit a bit;" he made two 2s and a 5 from one over of Howitt's, he followed that little lot up with another 5 and in all made 18 runs in eleven minutes. Mr Yardley had made 33 when a splendid catch – very low down – at point settled him, and by good luck, and hitting so hard that his score included a 6, two 5s and five 4s, Mr Cobden took his bat out for 73, the MCC innings being over at twenty minutes past five for 338 runs, the wickets having fallen as follows:

1/161 2/171 3/171 4/184 5/203 6/253 7/254 8/287 9/335 10/338

Then at a quarter to six was commenced the now famous innings of Middlesex and in such striking contrast to the commencement of MCC's, that although Mr Wilkinson got the first ball past the pavilion for 5, the third ball delivered bowled Mr Walker, and the first Middlesex wicket was down for 5 runs; then – at ten minutes to six — Mr Hadow commenced his innings. He and Mr Wilkinson played well and appeared "set" for that evening, when, just prior to "time" being called, Mr Wilkinson was had at wicket, the first day's cricket closing with the Middlesex score as under:

Mr Wilkinson c Biddulph b Riddell	37
Mr I. D. Walker b Farrands	0
Mr Hadow not out	41
B 2, l-b 1	3
	81

On the Tuesday at 12.20 Mr Hadow and Mr Pauncefote renewed the Middlesex innings. Both gentleman "played" great cricket, Mr Hadow "hitting" splendidly; in ten minutes he had increased his score by 15 runs; at twenty eight minutes to one the 100 was up, then Farrands was succeeded by Mr Riddell, Mr Grace bowled v Shaw and Mr Thornton went on v Mr Riddell; but the MCC bowling was then thoroughly mastered and the "hitting" of Mr Hadow a masterpiece. At ten minutes to two Mr Hadow had made 101 (the score 164), eighteen minutes past two the 200 was hoisted and when dinner was called at 2.30 the score was at 216 for two wickets – Mr Hadow 122, and Mr Pauncefote 45. Heavy rain then fell; however, at 3.20 the innings was renewed, but at 3.30 Mr Pauncefote's finely played score was finished by a cool and clever catch by Smith down by the billiard room door, so many as 152 runs having been put on since the fall of the preceding (the second) wicket. Mr Green and Mr Hadow then made the score 300 for three wickets, but before another run was made Farrands bowled Mr Green. At 5.30 a cut for 3 made Mr Hadow's score 200 (the Middlesex score then at 344 for four wickets), but at a quarter to six a catch at long-on by Mr Yardley ended Mr Hadow's innings for 217 runs, the greatest score but one ever made in a first-class match at Lord's. In at ten minutes to six on Monday, with the score at 5 for one wicket, Mr Hadow was out at a quarter to six on the Tuesday, the score at 370 for five wickets. During his innings on Tuesday play was frequently interrupted by rain showers, but his "hitting" was grand and acknowledged by all to have been the finest seen at Lord's by living man, so cool, so clean, so well timed, and so hard was it; and as to Mr Hadow's defence, how steady and perfect that was can be understood from the fact that notwithstanding Alfred Shaw, Farrands, Mr Grace, Mr Cobden, Mr Riddell, and three others, were one or the other pounding away at his stumps for more than five and a half hours, not one of them could bowl him. That his innings was a chanceless one cannot be said, for when he had made 195 runs, he was missed at wicket by Biddulph and at 200 he was missed at square-leg by Smith. Mr Hadow was so lame that during the greater portion of his great innings he had a man to run for him; his hits included four 5s (all off drives), sixteen 4s and – but the following is a faithful record of the hits as consecutively made by Mr Hadow in his memorable innings of 217 runs:

2-3-1-1-1-1-1-2-4-2-3-4-4-1-3-1-1-1-5-1-2-1-2-3-4-2-2-2-1-1-2-4
1-1-4-3-1-1-4-2-4-1-1-1-1-3-3-2-4-1-1-1-1-1-4-5-3-3-1-2-3-4-2-1
1-1-4-1-1-2-1-3-3-1-5-3-1-2-5-3-3-3-4-4-2-4-2-3-2-1-2-2-2-4-3-1

After Mr Hadow left 115 runs were added to the Middlesex score, the MCC men being fagged and thoroughly used up by their long outing that showery afternoon did not field at all well, and runs were rapidly piled up by the Middlesex men. At 6.20 the 400 was up with only six wickets down, but then Mr Strachan was cleverly had at short-left the eighth wicket went at 432, and the ninth at 441. Then it was thought the last wicket would quickly succumb, but there was "no rest for the weary" that evening, as Howitt and Mr Bissett slashed away in their own peculiar hard and fast form. Mr Bissett scored 8 for a drive, Howitt was missed stumping when he had scored 13, and although they played up to 7.30, the tired MCC men could not finish off the innings that evening, play closing with the score at 485 with a wicket to go down, the result of the two days' cricket being:

19 wickets down .... 823 runs scored!!

However, the innings was practically over that evening, for the first ball bowled on the Wednesday Howitt skied; it was easily caught by Price (fielding for Mr Filgate), and so at last was this great innings ended for 485 runs, the wickets having fallen in the following order:

1/5 2/81 3/233 4/300 5/370 6/394 7/400 8/432 9/441 10/485

The showers that fell on Tuesday afternoon and evening were succeeded by a soaking wet night and those best acquainted with the working of the old turf foretold there would be no more long scoring in that match; nor was there, for the wickets that prior to the rain were lively and favourable to batsmen, were on Wednesday dead and all in favour of bowlers and so successful was the slow bowling of Mr E. Rutter that morning, that the eleven who on the Monday occupied the wickets from 12.15 until twenty-three minutes past five and scored 338 runs, were on the Wednesday all got out in two hours for 92 and thereby Middlesex won this wonderful and memorable match by one innings and 55 runs. The number of wickets down in the match were 29, the number of runs made 915 (875 from the bat) and the number of balls bowled 1847. The whole of the hits booked "in the match" are: – One 8, one 7, one 6, fourteen 5s, forty-seven 4s, eighty 3s, seventy-seven 2s and 202 singles. Throughout the country last season Mr Hadow's 217 formed the principal conversational topic among all classes of cricketers and for very many a season yet to come will this great hitting match between Middlesex and Marylebone form one of the most remarkable pages in the history of cricket.

MCC and Ground

W. G. Grace Esq. b Howitt	88	– c Brune b Rutter	10
John Smith c and b Rutter	81	– c Howitt b Rutter	20
C. R. Filgate Esq. b Howitt	10	– b Howitt	16
J. W. Dale Esq. c I. D. Walker b Howitt	0	– c Strachan b Howitt	5
W. Yardley Esq. c V. E. Walker b Strachan	33	– b Howitt	3
C. I. Thornton Esq. c Strachan b Rutter	18	– absent	—
F. C. Cobden Esq. not out	73	– c Pauncefote b Rutter	23
E. M. Riddell Esq. b Brune	0	– c and b Rutter	4
Alfred Shaw b Howitt	15	– c I. D. Walker b Rutter	2
Biddulph c Bissett b Brune	9	– c I. D. Walker b Rutter	0
Farrands st Bissett b Rutter	3	– not out	6
B 4, l-b 1, w 3	8	B 3	3
	338		92

Middlesex

A. J. Wilkinson Esq. c Biddulph b Riddell	37	V. E. Walker Esq. b Farrands	20
I. D. Walker Esq. b Farrands	0	E. Rutter Esq. b Farrands	12
W. H. Hadow Esq. c Yardley b Alfred Shaw	217	R. Bissett Esq. not out	28
B. Pauncefote Esq. c Smith b Farrands	55	Howitt c Price (for Filgate) b Farrands	22
C. E. Green Esq. b Farrands	25	B 15, l-b 7, w 7	29
G. Strachan Esq. c Alfred Shaw b Cobden	33		
C. J. Brune Esq. c Cobden b Alfred Shaw	7		485

Middlesex Bowling

	Overs	Mdns	Runs	Wkts	Overs	Mdns	Runs	Wkts
Howitt	44	10	131	4	18.2	9	25	3
Mr Rutter	43	20	84	3	35	20	43	6
Mr Strachan	29	10	57	1	17	6	21	—
Mr Brune	20	6	58	2				

MCC Bowling

	Overs	Mdns	Runs	Wkts
Farrands	85.1	34	171	6
Shaw	83	42	114	2
Mr Grace	34	13	51	—
Mr Cobden	16	6	30	1
Mr Riddell	15	4	33	1
Mr Thornton	10	3	23	—
Mr Yardley	7	—	24	—
Mr Dale	5	3	10	—

Umpires: Thos. Hearne and Wootton.

THE THREE LARGEST INNINGS YET PLAYED AT LORD'S

In 1820	In 1815	In 1871
MCC .473	Epsom .476	Middlesex .485
(Mr W. W. Ward, 278)	(Mr Ladbrooke, 116; Mr Woodbridge, 107)	(Mr Hadow, 217)

MCC AND GROUND v HUNTINGDONSHIRE

Played at Lord's, July 31 and August 1, 1871

This match was over at a quarter past four on the second day, the Club the winners by an innings and 50 runs; the three ground-men – Hearne, Price, and West – having made 187 runs, or more than were made from the bat in the Shire's two innings. Mr Tobin and Mr Harbord made 23 before the first Huntingdonshire wicket fell and 46 runs were scored when their fourth wicket went, but the fifth, sixth, seventh and eighth all fell at 55 and the innings ended for 58. In the Shire's second innings Mr Harbord and Mr Fowler increased the score from 62 for five wickets to 111 for 6, but the eleven were out for 139. MCC did not commence their innings very hopefully, as they had lost three wickets when 29 runs had been made; but Hearne and Price put more than 100 runs on for the next wicket, as the score was at 137 when Price was out for 54, an innings that included six 4s and five 3s. From 174 Hearne and West increased the score to 235 and the Club's innings ended for 247, Hearne having made 108 by a leg-hit to the bat stacks for 6 (lost ball cried when 5 had been run), a 5, four 4s, etc. The Rev. H. Harbord played two good innings for Huntingdonshire; his 44 included a hit for 5 and two 4s.

Huntingdonshire

F. Tobin Esq. lbw b Hearne	13	– lbw b Price	12
J. Linton Esq. st Round b Hearne	8	– b Price	4
Rev. H. Harbord c and b Hearne	20	– b West	44
F. Safford Esq. b Hearne	1	– run out	3
W. Vyse Esq. b Price	8	– b Price	11
S. Pearson Esq. c Round b Price	2	– c Price	7
A. Tillard Esq. c and b Price	0	– not out	0
T. F. Fowler Esq. c Round b Price	0	– b Price	23
J. Ponsonby Esq. b Price	0	– b West	8
C. Burnett Esq. b Hearne	1	– c and b Price	9
H. Nixon not out	2	– c and b Price	6
L-b 3	3	B 8, l-b 3, w 1	12
	58		139

MCC and Ground

A. F. Jeffreys Esq. c Burnett b Nixon	5
H. J. Hill Esq. run out	7
J. S. Udal Esq. c Vyse b Burnett	17
Thomas Hearne c Salford b Nixon	108
Walter Price c Fowler b Nixon	54
A. R. Hawkins Esq. c Ponsonby b Nixon	15
J. Round Esq. b Nixon	2
G. Wright Esq. c Harbord b Nixon	0
G. A. Dawson Esq. b Nixon	0
John West c Fowler b Nixon	25
G. A. Reid Esq. not out	7
B 4, l-b 2, w 1	7
	247

MCC Bowling

	Overs	Mdns	Runs	Wkts	Overs	Mdns	Runs	Wkts
Hearne	26	15	19	5	26	8	49	—
Price	25.3	12	36	5	42.2	22	51	7
West					16	8	27	2

Huntingdonshire Bowling

Nixon (the bowler at Cambridge) bowled 54 overs and three balls (24 Maiden overs) for 76 runs and eight wickets, but the remainder of the Huntingdonshire bowling could not be accurately ascertained.

Umpires: Jordan and Barber.

THE CANTERBURY WEEK

August 10th, 1871

Thursday – The Ladies' Day – was one of those bright, cloudless, hot days, that in August last so frequently gladdened the hearts of farmers, tourists and pleasure-seekers. When the cricket commenced the company present hardly warranted expectations of an assemblage up to the usual Thursday magnitude, but from noon to four p.m. visitors arrived in large numbers. Four-in-hands skilfully tooled, old fashioned family carriages whisked along in the old fashioned 4-horse postillion form, new fashioned breaks and waggonettes, dashing dog-carts, tandems, 'busses and other vehicles, all of them fully, most of them fairly, freighted, rattled up the incline of the fine old ground one after the other in such numbers, that when the rush was over and all were settled in picturesque groups, when the little slope was covered by brightly toileted ladies, when the promenade was thronged by a gay company and when the ring around the ground was fully formed, it was unanimously acknowledged that the gathering was the gayest, the most numerous and influential ever seen at a cricket match at St. Lawrence. Truly was this "The Ladies' Day," for of the 7000 visitors present "the better half" were ladies, whose presence so very much enhanced the beauty of that charming, animated picture of English summer life.

"THE BIG WICKETS"

THE FIRST ELEVEN OF MCC AND GROUND v THE NEXT TWENTY

Played at Lord's, May 9, 1872

This was an experimental match, wherein wickets were used one inch higher, one inch wider, and somewhat thicker than the orthodox 27 by eight. Rylott was the only bowler who hit the big (and ugly) wickets in the Eleven's innings, but Alfred Shaw bowled eight of "The next Twenty". The extra inches did not in the least affect the batting of Mr Grace or Mr Dale, who commenced the Eleven's innings and made 63 runs before a wicket fell, Mr Dale then being had at wicket for a splendidly played 31, and Mr Grace being out at 75 through an admirably waited-for catch at deep square-leg by Mr Udal. A fine ball indeed bowled John Smith, but the other batsmen – at their best – lacked form to fairly test the experiment. Rylott bowled out and out well, all the runs scored from him being singles barring a 4 to leg by Mr Jeffreys. Alfred Shaw's bowling "worked" in capital form, as he had eleven wickets out of the nineteen, and wound up so successfully that he took Barratt's, Mike Flanagan's, and Clayton's wickets with the last three balls he delivered; Shaw's last four overs (of five balls) being bowled for 2 runs (singles), and six wickets. Mr Grace hit a ball from Barratt to square-leg over the Grand Stand for 6; and in Mr Dale's very finely "played" 31 there was a splendid on-drive to the Armoury for 5, and an equally good hit to square-leg for 4. The early portion of the match was played to an accompaniment of thunder, and so piercingly cold and rheumatically strong did the wind blow, that when, at ten minutes past five, Alfred Shaw had so summarily settled the tail of "The Twenty," it was wisely resolved to play no more in such weather, so, to the gratifying comfort of all, the big sticks were forthwith pulled up, and the experimental match ended with the following score:

The Eleven

W. G. Grace Esq. c Udal b Barratt	41
J. W. Dale Esq. c Biddulph b Barratt	31
C. P. Coote Esq. run out	2
John Smith b Rylott	0
E. G. Sutton Esq. b Rylott	6
C. J. Brune Esq. c Eldon b Barratt	2
A. F. Jeffreys Esq. c Flanagan b Barratt	5
John West c and b Rylott	1
W. M. Rose Esq. st Biddulph b Barratt	0
Alfred Shaw b Rylott	5
F. Farrands not out	3
B 2, w 1	3
	99

The Twenty

A. E. Crafter Esq. b Alfred Shaw	9
W. Churchill Esq. run out	4
Capt. Kenyon Slaney b Rose	2
Capt. Beecher c Brune b Rose	3
Visc. Bernard b Alfred Shaw	0
J. S. Udal Esq. c Dale b Rose	14
Rylott b Alfred Shaw	0
R. A. FitzGerald Esq. b Alfred Shaw	5
Capt. Battye b Rose	1
E. A. Bullock Esq. st Grace b Rose	1
H. Brand Esq. b Alfred Shaw	1
Earl of Eldon c and b Rose	2
Hon. E. Byng c and b Alfred Shaw	2
A. Guest Esq. b Alfred Shaw	0
R. Ward Esq. b Rose	1
J. P. Salomons Esq. b Alfred Shaw	0
Biddulph not out	1
Barratt c and b Alfred Shaw	0
Flanagan b Alfred Shaw	0
R. Clayton c Grace b Alfred Shaw	0
	46

The Bowling of The Twenty

	Overs	Mdns	Runs	Wkts
Rylott	18.3	8	15	4
Barratt	19	4	45	5
Flanagan	9	4	20	—
Clayton	9	3	16	—

The Bowling of The Eleven

	Overs	Mdns	Runs	Wkts
A. Shaw	19	5	25	11
Mr Rose	18	8	21	7

(Being a one day match they bowled 5 balls per over.)

Umpires: Walter Price and G. Nixon (Cambs.).

MCC AND GROUND v THE COUNTY OF SURREY

Played at Lord's, May 14, 1872

This was the most remarkable match of the MCC season. Seven MCC wickets, including the crack's being got rid of before a run was scored. Eight 0's were booked in that innings of MCC's, whose Eleven were out in three-quarters of an hour for a total of 16 runs. 19 was the highest score made in the match, which was commenced at ten past twelve, and concluded at twenty minutes to seven; the whole number of runs made in the match being 175, and that, too, notwithstanding such batsmen as Mr W. Grace, Jupp, John Smith, Richard Humphrey, Pooley, T. Hearne, T. Humphrey, and Mr L. S. Howell had played their two innings.

Incessant rain from dawn to dusk on the 13th (the day set to commence the match) necessitated a postponement until the following day, when on dead, deceitful playing wickets, and in a queer light for batting, Mr W. Grace and John Smith commenced (!) MCC's marvellous little innings of 16 runs, wherein seven of the wickets (including the crack's) went down before a run was scored in this form:– To the fourth ball delivered Mr Grace was lbw; from the sixth ball Smith was caught out by long-stop; the fifteenth ball shot down Mr Coote's wicket, and the twenty-second bowled Shaw. From the twenty-third ball Mr Onslow was smartly had at mid-off; the thirty-fifth thoroughly beat and bowled Mr Brune, and the very next ball slick bowled Hearne; seven wickets – and good ones too – in this way falling in twenty-five minutes before a run was scored; the bowling at that phase of the match standing in the score books in the following unique form:–

Southerton	. . . w	. . . .	. . . .	. . . .	. . w w
Marten	. w . .	. . w .	. w w .	. . . .	

Captain Beecher then made a 2 from the first ball of Marten's fifth over, but in Southerton's sixth over (another maiden) a clever catch by Pooley got rid of Biddulph; then Captain Beecher made his score 8, when a truly splendid left-hand catch – low down – by Marten settled him; Captain Beecher (ninth man out) having made all the runs (8) then scored for the Club. When Rylott and Howitt had doubled the score Marten bowled Howitt, and so, in exactly forty-five minutes, were the MCC. Eleven out for an innings of 16 runs, their wickets having fallen in the following curious form:–

1/0 2/0 3/0 4/0 5/0 6/0 7/0 8/2 9/8 10/16

At ten minutes past one the Surrey innings was commenced; at 2.30 it was concluded for 49 runs, made from 46 overs (less one ball).

At five minutes past three, the second innings of MCC was commenced by Mr Grace and Mr Onslow; with the score at 21, Mr Onslow was bowled, and at 22, Mr Grace was bowled. John Smith made 19 – the top score in the match; but at 5.30, the innings was over for 71 runs, made from 77 overs (less one ball).

At a quarter to six, Jupp and R. Humphrey commenced Surrey's second innings, and at twenty minutes to seven, the county had won by five wickets; but if Captain Beecher had not missed R. Humphrey when he had scored only 3 runs, and Mr Howell when he had scored but 2, the probability was the match would have been a very close affair.

MCC and Ground

W. G. Grace Esq. lbw b Southerton	0	– b Southerton	11
John Smith c Jupp b Marten	0	– st Pooley b Southerton	19
C. P. Coote Esq. b Marten	0	– b Strachan	9
C. J. Brune Esq. b Southerton	0	– c Howell b Southerton	6
Alfred Shaw b Marten	0	– c Jupp b Southerton	8
D. R. Onslow Esq. c Strachan b Marten	0	– b Southerton	10
Capt. Beecher c and b Marten	8	– b Hall	5
T. Hearne sen. b Southerton	0	– st Pooley b Southerton	0
Biddulph c Pooley b Southerton	0	– b Strachan	2
Rylott not out	6	– st Pooley b Southerton	0
Howitt b Marten	2	– not out	0
		W 1	1
	16		71

Surrey

Jupp b Alfred Shaw	4	– c Grace b Howitt	3
Richard Humphrey run out	7	– not out	12
T. Palmer c Grace b Rylott	2	– b Howitt	1
Pooley c Biddulph b Howitt	12	– c and b Howitt	12
G. Strachan, Esq. run out	5	– c Rylott b Alfred Shaw	1
Thomas Humphrey c and b Rylott	3	– c Beecher b Howitt	0
L. S. Howell Esq. b Howitt	7	– not out	9
C. Hall b Howitt	4		
Wheeler run out	3		
W. Marten c and b Howitt	1		
Southerton not out	0		
B 1	1	Lb 1	1
	49		39

Surrey Bowling

	Overs	Mdns	Runs	Wkts	Overs	Mdns	Runs	Wkts
Southerton	9	6	5	4	38.3	22	38	7
Marten	9	5	11	6	21	13	21	—
Mr Strachen					10	7	7	2
Hall					7	4	4	1

MCC Bowling

	Overs	Mdns	Runs	Wkts	Overs	Mdns	Runs	Wkts
A. Shaw	23	14	18	1	17	5	23	1
Rylott	14	5	24	2				
Howitt	8.3	5	6	4	17	7	15	4

Umpires: H. Royston and G. Wootton.

ENGLAND v NOTTINGHAMSHIRE AND YORKSHIRE

Played at Lord's, July 8 and 9, 1872

"Mr Grace First: – The Rest No Where." – Such was the brief emphatic verdict pronounced by an old cricketer on the wonderful innings played by the great batsman in this match. This record requires a more extended notice of this extraordinary "bit of batting", and to the best of the compiler's ability it shall have one.

The match was one of the novelties of the MCC season, and doubtless would have attracted larger audiences had the weather been more favourable and each side played its full strength; but the weather was dull, cold, and wet. Daft did not play for The Counties, and other engagements prevented Mr I. D. Walker, Mr Yardley, Mr Hornby and Mr Ottaway playing for England. At 12.15 Mr W. Grace and Jupp opened England's innings to the bowling of J. C. Shaw and Hill, and when one run only had been scored Pinder stumped Jupp, who was succeeded by young Humphrey; he stayed well, and played well; and despite J. C. Shaw, Hill, Emmett, Alfred Shaw and McIntyre, all took a turn at him, he did his share in increasing the score from 1 to 77, when McIntyre bowled him (off his leg) for 34 – in scoring which Humphrey had made four 4s. Carpenter was next man in; he and the crack rapidly made up the 100, and then so rapidly added another half-hundred that when luncheon time – 2.30 – came the score boards told the following tale:— two wickets down, 150 runs scored, Mr Grace 87 not out, and Carpenter 29 not out. (78 overs had then been bowled). On renewing play they made the score 177, when Carpenter was had by the wicket-keeper for 36 – the second highest score made for England, and one that included a 4 to leg from McIntyre, and a very fine off-drive for 4 to the wood stacks from J. C. Shaw. Mr F. Grace had made 6 only when he was caught out at point, the score at 197; and when Pooley had made a dozen he was bowled off his thigh by McIntyre, half the wickets then being down and 225 runs scored. Then Roger Iddison went on with lobs, and with the first six of these he had three wickets; the first, a full pitch, getting Smith caught out at short-leg, the fifth causing Tom Hearne to be had at point, and from the following ball Lillywhite was "c and b;" of course Roger was jubilant at such success – what bowler would not be? But his next batch of lobs was tremendously thrashed by Mr Grace, who by a 2, a 6 (2 overthrow), a 2, and a 3 actually made 13 runs from that over. However, at 289 Southerton was grandly stumped by Pinder (who took the ball leg side), and at 290 Rylott was c and b, and so the innings ended at twelve minutes past five, the great batsman not out 170.

Mr W. Grace was first man in at a quarter past twelve; when 100 runs had been made, at five minutes to two, Mr Grace had made 51; (when he had scored 72 he was nearly had at short-leg by Emmett, and when his score was 141 the same man nearly had him at point); when the 200 runs were hoisted Mr Grace's score was 124; when half the wickets were down for 225 he had made 135; when the eighth man was out, and the score at 264, Mr Grace had made 151 of those runs, and when the innings was up with the total 290 – 283 from the bat, Mr Grace had scored 170, or 57 more than his 10 colleagues had collectively contributed. He commenced that innings with a single from J. C. S.; he concluded it with a drive for 4 from Iddison. The hits that made up this wonderful innings of 170 runs, were – 31 singles, seventeen 2s, fourteen 3s, nine 4s, three 5s and two 6s – one a splendid straight drive to the northern wall from Emmett. The 5s were all drives and great ones, two from Alfred Shaw and one from Emmett, and the nine 4s included five drives; so those not present can readily realise what a splendid, magnificant driving display this 170 of the great batsman's was, and how lustily and long he was cheered by those that were present.

The Counties' first innings was commenced by Bignall and Emmett to the bowling of Southerton and Rylott. After making two singles, a 2, a 3, and a 4, Emmett lifted two successively bowled balls high to square-leg, where Hearne missed the first and caught the second, and as Southerton immediately after bowled Rowbotham there were two wickets down for 14 runs (the first fell at 13). Oscroft and Bignall then made the score 89, when play ceased for the day – Bignall not out 34, Oscroft not out 33.

On Tuesday the two Notts men renewed the innings to the bowling of the two Sussex men – Southerton and Lillywhite, and after being twenty minutes at wickets for two singles, Oscroft was had at slip – the score 103; at 104 Lockwood was bowled, and at 105 McIntyre was had at wicket. Bignall and Iddison made it 134, when a catch at long-field settled Bignall for a hard hitting innings of 74 runs; Bignall was first man in, and sixth out with the score 134; he was missed by Mr F. Grace when he had made 26, and subsequently he hoisted one or two that should have been secured but were not; his hits included six 4s, principally drives. Alfred Shaw was bowled at 136, but Iddison and Hill made the score 157, when both had to leave; the two last of the Counties' men – Pinder and J. C. Shaw – then merrily rattled the runs up to 175. J. C. by two 4s and a 3 (all from Rylott) making eleven in eight hits, when he was bowled – the innings ending for 175; Southerton having a hand in the break up of eight of the 10 wickets. At twenty-two minutes past two the second innings of the Counties was started by Bignall and Rowbotham, but a heavy rainfall from 2.30 until 3.30 made the ground queer all round for cricket; however, they went at it again at 4 o'clock; Rowbotham was done with at 37, and at 72 Bignall was had at cover-point – he having made 47 runs in fifty-eight minutes; his brace of innings being the two highest made for the Counties. Lockwood and Oscroft, by excellent cricket, then made the score 104, when Oscroft had to leave; and when Lockwood had made 33 (so steadily that his hits included so many as 17 singles) five wickets fell with astounding rapidity; Lockwood was snapped at wicket with the score at 118, Iddison bowled and McIntyre caught out at 119, and Alfred Shaw and Hill settled at long-off and slip at 120. Then Pinder and Emmett rapidly increased the score to 163, when Pinder was caught out at long-on, and at 168 Southerton bowled J. C. Shaw, thereby ending the innings at nine minutes to seven – Emmett not out 27; a hard driving innings that included three 4s and three 3s.

England then required 54 runs to win the match; they commenced at three minutes past seven, and being desirous of finishing that evening they played on to the – at Lord's – unprecedentedly late time of five minutes to eight, when England had won by nine wickets.

England

W. G. Grace Esq. (1st man in), not out	170		
Jupp st Pinder b J. C. Shaw	0		
Richard Humphrey b McIntyre	34	– not out	16
R. Carpenter c Pinder b Alfred Shaw	36		
G. F. Grace Esq. c Emmett b Alfred Shaw	6	– not out	11
Pooley b McIntyre	12		
John Smith c J. C. Shaw b Iddison	10		
Thos Hearne sen. c Alfred Shaw b Iddison	10		
James Lillywhite c and b Iddison	0	– st Pinder b Alfred Shaw	29
Southerton st Pinder b McIntyre	5		
Rylott c and b J. C. Shaw	0		
B 5, lb 2	7		
	290		56

Nottinghamshire and Yorkshire

Bignall c F. Grace b Southerton	74	– c Humphrey b Southerton	47
Emmett c Hearne b Southerton	11	– not out	27
Rowbotham b Southerton	0	– c Carpenter b Southerton	17
Wm Oscroft c Southerton b Lillywhite	35	– st Pooley b Southerton	15
Ephraim Lockwood b Southerton	0	– c Pooley b Lillywhite	33
Martin McIntyre c Pooley b Lillywhite	0	– b Lillywhite	5
Roger Iddison c Southerton b Lillywhite	16	– b Southerton	0
Alfred Shaw b Lillywhite	0	– c W. Grace b Southerton	1
Allen Hill c Southerton b Rylott	9	– c F. Grace b Lillywhite	0
Pinder not out	7	– c F. Grace b Southerton	15
J. C. Shaw b Southerton	11	– b Southerton	5
B 9, l-b 2, w 1	12	B 1, l-b 2	3
	175		168

The Counties Bowling

	Overs	Mdns	Runs	Wkts	Overs	Mdns	Runs	Wkts
Alfred Shaw	36	18	58	2	16	7	28	1
J. C. Shaw	31	11	67	2	15.3	7	28	—
McIntyre	30	9	47	3				
Emmett	21	4	60	—				
Hill	11	2	25	—				
Iddison	4	—	26	3				

England Bowling

	Overs	Mdns	Runs	Wkts	Overs	Mdns	Runs	Wkts
Southerton	53.1	28	66	5	47.1	13	84	7
Lillywhite	32	16	37	4	25	8	48	3
Rylott	16	5	36	1	22	6	33	—
Mr F. Grace	12	5	20	—				
Hearne	3	2	4	—				

Umpires: Wootton and Barratt.

ETON v HARROW

Played at Lord's July 12 and 13, 1872

Never before was congregated on Lord's Ground so numerous and brilliant a company as that which on the 12th of last July crushed and crowded on to that famous cricket arena to witness the first day's play in this, "the fashionable match of the season." Every seat in the spacious grand stand had been secured several days prior to the match, and up to the close of the day preceding, applications for "seats in the stand" were continuously arriving. On "the day before the battle commenced," so extensive a use had been made of members' privileges in regard to standing room for their carriages, and so numerous had been the applications from non-members for space for their vehicles, that every available foot of the old ground set apart for carriage standing was secured; so, in order to lessen public disappointment as much as possible, the Committee caused to be inserted in the morning journals of Friday the following:

Notice.

"In consequence of the great number of applications for carriages on the part of the members, the Committee regret that they will be unable to accommodate any more visitors' carriages to-day at Lord's Ground.

By order of the Committee,

Lord's Ground, July 12 R. A. FitzGerald, Secretary, MCC"

The crush at the gates on the first day was great and lasting beyond all precedent, the crowd waiting their turn to pay and pass on to the ground extending in a line some distance up St. John's Wood Road, and for hours the "clack" "clack" of the turnstiles resounded as rapidly and as regularly as the men in the two boxes could take the admission shillings. On the Saturday, the storms that fell at mid-day doubtless deterred hundreds from visiting Lord's; but when all was over, the tell-tales notified that

On the Friday,	and	On the Saturday,
16,450 visitors had paid and passed through the turnstiles		11,005 visitors had paid and passed through the turnstiles

The number that paid on the Friday exceeded by nearly 3,000 those that paid on the first day of the match in 1871, and although the number paying on the second day was about 130 fewer than on the second day in '71, the aggregate numbers that paid on the two days was considerably greater, and by those best qualified to ascertain, it was computed that – Club members and carriage company included – there were 38,000 visitors on Lord's Ground during the two days of the Eton and Harrow match of 1872.

Friday was a superb day for cricket and other out-door pleasures, and when about 5.30 that afternoon The Prince and Princess of Wales and Prince Arthur came on the ground, the scene at old Lord's was indeed "splendid." Grand stand, pavilion, carriages, and the space between the carriages and ropes set apart for visitors on foot were all as crowded as they possibly could be. The four-in-hand enclosure at the top end of the pavilion was packed with drags, not one of which had room for another outside passenger; and stand, drags, and carriages were all made bright and glorious by a crowd and wealth of brilliantly attired beauteous women, such as can be seen nowhere out of grumbling but glorious Old England. Some disturbance after the conclusion of the match led to the publication of the following letter in Bell's Life in London of July 19th:

> "Mr Editor: The committee regret that notwithstanding all their efforts to prevent a scene of confusion at the termination of the Schools match, their efforts were frustrated by the unseemly conduct of some persons on the ground. Such scenes as those witnessed on Saturday would not occur if the partisans of both schools would assist the authorities in checking the immoderate expression of feeling at the conclusion of the match. The committee appeal to the old and young members of the two schools to assist them in future in preventing a repetition of such disorder which must inevitably end in a discontinuance of the match.
>
> By order of the committee,
>
> R. A. FitzGerald, Secretary, MCC"

Etonians do not reckon this match as one of the regular series: Harrovians argue that it should be so reckoned.

THE CANTERBURY WEEK

August 6th, 7th, 8th, 9th, 10th, 1872

The Canterbury Week of 1872 was commenced in a rain storm, continued in a thunder storm and concluded in a wind storm. That week's weather will not easily be forgotten by "the strangers that were within the gates" of the old clerical city. On Monday, the fifth (the Bank Holiday?), it rained so persistently the whole day, that no cricket was played. On Thursday, the eighth, a rain storm in the morning so swamped the ground that fresh wickets had to be pitched to continue the match commenced the preceding day, and visitors on the ground that Thursday partook of luncheon to the accompaniments of fierce rainfalls, vivid lightning flashes, and distant thunder peals; and the week's cricket was tempestuously wound up on the afternoon of Saturday, the tenth, with a characteristically strong combination of wind and wet. But this is only one side of the picture; per contra, there was a pleasant day on Tuesday, the sixth, an agreeably fine afternoon and evening on "The Ladies' Day", and an enjoyably bright day on Friday, the ninth, – the large companies present on the ground when it was fine unmistakably indicating that, had all been bright and fair, the attendance in 1872 would have – in numbers and brilliancy – surpassed the gay gatherings on St. Lawrence's Ground of all preceding Canterbury Cricket Weeks. But unpleasant weather was not the only disappointment visitors suffered – several cricketing celebrities announced to play could not. Dr E. M. Grace was unable to journey south (the Doctor is a great favourite at Canterbury); Mr Dale could not play; Mr Mitchell was too unwell to take part in the great match; the visit to Canada prevented several promised visits to Canterbury; Mr W. Grace was compelled to leave ere his match was finished; and the two crack slow bowlers of England – Southerton and Alfred Shaw – were absent through illness. These important voids in the teams for the match of the week were filled by Mr Tennent, Hearne, Bignall, Charlwood, Morley and Andrew Greenwood, the two last named being "Colts at Canterbury"; and it is a pleasure to have to record that both Colts made successful débuts on the famous old ground. But why Charlwood was left out of the originally selected South Eleven the cricketing public could not understand, for few, very few, excel him as a run-getter and run-saver combined. However, the ranks were duly filled up and all were ready to commence the annual Canterbury Cricket Autumn Manoeuvres.

On Monday morning rain fell from morn to eve and cricket on that day was so obviously impracticable, that they did not pitch the wickets; but

On Tuesday the weather was favourable and in the afternoon the attendance up at St. Lawrence was large, fashionable and influential, many of the magnates of the county being present, including an unusually large number of ladies, whose bright and many coloured costumes set the pleasantly located ground off in its best and most attractive form. The stiff breeze from the west that had blown over the ground throughout the morning sufficiently counteracted the effects of Monday's heavy rainfalls, to enable them to commence, at ten minutes past eleven, cricket for the week with

NORTH v SOUTH

The South commenced the batting with Jupp and R. Humphrey, the North bowlers at starting being J. C. Shaw and Lockwood. (Here it is as well to state that all hits to the seated visitors counted 4 and were not run out, hence so very many 4s were made.) From the third ball delivered Humphrey was run out, and the seventh ball glanced from Jupp's thigh and whipped the off bail from his wicket, the first Southern wicket going with the score 0, and the second for 4 (a leg-hit by Jupp). Mr Fryer and Mr I. D. Walker stayed; Morley went on to bowl v Lockwood, and the score to 37, when Shaw bowled down the middle stump of Mr Walker's wicket. Then a stirring Kentish cheer notified Mr Thornton's walk to the wickets and "I hope he will do 50", exclaimed one of the many admirers of hard hitting present; but the 50 did not come off, for when, by a brace of 4's and a 2 (all leg-hits and all from J. C. Shaw) Mr Thornton had made 10 runs in five minutes, Shaw bowled him. On Charlwood going to Mr Fryer's aid, the North bowling was mastered. Morley was succeeded by Emmett, Shaw gave up the ball to McIntyre and as 13 runs were made from three overs of Emmett's, he was supplanted by Lockwood; nevertheless, the score increased to 105, when Charlwood was smartly had at wicket by Pinder for 20. Mr Grace having arrived, then went in (the score at five wickets down for 105 runs); but when only three more runs had been made, Mr Fryer was easily had at cover-point for 55, an innings that eminently merited the hearty applause that was awarded it from all on the ground. It was twelve minutes past eleven before a run was scored for the South, Mr Fryer was sixth out at twelve minutes to one with the score at 108; his 55 included eleven 4s – eight of those 4s being successive hits and there can be no doubt that bowling and fielding being duly considered, this 55 was the best amateur innings played during the week. A clever – a very clever catch at mid-off, by Daft, soon settled Pooley and the second ball Hearne received he played on. Mr Grace had a life at leg from Mr Tennent, but was had at long-on, by Emmett, for a badly played 15. Then four more runs only were made when a very fine left-hand catch – low down – at point, by Carpenter, settled Willsher and finished the South's innings for 131 runs. The wickets fell as follows:

1/0 2/4 3/37 4/47 5/105 6/108 7/122 8/124 9/127 10/131

Daft's fielding was excellent and so was Carpenter's but the cream of the field work in that innings was Greenwood's at long-field; it was really brilliant, and saved the North many runs.

The North's innings was commenced at twenty minutes to two by Bignall and Lockwood, the Southern bowlers being Mr Fryer (round arm medium) and Lillywhite. When Bignall had made 8 runs he gave a chance that both Charlwood and Mr Grace went after; Charlwood let it alone, Mr Grace waited for and missed it; but when he made 18

Bignall was bowled by Lillywhite, who thus inaugurated the somewhat unusual bowling feat of obtaining all the ten wickets of an innings in a top class match. The score was at 34 when Bignall left and Greenwood faced Lockwood, but it was more than three times 34 when those two clipping little Yorkshire batsmen were separated. Greenwood hit freely and scored rapidly; opening with a single, he followed that up with four successive 4s, then he was missed by Mr Grace at mid-off; subsequently he made six more 4s, – four of them successive and very fine hits, and in all he had made 52, when a thorough good catch (so well was it judged and so patiently waited for) at long-field, by Mr Thornton, settled him; how hard Greenwood hit can be realised from the fact that his 52 included ten 4s and how rapidly he scored, as easily estimated, by the knowledge that he made 52 out of the 79 runs scored whilst he was at wickets. Daft was welcomed to wickets with an earnest cheer that told how pleased the men of Kent were to see him once more in flannel on their historically famous cricket ground; he was twenty three minutes before he scored and at 149 lost Lockwood, who was very cleverly had at wicket for 68 – the highest score in the match and one of the most scientific batting displays of the week. First man in Lockwood was third out, the score at 149; Mr Fryer, Lillywhite, Willsher and Mr W. Grace bowled to him; he played them all correctly, and hit them just when and how they should have been hit; he gave no chance until he was settled by a catch at wicket that very few keepers would have secured; his hits included seven 4s – legs, drives and cuts – and when all was over it was the general opinion that the best "played" innings of the week was Lockwood's 68. But neither the fine batting nor the effective scoring of the Northerners was over when little Lockwood left, as on Carpenter taking the vacant wicket he and Daft made another great stand; they scored slowly at first, but eventually hit freely and finely, and despite the bowling of Lillywhite, Mr Grace, Hearne, Willsher, Mr Fryer, Mr Thornton and Mr Walker they put on 113 runs after the fall of the preceding wicket, then – on Lillywhite resuming bowling – Daft was had at wicket for 64. Ther score was at 113 for two wickets when Daft went in at twenty minutes to four; it was 262 for four wickets when he was out at eight minutes to six for 64 – a very finely played innings that included five 4s and 16 singles. Mr Tennent was bowled at 264, and at 275 another well-judged catch at long-field by Mr Thornton settled Carpenter, so many as 126 runs having been made during his stay; his 54 was an especially fine leg-hitting innings that included nine 4s – five of them leg hits; both Daft and Carpenter were heartily cheered. An exceeding clever catch by Humphrey settled McIntyre at 278. The two Yorkshiremen, Emmett and Pinder, then scored so merrily that when Pinder was had at point for 18, the score was 311; then Morley was bowled; shortly after the first day's cricket ended, there having been nineteen wickets got rid of and 441 runs scored that day; the North innings standing at 313 for nine wickets – Emmett not out 24, J. C. Shaw not out 2.

On Wednesday a showery morning was succeeded by a fine afternoon, and the attendance on the ground was equal to that on any off-day of previous "weeks". They resumed the cricket at sixteen minutes to twelve and when eight minutes had been played off the reel of time, Mr Walker, at mid-off, caught out Shaw and so ended the North's innings for 319 runs – Emmett not out 27, a hard hitting score. The wickets fell in this form:

1/34 2/113 3/149 4/262 5/264 6/275 7/278 8/311 9/311 10/319

The whole of the ten wickets – three bowled – fell to James Lillywhite's bowling. There was some good fielding by Mr Thornton, Mr Walker, Pooley and Jupp but there was also fielding the reverse of good, Mr Grace being quite out of form in bowling, batting and fielding.

The South's second innings was commenced at eighteen minutes past twelve; the necessary absence of Mr Grace on account of his leaving Liverpool for Canada early the following day, causing general regret. Jupp and Humphrey began the batting to the bowling of McIntyre and Lockwood, but when 23 runs had been made from sixteen overs McIntyre resigned the ball to Morley, who was in such capital form that his first thirteen overs (ten maidens – six in succession) were bowled for 7 runs and a wicket, he then having clean bowled Jupp, who had been one hour and ten minutes scoring his 21 runs, an innings that included three very fine cuts for 4 each – one from McIntyre, one from Morley and one from J. C. Shaw. Mr Fryer was not in form and when he had made two 3s and a 2, J. C. Shaw clean bowled him. Mr Walker made a single and a cut for 4 when he was had where he himself has put an end to many a good cricketer's innings; and when J. C. Shaw bowled Humphrey for 28 there were 4 of the South's best wickets down for 66 runs. Mr Thornton began with a sensationally big on-drive from Morley into the old hop garden for 4; he followed that up by another on-drive for 4 from Morley, who then bowled him, and half the wickets were down for 77 runs. Pooley and Charlwood then rapidly hit the score to 104, when Charlwood was easily c and b for 22 and Hearne had at cover-point for 0. Lillywhite then rattled away in his usual hard and fast form and the score was up to 124 when Lockwood – by a rare bit of fielding – threw down the wicket and Pooley was run out for 18. Mr Grace being away, Willsher was last man in; he made a 2 and was then again caught out, this time easily, at point by Carpenter, and so, at about twenty minutes to four the innings was ended for 142 and the North had won by an innings and 46 runs, Lillywhite not out 29 – a hard hitting innings that included five 4s. (The part played by Lillywhite in this match was a curious one – not out both innings with the bat and all the North wickets with his bowling.) The wickets fell as under:

1/42 2/57 3/65 4/66 5/77 6/104 7/104 8/124 9/142

Morley's bowling in this match was excellent for a Colt on a strange ground and against such a team of top-class batsmen; his first thirteen overs were sent in for 7 runs and a wicket and the last twenty-two balls he bowled were all maidens, the actual last ball having a wicket. Lockwood bowled well, so did Willsher, who at one time sent in eight successive overs for a hit for 3; but the prominent bowling feature of the match was Lillywhite's monopoly of the North men's wickets.

The South

Jupp b Lockwood	4	– b Morley	21
Richard Humphrey run out	0	– b J. C. Shaw	28
F. E. R. Fryer Esq. c Greenwood b McIntyre	55	– b J. C. Shaw	8
I. D. Walker Esq. b J. C. Shaw	16	– c Daft b J. C. Shaw	5
C. I. Thornton Esq. b J. C. Shaw	10	– b Morley	8
H. Charlwood c Pinder b McIntyre	20	– c and b Morley	22
W. G. Grace Esq. c Emmett b Lockwood	15	– absent (off for Canada)	—
Pooley c Daft b McIntyre	7	– run out	18
T. Hearne sen. b Lockwood	0	– c Greenwood b Morley	0
James Lillywhite not out	1	– not out	29
Willsher c Carpenter b McIntyre	3	– c Carpenter b Morley	2
		B 1	1
	131		142

The North

Bignall b Lillywhite	18
Ephraim Lockwood c Pooley b Lillywhite	68
Andrew Greenwood c Thornton b Lillywhite.	52
Richard Daft c Pooley b Lillywhite	64
R. Carpenter c Thornton b Lillywhite	57
H. N. Tennent Esq. b Lillywhite	1
Emmett not out	27
Martin McIntyre c Humphrey b Lillywhite	1
Pinder c Fryer b Lillywhite	18
F. Morley b Lillywhite	0
J. C. Shaw c Walker b Lillywhite	3
B 7, l-b, 3	10
	319

North Bowling

	Overs	Mdns	Runs	Wkts	Overs	Mdns	Runs	Wkts
Lockwood	23	9	30	3	18	10	15	—
J. C. Shaw	20	11	33	2	25	9	58	3
McIntyre	17.2	6	29	4	10	3	18	—
Morley	11	5	23	—	37.3	22	50	5
Emmett	3	—	13	—				

South Bowling

	Overs	Mdns	Runs	Wkts	
Lillywhite	60.2	22	120	10	(All 10 wickets).
Willsher	37	21	40	—	
Mr Fryer	29	7	59	—	
Mr Grace	15	4	28	—	
Hearne	12	5	13	—	
Mr Walker	13	4	25	—	
Mr Thornton	7	3	15	—	

Umpires: Fryer and Goodhew.

Fresh wickets were then pitched, and on them, at twenty minutes past four, they commenced the second match.

MCC AND GROUND v NORFOLK AND NORWICH CLUB

Played at Norwich, August 22, 23, 1872

This match was played in compliment to George Figg, who for more than 20 years had been engaged as bowler to the Norwich Club; who in his time was one of the straightest bowlers that ever hit a middle stump and who, throughout a long professional career, merited and obtained the good wishes and respect of all classes of cricketers.

There were no high scores made in the match, the bowling and fielding being too good for that. Wootton was again in force, taking thirteen wickets – six bowled – in the match; but the feature with the ball was the bowling of young Mr Davies – a lad not seventeen years old – who bowled forty-seven overs for 47 runs and six MCC wickets – four "bowled". His fellow students of the Grammar School were so elated at their comrade's success that they hoisted him shoulder high and carried him in triumph round the ground. In the words of one of the MCC professionals "Mr Davies' bowling was very good for a boy only sixteen years old". Mr B. Preston (one of the Cambridge Eleven of 1869) made the highest score in the match – 36 for Norfolk; nevertheless MCC and Ground won by four wickets.

Norfolk and Norwich

First innings		Second innings	
W. Collyer Esq. b Price	3	lbw b Price	3
Rev. R. T. Scott lbw b Wootton	8	c Biddulph b Price	6
E. P. Ash Esq. c Hearne b Price	1	b Wootton	4
B. Preston Esq. c Duncan b Wootton	36	lbw b Wootton	8
G. H. Tuck Esq. c Price b Wootton	3	b Wootton	5
E. L. Fellowes Esq. c Price b Wootton	0	b Wootton	10
C. Pattison Esq. c Biddulph b Wootton	6	b Price	23
Rev. E. R. Chute b Hearne	14	c Brockbank b Price	11
Rev. T. S. Curteis b Hearne	9	st Biddulph b Wootton	0
F. C. Davies Esq. not out	7	b Wootton	2
E. H. Willett Esq. b Wootton	0	not out	4
S. G. Buxton Esq. c Roxburgh b Hearne	0	b Wootton	3
L-b 1	1	L-b 1	1
	88		80

MCC and Ground

First innings		Second innings	
H. W. Turner Esq. c and b Davies	14	b Fellowes	10
Biddulph b Curteis	1		
W. Vyse Esq. b Davies	20	c Tuck b Fellows	10
T. Hearne sen. b Fellows	12	c Ash b Fellowes	0
A. S. Duncan Esq. c Willett b Fellowes	1	c and b Fellowes	6
Walter Price c Chute b Willett	14	b Willett	5
J. Brockbank Esq. b Davies	18	not out	16
Wootton c Ash b Davies	8	not out	2
F. Roxburgh Esq. b Davies	0		
A. R. Upcher Esq. b Davies	0		
J. Perkins Esq. lbw b Fellowes	9		
P. W. Taylor Esq. not out	3	b Davies	5
B 3, l-b 2, w 3	8	B 6, w 1	7
	108		61

MCC Bowling

	Overs	Mdns	Runs	Wkts	Overs	Mdns	Runs	Wkts
Wootton	36	18	29	6	32.3	13	46	7
Price	25	11	32	2	36	25	25	4
Hearne	10.3	1	26	3	4	—	8	—

Norfolk and Norwich Bowling

	Overs	Mdns	Runs	Wkts	Overs	Mdns	Runs	Wkts
Mr. Davies	37	13	33	5	10	4	14	1
Mr Fellowes	20.1	9	38	3	9	4	21	4
Mr Willett	10	4	7	1	6	3	10	1
Mr Curteis	7	—	22	1				
Mr Collyer					8	4	9	—

Umpires: Bareham and Burgess.

KENT v SUSSEX

Played at Lord's, June 9, 10, 1873

Prior to the commencement of the 1873 season, The Marylebone Club, with the praiseworthy purpose of increasing the popularity of County Cricket, offered a County Champion Cup for annual competition by recognised County Elevens on the neutral ground at Lord's. Sufficient of the Counties agreed to compete to promise these fights for the Championship becoming an interesting series of struggles, but subsequently several of the Counties' authorities declined to contend, and consequently MCC withdrew for that season their offer, and the Cup contests did not come off. However, Kent and Sussex agreed to have their round at Lord's, and on dangerously bad wickets they fought out the old fight, when Kent won by 52 runs. A new and very fast bowler in Mr Coles, battering and bruising several of the Sussex men, and finally disabling George Humphreys, who had, however, previously played a particularly plucky and good not out innings of 32 runs, making 20 of those runs from the tear-away bowling. Mr Coles had ten Sussex wickets – eight bowled; and Kent's rare old bowler, Willsher, was in such force in Sussex's first innings that he got four wickets at the rate of 4 runs per wicket, and finished his bowling that innings with ten consecutive maiden overs that included a couple of wickets. The match was over before two o'clock on the second day.

Kent

W. Penn Esq. b Fillery	5	– b Fillery	5
William McCanlis b Fillery	26	– b Lillywhite	0
W. Yardley Esq. b Fillery	13	– st Phillips b Lillywhite	15
Lord Harris b Lillywhite	11	– c and b Fillery	4
G. E. Coles Esq. (colt) b Fillery	3	– b Lillywhite	17
H. J. Hayman Esq. (colt) b Lillywhite	1	– b Lillywhite	1
J. C. Crawford Esq. c Phillips b Lillywhite	35	– b Lillywhite	6
Henty b Lillywhite	0	– b Fillery	0
Croxford b Lillywhite	0	– c W. Humphreys b Fillery	11
Willsher not out	13	– st Phillips b Lillywhite	8
R. Palmer (colt) b Fillery	8	– not out	0
B 4, l-b 3	7	B 6, l-b 2	8
	122		75

Sussex

Walter Humphreys b Coles	1	– c Hayman b Croxford	8
H. Killick b Willsher	0	– c Penn b Croxford	6
Fillery b Willsher	15	– b Coles	14
H. Charlwood b Coles	7	– run out	10
H. Phillips hit wkt b Willsher	1	– c Henty b Willsher	6
George Humphreys b Coles	3	– not out (retired, hurt by Mr Coles' bowling).	32
A. A. Reed b Coles	7	– c Yardley b Coles	3
James Lillywhite b Coles	0	– c sub b Coles	6
G. Lynn b Coles	3	– run out	5
Davey not out	1	– not out	0
J. Skinner c and b Willsher	1	– b Coles	0
B 4, l-b 2	6	B 7, l-b 3	10
	45		100

Sussex Bowling

	Overs	Mdns	Runs	Wkts	Overs	Mdns	Runs	Wkts
Fillery	33.1	11	70	5	25.3	14	24	4
Lillywhite	33	17	45	5	26	13	43	6

Kent Bowling

	Overs	Mdns	Runs	Wkts	Overs	Mdns	Runs	Wkts
Willsher	17.3	11	16	4	14	9	19	1
Mr Coles	17	6	23	6	24.2	7	47	4
Croxford					9	2	24	2

Umpires: T. Hearne sen. and Biddulph.

Subsequent to this match, the preparation of the wickets at Lord's were left to the superintendence of the Umpires, who were selected a week prior to a match being played; the results were good wickets for the remainder of the season.

MCC AND GROUND v CAMBRIDGE UNIVERSITY

Played at Lord's, June 16, 17, 1873

Mr Longman played markedly good, true cricket, cutting and hitting to leg very finely. His seventy-five minutes at wickets for 47 runs was a capital display, Alfred Shaw's fine bowling compelling Mr Longman to play all he knew to keep up his sticks; he did keep them up until the Chapel clock struck seven, but then one more over was bowled, and with the last ball to be delivered that evening Shaw bowled Mr Longman. Mr Fryer hit well for his 29, and Mr Tabor and Mr Blacker both played steadily and well for 20 and 15. Alfred Shaw bowled 76 overs for 68 runs and nine wickets – seven bowled. In the 'Varsity's first innings Shaw's last nineteen overs were bowled for 13 runs and two wickets; and in their second innings Shaw commenced with nine successive maiden overs, one of which included a wicket. Rylott had ten wickets – seven bowled. Mr Yardley made 18 runs in fifteen minutes; his 51 included a couple of big on drives for 5 each, and four 4s to leg. The 'Varsity Eleven were defeated by five wickets.

Cambridge

G. H. Longman Esq. b Rylott	43	– b Alfred Shaw	47
A. S. Tabor Esq. run out	20	– b Alfred Shaw	0
W. Blacker Esq. b Rylott	6	– b Alfred Shaw	15
T. Latham Esq. st Biddulph b Rylott	11	– not out	19
G. E. Jeffery Esq. b Rylott	11	– b Rylott	1
F. E. R. Fryer Esq. b Alfred Shaw	0	– b Alfred Shaw	29
H. A. Hamilton Esq. c and b Alfred Shaw	9	– c and b Alfred Shaw	2
C. Tillard Esq. b Rylott	5	– b Rylott	4
G. Macan Esq. c Alfred Shaw b Rylott	0	– b Alfred Shaw	3
H. M. Sims Esq. not out	1	– b Alfred Shaw	0
F. Price Esq. b Rylott	0	– c Biddulph b Rylott	2
B 1	1	B 2, l-b 4	6
	107		128

MCC and Ground

Capt. Rowley c Price b Sims	1 – not out	7
C. P. Coote Esq. b Jeffery	22 – b Sims	5
W. Yardley Esq. b Sims	18 – c Sims b Hamilton	51
C. Booth Esq. b Jeffery	20 – b Jeffery	19
R. D. Balfour Esq. c and b Jeffery	2 – run out	1
Rylott c Sims b Jeffery	26 – b Jeffery	6
R. E. Tomkinson Esq. lbw b Sims	6 – not out	10
Alfred Shaw c Macan b Sims	0	
Biddulph b Jeffery	4	
G. Nixon (Cambs.) not out	15	
Farrands b Jeffery	5	
B 6, l-b 6	12	B 4, l-b 2, w 2 8
	131	107

MCC Bowling

	Overs	Mdns	Runs	Wkts	Overs	Mdns	Runs	Wkts
A. Shaw	37	21	37	2	39	23	31	7
Rylott	30	13	46	7	31	11	65	3
Farrands	7	—	23	—	9	1	26	—

University Bowling

	Overs	Mdns	Runs	Wkts	Overs	Mdns	Runs	Wkts
Mr Jeffery	37.3	16	57	6	21.1	10	32	2
Mr Sims	32	13	47	4	16	4	36	1
Mr Tillard	10	6	15	—	7	3	14	—
Mr Hamilton					6	2	11	1
Mr Price					6	4	6	—

Umpires: Wootton and Walter Price.

MCC AND GROUND v OXFORD UNIVERSITY (12 a-side)

Played at Lord's, June 19, 20, 1873

This match commenced awkwardly for Oxford, inasmuch as with the second ball delivered Alfred Shaw bowled Mr Ottaway, and with his seventh ball Shaw bowled Mr Wallroth, both wickets falling when only one run was scored; and when but 47 runs only had been booked so many as eight wickets had fallen; then Mr Nepean and Mr Butler rapidly hit the score to 100, when Mr Butler was bowled by Shaw, who, at 109, bowled Mr Nepean for 49, an innings marked by well-timed, clean, and hard hitting, especially his driving to the on, as those hits included a 6 from Rylott (a splendid smack that), two 4s, a couple of 3s, etc. Mr Law played well; his one hour's hitting for 39 included a remarkably fine off-drive for 5 from Rylott, and some capital cutting. Alfred Shaw was again in form with the ball, as, notwithstanding Mr Wallroth made a splendid drive for 5, and Mr Game a ditto for 6, from one over of his bowling. Shaw bowled in the match 88 overs (less one ball) for 85 runs and eleven wickets – eight bowled. Rylott had ten wickets – six bowled. When the Oxonians bowled their superiority to the Cantabs became manifest. Mr Maude's left-hand slows started successfully, as with the first ball he delivered he bowled Mr Coote, and with the score at 26 he bowled Mr Yardley. In all that innings Mr Maude had four wickets at the rate of 6½ runs per wicket. The other Freshman bowler – Mr Boyle – was not tried until nearly 60 runs had been made for four wickets; then his great pace quickly told, as in his fifth over he bowled two wickets, in his seventh over he bowled another, and in his twelfth over he bowled one more. In the Club's second innings Mr Boyle's bowling had seven wickets – five bowled, but he bowled as many wide balls as he gained wickets. Oxford won the match by 40 runs.

Oxford

C. J. Ottaway Esq. b Alfred Shaw	0	– c Rylott b Brune	18
W. Law Esq. c Booth b Rylott	20	– b Alfred Shaw	39
C. A. Wallroth Esq. b Alfred Shaw	0	– c Barry b Alfred Shaw	9
W. H. Game Esq. b Rylott	14	– b Rylott	7
Lord Harris b Rylott	2	– b Alfred Shaw	0
C. E. B. Nepean Esq. b Alfred Shaw	49	– c Yardley b Rylott	11
E. S. Garnier Esq. b Rylott	0	– b Rylott	2
C. K. Francis Esq. c Biddulph b Rylott	0	– b Rylott	0
D. Campbell Esq. c and b Alfred Shaw	3	– lbw b Alfred Shaw	6
S. E. Butler Esq. b Alfred Shaw	17	– not out	13
C. W. Boyle Esq. not out	11	– b Alfred Shaw	7
J. Maude Esq. st Biddulph b Rylott	4	– b Alfred Shaw	1
B 2	2	B 2, l-b 2	4
	122		117

MCC and Ground

C. P. Coote Esq. b Maude	0	– b Butler	4
A. H. Smith-Barry Esq. c Ottaway b Butler	9	– b Boyle	0
W. Yardley Esq. b Maude	16	– b Boyle	1
C. Booth Esq. c Ottaway b Maude	2	– b Butler	21
A. W. Herbert Esq. b Francis	13	– b Boyle	14
C. J. Brune Esq. b Boyle	18	– c Butler b Boyle	4
G. Strachan Esq. b Francis	1	– b Butler	20
Rylott b Boyle	0	– run out	0
R. E. Tomkinson Esq. b Boyle	4	– c Game b Boyle	9
Alfred Shaw not out	13	– b Boyle	0
Biddulph b Boyle	8	– not out	6
Farrands st Nepean b Maude	6	– b Boyle	2
B 2, l-b 4, w 3	9	B 10, l-b 1, w 8	19
	99		100

MCC Bowling

	Overs	Mdns	Runs	Wkts	Overs	Mdns	Runs	Wkts
A. Shaw	41	21	41	5	46.3	27	44	6
Rylott	36.1	14	67	6	42	19	52	4
Farrands	5	—	12	—	4	1	13	—
Mr Brune					2	—	4	1

University Bowling

	Overs	Mdns	Runs	Wkts	Overs	Mdns	Runs	Wkts
Mr Maude	34	21	27	4	12	6	12	—
Mr Butler	31	18	26	1	37	21	36	3
Mr Francis	17	8	25	2				
Mr Boyle	14	7	12	4	24.3	10	33	7

Umpires: T. Hearne sen. and John West.

The averages in these two test matches resulted as under:

Batting

Cambridge averaged a trifle under 11 runs per wicket.
Oxford averaged a trifle under 11 runs per wicket.

Bowling

	Overs	Mdns	Runs	Wkts	
Cambridge	136	58	218	15	9 bowled.
Oxford	169.3	91	171	21	– 16 bowled.

MCC AND GROUND v STAFFORDSHIRE (12 a-side)

Played at Lord's, July 14, 15, 1873

Notwithstanding the Staffordshire twelve included Hughes the slow bowler, and Mr Lines the wicket-keeper of Hertfordshire, the MCC dozen won by an innings and 99 runs; Mr Udal and Mr W. G. Grace making 15 more runs between them than the Staffordshire twelve did in their two innings. Hughes's slow bowling had nine MCC wickets, and a glance at the MCC bowling figures will tell how successful were the attacks of Wootton and Mr Grace on the Staffordshire stumps. Wootton's bowling in the Shire's first innings being extraordinarily successful, bowling sixteen over (twelve maidens) for 6 runs (all singles) and five wickets.

MCC and Ground

W. G. Grace Esq. c Compson b Hughes ...	67
A. H. Smith-Barry Esq. c Brown b Hughes .	4
E. G. Sutton Esq. c Burnett b Hughes	6
W. L. Davidson Esq. b Hughes	6
E. Bird Esq. c Compson b Hughes	2
W. A. Greenwood Esq. b Hughes	5
J. S. Udal Esq. b Clarke	72
T. Parkin Esq. c Hurst b Ford	10
A. W. Anstruther, Esq. c Lines b Hughes ..	0
Wootton st Lines b Hughes	29
Davey c Burnett b Hughes	4
Geo. Nixon (Cambs) not out	3
B 7, l-b 7, w 1	15
	223

Staffordshire

Hughes c Davey b Grace	3	– c Greenwood b Grace	4
J. Brown Esq. c Grace b Wootton	0	– c and b Grace	1
H. E. Compson Esq. b Wootton	0	– c Bird b Grace	2
Mr Lines c Bird b Grace	8	– c Bird b Wootton	23
E. Hurst Esq. c and b Grace	2	– c Sutton b Wootton	0
G. F. Rendall Esq. lbw b Grace	3	– st Davey b Grace	2
E. W. Burnett Esq. b Grace	8	– not out	13
J. B. Cope Esq. b Wootton	1	– b Wootton	12
Ford b Wootton	0	– c Udal b Grace	12
Clarke run out	2	– c Davidson b Grace	4
J. W. Bullock Esq. b Wootton	3	– c Barry b Grace	4
Tranter not out	1	– run out	0
B 7, l-b 2	9	B 5, l-b 2	7
	40		84

Umpires: Walter Price and Biddulph.

Staffordshire Bowling

	Overs	Mdns	Runs	Wkts
Hughes	47.1	17	82	9
Tranter	26	7	65	—
Ford	9	—	32	1
Clarke	7	4	8	1
Mr Cope	5	2	21	—

MCC Bowling

	Overs	Mdns	Runs	Wkts	Overs	Mdns	Runs	Wkts
Mr Grace	17	5	25	5	38	16	53	7
Wootton	16.1	12	6	5	38	29	24	3

THE CANTERBURY WEEK

August 4, 5, 6, 7, 8, 9, 1873

The Canterbury Cricket Week of 1873 was favoured with a bright, breezy, warm, enjoyable "Bank Holiday" to commence with on the Monday; a brilliantly fine "Ladies' Day" on the Thursday; a burning hot and glorious corn-ripening sun on the Friday, and fairly pleasant weather on the other days.

The clerical, staid, quiet, quaint old "City of the Men of Kent" was, from Monday morn until Saturday eve, dressed up in an unwonted gay form, the whole length of the ancient High Street being ablaze with flags: scarce a house in that long, narrow, and historically interesting thoroughfare but what had its bits of bunting blowing in the breeze, and at about every two score yards or so a string of flags of all colours streamed across the street. The Union Jack; the rampant White Horse of Kent; the famous old buff and blue of politics; the gorgeous red, black, and gold of "I Zingari"; the sombre black and blue of Kent's "Band of Brothers"; the scarlet and black of "The Knickerbocker's"; the ever popular red and gold of MCC; the dark blue of Oxford; the light blue of Cambridge; the blue and yellow of the RA; and lots of other banners crowdedly covered the house fronts in the High Street, and as the strong wind fluttered them they seemed to cheerily wave welcomes to all comers to The Canterbury Week of 1873.

The attendance up at breezy old St Lawrence was unprecedentedly large on the Monday; very good on the Tuesday; middling ditto on the Wednesday; numerically large beyond all preceding "Ladies' Day" on the Thursday; but slack on the Friday and on the Saturday.

The wickets were – thanks to the exertions of Mr Ladd and his men – in quite top class form, and as good wickets are one of the essentialities of good cricket, there was "good cricket"; albeit constant attendants at past year's "week's" fancied they had seen better, especially when they remembered the cricket of '68, which poor Fuller Pilch pronounced to have been "the best he had ever seen played at Canterbury".

As to run getting in 1873 there was plenty of that, as the six day's hitting averaged 319 runs per day, and over 20 runs per wicket.

GENTLEMEN OF MCC v THE COUNTY OF KENT (12 a-side)

This, the second match in "the week's" programme, was commenced at five o'clock on Wednesday. Kent began the batting; the only item of interest in that evening's play being the tremendous thwacking Mr W. Penn gave to Mr W. G. Grace's bowling – one on-drive pitched outside the boundary, and was the highest hit in the week's cricket, and three smacks to square-leg were such stingers that all three pitched in the upper field – two by the side of the military band stand, the other (a magnificent hit) was sent flying clear over the long rough-weather marquee by the side of the music stand. When "time" was called that evening Kent had lost eight wickets, and scored 130 runs.

(There had been 1,056 runs scored up to the close of Wednesday's play.)

On Thursday – "The Ladies' Day" – the only noteworthy cricket incident that cropped up was Mr W. Grace being easily caught out at slip, by Willsher, when he had scored only one run. None of the MCC twelve scored largely that day, nevertheless, as eight of them made doubles, the Club was ahead of the County by 65 runs on the first innings. The Kent men then went on with their second innings, and when they had lost four wickets and scored 65 runs the cricket for the great day ended, there having been 1,338 runs scored in the four days' cricket.

Friday was a blazing hot day. Lord Harris again hit well, making 42 runs, including five 4s – three of them successive hits from the bowling of Mr W. G. Grace. Croxford made 26, but at 1.30 the County Twelve were out for 171, so the Club had 107 runs to score to win. Mr W. Grace and Mr Griffiths commenced the innings, and before Mr Grace had made a run he gave a chance from Mr Lipscomb's bowling to mid-on, which Mr Penn missed, and thus Kent's "burly bowler" lost the credit of capturing the crack in both innings; and the end was that at 4.30 MCC had won the match by nine wickets – Mr W. G. Grace not out 57.

Kent

William McCanlis b W. Grace	3	– c and b W. Grace	16
W. Yardley Esq. b Appleby	29	– c Mitchell b Appleby	1
W. W. Rodger Esq. c and b W. Grace	9	– b W. Grace	3
W. Penn Esq. c Pickering b J. Ponsonby	29	– c Marriott b W. Grace	21
Lord Harris c Pickering b Appleby	4	– c Ponsonby b W. Grace	42
F. Stokes Esq. b Appleby	4	– c Sutherland b W. Grace	4
E. A. White Esq. b J. Ponsonby	0	– c and b W. Grace	13
Croxford b Appleby	37	– b W. Grace	26
George Bennett c Sutherland b W. Grace	8	– st Mitchell b W. Grace	14
Henty b W. Grace	11	– c Pickering b W. Grace	1
Willsher not out	6	– not out	6
R. Lipscomb Esq. c Appleby b W. Grace	0	– c Sutherland b W. Grace	5
W 1	1	B 17, l-b 2	19
	141		171

MCC

W. G. Grace Esq. c Willsher b Lipscomb	1	– not ut	57
A. S. Griffiths Esq. c McCanlis b Lipscomb	8	– b Willsher	2
L. S. Howell Esq. c Henty b Willsher	9	– not out	26
A. Appleby Esq. c Croxford b Bennett	21		
R. A. H. Mitchell Esq. b Bennett	25		
C. Marriott Esq. lbw b Lipscomb	13		
F. P. U. Pickering Esq. b Stokes	22		
J. H. Ponsonby Esq. b Willsher	27	– b Lipscomb	17
H. B. Sutherland Esq. b Bennett	22		
H. N. Tennent Esq. b Stokes	0		
E. O. Wilkinson Esq. not out	22		
Capt. Oldfield st Henty b McCanlis	19		
B 10, l-b 5, w 2	17	B 4, l-b 1	5
	206		107

MCC Bowling

	Overs	Mdns	Runs	Wkts	Overs	Mdns	Runs	Wkts
Mr Appleby	35	19	50	4	20	13	13	1
Mr W. Grace	20.2	9	55	5	46	15	92	10
Mr J. Ponsonby	15	4	35	2	6	1	14	—
Mr Sutherland					19	9	23	—
Capt. Oldfield					13	7	10	—

Kent Bowling

	Overs	Mdns	Runs	Wkts	Overs	Mdns	Runs	Wkts
Willsher	37	18	46	2	16	5	28	1
Mr Lipscomb	34	15	57	3	18	6	38	1
Bennett	26	8	51	3				
Mr Stokes	22	13	20	2	5	1	17	—
Croxford	5	3	5	—				
McCanlis	3	—	10	1	5	1	19	—

Umpires: W. H. Fryer and F. Farrands.

(Mr W. G. Grace's bowling had fifteen Kent wickets – ten in one innings.)

MCC AND GROUND v THE NORTH OF ENGLAND

Played at Lord's, June 1, 2, 1874

Alfred Shaw's bowling obtained all the ten wickets in the North's first innings of this revived contest. In any match this is a great bowling feat to bring off, but in a first-class affair like this, wherein the ten include such wickets as Mr A. N. Hornby's, Oscroft's, Lockwood's and Greenwood's, it is a remarkable bit of bowling deserving special notice in all records of the game. Four of the ten wickets were bowled; two were caught out at slip; one at long on; one at point; and the other two were captured at wicket. The identical ball wherewith Shaw obtained the ten wickets was handsomely and appropriately mounted at the expense of MCC, and presented to Alfred as a memento of the Club's appreciation of his successful bowling; Shaw is properly proud of the present, which will be carefully preserved by him as a family heirloom, and as an incentive to the Alfred Shaw's of the future to "go and do likewise".

MCC and Ground v The North was first played in 1840, when the Northmen were victorious by two wickets. For eight successive years the match was annually played, but in 1849 it was put on one side for the more interesting, the more popular, and the better match of North v South.

The revival last June was played in bright, hot weather, but did not prove attractive. Mr Hornby was the highest scorer in the match; he batted very finely; was first man in in the North's first innings and second out, having made 53 out of the 99 then scored, but having badly injured his hand in fielding he did not go in until the eighth wicket had fallen (score at 63) in the North's second innings, and then (although evidently batting in great pain) took his bat out for 21. Mr W. G. Grace was top scorer for the Club; a splendid catch by Greenwood at long on ended Mr Grace's first innings for 43 – out of 63 then scored; and in MCC's second innings Greenwood – at mid-off – made another superb catch that settled Mr Coote before a run was booked. J. C. Shaw made two very fine c and b's in the Club's second go. Mr Penn hit two good scored for MCC; his second innings included a splendid on drive for 5 and a capital cut for 4 from J. C. Shaw's bowling. Lockwood's 38 was a fine innings, and so were Oscroft's 24 and 28. Mr Buller was hurt when playing his first innings, and was unable to bat in the Club's second innings, wherein Hill's bowling was so very fine that he sent in 27 overs (less one ball) for 20 runs and two wickets, his last thirteen overs being bowled for 6 runs and the two wickets. The North won by 45 runs.

The North

A. N. Hornby Esq. c Buller b Alfred Shaw	53	– not out	21
Andrew Greenwood b Alfred Shaw	4	– c Biddulph b Alfred Shaw	9
Ephraim Lockwood c Grace b Alfred Shaw	38	– b Morley	0
William Oscroft b Alfred Shaw	24	– c Biddulph b Morley	28
H. Reynolds (Notts.) b Alfred Shaw	13	– b Alfred Shaw	0
T. Emmett c Grace b Alfred Shaw	13	– b Morley	7
W. Clark (Notts.) c Coote b Alfred Shaw	4	– b Morley	8
Allen Hill st Biddulph b Alfred Shaw	1	– b Morley	0
T. Plumb not out	7	– c Crooke b Alfred Shaw	7
M. McIntyre c Biddulph b Alfred Shaw	11	– c Grace b Clayton	21
J. C. Shaw b Alfred Shaw	0	– b Clayton	2
B 6, l-b 1	7	B 2, l-b 1	3
	175		106

MCC and Ground

W. G. Grace Esq. c Greenwood b Lockwood	43	– b J. C. Shaw	12
C. P. Coote Esq. b J. C. Shaw	1	– c Greenwood b J. C. Shaw	0
C. Marriott Esq. b Hill	23	– c and b J. C. Shaw	5
C. F. Buller Esq. not out	24	– hurt – did not bat	
F. J. Crooke Esq. st Plumb b Hill	3	– b Lockwood	27
G. E. Bird Esq. b Emmett	10	– c and b J. C. Shaw	4
W. Penn Esq. c Reynolds b Emmett	23	– c Clark b Lockwood	14
Alfred Shaw c J. C. Shaw b Lockwood	3	– b Hill	3
R. Clayton b Lockwood	1	– not out	7
Biddulph c Reynolds b Emmett	4	– b J. C. Shaw	4
Morley b Emmett	4	– b Hill	3
B 9, l-b 4, n-b 2	15	L-b 3	3
	154		82

MCC Bowling

	Overs	Mdns	Runs	Wkts	Overs	Mdns	Runs	Wkts
A. Shaw	36.2	8	73	10	35	14	43	3
Morley	24	8	49	—	29	13	48	5
Mr W. Grace	22	7	35	—	6	3	3	—
Clayton	7	3	11	—	3.3	—	9	2

North Bowling

	Overs	Mdns	Runs	Wkts	Overs	Mdns	Runs	Wkts
J. C. Shaw	27	10	38	1	22	10	44	5
Hill	25	10	34	2	26.3	14	20	2
Emmett	24	9	32	4				
Lockwood	22	10	35	3	5	1	15	2

Umpires: Thos Hearne sen. and Walter Price.

ETON v HARROW

Played at Lord's, July 10, 11, 1874

Shortly after the termination of the Eton and Harrow match of 1873 it was rumoured that the admission charges to the ground would, in all probability, be increased at the 1874 match. A proposition to that effect was advanced at the Club's annual May meeting; it was subsequently discussed by the Committee, and the result was the publication in the usual cricket chronicles of the following announcement:

ETON v HARROW

To The Editor

"Sir, – I am instructed to ask you to publish the following resolution, passed at a meeting of committee on June 8 last:

Resolved – 'That it is desirable to make arrangements for diminishing the number of persons at the Eton and Harrow match, on July 10 and 11, and that, with that view, the price of admission on that occasion for each person on foot be raised from 1s. to 2s. 6d.'

It was also resolved – 'That the masters and boys of each school be admitted free, by tickets.'

I am, your obedient servant,

R. A. FitzGerald, Secretary, MCC"

Lord's Ground, NW

So numerous were the applications for carriage standings, that a week prior to the match the Secretary found it necessary to issue a public notice, of which the following formed parts:

CARRIAGE ARRANGEMENTS

"No further application for carriage tickets can be entertained. The Secretary has issued as many tickets as the space at his disposal admits of.

Members' carriages will be admitted by ticket on Thursday, July 9, from 10 a.m. to 7 p.m., to take up position on the ground.

The Committee particularly request that at the conclusion of the Eton and Harrow match everybody present on the ground will abstain from undue exhibition of party feeling. The co-operation of the members of the club is earnestly solicited to carry out this resolution. Hoisting is strictly prohibited.

By order of the Committee.

R. A. FitzGerald, Secretary, MCC"

The seats in the Grand Stand had all been secured a week prior to the match, and as the demand for more seats continued numerous and pressing, a temporary stand was erected at the east end of the grand, and all the seats in the temporary were quickly secured. Over 400 carriages of the members of the club entered and were admirably positioned on the ground during the day prior to the match, and the official records of the numbers of visitors who paid the 2s. 6d. and passed through the turnstiles on to the ground during the two match days, were:

9,039 on the Friday, and 6,325 on the Saturday.

On the Friday the weather was bright and hot, very hot, and the closely packed human ring that encircled the cricketers, the fair-ly, fashionably, and fully occupied seats on the new embankment, and the wealth of beauty and rank that filled and graced the two Grand Stands and the 430 carriages, eloquently told that Eton v Harrow at Lord's was still the great event of the London fashionable season, and that for aught it would have affected the wonderful attraction of the match, the admission charge might as well have been raised to half-a-guinea as to half-a-crown.

THE LATE ETON AND HARROW MATCH

To The Editor of *Bell's Life in London*

"Sir, – I shall feel obliged by your publishing the following facts in connection with the late Eton and Harrow match. Numerous unauthenticated statements have appeared in the papers, and in justice to MCC I trust you will permit me to correct them:

1. No money was taken for any carriage taking up position on the ground.
2. 430 carriages belonging to members only were admitted.
3. 9,039 persons paid admission on the first day, 6,325 persons on the second day; in 1873 15,808 persons paid admission on the first day, and 11,214 persons on the second day.
4. 1,000 free passes were sent to each school, and upwards of 1,000 tickets, each admitting four persons, were allotted to the members; 6,000 persons may fairly be computed to have had free admission to the ground on each day of the match.

The admirable order preserved by this assembly, and the kind attention shown by all persons to the published regulations of the Committee, eminently deserve a public recognition. The increased tariff of admission fulfilled the expectations of the Committee; it not only tended to check the attendance by several thousands, but it was especially conducive to the good order that prevailed.

In grateful acknowledgment of the help I personally derived from the visitors themselves.

I remain, your obedient servant,

R. A. FitzGerald, Secretary, MCC"

THE AMERICAN BASE BALL PLAYERS IN ENGLAND, 1874

Twenty-two base ball players from America visited England at the back end of the cricket season, 1874, "their mission" – it was semi-officially stated – "being to give the English a practical insight into the workings of base ball." The twenty-two comprised eleven members of the Boston (red stockings) and eleven of the Philadelphia Athletes (blue stockings), the two leading base ball clubs in the United States, where the game holds the same high and popular national position cricket does in England. The visitors' stay in this country was limited to one month. They quickly got to work, making their first appearance in flannel on an English ground the 30th of July, at Edgehill, the ground of the Liverpool Cricket Club. They were a finely-framed, powerful set of men and, although "Base Ball" did not take the popular fancy here, the splendid long-distance throwing and truly magnificent out-fielding of the Americans at once won the full and heartily-expressed admiration of Englishmen, who frankly and freely acknowledged the Americans' superiority to the generality of English fielders.

Nine Bostons v Nine Athletics played, with varying success, base ball matches on the Liverpool Club's cricket ground at Edgehill; on the Manchester Club's ground at Old Trafford; on the Marylebone Club's ground, "Lord's"; on Prince's ground, at Belgravia; on the Richmond Club's ground in the Old Deer Park, Richmond; at the Crystal Palace, Sydenham; on the Surrey County Club's ground, "The Oval"; on the Yorkshire County ground, Sheffield; and at Dublin.

THE AMERICANS AT CRICKET

At several of the above grounds the Americans supplemented their base ball exhibitions with cricket matches. Not one of the English teams pitted against the strangers embodies the strength of the club they represented – indeed, some of them were very weak teams – and the Americans having one or two good bowlers, several plucky hard-hitters and a team of good fielders, they had the best of every match they played. The matches at Lord's, at Prince's and on the Oval, will be found full-scored on preceding pages. The following is a summary of the

RESULTS OF THE CRICKET MATCHES PLAYED BY THE AMERICANS IN ENGLAND IN 1874

When and Where	Matches and Scores			Results
August 3, 4 At Lord's	The Americans (18)	107	—	
	Gentlemen of MCC (12)	105	—	
August 6, 7 At Prince's	The Americans (18)	110	—	Americans won by an innings and 50 runs
	Prince's Club and Ground (11)	21	39	
August 8 At Richmond	The Americans (22)	*45	—	* Only 6 wkts down
	Richmond Club (13)	108	—	
August 13, 14 At The Oval	The Americans (18)	100	111	* 4 wkts were down for the 2 runs
	Surrey Club and Ground (11) .	27	*2	
August 15, 17 At Sheffield	The Americans (18)	130	—	Americans won by an innings and 42 runs
	Sheffield Town (12)	43	45	
August 22, 24, 25 At Dublin	The Americans (19)	71	94	The Americans won by 86 runs
	Ireland (12)	47	32	

The Americans left Ireland for America on Wednesday the 26th of August, 1874.

THE AMERICANS AT LORD'S

Considerable interest was excited in cricketing circles last summer by public announcements that representative teams of the two leading Base Ball Clubs of America would, at the back end of our cricket season visit England and by playing their national game on our principal cricket grounds, endeavour to acclimatise that game in this country. The interest created by this announcement was increased by the statement that the Americans had also (but somewhat reluctantly) agreed to play a cricket match against an English Club team on each ground they played their base ball match on. Of course Lord's was one of the grounds selected for these displays and respecting this visit of the Americans to head quarters, the following announcement was published:

ELEVEN GENTLEMEN OF MCC v EIGHTEEN GENTLEMEN OF AMERICA

"August 3, 4, 5, 1874. – The Committee of the Marylebone Club have granted the use of Lord's Ground during the above days to the American gentlemen, who intend to give an exhibition of their prowess at cricket as well as their national game of base ball. The proceeds of the match will be handed over to the American gentlemen, to meet the large expenditure incurred by their visit to England. The programme will be as follows:

On Monday, August 3, a match will commence between Eleven Gentlemen of MCC and Eighteen of America.

Play will be suspended at 3 p.m. on Monday, August 3, when two selected nines (Americans) will commence a game of base ball.

The cricket match will be resumed on Tuesday morning, August 4 and at its conclusion a second match of base ball will be commenced, the sides to be selected, as may be arranged, between a mixed English and American nine.

A dinner will be given at the Tavern, Lord's Ground, at 8 p.m. on August 3, to which the visitors and other distinguished Americans will be invited by the MCC.

Members of the MCC who may wish to be present at the dinner are requested to give early notice of their intention to the Secretary of the MCC. Dinner tickets £1 1s. each. The chair will be taken by the president of the club, the Marquis of Hamilton.

The admission to the ground on each day of the match will be 1s. for persons on foot; 2s. 6d. will be charged for each carriage. Admission to the Grand Stand 1s. The members' enclosure will be reserved for visitors introduced by the members of the club.

By order of the Committee,

R. A. FitzGerald, Sec. MCC"

Monday, August 3rd, was one of our Bank Holidays and, fortunately, a day of splendid weather, but, unfortunately, it was also the opening day of the annual Canterbury Cricket Week; nevertheless, there was a large company present to welcome the strangers to Lord's, so many as 3,580 having paid the 1s. and passed on to the old ground that day.

Prior, to the commencement of the cricket match, the Americans surprised and delighted the company with a display of their ball-throwing and catching abilities; the great height and distance they threw was marvellous and their correct judging, cool, clever waiting for, and easy catch of the ball from those big throws, was really wonderful; each throw and catch eliciting a hearty cheer. Having evidently greatly gratified the company with this display, they turned out at 12.25 to commence the cricket match:

12 GENTLEMEN OF MCC v 18 OF AMERICA

The MCC batting was commenced by Mr Alfred Lubbock and Mr Courtenay, to the bowling of H. Wright (medium round) and McBride (fast underhand) who took three strides to the wicket and then let fly a tremendously fast grubber that rarely rose from the ground an inch after it pitched; this kind of bowling quickly settled Mr Courtenay and Mr Round and at first somewhat stuck up Mr Alfred Lubbock, who, however, soon got into something like his old fine form of play, scored 24 runs, and was then clean bowled by H. Wright. Mr Lubbock left with the score at 34 and at 41 a clever catch at point settled Mr Lucas for 12. One more run was scored and then – at five minutes past two – they retired to luncheon and preparations were forthwith made for commencing:

THE BASE BALL MATCH

ATHLETIC CLUB 9 v BOSTON CLUB 9

The Boston men were the Base Ball champions of America and The Athletics (of Philadelphia) the ex-champions. The marking out the diamond-shaped base ground, and the subsequent play of the sides was watched with marked interest by the audience, but they had not proceeded far with the match before many of the spectators were impressed with the idea that they were witnessing a modernised, manly – and unquestionably an improved – edition of that most enjoyable old game of their boyhood — Rounders, the most patent differences being: – a cricket-sized ball is used at base ball, instead of a ball of tennis size, as at rounders; throwing the ball at the striker when running from base to base is allowed at rounders, but is properly barred at base ball; and instead of the ball being struck with a stick of broom-handle thickness held in one hand, as at rounders, it is at base ball struck by a formidably-sized club, clutched and wielded by both hands, a form of play that, to become efficient in, evidently requires lengthened practice and much skill.

The play proceeded to the evident advantage of the Bostonians all through; and after a contest of two hours and ten minutes' duration, the Boston Champions won by 27 to 7, the following being the score, as published in *Bell's Life*:

Athletics

	Runs	First Base hits	Put out	Assisted to put out
McMullen (centre field)	1	3	4	0
McGeary (short stop)	1	1	1	5
Anson (first base)	1	3	10	0
McBride (pitcher)	1	2	0	0
Murnan (right field)	1	2	2	0
Batten (second base)	1	2	3	2
Sutton (third base)	1	1	0	3
Clapp (catcher)	0	1	6	1
Gedney (left field)	0	2	1	0
Totals	7	17	27	11

Bostons

	Runs	First Base hits	Put out	Assisted to put out
C. Wright (short stop)	4	4	4	0
Barnes (second base)	4	2	3	5
Spalding (pitcher)	4	4	0	0
McKey (catcher)	3	4	4	0
Leonard (left field)	2	3	1	0
O'Rouke (first base)	2	2	7	0
H. Wright (centre field)	1	2	5	0
Hall (right field)	1	3	0	0
Schafer (third base)	3	1	3	2
Totals	24	25	27	7

Runs Scored in Each Innings

										Totals
Athletics ...	3	0	0	0	1	1	1	0	1	7
Boston	3	7	4	0	5	0	5	0	0	24

Bases by errors: Boston 9 times, Athletics 1. Runs earned: Athletics 6, Bostons 11. Umpire, Mr Thomas Beales, of the Boston Club. Duration of game, two hours ten minutes.

Play in the cricket match was resumed at 6 o'clock, Mr V. E. Walker and Mr Bird continuing the MCC batting. Mr V. E. Walker hit freely and got well hold of the bowling, but was at last settled by a good ball from H. Wright and was out for 27 – the highest score hit in the match. Then play ceased for the day, the MCC score standing at 88 for five wickets, Mr Bird not out, 15. The Americans fielded very smartly and effectively before luncheon, but subsequent to their base ball struggle their fielding was loose and ineffective.

In the evening the Americans were entertained at dinner by the Marylebone Club, the President of the Club, the Marquis of Hamilton, presiding, supported by the Treasurer, Mr R. Burgoyne and the Secretary, Mr R. A. FitzGerald. It was understood that 50 gentlemen sat down to dinner.

Tuesday, August 4th, was a woeful wet day, so wet that play in the cricket match could not be resumed until 2.30 and then under such difficulties to the batsmen that twelve overs sufficed, to finish off the MCC innings, which had become part of cricket history by 3 o'clock, the wickets having fallen as under:

1/2 2/8 3/34 4/41 5/88 6/90 7/92 8/92 9/102 10/105 11/105

The Americans then batted to the bowling of Mr Appleby and Mr Rose. Most of the strangers went in for hard hitting, Mr Spalding heading the lot with 23, an innings that included a splendid on-drive down to Dark's house and two or three other hard cracks. They had made up 73 runs for ten wickets when a fierce rainstorm of twenty minutes' duration literally swamped the ground; however, being desirous of finishing off that innings and then closing the match, they went at it again later on and the finish was so close and exciting, that when the Americans had only two wickets to fall, they wanted 6 runs to defeat MCC's total; when they had only one wicket to fall they wanted 3 runs; and when their last man was caught out they were two runs ahead of MCC, a result they were evidently proud of and justly so, for this MCC 12 was undoubtedly the best English team the Americans met at cricket throughout their brief tour. The American wickets fell as follows:

1/2 2/9 3/23 4/34 5/38 6/41 7/56 8/68 9/71
10/73 11/87 12/87 13/87 14/91 15/100 16/103 17/107

The match was not played out.

MCC

C. Courtenav b McBride	0	*E. Lubbock b G. Wright	0
*A. Lubbock b H. Wright	24	*R. A. FitzGerald c Hall b G. Wright	4
J. Round b McBride	0	*W. M. Rose b G. Wright	0
A. C. Lucas c Schafer b McBride	12	*A. Appleby not out	0
G. E. Bird c McVey b H. Wright	15		
V. E. Walker b H. Wright	27	B 9, l-b 3, w 2	14
A. Anstruther c Batten b G. Wright	0		
*F. P. U. Pickering b H. Wright	9		105

America

H. Wright b Rose	2	J. O'Rourke b E. Lubbock	4
J. D. McBride b Rose	5	J. Sensenderfer b Pickering	0
A. G. Spalding b Appleby	23	T. Batten c Appleby b Pickering	4
W. Anson c FitzGerald b Rose	2	J. McMullen b Pickering	5
R. C. Barnes b Pickering	5	G. Hall c Round b Pickering	5
G. Wright b Rose	12	H. C. Schafer c A. Lubbock b Pickering	5
E. B. Sutton b Pickering	3	G. Beales not out	1
W. Fisher run out	3		
A. J. Leonard b Rose	13	B 2, l-b 2, w 1	5
S. Wright c A. Lubbock b E. Lubbock	0		
C. A. McVey b Pickering	10		107

* Played in America in 1872.

American Bowling

	Overs	Mdns	Runs	Wkts
H. Wright	52	32	43	4
McBride	37	19	34	3
G. Wright	16	9	14	4

MCC Bowling

	Overs	Mdns	Runs	Wkts
Pickering	15.3	4	23	8
Appleby	15	4	26	1
Rose.............	12	3	35	5
E. Lubbock	8	4	13	2

Umpires: Walter Price and F. Farrands.

THE CANTERBURY WEEK

August 3rd, 4th, 5th, 6th, 7th and 8th, 1874

The Canterbury Cricket Week of 1874 was reported to have been the most successful "week" yet played. The weather on the two important days – Monday and Thursday – was most fortunately favourable and the attendances numerous and brilliant beyond precedent. The new match – Kent and Gloucestershire v the Rest of England – that formed the prominent item in the cricket programme has (it was stated) by its success "become a great fact". The two county balls were crowdedly patronised by the beauty, rank and fashion of the county. "The great concomitant of cricket in the Canterbury week", The Old Stager's Theatricals, were "blazes of triumphs", and, beyond and above all, the great star of the cricketing world, the most wonderful batsmen of all times, shone with unwonted batting brilliancy, for, as the journals of the period eloquently recorded, in the only three innings he played in the Canterbury Week of 1874.

Mr. W. G. GRACE scored 94, 121 and 123!!!

MCC AND GROUND v MARLBOROUGH COLLEGE

Played at Marlborough, July 17, 1874

In this match the three MCC professionals – Farrands, Nixon and Scotton, incautiously travelled past the station they should have landed at, consequently they were not "up to time" for MCC's first innings, which the "Marlbro' Boys" finished off for 43 runs, the first five wickets being down with only 19 runs scored. MCC's second innings was of far better form, as it totalled 150 runs; of these, Mr A. F. Lucas made 39, including a 6 and three 4s; Mr G. A. Hodgson made 28, a 6 figuring among his hits; and Nixon (of Cambs.) made 24 by three singles, a couple of 3s, a 4, a 5 and a 6. A large quantity of big hits were made by the "Marlbro' Boys," to wit: F. H. Lee's 27 included a 7 and a 6; there was a 7, a 5 and a 4 in A. C. Sim's 32; P. R. Armstrong's 28 included three 5s and a 4; A. G. Steel's 10 was a two-hit innings, a 4 and a 6; in A. P. Wickham's 24 and 12 (not out) there was a 6, a 5 and a couple of 4s; and in A. J. S. Sambourne's 17 and 13 there was a 6 and a couple of 3s. So with all this big hitting there is nothing surprising in the fact that Marlborough College beat Marylebone Club and Ground by nine wickets. Totals: MCC and Ground (only eight men batted), 43 and 150; Marlborough College 166 and (one wicket down) 28.

NORTH v SOUTH

Played at Lord's, May 17, 1875
(for the benefit of the MCC Professional Fund)

The Whit Monday of 1875 was most enjoyably fine, the bright, hot sun that beamed down upon the millions of holiday folks out that day pleasure taking, being agreeably tempered by a cool and brisk breeze from the east. "Lord's" was thronged, so many as 8,342 having paid for admission to the old ground, which, as evening drew near, presented all the familiarly free and easy appearance of a great match day on a great holiday. The pavilion seats and roof had a much larger number of occupants than had ever been seen thereon at preceding Whit Monday matches. The grand stand was largely patronized. The tavern balcony was as full as the many bottles of champagne that were uncorked there on that day. The wall top of Mr. Frank Dark's garden wall was covered by those "who could climb and did not fear to fall". "The reporters' stall" was filled by an unusually large number of "the gentlemen of the press;" and around the ground the people sat, or stood, five or six deep, crowding in front of the score box throughout the afternoon and evening as they were never before allowed to crowd and, it is to be hoped, will never again be allowed to crowd; for the angry disputations, the noisy chaff, the frequent question asking to the scorers and the (at times) interception of all sight of the wickets by that upstanding throng of men – some of them six-footers – rendered the perfect fulfilment of the scorers' duties next door to an impossibility.

The match – as a fair trial of the cricketing strength of North and South – was a thorough failure, owing to the absence of many of the best cricketers of the North. Mr. A. N. Hornby did not play; Richard Daft, William Oscroft, Martin McIntyre, J. C. Shaw, Mycroft, Flint and Frost were playing at Nottingham in the Notts. v Derbyshire match; Ephraim Lockwood, Andrew Greenwood, Pinder, Allen Hill, Emmett, and Ulyett were playing against a Twenty-two at Hallam (or thereabouts); Watson – the Southerton of the North – was playing at Old Trafford; Rylott was absent; and F. Randon was playing at Leicester. So the North team had to be made up from men engaged on the ground, colts, veterans, etc.; consequently the surprise was not that the Northerners were so emphatically licked, but that they were enabled to get that very strong batting Eleven of the South out for an innings of 123 runs.

The North won choice, and were the first to bat; they lost a wicket when 6 runs only had been scored, another when 8 were booked, a third at 16, their fourth at 17, their fifth at 22 and their sixth at 29; then the Yorkshire colt – A. Marshall (a free hitter) – and Alfred Shaw made a bit of a stand, brought on Mr F. Grace to bowl v Mr W. Grace, and had hit the score to 48, when the colt collapsed for 13. Clayton then got hold of one or two, but left at 64; and at 75 Biddulph was stumped! all the nine wickets down having fallen to the bowling of Southerton, who had a wicket to perform on that suited him to a nicety, and who bowled with such skill and success, that a moiety of his overs were maidens and his nine wickets were obtained at a trifle over 3 runs per wicket. All hoped "The Mitcham Figaro," as his pen-and-ink friends term Southerton, would complete the innings by obtaining the 10th wicket, but fate foiled him, for that wicket (Morley's) was splendidly run out by Mr W. Grace and thereby the innings was finished at five minutes to two for 90 runs, Alfred Shaw taking his bat out for 26, a bit of batting that brought out a lot of lusty cheering from the holiday lads, some hundreds of whom triumphantly escorted Alfred from the wickets to the players' room.

At ten minutes past two, Mr W. Grace and Jupp commenced the South's innings to the bowling of Alfred Shaw and Morley. When 3 byes only had been scored, Shaw clean bowled Jupp for 0. Mr W. Grace and Mr Gilbert then made the score 20, when "dinner" (at 2.30) was called. After dinner, Mr Gilbert was had at mid-off, the score still at 20; and at 33, Mr W. Grace hit out at one from Morley, the bat swinging out of his hands a distance of 40 yards from the wicket to mid-on and the ball going to cover-slip, where it was caught by Rawlinson, the crack being thus curiously out for a hard earned 9. Before another run was made Mr Renny-Tailyour was bowled; Mr F. Grace and Charlwood then increased the score to 59, when Biddulph snapped Mr F. Grace for 22. At 70, both Mr Hadow and Richard Humphrey were bowled by Morley; and when, at 76, Biddulph settled Charlwood for 24 and eight wickets had gone down, the visitors began to fancy the Northmen would after all make a match of it, in so far as the first innings went. But on Pooley and Pearce (from Herts.) getting together, a stand was made and the score increased to 103, when Shaw bowled Pooley for 22, an innings that testified to the old Pooley form being still in full vigour. Southerton then stayed until Pearce had, in really good style, increased the score to 123, when Biddulph caught out the young man from Herts. for 21; and so the innings ended at five minutes to five, the match being then half played out with an advantage of 33 runs to the South.

The North's second innings was indeed a brief affair; commenced at 5.12, it was done with at 6.40. Mr C. Booth and Hicks began the batting to the bowling of Southerton and Mr W. Grace; they had made 17 runs before the first wicket (Mr Booth's) fell, but at 25, the second and third both went; at 37, the fourth wicket fell and at 42, half the wickets had gone. Bold, resolute, hard – aye and good – hitting by Clayton was the main reason why the sixth wicket stood up until the score reached 64, but before another run had been made, the seventh went; the eighth collapsed at 65 and the ninth at 66, Clayton being then very cleverly caught out by Mr W. Grace for 27, a hard driving innings and the largest score hit for the North in the match. Morley then had a go at one or two, but was stumped for 5 and so the innings ended for 72, leaving the Southerners only 40 to make to win. It was then twenty minutes to seven and under the impression there would be no more play that day, hundreds of visitors left the ground and thereby lost a brief but busy bit of batting. A consulation was held and a decision to play out the match that evening promptly come to; the clear-the-ground bell rang out forthwith, the people settled down in their places and at 6.50 out came Mr W. Grace and Jupp to get the 40 runs. They got them in dashing form. The bowlers were Alfred Shaw and Morley. Jupp commenced with a 3, a single was then overthrown into a 5, a 3 followed that and in this way the first 20 runs were made from 6 overs; then Mr Grace made a 4, a 4 and a 2 (all on-drives) from one over of Alfred Shaw's; and when nine overs had been bowled, 31 runs had been made; 5 more runs were made from the next over and 5 more from the following four balls and so the match was won, the 41 runs having been made from eleven overs, in exactly fifteen minutes and thus was this uninteresting "North v South" match played out in one day, the South the winners by ten wickets — Jupp, not out 13, Mr W. Grace, not out, 28.

The North

J. Hicks b Southerton	9	– lbw b W. G. Grace	9
F. Wyld c Hadow b Southerton	6	– b Southerton	6
E. B. Rawlinson b Southerton	0	– st Pooley b W. G. Grace	3
C. Booth Esq. b Southerton	2	– lbw b Southerton	8
R. Wright b Southerton	5	– b Southerton	4
J. Taylor c Pooley b Southerton	3	– b Southerton	0
A. Marshall b Southerton	13	– not out	3
Alfred Shaw not out	26	– b Southerton	4
R. Clayton c Jupp b Southerton	9	– c W. G. Grace b Southerton	27
Biddulph st Pooley b Southerton	2	– c T. Pearce b W. G. Grace	0
F. Morley run out	8	– st Pooley b Southerton	5
B 4, l-b 3	7	B 1, l-b 2	3
	90		72

The South

W. G. Grace Esq. c Rawlinson b Morley	9	– not out	28
H. Jupp b Alfred Shaw	0	– not out	13
W. Gilbert Esq. c Clayton b Morley	9		
G. F. Grace Esq. c Biddulph b Alfred Shaw	22		
H. W. Renny-Tailyour Esq. b Morley	0		
H. Carlwood c Biddulph b Alfred Shaw	24		
W. H. Hadow Esq. b Morley	3		
Richard Humphrey b Morley	0		
E. Pooley b Alfred Shaw	22		
T. Pearce c Biddulph b Marshall	21		
Southerton not out	4		
B 3, l-b 6	9		
	123		41

South Bowling

	Overs	Mdns	Runs	Wkts	Overs	Mdns	Runs	Wkts
Southerton	29	15	30	9	23.2	12	22	7
Mr W. G. Grace ...	17.3	6	25	—	23	6	47	3
Mr G. F. Grace	12	2	28	—				

North Bowling

	Overs	Mdns	Runs	Wkts	Overs	Mdns	Runs	Wkts
A. Shaw	43	26	52	4	6	1	24	—
Morley	38	20	55	5	5	2	17	—
A. Marshall	4.3	2	7	1				

Umpires: F. Farrands and Nixon.

GENTLEMEN OF MCC v THE ROYAL ARTILLERY

Played at Lord's, June 3, 4, 1875

Two quiet days at Lord's were enjoyed by the few visitors who witnessed the cricket in this match – the oldest now played by MCC. Barring a few (then) welcome summer showers, the weather was bright and hot and the happy absence of crowd, cads, card-criers and other unpleasantries necessarily suffered at a great match, increased the enjoyment, which would have been thorough had better out-cricket been played by both teams, especially by the gunners.

ALFRED SHAW's MAGNIFICENT BIT OF BOWLING

41 overs (36 maidens) for 7 runs and seven wickets — 6 bowled

MCC AND GROUND v NOTTINGHAMSHIRE

Played at Lord's, June 14, 15, 1875

Wind and weather alone considered, this was the most un-enjoyable match ever played out at Lord's, for throughout those two days the wind blew big and bitter blasts from the WSW, so cold that the air was more fitting for Ulsters and mid-winter than summer suits and midsummer and so strong that — in addition to other casualties — the wind broke clean in half the trunk of a full-sized sturdy elm tree that stood at that end of the Regent's Park nearest to Lord's Ground.

The attendances included most of the familiar faces seen on London grounds when a great match is being played by first-class cricketers, a strong contingent of "cricket critics" (grey beards and smooth chins) and a fairly large number of members; and if the gatherings were not, numerically, up to the form such a match deserved, that must be debited to the exceedingly ungenial cricketing weather; as it was 1,214 paid for admission the first day, and 1,439 on the second, and there can be no doubt but that had the match days been favoured with those sunny skies and seasonable warmth, cricketers – and all other men – naturally expect in "leafy June", the ground would have been largely attended, especially as it was Richard Daft's first match in London that season.

The batting was unequal and most certainly did not master the bowling, notwithstanding so many of the batting cracks of the period played. Only 440 runs were scored for the forty wickets down. Mr W. Grace was one hour at wickets scoring his 10 runs and one hour and ten minutes making his 35; he was thoroughly put on his defence by Alfred Shaw and one of the few batting treats of the match was the defence of Mr W. Grace against the rare bowling of Alfred Shaw; over after over was played in truly great form, shooters being got down upon with marvellous sharpness, but those enjoyable struggles between ball and bat ended in victories to Shaw, who clean bowled the crack in each innings. In his innings of 10 Mr Grace made only 3 runs (all singles) from Alfred Shaw's bowling and in his second innings of 35 runs only three of them (all singles) were obtained from Shaw's bowling. Mr I. D. Walker was one hour scoring his 13 runs, including a splendid cut down the ground for 5 from McIntyre and Mr I. D. was nearly an hour making his 12 runs all of which were from McIntyre's bowling. Mr Hadow was precisely thirty-eight minutes at wickets for his first innings of one run and in his second he went in fourth wicket down and took his bat out for 8, so it can be readily imagined how very carefully Mr Hadow played. Mr Webbe (the colt from Oxford) was undeservedly out in his second innings, being called by Mr Grace to a desperately sharp run and being splendidly thrown out from cover-point by Wyld. Mr Duncan (the colt from Cambridge) played with much steadiness a not out innings of 18 runs, made by five 2s and eight singles and equally steady was the batting of Mr Ridley during his one hour's play for 15 runs. Clayton hit as Clayton usually does when they let him stay – i.e., freely and hard, though for all that his 22 took him forty minutes to knock together. But the best batting for MCC – and in the match – was Mr Buller's 45; that was a brilliant display of truly fine all round hitting, comprising a superb on-drive up to the NE corner of the ground for 5 from Oscroft's bowling, four 4s – off-drive and cut from J. C. Shaw, on-drive from Oscroft and a magnificent leg hit from Morley, the ball pitching about a dozen yards from the racket court; in addition to those hits Mr Buller made seven 3s, three of them from Alfred Shaw's bowling; but although Mr Buller made three 4s, a 3 and two singles in his 17, he did not score one of those runs from Alfred Shaw. Mr Renny-Tailyour's 6 was a one hit innings – a grand on-drive from Morley, who shortly retaliated by clean bowling his man and with the following ball he as brilliantly bowled Mr Duncan. The Nottinghamshire innings was productive of further proof of good batting promise in Arthur Shrewsbury, who stayed forty minutes at wickets for 8 runs against the bowling of Mr Grace and Mr Ridley. None played the Oxford lobs in better form than this lad, who is not 21 years old, but who possesses the confidence of a veteran and shaped in a form that foretells a prominent batting career in the cricket of the future. Martin McIntyre was exactly one hour and ten minutes making his 41, the highest Notts. score; he played with unusual steadiness; he was missed at short-leg by Mr Duncan when he made 22 and finished his innings with a very fine drive up the ground for 4 – the only 4 he made, his other hits being one 3, eleven 2s and 12 singles. Daft appeared somewhat nervous on commencing his first innings and was some time ere he settled down; he was ninety-five minutes at wickets for his 25 runs, which were not made in "his old form" as reported; but in his second innings he quickly got into something like that "old form", played all the MCC bowling with his usual ease, grace and skill, saw seven wickets fall, the score increased from 4 to 75 and took his bat out for 35, an innings that included three good drives for 4 each and – his last hit – a superb off-drive from Mr W. Grace's bowling for 5.

The fielding of Mr Herbert at leg and long-off, of Mr Renny-Tailyour at square-leg and of Selby at cover-slip and long-off was A1; the very fine form in which they flew over ground after the ball and saved runs elicited frequent, loud and deserved cheering. But the cream of the fielding was the effective way in which Mr Ridley, Alfred Shaw, Morley and Mr W. Grace fielded their own bowling; that was indeed fine and enjoyable cricket, and atoned for several shortcomings in the field by others.

The bowling was very remarkable. McIntyre ended the play before dinner on the first day by bowling Lord Harris with a brilliant bailer – a better ball was never bowled; but on the second day Mc. commenced with an over that included two wides, a hit for 4 and a 2.

Morley, on the first day, started with six successive maiden overs; on the second day, one of his overs was finished off with a hit for 6, but in his following over he clean bowled two wickets. Mr Ridley, on the first day, bowled three wickets in five successive balls; on the second day he started with seven overs for one run and two wickets and finished with ten overs and three balls for five runs and two wickets. Mr W. Grace, in the match, bowled 83 overs for 86 runs and nine wickets; and although Mr Hadow failed to floor a wicket, only four of his 14 overs were hit. But successful as some of those bowlers undoubtedly were, all of them were entirely put into shade by the brilliant ball work done in the match by

ALFRED SHAW,

who, all told, bowled 95 overs (71 maidens) for 46 runs and nine wickets – averaging in the match less than half a run per over for 95 overs, and a shade over 5 runs per wicket for nine wickets.

Alfred commenced the bowling on the first day with a maiden over; two singles were scored from his second over and one from his third; then he bowled seven overs for one run and a wicket and when dinner was called at 2.30, he had bowled 44 overs (31 maidens) for 27 runs and two wickets; after dinner, he was hit a bit and they scored a 2 from each of his last overs; nevertheless, his bowling in that innings totalled up

Overs	Mdns	Runs	Wkts
54	35	39	2

If the reader runs his eye down the names of the eleven MCC batsmen, he will see they include several of Gentlemen of England status and some of the most accomplished batsmen and finest hitters of the period, making the above a most successful bit of bowling; but it was as nothing to what followed from the clever right hand of the same great master of the ball, who, in the old Club's second innings, actually bowled

Overs	Mdns	Runs	Wkts	
41.2	36	7	7	(six bowled)

Such marvellous bowling as this to such high-class batsmen has no equal in the history of the game. It brought out the full defensive powers of Mr W. Grace, Mr I. D. Walker, Mr Hadow, Mr Ridley and Mr Buller; none of these great hitters being able to get the ball away for runs and during their stay at wickets the attack from Alfred Shaw and their defence was indeed "splendid cricket," that will long be remembered with admiration by those who sat out that bitterly cold, boisterous, but memorable Tuesday at Lord's. To worthily portray on paper the many rare excellencies of Alfred Shaw's bowling in that second innings of MCC's is wholly beyond the power of the compiler of this little book, but he will give those who missed witnessing it an opportunity of estimating its excellence and success by the following full and careful chronicle of every ball bowled by Alfred Shaw in MCC's second innings:

. . . . 1 . . . . .
. . . . 1 . . . . w . . . . . . 1 . . . . .
. . . . 1 1 . w . . . . . . w . . . .
. . . . . . w (Dinner) . . . . w . . . .
. . . . w 2 . . . . w

The 2 hit (scored by Clayton) was a pure fluke, and so was one of the singles; bearing this in mind, considering that this bowling was delivered to some of the most skilled batsmen of the day, remembering also that six of their wickets were clean bowled, it will be conceded that those 41 overs and two balls for 7 runs and seven wickets by Alfred Shaw is the most wonderful display of the mastery of the ball over the bat ever delivered by bowler. Nevertheless, MCC won the match by 62 runs.

MCC and Ground

W. G. Grace Esq. b Alfred Shaw	10	– b Alfred Shaw	35
I. D. Walker Esq. b Alfred Shaw	13	– st Biddulph b Alfred Shaw	12
W. H. Hadow Esq. b Martin McIntyre	1	– not out	8
A. W. Ridley Esq. b William Oscroft	15	– b Alfred Shaw	8
C. F. Buller Esq. c Alfred Shaw b Morley	54	– b Alfred Shaw	17
A. J. Webbe Esq. b William Oscroft	0	– run out	0
Lord Harris b Martin McIntyre	3	– b Alfred Shaw	0
H. W. Renny-Tailyour Esq. c Alfred Shaw b Martin McIntyre.	4	– b Morley	6
A. S. Duncan Esq. not out	18	– b Morley	0
A. W. Herbert Esq. b Martin McIntyre	0	– b Alfred Shaw	0
R. Clayton c and b William Oscroft	22	– b Alfred Shaw	2
B 7, l-b 4, w 2	13	B 1, l-b 6, w 3	10
	153		93

Nottinghamshire

William Oscroft lbw b W. G. Grace	4	– b W. G. Grace	3
F. Wyld b Clayton	6	– b Ridley	0
Arthur Shrewsbury b W. G. Grace	3	– c and b W. G. Grace	8
Richard Daft c and b W. G. Grace	25	– not out	35
Martin McIntyre c Harris b W. G. Grace	41	– c I. D. Walker b Ridley	4
J. Selby not out	15	– c W. G. Grace b Ridley	1
Alfred Shaw c Hadow b Ridley	5	– st Webbe b W. G. Grace	7
William Shrewsbury b Ridley	0	– b W. G. Grace	5
Biddulph b Ridley	0	– b W. G. Grace	0
F. Morley c and b Ridley	9	– c and b Ridley	6
J. C. Shaw b Ridley	3	– c and b Ridley	5
B 2, l-b 1	3	B 1	1
	114		75

Nottinghamshire Bowling

	Overs	Mdns	Runs	Wkts	Overs	Mdns	Runs	Wkts
Alfred Shaw	45	35	39	2	41.2	36	7	7
M McIntyre	39	18	48	4	10	2	35	—
Morley	21	13	20	1	25	13	30	2
W. Oscroft	13.3	6	19	3	6	1	16	—
J. C. Shaw	6	2	14	—				

MCC and Ground Bowling

	Overs	Mdns	Runs	Wkts.	Overs	Mdns	Runs	Wkts
Mr W. Grace	45	20	43	4	38	18	43	5
Clayton	18	6	28	1				
Mr Ridley	14.1	8	15	5	38.3	24	31	5
Mr W. Hadow	14	10	13	—				
Mr R.-Tailyour	8	3	12	—				

Umpires: John West and Nixon.

OXFORD CIRCUIT v MIDLAND CIRCUIT

Played at Lord's, June 23, 1875

This one day match is noticed here to record – "In Mr Atkinson's 31 were a square-leg hit out of the ground for 6 past the grand stand, and an on-drive into the corner below the pavilion, for which 9 runs were made before the ball was returned." – *Bell's Life*, July 3.

Result – Midland Circuit 264; Oxford Circuit 71, and (one wicket down) 64.

OXFORD v CAMBRIDGE

Played at Lord's, June 28, 29, 30, 1875

This was the 41st cricket match played by Oxford and Cambridge Elevens, and inasmuch as each University was credited with nineteen victories, a more than usually strong interest was felt in the result of the 1875 struggle, which will long be remembered for the unprecedentedly large attandance on the second day; for the magnificent catch made by the Oxford colt, Mr A. J. Webbe; for the plucky, stirring form in which the Cambridge men brought up their second innings' score so near to victory; and for that never-to-be-forgotten last ball bowled by Mr Ridley, which so excitingly won the match for Oxford by 6 runs. As to the attendances, those tellers of truth, "the turnstiles", registered the following:

On the Monday,	On the Tuesday,	On the Wednesday,
7,388 paid.	12,697 paid.	5,002 paid.

That is to say, 25,087 persons paid 1s. to witness the Oxford v Cambridge match of 1875 played at Lord's.

On Monday, the first day, rain discouragingly fell from day-break to mid-day. At 1.20 it ceased raining for a brief while; this lull was followed by ten minutes of fierce rainfall; then a gleam of sunshine broke through the huge rain clouds, the foul weather passed away for a time, the coin was spun, Oxford won choice, the tarpaulin covers were taken off the carefully prepared wickets, and at ten minutes past two, this memorable cricket "battle of the blues" was commenced – Mr A. J. Webbe and Mr T. W. Lang batting for Oxford, Mr C. M. Sharpe and Mr H. M. Sims bowling for Cambridge, whose wicket-keeper was Mr Hamilton. Mr Sharpe set the ball rolling with a maiden over from the pavilion end wicket, each of the four balls being played well to the off by Mr Webbe; a bye was made from the first ball bowled by Mr Sims, the third ball being hit to square-leg for 3 by Mr Webbe, and so the match was got well under way. They had made 30 runs from seventeen overs when Mr Patterson's slows were tried v Mr Sims's fasts. They had made 40 runs from 26 overs when Mr Webbe was twice let off at slip by Mr Sims, and Mr Lang was missed being stumped by Mr Hamilton. They had made 67 runs from 47 overs when Mr Greenfield's lobs were tried for three overs, and they had made 86 runs when a capital catch at cover-slip settled Mr Webbe for 55, the highest score made in the match. (Mr Lang had then made 22.) There was some excellent leg-hitting in Mr Webbe's 55, which included seven 4s (four to leg), and five 3s (three to leg). Mr Campbell was also had at cover-slip by Mr Smith, and then a roar of Oxford cheers greeted Mr Ridley's walk to the wickets. From the first hit he made, Mr Ridley nearly ran himself out, but escaping that very close shave, steady play ensued, and the score was slowly increased to 133, when Mr Sims bowled Mr Lang, who had been two hours and seventeen minutes scoring his 45 runs, made by two 4s, five 3s (four of them neat, clean cuts), three 2s and sixteen singles. Mr Pulman was next man in, but heavy rain then fell and interrupted play for a full hour, the thousands of opened umbrellas that covered the patient British public, who sat and stood the downpour out all round the ground, forming a strange and curious cricket ground sight. At 5.30, they resumed play, the weather still threatening and the light bad. Mr Sharpe and Mr Patterson went on with the bowling, and when 7 more runs had been slowly added, a ringing Cambridge shout told Mr Patterson had bowled the Oxford captain for 21. Another 7 runs were made, and then another catch at cover-slip by Mr

Smith settled Mr Briggs, after which (the light very bad) the Oxford wickets went down so fast that when "time" was called at seven o'clock, the score stood at 188 for seven wickets down – Mr Pulman not out 19, Mr Game not out 2.

On Tuesday, the second day, the weather was favourable, and such was the interest felt in the match, that the attendance was the largest yet seen at an Inter-University cricket contest, over £600 being taken at the gates that day for admission to the ground, which in the afternoon presented a pleasantly animated scene. The roofs of a large number of drags clustered up by "Knatchbull's corner" were charmingly freighted by those "fair flowers of society" whose presence so brightly grace any assemblage. The grand stand was full, the pavilion seats and roof were crowded, two rows of people sat on the turf inside the roped arena, and outside it they stood crowded and crammed together six deep all round the ground. On the tops of all walls commanding a sight men clustered as closely as they could, and, indeed, every available spot that afforded a view of the cricket had its occupants by some of the 12,000 visitors, who on that day paid and passed on to the old ground.

Play was resumed at a quarter past eleven. At twenty-three minutes to twelve, the innings was over for 200 runs, the last man out being Mr Pulman, who was had at slip for 25, a patient, careful, excellent, and very useful batting display. The wickets went down as follows:

86 for one Mr Webbe	90 for two Mr Campbell	133 for three Mr Lang	140 for four Mr Ridley	147 for five Mr Briggs
150 for six Mr Royle	186 for seven Mr Buckland	193 for eight Mr Game	195 for nine Mr Tylecote	200 for ten Mr Pulman

Cambridge batting was commenced at 11.53 by Mr A. P. Lucas and Mr F. J. Greenfield to the bowling of Mr Kelcey and Mr Lang; the wicket being looked after by Mr Tylecote. When twenty overs had been bowled for 21 runs, only 6 of those runs (a 4 and a 2) had been made from Mr Kelcey's bowling, but soon after a fine straight drive by Mr Greenfield from "a Kelcey" sent the ball bounding into the pavilion; then a catch at point settled Mr Greenfield for 12, the score at 27 from 24 overs. An encouraging cheer greet Mr Longman's walk to wickets, a compliment the Cambridge captain repayed by playing an innings of 40 runs. At 39 a catch at point finished Mr Lucas's innings for 19 runs; thereupon Mr Blacker faced his captain, and the cricket was excellent, good batting being countered by good fielding; the bowling was frequently changed, Mr Kelcey, Mr Lang, Mr Ridley, Mr Kelcey (again), Mr Buckland, and Mr Royle all taking a turn with the ball, which was then ably mastered by the bat, and the score slowly, but skilfully played up to 93, when Buckland bowled Blacker for 19, and at 102 Longman was had at point for 40 – the highest score made in the match for Cambridge. Then Mr Sims hit wicket, Mr Macan was bowled, and Mr Lyttelton very finely c and b by Mr Lang who just reached the ball; Mr Lyttelton's 23 included some free, hard hitting, five consecutive hits by him being a 3 (cut), a 2 (leg hit), a 4 (drive to the embankment), a 3 (drive to the pavilion), and a 4 (leg hit). Mr Patterson's 12 included a hard drive for 4, but the others did but little, and at a quarter to four the innings was over for 163 runs, the wickets having fallen as under:

27 for one Mr Greenfield	39 for two Mr Lucas	93 for three Mr Blacker	102 for four Mr Longman	131 for five Mr Sims
135 for six Mr Macan	136 for seven Mr Lyttelton	144 for eight Mr Smith	152 for nine Mr Patterson	163 for ten Mr Hamilton

Oxford's second was started at eight minutes past four by Mr Webbe and Mr Lang, to the bowling of Mr Sharpe and Mr Patterson, and as Mr Sharpe captured both Mr Lang's and Mr Campbell's wickets with the score at 5 only, and Mr Smith at cover point had

Mr Ridley with the score at 16, the roar of Cambridge cheers that rang out as each wicket collapsed was something to hear and remember; cheers that were repeated with threefold vigour when at 34 Mr Sims ran from slip to short leg and finely – very finely – caught out Mr Webbe for 21, fifteen of which runs were made by a 3 and three 4s. Then, by careful play, Mr Pulman and Mr Briggs brought on a bowling change, and added 30 runs to the score, when Mr Briggs was bowled by a lob; and when 10 more runs had been made Mr Pulman was stumped for 30 – another carefully played, good, and very useful innings of 80 minutes' duration; there was a cut for 3, a leg hit for 4, and two drives for 4 each in Mr Pulman's 30. Mr Game was fortunate in being missed when he had made 3 only, and in having a single made into a 5 by an overthrow by Mr Lyttelton, but when he had made 22 a splendid one hand catch at mid-on by Mr Lucas settled Mr Game. The next ball delivered bowled Mr Buckland, and when 9 more runs were made the stumper had Mr Royle, a tumult of cheers for Cambridge welcoming the capture of each wicket. Mr Kelcey was last man in; by a 2, a single, and a couple of hard thwacks for 4 each he quickly made 11, but then he lifted one that Mr Patterson caught, and so – at a quarter to seven – Oxford's second was over for 137 runs, the wickets having gone down as follows:

5 for one Mr Lang	5 for two Mr Campbell	16 for three Mr Ridley	34 for four Mr Webbe	64 for five Mr Briggs
74 for six Mr Pulman	109 for seven Mr Game	109 for eight Mr Buckland	121 for nine Mr Royle	137 for ten Mr Kelcey

On the completion of the innings the ground was covered with visitors, hundreds of whom left under the impression play for the day was ended; but in due time the clear-the-ground bell rang sharply, the wickets were promptly rolled, Mr Sharpe and Mr Hamilton took their places at the wickets, and Mr Lang commenced the bowling in Cambridge's second innings. The first ball delivered Mr Sharpe hit well to leg for 4; the remaining three balls he "played", and when that one over was over "time" was called, and the second day's play ended with the match standing for the morrow at the interesting phase of:

Cambridge 171 to win, with ten wickets to fall.

On Wednesday, the third day, the weather was not promising, heavily charged rain-clouds rapidly rolling up from the SW and darkening the ground; however, they travelled further, so Lord's escaped for a time the deluge they threatened, and at ten minutes past twelve, a loud cheer greeted the appearance of the two not out Cantabs, who resumed their innings to the bowling of Mr Buckland and Mr Lang. Scoring commenced with 2 for an overthrow by Mr Royle, who fell in fielding the ball and was over-anxious in shying it in. Then a 4 to leg by Mr Sharpe from the first ball bowled by Mr Lang elicited a salvo of Cambridge cheers; but sharp, very sharp, runs for singles, brought out earnest and requisite warnings of "Steady", "Steady", from the pavilion. Nevertheless, runs were rapidly made, and "20" hoisted on the boards was welcomed with shouts for Cambridge, vigorously countered by cheers for Oxford, when, at 21, an earnest, sharp "How's that?" was answered "Out" by the umpire, and Mr Hamilton left "lbw" for 11. Mr Lucas began with a 4 to leg, but in the following over he was bowled, and with the score at 26 for two wickets, Mr Longman went in, a loud Cambridge cheer welcoming the captain; the score slowly rose, but Mr Lang not being on the spot, he was relieved by Mr Ridley, who bowled three overs for 11 runs, and then judiciously thinking that enough for the present, gave the ball to Mr Royle, who bowled fourteen balls without a run being made from him, and with the fifteenth ball he bowled Mr Sharpe for a well-played 29, that included three 4s (leg-hits and a cut), and a drive for 3. Mr Blacker "hit on" at 67, and at 76 a shooter bowled Mr Longman for 23, a sterling good innings. There were then five wickets down and Cambridge 95 runs from winning, the look out then being somewhat cheering for Oxford; but on the Hon. E. Lyttelton facing Mr Greenfield, Cambridge hopes rose high, especially when Mr Lyttelton was missed by Mr Lang, and a snick for 3 caused the 100 to be hoisted; but at 101, Mr Greenfield was caught out from a skyer. Mr Sims then went in, and Mr Lang was again unfortunate in missing Mr Lyttelton, who, however, was shortly after settled by a catch at the top of the ground, so splendidly achieved that the spectators evinced their delight thereat in three distinct peals of applause. Mr Lyttelton hit the ball very finely to square-leg forward; Mr Webbe dashed after the ball in front of the people for full twenty yards, and whilst running at top speed, sprang up and clutched the ball in great form. That was indeed "a brilliant bit of fielding", and so long as 'Varsity cricketers gossipingly play their matches over again, so long must both blues recall with high praise Webbe's great catch that settled Lyttelton in the 1875 match. The score was at 114 when Mr Lyttelton left, and at 128 (at ten past 2), rain stopped play until 3.35; then Mr Sims and Mr Patterson hit so determinedly, and the wet, slippery ground caused the Oxford men to field so unfortunately, that the runs were rapidly being hit off. At ten minutes to four, the 150 was up, and when five minutes more had passed away, the 160 was hoisted, the cheering for Cambridge all this time, as hit after hit rapidly rubbed off the runs, was loud and protracted. One more run was scored, and then Mr Ridley took the ball, and – but, perhaps, how excitingly the match was worked off will be best told by the following record of what took place:

At 161 for seven – or 14 to win – Mr Ridley bowled Mr Buckland.
With the first ball he delivered, Mr Ridley bowled Mr Patterson .... 14 to win.
At 161 for eight Mr Macan went in; he made a single .... 13 to win.
Mr Sims then drove one from Mr Ridley for 4 .... 9 to win.

(Then Mr. Lang bowled v Mr Royle.)

A leg-bye from Mr Lang's bowling made it .... 8 to win.
A no-ball bowled by Mr Lang made it .... 7 to win.
An especially fine catch at long-on by Mr Pulman (Mr Sims out) left it one wicket to fall and .... 7 to win.

So the score was 168 for nine when the last of the Cantabs – Mr Smith – went in. He did not appear confident, but stopped two balls bowled by Mr Ridley, who then tossed in one that clean bowled Mr S., and that ball, at four minutes past four, won Oxford the 41st match by 6 runs.

Thereupon the Oxford Eleven threw up their caps in token of their gratification at gaining this much coveted victory. Thousands of excited men rushed to the pavilion front and roared for "Ridley", "Ridley". The longer they stayed the more vigorous became their shouts. At last Mr Ridley came and bowed his thanks, but that would not do, so he was forced down the steps on to the turf; there he was hoisted on to men's shoulders, and – pushing through the roaring crowd – they carried him to and from the wickets with all the wild enthusiasm of other days. So ended this memorable contest, which Oxonians will ever recall as "Ridley's match", with as much pleasure as Cantabs refer to the 1870 contest as "Cobden's match".

Oxford

*A. J. Webbe Esq. c Smith b Sharpe	55	– c Blacker b Sharpe	21
T. W. Lang Esq. b Sims	45	– c and b Sharpe	2
D. Campbell Esq. c Smith b Sharpe	1	– b Sharpe	0
A. W. Ridley Esq. (Captain) b Patterson	21	– c Smith b Patterson	2
*R. Briggs Esq. c Smith b Sharpe	2	– b Greenfield	12
W. W. Pulman Esq. c Blacker b Sharpe	25	– st Hamilton b Sharpe	30
*V. Royle Esq. b Patterson	1	– st Hamilton b Sharpe	21
*F. M. Buckland Esq. b Sims	22	– b Patterson	0
W. H. Game Esq. st Hamilton b Patterson	5	– c Lucas b Patterson	22
H. G. Tylecote Esq. c Greenfield b Sharp	1	– not out	12
W. Foord-Kelcey Esq. not out	2	– c Patterson b Sharpe	11
B 15, l-b 3, w 2	20	B 4	4
	200		137

Cambridge

F. J. Greenfield Esq. c Ridley b Kelcey	12	– c Campbell b Royle	14
*A. P. Lucas Esq. c Buckland b Ridley	19	– b Buckland	5
G. H. Longman Esq. (Captain) c Ridley b Buckland	40	– b Royle	23
W. Blacker Esq. b Buckland	19	– b Royle	1
*Hon. E. Lyttelton c and b Lang	23	– c Webbe b Buckland	20
H. M. Sims Esq. hit wkt b Lang	5	– c Pulman b Lang	39
G. Macan Esq. b Lang	2	– not out	1
*W. S. Patterson Esq. c Ridley b Buckland	12	– b Ridley	18
*A. F. Smith Esq. c Royle b Lang	3	– b Ridley	0
*C. M. Sharpe Esq. not out	6	– b Royle	29
H. A. Hamilton Esq. st Tylecote b Lang	5	– lbw b Lang	11
B 10, l-b 7	17	B 1, l-b 4, n-b 2	7
	163		168

* Their first year in the Eleven.

Cambridge Bowling

	Overs	Mdns	Runs	Wkts	Overs	Mdns	Runs	Wkts
Mr Sharpe	68.2	29	89	5	37	14	66	6
Mr Patterson	41	21	51	3	34	12	44	3
Mr Sims	26	10	30	2	5	1	14	—
Mr Greenfield	7	3	10	—	7	2	9	1

Oxford Bowling

	Overs	Mdns	Runs	Wkts	Overs	Mdns	Runs	Wkts
Mr Lang	35	15	35	5	14	2	33	2
Mr Kelcey	30	17	48	1	15	4	23	—
Mr Buckland	28	12	34	3	22	8	38	2
Mr Ridley	20	9	21	1	4.3	1	16	2
Mr Royle	7	3	8	—	28	7	51	4

Umpires: F. Morley and F. Wyld.

RESULTS OF PAST INTER-UNIVERSITY CRICKET MATCHES

Won by Oxford			Won by Cambridge		
Year	Where	How won	Year	Where	How won
1829	Oxford	115 runs	1839	Lord's	One innings and 125 runs
1836	Lord's	121 runs	1840	Lord's	63 runs
1838	Lord's	98 runs	1841	Lord's	8 runs
1846	Oxford	Three wickets	1842	Lord's	162 runs
1848	Oxford	23 runs	1843	Oxford	54 runs
1850	Oxford	127 runs	1845	Lord's	Six wickets
1852	Lord's	One innings and 77 runs	1847	Lord's	138 runs
1853	Lord's	One innings and 19 runs	1849	Lord's	Three wickets
1854	Lord's	One innings and 18 runs	1851	Lord's	One innings and 4 runs
1855	Lord's	Three wickets	1856	Lord's	Three wickets
1857	Lord's	81 runs	1859	Lord's	28 runs
1858	Lord's	One innings and 38 runs	1860	Lord's	Three wickets
1863	Lord's	Eight wickets	1861	Lord's	133 runs
1864	Lord's	Four wickets	1862	Lord's	Eight wickets
1865	Lord's	114 runs	1867	Lord's	Five wickets
1866	Lord's	12 runs	1868	Lord's	168 runs
1871	Lord's	Eight wickets	1869	Lord's	58 runs
1873	Lord's	Three wickets	1870	Lord's	2 runs
1874	Lord's	One innings and 92 runs	1872	Lord's	One innings and 166 runs
1875	Lord's	6 runs			

Unfinished matches	1827	Lord's	Oxford 1st inns. 258	Cambridge 1st inns. 92	Rain
	1844	Lord's	Oxford 1st inns. 96	Cambridge 1st inns. 69	both years

Summary – 41 matches played. Oxford won 20. Cambridge won 19. 2 unfinished.

Cambridge's 338 (in 1872) and Oxford's 297 (in 1853) are the two highest totals yet made in these matches.

Mr Yardley's 130 (in 1872), and 100 (in 1870) are the two highest individual scores yet hit in these matches.

PUBLIC ATTENDANCES AT THE OXFORD AND CAMBRIDGE MATCHES OF 1871, 1872, 1873, 1874 AND 1875

The turnstiles at the entrance gates at Lord's were first used in 1871. Those unerring reporters (the turnstiles) recorded the following as the numbers who had paid and passed on to the ground at the last five Oxford v Cambridge matches:

	On the Monday	On the Tuesday	On the Wednesday	Total the 2 days
1871	9,195	7,964	—	17,159
1872	10,283	4,905	—	15,189
1873	10,153	7,178	—	17,331
1874	8,946	4,161	—	13,107
1875	7,388	12,697	4,902	(3 days) 24,987

In 1871 the match was concluded at 1.30; in 1872 at five minutes to four; in 1873 at 5.30; in 1874 at 1.30 (on the second days), and in 1875 at four minutes past four on the third day.

N.B. – "The Cricketers' Almanack" for 1865 contains the full scores of all Oxford v Cambridge matches played up to that date, from when each successive Almanack contains the full score of the preceding year's match. All the volumes are on sale.

ETON v HARROW

Played at Lord's, July 9, 10, 1875

That Eton v Harrow maintains its popular position in fashionable society as "the match of the season", was abundantly proved by the facts that all the seats in The Grand Stand at Lord's were secured so early that the MCC Committee resolved to have erected another Stand (larger than the temporary Grand Stand of 1874), and that a clear week prior to the match the following notice was issues via the public press:

"The whole available space having been filled up, no further applications for carriage or enclosure tickets can be entertained"

Lord's Ground, July 1. R. A. FitzGerald, Secretary, MCC"

The little row of cosy boxes fronting "Lord's Ground Hotel" were eagerly and early engaged, and there was not a window in the few villas commanding a view of the famous "battle-field of the young blues", that had not, by invitation or otherwise, been secured some time previously. In fact every concluded arrangement foreshadowed (weather permitting) an unprecedentedly large and brilliant gathering at the '75 match; but the weather did not permit, for on the first day rain fell with a persistency and fluency rarely, if ever, equalled even at Eton and Harrow matches; and, although it was pleasantly fine on the second day, Friday's moisture had somewhat damped the fashionable ardour, and the results were – attendances not equal to expectations, and an unfinished match. As to the attendances, the numbers registered on the tell-tales at the two gates told that:

On the Wet Friday,	and	On the Fine Saturday
3,540 paid 2s. 6d. for admission.		9,982 paid 2s. 6d. for admission.

The numbers in the grand stands were estimated at (about) 850 on the first day and (about) 750 on the second day, and it was calculated that (about) 450 carriages belonging to members of MCC crowdedly filled the space allotted for vehicles.

THE CANTERBURY WEEK

August 2, 3, 4, 5, 6, 7, 1875

"Admission on Monday and Tuesday, 1s." This was the only novelty in the official programme for The Canterbury Cricket Week of 1875. There was the same unmeaning, uninteresting match that was played in 1874 to lead off the week's cricket. There was the same excellent twelve-a-side contest between The County of Kent and The Gentlemen of MCC for the second match that has so appropriately formed the centre piece in several prior programmes, and to wind up the cricket of "the week", ther was the old Red, Black and Gold match of I Zingari v The Gentlemen of Kent that (in compliment to "I.Z.", some of whose members originated "The Week"), has for so long a period held position as third match.

There was pleasantly played military music up on the ground each afternoon, and the usual theatricals or county balls down in the city each night. Flags in profusion fluttered from the outward walls of most of the houses in "The High", "St. George's", and "The Parade", and the fashionably familiar tri-coloured ribbon of "I.Z." appeared to be as popular a necessity in shop windows, and elsewhere, as heretofore. Strangers who visited St. Lawrence for the first time, and enjoyed the game in the sunshine of the Bank Holiday, left the clerical city with delighted impressions of the pleasantly situated old ground, and of the cricket played that day thereon; but old hands at "The Week" who stayed it out to the stormy end, left with an impression that their 1875 pilgrimage lacked the thorough enjoyment of the old "weeks" when the principal match not only interested all Kent but all England.

GREAT SCORING BY A CLIFTON COLLEGIAN

Played at Clifton College, June 23, 1875

Mr R. E. Bush, caught out, 80, and (first man in) not out, 228

It will not be out of place to record here some wonderful scoring by the Clifton Captain in a match played on the C.C. ground last season. The match was "South Town v Brown's", a college contest, concluded on the 23rd June. Mr R. E. Bush was first man in both innings; his 80 runs (out of 116 from the bat!) were made by two 6s, one 5, four 4s, six 3s, five 2s, and nineteen singles. His 228 not out comprised seven 6s, six 5s, nine 4s, twenty-one 3s, nine 2s, and thirty-nine singles. It will thus be seen Mr R. E. Bush scored 308 runs in a match, and was only once out; and that in his second innings he made 108 runs in 22 hits! In his big innings Mr R. E. Bush gave but two chances, and they were both between his scoring 104 and 120. Between the falls of the fourth and fifth wickets Mr F. Bryant (who made 107) and Mr R. E. Bush put on 252 runs! The rest of their side made only 10 runs between them, consequently there was no "double". Just fancy an innings of 379 runs with no double figure score in it! If this be not "a cricket curiosity", what is? To render this record complete, the full score is here given of the two innings played for:

South Town

R. E. Bush c Cooper b H. Evershed	80	– (first man in) not out	228
S. D. Piers hit wkt b Spence	0	– b Spence	1
F. Leir b Spence	0	– b Spence	2
C. Haynes b Spence	11	– b H. Evershed	0
J. P. Bush b H. Evershed	0	– b H. Evershed	0
F. Bryant b Spence	8	– b Spence	107
J. E. Bush b Spence	12	– b H. Evershed	6
J. Evans	5	– b Spence	1
A. G. Hobart b H. Evershed	0	– c and b Spence	0
J. F. Evans b Spence	0	– lbw b Spence	0
K. O. Young not out	0	– b Spence	0
Extras	21	Extras	34
	137		379

THE LARGEST INNINGS EVER SCORED – 724 RUNS FOR EIGHT WICKETS

ROYAL ENGINEERS v I ZINGARI

Played at Chatham, August 20, 21, 1875

In recording this very "extraordinary innings", one who ought to know all about it stated in *Bell's Life* – "The weather on both days was splendid", and "the wicket was simply perfect for the batsman, and impossible for the bowler".

About noon on Friday, August the 20th, The Royal Engineers commenced the batting; when play ceased that evening the Royal Engineers score stood thus:

L. K. Scott Esq. not out	142
Hon. M. G. Talbot not out	153
B 8, l-b 4, w 13	25
(no wicket down)	320

On the Saturday the two batsmen increased the score to 356, when Mr Talbot was run out for 172, the 356 being the greatest number of runs (by 73) ever scored before a first wicket fell. On Mr Talbot's leaving, Mr Scott and Mr Renny-Tailyour made the score 395, when both left, Mr Scott having had a very busy time of it between wickets. When the fifth wicket fell the runs averaged 102 per wicket, and when "time" was called on that Saturday evening, and the stumps finally drawn, there had been ten and a half hours' cricket played, 1,224 balls bowled by I Zingari, and 724 runs (including 55 extras) scored, and eight wickets lost by Royal Engineers, the two days' cricket resulting in the following "extraordinary innings" hit by

The Royal Engineers

L. K. Scott Esq. c Kemp b Crutchley	164
Hon. M. G. Talbot run out	172
H. W. Renny-Tailyour Esq. b Fryer	26
L. B. Friend Esq. b Crutchley	1
W. H. Stafford Esq. c Fellows b Crutchley	58
F. T. Maxwell Esq. b Fryer	64
P. G. Von Donop Esq. run out	101
H. Mitchell Esq. c Balfour b Russell	62
C. V. W. Stratford Esq. not out	21
B 21, l-b 12, w 22	55
(8 wkts)	724

Captain Fellowes, E. S. E. Childers Esq. and H. E. Abbott Esq. did not bat.

The eight wickets fell in the following order:

1/356 2/395 3/395 4/399 5/511 6/523 7/669 8/724

I Zingari Bowling

	Balls	Mdns	Runs	Wkts		Balls	Mdns	Runs	Wkts
*Mr F. E. R. Fryer	364	35	154	2	*Hon. S. Ponsonby-Fane	48	2	31	—
Mr P. Crutchley ..	352	19	228	3	Lord E. Somerset .	44	1	28	—
Mr G. Russell	184	14	114	1	*Mr R. D. Balfour	32	4	17	—
*Mr C. Kemp	120	8	65	—					
*Mr H. Fellows ...	80	8	32	—					

* Mr Fryer bowled one wide ball; Mr Kemp bowled six wides; Mr H. Fellows bowled two wides; Hon. S. Ponsonby-Fane bowled ten wides, and Mr Balfour bowled three wides.

The three I Zingari who did not bowl were: Captain Inge, Mr J. Langley, and Mr C. Mills.

As to the hitting of The Royal Engineers, that will be best understood from the following record compiled from the score sheet:

Mr Scott's 164 was made by one 5, nine 4s, eighteen 3s, sixteen 2s, and 37 singles.

Hon. M. Talbot's 172 was made by three 5s, seven 4s, eight 3s, thirty 2s, and 45 singles.

Mr Renny-Tailyour's 26 was made by one 8, one 4, five 2s, and four singles.

Mr Stafford's 58 was made by one 6, two 4s, five 3s, seven 2s, and twelve singles.

Mr Maxwell's 64 was made by three 4s, two 3s, twelve 2s, and 22 singles.

Mr Von Donop's 101 was made by one 7, two 6s, one 5, one 4, eight 3s, sixteen 2s, and seventeen singles.

Mr Mitchell's 62 was made by three 5s, five 4s, four 3s, one 2, and fifteen singles.

Mr Stratford's 21 was made by three 3s, five 2s, and two singles.

The total hits made in this wondrous large innings were: One 8, one 7, three 6s, eight 5s, twenty-eight 4s, forty-eight 3s, ninety-two 2s, and 156 singles.

Respecting the fielding of I Zingari, *Bell's Life* stated "The fielding, even to the last, was good and spirited, and in many respects brilliant, and though there were some mischances in the latter part of the innings, nearly 500 runs were scored before a chance to hand was missed in the field."

THE CANTERBURY WEEK

August 7, 8, 9, 10, 11, 12, 1876

The charge of one shilling admission to the ground on each of the six days; splendid sunny summer weather from Monday morn to Saturday eve; large and brilliant assemblages on the cricket ground; wickets rolled to unsurpassable smoothness by a steam roller(!); innings by sides of 557 (for nine wickets) – 473 – 355 – 345 – 226 – 206 – (for eight wickets) – and 144 runs; individual scores of 344(!) – 154 – 143 – 109 – 91 – 84 – 63 – 58 – 57 not out – and 52 runs; 2,328 runs scored, but no match finished, and the old I Zingari match not even commenced, are the facts and features that will render The Canterbury Cricket Week of 1876 the most famous yet played.

The two County Balls appear to have been as numerously attended by the fair maids, matrons, and magnates of the county as heretofore; and "The Old Stagers" drew to the little theatre as large, light-hearted, laughing audience as they ever attracted since "the theatricals" of "The O.S." were first played in the old theatre in 1842.

The cricket programme for "The Week" was: Kent and Gloucestershire v England, Gentlemen of MCC v The County of Kent, and Gentlemen of Kent v I Zingari; but committees propose and batsmen (aided by steam-rolled wickets) dispose of these matters; and unprecedentedly large scoring not only prevented either of the two matches commenced being concluded, but wholly pushed the old I Zingari match out of the programme. Thursday ("The Ladies' Day") was – as a "ladies' day" should be – bright and beautiful; and the scene presented on the historically famous old ground must have been magnificent. *The Kent Herald* stated: "The attendance is said to have numbered 7,000; and the effect of the charming costumes of the ladies made altogether a brilliant scene." *The Sportsman* chronicled the gathering this-wise: "On the slope at the upper side of the ground, under the famous 'Tree', the ladies mustered in greater force than ever, and at this spot the spectators were six and seven deep. . . . Splendid weather, the large expanse of ground in every part occupied by an appreciative assemblage, in which were some of the fairest and comeliest faces to be seen at any event during the cricket season." And *Bell's Life* remarked: "The ladies' day was very grand, nothing like it having been seen on any previous gathering ... that brilliant display of Kentish grace, beauty and fashion which can only be seen, even at Canterbury, on the Thursday of 'The Week'".

And so on, in those polite and pretty phrases so natural to "cricket critics", did other "special correspondents" sing high praises of "The Ladies' Day" of 1876. The cricket played on that day commenced with the 12-a-side match:

THE COUNTY OF KENT v THE GENTLEMEN OF MCC

A marvellous run-getting match, which – like its predecessor – three days of splendid cricketing weather was insufficient to play out. Kent commenced the batting in this wonderful match at noon and when the stumps were drawn at ten minutes to seven the Kent batsmen were still pegging away at the MCC bowling. Mr W. Yardley began his hitting when the score was at 41 for two wickets; he was bowled for 47 when the score was at 177 for four wickets. Young George Hearne (son of George) began his innings when the score stood at 256 for six wickets. When play ceased for the day young George had made 51 not out. But Kent's hero on that ladies' day was Lord Harris, who went to wickets with the score at 70 runs for three wickets, stayed until 304 had been scored and then was caught out at mid-off for 154 – "the longest score", wrote the chroniclers, "the Kentish Captain has yet made in a first-class match". The hits made by Lord Harris were 28 singles, nine 2s, four 3s and twenty-four 4s, or 96 by fourers! so it can well be believed that "his hitting was especially hard", as chronicled, and doubtless his innings was "a brilliant display", for assuredly Lord Harris was never in finer hitting form than he was throughout the great scoring season – 1876. That day of hard hitting closed with Kent having scored 453 runs and lost ten wickets; George Hearne, not out 51; Henty, not out 6.

Friday was as lovely as had been the Thursday, but the attendance was slack. Play was resumed at ten to twelve. In ten minutes the innings was over and young Hearne not out 57 – an innings played so well as to earn him the applause of all on the ground. "Mr Grace and the other members of MCC joining in encouraging the lad, who was also subsequently rewarded by the County Club." Nine MCC bowlers were tried that innings. They bowled 195 overs and two balls for the 473 scored; so the quality of the bowling can be better imagined than described.

MCC batting was commenced at 12.25; by 4.20 their innings was over for 144 runs. Mr Lucas was bowled with the score at 13; Mr Grace was caught out for 17 (all the runs then scored), and the innings was wound up by the lad.

	Overs	Mdns	Runs	Wkts
Hearne	4.1	4	none	3

Young George Hearne had, so far in the match, framed so well that he had scored 57 not out; caught out Mr W. Grace for 17 runs and bowled the above rare bit of bowling; and considering he had only just turned his twentieth year, it must be admitted a wonderfully good all round performance of the little lad's.

With the large lot of 329 runs to hit off ere they could make a start from Kent's first innings, the MCC men commenced their "follow on" at five minutes to five with Mr W. Grace and Mr Lucas. With the score at 7 only Mr Lucas was out and the previously seeming hopeless task appeared still more hopeless; but then Mr Grace started his wonderful hitting in such form that he made 20 runs from two successive over of Hearne's; had brought the score to 100 in forty-five minutes; and when the stumps were drawn at 6.45 he (by hitting almost unexampled in its brilliant severity) had in 110 minutes raised the score to the following hopeful phase:

Mr W. G. Grace not out	133
Mr A. P. Lucas c Thomson b Hearne	7
Mr H. N. Tennent c Penn b Absolom	12
Mr G. Bird b Foord-Kelcey	13
Mr L. S. Howell c Shaw b Thornton	30
Mr P. Crutchley not out	5
Extras	17
	(4 wkts) 217

(Mr Grace and Mr Howell had increased the score from 125 for three wickets, to 203 for four.)

Saturday was the last day of "the Week", and Mr Grace's day; for on that day he completed the largest innings ever played for MCC, made three-fifths of the runs in the largest innings ever scored on the Canterbury ground and had – according to *The Kent Herald* – "completely settled the Kentish Twelve".

The day was intensely hot and so was the hitting of the MCC two – Mr W. Grace and Mr Crutchley – who resumed their innings at noon and were not parted until late in the afternoon when they had increased the score by 227 runs! as Mr Crutchley went to wickets with the score at 203 and was out for 84 with it at 430. There were then five wickets down at an average of 86 runs per wicket and Mr Grace as full of fine hitting as he had been at any phase of this great display, and he kept on hitting, scoring and fagging the field until near the end, for he was not out until 546 runs had been scored, and play finally ceased when the score was at 557, nine wickets having then fallen. Then "time" was up for the Canterbury Week of 1876; and this stupendous run-getting match was drawn; nineteen different bowlers having bowled therein; 1999 balls bowled; 1099 runs from the bat and 75 extras scored and thirty one wickets having fallen.

Mr W. Grace commenced MCC's second innings; he was six hours and twenty minutes at wickets, and had scored 344 runs out of the 546 booked, when he was caught out at mid-off, *Bell's Life* stating – "He scored those 344 runs without positively giving a chance." His hits consisted of 76 singles, twenty 2s, eight 3s and fifty-one 4s (204 runs by fourers in one innings!).

Kent

V. K. Shaw Esq. b Clarke	17
C. A. Absolom Esq. b W. Grace	10
W. B. Pattison Esq. c and b Clarke	20
W. Yardley Esq. b Meares	47
Lord Harris c Meares b Crutchley	154
F. Penn Esq. run out	0
F. A. Mackinnon Esq. c and b W. Grace	23
Geo. Hearne jun. (son of George) not out	57
H. Thomson Esq. c Clarke b W. Grace	27
W. Foord-Kelcey Esq. b W. Grace	31
Capt. Fellowes c Goldney b Crutchley	32
Henty b Meares	19
B 28, l-b 4, w 4	36
	473

MCC

W. G. Grace Esq. c Hearne b Thomson	17	– c V. K. Shaw b Harris 344
A. P. Lucas Esq. b Absolom	0	– c Thomson b Hearne 7
G Bird Esq. c Henty b Fellowes	4	– b Foord-Kelcey 18
J. Turner Esq. c Absolom b Fellowes	15	– b Harris 15
W. Hay Esq. b Hearne	12	
C. C. Clarke Esq. c Absolom b Fellowes	19	– c Hearne b Harris 12
L. S. Howell Esq. b Foord-Kelcey	34	– c V. K. Shaw b Thomson 30
C. E. Cottrell Esq. b Fellowes	17	– c Thomson b Harris 10
Capt. Meares c and b Hearne	14	– not out 0
G. H. Goldney Esq. b Fellowes	0	– not out 0
H. N. Tennent Esq. st Henty b Hearne	3	– c Penn b Absolom 12
P. C. Crutchley Esq. not out	0	– c Pattison b Absolom 84
B 3, l-b 1, w 5	9	B 14, l-b 11, w 5 30
	144	557

MCC Bowling

	Overs	Mdns	Runs	Wkts
Mr W. Grace	77	32	116	4
Capt. Meares	32.2	9	85	2
Mr Crutchley	24	6	68	2
Mr Clarke	20	8	50	2
Mr Cottrell	19	4	49	—
Mr Goldney	9	1	30	—
Mr Lucas	6	—	19	—
Mr Tennent	6	2	20	—
Mr Bird	2	2	—	—

Kent Bowling

	Overs	Mdns	Runs	Wkts	Overs	Mdns	Runs	Wkts
Capt. Fellowes	41	22	50	5	28	6	63	—
Mr Absolom	32	15	42	1	39	12	105	2
Mr Kelcey	14	9	24	1	40	11	84	1
Mr Thomson	7	3	14	1	20	5	52	1
G. Hearne jun.	4.1	4	—	3	35	9	91	1
Mr Penn	4	2	5	—	7	—	25	—
Lord Harris					19	6	59	4
Mr Yardley					8	—	27	—
Mr V. K. Shaw					4	2	14	—
Henty					2	—	7	—

Umpires: T. Hearne sen. and E. Willsher.

MCC AND GROUND v HAMPSHIRE

Played at Lord's May 3, 4, 1877

The revival of this old match, first played in 1797, made a capital start for the MCC season of 1877; and had not that nipping north-easter blew so unseasonably cold during the play, the opening match would have been most enjoyable. Young George Hearne (son of George) and John Wheeler, of Notts., played their first MCC match on this occasion, and Mr D. W. J. Duncan played his first match at Lord's. Mr Duncan played a good first; Young Hearne, Flanagan, Morley, Rylott and Wheeler all took a turn at him and he played all of them well; his hits included two 4's and a fine square-leg crack down to the Hotel, from Flanagan, for 6, but old Mike squared all that up by bowling Mr Duncan. Flanagan also made a splendid one-hand catch (not more than four inches from the ground), that summarily settled Galpin. Mr Duncan and Mr Jeffreys increased Hampshire's score from 29 to 111, when Young Hearne bowled Mr Jeffreys for 51 – a good hitting display. For MCC, Mr Russel and Mr Richardson increased the runs from 7 to 119, when Mr Richardson was bowled for 42, and at 126 Mr Russel was bowled for 73, an innings that included seven 4's. Mr E. F. S. Tylecote played well for 34; Morley hit hard for 18; and MCC won by nine wickets. The few visitors present being thankful all was over, unanimously agreeing a colder wind had never blew at cricket than had blown across Lord's ground throughout this match. Ugh! it was cold.

MCC AND GROUND v ENGLAND

Played at Lord's, May 14, 15 1877

First played in 1792, the revival of this match created some interest among the London cricketing public; but wretched wet weather on the first day discounted all that, broke up the wickets, and knocked the second day's play into cocked hats, one eleven being out for 36 runs, the other for 26, a 10 being the only double-figure score made in their second innings by those twenty-two men – some of them the finest bats in England. The MCC team was an especially strong batting team; but on the soft wickets they could do but little, for, although five of them made double figures, Mr Russel's 24 was highest score in their first innings, and the lot were out for 114, Watson's slows having seven wickets (three bowled) for 39 runs. Then – at 5.30 – England batted. At 14 Mr F. Grace was caught out, at 48 Mr Gilbert was stumped and at 68 Shrewsbury was out, whereupon play ceased for the day, Barlow (in with the score at 14) not out, 32 – a real good bit of batting, played under great difficulties, his fine forward play smothering danger balls delighting all who admire science v slogging. That day's cricket resulted in 598 balls having been bowled, 182 runs scored, and thirteen wickets captured.

On the Tuesday it rained hard up to ten o'clock, making the wickets as pasty as uncooked pudding crust. After ten a clear sky, a bright sun and a keen, health-blowing air formed an enjoyable contrast to Monday's gloom and wet; but the top of the ground dried rapidly, the cut-up wickets played the more falsely the more they were played on; and the numerous visitors present that afternoon witnessed one strong batting team got out in seventy minutes for 36 runs and an England team used up in another seventy minutes for 26 runs!

The England team went on with their first innings at noon. Barlow was out at 88, his 37 being a really finely played innings. The lot were out for 100.

Then came the two memorable short time innings, wherein twenty-two of the front-rank cricketers of the country were got out in 140 minutes for 62 runs (59 from the bat). At 1.40 MCC's second was commenced; at 2.50 they were all out for 36 runs (33 from the bat), Mr Ridley's 7 being top score! This was a queer innings, but a queerer remained to be played, for at 3.48 the England men commenced their second, and at 4.55 they were all out for 26, their highest score being 10 by Mr. Gilbert, who was sixty-two minutes at wickets making these 10 runs. When only 12 runs had been scored six wickets had fallen,

W. Mycroft having then bowled eight overs for 4 runs and six wickets.

Mycroft had been helped by some clinking good fielding, but he bowled well, and MCC and Ground won the match by 24 runs. The following score of 44 innings played by twenty-two such cricketers at an average of a trifle over 6 runs per innings is a curiosity:

MCC and Ground

A. N. Hornby Esq. c Gilbert b Watson	15	– b Watson	4
W. G. Grace Esq. b Watson	11	– c Shrewsbury b Lockwood	6
F. Penn Esq. run out	19	– b Watson	3
A. W. Ridley Esq. b Tye	10	– c Tye b Watson	7
C. E. Green Esq. c Pinder b Watson	15	– c Barlow b Watson	3
J. S. Russel Esq. b Watson	24	– b Watson	5
T. S. Pearson Esq. c Gilbert b Watson	2	– c Pinder b Lockwood	1
F. Wyld b Watson	3	– not out	1
C. E. Buller Esq. b Lockwood	5	– c Pinder b Watson	0
F. Morley not out	4	– c Pinder b Lockwood	0
W. Mycroft c Lockwood b Watson	2	– st Pinder b Watson	3
B 1, l-b 2, w 1	4	B 2, l-b 1	3
	114		36

England

G. F. Grace Esq. c Buller b W. Grace	10 – c and b W. Mycroft	0
W. Gilbert Esq. st Wyld b Ridley	13 – c Green b Morley	10
R. G. Barlow c Wyld b Pearson	37 – st Wyld b W. Mycroft	0
Arthur Shrewsbury c Wheeler (for Hornby) b Morley	12 – c Green b W. Mycroft	2
Ephraim Lockwood b Pearson	3 – b W. Mycroft	0
William Oscroft c Buller b Pearson	0 – hit wkt b W. Mycroft	4
William Barnes run out	0 – c W. Grace b W. Mycroft	0
R. Fillery b Morley	0 – not out	0
A. Watson b Pearson	3 – c W. Grace b Morley	7
George Pinder c and b W. Grace	13 – b Morley	3
John Tye not out	7 – c W. Grace b Morley	0
B 2	2	
	100	26

England Bowling

	Overs	Mdns	Runs	Wkts	Overs	Mdns	Runs	Wkts
Watson	42.3	20	39	7	20.1	16	10	7
Mr Gilbert	13	3	22	—				
Tye	12	3	21	1				
Fillery	11	1	23	—				
Lockwood	6	3	5	1	21	10	23	3

MCC Bowling

	Overs	Mdns	Runs	Wkts	Overs	Mdns	Runs	Wkts
Mr W. Grace	38.1	21	27	2	5	2	5	—
Mr Pearson	24	14	16	4				
Morley	17	9	15	2	10	6	9	4
Mr Ridley	16	3	24	1				
W. Mycroft	15	6	16	—	15	9	12	6

Umpires: F. Farrands and Thomas Hearne sen.

MCC AND GROUND v OXFORD UNIVERSITY

Played at Cowley Marsh, Oxford, May 21, 1877

This match was played out in one day and notwithstanding only 171 runs were made in the match MCC won by an innings and 77 runs. The match was played in the memorable wet season and the wickets were of bad form; one end playing very badly. In the first innings the Oxford men played without their Captain's aid and could not get into their form on such wickets; in fact they were got out for two surprisingly small totals of 12 and 35. But that little innings of a dozen runs was made from 174 balls bowled, and took them near upon two hours to play, so the runs scored must have been greatly out of proportion to the cricket played. The wickets in that jewel of a small innings fell as follows:

1/1 2/1 3/1 4/8 5/8 6/8 7/8 8/12 9/12

The only hits made were one 3, three 2s and three singles. In Oxford's second innings, Mr Savory made eight by a 6 and a 2; Mr H. R. Webbe ten by a 2, a 3 and a 5; Mr A. J. Webbe six by a 2 and a 4; and Mr E. Wallington six by a couple of 3s. The wickets in that innings fell this wise:

1/8 2/17 3/17 4/20 5/27 6/27 7/27 8/27 9/27 10/35

In Oxford's two innings Morley bowled 33 overs and one ball for 14 runs and thirteen wickets – nine bowled. Mr I. D. Walker and Mr A. N. Hornby commenced MCC's innings, and before they were parted had made 51, or four more runs than were scored in Oxford's two innings. Mr Hornby's 30 included a 5, a 4 and two 3s; Mr I. D. Walker's 23 also included a 5; and there was a hit for 4 and six 3s in Wyld's 36, the highest innings hit in this very curious match, of which the following is the score:

Oxford

H. G. Tylecote Esq. b Rylott	0	– b Clayton	0
H. R. Webbe Esq. b Morley	1	– c I. D. Walker b Morley	10
E. T. Hirst Esq. b Morley	0	– b Morley	0
E. W. Wallington Esq. not out	7	– b Clayton	6
H. Fowler Esq. b Morley	4	– st Wyld b Morley	0
A. Pearson Esq. b Morley	0	– c Rylott b Morley	4
H. J. B. Hollings Esq. b Morley	0	– b Clayton	0
J. H. Savory Esq. b Morley	0	– not out	8
C. E. Horner Esq. c I. D. Walker b Morley	0	– b Morley	0
F. G. Jellicoe Esq. b Rylott	0	– b Morley	0
A. J. Webbe Esq. absent		– c Barnes b Clayton	6
		B 1	1
	12		35

MCC and Ground

I. D. Walker Esq. c Fowler b H. G. Tylecote	23	H. Tubb Esq. b H. G. Tylecote	8
A. N. Hornby Esq. b H. G. Tylecote	30	R. Clayton b H. G. Tylecote	2
F. Wyld c Fowler b H. G. Tylecote	36	Rylott c Pearson b H. G. Tylecote	0
R. T. Richardson Esq. c H. G. Tylecote b Jellicoe.	8	Morley not out	0
T. S. Dury, Esq. c and b H. G. Tylecote	0	B 2, l-b 1, n-b 1	4
W. Evetts Esq. c A. J. Webbe b Jellicoe	7		
A. S. Barnes Esq. c and b H. G. Tylecote	6		124

MCC Bowling

	Overs	Mdns	Runs	Wkts	Overs	Mdns	Runs	Wkts
Morley	22	18	6	7	11.1	9	8	6
Rylott	21.2	18	6	2				
Clayton					11	5	26	4

Oxford Bowling

	Overs	Mdns	Runs	Wkts
Mr Tylecote	27.2	10	51	8
Mr Jellicoe	19	7	34	2
Mr Pearson	16	10	16	—
Mr Horner	9	3	19	—

Umpires: Nixon (of Cambs.) and George Howitt.

MCC AND GROUND v DERBYSHIRE

Played at Lord's, May 28, 29, 1877

Played in a gale of wind and finished off (at 6.35) by a storm of rain. Such were the weather characteristics of the first day's play in this match. Old Boreas blew his biggest breath behind W. Mycroft, who appeared to revel in the wind's riot, and bowled in such top class form that at one time he bowled down five wickets in nine balls, three of the five in one over, the fifth, sixth, seventh, eighth and ninth MCC wickets all falling to W. Mycroft's bowling with the score at 91. Mr W. Grace was in form with the bat on that tempestuous Monday, as in MCC's first he made 35 out of the 46 scored for the Club when he was out, and when the rain storm stayed play for that day, he had made 20 not out of the 32 then booked in MCC's second innings. Mr Russel stayed long and played well for 10; and young George Hearne (son of old George) played well and hit so successfully, especially to leg, that he made 21, including three 4s from Mycroft. Mr Turner was fourth man in and tenth out and Morley was not out 15 including two 4s (drives). Some of the Midland men hit hard; Regan's 20 included two 3s, a 4 and a drive down to the trees for 5 – all from Morley, who appeared to be beaten by the gale. Platts' 28 included two 4s and a big drive for 5 and when the Shire's first innings stood at 112 – or the tie – Mycroft thumped one for 5 and was then bowled the innings ending with Derby 5 runs on.

The second day was breezy, cold and showery. Mr Grace made his score 48 (out of 84) when he was caught out, close to the pavilion, by Mr R. P. Smith, hit and catch thoroughly warranting the hearty cheer of "Well done both" that rang out from an old looker on. Mr Grace's innings included two 6s and a 5 – all splendid on drives from Mycroft. Mr Turner was wonderfully well caught out (so low down) at point by Mr R. P. Smith. Wheeler played well for 18 and "Little George" again did doubles; the result of the MCC batting being Derbyshire had 119 to score to win. The two Mr Smiths played with much care and skill. One of the professionals hit the ball into the printing shop, but none of the others could successfully tackle Mr Grace's bowling, which, backed up by fine fielding, took eight of the ten wickets, and so, at five o'clock on that day before the Derby, Derbyshire was defeated by 40 runs.

MCC and Ground

J. S. Russel Esq. hit wkt b W. Mycroft	10	– b W. Mycroft	11
W. G. Grace Esq. c A. Smith b Jackson	35	– c R. P. Smith b A. Hind	48
F. Wyld b W. Mycroft	2	– b W. Mycroft	0
J. Turner Esq. b W. Mycroft	23	– c R. P. Smith b W. Mycroft	2
John Wheeler b Jackson	1	– b W. Mycroft	18
G. G. Hearne jun. (son of George) b W. Mycroft	21	– b Jackson	15
A. S. Barnes Esq. b W. Mycroft	0	– b A. Hind	7
F. S. Miller Esq. b W. Mycroft	0	– b A. Hind	8
R. Clayton b W. Mycroft	0	– b A. Hind	0
Rylott b W. Mycroft	0	– not out	5
F. Morley not out	15	– b W. Mycroft	1
B 1, l-b 4	5	B 8	8
	112		123

Derbyshire

J. Smith Esq. b Morley	15	– c Rylott b W. Grace	22
Rigley b W. Grace	14	– c Miller b W. Grace	2
R. P. Smith Esq. c and b W. Grace	3	– b W. Grace	19
Frost b W. Grace	0	– c Wyld b W. Grace	4
Amos Hind, c Wyld b W. Grace	7	– hit wkt b Rylott	3
Regan c Rylott b W. Grace	20	– c Wheeler b W. Grace	9
J. Platts c and b Morley	28	– c Wyld b Rylott	7
Foster c Miller b W. Grace	6	– not out	9
Jackson not out	17	– c Russel b W. Grace	3
A. Smith b Clayton	0	– st Wyld b W. Grace	0
W. Mycroft b Morley	5	– lbw b W. Grace	0
B 1, l-b 1	2		
	117		78

Derbyshire Bowling

	Overs	Mdns	Runs	Wkts	Overs	Mdns	Runs	Wkts
W. Mycroft	46.2	26	47	8	34.2	16	57	5
Platts	26	10	41	—	10	2	22	—
Jackson	20	9	19	2	17	6	27	1
A. Hind					15	10	9	4

MCC Bowling

	Overs	Mdns	Runs	Wkts	Overs	Mdns	Runs	Wkts
Mr W. Grace	32	11	55	6	41.2	17	54	8
Morley	31.1	14	40	3	19	13	9	—
Clayton	19	13	20	1				
Rylott					21	11	15	2

Umpires: Thomas Hearne sen. and F. Farrands.

OXFORD v CAMBRIDGE

Played at Lord's, June 25, 26, 1877

That it was 50 years since the first Oxford v Cambridge match had been played and that of the 42 matches then chronicled in cricket history, each University had won 20, were incidents that invested the 1877 match with more than usual attraction to past and present men, the interest in the year's contest being further enhanced by the public announcement that more than 100 gentlemen who had played their parts in past Inter-University matches would assemble and quietly celebrate "The Jubilee Year" by a Jubilee dinner in London. All this led to such a gathering of University cricketers as had never before been seen at one match, and to the happy meeting of many old 'Varsity friends who had been separated for so many years, and who, meeting on the old battle-field, "fought their old battles o'er again", pleasantly turning over memory's pages in their book of University life, and feeling young again in their pleasant gossip about how matches were played, lost or won in their times. And to those wholly unconnected with the Universities, but whose pleasure or duties had caused them to look on "Cricket at Lord's" for the part quarter of a century the sight was indeed one to call up cricket of other times, for none could move a score yards around the thronged ground without catching sight of some man who had in the past twenty years or so, by his deeds with bat or ball, made his name famous in University or other cricket at Lord's. As to the public, they were present in thousands, for the official record of those who passed the pay boxes to witness the 1877 match notifies

11,691 paid on the Monday.........and.........10,281 on the Tuesday.

It is perfectly true that those 21,000 admittants were 6,000 fewer than paid on the Monday and Tuesday of the 1876 match; but for all that it was stated by those in a position to know that the attendances at the 1877 match were unprecedentedly large, the numbers of members and their friends present being so greatly in excess of previous occasions. But there was a palpable decrease of carriages, the thick clusters of drags, with their fair freights, that used to form so bright and charming a background to this pleasant cricket picture, being few, very few at this match. A new erection, in the form of four rows of fixed seats, extending, in semi-circular shape; from the eastern end of the Grand Stand to the little chesnut trees, afforded, on payment, extra sitting accommodation to many; but it also most unpopularly contracted the comfort of that portion of the public who, having paid for admission to the ground, did not think it proper to have to pay again for sitting room on a portion of the ground that had previously been free to all who came sufficiently early to find vacant seats. Those four rows of seats, their fellows at the opposite corner, the embankment seats down by the SW nook, the Pavilion, and the Grand Stand were eventually all crowded, and when, at about 4.30 on the Tuesday, the sun briefly beamed down on the old ground, it brightened up a sight that will not easily fade away from the memories of those placed in a position to fully enjoy the pleasure of witnessing it.

"Play" was called at noon on the Monday, the Cambridge batting being then commenced by Mr A. P. Lucas and the Hon. A. Lyttelton, to the bowling of Mr Jellicoe and Mr H. G. Tylecote, the wicket being kept by Mr Fowler. A single was made from Mr Jellicoe's first over, and a 4 to leg from Mr Tylecote's first, whereat Cambridge partisans rejoiced and more loudly so when another 4 to leg was made from Mr Tylecote, who, however, with the following ball clean bowled Mr A. Lyttleton, a roar of Oxford cheers greeting a good man going with the score at 10 only. Mr Patterson took the vacant wicket and thence so close was the bowling and careful the batting, that Mr Tylecote bowled ten overs for five singles, and Mr Jellicoe nine successive maidens; but when forty overs had been bowled for 43 runs, Mr Jellicoe was succeeded by Mr Buckland. Then another wicket quickly gave way, as, when 46 runs had been made, Mr Patterson was lbw to Mr Tylecote for 20, carefully and well made by a cut for 4 from Mr Jellicoe, a couple of 2s and twelve singles. The Hon. E. Lyttelton made a cut for 3 and drive for 4 when Mr Buckland bowled him, a shout of Oxford cheers welcoming three good wickets down for 59 runs. Then Mr D. Q. Steel went in, made a 2, a 4 and a single from one over of Mr Tylecote's, and in all 9, when a catch at cover point settled him. Mr L. K. Jarvis made 3, and then skied one that was well judged and well taken at square leg by Mr A. D. Greene, who fielded finely throughout. When luncheon was called at two o'clock Oxford had bowled 76 overs, Cambridge had scored 83 runs, and lost five wickets, and Mr Lucas had made 32 not out.

At 2.30, Mr Lucas and Mr Mellor resumed the Cambridge batting to the bowling of Mr Jellicoe and Mr Tylecote. They had made the score 94 when a good catch at point settled Mr Mellor for 5, and before another run was scored a shooter bowled Mr Pigg. Then Mr Lucas and Mr Schultz made a stand increasing the score to 123, when Mr Buckland bowled again, and he not only bowled Mr Schultz for 18, but immediately after caught out Mr Bury at mid on. Then the last of the light blues, Mr Luddington, went to the aid of Mr Lucas, whose fine defence all had admired, and all hoped he would stay it out to the end; but not so, for after a few more overs had been delivered, he played one back that was easily secured by the bowler; and so, at twenty minutes to four, was the innings ended for 134 runs. Mr Lucas was first man in and last out; he had been three hours and ten minutes at wickets making his 54 runs, against 116 overs of straight bowling, and some very fine fielding. His hits included four 4s (three to leg and one off drive); but it was his skilled and splendid defence that won Mr Lucas that burst of earnest applause that so pleasantly rang out all round the ground as he returned to the pavilion. He had "played the game" coolly and truly, and thereby he won the goodwill of all. The wickets fell as follows:

1/10 2/46 3/59 4/71 5/82 6/94 7/94 8/130 9/131 10/134

134 was an unexpectedly small innings for an Eleven who had won, and justly so, so great a run-getting fame; all appeared surprised at so mild a total; still but few thought of the result being otherwise than successful for Cambridge, who, it was generally fancied, should make it a winning game in their second innings; but there were some who did not believe the Oxford Eleven were nearly so inefficient as rumoured, and who thought there was no just ground for the "they are not in it" opinion so pompously and so pertinaciously pronounced by a majority of men.

The Oxford batting was commenced at five minutes past four, by the brothers Webbe, to the bowling of Mr Patterson and Mr Luddington, the wicket being kept by the Hon. A. Lyttelton. Mr Patterson began the Cambridge bowling with a maiden over, and Mr H. R. Webbe started the Oxford batting with a capital cut for 4, shouts and counter shouts greeting each successful opening. Thence the Cambridge partisans had, for some time, the shouting all to themselves, so surprisingly rapidly did the Oxford wickets fall. With the score at 5 only, Mr Luddington bowled Mr A. J. Webbe; at 13 Mr H. R. Webbe rushed out to a slow, missed it, and was stumped; and from the following ball Mr Heath was clean bowled. Then it was, at 13 runs for three wickets, that Mr Buckland went in, and literally won the match for Oxford; but it was not until three more wickets had fallen, that he had a staying mate to help him; for when but 25 runs had been scored, Mr Wallington was bowled by Mr Luddington, who at 30 also bowled Mr Savory; and at 31 Mr Patterson bowled Mr Greene; the Cambridge partisans' rejoicing at all this being hearty and hopeful. But then Mr H. G. Tylecote faced Mr Buckland and one of the best stands (because it was a winning one) ever made in an inter-University match was effected. The score was hit by those gentlemen to 50, when Mr Luddington gave way to Mr Jarvis, whose lobs being unsuccessful, were put on one side for Mr Luddington's fasts again; yet the score rose rapidly and when, at eighteen minutes to six, four byes caused the markers to hoist the 100, the cheering for Oxford was lusty, loud and long. Still yet the score was increased, but no wicket fell. 110 was up, when Mr Lucas bowled v Mr Patterson, but thereabouts the Cambridge fielding was very faulty, and by six o'clock 100 runs had been made since the sixth wicket fell; and when, ten minutes subsequently, a 4 by Mr Buckland put Oxford's score one run ahead of Cambridge's total, there rang out such a joyous, thrilling, Oxford shout that must long be remembered by all who heard it, for it was the cheer of the day. All this time Mr Buckland had been batting with an ease and success that elicited repeated cheers; bowling changes occurred without effecting a change in the batsmen, until, at 6.30, when the score had reached, 173, then one more bowling change caused Mr Tylecote to be caught out at wicket for 39, a most valuable lot of runs, made at the right time, for it was the successful stand then made that really won this memorable Oxford victory. There had then been 142 runs scored since the fall of the preceding wicket, and 22 more had been added when Mr Luddington bowled Mr Fowler for 10. Mr Pearson stayed until 206 had been booked; then the slow bowler bowled him for 9. Mr Jellicoe was last man in; he stayed out the few minutes left for play, and, accompanied by a tumult of Oxford cheers, "time" was called, with the score at 212 for nine wickets.

Mr Buckland not out 117

On the Tuesday play was resumed at 11.40. A bye was run, and Mr Jellicoe made a single, but was then caught out at point, and so the Oxford innings ended for 214, Mr Buckland taking his bat out for 117, a great batting feat that justly won him great applause, none of the cheering thousands then on the ground applauding more heartily than the Cambridge Eleven. Mr Buckland was at wickets whilst Oxford's score was increased by 201 runs; his 117 is the second largest score yet made in these matches, and the largest ever scored for Oxford; it was a good hitting display that included nineteen 4s and twenty-two singles; and it is an innings that will always be memorable as having, in 1877, won the conquering match for Oxford. The wickets fell as follows:

1/5 2/13 3/13 4/25 5/30 6/31 7/173 8/195 9/206 10/214

The Oxford innings ended at a quarter to twelve, but rain prevented the second innings of Cambridge commencing until 1.40, the ground in the meantime presenting a curious sight with the hundreds of closely packed opened umbrellas covering the seated visitors determined to sit and see the end of it. At twenty to two Cambridge, with a leeway of 80 runs to make up, commenced their second innings with Mr Lucas and the Hon. A. Lyttelton to the bowling of Mr Jellicoe and Mr Tylecote, who were efficiently backed up by some really splendid fielding. When fifteen balls had been bowled for 9 runs a truly superb catch (low down) at short-leg by Mr Jellicoe got rid of Mr A. Lyttelton for 6; and when only 18 had been scored, Mr Tylecote bowled Mr Lucas for 8. Then Mr Patterson and the Hon. E. Lyttelton were batting, but at 20 runs (from twelve overs) luncheon was called, and, although rain fell in the meantime, rendering the wickets more difficult to play on, they resumed play at 3 o'clock, but, with the score at 30, Mr Patterson was bowled by Mr Jellicoe, who, at 45, with a fine ball also bowled Mr E. Lyttelton, whose 16 included a cut for 3 and two 4s (leg hit and drive). Mr Steel and Mr Jarvis then hit the score to 75, when Mr Buckland bowled v Mr Jellicoe. A huge hit to square-leg for 4 by Mr Jarvis made the score 80, and somewhat brightened up the fast fading hopes of Cambridge partisans; but when 6 more runs had been made a smart catch at wicket by Mr Fowler settled Mr Steel for 21, half the wickets being then down, and Cambridge but 6 runs on. Mr Mellor was next man in, but at 97 Mr Jarvis played badly at a ball that clean bowled him for 30, the highest score in that innings, and the second highest Cambridge score in the match. Mr Jarvis had shown hard hitting in his 30, which included five 4s, three of them good cuts; the other two were hard cracks to square leg. At 101 Mr Greene, at long-off, very finely caught out Mr Pigg; at 106 Mr Schultz was had at mid-wicket, and 3 runs later on Mr Greene grandly caught out Mr Bury at deep square-leg, this splendid sample of fine fielding eliciting rounds of ringing cheers, the fielder having to run some distance to get to the ball, and taking it sideways while sprinting at full speed. That was indeed "a rare catch". Mr Luddington was last man in; he and Mr Mellor stayed and increased the score by 17 runs, but then Mr Luddington was easily c and b, and so at twenty-five to five the innings ended at 126, or 46 on, the wickets having gone down as follows:

1/9 2/18 3/30 4/45 5/86 6/97 7/101 8/106 9/109 10/126

This innings over, the visitors crowded on to the playing portion of the ground in great numbers; in fact, Lord's ground was then literally covered by the fashionable throng. The gaily dressed ladies slowly promenading; the thickly packed crowd swaying to and fro in front of the Pavilion; the mass of people outside the ropes down at the bottom of the ground, perforce moving onwards at a snail's pace, and at times coming to a dead block, unable to move either way; and the chock at the top of the ground when the police mandate rang out, "Clear the ground", "Clear the ground there", "Ladies, do pray clear the ground", formed a sight that those who were in a position to look down on never can forget, for truly said a 20-years' regular attendant at Lord's, "It is a sight that never had an equal on a cricket-ground."

But at last the entreaties of the police cleared the ground sufficiently to finish off the match; and at five o'clock the brothers Webbe were lustily cheered as they walked to the wickets to hit off the required 47 runs, and thereby square up the ill-fortune attending their first innings. They hit freely and finely, and although they failed to score much from Mr Patterson's slows, they punished the fast bowling so severely that in thirty-eight minutes they had made the 47 runs, and Oxford had won the conquering match by ten wickets, Mr A. J. Webbe, not out, 27, by one 5 (4 from an overthrow), one 4, two 3s, three 2s and six singles, and Mr H. R. Webbe, not out 18, by three 4s, one 3 and four singles. So ended the 43rd Inter-University match, the brightest and best cricket features in which were: the successful batting and bowling of Mr Buckland, the splendid defence of Mr Lucas and the magnificient fielding of the Oxford men in the second innings of Cambridge.

Cambridge

A. P. Lucas Esq. c and b H. G. Tylecote	54	– b H. G. Tylecote	8
Hon. A. Lyttelton b H. G. Tylecote	4	– c Jellicoe b H. G. Tylecote	6
W. S. Patterson Esq. (Capt.) lbw b H. G. Tylecote	20	– b Jellicoe	7
Hon. E. Lyttelton b Buckland	7	– b Jellicoe	16
D. Q. Steel Esq. c Savory b Buckland	9	– c Fowler b Buckland	21
*L. K. Jarvis Esq. c Greene b H. G. Tylecote	3	– b Buckland	30
*F. H. Mellor Esq. c H. G. Tylecote b Jellicoe	5	– not out	15
*H. Pigg Esq. b Jellicoe	0	– c Greene b Buckland	2
*S. S. Schultz Esq. b Buckland	18	– c Wallington b Buckland	2
*L. Bury Esq. c Buckland b H. G. Tylecote	1	– c Greene b H. G. Tylecote	2
H. T. Luddington Esq. not out	1	– c and b H. G. Tylecote	12
B 12	12	B 3, 1-b 2	5
	134		126

Oxford

A. J. Webbe, Esq. (Capt.) b Luddington	0	– not out	27
*H. R. Webbe, Esq. st A. Lyttelton b Patterson	9	– not out	19
*E. W. Wallington Esq. b Luddington	15		
A. H. Heath, Esq. b Patterson	0		
F. M. Buckland Esq. not out	117		
*A. D. Greene Esq. b Patterson	5		
*J. H. Savory Esq. b Luddington	0		
H. G. Tylecote Esq. c A. Lyttelton b Luddington	39		
*H. Fowler Esq. b Luddington	10		
A. W. Pearson Esq. b Patterson	9		
*F. G. Jellicoe Esq. c Mellor b Patterson	1		
B 8, l-b 1	9	N-b 1	1
	214		47

* Their first year in the Elevens.

Oxford Bowling

	Overs	Mdns	Runs	Wkts	Overs	Mdns	Runs	Wkts
Mr Tylecote	58	30	71	5	35	13	51	4
Mr Jellicoe	34	19	28	2	22	8	41	2
Mr Buckland	24	13	23	3	13	2	29	4

Cambridge Bowling

	Overs	Mdns	Runs	Wkts	Overs	Mdns	Runs	Wkts
Mr Patterson	37.1	19	41	5	10	6	9	—
Mr Luddington	27	5	90	5	6	1	24	—
Mr Lucas	11	4	16	—				
Mr Schultz	9	2	40	—	3.2	1	13	—
Mr Jarvis	4	1	9	—				
Mr Pigg	2	—	9	—				

Umpires: F. Farrands and John West.

MARLBOROUGH COLLEGE v RUGBY SCHOOL

Played at Lord's, July 25, 26, 1877

A fairly numerous and very select company, comprising many ladies and several "past" Blues of either school, assembled on the old ground at the above date to witness the commencement of this annual cricket contest – unquestionably the most enjoyable Public Schools match now played on London grounds, there being a welcome absence of that crowding, crushing, and other accompanyings so prevalent at some similar matches. Here good cricket was met with earnest applause that never ran riot into noise, and wides, misfielded balls, or other mishaps to which all cricketers are subject, were condemned with a severe silence that appeared to be more keenly felt by the unfortunate youngsters than all the rough and rude "Oh's" ever screamed out at a PS match.

Play commenced at 11.30 on good wickets, Marlborough starting the batting with Wilson and Hayes to the bowling of Jones (fast) and Gaddum, whose left-hand slow rounds had at times a bit of a break on them that enforced careful play on the batsmen. A miss at point before a run was scored did not go for much, as, when but 12 runs had been scored, the batsman, Hayes, was caught out at mid-off for 4, and when 31 had been booked, Grainger was had by mid-on for 10. Then a hearty Marlburian cheer welcomed Steel's walk to the wickets, and great expectations were held that the popular Captain, who in the '76 match made 84 and 28 runs, and took ten Rugby wickets, would on this occasion accomplish an equally brilliant success; but those expectants were on that day fated to ruthless disappointment, for a real good ball by Jones – the very best he bowled in the match – broke in from the off and clean bowled Steel for 0. "That ball would have bowled the best bat in England", exclaimed an old Public School cricketer. F. M. Lucas (left-hand) then made a single, a 3 to square leg, and a big off-drive past the trees, from Jones, for 7, when he was caught out at slip. Napier and Weston hit the score from 54 to 83, when a smart – a very smart – stump out by Speed ended Weston's innings for 42, his hits including three 3s and four good cuts for 4 each. "Half the wickets down for 83 runs is hardly enough", said old Charley Brampton (the excellent and faithful cricket coach of the Marlburians); but what "Bram" thought of it when the whole team were out for 108 this compiler knoweth not. Anyhow, so it occurred, the sixth, seventh, eighth wickets all falling at 88, the ninth (Napier's) at 105 and the tenth when 3 more runs had been made. The innings was over at twenty-five minutes to two.

Rugby batting was commenced by Leslie and FitzGerald, to the bowling of Wilson (fast) and Steel, whose round-arm slows, with a very high curve, had the good fortune to be aided and abetted by some of the smartest wicket-keeping ever seen at these matches. When the score was at 5 only, Alston stumped FitzGerald; at 37 Alston stumped Capron; at 43 Alston caught out Leslie (who had played and hit well, especially to leg); and at 45 Alston stumped Bailey, all four wickets then down having been captured by Alston from Steel's bowling. Evelyn and Speed then increased the score to 83, when Evelyn was out for a steadily played 13 and Stokes was smartly run out. With six wickets down and 83 runs scored, Rugby was thought to be well on the road to a majority on the innings, especially so when their score was up to 102 when their seventh wicket fell; but cricket casualties are at times cruelly disappointing and so they were hereabouts to Rugbæins, for at 104 the eighth was run out and at 105 Steel clean bowled the remaining two and so at 4.30 half the match had been played, Marlborough 3 runs on.

Marlborough's second innings was commenced at a quarter to five. When only 5 runs had been scored, Jones bowled Hayes for 3; but on Grainger going in, Wilson hit so freely that 49 had been made when mid-wicket settled Grainger for 8. Then Wilson was faced by Steel, who brilliantly made amends for "that awful 0" of the morning by hitting all bowlers all round in excellent form. He was so ably supported by Wilson that at 6.25 the 100 was up; and when, after various bowling changes, Gaddum at a quarter to seven was put on again and with the first ball he delivered bowled Wilson for 51, the score stood at 129 for three wickets. Wilson's 51 was another well-played score that was deservedly applauded. Lucas had a life at long-on, but found death at short-slip and so the fourth wicket fell at 135, whereupon Napier went to Steel's aid and those two played up to "time," the score then standing at 150 for four wickets, Napier, not out, 4, Steel, not out, 72. A hearty reception was given to the Captain on his return to the pavilion.

A thorough wet night was succeeded by a morning of showers and an afternoon of sunshine, the ground on Thursday being again largely and influentially attended. Play was resumed at 11.25 and the score – aided by much misfielding – was rapidly increased to 198, when Napier was settled by mid-off for 24. S. Leach was out at 202 and Alston at 218, but the score was up to 231 when a catch at mid-wicket finished Steel's innings for 128, a fine display of hitting, especially on the leg-side, but an innings that was so far fortunate that it included three misses – two at wicket. Steel went in with the score at 49 for two wickets; he was eighth out, the score at 231, so 182 runs were scored whilst he was batting. His 128 was made by seven 4s, ten 3s, twenty-one 2s and 28 singles. All on the ground joined in the applause that greeted Steel's return to the pavilion. H. Leach and Womersley made the score 264 and a catch at point ended the innings at 1.30 for 266.

The second innings of Rugby was commenced at six minutes to two and at 4 o'clock (luncheon time included) was over for 73 runs. The first wicket fell with the score at 4; the figures were 12 for one wicket when they luncheoned; the score was 15 when wicket No. 2 fell, at 17 when the third and fourth fell and at 18 when the fifth fell. Four of these five wickets had fallen to Steel's bowling, three of the four to the combined efforts of Steel and Alston, the latter keeping wicket in really fine form. The sixth wicket also fell to Steel and

Alston, the score then standing at 33. Napier's bowling then had the seventh and eighth, with the score at 52 and 53 respectively. When 71 runs were scored, Steel, at point, caught out Gaddum for 14 and 73 the last wicket went down to Steel's bowling, the match being thus won by Marlborough by 196 runs, A. G. Steel having scored 0 and 128, obtained twelve wickets for 59 runs, caught out another man and saved ever so many runs at point. It will be seen that in the match Alston stumped six and caught two – all eight wickets from Steel's bowling.

Marlborough

*C. P. Wilson st Speed b Gaddum	42	– b Gaddum	51
S. H. Hayes c Brierly b Gaddum	4	– c Jones	3
*C. E. Grainger c FitzGerald b Jones	10	– c Bailey b Gaddum	8
*A. G. Steel (Captain) b Jones	0	– c Brierley b Leggatt	128
*F. M. Lucas c Bailey b Gaddum	11	– c Jones b Gaddum	4
J. R. Napier b Gaddum	28	– c Evelyn b Gaddum	24
S. H. Leach b Jones	3	– c Leggatt b Gaddum	1
G. H. Alston b Jones	0	– b Leggatt	1
D. Womersley c Speed b Gaddum	0	– hit wkt b Leslie	21
H. Leach st Speed b Gaddum	3	– not out	9
P. Hardy not out	0	– c sub. b Leslie	0
B 3, l-b 1, w 3	7	B 2, l-b 2, w 12	16
	108		266

Rugby

C. F. H. Leslie c Alston b A. G. Steel	28	– hit wkt b A. G. Steel	5
R. FitzGerald st Alston b A. G. Steel	0	– st Alston b A. G. Steel	13
F. W. Capron st Alston b A. G. Steel	10	– c S. H. Leach b A. G. Steel	10
*F. S. Evelyn c Hayes b Wilson	13	– c S. H. Leach b Wilson	0
A. J. Bailey st Alston b A. G. Steel	0	– c Alston b A. G. Steel	0
*F. E. Speed (Captain) not out	22	– st Alston b A. G. Steel	1
T. A. Stokes run out	0	– st Alston b A. G. Steel	9
*S. E. Jones b Napier	14	– b Napier	17
E. Brierley run out	0	– c and b Napier	0
F. S. Gaddum b A. G. Steel	0	– c A. G. Steel b Wilson	14
C. Leggatt b A. G. Steel	0	– not out	0
B 10, l-b 7, w 1	18	L-b 1, w 3	4
	105		73

* Played in the 1876 match.

Rugby Bowling

	Overs	Mdns	Runs	Wkts	Overs	Mdns	Runs	Wkts
Gaddum	33.1	16	31	6	84	26	91	5
Jones	28	12	43	4	38	14	80	1
Leggatt	11	6	19	—	27	13	39	2
Leslie	6	2	8	—	21	6	32	2
FitzGerald					1	—	8	—

Marlborough Bowling

	Overs	Mdns	Runs	Wkts	Overs	Mdns	Runs	Wkts
A. G. Steel	37	18	35	6	30.2	14	24	6
Wilson	24	12	32	1	21	7	28	2
Napier	13	8	12	1	9	3	17	2
F. M. Lucas	3	2	8					

Umpires: F. Farrands and Nixon (Cambs.).

RESULTS OF PAST RUGBY v MARLBOROUGH MATCHES

Year	Who and How won	Where	Year	Who and How won	Where
1855	Rugby by ten wickets	Lord's	1868	Rugby by 1 in. and 133 r. .	Rugby
1856	Rugby by five wickets	Lord's	1869	Rugby by 179 runs	Lord's
1857	Rugby by 1 in. and 83 r. . .	The Oval	1870	Rugby by five wickets	Marlbro.
1860	Rugby by 1 in. and 50 r. . .	Lord's	1871	Marlbro. by 68 runs	Lord's
1862	Marlbro. by 1 in. and 17 r.	Lord's	1872	Marlbro. by nine wickets . .	Lord's
1863	Rugby by 83 runs	The Oval	1873	Rugby by eight wickets . . .	Lord's
1864	Rugby by 1 in. and 33 r. . .	Islington	1874	Rugby by five wickets	Lord's
1865	Rugby by nine wickets . . .	Lord's	1875	Rugby by 1 in. and 35 r. . .	Lord's
1866	Unfinished	Lord's	1876	Marlbro. by five wickets . .	Lord's
1867	Rugby by six wickets	The Oval	1877	Marlbro. by 196 runs	Lord's

THE CANTERBURY WEEK

August 6th, 7th, 8th, 9th, 10th, 11th, 1877

The Canterbury Cricket Week of 1877 was commenced on the Bank Holiday in splended weather, but for the remainder of the week success had to fight against weather of bad form; nevertheless, the attendances on the great days were excellent, the best authority on this subject stating the assemblage on the showery and rough Thursday was the largest that had ever gathered together there on a "Ladies' Day". All agreed that, in high character and county influence, the gatherings of 1877 on old "St. Lawrence" were never surpassed. The daily admission charge was one shilling throughout the week and daily were the ladies gratified by "music's sweet sounds" being sent forth by the Royal Artillery or the Cavalry Depôt bands, and had the weather kept at fair after Monday, there can be no doubt but that "the week" of 1877 would have been far away the most successful ever played at Canterbury, as the county balls were brilliantly patronised and the theatre nightly crowded by the maids, matrons and men, who form the far-famed Aristocracy of Kent.

"KENT AGAINST ALL THE WORLD"

An epilogue usually finishes up the dramatic performances of "The Week". In the epilogue spoken in the theatre on the conclusion of the 1877 performances Lord Harris had to utter his indignant protest against all "obstructives", cricketing or otherwise; and thus his lordship spoke:

"Hold! I protest, for here I represent
  All – MCC, I Zingari and Kent.
Ne'er shall such trivial, childish schemes be found
  To desecrate our famed St. Lawrence Ground.
There, let Kent's white-horse banner be unfurled
Against All England – aye, 'gainst All The World."

THE MARYLEBONE CLUB IN 1878

Patron – HRH THE PRINCE OF WALES

President – LORD FITZHARDINGE

Treasurer – T. BURGOYNE, ESQ.

Trustees – EARL DUDLEY, EARL SEFTON, HON. F. PONSONBY, R. BROUGHTON, ESQ., W. NICHOLSON, ESQ.

The Committee (including Trustees) – Lord Harris, Lord Lyttelton, Hon. Spencer Ponsonby-Fane, Viscount Lewisham MP, Hon. E. Chandos Leigh, Col Taswell, Capt. Kenyon-Slaney, R. C. Antrobus Esq., S. Bircham Esq., C. E. Boyle Esq., J. M. Heathcote Esq., F. Lee Esq., T. Ratliff Esq., A. W. Ridley Esq., V. E. Walker Esq. and G. H. Wood Esq.

Assistant Secretary and Clerk to the Committee – MR J. MURDOCH

Professional Bowlers engaged at Lord's in 1878 – Thomas Hearne, sen., (Captain), Alfred Shaw, F. Farrands, John West, M. Flanagan, Walter Price, R. Clayton, Nixon (of Cambs.), A. Rylott, F. Randon, F. Morley, F. Wyld, W. Mycroft, T. Mycroft, G. G. Hearne, jun. (son of George), M. Sherwin, John Wheeler, Wilfred Flowers, George McCanlis and William Hearn (of Herts.).

Ground Supt. – P. Pearce

Tennis Master – Geo. Lambert (Champion)

THE ANNUAL MEETING

The 91st Anniversary Meeting of the Marylebone Club was held at Lord's on Wednesday, the 1st of May, 1878, T. Burgoyne, Esq. (The Treasurer), in the chair. The Secretary, H. Perkins, Esq., read the report, the most publicly-interesting items of which were as follows, as extracted from *Bell's Life* of May the 4th. "A sum of £4,428 was received from matches last season and £2,385 expended.' . . . 'Last year the total number of members, including those on the abroad list, amounted to 2.304 and there are now no less than 443 candidates for membership.' . . . 'Since last season a new lodge, a new workshop, a new storeroom, stable, etc., have been erected at a cost of about £1,000; and all buildings and other property of the Club are in good repair.' . . . 'The question of the admission of carriages at the Eton and Harrow match is becoming a difficult one. Last year many members were refused carriage tickets owing to want of space; and if the number of applications for carriage tickets goes on increasing, the admission of carriages may have to be stopped altogether. It having come to the knowledge of the committee last season that carriage tickets were in several cases disposed of to persons who were not members of the Club, the committee desire to remind members that carriage tickets are not transferrable and that it is most unjust that strangers should have carriage tickets when many members cannot obtain them.' . . . 'Since last year three more volumes of Scores and Biographies have been published, bringing the records of Cricket up to the end of 1870.' "

THE DINNER

The annual dinner took place at Lord's Hotel at 7.30. The President, the Duke of Beaufort, took the chair. The noble President nominated Lord Fitzhardinge as his successor. The usual loyal, and MCC, toasts were given and honoured and so was satisfactorily passed away one more first Wednesday in May by the leading men of the Marylebone Cricket Club.

THE GROUND

Due consideration being given to the extremely wet spring that cricket-ground keepers had to contend against in 1878, high praise is due to Peter Pearce for the excellent form into which he had worked the old ground. Five-and-twenty years attendance at Lord's fails to bring to mind the old battle-field looking so smooth, so firm, so well covered with herbage, so free from spots and blotches, so green, or so apparently fit for the fights of a season, as it appeared on the 2nd of May, when it was indeed "in high class condition." but the frequent and heavy rainstorms that subsequently fell materially discounted the care, skill and labour that had been lavished and – for a time – the mucky, messy, muddy wickets played old scratch with true cricket, and upset all calculations and anticipations, excepting those of slow bowlers, whose efforts were almost irresistible on the slippery pasty turf that cricket was, unavoidably, played on during that most miserable month of May, nineteen of whose thirty-one days were thorough wet ones. Moreover two-thirds of June was – for enjoyable cricket – as miserable as the May days, for, up to the 20th, scarce a day of "the leafy month" passed away without copious rain-storms pelting down, drenching the old ground and making the cricketing community as miserable as maniacs; but all things come to those who can wait, and on the 20th, 21st and 22nd of June the sun shone out with true summer brilliancy and heat, and all were then hopeful that thenceforth fair weather, good wickets, good cricket and good attendances, would be the rule at Lord's Ground in 1878.

NORTH v SOUTH

Played at Lord's, June 10, 11 and 12, 1878, for the benefit of the MCC Professional Cricketers' Fund. – Whit Monday, 1878, broke bright, breezy and hopeful for the enjoyment of the holiday folks and up to the early afternoon of that day the people streamed up St. John's Wood Road to Lord's so continuously, that – notwithstanding a showery stormy afternoon, that undoubtedly lessened the attendance – the official return stated

10,858 paid their 6d. for admission.

Lord's Ground on that day was indeed a sight, the equal of which had never been seen on a Whit-Monday. The people thronged the Grand Stand – they crowded to inconvenience the players' seats at the north end of the pavilion – they filled to an inch the embankment seats at the NE and SW corners – they completely blocked up the Tavern steps – they sat as closely together as they could sit on the garden wall tops – every window looking on the ground was filled with lookers on, and not only did the visitors stand five or six deep behind the ring, but at top and bottom of the ground, they swarmed in hundreds before the ring, thereby materially contracting the fielding space and rendering "hits to the people" not worth more than half the runs they were booked for. But for all that, the 10,000 present were, as a rule, a jolly and good tempered crowd; and when Mr W. G. Grace went to and entreated them, in his well known bland and courteous manner, to get back a bit and give a little more fielding space, they laughed at, chaffed and shook hands with the crack in the most enjoyable, merry and free and easy form; and by this and other ways practically proved that "the enlightened foreigner" who wrote "the English took their pleasures churlishly", knew nothing about the matter, and wrote a famous fib.

MCC AND GROUND v CAMBRIDGE UNIVERSITY

Played at Lord's, June 25, 26, 27, 1878

An astonishing and altogether unparalled triumph was gained by the University eleven, Cambridge actually obtaining the 507 runs set them to win in the last innings, with three wickets to spare. As all previous attempts to make 400 under similar circumstances had failed, the Cambridge men are to be heartily congratulated upon what must rank as one of the most remarkable performances on record. The early part of the match did not give promise of anything out of the common, for on the Thursday twenty-two wickets went down for an aggregate of 337, the Light Blues leaving off at a considerable disadvantage. On the Friday, the game went even more decidely in favour of the MCC, for despite the fact that Davenport was unable to bat, their remaining seven wickets added 391 runs and Cambridge were left with 507 to win. Of these, 98 were obtained for the loss of two wickets before stumps were pulled up. It was on Saturday that the most surprising cricket took place, Druce and Wilson who had come together at 38, raised the total to 280 and this stand, of course, made the victory possible. The rest of the innings was notworthy for the brilliancy exhibited by Marriott and Bray, who became partners when 118 runs were required and hit them off in 75 minutes. In the three days, 1,235 were scored for thirty-six wickets.

MCC and Ground

H. Carpenter b Gray	37	c Gray b Grace	161
A. Hearne c Marriott b Gray	3	b Gray	5
A. E. Trott b Gray	5	b Shine	14
G. Davenport b Shine	18	absent hurt	0
Mr C. H. Hulls b Shine	0	b Druce	30
Mr R. W. Nicholls c Bray b Gray	10	c Burnup b Marriott	59
Mr H. E. Symes-Thompson c and b Shine	6	b Marriott	0
Mr R. J. Burrell c Stogdon b Shine	16	c Stogdon b Marriott	19
W. Mead c Bray b Burnup	12	not out	46
F. Martin not out	14	c Bray b Marriott	36
Mr F. A. Phillips c Stogdon b Gray	3	c Shine b Mitchell	74
B 10	10	B 30, l-b 3, w 5, n-b 1	39
	134		483

Cambridge University

Mr C. J. Burnup b Trott	25	c Phillips b Martin	26
Mr W. G. Grace jun. b Martin	26	b Trott	0
Mr H. H. Marriott b Martin	0	not out	146
Mr N. F. Druce c Carpenter b Trott	13	b Mead	146
Mr C. E. M. Wilson b Martin	6	c and b Martin	82
Mr W. M'G. Hemingway b Trott	4	b Trott	12
Mr F. Mitchell b Trott	4	c Hulls b Martin	7
Mr. J. H. Stogdon b Trott	15	c Nicholls b Hearne	8
Mr E. H. Bray c Martin b Trott	3	not out	32
Mr E. B. Shine c Nicholls b Martin	14		
Mr H. Gray not out	0		
B 1	1	B 45, l-b 3	48
	111		507

Cambridge University Bowling

	Overs	Mdns	Runs	Wkts	Overs	Mdns	Runs	Wkts
Gray	18.4	3	62	5	24	3	87	1
Wilson	5	1	11	0				
Shine	15	5	48	4	18	6	55	1
Burnup	3	0	3	1	13	0	61	0
Mitchell					18	7	87	1
Druce					16	1	60	1
Grace					27	5	84	1
Marriott					20.1	1	60	4

MCC and Ground Bowling

	Overs	Mdns	Runs	Wkts	Overs	Mdns	Runs	Wkts
Mead	7	2	19	0	50.2	11	147	1
Martin	28	12	32	4	65	29	109	3
Trott	22.2	7	59	6	38	8	120	2
Hearne					29	6	66	1
Carpenter					7	1	17	0

Umpires: W. Barnes and R. Clayton.

THE CANTERBURY WEEK

August 5th, 6th, 7th, 8th, 9th, 10th, 1878

The Canterbury Week of 1878 was praised by the press as "The most successful ever played." The cricket critics praised nearly every body and every thing connected with that "week". Never before were those eminent gentlemen so unanimous in awarding all round praise as on this occasion. They praised the ground; they praised the ground's surroundings; they praised the weather; they praised "The White Horse of Kent"; they praised the wickets; they praised the cricket; they praised Lord Harris, the Captain; they praised George Hearne, the Professional; they praised Mr de C. Baker, the Manager; they praised Superintendent Davies, of the City police; they praised the military bands that played; they praised the many-headed multitude who thronged the ground on that Bank-holiday; they praised the 15,000 visitors said to be present on the Ladies' Day; they praised the many and varied turn-outs that were driven on to the ground and gave so much dash and life to that splendid County gathering; they praised the charmingly attired group that, for the nonce, made beautiful the base of "The Ladies' Tree", and their manly minds and courteous pens did not fail to praise the fair maids and matrons of Kent, whose presence in unusually large numbers made perfect that splendid cricketing picture witnessed no where else but at old St. Lawrence on "The Ladies' Day".

ALFRED SHAW'S MATCH

NORTH v SOUTH

Played at Lords, June 3, 4, 1879

Alfred Shaw is so deservedly popular among all classes of cricketers that the Whit-Monday, Tuesday and Wednesday North v South match so kindly set apart by the MCC authorities for his benefit, was looked forward to as the event of the 1879 cricketing season. We all like him, and we all wished him fair weather, because we all knew if he was favoured with that, large attendances would be sure to be present, men of much experience in these matches giving their opinion that a fine Whit-Monday would result in at least

12,000 visitors being on the old ground that day, and when it is borne in mind that near upon 11,000 were on the ground at the same match on the fine Whit-Monday of 1878, none can say 12,000 was an over estimate for Alfred's day had it been fine; but it was not fine; *per contra*, it was foul, very foul, for it rained heavily throughout that day, evening, and night; it was the most dismal, dreary, depressing, drenchingly wet Whit-Monday the oldest holiday maker could remember; not one gleam of hope shone throughout that wretched day; all was rain, rain, rain; success was soakingly swamped out from all the many outdoor amusements arranged to attract the holiday thousands. No cricket could possibly be played at Lord's ground, and of the 1,105 cricket enthusiasts who paid their admission 6d. on that wretchedly wet day, all – or all who chose to ask for them – received re-admission checks for the Tuesday or Wednesday.

Whit-Tuesday was another wet day, but not so wet as that miserably memorable Monday. 1,910 paid for admission, and although the wickets were wholly unfit for cricket, it was agreed to play to satisfy the visitors, so a commencement was made at 2.45, and as the cracks of the period came on to the ground flannelled for the fray they were received with hearty cheers, Mr Hornby, Ulyett, Emmett, Mr Lucas, Mr Penn and Lord Harris being all greeted with especial heartiness. The North first batted, and Daft being had at slip from the first ball bowled, truly foretold how dead the wickets were against great scoring. With the score at 15 Lockwood was out for 10; Ulyett was the next to go, and at 48 Mr Hornby was bowled for 20, and Mr A. G. Steel for 3, and indeed no stand was made until eight wickets had gone for 61 runs; then Alfred Shaw and Pinder hit the score to 87, when Alfred was out for 12, vigorous cheers greeting Shaw's advance to and retreat from the wickets. Morley stayed whilst Pinder had a few more "goes at her"; then F. M. was bowled, and the innings ended at 5.20 for 92 runs, Pinder taking out his bat for 21, the largest score hit that day. At 5.35 the South's innings was commenced by Mr W. G. Grace and Mr A. P. Lucas, to the bowling of Morley and Alfred Shaw, and Alfred's third over was so frightfully knocked about that fifteen runs were actually scored from three of those four balls, thus: the first ball Mr Lucas drove to the ropes for 3; the second ball Mr W. Grace sent into Dark's garden for 6, though it should be stated that the wickets were pitched unusually low down the ground owing to the very wet state of all the upper portion. But (that 15 runs from three balls of an over notwithstanding) when 26 had been scored both wickets fell, Mr Grace being caught out at slip for 18, and Mr Lucas at short leg for 7. Then Alfred Shaw's bowling worked and wickets went down rapidly; at 29 Shaw bowled Mr Hadow; at 30 Shaw bowled Mr F. Penn; at 38 Shaw bowled the Hon. E. Lyttelton; and at 44 a clever left hand catch at point from Shaw's bowling got rid of Lord Harris. Then Mr Ridley and young George Hearne played up to "time", when the South score stood at 54 for six wickets, Shaw's bowling having taken five of those wickets, an enjoyable revenge for that fifteen runs from three balls' affair.

Whit-Wednesday was a fair weather day, and 3,262 paid for admission. The wickets had dried a bit, but still played false, and the South's innings was soon finished off for 80, Mr A. G. Steel's bowling taking three wickets for 6 runs; but it must be borne in mind that the South did not play full strength, as, owing to other engagements, neither the Hon. A. Lyttelton, Mr G. F. Grace, Mr J. Shuter, nor Jupp could play, and Pooley was put out of count by an injured foot. The South's innings was over at 12.30. Mr Hornby and Lockwood started the North's second innings at 12.50, the bowlers being Mr W. Grace and Mr Lucas. When 8 runs had been made, Lockwood was bowled for 5; then Ulyett went to wickets, and so good a stand did Mr Hornby and he make that when a 'ticer got Mr Hornby stumped for 27, the score was at 40. Selby made no sign, and was out of it at 43. At 51 Mr Steel was lbw, and at 62 Mr Lucas bowled Daft. Shrewsbury then stayed with Ulyett up to 80, when a catch at long-field by Hearn (of Hertfordshire) settled Shrewsbury for 3. At 86 Emmett was run out; at 88 Mr Penn settled Pinder; at 90 Shaw was had by mid-off; and at ten minutes to four Mr Ridley ended the innings by stumping Morley, Ulyett taking his bat out for 41, not only the largest score hit in the match, but a very fine innings. It was five minutes past four when the South's second innings was commenced by Lord Harris and Mr W. Grace. 106 runs were required to win, but Alfred

Shaw's bowling was so wonderfully good and successful that but three more than half that number of runs were made. When one run only was made Mr Grace was finely caught out at long-field from Shaw's bowling. Lord Harris and Mr Lucas then hit the score to 27, when Shaw bowled his lordship for 15. At 33 Shaw bowled the Hon. E. Lyttelton; at 40 a superb catch by Ulyett at long-on got rid of Mr Lucas for 18; and at 48 Mr F. Penn's, Mr Hadow's, and George Hearne's wickets all fell to Alfred Shaw's bowling, two of the three being bowled. Mr Stratford was not equal to the occasion, and when Pinder had stumped him there were eight wickets down, all those eight wickets having fallen to Alfred Shaw's bowling! Then the end was close at hand, as with successive balls Morley bowled Mr Ridley and F. Steele, the innings being finished at 6.15 for 56 runs, the North the winners of the match by 49, a result mainly due to the fine hitting of Ulyett and the splendid bowling of Shaw, who, in that second innings of the South's, bowled

43 overs (30 maidens) for 21 runs and eight wickets – four bowled.

So ended Alfred Shaw's match – a match that will be memorable in cricket history from the foul weather preventing cricket being played on the Whit-Monday (an unprecedented fact at Lord's), and for the very fine bowling of Shaw.

The North

Richard Daft c Stratford b W. Grace	0	– b A. P. Lucas	4
A. N. Hornby Esq. b W. Grace	20	– st Ridley b Stratford	27
Ephraim Lockwood c Steele b Stratford	10	– b W. Grace	5
George Ulyett b W. Grace	10	– not out	41
A. G. Steel Esq. b A. P. Lucas	3	– lbw b Steele	6
J. Selby hit wkt b W. Grace	6	– b Steele	0
Arthur Shrewsbury b A. P. Lucas	0	– c W. Hearn b W. Grace	3
T. Emmett run out	3	– run out	2
Alfred Shaw c E. Lyttelton b G. G. Hearne	12	– c G. G. Hearne b A. P. Lucas	0
George Pinder not out	21	– c F. Penn b W. Grace	2
F. Morley b W. Grace	1	– st Ridley b A. P. Lucas	1
B 4, l-b 2	6	B 2	2
	92		93

The South

W. G. Grace Esq. c Ulyett b Morley	18	– c Selby b Alfred Shaw	1
A. P. Lucas Esq. c Shrewsbury b Alfred Shaw	7	– c Ulyett b Alfred Shaw	18
W. H. Hadow Esq. b Alfred Shaw	0	– b Alfred Shaw	0
F. Penn Esq. b Alfred Shaw	2	– b Alfred Shaw	10
A. W. Ridley Esq. b A. G. Steel	20	– b Morley	8
Hon. E. Lyttelton b Alfred Shaw	7	– b Alfred Shaw	2
Lord Harris c Hornby b Alfred Shaw	3	– b Alfred Shaw	15
G. G. Hearne jun. c Selby b A. G. Steel	12	– c Lockwood b Alfred Shaw	0
A. H. Stratford Esq. not out	1	– st Pinder b Alfred Shaw	2
William Hearn b Alfred Shaw	0	– not out	0
F. Steele c Emmett b A. G. Steel	3	– b Morley	0
B 7	7		
	80		56

South Bowling

	Overs	Mdns	Runs	Wkts	Overs	Mdns	Runs	Wkts
Mr W. Grace	34.3	17	27	5	26	9	37	3
Mr A. P. Lucas	20	6	24	2	24	12	22	3
Mr Stratford	17	7	21	1	10	5	9	1
G. G. Hearne	11	5	14	1	2	—	12	—
F. Steele					9	4	11	2

North Bowling

	Overs	Mdns	Runs	Wkts	Overs	Mdns	Runs	Wkts
A. Shaw	33	20	39	6	43	30	21	8
Morley	23	6	28	1	31.3	17	21	2
Mr A. G. Steel	9.1	5	6	3	11	3	14	—

Umpires: F. Farrands and F. Wyld.

A GENEROUS OFFER

The newspapers of the Saturday subsequent to the above match gratifyingly announced that in consequence of the unfavourable weather of Whit-Monday and Tuesday, it had been decided to give Shaw the proceeds (less the expenses) of the complimentary match to Mr W. G. Grace, then to be played on the 21st, etc., of July. It is understood that Mr W. Grace sent a letter to the MCC Committee stating that as the weather at Shaw's match had been so disastrous he should be pleased if the MCC would sanction the proceeds of his complimentary match being added (less the expenses) as a subscription to Alfred Shaw's lists. The compiler of this book feels gratification in chronicling on the pages of "*Wisden*" so generous an action to a worthy comrade and opponent in very many finely fought out and celebrated cricket battles.

MCC AND GROUND v HERTFORDSHIRE

Played at Royston, July 3, 4, 1879

The Hertfordshire Men had a fair chance of winning this match, wanting only 60 runs to win when they commenced their second innings, but the extraordinary bowling of William Mycroft entirely upset that chance (as it would have upset any other County's chance) by delivering 21 overs (15 maidens) for 8 runs and nine wickets, four bowled. Every ball of those 21 overs bowled by Mycroft would have been (with pleasure) chronicled here by the Compiler of this book, who, however, failed in obtaining the necessary particulars. Not being able to do that, he will here give how the wickets fell in that innings of 23 runs (19 from the bat) made by Hertfordshire:

1/2 2/10 3/10 4/10 5/11 6/11 7/15 8/17 9/23 10/23

W. Mycroft won the match for MCC by 36 runs.

MCC and Ground

A. S. Barnes Esq. b C. Pigg	3	– c Hughes b H. Pigg	4
Hon. W. N. Hood b Titchmarsh	0	– b H. Pigg	8
Capt. D. Roebuck not out	12	– c and b Titchmarsh	11
F. W. Bennet Esq. b Titchmarsh	0	– b H. Pigg	5
W. Flowers b Titchmarsh	6	– b John Hughes	18
A. C. MacPherson Esq. c Titchmarsh b C. Pigg	11	– c T. Pearce b H. Pigg	3
W. Barnes not out	31	– run out	14
M. C. Clarke Esq. b H. Pigg	1	– c Dale b John Hughes	9
E. T. Welman Esq. c W. Hearn b H. Pigg	15	– c T. Pearce b H. Pigg	8
J. E. Phillips Esq. c Titchmarsh b Dale	18	– b John Hughes	2
W. Mycroft b Titchmarsh	2	– not out	6
		B 6	6
	99		94

Hertfordshire

T. Pearce b Flowers	20	– b W. Mycroft	2
H. A. Taylor Esq. b Flowers	6	– b W. Mycroft	0
William Hearn c M. C. Clarke b W. Mycroft	15	– b W. Mycroft	4
H. Pigg Esq. c Bennett b Hood	36	– c Roebuck b W. Mycroft	0
C. Pigg Esq. b Flowers	25	– c Roebuck b W. Mycroft	0
W. H. Heale Esq. b Flowers	3	– b Flowers	1
R. Porter Esq. c Roebuck b Flowers	2	– not out	4
V. E. Titchmarsh Esq. b W. Mycroft	6	– c Flowers b W. Mycroft	4
Rev. T. G. Dale b W. Mycroft	1	– st Roebuck b W. Mycroft	2
C. E. Keyser Esq. b Flowers	3	– c Bennett b W. Mycroft	2
John Hughes not out	5	– b W. Mycroft	0
B 6, l-b 4, w 2	12	B 2, l-b 2	4
	134		23

Hertfordshire Bowling

	Overs	Mdns	Runs	Wkts	Overs	Mdns	Runs	Wkts
Mr Titchmarsh	19.1	6	32	4	19	11	18	1
Mr C. Pigg	15	3	27	2				
Hughes	13	6	11	—	46	24	33	3
Mr H. Pigg	13	6	19	2	26.3	10	37	5
Mr Dale	4	—	10	1				

MCC Bowling

	Overs	Mdns	Runs	Wkts	Overs	Mdns	Runs	Wkts
Flowers	35	15	45	6	20	13	11	1
W. Mycroft	26	11	36	3	21	15	8	9
Barnes	13	3	28	—				
Hon. W. Hood	8	3	13	1				

OVER THIRTY v UNDER THIRTY

Played at Lord's, July 22, 23, 1879

It is admitted beyond all dispute that Mr W. G. Grace is the greatest cricketer "the world e'er saw". Whatever may be the prejudices of those whose memories carry them back to the heroes of the last generation, even they give way, and yield the palm to the Gloucestershire captain. This being so, and considering the impetus which his reputation has given to the game, it was only natural that his admirers should wish to pay him a tribute more substantial than mere praise. Subscriptions were, therefore, invited in the season of 1877, and the outcome of this was the presentation of a testimonial, and a sum of money, to which were to be added the proceeds of the above match, played at Lord's on July 21, 22, and 23. A disappointment, however, had befallen Shaw on account of the weather being so unfavourable on the occasion of his benefit match – North v South. Earlier in the season, and with a generosity which met with hearty approval on all hands, Mr Grace asked that the match intended for himself should be devoted to Shaw. But, alas! the elements were even more perverse on the days intended for the Over Thirty v Under Thirty match than they had been on the occasion of North v South, and so far as Shaw was concerned little benefit was reaped from it. There is a rumour afloat, however, that another fixture will be given to the clever and deserving Nottinghamshire cricketer. Let us hope it may prove true.

Two exceedingly good teams had been selected to take part in the match, and large attendances were anticipated. The first day, Monday, proved a blank. So wet were the wickets, and moist the atmosphere generally, that not a ball was bowled. Even on Tuesday it was so bad that a beginning could not be made until a quarter past one. Under Thirty, who had won the toss, then deputed the Hon. A. Lyttelton and Barlow to oppose Mycroft and Shaw. Out of the first 16 runs registered Mr Lyttelton claimed 15, and was then clean bowled. Mr F. Penn made one run less than his predecessor, and succumbed to a catch at slip. Now occurred the interval for luncheon, when the presentation (a notice of which immediately follows this match) was made to Mr W. G. Grace. Soon after play was resumed rain fell so heavily that a delay of nearly half an hour was caused. Mr G. F. Grace, who went in third wicket down, saw the dismissal of the remainder of his side for a well-played 35. It was rather unfortunate that Mr W. G. Grace (who, with the "Doctor", went in first for Over Thirty) should have been clean-bowled with the unenviable cypher affixed to his name on an occasion when he would probably liked to have shown to advantage. But such was his fate. The second wicket, however, was not so easily captured. Mr F. Townsend joined Mr E. M. Grace. So speedily did they put together runs that the attacking division became alarmed. The bowled was changed and re-changed, but without effect on the obstinate pair, who kept up their wickets until the close of the day, and had placed the creditable number of 78 runs on the score sheet.

There was a marked improvement in the weather on the third day, Wednesday, but the wicket proved much more difficult. The obstinate pair were soon separated, Mr Townsend being caught at slip. Selby, who came next, was sent back scoreless, and at 103 Mr E. M. Grace was dismissed through a clever catch by Ulyett at long-field-off. Four wickets were now down. Oscroft (22) and Wild (not out 14) were the only remaining two who made any pretensions to a stand, and at ten minutes past one the innings terminated for 138. With a deficit of 27 the Juniors entered on their second trial. Mr W. G. Grace compensated in great measure for his poor batting by showing some excellent bowling. When only a single had been made he induced the Hon. A. Lyttelton to return him the ball, while with an additional 5 runs he caused his brother, Mr G. F. Grace, to lodge it in the hands of the wicket-keeper. Barlow played a patient and effective innings for 26, and his efforts were seconded a little by Mr F. Penn and Ulyett, but the others evinced a lamentable inability to play to the bowling, and the last wicket only realised 80 runs. The "old uns" now had the easy task of getting 54 to win. Mr E. M. Grace again hit away in a style which showed that he meant business; and at 5.25 Selby made the winning hit, the "Doctor" carrying out his bat. Over Thirty, as may be seen from the score, won by seven wickets.

Under Thirty

R. G. Barlow b Alfred Shaw	15	– c Selby b W. Grace	26
Hon. A. Lyttelton b Alfred Shaw	15	– c and b W. Grace	0
F. Penn Esq. c Alfred Shaw b W. Grace	14	– c E. Pooley b W. Mycroft	11
George Ulyett c Alfred Shaw b W. Grace	7	– c Selby b W. Grace	12
G. F. Grace Esq. not out	35	– c E. Pooley b W. Grace	5
V. Royle Esq. c Daft b Alfred Shaw	2	– c Daft b W. Grace	0
Hon. Ivo Bligh st E. Pooley b Alfred Shaw	7	– c Alfred Shaw b W. Grace	3
W. Bates b W. Mycroft	10	– c Daft b Alfred Shaw	5
W. Barnes b W. Mycroft	4	– b Alfred Shaw	8
G. G. Hearne jun. b W. Grace	0	– not out	1
F. Morley b W. Mycroft	0	– c W. Grace b Alfred Shaw	1
B 1, l-b 1	2	B 7, l-b 1	8
	111		80

Over Thirty

Dr W. G. Grace b Morley	0 – c Royle b Bates	7
Dr E. M. Grace c Ulyett b Morley	40 – not out	33
F. Townsend Esq. c Morley b Bates	43 – b Morley	6
J. Selby b Morley	0 – not out	2
William Oscroft c A. Lyttelton b Morley	22	
Richard Daft c Hearne b Barlow	1 – b Bates	4
T. Emmett c Morley b Barlow	7	
F. Wyld not out	14	
Alfred Shaw b Barlow	4	
E. Pooley c Bligh b Barlow	0	
W. Mycroft c Royle b Barlow	0	
B 3, l-b 3, w 1	7	B 1, l-b 1 2
	138	54

The Bowling of "The Old Un's"

	Overs	Mdns	Runs	Wkts	Overs	Mdns	Runs	Wkts
A. Shaw	36	20	34	4	18.2	12	21	3
Mr W. Grace	35	10	55	3	46	30	32	6
W. Mycroft	17.2	7	30	3	30	20	19	1

The Bowling of "The Young Un's"

	Overs	Mdns	Runs	Wkts	Overs	Mdns	Runs	Wkts
Morley	46	20	57	4	13	7	14	1
Barlow	33.2	20	21	5	3	1	17	—
Bates	18	9	30	1	9.3	1	21	2
Barnes	8	3	13	—				

Umpires: F. Farrands and Nixon (Cambs.).

PRESENTATION TO MR W. G. GRACE

The presentation to which allusion has been made above took place at the most appropriate spot which could have been selected – viz., in front of the pavilion at Lord's. It consisted of a sum of money and a marble clock, bearing this inscription: – "Presented to W. G. Grace, on July 22nd, 1879, on the occasion of the match Over Thirty v Under Thirty, played in his honour at Lord's", and two bronze ornaments representing Egyptian obelisks.

Lord Fitzhardinge, who had kindly undertaken to make the presentation, regretted his inability to control the weather, as he thought there were few such interesting occasions as that which had brought them together. Referring to the testimonial, his Lordship said that the original idea had been to purchase a practice for Mr Grace; but he had talked the matter over with the Duke of Beaufort, and they thought that Mr Grace was old enough and strong enough to take care of himself – (laughter and cheers) – and they would leave him to choose a practice for himself. The total amount, deducting expenses, which would be placed to Mr Grace's credit, including the value of the clock and the ornaments, was about £1,400 (cheers). He had, accordingly, great pleasure in presenting this testimonial to Mr Grace, and he could only say, on behalf of the people of Gloucestershire, that they wished him as much success in his profession as he had reaped in the cricket field (loud cheers).

Mr W. G. Grace, after stating that he was not a speech-maker, made a short and appropriate reply, in which he thanked them all for the manner in which they had got up the testimonial. It had far exceeded his expectations, and whenever he looked at the clock he should remember the occasion on which it was presented to him.

Lord Charles Russell, who had been asked as one of the oldest members of the Marylebone Club to say a few words on the occasion, said "he was not satisfied with the amount. He thought £1,400 was an odd sum to present to any one, and he pledge his word it would be £1,500 before they were done with it. He was an old cricketer, and the enjoyment he had had in the cricket-field for many years past was in seeing Mr Grace play cricket. He looked upon cricket as the sport of the people, from the prince to the peasant, he was delighted to see that it was increasing in popularity year by year, and that in some respects also it was being better played. He had seen better bowling than was seen now. He had certainly seen greater men in that department of the game than Mr Grace, but he would say, with a clear conscience, that he had never seen a better field – (cheers) – and he had never seen anyone approach him as a batsman. (Cheers.) More than agility was wanted in playing cricket. The game must be played with head and heart, and in that respect Mr Grace was eminently prominent. He had often seen an England Eleven playing an up-hill game steadily and well; a sudden change had placed the game in their favour, and a change came over the field, such as there would be were the sun now to break out over their heads. Looking at Mr Grace's playing, he was never able to tell whether that gentleman was playing a winning or a losing game. He had never seen the slightest luke-warmness or inertness in him in the field. (Cheers.) If they wanted to see Mr Grace play cricket, he would ask them to look at him playing one ball. They all knew the miserably tame effect of the ball hitting the bat instead of the bat hitting the ball, whether acting on the defensive or offensive. In playing a ball, Mr Grace put every muscle into it, from the sole of his foot to the crown of his head (laughter); and just as he played one ball so he played cricket. He was heart and soul in it. He had never heard a bell ring for cricketers to go into the field, but Mr Grace was in first. And that was a great matter in cricket playing. The game was a game of laws and regulations. If they relaxed these, then it became merely a pastime fit for young men who had nothing else to do, or some middle-aged men who wanted to get an appetite. (Laughter and cheers.) The Marylebone Cricket Club held its ground for the practice and promotion of good sound cricket, and it was for that reason they had such great delight in taking part in this testimonial to Mr Grace, who was in every respect of the word a thorough cricketer. (Loud cheers.) Allusion had been made to HRH the Prince of Wales having joined the subscribers; it might be presumption in him to speculate on his Royal Highness's motives for doing so, but he must hazard an opinion that HRH was grateful to Mr Grace for affording him an opportunity of showing his respect for the one great game of the people, requiring in those who play it the national essentials of patience, fortitude, and pluck, and fostering the respect for law and love of fair play which are characteristic of us English people. (Loud cheers.)

HUNTSMEN OF ENGLAND v JOCKEYS

Played at Lord's, May 29, 1880

The proceeds of the match were divided between the Hunt Servants' Benefit Society and the Bentinck Benevolent Fund. Fine weather and a large attendance ensured a substantial addition to the funds of two deserving charities. Thirteen a side played and the result was a draw. For the Huntsmen G. Summers scored 4 and 17; Jas. Bailey, 1 and 29; G. Champion, 19 and 9; R. Summers, 6 and 20; Tom Goddard, 0 and 16; and R. Roake, 12 and 4. For the Jockeys Captain Middleton was top scorer with 58; R. I'Anson contributed 20; Mr R. Shaw, 15; and Tom Cannon and T. McGeorge, 12 each.

Huntsmen, 66 and 114 for ten; Jockeys 152.

MCC AND GROUND v FIFTEEN CANADIANS

Played at Lord's, June 10, 1880

If fifty Canadians of the calibre of this fifteen had been brought into the field it is possible, even probable, that MCC would still have been victorious, so miserable was the display made by the visitors. H. Lemmon, who scored 14 not out, and G. F. Hall, 13, were the only two who managed to reach double figures, while no less than six of the Canadians figured with "a pair of them". In the first innings of the visitors, Morley bowled 21 overs (sixteen maidens) for 10 runs and eight wickets, and in the two innings Shaw bowled 37 overs and 3 balls (21 maidens) for 40 runs and fifteen wickets. The "hat trick" was twice accomplished in this match – by Morley in the first innings, and by Shaw in the second. There was absolutely nothing either in the batting, bowling, or fielding of the visitors calling for praise. For MCC Mr I. D. Walker contributed 35; George Ulyett, 30; Mr G. F. Vernon, 27; Mr C. I. Thornton, 22; and Morley, 21. The match occupied but one day, and was concluded at 6.35, MCC being the winners by an innings and 123 runs.

MCC and Ground 192; The Canadians (14 batted), 33 and 36.

THE CANTERBURY WEEK

I ZINGARI v GENTLEMEN OF ENGLAND

Played on the St. Lawrence Ground, August 5, 1881

This one day match, and the last of the week, was commenced on Friday. The I Zingari was much the stronger team, and hit up a big score against the weak bowling of the opposite side, for whom Mr J. Patterson was the most successful bowler, taking six wickets for 92 runs. Mr Lyttelton's innings was the feature of the match. The Gentlemen of England showed very poor form, Mr Cottrell taking six of their wickets for 32 runs. At the conclusion of the innings of the Gentlemen of England the match was abandoned.

I Zingari

Hon. A. Lyttelton b Robertson	91
Hon. Ivo Bligh c Blaxland b Patterson	9
Hon. E. Lyttelton b Patterson	32
H. W. Renny-Tailyour Esq. c Vernon b Robertson	40
C. E. Cottrell Esq. c Malden b Vernon	43
C. C. Clarke Esq. c Tylecote b Patterson	6
R. A. H. Mitchell Esq. not out	41
Lord Throwley c Kemp b Patterson	1
W. Yardley Esq. b Patterson	6
F. G. Randolph Esq. st Kemp b Robertson	0
Hon. R. Dillon lbw b Patterson	0
B 12, l-b 9	21
	290

Gentlemen of England

E. F. S. Tylecote Esq. lbw b Clarke	5
E. Knight Esq. c Bligh b Cottrell	3
B. Blaxland Esq. b Cottrell	0
Webber-Smith Esq. b Clarke	18
P. Malden Esq. c Bligh b Cottrell	0
M. C. Kemp Esq. c Randolph b Clarke	0
J. Patterson Esq. b Clarke	0
J. Robertson Esq. c Lyttelton b Cottrell	12
G. F. Vernon Esq. b Cottrell	14
F. A. Mackinnon Esq. c Bligh b Cottrell	7
W. Foord-Kelcey Esq. not out	0
B 9	9
	68

England Bowling

	Overs	Mdns	Runs	Wkts
Mr Patterson	50.1	22	92	6
Mr Foord-Kelcey	24	7	61	—
Mr Robertson	29	12	63	3
Mr Vernon	9	1	32	1
Mr Malden	5	2	11	—
Mr Blaxland	2	—	10	—

I Zingari Bowling

	Overs	Mdns	Runs	Wkts
Mr Cottrell	11.2	3	32	6
Mr Clarke	11	—	27	4

The "Old Stagers" met with great success, the programme being "The Charming Woman", "Out of Light", "Tit for Tat", "A Thumping Legacy", and "Hester's Mystery". Lord Harris's absence was feelingly alluded to in the original epilogue, which concludes the Canterbury Week, in the following lines:

"Our pleasure's tainted by one heavy grief –
The absence of our former cricket chief,
For all the pluck with which he strove to raise
Her cricket to the height of former days
Kent owes to him – that is no empty platitude –
A deep and everlasting debt of gratitude;
'Tis sad his dear familiar face to miss,
But we must consolation seek in this;
Though him and us a cruel distance parts,
We are in his as he in all our hearts."

On Wednesday and Thursday the usual balls took place at the Freemasons' Hall, where dancing was kept up with great zeal to the strains of Gates's band.

A PARTNERSHIP PRODUCING 454 RUNS!

MCC AND GROUND v LEICESTERSHIRE

Played at Lord's, June 1, 2, 1882

The whole of the interest in this match centred in the extraordinary batting performances of Barnes and Midwinter, whose long partnership left all previous records of the kind far behind. The longest stand ever before made was that by Messrs G. F. Grace and I. D. Walker, for the Gentlemen of the South v the Gentlemen of the North, at Beeston, Nottinghamshire, in 1870, who scored 288 while they were together (Mr Grace making 189 and Mr Walker 179), and thus eclipsed the previous best on record of 283 for the first wicket made by Messrs W. G. Grace and B. B. Cooper for the Gentlemen of the South v the Players of the South, at Kennington Oval, in 1869, Mr Grace scoring 180, and Mr Cooper 101.

Barnes went in with the score at one for the first wicket (Mr Booth's), and when Mr Russel was bowled at 19, he was joined by Midwinter at about ten minutes past four. When play ceased for the day, at seven o'clock, they were still together, the total being 283, Barnes 146 not out and Midwinter 120 not out, their partnership having then produced 264 runs. Up to that time they had scored at the rate of nearly 100 runs per hour. Midwinter had not given a single chance, and his 120 not out consisted of a splendid square-leg hit for 6 (the ball bounding from the roof of the grand stand clean out of the ground), eight 4s, ten 3s, eleven 2s, and thirty singles. Barnes narrowly escaped stumping when he had scored about 20, gave a somewhat hard chance to point when he had made 110, and another to the bowler when his score stood at 126; and his 146 not out was made up of a big on-drive for 6 (past the new dining pavilion), two 5s, twelve 4s, fourteen 3s, six 2s and 28 singles.

The game was continued at 11.40 on the Friday, and at the luncheon interval Barnes and Midwinter were still in, the former having made 264 and the latter 186. On resuming, a very few minutes' play sufficed to bring the longest stand on record to an end, Barnes being caught at mid-off for 266. Only one more run was added before Midwinter was caught at extra-cover point. The pair were at the wickets within a few minutes of five and a half hours, scoring at the rate of more than 80 runs per hour, and raising the score from 19 for two wickets to 473 for three. Barnes' previous best score was 143 for Nottinghamshire v Gloucestershire, at Cheltenham, in 1880, and his 266 is the second highest individual score made at Lord's, Mr Ward's 278 in 1820 being the biggest innings made on the old ground. When little more than a boy, Midwinter played an innings of 256 at Bendigo, Sandhurst, Victoria, but his 187 is the highest score he has made in England. He gave one chance when he had made 130, and Barnes also had another life on the Friday. Their hits were as follow:

	6s	5s	4s	3s	2s	Singles
Barnes	1	4	26	20	15	46
Midwinter	1	1	12	15	22	39

Of the batting of the two men a critic observes, "Midwinter's 187 was perhaps a more sound innings, but his hitting was not so severe. It would be difficult, however, to say which was the better – the Australians's off-driving or Barnes' leg-hitting." The MCC total of 548 is the highest score a side has made at Lord's, the next best being the 485 by Middlesex against the MCC in 1871.

It will be seen that Parnham's trundling was by far the most successful for Leicestershire, and when that bowler's subsequent splendid performances against the Australians are considered the effect is greatly to enhance the merit of the extraordinary batting of Barnes and Midwinter.

The match, being limited to two days, resulted in a draw.

Leicestershire

J. Wheeler c Bencraft b Barnes	13	c Willett b Midwinter	37
F. Turner c Barnes b Midwinter	21	c Willett b Rylott	8
A. W. Crofts Esq. c Bencraft b Barnes	16	run out	7
C. Marriott Esq. c Willett b Midwinter	25	b Barnes	1
C. Wright Esq. b Midwinter	0	c Rylott b Midwinter	5
C. Panter c Barnes b Midwinter	0	not out	46
Rev. G. S. Marriott c Maynard b Rylott	40	run out	25
J. Parnham c and b Rylott	19	b Rylott	14
R. W. G. Stainton Esq. run out	7	c Bencraft b Midwinter	4
W. Bottomore c Maynard b Barnes	0	not out	11
W. Garner not out	0		
B 5, l-b 5, n-b 1	11	L-b 5, n-b 1	6
	152		164

MCC and Ground

C. Booth Esq. c Wheeler b Parnham	0
J. S. Russel Esq. b Bottomore	11
W. Barnes c Panter b Parnham	266
W. Midwinter c G. S. Marriott b Parnham	187
J. Turner Esq. b Bottomore	0
W. Flowers c Panter b Parnham	15
H. Maynard Esq. c Turner b Wright	23
R. Bencraft Esq. c Panter b Parnham	2
J. Carrick Esq. b Parnham	18
F. S. Willett Esq. c Crofts b Parnham	5
A. Rylott not out	6
B 8, l-b 3, w 2	15
	548

MCC Bowling

	Overs	Mdns	Runs	Wkts	Overs	Mdns	Runs	Wkts
Flowers	18	5	39	—	24	4	59	—
Rylott	23.2	9	27	2	22	12	37	2
Barnes	20	5	44	3	7	2	17	1
Midwinter	21	12	31	4	24	6	45	3

Leicestershire Bowling

	Overs	Mdns	Runs	Wkts		Overs	Mdns	Runs	Wkts
Parnham	83.3	23	174	7	Wheeler	16	1	46	—
Bottomore	49	17	106	2	Mr C. Marriott	2	—	10	—
Garner	13	3	31	—	Panter	3	—	11	—
Rev. G. S. Marriott	16	4	52	—	Turner	19	7	42	—
Mr Wright	28	7	61	1					

Umpires: W. Price and M. Sherwin.

MCC AND GROUND v NOTTINGHAMSHIRE

Played at Lord's, June 15, 16, 1882

This match produced some extraordinary cricket and a most exciting finish, and afforded an instance of a weak eleven making a most gallant bid for victory against a strong one. The wicket was slow and difficult and when time was called on the first day the MCC had scored an innings of 136 and Notts had lost five wickets for 71 runs, the features of the play being the good batting of Scotton (52) and Oscroft (49 not out) and the bowling of Shaw and Morley. Shaw bowled 35 maidens out of 40 overs without taking a wicket and Morley, who went on late, took five wickets for 25 runs.

Play was resumed at twenty-five minutes to twelve on the Friday. Oscroft added eight runs to his overnight total and the innings closed for 117, or 19 runs to the bad, Mills and Sherwin putting on 30 while they were together. On the MCC men going in again, Mr. Leslie and Scotton, by capital cricket, raised the score from 14 for two wickets to 78 for three and Hearn and Fothergill also rendered material assistance in carrying the total to 144. Attewell's bowling in that innings – ten overs (nine maidens) for 2 runs and three wickets – is a curiosity.

The innings closed at 5.10 and previous to the Notts men going in for the necessary 164 runs, it was arranged that play should be continued till 7.30 if there were any chance of concluding the match that evening; and later on it was decided to further prolong the play when it was thought the game would be finished in a fair light. There seemed little doubt of that when wicket after wicket fell in rapid succession and seven were down for 54 runs. Mills then became the partner of Barnes, who had been batting admirably and these two put on no fewer than 99 runs before Fothergill bowled the former for 59, made by very plucky and vigorous batting, his hits consisting of one 5, five 4s, three 3s, nine 2s and only seven singles. With 11 runs required to win, Sherwin came in, but in attempting a short run lost his wicket; and Morley, the last man, joined Barnes, the county wanting five runs to ensure victory. Each man hit a single and then Morley scored a 3 from Rylott and won the match for Notts by one wicket at eight minutes to eight, in semi-darkness and amid great enthusiasm. Barnes carried out his bat for a first-class 66, made up of a 5, five 4s, four 3s, three 2s and 23 singles.

MCC and Ground

C. Booth Esq. run out	12	– c Oscroft b Morley	1
J. S. Russel Esq. b Wright	5	– st Sherwin b Morley	9
C. F. H. Leslie Esq. b Wright	0	– b Shaw	38
W. Scotton c Butler b Morley	52	– run out	27
F. E. Speed Esq. b Morley	16	– c Sherwin b Shaw	11
J. Carrick Esq. b Attewell	10	– lbw b Shaw	3
W. Hearn c Shaw b Morley	1	– b Shaw	21
A. J. Fothergill b Morley	6	– b Attewell	16
F. Wyld c Sherwin b Morley	9	– c Shaw b Attewell	0
A. Rylott b Mills	14	– c Sherwin b Attewell	0
W. A. Woof not out	0	– not out	4
B 7, l-b 4	11	B 11, l-b 2, n-b 1	14
	136		144

Nottinghamshire

A. Shrewsbury c Leslie b Fothergill	1	– b Fothergill	4
W. Oscroft c Hearn b Woof	57	– c Wyld b Fothergill	1
W. Barnes b Fothergill	8	– not out	66
J. Selby c Wyld b Fothergill	0	– lbw b Woof	4
F. Butler c Leslie b Rylott	7	– b Woof	2
W. Attewell b Woof	3	– c Booth b Woof	6
W. Wright b Woof	2	– c Russel b Woof	1
A. Shaw c Woof b Rylott	3	– b Woof	3
E. Mills c Scotton b Woof	12	– b Fothergill	59
M. Sherwin not out	15	– run out	2
F. Morley b Fothergill	1	– not out	4
B 5, l-b 3	8	B 7, l-b 3, n-b 2	12
	117		164

Nottinghamshire Bowling

	Overs	Mdns	Runs	Wkts	Overs	Mdns	Runs	Wkts
Shaw	40	35	7	—	41.3	22	34	—
Wright	28	11	50	2	22	13	28	—
Mills	16.2	9	15	1	13	7	10	—
Barnes	10	4	16	—	4	1	15	—
Attewell	12	6	12	1	10	9	2	3
Morley	35	26	25	5	47	26	41	2

MCC Bowling

	Overs	Mdns	Runs	Wkts	Overs	Mdns	Runs	Wkts
Rylott	32	17	35	2	10	2	24	—
Fothergill	28.3	12	37	4	32	10	64	3
Woof	25	9	37	4	30	8	64	5
Scotton					1	1	—	—

Umpires: T. Hearne and W. Price.

THE CANTERBURY WEEK

August 7, 8, 9, 10, 11, 1882

By the unanimous vote of the cricket critics, a verdict of "Best of all" was recorded of the "Canterbury Week" of 1882. The matches selected were both novelties, it being the only occassion on which an Australian team had played on the old St. Lawrence Ground; and Kent had never before played a County in their second match. The Committee of the Kent County Club are heartily to be congratulated on the success attending such radical changes in the constitution of the programme and the best thanks of the cricketing public are due to Mr de Chair Baker (for forty years the manager of the "Week") and to Mr J. J. Lancaster (the Assistant-Secretary of the Kent CCC), for the admirable way in which all arrangements were carried out.

Monday was fine and warm. All the hotels in the old city were full, the streets more crowded than ever and the display of bunting more plentiful than on any previous occasion. A special point of attraction was a jeweller's window in which were exhibited a pair of silver candelabra, representing oak trees, beneath which stood a group of cricketers and on the pedestal of which appeared the inscription: – "Presented to Lord Harris by upwards of seven hundred subscribers, as a mark of their appreciation of the services rendered by him to the cause of County Cricket. August, 1882". On the cricket ground a treble row of seats replaced the single row of benches and thirty-nine tents were well filled with the subscribers to County cricket. 4,360 spectators paid at the gates and about 1,000 more were admitted with subscription tickets. Play was started precisely at noon and at two o'clock the Australians were entertained at lunch in the Corporation tent on the ground by Mr G. A. Friend, the mayor of Canterbury, who proposed the toast of "The Australian Cricketers", to which Mr Murdoch briefly responded. At the call of time the Australians had played an innings of 307 and Kent had lost six wickets for 81 runs. In the evening the comedy of "Friends or Foes" was given at the theatre and was well received.

Tuesday was gloriously fine and "the crowd was never so large at Canterbury before on any day of any week". Messrs Tylecote, Wilson and Patterson batted in magnificent form and when stumps were drawn for the day Kent had completed their second innings and the Australians had scored 21 towards the 81 required to win, without losing a wicket. The amusements of the day were brought to a conclusion by the performance at the theatre of a new comedy "Time will Tell".

On Wednesday a slight shower fell about ten o'clock, but the day was otherwise fine though dull. Kent suffered a seven wickets' defeat and to fill up the afternoon a scratch match "Band of Brothers" v "The World" was played. The most interesting episode of the day, however, was the presentation to Lord Harris of the handsome pair of candelabra already referred to. Space will not allow of the speeches appearing in Wisden's in full and the following abridged account of the proceedings, taken from the *Daily Chronicle*, must therefore suffice:

"At about half-past two the presentation to Lord Harris was made in front of the tent occupied by Mrs Mackinnon. The company in the field had considerably increased in numbers, most of the notabilities and all the cricketers both gentlemen and professionals, of the county and the colonials, with many ladies, being present in and about the tent, while the general public assembled in front. Pleased expectation was on every face when Earl Darnley, president for the year of the Kent County Club, made the presentation in a neat and graceful speech. His Lordship spoke of what he called the golden age of Kentish cricket – the days of Wenman, Felix, Hillyer, Fuller Pilch, and Alfred Mynn and went on to say that after the disappearance of those celebrities there was a less brilliant period. It was at this time that Lord Harris, by general desire and universal approval, took the lead in Kent cricket. In three or four years he succeeded in organizing and bringing into the field a team able to hold its own against almost any other county in England. If that success had not been maintained, it was not through any fault on the part of Lord Harris, who, besides being captain in the field, undertook for several years the management of the matches, and this was a public recognition of his services to Kentish cricket. Lord Darnley then removed the Kentish flag, which had covered the testimonial and formally presented the handsome pair of silver candelabra, which were specially and very appropriately designed and inscribed. There was considerable applause, which was renewed on its being stated that there were more than 700 subscribers to the fund. Lord Darnley, on behalf of the same subscribers, afterwards presented a silver inkstand to Lady Harris, with the good-natured remark that it could never hold ink enough to express all the good wishes they entertained towards her. Earl Darnley spoke for fully ten minutes; and then Lord Harris came forward to return thanks. He was at first somewhat nervous, but as he proceeded, every telling point was taken up by the audience and warmly applauded. He expressed great pleasure at their token of approval, which, however, he felt he had done little to deserve, but he could fairly say that in playing the game he loved best he had never forgotten that he had done so for the honour of Kent. He was trustful that the energy which was so apparent of late amongst the cricketers of the county would be productive of good results in the future and anything which he could do to further the interests of the noble game they might rely upon being done. On the conclusion of his speech three hearty cheers were given for Kent and its cricketers; and Lord Harris again came forward and asked for three cheers for the Australians. They were given with hearty aplomb, in the manner known as Kentish fire, led by Lord Harris himself. Among the company I noticed Lady Harris, Mrs Mackinson, Earl Sondes, the Hon. Ivo Bligh, Lord Throwley, the Hon.

Spencer Ponsonby-Fane, the Hon. F. Cavendish Bentinck, the Rev C. E. Nepean, Rev. C. Randolph, Colonel Laurie, Captain Lambert and Messrs. A. Douglas, M.P., W. Foord-Kelcey, W. W. Knight, Alfred Donne, M. C. Kemp, S. P. Jones and G. A. Friend, Mayor of Canterbury."

In the evening the Mayor presided at a smoking concert given by the St. Lawrence Amateur Musical Society, at the "Odd Fellows Hall", at which the Colonists attended. This was followed by the usual ball at St. Margaret's Music Hall.

Thursday – the Ladies' Day – proved dull and cloudy throughout, but the attendance was nevertheless as large and brilliant as in any previous year. The second match of the week – Kent v Middlesex – was commenced and when play ceased for the day Middlesex had scored an innings of 338 and Kent had lost three of their best wickets for 81 runs. In the evening the performance of "Friends and Foes" was repeated, followed by the Farce "If I had £1,000 a year".

Friday, the concluding day of the week, was a perfect day for cricket. Lord Harris batted magnificently, but could not avert a crushing defeat by ten wickets. At twenty-eight minutes past six the match was over and the most successful "Week" ever held at Canterbury was brought to a conclusion by a repetition of "Time tries all", followed by another ball at the Music Hall. The Bands of the Royal Artillery and Cavalry Depôt played selections of music on alternate days.

MCC AND GROUND v EASTBOURNE

Played on the Eastbourne Cricket Ground (South Fields), June 9, 1883

The only remarkable feature of this match was the bowling of Jesse Hide, who obtained the whole of the ten wickets – nine bowled – in the first innings of the MCC at a cost of only 11 runs, his analysis reading fourteen overs and three balls (eight maidens) for 11 runs and ten wickets. That innings must be given in full:

MCC and Ground

R. M. Curteis Esq. b Jesse Hide	0
J. W. Blundell Esq. b Jesse Hide	14
W. P. Burn Esq b Jesse Hide	1
G. G. Hearne b Jesse Hide	10
John Wheeler b Jesse Hide	0
J. E. A. Greatorex Esq. c Bergg b Jesse Hide	21
A. Ireland Esq. b Jesse Hide	0
A. Lamond Esq. b Jesse Hide	3
W. A. Woof not out	1
A. W. Owen Esq. b Jesse Hide	0
H. Curteis Esq. b Jesse Hide	3
B 8	8
	61

In the second innings of the visitors Mr Greatorex scored 44; Mr R. M. Curteis, 20 not out; Wheeler, 14; and four other batsmen 14 between them, but of the six wickets which fell only two were obtained by Hide. The highest scorers for Eastbourne were Mr R. Hart, 15 and 28; Rev. H. Von E. Scott, 35 and 2; Mr S. H. Reed, 0 and 27 not out; Mr L. Jeffery, 0 and 19; Dr. C. N. Hayman, 18 and 0; and Jesse Hide, 2 and 10. The game resulted in a draw. Totals: – MCC and Ground, 61 and (six wickets down) 96. Eastbourne, 92 and 110.

THE LARGEST INNINGS OF THE SEASON
MCC AND GROUND v ARDINGLY COLLEGE

Played on the Ardingly College Ground, June 11, 1883

The innings of 672 made by the College in this match was the largest scored in England during the season of 1883, and apart from this was remarkable for the extraordinary rate at which the runs were put on. Play began at 12 o'clock and ceased at 6.45, the luncheon interval occupying three-quarters of an hour. Thus 672 runs were made in six hours, or at the rate of 112 per hour! The score stood at 112 when the first wicket fell and during the partnership of Messrs Blackman and Brann 307 runs were added to the total. Only two instances are recorded where two batsmen have succeeded in putting on a greater number of runs for a wicket and both occurred in the year 1882. At Rickling Green, on August 4 and 5, Messrs A. H. Trevor and G. F. Vernon put on 605 runs for the second wicket; and at Lord's, on June 1 and 2, the partnership of Barnes and Midwinter resulted in a total of 454 runs being added for the third wicket.

Mr W. Blackman had three escapes before being finally caught. The first occurred when he had made 20; the second when his score reached 45; and the third when he had compiled 126. G. G. Hearne was included in the visitors' team, but owing to an injury he received at Eastbourne the previous Saturday was unable to bowl much and the little he did proved ineffective. The MCC did not bat.

Ardingly College

W. Blackman c Thornton b Borrodaile	277
W. M. Thompson st Hilton b Burn	29
J. Phillips b Jeffrey	3
W. Newham c Burn b Thornton	50
G. Brann c Hilton b Maude	176
C. Marshall run out	10
A. C. Seymour c and b Maude	21
F. K. Hilton c Hearne b Maude	25
A. E. Palmer b Maude	27
A. H. Besant b Maude	0
S. Mooré not out	0
B 39, l-b 12, w3	54
	672

MCC AND GROUND v LANCASHIRE

Played at Lord's, June 11, 12, 1883

This match, full of incident and variety, ended in a brilliant victory for Lancashire by ten wickets. The MCC had first innings, and their first two wickets put on 78 runs, while the last eight were disposed of for 73. Per contra the first eight Lancashire wickets fell for 90 runs, while the last two added no fewer than 70. Flowers for the one, and Watson for the other, each made 45, the latter carrying his bat. Each played admirable cricket and each made seven 4s. Barlow was run out in a singular manner. He hit a ball to mid-off, where it was fielded by Mr Russel. There was no chance of a run and Barlow, thinking the ball would be returned to the bowler, went beyond his crease to pat the ground. Mr Russel then threw the ball to Sherwin, who put down the wicket. The match was a capital one on the first innings, but the fifty-five minutes' play before the call of time on the Monday entirely changed the aspect of the game, as six of the best bats on the MCC side were dismissed for 47 runs and the ultimate result left in little or no doubt.

When the game was resumed on the Tuesday the overnight not outs, Gunn and Mr Russel, put on 22 runs and then a change of bowling was tried, Watson, who had started with Barlow, crossing over to the pavilion end and Nash going on at the nursery wicket. The effect was immediate and extraordinary, as in 21 balls and at a cost of only five runs, Nash finished off the innings by taking the remaining four wickets. Then followed the most remarkable cricket in this match of many changes. Lancashire had 72 to get to win and in fifty-five minutes Mr Hornby and Barlow hit off the runs without the loss of a wicket. Mr Hornby began with unusual care, but when 12 runs had been totalled from ten overs, he batted with great freedom and scored 41 out of the last 54 runs made.

MCC and Ground

Dr W. G. Grace b Nash	31	– c Haigh b Barlow	0
J. G. Walker Esq. c Watson b Barlow	28	– c Watson b Barlow	0
W. Barnes c Watson b Barlow	18	– b Watson	20
W. Flowers b Nash	45	– c Robinson b Barlow	8
W. Hearn c Pilling b Barlow	2	– c Nash b Watson	1
T. C. O'Brien Esq. c and b Nash	0	– lbw b Watson	0
W. Gunn b Nash	5	– c Pilling b Nash	27
J. S. Russel Esq. c Haigh b Barlow	14	– c Pilling b Nash	14
A. Rylott b Barlow	0	– c Crossland b Nash	2
M. Sherwin not out	0	– not out	6
F. Morley run out	3	– c Hornby b Nash	0
B 5	5	B 1, l-b 1	2
	151		80

Lancashire

A. N. Hornby Esq. c Gunn b Flowers	28	– not out	52
R. G. Barlow run out	0	– not out	22
E. Roper Esq. c Sherwin b Morley	3		
W. Robinson c Sherwin b Flowers	19		
S. M. Crosfield Esq. c Rylott b Flowers	0		
J. Briggs b Flowers	13		
C. Haigh Esq. c O'Brien b Grace	9		
A. Watson not out	45		
J. Crossland b Flowers	7		
R. Pilling c and b Barnes	22		
G. Nash b Barnes	7		
B 2, l-b 5	7	B 1	1
	160		75

Lancashire Bowling

	Overs	Mdns	Runs	Wkts	Overs	Mdns	Runs	Wkts
Barlow	39.1	18	65	5	24	10	47	3
Watson	24	14	27	—	30	16	26	3
Crossland	3	—	12	—				
Nash	18	7	42	4	5.1	2	5	4

MCC Bowling

	Overs	Mdns	Runs	Wkts	Overs	Mdns	Runs	Wkts
Morley	23	10	34	1	2.2	—	15	—
Rylott	11	4	36	—	5	—	14	—
Flowers	20	6	44	5	14	5	15	—
Dr W. G. Grace	12	6	23	1	6	—	14	—
Barnes	8.3	2	16	2	6	2	16	—

Umpires: F. H. Farrands and F. Wyld.

MCC AND GROUND v YORKSHIRE

Played at Scarborough, August 30, 31, September 1, 1883

This was the second fixture of the Scarborough Festival and resulted in a draw, the visitors wanting 206 runs to win with eight wickets to fall. The match was full of incident and variety. Owing to the late arrival of some of the players, a start was not effected until 12.45 on the opening day and the Yorkshiremen, who were successful in the toss, were batting until just before the call of time. The first five wickets were obtained for 59 and then, by some especially brilliant hitting by Bates and sound and steady batting by

Emmett, the score was taken to 125 before the former was caught at the wicket, having, by nine 4s, five 3s, five 2s and 14 singles, made 75 out of 112 put on while he was in, a performance for which he was loudly cheered on his retirement. The eighth wicket fell at 132 and it seemed as though the innings would soon be over, but Peate and Peel offered a most determined resistance to the visitors' bowling. Peate hit in capital style while his partner played most patiently, with the result that 88 runs were put on before the former was dismissed for a very freely-hit 60, which included a 6, five 4s, three 3s and five 2s.

A curious feature of the second day's play was that the last five batsmen on the visitors' side drew lots to determine the order of going in and it was during the stay of the last four that the most interesting cricket of the innings was witnessed. Three wickets fell for 14 runs and in spite of some good batting by Gunn, the seventh was disposed of when only 65 runs had been totalled. Then Messrs Paravicini and Schultz became partners and by very fine cricket put on 118 runs before a separation was effected. As a wind up to the innings Mr. Vernon scored 32 out of the last 40 runs, making 16 in one over from Bates. At the conclusion of the second day's play the Yorkshiremen had scored 39 in their second innings without losing a wicket, Ulyett having contributed 28 while Mr Lumb made 5.

On the concluding day of the match Ulyett hit away in most brilliant style and by two 6s (drives out of the ground), ten 4s, eight 2s and sixteen singles, made no fewer than 84 out of the first 131 runs. Lockwood also played very fine cricket, hitting hard at times, besides showing excellent defence. He went in when three wickets had fallen for 131 and was eighth out with the score at 262, neither of the last two wickets adding a run. His hits were six 4s, six 3s, eight 2s and twenty-one singles. The MCC went in a second time wanting 269 to win with only fifty minutes left for play. Two wickets fell very quickly and then Mr. Wright and Flowers played out time.

Yorkshire

G. Ulyett c Schulz b Barnes	5	– b Hearne	84
E. Lumb Esq. c Wright b Allcock	2	– b Flowers	6
Hon. M. B. Hawke c Wright b Barnes	25	– c Wright b Allcock	22
W. Bates c Wright b Barnes	75	– b Hearne	13
E. Lockwood c Hearne b Gunn	2	– lbw b Gunn	79
E. T. Hirst Esq. c Wright b Barnes	0	– c Allcock b Barnes	24
T. Emmett b Barnes	19	– c Barnes b Daft	0
H. E. Rhodes Esq. c Schultz b Barnes	0	– b Barnes	8
R. Peel c Thornton b Paravicini	21	– c sub. b Gunn	12
E. Peate c Wright b Gunn	60	– c Paravicini b Gunn	0
G. A. B. Leatham Esq. not out	4	– not out	0
B 13, l-b 2	15	B 12, l-b 2	14
	223		262

MCC and Ground

C. I. Thornton Esq. c Leatham b Emmett	6		
R. Daft Esq. b Emmett	2		
W. Barnes b Peate	2	– b Emmett	2
W. Gunn b Emmett	25		
G. G. Hearne c Leatham b Peate	5		
W. Flowers b Peate	14	– not out	31
C. H. Allcock Esq. b Peate	0	– c Hawke b Peate	0
P. J. de Paravicini Esq. c Bates b Emmett	60		
S. S. Schultz Esq. run out	51		
C. W. Wright Esq. not out	7	– not out	27
G. F. Vernon Esq. c Lumb b Emmett	32		
B 13, l-b 4, w 1	18	L-b 3	3
	222		63

MCC Bowling

	Overs	Mdns	Runs	Wkts	Overs	Mdns	Runs	Wkts
Mr Allcock	32	15	45	1	12	6	21	1
Barnes	34	14	64	6	39	13	83	2
Gunn	20	10	26	2	18.1	11	16	3
Flowers	17	8	31	—	45	16	77	1
Mr Daft	7	—	19	—	11	4	24	1
Hearne	7	4	6	—	21	11	27	2
Mr Thornton	3	—	11	—				
Mr Schultz	5	1	11	—				
Mr Paravicini	4.2	4	—	1	4	4	—	—

Yorkshire Bowling

	Overs	Mdns	Runs	Wkts	Overs	Mdns	Runs	Wkts
Peate	39	21	40	4	10	2	23	1
Emmett	43.3	19	81	5	12	4	30	1
Bates	12	3	42	—				
Ulyett	8	1	23	—				
Peel	8	3	18	—	5	2	7	—
Lockwood					3	3	—	—

Umpires: F. Wyld and J. King.

MCC AND GROUND v NOTTINGHAMSHIRE

Played at Nottingham, September 13, 14, 15, 1883

For the second time in the season of 1883 a very moderate team of the leading club succeeded in defeating Nottinghamshire, who, however, on this occasion were not represented by quite their full strength. Selby and Mr C. W. Wright were not in the eleven, and Attewell and Scotton were opposed to them. The home team, however, had no cause to complain of the cricket played by the substitutes, as Mills contributed the highest individual innings in the match; Mr J. A. Dixon tied with Shrewsbury as second highest scorer for Notts.; Shacklock took four wickets for 18 runs in the second innings of the MCC, and Smith was highest scorer in the very brief first innings of the home team. The feature of the match was the dismissal of Notts. in their first innings for 23 runs, the smallest total recorded during the season in a first-class match and one of the most remarkable cricket curiosities of the year.

The MCC won the toss and went in to bat at 12.20. Mr W. J. Ford hit hard and W. Hearn played excellent cricket. 90 appeared on the board with only four wickets down, and there seemed every chance of a good score being made. At this point, however, a remarkable change occurred. With the total at 91, W. Hearn was caught at cover-point, and the remaining five wickets fell for an addition of only 8 runs. Then the Notts. men went to the wickets and played their memorably brief innings of 23, the result of an hour and ten minutes' batting. When two runs had been made Shrewsbury was caught at extra mid-off, after being missed by Mr Ford at point and by Mr Russel at mid-on. With the score at 3, no fewer than four wickets fell. Barnes was bowled, Mr Dixon played a ball on to his wicket, Flowers was caught at mid-off and Shacklock caught behind the bowler. Thus ten wickets – five on each side – had fallen in succession for 11 runs! With the total at 7 Gunn was bowled and at 10 Wright was caught at slip and it seemed by no means impossible that Notts. would have to follow their innings. Mills and Smith, however, put on 9 runs while they were together and such a disgrace was ultimately averted. Before Smith had made a run, a ball bowled by Woof hit his leg and was caught at slip by Rylott, who thinking he played the ball, appealed for the catch. Had the bowler appealed for leg-before-wicket, the umpire – Selby – would have given him out. The two catches by W. Hearn which got rid of Shrewsbury and Flowers were both very brilliant ones, the fieldsman in both instances running sideways and taking the ball close to the ground. The bowling of Rylott and Woof was of a truly sensational character, and in the score book assumed the following form:

Rylott	. . . .	. . . .	. . . .	. . . .	. . . w	. w . .
	. . . .	. . . .	. 1 . w	. . . .	. . . .	. 1 . .
	. 1 . 1	. . . .	. . . .	. . . .	. . 2 .	. 1 w
Woof	1 . . .	. . . .	. . . .	. . . .	. . . w	. . ww
	. . . .	. . . .	. . . 1	. . . .	. 1 . 2	. . w 3
	. 3 . .	. . 1 .	. . . .	. . 1 .	w . . .	

A run was scored from the fifth ball and then sixty more were bowled before another was made. But in those sixty-five balls five wickets were taken.

The MCC began their second innings with 76 runs in hand and when 13 had been totalled, stumps were drawn for the day, F. Hearne being 9 not out and Scotton, 3 not out. In continuing the innings on the Friday F. Hearne was out with the total at 19, and then his successor, Mr Ford, hit with so much freedom that he scored 28 out of 32 before he was dismissed by a very smart piece of fielding. G. G. Hearne, W. Hearn and Scotton played good and patient cricket and Mr Russel and Attewell scored freely. With the total at 115 Shacklock relieved Shaw and the change was attended with great success, only 34 more runs being scored for the loss of the remaining five wickets. Nottingham were set the task of scoring 226 runs to win. Shrewsbury and Mr Dixon began and put on 29 before they were parted. Then followed another complete and remarkable collapse, six more wickets falling for only 17 runs. At the call of time the total was 52, Wright and Mills being the not out men, with 4 each.

The match was finished off at 1.5 on the third day, the visitors winning by 121 runs. Mills made a determined effort to turn the tide of victory, his vigorously-hit 34 including five 4s and four 2s. The committee of the Notts. CC gave the proceeds of the match for division among the county team.

MCC and Ground

W. J. Ford Esq. c Mills b Shacklock	23	– run out	28
G. G. Hearne run out	2	– b Flowers	13
W. H. Scotton c Gunn b Flowers	12	– b Flowers	18
W. Hearn c Barnes b Wright	33	– c Wright b Shaw	14
W. Attewell b Flowers	3	– b Shacklock	20
F. Hearne not out	12	– c and b Wright	15
J. S. Russel Esq. b Wright	1	– c Smith b Shacklock	18
A. J. Fothergill c Sherwin b Wright	0	– b Shacklock	0
W. A. Woof b Wright	2	– not out	5
A. Rylott c Shaw b Wright	0	– b Shacklock	2
T. Mycroft c Shaw b Flowers	2	– c Wright b Flowers	11
B 6, l-b 3	9	B 3, l-b 2	5
	99		149

Nottinghamshire

J. A. Dixon Esq b Rylott	1	– c Mycroft b Fothergill	14
A. Shrewsbury c W. Hearn b Rylott	0	– b Woof	14
W. Barnes b Woof	0	– b Fothergill	12
W. Flowers c W. Hearn b Woof	0	– lbw b Woof	1
W. Gunn b Rylott	0	– c Woof b Fothergill	1
F. Shacklock c Fothergill b Woof	0	– c G. G. Hearne b Fothergill	0
A. Smith b Woof	8	– c G. G. Hearne b Fothergill	1
W. Wright c Rylott b Woof	2	– c sub. b Woof	4
E. Mills run out	5	– c Mycroft b G. G. Hearne	34
A. Shaw not out	4	– not out	13
M. Sherwin c Mycroft b Rylott	0	– b G. G. Hearne	9
L-b 3	3	N-b 1	1
	23		104

Nottinghamshire Bowling

	Overs	Mdns	Runs	Wkts	Overs	Mdns	Runs	Wkts
Wright	33	19	26	5	13	4	25	1
Shacklock	20	10	30	1	9.1	2	18	4
Flowers	29	13	28	3	42	15	48	3
Gunn	9	6	6	—	2	—	6	—
Shaw					47	29	47	1

MCC Bowling

	Overs	Mdns	Runs	Wkts	Overs	Mdns	Runs	Wkts
Rylott	17.3	13	7	4	18	6	22	—
Woof	17	10	13	5	29	12	40	2
Fothergill					21	10	30	5
G. G. Hearne					6.3	2	11	2

Umpires: J. Selby and F. H. Farrands.

ELEVEN OF THE NORTH v ELEVEN OF THE SOUTH

Played at Lord's, June 2, 3, 1884

With seven of the leading counties engaged, and the Gentlemen of England playing Cambridge University, representative teams could not possibly be obtained for this match. Nevertheless, the weather being fine, a very large crowd witnessed the play on the opening day. The Southerners batted first, and the bowling of Crossland was the feature of the innings. Though his reception by many of the spectators was not of the most cordial description, his success in taking seven wickets – six bowled – for 45 runs, was received with enthusiasm by the partisans of the northerners. The innings lasted two hours and twenty minutes, and though only 120 runs were scored from the bat, seven of the eleven got into double figures. The innings of the North occupied only an hour and forty minutes. Gregg, the Gloucestershire fast bowler, and Wood-Sims, shared the honours of the innings. Gregg took six wickets for 47 runs, and Wood-Sims, by good, clean, and very free hitting, scored 39 out of 43 runs put on after he came in. On going in a second time, with an advantage of 39 runs, the South lost Dr Grace and Mr Welman for 15 runs. Then Messrs Gilbert and Fowler added 37 runs, and Messrs Sainsbury and Gilbert afterwards carried the score to 95, the day's play ceasing with the score at 106 for four wickets, Mr Sainsbury, not out 29, and W. Hearn not out 5.

Before a very small company the second innings of the South came to a speedy conclusion when play was resumed on the Tuesday, and the last six wickets only added 24 runs to the overnight score. Crossland carried all before him, but his style of bowling again met with signs of disapproval. The North were set the task of getting 170 to win, but four wickets fell for 13 runs, and except for some spirited hitting by Brown and careful play by Davenport, the batting was very poor. The two put on 56 runs, and Brown's 43 included six 4s. The innings closed for 103 at 12.20, and the South won the match by 66 runs.

The South

Dr W. G. Grace b Crossland	11	– b Mycroft	4
W. R. Gilbert Esq. b Shilton	22	– b Crossland	34
W. H. Fowler Esq. b Crossland	11	– c Shilton b Mycroft	21
E. Sainsbury Esq. c Brown b Mycroft	3	– c Hornby b Mycroft	29
W. Hearn b Crossland	18	– b Crossland	8
J. Jones b Crossland	21	– b Crossland	1
T. Gregg b Crossland	0	– b Crossland	1
A. J. Fothergill c Price b Crossland	12	– not out	10
F. T. Welman Esq. not out	17	– c Wardall b Crossland	5
E. A. Parke Esq. b Crossland	0	– b Crossland	0
W. A. Woof c Emmett b Brown	5	– c Price b Crossland	3
B 2, l-b 8	10	B 14	14
	130		130

The North

A. N. Hornby Esq. c Fothergill b Gregg	1	– b Gregg	6
A. Price b Woof	4	– b Gregg	4
T. Wardall b Gregg	0	– b Grace	2
G. Davenport c Grace b Gregg	12	– b Gilbert	14
L. O. Lindley Esq. b Gregg	22	– b Gregg	0
S. Brown b Grace	4	– c Woof b Gilbert	43
J. E. Shilton b Gregg	1	– c Woof b Grace	8
H. Emmett b Gregg	0	– not out	4
W. Wood-Sims not out	39	– c Parke b Gilbert	14
J. Crossland hit wkt b Grace	0	– b Grace	4
W. Mycroft c Welman b Woof	2	– c Gregg b Gilbert	3
B 6	6	L-b 1	1
	91		103

Northern Bowling

	Overs	Mdns	Runs	Wkts	Overs	Mdns	Runs	Wkts
Crossland	30	11	45	7	25.2	8	35	7
Mycroft	21	11	28	1	27	13	33	3
Shilton	11	7	16	1	7	1	18	—
Brown	20	11	31	1	10	5	20	—
Wardall					5	2	10	—

Southern Bowling

	Overs	Mdns	Runs	Wkts	Overs	Mdns	Runs	Wkts
Woof	11.1	4	15	2	12	6	15	—
Gregg	27	13	47	6	11	2	32	3
Dr Grace	18	8	23	2	21	12	28	3
Fothergill					3	—	12	—
Mr Gilbert					12.3	6	15	4

Umpires: F. H. Farrands and G. Hay.

MCC AND GROUND v CAMBRIDGE UNIVERSITY

Played at Lord's, June 23, 24, 1884

The victory of the MCC in this the last of the Cambridge trial matches, was the triumph of one man, and the splendid all-round cricket played by Wilfred Flowers, the Nottinghamshire professional, will be found to have few parallels in the history of the game. The University secured first innings, but mainly through the extraordinarily successful bowling of Flowers, who sent down 51 overs for 20 runs and six wickets, the whole side were dismissed for 74, 24 of which were contributed by Mr Paravicini, who scored the whole of the last 19 runs made in the innings. When the MCC went in to bat Mr Wilson scored 22 out of 30, and was then run out. Barnes was bowled at 41, and then Flowers commenced his very brilliant innings at 4.30. Up to this time only 115 runs had been scored in three and a half hours, and thirteen wickets had fallen, but owing to the remarkable freedom with which Flowers hit all the bowling, no fewer than 179 runs were put on in the space of two and a half hours for the loss of six wickets. Flowers actually scored 122 while his various partners made 35. He was out with the total at 201, and his magnificent innings – made without a chance until he had scored his hundred – consisted of eighteen 4s, mostly hard drives, five 3s, eight 2s, and nineteen singles. At the call of time on the first day the MCC had scored 220 for the loss eight wickets, Mr D. G. Spiro, who had rendered Flowers such good service, being the not out man with 43 to his credit.

The MCC innings was quickly brought to a conclusion when play was resumed on the second day, the remaining three wickets being disposed of for an addition of 9 runs. Mr Spiro's 47 was a well-hit innings. Cambridge went in for the second time 155 runs to the bad, and Messrs Wright and Bainbridge were both out when only four runs had been totalled. Mr Turner made 20 by free hitting and was out at 30, Mr Mansfield following at 31. Mr de Paravicini left at 43, and Mr Studd at 62, and 93 runs were wanted to save a single innings defeat, with only five wickets to fall. Messrs Powell and Greatorex stayed until 90 was reached, and Messrs Rock and Marchant made a short stand, but all were out for 126, and the MCC won the match by an innings and 29 runs. It will be seen that twelve a side batted (though only eleven fielded), and that in the second innings of Cambridge, Flowers wound up his splendid work in this match by taking eight of the eleven wickets at a cost of 60 runs.

Cambridge University

C. W. Wright Esq. b Flowers	8	– c Barnes b Flowers	0
H. W. Bainbridge Esq. b Flowers	7	– b Woof	3
E. O. Powell Esq. b Woof	3	– c Robertson b Woof	24
J. E. K. Studd Esq. c Barnes b Woof	11	– b Flowers	13
T. Greatorex Esq. b Woof	3	– c Wilson b Flowers	24
F. Marchant Esq. b Woof	14	– lbw b Flowers	12
Hon. J. Mansfield b Flowers	1	– st Sherwin b Flowers	7
P. J. de Paravicini Esq. c Flowers b Woof	24	– lbw b Flowers	6
J. A. Turner Esq. b Flowers	1	– st Sherwin b Flowers	20
C. W. Rock Esq. b Flowers	0	– not out	13
C. A. Smith Esq. b Flowers	0	– c Sherwin b Flowers	0
H. G. Topham Esq. not out	0	– c Sherwin b Woof	0
B 2	2	B 2, l-b 2	4
	74		126

MCC and Ground

C. Wilson Esq. run out	22	D. G. Spiro Esq. b Turner	47
W. H. Scotton b Rock	12	J. Robertson Esq. b Rock	1
W. Barnes b Smith	6	Rev. R. T. Thornton b Turner	1
W. Flowers c Turner b Smith	122	W. A. Woof b Rock	0
F. E. Allsopp Esq. b Topham	0	M. Sherwin not out	0
Hon. M. B. Hawke b Smith	8	B 4, l-b 5	9
G. F. Vernon Esq. c de Paravicini b Topham.	1		229

MCC Bowling

	Overs	Mdns	Runs	Wkts	Overs	Mdns	Runs	Wkts
Woof	51.2	29	52	5	41	18	55	3
Flowers	51	39	20	6	48	21	60	8
Barnes					6	3	7	—

Cambridge Bowling

	Overs	Mdns	Runs	Wkts
Mr Rock	53	29	68	3
Mr Topham	27	8	68	2
Mr Smith	27	10	50	3
Mr Bainbridge	5	2	7	—
Mr Turner	13	7	15	2
Mr de Paravicini ...	5	1	12	—

Umpires: R. Clayton and W. Mycroft.

MCC AND GROUND v YORKSHIRE

Played at Scarborough, September 8, 9, 10, 1884

Thanks to the splendid batting of Ulyett in the second innings of the Yorkshiremen, and, subsequently, to the fine bowling of the veteran Emmett, the north countrymen, after having all the worst of the game on the opening day, succeeded in defeating a strong team of the premier club by 42 runs. Owing to somewhat heavy rain on the previous Saturday the wicket was heavy when Yorkshire went in to bat at 12.25 on the Monday, and the bowling of Barnes and Flowers proved so effective that no change was found necessary during the innings, which closed at 3.30. Ulyett made 21 out of 27, when he slipped in stepping out to Flowers and was stumped. Mr Leadbeater played most carefully and well for 18 not out, and was in while 48 runs were scored. Peate made his 18 in six hits. When the MCC went in Mr Thornton was bowled without scoring, and at 29 Mr Wright was dismissed in the same way. Barnes batted very finely, and out of the first 40 runs had actually scored 35. At the call of time MCC had made 112 for the loss of four wickets, Mr W. H. Hadow being 29 not out, and Mr Schultz 16 not out.

The MCC went on with their innings at 12.15, and the last wicket fell at ten minutes to two. At three o'clock Mr Hawke and Hall opened the second innings of Yorkshire. Mr Hawke scored 18 out of the first 19 runs and was then caught. Ulyett then joined Hall and commenced to hit most brilliantly, and after Grimshaw had succeeded Hall runs were put on at a great rate, Ulyett, among many other fine hits, making one grand drive out of the ground for 6. Stumps were drawn ten minutes earlier than usual in consequence of rain, and the score at the close of the day's play stood at 169 for two wickets, Ulyett, not out, 99, and Grimshaw, not out, 29. When he had made 93 Ulyett gave a chance to Flowers, which, owing to the bad light, was not accepted. Mr Schultz strained his leg so severely during the Yorkshire innings that he had to retire, and a substitute came out in his place.

Soon after the not outs resumed on the Wednesday Ulyett made another hit out of the ground, this time off Flowers' bowling. Grimshaw was out with the score at 198 for a capital innings of 43, his partnership with Ulyett having yielded no fewer than 109 runs. Ulyett continued to bat in his best form, but his various partners were soon dismissed. Hunter got back to the ground too late to go in, and the innings closed for 248, Ulyett carrying his bat for a magnificent score of 146, made with the one chance mentioned, and consisting of three 6s, fourteen 4s, three 3s, twenty-two 2s, and 21 singles. When MCC went in to try and get 152 runs to win, only two hours and thirty-five minutes remained for play. Three wickets fell for 24 runs, and though a stand was made by Barnes and Mr Hadow, and another by Gunn and Flowers, the last wicket fell at a quarter to six, and Yorkshire gained a well-earned victory. Mr Schultz, owing to his accident, was unable to go in.

Yorkshire

G. Ulyett st Wright b Flowers	21	– not out	146
L. Hall b Barnes	9	– c Sherwin b Flowers	20
E. Lockwood c and b Barnes	2	– c Hadow b Barnes	0
I. Grimshaw b Barnes	0	– c Sherwin b Attewell	43
W. Bates c and b Barnes	14	– run out	2
Hon. M. B. Hawke c Scotton b Flowers	2	– c Gunn b Flowers	18
J. Hunter b Barnes	3	– absent	
H. Leadbeater Esq. not out	18	– b Barnes	6
R. Peel b Flowers	9	– lbw b Attewell	5
T. Emmett st Wright b Flowers	0	– st Sherwin b Attewell	0
E. Peate c sub b Flowers	18	– st Sherwin b Attewell	4
		B 2, l-b 2	4
	96		248

MCC and Ground

C. I. Thornton Esq. b Peate	0	– lbw b Emmett	17
C. W. Wright Esq. b Emmett	3	– st Hunter b Emmett	5
W. Barnes run out	44	– b Peel	25
W. H. Scotton c Lockwood b Emmett	16	– c Ulyett b Emmett	0
W. H. Hadow Esq. b Emmett	37	– st Hunter b Peel	12
S. S. Schultz Esq. c Peate b Emmett	20	– absent (hurt)	
W. Gunn c Bates b Peel	15	– b Emmett	20
W. Flowers b Peel	5	– c Hall b Emmett	23
P. J. de Paravicini Esq. c Grimshaw b Peate	11	– b Emmett	2
W. Attewell not out	16	– c Leadbeater b Peate	4
M. Sherwin b Peel	5	– not out	0
B 10, l-b 2, w 2	14	B 7, w 1	8
	186		116

MCC Bowling

	Overs	Mdns	Runs	Wkts	Overs	Mdns	Runs	Wkts
Flowers	36	15	58	5	21	5	55	2
Barnes	35	21	38	5	54	29	77	2
Attewell					66.1	30	81	4
Gunn					7	1	19	—
Mr Paravicini					7	2	9	—
Mr Thornton					2	1	3	—

Yorkshire Bowling

	Overs	Mdns	Runs	Wkts	Overs	Mdns	Runs	Wkts
Peate	53	27	55	2	20	5	35	1
Ulyett	6	4	11	—				
Emmett	42	19	61	4	28	14	31	6
Bates	7	3	16	—	10	4	20	—
Peel	27	16	25	3	17	10	22	2
Mr Leadbeater	1	—	4	—				

Umpires: F. Wyld and King.

SMOKERS v NON-SMOKERS

Played at Lord's, September 15, 16, 1884

This match was played for the benefit of the Cricketers' Fund Friendly Society, and, contrary to the anticipations of many, proved one of the most attractive contests of the season. Though it only occupied two days, no less a sum than £561 16s. 6d. was handed to the treasurer of the Fund after all the expenses were paid. The match owed its origin to Mr V. E. Walker, whose desire was in the first place to promote the welfare of a very deserving charity, and in the second to see members of the redoubtable Australian team opposed to each other. That this object was effected a glance at the score will show, Spofforth, Palmer, M'Donnell and Giffen appearing on the side of the Smokers, while Murdoch, Bannerman, Bonnor and Scott were found in the ranks of the Non-smokers. The sides were not so strong as could have been wished, as several prominent amateurs were unavoidably absent, and owing to the early departure of Shaw and Shrewsbury's team for the Antipodes, many of the most celebrated professionals were prevented from taking part in the match. The two elevens, however, were undoubtedly strong, though the Smokers laboured under the disadvantage of going into the field without a thoroughly reliable wicket-keeper, Blackham, owing to a bad hand, being unable to render any assistance. Bonnor's remarkable hitting was of course the feature of the match. His 124 is the highest score he has made in England, and the manner in which he punished the bowling of Spofforth was perhaps the most extraordinary part of it. The great bowler had certainly never been hit with such astonishing freedom in this country before.

The Non-smokers were successful in the toss, and W. G. Grace and Bannerman opened the innings a few minutes after 12. Grace was caught and bowled at 27, and Murdoch bowled at 34. Bonnor then commenced his remarkable innings. He lost Bannerman at 38, but with Barlow as a partner the aspect of the game was soon changed. Both batted with care for several overs, but at length Bonnor commenced to hit out in splendid style, Spofforth being most severely punished. When he had made 44 he was missed by the wicket-keeper standing back. At lunch time he had made 63, and Barlow 25, and the total stood at 125. On resumption of play runs came just as fast, and at 3.20 Bonnor completed his 100 with a big off-drive for 6 off Spofforth, which was followed by a couple of 4s off the same bowler, the second pitching on to the roof of the pavilion. At last, with the score at 190, he was caught at slip off Peate, having scored 124 out of 156 put on while he was in, by one 6, sixteen 4s, seven 3s, ten 2s, and only thirteen singles. E. M. Grace was bowled at 215, and Barlow's admirably-played innings came to an end at 223. Scott and Walter Wright both left at 229, and after making 20 in a very short time O'Brien was caught, and Pilling failing to add to the score, the innings terminated for 250. The bowling of Peate in the latter part of the innings was extraordinarily successful. He went on for Emmett at 189, and in 13 overs, six of which were maidens, he took six wickets for 10 runs, besides having several chances missed off him. The Smokers went in at ten minutes to five in a bad light, and when play ceased for the day had lost Thornton, M'Donnell, Giffen and Lord Harris for only 25 runs.

The game was continued at 11.40 on the second day, which, like the Monday, proved fine and exceptionally warm for the time of year. Bowden joined Gunn, and by good cricket, the overnight total was increased by 51 runs. Then three wickets fell together, Bowden being run out, and Gunn and Christopherson bowled. Palmer was bowled at 84, and after Clarke and Emmett had made a short stand the end soon came, and the Smokers being 129 runs in arrears were compelled to follow their innings. They commenced directly after luncheon, Clarke and M'Donnell facing the bowling of Grace and Christopherson. M'Donnell was missed when he had made 8, and with the total at 26 was clean bowled by Grace for the second time in the match. Clarke was caught at 45, and Giffen, after giving a hard chance to the wicket-keeper, was bowled. Lord Harris was clean bowled and Bowden caught, the fifth wicket falling with only 54 runs scored. Thornton and Gunn then became associated, and some capital cricket was witnessed, the former hitting with characteristic freedom, while the latter exhibited great care and patience. Exactly 50 runs were added before a very good chance got rid of Thornton, and after his departure Gunn could get no one to stay with him, and eventually carried out his bat for a thoroughly well-played 43. It will be seen that Grace in the first innings of the Smokers, and Barlow in their second, bowled with great effect, each taking five wickets with a remarkably good analysis. It wanted twenty minutes to six when the innings was over, and though the light was getting very bad, it was decided that the 14 runs the Non-smokers required to win should be hit off that evening. Christopherson was caught after making 8, but no other loss was experienced, and the Non-smokers won the match easily by nine wickets. With the conclusion of the contest the busiest season on record, so far as first-class cricket was concerned, came to an end.

Non-Smokers

W. G. Grace c and b Palmer	10	
A. C. Bannerman lbw b Spofforth	22	
W. L. Murdoch b Palmer	4	
G. J. Bonnor c Harris b Peate	124	
R. G. Barlow c Giffen b Peate	39	
E. M. Grace b Peate	10	– not out 1
H. J. H. Scott c Harris b Peate	4	
T. C. O'Brien c Emmett b Peate	20	– not out 6
W. Wright b Peate	0	
S. Christopherson not out	2	– c Gunn b Peate 8
R. Pilling b Spofforth	0	
B 14, l-b 1	15	
	250	15

Smokers

C. I. Thornton c Pilling b Barlow	5	– c O'Brien b Bonnor 27
P. S. M'Donnell b W. G. Grace	7	– b W. G. Grace 14
G. Giffen c and b W. G. Grace	6	– b Barlow 15
Lord Harris c E. M. Grace b W. G. Grace	0	– b Barlow 5
W. Gunn b Christopherson	18	– not out 43
M. P. Bowden run out	29	– c Wright b Barlow 0
G. E. Palmer run out	0	– st Pilling b Wright 4
F. R. Spofforth b Christopherson	0	– c E. M. Grace b W. G. Grace 5
C. C. Clarke not out	20	– c Pilling b W. G. Grace 19
T. Emmett c Bannerman b W. G. Grace	7	– b Barlow 7
E. Peate c Pilling b W. G. Grace	2	– c E. M. Grace b Barlow 1
B 9, l-b 8	17	B 10, l-b 2 12
	111	152

The Bowling of the Smokers

	Overs	Mdns	Runs	Wkts	Overs	Mdns	Runs	Wkts
Palmer	33	11	68	2	1	—	2	—
Emmett	22	10	23	—				
Spofforth	36.1	14	87	2	2.3	2	3	—
Peate	23	10	30	6	1	—	10	1
Giffen	7	2	18	—				
Thornton	6	3	9	—				

The Bowling of the Non-Smokers

	Overs	Mdns	Runs	Wkts	Overs	Mdns	Runs	Wkts
Barlow	35	20	34	1	27.3	16	24	5
W. G. Grace	34	19	29	5	26	7	63	3
Wright	14	10	5	—	8	4	9	1
Christopherson	13	6	26	2	17	7	28	—
Bonnor					8	3	16	1

Umpires: T. Hearne and E. Willsher.

MCC AND GROUND v NOTTINGHAMSHIRE

Played at Lord's, May 28, 29, 1885

To the brilliant all-round cricket played by Dr W. G. Grace in this match the crushing defeat of the powerful Nottinghamshire Eleven by an innings and 59 runs was mainly due. Shrewsbury and Attewell were absent from the visiting team, but it was generally expected that the county eleven would still be strong enough to more than hold their own against the moderate side opposed to them. The wicket was in fairly good condition, though it had not thoroughly recovered from the heavy rain of the previous Monday, and it gave the bowlers some little assistance, and now and then the ball got up awkwardly. Nottinghamshire had first innings, and going in at five minutes after noon, were all out half an hour after luncheon for 96. Scotton was at wickets an hour for 10 runs; Barnes was caught and bowled from the first ball he received, and Flowers was unlucky in being run out before he had a chance to score. Mr H. B. Daft, son of the famous Richard Daft, made his début in the County Eleven, and was the highest scorer on his side. Selby and Gunn played well; but on the whole the batting was feeble. William Hearn's splendid fielding was quite a feature of the match, and he made two very fine catches at deep-square leg. When the MCC went in to bat Selby took Shrewsbury's place at point, but being unused to the position made several mistakes, for which Nottinghamshire had to pay dearly. Messrs Grace and Russel put on 54 runs for the first wicket, but at starting the Gloucestershire captain did not seem quite at home, and gave three difficult chances. Afterwards, however, he played in his old form, although he scored rather more slowly than usual. The Nottinghamshire total was passed for the loss of but two wickets. Dr Grace, after being in for two hours and a quarter for 61 out of 109, was bowled, his chief hits being three 4s, a 3 and eleven 2s. Mr G. B. Studd gave a couple of chances late in the day, but his innings was characterised by much of his old brilliancy. Mr Ross batted in good form for his 40, his hitting on the off-side being especially good. When stumps were drawn for the day the MCC had scored 173 for the loss of seven wickets, Davenport not out 6.

There was a good deal of rain overnight, and the hot sun on Friday morning rendered the wicket slow and treacherous. The bowlers therefore had matters all their own way. Flowers took the last three MCC wickets, only three runs being scored off him. Nottinghamshire began their second innings at ten minutes to one, Dr Grace bowling from the Pavilion wicket, where Flowers had met with so much success. Scotton was in an hour and twenty minutes for 12, and Mr Daft played very steadily and well for 10 not out, but the other batsmen only offered the feeblest resistance to the bowling of Dr Grace, and in two hours the innings closed for 44, and the MCC gained an easy victory. In scoring 63 and taking sixteen wickets at a cost of only 60 runs in such a match, Dr Grace achieved one of the greatest successes attached to his name.

Nottinghamshire

J. A. Dixon Esq. c Newton b Fothergill	13	– b Mycroft	0
W. H. Scotton c Fothergill b Grace	10	– c Mycroft b Grace	12
W. Barnes c and b Grace	0	– b Grace	2
W. Gunn c Hearn b Grace	14	– c Studd b Grace	3
W. Flowers run out	0	– c Welman b Grace	1
H. B. Daft Esq. b Grace	23	– not out	10
J. Selby c Hearn b Grace	15	– c Welman b Grace	0
W. Wright c Welman b Grace	4	– b Grace	4
C. Shore not out	6	– b Grace	2
A. Shaw c Fothergill b Grace	9	– b Grace	0
M. Sherwin b Mycroft	0	– c Mycroft b Grace	7
B 2	2	B 3	3
	96		44

MCC and Ground

Dr W. G. Grace b Gunn	63	G. Davenport not out	19
J. S. Russel Esq. hit wkt b Flowers	19	F. T. Welman Esq. b Flowers	4
W. Hearn c Dixon b Barnes	3	V. A. Titchmarsh c Gunn b Flowers	7
G. B. Studd Esq. c Scotton b Gunn	28	W. Mycroft b Flowers	2
S. C. Newton Esq. b Wright	2	B 5, l-b 2	7
H. Ross Esq. c Sherwin b Shore	40		
A. J. Fothergill b Wright	5		199

MCC Bowling

	Overs	Mdns	Runs	Wkts	Overs	Mdns	Runs	Wkts
Fothergill	28	13	40	1				
Dr W. G. Grace	43	26	40	7	35.1	25	20	9
Mycroft	15.3	9	14	1	35	23	21	1

Nottinghamshire Bowling

	Overs	Mdns	Runs	Wkts
Flowers	58.3	39	35	4
Wright	26	9	37	2
Barnes	20	8	23	1
Shore	36	16	52	1
Gunn	19	6	27	2
Mr Dixon	6	3	9	—
Mr Daft	11	5	9	—

MCC AND GROUND v LANCASHIRE

Played at Lord's, July 20, 21, 1885

This match terminated in an unexpectedly easy and brilliant victory for Lancashire. Beyond the free hitting of Mr E. C. Hornby there was nothing at all remarkable in the batting on the opening day, the feature of which was the bowling of Briggs for the county, and of W. Mycroft for MCC. The home team went in first and were all dimissed in a little over two hours for 122, Dr W. G. Grace and Mr P. J. de Paravicini being the only batsmen to make anything of a stand. A reference to Briggs' analysis will show that the greatest difficult was experienced in scoring from his bowling. The Lancashire innings was a complete contrast to that of the MCC inasmuch as the collapse came in the latter part of the Club's batting, whereas the County did so badly at starting that seven of their best batsmen were out for 38 runs. This result had been brought about by the extraordinary bowling of Mycroft, who at the fall of the seventh wicket had sent down fourteen overs (ten maidens) for 10 runs and the whole seven wickets. Then came a complete change in the aspect of the game. Mr E. C. Hornby batted with rare pluck and determination, and hit the bowling to all parts of the field. Several of his hits were lofty, but none of them went to hand, and he fully deserved the hearty congratulations he received on his admirable achievement. While he was in 94 runs were added to the total, and of this number he scored 64 by eleven 4s, three 3s, two 2s, and seven singles, and it was entirely owing to him that Lancashire were able to head their opponents' score. In spite of the free hitting of Mr Hornby, Mycroft still had an excellent analysis when the innings closed. A serious disaster befell the MCC directly they started their second innings, as Dr Grace, of whom so much is always expected, was again given out leg-before-wicket, this time before he had scored. A good stand was then made by Messrs Russel and Buckland, several changes in the bowling being made before the later was got rid of for a well-played 20. Mr Russel stayed until the total reached 68, when he was easily caught at slip for a good innings of 34. Messrs Newton and Paravicini then played up capitally, and took the score to 108 before the latter was bowled for another very useful innings. Play then ceased for the day, Mr Newton being not out 20.

Mr Newton continued to play very fine cricket when the game was continued on the second day, and it was mainly owing to his efforts that the home side put together so good a score. He had gone in on the Monday evening when the score was 43 for two wickets, and was batting on the Tuesday until the total reached 233, when he was eighth out. Of the 190 runs added during his stay at the wicket he made 86, giving, apparently, only one chance, and that of stumping, when his score stood at 48. Nine 4s, four 3s, and eight 2s were his principal hits. Mr Baines helped him to raise the total from 130 to 192, but the others did little, and the innings closed at 1.35 for 236, leaving Lancashire with 227 runs to get to win. Commencing this task, Lancashire had ten minutes' batting before the interval. Afterwards Barlow and Bower made 37 runs for the first wicket, the latter, with a square-leg hit, putting the ball through a pane of glass in the tennis-court. Mr Lancashire became Barlow's partner at the fall of the first wicket, and these two, offering a grand resistance to the bowling, stayed together until the match was virtually won. In all they scored 188 runs for the second wicket, the total being 225 when Barlow was out lbw. He hit ten 4s, nine 3s, and ten 2s in his 117, and was at the wickets for three hours and five minutes. This innings was the largest Barlow had ever played for his county in a first-class match. Great praise was due to Mr Lancashire, who, except for a sharp chance to slip when he had made 28, played very fine cricket. He went in at 37, and stayed until the match was won, making nine 4s, six 3s, and five 2s in his 76 not out. The match ended at a quarter to six, Lancashire gaining a splendid victory with eight wickets to spare.

MCC and Ground

Dr W. G. Grace lbw b Briggs	37	– lbw b Watson	0
J. S. Russel Esq. run out	4	– c Appleby b Briggs	34
E. H. Buckland Esq. b Watson	0	– lbw b Briggs	20
P. J. de Paravicini Esq. c and b Briggs	28	– b Briggs	27
S. C. Newton Esq. c Appleby b Briggs	15	– c Lancashire b Briggs	86
A. M. Inglis Esq. c Pilling b Briggs	11	– c E. C. Hornby b Briggs	12
M. T. Baines Esq. b Watson	1	– c Appleby b Briggs	23
F. T. Welman Esq. c E. C. Hornby b Watson	0	– c E. Hornby b Watson	10
V. A. Titchmarsh b Briggs	8	– c Bower b Watson	2
H. Pickett c Yates b Briggs	2	– b Appleby	3
W. Mycroft not out	4	– not out	1
B 4, l-b 7, n-b 1	12	B 9, l-b 9	18
	122		236

Lancashire

A. N. Hornby Esq. c Newton b Mycroft	1		
R. G. Barlow b Mycroft	1	– lbw b Grace	117
O. P. Lancashire Esq. c Welman b Mycroft	4	– not out	76
J. Briggs b Mycroft	20	– not out	0
G. M. Kemp Esq. b Mycroft	0		
J. Bower b Mycroft	0	– c Welman b Grace	19
A. Watson c Buckland b Mycroft	15		
G. Yates b Mycroft	9		
E. C. Hornby Esq. c Welman b Grace	64		
A. Appleby Esq. c Newton b Pickett	12		
R. Pilling not out	2		
L-b 4	4	B 11, l-b 5, w 1	17
	132		229

Lancashire Bowling

	Overs	Mdns	Runs	Wkts	Overs	Mdns	Runs	Wkts
Watson	28	13	31	3	38	18	56	3
Barlow	16	7	37	—	16	3	31	—
Briggs	21	14	28	6	41	15	76	6
Mr Appleby	10	4	19	—	29	11	42	1
Mr E. C. Hornby ...					5	2	6	—
Yates					3	—	7	—

MCC Bowling

	Overs	Mdns	Runs	Wkts	Overs	Mdns	Runs	Wkts
Dr Grace	21.2	8	52	1	37	14	72	2
Mycroft	28	15	45	8	46	19	49	—
Pickett	8	1	26	1	6	1	13	—
Mr Buckland	1	—	5	—	11	4	15	—
Titchmarsh					8	3	25	—
Mr Newton					3	—	16	—
Mr Paravicini					8	2	22	—

THE HIGHEST INNINGS EVER SCORED ON LORD'S GROUND

MCC AND GROUND v NORFOLK

Played at Lord's, July 24, 25, 1885

Norfolk had first innings, the brothers L. K. and C. J. E. Jarvis commencing the batting. Both played carefully at starting, only 10 runs being made in the first twenty minutes; but after this the rate of scoring increased, and at 1.20, or after an hour and a quarter's play, the 100 went up. The batsmen were then thoroughly set, and they treated all the bowlers pretty much alike. Mr L. K. Jarvis had a narrow escape of being run out when he had scored 67. The ball was thrown to Wheeler, the wicket-keeper, but he failed to remove the bails before the batsman got home. The 200 appeared at 3.15, and then Mr C. J. E. Jarvis was missed at long-on by Mr Turner. The mistake made little difference, however, as, with three runs added to his individual score, he was very finely caught at point with the total at 241. The chief hits in Mr C. J. E. Jarvis' splendid innings of 130 were a 5, eighteen 4s, five 3s, and eight 2s. The partnership for the first wicket lasted two hours and forty-five minutes, and the bowling was fifteen times changed. Hansell joined Mr L. K. Jarvis, and again the Club bowling was completely mastered for over an hour. When the association of the two batsman had realised 113 runs, Mr L. K. Jarvis, like his brother, fell a victim to William Hearn at point, the fieldsman taking the ball in brilliant style with one hand. Mr Jarvis made no mistake while scoring his magnificent inings of 181. He was at the wickets three hours and three-quarters, and his figures were twenty-one 4s, five 3s, twenty-one 2s and forty singles. With only two wickets down for 354, Hansell was joined by Mr C. L. Kennaway, and another long stand was made. The professional gave a possible chance to Hearn at point, when he had made 62, but otherwise the batting continued to be of a high order. The 400 went up at 5.25, and at six o'clock 450 appeared, Hansell completing his hundred five minutes later, the total then being 467. At half-past six 500 runs had been scored for the loss of only two wickets, but at 509 Hansell was caught in the long-field for an admirable innings of 136. He had been batting three hours, and his hits included seventeen 4s, ten 3s, and twelve 2s. Mr Kennaway was caught at the wicket at 514, and when stumps were drawn for the day, the score stood in the following extra-ordinary form:

Norfolk

L. K. Jarvis Esq. c Hearn b Price	181
C. J. E. Jarvis Esq. c Hearn b Smith	130
Hansell c Hay b C. Wilson	136
Rev. C. L. Kennaway, c Wheeler b Mycroft	39
C. H. Morton Esq. not out	5
H. Birkbeck Esq. not out	10
B 15, l-b 11	26
	(4 wkts) 527

This huge total was the result of six hours and five minutes' play, during which time nine bowlers were tried, and had it not been for an injured leg, W. Hearn would also have been put on.

Going on with the innings at 11.30 on the Friday, the not outs carried the score to 563, when Mr Morton was caught at the wickets. Mr Wickham was caught without scoring at 574, and Mr "Blunt" was clean bowled at 590. Mr Patteson became Mr Birkbeck's partner, and the sixth hundred was recorded at 12.40. Mr Patteson scored very freely, contributing 31 out of the 37 runs put on during his stay. The seventh wicket fell at 627, and 30 more runs were added before Mr Gee was caught at mid-off. Rudd, the last man, was stumped after scoring 19, and so brought this historical innings to a close at ten minutes to two. Mr Birkbeck carried his bat for 89, and with the exception of a chance to the wicket-keeper when he had made 37, his innings was a very good one, and included seven 4s, seven 3s, and eight 2s. The MCC commenced batting directly after luncheon, with Messrs Seymour and Turner, and from the start runs were put on very rapidly. The bowling was frequently changed, but the 100 went up after an hour and a half's play, and it was not until the total reached 162 that the first wicket fell, Mr Seymour being bowled by a shooter. No stand worth mentioning was then made until towards the end of the day. Hearn played a ball on to his wicket at 181; Mr C. Wilson was bowled at 192; and Mr Turner was caught at the wicket at 196 for a capital 86, which included nine 4s. The 200 was posted at ten minutes to six, and with 19 runs added Wheeler was caught at the wicket. Mr "C. Smith" was bowled at 246, and then Price and Mr C. J. Wilson offered a stubborn resistance, which lasted until time was called, and the match, limited to two days, abandoned as a draw. In all 992 runs were scored in this match for the loss of sixteen wickets, giving an average of exactly 62 runs per wicket.

Norfolk

L. K. Jarvis Esq. c Hearn b Price	181
C. J. E. Jarvis Esq. c Hearn b Smith	130
Hansell c Hay b C. Wilson	136
Rev. C. L. Kennaway c Wheeler b Mycroft	39
C. H. Morton Esq. c Wheeler b Mycroft	16
H. Birkbeck Esq. not out	89
Rev. A. P. Wickham c Mycroft b Fothergill	0
J. "Blunt" Esq. b Fothergill	2
F. E. Patteson Esq. st Wheeler b C. Wilson	31
A. M. Gee Esq. c Smith b Mycroft	14
Rudd st Wheeler b C. Wilson	19
B 26, l-b 12	38
	695

MCC and Ground

C. R. Seymour Esq. b Morton	75
J. Turner Esq. c Wickham b C. J. E. Jarvis	86
W. Hearn b C. J. E. Jarvis	12
C. Wilson Esq. b Morton	11
J. Wheeler c Wickham b C. J. E. Jarvis	11
"C. Smith" Esq. b Morton	13
S. J. Wilson Esq. not out	48
F. Price not out	24
B 7, l-b 10	17
	297

A. J. Fothergill, G. Hay and W. Mycroft did not bat.

MCC Bowling

	Overs	Mdns	Runs	Wkts		Overs	Mdns	Runs	Wkts
W. Mycroft	91	41	154	3	Hay	34	7	87	—
Fothergill	57	20	117	2	F. Price	14	2	49	1
Mr S. L. Wilson ..	3	—	7	—	Mr J. Turner	6	1	27	—
Mr C. Wilson	60.3	20	129	3	Wheeler	8	1	31	—
Mr C. Smith	39	3	56	1					

Norfolk Bowling

	Overs	Mdns	Runs	Wkts		Overs	Mdns	Runs	Wkts
Hansell	28	10	51	—	Rev. Kennaway ..	3	1	3	—
Rudd	26	6	48	—	Mr C. J. E. Jarvis .	46	11	97	3
Mr C. H. Morton .	32	12	62	3	Mr A. M. Jee	9	1	19	—

MCC AND GROUND v STAFFORDSHIRE

Played at Stoke, August 5, 6, 1885

The bowling of the Staffordshire professional, Briscoe, was certainly the feature of this match, which the County won by 111 runs. In all, Briscoe captured fourteen wickets at a cost of only 81 runs.

Staffordshire

A. H. Heath Esq. c Wyld b Clayton	34	– run out	21
Brooks c Trafford b Clayton	33	– c Clayton b Fothergill	3
F. R. Twemlow Esq. c Trafford b Heath	16	– b Fothergill	0
Lord Anson c Trafford b Fothergill	3	– b Clayton	6
Rev. S. C. Voules c Trafford b Heath	10	– c Mainwaring b Clayton	33
H. Fishwick Esq. not out	5	– hit wkt b West	25
W. H. Allerton Esq. c Clayton	8	– b Fothergill	16
F. Stokes Esq. st Wyld b Heath	0	– run out	17
Briscoe c Heath b West	6	– b Fothergill	2
Johnson c Savory b West	6	– not out	1
Burrows b Clayton	0	– c Fitzherbert b Heath	10
Extras	23	Extras	18
	144		149

MCC and Ground

A. J. Fothergill b Briscoe	5	– st Brooks b Johnson	12
E. Rodriquez Esq. b Briscoe	12	– b Allerton	24
F. Wyld c and b Johnson	1	– b Briscoe	1
C. E. de Trafford Esq. b Johnson	0	– not out	9
J. West c Allerton b Briscoe	2	– c Brooks b Briscoe	0
J. H. Savory Esq. b Briscoe	23	– b Johnson	19
E. Clayton c Lord Anson b Johnson	35	– b Briscoe	3
Rev. F. Mainwaring c Allerton b Briscoe	7	– c Brooks b Briscoe	1
B. J. Fitzherbert Esq. c Brooks b Briscoe	10	– b Briscoe	2
Rev. C. Nankleyn b Briscoe	0	– b Briscoe	0
J. Heath Esq. not out	2	– c Allerton b Briscoe	0
Extras	11	Extras	3
	108		74

MCC Bowling

	Overs	Mdns	Runs	Wkts	Overs	Mdns	Runs	Wkts
Fothergill	27	11	34	1	27.1	10	58	4
Clayton	31	13	48	4	16	5	30	2
West	15.3	7	26	2	9	2	23	1
Rev. F. Mainwaring .	3	—	7	—				
Mr Heath	8	5	6	3	7	1	14	2
Mr Savory					2	—	6	—

Staffordshire Bowling

	Overs	Mdns	Runs	Wkts	Overs	Mdns	Runs	Wkts
Briscoe	22	8	42	7	20	10	39	7
Johnson	24	10	39	3	16	5	23	2
Mr Fishwick	4	—	16	—				
Mr Allerton					4	2	9	1

A RECORD

MCC AND GROUND v RUTLAND

Played at Lord's, August 10, 11, 1885

No fewer than 645 runs were scored for twelve wickets on the second day of this match. This number surpasses by exactly 100 runs the previous record for one day's batting on the St. John's Wood ground. At the close of the first day's play there was little difference in the position of the two sides, the MCC being 73 runs ahead of their opponents, who had four wickets to fall. Barnes played finely for his 83, and hit thirteen 4s, one 3 and six 2s. At the luncheon interval the total stood at 226 for five wickets, but nothing of a stand was made afterwards and the innings closed at 3.30. When the visitors went in, 52 runs were put on for the first wicket, and the total was taken to 131 before the second batsman was out. At the call of time the total was 207 for six wickets. Mr R. Finch, not out 0. Drake's innings of 67 included one 5 (all run out), ten 4s, one 3 and five 2s; and Mr Furley's 56, five 4s, five 3s and seven 2s.

Next morning the remaining four wickets fell for two runs and the MCC, going in for the second time, remained at the wickets the rest of the day, scoring 643 for the loss of eight wickets, and were consequently 712 runs ahead at the finish, with two wickets to fall. Mr Hattersley-Smith, in his 132, hit twenty-one 4s, four 3s and nine 2s, and Mr Maude's 141 included one 5, twenty-two 4s, five 3s and twelve 2s. Barnes made a 5, sixteen 4s, a 3 and four 2s; Flowers, fifteen 4s, two 3s and six 2s; and Mr Robertson twelve 4s, two 3s and six 2s. The MCC went in at ten minutes past twelve, and, deducting the luncheon interval, the innings lasted five hours and thirty-five minutes, the runs therefore being put on at the rate of about 116 an hour. Stumps were finally pulled up at half-past six, and ten minutes before that time Mr Maude hit a ball on to the roof of the tennis court. The match, being limited to two days, ended in a draw.

The wickets fell as under:

1/81 2/214 2/234 4/279 5/447 6/456 7/531 8/643

MCC and Ground

J. S. Russel Esq. c Neilson b Drake	16 – c Norman b Finch	31
W. Barnes c Tuck b Norman	83 – c Neilson b R. Eaton	91
W. Flowers b R. Eaton	6 – b Finch	90
Rev. P. Hattersley-Smith b Furley	38 – b H. Eaton	132
W. F. Thompson Esq. c Moss b Furley	30 – b Norman	14
J. Robertson Esq. b R. Eaton	45 – c Drake b Norman	80
F. W. Maude Esq. b Drake	32 – c Arnsby b Finch	141
A. J. Fothergill c Eaton b Furley	11 – c Finch b Arnsby	20
M. Sherwin not out	6 – not out	23
W. Philips Esq. b Furley	0	
A. James Esq. b Drake	0	
B 8, l-b 3	11	B 5, l-b 10, w 6 21
	278	643

Rutland

Rev. A. J. Tuck b Barnes	28	Moss c and b Flowers	0
W. F. Neilson Esq. c Sherwin b Fothergill	38	S. Arnsby Esq. b Robertson	1
Drake b Robertson	67	A. P. Norman Esq. b Flowers	0
J. Furley Esq. lbw b Robertson	56	R. Eaton Esq. not out	0
E. Hanbury Esq. b Fothergill	0	B 2, l-b 3	5
H. Eaton Esq. c Sherwin b Flowers	13		
H. R. Finch Esq. b Flowers	1		209

Rutland Bowling

	Overs	Mdns	Runs	Wkts	Overs	Mdns	Runs	Wkts
Mr R. Eaton	21	4	63	2	26	7	95	1
Drake	23.3	5	56	3	38	6	103	—
Mr Furley	27	7	73	4	5	1	7	—
Mr Arnsby	6	2	16	—	18	3	66	1
Mr Finch	12	3	33	—	26.1	3	116	3
Mr Norman	8	2	26	1	39	11	109	2
Moss					9	1	40	—
Mr H Eaton					19	3	68	1
Mr Neilson					7	2	18	—

MCC Bowling

	Overs	Mdns	Runs	Wkts
Flowers	31	14	55	4
Fothergill	21	9	49	2
Barnes	22	6	53	1
Mr Maude	10	4	13	—
Mr Robertson	15.2	5	34	3

MCC AND GROUND v LANCASHIRE

Played at Lord's, May 18, 1886

This match was one of the few instances in first-class cricket of a game between two strong sides being begun and finished off in a single day. As may be supposed, the cause of such small scoring on both sides was the very treacherous state of the ground. Rain had been falling heavily on the Sunday, and not a ball could be bowled on the day fixed for the start – Monday, May 17. On the Tuesday morning the sun shone out brilliantly, and certainly for the first half of the day the wicket was almost unplayable. After luncheon the condition of the ground certainly improved, but at no time could the wicket be considered easy. During the day no fewer than thirty-four wickets fell for 246 runs – an average of just over 7 runs a wicket. Despite the small scoring the cricket throughout the day was most interesting, and the result was in doubt up to within an hour of the finish.

Going in first the MCC fared very badly against the admirable bowling of Watson and Briggs, and were dismissed for the paltry total of 30, Mr Hadow alone reaching double figures. The bowling analyses of Watson and Briggs deserve more than passing mention. The innings of Lancashire was little less remarkable than that of the MCC. Two men scored double figures, but the others could do next to nothing with the bowling of Rylott and Wootton. Ten minutes before luncheon the whole side were out for 53, or only 23 runs to the good. Rylott's seven wickets cost him just over 3 runs each. As the ground became a little better it was only natural that the MCC total in the second innings should have been a larger one. However, the innings only lasted an hour and forty minutes, and the total reached 92, five members of the team making 74 of this number between them. With 70 runs to get to win Lancashire went in for the second time at about ten minutes to five. Mr Hornby played quite the right game on the treacherous wicket, and it was mainly to his confidence and judgment that Lancashire owed their victory. While he was in, Mr Hornby made 50 out of 60, and among his hits were six 3s and seven 2s. The runs were hit off by six o'clock, and Lancashire were left the winners of a sensational game by six wickets.

MCC and Ground

J. E. West c and b Watson	4	– run out	11
Davenport run out	1	– c Robinson b Watson	13
G. G. Hearne c Hornby b Watson	4	– b Barlow	7
W. Chatterton c Briggs b Watson	5	– b Watson	0
F. Hearne c Barlow b Watson	0	– c and b Watson	19
Mr E. M. Hadow hit wkt b Briggs	10	– b Barlow	1
Fothergill c Hornby b Watson	0	– c Haigh b Watson	13
Mr E. A. Leatham c Roper b Watson	0	– c and b Barlow	18
Mr F. T. Welman lbw b Briggs	0	– c and b Barlow	0
Wootton b Briggs	1	– b Barlow	0
Rylott not out	1	– not out	3
B 3, l-b 1	4	B 6, l-b 1	7
	30		92

Lancashire

Mr A. N. Hornby c G. G. Hearne b Rylott	9	– lbw b Wootton	50
Barlow b Wootton	0	– c Rylott b Wootton	2
Briggs b Wootton	5	– b Rylott	11
Mr O. P. Lancashire c G. G. Hearne b Rylott	11	– c and b Rylott	0
Mr G. Kemp b Rylott	3	– not out	5
Mr E. Roper b Rylott	0	– not out	1
Mr C. H. Haigh c G. G. Hearne b Wootton	1		
Robinson c Chatterton b Rylott	2		
Yates c Hadow b Rylott	8		
Watson c Welman b Rylott	10		
Pilling not out	4		
		L-b 2	2
	53		71

Lancashire Bowling

	Overs	Mdns	Runs	Wkts	Overs	Mdns	Runs	Wkts
Watson	15	10	8	6	29	9	46	4
Briggs	14.3	7	18	3	6	1	16	—
Barlow					25.1	10	23	5

MCC Bowling

	Overs	Mdns	Runs	Wkts	Overs	Mdns	Runs	Wkts
Rylott	22.1	11	22	7	20	4	28	2
Wootton	22	7	31	3	9	4	10	2
G. G. Hearne					6	1	19	—
West					3	1	12	—

MCC AND GROUND v PARSEES

Played at Lord's, May 27, 28, 1886

For this match the Marylebone Club put an altogether unnecessarily strong team into the field to oppose the Parsees, and there was really no serious interest in the game. From the first it was seen that the Parsees were utterly overmatched, and had not the smallest chance of success. Their notions of bowling and fielding were at that time of the most elementary description. It should be stated, however, that Mr W. G. Grace played at the request of the Parsees, who were anxious to have the champion on the opposing side once during their tour. Lord Harris was also asked to play as a compliment, but was prevented from doing so by parliamentary engagements. On the first day rain prevented any play taking place until half-past three, and from that time until the drawing of stumps at half-past six the Englishmen were batting, scoring in the three hours 200 runs for the loss of five wickets – an average of just under 70 runs an hour. Mr W. G. Grace's 65 included two 4s, ten 3s, one 2 and twenty-five singles, while Mr I. D. Walker, who gave about four chances, hit one 4, five 3s and eight 2s.

On the second day Mr W. Lindsay, an old member of the Surrey eleven, hit freely and well for 74, and among his figures were one 5, one 4, seven 3s and eight 2s. The innings closed for 313. Although the Parsees had done so badly in bowling and fielding, the spectators were hardly prepared for the poor batting display that was given. Between twenty minutes to three and ten minutes to six the Parsees were twice got rid of for a gross total of 89 runs. In the first innings they could do nothing at all with the bowling of Messrs Grace and Robertson, the score only reaching 23, and in the second innings they did little better against Mr Walker's lobs and Mr Grace. Mr Morinas certainly batted in fair form for 10 and 28 not out, but in the two innings there were only a couple of other double figure scores. It was certainly hard to put the Parsees against such a powerful MCC eleven, and their poor performance was perhaps judged a little too harshly.

MCC and Ground

Mr W. G. Grace c Balla b Major	65	Mr F. T. Welman b Bhedwar	25
Mr I. D. Walker b Major	51	Mr C. W. L. Bulpett c Major b Framjee ...	4
Mr H. Ross b Major	14	Mr H. Smith-Turberville not out	12
Mr J. S. Russel b Major	22	Rev. A. Carter b Patel	5
Mr R. G. Hargreaves b Major	0	B 8, l-b 3, w 2	13
Mr W. Lindsay b Bhedwar	74		
Mr J. Robertson b Framjee	28		313

Parsees

Mr P. Dastur c Carter b Grace	2 – b Walker	0
Mr B. B. Baria b Grace	4 – b Walker	0
Mr J. M. Morinas c Ross b Grace	10 – not out	28
Mr M. Framjee b Robertson	3 – b Grace	0
Mr a. C. Major b Robertson	0 – c Grace b Bulpett	11
Mr D. H. Patell b Grace	0 – c Grace b Walker	6
Mr B. P. Bala b Grace	1 – b Grace	2
Mr S. N. Bhedwar c Ross b Grace	0 – c Robertson b Grace	6
Mr S. Harver b Robertson	0 – c and b Grace	10
Mr A. E. Liboovalla c Hargreaves b Grace	1 – b Walker	0
Mr D. D. Khambatta not out	1 – c Smith-Turberville b Walker	0
B 1	1 B 3	3
	23	66

Parsee Bowling

	Overs	Mdns	Runs	Wkts
Mr Patel	37	10	57	1
Mr Framjee	39	12	74	2
Mr Bhedwar	13	1	31	2
Mr Kambatta	9	—	47	—
Mr Major	36	7	91	5

MCC Bowling

	Overs	Mdns	Runs	Wkts	Overs	Mdns	Runs	Wkts
Mr Grace	19.1	8	18	7	16.1	6	26	4
Mr Robertson	19	16	4	3				
Mr Walker					34	19	28	5
Mr Bulpett					17	13	9	1

Umpires: Price and Wheeler.

OXFORD UNIVERSITY v CAMBRIDGE UNIVERSITY

Played at Lord's, July 5, 6, 7, 1886

In the University teams that went into the field at Lord's on the 5th July, there were eight men new to the match, and curiously enough four belonged to each side – Messrs Rashleigh, Hewett, Cobb and Arnall-Thompson for Oxford and Messrs Thomas, Orford, and Dorman and the Hon. C. M. Knatchbull-Hugessen for Cambridge. Of these eight gentlemen, Messrs Rashleigh and Thomas were the only freshmen. Previous to the match public opinion was decidedly in favour of Cambridge, though the reputation gained by the Light Blues in their earlier trial matches had been seriously tarnished by a bad performance against Surrey at the Oval. Oxford had played a very close game on a bad wicket against the Australians, and on another bad wicket had, in the absence of Messrs W. W. Read and W. E. Roller, gained a well-earned victory against Surrey; but with the grounds in good order their bowling had proved very harmless, and the chief batsmen of the team had certainly not played up to the form expected of them. The great point in Cambridge's favour was certainly the presence of Mr. Rock, who was bowling his best at this period of the season, and who certainly ranked higher last year than any other amateur bowler. Though the general election was in progress at the time of the match, there was a very large attendance of the public, 9,299 paying for admission on the first day, 9.014 on the second day, and 3,823 on the Wednesday. These figures contrast unfavourably with the records of several previous years, but we are not inclined to think that the interest in the contest has suffered any diminution.

Oxford won the toss on the Monday and in delightfully fine weather went in to bat at a few minutes past twelve. It cannot be said that they gave at all a first-rate display of batting but in excuse for their comparative failure it should be stated that the wicket, having been too recently watered, played much slower than might have been expected, the ball every now and then getting up very awkwardly. The early play was very slow indeed, only 83 runs being scored before luncheon in more than an hour and fifty minutes for the loss of four batsmen. Buckland was bowled at 19, Key was bowled at 25, Page smartly taken at forward short-leg at 54, and Brain caught at the wicket at 79. While Page was in he hit a ball back to Rock, the bowler, who appealed confidently for the catch. Farrands, the umpire at the bowler's end, however, was quite unable to see what had happened, and therefore could not give a decision. He referred the matter to the other umpire, Wheeler, but the latter's view of the catch had also been impeded by fieldsmen, and after a little discussion, the catch, to the evident dissatisfaction of the Cambridge men, was disallowed. Rashleigh, who was batting nearly an hour and three-quarters for 21, was bowled after luncheon, and when Oxford's sixth wicket fell, the total was only 94. Hildyard left at 116 and Arnall-Thompson at 132, Oxford's position then being a very unfavourable one. At this point, however, Cobb found a most valuable partner in Cochrane, and the two batsmen while they were together put on 40 runs. Cobb, whose death in the autumn after his return from America came with such a shock to his friends, was the last man out, being stumped through the ball rebounding from the wicket-keeper's pads. His very pluckily hit 50 – an invaluable innings for Oxford – comprised five 4s a 3 and five 2s. Rock and Toppin bowled exceedingly well, the former being on at the Pavilion end for three hours and a half before he was changed. During the whole innings he was only off while 9 runs were being scored. Cambridge went in at about ten minutes past five and so excellent a start was made by Buxton and Bainbridge that Cambridge's prospects looked very good indeed. Sixty-four runs had been rapidly scored, when, in hitting to leg, Buxton was caught at cover slip. Then came a great change in the game, Cochrane going on bowling for the second time at the Nursery end and proving very successful. With the score at 73, he clean bowled Kemp, the crack batsman, and at 84 with successive balls he got Bainbridge caught at point, and bowled Turner with a fast yorker. From the point when he went on the second time up to the drawing of stumps, Cochrane sent down twelve overs five maidens for 15 runs and three wickets. Bainbridge's 44 was the best innings of the day, and included four 4s, three 3s and six 2s. When time was called the Cambridge score stood at 95 for four wickets, Rock and Thomas being the not outs.

The second day of the match was as sensational as the first day had been uneventful. In three particulars the records of previous matches between Oxford and Cambridge were beaten – in the first place, Mr Yardley's great innings of 130 in 1872, which had stood on record as the highest individual innings ever made in the whole series of matches, was surpassed by Mr Key; in the second place, a larger number of runs was made for the first wicket than had ever before been obtained; and for the first and only time in fifty-two matches there were two individual scores of over 100 obtained in the same innings. Playing very indifferently on a beautiful wicket, the Cambridge men completed their first innings for 156, six wickets thus going down for 61 runs. The Oxford bowling was fairly good, but not of such a character as to account for the collapse. It was twenty minutes past one when Key and Rashleigh opened Oxford's second innings, and began a partnership unprecedented in the history of the match. At lunch time the score stood at 49; at half-past three, the innings having lasted an hour and twenty-five minutes, the 100 went up; the 150 was reached at a few minutes past four and at twenty-five minutes to five, amid, perhaps the heartiest cheering heard last season at Lord's ground, the 200 went up without the loss of a wicket. Only three times before had even 100 been put up by the first pair of batsmen – viz., 104 by G. H. Longman and A. S. Tabor, for Cambridge, in 1872; 117 by A. P. Lucas and Alfred Lyttelton, for Cambridge, in 1878; and 152 by Bainbridge and C. W. Wright, for Cambridge, in 1885. Key and Rashleigh went on hitting for some time longer, but, at last, with the total at 243, a number which had been obtained in rather more than two hours and fifty minutes, Key was caught at long off. Out of these 243 runs, Key made exactly 143, thus beating Mr Yardley's record by 13. His splendidly hit innings comprised a 6 (4 for an overthrow), fifteen 4s, four 3s, twenty 2s and twenty-five singles. With his total at 67, he made a boundary hit which might have been a catch had the fieldsman judged the ball better, and, about half way through his innings, he made one or two lofty strokes which fell harmless; but these were only small blemishes in a very remarkable display. Rashleigh did not stay long after his partner left, and was easily caught and bowled at 257. He was at the wickets altogether for three hours and a quarter, his innings of 107 being made up by fifteen 4s, five 3s, three 2s and twenty-six singles. Up to the time of obtaining his 100, Rashleigh played wonderfully good cricket, his only mistake being a clear chance to Knatchbull-Hugessen at mid-on when he had made 46. After getting his 100, however, and being, we understood, excessively fatigued, he hit out recklessly, as if anxious to finish his innings. Rashleigh is the only batsman who has ever played an innings of 100 in his first Oxford and Cambridge match, and the honour was well earned by first-rate cricket. Having made so many runs as to put defeat almost out of the question, the Oxford men had instructions to play a freer game than they would otherwise have done, and be out, if possible, by seven o'clock. In attempting to play a false game, however, they exceeded their instructions, and the last seven wickets going down for 47 runs, the innings was all over by twenty minutes past six for 304. With 340 runs to get to win the match, Cambridge went in at rather less than twenty minutes to seven. Rock and Orford being selected to open the innings. Fourteen overs were sent down by five bowlers for a bye, and then stumps were drawn for the day.

Up to a certain time on the Wednesday the Cambridge men made so brilliant a struggle, that up to five o'clock it seemed by no means certain they would be beaten. Orford was bowled at 19, and Kemp, who, we believe, was indisposed, and certainly out of form, was caught at the wicket at 48. Then Bainbridge joined Rock, and a most stubborn resistance was offered. Only 90 runs were obtained in the two hours and twenty-five minutes before luncheon, and directly after the interval Rock was bowled for 27. He was at the wickets altogether two hours and fifty-five minutes and did not give a chance. Turner was out at 140, and Buxton joined Bainbridge. The new batsman was missed at mid-on, and also gave a hard chance of being caught and bowled. So long as he stayed in with Bainbridge Cambridge had good hopes of saving the game. However, at 196 Bainbridge was caught at mid-off, and after his dismissal the batting broke down so hopelessly that the remaining five wickets fell for 10 runs, the side being all out shortly before six o'clock for 206, and Oxford winning the match by 133 runs. Bainbridge's 79, which included seven 4s, two 3s and twelve 2s, was a masterly innings, and, certainly, by scoring in the whole match 123 runs the Cambridge captain finished his University career most brilliantly. Buckland went on bowling for the last time with the score at 176, and actually took five wickets in twenty overs and a ball at a cost of only 14 runs. In the whole innings 19 runs were hit from him. The general opinion, in which we thoroughly concur, was that a balance of 133 runs did not properly represent the difference between the two elevens, the extraordinary stand made on the second day by Key and Rashleigh upsetting all calculations. At the same time it would be quite unfair to take away from the credit fairly due to the winners. Page captained Oxford extremely well, changing his bowling on the last day with consummate judgment.

Oxford

	First innings		Second innings	
Mr K. J. Key b Toppin	6	–	c Marchant b Rock	143
Mr E. H. Buckland b Rock	15	–	b Rock	3
Mr W. Rashleigh b Rock	21	–	c and b Rock	107
Mr H. V. Page c Kemp b Rock	20	–	c Rock b Bainbridge	2
Mr J. H. Brain c Orford b Rock	17	–	c Bainbridge b Rock	8
Mr L. D. Hildyard b Toppin	12	–	lbw b Bainbridge	5
Mr H. T. Hewett b Rock	0	–	b Bainbridge	7
Mr A. R. Cobb st Orford b Toppin	50	–	c Knatchbull-Huggessen b Rock	9
Mr H. T. Arnall-Thompson b Toppin	6	–	b Toppin	4
Mr A. H. J. Cochrane c Rock b Buxton	6	–	c Turner b Dorman	7
Mr H. O. Whitby not out	11	–	not out	0
B 20, l-b 6, w 1	27		B 6, l-b 1, w 2	9
	191			304

Cambridge

	First innings		Second innings	
Mr C. D. Buxton c Arnall-Thompson b Page	30	–	c Cobb b Buckland	27
Mr H. W. Bainbridge c Hildyard b Cochrane	44	–	c Arnall-Thompson b Buckland	79
Mr G. Kemp b Cochrane	5	–	c Cobb b Whitby	19
Mr C. W. Rock run out	20	–	b Whitby	27
Mr J. A. Turner b Cochrane	0	–	c Brain b Cochrane	21
Mr F. Thomas lbw b Arnall-Thompson	13	–	c Page b Buckland	1
Mr F. Marchant lbw b Whitby	20	–	b Arnall-Thompson	3
Mr C. Toppin b Whitby	8	–	c Cobb b Buckland	2
Mr L. Orford c Cobb b Whitby	8	–	b Arnall-Thompson	15
Hon. C. M. Knatchbull-Hugessen c Cobb b Arnall-Thompson.	0	–	not out	0
Mr A. W. Dorman not out	0	–	b Buckland	4
B 5, l-b 3	8		B 4, l-b 2, w 2	8
	156			206

Cambridge Bowling

	Overs	Mdns	Runs	Wkts	Overs	Mdns	Runs	Wkts
Mr Rock	59	35	72	5	50	20	76	5
Mr Topping	41.1	13	62	4	16	1	57	1
Mr Dorman	16	10	16	0	20.3	3	64	1
Mr Buxton	7	2	14	1	8	2	40	—
Mr Turner					21	8	34	—
Mr Bainbridge					17	5	24	3

Oxford Bowling

	Overs	Mdns	Runs	Wkts	Overs	Mdns	Runs	Wkts
Mr Whitby	28.3	8	52	3	41	21	55	2
Mr Cochrane	32	14	52	3	32	13	50	1
Mr Page	20	9	23	1	40	22	34	—
Mr Arnall-Thompson	27	19	21	2	52	36	31	2
Mr Brain					2	2	0	—
Mr Buckland					28.1	21	19	5

Umpires: Farrands and Wheeler.

RESULTS OF PAST UNIVERSITY MATCHES

1829. Oxford won by 115 runs.
1836. Oxford won by 121 runs.
1938. Oxford won by 98 runs.
1839. Cambride won in one innings and 125 runs.
1840. Cambridge won by 63 runs.
1841. Cambridge won by 8 runs.
1842. Cambridge won by 162 runs.
1843. Cambridge won by 54 runs.
1845. Cambridge won by 6 wickets.
1846. Oxford won by 3 wickets.
1847. Cambridge won by 138 runs.
1848. Oxford won by 23 runs.
1849. Cambridge won by 3 wickets.
1850. Oxford won by 127 runs.
1851. Cambridge won in one innings and 4 runs.
1852. Oxford won in one innings and 77 runs.
1853. Oxford won in one innings and 19 runs.
1854. Oxford won in one innings and 8 runs.
1855. Oxford won by 3 wickets.
1856. Cambridge won by 3 wickets.
1857. Oxford won by 81 runs.
1858. Oxford won in one innings and 33 runs.
1859. Cambridge won by 28 runs.
1860. Cambridge won by 3 wickets.
1861. Cambridge won by 133 runs.
1862. Cambridge won by 8 wickets.
1863. Oxford won by 8 wickets.
1864. Oxford won by 4 wickets.
1865. Oxford won by 114 runs.
1866. Oxford won by 13 runs.
1867. Cambridge won by 5 wickets.
1868. Cambridge won by 168 runs.
1869. Cambridge won by 58 runs.
1870. Cambridge won by 2 runs.
1871. Oxford won by 8 wickets.
1872. Cambridge won by an innings and 166 runs.
1873. Oxford won by 3 wickets.
1974. Oxford won in one innings and 92 runs.
1875. Oxford won by 6 runs.
1876. Cambridge won by 9 wickets.
1877. Oxford won by 10 wickets.
1878. Cambridge won by 238 runs.
1879. Cambridge won by 9 wickets.
1880. Cambridge won by 115 runs.
1881. Oxford won by 135 runs.
1882. Cambridge won by 7 wickets.
1883. Cambridge won by 7 wickets.
1884. Oxford won by 7 wickets.
1885. Cambridge won by 7 wickets.
1886. Oxford won by 133 runs.

Unfinished matches	1827	Lord's	Oxford 1st innings 258	Cambridge 1st innings 92	Rain both years
	1844	Lord's	Oxford 1st innings 96	Cambridge 1st innings 69	

Summary – 52 matches played. Cambridge won 26. Oxford 24. 2 unfinished.

Cambridge's 388 (in 1872), Oxford's 306 (in 1881), Oxford's 304 (in 1886) and Cambridge's 302 (in 1876), are the four highest innings yet made in these matches.

RUGBY v MARLBOROUGH

Played at Lord's, July 28, 29, 1886

This proved to be one of the most interesting and well-contested of the public school matches played during the season of 1886, and it was made specially remarkable by a very singular incident which occurred late on the second afternoon. When Kitcat, the Marlborough captain, was disposed of it was discovered that Bengough, the Rugby captain, had by some oversight been allowed to go on twice at each end and in his first over from the pavilion wicket (the second time he had been on at that end) he got Kitcat caught at cover point. A long discussion ensued; but it was decided by the umpires that Kitcat, having been fairly caught, could not go in again. As a result, however, on the objection of the Marlborough captain, Bengough was not allowed to bowl another ball in the innings after he had completed his over. The affair gave rise to a great deal of correspondence, and indeed it was not thoroughly settled at the time whether or not the umpires had acted rightly. Of course it was a clear oversight on the part of the umpires that Bengough went on at this wrong end, but the universal opinion afterwards was that Kitcat having been fairly caught, the umpires had no option but to give him out.

On the first day Rugby won the toss and scored 163, G. H. R. Wilson, a very small cricketer, playing in capital form for 36, and W. Bowden-Smith and F. E. Gaddum showing about the best form of the others. This total of 163 was headed by Marlborough by 8 runs, S. B. Prest and F. J. Poynton playing exceedingly well for their respective scores. R. H. Wilson (fast right) bowled remarkably well at the start of the innings but did not last. Bengough, the captain, effected a remarkable catch off his own bowling in dismissing Kitcat. Going in a second time Rugby lost four wickets for 47 runs, so that the chances of the game seemed rather in favour of Marlborough, Rugby being only 39 runs ahead with six wickets to fall.

On the second day the interest in the game was maintained right up to the finish. Thanks mainly to a very finely played innings of 95 by H. Bowden-Smith, and an excellent 48 by H. C. Bradby, the total in the second innings of Rugby reached 240. Bowden-Smith's invaluable 95 included ten 4s, five 3s and six 2s. He and Bradby put on 81 during their partnership. Marlborough wanted 233 runs to win, and though the boys made an admirable and plucky attempt to save the game, their last wicket fell for 195, and so Rugby were left with a most creditable and hard-earned victory by 37 runs. On all hands it was admitted that both teams were above the average. It will be seen that in the second innings of Marlborough no fewer than eight members of the team got into double figures, Poynton's 47 being the best display of cricket on the side.

Rugby

Mr H. C. Bradby c Robertson b Nockolds	2	– run out	48
Mr R. G. Lewis b Robertson	4	– b Nockfolds	0
Mr F. E. Gaddum c Browning b Nockolds	28	– run out	7
Mr G. H. R. Wilson b Nockolds	36	– b Sale	2
Mr G. F. Jackson b Sale	5	– b Nockolds	31
Mr W. Bowden-Smith not out	31	– c and b Nockolds	13
Mr R. H. Wilson b Nockolds	2	– c Browning b Sale	3
Mr C. W. Bengough b Robertson	6	– run out	18
Mr H. Bowden-Smith c Browning b Nockolds	21	– c Browning b Poynton	95
Mr B. H. Milne b Nockolds	15	– c Robertson b Sale	5
Mr A. W. Dixon b Nockolds	0	– not out	5
B 10, l-b 3	13	B 5, l-b 5, w 3	13
	163		240

Marlborough

Mr F. H. Browning b R. H. Wilson	3	– not out	15
Mr W. L. Rowell b R. H. Wilson	1	– c Milne b R. H. Wilson	20
Mr F. J. Poynton b R. H. Wilson	30	– c W. Bowden-Smith b R. H. Wilson	47
Mr S. A. P. Kitcat c and b Bengough	12	– c W. Bowden-Smith b Bengough	27
Mr F. B. Prest c Milne b R. H. Wilson	37	– b R. H. Wilson	35
Mr W. W. Sale b R. H. Wilson	0	– b R. H. Wilson	10
Mr H. de L. Houseman b Bengough	28	– c Bradbury b Lewis	14
Mr H. M. Barnes run out	20	– b Bengough	16
Mr E. M. Dawson-Thomas b Bengough	16	– st Milne b Gaddum	2
Mr W. H. Robertson b Bengough	7	– c Milne b R. H. Wilson	16
Mr A. G. Nockolds run out	0	– b Lewis	7
B 7, l-b 10	17	B 8, l-b 7, w 1	16
	171		225

Marlborough Bowling

	Overs	Mdns	Runs	Wkts	Overs	Mdns	Runs	Wkts
Robertson	19	7	43	2	10	1	22	0
Nockolds	32.3	16	45	7	42	20	68	3
Dawson-Thomas	21	12	13	0	24	10	43	0
Poynton	14	8	16	0	13.2	2	22	1
Barnes	10	3	21	0	3	0	10	0
Sale	13	8	7	1	19	6	38	3
Kitcat	2	1	5	0	4	0	11	0
Houseman					6	3	13	0

Rugby Bowling

	Overs	Mdns	Runs	Wkts	Overs	Mdns	Runs	Wkts
Bengough	36	18	64	4	42	24	49	2
R. H. Wilson	40	24	50	5	64	41	72	5
Dixon	15	5	26	0	7	3	12	0
Lewis	14	9	14	0	29.1	14	36	2
Gaddum					4	2	10	1

MCC AND GROUND v SUSSEX

Played at Lord's, May 19, 20, 21, 1887

In the absence of Messrs F. M. Lucas, Newham and Thomas, Sussex had a weak batting team in the annual match with the MCC, but, apart from one or two players, the Club side was a very good one, Mr Grace's services being again available. The opening day was very wet, cricket being practicable for only three hours and a quarter. There were three interruptions before luncheon, and there was no play after a quarter-past five. The Club went in at ten minutes past twelve, the one feature of the innings being Mr Grace's play. The great batsman went in first, and took out his bat for 81, his fine innings, which last two hours and a quarter, comprising three 4s, six 3s, fourteen 2s and twenty-three singles. Mr Grace made so large a proportion of the runs from the bat that his ten colleagues only got 37 between them, six batsmen being dismissed without scoring. When rain stopped play, Sussex had made 54 for one wicket, Tester being not out 21, and Mr Cotterill not out 7. Quaife played uncommonly well for his 23.

Friday was a miserable day, storms of hail and rain interrupting the game half a dozen times. The sun shone out between the showers, but the air was very cold. The rain overnight had seriously affected the ground, and there was no long scoring. Sussex's innings closed for 119, Mr Grace following up his success as a batsman by taking seven wickets for 53 runs. Going in a second time with a majority of nine in their favour, the Club lost two wickets before luncheon for 37. Mr Grace's 18 included a square-leg hit over the tennis court, for which, after some discussion, six runs were allowed. It was a good hit, but not a very exceptional one, the wickets having been pitched some distance from the centre of the ground. After luncheon the Club did very badly, and seven wickets were down for 83. Thanks, however, to Mr Russel's good cricket, the total in the end reached 125. With 135 to get to win, Sussex went in at a quarter to six, and, with the ground decidedly easier than it had been in the early part of the day, Tester and Quaife scored 46 for the first wicket. Quaife again batted in capital form, and foreshadowed the brilliant cricket he showed for Sussex later in the summer. At the call of time the score was 65 for two wickets, or only 70 runs to win.

On the Saturday the game was finished off by five-and-twenty minutes to three, the weather being again wretched, and rain causing two interruptions. Thanks in a great measure to Walter Humphrey's batting, at the finish Sussex won by four wickets. The MCC lost a good deal through bad wicket-keeping, Mr C. W. Wright being sadly at fault. This gentleman, however, had only just resumed cricket after a long interval caused by an accident while steeplechasing, and could hardly be expected to excel.

MCC and Ground

Mr W. G. Grace not out	81	– b J. Hide	18
Mr F. E. Lacey b A. Hide	0	– b Smith	29
G. G. Hearne c Humphreys b J. Hide	0	– run out	15
Rev. R. T. Thornton b A. Hide	16	– b Smith	5
Mr C. W. Wright b A. Hide	0	– c Phillips b A. Hide	5
Mr H. Ross lbw b J. Hide	0	– c J. Hide b Smith	6
W. Attewell c Humphreys b J. Hide	8	– b Smith	0
Mr J. S. Russel lbw b Smith	8	– b Bean	27
Mr H. D. Littlewood c Smith b Bean	5	– c Phillips b Tester	8
H. Pickett run out	0	– st Phillips b Tester	4
J. Wootton c A. Hide b Smith	0	– not out	3
B 7, l-b 3	10	B 3, l-b 1, w 1	5
	128		125

Sussex

W. Tester c Wright b Grace	23	– b Grace	4
W. Quaife c Lacey b Grace	23	– b Hearne	38
Mr G. H. Cotterill c Attewell b Grace	7	– c Wright b Pickett	19
Hollands b Grace	10	– c Ross (sub) b Attewell	6
J. Hide c Lacey b Grace	5	– b Attewell	17
G. Bean c Grace b Attewell	0	– not out	13
W. Humphreys c Wootton b Grace	2	– not out	17
H. Tebay b Grace	6	– c Grace b Attewell	6
Mr C. A. Smith not out	16		
H. Phillips c Grace b Wootton	13		
A. Hide c Thornton b Attewell	2		
B 9, l-b 3	12	B 7	7
	119		137

Sussex Bowling

	Overs	Mdns	Runs	Wkts	Overs	Mdns	Runs	Wkts
J. Hide	27	11	52	3	21	9	33	1
A. Hide	30	12	38	3	7	1	18	1
Mr Smith	12.2	3	20	2	15	6	27	4
Bean	9	4	8	1	13	5	14	1
Tester					24.3	10	28	2

MCC and Ground Bowling

	Overs	Mdns	Runs	Wkts	Overs	Mdns	Runs	Wkts
Wootton	15	7	19	1	22.1	7	44	—
Pickett	8	2	16	—	15	7	18	1
Mr Grace	42	17	53	7	19	10	20	1
Attewell	36.3	24	19	2	41	23	37	3
Hearne					15	10	11	1

Umpires: Wild and W. Hearn.

THE MCC CENTENARY WEEK

MCC AND GROUND v ENGLAND

Played at Lord's, June 13, 14, 15, 1887

It was in every way fitting that the MCC should celebrate its centenary on a large scale, and it is not easy to say what better fixture could have been selected for the opening of the week than the Club and Ground against England. The one disadvantage was the fact that the Club includes in its ranks so many of the prominent gentlemen players of the day that the only amateurs for whom places could be found in the England eleven were Mr W. W. Read and Mr Stoddart. Even at this time Mr Stoddart was up for election to the Club, and a few weeks later he could not have been chosen. The general public showed a lively interest in the celebration, and on the opening day there was a very fine assemblage at Lord's, the number paying at the gates being 5,992, and the full company being estimated at about 8,000. Both sides were very strong, but, as events proved, the MCC committee would have done much better to have left out one of the batsmen from their side and played either Attewell or Wootton. The want of another good bowler was sadly felt before the game came to an end. Winning the toss, the MCC went in first in magnificent weather at five minutes after twelve and, as the wicket was in capital condition, there seemed every prospect of some high scoring. Lohmann, however, bowling from the Pavilion end, found a spot to help him, and the early play was disastrous. Mr Hornby was caught and bowled at 19; Mr Grace at 23 played forward at rather a short ball from Lohmann and was clean bowled; and before a run had been added, Mr Webbe, from a bad stroke, was splendidly caught at cover-point by Briggs, who took the ball with one hand while running at full speed. Barnes and Gunn stayed together for some little time, but the former was bowled at 36. A very fine ball dismissed George Hearne at 52, and just afterwards Mr J. G. Walker was brilliantly caught at slip, six of the best MCC wickets being then down for 55 runs. The remaining batsmen played up well and gave Gunn some valuable help, but by a quarter-past four the innings was all over for 175, the last four wickets having thus put on 120 runs. Gunn was out very unluckily, a ball from Lohmann going off his bat on to his legs and then into his wicket. He hit three 4s, three 3s and twelve 2s in his 61 and, though somewhat over-cautious in the early part of his innings, played admirable cricket. Lohmann, it will be seen, took six wickets for 62 runs – a very fine performance. Shrewsbury and Mr Stoddart commenced England's innings at twenty-five minutes to five and when seven o'clock came they were still together, the amateur being not out 111, Shrewsbury not out 70 and the total 196 for no wicket. Both batsmen played magnificently, but Mr Stoddart had one great piece of good fortune. When he had scored 13, and the total was 32, he drove a ball back to Mr Grace, who half-stopped it, and having taken all the force out of the hit, put it up to mid-off. Under ordinary circumstances Mr Webbe would have had a certain catch, but with a strong sun shining full in his eyes, he lost sight of the ball, which hit his face and fell to the ground. The 100 went up when the innings had lasted exactly an hour and a half, and at the end of two hours' batting the total was 147, the bowling by this time having been completely mastered. Mr Stoddart completed his 100 at ten minutes to seven, having then been at the wickets for two hours and a quarter; and five minutes before the call of time the MCC total was passed without a wicket being down. In the last twelve minutes of play no fewer than 33 runs were scored, Shrewsbury, who had previously been playing with great caution, making four 4s in quick succession.

On the second morning the two batsmen resumed their innings, and were not separated until the score had reached 266, only 17 runs short of the great score made by Messrs W. G. Grace and Cooper for the first wicket at Kennington Oval in 1869. Mr Stoddart was the first out, having scored, in three hours and forty minutes, 151 – the highest innings he has ever played in a first-class match. His figures were nineteen 4s, five 3s, ten 2s and forty singles. Except the chance referred to above, his only mistake was a very difficult catch to

Sherwin at the wicket, and on the whole the display was one of the finest he has ever given. With such an extraordinary start the other England batsmen had a very easy task, and it was not until ten minutes to six that the innings closed, the total being 514 – the largest score ever made at Lord's in a match of first-rate importance. Shrewsbury exceeded Mr Stoddart's score by a single run and was the fourth man out – caught at slip off Rawlin's bowling. He gave a hard chance at the wicket when he had made 87 and was badly missed by Mr Grace at point when he had made 100, but otherwise his innings was a masterly one both for defence and hitting. His figures were fifteen 4s, eleven 3s, eleven 2s and thirty-seven singles and he was at the wickets altogether five hours and a quarter. Mr W. W. Read, in his brilliant 74, hit a 5, seven 4s, two 3s, and nine 2s, and Ulyett was also seen to advantage. Mr Hornby did not manage his bowlers with so much judgment as might have been expected and put a tremendous amount of work upon Rawlin, Barnes and Flowers. Barnes, it will be seen, was by far the most successful. In connection with a record score in first-class matches at Lord's, it may be of interest to give the falls of the wickets:

1/266 2/266 3/312 4/369 5/430 6/461 7/461 8/489 9/514 10/514

Three times during the innings, it will be noticed, two wickets fell at the same total. The exact time of the innings, deducting all intervals, was seven hours and three-quarters. Wanting no fewer than 339 runs to save a single-innings' defeat, the MCC had fifty minutes' batting before the drawing of stumps, and lost Mr Webbe's wicket for 58 runs. Mr. Grace being not out 34 and Gunn not out 6, at seven o'clock. The attendance of the public was even larger than on the opening day, 6,176 people paying for admission at the gates.

On the Wednesday play was resumed at twenty minutes to twelve and just after two o'clock the MCC were all out for 222, England winning the match by an innings and 117 runs. Mr Grace only added 11 to his overnight score before being easily caught and bowled, but some capital batting was shown by Barnes and Flowers, who hit the score from 116 to 190. Mr Hornby, who was lame, did not go in until eight wickets had fallen.

MCC and Ground

Mr W. G. Grace b Lohmann	5	– c and b Briggs	45
Mr A. N. Hornby c and b Briggs	16	– b Bates	6
W. Barnes b Briggs	8	– c and b Bates	53
Mr A. J. Webbe c Briggs b Lohmann	0	– c Pilling b Bates	14
W. Gunn b Lohmann	61	– c Shrewsbury b Briggs	10
G. G. Hearne b Briggs	8	– c Barlow b Lohmann	6
Mr J. G. Walker c Hall b Lohmann	3	– b Briggs	25
Hon. M. B. Hawke b Lohmann	16	– b Briggs	10
W. Flowers b Lohmann	19	– c Lohmann b Bates	43
J. T. Rawlin not out	18	– c W. Read b Bates	4
M. Sherwin b Bates	17	– not out	1
B 3, w 1	4	B 4, l-b 1	5
	175		222

England

A. Shrewsbury c Barnes b Rawlin	152	L. Hall c Webbe b Barnes	0
Mr A. E. Stoddart c and b Rawlin	151	J. Briggs b Barnes	9
R. G. Barlow lbw b Rawlin	0	G. Lohmann not out	9
M. Read c Sherwin b Flowers	25	R. Pilling c Gunn b Barnes	0
Mr W. W. Read c Webbe b Barnes	74	B 8, l-b 12	20
W. Bates c Hornby b Barnes	28		
G. Ulyett c Sherwin b Barnes	46		514

England Bowling

	Overs	Mdns	Runs	Wkts	Overs	Mdns	Runs	Wkts
Lohmann	57	29	62	6	32	13	60	1
Briggs	55	22	84	3	39	8	77	4
Bates	5	2	5	1	28.3	15	46	5
Barlow	2	2	0	0				
Ulyett	8	3	20	0	21	8	34	0

MCC and Ground Bowling

	Overs	Mdns	Runs	Wkts
Barnes	74.2	30	126	6
Rawlin	90	39	140	3
Mr W. G. Grace ...	36	16	65	0
Flowers	74	29	122	1
Hearne	9	3	19	0
Mr Webbe	13	5	22	0

Umpires: John West and T. Mycroft.

THE CENTENARY OF THE MARYLEBONE CLUB

Banquet at Lord's

On Wednesday, June 15th, 1887, the Centenary banquet of the Marylebone Club was held in the Tennis Court at Lord's Cricket Ground. The Hon. E. Chandos Leigh (president) occupied the chair and the company present included the French Ambassador (M. Waddington), the Right Hon. G. J. Goschen, MP, the Duke of Abercorn, Lord Latham, Lord G. Hamilton, MP, Lord Bessborough, Lord Clarendon, Lord Willoughby de Broke, Lord Londesborough, Lord Oxenbridge, Lord Darnley, Lord Winterton, Lord Downe, Lord Wenlock, Lord Lyttelton, Lord Belper, Lord Harris, Sir W. Hart-Dyke, MP, Sir A. L. Smith, Sir G. Berry, Sir Saul Samuel, Sir J. F. Garrick, Sir J. Chitty, Hon. W. Monk Jervis, Hon. Sir S. Ponsonby-Fane, Hon. E. Stanhope, MP, Hon. Alfred Lyttelton, Rev. T. A. Anson, Rev. G. J. Boudier, Rev. J. Hornby, Mr R. Broughton, Mr J. L. Baldwin, Mr W. Nicholson, Mr R. A. H. Mitchell, Mr C. E. Green Mr A. Rutter, Rev. V. Royle, Mr W. N. Roe, Mr T. C. O'Brien, Mr J. G. Walker, Mr E. F. S. Tylecote, Mr J. Shuter, Mr W. W. Read, Mr W. G. Grace, Mr H. Perkins, Mr A. N. Hornby, Mr A. J. Webbe, Mr I. D. Walker, Mr W. H. Patterson, Mr A. W. Ridley, Mr A. Appleby, Mr D. Buchanan, Mr V. E. Walker, Mr W. H. Hadow, Mr Courtney Boyle, etc. After the loyal toasts had been duly honoured, Mr. Justice Chitty proposed "The Houses of Lords and Commons", coupled with the names of the Duke of Abercorn and the Right Hon. G. J. Goschen, the Chancellor of the Exchequer.

Mr Goschen, who was received with loud applause, remarked that it was extremely kind to give so cordial a reception to one whose only feat in the cricket field was recorded by Mr Justice Chitty. It was in a single-wicket match and as it was a true anecdote of his early years he did not feel called upon to deny it. He had been asked to return thanks for the House of Commons, and it had been most properly observed that this was not a political toast. Any introduction of politics at a gathering of this kind would remind one of the bore who came up to a cricket match at Lord's and made some remarks upon what was going on in the House of Commons. They knew what a reception he would have if he were to say "The Ministry are out". (Laughter.) In the course of an excellent speech the right Hon. gentleman went on to say that, however important the matters might be which engaged his attention as a politician, there was one part of the daily paper to which he invariably directed his attention the first thing in the morning, and that was the part containing the scores of the cricket matches in course of progress.

The Earl of Bessborough then proposed "Success to Cricket and the MCC", tracing in the course of his speech the career of the Club from its earliest beginnings.

The Chairman responded and Lord Lathom proposed "The Distinguished Visitors", to which toast M. Waddington and Sir Saul Samuel replied.

Viscount Lewisham, MP, then proposed "The Great Army of Cricketers", to which there were six responses: "The Church" (the Rev. Dr Hornby, Provost of Eton), "The Army" (the Right Hon. E. Stanhope, MP), "The Navy" (the Right Hon. Lord George Hamilton, MP), "The Bench and the Bar" (the Hon. Mr Justice A. L. Smith), "Medicine" (Mr W. G. Grace), and "the Cricket Counties" (Lord Harris).

After his response to this toast, Lord Harris proposed the last toast of the evening, "The Press", and in so doing bore full and generous testimony to the careful accuracy with which cricket matches were recorded in the papers, and to the large share with the Press had in promoting the popularity of the national game. Then, with the toast, "Our Next Merry Meeting", a memorable evening came to an end.

MCC AND GROUND v CAMBRIDGE UNIVERSITY

Played at Lord's, June 27, 28, 29, 1887

The Marylebone Club put a very strong team in the field against Cambridge University, the occasion being the last trial match of the Light Blues prior to their meeting with Oxford. With bowlers like Barnes, Pougher, Attewell and Mr Grace, the Cantabs naturally found run-getting very difficult, but the wicket was in such good condition as to afford practically no excuse for the poor display made by the undergraduates on the opening day. Barnes, bowling in rare form, dismissed the five most likely run-getters on the side, but after the luncheon interval Mr Grace got three wickets, two of them leg before, and then a very tame innings was brought to a sensational finish, Pougher bowling Mr Ford, Mr Hale, and Mr Toppin with the first three balls he delivered at his second trial. A word of praise is due to Mr Marchant, the captain, who made 45 by good and stylish cricket. Twelve men played on each side, but only eleven fielded. It is worthy of remark that Mr Crawley, who in the University contest gained so much distinction, did not field in the first innings of the MCC. Going in against the Cambridge total of 143, the Club headed this score by 26 runs for the loss of four wickets before the call of time. Mr Grace and Mr Webbe made 68 runs in less than an hour, and later in the day there was some capital batting by Mr Morton Lucas and Mr Thornton, who were not out respectively with 17 and 26 at the drawing of stumps.

The poor display of the Cantabs on the opening day exercised a very prejudicial effect upon the attendance on the Tuesday, but as a matter of fact the cricket was of the most interesting description. The bowling of the Light Blues on the opening day had been very tame stuff, and their fielding had left a good deal to be desired, but on the Tuesday morning they got six more wickets down for the addition of only 32 runs. Pougher and Mr Studd, however, put on 50 runs in an hour before the innings closed, and Cambridge were 117 runs in arrear. Mr Ford had a capital bowling analysis, and indeed gave promise of much greater ability than he afterwards displayed. This time the undergraduates fully redeemed their reputation as batsmen, every one of the first eight members of the team achieving some degree of success. Mr Marchant hit so hard in company with Mr Thomas that at one time 50 runs were obtained in twenty minutes, and after the Cambridge captain, whose 36 included seven 4s, was leg before, Mr Sutthery and Mr Thomas punished the Marylebone bowling very severely. The Etonian, one of the most graceful of batsmen, was seen at his best in scoring 48, and Mr Sutthery, though scarcely so stylish, hit in fine form. So free was the batting that after the interval 126 runs were obtained in eighty minutes. Mr Sutthery made 45 out of 47 added for the fourth wicket, that gentleman's dashing 72, which was scored in an hour and a half, including eight 4s, three 3s and nine 2s. Mention should also be made of Mr Buxton, who was at the wickets half an hour without making a run and then made 41 in good style. Just before seven o'clock the innings came to an end for 294, the last five wickets having fallen for 44.

On the third day the MCC with an innings to play required 178 runs to gain a victory. Against the moderate bowling of the Cantabs this task seemed fairly easy, but no one could have expected so decisive a result as was actually obtained. It was one of Mr Grace's best days, and out of 167 runs obtained from the bat the great cricketer obtained no fewer than 116, being not out when the match was won. Mr Webbe commenced the innings with Mr Grace and the pair scored the first 77 runs in about a hundred minutes. The Middlesex captain was then dismissed, and Mr Lucas confining himself for the most part to defensive cricket, the interest in the remainder of the match centred in Mr Grace's batting. The Gloucestershire captain completed his 50 with the total at 74, and reached his 100 with the score at 145. He hit in grand style all round the wicket, and one big drive pitched on the upper part of the Pavilion. His innings, one of the most finished he played during the season, lasted two hours and fifty minutes and included thirteen 4s, five 3s and nine 2s. The victory, with ten wickets to spare, gained by the MCC, was due to exceptionally fine batting and the first innings failure on the part of Cambridge.

Cambridge University

Mr C. D. Buxton b Barnes	9	– c and b Attewell	41
Mr F. Marchant b Barnes	45	– lbw b Grace	36
Mr F. Thomas b Barnes	5	– c Welman b Webbe	48
Mr A. M. Sutthery b Barnes	9	– c A. P. Lucas b Grace	72
Mr F. G. J. Ford c Pougher b Barnes	0	– b Attewell	26
Mr E. Crawley lbw b Grace	16	– not out	19
Mr W. C. Bridgeman lbw b Grace	21	– lbw b Grace	12
Mr L. Martineau not out	22	– c Grace b Barnes	16
Mr F. Meyrick-Jones b Grace	0	– lbw b Attewell	0
Mr L. Orford b Pougher	2	– b Barnes	7
Mr H. Hale b Pougher	0	– b Attewell	3
Mr C. Toppin b Pougher	0	– c and b Pougher	4
B 7, l-b 7	14	B 5, l-b 5	10
	143		294

MCC and Ground

Mr W. G. Grace lbw b Ford	31	– not out	116
Mr A. J. Webbe c Ford b Martineau	33	– c Ford b Sutthery	22
Mr A. P. Lucas b Ford	12	– not out	29
Mr M. P. Lucas b Ford	50		
W. Barnes b Toppin	11		
Rev. R. T. Thornton c Orford b Ford	26		
Mr C. W. Wright b Hale	0		
W. Attewell c Ford b Hale	0		
Mr A. H. Studd b Ford	32		
Mr J. Eyre c Thomas b Ford	9		
Mr F. T. Welman b Toppin	3		
A. D. Pougher not out	32		
B 15, l-b 3, w 3	21	B 6, l-b 5	11
	260		178

MCC and Ground Bowling

	Overs	Mdns	Runs	Wkts	Overs	Mdns	Runs	Wkts
Barnes	47	28	55	5	38	17	85	2
Attewell	12	4	24	0	41	17	78	4
Pougher	13.3	8	18	3	23.2	6	48	1
Mr Grace	29	18	19	3	27	12	47	3
Mr Webbe	7	4	13	0	12	6	11	1
A. P. Lucas					8	1	15	0

Cambridge University Bowling

	Overs	Mdns	Runs	Wkts	Overs	Mdns	Runs	Wkts
Mr Hale	34	13	54	2	15	7	22	0
Mr Sutthery	27	9	44	0	18	12	21	1
Mr Martineau	16	6	29	1	6	2	17	0
Mr Ford	43.2	21	57	6	31.3	10	49	0
Mr Toppin	26	3	46	2	12	1	33	0
Mr Buxton	20	14	9	0	11	6	11	0
Marchant					7	3	14	0

Umpires: Clayton and Hay.

MCC AND GROUND v OXFORD UNIVERSITY

Played at Lord's, June, 30, July 1, 1887

The annual two days' match played by the Oxford eleven against the Marylebone Club is far too close to the great struggle with Cambridge for the Dark Blues to really extend themselves, and for some years past little interest has attached to the fixture. The fact of the game being limited to two days also detracts from its importance. Mr Philipson was allowed to rest, and his place was taken by Mr Lyon, but in other respects the Oxford eleven was the same that during the following week gained so brilliant a victory over Cambridge. The Marylebone team was not nearly so strong as that which had beaten Cambridge, but with Pougher, Rawlin, Chatterton, and Rylott the bowling had plenty of variety, and the Oxonians were occupied from a few minutes past twelve until ten minutes to five in making a total of 193. For 32 and 27 respectively Mr Key and Mr Rashleigh batted in good style, but they never got the upper hand of the bowling. After seven wickets had fallen for 119, Lord George Scott, who had not previously been included in the eleven, joined Mr Ricketts, and the pair added 60 runs for the eighth wicket. Going in to bat at ten minutes past five, the MCC fared so indifferently against the bowling of Messrs Foster and Buckland that two wickets were down for 5 runs and five for 53. As there were no prominent batsmen to assist Chatterton there seemed every probability of a follow-on, but Rawlin afforded his fellow-professional excellent assistance, and despite all that the Oxonians could do no other wicket fell before the call of time, when the total had been raised to 124, Chatterton being not out with 61 and Rawlin not out 31.

On the second day the Marylebone innings was finished off in an hour and twenty minutes for the addition of 75 runs. Chatterton only added 5 runs to his overnight score and Rawlin also made his innings into 66, this being the first real batting success of the latter professional at Lord's. The second innings of Oxford occupied the rest of the day, and lasted from a quarter-past one until half-past six, the total amounting to 249. There was some heavy scoring at first, 174 runs being made for the first three wickets. Messrs Gresson and Nepean put on 80 while together, the former, who was out at 129, contributing an admirable 70, made up by nine 4s, four 3s, six 2s, and singles. Mr Rashleigh hit in very brilliant form for 55, making at one time three 4s from successive balls, and later on Lord George Scott achieved so much success that he was chosen to fill the place rendered vacant through the injury suffered by Mr Wreford-Brown. When the match was left drawn, the MCC with an innings to play wanted 244 runs to gain a victory.

Oxford University

Mr F. H. Gresson c Mycroft b Rawlin	18 – b Pougher	70
Mr E. A. Nepean b Pougher	10 – c Whitfeld b Arnall-Thompson	33
Mr W. Rashleigh c Studd b Pougher	27 – c Thompson b Rylott	55
Mr H. W. Forster c Mycroft b Pougher	6 – c and b Rylott	1
Mr K. J. Key c Chatterton b Rawlin	32 – b Rylott	4
Mr J. H. Brain b Rawlin	8 – c Greatorex b Pougher	16
Mr E. H. Buckland c Whitfeld b Chatterton	12 – absent	0
Mr G. W. Ricketts lbw b Pougher	39 – c Wynyard b Rylott	16
Lord George Scott b Pougher	21 – not out	42
Mr H. O. Whitby not out	14 – b Pougher	4
Mr H. Lyon c Mycroft b Rylott	0 – b Pougher	0
B 1, l-b 5	6 B 1, l-b 7	8
	193	249

MCC and Ground

Mr C. W. Wright b Forster	15	A. D. Pougher c sub. b Gresson	6
Mr H. Whitfeld b Forster	2	Mr H. T. Arnall-Thompson b Gresson	1
Mr E. G. Wynyard c Lyon b Buckland	0	T. Mycroft not out	20
W. Chatterton c Brain b Gresson	66	A. Rylott c Gresson b Nepean	0
Mr A. H. Studd b Buckland	2	B 10, l-b 7, w 2	19
Mr T. Greatorex c Ricketts b Nepean	2		
J. T. Rawlin b Nepean	66		199

MCC and Ground Bowling

	Overs	Mdns	Runs	Wkts	Overs	Mdns	Runs	Wkts
Chatterton	29	14	43	1	22	11	26	0
Rawlin	55	34	54	3	27	11	50	0
Pougher	49	27	70	5	44	22	59	4
Rylott	22.3	15	20	1	46	26	57	4
Mr Arnall-Thompson					26	12	49	1

Oxford University Bowling

	Overs	Mdns	Runs	Wkts
Mr Buckland	33	16	36	2
Mr Forster	17	6	38	2
Mr Nepean	12	3	36	3
Mr Whitby	23	10	32	0
Mr Ricketts	4	1	3	0
Mr Gresson	19	6	35	3

Umpires: Farrands and Titchmarsh.

THE REFORMS OF 1889

At their meeting last May the Marylebone Club adopted some changes in the laws of cricket, and the game was everywhere played last summer under the new conditions. The Authorised Laws as they now stand and a report of the meeting at which the reforms were carried, will be found elsewhere in this Almanack. What was done was, briefly, to made the Over consist of five balls instead of four, to permit a bowler to change ends as often as he pleased, and to empower the captain of the batting side to declare the innings at an end whenever he chose to do so. There were, of course, some qualifications. Thus, although a bowler is now allowed to change ends as often as he likes – which practically means as often as the captain of his side likes – he may not bowl two overs in succession. Again, although what has been generally called the closure can be applied at any time in a one-day match, it can only be put into force on the last day of a match arranged for more than one day. Naturally these changes caused a good deal of discussion. The closure was only, I think, applied about half-a-dozen times in important matches, but the other alterations affected every match except the comparatively few games where the bowlers put out the opposing sides in the fashion that Turner and Ferris accustomed us to in the May of 1888. Amateurs and professionals alike expressed their views pretty freely on the alterations that had been carried out, and, except on the part of those good, worthy people who never can see good in any change, the opinions were for the most part strongly favourable. Still there was evidently a good deal of opposition and I thought it might interest the readers of Wisden's Almanack if I could obtain from captains of great elevens and from famous cricketers generally their ideas on how the new laws had worked and were likely to work. I accordingly asked the following questions:

1. Do you think the change to five balls per over has worked well?
2. If not, will you state your objection?
3. Do you think the change has worked well which prevents a man bowling two overs in succession, and, therefore, does not allow bowlers to change ends without someone else bowling an odd over? Would it not suffice, at any rate in matches extending over more than one day, if the restriction were upon his bowling more than two overs in succession?
4. Do you think the closure rule likely to work well?

Very courteous and frank answers were received from nearly all the gentlemen and players written to, and as it is far better that they should speak for themselves than that I should attempt to classify their views, I have published below this most interesting collection of expert opinion on cricket subjects. I ought, perhaps, to say that the reasons why the questions were framed as they appear were: (1) because some people said the bowlers would be overtired by bowling five balls in succession instead of four; (2) because some few persons had told me that the proper and ideal over consisted of six balls; (3) because, when you wanted your present bowlers to change ends, I considered it very awkward to have to call upon another man to bowl an odd over, and because I thought that in matches extending over more than one day there would be little risk in allowing two successive overs to one man; and (4) because the closure seemed likely to diminish the number of drawn matches and to give victory to the stronger and better team; but, further, because there seemed a want of knowledge among public cricketers of the fact that in some one-day matches the law had been abused. Instances were brought to my knowledge in which captains had closed their innings when their score was less than that of the other side, and had done other things that I do not think were contemplated by the framers of the law. There were other questions that I asked of the experts, but, as they do not relate to the reforms of the year, I have dealt with them, and with the answers to them, in another article. My esteemed friend, Bob Thoms, has, with the wilfulness of youth, mixed all the ingredients together, but still, I think, his jottings will be found interesting in what he has characteristically said as well as in what he has judiciously left unsaid. Without further preface I publish the answers I received:

Mr I. D. Walker thinks well of the change to five balls per over and of the closure rule; while as to bowlers changing ends, he says, "The objection to a man bowling two overs in succession with unlimited change of ends is, that it would be possible for a man to bowl eight overs out of eleven, which is too large a proportion".

Mr W. H. Patterson expresses his approval of the five balls per over and of the closure rule, but does not see much practical good in the suggestion as to changing ends.

C. K. Pullin approves of the increase of the over to five balls, as it saves time; and he points out that a man might bowl four overs out of five if the suggestion were adopted that he might bowl two overs in succession and change ends as often as he liked. This experienced umpire does not think the closure rule ought to apply to one-day matches.

John Beaumont is opposed to the increase of the over from four balls to five, as it gives fast bowlers too much work. He, however, approves of the other new laws, as to changing ends and declaring an innings over.

Mr J. A. Dixon believes the extra ball to the over saved a lot of time and made very little difference, even to fast bowlers. He therefore supports the new law, and so he does the closure rule. As to changing ends, Mr Dixon thinks the new regulation acted fairly well, although the odd over was a difficulty sometimes. The suggestion to allow two overs in succession would be open to abuse, and he prefers the rule as it is.

Mr C. Pigg is in favour of all the new laws – the increase to five balls, the changing of ends, and the closure.

Tom Hearne, the veteran chief of the ground staff at Lord's, also says emphatically "yes" to these three questions.

The Hon. Ivo Bligh, in his individual capacity, of course, and not as secretary to the County Council, also gives an unqualified assent to the new laws of 1889.

Mr W. G. Grace supports the increase to five balls per over; and, on the subject of changing ends, says, "Certainly; if a bowler can change ends as often as he likes you must restrict him not to bowl two overs in succession, or he could bowl four overs out of five." Asked, however, if the closure rule is likely to work well, the Champion says, "Certainly not, as it may lead to disagreement".

W. Attewell favours the increase in the length of the over, believes in the closure and thinks a bowler ought to be allowed to bowl two overs in succession.

Mr S. M. J. Woods says the new law as to bowlers changing ends has done no harm, and he approves of the longer over and the legal closing of an innings.

Mr A. G. Steel thinks the change to five balls an over is a great improvement. As to changing ends he makes the following suggestion, which in my judgment is well worth consideration as a way of avoiding the present awkwardness and yet preventing any abuse of the law: "I think the best rule would be to allow a bowler to change ends as often as he likes, so long as he does not bowl two overs in succession more than once in an innings; three overs consecutively never to be allowed". Then, as to whether the closure rule is likely to work well, Mr Steel says, "Yes, in three-day matches. In one-day matches I, for one, would hesitate to use it. The good bats get an innings and not the others. Lawn-tennis is already in many places a formidable rival to cricket; we cricketers should not help it."

Louis Hall likes the increase of the over to five balls, and is in favour of the changing-ends rule as it is at present. He thinks the closure rule will work well, as it will cause more excitement in trying to finish matches, which is what the public enjoy.

H. H. Stephenson thinks the change to five balls per over a good one, and likely to work well. As to the closure, he likes what he has seen of it, but does not care to say much on the subject until another cricket season. Stephenson expresses no opinion on the question of bowlers changing ends, and in a letter to me says he is not enough connected with county cricket now to answer all my questions. On the subject of the approaching Australian visit, however, the Surrey veteran is enthusiastic. He says, "The Australians have done much good to cricket in this country. They have taught us several valuable lessons and they have 'mettled' our cricketers up and put great life into the game. I am sure they will be well supported by the cricket public of the country". It is refreshing to read this from the man who was captain of the first English cricket team that went to Australia, in 1861; the man who was in his prime, a great batsman, a most difficult bowler, and an accomplished wicket-keeper, when I, as a boy, used to be taken to see cricket at the Oval; and I have been scribbling about the game now for nearly twenty years!

Robert Peel considers the increase of the over to five balls is an advantage; he believes in the closure, and would "advocate a bowler being allowed to bowl two successive overs, one at each end".

Mr Harry Thornber, of Cheshire, thinks well of the closure and the longer over; and, as to changing ends, "would prefer that a bowler be allowed to bowl two overs in succession, so long as he did not do it more than twice in one innings". [This is a variant of Mr Steel's suggestion. – C. F. P.]

Lord Harris has not noticed any disadvantage from the increased length of the over. He thinks the closure rule is likely to work well; and regards it as inconvenient that bowlers are not allowed to bowl two consecutive overs.

Mr A. H. Heath favours the over of five balls, can see no objection to the new law about bowlers changing ends and approves of the closure, "as the captain can always use his discretion, while if he applied the rule without due consideration for his side he would be supplanted".

R. G. Barlow thinks well of the closure and the increase in the length of over, but believes the old rule is preferable which allowed a man to bowl two overs in succession, but only permitted him to change ends twice.

Mr H. W. Bainbridge says the change to five balls per over seems to him a success, the additional strain on the bowlers not being very apparent. He likes the closure, but thinks the rule as to changing ends is not satisfactory as it stands. He remarks, "A bowler should be prevented bowling more than two consecutive overs. I do not think any further restriction is necessary".

Mr F. E. Lacey regards the increase of the over to five balls as an advantageous change, and believes the closure rule will work well. As to the bowling question the Hampshire batsman says: "This is a change that is especially felt in country cricket, where victory often depends on the local professional. In the interests of cricket generally I think the change is a good one and that it tends to reduce the power of the one good bowler".

W. Chatterton quite agrees with the present rule as to changing ends, believes in the longer over and thinks the closure will work well.

Mr C. I. Thornton thinks well of the bowling of five balls instead of four every over, because it saves time. As to changing ends, he "would put the restriction at two overs instead of one"; and on the closure question says, "I think it hard to put a side in the position that they cannot win and may lose".

Mr R. A. H. Mitchell approves the increase of the over to five balls, and says he has long wished it. He also thinks well of the closure rule: while on the question of bowlers changing ends, the famous Old Oxonian says, "I tried to get this change introduced twenty years ago, and approve of it. I approve of the rule as it now stands without further alteration."

G. A. Lohmann believes the change to five balls per over has certainly worked well, from the spectators' point of view. He favours the other new laws as to closing an innings and changing ends.

G. G. Hearne likes the increase of the over from four balls to five and also the power to legally close an innings. He would not allow a bowler to bowl more than two overs in succession.

In sending me his answers, Mr I. D. Walker said he thought that, on some points at any rate, there would be much difference of opinion among my correspondents. He has proved quite correct in that surmise, but the experiment was worth trying, if only for the general favour expressed for the longer over, the dangers shown to exist of the closure rule being abused in one-day matches and the suggestion of Mr A. G. Steel as to how bowlers should be restricted as to changing ends.

C. F. P.

GENTLEMEN OF MCC v ROYAL ARTILLERY

Played at Lord's, June 13, 14, 1889

In this fixture the MCC had the advantage of Mr W. G. Grace's services, but in the absence of their professionals they were naturally weak in bowling. Under the circumstances the Artillery won by 160 runs. The victory was clearly due to the superb batting performance of Bombardier Barton, who scored 91 out of 167 in the first innings, and 102 out of 173 in the second. Besides this remarkable achievement, Barton took six wickets for 53 runs, and altogether fairly earned the trial he subsequently obtained for Kent.

Royal Artillery

Capt. King c Robertson b Grace	27	– b Shand	18
Mr J. Haggard c Farmer b Shand	1	– b Shand	6
Bombardier Barton c Russel b Shand	91	– c Robertson b Shand	102
Capt. Curteis (captain) lbw b Grace	9	– b Shand	0
Mr H. De Rougemont b Shand	0	– b Cobbald	0
Mr P. H. Dorchill b Grace	7	– b Farmer	0
Bombardier Osmond b Grace	0	– hit wkt b Grace	9
Mr A. C. Currie b Grace	4	– b Grace	7
Capt. Fox lbw b Shand	14	– hit wkt b Farmer	3
Major Davidson not out	4	– lbw b Shand	11
Mr H. Calley b Shand	0	– not out	0
B 10	10	B 8, l-b 8, w 1	17
	167		173

Gentlemen of MCC

Mr J. S. Russel c and b Currie	41	– b Barton	9
Mr D. D. Pontifex c Osmond b King	11	– b Currie	2
Mr H. Ross b Barton	1	– c and b Currie	0
Mr J. Robertson c Osmond b Barton	12	– c Barton b Currie	2
Mr W. G. Grace (captain) c Dorehill b Currie	18	– b Currie	9
Mr J. H. Farmer b Currie	3	– b Barton	5
Major J. C. Ker-Fox c Davidson b King	5	– not out	2
Mr W. R. Collins c and b Currie	9	– b Barton	4
Mr C. S. W. Cobbold not out	11	– b Barton	10
Mr F. L. Shand b Dorehill	10	– c Haggard b Currie	0
Mr F. T. Welman b King	8	– c Rougemont b Currie	6
B 3, l-b 1	4	B 6, l-b 1	7
	124		56

MCC AND GROUND v NORTHUMBERLAND

Played at Lord's, August 9, 10, 1889

This was one of the most remarkable matches of the season, for in it Gunn and Attewell accomplished an extraordinary batting performance, putting on no fewer than 419 runs during their partnership. They got together when the score was 9 for one wicket, and after raising the total to 325 without being parted on the first day, they increased it to 428 on the second, and then, on Attewell being caught, the innings was declared at an end. A fitting sequel to this achievement was the dismissal of the County eleven twice for 141 and 117 respectively, which gave the MCC a single innings victory with 170 runs to spare. Gunn's not out innings of 219 contained thirty-three 4s, seven 3s and eighteen 2s, while

Attewell's 200, which is the highest score he had ever made, included twenty-three 4s, eleven 3s, and seventeen 2s. Except the 454 put on by Barnes and Midwinter for the MCC against Leicestershire in June 1882, this stand by Gunn and Attewell is, we believe, the longest ever made at Lord's.

MCC and Ground

Gunn not out	219
Mr W. Brodrick-Cloete b Palmer	1
Attewell c Palmer b Ogilvie	200
B 6, l-b 1, w 1	8
(2 wkts dec.)	428

Messrs C. M. Thring, H. Awdry, J. H. Farmer, Capt. M. G. Wilkinson, Messrs T. S. Sidney, and F. Furner, Shacklock and Carlin did not bat.

Northumberland

Mr C. F. Cumberlege c Carlin b Shacklock	0	– b Attewell	2
Mr H. Phillipson b Shacklock	2	– c Awdry b Shacklock	21
Mr J. Hansell run out	28	– lbw b Attewell	0
Bookless b Shacklock	0	– c Carlin b Shacklock	16
Mr J. F. Ogilvie b Shacklock	3	– b Attewell	20
Rev. E. W. R. Walters not out	64	– st Carlin b Attewell	0
Mr S. J. Crawford b Shacklock	9	– c Cloete b Attewell	20
Lieut. Baker b Shacklock	10	– b Shacklock	1
Mr L. H. Palmer b Shacklock	0	– lbw b Attewell	0
Mr F. Latimer b Shacklock	1	– b Gunn	20
Mr C. Latimer b Attewell	14	– not out	6
B 9, l-b 1	10	B 8, l-b 3	11
	141		117

Umpires: J. West and Parnham.

MCC AND GROUND v SUSSEX

Played at Lord's, May 12, 13, 1890

The rain in the latter portion of the previous week and during the early part of Monday had so thoroughly saturated the ground that it seemed extremely likely the commencement of this fixture would have to be postponed. However, on Monday afternoon the weather cleared up, and though it was found impossible to start until twenty minutes to four, so much progress was made that the MCC completed an innings of 57, and Sussex were all dismissed for 41. The features of the play were the splendid bowling of Jesse Hide and Bean for one side and of Martin and Attewell for the other. Hide created something like a sensation by taking four wickets – those of Flowers, Mr Ford, Mr Wright and Mr Russel – in one over. On Tuesday the wicket proved quite as difficult as before, and the bowlers again had matters so much their own way that Hide and Mr C. A. Smith dismissed the MCC in the second innings for 41, and then Attewell and Martin got rid of six Sussex men before the county could make the 53 required to win. The whole match occupied barely four hours, and altogether thirty-six wickets fell for 187 runs. Hide and Attewell each took nine wickets, the former for just over 4 runs each, and Attewell for just under 4 runs, but Mr C. A. Smith, who obtained seven wickets for 16 runs, did absolutely the best performance in the match. Only two men made double figures and thirteen batsmen failed to score at all.

MCC and Ground

Mr A. N. Hornby c Butt b Hide	45	– c Tebay b Smith	8
W. Gunn b Bean	2	– run out	0
W. Barnes c and b Hide	0	– c Tebay b Hide	1
W. Chatterton b Bean	4	– b Hide	5
W. Flowers c Charlwood b Hide	3	– b Smith	5
Mr W. J. Ford c Tebay b Hide	0	– b Smith	4
Mr C. W. Wright c Charlwood b Hide	0	– not out	5
Mr J. S. Russel c and b Hide	0	– c Quaife b Smith	1
W. Attewell c Tebay b Bean	0	– c and b Smith	0
F. Martin not out	2	– c Humphreys b Smith	1
M. Sherwin c Charlwood b Hide	0	– b Smith	3
B 1	1	B 3	3
	57		36

Sussex

W. Quaife b Attewell	4	– not out	6
G. Bean c and b Martin	8	– c Gunn b Attewell	33
Mr E. J. McCormick b Martin	8	– b Martin	0
J. Hide c Hornby b Martin	0	– c Gunn b Attewell	3
Mr W. Newham c Ford b Martin	1	– c Sherwin b Attewell	2
H. Tebay c Chatterton b Martin	6	– c Barnes b Attewell	4
Charlwood b Attewell	6	– b Attewell	4
Mr C. A. Smith c Chatterton b Martin	7	– not out	1
W. Humphreys b Attewell	0		
H. Butt c Gunn b Attewell	0		
F. Gibb not out	0		
B 1	1		
	41		53

Sussex Bowling

	Overs	Mdns	Runs	Wkts	Overs	Mdns	Runs	Wkts
Hide	11	0	22	7	12	6	17	2
Bean	11	2	34	3				
Mr Smith					12	4	16	7

MCC and Ground Bowling

	Overs	Mdns	Runs	Wkts	Overs	Mdns	Runs	Wkts
Martin	15	7	20	6	4	1	23	1
Attewell	14.4	6	20	4	7.3	1	15	5
Flowers					5	0	15	0

Umpires: G. Hay and W. Scotton.

MCC AND GROUND v NOTTINGHAMSHIRE

Played at Lord's, June 1, 1891

After nearly a fortnight of bad weather there was a hot sun shining on the soft ground at Lord's when this match commenced, and the spectators present were fully prepared to see some curious cricket, though few could have anticipated that the game would begin and end in the single day. Such, however, proved to be the case. Mr Grace on winning the toss put Notts. in, and the county, weakened by the absence of Arthur Shrewsbury and Mr Dixon, failed so completely that they were all dismissed by Mr Ferris and Rawlin in the course of twenty-five overs for the paltry score of 21. Seven members of the team failed to get a run between them, and Mr C. W. Wright, though he only obtained 5, alone showed any ability against the bowling. Poor as was the total, it will be noticed that there were six extras. When the Club went in some far superior batting was witnessed, though certainly the ground had slightly improved. Mr Grace and Mr Ferris made 37 for the first partnership, and Mr Pope and Mr Murdoch 33 for the third, while a useful contribution later on by Davidson helped the total to 127 before all the side were got rid of. The county had a balance of 106 against them, and though they did better than before they only made 69, and in the end were beaten in an innings with 37 runs to spare. Mr Wright, as at the first attempt, batted capitally, and he and William Attewell actually put together 37 for the first wicket, but no one else reached double figures and there were four more "duck's eggs". The victory was a memorable one for the MCC, and the honours were fairly borne off by the four Australians playing. Messrs Ferris, Pope, and Murdoch made 68 runs between them, and the first named in addition took eleven wickets for 32 runs, while James Phillips obtained five wickets in the second innings for 30 runs.

Nottinghamshire

Mr C. W. Wright b Ferris	5	– lbw b Phillips	39
W. Flowers c and b Rawlin	3	– c Foley b Ferris	3
W. Gunn b Rawlin	0	– lbw b Phillips	7
W. Barnes c Murdoch b Rawlin	0	– b Phillips	2
H. B. Daft c Grace b Rawlin	0	– c Grace b Ferris	1
Mr O. Redgate c and b Ferris	3	– b Ferris	0
W. Attewell c Grace b Ferris	0	– c Whiteside b Ferris	16
J. Wharmby c Phillips b Ferris	0	– c Rawlin b Ferris	0
T. Attewell c Rawlin b Ferris	0	– b Phillips	0
M. Sherwin not out	4	– b Phillips	0
F. Needham b Ferris	0	– not out	1
B 4, l-b 2	6		
	21		69

MCC and Ground

Mr W. G. Grace c and b W. Attewell	18
Mr J. J. Ferris lbw b Flowers	16
Mr R. J. Pope b Redgate	31
Mr W. L. Murdoch b Barnes	21
W. Chatterton b Needham	6
Mr C. P. Foley b Needham	0
G. Davidson b W. Attewell	18
Mr A. H. Heath not out	2
J. T. Rawlin c W. Attewell b Redgate	1
J. Phillips b Redgate	3
J. P. Whiteside lbw b W. Attewell	3
B 4, l-b 3, n-b 1	8
	127

MCC and Ground Bowling

	Overs	Mdns	Runs	Wkts	Overs	Mdns	Runs	Wkts
Ferris	13	7	7	6	17	8	25	5
Rawlin	12	8	8	4	6	1	14	0
Phillips					10.4	2	30	5

Nottinghamshire Bowling

	Overs	Mdns	Runs	Wkts
W. Attewell	30.3	16	28	3
Barnes	17	6	29	1
Wharmby	1	0	4	0
Flowers	12	3	21	1
Needham	10	4	17	2
T. Attewell	4	0	12	0
Redgate	6	1	8	3

Umpires: A. Rylott and W. Mycroft.

OXFORD v CAMBRIDGE

Played at Lord's, June 29, 30, 1891

The trial games of the two Universities proved conclusively the immense superiority of Cambridge, but the prestige of the match was sufficient to ensure a big attendance, 10,218 people paying for admission on the first day, and 9,077 on the second. These figures, however, large as they are, give a very inadequate idea of the number of people present, the company on the opening day being estimated by the MCC authorities at something between 17,000 and 18,000. Fortunately for the crowds of visitors the match, after being altogether one-sided in its early stages, proved singularly exciting on the second afternoon, the finish indeed being the closest since the memorable match in 1875, when Oxford won by six runs. Cambridge in the end won by two wickets, but without any disparagement to the Oxford men, who played an up-hill game with the utmost resolution, we cannot think that this result represented with any approach to accuracy the real difference between the two sides. Had the elevens met three times under even conditions we are firmly of opinion that victory would always have rested with Cambridge. Each side started the match with eight "old blues," but before luncheon on the first day the Hon. F. J. N. Thesiger, in trying to field a ball, slipped down and sprained his hand. As he was unable to go on playing the Cambridge captain courteously allowed his place to be taken by T. B. Case, a senior from Winchester and a son of the Mr T. B. Case who played in the great Oxford elevens of 1864 and 1865 under Mr R. A. H. Mitchell's captaincy. The other new comers in the Oxford eleven were A. J. Boger, a freshman from Winchester, W. H. Brain, the wicket-keeper, a senior from Clifton, and H. D. Watson, a senior from Harrow. The new men in the Cambridge eleven were W. I. Rowell, of Marlborough, G. J. V. Weigall – both seniors – and C. M. Wells, a freshman from Dulwich College. The eleventh place had been left open up to the morning of the match, the choice laying between C. P. Foley, of the 1890 team, and the famous Rugby football player Martin Scott. The weather being fine and the wicket hard the preference was given to Foley, whose nerve and experience proved invaluable in the last stage of the game.

On the opening day the superiority of Cambridge was clearly demonstrated, the Light Blues playing an innings of 210, and then getting seven Oxford wickets down for 88. It cannot be said that the Cambridge batting came up to expectation, the early play indeed being of a very disappointing character. Possibly a couple of showers which fell during the first hour and drove the players to the pavilion had some effect on the pitch, but anyway there were four of the best wickets down for 38, and five for 61. The turning point of the innings came with the partnership of Hill and McGregor, who put on 69 runs while they were together, and saved their side from failure. Hill headed the score with 62, the result of nearly two hours' batting. Apart from a chance to Wilson at cover-slip when he had made 14, there was very little fault to be found with his invaluable innings. He hit eight 4s, a 3, five 2s, and seventeen singles. Streatfeild also played quite up to his form. The best cricket of the day was certainly seen between a quarter-past five and seven o'clock, when Oxford were in, the bowling of Woods, the wicket-keeping of McGregor, and the batting of Llewelyn being of an excellence altogether exceptional. Woods bowled faster and perhaps better than he ever bowled before, but Llewelyn played him with the utmost confidence, and McGregor took his fastest balls in a style that not even Blackham could have surpassed. Apart from Llewelyn and Smith, the Oxford batsmen found Woods' pace far too much for them, and at the call of time seven wickets, as we have already said, were down for 88. Llewelyn was batting an hour and twenty-five minutes for his 38, and considering the bowling he had to face, his innings was certainly the best of the day.

On the second morning Oxford went on batting at twenty minutes to twelve, and so difficult did the batsmen find the task of making runs that, though the completion of the innings lasted three-quarters of an hour, the overnight score was only increased by 20, the total thus reaching 108. Woods in this innings took seven wickets for 60 runs – a splendid average on a hard ground – and was seen at his very best. Being 102 behind, Oxford had necessarily to follow on, and up to a certain point there was nothing in the cricket that gave promise of a close finish, Oxford, with five of their best wickets down, still requiring 21 runs to avoid a single innings defeat. A great change, however, came with the partnership of Wilson and Smith, who got together at twenty minutes past three, and by some very brilliant hitting added 47 runs to the score. With two wickets to fall Oxford were only 34 runs ahead, but Brain and Berkeley stayed so long that the ninth wicket added 23 runs and the tenth 32, the result being that the score reached 191, or 89 to the good. Wilson's 53 – the highest score made for Oxford and in every way an admirable display of cricket – included a late cut for 5, four 4s, two 3s, and four 2s. He was at the wickets an hour and forty minutes, and it would not be easy to overpraise his batting. Woods in this innings took four wickets for 72 runs, and it seemed to be the general opinion that he had somewhat over-exerted himself on the opening day. Cambridge had only 90 runs to get to win, and had they been able to start fresh in the morning there is little doubt that they would have made the runs very easily. As it was, however, they had to go in after several hours' hard work in the field, and experienced judges of the game were quite prepared to find the task a far heavier one than it looked on paper. The start was unfortunate for Cambridge, Rowell being bowled in the second over when only a single run had been scored, and Weigall being out in the same way with the total at 12. However, with Douglas and Foley together, matters went much better, and for the third or fourth time during the day the match looked as good as over. Runs came at a good pace, and the score was carried to 47, or only 43 to win, with eight wickets to go down. Then as a sort of forlorn hope the Oxford captain made a change of bowling, putting Berkeley on at the pavilion end in place of Smith. This change, as it happened, had astonishing results, and made the last part of the match intensely interesting. In his first over without any addition to the score Berkeley clean bowled Douglas. Foley, who was playing very fine cricket, was then joined by Hill, and by slow degrees the total was carried to 60, or 30 to win. At this point Hill was caught at slip, and Jackson, who followed in, was bowled at 67, Cambridge with five wickets to go down still requiring 23 runs to win. McGregor at half-past six became Foley's partner, and when the score had been raised to 78, or only 12 to get with five wickets to fall, the match seemed a certainty. At this total, however, a catch in the slips got rid of Foley. Streatfeild then joined McGregor, and seven of the twelve runs required were quickly obtained. However, at 88, or only two runs to win, Streatfeild was bowled, and with the game a tie a yorker from Berkeley dismissed McGregor. Though all chance of Oxford's winning had departed excitement ran high as Woods left the pavilion. That famous cricketer quickly settled the matter, driving the first ball he received to the boundary and so winning the match for Cambridge by two wickets. The Light Blues owed a great deal to Foley, as but for his coolness and confidence at a very critical time there is no saying what might have happened.

Cambridge

Mr R. N. Douglas b Bassett	4	– b Berkeley	15
Mr W. I. Rowell b Bassett	3	– b Smith	1
Mr G. J. V. Weigall c Palairet b Smith	11	– b Bassett	2
Mr C. P. Foley b Smith	12	– c Boger b Berkeley	41
Mr A. J. L. Hill c Brain b Smith	62	– c Berkeley b Bassett	4
Mr F. S. Jackson b Bassett	10	– b Berkeley	2
Mr G. McGregor b Berkeley	29	– b Berkeley	8
Mr E. C. Streatfeild b Berkeley	36	– b Berkeley	8
Mr C. M. Wells st Brain b Bassett	11	– not out	0
Mr S. M. J. Woods b Smith	0	– not out	4
Mr D. L. A. Jephson not out	10	B 8	8
B 13, l-b 7, n-b 2	22		
	210		93

Oxford

Mr W. D. Llewelyn b Hill	38	– c Douglas b Woods	24
Mr H. D. Watson c Streatfeild b Woods	7	– c Weigall b Woods	17
Mr M. R. Jardine b Woods	0	– c Hill b Streatfeild	15
Mr L. C. H. Palairet c McGregor b Jackson	2	– c Streatfeild b Woods	11
Mr T. B. Case c Rowell b Woods	5	– run out	2
Mr G. L. Wilson c and b Woods	0	– b Streatfeild	53
Mr E. Smith b Woods	16	– c Jephson b Woods	32
Mr A. J. Boger run out	4	– c Jackson b Wells	5
Mr H. Bassett b Woods	15	– c Streatfeild b Jackson	0
Jr W. H. Brain c and b Woods	6	– c Jephson b Wells	7
Mr G. F. H. Berkeley not out	7	– not out	8
B 5, l-b 3	8	B 4, l-b 8, w 3, n-b 2	17
	108		191

Oxford Bowling

	Overs	Mdns	Runs	Wkts	Overs	Mdns	Runs	Wkts
Mr Bassett	37	13	71	4	22	4	44	2
Mr Smith	30	4	81	4	9	4	21	1
Mr Berkeley	16	3	23	2	12.3	5	20	5
Mr Wilson	9	2	13	—				

Cambridge Bowling

	Overs	Mdns	Runs	Wkts	Overs	Mdns	Runs	Wkts
Mr Woods	35.3	14	60	7	32	6	72	4
Mr Jackson	21	9	24	1	22	9	46	1
Mr Hill	14	6	16	1	4	0	12	0
Mr Wells					10	4	18	2
Mr Streatfeild					15.2	4	26	2

Umpires: J. Phillips and W. A. J. West.

MR S. M. J. WOODS IN THE OXFORD AND CAMBRIDGE MATCH

Mr S. M. J. Woods, who, in 1891, played for the last time for Cambridge, bowled so finely during his four years that his performances are quite worthy of special reference. We give accordingly his seven analyses for the four matches, the first of which was drawn in favour of Cambridge, while the other three all resulted in victories for the Light Blues:

	Overs	Mdns	Runs	Wkts
1888	39	23	48	6
1889	20.4	7	42	6
1889	24.3	8	40	5
1890	14.3	5	25	4
1890	16.4	7	31	4
1891	35.3	14	60	7
1891	32	6	72	4

In all, therefore, he took thirty-six wickets for 318 runs.

MCC AND GROUND v LANCASHIRE

Played at Lord's, May 11, 12, 1893

While the county put practically their best eleven into the field, the Marylebone Club had a very weak batting team, so many of their amateurs failing them that they had to enlist the services of nine members of the ground staff. Notwithstanding this disadvantage, however, the MCC held their own on the first day, and on the second afternoon actually won an exciting match by one wicket. On Thursday Lancashire went in first, and, after losing two wickets for 7 runs, raised the total to 59 before the third man was out, but in the end the innings only amounted to 138. Poor as was this score, the Club, with four batsmen out for 27, did not look like heading it at one time, but, thanks largely to Rawlin and Davidson, whose partnership yielded 52, a score of 155 was reached, Rawlin obtaining 65 of these, in an hour and three-quarters, by four 4s, three 3s, eight 2s, and twenty-four singles. Oakley, a medium-paced left-handed bowler, justified his first appearance for the county by taking four wickets for 33. Subsequently Lancashire scored 13 without loss before stumps were drawn. On Friday, Rawlin followed up his batting success by some very fine bowling, and Lancashire were all dismissed for 119, Baker and Tinsley being the only successful batsmen. This left the MCC 103 to make, but, despite a splendid display on the part of Mr Foley, eight wickets went down for 41 runs, and the county's triumph seemed assured. On J. T. Hearne joining the old Cambridge cricketer, however, a complete and remarkable change took place. The professional ought to have been run out almost directly, and this mistake cost Lancashire the match. Mr Foley played as well as at any period in his career, and Hearne gave him most valuable assistance. Briggs and Mold were knocked off in favour of Oakley and Smith, who in turn gave way to the original bowlers, but it was not until the game was a tie – 102 – that Hearne was bowled. Then Martin came in and made the winning hit. The chief credit of the victory belonged to Mr Foley, who carried his bat through the innings for a magnificent 62. He played the excellent bowling with the greatest skill and confidence the whole time, and hit seven 4s, five 3s, and three 2s.

Lancashire

A. Ward b J. T. Hearne	0	– b J. T. Hearne	22
F. H. Sugg run out	0	– b Rawlin	3
A. Smith c Storer b Davidson	41	– b J. T. Hearne	0
J. Briggs c A. Hearne b Rawlin	32	– b Rawlin	0
G. R. Baker c Carpenter b Davidson	21	– b Rawlin	30
A. Tinsley not out	20	– c Storer b A. Hearne	23
Mr S. M. Crosfield b Martin	3	– c A. Hearne b Davidson	1
Mr A. T. Kemble c Ford b Martin	0	– b Rawlin	3
W. Oakley c and b Martin	2	– b Rawlin	0
A. Watson b Davidson	2	– not out	18
A. Mold c Moss b Martin	9	– c A. Hearne b Davidson	9
B 6, l-b 2	8	B 9, l-b 1	10
	138		119

MCC and Ground

A. Hearne b Mold	0 – b Mold	0
Mr C. P. Foley b Oakley	9 – not out	62
G. Davidson b Briggs	43 – b Mold	5
W. Storer c Sugg b Oakley	0 – c Watson b Mold	6
H. Carpenter b Mold	0 – b Mold	0
J. T. Rawlin c and b Oakley	65 – c Baker b Mold	1
Mr F. G. J. Ford b Mold	14 – b Briggs	2
Moss c Kemble b Watson	3 – b Briggs	4
J. E. West c Briggs b Oakley	9 – b Briggs	0
J. T. Hearne run out	0 – b Mold	19
F. Martin not out	3 – not out	3
B 7, l-b 2	9 B 1, l-b 2	3
	155	105

MCC Bowling

	Overs	Mdns	Runs	Wkts	Overs	Mdns	Runs	Wkts
J. T. Hearne	10	3	26	1	19	10	29	2
Martin	35	13	51	4	6	2	13	0
Davidson	18	8	36	3	12.3	3	29	2
Rawlin	11	4	17	1	21	5	35	5
A. Hearne					3	2	3	1

Lancashire Bowling

	Overs	Mdns	Runs	Wkts	Overs	Mdns	Runs	Wkts
Mold	24	7	57	3	25.3	7	57	6
Oakley	20.4	11	33	4	4	1	5	0
Watson	12	3	19	1				
Briggs	15	4	37	1	23	13	36	3
Smith					2	0	4	0

Umpires: R. Clayton and A. Rylott.

M.C.C. AND GROUND v SUSSEX

Played at Lord's, May 15, 16, 17, 1893

Unlike the team in the Lancashire match, the eleven representing the MCC against Sussex was exceedingly powerful in batting, but decidedly weak in bowling. On Sussex winning the toss, there was a fine exhibition of free cricket, and altogether on the first day 406 runs were scored for the loss of ten wickets. At the outset Sussex did fairly well, but with three men out for 79 quite an ordinary score seemed in prospect. However, it was then that Mr Brann came in, and accomplished one of the finest pieces of hitting of the season. During a stay of less than two hours he made 137 out of 177. He batted in most vigorous and fearless fashion, scoring his 100 in a little over an hour and a half. His figures included eighteen 4s, eight 3s and eight 2s. His performance dwarfed everything else done on the side, but Marlow, Mr Murdoch, and Mr Newham played well, and Tate and Lowe added 61 runs for the tenth wicket. In the last hour of the day Stoddart and Foley scored 89 for the MCC, the former by brilliant cricket making 61. On Tuesday the rain, which had only threatened on the previous day, fell and delayed play from one o'clock until past three. Before it came on, however, the overnight not outs had raised the Club total to 95, and Gunn and Mr Foley carried the figures to 206. After the rain the ground became more difficult, and runs were much harder to get. Mr Foley left with the addition of two runs, but Gunn was not dismissed until the total reached 324. His correct and stylish display occupied two hours and fifty minutes, and included a 5, fifteen 4s, two 3s, and seven 2s. Stoddart hit ten 4s and Foley nine. Flowers and Moorhouse alone of the others met with any success, and the innings finished for 345, the last five wickets falling for 21 runs. Sussex lost a wicket in their second attempt for 25 runs before the call of time. Unfortunately, the prospects of a good finish on the Wednesday were spoiled by the weather, only about half an hour's play being possible. In that time two more men were dismissed, and the figures raised to 41. The game was abandoned as a draw in favour of the MCC, Sussex being only 13 runs on with three good wickets down.

Sussex

G. Bean st Sherwin b Attewell	0	– st Sherwin b Attewell	13
F. W. Marlow st Sherwin b Flowers	21	– b Attewell	4
Mr W. L. Murdoch b Moorhouse	25	– b Flowers	10
Mr W. Newham b Attewell	35	– not out	14
Mr G. Brann st Sherwin b Attewell	137	– not out	0
Mr C. A. Smith b Moorhouse	9		
F. H. Guttridge c Stoddart b Moorhouse	0		
W. Humphreys c Sherwin b Moorhouse	8		
H. Butt b Ford	5		
F. W. Tate not out	48		
J. Lowe b Flowers	20		
B 5, l-b 4	9		
	317		41

MCC and Ground

Mr A. E. Stoddart c Humphreys b Bean	62	Mr F. G. J. Ford c Tate b Guttridge	1
Mr C. P. Foley c Butt b Smith	69	W. Attewell not out	3
W. Gunn c Newham b Lowe	124	Mr M. F. Maclean c and b Guttridge	2
W. Barnes b Bean	9	M. Sherwin b Guttridge	0
W. Flowers c Humphreys b Guttridge	41	B 1, l-b 3	4
R. Moorhouse c Bean b Lowe	30		
Rev R. T. Thornton c Smith b Lowe	0		345

MCC and Ground Bowling

	Overs	Mdns	Runs	Wkts	Overs	Mdns	Runs	Wkts
Attewell	46	16	72	3	21	12	21	2
Flowers	35.4	12	87	2	17	10	17	1
Moorhouse	22	12	40	4	4	3	3	0
Barnes	7	3	15	0				
Ford	13	3	49	1				
Maclean	3	0	14	0				
Thornton	3	0	20	0				
Stoddart	4	1	11	0				

Sussex Bowling

	Overs	Mdns	Runs	Wkts
Tate	16	5	46	0
Lowe	19	2	66	3
Guttridge	20	6	50	4
Humphreys	12	0	46	0
Smith	20	6	50	1
Bean	28	16	61	2
Brann	5	0	22	0

OXFORD v CAMBRIDGE

Played at Lord's, July 3, 4, 1893

By comparison with the wonderful game in the previous year, the Oxford and Cambridge match of 1893 was very tame and uneventful. There was one incident, however – with which we shall have occasion for talk further on – that caused a great deal of discussion in all cricket circles, and brought the question of an alteration of rule affecting the follow-on into the region of practical politics. The contest finished towards the close of the second afternoon, Cambridge winning by the enormous majority of 266 runs. That they had very much the stronger side at every point could not be doubted by anyone who watched the cricket, but it is equally certain that the Oxford men played very much below the form that might reasonably have been expected of a team that had only a few weeks before made a close and highly creditable fight against the Australians. On the Cambridge side there were no fewer than eight members of the eleven that had suffered defeat in 1892, the places of G. J. V. Weigall, R. N. Douglas, and D. L. A. Jephson being taken by T. N. Perkins, A. O. Jones, and the young Indian cricketer, Ranjitsinhji. The three new men, it may be mentioned, were all Seniors. Oxford made five changes from the victorious eleven of a twelvemonth before, R. C. N. Palairet, R. W. Rice, G. J. Mordaunt, H. Leveson-Gower, and L. C. V. Bathurst appearing in place of M. R. Jardine, F. A. Phillips, T. B. Case, V. T. Hill, and R. T. Jones. R. C. N. Palairet, Rice, and Bathurst were Seniors, and Mordaunt (Wellington) and Leveson-Gower (Winchester) Freshmen. The match did not show any sign of declining interest, 11,090 people paying for admission on the first day, and 11,466 on the Tuesday. According to the estimate of the MCC officials the full attendance numbered close upon 19,000 on the first day, and not far short of 20,000 on the second. The opening day's cricket was not by any means in accordance with expectation. The weather was fine all the afternoon, and as batsmen all through May and June had been making any number of runs at Lord's it was naturally thought that the scoring would be high. As it turned out, however, an innings was completed on each side for an aggregate of 287, Cambridge making 182 and Oxford 105. From the start of play to the drawing of stumps the ball beat the bat in a way for which no one was prepared, and the general opinion was that the long-continued sunshine of the two previous months had caused the turf to become slightly crumbled. In view of what Cambridge did in their second innings, it is probable that the batting was to some extent at fault, but we cannot believe that the wicket was so easy as those that had been used in the earlier matches. Cambridge led off with every prospect of making a far better score than 182, Jackson and Douglas, the first pair of batsmen, staying together for forty minutes and obtaining 56 runs before they were separated. The partnership was closed by a superb piece of cricket, Bathurst at mid-off catching Douglas in a marvellous way with one hand, from a hard drive. Nothing in the whole match was better than this. Jackson, after playing a capital innings of 38, hit one of Wood's lobs back to the bowler, and from the time he left the Cambridge batting seemed to lose all spirit. Between a quarter-past one and two o'clock three more wickets went down for an addition of only 30 runs, and at the luncheon interval the total with five men out stood at 110. On the game being resumed, Streatfeild hit in capital form for 30, but he received very little support, and by four o'clock the innings was all over. Berkeley bowled wonderfully well taking five wickets at a cost of only 38 runs. After luncheon he was brilliantly successful, four of the last five wickets falling to him at a very small cost. It was not generally thought that Cambridge had made enough runs, but when Oxford went in it was soon seen that 182 was going to be a winning score. L. C. H. Palairet and Rice put on 23 together for the second wicket, but after they had been separated at 29 the Cambridge bowlers had everything their own way. L. C. H. Palairet, who was out fifth at 58, was at the wickets seventy minutes for his 32, his being the only batting in the innings that was in any degree noteworthy. Nine wickets were down for 95, and then on Wilson, the last man, joining Brain, an incident occurred which is likely to be talked about for a good many years to come. Three runs were added, making the score 98, or 84 short of Cambridge's total, and Oxford thus required only 5 runs to save the follow-on. The two batsmen were then seen to consult together between the wickets, and it was at once evident to those who had grasped the situation that the Dark Blues were going to throw away a wicket in order that their side might go in again. Had one of them acted on his own account, it is probable that the object would have been gained, but Wells, who was bowling from the Pavilion end, saw at once what was intended and promptly set to work to frustrate it. Going over the crease, he bowled a ball wide to the boundary, and then after an unsuccessful effort to bowl a wide all along the ground, sent another round-arm ball to the ropes, thus giving away eight runs, but preventing Oxford from going in a second time. The incident gave rise to a great deal of talk and discussion, to say nothing of special articles in various newspapers. We are inclined to think, however, that in some quarters the matter was treated far too seriously, the point being overlooked that all the players immediately concerned were actuated entirely by the desire to do the best thing possible for their side. Particularly would we wish to exonerate Wells from all blame. He saw clearly that Oxford, with the idea of securing an advantage, meant to throw away a wicket, and we hold that he was perfectly justified in taking any means to prevent them that the law permitted. Whatever may be thought of the incident, it had the immediate effect of bringing the question of the follow-on under the consideration of the MCC Committee. Immediately after the follow-on had been prevented, Oxford's innings closed for 106, and the day's cricket came to an end. Wells, who was unchanged at the Pavilion end, bowled exceptionally well, and took five wickets for 39 runs.

As Cambridge had secured a lead of 79, it was felt that, unless they failed very badly in their second innings, they had the match in their hands, and this view was abundantly borne out by the result. Going in soon after half-past eleven on the second morning, Cambridge lost Douglas with the score at 23, but with Jackson and Latham together the best batting in the match was seen. Jackson played very brilliantly and made so large a proportion of the runs that when at last he was bowled in jumping out to drive Berkeley, he had scored 57 out of 74, his innings including no fewer than ten 4s. Latham, who scored with much greater freedom after Jackson's departure, played a splendid innings of 54 but he did not receive much support, and at lunch time seven wickets were down for 153. Then on a fresh start being made – shortly before three o'clock – some cricket was shown entirely different in character to anything else seen in the game, Perkins and Gay hitting with such extraordinary freedom that in the course of half an hour they added 71 to the score. While they were sending the ball all over the field it was difficult to understand why the batting on the previous day should have been so cramped and cautious. Perkins was out at last with the total at 224 – the eighth wicket having put on 77 runs – and at ten minutes to four the innings came to an end for 254, no fewer than 101 runs having been obtained after luncheon in sixty-five minutes. Berkeley again bowled very well, and with four wickets for 56 runs made his aggregate for the match nine wickets for 94 – a capital performance. Oxford were left with 331 to get to win, and on a wicket that had certainly somewhat crumbled it was felt that they had no chance of success. For the deplorable exhibition of batting that they gave, however, no one could have been prepared. Nothing so feeble has been seen in the University match since A. G. Steel and P. H. Morton got rid of Oxford in 1878 for a total of 32. Fry, who went in second wicket down with the score at 7, and was out eighth at 55, did his best to redeem the credit of the side, but, apart from his batting and some patient play by Rice, the cricket was melancholy in the extreme. After five wickets had fallen for 52, Jackson, who had been sharing the bowling with Wells, put on Streatfeild and Bromley-Davenport, and these two bowlers met with such success that in a little more than a quarter of an hour the last five wickets went down for an addition of only 12 runs. The result had been so long foreseen that the match ended very quietly, but the Cambridge eleven received some well-deserved cheers as they walked back to the Pavilion. Bromley-Davenport had the extraordinary bowling record in the game of five wickets for 11 runs – two for 9 and three for 2. With this match F. S. Jackson brought his career as a University cricketer to a brilliantly successful conclusion. Not only did he captain the winning side, but he had the satisfaction of playing the highest individual innings and making the largest aggregate of runs.

Cambridge

Batsman	First innings		Second innings	
Mr F. S. Jackson (*Harrow and Trinity*), c and b Wood	38	–	b Berkeley	57
Mr J. Douglas (*Dulwich and Selwyn*), c Bathurst b Wilson	25	–	b Berkeley	4
Mr P. H. Latham (*Malvern and Pembroke*), c L. C. H. Palairet b Fry	21	–	c Bathurst b Berkeley	54
Mr K. S. Ranjitsinhji (*Trinity*) b Berkeley	9	–	c Wilson b Bathurst	0
Mr A. J. L. Hill (*Marlborough and Jesus*) b Fry	1	–	c Brain b Bathurst	8
Mr E. C. Streatfeild (*Charterhouse and Pembroke*) c Brain b Berkeley	30	–	c Brain b Wilson	0
Mr C. M. Wells (*Dulwich and Trinity*) c Brain b Berkeley	8	–	c Leveson-Gower b Fry	7
Mr T. N. Perkins (*Leatherhead and Jesus*) c Brain b Bathurst	18	–	b Wilson	37
Mr L. H. Gay (*Brighton and Clare*) b Berkeley	6	–	b Bathurst	37
Mr A. O. Jones (*Bedford Modern and Jesus*) b Berkeley	2	–	not out	16
Mr H. R. Bromley-Davenport (*Eton and Trinity Hall*), not out	2	–	b Berkeley	9
B 11, l-b 9, w 2	22		B 18, l-b 5, w 2	25
	182			254

Oxford

Batsman	First innings		Second innings	
Mr L. C. H. Palairet (*Repton and Oriel*) c Gay b Davenport	32	–	b Jackson	2
Mr R. C. N. Palairet (*Repton and Oriel*) c Hill b Wells	4	–	lbw b Wells	2
Mr R. W. Rice (*Cardiff and Jesus*) c Ranjitsinhji b Jackson	7	–	c Gay b Wells	12
Mr C. B. Fry (*Repton and Wadham*) b Wells	7	–	c Davenport b Streatfeild	31
Mr G. J. Mordaunt (*Wellington and University*) b Wells	1	–	c Jones b Jackson	5
Mr H. D. G. Leveson-Gower (*Winchester and Magdalen*) lbw b Wells	12	–	b Jackson	5
Mr L. C. V. Bathurst (*Radley and Trinity*) c Gay b Streatfeild	6	–	b Davenport	2
Mr J. B. Wood (*Marlborough and Balliol*) c Ranjitsinhji b Davenport	0	–	b Davenport	0
Mr W. H. Brain (*Clifton and Oriel*) not out	10	–	c Ranjitsinhji b Davenport	0
Mr G. F. H. Berkeley (*Wellington and Keble*) c Hill b Wells	14	–	not out	1
Mr T. S. B. Wilson (*Bath and Trinity*) st Gay b Streatfeild	0	–	b Streatfeild	0
B 2, l-b 2, w 4, n-b 5	13		B 3, l-b 1	4
	106			64

Oxford Bowling

	Overs	Mdns	Runs	Wkts	Overs	Mdns	Runs	Wkts
Berkeley	30	12	38	5	25	11	56	4
Wood	14	2	42	1	7	0	27	0
Wilson	11	1	26	1	22	5	52	2
Bathurst	16	7	27	1	19	7	68	3
Fry	9	0	27	2	11	4	23	1
Leveson-Gower					1	0	3	0

Cambridge Bowling

	Overs	Mdns	Runs	Wkts	Overs	Mdns	Runs	Wkts
Wells	34	19	39	5	23	10	27	2
Jackson	14	4	35	1	23	12	22	3
Bromley-Davenport .	11	7	9	2	4	2	2	3
Streatfeild	8.3	4	10	2	4.4	1	9	2

Umpires: W. Heane and J. Phillips.

THE "FOLLOW ON." [1893]

The much-discussed incident in the Oxford and Cambridge match last season brought into sudden prominence the question of the advisability of some alteration being made in the present law which governs the follow on. Up till within a comparatively recent period it was generally regarded as a distinct advantage to gain a lead of 80 or more runs on the first innings, and so compel the opposing side to go in for the second time; but there has gradually come about a marked change of opinion on this point, captains having found that on the carefully-prepared wickets to which we are accustomed at the present day there is considerable risk in having to bowl and field through two innings in succession. So far as I am aware, the desirability of some change in the law was first broached in Australia, where the big matches are played through to a finish, irrespective of the number of days they may occupy, and where, moreover, the dryness of the grounds made the question more pressing than up to last season it had been with us. Indeed, little attention had been given to the matter in England until the occasion of the Oxford and Cambridge match in July, when Oxford's attempt to secure a follow on and Mr C. M. Wells's successful endeavours to frustrate their intention set all cricketing England talking upon the subject. Thinking that a free discussion on the point would be of interest to the readers of *Wisden's Almanack*, I communicated with a large number of prominent players and other first-rate authorities, whose various views may be found in the following pages. As might have been expected, I found considerable diversity of opinion existing. – S. H. P.

Mr E. M. Grace says:– "The rule about the 'follow on' was no doubt made with the idea that the apparently winning side should still have an advantage, and the same thing follows about declaring the innings over. I think it would be a good alteration in the rule if the leading side should have the option of doing which they thought best. This would prevent both the bowlers from bowling wides and the batsman from trying to get out. And in one-day matches it would prevent such a case as this. Say A. is playing B. A. makes 121 runs, and when B. has made 60 he has one, two, or three wickets to fall, as the case might be. B.'s captain says, 'Our innings is over,' and, as the law now is, B.'s side go on batting, instead of, perhaps, having to field the rest of the day."

Mr R. A. H. Mitchell writes:– "I think the best solution of the difficulty is to abolish the 'follow on' altogether, and to allow the closure to be applied at any time, instead of restricting it to the last day of the match. Gate-money considerations may cause some objection to be raised to this, but they ought not to outweigh the interests of sport. When the present rule was made, there was not power, as now, to close the innings. In one-day matches I would let the rule stand as it is now for many obvious reasons. Some have proposed that the side which is 80 or more runs ahead at the close of the first innings shall have the option of putting the other side in, or going in again themselves. This, I think, would be very unfair. The side that has the advantage has already won the toss, and possibly gained this advantage thereby. The option would again give them the choice of going in first or second, as their interests decided. In this way you would increase the value of winning the toss. Now, most people think that the advantage is already unduly great. You might, of course, raise the number from 80 to 100, 120, or 150, or fix a percentage to decide whether a side is to follow on, but I do not think this would be so satisfactory."

Mr Richard Daft says:– "I think the 'follow on' rule should be done away with now that the declaring rule has come in."

Mr A. P. Lucas writes:– "With regard to the 'follow on' rule, I do not see how it can be altered. I do not think the number of runs a side is behind ought to be increased so that they must follow on, as it would be putting them to a greater disadvantage than they are now. Generally the side winning the toss has a great advantage, and therefore I think the other side ought to have some advantage if possible. It sometimes happens that the side going in first have a good hard wicket to bat on, and then there is some rain, so that the side which lost the toss have a wet wicket to bat on, and so have to follow on. By the time their second innings is finished the wicket is fast again, and the other side have a great advantage. In a case like this I do not think the side winning the toss ought to have so great an advantage. The only way to avoid this would be to do away with the 'follow on' altogether, and this I should like to see done. Now that the closure rule is in force I do not think the following on rule is needed. I cannot help thinking that the closure might be applied on the second day of a match instead of the third."

Mr John Shuter, one of the very few cricketers who are in favour of letting the matter stand exactly as it does, writes:– "I am very strongly of opinion that the present law in connection with the 'follow on' needs no alteration. I think I am correct in stating that in the very large majority of cases the side which follows on loses the match. For this reason alone the present law must be a good one. Any change in the law in the direction of abolishing the compulsory part of the 'follow on' would, in all probability, tend to an increase in the number of drawn matches – a result which is most undesirable."

The Hon. Ivo Bligh says:– "I hold the opinion strongly that the rule *re* 'following on' should be altered, making it optional for the side who have the lead whether they make the others follow on or not."

Mr J. A. Dixon is of the same opinion as Mr Bligh. He writes:– "I am in favour of an alteration in the present rule to the effect that the 'follow on' shall be at the option of the side batting first and scoring 80 runs more than their opponents."

Mr H. T. Hewett says:– "I should like to see the 'follow on' entirely abolished and Law 54 amended so as to empower a side to close their innings at any period of the match, and, should occasion arise, to waive their claim to a second innings."

Mr F. S. Jackson, who was captain of the Cambridge team in 1893, had necessarily a strong personal interest in the matter. He says:– "The present rule, '80 runs behind, follow on,' is out of date, and that for two reasons – (1) a new rule has been introduced enabling the captains to declare an innings on the last day of a match at an end; (2) the grounds are too good, and give too much advantage, in my opinion, to the side 80 runs behind on the first innings. This is my proposal: To make the number of runs behind 90, and make it optional for the captain of the side with 90 runs advantage either to go in himself – having in view, of course, the declaring of his innings at an end – or put the other side in again, which, of course, he would do if he saw any advantage. You would thus do away with such a forced fiasco as a 4 no-ball, a 4 wide, etc., as in the 'Varsity match of 1893. I very much want to hear other views on the subject."

The veteran Robert Carpenter is another of the supporters of the "optional" theory. He writes:– "In my opinion the granting to that side who have placed their opponents 80 runs behind on the first innings the option of going in themselves or making the others follow on would do go, it being a harmless alteration of the law. It would be difficult to frame a law to keep cricketers from playing as suited them best, according to how the match stood, but this giving choice would do away with certain loose play connected with the 'follow on.' "

Robert Thoms, the most experienced of umpires, and an old and valued correspondent of *Wisden*, is also in favour of letting the "follow on" be at the option of the side which has gained a lead of 80 or more on the first innings, his view, though expressed at greater length, being identical with that of Carpenter. He says:– "Like the closure, which latterly was added to the laws, I am inclined to think it would be beneficial if our cricket legislators – the Marylebone Club – were to modify Law 53 as to the 'follow on,' by giving the option of choice to the side holding the lead of whether they will put their opponents in the minority of 80 on the first innings in again, or whether they would go in for their second innings themselves instead. Having on many occasions seen false play arise – attached to this 'follow on' business – wherein bowlers and fieldsmen don't try to get the batsmen out, but rather to let them get runs, and *vice versa* – batsmen wilfully getting themselves out – leads me to believe that if the law were qualified – to render it optional – as above stated, it would, like the 'closure,' do away with a loophole that tends at times to bring forth unseemly play in the cricket ground. Not that, if even this alteration be granted, it will stop other 'subterfuges' from occasionally cropping up. For in cricket, as in every other game, *finesse* will be resorted to in the hope of averting defeat. But that I need not dwell on, for the grand old game is played with the greatest keenness and integrity, and this matter of alteration – to be or not to be – will be decided by the MCC, who are ever watchful for the best interests of our national game."

Mr W. Newham says:– "My opinion is that the side holding the advantage of the 80 runs lead should have the option of either going in themselves or sending their opponents in the second time. My reason for taking such a view as this is that, under ordinary circumstances, this advantage would not be gained until some time on the second day of the match, so that the side having this lead could bat for the remainder of the day, and then, taking advantage of the closure rule, would be able to send in their opponents as soon as they wished on the third day."

Mr M. C. Kemp writes:– "I am in favour of any change in the law with regard to the 'follow on' which will be likely to reduce the number of drawn games, and not give the side which follows on an advantage to which its failure to avert the follow on does not entitle it. I am in favour of raising the number of runs considerably – up to 120 if necessary. If the present number, 80, be retained, the question of the 'follow on' should, in my opinion, be left to the decision of the captain of the side which has the lead of 80 runs. I should also have no objection to seeing a captain empowered to declare his innings over on the second day if his side have, in his opinion, made a sufficient number of runs. This, I fancy, would diminish the number of drawn games due to one side making a phenomenal score, and not leaving themselves time to get their opponents out."

Mr C. W. Wright shares Mr Shuter's opinion that the law should remain unchanged. He says:– "Of course there are distinctly two sides to the question of the 'follow on.' In the first place I don't think the question would have arisen if the past had not been an exceptional season for hard wickets and batsmen, and the unfortunate incident had not occurred in the 'Varsity match. We all know that after getting a big score – say, 280 – when the opposite side goes in and makes 290, it seems very hard to have to go on bowling and fielding when tired out, but then that depends solely on the toss. If you alter the rule, and say the fielding side shall have the choice whether they bat or make the other side follow on, you give a distinct advantage to the stronger side over the weaker, which isn't fair. For instance, in our ordinary English summer this may happen at any time:– Notts. v Yorkshire, Monday, July 1st. Notts. win the toss; go in on a good, slow wicket (weather threatening); make 160; all out at 4.30. Yorkshire go in; make 20 for two wickets when down comes the rain. It also rains early Tuesday morning. At ten o'clock out comes a blazing sun; Yorkshire have a piece of bird-lime to bat on at first; never recover themselves, though the wicket improves, and are all out for 70 (90 behind). The wicket rolls out plumb. It is a monstrous thing that Notts. should have the option of going in to bat on a plumb wicket after Yorkshire have had all the bad luck of losing the toss and in the matter of weather. To go on: Notts go in again; make 260 for six wickets at lunch on Wednesday; declare; put Yorkshire in, with 350 to win. Notts. cannot lose, and have ample time to get Yorkshire out fourth innings on the worn wicket. Yorkshire in this case may be a better side than Notts., and yet are robbed of the match through the weather and not being allowed to follow on. My illustration is, of course, rather far-fetched, but still you will see the gist of my argument, and on the whole, I think, the law ought to remain as it is."

The Hon. Edward Lyttelton writes:– "In my opinion the 60 and 80 runs should be 100 and 150 to constitute the difference between two totals necessary for a 'follow on,' in a one day's and two (three) days' match respectively. I should reserve the option to the side which lost the toss, both of following on and of making the enemy follow on. The result would be that it would not often occur; but with the rule of closing the innings it would not often be required."

Mr George Marsham, of the Kent County Club, writes:– "I am of opinion that the closure should be allowed at any time on the second or third day of a county match. I think this matter is closely connected with the 'follow on,' which I should do away with altogether, unless the number of runs be altered to some percentage to be agreed upon after due consideration."

Mr C. M. Wells, whose action in the University match – so unjustly blamed in some quarters – brought the question into prominence, writes:– "I feel very strongly that some change should be made in the rule for 'following on.' Surely it is not right that the side following on should thereby gain a distinct advantage, as happens not infrequently; for example, in the Australian match against Cambridge University, when the former being about 90 runs behind on the first innings, followed on and batted against tired bowling on a perfect wicket, with the result that they piled up a large score and made the 'Varsity take fourth innings on a crumbled wicket. I think that the simplest alteration would be as follows:– If one side A is 80 runs behind another side B on the first innings, then the captain of B shall have the power to decide whether A shall follow on or his own side take their second innings."

James Lillywhite says:– "With regard to the 'following on' law when a side is 80 runs behind, my opinion is that the side 80 runs to the good should have the choice of again sending their opponents to the wickets or batting again themselves, whichever in their judgment was thought best, so that the advantage gained, probably by superior play under even conditions, should not be so often lost by having to bat last on a worn wicket, or, perhaps worse, a sticky one, after a wet night. By the leading team having the option of doing this the farce that we sometimes see of one side trying to get out, and the other trying to allow them to get a few more runs, will be stopped, and the difficulty, I think, surmounted. I think 80 runs a fair margin."

William Attewell says:– "My opinion on the 'follow on' is that it ought to be at the option of the side which has gained the lead, and I would keep the number of runs at 80 as at present."

John Briggs:– "As regards the 'follow on' at cricket, my opinion is that it ought to be altered. Suppose Notts. are playing against Lancashire, and Lancashire make, say, over 300 runs. Notts. go in on a good wicket, and make the runs, less 83; they would, as the rule stands, follow on to their advantage, bowlers being tired. Notts. then make a very good score against loose bowling, and as a matter of fact have the best of the game. I think in this case Lancashire should have the choice to bat or send Notts. in again. I do not know if anyone else will fall in with my views, but I should like the change to come into force."

Maurice Read writes:– "As regards the 'follow on,' I think that if there is anything that can be done to further the interest of the game, it should be done, and there is no doubt there will be a great deal said about 'following on,' as I see the question is to be brought up at Lord's. I think in the event of a side failing to save the follow on, the opposing captain should be allowed to go in or send his opponents in, because I have often known it happen that it has been much better for a side not to give the follow on after having lost their best bats, and with the wicket still good, and the consequence is that only wanting a few runs to save the follow, and the last man going in, he, as is so often the case, has orders to get out. Perhaps it might be altered to advantage by making the number higher – instead of 80 runs make it more."

The Hon. R. H. Lyttelton, discussing the question more fully than any of my other correspondents, and also taking an entirely independent view, writes as follows:– "The number of runs a side have to be behind in order to follow their innings is 80. This rule holds good in Australia, where there is comparatively an equable climate and the wickets are generally easy, and in England, where the wickets are sometimes in favour of batsmen and sometimes in favour of bowlers, seldom equally divided between the two. Twenty-five years ago a side that won the toss on a good wicket were happy when they got 180 runs, and got their opponents out for 100 in their first innings. But if on following their innings their opponents secured 150, they would have put the first side in for 70 runs to win, and in those days that was a sufficient number to keep up the interest of the match. Now in a year like 1893 the first innings of the side that wins the toss realises 300, the other side gets 220, and follows on and gets 230. The wicket, even on Lord's or Fenner's, has now begun to show some signs of wear and tear, the side that won the toss have fielded out for 450 runs and the odds are about even that they will not get 150 runs to win the match. But suppose the side that went in second saved the follow by one run, the first side with a light heart would go in again with a majority of 79, and would very likely knock up 200 runs and stand to win the match. There can be no doubt that if 80 runs was a fair number twenty-five years ago, it is too few now on hard wickets favouring the batsmen. But on soft, tricky wickets, favouring the bowlers, it is too many, for if ever a bet is safe at cricket it is, on such wickets, to back the side that is 50 or even 40 runs ahead at the end of the first innings. On such wickets 50 runs behind would be fairer than 80 to follow on. What, if any, is the remedy for these inconsistencies? It is rumoured that the law is to be altered whereby the side that is 80 runs ahead on the first innings is to have the option of making the other side follow on or go in themselves. One great objection there is to this amended rule, and that is that it adds another to the already formidable number of advantages gained by winning the toss. But speaking with a measure of reserve, I think it would be worth while to try the experiment of amending the rule in this way; if it did not answer it could be repealed. But I also think there must be a limit each way. On hard, easy wickets perhaps 120 runs behind would be a fairer number than 80; on soft, difficult wickets 50 would be enough. But it seems ridiculous to have one fixed number for all countries, climates, and wickets, and though I am by no means sure that the change would, in the long run, be beneficial, I think it might be tried, for at any rate it would abolish the fixed quantity absurdity."

Mr W. G. Grace, Mr A. E. Stoddart, and William Gunn preferred not to express any opinion on the point.

Mr V. E. Walker writes:– "Being on the committee of the MCC, who are now discussing the 'follow on' rule, I do not wish my private opinions to appear, but I shall read with interest the opinions you propose to publish in *Wisden*."

Mr Henry Perkins, the secretary of the MCC, expressed no personal opinion on the matter, but stated that the committee of the MCC have already taken the opinion of leading cricketers as to the desirability of amending Law 53, and will bring the question before the general meeting of the club on May 2, 1894.

GOVERNMENT v OPPOSITION

Played at Lord's, July 29, 1893

A match between members of Parliament representing respectively the Government and Opposition was played, but did not prove the attraction expected. However, the weather was most unfavourable. The Opposition, which included several well known cricketers, won very easily, declaring their innings at an end when three wickets had fallen for 243 runs.

Government

Mr J. A. Pease b Forster	4 – c Whitelaw b Forster	7
Mr J. F. Leese b Beckett	22 – c Chelsea b Forster	6
Hon. Mark F. Napier c Walrond b Forster	40 – not out	14
Mr H. J. Gladstone b Chelsea	12	
Mr George Newnes st Davenport b Forster	4	
Mr A. E. Hutton c Walrond b Forster	4	
Mr William Allen c Chelsea b Forster	3	
Mr R. K. Causton b Forster	2	
Mr C. E. H. Hobhouse st Davenport b Forster	4	
Mr J. M. Paulton not out	1	
Mr R. T. Reid absent	0 – b Chelsea	11
B 5, l-b 2, w 1	8 L-b 1, w 1, n-b 1	3
	104	41

Opposition

Mr H. W. Forster c Allen b Napier	81
Viscount Curzon st Reid b Allen	97
Viscount Chelsea c Reid b Napier	44
Mr Walter Long not out	9
B 5, l-b 1, w 6	12
(3 wkts dec.)	243

Mr W. Bromley-Davenport, Mr Ernest W. Beckett, Hon. Sidney Herbert, Mr A. F. Jeffreys, Captain Grice-Hutchinson, Mr G. Whitelaw and Sir William Walrond did not bat.

Opposition Bowling

	Overs	Mdns	Runs	Wkts	Overs	Mdns	Runs	Wkts
Forster	17.3	3	49	7	13	5	17	2
Beckett	11	2	32	1	6	2	12	0
Chelsea	6	1	15	1	6	4	9	1

Government Bowling

	Overs	Mdns	Runs	Wkts
Gladstone	12	1	44	0
Napier	15	2	78	2
Pease	16	1	85	0
Allen	2.3	0	10	1
Hobhouse	4	0	14	0

Umpires: W. Price and T. Mycroft.

MCC AND GROUND v SUSSEX

Played at Lord's, May 9, 10, 11, 1895

This was a splendidly contested match from start to finish, and one in which the County, though the losing side, deserved as much credit as the winners. It was a batsmen's triumph throughout, those who especially distinguished themselves being the veteran champion,

W. G. Grace, who scored his first hundred for the season, K. S. Ranjitsinhji, who, making his initial appearance for Sussex, made 77 not out and 150, Storer, who batted finely in each innings, C. W. Wright, C. Heseltine, George Brann, A. Collins, and Butt. The first stage went in favour of the Club, who completed an innings of 293 and dismissed five Sussex batsmen for 124, so that afterwards the visitors were always playing an uphill game. Friday's cricket resulted in the MCC increasing their advantage, getting rid of their remaining opponents for an additional 95 runs and then getting 330, a state of affairs which left Sussex to make the enormous number of 405. This they failed to do, but though beaten they were far from disgraced, for, thanks to the brilliant batting of Ranjitsinhji, whose 150 was his first three-figure innings in important cricket, and the plucky stand of 96 made by Collins and Butt for the last partnership, the Sussex total only fell 20 short of the requisite number, the Club ultimately winning a remarkable match by 19 runs. During the three days 1,227 runs were obtained.

MCC and Ground

Mr W. G. Grace c Ranjitsinhji b Butcher	13	– c Brann b Ranjitsinhji	103
Mr C. W. Wright c and b Collins	24	– run out	53
W. Flowers c Butt b Collins	12	– b Ranjitsinhji	25
A. Hearne b Butcher	20	– b Ranjitsinhji	0
W. Storer run out	82	– b Ranjitsinhji	65
Mr C. Heseltine c Newham b Braun	74	– c Heasman b Ranjitsinhji	5
Mr Neville Leese b Butcher	36	– b J. Bean	17
Mr A. Knowles b Collins	16	– st Butt b Ranjitsinhji	4
Mr A. N. Hornby not out	2	– c Butt b Butcher	25
F. Martin b Collins	0	– c Ranjitsinhji b J. Bean	20
J. T. Hearne b Collins	2	– not out	0
B 7, l-b 5	12	B 11, l-b 2	13
	293		330

Sussex

G. Bean c Heseltine b J. T. Hearne	7	– b J. T. Hearne	0
F. W. Marlow b Martin	26	– b Martin	28
Mr W. L. Murdoch c Knowles b A. Hearne	31	– b J. T. Hearne	9
Mr W. Newham lbw b Martin	22	– c Grace b Martin	5
K. S. Ranjitsinhji not out	77	– b Grace	150
Mr W. G. Heasman c J. T. Hearne b Flowers	1	– st Storer b Heseltine	43
Mr G. Brann b Martin	48	– b Martin	28
J. Bean b J. T. Hearne	5	– lbw b Grace	0
A. Butcher run out	1	– lbw b Martin	6
Mr A. Collins b J. T. Hearne	0	– b Martin	47
H. Butt c Storer b Martin	0	– not out	64
B 1	1	L-b 5	5
	219		385

Sussex Bowling

	Overs	Mdns	Runs	Wkts	Overs	Mdns	Runs	Wkts
Collins	30.4	10	61	5	19	2	67	0
Butcher	42	15	107	3	34	8	76	1
J. Bean	3	0	22	0	9.3	4	16	2
G. Bean	9	0	40	0	5	0	20	0
Brann	12	2	33	1	5	2	10	0
Ranjitsinhji	6	1	18	0	32	8	109	6
Marlow					3	1	8	0
Heasman					2	0	11	0

MCC and Ground Bowling

	Overs	Mdns	Runs	Wkts	Overs	Mdns	Runs	Wkts
Martin	39.3	9	88	4	56.1	20	123	5
J. T. Hearne	43	23	64	3	35	12	91	2
A. Hearne	10	2	29	1	14	5	41	0
Flowers	2	0	7	1	7	0	31	0
Heseltine	4	0	30	0	18	3	52	1
Grace					13	2	42	2

Umpires: V. A. Titchmarsh and J. E. West.

I ZINGARI v GENTLEMEN OF ENGLAND

Played at Lord's, June 20, 21, 22, 1895

For the match arranged to commemorate their Jubilee, the Zingari put a splendidly powerful side into the field, while, on paper, that of the Gentlemen of England was far from representative; but, despite the absence of several famous names, the latter unexpectedly proved the stronger, and defeated the Zingari in decisive fashion by ten wickets. It was a batsman's match all through, and partly for that reason, and partly from the fact that it was contested in delightful weather, drew large and appreciative crowds on each of the three days over which it extended. Among those who were present, and subsequently photographed with the Zingari eleven, were Mr. John Loraine Baldwin and the Hon. Spencer Ponsonby-Fane, two of the original founders of the famous amateur organisation. At the outset the Gentlemen had none of the best of the game, for at the end of the first day, after getting rid of their opponents for 289, they had five wickets down for 148. On Friday the Gentlemen increased their total to 411, and as the others scored 224 for the loss of five wickets there was still every reason to hope for an interesting finish; but on Saturday the Zingari batting broke down, and, the innings closing for 293, the Gentlemen were left with 172 to win. Though it was generally thought that number would be obtained, few people could have expected the feat would be accomplished without loss. However, W. G. Grace and Sellers set about the task with remarkable spirit and determination, and actually hit the runs off in an hour and three-quarters. Grace had the satisfaction of making 101, the fourth of his three-figure innings at Lord's. In the whole match 1,165 runs were scored for thirty wickets.

I Zingari

Mr H. T. Hewett st MacGregor b Grace sen.	51	– b Fry	22
Mr F. S. Jackson c Grace jun. b Fry	34	– c Grace sen. b Grace jun.	23
Mr A. E. Stoddart c MacGregor b Fry	38	– c Hill b Massie	92
Mr G. J. Mordaunt b Fry	19	– b Massie	42
Captain E. G. Wynyard c Hill b Grace jun.	56	– c and b Fry	51
Sir T. C. O'Brien c Hill b Fry	20	– c Grace sen. b Hill	5
Mr G. F. Vernon b Fry	0	– c MacGregor b Hill	17
Mr A. G. Steel not out	38	– lbw b Fry	14
Mr L. C. V. Bathurst b Burnup	4	– b Fry	6
Mr H. Philipson b Burnup	15	– not out	8
Mr H. R. B. Davenport c and b Burnup	1	– c MacGregor b Fry	0
B 7, l-b 4, w 1, n-b 1	13	B 8, l-b 1, w 4	13
	289		293

Gentlemen of England

Mr W. G. Grace b Steel	34	– not out 101
Mr A. Sellers c Philipson b Davenport	10	– not out 70
Mr R. S. Lucas c Mordaunt b Steel	18	
Mr R. W. Rice lbw b Bathurst	1	
Mr C. B. Fry b Jackson	43	
Mr H. H. Massie c Vernon b Jackson	26	
Mr W. G. Grace jun. c Stoddart b Steel	79	
Mr V. T. Hill c Mordaunt b Davenport	73	
Mr C. J. Burnup not out	66	
Mr G. MacGregor c Hewett b Davenport	21	
Mr A. T. Kemble b Bathurst	30	
B 4, l-b 2, w 3, n-b 1	10	W 1 1
	411	172

Gentlemen of England Bowling

	Overs	Mdns	Runs	Wkts	Overs	Mdns	Runs	Wkts
Burnup	23.4	5	82	3	12	5	34	0
Grace, jun.	12	2	40	1	11	3	30	1
Fry	27	6	75	5	26.4	2	102	5
Grace, sen.	16	0	79	1	5	1	20	0
Massie					14	2	39	2
Hill					22	8	55	2

I Zingari Bowling

	Overs	Mdns	Runs	Wkts	Overs	Mdns	Runs	Wkts
Jackson	39	16	96	2	15	6	40	0
Bromley-Davenport	35	7	100	3	6	0	32	0
Steel	28	0	92	3	7	1	17	0
Bathurst	21.2	4	53	2	11	0	46	0
Stoddart	15	4	38	0	8.1	2	36	0
Wynyard	5	2	22	0				

Umpires: W. Hearn and W. A. J. West.

OXFORD v CAMBRIDGE

Played at Lord's, July 2, 3, 4, 1896

In one respect at least, the University engagement of 1896, was the most remarkable of the series, the Oxford eleven being left to get 330 in the last innings, and hitting off the runs for the loss of six wickets. No such feat had ever been performed before in the University match, and the Oxford eleven deserve all possible credit for establishing a new and startling record. It is not so much, however, for this exceptional performance, as for the much discussed incident in regard to the follow-on rule, that the Oxford and Cambridge match of 1896 will be remembered. When the MCC, yielding to the fears of some famous players, rejected a drastic alteration of law 53, and contented themselves with increasing from 80 to 120 the number of runs, involving a follow-on, it was easy to foresee that, given the same circumstances, the incident which caused so much angry discussion in the University match of 1893 would inevitably be repeated. After an interval of three years, Mr Frank Mitchell, as captain of the Cambridge eleven, followed the example set him in 1893 by Mr F. S. Jackson, and by palpably giving away runs to prevent his opponents from following on, forced the MCC to reconsider the whole question. Cambridge occupied nearly the whole of the first day in scoring 319, some admirable cricket of a very steady kind being shown by Burnup and Wilson, and at about a quarter to four on the Friday, they were leading on the first innings by 131 runs, with only one Oxford wicket to go down. Rightly or wrongly, Mitchell judged that it would be better for his own side to go in again than to field for the rest of the afternoon, and E. B. Shine, who was then bowling at the Pavilion wicket, settled the matter by sending three balls – two of them no balls – to the boundary for four each. These twelve runs deprived Oxford of the chance of following on, and immediately afterwards the Dark Blues' innings closed for 202 or 117 behind. As they left the field, the Cambridge eleven came in for a very hostile demonstration at the hands of the public, and inside the Pavilion matters were still worse, scores of members of the MCC protesting in the most vigorous fashion against the policy that Frank Mitchell had adopted. In our opinion this display of passion was altogether illogical and uncalled for. We defended F. S. Jackson and C. M. Wells for what they did in the match of 1893, and believing that even in its amended form, law 53 is ill-adapted to modern cricket, we think Mitchell was quite entitled, in the interests of his side, to take the course he did. The incident gave rise to a long correspondence in the columns of *The Times*, and to show the difference of opinion that existed amongst the best authorities, diametrically opposite views were expressed by Lord Cobham and his younger brother, Edward Lyttelton. Lord Cobham strongly supported Mitchell's action, and Edward Lyttelton as strenuously opposed it.

Whether or not the angry demonstration they provoked, unnerved the Cambridge batsmen, we cannot say, but on going in for the second time they started very badly. Cunliffe and Hartley bowled in splendid form, the former continually making the ball go down the hill with his arm, and when the sixth Cambridge wicket fell the score had only reached 61. N. F. Druce, however, came to the rescue of his side with a splendid innings, and received such valuable help from Bray that when rain came on and stopped play at twenty minutes to seven, the total had reached 154 with eight men out. Cambridge thus had considerably the best of the game, being 271 runs ahead with two wickets to fall. It was feared that the rain, which fell for some little time after the drawing of stumps, would spoil the ground, but as a matter of fact, it had just the contrary effect, the wicket, which had shown some slight signs of crumbling, rolling out better than ever on the Saturday morning. Cambridge carried their score to 212 and so set Oxford the tremendous task of getting 330 in the last innings. How brilliantly this task was accomplished is now a matter of cricket history. Up to a certain point they seemed to have no chance of victory, Mordaunt, Warner and Foster being out for 60 runs. The turning point came with the partnership of G. O. Smith and Pilkington, and once on the road to victory, the Oxford men never looked back. Cambridge made two or three mistakes in the field, but as to the fine quality of the batting there could not be two opinions. Pilkington, in about an hour and a quarter, helped to put on 84 for the fourth wicket, and then, during an hour and three quarters of gradually increasing excitement, Smith and Leveson-Gower added 97 runs together, the latter being caught at the wicket with the total at 241. Eighty-nine runs were then wanted with five wickets to go down, and any little accident might have turned the scale in Cambridge's favour. Smith, however, found an invaluable partner in Bardswell, and between them the two batsmen made Oxford's success certain. Smith, who up to a certain point had played with scrupulous care, hit out most brilliantly, and in less than an hour 87 runs were put on. Then, with only two runs wanted to win, Smith, overcome by the excitement of the moment, jumped out to drive one of Cobbold's slows and was easily caught at slip. On his departure, Waddy joined Bardswell and a couple of singles gave Oxford the victory by four wickets, Bardswell, in making the winning hit, being missed in the long field by Burnup. G. O. Smith was congratulated on all hands upon his magnificent innings of 132.

Cambridge

	1st inns		2nd inns	
Mr C. J. Burnup (*Malvern and Clare*) c Mordaunt b Hartley	80	– c and b Hartley	11
Mr W. G. Grace jun. (*Clifton and Pembroke*) b Hartley	0	– b Cunliffe	1
Mr H. H. Marriott (*Malvern and Clare*) c Warner b Hartley	16	– b Cunliffe	1
Mr N. F. Druce (*Marlborough and Trinity*) c Smith b Cunliffe	14	– c Pilkington b Waddy	72
Mr C. E. M. Wilson (*Uppingham and Trinity*) c Cunliffe b Hartley	80	– c Lewis b Hartley	2
Mr W. M'G. Hemingway (*Uppingham and Kings'*) c and b Hartley	26	– b Cunliffe	12
Mr F. Mitchell (*St. Peter's, York and Caius*) c Leveson-Gower b Hartley	26	– b Cunliffe	4
Mr G. L. Jessop (*Private and Christ's*) c Mordaunt b Hartley	0	– st Lewis b Hartley	19
Mr E. H. Bray (*Charterhouse and Trinity*) c Pilkington b Cunliffe	49	– c Lewis b Waddy	41
Mr P. W. Cobbold (*Eton and Trinity*) b Hartley	10	– not out	23
Mr E. B. Shine (*Private and Selwyn*) not out	10	– c Hartley b Waddy	16
B 4, l-b 1, w 2, n-b 1	8	B 5, w 1, n-b 5	11
	319		212

Oxford

	1st inns		2nd inns
Mr P. F. Warner (*Rugby and Oriel*) run out	10	– run out	17
Mr G. J. Mordaunt (*Wellington and University*) b Jessop	26	– b Jessop	9
Mr H. K. Foster (*Malvern and Trinity*) b Wilson	11	– c and b Cobbold	34
Mr G. O. Smith (*Charterhouse and Keble*) c Bray b Wilson	37	– c Mitchell b Cobbold	132
Mr C. C. Pilkington (*Eton and Magdalen*) b Jessop	4	– c and b Jessop	44
Mr H. D. G. Leveson-Gower (*Winchester and Magdalen*) b Jessop	26	– c Bray b Shine	41
Mr G. R. Bardswell (*Uppingham and Oriel*) c and b Cobbold	0	– not out	33
Mr P. S. Waddy (*Paramatta and Balliol*) st Bray b Cobbold	0	– not out	1
Mr J. C. Hartley (*Tonbridge and Brasenose*) c Marriott b Wilson	43		
Mr F. H. E. Cunliffe (*Eton and New*) b Shine	12		
Mr R. P. Lewis (*Winchester and University*) not out	0		
B 12, l-b 4, n-b 8	24	B 6, l-b 6, w 6, n-b 1	19
	202		330

Oxford Bowling

	Overs	Mdns	Runs	Wkts	Overs	Mdns	Runs	Wkts
Cunliffe	55	25	87	2	33	11	93	4
Hartley	59.3	13	161	8	30	3	78	3
Waddy	24	10	35	0	11	3	28	3
Pilkington	29	19	24	0	3	1	2	0
Leveson-Gower	2	0	4	0				

Cambridge Bowling

	Overs	Mdns	Runs	Wkts	Overs	Mdns	Runs	Wkts
Jessop	37	15	75	3	30	8	98	2
Wilson	37	19	48	3	42	20	50	0
Shine	12.3	4	29	1	20	9	41	1
Cobbold	11	2	26	2	44.4	7	96	2
Burnup					2	0	3	0
Druce					7	2	11	0
Mitchell					2	1	12	0

Umpires: W. Hearn and W. A. J. West.

MCC AND GROUND v SUSSEX

Played at Lord's, May 3, 4, 1899

Apart from the absence of Ranjitsinhji, Sussex put about their best side into the field at Lord's for the opening fixture on the MCC programme. The Club – on paper at any rate – were deficient in batting strength, but that fact did not prevent them from winning in very handsome fashion, thanks in a great measure, to the brilliant all-round cricket of Albert Trott. Sussex at the outset looked like securing a big advantage for 91 runs were obtained before the first wicket fell. C. B. Fry scored 98 out of 150 by resolute cricket, but from the moment he left, Hearne and Trott carried all before them and the innings only realised 178. Against that total the MCC fared none too well for Trott alone showed any ability to cope with the excellent bowling of Tate, and the county were able to secure a lead of 30 runs on the first innings. However, Trott and Hearne were even more effective on the second day, and with Sussex out for 97 the Club only required 131 to win. That number was obtained for the loss of five wickets – Trott again carrying off the batting honours. In the whole match the Anglo-Australian scored 133 runs and took 11 wickets for 113 runs, so that his share in the victory was immense. Hearne with nine wickets for 98, Tate with 10 for 117, and C. B. Fry, who made 118 runs, all accomplished noteworthy performances in match which, owing to the cold weather, scarcely attracted the public attention it deserved.

Sussex

Mr C. B. Fry c and b Trott	98	– lbw b J. T. Hearne	20
Mr G. Brann b Trott	24	– b Trott	11
F. W. Marlow b Trott	12	– b J. T. Hearne	11
Mr W. Newham b J. T. Hearne	0	– lbw b Trott	4
Mr C. L. A. Smith c and b J. T. Hearne	0	– b Trott	4
Mr W. L. Murdoch b Trott	2	– st Huish b J. T. Hearne	1
F. Parris b J. T. Hearne	0	– lbw b J. T. Hearne	9
E. H. Killick not out	7	– b Trott	5
H. R. Butt b Trott	0	– not out	12
F. W. Tate b J. T. Hearne	3	– c Huish b J. T. Hearne	9
C. H. G. Bland c de Trafford b Trott	14	– c Foley b Trott	3
B 12, l-b 6	18	B 6, l-b 2	8
	178		97

MCC and Ground

Mr C. E. de Trafford b Tate	4 – c Butt b Parris	17
Mr C. J. Burnup b Bland	6 – lbw b Tate	0
A. Hearne b Tate	10 – b Tate	2
Mr C. P. Foley b Tate	3 – not out	23
A. E. Trott b Tate	64 – b Tate	69
Mr S. M. Tindall b Tate	15 – b Tate	0
L. Whitehead b Tate	4 – not out	16
Mr F. B. May b Parris	2	
J. T. Hearne c Tate b Parris	4	
F. Martin b Parris	10	
F. H. Huish not out	4	
B 16, l-b 3	19	B 5, l-b 1 6
	145	133

MCC Bowling

	Overs	Mdns	Runs	Wkts	Overs	Mdns	Runs	Wkts
J. T. Hearne	26	7	65	4	19	7	33	5
Martin	6	3	16	0				
Trott	30.4	12	57	6	18.1	3	56	5
A. Hearne	11	3	22	0				

Sussex Bowling

	Overs	Mdns	Runs	Wkts	Overs	Mdns	Runs	Wkts
Tate	24	5	72	6	15	5	45	4
Bland	14	4	33	1	11	4	34	0
Parris	11.1	4	21	3	9	2	44	1
Killick	2	2	0	0	1	0	4	0

Umpires: F. Farrands and T. Mycroft.

MCC AND GROUND v LEICESTERSHIRE

Played at Lord's, May 15, 16, 17, 1899

After the first stage, which was considerably curtailed on account of the state of the wicket, batsmen were always at a disadvantage, and on the last day the bowlers on both sides were simply unplayable. Thus the innings of 192 put together by the MCC on Monday afternoon proved an important factor in the result. Tuesday's cricket was also interfered with by the weather, which prevented any progress after luncheon, but with the ground affected by the sun on Wednesday, there was never any doubt about a definite result being arrived at. Woodcock, who was in wonderful form with the ball, only just missed the distinction of taking all ten wickets in the second innings. When it is stated that he secured fourteen wickets for 72 runs, it will be readily understood that he was most unfortunate to be on the losing side. As it was Leicestershire were only set 123 to win, but Mead and Trott dismissed them for 30 and MCC won by 92. Mead's ten wickets in the match cost only 63. Trott was scarcely less successful in securing the other ten wickets for 69.

MCC and Ground

Mr H. B. Hayman b King	1 – b Woodcock	4
H. Carpenter c Pougher b King	0 – b Woodcock	9
R. Moorhouse b Woodcock	34 – b Woodcock	0
A. E. Trott b Agar	15 – b Woodcock	8
Mr A. F. Somerset b Woodcock	55 – not out	26
Mr L. C. V. Bathurst not out	41 – c and b King	1
Hon. J. S. R. Tufton b Woodcock	4 – b Woodcock	5
T. M. Russell b King	12 – c and b Woodcock	0
W. Mead b King	19 – b Woodcock	1
H. Young c Geeson b Woodcock	9 – b Woodcock	1
B. Cranfield b Woodcock	0 – b Woodcock	0
B 2	2 B 2	2
	192	57

Leicestershire

A. E. Knight b Mead	2 – b Mead	1
L. Brown b Trott	18 – b Mead	2
Mr C. J. B. Wood b Mead	0 – b Mead	11
A. D. Pougher b Mead	29 – b Trott	0
J. King not out	46 – c Bathurst b Trott	2
Mr C. E. de Trafford b Trott	9 – b Trott	2
S. Coe b Trott	0 – not out	4
Agar b Trott	1 – b Trott	0
F. Geeson lbw b Mead	2 – b Mead	3
A. Woodcock b Mead	7 – st Russell b Trott	1
J. P. Whiteside b Mead	0 – b Trott	4
B 5, l-b 7, w 1	13	
	127	30

Leicestershire Bowling

	Overs	Mdns	Runs	Wkts	Overs	Mdns	Runs	Wkts
Agar	11	2	27	1				
King	26	6	61	4	21	8	27	1
Pougher	5	0	24	0				
Coe	11	5	25	0				
Woodcock	17	5	44	5	22	11	28	9
Geeson	6	2	9	0				
Wood	1	1	0	0				

MCC Bowling

	Overs	Mdns	Runs	Wkts	Overs	Mdns	Runs	Wkts
Young	7	1	12	0				
Mead	23	6	54	6	12	9	9	4
Trott	18	2	48	4	11.3	7	21	6

Umpires: T. Mycroft and W. A. J. West.

THE COUNTY MATCHES

Most students of cricket history sense that 1864 was the year in which the game finally moved out of its medieval period into an era recognisably modern. That Wisden should happen to have made its debut in that year is more than a coincidence, for the appearance of a regular publication which codified the rapidly increasing amount of cricket activity was a clerical analogue to the advance of the game in two vitally important areas. In 1864 overarm bowling was legalised, the teenager W. G. Grace scored a century for South Wales against the Gentlemen of Sussex at Hove, and some people began for the first time to think of the counties as competing units vying for some sort of crown, which, however nebulous, appears to have been thought worth the winning. If the institution of overarm bowling and the advent of Grace are seen as a technical watershed, then the emergence of the idea of a county championship becomes equally important as a device for crystallising the appeal of cricket as a spectator sport.

This is not to say that a county championship, or anything remotely approaching it, existed as early as 1864. In fact, so confused is the early history of the competition, and so gradual was its evolution, that for a century now rival historians have been repudiating each other's theories. Perhaps the simplest way of creating a coher nt picture is to quote the opening paragraph of an essay on the subject which appeared in the 1963 centenary edition of Wisden, written by Rowland Bowen:

> The first year of Wisden – 1864 – saw also the first mention of a County Champion in the regular series. It does not matter that this was not a strictly contemporary reference – it occurred twenty-three years later when Surrey were again Champions.

What Bowen means by this curious remark is that when Surrey won the title in 1887, "somebody remembered that Surrey were champions for the first time since 1864". Bowen goes on to record that the earliest contemporary reference occurs in December 1866, when the Nottinghamshire Committee discussed their team's fortunes during the previous season. By 1870 the popular press was publishing, on its own initiative, and in the face of a steely indifference from the MCC, lists of the counties based on a system of the smallest number of matches lost. A further claim on behalf of 1870 as the first season in which people began to think of the counties in terms of some order of merit is that Grace, in his *Cricketing Reminiscences and Personal Recollections*, provides tables of what he calls "Inter-County Cricket" starting from 1870.

The first formal attempt to regularise the championship came on 11 December, 1872, when delegates from the counties met in London to draw up a set of rules. In June 1873 these rules were formally adopted, although it was not until 1911 that Wisden decided to publish a list of champions beginning with 1873. Wisden's decision notwithstanding, we are not to imagine that the county matches of 1873 and the following seasons bore the slightest resemblance to the championship as it later came to be known. For at least thirteen seasons after the deliberations of the 1872 committee, a championship list appeared only through the diligence of the newspapers, and although from 1873 laws existed for the qualification of players, not until 1887 and the advent of the County Cricket Council were these laws firmly established and some definition attempted of what constituted a first-class county. Indeed, so much contention centred around this vexed question of which counties comprised the elite, that the Council's recommendation in 1890 that there should be three groups of counties, with promotion and relegation, was rejected out of hand, at which point the Council tactfully committed suicide.

Not until the meeting of county secretaries in 1889 was the championship converted into a legal reality, and in the following year a system was adopted of deciding the championship by subtracting the losses from the wins and ignoring drawn matches altogether, an example of Victorian pragmatism making a comic contrast with the byzantine mathematical lunacies in which the first-class game was to become embroiled a century later. Throughout the 1880s, public interest in the championship grew to such a point that even the MCC was finally obliged to acknowledge it, although it was not until 1903 that an advisory committee under the aegis of the MCC was brought into existence. The battles over qualification of players had already been joined; as early as 1886 Lord Harris had demanded that the residential qualification should be reduced from two years to one, on the grounds that otherwise a player unfortunate enough to have been born, through no fault of his mother's, in a minor county, would be excluded from the game for too long a period. The motion was defeated, and the two-year period gradually became transmuted into holy writ.

It is apparent from the dramatic contrasts in bulk between the entries in this volume dedicated to the respective counties that each of them fought its way to first-class status at its own rate. At the beginning of the period the Big Seven were Kent, Lancashire, Middlesex, Nottinghamshire, Surrey, Sussex and Yorkshire, with Derbyshire, Hampshire and later Somerset hovering on the rim of full first-class recognition. (Derbyshire actually enjoyed this status, lost it, and later regained it; Somerset virtually forced itself in by its own efforts, enjoying a brilliant year in 1890, and finishing as high as third in its first season in the championship a year later.) In 1895 the championship began to take on a contemporary appearance with the admission of Derbyshire, Essex, Hampshire, Leicestershire and Warwickshire. (Other aspects of 1895 which mark it as a turning-point are the sudden increase in run-making and the parallel increase in the rate of run-making. Grace made his one thousand runs in May at the start of the season, and later in the summer A. C. Maclaren scored the only quadruple century in the championship's history. Finally, in 1899, the domination of the Minor County Championship by Worcestershire made inevitable that county's promotion to first-class status, a triumph due mainly to the efforts of two prodigious brotherhoods, the Lytteltons of Hagley Hall, who from the middle of the nineteenth century have provided the county with patrons, presidents, captains and players; and the amazing Fosters, the seven sons of the Reverend H. Foster, a housemaster at Malvern College. The greatest of all the Fosters, Reginald Erskine, still holds the record for the highest innings by an Englishman in a test match against Australia in Australia, and is never likely to be challenged as the only Englishman ever to captain his country at full international level at Cricket and Association Football. It is debatable, however, if he was much more remarkable as a sporting original than his elder brother Henry Knollys, who captained the county in its first years in the championship, was Amateur Rackets Champion of England at 21, and who never represented England at cricket simply because he did not choose to. The impact on Worcestershire cricket of the Fosters was prodigious (Fostershire), and perhaps the simplest way to convey its effect is to refer the reader to the sole Worcestershire entry in this volume, recording the extraordinary exploits of two of the Reverend Foster's sons in the match against Hampshire in July, 1900.

With the rise of Worcestershire, the championship was virtually fully formed, leaving only Northamptonshire (1907) and Glamorgan (1921) still to be drafted. What was vital about this increase in size and formalising of procedure in the county championship was that by vastly increasing the number of three-day competitive matches, it not only increased cricket's newsworthiness by intensifying public interest, but it lessened the odds against the occurrence of those freaklish and whimsical events in which cricket is so much richer than any other game. In other words, the existence of a large number of clubs pursuing a tangible prize in intensely competitive spirit, provided the perfect cockpit for the expression of individual personality in the context of a team game. No satirist, no social historian, no comedian would ever dare invent many of the incidents recorded so primly by the editors of Wisden, and it is striking, though perhaps not surprising, that so many of these happenings should centre about the figure of W. G. Grace.

The reader will discover, for example, that in the course of the county championship pageant described by this volume, the Doctor had to be provided with police protection, was carried shoulder-high from the ground, was on the field of play for every minute of all three days, made an offer to A. C. Maclaren to continue a match on a new pitch, witnessed a hat-trick of stumpings, scored his hundredth hundred, played against Yorkshire in a match of which the almanack cryptically remarks that the Yorkshireman Peel "had to go away", was the central figure in a bereavement which caused a match to be abandoned, and saved the life of a fellow-cricketer in mid-match. Wisden's account of this incident, in the game at Old Trafford between Lancashire and Gloucestershire in July 1887, does not quite make clear the extent to which the injured player owed his life to Grace, for which reason the account of the victim, A. C. M. Croome, is especially revealing:

> "It is, in all human probability, due to W. G. Grace that I survive to write my reminiscences of him, for he saved my life at Manchester in 1887. I ran into the railings in front of the Old Trafford pavilion while trying to save a boundary hit, and fell on the spikes, one of which made a deep wound in my throat. They had to send out for a needle and thread to sew it up, and for nearly half an hour W. G. held the edges of the wound together. It was of vital importance that the injured part should be kept absolutely still, and his hand never shook all that time. I should have known if there had been any twitching of finger and thumb, for I was conscious most of the time and the nerves of my neck and face were severely bruised. It would have been a remarkable feat of endurance under any circumstances, but the Old Man had been fielding out for over four hundred runs and had done his share of bowling, evidence of W. G.'s amazing stamina."

The perils facing the county cricketer of the Victorian era were not always so formidable, although it is faintly alarming that on one occasion an Essex player should have been obliged to retire because of a mosquito bite. There were always dangers of a more convivial kind, as in the Sussex v Kent match where one of batsmen took too leisurely a view of the luncheon interval. Was something of a similar nature the cause of the peculiarly truncated condition of the Somerset side against Hampshire in 1885? Wisden does not say, nor does it define the nature of the military crisis which obliged Hampshire to field a team with no Army officers against Yorkshire in 1898. National considerations of a different kind intruded on the Middlesex v Kent game of 1887, where play was suspended for a while as a mark of respect for the Queen, busy celebrating her Jubilee. In one match against Leicestershire Tom Hayward achieved the apparently impossible feat of taking three wickets for no runs without bowling a maiden over, but even this was surpassed by G. R. Baker of Lancashire who, if Wisden is to be believed, contrived in a match against Somerset at Taunton to bowl five overs of which eight were maidens. Once in a Nottinghamshire v Middlesex contest the ball was fielded by the bowler's hat, and it was not long after that incident that Arthur Shrewsbury declined to captain the side against Surrey, once again for reasons not specified. Jessop is found treating Tom Richardson "as though he was medium-pace", and while playing against Yorkshire, Lilley the Warwickshire wicket-keeper, was given out for hitting the ball twice. One of the most fulsome reports in the entire volume, of a match between Kent and Middlesex in the 1880s, achieves heights of Pooteresque incongruity by incorporating a magniloquent account of a presentation to a gentleman for managing the Canterbury Week. Reporting the Gloucestershire v Surrey match at Cheltenham in 1874, Wisden, in discussing the morality of Dr E. M. Grace's field positioning, reflects that "the Doctor has always been famous for this kind of daring pointwork, the surprise being that he had hitherto fortunately escaped enriching his profession with a case of broken head." And having achieved this Leacockian reflection on the fate of a sporting coroner, the writer of the report, searching for a suitable way to take his leave, is obliged to resort to William Shakespeare; perhaps this was no less than the due of the only man ever to score a century when opening the batting for the World. (See the match at the Oval, August 28, 1867).

It is this multiplicity of small miracles, intermingled with feats of individual and team prowess to comprise the history of the County Championship, which makes the emergent Wisden so captivating a collation. No doubt other journals and almanacks might have provided more comprehensive reports – and it is significant in this regard that more than once Wisden reports *Bell's London Life* verbatim – but no other publication held firm for anything like as long, and none ever quite aspired to that magisterial authority which Wisden assumed with the arrival of the Pardons. And in savouring the memorable moments in the section, it is as well to remember that whether countenancing the high jinks of the Graces at one end of the period, or marvelling at the swashbuckling of Major Poore at the other, the reader, in studying the county entries, is contemplating that section of the almanack which has always comprised by far the largest proportion of its total number of pages. Just as the heart of English cricket has always been its County Championship, so the heart of Wisden has always been its section reporting the events within the championship.

Benny Green

DERBYSHIRE

SIXTEEN OF DERBYSHIRE v ELEVEN OF NOTTINGHAMSHIRE

Played at Wirksworth, Derbyshire, September 4, 5, 1873

This match was that wherein Eleven of Nottinghamshire were all got out fair and square for an innings of 14 runs. The MCC matches in Scotland being then in play, neither Alfred Shaw nor Biddulph could be spared, their vacancies being filled by Mr Tolley and G. Martin (wicket-keeper), and Mr Clifton played v Mr Royle. The loss of Alfred Shaw's bowling (the ground being dead) was bad for Nottinghamshire, but that had nothing to do with the 14 runs' innings, and as those that were bowled in that curiously small affair were clean bowled, and as the others were caught out where, in all probability, men would have been, had only Eleven been fielding, this 14 must remain one of those unexplainable cricket collapses that help to form "the glorious, etc., etc." of the game; for, to set it down as Nottinghamshire's form, would be absurd and unjust. The wickets in that innings fell as under:

1/1 2/1 3/1 4/10 5/11 6/11 7/12 8/12 9/12 10/14

The number of overs bowled in that innings were thirty-two (twenty-two maidens). Three of the wickets were bowled; three were c and b by Flint; Daft was wonderfully well taken with one hand by Platts at mid-off; and McIntyre by Smith at mid-on. The two Derbyshire bowlers whose bowling effected this feat, were Flint and Mycroft. Flint is a round-arm slow bowler, and Mycroft, left-hand fast, who varies his pitch and pace, and arranges his field with much judgment. (Mycroft, in 1872, bowled seventy-five overs (fifty-two maidens) for 50 runs and eight wickets, in an innings played by Geo. Parr's Eleven.)

In their second innings the Nottinghamshire Eleven made a fair stand, but the end was, the Sixteen of Derbyshire won by an innings and 8 runs.

The Sixteen of Derbyshire

J. Smith (Derby) c Selby b J. C. Shaw	5
W. Rigley c Oscroft b Daft	15
S. Richardson Esq. run out	21
G. Frost b Oscroft	15
Rev. R. C. Moncrieff b Oscroft	0
R. P. Smith Esq. b Oscroft	2
T. Foster c McIntyre b J. C. Shaw	0
J. Frost b Morley	2
J. Howarth b Morley	7
R. Allsopp Esq. c Martin b Daft	22
J. Flint b J. C. Shaw	12
J. Platts b J. C. Shaw	1
W. Hickton run out	3
W. Allen c and b J. C. Shaw	2
W. Mycroft b J. C. Shaw	2
E. Tatlow not out	0
B 2, l-b 3	5
	114

The Eleven of Nottinghamshire

Bignall b Flint	0	– b Mycroft	3
F. Wyld b Mycroft	1	– hit wkt b Flint	11
Mr C. Clifton c and b Flint	0	– st Richardson b Flint	0
William Oscroft c Flint b Mycroft	4	– c Flint b Mycroft	12
Richard Daft c Platts b Mycroft	5	– st Richardson b Flint	0
R. Tolley Esq. c and b Flint	0	– c and b Flint	0
J. Selby lbw b Mycroft	0	– not out	14
Martin McIntyre c J. Smith b Flint	1	– b Hicton	23
G. Martin c and b Flint	0	– run out	23
Morley not out	0	– b Hickton	0
J. C. Shaw b Flint	2	– b Platts	3
B 1	1	B 3	3
	14		92

Nottinghamshire Bowling

	Overs	Mdns	Runs	Wkts
J. C. Shaw	48.1	23	40	6
Morley	40	28	20	2
Daft	14	2	33	2
McIntyre	9	5	7	—
Oscroft	7	3	9	3

Derbyshire Bowling

	Overs	Mdns	Runs	Wkts	Overs	Mdns	Runs	Wkts
Flint	16	10	7	6	26	9	44	4
Mycroft	16	12	6	4	28	9	34	2
Platts					6	4	5	1
Hickton					5	3	6	2

Umpires: E. Horrobin and W. H. Luck.

DERBYSHIRE v KENT

Played at Wirksworth, July 13, 14, 1874

In this match the forty wickets were down for 233 runs – Kent going for a first innings of 25 runs, and Derbyshire for a second of 36 runs. Geo. Frost's 37 for Derbyshire was the largest score made in the match, and William McCanlis's 28 the largest for the Southerners. Kent's first innings of 25 runs was a remarkable affair, only twenty-three overs were bowled by Flint and Mycroft, the latter bowling eleven overs (eight maidens) for 8 runs and five wickets – four bowled. The wickets fell this wise:

1/12 2/12 3/13 4/13 5/13 6/18 7/18 8/18 9/19 10/25 – from 23 overs

Willsher was in good form with the ball; he had thirteen wickets in the match – eight bowled, his bowling averaging four and a half runs per wicket. When play closed on the first day, Derbyshire's 97, and Kent's 25, had been booked, and there seven wickets down for 22 runs in Derbyshire's second; 17 of those 22 runs were made by Frost, and 2 more by the not out man, so the other six men out averaged a half a run per man! Altogether this was a remarkable match for County elevens to play, and perhaps the most remarkable feature of this remarkable match was:

Mycroft bowled fifty overs (thirty-eight maidens) for 23 runs and eight wickets – seven bowled. Derbyshire won by 33 runs.

Derbyshire

R. P. Smith Esq. lbw b Remnant	5	– b Willsher	3
G. Frost c and b Draper	37	– c Henty b Willsher	17
J. Frost c G. McCanlis b Willsher	18	– b Willsher	1
W. G. Curgenven Esq. b Willsher	5	– b Draper	0
J. Platts c Remnant b Draper	16	– b Willsher	0
W. J. Humble Esq. b Draper	7	– b Willsher	0
J. Tye b Willsher	3	– b Draper	7
W. Boden Esq. not out	2	– c Byas b Willsher	0
J. Flint b Willsher	4	– c Draper b Willsher	2
W. Mycroft c Hodgson b Willsher	0	– not out	0
J. Cooke b Willsher	0	– b Draper	6
	97		36

Kent

William McCanlis c Platts b Flint	6	– c Smith b Platts	28
Capt. Swinford b Mycroft	6	– b Mycroft	1
Remnant run out	1	– c Humble b Flint	11
Rev. G. H. Hodgson c J. Frost b Mycroft	0	– b Mycroft	4
Geo. McCanlis b Mycroft	0	– b Flint	2
Draper b Mycroft	0	– b Mycroft	3
Croxford lbw b Flint	3	– b Platts	0
J. E. Byas Esq. b Mycroft	0	– run out	2
Willsher c G. Frost b Flint	7	– c Platts b Flint	9
Henty c J. Frost b Flint	0	– not out	7
R. Palmer not out	0	– b Flint	5
		B 1, l-b 2	3
	25		75

Kent Bowling

	Overs	Mdns	Runs	Wkts	Overs	Mdns	Runs	Wkts
Willsher	35	18	36	6	16	7	22	7
Draper	18	9	22	3	17	11	14	3
Remnant	16	2	39	1				

Derbyshire Bowling

	Overs	Mdns	Runs	Wkts	Overs	Mdns	Runs	Wkts
Flint	12	6	17	4	27	9	35	4
Mycroft	11	8	8	5	39	30	15	3
Platts					12	5	22	2

Umpires: R. C. Tinley and Fryer.

DERBYSHIRE v NOTTINGHAMSHIRE

Played at Derby, August 18, 19, 1879

Derbyshire had shown such good form against Yorkshire, that it was generally anticipated they might score a notch against Nottinghamshire. The contrary to this, however, took place. The home team led off the batting, but only two gained the dignity of double figures, and the whole lot were dismissed for 59. The batting of Nottinghamshire was not very brilliant but they managed to leave their opponents 51 to avert a single innings' defeat. Their second venture, however, proved even more disastrous than the first had been. J. Platts headed the list with 8 runs, and the whole eleven were got rid of for 36. Morley's bowling was very fine; in each innings he took seven wickets, thus:

Morley sixty-one overs (thirty-nine maidens), 53 runs, fourteen wickets.

Nottinghamshire won by an innings and 15 runs.

Derbyshire

	First innings	Second innings	
A. Shuker Esq. b Shaw	0	b Morley	6
W. Rigley run out	1	b Shaw	2
T. Foster b Morley	13	b Morley	1
R. P. Smith Esq. b Morley	13	b Morley	0
A. M. Wood Esq. c Scotton b Morley	9	c Shaw b Morley	5
J. Platts b Morley	3	b Morley	8
J. Marlow b Morley	4	lbw b Shaw	0
A. W. Cursham Esq. lbw b Morley	5	st Wyld b Shaw	1
G. Hay b Morley	4	not out	8
A. Smith not out	0	b Morley	3
W. Mycroft b Shaw	1	b Morley	2
B 4, l-b 2	6		
	59		36

Nottinghamshire

W. Oscroft c Rigley b Mycroft	10
A. Shrewsbury b Platts	27
J. Selby b Hay	7
W. Scotton c Mycroft b Marlow	13
W. Barnes c Hay b Marlow	4
W. Flowers c and b Marlow	0
A. Shaw c Wood b Platts	5
F. Wild c Hay b Mycroft	26
W. Wright not out	3
W. Shrewsbury c A. Smith b Mycroft	0
F. Morley c A. Smith b Mycroft	6
B 7, l-b 2	9
	110

Nottinghamshire Bowling

	Overs	Mdns	Runs	Wkts	Overs	Mdns	Runs	Wkts
Shaw	35.3	22	20	2	26	13	15	3
Morley	35	21	32	7	26	18	21	7

Derbyshire Bowling

	Overs	Mdns	Runs	Wkts
Mycroft	32.3	20	33	4
Hay	48	30	40	1
Marlow	16	12	11	3
Platts	12	6	17	2

DERBYSHIRE v YORKSHIRE

Played at Derby, August 13, 14, 1888

For the first time for more than three years Derbyshire beat an important county, but Yorkshire lacked the services of their two best cricketers in Ulyett and Peel. The seven wickets' victory was chiefly brought about by Hulme's wonderful bowling, the young left-hander being credited with fifteen wickets in the match at a cost of only 70 runs. Derbyshire had an advantage of 14 on first innings, and then, dismissing their opponents for a small total, only required 83 to win. Mr Wright and Chatterton hit freely, and the necessary runs were obtained for the loss of three wickets.

Yorkshire

L. Hall run out	40	– c Storer b Hulme	2
J. M. Preston c Wright b Hulme	16	– b Hulme	49
F. Lee lbw b Hulme	4	– b Hulme	10
Lord Hawke c Wright b Walker	7	– not out	9
E. Wainwright B Hulme	0	– b Hulme	0
Thewlis c Chatterton b Hulme	8	– c Davidson b Hulme	4
S. Wade b Hulme	0	– c Chatterton b Hulme	1
Pride not out	24	– b Cropper	3
Mr A. W. Dixon b Hulme	0	– run out	1
R. Moorhouse lbw b Hulme	2	– run out	0
W. Middlebrook b Hulme	0	– lbw b Hulme	5
B 11, l-b 3	14	B 7, l-b 5	12
	115		96

Derbyshire

Mr G. G. Walker st Pride b Wade	4		
W. Sugg c Pride b Preston	0	– b Preston	6
W. Cropper b Preston	17	– b Preston	0
G. Davidson b Preston	13	– lbw b Wainwright	15
W. Chatterton b Middlebrook	34	– not out	13
Mr W. H. Hodges b Middlebrook	5		
Mr E. Evershed b Preston	13		
Mr L. G. Wright c Thewlis b Middlebrook	11	– not out	35
Storer b Middlebrook	8		
Hall not out	4		
J. Hulme run out	4		
B 14, l-b 2	16	B 11, l-b 2, n-b 1	14
	129		83

Derbyshire Bowling

	Overs	Mdns	Runs	Wkts	Overs	Mdns	Runs	Wkts
Walker	29	14	40	1	4	1	12	—
Davidson	23	12	26	—	10	5	10	—
Hulme	26	11	30	8	25.3	11	40	7
Cropper	2	—	5	—	25	14	16	1
Hall					1	—	2	—
Chatterton					7	4	4	—

Yorkshire Bowling

	Overs	Mdns	Runs	Wkts	Overs	Mdns	Runs	Wkts
Preston	35	18	51	4	15	7	21	2
Wade	16	8	22	1	6	2	13	0
Middlebrook	28	12	29	4	12	5	19	0
Wainwright	5	1	10	0	11.1	4	15	1
Dixon	1	0	1	0	2	1	1	0

DERBYSHIRE v YORKSHIRE

Played at Derby, June 25, 26, 27, 1896

Distinctly the feature of the match was the wonderful batting of William Storer, who playing in his finest form accomplished the exceptional performance of scoring two separate innings of 100 in the same game. The Derbyshire men had an uphill task – Yorkshire's first total amounting to 416 – but their batting was equal to anything done by the county last season, and at the finish they had rather the best of the draw. In addition to Storer's great achievement, Bagshaw, Evershed, Davidson and Hulme played remarkably well, the Yorkshire bowling being severely punished.

Yorkshire

Mr F. S. Jackson lbw b Porter	51		
J. Tunnicliffe c Storer b Davidson	49	– b Purdy	25
J. T. Brown c Evershed b Davidson	12	– not out	18
D. Denton c Porter b Davidson	48		
R. Moorhouse c Hulme b Porter	42		
E. Wainwright b Davidson	54		
R. Peel b Storer	49		
G. H. Hirst c Porter b Hulme	68		
Lord Hawke b Hulme	21		
Mr F. W. Milligan not out	7		
D. Hunter b Hulme	0		
B 7, l-b 8	15		
	416		43

Derbyshire

Mr S. H. Evershed c Hunter b Milligan	38	– b Wainwright	85
Mr L. G. Wright c Tunnicliffe b Milligan	27	– b Hirst	9
H. Bagshaw c Jackson b Wainwright	10	– b Hirst	115
W. Chatterton c Jackson b Milligan	15	– c Hunter b Peel	29
G. Davidson c Hawke b Peel	45	– b Hirst	29
W. Storer c Jackson b Brown	100	– not out	100
W. Sugg c Milligan b Hirst	7	– c Jackson b Hirst	15
J. H. Purdy b Hirst	1	– b Peel	0
Mr G. A. Marsden c and b Brown	35	– c and b Brown	2
J. Hulme c Tunnicliffe b Brown	0	– not out	51
G. Porter not out	0		
B 2, l-b 1	3	B 12, l-b 3	15
	281	(8 wkts dec.)	450

Derbyshire Bowling

	Overs	Mdns	Runs	Wkts	Overs	Mdns	Runs	Wkts
Davidson	58	23	93	4	6	1	23	—
Hulme	41.3	13	109	3				
Porter	30	10	77	2	12	9	9	—
Bagshaw	5	2	17	—				
Purdy	7	2	25	—	6.3	2	11	1
Sugg	5	—	20	—				
Storer	13	—	49	1				
Chatterton	3	1	11	—				

Yorkshire Bowling

	Overs	Mdns	Runs	Wkts	Overs	Mdns	Runs	Wkts
Wainwright	31	10	61	1	23	2	86	1
Jackson	29	8	68	—	16	4	42	—
Hirst	17	3	47	2	36	7	113	4
Peel	26	9	41	1	22	6	61	2
Milligan	17	3	45	3	5	1	35	—
Brown	5.4	1	16	3	14	4	49	1
Denton					11	1	44	—
Moorhouse					1	—	5	—

Umpires: M. Sherwin and A. Young.

DERBYSHIRE v HAMPSHIRE

Played at Derby, August 1, 2, 3, 1898

Though they failed to beat Hampshire, Derbyshire have every reason to look back upon the match with satisfaction for in scoring a remarkable innings of 645 they established a record for their County ground, while with four men on the side making hundreds, a feat was accomplished that previously had only been done once in first-class cricket – by Yorkshire in 1896 against Warwickshire. Wright obtained 134 in three hours and a quarter, Storer exactly 100 in an hour less, Chatterton 142 in three hours and George Davidson 108 in two hours fifty minutes. In every case the displays were remarkably free from error, the only chances apparently being difficult ones by Storer and Chatterton. Hampshire made a disastrous start and lost half their wickets for 31 runs but Poore and Lee added 110, the former carrying out his bat for 121 when the first innings ended for 240. It was reserved for Quinton to make the sixth hundred in the game and, with the help of some rain which curtailed the final stage, to save his side from defeat. The draw was of course immensely in favour of Derbyshire.

Derbyshire

Mr L. G. Wright c Barrett b Webb 134
Mr S. H. Evershed b Steele 67
H. Bagshaw c Barton b Steele 19
W. Storer c Bennett b Martin 100
W. Chatterton c and b Quinton 142
G. Davidson c Steele b Quinton 108
W. Sugg c Martin b Quinton 33
Mr E. M. Ashcroft c Webb b Quinton 10
Mr A Charlesworth c Poore b Lee 4
F. Davidson not out 0
J. Hancock c Bennett b Quinton 0
B 11, l-b 11, w 1, n-b 5 28

645

Hampshire

	1st innings		2nd innings
V. Barton b G. Davidson	5	– c Storer b F. Davidson	2
Mr E. I. M. Barrett c Storer b G. Davidson	18		
A. Webb c Chatterton b G. Davidson	5	– lbw b F. Davidson	51
Capt. F. W. D. Quinton c Evershed b G. Davidson ..	0	– not out	101
Major R. M. Poore not out	121	– b F. Davidson	15
Mr E. A. English c Chatterton b G. Davidson	0	– not out	14
Mr E. C. Lee b F. Davidson	44		
Mr D. A. Steele b Chatterton	17		
Mr R. A. Bennett b Chatterton	4	– b G. Davidson	16
E. Tate c Evershed b Storer	15		
Martin c F. Davidson b G. Davidson	3		
B 6, l-b 2	8	B 26, l-b 3, w 1, n-b 3	33
	240		232

Hampshire Bowling

	Overs	Mdns	Runs	Wkts
Tate	39	7	118	—
Martin	33	6	109	1
Steele	37	8	109	2
Lee	21	4	58	1
Quinton	21	—	93	5
Webb	30	4	91	1
English	4	1	16	—
Barton	6	—	23	—

Derbyshire Bowling

	Overs	Mdns	Runs	Wkts	Overs	Mdns	Runs	Wkts
G. Davidson	31.4	14	42	6	42	19	73	1
F. Davidson	31	12	68	1	36	20	42	3
Storer	19	—	77	1	5	—	16	—
Hancock	6	—	23	—	14	1	36	—
Chatterton	7	2	22	2				
Sugg					10	1	26	—
Bagshaw					4	1	6	0

Umpires: A. F. Smith and A. A. White.

DERBYSHIRE v YORKSHIRE

For W. Sugg's Benefit

Played at Chesterfield, August 18, 19, 20, 1898

This game will live long in the memories of those who were fortunate enough to witness it, for Brown and Tunnicliffe, commencing Yorkshire's innings on the Thursday, were not parted for five hours and five minutes, their stand lasting until Friday and producing the unprecedented number of 554. Needless to say this remarkable achievement completely eclipsed all previous records in important cricket, not only for the first, but for any wicket. Tunnicliffe was out first and Brown, having reached his 300, knocked his wicket down. Subsequently the other batsmen threw away their wickets in the most sportsmanlike fashion in order to give their side time to win, and the innings realised 662. Derbyshire had a somewhat worn pitch to bat on, and were got out for 118 and 157, ultimately suffering an overwhelming defeat by an innings and 387 runs. Brown gave four chances during the five hours and ten minutes he was batting, and hit forty-eight 4s, six 3s and nineteen 2s. Tunnicliffe was five minutes less making his 243, his figures including forty-eight 4s, three 3s and seven 2s. The proceeds of the match amounted to £340.

Yorkshire

J. T. Brown hit wkt b Storer	300
J. Tunnicliffe c F. Davidson b Storer	243
Lord Hawke c Walker b Storer	14
D. Denton b F. Davidson	45
G. H. Hirst c G. Davidson b Walker	0
Mr F. S. Jackson c Storer b Walker	14
W. Rhodes c Storer b Walker	6
Mr F. W. Milligan c Chatterton b F. Davidson	4
Mr Ernest Smith c Storer b Walker	4
S. Haigh c Ashcroft b F. Davidson	13
D. Hunter not out	0
B 14, l-b 4, n-b 1	19
	662

Derbyshire

Mr S. H. Evershed c Hunter b Jackson	18	– b Smith	12
Mr L. G. Wright c Hawke b Hirst	0	– st Hunter b Rhodes	5
H Bagshaw c Haigh b Jackson	20	– b Jackson	2
W. Storer c Denton b Milligan	13	– c Rhodes b Jackson	25
W. Chatterton b Milligan	6	– c and b Rhodes	54
G. Davidson b Jackson	36	– lbw b Jackson	2
Mr E. M. Ashcroft c Hunter b Jackson	1	– not out	21
W. Sugg c Brown b Smith	8	– b Rhodes	3
F. Davidson c Haigh b Smith	3	– retired	5
Mr A. Charlesworth c Haigh b Rhodes	7	– absent hurt	—
Mr G. G. Walker not out	0	– b Haigh	7
B 5, l-b 1	6	B 15, l-b 6	21
	118		157

Derbyshire Bowling

	Overs	Mdns	Runs	Wkts
G. Davidson	1	—	3	—
Walker	55	11	199	4
F. Davidson	39.3	9	133	3
Sugg	5	—	27	—
Bagshaw	11	1	50	—
Storer	26	1	142	3
Ashcroft	6	1	21	—
Evershed	3	—	13	—
Wright	3	—	24	—
Charlesworth	7	1	31	—

Yorkshire Bowling

	Overs	Mdns	Runs	Wkts	Overs	Mdns	Runs	Wkts
Hirst	10	3	19	1				
Jackson	28	12	52	4	37	22	26	3
Milligan	12	3	36	2	4	2	6	—
Smith	7.1	6	5	2	21	10	35	1
Rhodes	1	1	—	1	29	13	47	3
Brown					4	1	9	—
Haigh					7.1	4	13	1

Umpires: H. Holmes and J. H. Holmes.

ESSEX

ESSEX v LEICESTERSHIRE

Played at Leyton, June 3, 4, 5, 1895

In the opening of this fixture Pickett accomplished the rare feat of taking all ten wickets in an innings. The ground was fast and inclined to be fiery, but it was a remarkable achievement, and the spectators marked their appreciation of it by making an impromptu collection for the popular professional, which realised nearly £20. It was indeed bad luck for a bowler, after earning such a record, to be on the losing side, but, mainly owing to the bowling of Pougher and Woodcock, Leicestershire won an extremely interesting game early on the third day by 75 runs. The batting honours in a comparatively small scoring match were carried off by de Trafford and Chapman for the winners, and by McGahey for the losers. The Essex batting, it will be seen, completely broke down at the finish.

Leicestershire

M. Chapman b Pickett	14	– c Mead b Kortright	56
J. Holland c Russell b Pickett	1	– b Pickett	4
W. Tomlin b Pickett	9	– b Owen	28
A. D. Pougher c Russell b Pickett	10	– c Russell b Kortright	7
Mr C. C. Stone b Pickett	0	– b Kortright	0
Mr C. E. de Trafford c Kortright b Pickett	29	– b Kortright	44
F. Geeson c Mead b Pickett	4	– b Kortright	9
Mr D. Lorrimer b Pickett	0	– b Kortright	8
A. Woodcock b Pickett	20	– c Hailey b Kortright	14
King not out	12	– b Kortright	3
J. P. Whiteside b Pickett	7	– not out	6
L-b 5	5	L-b 11	11
	111		190

Essex

Mr H. G. Owen b Woodcock	1	– c Holland b Geeson	18
H. Carpenter b Woodcock	2	– c Chapman b Woodcock	17
Mr G. F. Higgins c Tomlin b Pougher	3	– c King b Geeson	6
Mr C. McGahey b Pougher	27	– b Woodcock	54
Mr H. Hailey c Geeson b Pougher	2	– b Woodcock	0
Mr A. P. Lucas b Woodcock	0	– b Woodcock	3
J. Burns c Whiteside b Pougher	37	– lbw b Woodcock	6
T. M. Russell b Woodcock	0	– b Woodcock	0
Mr C. J. Kortright b Woodcock	0	– not out	7
W. Mead not out	25	– c Geeson b Pougher	7
H. Pickett b Pougher	0	– c Holland b Woodcock	3
B 6	6	B 1, l-b 1	2
	103		123

Essex Bowling

	Overs	Mdns	Runs	Wkts	Overs	Mdns	Runs	Wkts
Mead	21	4	50	—	41	23	63	—
Pickett	27	11	32	10	13	3	41	1
Kortright	6	2	24	—	36.3	10	63	8
Carpenter					7	2	8	—
Owen					8	5	4	1

Leicestershire Bowling

	Overs	Mdns	Runs	Wkts	Overs	Mdns	Runs	Wkts
Pougher	23.4	11	29	5	24	15	39	1
Woodcock	20	3	53	5	24.1	7	62	7
Geeson	3	—	15	—	13	8	10	2
King					4	1	10	—

Umpires: Draper and Clements.

ESSEX v LEICESTERSHIRE

Played at Leyton, May 25, 26, 27, 1896

Whatever chance of success Leicestershire might have had was lost on the second day, for Essex gained a big advantage then, and despite the Midland's side subsequent improvement, always afterwards held the upper hand, winning in the end by seven wickets. The visitors gave a poor display to begin with, only obtaining 141, and against this Essex scored 126 for the loss of half their wickets. On the following day, thanks to the splendid cricket of Owen and in a lesser degree of Mead and Pickett, the Essex total reached 285. When Leicestershire went in again they gave a much better exhibition. Pougher, assisted by some luck, scored 70, and the aggregate of 225 was assisted by a large number of extras, Russell being incapacitated from keeping wicket. The result however was never in doubt, and Essex won easily on Wednesday with seven wickets in hand. Mead had a large share in the triumph, dismissing fourteen batsmen for 132 runs.

Leicestershire

Mr C. E. de Trafford b Kortright	0	– b Mead	1
Mr A. Lorrimer c Kortright b Mead	8	– c and b Mead	46
J. Holland c Pickett b Mead	31	– c Kortright b Mead	19
Knight b Kortright	5	– c Bull b Mead	5
A. D. Pougher c Russell b Pickett	38	– b Mead	70
W. Tomlin c Kortright b Mead	3	– b Mead	11
Brown b Pickett	5	– b Mead	6
F. Geeson c Carpenter b Mead	3	– b Pickett	3
Coe not out	27	– c sub b Mead	19
A. Woodcock b Pickett	0	– not out	9
J. P. Whiteside b Mead	14	– c sub b Mead	0
B 2, l-b 5	7	B 33, l-b 3	36
	141		225

Essex

Major Orman st Whiteside b Pougher	4		
H. Carpenter b Geeson	22	– c Tomlin b Woodcock	6
Mr P. Perrin b Woodcock	52	– not out	37
Mr C. McGahey c Geeson b Pougher	14	– st Whiteside b Pougher	5
Mr H. G. Owen c Holland b Pougher	82	– not out	0
Mr C. J. Kortright b Pougher	0		
T. M. Russell b Woodcock	2		
Mr C. G. Littlehales b Pougher	7	– c Whiteside b Pougher	21
Mr F. G. Bull b Woodcock	8		
W. Mead c Pougher b Geeson	41		
H. Pickett not out	26		
B 24, l-b 3	27	B 10 l-b 3	13
	285		82

Essex Bowling

	Overs	Mdns	Runs	Wkts	Overs	Mdns	Runs	Wkts
Kortright	18	6	36	2	14	3	39	—
Mead	31.3	9	57	5	33.3	9	75	9
Pickett	17	3	41	3	12	—	52	1
Bull	2	2	—	—	8	3	23	—

Leicestershire Bowling

	Overs	Mdns	Runs	Wkts	Overs	Mdns	Runs	Wkts
Woodcock	27	5	83	3	10	1	18	1
Pougher	40.4	18	77	5	20.1	6	37	2
Geeson	23	8	64	2	11	5	14	—
Coe	13	1	33	—				
Brown	1	—	1	—				

Umpires: J. Street and V. A. Titchmarsh.

ESSEX v LANCASHIRE

Played at Leyton, August 5, 6, 7, 1897

With a victory over Lancashire by six wickets, the Essex eleven gained their greatest triumph in 1897. From first to last it was a splendid game and the victory was fairly earned by first-rate all round cricket. On the opening day, Perrin and McGahey played very finely together, putting on 129 runs in a trifle over two hours; while in the last innings, with the wicket a little broken at one end, and helping Briggs considerably, Carpenter gave so splendid a display that on a collection being made for him a sum of £43 10s. was subscribed. Bull, however, by taking fourteen wickets, had a bigger share in the victory than any of the batsmen. Frank Sugg's batting for Lancashire was superb.

Essex

Mr F. L. Fane c Smith b Briggs	14	– c Smith b Briggs	5
H. Carpenter b Mold	4	– not out	57
Mr P. Perrin c Ellis b Cuttell	67	– c Smith b Cuttell	17
Mr C. McGahey c Hornby b Ellis	87	– b Briggs	14
Mr A. J. Turner st Smith b Briggs	49	– lbw b Briggs	10
T. M. Russell c Smith b Cuttell	0	– not out	13
Mr H. G. Owen c Ellis b Cuttell	10		
Mr C. J. Kortright c Hornby b Briggs	20		
W. Mead c Hornby b Briggs	16		
Mr F. G. Bull not out	0		
H. Pickett c Mold b Briggs	4		
B 11, l-b 8	19	B 6, l-b 9	15
	290		131

Lancashire

Mr A. C. Maclaren c Kortright b Bull	33 – b Bull	3
A. Ward c Kortright b Bull	9 – lbw b Bull	68
F. H. Sugg not out	88 – c Russell b Bull	81
G. R. Baker c Kortright b Bull	5 – c Russell b Mead	22
C. Smith c Turner b Bull	6 – c Kortright b Bull	30
J. Ellis b Kortright	5 – b Kortright	5
J. Briggs b Kortright	0 – c and b Bull	15
W. R. Cuttell st Russell b Bull	5 – c Russell b Kortright	4
A. Hallam c Mead b Kortright	1 – st Russell b Bull	0
Mr A. N. Hornby lbw b Bull	1 – not out	1
A. Mold hit wkt b Bull	5 – b Bull	13
B 5, l-b 5	10 B 1, l-b 5, w 3	9
	168	251

Lancashire Bowling

	Overs	Mdns	Runs	Wkts	Overs	Mdns	Runs	Wkts
Mold	25	9	69	1	1	—	1	—
Briggs	35.3	7	77	5	28	12	42	3
Cuttell	25	7	48	3	18.2	4	45	1
Hallam	22	5	55	—	8	—	28	—
Ellis	8	3	22	—				

Essex Bowling

	Overs	Mdns	Runs	Wkts	Overs	Mdns	Runs	Wkts
Kortright	22	2	80	3	23	7	44	2
Bull	23.4	3	63	7	58.1	21	113	7
Mead	2	—	15	—	21	8	41	1
Pickett					29	11	44	—

Umpires: W. Hearn and G. Hay.

ESSEX v DERBYSHIRE

Played at Leyton, June 20, 21, 1898

Essex gained a most creditable victory by 129 runs, play being prolonged on the Tuesday for twenty-five minutes beyond the usual time for drawing stumps in order that the match might not run into the third day. Though Essex as a team showed much the finer cricket, however, the personal honours of the match clearly rested with George Davidson, who took in all fifteen wickets for 116 runs – seven for 42 and eight for 74. The pitch was not in first rate condition, but Davidson bowled exceptionally well, his length being a marvel of accuracy. Essex were weakened in batting by the absence of A. P. Lucas and A. J. Turner. Owen's first innings of 61 lasted a couple of hours and was a very fine display, and Carpenter was seen to advantage on both days.

Essex

Mr H. G. Owen c F. Davidson b Bestwick	61 – c G. Davidson b Hancock	10
H. Carpenter c and b Bestwick	34 – b G. Davidson	53
Mr P. Perrin b G. Davidson	17 – b G. Davidson	20
Mr C. McGahey b G. Davidson	19 – b Hancock	36
Mr F. Street c and b G. Davidson	6 – b G. Davidson	3
Mr J. W. Bonner c F. Davidson b G. Davidson	1 – c F. Davidson b G. Davidson	3
Mr C. J. Kortright c F. Davidson b G. Davidson	9 – b G. Davidson	14
T. M. Russell b G. Davidson	0 – b G. Davidson	30
W. Mead not out	18 – c Storer b G. Davidson	5
Mr F. G. Bull c Storer b F. Davidson	11 – c Chatterton b G. Davidson	4
Young b G. Davidson	0 – not out	0
B 11, l-b 1, w 1, n-b 2	15 B 4, l-b 6, w 1, n-b 3	14
	191	192

Derbyshire

Mr L. G. Wright c Kortright b Bull	9 – c Russell b Kortright	5
Mr S. H. Evershed st Russell b Bull	13 – c Owen b Bull	5
H. Bagshaw c Perrin b Mead	31 – c Mead b Bull	29
W. Chatterton b Bull	16 – c Perrin b Bull	0
W. Storer lbw b Young	27 – c Mead b Young	41
G. Davidson c Russell b Mead	0 – c Russell b Young	35
W. Sugg b Young	22 – b Kortright	0
Ellis b Kortright	4 – b Young	1
F. Davidson b Kortright	0 – not out	0
J. Hancock not out	3 – b Kortright	0
W. Bestwick b Kortright	5 – b Kortright	0
B 4	4 B 2, l-b 2	4
	134	120

Derbyshire Bowling

	Overs	Mdns	Runs	Wkts	Overs	Mdns	Runs	Wkts
G. Davidson	46.3	30	42	7	37.4	12	74	8
Hancock	13	1	47	0	13	2	37	2
F. Davidson	14	5	29	1	24	11	47	0
Chatterton	6	1	26	0	6	2	8	0
Bestwick	15	4	32	2	6	1	12	0

Essex Bowling

	Overs	Mdns	Runs	Wkts	Overs	Mdns	Runs	Wkts
Kortright	12.4	2	48	3	19	4	55	4
Bull	15	1	50	3	18	7	35	3
Mead	7	0	24	2	6	4	2	0
Young	4	1	8	2	18	8	24	3

Umpires: R. Clayton and G. Burton.

ESSEX v GLOUCESTERSHIRE

Played at Leyton, July 7, 8, 9, 1898

This was one of the closest matches of the season, Gloucestershire just getting home on the third morning by one wicket. It was unfortunate that so fine a game should have been marred by ill-feeling, but it is no secret that the Essex eleven were greatly incensed at much that happened after the first day, complaining bitterly of more than one decision. Mr Grace had never before appeared at Leyton in a county match and he marked the occasion by giving an astonishing display of all-round cricket on the opening day, taking seven wickets for 44 runs and then playing an innings of 126 with which not the slightest fault could be found. He was batting for three hours and ten minutes and scored his 126 out of a total of 203. The close of the game was intensely exciting, two runs being wanted by Gloucestershire when Roberts, the last man, went in. Next to Grace's all-round cricket, Kortright's terrific bowling was clearly the feature of the game.

Essex

Mr H. G. Owen b Grace	10	– b Townsend	0
H. Carpenter b Jessop	14	– c Brown b Wrathall	54
Mr P. Perrin c and b Grace	7	– c Grace b Wright	81
Mr C. McGahey b Grace	0	– b Brown	1
Mr A. J. Turner st Board b Grace	9	– lbw b Townsend	39
Mr A. P. Lucas c Board b Jessop	31	– c Board b Brown	22
T. M. Russell c Board b Roberts	0	– st Board b Wright	10
Mr C. J. Kortright lbw b Grace	2	– c Brown b Wright	4
W. Mead c Champain b Grace	34	– c Jessop b Wright	12
Mr F. G. Bull st Board b Grace	14	– not out	7
Young not out	2	– b Jessop	11
B 4, l-b 1	5	Extras	9
	128		250

Gloucestershire

Mr W. G. Grace c Russell b Bull	126	– b Kortright	49
H. Wrathall c Russell b Kortright	0	– c Carpenter b Mead	4
Mr W. Troup c Kortright b Mead	3	– b Kortright	0
Mr C. O. H. Sewell c Russell b Mead	5	– c Lucas b Kortright	34
Mr C. L. Townsend b Mead	51	– b Kortright	15
Mr F. H. B. Champain c and b Kortright	13	– c Russell b Mead	24
Mr G. L. Jessop b Kortright	10	– not out	14
Mr W. S. A. Brown b Kortright	5	– b Kortright	1
J. H. Board not out	1	– b Kortright	0
Mr E. C. Wright b Kortright	0	– lbw b Kortright	0
F. G. Roberts b Bull	0	– not out	1
B 13, l-b 3, n-b 1	17	B 8, l-b 1	9
	231		151

Gloucestershire Bowling

	Overs	Mdns	Runs	Wkts	Overs	Mdns	Runs	Wkts
Jessop	16	3	37	2	13.2	2	41	1
Townsend	6	1	18	0	13	3	39	2
Grace	16.1	4	44	7	20	9	25	0
Roberts	7	1	24	1	7	1	20	0
Brown					26	8	52	2
Wrathall					9	0	32	1
Wright					15	3	32	4

Essex Bowling

	Overs	Mdns	Runs	Wkts	Overs	Mdns	Runs	Wkts
Kortright	24	8	41	5	20.3	5	57	7
Bull	16	4	47	2	14	4	49	0
Mead	21	6	45	3	10	8	23	2
Young	14	4	38	0	6	1	13	0
McGahey	3	0	20	0				
Carpenter	5	2	12	0				
Turner	5	2	11	0				

Umpires: G. Burton and A. Chester.

ESSEX v YORKSHIRE

Played at Leyton, May 25, 26, 1899

In this match, at the end of Whitsun week, the Essex eleven cut a very sorry figure. Indeed, apart from the fine bowling of Walter Mead, there was nothing in the game upon which they could look back with satisfaction. Not one of their batsmen could make headway against Rhodes on a slow wicket, while on the other hand the Yorkshire team – favoured by the fact that the ground was at starting too soft to be difficult – scored uncommonly well. Rhodes gave a very significant suggestion of what sort of a bowler he would be if ever he should be favoured with a wet season by taking fifteen wickets for 56 runs. This is one of the biggest things he has ever done. Yorkshire won the match by 241 runs.

Yorkshire

J. Tunnicliffe c and b Mead	14	– b Mead	27
J. T. Brown b Mead	16	– b Mead	40
Mr F. S. Jackson c Russell b Young	28	– b Mead	23
Mr F. Mitchell b Reeves	10	– b Mead	8
D. Denton c Carpenter b Mead	33	– b Bull	37
E. Wainwright b Mead	51	– c McGahey b Mead	12
G. H. Hirst lbw b Mead	6	– c Perrin b Young	4
S. Haigh c Reeves b Mead	0	– b Mead	30
Lord Hawke c Mead b Young	0	– b Mead	0
W. Rhodes lbw b Mead	3	– b Ayres	8
D. Hunter not out	0	– not out	2
B 3, l-b 8	11	L-b 1	1
	172		192

Essex

Mr H. G. Owen b Rhodes	0	– b Haigh	3
H. Carpenter b Rhodes	1	– st Hunter b Rhodes	17
Mr P. Perrin b Rhodes	11	– c and b Haigh	8
Mr C. McGahey b Rhodes	8	– b Rhodes	0
Mr A. J. Turner b Rhodes	0	– b Haigh	12
G. Ayres c Wainwright b Rhodes	0	– st Hunter b Rhodes	0
T. M. Russell c Hirst b Rhodes	3	– b Haigh	0
W. Reeves c Denton b Rhodes	12	– st Hunter b Rhodes	2
W. Mead b Jackson	12	– b Rhodes	1
Mr F. G. Bull b Rhodes	4	– c Jackson b Rhodes	6
H. Young not out	3	– not out	5
B 2, l-b 3	5	B 8, l-b 2	10
	59		64

Essex Bowling

	Overs	Mdns	Runs	Wkts	Overs	Mdns	Runs	Wkts
Mead	36.1	18	37	7	38.2	11	90	7
Young	22	4	56	2	20	8	55	1
Bull	17	5	43	0	16	3	33	1
Reeves	6	1	21	1	4	2	11	0
Ayres	1	0	4	0	3	1	2	1

Yorkshire Bowling

	Overs	Mdns	Runs	Wkts	Overs	Mdns	Runs	Wkts
Rhodes	15.2	6	28	9	16.3	4	28	6
Jackson	15	5	26	1				
Haigh					16	5	26	4

Umpires: J. J. Tuck and W. Hearn.

ESSEX v SURREY

Played at Leyton, July 13, 14, 1899

This was the great catastrophe of the Essex season. Going in first on a wicket that, owing to some strange blunder, had been very much over-watered, Essex were all out in an hour and a quarter for 37, thus practically losing the match before lunch on the first day. In the second innings W. M. Turner and the colt Buckenham made a most plucky effort, putting on 96 runs together in seventy minutes for the seventh wicket, but their labours were quite fruitless. It was a great disappointment that the most interesting county match of the Leyton season should have been so completely spoiled. The Surrey men played their winning game very well, Lockwood as a bowler carrying off the chief honours. Surrey won by nine wickets.

Essex

Mr H. G. Owen c Lees b Brockwell	10	– c Wood b Lockwood	3
H. Carpenter b Brockwell	2	– c Key b Lockwood	11
Mr P. Perrin c H. B. Richardson b Brockwell	7	– b Lockwood	0
Mr C. McGahey c Wood b Lockwood	9	– c Lees b T. Richardson	15
Mr A. P. Lucas c Knox b Lockwood	1	– c Wood b T. Richardson	7
Mr W. M. Turner b Lockwood	0	– c Hayward b Lockwood	65
T. M. Russell b Brockwell	0	– b Lockwood	6
Buckenham b Lockwood	3	– c Wood b T. Richardson	41
Mr F. G. Bull c Knox b Lockwood	0	– c Brockwell b Lees	13
H. Young not out	5	– run out	4
W. Mead c Brockwell b Lockwood	0	– not out	0
		B 5, l-b 1	6
	37		176

Surrey

	First innings		Second innings	
W. Brockwell c Lucas b Mead	19	–	not out	23
R. Abel b Young	10	–	c Turner b Young	11
Mr F. P. Knox b Young	11	–	not out	29
Mr D. L. A. Jephson run out	18			
T. Hayward run out	6			
W. H. Lockwood c Mead b Young	0			
Mr H. B. Richardson c Carpenter b Bull	39			
H. Wood c Russell b Young	8			
Mr K. J. Key st Russell b Bull	29			
W. Lees not out	0			
T. Richardson b Bull	3			
B 3	3		B 4, l-b 3	7
	146			70

Surrey Bowling

	Overs	Mdns	Runs	Wkts	Overs	Mdns	Runs	Wkts
Brockwell	11	5	19	4	9	2	27	0
Lockwood	10.3	3	18	6	23	2	70	5
Richardson					21	5	38	3
Jephson					2	0	11	0
Lees					4.4	1	10	1
Knox					3	0	14	0

Essex Bowling

	Overs	Mdns	Runs	Wkts	Overs	Mdns	Runs	Wkts
Young	26	8	64	4	8.2	0	22	1
Buckenham	8	1	25	0	1	0	10	0
Mead	20	7	42	1	7	3	21	0
Bull	2.4	0	12	3	3	0	10	0

Umpires: W. Shrewsbury and A. Young.

ESSEX v GLOUCESTERSHIRE

Played at Leyton, August 3, 4, 5, 1899

The Gloucestershire eleven gave a fine display of all-round cricket and richly deserved their victory by an innings and three runs. Townsend's wonderful batting was followed up by bowling scarcely less admirable, Paish being seen at almost his best. Townsend was at the wickets for five hours and three quarters, going in with the score at 41. During his long stay he did not, so far as could be seen, give a chance and so complete was his mastery over the bowling that he was only once or twice beaten by the ball. Though, to a large extent defensive in character, his innings included seventeen 4s. As the wicket was one of the firmest prepared at Leyton during the season, Essex might have been expected to score heavily but Fane – in great form in August – alone did anything out of the common. He played with great steadiness, batting two hours for his 48 and three for his 65. Essex could no doubt have saved the single innings defeat if they had not been a man short on Saturday. Russell's arm was so swollen – from the effect of a mosquito bite – that he could not go in.

Gloucestershire

Mr R. W. Rice st Russell b Bull	6
H. Wrathall c Street b Young	34
Mr C. L. Townsend not out	181
Mr F. H. B. Champain c Russell b Mead	13
Mr C. O. H. Sewell c Perrin b Bull	23
Mr W. Troup b Young	54
Mr G. L. Jessop b McGahey	84
Mr W. S. A. Brown c Russell b Perrin	14
A. Paish c Russell b Young	0
Boroughs b Mead	25
F. G. Roberts c Perrin b Mead	3
B 3, w 1	4
	441

Essex

Mr F. L. Fane c and b Townsend	48	– c Townsend b Paish	65
H. Carpenter c Jessop b Roberts	34	– c Brown b Paish	26
Mr P. Perrin c Brown b Townsend	37	– c Sewell b Paish	23
Mr C. McGahey b Roberts	9	– lbw b Paish	13
Mr A. P. Lucas not out	39	– b Brown	1
Mr F. Street c and b Townsend	14	– b Brown	0
Mr H. G. Owen b Townsend	3	– not out	24
T. M. Russell run out	2	– absent	0
H. Young c Townsend b Roberts	0	– st Boroughs b Townsend	39
Mr F. G. Bull c and b Paish	19	– c Champain b Paish	0
W. Mead c Jessop b Paish	0	– st Boroughs b Paish	7
B 10, w 1, n-b 4	15	B 11, l-b 6, w 2, n-b 1	20
	220		218

Essex Bowling

	Overs	Mdns	Runs	Wkts
Bull	61	16	158	2
Young	48	9	126	3
Mead	30.3	10	59	3
McGahey	9	1	42	1
Carpenter	8	4	13	0
Street	2	0	14	0
Owen	2	0	14	0
Perrin	3	0	11	1

Gloucestershire Bowling

	Overs	Mdns	Runs	Wkts	Overs	Mdns	Runs	Wkts
Jessop	29	4	68	0	22	5	53	0
Paish	16.3	4	40	2	31.2	10	67	6
Roberts	20	9	33	3	20	11	31	0
Townsend	24	2	64	4	12	3	30	1
Brown					15	9	17	2

Umpires: R. Clayton and W. Hearn.

GLOUCESTERSHIRE

GLOUCESTERSHIRE v NOTTINGHAMSHIRE

Played at Clifton College, August 22, 23, 24, 1872

As Mr W. G. Grace was in Canada when this match was played and neither Mr Strachan, Mr Filgate, nor Mr Brice were able to play, it was thought by many that Gloucestershire would suffer an emphatic defeat. Not so, for when the play, in those memorable three days at Clifton, had become part of cricket history, the Gloucestershire men had made 484 runs for the loss of fourteen wickets and had much the best of the drawn match, wherein 723 runs had been scored with only 24 of the forty wickets down.

The weather was superb during the three days and the attendances large, fashionable and influential. The wickets were like the weather and the batting of the cracks so brilliantly effective that three of them scored 427 runs, so many as 279 of those runs being made in three not out innings; indeed the two Gloucestershire v Nottinghamshire matches in 1872 were so unprecedently prolific in runs to not out innings as to merit their special record here:

At Nottingham		At Clifton	
J. Selby	not out 128	Mr G. F. Grace, 1st innings ..	not out 115
Mr Strachan	not out 27	Mr G. F. Grace, 2nd innings .	not out 72
		R. Daft	not out 92
		Mr Bush	not out 13

447 runs to the not out innings of two such matches in one season is a batting feature, we think, without parallel in the history of County cricket.

Dr E. M. Grace and Mr Matthews opened the Gloucestershire batting to the bowling of J. C. Shaw and McIntyre, who, with the remainder of the Midland Eleven, had travelled over night from Sheffield and were consequently too rest-robbed and wearied to play up to their true form. The Doctor and Mr Matthews had made 68 runs (Dr Grace 42) when luncheon was called – no wicket down; but from the second ball afterwards delivered Mr Matthews was had at wicket. Mr Townsend made 15 whilst the Doctor done the rest of the work in hitting the score to 129, when Mr Townsend "played on"; then it was Mr G. F. Grace faced his brother, and the score was rapidly hit to 170, when Dr Grace was smartly caught out at wicket for 108, the result of two hours and twenty minutes hitting that included 28 singles, four 2s, four 3s and so many as fifteen 4s. Mr E. K. Browne and Mr G. F. Grace continued the fast scoring up to 214, when the Cheltenham Captain was captured at wicket and at 216 Wyld also had Mr Fewings. Mr Bush made 11, including a 5 from Daft, when he was bowled by Morley; and when the stumps were drawn for the day, at 6.30, the Gloucestershire innings were this shape:

six wickets down .... 264 runs scored.
Mr G. F. Grace, not out 77. Mr Lang, not out 6.

On Friday play was resumed about noon; Selby keeping wicket v Wyld, whose hand was damaged. At 268 Mr Lang was out; at 287 Mr Fox was stumped (Mr G. F. Grace then having made 98). At 289 Morley bowled Mr Carter, and when Barnes had bowled Mr Miles the innings was finished at 1.27 for 317 runs; Mr G. F. Grace not out 115, a fine innings that was made by 24 singles, five 2s, seven 3s and fifteen 4s; Mr G. F. made 115 of the 188 runs whilst he was at wickets. The wickets fell as follows:

1/69 2/129 3/169 4/214 5/216 6/245 7/268 8/287 9/289 10/317

The Notts. men commenced batting at twenty minutes to two; Bignall was bowled with the score at 3; Wyld was bowled at 19; and at 26, Oscroft played the ball on. Daft and

Selby then made a slight stand, but at 54, Selby was out. From 54, Daft and McIntyre increased the score to 81, when the Doctor bowled McIntyre. Daft (playing in his best form) was then faced by Barnes and – the Colt batting steadily and well – 50 runs were added to the score, but at 131, Mr Lang bowled Barnes for 33 – the second highest Notts. score and a thorough good bit of batting that included four 4s. Seaton was bowled at 166, and Reynolds at 179, whereupon the second day's cricket closed with the Notts. score at follows:

eight wickets down .... 179 runs scored.
Daft, not out .... 61.

On Saturday the attendance was a glorious one all round, numbering close on to 8,000. Daft and Morley resumed the hitting and had made the score 195, when Mr Lang bowled Morley; and as J. C. Shaw was the last man it was thought the innings would soon be up; not it, for J. C. stayed so stubbornly that he enabled Daft to materially increase the score until Shaw was bowled for 9, and the innings ended at a trifle before two for 239 runs – every one of the ten Notts. wickets having been bowled down. Daft was altogether about five hours at wickets; he went in with the score at 19 for two wickets, so 220 runs were made during his stay; his 92 not out included eleven 2s, one 3, five 4s and consequently so many as forty-seven singles. Notts. having just escaped following on, the Gloucestershire second innings was commenced at 3.10. Dr Grace made 40 runs in sixty minutes, when he was had at long-field, the score at 59. Mr G. F. Grace then went in, but at 63, a capital catch by Reynolds settled Mr Matthews; at 112, Mr Browne was stumped. Mr Fewings was unfortunate, but Mr Bush and Mr G. F. Grace stayed until the stumps were drawn at six o'clock; the match drawn, Mr Bush not out 13 and the score book showing the following wonderfully successful batting exploit:

Mr G. F. Grace not out 115 and not out 72.

In Mr G. F. Grace's 72 there were eight 4s and a great square-leg hit for 5 from Shaw. The result of the three day's cricket was the following score:

Gloucestershire

Dr E. M. Grace c Wyld b Barnes	108	– c Daft b J. C. Shaw	40
T. G. Matthews, Esq. c Wyld b Daft	21	– c Reynolds b J. C. Shaw	18
F. Townsend Esq. b Morley	15		
G. F. Grace Esq. not out	115	– not out	72
E. K. Browne Esq. c Wyld b Daft	19	– st Selby b Daft	16
J. Fewings Esq. st Wyld b Daft	1	– c McIntyre b Oscroft	0
J. A. Bush Esq. b Morley	11	– not out	13
T. W. Lang Esq. c Barnes b J. C. Shaw	6		
J. C. K. Fox Esq. st Selby b Morley	2		
F. A. Carter Esq. b Morley	1		
R. F. Miles Esq. b Barnes	10		
L-b 5, w 2, n-b 1	8	B 3, l-b 4, w 1	8
	317		167

Nottinghamshire

Bignall b F. Grace	2	J. Seaton b E. Grace	18
Wm. Oscroft b F. Grace	17	H. Reynolds b Browne	8
Wyld b F. Grace	4	F. Morley b Lang	8
Richard Daft not out	92	J. C. Shaw b Lang	9
J. Selby b F. Grace	18	B 11, l-b 1, w 3	15
Martin McIntyre b E. Grace	15		
T. Barnes b Lang	33		239

Nottinghamshire Bowling

	Overs	Mdns	Runs	Wkts	Overs	Mdns	Runs	Wkts
Morley	73	36	84	4	13	5	24	—
J. C. Shaw	50	22	103	1	31	12	56	2
Daft	22	3	68	3	13	2	35	1
McIntyre	12	4	31	—	20	9	23	—
Barnes	6	1	23	2				
Oscroft					10	2	21	1

Gloucestershire Bowling

	Overs	Mdns	Runs	Wkts
Mr F. Grace	90	39	81	4
Mr Lang	63	36	65	3
Dr Grace	40	12	49	2
Mr Miles	26	6	22	—
Mr Browne	4	2	7	1

Umpires: Pullin and Luck.

THE THREE BROTHERS GRACE ON THE 22nd OF AUGUST, 1872

A coincidence worthy of record here is, that on the day the above match was commenced – the 22nd of August – all the three brothers Grace scored largely, thus,

At Clifton,	At Clifton,	In Canada,
Dr Grace scored 108.	Mr G. F. Grace scored 77 not out. (A portion of his innings of 115 runs.)	Mr W. G. Grace scored 81.

GLOUCESTERSHIRE v SURREY

Played at Cheltenham, August 24, 25, 1874

Surrey's innings of 27 runs is the smallest ever played by a Surrey County Eleven; 6 was the largest score made and only 100 balls were bowled in that innings, which was of fifty-five minutes' duration, the bowling of Mr W. G. and Mr G. F. Grace getting the lot out at a cost of a trifle over one run per over and two and a half per wicket. But the wickets were not in good order, the report stating "the excessive use of the heavy roller had made the turf rather rotten". That something was wrong with the wickets may readily be inferred from the fact that notwithstanding such hitters as "The Three Graces", Jupp, Pooley, Humphrey, Mr Crooke, Swann, Mr Townsend, Mr Gordon, etc. played, 27 by Mr W. Grace was the largest score hit and only 224 runs were made in the match, which was won by Gloucestershire by an innings and 24 runs, thus squaring up the defeat Surrey gave them in June. Dr Grace was very effective at point, taking five wickets thereat, finishing off the last three of Surrey in great form, one record stating : "The Doctor, standing resolutely close up at point, took the remaining batsmen one after the other almost off their bats". But Dr Grace always was famous for this kind of daring point-work, the surprise being that he has hitherto fortunately escaped enriching his profession with a case of broken head; however, "All's well that ends well".

Surrey

H. Jupp c E. Grace b F. Grace	2	– lbw b W. Grace	0
Richard Humphrey b W. Grace	2	– c and b W. Grace	21
Swann st Bush b W. Grace	0	– c E. Grace b W. Grace	5
W. Read Esq. c Halford b W. Grace	0	– b W. Grace	2
Pooley c E. Grace b F. Grace	3	– c Halford b Lang	15
G. Strachan Esq. lbw b W. Grace	6	– c and b W. Grace	1
Geo. Clifford b F. Grace	1	– c and b Lang	1
Freeman not out	5	– c E. Grace b W. Grace	7
W. Carter c Bush b W. Grace	5	– c E. Grace b Lang	1
Southerton b W. Grace	2	– c E. Grace b W. Grace	17
James Street c Gordon b W. Grace	0	– not out	1
L-b 1	1	N-b 2	2
	27		73

Gloucestershire

W. G. Grace Esq. c Freeman b Southerton	27	E. M. Knapp Esq. run out	0
Dr E. M. Grace c Street b Clifford	10	F. G. Monkland Esq. lbw b Street	19
F. Townsend Esq. c Carter b Clifford	16	G. Halford Esq. not out	1
G. F. Grace Esq. st Pooley b Southerton	0	J. A. Bush Esq. c Freeman b Southerton	6
C. Gordon c sub. b Southerton	12	B 1, l-b 2	3
F. J. Crooke Esq. c Freeman b Southerton	20		
T. W. Lang Esq. c and b Southerton	10		124

Gloucestershire Bowling

	Overs	Mdns	Runs	Wkts	Overs	Mdns	Runs	Wkts
Mr W. Grace	13	4	18	7	25	7	48	7
Mr F. Grace	12	7	8	3	9	2	12	—
Mr Lang					15.2	7	11	3

Surrey Bowling

	Overs	Mdns	Runs	Wkts
Southerton	27.2	11	43	6
Clifford	17	4	47	2
Street	10	2	31	1

Umpires: Pullin and Thomas Humphrey.

GLOUCESTERSHIRE v SUSSEX

Played at Cheltenham, August 23, 24, 25, 1875

Dr E. M. Grace was front rank man for Gloucestershire in this match, for "The Doctor" scored 65 and 71, had five wickets with his bowling and caught out another.

Dr Grace and Mr W. Grace began the batting; when 23 runs had been made Lillywhite bowled Mr W. Grace for five singles. "The Doctor" was missed by Humphreys when he had made 34; he then hit away until he had made 65, when, wrote the critic, "Dr Grace drove a ball back tremendously hard, which Lillywhite caught splendidly, the grand catch eliciting loud applause, as did Dr Grace's innings". Dr Grace's 65 included three 3s, four 4s and two 5s (leg hits). "The Doctor" was sixth out the score at 110 and when seven wickets had fallen and 127 runs scored Mr Greenfield bowled, and with such success that he delivered three overs for one run and three wickets, all bowled and so summarily ended that innings.

Mr Greenfield and Mr Cotterill started the Sussex hitting to the bowling of Mr W. Grace and Mr Miles. Mr Cotterill did defence, Mr Greenfield defiance, and so successful were both that when one hour and twenty minutes had been played away Mr Greenfield had made over 70 runs and Mr Cotterill was had at wicket for 13, the score then standing at 91 for one wicket, the day's play ending with Sussex having scored 110 runs for two wickets, Mr Greenfield not out 79, Charlwood not out 9.

On the morrow Mr Greenfield was easily got rid of by mid-off, the score at 118; Mr Greenfield's 79 was made by a fine drive from Mr F. Grace for 5, seven 4s, four 3s, etc. Charlwood made 41 (including six 4s); Mr Winslow 22; and Lillywhite 19 not out, the innings closing for 204 runs, or 74 on.

Gloucestershire's second was commenced by Dr Grace and Mr W. Grace; they had made 53 runs when Mr W. G. was out for 19, but the Doctor was not done with until 122 had been scored; then he was stumped for 71, a dashing display of batting that included a chance to long-on when he had made 34 and eight 4s. Others scored, and when the stumps were drawn for the day four wickets had fallen and 171 runs had been scored.

On the third day 63 more runs were made for the Shire, Mr Monkland making 29, and Mr A. H. Heath (then of Clifton College, now of Oxford University) 25; the innings closed for 234 runs made from 124 Sussex overs.

Sussex then had 161 runs to score to win; they lost a wicket (Lillywhite's) at 14 and another (Humphreys') at 16; then Mr Cotterill and Mr Greenfield were together and by good batting they increased the score to 72, when a catch at mid-off settled Mr Greenfield for 29. At 96 Charlwood and Mr Cotterill both left, the former for 14 and latter for 37; and at 98 Mr Winslow, Mr Kennedy and Mr Soames were all three out. At 102 Fillery was run out and Mr Smith the last man of Sussex went in and wrote a critic in the *Sportsman*, "the Gloucestershire fielding was very smart"; for continued the critic, "W. G. now took up a very unusual position, confronting Mr Smith, and not more than four yards from him, just out of the bowlers' line, a circumstance calculated to intimidate and embarrass a batsman. He gave Phillips a wider berth". *Bell's Life* also noticed the same "incident", stating "Mr W. G. Grace had been fielding right in front of the batsman in a most unusual way". However and for all that, Phillips and Mr Smith increased the score to 120, when Mr F. Grace at cover point caught out Phillips; so Gloucestershire won the match by 40 runs.

Gloucestershire

Dr E. M. Grace c and b Lillywhite	65	– st H. Phillips b Greenfield	71
W. G. Grace Esq. b Lillywhite	5	– c and b Lillywhite	19
F. Townsend Esq. c Fillery b A. Smith	2	– c Winslow b Fillery	37
G. F. Grace Esq. b A. Smith	16	– b A. Smith	22
G. N. Wyatt Esq. c Charlwood b Lillywhite	1	– c Kennedy b Fillery	3
A. H. Heath Esq. b Lillywhite	0	– c H. Phillips b Lillywhite	25
Capt. Kington c Fillery b A. Smith	17	– c Charlwood b Greenfield	4
T. G. Matthews Esq. b Greenfield	7	– b Greenfield	1
F. G. Monkland Esq. not out	11	– c Humphreys b A. Smith	29
J. A. Bush Esq. b Greenfield	2	– not out	8
F. Miles Esq. b Greenfield	0	– c H. Phillips b Lillywhite	3
B 4	4	B 2, l-b 9, w 1	12
	130		234

Sussex

J. M. Cotterill Esq. c J. Bush b F. M. Grace	13 – b E. M. Grace	37
F. J. Greenfield Esq. c Townsend b W. Grace	79 – c W. Grace b Miles	29
W. Humphreys c Monkland b E. M. Grace	2 – hit wkt b W. Grace	1
H. Charlwood b F. Grace	41 – c E. M. Grace b Miles	14
Fillery c J. Bush b Miles	5 – run out	0
L. Winslow Esq. c and b W. Grace	22 – c W. Grace b Miles	2
James Lillywhite not out	19 – c J. Bush b W. Grace	8
C. M. Kennedy Esq. lbw b F. Grace	6 – c Miles b E. M. Grace	0
W. A. Soames Esq. st J. Bush b W. Grace	0 – c W. Grace b E. M. Grace	0
Henry Phillips run out	2 – c F. Grace b Miles	16
Arthur Smith Esq. c J. Bush b W. Grace	2 – not out	6
B 4, l-b 4, w 5	13 B 6, l-b 1	7
	204	120

Sussex Bowling

	Overs	Mdns	Runs	Wkts	Overs	Mdns	Runs	Wkts
Lillywhite	37	16	33	4	48.2	18	69	3
Mr A. Smith	25	6	47	3	23	13	30	2
Fillery	16	1	45	—	30	7	70	2
Mr Greenfield	3	2	1	3	18	4	40	3
Mr Winslow					5	1	13	—

Gloucestershire Bowling

	Overs	Mdns	Runs	Wkts	Overs	Mdns	Runs	Wkts
Mr W. Grace	57.1	23	71	4	27	9	49	2
Mr Miles	41	17	58	1	25	13	18	4
Mr F. Grace	26	11	42	2	15	2	26	—
Dr E. M. Grace	10	3	20	2	15	6	20	3

Umpires: C. K. Pullin and another.

GLOUCESTERSHIRE v SURREY

Played at Clifton, August 26, 27, 28, 1875

Mr G. F. Grace hit an 180 runs not out innings in this match, and thereby not only scored more runs than did the whole Surrey Eleven with the bat in either of their innings, but he made the largest Gloucestershire score of the season, and the second highest "County" innings of 1875.

The visiting Eleven did not include Mr A. P. Lucas, Mr Read, Mr Game, or the Captain, Mr Strachan; consequently the batting and fielding power of old Surrey was materially weakened. The batting was commenced by Surrey. Jupp was thirty minutes at wickets for 8 runs; Elliott played well for 32, as did Swann for 28, but although Pooley added 24, the ninth wicket had fallen with the score at 117; then Southerton went to Richard Humphrey's aid, and notwithstanding Mr Miles, Mr W. Grace, Dr E. M. Grace, and Mr G. F. Grace all took a turn at bowling, R. H. and J. S. hit the score to 181, when Humphrey lifted one from "The Doctor" and was out for 39, Southerton not out 33.

Gloucestershire batting was commenced by Mr W. Grace and Mr R. E. Bush, and Surrey bowling by Southerton and Street. Mr W. Grace's innings was brief and busy, for when 23 runs only had been scored Mr W. Grace was out for 21, made in twelve minutes by a square-leg hit out of the ground from Street for 6, two 4s, etc. Mr Townsend and Mr R. E. Bush then made the score 33, when an "incident" occurred which was thus described in *The Sportsman*: – "At 33 the ball had been just returned whilst a run was made; both men got in their ground, but Mr Bush stepped over the crease, and was standing outside, when Pooley signalled to Street to shy the ball down. He did so, and Pooley put the wicket down, and on appeal the Surrey umpire decided that Mr Bush was run out. The affair gave rise to considerable dispute, and a great deal of angry contention, it being alleged that the ball was out of play at the time." (It is deplorable that cricketers and spectators so frequently ignore the fact that Rule XXXVI explicitly states – "The Umpires are the sole judges of fair or unfair play, and all disputes shall be determined by them." Play was stopped for a while by this "incident"; on resuming Mr F. Grace batted, but with the score at 38 cricket ceased for the day.

The next day Mr F. Grace and Mr Townsend increased the score to 105, when a good ball from Southerton bowled Mr Townsend for 42. Dr Grace then made 28, when he was stumped, the score at 198; none others stayed with Mr F. Grace excepting Mr Monkland, who went in with the score at 221, and out at 333, having made 59 by a square leg-hit for five from Street, eight 4s, etc. The others were quickly done for, and at 5.30 the innings was over for 369; Mr F. Grace 180 not out. The wickets went down this-wise:

1/23 2/33 3/105 4/198 5/221 6/221 7/333 8/348 9/349 10/369

Mr G. F. Grace went to wickets on the evening of the first day when the score was at 33 for two wickets; he played all through the remainder of the innings, and at 5.30 the following day he was not out 180, one report describing his score: "a magnificent innings made by hitting brilliant in the extreme"; another recorded it as "a splendid display of batting made without the shadow of a chance". Mr F. Grace's hits were forty-three singles, fifteen 2s, four 3s, twenty 4s and three 5s (drive from Southerton, and leg-hits from Street and Southerton). Surrey then scored a second innings of 104 runs, so Gloucestershire won by an innings and 84 runs.

Surrey

W. Charman Esq. c Townsend b W. Grace	4	– c Townsend b E. M. Grace	7
H. Jupp c F. Grace b Miles	8	– not out	13
G. Elliott c F. Grace b Miles	32	– c Townsend b Miles	6
J. Swann c Monkland b Miles	28	– st J. Bush b E. M. Grace	0
Potter st J. Bush b W. Grace	3	– b E. M. Grace	11
Pooley c and b W. Grace	24	– b E. M. Grace	29
R. Humphrey c Townsend b E. M. Grace	39	– run out	14
Freeman b W. Grace	0	– b W. Grace	0
W. C. Wheeler c Heath b W. Grace	0	– c J. Bush b E. M. Grace	13
James Street c Heath b W. Grace	1	– b E. M. Grace	4
Southerton not out	33	– b E. M. Grace	0
B 2, l-b 1, w 6	9	B 4, l-b 2, w 1	7
	181		104

Gloucestershire

W. G. Grace Esq. c Pooley b Southerton	21	F. G. Monkland Esq. lbw b Freeman	59
R. E. Bush Esq. run out	7	T. G. Matthews Esq. run out	1
F. Townsend Esq. b Southerton	42	J. A. Bush Esq. n Southerton	1
G. F. Grace Esq. not out	180	R. F. Miles Esq. b Southerton	11
Dr E. M. Grace st Pooley b Southerton	28	B 11, l-b 4	15
A. H. Heath Esq. b Southerton	4		
G. N. Wyatt Esq. b Southerton	0		369

Gloucestershire Bowling

	Overs	Mdns	Runs	Wkts	Overs	Mdns	Runs	Wkts
Mr Miles	46	13	71	3	23	12	26	1
Mr W. Grace	45	18	70	6	12	4	25	1
Dr Grace	18.2	11	16	1	25	9	46	7
Mr F. Grace	9	4	15	—				

Surrey Bowling

	Overs	Mdns	Runs	Wkts
Southerton	58.1	25	76	7
Street	45	12	99	—
Potter	22	7	51	—
Mr Charman	15	8	24	—
Pooley	11	—	34	—
Wheeler	9	3	17	—
Elliott	8	3	20	—
Freeman	5	—	22	1
Swan	4	1	11	—

Umpires: C. K. Pullin and W. Mortlock.

GLOUCESTERSHIRE BOWLING IN 1875

	Overs	Mdns	Runs	Wides	Wkts (caught)	Wkts (bowled)	Total wkts
*Mr W. G. Grace .	568.2	256	792	2	36	7	54
*Mr R. F. Miles . . .	365.2	164	438	22	20	4	25
*Mr G. F. Grace . .	338	137	492	1	7	14	22
*Dr E. M. Grace . .	102.2	47	147	—	8	6	15
Mr Townsend	30	6	60	—	1	2	3
Mr Brotherhood . .	30	9	67	—	—	2	2
*Mr C. Gordon . . .	22.3	6	46	—	1	—	2

Mr Crooke bowled four overs for 12 runs; and Mr Wyatt bowled three overs for 4 runs and a wicket.

* From Mr W Grace's bowling six were lbw, four were stumped, and one hit wicket; from Mr Miles' bowling one was stumped; from Mr F. Grace's bowling one was lbw; from Dr Grace's bowling one was stumped; and from Mr Gordon's bowling one was stumped.

Gloucestershire wicket-keeping in 1875; Mr J. A. Bush stumped seven and caught out nineteen.

GLOUCESTERSHIRE BATTING IN 1875

	Matches	Inns	Not outs	Times bowled	Times caught	Highest Inns	Runs	Avge
Mr W. G. Grace . .	8	14	—	4	7	119	541	38.9
Dr E. M. Grace . . .	4	6	—	1	3	71	214	35.4
Mr G. F. Grace . . .	8	14	2	6	6	180*	430	35.1
Mr F. Townsend . .	7	12	—	3	7	84	289	24.1
Mr F. G. Monkland	8	14	3	4	4	59	208	18.1
Mr G. N. Wyatt . . .	7	13	—	6	7	37	148	11.5
Mr J. A. Bush	8	14	5	4	3	22*	88	9.7
Mr R. E. Bush	5	8	—	4	1	32	73	9.1
Mr T. G. Matthews	8	14	—	5	6	23	105	7.7
Mr A. H. Heath . . .	6	10	—	6	4	25	52	5.2
Mr R. F. Miles	6	10	1	4	2	11	26	2.8
Mr Brotherhood . .	3	6	2	4	—	2	3	0.3

The following played in two matches only: Mr F. J. Crooke, 14, 14, 0, 36; Mr E. C. B. Ford, 2, 0, 12, 12; Mr C. Gordon, 4, 0, 0, 3.

The following played in one match only: Mr F. Baker 27, 4; Captain Kington, 17, 4; Mr E. Smith, 12; Mr H. Jenner-Fust, 1, 0*.

* *Signifies not out.*

GLOUCESTERSHIRE'S SUMMARY FOR 1875

Victories	Defeats
Gloucestershire defeated Yorkshire by 122 runs.	Surrey defeated Gloucestershire by 26 runs.
Gloucestershire defeated Sussex by 40 runs.	Sussex defeated Gloucestershire by seven wickets.
Gloucestershire defeated Surrey by an innings and 84 runs.	Nottinghamshire defeated Gloucestershire by three wickets.
	Yorkshire defeated Gloucestershire by seven wickets.

Drawn – Gloucestershire v Nottinghamshire. – Gloucestershire 289; Nottinghamshire 192 and 21 for one wicket.

GLOUCESTERSHIRE v YORKSHIRE

Played on the Cheltenham College Ground, August 17, 18, 19, 1876

"A best on record" was made by Mr W. G. Grace in this match; that is to say his 318 not out is the largest score ever hit in a County v County contest. The match was commenced at 12.30 by Mr W. G. Grace and Dr E. M. Grace starting the Gloucestershire innings to the bowling of Hill and Armitage. Dr Grace left at 29; Mr Gilbert at 160; Mr Townsend at 167; and Mr G. F. Grace at 168. Then Mr Moberley and Mr W. G. Grace stayed and hit so grandly that when "time" was up that day the Gloucestershire score stood in this form:

Mr W. G. Grace not out	216
Dr E. M. Grace caught out	5
Mr W. Gilbert bowled	40
Mr F. Townsend stumped	0
Mr G. F. Grace bowled	0
Mr W. O. Moberley not out	73
Extras	19
	(4 wkts) 353

On the second day rain fell, preventing play commencing until one o'clock; then the two not outs increased the score to 429 when cover point caught out Mr Moberley for 103, so many as 261 runs having been added to the score since the fall of the preceding wicket. The sixth, seventh, eighth and ninth wickets fell quickly; but Mr J. A. Bush, the last man in, was so troublesome that he and Mr W. Grace hit the score from 466 to 528 before the end came by Ulyett bowling Mr Bush for 32.

Mr W. G. Grace commenced the innings at 12.30 on the Thursday; when the innings finished, at ten minutes to four on the Friday, Mr W. G. Grace was the not out man, having made 318 out of the 528 (504 from the bat) runs scored. He was timed to have been about eight hours batting; he ran 524 times between wickets, and the hits he made were seventy-six singles, thirty 2s, twelve 3s, twenty-eight 4s (112 by fourers), three 5s, two 6s and a 7. One critic described this 318 "a wonderful innings"; and another as "played in his very best style with only one chance, and that was when he had made 201".

Mr Moberley's 103 was also highly praised, and stated to have been made by one 5, ten 4s, one 3, ten 2s and thirty-five singles.

Yorkshire hitting was commenced at 5.20 by Lockwood and Myers; the score was at 39 when Lockwood hit wicket, and play for that day ceased, Myers not out 16. On the third day they resumed play at 11.40, but at two o'clock a thunder and rain storm ended the match the Yorkshiremen having lost seven wickets and scored 127 runs, Myers (first man in) not out 46, made by excellent cricket. Emmett scored 39 by vigorous hitting, that included a cut for 5 and five 4s. The match was draw, 294 overs having been bowled, and 655 runs scored, for the seventeen wickets down.

Gloucestershire

W. G. Grace Esq. not out	318
Dr E. M. Grace c sub. b Armitage	5
W. Gilbert Esq. b Armitage	40
F. Townsend Esq. st Pinder b Armitage	0
G. F. Grace Esq. b Emmett	0
W. O. Moberley Esq. c Myers b Emmett	103
R. E. Bush Esq. c Lister b Clayton	0
C. R. Filgate Esq. b Clayton	1
E. J. Taylor Esq. run out	1
R. F. Miles Esq. b Clayton	4
J. A. Bush Esq. b Ulyett	32
B 12, l-b 8, w 4	24
	528

Yorkshire

Ephraim Lockwood hit wkt b W. Grace	23
Matthew Myers not out	46
B. Lister c J. A. Bush b Miles	1
D. Eastwood c W. Grace b Miles	4
George Ulyett c Filgate b W. Grace	4
Emmett b Gilbert	39
T. Armitage c F. Grace b Gilbert	1
Allen Hill run out	6
W 3	3
	127

A, Champion, R. Clayton and Pinder did not bat.

Yorkshire Bowling

	Overs	Mdns	Runs	Wkts
Clayton	57	18	122	3
Emmett	51	18	94	2
Armitage	31	3	100	3
Ulyett	25	7	64	1
Hill	16	2	64	—
Lockwood	14	2	35	—
Eastwood	12	4	21	—
Myers	4	2	4	—

Gloucestershire Bowling

	Overs	Mdns	Runs	Wkts
Mr W. Grace	36	17	48	2
Mr F. Grace	17	7	34	—
Mr Miles	15	8	23	2
Mr Gilbert	8	5	9	2
Mr Townsend	8	—	10	—

Umpires: C. K. Pullin and another.

TWO BROTHERS' BATTING ON THE SAME DAYS

At Knole Park, August 11, 12. Mr G. F. Grace, 213.	At Canterbury, August 11, 12. Mr W. G. Grace, 344.

THREE SUCCESSIVE INNINGS BY MR W. G. GRACE

344	177	318*
At Canterbury, August 11, 12.	At Clifton, August 14, 15.	At Cheltenham, August 17, 18.

FIVE INNINGS BY THREE BROTHERS IN ONE SEASON – 1876

400*	344	327*	318*	213
At Grimsby, by Mr W. G. Grace.	At Canterbury, by Mr W. G. Grace.	At Thornbury, by Dr E. M. Grace.	At Cheltenham, by Mr W. G. Grace.	At Knole Park, by Mr G. F. Grace.

* *Signifies not out.*

GLOUCESTERSHIRE v ENGLAND

Played on The Oval, July 26, 27, 1877

This was the novel match of the season, and which, it was the opinion of many, would have been more appropriately played at Clifton in aid of "The Grace Testimonial Fund". The admission charge each day was 1s., at which increase many a man present exercised his Briton's privilege of grumbling, but for all that the ground was well attended on the first day, and largely so on the second day, when – at 6.25 – the match concluded in favour of Gloucestershire by five wickets, but inasinuch as neither Mr I. D. Walker, Mr A. N. Hornby, Richard Daft, Mr A. J. Webbe, Watson, Barlow, Oscroft, Morley, nor Ulyett played, it can hardly be fairly stated "England" was defeated. Gloucestershire admittedly played full strength, with the exception of Mr J. A. Bush, whose absence was caused by the dangerous illness of his father, but whose place behind the wickets was ably filled by Captain Kingscote, who, in 1877, "kept" in a form fit for any match.

Rain fell steadily and soakingly up to 11 o'clock of the morning set for commencing the match; nevertheless they went at it at 12.30, Mr W. Grace winning choice of in or out, sending the England men in to bat on wickets so heavy that it was simply impossible to make great scores; and so, notwithstanding Mr Lucas by two hours' careful cricket made 24, and Arthur Shrewsbury by a 6 to leg, two 4s, etc., made 25, good bowling, good fielding, and queer playing wickets got this England Eleven out for 79 runs from the bat. Gloucestershire then began batting, and fared even worse in run getting than did their opponents. At 19, Mr W. Grace was out for 9, and Mr Townsend for 0; Mr F. Grace then went in, and saw all the remaining men of his side out, the innings ending for 78 runs – 75 from the bat, Mr F. Grace, not out, 27. In this innings Mycroft's bowling had six wickets – two bowled – for 21 runs, and Barratt's four wickets for 33 runs. At 6.12 that evening England's second innings was commenced on cut up wickets, and in a bad light. When only 7 runs had been scored, Jupp was caught out – at the third try – by Mr Monkland, but Lockwood and Mr Cotterill played up to time when the score stood at 37 for one wicket, Mr Cotterill, not out, 19, Lockwood, not out, 15.

On the Friday – a bright hot day – the cricket was resumed at 12.15. At 46, Mr Cotterill was bowled for 23; Shrewsbury then went in, and, with Lockwood, played with great care, as Midwinter was bowling in real fine form, and so the score slowly rose to 76, when a very fine catch by Dr E. M. Grace at point settled Lockwood for 41 – the largest score hit for England in the match; a 5 drive from Mr Miles, and a 4 (square leg) from Mr W. Grace, being the Yorkshireman's principal hits. Mr Lucas's 18 included a dozen singles, and Pooley's 17 two 4s and a 3, but the others did but little, and at ten minutes to four they were all out for 123. The wickets were then well rolled, and at 1.15 the Gloucestershire men set about their task of scoring the 129 runs they wanted to win. Mr W. Grace and Mr Gilbert began the batting; they made 57 before they were parted by Mr W. Grace being had, at the second try, by Mycroft at point for 31, 20 of those runs being made by 4s; at 29, Mr Gilbert was stumped for 25, mainly made by a drive past the tree for 5, and three 4s; then in one hour and a quarter Mr Townsend made 43, not out, winning the match by a spanking off-drive for 5 from Barratt; and so it was that Gloucestershire won by five wickets.

"England"

	First innings		Second innings	
A. P. Lucas Esq. b Midwinter	24	–	not out	18
H. Jupp c W. Grace b Midwinter	5	–	c Fairbanks b W. Grace	1
J. M. Cotterill Esq. c Midwinter b W. Grace	1	–	b W. Grace	23
Ephraim Lockwood b Midwinter	5	–	c E. M. Grace b Miles	41
Arthur Shrewsbury c Kingscote b W. Grace	25	–	lbw b Midwinter	7
F. Penn, Esq. b Midwinter	11	–	c Kingscote b Midwinter	5
J. Furley Esq. st Kingscote b W. Grace	3	–	run out	0
E. Pooley c W. Grace b Midwinter	1	–	c Moberley b Midwinter	17
Emmett c W. Grace b Midwinter	0	–	c Gilbert b W. Grace	3
Barratt not out	3	–	c and b W. Grace	0
W. Mycroft lbw b Midwinter	1	–	st Kingscote b Midwinter	1
B 3, l-b 1	4		B 7	7
	83			123

Gloucestershire

	First innings		Second innings	
W. G. Grace Esq. c Emmett b W. Mycroft	9	–	c W. Mycroft b Emmett	31
W. Gilbert, Esq. c Shrewsbury b W. Mycroft	19	–	st E. Pooley b A. P. Lucas	25
F. Townsend Esq. c E. Pooley b W. Mycroft	0	–	not out	43
G. F. Grace Esq. not out	27	–	b Barratt	16
Dr E. M. Grace c E. Lockwood b W. Mycroft	10	–	c E. Pooley b Emmett	7
W. O. Moberley Esq. c F. Penn b Barratt	2	–	b Emmett	0
W. Fairbanks Esq. st E. Pooley b Barratt	0	–	not out	0
W. Midwinter c A. P. Lucas b Barratt	1			
F. G. Monkland Esq. st E. Pooley b Barratt	0			
Captain Kingscote b W. Mycroft	4			
R. F. Miles Esq. b W. Mycroft	3			
L-b 1, w 1, n-b 1	3		B 7	7
	78			129

Gloucestershire Bowling

	Overs	Mdns	Runs	Wkts	Overs	Mdns	Runs	Wkts
Mr W. Grace	47	28	37	3	43	25	46	4
Midwinter	39.2	23	35	7	66.3	39	46	4
Dr. E. M. Grace	8	3	7	—				
Mr Miles					13	9	8	1
Mr Townsend					10	4	16	—

England Bowling

	Overs	Mdns	Runs	Wkts	Overs	Mdns	Runs	Wkts
W. Mycroft	26.1	17	21	6	19	7	42	—
Barratt	18	5	33	4	15.2	4	37	1
Mr A. P. Lucas	10	4	21	—	12	4	19	1
Emmett					18	9	24	3

Umpires: Southerton and C. K. Pullin.

THE GRACE TESTIMONIAL FUND

On the 7th of February, 1877, a public meeting was held in Berkeley Castle, Gloucestershire, for the purpose of making the necessary preliminary arrangements for the formation of a "Grace Testimonial Fund", in recognition of the great and wonderful all-round cricketing abilities displayed by Mr W. G. Grace throughout his extraordinary career. An influential meeting was presided over by Lord Fitzhardinge, to whom is due, we believe, the honour of originating this movement. The committee was (it was understood) formed; Lord Fitzhardinge was appointed treasurer; a subscription was started, which was headed with £25 by Lord Fitzhardinge; and among other encouraging communications the following letters were read:

Lord's, December 16, 1876

"My Lord,

The question of presenting W. G. Grace with a testimonial as a recognition of his great exploits as a cricketer was discussed at a Committee Meeting of the Marylebone Club last Monday, and it was unanimously resolved that the time had arrived for presenting such a testimonial. I have offered to act as secretary of the fund in London. I hear that your lordship takes an interest in this matter; if so, will you kindly inform me what plan you would advise? My idea is that a committee should be formed, consisting of influential persons from all parts of the country.

Henry Perkins, Sec. MCC"

Badminton, January 21, 1877.

"I believe I am to be President of the Marylebone Club this year, and I have been in correspondence with the Secretary for the last six weeks about a subscription for W. G. Grace. The Committee of MCC think, as he has played so much for them, they ought to start it, and make it an All-England rather than a local subscription. Of course, his own County will be likely to be more keen about it than others; but it will be a much larger affair under the auspices of the MCC. I tell them when they see how much they can get, that a small piece of plate and a large purse will be the most useful form it can take. Yours truly,

Beaufort"

Then at one of the MCC Committee Meetings, held in May, at Lord's, the following resolution was unanimously carried, and was made public in the cricketing journals:

"That taking into consideration the extraordinary play of Mr W. G. Grace, and his great services to cricket, the Committee of the MCC are of opinion that the proposal of the President (The Duke of Beaufort) to present a national testimonial to Mr Grace ought to be supported, and that the Secretary of the MCC should communicate with the various County and other cricket clubs, and endeavour to bring together representatives from each, who may confer with the MCC Committee as to the best means of carrying out the object in view. Secretaries of all clubs are requested to communicate their views to the Secretary MCC, Lord's".

Whether the sensible suggestion of the Duke of Beaufort will be acted upon or not, or what has been the result of the above, this compiler does not know at present time of writing (October 10, 1877); in fact, but little was then known by outsiders as to the progress of the fund; for all that had come to public knowledge at that time was: The Marylebone Club had magnificently headed an MCC list with 100 guineas; that that subscription had been splendidly backed up by one of £25 from the Cambridge University Cricket Club, and another of £25 from the Duke of Beaufort; that I Zingari had started an IZ subscription list; that the Surrey Club had subscribed £50; and that, at a Gloucestershire CCC Committee meeting, held last March, it was resolved the proceeds of the Gloucestershire v Yorkshire match, to be played at Clifton, in August, 1877, should be given to the Fund. Doubtless there are many other additions to this list, unknown to the Compiler of this book, who gives himself the pleasure of wishing every possible success to "The Grace Testimonial Fund".

BATS v BROOMSTICKS

The abrupt and early termination of the match on August 15, 1877, was the cause of a fill-up-the-time match being arranged for the Gloucestershire Eleven with broomsticks, to play Eleven of Cheltenham with bats. The broomsticks made a first innings of 290 runs; of those runs

Dr E. M. Grace made 103, and Midwinter 58.

The batsmen had lost two wickets and scored 50 runs, when time was up.

GLOUCESTERSHIRE v SURREY

Played at Cirencester, August 29, 30, 1879

With this match the county season was brought to a doleful conclusion. As it commenced, so it ended, wet weather prevailing on the two first days of the above-titled contest; and, although a fine Saturday was experienced, there was not then time to bring matters to a definite issue. On Thursday no play was practicable, and on the following day rain upset the arrangements that had been made for an early start. Surrey were first to the wickets, which were in anything but good order. Mr Read played an excellent innings; Blamires and Jupp also rendered yeoman service, and at the finish the score was not so bad as had been anticipated. On behalf of the home team Mr Townsend and Midwinter batted in good style; but their score fell one short of Surrey's. In the second venture the visitors made a very sad beginning, Jupp, Mr Lindsay, and Mr Read being disposed of with the score at 13 only. Mr Shuter, who came next, narrowly escaped being caught. He then twice hit the ball over the pavilion into a plantation beyond, and each time secured 6 runs. Having obtained 44 out of 67 made while he was batting, Mr Shuter retired clean bowled, his finely-hit contribution including two 4s, a 3, and six 2s. The remainder of the innings can be only described by the word collapse. But 11 runs were realised for the loss of six wickets, five of which were clean bowled by Mr W. G. Grace. As it was 5.20 when the innings closed, and all interest in the match had evaporated, it was agreed to draw stumps.

Surrey

J. Shuter Esq. c and b W. G. Grace	14	– b G. F. Grace	44
Jupp c Gribble b Gilbert	20	– c Moberley b Midwinter	1
W. W. Read Esq. c G. F. Grace b W. G. Grace	48	– b W. G. Grace	5
W. Lindsay Esq. b W. G. Grace	3	– c Gribble b W. G. Grace	0
C. W. Burls Esq. c E. M. Grace b W. G. Grace	8	– b G. F. Grace	13
Humphrey c Gribble b W. G. Grace	17	– b W. G. Grace	1
Potter c Moberley b W. G. Grace	11	– b W. G. Grace	0
Pooley c E. M. Grace b W. G. Grace	2	– b W. G. Grace	8
Blamires not out	22	– b W. G. Grace	0
Southerton c G. F. Grace b W. G. Grace	2	– b W. G. Grace	1
Barratt c E. M. Grace b Midwinter	5	– not out	0
B 2, w 1	3	B 6	6
	155		79

Gloucestershire

W. G. Grace Esq. c Barratt b Blamires	10
W. R. Gilbert Esq. c Southerton b Blamires	21
Midwinter c Read b Barratt	24
E. M. Grace Esq. b Blamires	7
W. O. Moberley Esq. c Potter b Blamires	8
G. F. Grace Esq. c Lindsay b Blamires	8
F. Townsend Esq. hit wkt b Blamires	48
W. Fairbanks Esq. c Potter b Barratt	12
Rev. P. Hattersley-Smith b Southerton	7
J. Cranston Esq. not out	4
H. W. R. Gribble Esq. c Shuter b Blamires	2
B 1, l-b 2	3
	154

Gloucestershire Bowling

	Overs	Mdns	Runs	Wkts	Overs	Mdns	Runs	Wkts
Mr W. G. Grace ...	62	20	81	8	21.2	10	35	7
Midwinter	35.2	17	34	1	15	5	13	1
Mr Gilbert	24	12	28	1	5	3	8	—
Mr G. F. Grace	2	1	1	—	16	8	17	2
Mr E. M. Grace	4	1	7	—				

Surrey Bowling

	Overs	Mdns	Runs	Wkts
Southerton	54	27	52	1
Blamires	50.1	26	59	7
Potter	8	2	17	—
Barratt	12	2	23	2

Umpires: Pullin and Caffyn.

GLOUCESTERSHIRE v MIDDLESEX

Played at Clifton, August 16, 17, 18, 1883

Though not the longest on record, the marvellous stand made by the Hon. Alfred Lyttelton and Mr I. D. Walker in this match was without precedent in a first class contest, and may be regarded as the most remarkable batting performance of the year. The toss resulted favourably for Middlesex, and Messrs Webbe and Walker opened the innings for the visitors. Only eight runs were scored, however, before the former was bowled by Woof. Then Mr Lyttelton joined the Middlesex captain, and an absolute mastery was obtained over the Gloucestershire bowling. Both batsmen played steadily for about half-an-hour, but after that the rate of scoring considerably increased, and at lunch time the total was 106. On the game being resumed runs were put on at a truly extraordinary pace, 226 being added in an hour and three-quarters. The cricket, though brilliant in the extreme, was not without fault, however, as Mr Lyttelton was missed at the wicket, and Mr Walker, besides giving two chances of stumping, might have been caught in the long field. With the score at 332 a separation was at last effected, Mr Walker being caught at long-off for a splendidly-hit innings of 145, comprising two 6s, seventeen 4s, four 3s, fourteen 2s, and 25 singles.

Mr Walker and the Hon. Alfred Lyttelton had put on 324 runs for the second wicket.

Mr Lyttelton did not stay long after Mr Walker's dismissal, as at 347 he was caught off Woof for a grand innings of 181, made with two chances, and consisting of one 6, twenty-one 4s, five 3s, nineteen 2s, and 38 singles. When stumps were drawn for the day the score stood as under:

Middlesex

A. J. Webbe Esq. b Woof	4
I. D. Walker Esq. c W. G. Grace b Woof	145
Hon. A. Lyttelton c Cranston b Woof	181
C. T. Studd Esq. not out	57
T. S. Pearson Esq. b Townsend	36
G. B. Studd Esq. st Moberly b Townsend	0
G. F. Vernon Esq. not out	11
Extras	13
	(5 wkts) 447

Exactly 90 runs were added to the overnight score when the game was resumed on the Friday. Mr C. T. Studd was the eighth man out, with the total at 520, and he had been in while 188 runs had been put on. He played very finely the whole time of his stay at the wickets, and his 91 was made up of eight 4s, four 3s, sixteen 2s, and 15 singles. Gloucestershire began badly, as Dr E. M. Grace was out in the first over. Dr W. G. Grace and Mr Moberly then carried the score to 85, when the Gloucestershire captain was bowled. He had played with extreme caution, his first 12 runs taking him fifty-five minutes to make. Mr Moberly's 53 were made in his best style, and at the call of time the total was 181 for seven wickets, Mr Gilbert, not out 36, and Mr Fairbanks, not out 10.

On the Saturday the first innings of Gloucestershire was finished off for an addition of only 8 runs, and wanting no fewer than 348 to save a single innings defeat, the home team followed on. Dr W. G. Grace and Woof began, and when only 75 runs had been scored, Woof, Mr Moberly, Dr E. M. Grace, Mr Cranston, and Mr Townsend were all out, and anything but defeat for their side seemed impossible. But on Mr Gilbert joining his captain a determined stand was made, and 95 runs were added before Mr Grace was caught at the wicket. Both batsmen played with great steadiness and determination, Mr Grace especially showing conspicuous care, patience, and judgment. He was batting for three hours and a quarter, and his hits were five 4s, six 3s, nine 2s, and 29 singles. Mr Gilbert, who had been missed when he had scored 50, and gave another chance just before he was out, was caught at long-on for 79, an exceedingly good innings despite the mistakes. Nine 4s and three 3s were included in his score. The finish of the match proved very exciting, as Mr Page, the last man, went in when only ten minutes remained for play. He and Mr Fairbanks succeeded in keeping their wickets intact, and Gloucestershire, therefore, just escaped a crushing defeat, as they were still 114 runs to the bad and had only one wicket to fall.

Middlesex

A. J. Webbe Esq. b Woof	4
I. D. Walker Esq. c W. G. Grace b Woof	145
Hon. A. Lyttelton c Cranston b Woof	181
C. T. Studd Esq. c Moberly, b W. G. Grace	91
T. S. Pearson Esq. b Townsend	36
G. B. Studd Esq. st Moberly b Townsend	0
G. F. Vernon Esq. c Gilbert b Townsend	38
J. E. K. Studd Esq. c and b Townsend	2
P. J. de Paravicini Esq. c Gilbert b Townsend	14
J. Robertson Esq. b Townsend	11
G. Burton not out	0
B 8, l-b 7	15
	537

Gloucestershire

Dr W. G. Grace b Robertson	36	– c Lyttelton b Burton	85
Dr E. M. Grace st Lyttelton b C. T. Studd	0	– c Lyttelton b Robertson	20
W. O. Moberly Esq. c Paravicini b Burton	53	– b C. T. Studd	2
F. Townsend Esq. st Lyttelton b Burton	6	– b C. T. Studd	0
J. Cranston Esq. c Pearson b Robertson	9	– hit wkt b Walker	12
W. R. Gilbert Esq. b C. T. Studd	36	– c J. E. K. Studd b Burton	79
W. O. Vizard Esq. lbw b C. T. Studd	7	– c Burton b C. T. Studd	2
J. H. Brain Esq. c G. B. Studd b Walker	17	– b C. T. Studd	13
W. Fairbanks Esq. run out	12	– not out	10
H. V. Page Esq. b Walker	2	– not out	7
W. A. Woof not out	4	– b Walker	0
B 7	7	B 4	4
	189		234

Gloucestershire Bowling

	Overs	Mdns	Runs	Wkts
Dr W. G. Grace	63	21	154	1
Woof	54	20	127	3
Mr Page	33	9	77	—
Dr E. M. Grace	5	1	13	—
Mr Gilbert	13	3	56	—
Mr Townsend	31.3	4	95	6

Middlesex Bowling

	Overs	Mdns	Runs	Wkts	Overs	Mdns	Runs	Wkts
Mr C. T. Studd	54	31	52	3	65	33	76	4
Burton	49	23	68	2	47	32	28	2
Mr Robertson	38	12	44	2	16	10	20	1
Mr Walker	11	5	15	2	27	6	61	2
Mr Pearson	2	—	3	—	5	—	12	—
Mr Paravicini					6	2	10	—
Mr J. E. K. Studd ...					4	1	12	—
Mr Webbe					4	—	11	—

Umpires: R. Carpenter and E. Henty.

GLOUCESTERSHIRE v SURREY

Played at Clifton, August 25, 26, 27, 1884

The last match of the Gloucestershire programme ended in a draw, and was productive of some of the most remarkable cricket played during the season. In all, 948 runs were scored for the loss of only twenty wickets, giving the extraordinary average of 47.8 per wicket. The average rate of scoring was 87 runs per hour, and though only an innings a-piece was played, no less than four batsmen reached treble figures. Surrey went in first, and when the day's play came to an end, they had scored 412 and had still four wickets to fall, only one chance having been missed. Mr Shuter and Mr W. W. Read played magnificent cricket, and while they were together, 189 runs were added. Neither made a mistake, and the character of their hitting can be judged by their figures. Mr Shuter's 101 consisted of twenty 4s, two 3s, three 2s, and only nine singles, while Mr Read's 135 was made up of a 6, fourteen 4s, seven 3s, twelve 2s, and 28 singles.

Chiefly through the good hitting of Abel the Surrey score ultimately reached 464, and after a shower of rain, Gloucestershire went in. The start was not a promising one, as both Dr E. M. Grace and Mr Townsend were dismissed by the time the total reached 26. When Mr Brain joined the Gloucestershire captain, however, some splendid batting was witnessed, and a mastery was obtained over the Surrey bowling, no fewer than 118 runs being added before Dr W. G. Grace was bowled for 66. The association of Mr Brain and Painter was productive of another prolonged resistance, 145 runs being put on before Mr Brain was at last dismissed for a very brilliant inings of 143, which included thirteen 4s. Painter had scored 98 when stumps were drawn, and he added 35 on the last day, his really admirable 133 containing a 5 and twenty-one 4s. Mr Brain's and Painter's innings were the highest they ever played for Gloucestershire.

Surrey

J. M. Read b W. G. Grace 8
M. P. Bowden Esq. st Bush b Woof 35
E. J. Diver Esq. b Woof 55
W. W. Read Esq. c and b Pullen 135
J. Shuter Esq. c Brain b Painter 101
R. Abel c W. G. Grace b Woof 60
K. J. Key Esq. lbw b W. G. Grace 10
G. Lohmann b Woof 25
G. Jones c Page b Woof 2
E. Barratt not out 11
C. E. Horner Esq. st Bush b W. G. Grace .. 0
B 17, l-b 4, w 1 22

464

Gloucestershire

Dr W. G. Grace b Abel	66	F. A. Curteis Esq. lbw b Barratt	0
Dr E. M. Grace c Kay b Horner	0	E. J. Taylor Esq. c Diver b Abel	33
F. Townsend Esq. b Barratt	13	J. A. Bush Esq. not out	20
J. H. Brain Esq. c Barratt b Abel	143	W. A. Woof b Horner	0
W. W. F. Pullen Esq. b Barratt	0	B 25, l-b 3, w 1	29
E. J. Painter b W. W. Read	133		
H. V. Page Esq. b Barratt	47		484

Gloucestershire Bowling

	Overs	Mdns	Runs	Wkts
Dr W. G. Grace	57.3	19	129	3
Woof	73	27	155	5
Mr Townsend	15	5	32	—
Mr Brain	9	—	41	—
Mr Curteis	4	1	14	—
Mr Page	8	2	28	—
Painter	14	4	32	1
Mr Pullen	10	4	11	1

Surrey Bowling

	Overs	Mdns	Runs	Wkts
Mr Horner	35.1	6	91	2
Barratt	57	13	179	4
Jones	6	1	23	—
Lohmann	16	5	42	—
Abel	15	5	38	3
J. M. Read	3	—	22	—
Mr Diver	3	—	13	—
Mr W. W. Read	15	3	33	1
Mr Key	3	1	14	—

Umpires: E. Willsher and H. Holmes.

GLOUCESTERSHIRE v NOTTINGHAMSHIRE

Played at Moreton-in-the-Marsh, June 28, 29, 30, 1886

A wonderful not-out score of 227 by Arthur Shrewsbury constituted the great feature of the first home match undertaken by the Gloucestershire eleven. Although not too well represented, Gloucestershire had distinctly the best of the first day's play, getting rid of Nottinghamshire for 124, and scoring 105 for the loss of two wickets. Mr W. G. Grace and Mr Hale bowled very well for the western county, and after Painter had hit up a vigorous 38, the brothers Grace kept together until the close of play, when the elder brother was not out 42, and the champion not out 16.

On the second day Mr E. M. Grace did not materially increase his score, but the greatest of cricketers showed splendid form, and when Gloucestershire's innings closed for 242 was not out 92 – a splendid display of batting, lasting for several hours, and including two 4s, ten 3s, and twelve 2s. Although Mr W. G. Grace received little support, except from Mr Croome, Gloucestershire led on the first innings by 118 runs. With these arrears to clear off, Nottinghamshire went in for the second time, and after Scotton had been dismissed at 32, Shrewsbury and Gunn placed the visitors 11 runs ahead, the score at the close of the day being 129, Shrewsbury not out 66, and Gunn not out 48.

Nottinghamshire stayed in the whole of the third day, their innings closing shortly before time for 430. Shrewsbury and Gunn raised the total to 193, their partnership, when the latter was bowled, having realised 161 runs. Shrewsbury's grand batting completely dwarfed the rest of the day's play. He was at the wickets for seven hours and three-quarters, and except for a sharp chance when he had made 120, and a bad miss in the long field when his score was 164, he made no mistake. His enormous score of 227 not out was made up of fifteen 4s, twelve 3s, thirty-four 2s, and sixty-three singles. It will not be out of place to say that this innings was the fourth of over two hundred played by the famous Nottinghamshire batsman. In 1882 at The Oval he made 207 against Surrey, two years later he scored 209 against Sussex, at Brighton, and in 1885 he surpassed these efforts with 224 not out against Middlesex at Lord's. When the match was left drawn, Gloucestershire had an innings to play, and wanted 313 runs to win.

Nottinghamshire

Shrewsbury c Heath b Hale	6	– not out	227
Scotton run out	23	– b Turner	8
Gunn b W. G. Grace	18	– b Painter	82
Flowers b Gregg	0	– c Radcliffe b W. G. Grace	39
Selby c Painter b Hale	11	– c E. M. Grace b W. G. Grace	0
Mr H. B. Daft lbw b W. G. Grace	11	– c W. G. Grace b E. M. Grace	21
Wright b W. G. Grace	14	– b Radcliffe	25
Attewell b Hale	0	– c Heath b Radcliffe	0
Shacklock c Croome b W. G. Grace	17	– b Radcliffe	7
Lockwood b Turner	3	– b Hale	6
Shewin not out	1	– c E. M. Grace b W. G. Grace	1
B 17, l-b 3	20	B 9, l-b 5	14
	124		430

Gloucestershire

Mr E. M. Grace b Attewell	44
Mr O. G. Radcliffe c Sherwin b Shacklock	4
Painter b Attewell	38
Mr W. G. Grace not out	92
Mr C. Wreford-Brown c Sherwin b Flowers	0
Mr H. Hale c Sherwin b Attewell	6
Mr G. Francis b Attewell	8
Gregg c and b Attewell	15
Mr W. Heath run out	0
Mr A. C. M. Croome run out	24
Mr C. Turner c Flowers b Attewell	0
B 7, l-b 4	11
	242

Gloucestershire Bowling

	Overs	Mdns	Runs	Wkts	Overs	Mdns	Runs	Wkts
Mr Turner	15	7	16	1	27	6	64	1
Mr W. G. Grace	33	22	23	4	72.3	32	86	3
Gregg	20	5	30	1	51	20	60	—
Mr Hale	29	17	35	3	18	7	35	1
Mr Wreford-Brown					19	7	29	—
Mr Radcliffe					31	13	66	3
Painter					20	7	34	1
Mr Croome					4	2	7	—
Mr E. M. Grace					14	5	35	1

Nottinghamshire Bowling

	Overs	Mdns	Runs	Wkts
Flowers	39	20	37	1
Wright	19	6	37	—
Attewell	72	36	99	6
Shacklock	15	6	33	1
Lockwood	21	10	25	—

GLOUCESTERSHIRE v YORKSHIRE

Played at Gloucester, June 30, July 1, 2, 1887

Yorkshire brought over the same eleven that had defeated Derbyshire, while Gloucestershire, although still without Mr Townsend, Mr Brain, Mr Page, and Woof, had a fairly good side. The weather was delightfully fine on the Thursday, when the brothers went in for Gloucestershire, Mr W. G. Grace having fortunately won the toss on the splendid wicket. The pair put on 43 runs for the first wicket, and then Mr Troup joined Mr W. G. Grace, the total being carried to 149 before they were parted. Mr Grace, who had been in for two hours and forty minutes, had put together a faultless innings of 92, in which were twelve 4s, two 3s, and five 2s. Mr Troup a youngster of seventeen from a private school at Redlands, near Bristol, kept in altogether for four hours, being out sixth at 242 for an admirable 62. He had played all the bowling with the coolness of a veteran, and was loudly cheered by the spectators and the Yorkshiremen themselves. Of the others, Messrs Radcliffe and Hale played well, and at the close of the day the latter was not out 35, and the total 301 for eight wickets.

On Friday some free hitting by Messrs Boughton and Cole quickly carried the total to 369, and then shortly before one o'clock the innings closed. Emmett had bowled extremely well in this innings, and Hunter kept wicket in his best form.

Ulyett and Hall made a sensational start for Yorkshire, the former hitting in his best form, and the latter, after beginning badly, batting steadily. Before they were separated, they made no fewer than 173 for the first wicket, Ulyett being then caught in the long field for a brilliant 104. He had only been batting for two hours and ten minutes, and, except for a chance at long-on when he had scored 63, did not make a mistake. His figures included fourteen 4s, three 3s, and eight 2s. Up to this point the innings promised to be a very long one, but a complete change came over it, and wickets fell so rapidly that nine were down for 286, when four runs were still wanted to avert the "follow on". This, however, was saved by the last two men, and the total reached 300. But for Bates's dashing innings of 84 – made as perhaps only that batsman can make runs – Yorkshire would have had to go in again. Bates scored his runs in an hour and a half by one 6, thirteen 4s, two 3s, and six 2s. Hall's steadily played 70 occupied two hours and thirty-five minutes, but it was not one of his best displays. Mr E. M. Grace took seven wickets with his lobs. Gloucestershire, with a useful advantage of 69, went in again for a few minutes, and made two runs without losing a wicket.

On Saturday the play before luncheon did not give promise of anything sensational, for at the interval seven wickets had fallen for 138 runs, Mr W. G. Grace being not out for an admirable 64. Soon after resuming another wicket fell, and eight being down for 146, it seemed just possible that Gloucestershire might lose, but then Mr Newnham joined his captain, and the pair completely mastered the bowling. Both hit with great brilliancy, Mr Grace, after completing his hundred, showing astonishing power. Before the separation came no fewer than 143 runs were added, the score having been nearly doubled in an hour and fifty minutes. Mr Newnham was out for a capital 56, in which were six 4s, three 3s, and three 2s. Mr Griffiths, the last batsman, stayed some time while Mr Grace continued his grand hitting, but he was at length got rid of, and the innings closed at 5.35 for 338. It having been previously agreed to close at six o'clock, it was not thought worthwhile for Yorkshire to go in again, so the match was left drawn much in favour of the home side, who were 407 runs on. Mr W. G. Grace's not out innings of 183 was a magnificent display without a blemish. He was batting five hours and twenty-five minutes, his hits being twenty-one 4s, four 3s, nineteen 2s, and forty-nine singles. Next to Mr Grace's batting the feature of the match was Hunter's wicket-keeping, the Yorkshireman making nine catches in the two innings.

Gloucestershire

Mr W. G. Grace b Peel	92	– not out	183
Mr E. M. Grace c Hunter b Bates	21	– c Hunter b Emmett	24
Mr W. Troup c Bates b Emmett	62	– b Peel	0
Mr W. W. F. Pullen b Peel	6	– c Hunter b Bates	7
Mr O. G. Radcliffe c Hunter b Emmett	40	– c Hunter b Bates	1
Mr G. Francis b Hall	7	– c Hunter b Peel	12
Mr H. Hale lbw b Emmett	41	– b Preston	11
Mr E. L. Griffiths c Hunter b Wade	5	– c Hunter b Emmett	15
Mr A. Newnham b Ulyett	5	– c Hunter b Bates	56
Mr H. J. Boughton b Preston	41	– b Emmett	9
Mr F. L. Cole not out	24	– b Preston	2
B 12, l-b 4, w 9	25	B 7, l-b 3, w 8	18
	369		338

Yorkshire

L. Hall b Radcliffe	70
G. Ulyett c Newnham b E. M. Grace	104
S. Wade b E. M. Grace	1
Hon. M. B. Hawke b W. G. Grace	3
W. Bates c Pullen b E. M. Grace	84
J. M. Preston c W. G. Grace b E. M. Grace	5
R. Peel c Newnham b E. M. Grace	0
T. Denton c Boughton b E. M. Grace	12
F. Lee c Francis b E. M. Grace	0
T. Emmett not out	10
J. Hunter b Newnham	3
B 4, l-b 4	8
	300

Yorkshire Bowling

	Overs	Mdns	Runs	Wkts	Overs	Mdns	Runs	Wkts
Ulyett	29	9	61	1	10	1	29	—
Peel	49	21	77	2	28	15	56	2
Bates	27	13	54	1	48	16	80	3
Emmett	58	35	55	3	49.2	26	61	3
Preston	22.1	10	33	1	29	7	60	2
Wade	33	11	45	1	5	2	18	—
Hall	9	1	19	1	3	—	18	—

Gloucestershire Bowling

	Overs	Mdns	Runs	Wkts
Mr W. G. Grace	27	12	48	1
Mr Newnham	27	12	47	1
Mr Hale	10	3	27	0
Mr Radcliffe	27	13	46	1
Mr E. M. Grace	35	7	120	7
Mr Troup	2	1	4	—

Umpires: Coward and Jupp.

GLOUCESTERSHIRE v NOTTINGHAMSHIRE

Played at Clifton, August 8, 9, 10, 1887

This proved a triumph for the Nottinghamshire eleven, who were seen to advantage at all points of the game. The wicket was extremely good at starting, but it did not wear quite so well as is usually the case at Clifton. Scotton made his reappearance in the Nottinghamshire eleven, and, except perhaps for the absence of Mr J. H. Brain, Gloucestershire had their full strength.

Nottinghamshire had the good fortune to win the toss, and they made excellent use of their opportunity. Shrewsbury arrived too late on the ground to go in first as usual, but a capital start was made in his absence. Gunn and Flowers played exceedingly good cricket, and put on 87 runs for the third wicket. Gunn, in his 66, hit nine 4s and five 2s; while included in Flowers's brilliant 76 were seven 4s, four 3s, and eight 2s. It was when the score was 135 that Shrewsbury came in and commenced an admirable innings. Seven wickets were down for 224, but such valuable assistance was accorded to Shrewsbury by Richardson and Shacklock that at the call of time the Nottinghamshire score was 356 for the loss of eight wickets. Shrewsbury was not out 109, this being his fifth innings of over 100 for his county during the season; and Shacklock not out 30.

On the following day, thanks mainly to some very brilliant hitting by Shacklock, the Nottinghamshire total ultimately reached 423. Shacklock's 71 included three square-leg hits out of the ground for 6, six 4s, three 3s, and five 2s. Shrewsbury took out his bat for a beautifully played 119, in which were five 4s, nine 3s, and sixteen 2s. The batting in the first innings of Gloucestershire presented few features of interest, and though the brothers Grace put on 52 runs for the first wicket, the whole side were out for 172. Messrs E. M. Grace and Griffiths showed the best form. Richardson was by far the most successful bowler for Nottinghamshire, taking five wickets for 43 runs. Going in a second time against a majority of 251, Gloucestershire before the close of play scored 43 for the loss of two wickets. Mr W. G. Grace was not out 32.

Not very much interest remained in Wednesday's play, as scarcely a doubt could be felt as to the ultimate success of Nottinghamshire. Mr W. G. Grace certainly played a fine, though not a faultless, innings of 113 not out, but even his batting could not save his side from a crushing defeat. Except Mr Grace, no man on the Gloucestershire side scored more than 30, and the last wicket fell for 186, leaving Nottinghamshire with a decisive victory by an innings and 65 runs. The chief hits of Mr W. G. Grace's 113, which occupied over four hours, were a 5, eleven 4s, four 3s, and ten 2s. In the second innings of Gloucestershire Barnes bowled very finely and took five wickets for 31 runs.

Nottinghamshire

W. Scotton c Woof b Page	10	Mr H. B. Daft c W. G. Grace b Hale	3
W. Gunn c Woof b W. G. Grace	66	W. Attewell b Woof	4
W. Barnes b W. G. Grace	12	F. Richardson run out	29
W. Flowers b Woof	76	F. Shacklock c W. G. Grace b Radcliffe	71
A. Shrewsbury not out	119	B 7, l-b 10	17
Mr J. A. Dixon c Woof b Hale	5		
M. Sherwin b Page	11		423

Gloucestershire

Mr W. G. Grace b Richardson	19	– not out 113
Mr E. M. Grace b Shacklock	42	– c Shacklock b Richardson 0
Mr W. W. F. Pullen c Sherwin b Richardson	10	– b Flowers 30
Mr O. G. Radcliffe c Richardson b Shacklock	15	– b Barnes 9
Mr F. Townsend c Flowers b Richardson	13	– b Barnes 2
Mr H. V. Page c Sherwin b Shacklock	2	– b Barnes 12
J. Painter b Richardson	16	– b Attewell 2
Mr E. L. Griffiths not out	28	– b Barnes 0
W. A. Woof c Attewell b Richardson	12	– b Richardson 2
J. Roberts b Barnes	9	– c Barnes b Flowers 11
B 5, n-b 1	6	B 5 5
	172	186

Gloucestershire Bowling

	Overs	Mdns	Runs	Wkts
Roberts	19	6	50	—
Mr Page	51.2	21	76	2
Woof	55	31	45	2
Mr Townsend	6	—	17	—
Mr W. G. Grace	43	9	122	2
Mr Hale	28	9	53	2
Mr E. M. Grace	12	—	33	—
Mr Radcliffe	7	5	10	1

Nottinghamshire Bowling

	Overs	Mdns	Runs	Wkts	Overs	Mdns	Runs	Wkts
Attewell	15	11	39	1	48	19	57	1
Barnes	14	5	39	1	21	8	31	5
Shacklock	21	7	53	3	13	3	24	—
Richardson	37	18	43	5	42	22	43	2
Flowers	6	5	1	—	23.1	12	26	2

Umpires: Jupp and Platt.

GLOUCESTERSHIRE v KENT

Played at Clifton, August 25, 26, 27, 1887

The last fixture arranged by the Gloucestershire committee for the season was the return match with Kent, which followed immediately after the home side's contest with Middlesex at Clifton. Mr J. A. Bush made his reappearance for Gloucestershire, and Mr E. L. Griffiths stood out, while Kent brought down a powerful side. This was the first time a Kent team had ever played on the Clifton College ground. Mr W. G. Grace, after winning the toss, went in first with his brother, and the pair made so good a start that 127 runs were scored before the elder batsman was got rid of. Mr E. M. Grace, who had given a ridiculously easy chance when 32, made 70 in his usual unorthodox fashion, by four 4s, four 3s, seven 2s, and 28 singles. After he left, Mr W. G. Grace could find no one to stop with him, and he himself was run out, after a superb display, from the next ball after completing his 100. His innings was nearly faultless, and lasted two hours and fifty-five minutes, his figures including eleven 4s, six 3s and six 2s. The last part of the Gloucestershire innings, which closed just before time, was noteworthy for some splendid batting by Mr Page, who had not previously been seen to such advantage during the season. He carried out his bat for 61, having received some valuable assistance from Mr Peake.

Kent commenced their innings on Friday, but unfortunately the weather – delightfully fine on the first day – had changed, and very little cricket took place owing to rain. During the time play was possible, between twenty-five minutes past twelve and luncheon, the visitors made a good beginning, scoring 103 runs for the loss of but one wicket – Frank Hearne's. Subsequently rain fell again, and after one interruption it finally prevented any further progress after a quarter to four. By that time Messrs Rashleigh and Patterson, both of whom batted splendidly on the wet easy wicket, had raised the total to 144, the former being not out 47 and the latter not out 49.

Saturday's cricket was hardly expected to prove interesting, as there was little probability of the game reaching a definite conclusion, but the weather was fortunately fine again, and the large company present witnessed another grand batting performance by the champion. During the first part of the day Mr Rashleigh's batting was the feature of the cricket, that gentleman increasing his score from 47 to 108, an innings without a blemish excepting a chance at the wicket on the Friday. He hit one 5, nine 4s, seven 3s and ten 2s, and he was in altogether for four hours and twenty-five minutes. The last few Kentish batsmen went in for vigorous hitting, and as they got out quickly the inings closed at 3.25 for 317, or 40 runs on. When Gloucestershire went in a second time, two hours and twenty minutes remained for cricket, and the Graces once more made a good start. After Mr E. M. Grace left, Mr Pullen came in, and during his partnership with Mr W. G. Grace it began to look as if the latter had a chance of making his second hundred in the match. When Mr Pullen got out, about a quarter of an hour before time, Mr Grace still wanted 18 runs, but, hitting whenever the opportunity served, he managed to complete the hundred with a 4 to square-leg from the last ball but one of the day. He was most enthusiastically cheered at the close for a performance that, as we have said, has not been equalled in modern days in first-class matches except by himself. His second innings was absolutely faultless, and his figures included eleven 4s, six 3s, and eleven 2s. It was a performance in every way worthy of the great cricketer's reputation, and worthily wound up what proved to be his best season since 1876.

Gloucestershire

Mr W. G. Grace st Kemp b A. Hearne	101	– not out	103
Mr E. M. Grace b Martin	70	– c Patterson b Martin	29
Mr W. W. F. Pullen b A. Hearne	3	– c Kemp b Patterson	38
Mr O. G. Radcliffe b Wootton	0	– not out	1
Mr F. Townsend b Wootton	0		
Mr H. V. Page not out	61		
J. Painter b Wootton	8		
Mr E. Peake b Wilson	25		
Mr H. Hale st Kemp b Thornton	2		
Mr J. A. Bush c A. Hearne b Wootton	2		
J. Roberts b A. Hearne	0		
B 3, l-b 2	5	B 11	11
	277		182

Kent

Mr W. Rashleigh c Peake b Hale	108
F. Hearne run out	37
Mr W. H. Patterson c E. M. Grace b Peake	49
Lord Harris c Bush b Peake	6
Mr A. J. Thornton b Peake	10
Mr L. Wilson b Peake	0
A. Hearne c Bush b Page	10
Mr J. N. Tonge c W. G. Grace b Peake	38
Mr M. C. Kemp c Pullen b W. G. Grace	31
J. Wootton not out	0
F. Martin c Radcliffe b W. G. grace	3
B 14, l-b 11	25
	317

Kent Bowling

	Overs	Mdns	Runs	Wkts	Overs	Mdns	Runs	Wkts
A. Hearne	43	15	77	3	21	7	35	—
Wootton	52	16	80	4	19	5	28	—
Martin	21	7	44	1	13	2	26	1
Mr Wilson	14	5	26	1	15	6	25	—
F. Hearne	5	—	12	—				
Mr Thornton	12	3	22	1	8	2	22	—
Mr Tonge	4	2	11	—				
Mr Patterson					8	—	35	1

Gloucestershire Bowling

	Overs	Mdns	Runs	Wkts
Mr Peake	60	26	120	5
Roberts	38	17	60	—
Mr Page	25	12	29	1
Mr W. G. Grace	46.2	21	66	2
Mr E. M. Grace	7	3	5	—
Mr Hale	4	0	12	1

Umpires: Street and Panter.

GLOUCESTERSHIRE v KENT

Played at Moreton-in-the-Marsh, July 19, 20, 21, 1888

For the first time during the season Woof assisted Gloucestershire, and he and Roberts bowled with such astonishing success that Kent were dismissed in an hour and a half for the wretched total of 28. Lord Harris captained the visitors, who were, however, without the services of several of their best amateurs. On the slow wicket high scoring was not to be expected, but the Gloucestershire cricketers batted with far more determination than their opponents, and headed the total by 96. Alec Hearne bowled with great success, but his figures did not compare with those of Woof in the Kent innings, not to mention those of Roberts, whose analysis was a curiosity – 29 overs, 21 maidens, 8 runs, five wickets. Going in for the second time Kent fared scarcely any better than before, and at the drawing of stumps had half their wickets down for 19 runs. Next day only half a dozen overs were sent down before rain put a stop to cricket. The finish on the third day proved a very tame affair, the five outstanding Kent wickets falling in an hour and a half for the addition of 29 runs. Gloucestershire thus gained a very easy victory by 44 runs and an innings to spare. The great feature of the match was, of course, the bowling of the two left-handers, Roberts and Woof, the former of whom took nine wickets for 3 runs each, and the latter eleven at a cost of 4 runs each. Not often have Gloucestershire got a county out twice for 80 runs. On no other occasion were the Kent eleven seen to so little advantage.

Kent

F. Hearne b Woof	3	– b Woof	0
Mr A. J. Thornton c W. G. Grace b Woof	8	– c Pullen b Woof	1
G. G. Hearne c Pullen b Woof	0	– b Roberts	13
Mr C. J. M. Fox c Radcliffe b Woof	4	– c Radcliffe b Woof	6
Mr J. N. Tonge c Brain b Roberts	2	– b Roberts	5
A. Hearne b Roberts	0	– not out	4
W. Wright c Brain b Roberts	0	– c W. G. Grace b Roberts	0
Rev. R. T. Thornton b Woof	0	– c W. G. Grace b Roberts	7
Lord Harris b Roberts	0	– c Townsend b Woof	11
W. Hickmott not out	1	– lbw b Woof	1
J. Wootton b Roberts	8	– lbw b Woof	0
B 2	2	B 1, l-b 3	4
	28		52

Gloucestershire

Mr W. G. Grace c and b Wootton	16
Mr E. M. Grace b Wootton	8
Mr W. Troup c A. Hearne b Fox	5
Mr O. G. Radcliffe c R. T. Thornton b Wootton	12
Mr W. W. F. Pullen c Wootton b Wright	26
J. Painter c Hickmott b Fox	7
Mr F. Townsend b A. Hearne	5
Mr J. H. Brain c Wootton b A. Hearne	15
Mr G. Francis not out	16
W. A. Woof c Hickmott b A. Hearne	8
F. G. Roberts b A. Hearne	1
B 5	5
	124

Gloucestershire Bowling

	Overs	Mdns	Runs	Wkts	Overs	Mdns	Runs	Wkts
Woof	29	20	18	5	47	33	27	6
Roberts	29	21	8	5	36.3	23	19	4
Mr W. G. Grace					10	9	2	—

Kent Bowling

	Overs	Mdns	Runs	Wkts
Wright	25	12	27	1
Wootton	26	11	46	3
A. Hearne	19.3	5	31	4
Mr Fox	18	10	15	2

Umpires: Nicholas and Allan Hill.

GLOUCESTERSHIRE v YORKSHIRE

Played at Clifton, August 16, 17, 18, 1888

This was one of the heaviest scoring matches of the season, 1,053 runs being obtained in the course of three days for the loss of only twenty-nine wickets. Apart from the heavy scoring, it was rendered remarkable by the wonderful achievement on the part of Mr W. G. Grace, who, for the third time in his career, succeeded in making over 100 runs in each innings. The ground was in exceptionally good order, but that the feat also was exceptional is fully proved by the fact that no other cricketer within the last fifty years has ever succeeded in accomplishing it in a first-class match. Mr Grace did it in 1887 at Clifton against Kent, scoring 101 and 103 not out, while so long ago as 1868 he made 130 and 102 not out at Canterbury for South of the Thames against North of the Thames. While no one but Mr Grace has ever scored so well in a big match, the feat has been accomplished in minor engagements by Mr W. Townsend, Mr D. G. Spiro, and Mr F. W. Mande. To return to the match, we may say that Gloucestershire, after winning the toss, made a wretched start, losing Mr E. M. Grace, Mr Pullen, Mr Champain (the Cheltenham captain), and Painter for 26 runs, Peel and Preston taking two wickets each. At this point Mr Radcliffe came in, and rendered his captain such great assistance that 107 runs were put on for the fifth wicket; while after Mr Radcliffe's departure Mr W. G. Grace and Mr Brain took the score from 133 to 221. Mr Radcliffe was in nearly two hours, and Mr Brain, after a moderate start, hit very finely for his 47. It may be of interest to state that Mr Grace scored 50 out of 75, and reached his 100 when the total was 147. He was sixth out with the total at 221, having played an absolutely faultless innings of 148, which lasted three hours and a half, and was made up by sixteen 4s, eleven 3s, eight 2s and thirty-five singles. After Mr Grace's dismissal the innings was quickly finished off for 248, and Yorkshire in three-quarters of an hour lost two wickets for 35.

The Yorkshiremen monopolised the wicket during the second day, Hall, who was 8 not out overnight, increasing his score to 122 before the call of time. At the start he received very useful assistance from Wormald, who was played as wicket-keeper in place of Ellis, and who, by his batting, surprised almost as much as he delighted the Yorkshiremen. His style was not elegant, but he played with creditable judgment as well as showing considerable hitting power. In company with Hall he assisted to put on 130 runs for the third wicket. Preston and Wainwright both did fairly well, but with only two men to go in Yorkshire were still 7 runs behind when Wade joined Hall. From this point the north-countrymen speedily assumed the mastery, and at the drawing of stumps the total was 427 for eight wickets. Wade, who scored 68, was in while 116 runs were added, and Moorhouse hit so brilliantly that he made 70 runs in sixty-five minutes.

On Saturday morning the Yorkshire innings closed for 461, Moorhouse adding 16 runs to his total, and Hall carrying out his bat for a marvellously patient innings of 129. The Yorkshire professional was in a part of three days, his stay at the wickets extending over rather more than seven hours. Of course most batsmen during so long an innings would have scored far more largely upon so good a wicket as that of the Clifton College ground, but Hall played his own game, which, if perhaps not attractive on a fast ground, was of immense value to Yorkshire in the course of the season. He hit eleven 4s, nine 3s and thirteen 2s. With arrears of 213 to clear off, Gloucestershire commenced their second innings, and before Mr Grace left the score stood at 253. The Gloucestershire captain gave a chance at the wicket when he had only made 12, but in other respects his batting was masterly, and included in his splendid innings of 153, which lasted three hours and ten minutes, were twenty-two 4s, five 3s, twelve 2s and twenty-six singles. Mr Pullen and Mr Radcliffe were fairly successful, but of course Mr Grace's batting dwarfed everything else. But for his wonderful performance Gloucestershire would undoubtedly have been beaten. As it was the innings closed for 316, and at the finish Yorkshire, with all their wickets to fall, wanted only 76 runs to win. Yorkshire experienced a piece of very bad luck, Peel having to go away on the first day, so that he did not take his innings, while on the Saturday the want of his bowling was severely felt.

Gloucestershire

Mr W. G. Grace c Ulyett b Preston	148	– c Parratt b Ulyett	153
Mr E. M. Grace c Wormald b Peel	5	– c Wainwright b Preston	11
Mr W. W. F. Pullen c Wormald b Preston	1	– c and b Ulyett	37
Mr H. B. Champain b Preston	0	– b Wade	2
J. Painter c Wainwright b Peel	6	– c Parratt b Preston	31
Mr O. G. Radcliffe c and b Peel	31	– b Wade	20
Mr J. H. Brain c Moorhouse b Preston	47	– b Moorhouse	0
Mr F. Townsend b Preston	7	– c Wormald b Preston	19
Mr H. V. Page not out	0	– not out	15
Mr E. Peake c Moorhouse b Preston	0	– b Wainwright	10
W. A. Woof b Preston	0	– c Thewlis b Preston	5
B 2, l-b 1	3	B 7, l-b 2, w 1, n-b 3	13
	248		316

Yorkshire

L. Hall not out	129		
G. Ulyett b Woof	16		
Thewlis b Woof	0	– not out	2
Wormald c W. G. Grace b Peake	80		
J. M. Preston c Page b Townsend	23		
E. Wainwright b E. M. Grace	23		
Lord Hawke b Woof	4	– not out	21
Parratt b Woof	11		
S. Wade c Townsend b Woof	68		
R. Moorhouse c Brain b E. M. Grace	86		
R. Peel absent	0		
B 16, l-b 5	21	Extras	5
	461		28

Yorkshire Bowling

	Overs	Mdns	Runs	Wkts	Overs	Mdns	Runs	Wkts
Peel	53	21	80	3				
Preston	41	14	82	7	32.3	10	99	4
Parratt	9	5	12	—	22	8	51	—
Wainwright	9	—	29	—	34	9	69	1
Wade	10	2	17	—	22	6	43	2
Ulyett	6	2	14	—	19	8	30	2
Hall	3	—	11	—				
Moorhouse					11	6	11	1

Gloucestershire Bowling

	Overs	Mdns	Runs	Wkts	Overs	Mdns	Runs	Wkts
Mr Peake	64	27	124	1	6	—	20	—
Woof	96	64	87	5	5	4	3	—
Mr W. G. Grace	50	24	87	—				
Mr Townsend	13	3	32	1				
Mr Radcliffe	15	8	20	—				
Mr Page	13	8	17	—				
Mr E. M. Grace	20.3	1	62	2				
Mr Brain	2	—	11	—				

Umpires: Coward and Tuck.

GLOUCESTERSHIRE v LANCASHIRE

Played at Bristol, July 1, 2, 1889

Playing without their two bowlers, Woof and Roberts, Gloucestershire had but a small chance of defeating their northern rivals, and the team made a very bad show. Not only was their bowling freely punished, but their batting was poor, and in the second innings broke down completely. Going in first for Gloucestershire, who won the toss, the brothers Grace scored 47 before being separated, and then for the rest of the innings the bowlers held the upper hand. Painter was the only batsman to offer any serious resistance, and the whole side, though at the wickets three hours and a quarter, were put out for the moderate total of 145. When Lancashire went in the weak Gloucestershire bowling was hit to all parts of the field. Messrs Hornby and Eccles put on 68 runs in three-quarters of an hour, and afterwards Mr Eccles and Sugg added 62 in forty minutes, the professional playing brilliant cricket. On the second morning Albert Ward, Briggs and Paul scored with ease, and Lancashire's total in the end reached 327. Pilling, who had a finger split while wicket-keeping, was unable to bat. Being 182 runs behind, Gloucestershire were in a hopeless position, and on going in a second time, their batting collapsed so completely that the whole side were dismissed for 87, Lancashire being left with a victory by an innings and 95 runs. Mr W. G. Grace carried his bat through the innings, but he received little or no support.

Gloucestershire

Mr W. G. Grace c and b Watson	35	– not out	37
Mr E. M. Grace c Watson b Mold	14	– c Eccles b Mold	9
Mr J. H. Brain c Baker b Mold	16	– b Briggs	17
Mr W. W. F. Pullen c Mold b Watson	0	– c and b Briggs	0
Mr J. Cranston c Eccles b Mold	5	– b Watson	1
Mr O. G. Radcliffe b Watson	19	– c Paul b Briggs	11
J. Painter b Watson	32	– b Watson	3
Mr F. Townsend c Sugg b Watson	11	– b Briggs	5
Mr D. L. Evans c Hornby b Briggs	4	– b Briggs	0
T. Gregg run out	3	– b Briggs	0
Mr J. A. Bush not out	0	– b Briggs	3
B 6	6	B 1	1
	145		87

Lancashire

Mr A. N. Hornby lbw b W. G. Grace	39
Mr J. Eccles c Radcliffe b E. M. Grace	62
F. H. Sugg c Bush b Gregg	48
A. Ward c Cranston b E. M. Grace	53
Mr S. M. Crosfield b Gregg	0
J. Briggs c Bush b Radcliffe	40
A. Paul b Painter	60
G. R. Baker b E. M. Grace	7
A. Watson c Cranston b E. M. Grace	2
A. Mold not out	0
R. Pilling absent hurt	
B 8, l-b 8	16
	327

Lancashire Bowling

	Overs	Mdns	Runs	Wkts	Overs	Mdns	Runs	Wkts
Watson	50	29	70	5	31	18	28	2
Mold	39	15	57	3	14	3	36	1
Briggs	10	5	12	1	16.4	9	22	7

Gloucestershire Bowling

	Overs	Mdns	Runs	Wkts
Gregg	37	15	75	2
Mr Radcliffe	27	9	60	1
Mr W. G. Grace	27	11	68	1
Painter	15	5	32	1
Mr E. M. Grace	27.4	3	70	4
Mr Evans	1	—	6	—

Umpires: Tuck and Panter.

GLOUCESTERSHIRE v SURREY

Played at Cheltenham, August 19, 20, 21, 1889

The annual cricket week at Cheltenham opened with the return match with Surrey, who on the former meeting at The Oval had put the new rule of closing the innings into force, and beaten Gloucestershire by 250 runs. Gloucestershire put their best eleven into the field, but owing to a severe cold Mr John Shuter was unable to play, and his place was taken by Brockwell. Mr Grace won the toss and decided to go in first, but the wicket did not play at all well, and for some time Gloucestershire fared badly. Messrs Radcliffe, Pullen and Brain were disposed of for 13 runs, and with the score at 41 Mr W. G. Grace, who was at the wickets three-quarters of an hour for 12, was caught in the slips. Mr Page was bowled at 45, and six wickets were down. At this point Mr Townsend joined Mr Cranston, who had gone in at the fall of the third wicket, and was playing splendid cricket, and in twenty-five minutes the pair put on 40 runs. Mr Croome was Mr Cranston's next partner, and the score had been taken to 100, when just before two o'clock rain came on suddenly and stopped play. The downpour lasted until four o'clock, and it was twenty-five minutes to five before a resumption could be made. Mr Cranston then hit with great vigour, and received excellent support from Mr Croome, Woof and Roberts, who helped him respectively to put on 39, 41 and 36 runs, and it may be mentioned that the last four wickets actually added 156 runs to the score. Mr Cranston, who carried out his bat for 111, was at the wickets two hours and thirty-five minutes. He was missed twice in making his first 50, but despite these blemishes his innings under the circumstances was a remarkably fine one. His chief hits were nine 4s, nine 3s and thirteen 2s. With the close of Gloucestershire's innings play ceased for the day.

Rain fell during the night, but the game was resumed punctually at half-past eleven on Tuesday morning. The wicket was difficult, and, like the home team, Surrey started badly, losing Brockwell, Mr Key and Mr Read for 8 runs. To get rid of the two crack amateurs so cheaply was great good fortune; but instead of making the most of their chances the Gloucestershire team began to drop catches. Maurice Read, who had gone in first, was missed at point, and this mistake proved serious, as the professional afterwards hit with great power. Abel and Lohmann were soon got rid of, the fifth wicket falling at 36. A valuable stand was then made by Read and Henderson, but the former was twice missed by Mr Radcliffe, the second chance, when the batsman had made 48, being very easy. After this good luck Read hit with increased vigour, and despite bowling changes the score was taken to 124, or 88 for the partnership, before Henderson, who was missed when he had made 8, was got rid of. Read, after giving another chance, was stumped at 157. Although very lucky, his innings of 93 was of great value to his side. He was batting two hours and fifty minutes, and hit a 5, eight 4s, three 3s and fifteen 2s. In the end the Surrey total reached 183, or 18 runs behind. When Gloucestershire went in a second time an extremely good start was made, 70 going up on the board with only two wickets down. Then a great change came over the game, and when stumps were drawn for the day nine batsmen were out, and the score was only 107. This sudden collapse was mainly due to Brockwell, who, in one over, got rid of Messrs Cranston, E. M. Grace and Townsend.

Mr Radcliffe played a plucky, if not particularly good, innings of 63, and Mr W. G. Grace hit in fine style until taken by Maurice Read, who brought off a splendid running catch.

About eleven o'clock on the third morning rain fell for an hour, and afterwards there came another heavy downpour, and the wicket was so saturated that play could not be resumed until five minutes past four. Woof being bowled in the second over, the home team's innings closed for 107, the last seven wickets having fallen for 35 runs. Surrey were set 126 runs to get to win, and when they entered upon the task exactly a hundred minutes were left for play. As the ground was soft and slow the chances were against the feat being accomplished, but Maurice Read and Brockwell, who went in first, kept in front of the clock, scoring 31 in just over twenty minutes. Read was then dismissed, and Mr Key came in, and a great attempt was made to win the match. At five o'clock – or an hour left for play – 80 runs were required, but only 28 were scored in the half hour, and a draw looked certain. Then Mr Key, who had been missed in the long field, hit with remarkable energy, and of the 52 runs still wanted 38 were made in twenty-five minutes. A catch at mid-off then got rid of the old Oxonian, and as it was just within five minutes of time stumps were pulled up, and the game abandoned as a draw, greatly in favour of Surrey, who at the finish only wanted 14 runs to win, and had six wickets in hand. Though he failed to win the match, Mr Key deserved and received great praise for his splendid effort. He obtained his 58 in just over an hour, his chief hits being five 4s, three 3s and nine 2s.

Gloucestershire

Mr W. G. Grace c Abel b Lohmann	12	– c M. Read b Lohmann	20
Mr O. G. Radcliffe c Key b Beaumont	9	– lbw b Beaumont	63
Mr W. W. F. Pullen c M. Read b Beaumont	1	– c Abel b Beaumont	0
Mr J. H. Brain c Lohmann b Beaumont	0	– c M. Read b Brockwell	5
Mr J. Cranston not out	111	– c and b Brockwell	2
Mr E. M. Grace c Abel b Lohmann	0	– c Lohmann b Brockwell	0
Mr H. V. Page b Lohmann	0	– c Wood b Brockwell	2
Mr F. Townsend c M. Read b Lohmann	28	– b Brockwell	0
Mr A. C. M. Croome c and b Lohmann	6	– b Beaumont	4
W. A. Woof c Wood b Bowley	9	– b Beaumont	2
F. G. Roberts c Henderson b Lohmann	11	– not out	1
B 14	14	B 2, l-b 6	8
	201		107

Surrey

W. Brockwell c Page b Roberts	3	– c Croome b W. G. Grace	27
M. Read st Page b Woof	93	– c and b Woof	10
Mr K. J. Key b Woof	0	– c Townsend b Roberts	58
Mr W. W. Read lbw b Woof	0	– c sub b Woof	8
R. Abel c Brain b Woof	12	– not out	8
G. A. Lohmann c W. G. Grace b Woof	1		
R. Henderson c Radcliffe b Woof	31		
W. Lockwood c W. G. Grace b Roberts	14		
H. Wood not out	13		
J. Beaumont c and b Woof	1		
T. Bowley c Cranston b Roberts	10		
B 3, l-b 2	5	L-b 1	1
	183		112

Surrey Bowling

	Overs	Mdns	Runs	Wkts	Overs	Mdns	Runs	Wkts
Lohmann	32.1	15	68	6	12	2	37	1
Beaumont	31	8	93	3	19	10	25	4
Bowley	10	3	26	1	11	7	13	—
Brockwell					15	6	24	5

Gloucestershire Bowling

	Overs	Mdns	Runs	Wkts	Overs	Mdns	Runs	Wkts
Woof	38	13	71	7	24	3	66	2
Roberts	38.4	14	76	3	17.3	8	33	1
Mr Radcliffe	4	1	12	—				
Mr W. G. Grace	5	1	15	—	6	2	12	1
Mr Croome	1	—	4	—				
Mr Townsend	1	1	—	—				

Umpires: Chatterton and Veitch.

GLOUCESTERSHIRE v MIDDLESEX

Played at Cheltenham, August 22, 23, 24, 1889

In this, the second match of the Cheltenham week, some remarkable cricket was witnessed, as Middlesex, following on in a heavy minority, played so well afterwards as to be enabled to close their innings, and have the best of a drawn game. One change was made from the home team that opposed Surrey in the early part of the week, Painter taking the place of Mr Croome, while Middlesex, though not playing Mr L. H. Baemeister, were strongly represented. More rain had fallen during the night, and the weather on Thursday was cold and unsettled. Rain stopped the game for a quarter of an hour before lunch, and just before four o'clock a heavy shower fell, and prevented further play for the day. Cricket was only practicable for two hours and a half, and in that time Gloucestershire, who won the toss and went in first on the soft wicket, scored 146 runs for the loss of six wickets. The early batting gave no promise of a good score, as the first four wickets fell for 28 runs. Mr W. G. Grace, who had opened the innings, was then joined by Mr Townsend, and a much better appearance was put on the game, 90 runs being added before the latter was dismissed for an extremely useful, if not very well played, innings of 45. At the drawing of stumps Mr W. G. Grace was not out 63, and Painter not out 8. The champion started so carefully as to only score five singles in the first half hour, but he afterwards played admirable cricket, though he should have been caught by Burton at short slip when he had made 39.

There was more rain in the night, and the ground was very soft on Friday morning. Painter was soon dismissed, but Mr Grace and Mr Page gave the fieldsmen a lot of trouble, runs coming at a good pace. The former gave a fine display, and there was great cheering when, with the score at 233, he completed his hundred, having then been at the wickets four hours. At length Mr Page was caught at the wicket for a capital 43, the partnership for the eighth wicket having produced 83 runs. In the end Gloucestershire's total reached 282, Mr Grace carrying out his bat for a superb innings of 127. Except for the chance to Burton on Thursday, the great cricketer made no mistake during the four hours and a half he was batting, and his innings was in every way worthy of him. His chief hits were eleven 4s, four 3s and seventeen 2s. Middlesex went in for five minutes before lunch, and lost Mr Webbe's wicket before a run was scored. After the interval the game for some time went against the visitors, the third wicket falling at 30. Mr O'Brien and Mr Hadow showed brilliant cricket, and afterwards Mr Henery and Mr Vernon played pluckily, the 100 going up with only five wickets down. Mr Paravicini and West made a few good hits, but the visitors failed to save the follow-on, and were dismissed by half-past five for 178. In a minority of 104, Middlesex went in again, and in a quarter of an hour before the drawing of stumps Messrs Ford and Paravicini scored 11 runs.

During the early hours of Saturday morning rain fell heavily, and play could not be resumed until a quarter to twelve. Even then the ground was exceedingly soft, and by no means unfavourable to batsmen. When he had made 17 Mr Ford was missed at the wicket, and the mistake had serious results, as afterwards the Cantab hit in most brilliant style. With the score at 49 rain stopped play for twenty minutes, thus further handicapping the fieldsmen. On resuming, Mr Paravicini, who played steady cricket, was got rid of at

87, but Mr Stoddart, who came next, quickly settled down, and he and Mr Ford scored with great freedom. At lunch time the total was 138 for one wicket, and afterwards – rain during the interval having made the wicket easy again – runs came just as freely as before. At 171, however, Mr Ford was bowled for a splendidly hit 108. Though not faultless, his innings, which only occupied an hour and fifty minutes, was a fine display of free hitting, and undoubtedly saved Middlesex from defeat. Mr Ford's chief hits were ten 4s, five 3s and sixteen 2s. Mr Stoddart left at 176, his dashing 45 including eight 4s, and afterwards the batsmen continued to hit out. When seven wickets were down for 240, Mr Webbe declared the innings at an end, and put Gloucestershire in with 137 to get to win. As only seventy minutes were left for cricket, there was no time to obtain the runs, and Middlesex had little or no chance of getting Gloucestershire out. The usual order of going in was altered, and the result was that five wickets were lost for 48 runs before stumps were finally pulled up, and the match abandoned as a draw. As the game was left, Middlesex had the best of it, but under the circumstances no real superiority could be claimed.

Gloucestershire

Mr W. G. Grace not out	127		
Mr O. G. Radcliffe b Stoddart	9	– b Ford	10
Mr W. W. F. Pullen c Ford b Stoddart	4	– b Ford	0
Mr J. Cranston b Nepean	0	– not out	15
Mr J. H. Brain b Stoddart	1	– c Stoddart b Ford	1
Mr F. Townsend c Vernon b Ford	45	– not out	5
Mr E. M. Grace c Stoddart b Ford	10	– c Paravicini b Stoddart	4
J. Painter c West b Stoddart	17	– b Stoddart	11
Mr H. V. Page c West b Hadow	43		
F. G. Roberts c Ford b Nepean	3		
W. A. Woof c Burton b Stoddart	13		
B 7, l-b 2, n-b 1	10	L-b 2	2
	282		48

Middlesex

Mr A. J. Webbe c Townsend b Woof	0	– not out	0
Mr A. E. Stoddart c Townsend b Roberts	0	– st Page b Woof	45
Mr E. A. Nepean c Townsend b Woof	13	– c Cranston b Roberts	10
Mr T. C. O'Brien b W. G. Grace	24	– b Roberts	21
Mr E. M. Hadow c Page b W. G. Grace	40	– c and b Roberts	17
Mr P. J. T. Henery c E. M. Grace b Woof	30	– b Woof	5
Mr G. F. Vernon c Pullen b Townsend	32	– not out	9
Mr F. G. J. Ford b Townsend	7	– b Woof	108
Mr P. J. de Paravicini b Roberts	15	– c Townsend b Painter	20
J. E. West c Townsend b Woof	16		
G. Burton not out	0		
B 1	1	B 5	5
	178		(7 wkts dec.) 240

Middlesex Bowling

	Overs	Mdns	Runs	Wkts	Overs	Mdns	Runs	Wkts
Mr Nepean	23	4	47	2				
Mr Stoddart	34.3	7	97	5	14	5	25	2
Burton	16	5	28	—				
Mr Hadow	10	3	29	1				
Mr Ford	22	7	48	2	13	6	21	3
Mr Webbe	7	1	23	—				

Gloucestershire Bowling

	Overs	Mdns	Runs	Wkts	Overs	Mdns	Runs	Wkts
Roberts	22	8	36	2	23	2	86	3
Woof	28.4	5	89	4	28	4	80	3
Mr W. G. Grace	7	1	33	2	4	2	4	—
Mr Townsend	5	—	19	2	3	—	9	—
Mr Radcliffe					5	2	29	—
Painter					8	2	27	1

Umpires: Veitch and Tuck.

GLOUCESTERSHIRE v NOTTINGHAMSHIRE

Played at Clifton, August 14, 15, 16, 1890

Rain in the early part of the week and during the progress of this return match made the ground extremely difficult, and batsmen all through were seriously handicapped. The home team had the best of the opening day's play, and, maintaining their advantage to the end, won a highly interesting game by 42 runs. For their victory – the second in a fortnight over the famous Nottinghamshire eleven – Gloucestershire were mainly indebted to Mr W. G. Grace and Woof. On the second day the champion played superb cricket, going in second wicket down and taking out his bat for 70.

Gloucestershire

Mr W. G. Grace b Needham	2	– not out	70
Mr E. M. Grace c Shrewsbury b Attewell	27	– c Gunn b Flowers	7
Mr O. G. Radcliffe c Flowers b Attewell	4	– lbw b Attewell	32
Mr W. W. F. Pullen b Needham	1	– c Gunn b Barnes	6
Mr J. Cranston c Gunn b Attewell	17	– c Shrewsbury b Flowers	9
J. Painter b Needham	4	– st Carlin b Attewell	13
Mr F. Townsend b Needham	0	– b Attewell	3
Mr A. C. M. Croome c Needham b Attewell	15	– lbw b Attewell	7
Mr H. V. Page not out	4	– b Needham	12
W. A. Woof c Dixon b Attewell	0	– c Dixon b Attewell	4
F. G. Roberts c Gunn b Attewell	1	– hit wkt b Needham	1
L-b 2	2	B 5, l-b 1	6
	77		170

Nottinghamshire

A. Shrewsbury c W. G. Grace b Woof	14	– st Page b Woof	11
Mr J. A. Dixon lbw b W. G. Grace	11	– b Woof	4
W. Gunn c Townsend b W. G. Grace	3	– lbw b Radcliffe	14
F. Butler c E. M. Grace b Woof	0	– st Page b Woof	0
W. Barnes c W. G. Grace b Woof	4	– c W. G. Grace b Woof	0
W. Flowers c W. G. Grace b Woof	9	– c Croome b Woof	34
Mr H. B. Daft c and b Woof	0	– b W. G. Grace	12
W. Attewell c Townsend b W. G. Grace	1	– b Woof	25
F. Shacklock b Woof	6	– c Croome b Woof	15
J. Carlin not out	0	– not out	15
F. Needham c E. M. Grace b Woof	13	– b W. G. Grace	5
L-b 1	1	B 2, l-b 5, w 1	8
	62		143

Nottinghamshire Bowling

	Overs	Mdns	Runs	Wkts	Overs	Mdns	Runs	Wkts
Attewell	28	11	34	6	42	17	57	5
Needham	22	11	28	4	9	5	18	2
Shacklock	5	2	13	—				
Flowers					19	3	51	2
Barnes					18	6	38	1

Gloucestershire Bowling

	Overs	Mdns	Runs	Wkts	Overs	Mdns	Runs	Wkts
Woof	19.4	10	27	7	31	11	70	7
Roberts	4	—	14	—	2	—	6	—
Mr W. G. Grace	15	10	20	3	25.2	11	50	2
Mr Radcliffe					3	1	9	1

Umpires: Draper and Veitch.

GLOUCESTERSHIRE v LANCASHIRE

Played at Bristol, July 13, 14, 1891

Thanks to a fine innings of 124 by Arthur Smith, and some splendid bowling on a hard wicket by Mold, Lancashire gained a brilliant and decisive victory by an innings and 65 runs. Smith went in first wicket down at 13 and was ninth out at 289, being at the wickets three hours and forty minutes. This 124 was Smith's first three figure innings in an important match, and was in every way a fine display. Mold, who had accomplished a splendid performance at Taunton in the previous week, did a second great bowling feat, taking fourteen wickets for 95 runs, and in the two matches he obtained twenty-nine wickets for 226, or less than eight runs each. The Gloucestershire batting was extremely disappointing, though Mr E. M. Grace and Mr Radcliffe made an excellent start, scoring 76 runs for the first wicket at the outset of the match. Mr W. G. Grace batted well in the second innings, but was greatly hampered by an injury to his knee received a few days previously.

Gloucestershire

Mr E. M. Grace c Kemble b Mold	48	– lbw b Mold	9
Mr O. G. Radcliffe c Watson b Mold	54	– b Mold	14
Mr E. Sainsbury b Mold	0	– not out	18
J. Painter st Kemble b Smith	8	– b Mold	4
Mr W. W. F. Pullen b Smith	4	– c Briggs b Mold	21
Mr F. Townsend c Ward b Smith	0	– c and b Smith	0
Mr W. G. Grace c Kemble b Smith	3	– c Sugg b Watson	22
Mr H. W. Brown b Mold	0	– b Mold	1
W. A. Woof not out	4	– b Mold	0
F. G. Roberts b Mold	4	– c Hornby b Mold	0
J. H. Board b Mold	0	– b Mold	5
B 1, l-b 2	3	B 2, l-b 4	6
	128		110

Lancashire

R. G. Barlow lbw b Roberts	7
A. Ward st Board b Townsend	48
A. Smith b Roberts	124
F. H. Sugg c Roberts b Townsend	12
G. Yates c Sainsbury b Woof	40
J. Briggs b Woof	11
G. R. Baker c sub b Painter	18
Mr A. N. Hornby c Painter b Roberts	7
Mr A. T. Kemble b Brown	2
A. Watson b Woof	25
A. Mold not out	8
B 2, l-b 4	6
	303

Lancashire Bowling

	Overs	Mdns	Runs	Wkts	Overs	Mdns	Runs	Wkts
Mold	42	23	44	6	26	8	51	8
Briggs	13	3	32	—	8	1	19	—
Watson	7	3	16	—	4	1	3	1
Smith	28	15	33	4	21	8	31	1

Gloucestershire Bowling

	Overs	Mdns	Runs	Wkts
Roberts	40	13	67	3
Woof	43.3	15	88	3
Brown	21	3	60	1
Mr Townsend	8	—	35	2
Mr Radcliffe	2	—	13	—
Mr E. M. Grace	4	1	12	—
Painter	4	—	22	1

Umpires: Hill and Henty.

GLOUCESTERSHIRE v SOMERSETSHIRE

Played at Cheltenham, August 17, 18, 1891

Owing to rain there was rather less than two hours cricket on Monday, but the visitors made splendid use of their opportunity, scoring 142 runs for two wickets. All but four of this number were obtained during the partnership of Mr L. Palairet and Mr Challen, the latter of whom played resolute cricket for 79. On Tuesday Mr Palairet succeeded in completing his hundred, his innings, which was a capital display lasting three hours and a half. On going in to bat Gloucestershire completely failed to overcome the difficulties of the ground, and were put out in fifty minutes for 25, this being the smallest score obtained in a first-class county match during the season. The home men did much better at their second attempt, but were unable to avert a crushing defeat, Somersetshire winning by an innings and 130 runs.

Somersetshire

Mr L. C. Palairet c E. M. Grace b Woof	100
Mr H. T. Hewett b Woof	0
Mr J. B. Challen c Pullen b W. G. Grace	79
Mr S. M. J. Woods b W. G. Grace	13
Mr V. T. Hill b Woof	4
Mr A. E. Newton c Pullen b Woof	5
G. B. Nichols c Pullen b Woof	12
Mr W. N. Roe c Pullen b Woof	6
Mr R. C. N. Palairet c Groome b Woof	29
Mr C. J. Robinson c W. G. Grace b Woof	5
E. J. Tyler not out	0
L-b 1, w 1	2
	255

Gloucestershire

Mr W. G. Grace c Nichols b Tyler	4 – b Woods	12
Mr O. G. Radcliffe c Hewett b Tyler	0 – c Challen b Tyler	26
Mr H. V. Page st Newton b Tyler	0 – c Newton b Tyler	9
Mr E. M. Grace c Hill b Woods	0 – b Woods	5
J. Painter c and b Woods	7 – b Woods	11
Mr W. W. F. Pullen c Newton b Tyler	3 – c Robinson b Tyler	1
Mr A. C. M. Croome b Woods	0 – b Nichols	22
H. W. Murch c Robinson b Tyler	6 – b Tyler	7
W. A. Woof c Robinson b Woods	3 – b Tyler	0
F. G. Roberts b Woods	1 – run out	4
J. H. Board not out	0 – not out	3
B 1	1	
	25	100

Gloucestershire Bowling

	Overs	Mdns	Runs	Wkts
Woof	53.2	15	125	8
Mr W. G. Grace	37	8	82	2
Roberts	18	6	31	—
Murch	4	1	15	—

Somersetshire Bowling

	Overs	Mdns	Runs	Wkts	Overs	Mdns	Runs	Wkts
Mr Woods	7	3	14	5	16	3	32	3
Tyler	7	2	10	5	20	3	60	5
Nichols					4.2	—	8	1

Umpires: Carpenter and Street.

GLOUCESTERSHIRE IN 1893

In the latter part of the summer a remarkable young player was introduced into the eleven in the person of Mr C. L. Townsend, a son of Mr Frank Townsend, one of the old school of Gloucestershire cricketers. Both he and Mr W. G. Grace, jun. – the eldest son of the champion – while still at Clifton College, made their first appearance in county cricket, in the match against Middlesex on their own school ground, and for Mr Townsend there is unquestionably a future as a bowler. His first experience was not altogether satisfactory, as, on a good wicket and with indifferent support from the field, he met with severe treatment; but in the four games in which he took part he succeeded in taking twenty-one wickets for just over 23 runs each. For one so young – he is only seventeen and looks at least two years younger – he bowls with admirable judgment and is able to make the ball break either way. He, however, relied mainly on his leg break, and this he bowled with quite as much success as could be expected. At first sight this young bowler, with his slight build, gives the impression of being scarcely strong enough to stand the fatigue of a three days' match, but yet in his first outing in the field he sent down no fewer than seventy overs. There is little doubt that in Mr Townsend Gloucestershire have discovered a bowler of considerable natural talent, and his career will be followed with close interest.

Turning to the batting it is pleasant to again find Mr W. G. Grace occupying the post of honour. Though not so successful in county cricket as in 1892, when he scored 802 runs with an average of 36, the champion had a good season, his aggregate being 711, and his average 28. Satisfactory as these figures are, they do not convey an adequate impression of the splendidly consistent batting of the famous cricketer. He had a big share in the victories over Kent and Middlesex, scoring 46 and 42 not out against the former county, and 96 and 8 at Lord's. Against the Surrey bowlers at The Oval he carried his bat through the first innings for 61, and later in the season he played a fine innings of 75 in the return with Sussex, and scored 68 against Middlesex. Outside the county matches Mr Grace was even more successful, the admirable form he displayed in the many encounters with the Australians being quite a feature of a busy season. Playing for the Marylebone Club against Kent he made 128, this being his best score in important cricket in England since 1890. July, with some soft wickets, was a rather bad month for Mr Grace, but while the grounds were hard and firm he fully held his own with the best of the younger batsmen. Altogether in first-class cricket Mr Grace scored 1,609 runs with an average of 35.34, a remarkable record for a player who was at the zenith of his fame when most of his present-day rivals were still at school.

With regard to the other Gloucestershire batsmen a few words will suffice. Mr Ferris made a great advance, his aggregate rising from 350 to 687, and his average from 17.19 to 22.5, and he had the distinction of playing the only three-figure innings obtained for the county, scoring 106 against Sussex at Brighton. Mr Kitcat confirmed the good impression he made in the previous year, but Mr Rice was a disappointment. Against Nottinghamshire he scored 34 and 64 not out – an achievement that practically secured for him his Blue at Oxford – but afterwards he failed to maintain the admirable form he displayed in 1892. It may, however, be assumed that in the case of a young batsman with most approved methods, the falling off is merely temporary. A left-handed batsman and excellent field made his appearance in the county ranks in the person of Mr G. S. De Winton, who was seen at his best in an innings of 80 against Somerset at Cheltenham. Mr Radcliffe had a poor season, and Painter, though he played three or four brilliant innings, had to be content with modest results. During the latter part of the season, Mr W. H. Brain, of Oxford, a brother of Mr J. H. Brain, the old Gloucestershire cricketer, kept wicket, and acquitted himself with great credit. There is little further that need be said with regard to Gloucestershire cricket, but it is necessary to remark that the team did not work harmoniously together. It was quite an open secret that a spirit of mutiny prevailed, and matters went so far that at one point a crisis seemed imminent. Happily, however, good counsels prevailed, and the difficulties that had arisen were smoothed over. There is no doubt that, owing to the cause indicated, Gloucestershire suffered last season, and it is to be hoped that in future a better state of affairs will exist. In the latter part of the season. Mr W. G. Grace wrote to the Committee expressing his desire to give up the captaincy of the eleven, but in the autumn he withdrew his resignation.

GLOUCESTERSHIRE v MIDDLESEX

Played at Bristol August 10, 11, 12, 1893

In this game C. L. Townsend and W. G. Grace, jun. made their first appearance in county cricket, the former creating a favourable impression as a bowler. Several of the Middlesex batsmen did themselves full justice, and Gloucestershire fared tolerably well in the first innings. Following on, however, on a slow wicket, they offered a poor resistance to the admirable bowling of Rawlin, and Middlesex won easily by an innings and 98 runs. In taking twelve wickets for 79 runs Rawlin accomplished perhaps his best bowling feat in important cricket and as he also played a capital innings of 74 his share in the victory was considerable.

Middlesex

Mr A. E. Stoddart b Murch 75	Mr R. S. Lucas b Murch 0
Mr A. J. Webbe b Murch 5	Mr P. J. T. Henery b Murch 0
Mr C. P. Foley b Murch 72	J. T. Hearne st Brain b Townsend 1
Mr T. C. O'Brien c Ferris b Townsend 50	J. Phillips not out 19
Mr F. G. J. Ford c Luard b Murch 12	B 7 7
J. T. Rawlin b Murch 74	
Mr G. MacGregor c Murch b Townsend ... 68	385

Gloucestershire

Mr W. G. Grace b Ford	68 – c Webbe b Rawlin	3
Mr J. J. Ferris b Rawlin	22 – b Hearne	5
J. Painter c Ford b Hearne	1 – b Rawlin	9
Mr R. W. Rice run out	0 – b Rawlin	7
Mr C. L. Townsend b Rawlin	1 – b Rawlin	1
Mr W. G. Grace jun. c MacGregor b Rawlin	0 – c MacGregor b Hearne	11
Capt. A. H. Luard b Rawlin	34 – b Rawlin	2
Mr E. M. Grace c Hearne b Stoddart	4 – b Rawlin	10
Mr H. V. Page not out	30 – c MacGregor b Rawlin	0
Mr W. H. Brain c Ford b Stoddart	36 – not out	4
H. W. Murch c Rawlin b Ford	30 – b Rawlin	0
B 8, l-b 1	9	
	235	52

Gloucestershire Bowling

	Overs	Mdns	Runs	Wkts
Townsend	70	21	151	3
Murch	56.3	16	131	7
J. J. Ferris	5	—	14	—
W. Grace jun.	24	6	57	—
W. G. Grace	8	2	18	—
Page	2	—	7	0

Middlesex Bowling

	Overs	Mdns	Runs	Wkts	Overs	Mdns	Runs	Wkts
Hearne	28	11	68	1	20	9	23	2
Rawlin	33	14	50	4	19.1	8	29	8
Stoddart	23	5	54	2				
Ford	13.1	—	44	2				
Phillips	6	2	10	—				

Umpires: J. Wheeler and J. Street.

GLOUCESTERSHIRE v SOMERSET

Played at Cheltenham, August 14, 15, 16, 1893

After a close struggle on the first innings Somerset outplayed the home eleven and won by 127 runs. As the wicket was fiery all through the scoring was rather remarkable, and the achievements of Roe, Lionel Palairet and De Winton were of great merit, the last-named surpassing all his previous performances for his county. There was a sensational incident on the second afternoon, Townsend finishing off Somerset's second innings with the "hat" trick, and all three batsmen being stumped.

Somerset

Mr W. C. Hedley b Murch	8 – c Brain b Ferris	14
Mr L. C. H. Palairet b Roberts	27 – c Painter b Ferris	72
Mr J. B. Challen b Murch	14 – st Brain b W. G. Grace	30
Mr R. C. N. Palairet c Brain b Roberts	16 – c W. G. Grace b Roberts	39
Mr V. T. Hill b Roberts	0 – c Page b Murch	29
Mr W. N. Roe b Roberts	75 – not out	9
Mr H. T. Hewett c Page b Murch	0 – c Painter b Murch	33
Mr S. M. J. Woods st Brain b Townsend	26 – c De Winton b Townsend	22
Mr A. E. Newton c De Winton b Murch	13 – st Brain b Townsend	4
G. B. Nichols not out	9 – st Brain b Townsend	0
E. J. Tyler b Ferris	1 – st Brain b Townsend	0
B 8	8 B 15, l-b 3	18
	197	270

Gloucestershire

Mr J. J. Ferris b Nichols	32 – b Tyler	1
Mr R. W. Rice c and b Tyler	0 – c Roe b Tyler	2
Mr W. G. Grace jun. c Newton b Nichols	7 – c and b Woods	14
Mr G. S. De Winton lbw b Tyler	80 – run out	10
J. Painter c R. Palairet b Hedley	6 – c Newton b Woods	11
Mr E. M. Grace b Hedley	0 – c L. Palairet b Tyler	28
Mr H. V. Page c L. Palairet b Nichols	22 – b Nichols	40
Mr W. H. Brain c Wood b Tyler	5 – c Hewett b Tyler	17
Mr C. L. Townsend not out	1 – c R. Palairet b Tyler	4
H. W. Murch b Tyler	2 – c R. Palairet b Hedley	26
F. G. Roberts c Hill b Tyler	1 – not out	11
B 9, l-b 1	10 B10	10
	166	174

Gloucestershire Bowling

	Overs	Mdns	Runs	Wkts	Overs	Mdns	Runs	Wkts
Townsend	20	3	71	1	8	1	16	4
Murch	24	5	67	4	20	2	88	2
Roberts	17	2	43	4	15	3	44	1
Ferris	10.3	1	8	1	19	2	74	2
W. G. Grace					12	3	30	1

Somerset Bowling

	Overs	Mdns	Runs	Wkts	Overs	Mdns	Runs	Wkts
Tyler	33.2	12	39	5	36	10	71	5
Woods	13	2	32	—	21	4	46	2
Nichols	35	15	48	3	10	4	24	1
Hedley	23	8	37	2	7.2	2	23	1

Umpires: J. Street and S. Talboys.

GLOUCESTERSHIRE v SUSSEX

Played at Bristol, August 6, 7, 8, 1894

Owing to unfavourable weather the game could not be commenced on Monday, and an unpleasant episode occurred. Drenching rains on Sunday had left the ground very heavy, there was a further downpour on Monday, and at three o'clock, the umpires declaring the turf quite unfit for cricket, it was decided to postpone the start. In the meantime, however, some two or three thousand spectators had been admitted to the ground, and, on learning the decision, they behaved in a very unsportsmanlike manner. A number of them trampled on the playing portion of the ground, doing considerable damage, and Mr W. G. Grace and Mr Murdoch, the captains, were mobbed and had to be protected by the police. This regrettable incident points to the necessity of gate money not being taken until play has been definitely decided upon. On the Tuesday, Sussex, who went in first, occupied the whole of the day in completing a first innings of 302. The total was only 108 when the sixth wicket fell, but Fry and Butt then added 178 runs in two hours and a half. Fry's 109 occupied three hours, and was his first hundred for Sussex. The wicket on Wednesday helped the bowlers a good deal, and Gloucestershire were in a hopeless position. With the exception of W. G. Grace, Ferris and Rice, the home batsmen quite failed to overcome the difficulties of the situation, and Sussex won by an innings and 104 runs, their decisive success being attributable to the extremely effective bowling of Parris.

Sussex

Batsman	Runs
G. Bean c Townsend b Woof	12
F. W. Marlow b Townsend	32
Mr G. H. Arlington run out	11
Mr W. I. Murdoch b Townsend	20
Mr W. Newham b Jessop	7
Mr G. Brann lbw b Townsend	14
Mr C. B. Fry c Ferris b Roberts	109
H. Butt c Jessop b Townsend	65
F. Parris c Wrathall b Townsend	0
W. Humphreys not out	5
J. Hilton c Ferris b Townsend	9
B 11, l-b 5, n-b 2	18
	302

Gloucestershire

Batsman	1st inns	2nd inns	
Mr W. G. Grace c Murdoch b Parris	33	lbw b Parris	9
Mr J. J. Ferris b Hilton	9	not out	34
J. Painter b Parris	4	c Butt b Parris	18
Mr R. W. Rice c Newham b Hilton	38	b Parris	2
Mr C. L. Townsend c Bean b Parris	17	st Butt b Parris	0
Mr G. L. Jessop c Marlow b Parris	5	st Butt b Hilton	0
Mr E. M. Grace b Parris	3	c Bean b hilton	3
Mr H. V. Page c Humphreys b Hilton	5	b Parris	0
H. Wrathall lbw b Parris	0	c Arlington b Parris	3
W. A. Woof st Butt b Parris	1	c Newham b Parris	3
F. G. Roberts not out	2	st Butt b Parris	5
B 4	4		
	121		77

Gloucestershire Bowling

	Overs	Mdns	Runs	Wkts
Townsend	56.2	10	125	6
Woof	24	7	44	1
Roberts	33	16	55	1
Jessop	8	3	16	1
W. G. Grace	11	5	13	—
Ferris	8	2	31	—

Sussex Bowling

	Overs	Mdns	Runs	Wkts	Overs	Mdns	Runs	Wkts
Parris	41	16	70	7	22.3	9	28	8
Hilton	31.2	19	35	3	32	5	49	2
Brann	9	4	12	—				

Umpires: R. Carpenter and S. Talboys.

GLOUCESTERSHIRE v SOMERSET

Played at Bristol, May 16, 17, 18, 1895

Though Fowler and Lionel Palairet opened the match by scoring 205 for the first Somerset wicket Gloucestershire gained a brilliant victory by nine wickets. Everything in the game was dwarfed by Grace's big innings of 288, which was his hundredth three-figure score in important cricket. He was batting for five hours and twenty minutes without making a single mistake, his hitting at times being marked by all the vigour of his younger days. He was ninth out at 465, and among his hits were thirty-eight 4's, eleven 3's and twenty-nine 2's. Townsend played a fine innings, and helped his captain to put on 233 runs for the third wicket.

Somerset

Mr L. C. H. Palairet c Bracher b Roberts	80	– c Board b Murch	1
Mr G. Fowler st Board b Grace	118	– lbw b Townsend	33
Mr J. B. Challen b Grace	6	– c Wrathall b Townsend	16
Mr R. C. N. Palairet c Board b Murch	26	– c Roberts b Murch	23
Mr H. T. Stanley c Board b Murch	29	– b Murch	31
Mr S. M. J. Woods c Board b Murch	6	– c Painter b Murch	47
Mr D. L. Evans lbw b Grace	11	– c Board b Murch	2
G. B. Nichols c Board b Grace	0	– c Board b Murch	6
E. J. Tyler c Ferris b Grace	0	– not out	17
Rev. A. P. Wickham c Thomas b Murch	3	– b Murch	0
Mr J. Bucknell not out	10	– b Murch	0
B 5, l-b 6, w 3	14	B 9, w 4	13
	303		189

Gloucestershire

Mr W. G. Grace c Tyler b Woods	288		
Mr J. J. Ferris b Tyler	4		
Mr C. O. H. Sewell c and b Woods	2		
Mr C. L. Townsend lbw b Bucknell	95		
J. Painter lbw b Tyler	34		
H. Wrathall b Fowler	6	– not out	6
Mr E. L. Thomas b Woods	3	– lbw b Bucknell	12
Mr F. C. Bracher b Bucknell	20		
H. W. Murch c Stanley b Tyler	5		
J. H. Board not out	2	– not out	1
F. G. Roberts c sub b Tyler	9		
B 4, l-b 2	6		
	474		19

Gloucestershire Bowling

	Overs	Mdns	Runs	Wkts	Overs	Mdns	Runs	Wkts
Townsend	11	2	31	—	34	16	63	2
Roberts	29	7	51	1	13	2	29	—
Sewell	7	—	38	—				
Murch	35.2	14	72	4	44	16	68	8
Ferris	2	—	10	—				
Grace	45	16	87	5				
Wrathall					9	2	16	—

Somerset Bowling

	Overs	Mdns	Runs	Wkts	Overs	Mdns	Runs	Wkts
Tyler	42.4	7	160	4				
Woods	40	3	145	3				
Nichols	10	4	21	—				
Bucknell	17	2	68	2	4	1	5	1
Fowler	14	2	56	1	3.3	—	14	—
L. Palairet	4	—	18	—				

Umpires: J. Street and W. F. Collishaw.

GLOUCESTERSHIRE v NOTTINGHAMSHIRE

Played at Cheltenham, August 19, 20, 1895

In fulfilling their return engagement with Gloucestershire, the Nottinghamshire eleven had to take the field at a grave disadvantage. Both Shrewsbury and Gunn were unable to play, and, to add to the misfortunes of the side, Flowers, owing to the sudden death of his father, had to leave Cheltenham on the Monday afternoon. Under these circumstances it was not surprising that the Nottinghamshire men failed, being badly beaten by an innings and 93 runs. Winning the toss and going in first, Gloucestershire stayed at the wickets the whole of the first day, scoring 242 for seven wickets. The chief feature of the play was the admirable batting of Grace, who scored 113 not out. On the second morning he only added 6 to his score, being ninth out at 254, and the innings closed for 257. This was Grace's eighth hundred in first-class cricket during the season, and occupied him about five hours. The wicket, though dry, was very difficult, and, contrasted with the many failures in the match, the achievement of the champion was indeed remarkable. There is no need to comment on the batting of the visitors, who, with two or three exceptions, failed completely. Continuing his marvellous run of success, Townsend took thirteen wickets for 110 runs.

Gloucestershire

Mr W. G. Grace b Bennett	119	Mr H. V. Page b Attewell	9
Mr J. J. Ferris b Jones	9	J. Painter lbw b Attewell	15
H. Wrathall c and b Attewell	11	J. H. Board not out	3
Mr R. W. Rice b Attewell	21	F. G. Roberts c sub b Attewell	1
Mr C. O. H. Sewell c and b Attewell	8	B 12, l-b 5, n-b 1	18
Mr C. L. Townsend b Dixon	33		
Mr G. L. Jessop b Dixon	10		257

Nottinghamshire

Mr J. A. Dixon b Townsend	9	– c Board b Townsend	26
Mr A. O. Jones c Grace b Townsend	14	– c Board b Townsend	39
Mr P. W. Oscroft b Jessop	3	– c Ferris b Townsend	0
Mr C. W. Wright c Board b Jessop	0	– c Ferris b Townsend	4
R. Bagguley c and b Townsend	7	– c and b Townsend	2
H. B. Daft b Jessop	2	– not out	5
W. Attewell c Grace b Townsend	11	– c Page b Townsend	4
A. Longdon b Jessop	2	– st Board b Townsend	2
A. Wilkinson not out	7	– c Grace b Roberts	1
Mr A. R. Bennett st Board b Townsend	7	– lbw b Townsend	9
W. Flowers absent	0	– absent	0
B 3	3	B 7	7
	65		99

Nottinghamshire Bowling

	Overs	Mdns	Runs	Wkts
Bennett	30	11	55	1
Attewell	64	35	52	6
Jones	20	6	48	1
Wilkinson	9	4	17	—
Dixon	22	1	49	2
Flowers	2	—	17	—
Daft	1	—	1	—

Gloucestershire Bowling

	Overs	Mdns	Runs	Wkts	Overs	Mdns	Runs	Wkts
Townsend	20.3	6	43	5	19	2	67	8
Painter	5	2	10	—				
Jessop	15	12	9	4	8	4	12	—
Roberts					10	6	13	1

Umpires: L. Hall and J. Platts.

GLOUCESTERSHIRE v YORKSHIRE

Played at Cheltenham, August 22, 23, 24, 1895

The Gloucestershire eleven concluded a most successful week by a brilliant triumph over Yorkshire. Two days were occupied in completing an innings on each side, but with the wicket rendered slow by rain some remarkable cricket was witnessed on Saturday. In Yorkshire's second innings Brown and Tunnicliffe scored 66 for the first wicket, and when 90 went up with only one man out there seemed little likelihood of Yorkshire being beaten. Afterwards, however, Townsend bowled with astonishing success, and Yorkshire were put out for 143, the last eight wickets going down for 50 runs. Gloucestershire were set 146 runs to win, and light work was made of the task. Ferris played steadily, while the other batsmen, forced the game, and Gloucestershire won by seven wickets.

Yorkshire

J. T. Brown st Board b Townsend	13	c Board b Roberts	35
J. Tunnicliffe c Painter b Townsend	4	c and b Jessop	52
D. Denton c Painter b Roberts	39	c Sewell b Townsend	8
R. Moorhouse b Jessop	70	lbw b Townsend	1
R. Peel c Sewell b Townsend	31	c Jessop b Townsend	2
E. Wainwright c Painter b Townsend	8	c Jessop b Townsend	0
G. H. Hirst c Sewell b Townsend	2	c Board b Roberts	20
Mr E. Smith c Page b Townsend	27	c Sewell b Townsend	11
Lord Hawke not out	20	st Board b Townsend	0
J. Mounsey st Board b Townsend	2	c Jessop b Townsend	5
D. Hunter c Painter b Townsend	2	not out	0
L-b 2, n-b 1	3	B 5, l-b 2, n-b 2	9
	221		143

Gloucestershire

	First innings	Second innings	
Mr W. G. Grace b Peel	4	c and b Wainwright	38
Mr J. J. Ferris c Hunter b Wainwright	16	not out	40
H. Wrathall c Wainwright b Peel	4	c Tunnicliffe b Peel	26
Mr G. L. Jessop b Smith	63	not out	7
Mr R. W. Rice b Peel	15		
Mr C. O. H. Sewell c Moorhouse b Wainwright	50		
Mr C. L. Townsend c Peel b Brown	42		
Mr H. V. Page c Hunter b Brown	17		
J. Painter c Tunnicliffe b Hirst	3	c Smith b Brown	32
J. H. Board c Wainwright b Brown	1		
F. G. Roberts not out	0		
B 3, w 1	4	B 3, l-b 1	4
	219		147

Gloucestershire Bowling

	Overs	Mdns	Runs	Wkts	Overs	Mdns	Runs	Wkts
Townsend	32.4	4	130	8	24	5	54	7
Jessop	27	9	59	1	10	2	29	1
Roberts	9	3	16	1	21.3	11	32	2
Ferris	4	1	13	—				
Painter					8	2	19	—

Yorkshire Bowling

	Overs	Mdns	Runs	Wkts	Overs	Mdns	Runs	Wkts
Peel	32	12	56	3	23	11	34	1
Hirst	34	12	82	1	16	6	32	—
Smith	18	5	34	1	5	—	18	—
Wainwright	16	4	32	2	10	4	22	1
Brown	5.2	1	11	3	7	1	37	1

Umpires: H. Holmes and W. Clarke.

GLOUCESTERSHIRE v SURREY

Played at Clifton, August 26, 27, 28, 1895

Up to a late period in the match the chief question appeared to be whether Gloucestershire would succeed in forcing a win. Surrey, however, not only made themselves safe from defeat, but came very near gaining a victory. When Gloucestershire went in a second time only an hour remained for play. The order of going in was unwisely changed, with the result that seven wickets were lost for 37 runs, the steadiness of Ferris alone saving the side. This bad failure, of course, largely discounted the fine cricket the Gloucestershire men had shown in the early stages of the match.

Surrey

R. Abel b Roberts	38	– c Jessop b Townsend	39
M. Read st Board b Townsend	88	– c Jessop b Roberts	38
T. Hayward c Grace sen. b Townsend	4	– c Grace sen. b Painter	23
Holland c Grace jun. b Townsend	18	– c Board b Roberts	5
W. Brockwell c Board b Jessop	16	– not out	21
W. Lockwood b Townsend	5	– c and b Townsend	23
Mr H. D. G. Leveson-Gower st Board b Townsend	0	– c Board b Townsend	1
Mr K. J. Key run out	4	– c Wrathall b Townsend	13
G. Lohmann not out	2	– c Grace jun. b Painter	10
C. Marshall c Painter b Townsend	0	– c Painter b Townsend	11
T. Richardson b Townsend	2		
B 2, l-b 1, w 1, n-b 1	5	B 3, l-b 5, n-b 1	9
	182	(9 wkts dec.)	193

Gloucestershire

Mr W. G. Grace sen. c Marshall b Richardson	0		
Mr J. J. Ferris b Lockwood	58	– not out	22
H. Wrathall b Richardson	59	– c Abel b Richardson	0
Mr G. L. Jessop b Richardson	8	– not out	5
Mr R. W. Rice b Richardson	46	– b Richardson	2
Mr W. G. Grace jun. b Richardson	16	– b Lohmann	2
Mr C. L. Townsend c Lohmann b Richardson	18	– b Richardson	0
Mr C. O. H. Sewell c Key b Lohmann	5	– b Lohmann	0
J. Painter c Brockwell b Richardson	1	– b Richardson	4
J. H. Board not out	9	– b Lohmann	1
F. G. Roberts b Richardson	1		
B 17, l-b 5	22	L-b 1	1
	243		37

Gloucestershire Bowling

	Overs	Mdns	Runs	Wkts	Overs	Mdns	Runs	Wkts
Townsend	43.1	11	80	7	55.3	14	95	5
Jessop	26	8	57	1	7	2	14	—
Roberts	19	8	40	1	29	13	39	2
Grace jun.					5	4	3	—
Painter					23	11	33	2

Surrey Bowling

	Overs	Mdns	Runs	Wkts	Overs	Mdns	Runs	Wkts
Richardson	37	10	91	8	13	3	25	4
Lohmann	27	9	46	1	12	8	11	3
Lockwood	19	6	46	1				
Hayward	12	5	22	—				
Abel	5	2	16	—				

Umpires: H. Holmes and W. Clarke.

GLOUCESTERSHIRE v SOMERSET

Played at Bristol, May 7, 8, 9, 1896

After starting the match by losing four wickets for 39 runs, the Somerset eleven steadily gained the upper hand, and in the end won by 123 runs. The first move towards their ultimate success was made by Woods and Stanley, who in the first innings put on 165 runs in two hours, and of that number Woods scored 108 by brilliant hitting. Nichols was out in an unusual manner, attempting a run after hitting the ball a second time. On the second day, Woods played another characteristic innings of 52, but most of the Somerset batsmen were in difficulties with Grace's slows. Gloucestershire failed in batting, but of course the weakness of the side must be taken into consideration. Wrathall, however, greatly distinguished himself; on Friday, though lame, he scored 59 of the last 68 in ninety minutes, and on the last day in five minutes less time he hit up 70. While Wrathall stayed there seemed a chance of a close finish, but after he left Tyler carried all before him.

Somerset

	1st inns		2nd inns	
Mr G. Fowler b Roberts	8	–	b Grace	29
Mr L. C. H. Palairet b Roberts	5	–	b Grace	6
W. Sloman c Pritchard b Roberts	5	–	b Townsend	1
G. Robson c Board b Roberts	20	–	c Board b Grace	41
Mr H. T. Stanley b Grace	79	–	c and b Grace	3
Mr S. M. J. Woods lbw b Murch	108	–	b Grace	52
G. B. Nichols hit ball twice	10	–	c Board b Roberts	13
D. Smith run out	8	–	c Board b Grace	0
Dr F. J. Poynton c Murch b Grace	12	–	c Townsend b Grace	7
Rev. A. P. Wickham not out	0	–	b Townsend	8
E. J. Tyler b Grace	0	–	not out	8
B 3	3		B 2, l-b 3	5
	258			173

Gloucestershire

	1st inns		2nd inns	
Mr W. G. Grace b Tyler	17	–	c Palairet b Tyler	25
Mr J. W. S. Jellie lbw b Tyler	1	–	lbw b Tyler	0
Mr E. L. Thomas c Poynton b Woods	47	–	b Robson	2
J. H. Board c Robson b Tyler	0	–	c Woods b Tyler	30
Mr H. C. Pritchard b Woods	16	–	b Robson	4
Mr C. L. Townsend c Fowler b Tyler	8	–	c and b Tyler	13
H. Wrathall not out	59	–	c Poynton b Tyler	70
H. W. Murch b Robson	1	–	lbw b Tyler	4
Mr F. C. Bracher c Stanley b Tyler	1	–	c Fowler b Tyler	1
F. G. Roberts c Palairet b Woods	0	–	not out	3
G. Pepall c Nichols b Tyler	1	–	st Wickham b Tyler	0
B 2	2		B 3	3
	153			155

Gloucestershire Bowling

	Overs	Mdns	Runs	Wkts	Overs	Mdns	Runs	Wkts
Roberts	40	14	82	4	11	2	40	1
Murch	44	12	122	1				
Pepall	8	1	28	0				
Grace	18.4	9	23	3	22.2	5	59	7
Townsend					17	1	69	2

Somerset Bowling

	Overs	Mdns	Runs	Wkts	Overs	Mdns	Runs	Wkts
Tyler	33.2	14	50	6	28.1	9	2	8
Nichols	23	12	34	0	7	2	0	0
Fowler	2	0	2	0				
Woods	21	6	47	3	10	0	50	0
Robson	11	0	18	1	14	10	10	2

Umpires: A. F. Smith and A. Chester.

GLOUCESTERSHIRE v LANCASHIRE

Played at Bristol, June 25, 26, 27, 1896

Without the Cambridge cricketers and Sewell, Gloucestershire opposed Lancashire with a weak eleven, and the success of the northern county by an innings and 18 runs was scarcely surprising. Gloucestershire began well, Grace and Wrathall scoring 64 for the first wicket, but afterwards the batting broke down badly. At the close of the first day Lancashire had scored 97 for one wicket, and on Friday they increased their total to 389. The feature of the innings and indeed of the match, was the brilliant batting of Frank Sugg, who, going in first and being sixth out, scored 220 out of 335. He was missed at 112 and again at 143, but these were the only real mistakes in a remarkable display, which only occupied three hours and 40 minutes, and included thirty-three 4s, eight 3s and ten 2s. The closing stage of the match was rendered notable by Grace accomplishing the rare feat of carrying his bat through the innings. His 102 not out was a masterly display and in making his 100, he was greatly indebted to Roberts, the last man, who stayed for a half an hour while the champion made his last 18 runs. In this match Grace completed his 1,000 runs, and Townsend showed some return to form. Mold broke down after bowling two overs, and Rowley was also injured.

Gloucestershire

Mr W. G. Grace c Tyldesley b Briggs	51	– not out	102
H. Wrathall c I'Anson b Baker	44	– c Tyldesley b Paul	30
Mr C. L. Townsend c Benton b Baker	17	– c Paul b Briggs	38
Mr H. B. Champain c I'Anson b Baker	1	– c Smith b Briggs	28
J. H. Board c Smith b Baker	0	– c Rowley b Briggs	0
Mr A. Lamb c Paul b Briggs	8	– b Briggs	10
J. Painter b Baker	0	– st Smith b Briggs	9
Mr H. Jessop run out	0	– run out	3
Mr F. C. Bracher st Smith b Briggs	4	– c Sugg b Briggs	4
H. W. Murch b Baker	1	– absent hurt	0
F. G. Roberts not out	0	– c Smith b Briggs	0
B 4, l-b 3	7	B 12, l-b 1, w 1	14
	133		238

Lancashire

A. Ward b Townsend	27
F. H. Sugg c sub. b Townsend	220
C. Smith c Grace b Townsend	10
A. Paul st Board b Townsend	9
Mr C. H. Benton c Champain b Townsend	2
J. H. Tyldesley c Board b Murch	19
G. R. Baker c Board b Roberts	63
J. Briggs c Jessop b Townsend	19
J. I'Anson b Roberts	9
Mr E. Rowley not out	0
A. Mold absent hurt	0
B 8, w 3	11
	389

Lancashire Bowling

	Overs	Mdns	Runs	Wkts	Overs	Mdns	Runs	Wkts
Briggs	34	7	81	3	60.1	20	93	7
I'Anson	12	2	24	0	44	22	78	0
Mold	2	0	3	0				
Baker	22.1	13	18	6	22	11	30	0
Paul	1	1	0	0	7	1	23	1

Gloucestershire Bowling

	Overs	Mdns	Runs	Wkts
Roberts	42.2	12	125	2
Murch	12	2	44	1
Townsend	41	8	125	6
Painter	8	1	35	0
Lamb	4	0	32	0
Jessop	5	1	17	0

Umpires: J. J. Tuck and G. Littlewood.

GLOUCESTERSHIRE v SUSSEX

Played at Bristol, August 3, 4, 5, 1896

At Brighton in Whit-week, W. G. Grace scored 243 not out, and in the return he surpassed that achievement, playing a remarkable innings of 301. This was the highest individual score of the season, and the third best ever made by Grace in first-class matches. On Monday he scored 193 out of 341 for three wickets, and he was ninth out with the total at 548. He was at the wickets for eight hours and a half, and so grandly did he play, that he gave no actual chance. His great score was made up by twenty-nine 4s, sixteen 3s, twenty-seven 2s and eighty-five singles. Rice assisted him to add 211 runs for the second wicket, while Grace and Kitcat together scored 193 for the ninth partnership. Sussex began well, scoring 132 for three wickets, but on the third day their batting scarcely came up to expectation. Ranjitsinhji, Marlow and Newham played very well, the Indian trying hard in the second innings to save the match. There was quite an exciting finish, for less than a quarter of an hour remained when Gloucestershire secured a decisive victory by an innings and 123 runs.

Gloucestershire

Mr W. G. Grace sen. b Collins	301
Mr W. G. Grace jun. b Hartley	1
Mr R. W. Rice c Parris b Ranjitsinhji	84
Mr W. McG. Hemingway c Killick b Hartley	30
Mr C. L. Townsend c and b Tate	30
H. Wrathall c Parris b Tate	0
Mr C. O. H. Sewell b Parris	4
Mr G. L. Jessop lbw b Parris	2
J. H. Board c and b Parris	0
Mr S. A. P. Kitcat not out	77
F. G. Roberts c Parris b Killick	2
B 17, l-b 3	20
	551

Sussex

F. W. Marlow c Hemingway b Townsend	57	– c and b Townsend	21
E. H. Killick b Jessop	13	– b Jessop	20
K. S. Ranjitsinhji b Roberts	38	– c Grace jun. b Jessop	54
Mr W. L. Murdoch b Townsend	12	– run out	9
Mr W. Newham not out	63	– lbw b Grace sen.	11
G. Bean c Jessop b Townsend	8	– c Wrathall b Grace sen.	6
Mr A. Collins c and b Roberts	23	– not out	14
Mr J. C. Hartley c Grace sen. b Roberts	0	– b Grace sen.	0
F. Parris c Townsend b Grace sen.	1	– b Roberts	3
F. W. Tate b Roberts	4	– lbw b Roberts	30
Mr R. W. Fox b Roberts	9	– lbw b Townsend	0
B 13, l-b 5, w 1, n-b 3	22	B 6, l-b 1, n-b 3	10
	250		178

Sussex Bowling

	Overs	Mdns	Runs	Wkts
Tate	65	24	134	2
Hartley	37	5	115	2
Collins	48	7	48	1
Parris	63	30	103	3
Killick	32.2	11	57	1
Bean	13	4	34	0
Ranjitsinhji	12	1	40	1

Gloucestershire Bowling

	Overs	Mdns	Runs	Wkts	Overs	Mdns	Runs	Wkts
Townsend	27	4	88	3	26.3	3	67	2
Roberts	27	7	50	5	24	10	38	2
Jessop	19	4	52	1	14	7	40	2
Grace, sen.	10	3	30	1	19	11	23	3
Grace, jun.	4	0	8	0				

Umpires: G. Littlewood and A. Chester.

GLOUCESTERSHIRE IN 1897

Next to the captain, the most prominent and attractive figure on the Gloucestershire side was unquestionably Mr G. L. Jessop, who made a great advance in reputation and repeatedly startled the cricket world by remarkable displays of batting. In another part of the *Almanack* will be found a biographical notice of this brilliant young cricketer, who during 1897 quite rivalled the feats of such great hitters as Mr C. I. Thornton, G. J. Bonnor, H. H. Massie, and J. J. Lyons. Apart from observing that like Hayward of Surrey, and Hirst and Wainwright of Yorkshire, he had the distinction of scoring over a thousand runs and taking over a hundred wickets in first-class cricket, our comments here must be confined entirely to his doings with the Gloucestershire eleven. For the western county Mr Jessop scored 571 runs with an average of 28 while he took 58 wickets at a cost of just over 19 runs each, and was at the head of the bowling table. These bare figures, however, do not convey an adequate idea of his value to the side. His great merit rested in the fact that until he was disposed of no one could say what was likely to happen, as by his fierce and rapid hitting he was able in half an hour to completely change the fortunes of a game. He had many failures, often throwing away his wicket by sheer recklessness; but he had several memorable triumphs. Prior to 1897, Mr Jessop had never played an innings of three figures in first-class cricket, but last summer he exceeded the hundred on four occasions. Three of these big scores were obtained for the county and were – 101 against the Philadelphians, 126 against Warwickshire, and 101 against Yorkshire. The last-named innings was perhaps his most remarkable performance, as he obtained the 101 runs in the astonishingly short time of forty minutes. As he followed up his great innings by taking nine wickets, he had a big share in the victory over the northern county. Another display, to which attention may be specially directed, was a brilliantly hit 90, against the Somerset bowlers, at Clifton. Whether or not successful as a batsman or bowler, Mr Jessop was always a most dependable field, his work at times being quite brilliant, and, next to his captain, he was the greatest power on the side.

GLOUCESTERSHIRE v KENT

Played at Cheltenham, August 9, 10, 11, 1897

For two days this game was extremely well contested, but, on Wednesday, Gloucestershire gained the upper hand and won by 63 runs. There was some capital batting, but everything was dwarfed by the remarkable performance of the Malvern schoolboy, S. H. Day, who was playing his first county match. In making his 101, not out, he was at the wicket for three hours without giving a chance and hit eleven 4s. But for him, Kent would have cut a sorry figure in their second innings. In Kent's first innings, Stewart gave an admirable display, while Rice and Richardson on the opening day and Grace, senior, on Tuesday, did the best work for Gloucestershire.

Gloucestershire

Mr W. G. Grace b Hearne	11	– b Martin	58
Mr R. W. Rice c Shine b Wright	57	– b Mason	24
H. Wrathall b Hearne	0	– c Hearne b Shine	32
Mr F. H. B. Champain c Bradley b Wright	28	– c and b Martin	13
Mr G. L. Jessop b Wright	0	– st Huish b Wright	13
Mr C. L. Townsend b Bradley	5	– b Mason	25
J. H. Board c Marchant b Bradley	0	– b Martin	22
Mr A. G. Richardson c Marchant b Martin	51	– b Mason	13
Mr W. G. Grace jun. hit wkt b Easby	22	– c Bradley b Wright	25
Mr H. S. Goodwin not out	8	– c Hearne b Mason	0
Mr W. S. A. Brown b Shine	17	– not out	14
B 4, w 1, n-b 1	6	B 5, l-b 5	10
	205		249

Kent

Mr J. R. Mason c Grace jun. b Brown	19	– c Jessop b Brown	20
Alec Hearne b Brown	14	– st Board b Townsend	3
Mr S. H. Day b Jessop	8	– not out	101
F. Martin b Jessop	0	– b Townsend	7
W. Wright b Jessop	29	– b Jessop	5
J. Easby c Goodwin b Brown	5	– b Jessop	2
Mr H. C. Stewart c and b Townsend	64	– c Brown b Grace sen.	2
Mr F. Marchant c Champain b Brown	28	– c Grace sen. b Brown	37
Mr W. M. Bradley c Brown b Townsend	5	– c Grace jun. b Townsend	4
F. H. Huish b Townsend	5	– c Grace sen. b Townsend	0
Mr E. B. Shine not out	7	– b Jessop	5
B 1, l-b 9, w 1	11	B 13, l-b 2	15
	190		201

Kent Bowling

	Overs	Mdns	Runs	Wkts	Overs	Mdns	Runs	Wkts
Martin	26	10	50	1	30	11	60	3
Shine	29.2	16	46	1	28	8	51	1
Hearne	14	6	38	2				
Wright	13	6	28	3	9.3	1	35	2
Mason	8	3	12	0	23	10	49	4
Bradley	13	7	13	2	14	5	44	0
Easby	4	1	12	1	1	1	0	0

Gloucestershire Bowling

	Overs	Mdns	Runs	Wkts	Overs	Mdns	Runs	Wkts
Jessop	37	13	71	3	25.1	3	41	3
Townsend	12	0	49	3	26	6	69	4
Brown	33	19	39	4	15	7	35	2
Grace, jun.	7	4	8	0	5	1	16	0
Grace, sen.	5	1	12	0	15	3	25	1

Umpires: J. Street and J. Potter.

GLOUCESTERSHIRE v NOTTINGHAMSHIRE

Played at Bristol, June 9, 10, 11, 1897

The Gloucestershire eleven accomplished a notable batting performance, but stayed at the wickets too long to give themselves a fair chance of winning, their innings, which lasted ten hours and fifty minutes, not being terminated until six o'clock in the second afternoon. Grace and Rice put in 106 for the first wicket, Troup and Sewell 162 for the third, and Troup and Townsend 225 for the fourth. In first wicket down Troup was ninth out at 609, and he did not give a chance until 176. He was batting for eight hours and ten minutes. Sewell played very brilliantly, making his runs in less than two hours, while Townsend was at the wickets for three hours and a half. As was only to be expected, Gloucestershire failed to dispose of Nottinghamshire twice on the same day, the game ending in a draw.

Gloucestershire

Mr W. G. Grace c Pike b Wass	63
Mr R. W. Rice c Shrewsbury b Dench	42
Mr W. Troup b Attewell	180
Mr C. O. H. Sewell c Dixon b Guttridge	108
Mr C. L. Townsend b Attewell	134
Mr W. S. A. Brown lbw b Attewell	9
J. H. Board c Dixon b Attewell	1
H. Wrathall c Pike b Attewell	23
Mr C. B. Champain c Pike b Wass	1
H. W. Murch st Pike b Attewell	49
F. G. Roberts not out	3
B 8, l-b 4, w 9	21
	634

Nottinghamshire

Mr J. A. Dixon c Wrathall b Grace	40		
J. Gunn c Murch b Townsend	9		
A. Shrewsbury b Townsend	19	– not out	53
W. Gunn b Roberts	41	– not out	14
Mr A. O. Jones st Board b Wrathall	55		
C. E. Dench c Board b Brown	24		
W. Attewell st Board b Wrathall	23		
H. B. Daft not out	10	– c Board b Murch	13
A. Pike b Brown	0		
F. H. Guttridge lbw b Wrathall	0		
T. Wass run out	4		
B 4, n-b 1	4	B 2, n-b 1	3
	229		83

Nottinghamshire Bowling

	Overs	Mdns	Runs	Wkts
Wass	61	15	115	2
Attewell	82.2	33	143	6
Jones	21	2	59	0
J. Gunn	16	8	35	0
Daft	30	5	75	0
Guttridge	24	5	57	1
Dench	28	8	61	1
Dixon	22	10	41	0
W. Gunn	5	0	27	0

Gloucestershire Bowling

	Overs	Mdns	Runs	Wkts	Overs	Mdns	Runs	Wkts
Townsend	32	10	61	2				
Roberts	25	12	39	1	7	4	12	0
Grace	15	7	15	1				
Wrathall	32	5	58	3				
Brown	22	10	28	2	8	1	16	0
Champain	4	0	24	0				
Murch					16	2	52	1

Umpires: J. H. Holmes and J. J. Tuck.

GLOUCESTERSHIRE v WARWICKSHIRE

Played at Cheltenham, August 11, 12, 13, 1898

In this return match Gloucestershire, as at Birmingham, proved themselves the stronger side, and shortly after four o'clock on Saturday they gained a handsome win by five wickets. Townsend followed up his success against Kent by obtaining fifteen wickets for 205 runs, and in the course of the match he had the satisfaction of taking his hundredth wicket in first-class cricket during the season. In this game William Quaife's remarkable series of not-out innings came to an end, Grace in each innings neatly catching him at backward point. With the conditions favourable several batsmen were seen to advantage, Sewell's 71 being perhaps the best innings. At their second attempt Warwickshire lost five wickets before clearing off the arrears of 56, and afterwards they were always playing a losing game.

Warwickshire

W. Quaife c and b Townsend	6	– c and b Townsend	1
J. Devey c Board b Townsend	58	– b Jessop	1
Kinneir c Sewell b Jessop	29	– c Sewell b Jessop	14
W. G. Quaife c Grace b Townsend	3	– c Grace b Townsend	20
A. A. Lilley b Townsend	50	– c Hemingway b Townsend	48
Mr J. F. Byrne lbw b Townsend	1	– b Jessop	2
E. J. Diver c Board b Townsend	9	– c Jessop b Townsend	10
Mr A. C. S. Glover b Townsend	55	– c Grace b Townsend	32
S. Santall c Champain b Townsend	57	– lbw b Townsend	3
S. J. Whitehead not out	11	– not out	9
Field c Brown b Townsend	0	– b Jessop	1
B 7, l-b 2, n-b 2	11	B 10, n-b 2	12
	290		153

Gloucestershire

Mr R. W. Rice b Byrne	28 – not out	5
Mr W. S. A. Brown c Lilley b Whitehead	57 – b Byrne	14
Mr F. H. B. Champain c and b Kinneir	33 – c Santall b Whitehead	23
Mr C. L. Townsend b Whitehead	4 – c Lilley b Byrne	5
Mr C. O. H. Sewell c Field b Devey	71 – not out	1
Mr W. G. Grace c W. Quaife b Whitehead	34	
Mr W. Troup not out	31 – b Devey	39
Mr G. L. Jessop c Santall b Whitehead	26	
Mr W. McG. Hemingway c sub. b W. G. Quaife	24 – c W. G. Quaife b Whitehead	7
J. H. Board c W. Quaife b Whitehead	17	
H. Wrathall c Byrne b Field	7	
B 14	14 B 2, w 2, n-b 1	5
	346	99

Gloucestershire Bowling

	Overs	Mdns	Runs	Wkts	Overs	Mdns	Runs	Wkts
Townsend	46.4	8	128	9	31	4	77	6
Jessop	17	4	65	1	23.2	5	39	4
Brown	19	8	35	0	7	2	25	0
Grace	20	4	39	0				
Wrathall	4	1	12	0				

Warwickshire Bowling

	Overs	Mdns	Runs	Wkts	Overs	Mdns	Runs	Wkts
Field	28.4	5	76	1	3	1	6	0
Whitehead	40	10	107	5	14	3	44	2
Santall	32	12	71	0	9	3	17	0
Kinneir	7	4	14	1	1	0	5	0
Byrne	8	0	34	1	5	0	14	2
Devey	4	1	11	1	1.4	0	8	1
W. G. Quaife	3	0	19	1				

Umpires: R. Thoms and L. Hall.

GLOUCESTERSHIRE v ESSEX

Played at Clifton, August 15, 16, 1898

In this return match the luck was all against the Essex man. In the first place they were without A. J. Turner, and then A. P. Lucas, after making the journey, was compelled through indisposition to stand out of the match. Russell was also too unwell to keep wicket, though he batted on the second day. Further, after losing the toss, and fielding out the greater part of the day, Essex had to bat with the wicket rendered treacherous by brilliant sunshine following heavy rain during the night. Under these circumstances it was not surprising they were badly beaten, Gloucestershire winning in a single innings with eight runs to spare. Gloucestershire's innings occupied three hours and fifty minutes, and at one time looked like being an even more lengthy affair. At one point 180 was on the board with only three men out, but afterwards the batting broke down before the skilful bowling of Bull, who took six of the seven last wickets for 58 runs. Troup's innings of 100 was the event of the day, standing out prominently among a number of moderate scores.

His display occupied three hours and ten minutes, and was practically free from any real blemish. At the drawing of stumps on Monday, Essex had lost Owen and Perrin for 33 runs, and on the next day they had to face a hopeless task. With the pitch helping him greatly, Townsend bowled his slow leg breaks with fine effect, taking in the two innings 15 wickets for 141 runs.

Gloucestershire

Mr W. G. Grace b Mead	20
Mr W. Troup b Bull	100
Mr C. L. Townsend c Reeves b Mead	5
Mr C. O. H. Sewell lbw b Mead	31
Mr R. W. Rice b Bull	25
Mr G. L. Jessop c Carpenter b Bull	2
Mr A. G. Richardson b Bull	18
Mr W. G. Grace jun. c and b Bull	16
Mr W. S. A. Brown not out	14
J. H. Board b Bull	2
H. Wrathall c Fane b Mead	6
B 18, l-b 3	21
	260

Essex

H. Carpenter b Townsend	28 – b Townsend	3
Mr H. G. Owen c Brown b Townsend	0 – lbw b Townsend	29
Mr P. Perrin c Grace, jun. b Jessop	5 – b Jessop	37
Mr C. McGahey b Jessop	19 – c and b Townsend	19
Mr F. L. Fane b Townsend	2 – b Jessop	2
Mr C. J. Kortright c Grace, jun. b Townsend	4 – b Towsend	10
W. Reeves st Broard b Townsend	5 – c Brown b Townsend	0
E. Russell not out	15 – b Townsend	7
W. Mead c and b Townsend	0 – st Board b Townsend	15
Mr F. G. Bull b Townsend	17 – c Board b Jessop	20
Young c Brown b Townsend	3 – not out	0
L-b 6, n-b 1	7 B 2, l-b 1, n-b 2	5
	105	147

Essex Bowling

	Overs	Mdns	Runs	Wkts
Kortright	16	4	36	0
Bull	32	7	109	6
Mead	34.2	16	56	4
Young	13	4	23	0
Reeves	2	0	15	0

Gloucestershire Bowling

	Overs	Mdns	Runs	Wkts	Overs	Mdns	Runs	Wkts
Townsend	31.1	7	64	8	36	8	77	7
Jessop	22	8	25	2	25.3	11	51	3
Grace, sen.	2	0	2	0	4	2	6	0
Brown	7	3	7	0	6	1	8	0

Umpires: R. G. Barlow and W. A. J. West.

GLOUCESTERSHIRE v NOTTINGHAMSHIRE

Played at Bristol, June 8, 9, 10, 1899

After producing some exceptionally heavy scoring, 1166 runs being obtained for 25 wickets, this match ended in a draw. The first day's play was indeed remarkable, Notts. scoring 438 runs for two wickets. This was practically the work of Jones and Shrewsbury, who in four and a half hours scored 391 for the first wicket, this being the second highest partnership of the kind in important cricket. Jones, who was first out, had some luck late in his innings, but he gave a great display, which included thirty-two 4s. Shrewsbury was batting for an hour longer than the old Cantab, his superb innings being free from any serious blemish. The Notts. innings lasted seven hours and a half. Gloucestershire started badly, but thanks to Troup, Townsend and Cranston ran up a creditable total. Townsend played a great innings, which extended over four hours and a half, and was quite faultless. In Gloucestershire's second innings Dench dismissed Brown, Cranston, and Wrathall with successive balls, but Troup and Hale offered a stubborn resistance, raising the score from 77 to 193 without being separated.

Nottinghamshire

Batsman	Runs
A. Shrewsbury c and b Townsend	146
Mr A. O. Jones b Brown	250
W. Gunn b Townsend	38
Mr J. A. Dixon c Brown b Townsend	63
W. Attewell b Wrathall	57
F. H. Guttridge c Cranston b Paish	9
J. Gunn c and b Townsend	8
J. Iremonger c Thomas b Paish	6
T. Oates not out	8
C. E. Dench c Townsend b Paish	0
T. Wass c Wrathall b Townsend	6
B 6, l-b 3, w 7	16
	607

Gloucestershire

Batsman	First innings	Second innings	
J. H. Board c Guttridge b Wass	4	c sub. b Dench	10
H. Wrathall b Jones	16	b Dench	0
A. Paish b Wass	16		
Mr W. Troup lbw b Jones	56	not out	64
Mr C. L. Townsend lbw b Dixon	141	c sub. b Wass	31
Mr W. S. A. Brown b Jones	30	b Dench	8
Mr J. Cranston c Guttridge b Dixon	58	c Oates b Dench	0
W. H. Hale b Iremonger	0	not out	72
Mr J. Healing c sub b Dixon	9		
Mr E. L. Thomas c and b Dixon	15		
Mr J. Wilkinson not out	6		
B 3, l-b 5, w 6, n-b 1	15	B 5, l-b 1, w 1, n-b 1	8
	366		193

Gloucestershire Bowling

	Overs	Mdns	Runs	Wkts
Townsend	70.2	12	197	5
Wilkinson	13	0	69	0
Paish	49	11	145	3
Brown	47	22	81	1
Wrathall	18	3	83	1
Hale	3	0	16	0

Nottinghamshire Bowling

	Overs	Mdns	Runs	Wkts	Overs	Mdns	Runs	Wkts
Wass	33	13	75	2	18	10	20	1
Jones	26	0	86	3				
J. Gunn	14	6	27	0	2	3	7	0
Attewell	16	3	44	0	13	10	10	0
Iremonger	16	6	31	1	17	6	39	0
Guttridge	23	7	45	0	2	0	6	0
Dench	5	3	8	0	14	5	37	4
Dixon	15.2	6	35	4	20	3	66	0

Umpires: A. Young and W. Hearn.

GLOUCESTERSHIRE v KENT

Played at Bristol, July 17, 18, 19, 1899

The first day's play was tolerably even, Gloucestershire completing a first innings and Kent losing two wickets for 53. Champain played a capital innings, and when Gloucestershire had seven wickets down for 166, Board and Brown made a spirited stand. On the second day the home bowling was fairly collared, and Kent were not disposed of until shortly before the time for drawing stumps. Burnup, who had made 29 overnight, stayed until the total was 294; he was batting for four hours. Huish assisted Burnup to add 102 runs and Livesay helped to put on 113. In a minority of 150 Gloucestershire had an uphill fight before them on the Wednesday, but they proved quite equal to the occasion. Wrathall and Townsend scored 120 for the second wicket, and after this stand Gloucestershire had no difficulty in saving the game. Wrathall hit nineteen 4s in his 91. Townsend played a great innings.

Gloucestershire

Mr C. O. H. Sewell c sub. b Mason	13	– c Mason b Hearne	0
H. Wrathall b Martin	33	– c Hearne b Day	91
Mr C. L. Townsend b Hearne	26	– not out	152
Mr W. Troup c Huish b Hearne	23	– b Hearne	5
Mr F. H. B. Champain c Burnup b Martin	53	– b Blaker	37
Mr G. L. Jessop c Mason b Martin	13	– c Burnup b Martin	25
Mr F. N. Bird c Hearne b Martin	2	– not out	25
Mr W. S. A. Brown c Mason b Hearne	24		
J. H. Board c Blaker b Hearne	58		
A. Paish not out	1		
F. G. Roberts b Hearne	4		
B 5, l-b 1	6	B 7, l-b 2, w 1, n-b 2	12
	256		347

Kent

Mr C. J. Burnup c Sewell b Paish	150	Mr G. J. V. Weigall not out	55
A. Hearne lbw b Paish	0	Mr R. N. R. Blaker c Board b Roberts	34
Mr W. H. Patterson c Board b Townsend	13	F. Martin c Troup b Townsend	7
F. H. Huish b Wrathall	50	W. Wright c Jessop b Townsend	5
Mr S. H. Day lbw b Wrathall	11	B 10, l-b 8, n-b 4	22
Mr R. O'H. Livesay c Board b Townsend	55		
Mr J. R. Mason b Paish	4		406

Kent Bowling

	Overs	Mdns	Runs	Wkts	Overs	Mdns	Runs	Wkts
Wright	27	7	66	0				
Mason	24	9	67	1	22	7	66	0
Hearne	33.2	12	64	5	32	8	60	2
Martin	18	3	53	4	32	10	60	1
Patterson					14	5	31	0
Burnup					5	1	31	0
Day					6	0	20	1
Blaker					8	2	25	1
Huish					6	0	27	0
Weigall					1	0	8	0
Livesay					1	0	7	0

Gloucestershire Bowling

	Overs	Mdns	Runs	Wkts
Roberts	33	12	66	1
Paish	39	17	56	3
Jessop	31	8	69	0
Townsend	36.4	11	93	4
Wrathall	16	2	37	2
Brown	25	7	63	0

Umpires: R. Thoms and J. Moss.

GLOUCESTERSHIRE v SURREY

Played at Cheltenham, August 21, 22, 23, 1899

The chief features of this match were the splendid batting of Brockwell and the effective bowling of Paish and Lockwood. Brockwell's 167 only occupied him three hours and three-quarters, and though not faultless his innings was a fine piece of cricket. Pretty helped him to put on 101 runs. In the second innings Brockwell again showed the best form on the Surrey side. The Gloucestershire batting was disappointing, but with the pitch crumbling Lockwood made the ball fly about. Gloucestershire never looked like making the 297 runs required, Surrey winning by 140 runs. In this game Lockwood completed his thousand runs and obtained his hundredth wicket.

Surrey

First innings		Second innings	
R. Abel c Jessop b Paish	24	b Townsend	31
W. Brockwell c Townsend b Paish	167	c Jessop b Paish	50
E. G. Hayes c Brown b Roberts	13	c Townsend b Paish	25
Mr H. C. Pretty run out	31	c Brown b Paish	6
T. Hayward c and b Paish	10	c Rice b Paish	9
Mr D. L. A. Jepson c Rice b Paish	0	c Board b Paish	16
W. H. Lockwood c Roberts b Townsend	15	c Wrathall b Townsend	33
W. Lees c Jessop b Paish	14	c Wrathall b Paish	1
Mr K. J. Key c Wrathall b Paish	1	b Townsend	8
E. H. L. Nice c Wrathall b Paish	7	not out	17
A. Stedman not out	0	c Goodwin b Paish	8
B 7, w 3	10	B 7	7
	292		211

Gloucestershire

First innings		Second innings	
Mr R. W. Rice c Hayward b Lockwood	4	b Lockwood	5
H. Wrathall c Abel b Lockwood	20	b Lockwood	39
Mr C. L. Townsend b Lockwood	22	b Brockwell	13
Mr W. Troup b Lockwood	27	c Hayward b Lockwood	0
Mr G. L. Jessop b Lockwood	9	c Lees b Lockwood	22
J. H. Board c Lees b Lockwood	33	c Lees b Brockwell	10
Mr W. McG. Hemingway c Hayes b Lockwood	9	b Lockwood	2
Mr W. S. A. Brown lbw b Nice	5	c Pretty b Lockwood	17
Mr H. S. Goodwin c Brockwell b Lockwood	26	b Brockwell	8
A. Paish not out	36	b Nice	12
F. G. Roberts b Lockwood	0	not out	16
B 8, l-b 4, n-b 4	16	B 9, l-b 3	12
	207		156

Gloucestershire Bowling

	Overs	Mdns	Runs	Wkts	Overs	Mdns	Runs	Wkts
Jessop	6	1	15	0				
Townsend	21	1	74	1	28	6	66	3
Roberts	22	6	51	1	3	3	0	0
Paish	31.4	4	93	7	44.1	9	103	7
Brown	17	4	49	0	13	3	35	0

Surrey Bowling

	Overs	Mdns	Runs	Wkts	Overs	Mdns	Runs	Wkts
Lockwood	32	5	105	9	23	4	79	6
Nice	15	4	36	1	2.2	1	1	1
Lees	17	6	38	0				
Brockwell	2	0	4	0	25	8	64	3
Jephson	5	0	8	0				

Umpires: C. E. Richardson and E. Goodyear.

GLOUCESTERSHIRE v ESSEX

Played at Clifton, August 24, 25, 26, 1899

On the opening day Gloucestershire scored 299 for four wickets. Townsend and Troup raised the total from 31 to 290 and were together for nearly four hours. Troup did not give any chance in his 113 and hit seventeen 4s. With this score he completed his thousand runs. Townsend was 142 on Thursday evening, and on Friday he raised his score to 224 and carried out his bat. He was at the wickets for six hours and ten minutes and the only chance he gave was off the last ball he received. He hit twenty-eight 4s, eight 3s, and fifteen 2s, and in the course of his great innings displayed all his well-known skill. It was curious that in a total of over four hundred there should be no fewer than seven single figure scores, Townsend and Troup between them making 339. Essex began their first innings in an encouraging way, Fane and McGahey playing very well indeed, and at one point 150 was on the board with only three men out. Afterwards, however, the batting broke down. Following on in a minority of 202, Essex gave a lamentable display, and Gloucestershire won by an innings and 117 runs. Essex's second innings only occupied two hours and there was nothing in the condition of the ground to account for their failure.

Gloucestershire

Mr R. W. Rice c Ayres b Young	5
H. Wrathall b Young	6
Mr C. L. Townsend not out	224
Mr W. Troup c McGahey b Mead	115
Mr G. L. Jessop b Mead	6
J. H. Board b Young	2
Mr W. McG. Hemingway b Young	10
Mr W. S. A. Brown lbw b Reeves	20
Mr H. S. Goodwin b Mead	8
A. Paish c Fane b Bull	4
G. Pepall b Young	0
B 18, l-b 13, w 3, n-b 2	36
	436

Essex

Mr F. L. Fane b Paish	62	– c Board b Townsend	25
H. Carpenter b Jessop	24	– c Wrathall b Paish	5
Mr P. Perrin c and b Townsend	24	– st Board b Paish	0
Mr C. McGahey b Paish	49	– st Board b Paish	0
Mr A. P. Lucas b Paish	23	– c and b Brown	9
G. Ayres b Brown	1	– c Troup b Townsend	4
W. Reeves lbw b Paish	0	– c Paish b Townsend	1
H. Young lbw b Paish	0	– b Paish	26
Mr F. G. Bull not out	27	– c and b Townsend	3
W. Mead st Board b Paish	3	– not out	6
T. M. Russell absent ill		– absent ill	
B 10, l-b 9, w 1, n-b 1	21	B 1, w 5	6
	234		85

Essex Bowling

	Overs	Mdns	Runs	Wkts
Mead	52	20	105	3
Young	41.3	4	123	5
Bull	26	7	60	1
Reeves	24	6	70	1
McGahey	4	1	12	0
Ayres	2	0	10	0
Carpenter	3	1	9	0
Perrin	2	0	11	0

Gloucestershire Bowling

	Overs	Mdns	Runs	Wkts	Overs	Mdns	Runs	Wkts
Paish	28.3	10	98	6	26	11	47	4
Brown	21	5	48	1	14	11	10	1
Townsend	12	4	22	1	6.4	2	10	4
Pepall	9	5	17	0	6	3	12	0
Jessop	13	1	28	1				

Umpires: W. Richards and W. Shrewsbury.

HAMPSHIRE

HAMPSHIRE v DERBYSHIRE

Played at Southampton, July 24, 25, 1876

Mycroft's exceedingly successful bowling in this match will render the contest one of the most interesting played in County cricket history. The critics were loud in their praise of the Derbyshire left-hander's success; and well they might be, for his bowling had 17 of the 20 Hampshire wickets, 15 of the 17 being bowled; and he caught out another man, that catch crediting him with having had a hand in the downfall of all 10 wickets in Hampshire's first innings.

Mycroft commenced with taking two wickets in the first over he delivered, Hyslop playing the ball and kicking it into his wicket, and Mr Longman being well taken by the keeper. In his third over Mycroft bowled Mr Carter, whereupon Mr Ridley and Mr Booth played the score to 38, when Mycroft bowled Mr Booth. Soon after Mycroft bowled Mr Ridley, Mr Jeffreys, Holmes, and Mr Hargreaves, making 8 men out – all by Mycroft's bowling – for the 52 runs scored. Then Mycroft (at slip) caught out Tate; and when 10 more runs had been made he bowled Mr Foster; and so – in 90 minutes – did Mycroft get all 10 Hampshire men out for 63 runs, he having bowled in that innings: 21 overs and 3 balls (13 maidens) for 25 runs and 9 wickets – 8 bowled. His second innings bowling was not quite so astoundingly successful, but, backing up as it did his first, it was a marvel of success, though 50 runs appear to have been scored before that success set in; then Derby's left hand workęd, as at 51 Mycroft bowled Mr Carter; at 68 he bowled Mr Ridley; at 89 he bowled Mr Booth; at 92 he bowled Mr Longman; at 96 Mr Jeffreys played a Mycroft on; at 122 Holmes was had at point; at 130 Mr Foster was caught out at short-leg; and at 135 Tate was had at point – all three catches from Mycroft's bowling. There were then 9 wickets down, and 9 runs wanting by Hampshire to win, Mr Hargreaves well set, Galpin last man in, and the excitement of top quality, every run made being cheered in lusty form. When only three were required to win, Mycroft changed ends; but the first ball he there delivered Mr Hargreaves drove for 4; and so, despite Mycroft's rare success with the ball, Hampshire won by one wicket, "immense cheering" greeting the victory and Mr Hargreaves, who took his bat out for a well-played and winning 35, finishing up the brief and brilliant Hampshire season in splendid form.

Derbyshire

W. Rigley b Ridley	8	– b Ridley	22
J. Smith, Esq. c and b Galpin	17	– b Galpin	1
R. P. Smith Esq. c Tate b Galpin	1	– c Tate b Ridley	6
S. Richardson Esq. b Galpin	0	– c Hargreaves b Ridley	0
J. Platts st Hyslop b Ridley	28	– c Tate b Galpin	36
Amos Hind b Ridley	13	– st Hyslop b Ridley	3
T. Foster b Galpin	15	– c Foster b Ridley	11
W. G. Curgenven Esq. b Galpin	10	– b Galpin	3
A. Smith b Ridley	0	– not out	0
G. Hay not out	9	– st Hyslop b Ridley	3
W. Mycroft c Tate b Ridley	11	– b Galpin	4
L-b 3	3	L-b 2	2
	115		91

Hampshire

G. Carter Esq. b W. Mycroft	0	– b W. Mycroft	30
Hyslop b W. Mycroft	0	– c Hind b Platts	8
G. H. Longman Esq. c A. Smith b W. Mycroft	0	– b W. Mycroft	19
A. W. Ridley Esq. b W. Mycroft	24	– b W. Mycroft	13
C. Booth Esq. b W. Mycroft	14	– b W. Mycroft	12
R. Hargreaves Esq. b W. Mycroft	4	– not out	35
A. F. Jeffreys Esq. b W. Mycroft	4	– b W. Mycroft	3
H. Holmes b W. Mycroft	3	– c Richardson b W. Mycroft	8
H. Tate c W. Mycroft b Hay	0	– c Richardson b W. Mycroft	1
F. Foster Esq. b W. Mycroft	10	– c sub. b W. Mycroft	2
Galpin not out	4	– not out	1
		B 5, l-b 8	13
	63		145

Hampshire Bowling

	Overs	Mdns	Runs	Wkts	Overs	Mdns	Runs	Wkts
Galpin	34	16	42	5	23	7	40	4
Mr Ridley	33.2	10	70	5	26.1	11	37	6
Holmes					3	1	12	0

Derbyshire Bowling

	Overs	Mdns	Runs	Wkts	Overs	Mdns	Runs	Wkts
W. Mycroft	21.3	13	25	9	42.1	11	78	8
Hay	14	6	19	1				
Platts	7	3	19	0	11	4	22	1
Hind					26	9	32	0

HAMPSHIRE IN 1884

President – W. W. B. Beach, Esq., MP

Vice-Presidents – T. Chamberlayne, Esq., W. Nicholson, Esq., MP, and Capt. W. H. Eccles.

Captain – A. H. Wood, Esq.

Hon. Secretaries – Russell Bencraft, Esq., and Major J. Fellowes, RE

The inability of the Hampshire bowlers to prevent their opponents making long scores was the resaon the county lost three times as many matches as they won. There were several things, however, in connection with Hampshire cricket in 1884 which will render that season remarkable. In three of their matches an aggregate of over 1,000 runs was scored, and they thus gained an equal distinction with Kent in this respect. The innings of 645 scored against Somersetshire was the largest made in any county match during the season, and Hampshire also made scores of 414, 351, 307 and 294, while Mr F. E. Lacey's 211 was the highest individual innings hit in a county match during the year.

HAMPSHIRE v KENT

Played at Southampton, June 16, 17, 18, 1884

This was the second match played by Hampshire in 1884 which resulted in an aggregate of over 1000 runs being scored. The game was not concluded until nearly six o'clock on the third day, when Hampshire won by three wickets, 1,122 runs having been scored for 37 wickets, giving an average of 30.12 runs per wicket. Hampshire went in first, and were batting from 12.15 until about 5.15. As the total of their innings was 414, the runs were thus put on at the tremendous rate of 100 an hour. The feature of the innings was of course the splendid batting of Mr F. E. Lacey, who scored the highest innings made in a county match during the season. He was at the wickets only about three hours for his 211, and though the ground was small, and the boundary hits were easily obtained, the performance was a very remarkable one. Mr Lacey hit one 6, twenty-seven 4s and three 3s, and received capital support from Mr Bonham-Carter, Mr Ridley and Major Wallace. Kent lost three wickets that day for 67 runs, and time was then called, George Hearne being 32, not out, and Mr L. Wilson 2, not out.

Mr Mackinnon, Collins and Mr Wilson played up well when the Kent innings was resumed next morning, but they could not avert a follow-on. The visitors began their second innings 198 to the bad, but, thanks mainly to the fine hitting of Mr Mackinnon, the arrears were knocked off before the third wicket fell. Mr Mackinnon and Pentecost scored 61 for the first wicket, the latter's 38 being a capital innings. Frank Hearne failed to score, but on Mr Mackinnon and George Hearne coming together 115 more were put on before the latter was bowled for 38. When stumps were drawn for the day, the total stood at 219, Mr Mackinnon, not out, 109.

Mr Mackinnon was soon stumped for a fine innings of 115 when the match was continued on the last day, but Mr Thornton and Wootton batted exceedingly well, and in the end Hampshire had to go in again to get 147 to win, and with one exception the batsmen did very poorly. That exception was Mr Lacey, who followed up his grand innings of 211 by carrying his bat out for 92, and thus achieved one of the most remarkable batting performances ever recorded in a county match. He hit fifteen 4s and six 2s, and it was almost entirely due to his batting that Hampshire won the match.

Hampshire

L. Bonham-Carter Esq. c Wootton b Bligh	59	– b G. G. Hearne	3
C. Leat c Bligh b Wootton	4	– c H. Hearne b Wootton	5
G. H. Longman Esq. c Pentecost b Collins	5	– b G. G. Hearne	17
F. E. Lacey Esq. b G. G. Hearne	211	– not out	92
Major Wallace c Atkins b G. G. Hearne	24	– c F. Hearne b H. Hearne	2
H. Armstrong Esq. b Wootton	11	– b G. G. Hearne	5
C. Young c G. G. Hearne b Wootton	2	– c Pentecost b H. Hearne	12
A. B. Ridley Esq. lbw b Collins	41	– b H. Hearne	1
C. E. Currie Esq. b G. G. Hearne	17	– not out	9
W. Dible not out	30		
Major Fellowes b Bligh	2		
B 5, l-b 3	8	B 2	2
	414		148

Kent

Rev. R. T. Thornton b Dible	1	– c and b Dible	57
F. Hearne c Ridley b Armstrong	31	– c Young b Ridley	0
G. G. Hearne c Leat b Armstrong	42	– b Armstrong	38
L. Bligh Esq. c Dible b Young	0	– b Dible	3
L. Wilson Esq. c Leat b Armstrong	36	– c Leat b Dible	0
F. A. Mackinnon Esq. c Currie b Dible	47	– st Leat b Currie	115
J. Wootton lbw b Armstrong	5	– b Young	37
F. Atkins Esq. b Young	1	– c Fellowes b Currie	5
C. Collins run out	41	– c Leat b Young	2
H. Hearn lbw b Fellowes	1	– not out	10
J. Pentecost not out	6	– c Armstrong b Ridley	38
B 5	5	B 31, l-b 7, n-b 1	39
	216		344

Kent Bowling

	Overs	Mdns	Runs	Wkts	Overs	Mdns	Runs	Wkts
Wootton	57	17	99	3	27.3	12	59	1
H. Hearne	31	10	92	0	19	7	41	3
Collins	14	4	32	2	2	2	0	0
G. G. Hearne	28	5	82	3	37	17	46	3
F. Hearne	7	0	21	0				
Mr Bligh	15	3	44	2				
Mr Wilson	8	1	36	0				

Hampshire Bowling

	Overs	Mdns	Runs	Wkts	Overs	Mdns	Runs	Wkts
Young	53	21	93	2	46	18	94	2
Dible	36	18	48	2	28.1	10	36	3
Mr Currie	10	0	36	0	46	23	50	2
Mr Armstrong	18	9	19	4	19	4	49	1
Major Fellowes	15	10	15	1	20	11	29	0
Mr Ridley					14	6	30	2
Mr Lacey					8	4	12	0
Mr Longman					5	3	5	0

Umpires: H. Jupp and J. Lillywhite.

HAMPSHIRE v SURREY

Played at Southampton, July 21, 22, 1884

Surrey won this match by ten wickets, having to go in a second time to get a single run. Mr Shuter, Mr Roller, and Mr Key all played their highest innings for Surrey during the season in this match, and Mr Horner was seen to great advantage as a bowler, taking seven wickets in each innings, at a total cost of 137 runs. Surrey batted first, and their innings was chiefly remarkable for the extraordinary stand made by Mr Shuter and Mr Roller, who came together when the score stood at 38 for three wickets, and were not separated until they had put on exactly 200 runs. Mr Shuter played grand cricket, despite a couple of chances, and his innings of 125 included three 6s (drives), sixteen 4s, a 3, and six 2s. Mr Roller's well-played 69 contained nine 4s, a 3, and five 2s. Afterwards Mr Key hit hard and well for 53, and the innings closed at 4.35 for 324. When Hampshire went in they could make no stand against the bowling of Mr Horner, and lsot seven wickets for 90 runs before the call of time.

Next morning the last three wickets added 37, and the home team followed on in arrears to the extent of 197 runs. Mr Longman batted in excellent form for 78, his highest innings for his county during the season, and comprising ten 4's, a 3, and four 2's. Mr Armstrong scored eight 4's and a 2 in his 43, and Leat also hit well for 24.

Surrey

	First innings		Second innings
H. W. Bainbridge Esq. c Wood b Currie	7		
E. J. Diver Esq. c Feltham b Currie	10		
J. M. Read b Feltham	13		
J. Shuter Esq. c Bonham-Carter b Armstrong	125		
W. E. Roller Esq. b Armstrong	69		
R. Abel b Armstrong	2		
K. J. Key Esq. b Feltham	53	– not out	1
M. P. Bowden Esq. c and b Lacey	22		
H. Wood c and b Lacey	0	– not out	0
E. Barratt not out	3		
C. E. Horner Esq. b Feltham	0		
B 17, l-b 2, w 1	20		
	324		1

Hampshire

	First innings		Second innings
A. H. Wood Esq. c Shuter b Horner	11	– c Abel b Horner	12
L. Bonham-Carter Esq. b Horner	12	– c Abel b Horner	17
G. H. Longman Esq. c Abel b Horner	33	– c Read b Horner	78
F. E. Lacey Esq. c Read b Horner	0	– c Roller b Barratt	1
Rev G. J. Crowdy c Abel b Horner	18	– c Roller b Horner	8
C. Leat c Shuter b Horner	0	– c Wood b Roller	24
H. Armstrong Esq. b Barratt	4	– c Bainbridge b Horner	43
C. E. Currie Esq. c Read b Horner	12	– c Read b Horner	0
C. Young st Wood b Roller	20	– c Read b Roller	2
W. Dible not out	14	– c Read b Horner	4
W. Feltham c Bainbridge b Roller	0	– not out	0
B 2, w 1	3	B 7, n-b 1	8
	127		197

Hampshire Bowling

	Overs	Mdns	Runs	Wkts	Overs	Mdns	Runs	Wkts
Young	14	0	41	0				
Mr Currie	30	4	109	2				
Feltham	37.3	12	74	3	0.3	0	1	0
Mr Armstrong	18	8	43	3				
Dible	15	7	26	0				
Mr Lacey	6	1	11	2				

Surrey Bowling

	Overs	Mdns	Runs	Wkts	Overs	Mdns	Runs	Wkts
Barratt	33	11	64	1	30	12	51	1
Mr Horner	32	14	51	7	43	12	86	7
Mr Bainbridge	1	1	0	0	11	2	26	0
Mr Roller	3	1	9	2	13.1	5	26	2

Umpires: C. Payne and W. H. Luck.

HAMPSHIRE v SOMERSETSHIRE

Played at Southampton, August 7, 8, 9, 1884

This was the third match played by Hampshire during the season in which over 1000 runs were totalled, and the huge score of 645 was the highest innings compiled in any county match during the year, and the second highest in any match of importance ever scored in England, beating the total of 643 by the Australians against Sussex in 1882, and being only 5 runs less than the memorable 650 made against Hampshire by Surrey in 1883. Hampshire went in first, and the Somersetshire bowling was completely mastered at the outset. Messrs Lacey and Andrews began, and they were still together at lunch time, the score then being 127. On resuming, Mr Andrews was caught and bowled for 60, an innings which included nine 4s. Mr Longman came in and the score rose rapidly. At length Mr Lacey was bowled for an admirable innings of 100, in which there were no fewer than fourteen 4s. Mr Powell joined the Hampshire captain, and from this point runs were put on with great freedom. When Mr Longman was out for an excellent 52, Messrs Powell and Richards caused the score to rise faster than ever. At five o'clock the 300 went up, and soon after Mr Richards was caught, his 47 containing seven 4s. Mr Powell gave a chance soon after Mr Wood came in, and the mistake proved expensive, as that batsman was not out 106 when play came to an end for the day with the score 420 for 5 wickets, Mr Wood having been run out just previously to the call of time.

The last five wickets added 625 on the Friday. Mr Powell was joined by Mr Duncan, and the total was carried to 475 before Mr Powell was at last dismissed for 140. He had given a chance when he had made 102, but that was the only blemish in his highly meritorious innings, which contained the extraordinary proportion of twenty-five 4s. Mr Armstrong became Mr Duncan's partner, and the two batsmen added 99 runs for the seventh wicket. The total at lunch time was 644 for eight wickets, and there appeared every prospect of the historical Surrey score being passed, but the last two wickets fell with successive balls, and at 3.5 the innings closed for 645, Mr Duncan carrying out his bat for 87, the chief hits in which were thirteen 4s. Somersetshire on going in lost three wickets for 42 runs, and then Messrs Terry and Robinson put on 91 for the fourth, the former's 51 consisting of twelve 4s and three singles. When stumps were drawn for the day Somersetshire had lost 7 wickets, and scored 221 runs.

On the last day, mainly through the hitting of the Rev. F. Reed, the total of the first innings of Somersetshire reached 254. They followed on in a minority of 391, and the feature of the second innings was the very fine batting of Mr J. B. Challen, whose 93 was made with only one chance, and included nineteen 4s. Mr Trask and Mr Newton gave valuable assistance, but the side could not score heavily enough to bring about a draw, and Hampshire won the match by an innings and 169 runs.

Hampshire

F. E. Lacey Esq. b Winter	100	H. Armstrong Esq. c Winter b Newton	58
A. Andrews Esq. c and b Challen	60	E. Sheldrake Esq. b Winter	12
G. H. Longman Esq. c H. F. Reed b Trask	52	W. Dible b Hall	17
E. O. Powell Esq. run out	140	W. Feltham b Hall	0
A. C. Richards Esq. c H. F. Reed b Newton	47	B 34, lb 11, n-b 1	46
A. H. Wood Esq. run out	26		
D. Duncan Esq. not out	87		645

Somersetshire

E. Sainsbury Esq. c Longman b Dible	12 – b Dible	14
S. C. Newton Esq. c Andrews b Armstrong	18 – c Powell b Armstrong	31
J. B. Challen Esq. b Armstrong	11 – c Powell b Dible	93
F. W. Terry Esq. b Feltham	51 – run out	5
T. Robinson Esq. lbw b Lacey	57 – c Andrews b Dible	0
H. F. Reed Esq. b Feltham	0 – b Feltham	21
E. H. Hall Esq. b Feltham	0 – c Dible b Feltham	2
W. Trask Esq. c Powell b Feltham	14 – b Armstrong	45
Rev. F. Reed not out	57 – c Powell b Dible	4
F. Marks Esq. b Dible	2 – not out	0
C. Winter Esq. b Dible	4 – b Feltham	0
B 19, l-b 9	28 B 4, l-b 3	7
	254	222

Somersetshire Bowling

	Overs	Mdns	Runs	Wkts
Mr Winter	45	15	93	2
Mr Trask	61	23	126	1
Mr Robinson	21	5	60	0
Mr Hall	38.2	17	67	2
Mr Challen	45	17	92	1
Mr H. F. Read	5	1	21	0
Mr Sainsbury	18	3	55	0
Mr Marks	2	0	3	0
Rev. F. Read	18	4	28	0
Mr Newton	18	4	54	2

Hampshire Bowling

	Overs	Mdns	Runs	Wkts	Overs	Mdns	Runs	Wkts
Dible	19.2	7	45	3	32	12	78	4
Mr Armstrong	39	18	62	2	22	13	41	2
Mr Richards	15	4	33	0	18	7	34	0
Mr Sheldrake	11	6	19	0				
Feltham	24	9	54	4	22.3	9	41	3
Mr Lacey	9	5	13	1	3	0	21	0

Umpires: E. Henty and J. Street.

HAMPSHIRE v SURREY

Played at Southampton, July 6, 7, 1885

This was the fifth match which Hampshire lost by an innings. Surrey accomplished a remarkable batting performance on the opening day. Going in first on a beautiful wicket, they remained in for the whole of the day, and the total reached 390. The chief credit was due to Mr M. P. Bowden, who played a brilliant innings of 125. He went in fifth wicket down, and during his stay made 125 out of 214. He was batting for nearly two hours and a half, and did not give a chance. The vigour of his hitting may be easily judged from the following figures – one six (a splendid drive clean out of the ground), twenty 4s, four 3s, five 2s, and 17 singles. At the start of the innings Abel played excellent cricket, and made his 72 out of 132 while he was at the wickets. He gave a chance at mid-off just before his departure, but on the whole there was no fault to find with his performance. Among his hits were six 4s, seven 3s, and six 2s. Mr W. W. Read hit very well for 50, and Bowley rendered Mr Bowden some valuable assistance. In all, the innings which closed at ten minutes past six, lasted five hours, and the average rate of scoring was 78 runs an hour.

Hampshire went in at the commencement of Tuesday's play, and Mr F. E. Lacey, the old Cambridge University batsman, played good cricket, and scored 35 out of 51, but after this Lohmann bowled with remarkable success, and the whole side were out in less than two hours from the start for 104. Hampshire necessarily had to follow their innings, and this time they offered no resistance whatever to the Surrey bowling; the innings only lasted an hour and five minutes, and the total was 34, Surrey thus winning in one innings with 252 runs to spare. The wicket, it should be mentioned, was not in the same easy condition as on the opening day, as several balls kicked very awkwardly. In the first innings of Hampshire Beaumont only took one wicket for 31 runs, but in the second innings he actually took six wickets for 15 runs – an extraordinary performance in fine weather, even allowing for the worn wicket. His achievement, however, was less noteworthy than that of Lohmann, who took eight wickets in the first innings for 18 runs and four in the second for 16 runs, or 12 wickets in the match for less than three runs each.

Surrey

R. Abel c Leat b Willoughby	72
J. Shuter Esq. c Willoughby b Dible	2
K. J. Key Esq. c Heath b Willoughby	0
W. W. Read Esq. c Armstrong b Willoughby	50
J. M. Read c Lacey b Willoughby	14
E. J. Diver Esq. c and b Dible	34
M. P. Bowden Esq. lbw b Heath	125
G. A. Lohmann c Bencraft b Calder	22
J. Beaumont c and b Calder	3
T. Bowley c and b Heath	46
E. Barratt not out	16
B 2, l-b 4	6
	390

Hampshire

F. E. Lacey Esq. c Bowden b Lohmann	35	– c W. W. Read b Beaumont	7
A. B. Heath Esq. c and b Beaumont	10	– c J. M. Read b Lohmann	1
L. G. Bonham-Carter Esq. c Key b Lohmann	11	– c Shuter b Lohmann	0
C. Leat b Bowley	13	– c Abel b Beaumont	6
B. Bencraft Esq. c J. M. Read b Lohmann	1	– not out	6
H. Calder Esq. c and b Lohmann	14	– b Beaumont	8
J. Smith c Bowley b Lohmann	0	– c W. W. Read b Lohmann	1
A. H. Wood Esq. b Lohmann	1	– c Shuter b Lohmann	0
H. Armstrong Esq. not out	9	– c Diver b Beaumont	2
W. Dible b Lohmann	1	– b Beaumont	0
F. G. Willoughby c Abel b Lohmann	4	– c Key b Beaumont	0
B 1, l-b 4	5	B 1, l-b 2	3
	104		34

Hampshire Bowling

	Overs	Mdns	Runs	Wkts
Dible	49	23	85	2
Willoughby	38	11	95	4
Mr Lacey	11	3	26	0
Mr Armstrong	27	8	76	0
Mr Bonham-Carter	7	0	27	0
Mr Heath	11.1	2	28	2
Mr Calder	14	2	47	2

Surrey Bowling

	Overs	Mdns	Runs	Wkts	Overs	Mdns	Runs	Wkts
Beaumont	12	3	32	1	16.2	9	15	6
Barratt	8	3	12	0				
Bowley	22	10	37	1				
Lohmann	18.2	13	18	8	17	10	16	4

HAMPSHIRE v SOMERSETSHIRE

Played at Southampton, August 20, 21, 1885

The last of Hampshire's home matches ended in a victory over Somersetshire by eight wickets, the visitors playing only nine men. Somersetshire had first innings, and Mr O. G. Radcliffe, with a well-played 34, was highest scorer for the side. When Hampshire went in Messrs Powell, Duncan, Currie, Forster and Colonel Fellowes all played up well, and at the close of the innings the home team held an advantage of 45 runs. Mr Bastard bowled admirably throughout the innings, and took 8 wickets for 59 runs. Somersetshire went in again for a few minutes and scored 7 runs without loss.

The continuation of the innings on the Friday was alone remarkable for the capital innings of 62 played by Mr Winter, the figures being seven 4s, three 3s, five 2s and 15 singles. Mr Winter did not make a mistake throughout, and his score was the highest he had ever played for his county. Hampshire had 122 runs to make to win, and they accomplished the task in brilliant style, scoring the required number in an hour and thirty-five minutes, for the loss of only two wickets. Mr Calder hit a 5, five 4s, three 3s and two 2s in his 43; while Mr Powell, who carried out his bat for 54, had six 4s, five 3s and a 2 placed to his credit. The innings was a very good one, except for an easy chance when he had made 23.

Somersetshire

E. Sainsbury Esq. c Fellowes b Willoughby	9	– c and b Forster	10
O. G. Radcliffe Esq. run out	34	– c and b Dible	29
E. P. Spurway Esq. b Currie	10	– b Forster	1
W. N. Roe Esq. c Calder b Currie	12	– c Powell b Dible	1
H. F. Read Esq. c Fellowes b Currie	4	– c Willoughby b Dible	10
C. E. Winter Esq. b Dible	22	– b Dible	62
E. W. Bastard Esq. c and b Currie	0	– c Powell b Forster	3
E. H. Hall Esq. not out	14	– c and b Willoughby	23
E. G. Murdock Esq. b Dible	4	– not out	5
B 5, l-b 3	8	B 14, l-b 3, w 5	22
	117		166

Hampshire

R. G. Hargreaves Esq. c Murdock b Bastard	8	– run out	1
D. Duncan Esq. b Bastard	25	– not out	10
E. O. Powell Esq. c Sainsbury b Bastard	36	– not out	54
H. W. Forster Esq. c Spurway b Roe	20		
H. Calder Esq. b Bastard	10	– b Roe	43
W. Dible b Bastard	8		
H. J. Mordaunt Esq. b Roe	0		
C. Leat c sub. b Bastard	4		
C. E. Currie Esq. b Bastard	26		
Col. Fellowes b Bastard	22		
F. G. Willoughby not out	0		
B 1, l-b 2	3	B 12, l-b 3	15
	162		123

Hampshire Bowling

	Overs	Mdns	Runs	Wkts	Overs	Mdns	Runs	Wkts
Willoughby	12	6	21	1	20	8	36	1
Dible	34.3	21	32	2	32	18	43	4
Mr Currie	28	12	49	4	15	9	14	0
Col. Fellowes	5	1	7	0				
Mr Hargreaves					3	0	10	0
Mr Calder					12	4	19	0
Mr Forster					17.2	9	22	3

Somersetshire Bowling

	Overs	Mdns	Runs	Wkts	Overs	Mdns	Runs	Wkts
Mr Bastard	35	15	59	8	27	12	38	0
Mr Winter	7	2	35	0	2	1	4	0
Mr Hall	7	1	20	0	2	0	8	0
Mr Roe	19	10	37	2	26.3	13	42	1
Mr Sainsbury	1	0	8	0	1	0	3	0
Mr Read					2	0	13	0

HAMPSHIRE v NORFOLK

Played at Southampton, May 30, 31, 1887

In this, the first of the two matches between these counties, a great batting triumph was achieved on the opening day by the old Cambridge cricketer, Mr F. E. Lacey. Going in when Hampshire had lost one wicket for 12 runs, Mr Lacey carried out his bat for 323, the total of the side reaching 558. He was at the wickets for four hours and a half, and though his innings was not faultless it was a grand display of brilliant hitting, and included four 6s, two 5s, and thirty-seven 4s. This 323, it may be stated, is the highest individual score ever made in a county match. Dible helped Mr Lacey to put on 141 for the fourth wicket, and Mr Armstrong stayed while 159 runs were added for the fifth wicket. Before the call of time Norfolk lost two wickets for 31 runs.

On the second day Messrs Young and Armstrong soon finished off the remaining Norfolk batsmen, who had to follow on in a minority of 481 runs. The visitors batted better at their second attempt, but there was no real opposition to the fine bowling of Mr Currie. In the end the match terminated in a brilliant victory for Hampshire by no fewer than 342 runs with an innings to spare.

Hampshire

Mr L. G. Bonham-Carter c C. J. E. Jarvis b Rudd . 9
Mr A. Russell run out 27
Mr F. E. Lacey not out 323
Mr E. O. Powell run out 26
W. Dible c and b Rye 56
Mr H. Armstrong c C. J. E. Jarvis b Jee ... 74
Annett b Rye 0
C. Leat c Wickham b Rye 7
Mr C. E. Currie c Jee b Rudd 0
C. Young b Rye 9
Roberts c sub. b Rudd 13

B 9, l-b 5 14

558

Norfolk

Major F. A. Currie b Young	10 – b Currie	0
Mr C. J. E. Jarvis b Young	0 – c Leat b Annett	29
Hansell c Lacey b Young	30 – c Lacey b Currie	4
Mr L. K. Jarvis c Leat b Armstrong	7 – b Currie	21
Mr A. M. Jee c Leat b Armstrong	0 – c and b Currie	27
Mr P. H. Morton c Leat b Armstrong	5 – b Currie	7
Rev A. P. Wickham c Lacey b Young	1 – run out	15
Mr E. G. Buxton not out	8 – b Currie	0
Rye c Powell b Armstrong	0 – c Leat b Young	5
Mr P. Raikes b Young	10 – c Young b Currie	12
Rudd b Young	0 – not out	4
L-b 6	6 B 14, l-b 1	15
	77	139

Norfolk Bowling

	Overs	Mdns	Runs	Wkts
Mr Raikes	22	1	98	0
Rye	33	14	77	4
Mr C. J. E. Jarvis	20	4	64	0
Mr Morton	15	1	88	0
Mr Jee	15	1	72	1
Rudd	56.2	15	145	3

Hampshire Bowling

	Overs	Mdns	Runs	Wkts	Overs	Mdns	Runs	Wkts
Mr Armstrong	19	7	31	4				
Young	20	11	36	6	15.2	4	32	1
Mr Currie	1	0	4	0	33	14	51	7
Roberts					8	1	30	0
Annett					9	3	11	1

HAMPSHIRE v ESSEX

Played at Southampton, July 25, 26, 27, 1895

Drizzling rain prevented a start being made till half past four, and when Hampshire opened their innings the bowlers were placed at a great disadvantage, the wicket, though hard, being very wet. After the first hour, during which runs came freely, the game was contested under practically even conditions, and the home team, holding the upper hand throughout, eventually won by 171 runs. By far the most prominent features of the match were two marvellous bowling performances by Mead and Baldwin. Perhaps the better was that by the Essex professional, who in the two innings came out with the extraordinary record of seventeen wickets for 119 runs. His efforts, however, were all but equalled by

Baldwin, who, indeed, had a smaller average, dismissing thirteen men at a cost of 6 runs each. This was Hampshire's first victory in a county match since that over Derbyshire at the beginning of June.

Hampshire

Mr A. J. L. Hill b Owen	37	– lbw b Mead	3
V. Barton c Carpenter b Mead	79	– b Mead	3
Capt. Wynyard b Mead	10	– lbw b Mead	20
Mr R. A. Studd b Mead	0	– b Pickett	8
Mr H. F. Ward b Mead	10	– b Mead	10
J. Wootton c Kortright b Mead	9	– b Mead	2
F. E. Bacon c Carpenter b Bawtree	28	– b Mead	12
Dr R. Bencraft b Mead	35	– b Mead	0
T. Soar c Arkwright b Mead	30	– not out	37
Dean not out	0	– b Mead	1
H. Baldwin c Carpenter b Mead	2	– st Russell b Mead	32
B 2, l-b 4	6	B 8	8
	246		136

Essex

Mr H. G. Owen b Soar	24	– b Baldwin	0
H. Carpenter c Soar b Baldwin	1	– b Baldwin	14
Mr J. F. Bawtree b Wootton	6	– b Baldwin	3
Mr C. McGahey run out	0	– b Wootton	5
Mr A. P. Lucas c Wynyard b Soar	37	– lbw b Baldwin	0
J. Burns c Wootton b Baldwin	5	– b Soar	28
Mr C. J. Kortright b Baldwin	34	– not out	20
T. M. Russell c Bencraft b Baldwin	0	– b Baldwin	0
W. Mead c Wootton b Baldwin	0	– b Baldwin	6
Mr H. A. Arkwright b Baldwin	5	– b Baldwin	7
H. Pickett not out	5	– run out	0
B 10, l-b 1	11		
	128		83

Essex Bowling

	Overs	Mdns	Runs	Wkts	Overs	Mdns	Runs	Wkts
Kortright	15	3	37	0	6	1	17	0
Mead	47.2	20	67	8	30.1	12	52	9
Pickett	18	5	37	0	25	9	49	1
Arkwright	14	3	52	0				
Owen	10	0	28	1	3	0	10	0
Bawtree	5	1	16	1				
Carpenter	2	0	3	0				

Hampshire Bowling

	Overs	Mdns	Runs	Wkts	Overs	Mdns	Runs	Wkts
Baldwin	34.4	18	36	6	18.4	8	42	7
Wootton	20	8	40	1	7	1	21	1
Soar	15	4	41	2	11	4	20	1

Umpires: R. Clayton and Wickens.

HAMPSHIRE v SOMERSET

Played at Southampton, July 9, 10, 11, 1896

A magnificent innings of 292 by L. C. H. Palairet, gave Somerset an advantage which enabled them to win comfortably by eight wickets. The old Oxonian was batting for six hours and a half, and made very few mistakes, his cricket as usual being most correct and elegant. In the face of so large a total as 519, Hampshire did well to save the innings defeat. Webb and Quinton played admirably in the first innings, while after the follow on, with the ground still in capital run-getting order, Quinton, Bacon and Wootton, were seen to considerable advantage. In the course of the match, 1,065 runs were scored.

Somerset

Mr H. T. Stanley c Robson b Barton	5	– not out	4
Mr L. C. H. Palairet b Ward	292		
D. Smith b Wootton	19		
G. B. Nichols b Steele	22		
Mr R. C. N. Palairet b Steele	3	– not out	4
Mr S. M. J. Woods c Steele b Ward	30		
Mr V. T. Hill c Wynyard b Ward	22	– c Barton b Ward	5
Mr R. B. Porch run out	11		
G. Robson run out	54	– b Ward	0
Mr A. E. Newton not out	4		
E. J. Tyler b Barton	28		
B 18, l-b 9, n-b 2	29	W 1	1
	519		14

Hampshire

Mr H. F. Ward c Woods b Tyler	6	– c Newton b Nichols	32
Mr C. Robson c Robson b Tyler	1	– c R. Palairet b Woods	2
V. Barton b Woods	14	– b Nichols	7
A. Webb c Tyler b Woods	73	– c Newton b Tyler	8
Captain E. G. Wynyard c R. Palairet b Tyler	14	– c Hill b Tyler	6
Captain F. W. D. Quinton lbw b Hill	76	– b Woods	52
F. E. Bacon c Smith b Woods	0	– c Tyler b Nichols	47
Mr D. A. Steele st Newton b Tyler	48	– b Tyler	25
T. Soar c R. Palairet b Tyler	4	– run out	12
J. Wootton run out	14	– c R. Palairet b Tyler	53
H. Baldwin not out	6	– c Porch b Woods	2
B 5, w 1	6	B 14, l-b 8, w 2	24
	262		270

Hampshire Bowling

	Overs	Mdns	Runs	Wkts	Overs	Mdns	Runs	Wkts
Ward	19	4	38	3	2	0	7	2
Baldwin	37	8	116	0	2	0	6	0
Soar	24	5	89	0				
Barton	30.2	6	69	2				
Wootton	32	11	78	1				
Steele	22	2	65	2				
Wynyard	6	3	20	0				
Quinton	6	1	15	0				

Somerset Bowling

	Overs	Mdns	Runs	Wkts	Overs	Mdns	Runs	Wkts
Tyler	47	12	111	5	40	15	89	4
Woods	32.1	10	77	3	28.1	12	57	3
Nichols	10	3	14	0	23	16	17	0
L. Palairet	12	4	27	0	21	4	60	0
Robson	6	2	11	0	5	2	15	0
Hill	6	2	16	1	1	0	8	0

Umpires: J. Lillywhite and A. Chester.

HAMPSHIRE v YORKSHIRE

Played at Southampton, July 16, 17, 18, 1896

A grand innings of 268 by Captain Wynyard, which far surpassed anything previously done by the old Carthusian, was the great feature of this match. Thanks to this splendid effort, Hampshire seemed likely to beat their famous rivals till late on the third afternoon. By stubborn batting, however, Milligan, Mounsey, and Hirst, with some bad fielding to keep them, gradually saved their side from defeat, though at the close, with really only one wicket in hand they were but 27 runs to the good. During his long stay Wynyard only gave two chances, and after playing so finely it was extremely hard for him to see his county just robbed of a victory.

Hampshire

Mr H. F. Ward c Hunter b Peel	53
V. Barton b Haigh	14
Captain E. G. Wynyard c Moorhouse b Wainwright	268
Captain F. W. D. Quinton b Denton	57
A. Webb c Hirst b Haigh	21
Mr D. A. Steele b Wainwright	0
F. E. Bacon b Haigh	24
Mr J. M. Quinton b Wainwright	1
T. Soar not out	39
H. Baldwin b Peel	18
Passmore st Hunter b Peel	0
B 15, l-b 5	20
	515

Yorkshire

Lord Hawke c Capt. Quinton b Soar	7	– c Passmore b Soar	6
J. Tunnicliffe c Wynyard b Soar	7	– c J. M. Quinton b Baldwin	6
D. Denton c Passmore b Steele	35	– b Soar	2
E. Wainwright c Wynyard b Ward	26	– b Soar	6
R. Peel c Bacon b Soar	36	– b Soar	3
Mr F. W. Milligan st Passmore b Capt. Quinton	58	– c Bacon b Soar	52
J. Mounsey c Baldwin b Capt. Quinton	55	– c Capt. Quinton b Soar	64
G. H. Hirst c sub. b Ward	55	– b Soar	68
S. Haigh c Baldwin b Capt. Quinton	0	– not out	9
D. Hunter not out	5	– not out	10
R. Moorhouse absent hurt	0		
B 12, l-b 10, w 1	23	B 5, l-b 4	9
	307		235

Yorkshire Bowling

	Overs	Mdns	Runs	Wkts
Haigh	62	19	132	3
Hirst	40	18	70	0
Peel	55.4	19	119	3
Milligan	18	6	41	0
Wainwright	29	4	102	3
Mounsey	6	1	18	0
Moorhouse	5	1	10	0
Denton	5	3	3	1

Hampshire Bowling

	Overs	Mdns	Runs	Wkts	Overs	Mdns	Runs	Wkts
Baldwin	36	13	68	0	34	17	44	1
Soar	39	15	81	3	45	17	97	7
Steele	12	6	28	1	10	7	15	0
Ward	12	2	35	2	13	8	33	0
J. M. Quinton	6	4	14	0				
Capt. Quinton	17	2	42	3	9	3	21	0
Wynyard	3	0	16	0	4	1	16	0

Umpires: J. Street and H. Draper.

HAMPSHIRE v ESSEX

Played at Southampton, June 24, 25, 1897

After being completely out-played at all points of the game, Hampshire were beaten on the second afternoon by an innings and 87 runs. They had a weak side, and again had the misfortune to lose the toss when the wicket was all in favour of run-getting, but allowing for these circumstances it must be said that their batting was sadly disappointing and contrasted most unfavourably with that of the visitors. The Essex innings lasted nearly the whole of Thursday, the splendid total of 367 being reached. Carpenter and C. McGahey set the side a fine example by making 104 for the first wicket in sixty-five minutes, their batting being most brilliant and at lunch time the score was 156 with only McGahey out. There was something of a break-down after this, but A. J. Turner (whose first appearance it was for the county), C. J. Kortright and Mead gave A. P. Lucas most useful assistance. Carpenter's 73 was in every way admirably played. A curious incident happened when he had scored 67, an appeal for stumping being given against him, although neither of the bails had been removed. This fact had escaped the umpire's notice, but after some discussion, Carpenter was very properly allowed to continue his innings. In the last few minutes Hampshire scored four without loss, but on Friday they shaped very badly against the Essex bowlers, of whom F. G. Bull was specially difficult. Bowling unchanged through both innings, the young amateur took nine wickets for 147, a wonderful performance for a slow bowler on a hard wicket. Mead in the second innings took six wickets for 50, he and Bull being on unchanged.

Essex

H. Carpenter b Light	73
Mr C. McGahey b Heseltine	53
Mr P. Perrin c Baldwin b Heseltine	36
T. M. Russell c Heseltine b Light	16
Mr A. J. Turner c Robson b Webb	33
Mr A. P. Lucas c Light b Hill	70
Mr H. G. Owen b Webb	3
Mr C. J. Kortright c Barrett b Baldwin	24
W. Mead b Baldwin	41
Mr F. G. Bull c Robson b Hill	0
H. Pickett not out	5
B 11, w 2	13
	367

Hampshire

Mr D. A. Steele c Kortright b Bull	3	– lbw b Mead	9
T. Soar b Bull	8	– not out	0
V. Barton c Mead b Kortright	2	– b Mead	31
Mr E. I. M. Barrett b Kortright	4	– st Russell b Bull	6
A. Webb c McGahey b Bull	6	– b Mead	14
Mr A. J. L. Hill lbw b Mead	37	– b Mead	4
Mr C. Robson c Perrin b Bull	28	– b Bull	2
Mr R. A. Bennett b Mead	30	– c Perrin b Bull	27
Mr C. Heseltine c Russell b Bull	4	– b Mead	3
W. Light run out	14	– c Pickett b Bull	15
H. Baldwin not out	0	– c Lucas b Mead	15
B 6, l-b 4, w 1	11	B 4, l-b 3	7
	147		133

Hampshire Bowling

	Overs	Mdns	Runs	Wkts
Soar	19	2	74	0
Baldwin	42.4	15	87	2
Hill	14	3	48	2
Heseltine	20	7	37	2
Steele	10	1	29	0
Light	21	5	61	2
Webb	12	6	18	2

Essex Bowling

	Overs	Mdns	Runs	Wkts	Overs	Mdns	Runs	Wkts
Kortright	14	4	27	2				
Bull	29	6	71	5	29	7	76	4
Mead	15	4	38	2	28.4	7	50	6

Umpires: H. Draper and R. Clayton.

HAMPSHIRE v WARWICKSHIRE

Played at Southampton, August 12, 13, 14, 1897

Returning home after five out matches, Hampshire made a most creditable draw with Warwickshire. The game was chiefly remarkable for two exceptional partnerships. H. W. Bainbridge and W. G. Quaife started by scoring 288 for the first wicket and A. J. L. Hill and W. Andrew saving Hampshire adding 222. Earlier in the week, Hampshire had had the record stand for the first wicket made against them by Abel and Brockwell at the Oval, and their tired bowlers were further handicapped by the indisposition of Soar, who had to retire from the game. On the first day Bainbridge was the only man dismissed, the total runs scored being 324, but rain in the night considerably affected the wicket and the innings closed for 475, W. G. Quaife carrying his bat right through for 178. On the difficult pitch Hampshire were rapidly dismissed and following on they lost three wickets for 83, but then came the splendid partnership which made them secure.

Warwickshire

Mr H. W. Bainbridge st Wynyard b Baldwin	162
W. G. Quaife not out	178
Mr J. F. Byrne b Baldwin	38
E. J. Diver st Wynyard b Baldwin	0
W. Quaife c Wynyard b Hill	9
Mr A. C. S. Glover c Steele b Hill	0
S. J. Santall b Andrew	42
H. T. Pallett b Wynyard	15
T. Forester st Steele b Baldwin	3
Lord c Baldwin b Wynyard	6
A. A. Lilley absent ill	0
B 11, l-b 7, w 4, n-b 1	22
	475

Hampshire

Captain Wynyard c Byrne b Lord	67 – c Byrne b Lord	37
V. Barton c Bainbridge b Santall	27 – c Lilley b Pallett	4
Mr W. Andrew b Forester	1 – c and b Glover	106
A. Webb c Byrne b Santall	0 – b Forester	6
Mr A. J. L. Hill c Lilley b Forester	17 – c Lord b Forester	100
Mr F. E. Lacey c and b Forester	10 – not out	8
Mr D. A. Steele c and b Forester	3 – not out	1
Mr C. G. Ward b Santall	7	
H. Baldwin b Pallett	0	
Mr E. C. Lee not out	0 – c Bainbridge b Forester	32
T. Soar absent ill	0	
B 3, l-b 2	5 B 26, l-b 4	30
	137	324

Hampshire Bowling

	Overs	Mdns	Runs	Wkts
Soar	17	6	29	0
Baldwin	64	34	67	4
Andrew	29	7	66	1
Hill	26	3	69	2
Ward	8	1	42	0
Wynyard	10	3	28	2
Lee	9	1	25	0
Barton	6	4	8	0
Steele	18	3	68	0
Lacey	12	3	45	0
Webb	5	2	6	0

Warwickshire Bowling

	Overs	Mdns	Runs	Wkts	Overs	Mdns	Runs	Wkts
Santall	18.2	1	53	3	33	9	88	0
Lord	14	2	38	1	28	9	49	1
Forester	17	8	23	4	35	15	60	3
Pallett	8	2	18	1	28	11	42	1
Byrne					8	5	7	0
W. G. Quaife					3	0	13	0
Lilley					13	4	31	0
W. Quaife					3	1	3	0
Glover					3	2	1	1

Umpires: J. H. Holmes and W. A. Woof.

HAMPSHIRE v YORKSHIRE

(for H. Baldwin's benefit)

Played at Southampton, May 26, 27, 1898

After rain had prevented a ball being bowled on the opening day, the wicket proved so treacherous that between twelve o'clock and five minutes past six on Friday the game was finished off, Yorkshire doing a noteworthy performance in winning in one afternoon by an innings and 79 runs. With all their Army officers away the Hampshire batting proved lamentably weak on the soft ground which had caked on the top. In the two innings, which in the aggregate realised but 78 runs, only one man reached double figures and he was let off. Haigh carried off the bowling honours and no one could have turned such an opportunity to better account. Varying his pace skilfully, he got a wonderful break on the ball and had the batsmen completely at his mercy. His record for the match was extraordinary – fourteen wickets for 43 runs – and he hit the stumps no fewer than ten times. Between the two collapses of the home side Yorkshire put together the capital score of 157, in making which they were largely assisted by the weakness of the bowling opposed to them. Certainly the Hampshire men failed where Haigh succeeded so brilliantly, but still great credit belongs to Tunnicliffe for an admirable 58. He was in the whole of the time the innings lasted. Much disappointment was occasioned through the match being brought to such a summary conclusion, as it had been set aside as the benefit for the Hampshire bowler H. Baldwin.

Hampshire

Mr C. G. Ward c Denton b Haigh	6	– b Haigh	5
V. Barton b Haigh	7	– c Brown b Rhodes	3
Mr A. J. L. Hill c Jackson b Rhodes	0	– b Haigh	7
Mr W. Andrew b Haigh	0	– b Haigh	0
A. Webb c Jackson b Rhodes	0	– b Jackson	7
Mr B. Lamb c Rhodes b Haigh	0	– b Jackson	3
Mr C. Heseltine b Haigh	6	– not out	5
Mr D. A. Steele c Jackson b Haigh	10	– not out	0
Mr C. Robson not out	6	– b Haigh	0
H. Baldwin b Haigh	6	– b Haigh	0
E. Light b Haigh	0	– st Hunter b Haigh	4
L-b 1	1	L-b 2	2
	42		36

Yorkshire

J. T. Brown b Baldwin	4
J. Tunnicliffe b Baldwin	58
Mr F. S. Jackson b Andrew	9
D. Denton c Barton b Baldwin	3
E. Wainwright st Robson b Light	8
G. H. Hirst st Robson b Light	18
Mr F. W. Milligan c Barton b Hill	2
W. Rhodes c Andrew b Hill	28
Lord Hawke c Ward b Hill	0
S. Haigh c Lamb b Baldwin	17
D. Hunter not out	4
B 4, l-b 2	6
	157

Yorkshire Bowling

	Overs	Mdns	Runs	Wkts	Overs	Mdns	Runs	Wkts
Haigh	15.4	10	21	8	13.2	7	22	6
Rhodes	15	8	20	2	7	3	10	1
Jackson					6	4	2	2

Hampshire Bowling

	Overs	Mdns	Runs	Wkts
Andrew	15	4	30	1
Baldwin	12.1	1	37	4
Light	11	0	44	2
Hill	18	5	34	3
Heseltine	2	0	6	0

Umpires: W. A. J. West and J. Lillywhite.

HAMPSHIRE v SOMERSET

Played at Bournemouth, July 11, 12, 13, 1898

After having all the worst of the opening day's play Hampshire managed to snatch a victory by nine runs on the third morning. The result was the more remarkable as going in a second time 115 runs behind the home county actually lost four wickets for 16 runs. From that point everything went well with them and Somerset were set 128 to win. Half of these were obtained with only three men out on Tuesday, but on the following morning Tate made such use of a crumbling pitch as to take the last seven wickets for 25 runs, and thanks to him Hampshire won a remarkable match after a most exciting finish. Captain Hedley's 101 was a splendid and almost faultless display of free hitting. The match – the first in the Bournemouth Week – was a success financially.

Hampshire

Major R. M. Poore b Robson	57	– run out	8
A. Webb b Woods	12	– c Palairet b Robson	0
Mr W. Andrew c Newton b Gill	3	– b Hedley	0
Captain F. W. D. Quinton b Robson	7	– b Hedley	35
Mr A. J. L. Hill b Hedley	2	– b Robson	7
Mr E. C. Lee b Hedley	8	– b Hedley	27
Mr E. I. M. Barrett b Robson	0	– b Robson	48
Mr D. A. Steele b Robson	43	– b Tyler	19
Mr C. Heseltine lbw b Tyler	28	– c Robson b Tyler	47
Mr C. Robson not out	8	– not out	33
E. Tate b Robson	0	– c Hedley b Tyler	4
B 6, l-b 4	10	B 11, l-b 3	14
	178		242

Somerset

Mr L. C. H. Palairet c Steele b Tate	11	– b Heseltine	3
Captain W. C. Hedley b Tate	101	– c Hestine b Tate	10
Mr H. T. Stanley c Hill b Heseltine	0	– not out	38
Mr W. Trask b Quinton	46	– b Tate	0
Mr S. M. J. Woods c Webb b Tate	8	– b Tate	0
Lieut C. S. Hickley c Hill b Heseltine	32	– b Tate	13
Mr G. Fowler b Heseltine	24	– b Tate	8
E. Robson c Tate b Haseltine	13	– b Heseltine	13
Mr A. E. Newton c and b Heseltine	8	– c Quinton b Tate	9
E. J. Tyler c Poore b Andrew	28	– b Tate	20
G. Gill not out	7	– c Robinson b Tate	0
B 12, l-b 3	15	B 3, l-b 1	4
	293		118

Somerset Bowling

	Overs	Mdns	Runs	Wkts	Overs	Mdns	Runs	Wkts
Fowler	4	0	8	0				
Tyler	11	0	26	1	25	3	81	3
Gill	8	3	23	1	1	0	3	0
Woods	7	2	24	1	4	1	16	0
Robson	21.2	7	41	5	29	9	77	3
Hedley	15	4	46	2	25	9	51	3

Hampshire Bowling

	Overs	Mdns	Runs	Wkts	Overs	Mdns	Runs	Wkts
Heseltine	26	5	79	5	21	7	49	2
Tate	26	8	63	3	24.2	7	51	8
Hill	13	2	34	—				
Andrew	5.2	1	14	1	1	1	0	0
Lee	5	1	11	0				
Steele	10	1	30	0	3	0	12	0
Webb	1	0	4	0				
Quinton	10	1	43	1	1	0	2	0

Umpires: W. Shrewsbury and F. Johnson.

HAMPSHIRE IN 1899

President – Lord Aberdare.

Treasurer – Mr H. K. Grierson.

Hon. Secretary – Dr Russell Bencraft, 6, Anglesea Place, Southampton.

Captain – Captain E. G. Wynyard.

With a programme increased by fixtures with Worcestershire, Hampshire enjoyed a somewhat less disastrous season than in 1898, gaining four victories as against two, while strangely enough the remaining sixteen games were again equally divided into draws and defeats. Such a record does not suggest any exceptional merit in the side and it cannot be claimed that there was any – generally speaking – but the presence of two great players always left an element of doubt as to what might happen when Hampshire took the field. Major Poore and Captain Wynyard had always to be reckoned with when in the eleven, and had they been able to play throughout the summer the county would have undoubtedly held a higher position in the struggle for the Championship. The services of Captain Wynyard were enjoyed fairly regularly after the first three matches and that he was in as good form as ever his average of 49 testifies. Playing consistently well all through, Wynyard enjoyed one great triumph when at Taunton he scored 225. Another brilliant innings was his 108 against Worcestershire. His doings, however, were quite insignificant compared with those of Major Poore whose batting was phenomenal. In the previous summer Poore had proved himself a great acquisition to English cricket and for two months last season he was perhaps the most prominent man playing. Between the 12th of June and the 12th of August he scored 1399 runs in sixteen innings, with an average of 116.58. No one has ever approached such figures as these and it was not only in the matter of average that Major Poore distinguished himself. In his first match – that against Somerset at Portsmouth – he scored 104 and 119 not out and he followed up this rare feat of making two hundreds in a match with 111 against Lancashire at Southampton, adding his name to the list of those who have scored three consecutive hundreds. Nor did his successes end there. On four other occasions he exceeded the hundred and surpassed all his other performances by scoring 304 against Somerset in the same game in which Wynyard played his big innings. Moreover Poore never failed, his lowest score being 11 against Essex. Very naturally Poore's superb batting had its reward in his being included in the Gentlemen and Players' matches at The Oval and Lords. Unfortunately he did not do himself justice on either of the two great London grounds. Had he met with success, he would, no doubt, have had as a concluding triumph the honour of representing England against the Australians.

HAMPSHIRE v SOMERSET

Played at Portsmouth, June 12, 13, 14, 1899

A heavy scoring match, made famous by Major Poore scoring two innings of over a hundred, was drawn after three full day's cricket. Poore's performance was the more remarkable as it was his first appearance of the season in the Hampshire eleven. His 119 not out was a much more vigorous innings than his 104, occupying an hour less and including a five and fifteen 4s. Spens was his most useful assistant on each day their partnerships producing 109 on the Monday and 174 on the Wednesday. Hedley batted admirably for Somerset in each innings.

Hampshire

Mr C. Robson c Cranfield b Gill	24	– c Woods b Cranfield	33
V. Barcon c Cranfield b Woods	58	– lbw b Cranfield	9
Major R. M. Poore c Woods b Cranfield	104	– not out	119
Mr E. A. English b Robson	1	– c Nichols b Cranfield	0
Mr E. M. Sprot c Cranfield b Woods	13	– b Woods	21
Col. J. Spens c Woods b Hedley	74	– c Daniell b Stanley	71
Mr C. Heseltine b Gill	77		
Mr D. A. Steele b Gill	21		
H. Baldwin c Woods b Gill	4		
E. Tate b Gill	16	– b Stanley	2
T. Sutherland not out	0	– not out	0
B 4, l-b 2, n-b 1	7	B 11, l-b 2, n-b 1	14
	399	(6 wkts dec.)	269

Somerset

Mr H. T. Stanley c Robson b Baldwin	9	– b Heseltine	0
Mr W. Trask run out	41	– c Robson b Heseltine	16
E. Robson c Tate b Baldwin	52	– c Poore b Heseltine	14
Capt. W. C. Hedley lbw b Tate	92	– not out	75
Mr S. M. J. Woods c and b Baldwin	12	– b Steele	26
Mr H. W. Kettlewell c Tate b Baldwin	1	– not out	6
G. B. Nichols run out	28		
G. Gill lbw b Heseltine	10		
Mr J. Daniell c English b Baldwin	35		
B. Cranfield c Heseltine b Sprot	14		
Rev. A. P. Wickham not out	4		
B 9, l-b 5, w 5	19	B 1	1
	317		138

Somerset Bowling

	Overs	Mdns	Runs	Wkts	Overs	Mdns	Runs	Wkts
Cranfield	37	6	96	1	18	7	41	3
Gill	24.2	5	62	5	12	1	50	0
Nichols	21	6	60	0	4	1	11	0
Hedley	19	4	64	1	8	0	30	0
Woods	14	4	55	2	15	2	46	1
Stanley	3	0	18	0	4	1	11	2
Robson	13	3	37	1	13	3	36	0
Kettlewell					8	0	30	0

Hampshire Bowling

	Overs	Mdns	Runs	Wkts	Overs	Mdns	Runs	Wkts
Heseltine	16	6	42	1	20	10	31	3
Baldwin	39	16	71	5	35	18	35	0
Sutherland	13	2	39	0	5	1	19	0
Tate	24	9	36	1	5	4	2	0
Sprot	17	5	45	1	1	1	0	0
Steele	11	2	36	0	12	6	29	1
Spens	3	0	16	0				
English	7	1	13	0	3	2	7	0
Barton					2	0	14	0

Umpires: R. Thomas and J. Lillywhite.

HAMPSHIRE v LANCASHIRE

Played at Southampton, June 15, 16, 17, 1899

After gaining a big advantage on the Thursday Hampshire were completely outplayed and beaten by 71 runs. Apart from the way in which Lancashire recovered from a disastrous start the great feature of the match was the batting of Major Poore who scored his third successive hundred. On a good wicket Soar and Baldwin dismissed the visitors for 163 – a score Hampshire got within one of on the first day for the loss of three men. Poore, who with Robson had added 122, again played well the next morning, but Cuttell carried all before him taking six of the last seven wickets in sixteen overs for only 22. Going in a second time 92 runs behind, Lancashire showed very different form to that of the first innings. Albert Ward played with great caution and carried his bat through the innings. Wanting 246 to win Hampshire fared badly after Poore was out – the second to leave at 74 – Briggs bowling in his best form.

Lancashire

A. Ward b Baldwin	7	– not out	109
A. Paul b Soar	14	– b Soar	63
F. H. Sugg b Soar	9	– b Steele	25
J. Hallows c and b Baldwin	21	– c Robson b Baldwin	7
W. R. Cuttell c Radcliffe b Soar	4	– c Poore b Baldwin	3
Mr A. Eccles b Soar	20	– b Light	63
J. Sharp b Baldwin	28	– b Soar	2
J. Briggs not out	41	– b Soar	8
Mr G. R. Bardswell c Ward b Baldwin	5	– c and b Tate	31
C. Smith b Baldwin	4	– c Poore b Tate	0
A. Mold c Ward b Soar	4	– b Baldwin	6
B 2, l-b 1, n-b 3	6	B 19, n-b 1	20
	163		337

Hampshire

Mr C. Robson run out	60 – c Bardswell b Cuttell	38
V. Barton b Cuttell	1 – c Sharp b Cuttell	3
Major R. M. Poore st Smith b Briggs	111 – c Smith b Briggs	40
A. Webb c Hallows b Mold	5 – c Eccles b Mold	20
Mr A. H. Delme-Radcliffe c Bardswell b Cuttell	32 – c and b Briggs	4
Mr C. G. Ward c Smith b Cuttell	6 – c Cuttell b Briggs	1
T. Soar c Smith b Cuttell	23 – b Briggs	28
Mr D. A. Steele b Cuttell	12 – b Briggs	1
H. Baldwin c Smith b Cuttell	0 – lbw b Briggs	12
E. Light not out	1 – not out	6
E. Tate b Cuttell	0 – b Mold	5
B 1, l-b 3	4 – B 3, l-b 2, w 1	6
	255	174

Hampshire Bowling

	Overs	Mdns	Runs	Wkts	Overs	Mdns	Runs	Wkts
Baldwin	38	17	70	5	53.2	24	86	3
Soar	32.1	16	73	5	47	14	121	3
Steele	3	1	10	0	15	6	40	1
Tate	2	1	4	0	21	6	50	2
Light					8	3	20	1

Lancashire Bowling

	Overs	Mdns	Runs	Wkts	Overs	Mdns	Runs	Wkts
Mold	29	6	91	1	13	4	18	2
Cuttell	22	7	42	7	28	11	61	2
Hallows	12	3	28	0	3	1	9	0
Briggs	41	14	71	1	39	11	77	6
Ward	4	0	19	0				
Sugg					1	0	3	0

Umpires: W. Clarke and R. Thoms.

HAMPSHIRE v SURREY

Played at Portsmouth, June 29, 30, and July 1, 1899

Hampshire had the satisfaction of being the first county to beat Surrey, a well contested game ending in their gaining a victory by six wickets. With Hayward, Brockwell and Tom Richardson in attendance at Leeds where England were playing Australia, Surrey were necessarily at a considerable disadvantage but they more than held their own until a great innings by Major Poore turned the fortunes of the struggle. After a lamentable beginning, seven wickets being down for 44 runs, Surrey put together 200, Abel and Stoner stopping the collapse. Before stumps were drawn on the first day Hampshire lost four wickets for 88. Of these Poore had made 42 and – the last man out – his share of the total of 313 was a superbly played 175. For over four hours and a half he scored freely without making any mistake, and he hit a five and sixteen 4s. Rain greatly interfered with play on the Saturday.

Surrey

Mr D. L. A. Jephson c Quinton b Soar	5	c Quinton b Soar	13
E. G. Hayes c Robson b Heseltine	0	c Quinton b Soar	1
Mr H. G. D. Leveson-Gower c Robson b Soar	2	c Wynyard b Baldwin	21
R. Abel b Heseltine	50	b Heseltine	9
Mr H. B. Richardson b Steele	2	b Steele	38
W. H. Lockwood c Spens b Heseltine	3	c Steele b Tate	13
A. Stonor c Steele b Quinton	61	b Tate	1
Mr K. J. Key c Quinton b Steele	0	c Steele b Baldwin	18
W. Lees c Robson b Soar	6	c Heseltine b Tate	38
E. H. L. Nice c Steele b Soar	22	b Steele	10
H. Wood not out	34	not out	38
B 13, w 2	15	B 2, l-b 1, w 2, n-b 1	6
	200		206

Hampshire

Mr C. Robson b Lees	24	c Richardson b Lockwood	15
V. Barton c Wood b Lockwood	8	run out	12
Major R. M. Poore c Stonor b Jephson	175	not out	39
Captain F. W. D. Quinton c Nice b Lockwood	3	not out	5
Col. J. Spens b Lockwood	1	c Wood b Lockwood	7
Capt. E. G. Wynyard b Stonor	26	c Hayes b Lockwood	10
T. Soar c Abel b Jephson	11		
Mr C. Heseltine b Stonor	35		
H. Baldwin b Stonor	0		
Mr D. A. Steele b Nice	16		
E. Tate not out	0		
B 5, l-b 1, n-b 8	14	B 4, l-b 1, n-b 2	7
	313		95

Hampshire Bowling

	Overs	Mdns	Runs	Wkts	Overs	Mdns	Runs	Wkts
Heseltine	22	4	62	3	12	4	21	1
Baldwin	9	4	13	0	19	6	63	2
Soar	18	8	28	4	17	4	42	2
Steele	18	7	47	2	8.3	3	30	2
Quinton	6	1	34	1				
Tate	1	0	1	0	19	9	44	3

Surrey Bowling

	Overs	Mdns	Runs	Wkts	Overs	Mdns	Runs	Wkts
Lockwood	29	8	62	3	17.1	1	53	3
Nice	22	4	63	1	2	0	6	0
Lees	30	4	83	1	15	2	29	0
Stonor	14	1	59	3				
Jephson	10.4	0	32	2				

Umpires: J. Lillywhite and R. Thoms.

MAJOR ROBERT M. POORE

Major Robert M. Poore, beyond a doubt the most sensational batsman of the season of 1899 was born on the 20th of March, 1866, and is thus in his 34th year. To find any close parallel to his sudden jump to fame in the cricket world would be very difficult, for before the public became familiar with his name he had passed the age at which a good many of our amateurs give up first-class cricket for more serious occupations. Major Poore was, as regards cricket, the victim of circumstances, his military duties in India and South Africa keeping him out of this country at the time, when, had he not been in the Army, he would have been making his name. He was, however, later than most men in taking seriously to the game, and in an interview with him, which appeared in *Cricket* during the autumn it was stated that in order to make up for lost time he studied the Badminton Book as thoroughly as though he had had to get it up for an examination. While he was thus learning the theory of the game in all its branches he was getting plenty of practical experience on Indian cricket grounds. His name became known to English cricketers by reason of his fine batting against Lord Hawke's team in South Africa during the winter of 1895-96. He was then a lieutenant and was out at the Cape with his regiment. Twice against the English eleven he played a three figure innings, scoring 112 at Pietermaritzburg and 107 not out for Fifteen of Natal at Durham. In the latter case he was mainly instrumental in gaining a remarkable victory for his side, the Fifteen going in to get 228 in the last innings, and hitting off the runs for the loss of five wickets. His two hundreds made a great impression on the members of Lord Hawke's eleven, and very flattering things were said of him in the letters descriptive of the tour that were sent home from South Africa. Naturally, therefore, a good deal of interest was excited when it became known, before the season of 1898 commenced, that the new batsman – by this time a captain – was in England and would be seen in the cricket field. His first appearance at Lord's was highly successful, as against Lancashire on a soft wicket on the 9th of May, he scored 51 and had no small share in gaining the MCC a single innings victory. He had not yet accustomed himself to English wickets, and despite his enormous advantages of height and reach – he stands 6ft. 4in. – it was rather as a defensive than a hitting batsman that he impressed those who saw him play. Being qualified for Hampshire he played in eleven matches for that county in 1898, and did uncommonly well, coming out third in batting with an aggregate of 659 runs and an average of 34. His best scores were 121 not out against Derbyshire at Derby, and 107 against Essex at Leyton. Excellent as his cricket was, however, it scarcely foreshadowed the marvellous success that attended him in 1899. All his scores will be found fully set forth in later pages of *Wisden*, and it will be sufficient to say here that he headed the season's batting in first-class matches scoring 1551 runs with the wonderful average of 91. He went in twenty-one times, and his average, so far as can be recalled, has never been equalled in first-class cricket for so large a number of innings. For Hampshire his average was 116. He played an innings of 304 against Somerset, and made six other hundreds for his county – two of them against Somerset in one match. Unfortunately he had by reason of his military duties to give up cricket some time before the season was over. The one blot upon his summer's work was his comparative failure for Gentlemen against Players at the Oval and Lord's. At neither ground did he get sufficiently well set to play his true game. Major Poore has a style of his own, and seeing him for the first time it would be difficult, unless he had made a very big score, to properly gauge his merits. He is essentially a forward player, his enormous reach enabling him to smother many balls at which ordinary batsmen would have to play back. A certain stiffness of arm detracts from the appearance of his batting, but though his method may compare unfavourably with that of more finished players, there can be no doubt as to its effectiveness. He gets most of his runs in front of cover-point, driving with immense vigour and facility when once he has taken the measure of the bowling. In the finesse of batting he has many superiors, but for sheer power of forward play there are few men now before the public who can touch him. As a fieldsman he is a little handicapped by his great height, and at times finds some difficulty in getting down to the ball. Major Poore does not limit his activities to the game of cricket. He is one of the finest swordsmen in the army, having taken the highest honours in the Military Tournament at the Agricultural Hall, and beyond that he is a first-rate Polo player. Like many other cricketers who are in the army Major Poore left England for South Africa after the outbreak of the war.

KENT

KENT v NOTTINGHAMSHIRE

Played at Tunbridge, July 22, 23, 24, 1869

The wickets did not play well. Mr Yardley played the good and fast bowling of J. C. Shaw and McIntyre pluckily for his 24. Mr South Norton went in with the score at 67 for seven wickets and at 112 took his bat out for 30. For Nottinghamshire, Summers made 42 (a good innings). But the innings of the match was Bignall's, who went in with the score at 60 for three wickets, saw the other seven men go, and took his bat out for 116, an innings as praiseworthy for skilled defence as for brilliant hitting; his leg-hitting in that 116 was pronounced by good judges to have been equal to George Parr's in George's best days. £5 was presented to Bignall. In Kent's second innings Mr Thornton went in two wickets down, the score 14; he hit hard and scored fast, and was out for 76 with the score at 110 for seven wickets. It will be seen J. C. Shaw had eleven wickets. Nottinghamshire won by one innings and 25 runs.

Kent

L. A. White Esq. run out	8	– c McIntyre b J. C. Shaw	9
Willsher c Daft b J. C. Shaw	2	– c Wild b J. C. Shaw	2
W. Yardley Esq. b J. C. Shaw	24	– b J. C. Shaw	0
B. B. Cooper Esq. run out	7	– run out	8
M. A. Troughton Esq. c J. Oscroft b J. C. Shaw	0	– c Summers b J. C. Shaw	8
Bennett b J. C. Shaw	18	– run out	0
C. I. Thornton Esq. b Wootton	2	– c and b J. C. Shaw	76
W. W. Rodger Esq. b McIntyre	9	– c Wootton	2
W. S. Norton Esq. not out	30	– c Price b McIntyre	2
Marten b McIntyre	0	– c W. Oscroft b J. C. Shaw	0
Henty c McIntyre b J. C. Shaw	8	– not out	2
L-b 4	4	B 4, n-b 1	5
	112		114

Nottinghamshire

Wild c Norton b Marten	11
Summers b Bennett	42
W. Oscroft c Rodger b Marten	0
Richard Daft b Bennett	9
Bignall not out	116
J. Oscroft c Norton b Willsher	17
Walter Price b Bennett	29
Biddulph lbw b Bennett	3
W. McIntyre b Yardley	1
Wootton b Willsher	7
J. C. Shaw b Yardley	1
B 4, l-b 10, w 1	15
	251

Nottinghamshire Bowling

	Overs	Mdns	Runs	Wkts	Overs	Mdns	Runs	Wkts
J. C. Shaw	52	32	39	5	38.1	22	44	6
McIntyre	34	19	33	2	23	14	44	1
Wootton	23	11	27	1	15	6	21	1
Daft	4	1	6	—				
J. Oscroft	3	2	3	—				

Kent Bowling

	Overs	Mdns	Runs	Wkts
Willsher	61	26	88	2
Marten	45	13	81	2
Bennett	28	7	57	4
Mr Yardley	5	1	10	2

Umpires: Luck and James Grundy.

MR THORNTON'S HITTING FOR KENT IN 1869

When – in the Canterbury Week in 1866 – Mr Thornton (then an Etonian) was time after time sending the ball flying to square-leg clear over the long booth at the top of the Canterbury ground, there were those present who foretold a great "hitting" career for this young gentlemen, and as one who would in time become of great aid to his County. Others on that occasion decried what they termed "his too eager desire to hit", prophecying him early grief when he met first-class County bowling, unless he practised and "played" more on the defence. Well, three seasons have since then been played away, and those who witnessed Mr Thornton bat in 1866 and in 1869 cannot fail to have noticed a visible improvement (as in three years he was bound to improve) in his defence last season, and his powerful – astonishingly powerful – driving, on and off, has placed him among the prominent hitters of the time. Last year Mr Thornton was the largest scorer in the Universities match at Lord's; he hit the highest innings for his County against Nottinghamshire against Sussex, and against Surrey, scoring 310 runs in those three innings. The following are the innings hit for his County last season by Mr Thornton:

Where at	Match	1st Inns	2nd Inns
Crystal Palace .	Kent v Sussex	3	—
Tunbridge Wells	Kent v Sussex	10	124
Tunbridge	Kent v Nottinghamshire	2	76
Canterbury	Kent v MCC	18	44
The Oval	Kent v Surrey	11	110

Or 398 runs in nine innings. Average: 44 per innings,

FOR THE GENTLEMEN OF KENT

Brighton	Gentlemen of Kent v Gentlemen of Sussex	14	156*
Marlow	Gentlemen of Kent v Gentlemen of Bucks	3	—
Canterbury	Gentlemen of Kent v I Zingari	12	—

* *Signifies not out.*

All told, Mr Thornton played out twelve innings for Kent, scoring 583 runs.

Average: "nearly" 49 per innings.

FOR CAMBRIDGE UNIVERSITY

Cambridge	The University v MCC and Ground	21	28
Cambridge	University XVI v All England XI	12	13
Cambridge	The University v Gentlemen of England	8	13
Cambridge	The Univesity v Birkenhead Park Club	2	51
Lord's	The University v MCC and Ground	33	34
Lord's	Cambridge v Oxford	50	36

Result for the University: 301 runs in twelve innings. Average: 25 per innings.

For MCC and Ground v Surrey, Mr Thornton scored 0 and 26; for MCC and Ground v Northumberland hescored 9; for The Gentlemen (England) v The Players on The Oval 4 and 7; for The South v The North at Canterbury, 8; for The Gentlemen v The Players of the South, 2; and in The Bowlers' match on the Oval (against the Bowling of Southerton and Silcock), 38 and 7.

All the above reckoned give a total of 985 runs in 34 innings (one not out), averaging nearly 30 runs per innings.

In addition to the above, Mr Thornton scored 66 and 17 in the Cambridge University Freshmen's match, and 0 in one match and 67 in another at Scarborough, and various other innings of which the compiler of this book failed to obtain information.

KENT v NOTTINGHAMSHIRE

Played at Town Malling, June 3, 4, 1878

The inability of Lord Harris, Mr F. Penn, Mr Foord-Kelcey, and Mr Mackinnon to play, was a bad blow and sore discouragement to Kent, who played two fresh men in Mr Pearce and Mr Fulcher, those two gentlemen being the highest scorers in two remarkably brief innings, none appearing able to stand against the destructive Nottinghamshire bowling, Morley being in great form, taking seven wickets for 9 runs in Kent's first innings, and eight for 26 in their second, eight of those fifteen wickets having been bowled. But so far as batting went, there were only two in it among the Nottinghamshire Eleven, eight of whom made only 30 runs between them, but Richard Daft and Selby played fine innings, scoring 102 of the 132 runs (from the bat) made by their side, and so it was that Morley, Daft, and Selby won this match of 220 runs for Nottinghamshire by an innings and 48 runs.

Kent

C. A. Absolom Esq. c Daft b Morley	1	– b Morley	7
F. H. Mellor Esq. b Morley	0	– b Morley	0
A. W. Fulcher Esq. b Morley	13	– b Alfred Shaw	0
G. G. Hearne jun. (son of George) b Alfred Shaw	0	– b Morley	10
W. Pearce Esq. c Daft b Morley	8	– c Alfred Shaw b Morley	8
George Remnant b Morley	6	– c Flowers b Morley	0
H. Wood c Alfred Shaw b Morley	2	– b Alfred Shaw	2
A. Penn Esq. b Morley	4	– c Wyld b Morley	0
I. Ingram lbw b Alfred Shaw	0	– not out	9
Henty b Alfred Shaw	0	– c W. Oscroft b Morley	6
W. Yardley Esq. not out	2	– b Morley	6
		L-b 2	2
	36		50

Nottinghamshire

Richard Daft c Fulcher b G. Hearne jun.	52
William Oscroft c A. Penn b Pearce	0
Arthur Shrewsbury c Remnant b G. Hearne jun.	1
J. Selby c Mellor b A. Penn	50
F. Wyld b A. Penn	8
W. Barnes c Absolom b G. Hearne jun.	10
W. Flowers b A. Penn	2
Alfred Shaw not out	6
S. Hind c Mellor b G. Hearne jun.	0
R. Tolley Esq. hit wkt b A. Penn	0
Morley c A. Penn b G. Hearne jun	3
L-b 2	2
	134

Nottinghamshire Bowling

	Overs	Mdns	Runs	Wkts	Overs	Mdns	Runs	Wkts
A. Shaw	22	7	27	3	29	15	22	2
Morley	22	15	9	7	28.2	19	26	8

Kent Bowling

	Overs	Mdns	Runs	Wkts
G. Hearne jun.	42	22	49	5
Mr A. Penn	20.2	9	34	4
Mr Pearce	10	3	25	1
Remnant	6	1	8	—
Mr Absolsom	4	—	16	—

KENT v YORKSHIRE

Played at Canterbury, August 5, 6, 7, 1886

Naturally elated with their victory over the Australians in the first match of the Canterbury week, the Kent eleven were in the best spirits for their return match with Yorkshire, and having the good fortune to win the toss and go in first on a capital wicket, they stayed in the whole of the Thursday afternoon, and in making 273 runs only lost two batsmen – Mr W. H. Patterson and Frank Hearne. The latter played a very good innings of 41, but the heroes of the day were George Hearne and Mr Cecil Wilson, who became partners with the score at 80 for two wickets, and actually stopped in for the rest of the day, being not out 102 each at the drawing of stumps. The Ladies' Day was not favoured with the brightest weather, but there was a big attendance, and the fine performance of the home side of course gave immense satisfaction.

On the Friday morning Mr Wilson and Hearne were parted with the score at 304, the amateur being stumped for 127 – a splendid innings, which lasted altogether four hours and a quarter, and included thirteen 4s, five 3s and thirteen 2s. With the total at 304 for three wickets, one might have expected a score of 500, but with such wonderful effect did Emmett bowl that the last seven wickets actually went down for 31 runs, the whole side being out for 335. George Hearne was the fifth man out, his 117, which took five hours and a half to score, comprising ten 4s, eight 3s and twelve 2s. So far as we are aware, there was no fault whatever in his innings, and the only chance Mr Wilson gave was one at the wicket soon after he went in. The Yorkshiremen, on going in to bat, played so badly on the hard ground that, when the eighth wicket fell, the score was only 81. Then Hall, who from the start had been playing remarkably well, was joined by Emmett, and during their partnership the two batsmen carried the score to 172. Emmett worthily followed up his bowling success of the morning by scoring 48. Hall took out his bat for 74 – an innings in which his defence was as good as ever, and his hitting far more vigorous than is usual with him. He made eleven 4s, two 3s and four 2s. Having to follow on against a majority of 163, Yorkshire at the drawing of stumps had lost one wicket for 6 runs.

On the Saturday Yorkshire played up fairly well, the chief batting honours being again carried off by Hall, who went in, second wicket down, with the score at 27, and again took out his bat. He gave a chance to Herbert Hearne when he had made 28, but this was the only blemish in his innings. He hit this time eleven 4s, three 3s and four 2s. Certainly his performance of scoring 149 runs in the match without being dismissed in either innings must rank among the best batting achievements of the year. Kent had only 64 to get to win, and in an hour and a quarter the runs were hit off for four wickets, the county finishing up the Canterbury week of 1886 with a brilliant and thoroughly deserved victory. Mr Patterson scored 40 runs out of 62 – a very large proportion for him. It may here be mentioned that the proceeds of the week were £1,083, of which sum £474 went to the Kent County Club. The social features of the gathering were much the same as in previous years, the Old Stagers occupying the boards of the theatre on four evenings, and the usual county balls being held at the Music Hall.

Kent

	First innings		Second innings	
Mr W. H. Patterson lbw b Bates	16	–	st Crossland b Emmett	40
F. Hearne b Bates	41	–	c Peel b Emmett	6
G. G. Hearne b Ulyett	117	–	not out	0
Mr C. Wilson st Crossland b Emmett	127	–	b Emmett	0
Mr L. Wilson c Bates b Emmett	8	–	b Ulyett	10
Mr M. C. Kemp c Hall b Emmett	1	–	not out	2
Mr A. J. Thornton not out	12			
Mr F. Marchant b Emmett	0			
Wootton b Emmett	0			
A. Hearne c Crossland b Emmett	0			
H. Hearne c Crossland b Bates	1			
B 5, l-b 7	12		B 1, l-b 4, w 1	6
	335			64

Yorkshire

	First innings		Second innings	
Hall not out	74	–	not out	75
Bates c Wootton b A. Hearne	11	–	b Wootton	34
Ulyett b A. Hearne	10	–	c A. Hearne b Wootton	2
Hon. M. B. Hawke c Kemp b A. Hearne	0	–	c and b Wootton	15
Preston c C. Wilson b Wootton	1	–	run out	33
Mr E. Lumb c L. Wilson b A. Hearne	5	–	b A. Hearne	8
Peel c G. Hearne b A. Hearne	12	–	c F. Hearne b Wootton	18
Lee c Marchant b Wootton	2	–	b A. Hearne	4
Crossland c H. Hearne b A. Hearne	0	–	b A. Hearne	20
Emmett b Wootton	48	–	b G. G. Hearne	10
Peate st Kemp b Wootton	0	–	c C. Wilson b A. Hearne	4
B 8, l-b 1	9		B 2, l-b 1	3
	172			226

Yorkshire Bowling

	Overs	Mdns	Runs	Wkts	Overs	Mdns	Runs	Wkts
Bates	74.2	30	93	3	11	2	22	0
Emmett	59	33	62	6	25	17	20	3
Peate	54	34	38	0				
Preston	15	4	28	0				
Ulyett	29	13	52	1	14.3	8	16	1
Peel	29	17	35	0				
Hall	6	2	15	0				

Kent Bowling

	Overs	Mdns	Runs	Wkts	Overs	Mdns	Runs	Wkts
Wootton	51	18	75	4	58	30	103	4
A. Hearne	52	28	61	6	67.1	38	80	4
G. G. Hearne	7	2	10	0	18	14	10	1
H. Hearne	12	5	8	0	5	3	8	0
Mr Thornton	3	0	9	0	11	2	22	0

KENT v MIDDLESEX

Played at Gravesend, August 12, 13, 14, 1886

The return match between Kent and Middlesex on the Bat and Ball ground will be remembered for having produced some of the most sensational batting that was seen during the season of 1886. In the course of the three days twenty-five wickets fell, 1,027 runs were obtained, and there were four individual innings of over a hundred. The wicket had been more carefully looked after than was the case at Gravesend a few years back, and this fact, coupled with rather short boundaries, will of course account for a good deal of the run-getting, but still the hitting was altogether exceptional. Owing to an accident he had met with at Canterbury, Alec Hearne could not play for Kent, and the loss of his bowling was seriously felt. Winning the toss on the opening day, Kent did not fare nearly so well as might have been expected, and only scored 196, by far the best cricket being shown by the brothers Frank and George Hearne. The latter batsman's 53 was quite free from fault. Mr A. J. Webbe and Mr Stoddart started the Middlesex innings at twenty minutes to five, and at the call of time the total had reached 106 and they were still together.

Resuming their innings on the Friday morning the two batsmen increased the score to 205, and then at last Mr Webbe was dismissed for 103, an admirable innings which lasted three hours, and included eight 4s, seven 3s and eleven 2s. Mr Stoddart made 116 – his first hundred in an important match – and was batting three hours and a half, his chief hits being eight 4s, nine 3s and nine 2s. His innings was a remarkably fine one. Including this 116, Mr Stoddart's last four innings had realised 906 runs, one innings of course being his record score of 485. Mr J. G. Walker and Mr O'Brien played brilliant cricket for 79 and 88 not out respectively, and on the first innings Middlesex held a lead of 261 runs, a defeat for Kent seeming, of course, inevitable. At the drawing of stumps the home side had lost one wicket for 64, Frank Hearne being not out 36 and George Hearne not out 14.

On the Saturday morning came the most sensational part of the match, George and Frank Hearne obtaining a complete mastery over the weak bowling of Middlesex, and actually hitting the score up to 258 before they were separated, their partnership altogether producing 226 runs. Frank Hearne, who had never before made a hundred in a first-class match, was batting about five hours for his 142 – an innings which included sixteen 4s, eleven 3s and nine 2s. He played very finely all through, but gave a chance at slip when he had made 66, and a hard chance of being caught and bowled when his total was 101. After he left, Lord Harris and George Hearne made another long stand, and put on 108 runs for the third wicket. Lord Harris was then bowled for a well hit 76, and at 374, just on the drawing of stumps, George Hearne was also bowled, Mr M. C. Kemp in the meantime having been dismissed without scoring. George Hearne did not give a chance, and his innings of 126, which lasted six hours and twenty minutes, comprised twelve 4s, nine 3s, fourteen 2s and twenty-three singles. When the game was left drawn Kent had five wickets to fall, and were 113 runs ahead. Very rarely indeed can a side have gone in against such a number as 261 and left off in so good a position. The spectators were naturally delighted with the performance of the brothers Hearne, and a sum of over £12 was collected on the ground and presented to them.

Kent

F. Hearne c Danglish b Webbe	47	– c Burton b Robertson	142
Mr W. H. Patterson b Burton	3	– c Dauglish b Robertson	12
G. G. Hearne b Robertson	53	– b Robertson	126
Lord Harris c Stoddart b Burton	27	– b Webbe	76
Mr M. C. Kemp b Robertson	10	– b Webbe	0
Mr A. J. Thornton not out	25	– not out	0
Rev. R. T. Thornton b Robertson	3		
Mr F. Marchant c West b Burton	0		
Hickmott b Robertson	0		
Wootton c Robertson b Burton	13		
H. Hearne c Robertson b Burton	6		
B 8, w 1	9	B 14, l-b 2, w 2	18
	196		374

Middlesex

Mr A. J. Webbe c A. J. Thornton b F. Hearne	103
Mr A. E. Stoddart run out	116
Mr S. W. Scott c R. T. Thornton b Wootton	30
Mr J. G. Walker c H. Hearne b Wootton	79
Spillman c Marchant b Wootton	0
Mr T. C. O'Brien not out	88
West run out	4
Mr F. G. J. Ford b Marchant	0
Mr M. J. Daughlish b Wootton	1
Mr J. Robertson c Marchant b G. Hearne	3
Burton c Harris b A. J. Thornton	25
B 5, l-b 2, w 1	8
	457

Middlesex Bowling

	Overs	Mdns	Runs	Wkts	Overs	Mdns	Runs	Wkts
Burton	48.2	25	56	5	62	35	65	0
Mr Robertson	32	12	58	4	53.2	16	108	3
West	6	2	13	0	25	18	52	0
Mr Ford	8	3	20	0	27	14	35	0
Mr Webbe	18	5	40	1	49	30	52	2
Mr Stoddart					12	4	27	0
Mr Daughlish					3	1	13	0
Mr Walker					1	0	4	0

Kent Bowling

	Overs	Mdns	Runs	Wkts
Wootton	85	31	123	4
H. Hearne	28	5	75	0
G. G. Hearne	39	18	61	1
Mr A. J. Thornton	30.3	8	66	1
Lord Harris	6	0	14	0
Rev. R. T. Thornton	4	1	18	0
Mr Patterson	5	0	16	0
F. Hearne	17	4	48	1
Mr Marchant	10	3	28	1

KENT v YORKSHIRE

Played at Canterbury, August 1, 2, 3, 1887

In the absence of an Australian team the Kent authorities chose the return match with Yorkshire for the first item of the programme for the Canterbury week. A year earlier the game had produced a great triumph for the home side, who on the first day scored 273 runs for the loss of two wickets, and it was only fitting that this time the luck should have fallen to the share of the Yorkshiremen. As a matter of fact the latter completely eclipsed Kent's achievement of the previous year, and on the opening day obtained 305 runs for the loss of only one wicket. Three men – Ulyett, Hall, and Lee – shared in this great batting feat. The two first named began the innings, and at luncheon-time they were both together, and had put on 99 runs. Afterwards George Ulyett hit with tremendous vigour, and by twenty-five minutes past four he had finished his innings for 124, made by fourteen

4s, three 3s, ten 2s and thirty-nine singles. He gave one difficult chance after he had passed his hundred, and, like any man who plays so determined a game, he made several risky strokes, but speaking generally his innings was free from fault, and, in whatever you regarded, must rank very high amongst the many successes of the popular Yorkshire batsman. The total was then 169, Hall having made only 43. That professional was joined by Fred Lee, and when time was called at a quarter-past six the men were still together, Hall being not out 89, and Lee not out 82, the partnership having already added 136 runs. The Kent eleven never got loose or slack in their fielding, and a lot of the bowling was admirable, but so true and fast was the St. Laurence ground that not one of the many bowlers tried could make any impression.

The Tuesday's play was only less remarkable than that of the opening day. Hall and Lee went on with the Yorkshire batting at ten minutes past eleven, and each man succeeded in reaching his hundred. Altogether they raised the total to 355, the second wicket having added 186 runs. Hall's innings had lasted nearly seven hours, and as a display of stubborn defence could scarcely have been excelled, although the advisability of not punishing the bowling in a more determined fashion when the ground was so true might be seriously questioned. Lee was out third at 380, and, despite a chance given on Monday evening, his innings of 119, which included fifteen 4s, two 3s and nine 2s, was a very fine display of cricket. It may be interesting to our readers to mention the figures on the board at the falls of the first three wickets: – 169–1–124; 355–2–110; 380–3–119. Mr Hawke soon pulled a ball on to his wicket, but Bates and Peel punished the bowling with great severity, and put on 99 runs, Bates hitting up his 64 in an hour and a half. There were eight wickets down for 497, but Emmett and Wade stayed together for forty minutes – a course which was certainly not to be praised. Runs were then of no use to Yorkshire, and every minute they stayed in lessened their chances of ultimate success. Eventually this great innings closed for 559, having lasted as nearly as possible ten hours and ten minutes. Despite the excellence of the ground the run-getting was never really fast from the start to the finish. While it was being played ten members of the Kent eleven went on to bowl. With something over an hour left for play, Kent having nothing to play for beyond a draw, went in to bat, and, fatigued no doubt by their long fielding, were not seen to advantage. At the call of time they had lost four wickets for 51 runs.

Wade bowled with great success on the Wednesday morning, and Kent's innings was finished off in an hour and a quarter for 78 more runs, the full total being only 129. The home side were in a minority of no fewer than 430, and Frank Hearne being sent in with Mr Patterson, a really good start was made in the second innings. Both men batted very finely indeed, and, though eight changes were tried in the bowling, the score was 88 for no wicket at the interval, this stand largely contributing to avert a defeat for Kent. A little while afterwards Hearne was so badly hurt by a ball from Ulyett that for the remainder of his innings he was compelled to have a man to run for him. The accident, however, in no way interfered with the Kent professional's cricket; indeed, he rarely or never was seen to more advantage. Mr Patterson was out at 96, and Lord Harris and Mr Leslie Wilson being caught at the wicket in turn, and Mr Cecil Wilson run out, four wickets were down for 102. With Mr Marchant in, Hearne with his score at 68 gave Preston an easy chance at deep square leg. Preston missed the opportunity, and so no doubt lost his side a victory. The Cambridge captain was also let off, and the batsmen seizing their chances stayed together for over an hour, and in this time put on 85 runs. Then, with Alec Hearne and Frank Hearne together, there was another long stand, and all chance of finishing the game was at an end when, at length, Frank Hearne was caught at point for a sound and brilliant innings of 144 – the fourth three-figure score of the match. It was a big performance for the young Kent professional to surpass the scores of the three Yorkshiremen, especially when it is remembered that the greater part of his innings was played when he was in serious pain. In the end the match was left drawn, Kent being 153 runs behind with four wickets to fall. Of course the result was a moral victory for the Northerners, but the Kentish batsmen deserve considerable praise for offering so stubborn a resistance to the Yorkshire bowling.

Yorkshire

G. Ulyett c A. Hearne b Christopherson	124
L. Hall c Harris b L. Wilson	110
F. Lee b A. Hearne	119
Hon. M. B. Hawke b Christopherson	15
W. Bates c Kemp b Christopherson	64
R. Peel c Kemp b Christopherson	43
J. M. Preston c Kemp b Wootton	6
S. Wade c Wootton b F. Hearne	40
J. Denton b Wootton	1
T. Emmett run out	16
J. Hunter not out	0
B 10, l-b 11	21
	559

Kent

Mr F. Marchant c Bates b Ulyett	4 – c Hunter b Ulyett	26
Mr W. H. Patterson c Bates b Ulyett	14 – c Hall b Peel	39
F. Hearne c Hunter b Emmett	10 – c Hall b Peel	144
Rev. C. Wilson b Wade	0 – run out	3
Mr L. Wilson c Bates b Ulyett	39 – c Hunter b Ulyett	0
Lord Harris lbw b Wade	20 – c Hunter b Ulyett	1
A. Hearne b Wade	2 – not out	36
Mr M. C. Kemp b Wade	0 – not out	11
Mr S. Christopherson b Emmett	1	
J. Wootton b Bates	17	
F. Martin not out	19	
B 2, l-b 1	3 – B 11, l-b 5, w 1	17
	129	277

Kent Bowling

	Overs	Mdns	Runs	Wkts
Wootton	79	31	108	2
A. Hearne	82	29	131	1
Mr S. Christopherson	60	24	111	4
Martin	94	57	82	0
F. Hearne	24	13	32	1
Mr F. Marchant	13	5	21	0
Lord Harris	8	2	12	0
Mr C. Wilson	7	4	7	0
Mr L. Wilson	4	0	14	1
Mr W. H. Patterson	6	2	20	0

Yorkshire Bowling

	Overs	Mdns	Runs	Wkts	Overs	Mdns	Runs	Wkts
Emmett	32	18	38	2	17	8	28	0
Ulyett	21	7	49	3	24	12	40	3
Wade	21	8	37	4	31	12	56	0
Peel	2	1	2	0	51	33	45	2
Bates	0.2	0	0	1	19	4	47	0
Preston					10	7	17	0
Hall					7	0	26	0

KENT v MIDDLESEX

Played at Canterbury, August 4, 5, 6, 1887

A very strong Middlesex eleven reached Canterbury on the Wednesday evening, and commenced on Thursday the return match with Kent, for which county Lord Harris and the Rev. Cecil Wilson were unable to play, Mr Rashleigh and Mr Tonge taking their places. The home team went in and scored a fair, but by no means great, innings of 241. This number would usually be considered a creditable first innings against Middlesex bowling, but the wicket was on the present occasion so exceptionally true and easy that a larger score might have been looked for. Frank Hearne was neatly caught at slip before he got set, and Mr Patterson was out when he had only made 29 to a catch at point. Some first-class cricket was then shown by Mr Rashleigh and Mr Leslie Wilson, and at the luncheon interval both gentlemen were not out, the score being 126 for two wickets. On the game being continued, Mr Rashleigh was leg before wicket for 47 – an excellent innings without a chance, which included four 4s, three 3s and six 2s. The partnership had lasted an hour and forty minutes, and had increased the score by 88 runs. Mr Wilson was fifth out, and his 63 was certainly the best, as it was the highest, innings of the day. He gave no chance till just before he was out, and the catch which dismissed him was an exceedingly good one. He hit ten 4s, a three and five 2s. Loud cheers greeted him on his return to the dressing tent, and certainly his stylish, vigorous play earned the popular recognition. Mr Marchant was the only other batsman who did himself justice, and he was out very unluckily, the ball being played on to his foot and rolling into the wicket. The Middlesex bowling was chiefly remarkable for the success of Mr Webbe and the great steadiness shown by Burton. The visitors in fifty minutes made 54 runs before time was called, Mr Stoddart being not out 33, and Mr Webbe not out 13, at the drawing of stumps. The Middlesex captain might perhaps have been caught by Mr Tonge at deep slip when his score was 16. This Thursday was the Ladies' Day of the Canterbury Week, and was in every respect a triumph. The cricket, as we have been explaining, was good and even, the weather was delightful, and the attendance was larger than had ever been the case on this annual Kentish celebration. The most prominent feature of the day was the presentation to Mr W. de Chair Baker of the testimonial which had been subscribed in recognition of his long and successful management of the Canterbury Week. The presentation was made during the luncheon interval by Lord Sendes on behalf of the subscribers. His lordship informed Mr Baker that a cheque of about £130 had been lodged at the bank to be at his service, and in the course of a few kindly and well-chosen remarks stated that Mr Baker was a cricketer contemporary of Pilch, Felix, Wenman and Hillier, and that for more than forty years he had been the manager of their annual Week, giving in that capacity great satisfaction to all with whom he had come in contact. He wished that they might long have the advantage of Mr Baker's companionship and advice, and declared that he was only expressing the feeling of all subscribers when he said that they hoped Mr Baker would regard the cheque not from its mere money value, but as an expression of their united and hearty goodwill. Mr Baker returned thanks in a few words, and afterwards caused a letter to be published, in which he expressed his deep appreciation of the friendly feeling that had always been shown towards him. He had during many years taken great pleasure in watching cricket and in the advancement of cricket, and he was sure anything he could do for the success of the Week would always be with him a labour of love. The editor and writers of this Cricket Almanac wish to express on behalf of the press their complete concurrence in the goodwill that has been shown towards the kindly and genial manager of the pleasantest of cricket festivals.

On the second day (Friday) Mr A. J. Webbe pretty well monopolised the game. The attendance of spectators was of course nothing like it had been, but the weather was again magnificently fine. Mr Stoddart stayed with Mr Webbe till he had made 46, Mr Walker played a capital innings of 40, and five other gentlemen of the team reached double figures. But Mr Webbe stayed in until half-past five in the afternoon, and his innings then only ceased because there was no other batsman to stay in with him. His magnificent 192 not out consisted of thirty 4s, seven 3s, eleven 2s and twenty-nine singles, and lasted six hours and a quarter. At 53 he gave a chance to third man, but after that we saw no mistakes in his display, and his hitting during the later part of the innings was very severe. The whole Kent eleven except Messrs Rashleigh and Kemp went on to bowl, and Martin's performance, though he only took one wicket, his first for the Week by the way, was a creditable one. The Middlesex innings finished for 412, and Kent lost a wicket for 18 runs before the call of time.

On the Saturday Kent, who were 153 runs behind with nine wickets to go down, were batting all day, and at the close, when the game was left drawn, they had completed their second innings for 364. They were thus 193 runs to the good, and so had little the worst of the encounter. Mr Leslie Wilson played a second stylish and very good innings, in which were eight 4s, six 3s and nine 2s; but the chief credit belonged to Mr W. H. Patterson, who with Mr Wilson put on 147 runs, and was not dismissed until he had contributed 99 – a magnificent innings, including ten 4s, six 3s and eleven 2s. It was bad luck for Mr Patterson to just miss his hundred. Considering how fast the wicket was, the number of extras given was exceedingly small, and to Mr Kemp's credit be it recorded that in the long Middlesex innings he only let one ball pass him. Thus the second match of the Canterbury Week ended in a draw, and beyond all doubt the interest of the spectators was decreased by the unusually heavy scoring. Canterbury is notoriously a run-getting ground, and in fine weather, with somewhat easy boundaries, the score mounts up at a great pace. But it would be unfair as well an ungenerous to say anything against the executive because the wickets were – as indeed was the case – too good. The utmost care had been observed through the summer in keeping the centre free from the encroachments of local clubs, and the turf upon which the Yorkshire and Middlesex elevens met Kent was, so far as we could see and bear, altogether faultless. The wonderful spell of sunshine with which England was favoured in 1887 was in the midst of its glory during the first week in August, and naturally batsmen took advantage of their good luck. There was no waste of time throughout the Week, and the fact that the two matches were left drawn was certainly not due to any laxity on the part of the players.

Kent

Mr W. H. Patterson c Walker b Burton	29	– c Buckland b Webbe	99
J. Hearne c Buckland b Barton	5	– c Welman b Bucklnad	47
Mr W. Rashleigh lbw b Webbe	47	– c and b Buckland	31
Mr L. Wilson c and b Burton	63	– lbw b Robertson	79
Mr J. N. Tonge c Welman b Robertson	12	– c Stoddart b Buckland	8
Mr F. Marchant b Ford	24	– c Burton b Robertson	15
A. Hearne b Ford	17	– not out	24
Mr M. C. Kemp b Webbe	8	– b Webbe	16
Mr S. Christopherson b Ford	7	– c Stoddart b Burton	17
J. Wootton not out	5	– c Welman b Robertson	8
F. Martin c Stoddart b Webbe	15	– c Dunkley b Webbe	1
L-b 9	9	B 13, l-b 5, w 1	19
	241		364

Middlesex

Mr A. J. Webbe not out	192
Mr A. E. Stoddart lbw b Wootton	46
Mr J. G. Walker c Marchant b F. Hearne	40
Mr E. H. Buckland b Martin	34
Mr T. C. O'Brien c and b A. Hearne	25
Mr G. F. Vernon c A. Hearne b Marchant	19
Mr F. G. J. Ford b Marchant	4
G. Burton st Kemp b A. Hearne	25
Mr J. Robertson c A. Hearne b Christopherson	16
Mr F. T. Welman b Christopherson	0
Dunkley b Tonge	4
B 1, l-b 3, n-b 3	7
	412

Middlesex Bowling

	Overs	Mdns	Runs	Wkts	Overs	Mdns	Runs	Wkts
Burton	51	28	52	3	44	21	70	1
Dunkley	16	5	43	—	11	4	20	—
Mr Buckland	14	4	30	—	39	17	70	3
Mr Robertson	22	—	41	1	52	23	87	3
Mr Webbe	28.1	19	28	3	29.3	14	44	3
Mr Ford	12	3	38	3	16	7	37	—
Mr Stoddart					4	—	10	—
Mr O'Brien					1	—	7	—

Kent Bowling

	Overs	Mdns	Runs	Wkts
Mr Christopherson	40	14	87	2
Wootton	55	27	87	1
Martin	66	36	79	1
A. Hearne	33	14	65	2
Mr Tonge	8.1	1	18	1
F. Hearne	15	6	31	1
Mr Marchant	6	1	20	2
Mr Patterson	2	—	8	—
Mr L. Wilson	2	—	10	—

The Old Stagers held their forty-sixth season in the little theatre in High Street during the Week, playing on Monday and Thursday Sydney Grundy's excellent comedy "The Glass of Fashion," and on Tuesday and Friday the late Henry J. Byron's domestic drama "Daisy Farm." Though we do not profess to criticise theatrical performances in these pages, we must say that Captain Gooch played John Macadam in the comedy with great briskness and humour.

KENT v ESSEX

Played at Tonbridge, August 18, 19, 1887

This was the return match to that played at Leyton at the beginnings of the week, and for the second time Kent gained a single-innings' victory. Essex won the toss, but against the excellent bowling of Martin and Wootton only managed to put together a total of 90. It did not seem at one time as if this number would be reached, as six wickets were down for 23 runs, five batsmen being dismissed at that total. Mr R. P. Sewell, however, showed very good form for 32 not out, and found a useful partner in Pickett. Martin, it will be seen, obtained six Essex wickets at a cost of less than 7 runs apiece. Some very different batting was seen when Kent took their innings. The home team occupied the wickets for the remainder of the day, scoring 215 for the loss of six batsmen. Mr W. H. Patterson played superb cricket for 99 not out, his partner at the drawing of stumps being Mr M. C. Kemp with 20.

Three-quarters of an hour's play on Friday sufficed to bring the Kentish innings to a close, the total reaching 264. Mr W. H. Patterson increased his overnight score to 127, taking out his bat for that number. Altogether he was batting for four hours and a quarter, and his faultless innings included nine 4s, six 3s and fourteen 2s. It will be observed that no fewer than five batsmen were run out, and this, we should say, was the only occasion during the season on which such a curious thing happened. It should be stated, however, that Mr Patterson was chiefly to blame for this unprecedented thing, although, in justice to Essex, it must be admitted that their fielding was smart and accurate. The visitors went in a second time, with arrears of 174 to make up, but this task proved beyond their strength, though Mr Owen played a capital 35, and Bastow carried out his bat for an excellent 58, the chief hits of which were six 4s, three 3s and five 2s. The side were all out for 148, and Kent were left with a victory by an innings and 26 runs.

Essex

Mr C. E. Green b Wootton	10	– b Wootton	0
Mr H. G. Owen c Patterson b Martin	5	– b Wootton	35
Almond c A. Hearne b Martin	8	– b Wootton	5
Mr C. D. Buxton c Hickmott b Martin	0	– b Wootton	5
J. Bastow b Wootton	0	– not out	58
Mr W. Francis c F. Hearne b Martin	0	– c Tonge b Martin	4
Mr R. P. Sewell not out	32	– c Patterson b A. Hearne	12
Mr F. A. Bishop c Tonge b Martin	17	– b Wootton	11
Mr G. McEwen b Wootton	0	– b Wootton	4
H. Pickett b Wootton	14	– b Wootton	1
J. Bryan c Tonge b Martin	0	– b A. Hearne	6
B 4	4	B 3, l-b 4	7
	90		148

Kent

Mr F. M. Atkins run out	19	Mr M. C. Kemp c Bastow b Pickett	35
F. Hearne b Sewell	22	W. Hickmott run out	0
Mr W. H. Patterson not out	127	F. Martin b Sewell	4
Mr W. Rashleigh run out	21	J. Wootton run out	2
Mr J. N. Tonge c and b Pickett	5	B 1, l-b 6, w 1	8
A. Hearne b Owen	21		
Mr A. Young run out	0		264

Kent Bowling

	Overs	Mdns	Runs	Wkts	Overs	Mdns	Runs	Wkts
Martin	24.3	14	38	6	29	15	37	1
Wootton	24	13	48	4	50	20	70	7
A. Hearne					21	6	34	—

Essex Bowling

	Overs	Mdns	Runs	Wkts
Mr Bishop	36	12	74	—
Bryan	41	18	50	—
Pickett	58	25	66	2
Mr Sewell	20	9	32	2
Mr Buxton	15	7	23	—
Mr Owen	6	2	11	1

KENT v SUSSEX

Played at Tonbridge, August 2, 3, 1888

One of the most remarkable games played in a remarkable season. When the match looked an absolute certainty for Kent, Tate, by a wonderful bowling performance, almost succeeded in snatching a victory for Sussex, and it was this achievement of a comparatively unknown man which justifies us in dealing with the match fully. The contest was decided on the Angel Ground at Tonbridge, and took place just at the time when the condition of the grounds was giving the bowlers a tremendous amount of assistance. Both sides were extremely well represented, and had the wicket been in good condition no doubt some very long scoring would have been seen. As it was, rain had fallen almost incessantly for about a day and a half previous to the match, and at one time it was feared a start would be out of the question on the opening day. However, as the morning was bright and there was a strong drying wind, it was found possible to commence the game at twenty minutes to four, between which time and the drawing of stumps at half-past six considerable progress was made with the game. On winning the toss, Sussex decided to take first innings, and Mr F. H. Gresson, taking advantage of the wicket while it was at its easiest, rapidly hit up 22. His, however, proved to be the only double-figure score on the side, the other batsmen failing one after another before the admirable bowling of Martin and Wright, who remained unchanged throughout the short innings of Sussex, the total only amounting to 51. The last four wickets went down for 8 runs. About an hour remained for play when Kent went in to bat, and though three of the best men on the side were got rid of for 4 runs, the score at the call of time was 33 for five wickets, or 18 behind, with five wickets to go down.

On the Friday the weather was again fine, but the wicket was still all in favour of the bowlers. Those who were fortunate enough to be present will long remember the day's cricket. In the early morning Wright and Alec Hearne made an invaluable stand, putting on 31 runs for the ninth wicket, and this practically won the match for Kent. The Sussex bowling was not as good as it ought to have been, but nevertheless the two Kent professionals deserve great praise. The total reached 103, leaving Kent in a majority of 52. At the start of the second innings of Sussex the Kent bowling was hit about with the greatest freedom. The wicket played easily enough until the effects of the rolling had worn off. Mr Gresson and Quaife scored 35 for the first wicket, and it seemed as if Kent would have a hard task set them, but the last few batsmen failed completely before the bowling of Martin and Alec Hearne, and Sussex were all out for 96. Martin, in the two innings, took ten wickets at a cost of only 50 runs, and as he later on stayed in and made the winning hit, the county had great reason to be thankful for his services in the match. Kent were left with only 45 runs to get to win, and even though the wicket was becoming more and more difficult, it did not seem as if the number would cost more than four or five wickets at the outside. The Sussex men themselves thought they had no chance, but they played up, and especially at the finish, in a style that reflected the greatest credit on them. At the start of the second innings Mr Rashleigh made a useful 12, and even though runs were always hard to obtain, the score reached 41 for four wickets, or only 4 runs to win, with six wickets to fall. If ever there was a certainty at cricket it seemed to be then, but it was at this point that Tate went on to bowl, and brought about such an extraordinary change in the game. The young professional at once dismissed George Hearne, who had been batting very patiently, and, encouraged by this early success, bowled wonderfully well, the Kent batsmen seeming quite helpless against him. In quick succession he clean bowled Mr Marchant, Mr Fox, Alec Hearne and Walter Wright, and he had obtained his five wickets without a run being scored off him. The excitement, which had been gradually increasing, was at its height when Martin, the last man in, joined Mr Kemp, two runs being then wanted to win. Martin played the first ball he received a little way on the off side, and Mr Kemp brought off a desperately short run, making the game a tie. Again Mr Kemp started for and brought off what had hardly looked to be a possible run, and Kent won the match by one wicket. Had the winning hit gone to a smart fieldsman it is more than likely either Martin or Mr Kemp would have been run out, and the result would have been a tie. Tate's performance is almost without parallel in first-class cricket, and it was a pity for the young bowler that he was not able to crown his efforts by winning the match. He took five wickets – all of them clean bowled and most of them obtained by yorkers – at a cost of only one run. There was a great amount of cheering at the finish, and almost every one on the ground would have liked to see Sussex win after making such a grand fight. The uncertainty of cricket was never more clearly asserted. With 4 runs to win and six wickets to fall it scarcely seemed worth while to change the bowling, and yet the experiment almost turned what looked to be a certain defeat into a victory.

Sussex

Mr F. H. Gresson c Wilson b Wright	22	– b A. Hearne	18
W. A. Quaife c Marchant b Martin	4	– b Martin	10
Mr G. Brann c and b Martin	0	– c Wilson b A. Hearne	10
Mr W. Newham b Wright	0	– b A. Hearne	9
Mr J. M. Cotterill c Wright b Martin	5	– c G. Hearne b A. Hearne	3
J. Hide b Wright	3	– b Martin	1
W. Humphreys b Martin	5	– b A. Hearne	11
Mr C. A. Smith b Wright	1	– c Fox b Martin	8
A. Hide c Marchant b Martin	2	– b A. Hearne	7
F. W. Tate not out	0	– c G. Hearne b Martin	7
H. Phillips st Kemp b Martin	1	– not out	0
B 6, l-b 2	8	B 9, l-b 3	12
	51		96

Kent

Mr W. Rashleigh b J. Hide	0	– c Newham b A. Hide	12
Mr J. N. Tonge c A. Hide b J. Hide	0	– c Humphreys b A. Hide	2
Mr W. H. Patterson b J. Hide	4	– c Tate b A. Hide	7
Mr C. J. M. Fox c A. Hide b J. Hide	10	– b Tate	11
Mr L. Wilson lbw b A. Hide	12	– c Tate b A. Hide	0
G. G. Hearne lbw b J. Hide	1	– b Tate	7
Mr F. Marchant b A. Hide	13	– b Tate	0
W. Wright not out	8	– b Tate	1
Mr M. C. Kemp run out	7	– not out	0
A. Hearne b A. Hide	28	– b Tate	0
F. Martin b J. Hide	10	– not out	2
B 9, l-b 1	10	B 3	3
	103		45

Kent Bowling

	Overs	Mdns	Runs	Wkts	Overs	Mdns	Runs	Wkts
Martin	24.2	11	27	6	35	20	23	4
Wright	24	15	16	4	6	—	14	—
A. Hearne					29.2	11	47	6

Sussex Bowling

	Overs	Mdns	Runs	Wkts	Overs	Mdns	Runs	Wkts
A. Hide	42	24	46	3	26	14	21	4
J. Hide	37.2	21	33	6	22	14	20	0
Mr Smith	7	5	5	0				
Tate	13	7	9	—	4	3	1	5

Umpires: Jupp and Panter.

KENT v NOTTINGHAMSHIRE

Played at Beckenham, August 29, 30, 1889

Probably in no year since the competition between the first-class counties has been a recognised institution has there been so remarkable a climax to the struggle as occurred in the return match between Kent and Nottinghamshire. The game was the absolute last of the first-class county season, and, although fifty-two matches had already been decided, the issue of the competition depended upon the result of the match under notice. A heavy dew had fallen during the night before the match, and the Beckenham wicket, which never had a very good reputation for wearing well, was decidedly soft. At the start Mr Dixon was got rid of very cheaply, and a brilliant piece of fielding by Wright at mid-off disposed of Shrewsbury for 12. The Kent bowlers kept an excellent length, and neither Gunn nor Barnes, powerful hitters as they both are, succeeded in scoring at any pace. The latter indeed was at the wickets nearly an hour for 12, and Gunn, in first wicket down at 4 and out fourth at 94, was batting two hours and a quarter for his careful 40. Flowers was the only man on the side who displayed any approach to freedom, and towards the close of the innings Mr Fox bowled with remarkable success, the last six wickets falling for 40 runs. The Old Westminster man deceived more than one batsman in the pitch of the ball, but he was perhaps scarcely so difficult to play as Martin, who took four wickets for 50 runs. Kent had an hour's batting before the call of time, the score reaching 44 for the loss of the captain's wicket.

On Friday there was a general expectation that bowlers would carry all before them, for not only had the wicket worn considerably, but there was again a heavy dew. Kent at starting perhaps possessed a slight advantage, but in the course of an hour's cricket they lost six more wickets for an addition of only 29 runs. With seven wickets down for 73, and Attewell almost unplayable, there was every prospect that Kent would find themselves a good many runs behind on the first innings. Mr Kemp, a splendid man at a pinch, played a most plucky and characteristic innings of 28 not out, and, as he received fair support from Barton and Martin, the difference between the two counties when an innings had been finished on each side was only 16 runs. Attewell's bowling figures speak for themselves. Going in for three-quarters of an hour's cricket before lunch, Nottinghamshire lost Shrewsbury before a run had been scored, and Mr Dixon at 4, but then Gunn and Barnes, by great care, raised the score to 24. So far there was little reason to imagine that the game would be concluded that day, but on play being continued at ten minutes to three some of the most remarkable cricket of the season was witnessed. In fifty minutes Martin and Wright got the other eight Nottinghamshire wickets down for an addition of only 11 runs, Nottinghamshire being all out at ten minutes to four for 35 – the smallest score made by any first-class county during the summer. Martin's performance of taking seven wickets for 18 runs was not only the best thing he had ever done since he made a name, but was probably one of the finest pieces of bowling of the year. Walter Wright also deserves great praise. Kent were set only 52 runs to get to win, but Mr Patterson, the best man on the side, was out in the first over, and at the end of half an hour the score was only 11. Lord Harris, who had made ten of these runs, was then dismissed, and Attewell and Flowers bowling at their best, there were five wickets down for 15. Frank Hearne, who was at the wicket in company with his brother George, made a few good hits, but when he left at 25 Nottinghamshire certainly looked to have the match in hand. George Hearne had been playing with untiring patience, and in Bombardier Barton he found a wonderfully good partner. The Artilleryman showed a degree of confidence which would have done credit to a veteran, and, although once or twice rather over keen in running, played in a manner of which, considering the circumstances, any cricketer might have been proud. Amidst the increasing cheers of the spectators the 27 runs wanted were hit off, and at ten minutes past five Kent had gained a famous victory by four wickets. George Hearne carried out his bat for 14, the result of an hour and three quarters sterling cricket. Attewell for the losers bowled superbly, sending down twenty-five overs for 7 runs and four wickets, and his performance in the match of taking ten wickets for 60 runs deserved even more praise than it obtained. We may add that the play on the second day lasted exactly five hours, and that during that time twenty-five wickets went down for 162 runs, fourteen falling between ten minutes to three and ten minutes past five. We must not conclude our notice of this match without referring to a very pleasant incident during the luncheon interval, when Frank Hearne, compelled to leave England for a warmer climate on account of his health, was presented with a sum of nearly £150 by Mr F. A. Mackinnon, the president of the Kent County Club. Lord Harris added a few words in bearing testimony to Frank Hearne's good qualities, both as a man and as a cricketer.

Nottinghamshire

Mr J. A. Dixon c A. Hearne b Martin	2	– c Marchant b Martin	2
A. Shrewsbury c Wright b Martin	12	– c A. Hearne b Martin	0
W. Gunn c Kemp b Martin	40	– c Fox b Martin	17
W. Barnes b Barton	12	– b Martin	8
W. Flowers b Fox	26	– b Wright	0
W. Scotton c G. Hearne b Fox	10	– b Martin	4
W. Attewell b Fox	8	– b Wright	1
Mr H. B. Daft lbw b Martin	2	– st Kemp b Martin	0
F. Shacklock b Fox	0	– st Kemp b Martin	3
H. Richardson b Fox	13	– b Wright	0
M. Sherwin not out	7	– not out	0
B 1, l-b 1	2		
	134		35

Kent

Lord Harris b Shacklock	13	– b Attewell	10
Mr W. H. Patterson b Richardson	28	– c Shrewsbury b Attewell	0
G. G. Hearne b Attewell	16	– not out	14
Mr F. Marchant c Flowers b Attewell	9	– b Attewell	0
Mr C. J. M. Fox b Attewell	2	– b Flowers	1
A. Hearne c Barnes b Attewell	1	– lbw b Flowers	0
F. Hearne b Attewell	4	– c Shrewsbury b Attewell	9
Bombardier Barton b Shacklock	7	– not out	12
Mr M. C. Kemp not out	28		
F. Martin c Scotton b Flowers	9		
W. Wright b Attewell	1		
		B 7	7
	118		53

Kent Bowling

	Overs	Mdns	Runs	Wkts	Overs	Mdns	Runs	Wkts
Martin	55	30	50	4	22.1	15	18	7
Wright	24	12	26	—	13	8	7	3
Mr Fox	34.2	16	43	5	9	6	10	—
Barton	4	—	13	1				

Nottinghamshire Bowling

	Overs	Mdns	Runs	Wkts	Overs	Mdns	Runs	Wkts
Attewell	32.3	10	53	6	25	21	7	4
Richardson	30	17	36	1	7	4	13	—
Shacklock	11	5	16	2				
Barnes	1	—	6	—				
Flowers	2	—	7	1	18	10	26	2

Umpires: J. Street and C. K. Pullin.

KENT v GLOUCESTERSHIRE

Played at Maidstone, May 22, 23, 24, 1890

Gloucestershire were unable to put into the field their strongest eleven, but they made a creditable fight, and were only beaten by five wickets. The finish was productive of a good deal of excitement, as Kent, wanting 100 runs to win, lost three wickets for 28, and had Murch accepted a chance offered him by Mr Fox, there would have been four men out for 34. The match presented many features of interest, but certainly the best was Mr W. G. Grace's remarkable not out innings of 109.

Gloucestershire

Mr W. G. Grace not out	109	– b Wright	37
Mr H. H. Francis run out	2	– st Pentecost b Martin	1
Mr O. G. Radcliffe b Martin	11	– c Fox b Martin	20
Mr J. Cranston c Marchant b Christopherson	27	– c G. G. Hearne b Christopherson	12
J. Painter st Pentecost b Martin	46	– c A. Hearne b G. G. Hearne	83
Mr E. M. Grace c Wright b Martin	1	– c Daffen b Martin	18
Mr W. O. Vizard lbw b Fox	17	– b Wright	2
H. W. Murch lbw b Martin	2	– c A. Hearne b Christopherson	5
Mr H. W. Brown c A. Hearne b Martin	0	– c Martin b Wright	7
Mr G. S. de Winton b Martin	0	– c A. Hearne b Martin	19
F. G. Roberts c Pentecost b Martin	8	– not out	0
B 7, l-b 1	8	B 4, l-b 1	5
	231		209

Kent

Mr L. A. Hamilton c W. G. Grace b Roberts	11	– st Vizard b E. M. Grace	4
Mr A. Daffen b Murch	52	– c Vizard b Roberts	18
G. G. Hearne b Roberts	22	– not out	38
Mr F. Marchant b Roberts	41	– b Roberts	0
Mr C. J. M. Fox b E. M. Grace	58	– c and b Roberts	22
Mr L. Wilson b E. M. Grace	86	– c Vizard b Roberts	13
A. Hearne c and b E. M. Grace	16	– not out	4
Mr S. Christopherson c Vizard b Roberts	0		
W. Wright b E. M. Grace	6		
F. Martin c Radcliffe b Murch	17		
J. Pentecost not out	8		
B 21, l-b 3	24	B 3	3
	341		102

Kent Bowling

	Overs	Mdns	Runs	Wkts	Overs	Mdns	Runs	Wkts
Wright	30	10	59	—	33.3	15	61	3
Martin	52.4	23	62	7	39	16	70	4
Mr Fox	13	2	40	1	2	—	9	—
Mr Christopherson	17	3	40	1	15	5	37	2
A. Hearne	7	2	22	—	13	3	15	—
G. G. Hearne					9	3	12	1

Gloucestershire Bowling

	Overs	Mdns	Runs	Wkts	Overs	Mdns	Runs	Wkts
Roberts	53	18	115	4	24	12	36	4
Mr Brown	13	1	37	—				
Mr W. G. Grace ...	7	2	9	—	6	2	7	—
Mr Radcliffe	11	3	29	—				
Murch	26	8	68	2				
Mr E. M. Grace	19.2	3	45	4	19	5	56	1
Painter	7	—	14	—				

Umpires: Tuck and Coward.

KENT v SURREY

Played at Canterbury, August 7, 8, 9, 1890

With most praiseworthy generosity, the Kent committee set apart the second match of the Canterbury week for the benefit of George Hearne, and certainly no professional cricketer has ever received a more genuine recognition of years of faithful service to his county. The match in itself had peculiar interest, as it was the first time the Surrey team had ever taken part in the great Kentish festival, and it was most fortunate that the weather remained fine. Moreover, the game produced a splendid struggle, in which the interest of the spectators was thoroughly maintained right up to the time of the last ball on the Saturday night. George Hearne made his first appearance for Kent in 1875, and from that time he has been a regular member of the Kent eleven, last summer being his sixteenth season for the county. He joined the ground staff at Lord's in 1877, and appeared for the Marylebone Club in the memorable game against the first Australian team, which was begun and ended in one day. His best years were 1883 and 1886, in both of which seasons he averaged over 31 runs an innings. The Marylebone Club selected him to represent the Players against the Gentlemen at Lord's in 1884. Originally he was played almost entirely as a bowler, but later in his career he developed batting powers of a very high order, and his services as a bowler were only occasionally called into requisition. After the luncheon interval on the first day of the match there was a very happy idea that some old Kent cricketers should make a collection for him on the ground, and this was so cordially responded to that the amount realised came to £81 9s. Among those who assisted in making the collection were the Hon. Ivo Bligh, Mr George Marsham, Mr F. A. Mackinnon, Mr W. H. Patterson and Mr C. J. M. Fox. On the first day the number that paid for admission was 5,900, and the whole attendance was estimated at about 9,400. On the second day the number paying at the gates was 2,361, representing an estimated attendance of 3,200; and on the third just over 1,200 paid, and there were altogether about 2,000 on the ground – the largest attendance, we believe, that has ever been seen on the St. Lawrence ground on the Saturday of the cricket week. Everyone connected with Kent was highly delighted that Hearne should have had such a successful benefit.

The wicket was in excellent condition, and Mr Patterson was extremely fortunate in winning the toss for Kent. At first, however, it seemed as though very little use would be made of the advantage, for the best and most trusted batsmen on the Kent side failed one after another before the admirable bowling of Lohmann and Sharpe, backed up as it was by fielding of the best description. The score at the luncheon interval was 70 for five wickets, but on the resumption of play there was a very marked improvement in the batting, and Messrs Leslie Wilson, Marchant and Kemp rendered their side invaluable assistance. The prospects of Kent looked none too favourable when the seventh wicket fell at 102, but then came a splendid stand by Messrs Marchant and Kemp, the two men putting on 60 runs during their partnership for the eighth wicket. In the end the Kent total reached 177. Wood kept wicket admirably, and brought off three good catches. The commencement of the Surrey innings was quite sensational, as Mr Shuter was bowled off his leg before a run had been scored, and Lockwood, after making a 4 to leg, was clean bowled by Wright. On Mr Walter Read joining Abel matters were made to look much better for Surrey, and the two men remained together for an hour and ten minutes, during which time they put on 65 runs, Mr Read being at last out to a smart catch at short slip. Maurice Read and Abel were together when time was called for the day, the score being left at 73 for three wickets, or 104 behind with seven wickets to go down.

The weather on the second day compared unfavourably with that of Thursday, but, though rain threatened for some time, it did not interfere with the game until a quarter past five. Two more Surrey wickets soon fell, and there were five batsmen out for 73, but then came a most valuable stand by Henderson and Mr Key, the two men putting on 52 runs in forty minutes. Mr Roller left at 158, and at 172 Mr Key's capital innings of 52 was brought to a close by Alec Hearne, the Surrey amateur having his off stump bowled down in attempting a hit to the on. It seemed as though there would be very little difference between the two teams on the first innings, but Sharpe kept up his wicket while Lohmann hit in splendid style, forcing the game just at the right time, and in the end the Surrey score reached 215, or 38 runs to the good. At the commencement of their second innings the Kent team gave a very fine display of batting, which was, of course, wonderfully popular with the spectators. Alec Hearne and Mr L. A Hamilton obtained quite a mastery over the Surrey bowling, and put on 78 runs for the first wicket, while after the amateur's departure. Mr Leslie Wilson and Hearne put on runs at a great pace and took the score up to 153 before Mr Wilson was bowled for a brilliant innings of 42, which included eight boundary hits. Just after Mr Patterson had joined Alec Hearne, the Surrey bowlers were handicapped by the fact that a drizzling rain kept the ball wet and greasy. However, the Kent captain should have been out to an easy catch by Henderson at cover slip, and the mistake proved a costly one for Surrey. At a quarter past five, when the score stood at 158 for two wickets, rain came on so heavily that the players had to seek shelter. It appeared as though there could have been about twenty minutes' more cricket, but the umpires considered the ground was unfit, and drew the stumps. The close of the day's play left Kent with a very great advantage, as they were 120 runs to the good with eight wickets to fall.

On the Saturday batsmen had to play under totally different conditions, as the rain of the previous night was followed by bright sunshine, and all through the afternoon the bowlers were able to get a large amount of work on the ball. The cricket proved of a wonderfully interesting character, and the result was in doubt right up to the last ball of the day. The second innings of Kent was brought to a close in an unexpectedly rapid manner, Lohmann and Sharpe bowling with such great effect that the last eight wickets went down for the addition of 70 runs, the total thus reaching 228. Mr Patterson forced the game with considerable success, but in making his 46 he was favoured by a little luck. Alec Hearne failed to add a run to his overnight score of 72, which is the highest innings he has ever played for his county. He was altogether at the wickets for two hours and forty minutes without giving the slightest chance, the chief hits of his admirable innings being ten 4s, three 3s and five 2s. In the morning Lohmann did a remarkable piece of bowling, sending down twenty-two overs and a ball for 30 runs and five wickets. Surrey were left with 191 runs to get to win, and about three hours and fifty minutes remained for play. Even under favourable circumstances this would not have been an easy task, and, with the ground helping Martin and Wright, it was thought most probable that Kent would get their opponents out in time to win the match. Just at first there seemed a possibility that the runs might be obtained, as Lockwood, who went in first wicket down, hit freely and well for 40, and was the fourth man out at 68. After this, however, Martin and Wright bowled splendidly, and the Surrey men soon giving up the idea of winning, set themselves steadily to the task of saving the game. Their prospects looked anything but favourable, however, when the eighth wicket went down, and fifty minutes still remained for play. However, Lohmann played with great nerve at a critical time, and he and Wood defied the Kent bowlers for about forty minutes. Wood should have been caught at mid-off by Mr Patterson, and, had this chance been accepted, Kent would probably have been able to score a victory. The excitement was intense when Wood was got rid of about ten minutes before time, and Sharpe, the last man, walked to the wicket. Had Sharpe failed, the match was lost for Surrey, but he and Lohmann kept wonderfully cool, and remained in till the umpire called time at a quarter-past six. The last ball of the match, which was bowled by Martin, completely beat Sharpe, and went just about an inch above the wicket, so that Kent were extremely unlucky in being unable to wind up an admirable performance with a victory. At the finish Surrey wanted 42 runs to win and had only one wicket to fall, so that the draw was all in favour of Kent. Lohmann carried out his bat for 28, an innings which, considering the time it was played, was quite equal to any ordinary 60. When he first went in he made some fine hits, but after a time, realising that runs were of no value, he contented himself by playing a purely defensive game, and he was fully entitled to all the praise he received for saving the match for Surrey.

Kent

Mr L. A. Hamilton c Abel b Lohmann	1	– c Roller b Lockwood	39
A. Hearne c Wood b Lohmann	9	– c Wood b Lohmann	72
G. G. Hearne c Wood b Lohmann	4	– c Wood b Lohmann	0
Mr A. Daffen lbw b Sharpe	7	– not out	10
Mr W. H. Patterson c Roller b Lohmann	23	– c Abel b Sharpe	46
Mr C. J. M. Fox b Lohmann	10	– c Key b Lohmann	0
Mr L. Wilson c Wood b Sharpe	34	– b Sharpe	42
Mr F. Marchant c Abel b Sharpe	35	– c Sharpe b Lohmann	5
Mr M. C. Kemp not out	33	– b Sharpe	3
W. Wright b Henderson	1	– c Abel b Sharpe	0
F. Martin c Lohmann b Henderson	1	– c Roller b Lohmann	0
B 9	9	B 9, l-b 2	11
	177		228

Surrey

Mr J. Shuter b Wright	0	– b Martin	1
R. Abel b Wright	28	– c Patterson b Martin	13
W. Lockwood b Wright	4	– st Kemp b Martin	40
Mr W. W. Read c Patterson b A. Hearne	35	– b Wright	8
M. Read b Martin	0	– c and b Wright	4
Mr K. J. Key b A. Hearne	52	– st Kemp b Martin	13
R. Henderson c Kemp b Fox	18	– c Patterson b Martin	13
Mr W. E. Roller b G. G. Hearne	18	– b Martin	9
G. A. Lohmann b Martin	41	– not out	28
H. Wood b Wright	0	– c sub b Wright	8
J. W. Sharpe not out	9	– not out	0
B 7, l-b 2, n-b 1	10	B 11, l-b 1	12
	215		149

Surrey Bowling

	Overs	Mdns	Runs	Wkts	Overs	Mdns	Runs	Wkts
Lohmann	40	20	67	5	41.1	17	69	5
Sharpe	44	20	78	3	46	19	80	4
Henderson	7.3	—	8	2	12	6	12	—
Mr Roller	2	—	15	—	4	3	1	—
Mr W. W. Read					6	1	19	—
Lockwood					11	4	36	1

Kent Bowling

	Overs	Mdns	Runs	Wkts	Overs	Mdns	Runs	Wkts
Martin	31	13	44	2	57	26	62	6
Wright	34	13	85	4	56	26	75	3
Mr Fox	14	3	34	1				
A. Hearne	16	8	30	2				
G. G. Hearne	6	3	12	1				

Umpires: J. Veitch and F. Coward.

KENT v LANCASHIRE

Played at Tonbridge, July 11, 12, 13, 1892

Though the Tonbridge week had been in existence for two years, this was the first occasion on which the executive were able to arrange for two first-class matches. In the first contest, that against Lancashire, Kent suffered a most crushing defeat in a single innings with no fewer than 330 runs to spare, but though, under the most favourable circumstances, Kent could scarcely have proved successful against their formidable opponents, it must be confessed that the conditions were such as to give the side that won the toss an immense advantage. When the weather was fine and the ground in almost perfect condition, Lancashire went in first and, occupying the wickets for the whole of the first day, scored 484 runs for the loss of nine batsmen. Baker scored his first three figure innings for Lancashire, the chief hits of his admirable 109 being sixteen 4s, three 3s and seven 2s. The conditions were entirely altered by a very heavy shower of rain, which fell on the second morning at a few minutes after one o'clock, and delayed the game until twenty minutes past four. After that the wicket kicked terribly, and the Kent batsmen were practically helpless against the splendid bowling of Mold and Briggs. Only Mr Weigall proved able to offer any resistance, and the Kent totals amounted to but 97 and 57. In the whole match Mold had the wonderful record of thirteen wickets for 91 runs.

Lancashire

A. Ward lbw b Hearne	18
F. H. Sugg c Wilson b Wright	68
A. Smith b Hearne	62
J. Briggs run out	54
A. Tinsley c Fox b Hearne	44
Mr S. M. Crosfield b Hearne	38
G. R. Baker c Weigall b Le Fleming	109
G. Yates c Malden b Hearne	74
Mr A. T. Kemble b Le Fleming	0
A. Watson c Rashleigh b Wright	7
A. Mold not out	0
B 7, l-b 3	10
	484

Kent

Mr H. M. Braybrooke c Baker b Mold	1	c Yates b Mold	1
Mr W. Rashleigh b Briggs	8	c Smith b Mold	4
Mr G. J. V. Weigall c Kemble b Mold	38	b Mold	18
Mr L. Wilson b Mold b Briggs	12	b Mold	1
Mr J. Le Fleming b Briggs	5	c Crossfield b Briggs	1
Mr C. J. M. Fox c Baker b Briggs	15	c Kemble b Mold	0
Mr F. Marchant run out	2	b Mold	0
Mr E. Malden c Watson b Mold	5	b Mold	8
F. Martin run out	9	c Yates b Mold	7
W. Hearne c Smith b Mold	0	b Mold	5
W. Wright not out	0	not out	5
B 1, l-b 1	2	B 4, l-b 3	7
	97		57

Kent Bowling

	Overs	Mdns	Runs	Wkts
Martin	51	12	113	0
W. Hearne	49.1	11	138	5
Wright	34	9	85	2
Mr Fox	9	1	36	0
Mr Le Fleming	12	0	44	2
Mr Marchant	6	1	20	0
Mr Wilson	4	0	21	0
Mr Rashleigh	2	0	17	0

Lancashire Bowling

	Overs	Mdns	Runs	Wkts	Overs	Mdns	Runs	Wkts
Mold	29.2	8	62	4	15.3	4	29	9
Briggs	29	16	33	4	15	7	21	1

Umpires: Street and Goodyear.

KENT v GLOUCESTERSHIRE

Played at Canterbury, August 1, 2, 3, 1892

Though up to this point of the season the Kent eleven had fared disastrously – a victory over Sussex at Gravesend being the only set off against a long series of defeats – the supporters of the county were by no means without hope that the team would render a good account of themselves at Canterbury, as they had done on so many previous occasions. It must be admitted that to a very large extent these expectations were borne out, as during the Canterbury week Kent gained a remarkably well-earned victory over Gloucestershire and made a much harder fight against Nottinghamshire than anyone could have expected. After the dismal experiences of the Jubilee week in 1891 everyone was hoping that fine weather would favour the Festival of 1892. The start was anything but promising, as rain fell heavily on the Monday morning, and, though play went on from three o'clock until a quarter past six, the outlook was terribly depressing, and there was not a gleam of sunshine. As it turned out, however, the weather took a most pleasant change from this time, and for the remainder of the week no one could have wished to look on at cricket under more delightful conditions. For the second year in succession the veteran champion, W. G. Grace, was unable to captain Gloucestershire, and this naturally took a little of the interest out of the game. When the counties met earlier in the season at Bristol, Gloucestershire proved successful, after a very hard fight, and Kent were therefore most anxious for the opportunity of revenge. In addition to the absence of W. G. Grace, Gloucestershire lacked the services of Roberts, who had badly injured his thumb against Lancashire at Liverpool, and S. A. P. Kitcat, who was kept away by a business engagement; but, as a slight set-off against these misfortunes, Captain Luard – who made his appearance in the county eleven simultaneously with Kitcat – was able to play again. Kent were strongly represented, but Marchant, who had captained the eleven during the months of May, June, and July, stood out, as he had been meeting with almost uninterrupted ill-luck. Kemp had been rather unwell, so the position of wicket-keeper was given to Malden, of Tunbridge Wells. After the rain that had fallen in the morning, it was, of course, a decided advantage to win the toss, and this piece of good fortune fell to Kent. While the ground was wet, and the bowlers had to use a greasy ball, run-getting was a fairly easy matter, and Alec Hearne and Braybrooke utilised their opportunity in such excellent fashion, that they scored 44 runs in half an hour during their partnership for the first wicket. Later on, as the ground dried, the bowlers were able to get some work on the ball, and had the sun come out, Gloucestershire would probably have dismissed Kent long before the call of time. As it was dried gradually by the wind, the wicket never became so difficult as it would otherwise have done, and what the ball did it did slowly. At the same time the ball wanted careful watching, and, under the circumstances, no man could have played a better game for his side than Alec Hearne. At the close of the first day's play the score was 193 for seven wickets, Hearne being not out 98, and on the Tuesday, much to the delight of the spectators, the young professional succeeded in completing the first three-figure innings he had ever scored for his county. The total reached 256, and Alec Hearne carried out his bat for 116, a most admirable display of batting which extended over four hours and twenty minutes, and against which scarcely a mistake could be urged. The chief hits of his remarkalbe innings were fifteen 4s five 3s and thirteen 2s. As the ground was beginning to play very treacherously, Gloucestershire had a thankless task in facing a total of 256, and though the score was up to 29 with only one batsman out, the bowlers after this gained such a tremendous advantage that in less than an hour and a half the last nine Gloucestershire wickets went down for the addition of 62 runs, the total thus reaching 91. The visitors had to follow on against a majority of 165, and though some capital batting was shown by Radcliffe, Rice, and Painter, six wickets fell before the call of time for 106 runs. Thus, on the last morning, Gloucestershire, with four wickets to fall, wanted 59 runs to avoid a single innings defeat, but the conclusion of the game proved more interesting than might have been expected, and the end was not reached until half-past one. Thanks mainly to some plucky and vigorous hitting by Painter, the Gloucestershire total reached 188, which left Kent with only 24 runs to get to win. Light as this task appeared, however, the requisite number was not obtained until three good wickets had fallen, and so Kent's second victory of the season was gained by seven wickets. It may be mentioned here that during the Thursday afternoon a public collection was made for Alec Hearne, as a reward for his fine innings. The appeal was so liberally responded to that he was presented with £50, and cheques for £6 8s. each were given to Martin, Wright and Walter Hearne, the other professional members of the team.

Kent

Mr H. M. Braybrooke b Woof	20		
A. Hearne not out	116		
Mr G. J. V. Weigall c Page b Woof	11	– b Murch	4
Mr W. H. Patterson c and b Woof	2	– not out	0
Mr W. L. Knowles c Board b Ferris	0	– c Painter b Ferris	0
Mr L. Wilson b Woof	7	– not out	10
Mr C. J. M. Fox b Ferris	19	– b Murch	7
F. Martin c Croome b Woof	1		
W. Wright b Ferris	28		
Mr E. Malden b Ferris	11		
W. Hearne b Murch	21		
B 16, l-b 4	20	B 4	4
	256		25

Gloucestershire

Mr E. M. Grace c Braybrooke b W. Hearne	3	– c Fox b Martin	2
Mr R. W. Rice c Wilson b Martin	6	– b Wright	19
Mr J. J. Ferris b Martin	26	– c Martin b W. Hearne	1
Mr O. G. Radcliffe c Wilson b Martin	11	– c sub. b Martin	31
Capt. A. H. Luard run out	17	– c sub. b Martin	0
J. Painter b W. Hearne	0	– not out	65
Mr H. V. Page c Wilson b W. Hearne	15	– c W. Hearne b Wright	12
Mr A. C. M. Croome b Martin	0	– b W. Hearne	22
H. W. Murch b Martin	2	– c Wilson b W. Hearne	0
W. A. Woof not out	0	– b W. Hearne	7
J. H. Board b W. Hearne	2	– c Wilson b Martin	18
B 9	9	B 8, l-b 3	11
	91		188

Gloucestershire Bowling

	Overs	Mdns	Runs	Wkts	Overs	Mdns	Runs	Wkts
Mr Ferris	56	22	91	4	6	4	5	1
Murch	7.4	0	38	1	5.3	3	16	2
Woof	53	14	104	5				
Mr Croome	3	1	3	0				

Kent Bowling

	Overs	Mdns	Runs	Wkts	Overs	Mdns	Runs	Wkts
Martin	32	17	40	5	35.2	11	62	4
W. Hearne	28	14	41	4	28	7	84	4
Wright	3	2	1	0	7	1	31	2

Umpires: H. Holmes and T. Foster.

KENT v NOTTINGHAMSHIRE

Played at Canterbury, August 4, 5, 6, 1892

The second match of the Canterbury week produced a thoroughly interesting struggle. After the strain they had gone through in the great game against Surrey the Nottinghamshire men were certainly below their best. The success of Nottinghamshire was gained by 56 runs, but Kent looked to have a chance of making the 241 runs set them to win. Weigall, Marchant, and Wilson played so well that, with six wickets to fall, Kent were within a hundred runs of victory, but from this point Nottinghamshire carried everything before them. Shrewsbury played one of his best innings, and mention must be made of an incident which caused a good deal of comment. Kent thought they would have a better position by following on, but their attempts were frustrated by Attewell bowling a wide, which went to the boundary.

Nottinghamshire

A. Shrewsbury not out	111	– c A. Hearne b Wright	13
Mr A. O. Jones run out	7	– c A. Hearne b W. Hearne	10
W. Gunn c Kemp b Martin	8	– c Kemp b W. Hearne	35
W. Barnes b Wright	27	– lbw b W. Hearne	23
W. Flowers c A. Hearne b Wright	0	– b W. Hearne	11
W. Shacklock b Martin	14	– c Fox b W. Hearne	31
W. Attewell b Wright	1	– lbw b A. Hearne	8
Mr J. S. Robinson b W. Hearne	10	– c Martin b A. Hearne	16
H. B. Daft c A. Hearne b W. Hearne	13	– b W. Hearne	10
T. Attewell b W. Hearne	4	– c Marchant b W. Hearne	1
M. Sherwin b Wright	29	– not out	16
B 1, l-b 1	2	L-b 4	4
	226		178

Kent

	1st innings	2nd innings	
A. Hearne b W. Attewell	6	c Robins b W. Attewell	3
Mr F. Marchant b Shacklock	2	c Sherwin b Shacklock	34
Mr G. J. V. Weigall b Shacklock	10	c and b Flowers	63
Mr W. L. Knowles b Shacklock	12	b Shacklock	8
Mr W. H. Patterson lbw b W. Attewell	35	c Sherwin b Shacklock	1
Mr L. Wilson b Shacklock	6	lbw b Flowers	30
Mr C. J. M. Fox c T. Attewell b Shacklock	34	b Barnes	4
Mr M. C. Kemp c Sherwin b Shacklock	3	c Flowers b Barnes	12
F. Martin st Sherwin b W. Attewell	3	not out	12
W. Wright b Shacklock	23	c Sherwin b W. Attewell	5
W. Hearne not out	21	c Gunn b W. Attewell	2
B 4, l-b 1, w 4	9	B 8, l-b 2	10
	164		184

Kent Bowling

	Overs	Mdns	Runs	Wkts	Overs	Mdns	Runs	Wkts
Martin	39	16	79	2	29	13	48	0
W. Hearne	34	14	64	3	41	11	75	7
W. Wright	25.2	16	33	4	10	4	22	1
A. Hearne	20	5	48	0	22	13	29	2

Nottinghamshire Bowling

	Overs	Mdns	Runs	Wkts	Overs	Mdns	Runs	Wkts
W. Attewell	39	17	61	3	32.2	17	52	3
Shacklock	35.2	8	69	7	24	6	63	3
Flowers	7	1	14	0	22	7	42	2
Barnes	5	2	11	0	13	6	17	2

Umpires: A. F. Smith and T. Foster.

KENT v NOTTINGHAMSHIRE

Played at Maidstone, July 19, 20, 1894

Up to a certain time Kent looked to have an almost certain victory in prospect, as in the last innings they were left with only 66 runs to get to win. Though the wicket was very difficult after some heavy rain, it seemed most probable that Kent would obtain the number for the loss of four or five batsmen, but as it turned out only Alec Hearne and Marchant proved capable of offering any resistance to the splendid bowling of Flowers and Attewell, and the side were all out for 52, leaving Nottinghamshire with a brilliant, but altogether unexpected victory by 13 runs. It was generally thought that Marchant might with advantage have altered his order in the second innings, and it certainly seemed that he kept himself back too late. This was one of the best performances accomplished by Nottinghamshire last season, and it was really a remarkable thing to gain a victory after the side had been dismissed in the first innings for 47.

Nottinghamshire

Mr J. A. Dixon c Mason b Martin	3	– b W. Hearne	16
Mr R. H. Hewitt b Martin	0	– b W. Hearne	16
W. Flowers b W. Hearne	14	– b W. Hearne	0
W. Gunn run out	11	– b W. Hearne	49
Mr C. W. Wright b W. Hearne	1	– b W. Hearne	8
H. B. Daft c W. Hearne b Martin	1	– c Wilson b A. Hearne	3
Mr J. S. Robinson b Martin	1	– b A. Hearne	2
W. Attewell c Weigall b W. Hearne	7	– b W. Hearne	3
A. Pike b W. Hearne	0	– b W. Hearne	11
R. Bagguley not out	0	– st Atkins b Martin	0
R. J. Mee c Perkins b W. Hearne	2	– not out	0
B 7	7	B 15, l-b 5	20
	47		128

Kent

Mr J. R. Mason c Bagguley b Attewell	11	– c and b Attewell	0
A. Hearne b Flowers	5	– c Dixon b Attewell	23
Mr L. Wilson b Flowers	20	– b Flowers	1
Mr T. N. Perkins c Wright b Bagguley	45	– lbw b Attewell	3
Mr G. J. V. Weigall b Bagguley	9	– b Flowers	8
Mr W. H. Patterson b Attewell	4	– c and b Flowers	0
Mr F. M. Atkins c and b Attewell	0	– c Pike b Flowers	0
J. Easby b Bagguley	1	– b Flowers	0
Mr F. Marchant c Mee b Attewell	6	– not out	14
F. Martin run out	4	– b Flowers	3
W. Hearne not out	0	– c Hewitt b Flowers	0
B 5	5		
	110		52

Kent Bowling

	Overs	Mdns	Runs	Wkts	Overs	Mdns	Runs	Wkts
Martin	22	15	11	4	37	19	50	1
W. Hearne	21.3	9	29	5	41.4	19	43	7
A. Hearne					17	8	15	2

Nottinghamshire Bowling

	Overs	Mdns	Runs	Wkts	Overs	Mdns	Runs	Wkts
Attewell	17	4	41	4	16	7	28	3
Flowers	16	3	33	2	15.4	4	24	7
Bagguley	19	8	29	3				
Mee	4	3	2	0				

Umpires: F. Coward and J. Potter.

KENT IN 1895

The weeks at Tonbridge and Canterbury proved highly successful, though the latter festival was somewhat marred at the outset by bad weather. At Canterbury the Old Stagers, as usual, occupied the theatre in High Street, the pieces selected being "The Professor", a three-act farce, adapted from the German by Gerald Maxwell; and Mr R. C. Carton's comedy, "Liberty Hall". It was generally thought that the performance of "Liberty Hall" was one of the most complete ever given by the Old Stagers. The professional ladies assisting the amateurs were Miss Carlotta Addison, Miss Lizzie Henderson, Miss Dora de Winton, Miss Aileen O'Brien, and Miss Ethel Norton.

KENT v GLOUCESTERSHIRE

Played at Gravesend, May 23, 24, 25, 1895

This was certainly the most remarkable game played last season, affording the only instance in first-class cricket in England of a side winning after having to face a first innings of over 400. Up to luncheon time on the third day only an innings on each side had been got through, and the game looked almost certain to be drawn. The chief credit of Gloucestershire's victory by nine wickets was due to W. G. Grace, who scored 330 runs for once out, and was on the field during every ball of the match.

Kent

Mr F. Marchant b Grace	38	– c and b Painter	4
A. Hearne c Board b Kitcat	155	– not out	22
J. Easby c Thomas b Roberts	28	– b Roberts	17
Mr G. J. V. Weigall b Painter	74	– b Painter	1
G. G. Hearne b Murch	49	– b Painter	6
Mr J. R. Mason c Board b Roberts	21	– c Bracher b Painter	5
Mr G. C. Hubbard c and b Grace	36	– c Board b Painter	4
Mr P. Northcote not out	27	– b Roberts	0
Mr C. H. Hunter c Board b Murch	6	– c Board b Painter	4
W. Wright b Roberts	5	– b Painter	0
F. Martin b Murch	7	– b Roberts	12
B 17, l-b 2, n-b 5	24	L-b 1	1
	470		76

Gloucestershire

Mr W. G. Grace c Hubbard b A. Hearne	257	– not out	73
H. Wrathall b A. Hearne	13	– c sub b A. Hearne	2
Mr C. J. Francis c Hunter b Martin	8		
Mr C. O. H. Sewell st Hunter b Hubbard	14		
J. Painter c A. Hearne b Mason	40	– not out	31
H. W. Murch c Hubbard b G. Hearne	0		
Mr S. A. P. Kitcat b Martin	52		
Mr E. L. Thomas b A. Hearne	6		
Mr F. C. Bracher b A. Hearne	16		
J. H. Board c Mason b Northcote	17		
F. G. Roberts not out	8		
B 6, l-b 4, w 2	12		
	443		106

Gloucestershire Bowling

	Overs	Mdns	Runs	Wkts	Overs	Mdns	Runs	Wkts
Roberts	58	23	131	3	29	12	50	3
Grace	43	13	115	2				
Wrathall	12	3	36	0				
Sewell	10	2	48	0				
Kitcat	9	1	40	1				
Francis	2	0	11	0				
Painter	6	3	14	1	28	15	25	7
Murch	26.3	8	51	3				

Kent Bowling

	Overs	Mdns	Runs	Wkts	Overs	Mdns	Runs	Wkts
Martin	63	23	96	2	8	2	29	0
A. Hearne	56.3	15	93	4	11	2	38	1
Wright	23	6	67	0	2.2	0	15	0
Mason	30	9	54	1	2	0	9	0
Hubbard	6	0	25	1				
G. Hearne	23	10	41	1	4	1	15	0
Northcote	15	1	47	1				
Easby	3	1	8	0				

Umpires: R. Thoms and W. Clarke.

KENT v MIDDLESEX

Played at Tonbridge, June 15, 16, 17, 1896

The first match of the Tonbridge week, was noteworthy for one of the finest displays of hitting seen during the season. Rashleigh, the famous old Oxonian, made one of his rare appearances in first-class cricket, and in two hours and a half, actually scored 163 out of 201. His cutting was superb, and he sent the ball twenty-five times to the boundary. Despite this brilliant start – the score being up to 201 for two wickets – the batting afterwards broke down, and Kent were all out for 257. The fine display by Rashleigh and Mason, was followed up by some capital bowling on the part of Wright and Martin, and Kent had all the best of the match, when, unluckily for them, rain came on very heavily on the third morning, and caused the game to be abandoned as a draw. At the finish Middlesex wanted 317 to win, with seven wickets to fall, so they had little hope of averting defeat.

Kent

Mr J. R. Mason st MacGregor b Rawlin	66	– c and b Phillips	58
A. Hearne c and b Rawlin	0	– b Phillips	40
Rev. W. Rashleigh c MacGregor b Hearne	163	– b Hearne	4
Mr F. Marchant c Stoddart b Hearne	1	– b Hearne	0
Mr E. H. Simpson b Rawlin	3	– b Hearne	0
Mr G. J. V. Weigall c Stoddart b Rawlin	11	– b Phillips	79
J. Easby b Hearne	0	– c MacGregor b Phillips	55
Mr E. C. Mordaunt b Hearne	1	– c Thornton b Hearne	21
W. Wright c MacGregor b Hearne	0	– c O'Brien b Phillips	2
F. Martin not out	5	– c Webbe b Hearne	5
F. H. Huish b Hearne	3	– not out	4
B 2, l-b 2	4	B 9	9
	257		277

Middlesex

Mr A. E. Stoddart b Wright	41	– not out	9
Mr H. B. Hayman b Wright	11	– not out	17
Mr G. MacGregor b Martin	7		
Mr R. S. Lucas b Wright	11	– b Wright	1
J. T. Rawlin c Mordaunt b Martin	10		
Sir T. C. O'Brien c Weigall b Martin	30		
Mr A. J. Webbe b Wright	3		
Dr G. Thornton lbw b Hearne	23	– b Wright	3
J. Phillips c Weigall b Mason	23	– c Hearne b Wright	0
Mr H. R. Bromley-Davenport b Martin	1		
J. T. Hearne not out	15		
B 8, l-b 2, n-b 1	11	B 2	2
	185		32

Middlesex Bowling

	Overs	Mdns	Runs	Wkts	Overs	Mdns	Runs	Wkts
J. T. Hearne	35.1	16	75	6	45.4	9	105	5
Rawlin	32	3	101	4	10	3	31	0
Phillips	8	0	33	0	36	10	86	5
Thornton	3	0	21	0	1	0	4	0
Stoddart	5	0	19	0		1	15	0
Davenport	3	0	4	0	10	4	27	0

Kent Bowling

	Overs	Mdns	Runs	Wkts	Overs	Mdns	Runs	Wkts
Wright	36	13	72	4	6	1	23	3
Martin	33	9	80	4	6	4	7	0
A. Hearne	12	2	23	1				
Mason	0.4	0	0	1				

Umpires: J. Street and W. Hearn.

KENT v GLOUCESTERSHIRE

Played at Maidstone, May 27, 28, 1897

Neither side was at all well represented but the Gloucestershire men showed by far the better form at all points, their victory by nine wickets, being achieved in a most creditable and decisive fashion. Kent had first innings, but made so little use of their opportunity that they were dismissed for 127, and from this bad start they could never recover. Gloucestershire headed their opponents by 99 runs and afterwards always had the match well in hand. When the wicket was by no means easy, J. R. Mason played a really superb innings for Kent, but his efforts came much too late. The honours of Gloucestershire's success rested mainly with W. G. Grace and Roberts. The veteran champion played finely in both innings, scoring 87 runs for once out, and Roberts was peculiarly suited by the slope on the Maidstone ground.

Kent

Alec Hearne c Goodwin b Roberts	4	– c Grace b Townsend	10
Mr J. R. Mason b Grace	27	– c De Winton b Roberts	70
Mr H. H. Harrington c Grace b Roberts	4	– b Roberts	5
Mr H. C. Stewart c Painter b Roberts	0	– c Hale b Townsend	18
Mr G. J. V. Weigall b Roberts	3	– c Townsend b Roberts	17
F. Martin c Wrathall b Roberts	11	– b Roberts	10
Mr F. Marchant st Board b Townsend	33	– b Roberts	0
J. Easby c Goodwin b Roberts	1	– c Board b Roberts	37
W. Wright c Hale b Roberts	20	– not out	17
F. H. Huish not out	9	– c Wrathall b Roberts	5
F. Hunt c De Winton b Roberts	4	– b Townsend	5
B 6, l-b 5	11	B 6, l-b 3	9
	127		203

Gloucestershire

Mr W. G. Grace c Mason b Martin	31	– not out	55
Mr A. G. Richardson c Huish b Mason	40	– c Hearne b Hunt	17
H. Wrathall c Mason b Hunt	29		
Mr C. L. Townsend st Huish b Mason	9		
Mr H. S. Goodwin c Harington b Martin	27		
J. H. Board lbw b Mason	30		
Mr S. de Winton c Huish b Hunt	8		
J. Painter b Martin	24	– not out	21
W. H. Hale st Huish b Martin	21		
H. W. Murch c Huish b Martin	4		
F. G. Roberts not out	1		
B 11, l-b 1	12	B 1	1
	236		95

Gloucestershire Bowling

	Overs	Mdns	Runs	Wkts	Overs	Mdns	Runs	Wkts
Townsend	16	3	56	1	26	5	85	3
Roberts	27.3	13	40	8	30.2	11	83	7
Grace	12	5	20	1	4	0	12	0
Murch					2	0	9	0
Hale					2	1	5	0

Kent Bowling

	Overs	Mdns	Runs	Wkts	Overs	Mdns	Runs	Wkts
Wright	26	5	72	0	8.2	3	25	0
Martin	38.4	16	90	5	5	1	10	0
Hunt	20	5	36	2	10	3	13	1
Mason	15	7	26	3	16	6	40	0
Hearne					3	1	6	0

Umpires: R. Thoms and G. Hay.

KENT v LANCASHIRE

Played at Canterbury, August 2, 3, 4, 1897

The first match of the Canterbury week, though it attracted large crowds of spectators, undoubtedly suffered in interest from the fact of being so one-sided. At every point of the game the Kent men were over matched, their cricket being only redeemed from failure by the beautifully finished batting of Mason. Lancashire, who played a winning game to perfection, proved successful by an innings and 19 runs, the game coming to an end early on the third day. Beyond everything else, the match will be remembered for the magnificent batting of A. C. MacLaren, who, out of Lancashire's total of 399, scored no fewer than 244. The conditions were all in his favour, but it would be difficult to imagine a better display of skilful and high class cricket. He was batting just over five hours, and hit no fewer than 38 fours. The great feature of his play was the manner in which he, time after time, pulled short-pitched balls to the boundary. Briggs bowled with remarkable success, finding a broken spot to pitch on, and taking in the whole game, thirteen wickets for 135 runs.

Lancashire

Mr A. C. MacLaren c Bradley b Martin	244
Albert Ward c Mason b Bradley	49
F. H. Sugg c Wright b Martin	1
G. R. Baker c Huish b Martin	2
J. T. Tyldesley b Wright	22
C. Smith c Mordaunt b Wright	0
J. Briggs c Hearne b Shine	36
W. R. Cuttell c Hearne b Mason	3
A. Hallam c Shine b Mason	4
Mr A. N. Hornby not out	19
A. Mold b Bradley	7
B 4, l-b 6, w 2	12
	399

Kent

Mr J. R. Mason c Smith b Hallam	51	– c Smith b Cuttell	86
Alec Hearne c and b Briggs	51	– b Briggs	14
Mr F. Marchant c Smith b Briggs	1	– c Smith b Buttell	10
Mr R. O'H. Livesay b Hallam	2	– c Cuttell b Briggs	4
F. Martin c and b Briggs	32	– c Mold b Briggs	7
Mr G. J. Mordaunt lbw b Briggs	37	– st Smith b Briggs	14
Mr H. C. Stewart c Smith b Mold	0	– c Hornby b Cuttell	9
W. Wright b Briggs	13	– not out	6
Mr E. B. Shine c Mold b Briggs	3	– c Hornby b Briggs	7
F. H. Huish b Mold	0	– c and b Briggs	12
Mr W. M. Bradley not out	0	– b Briggs	0
B 9	9	B 11, l-b 1	12
	199		181

Kent Bowling

	Overs	Mdns	Runs	Wkts
Wright	22	4	70	2
Shine	18	3	55	1
Hearne	33	7	72	0
Bradley	34.3	9	111	2
Martin	17	5	39	3
Mason	10	2	40	2

Lancashire Bowling

	Overs	Mdns	Runs	Wkts	Overs	Mdns	Runs	Wkts
Mold	24.4	6	65	2	2	0	5	0
Cuttell	22	9	41	0	25	9	49	3
Briggs	32	13	55	6	43	14	80	7
Hallam	30	21	29	2	14	3	35	0

Umpires: J. Lillywhite and W. A. Woof.

KENT v SURREY

Played at Beckenham, August 16, 17, 1897

As had proved the case on several previous occasions, the wicket at Beckenham did not wear at all well and despite the number of good batsmen in the match, the highest total in the four innings was 213. The presence of Richardson on the side gave an immense advantage to the Surrey men, who had the best of the game throughout and won in handsome and decisive fashion by 156 runs. Richardson took full advantage of the opportunity afforded him, obtaining in the whole match fourteen wickets for 102 runs. Even allowing that the conditions were in his favour, this was an exceptionally fine performance. Brockwell had the distinction of making the highest individual score in the match and Key, Abel, Lees and Baldwin also did well. In Kent's second innings, Marchant and Martin made runs in good style under obvious difficulties.

Surrey

R. Abel st Huish b Martin	38	– b Shine	20
W. Brockwell c Day b Bradley	1	– c Wright b Bradley	50
T. Hayward b Shine	30	– c and b Shine	2
C. Baldwin c Mason b Bradley	27	– c Martin b Bradley	23
Mr H. B. Chinnery b Martin	3	– c Mason b Shine	0
Mr D. L. A. Jephson lbw b Martin	2	– b Bradley	2
Mr H. D. G. Leveson-Gower c Huish b Bradley	9	– b Shine	16
Mr K. J. Key c Mason b Bradley	21	– b Shine	40
W. Lees c Shine b Martin	27	– b Mason	23
H. Wood b Bradley	4	– c Stewart b Mason	14
T. Richardson not out	0	– not out	14
B 9	9	B 2, l-b 5, n-b 2	9
	171		213

Kent

Mr J. R. Mason b Richardson	27	– b Richardson	12
Hon. J. R. Tufton c Baldwin b Richardson	14	– b Hayward	18
Mr S. H. Day b Richardson	0	– absent	0
Mr H. C. Stewart b Richardson	9	– b Richardson	3
Mr G. J. Mordaunt b Richardson	4	– c Brockwell b Richardson	2
F. Martin not out	26	– c Brockwell b Hayward	27
W. Wright b Hayward	4	– b Hayward	0
Mr F. Marchant b Richardson	8	– c Wood b Richardson	31
Mr W. M. Bradley c Wood b Hayward	4	– b Richardson	0
Mr E. B. Shine c Jephson b Richardson	4	– c Baldwin b Richardson	15
F. H. Huish b Richardson	3	– not out	2
B 7, l-b 5, n-b 1	13	N-b 2	2
	116		112

Kent Bowling

	Overs	Mdns	Runs	Wkts	Overs	Mdns	Runs	Wkts
Wright	5	2	7	0				
Bradley	18.1	5	67	5	22	5	73	3
Shine	17	6	41	1	25.2	8	55	5
Mason	3	0	12	0	15	7	37	2
Martin	17	5	35	4	14	4	39	0

Surrey Bowling

	Overs	Mdns	Runs	Wkts	Overs	Mdns	Runs	Wkts
Richardson	27.3	11	49	8	16	5	53	6
Hayward	15	2	38	2	15.4	3	57	3
Lees	11	7	16	0				

Umpires: L. Hall and R. Clayton.

KENT v YORKSHIRE

Played at Tonbridge, August 21, 22, 23, 1899

Next to the victory over the Australians at Canterbury, this match was the great triumph of the Kent season. The Yorkshiremen were in first-rate form and had a great chance of carrying off the championship, but Kent, securing a big advantage on the opening day, beat them in brilliant fashion by eight wickets. Burnup was the hero of the match. His magnificent 171 – free from fault of any kind – was the innings of his life, and at the finish he won the game by scoring 65 not out in an hour and three quarters. Yorkshire practically lost the match on the first day by getting out on a hard wicket for 164. In their second innings Wainwright and Lord Hawke made a great effort, putting on 138 runs together for the eighth wicket.

Yorkshire

Mr F. S. Jackson b Mason	1	– c Huish b Hearne	33
J. Tunnicliffe c Hearne b Mason	0	– c Hearne b Bradley	5
D. Denton c Huish b Mason	0	– c Huish b Bradley	2
Mr F. Mitchell b Blythe	55	– b Hearne	15
E. Wainwright c Weigall b Bradley	19	– c Stewart b Mason	100
G. H. Hirst c Burnup b Bradley	60	– lbw b Hearne	15
Mr E. Smith c Mason b Bradley	4	– c Stewart b Hearne	21
S. Haigh not out	15	– c Huish b Bradley	18
Lord Hawke b Bradley	0	– b Hearne	81
W. Rhodes b Bradley	0	– not out	10
D. Hunter b Bradley	8	– b Blythe	5
L-b 1, n-b 1	2	B 11, l-b 8, n-b 1	20
	164		325

Kent

Mr C. J. Burnup c and b Smith	171	– not out	65
A. Hearne b Smith	9	– b Hirst	22
Mr S. H. Day c Hunter b Smith	12	– st Hunter b Rhodes	15
Mr T. N. Perkins c Hunter b Smith	47	– not out	17
Mr J. R. Mason b Smith	7		
Rev. W. Rashleigh run out	44		
Mr H. C. Stewart b Rhodes	21		
Mr. G. J. V. Weigall c Wainwright b Smith	22		
F. H. Huish b Rhodes	7		
Mr W. M. Bradley not out	9		
Blythe c Tunnicliffe b Rhodes	0		
B 9, l-b 8, w 2, n-b 1	20	B 5	5
	369		124

Kent Bowling

	Overs	Mdns	Runs	Wkts	Overs	Mdns	Runs	Wkts
Bradley	24.1	6	84	6	40	10	125	3
Mason	22	11	34	3	27	9	49	1
Hearne	11	4	19	0	34	8	66	5
Blythe	4	0	25	1	14.1	2	41	1
Burnup	1	1	0	0	9	2	24	0

Yorkshire Bowling

	Overs	Mdns	Runs	Wkts	Overs	Mdns	Runs	Wkts
Rhodes	46.4	19	90	3	15	4	27	1
Smith	50	11	120	6	17.2	4	52	0
Hirst	17	4	35	0	13	8	23	1
Wainwright	10	3	27	0	6	3	17	0
Jackson	14	3	46	0				
Haigh	11	1	31	0				

Umpires: V. A. Titchmarsh and W. A. Woof.

LANCASHIRE

LANCASHIRE IN 1876

(*The County of Lancaster Cricket Club was formed in 1864.*)

President – The Earl of Sefton

Vice-Presidents – Earl Derby, Earl Ellesmere, Lord Skelmersdale, C. Turner Esq. MP and the Right Hon. R. A. Cross MP

Fifteen Gentlemen of Lancashire form the Committee.

Hon. Sec. – S. H. Swire Esq. *Treasurer* – E. Challender Esq.

Assistant Sec. and Collector – F. Reynolds, Manchester Cricket Ground, Stretford, Manchester

The Lancashire Season of 1876 consisted of out and home matches with Nottinghamshire, Derbyshire, Kent, Yorkshire and Sussex. They won five and lost five, some of the matches being very closely contested, notably the match against the Yorkshiremen at Sheffield, which "The Blades" won by 18 runs; the match at Brighton, which the Lancashire men won by 12 runs; and the return match at Old Trafford, which the Nottinghamshire men won by one wicket. The Yorkshiremen twice defeated Lancashire, and Lancashire twice defeated Derbyshire. Both Sussex matches were keenly contested, ending in trick and tie; and if Kent easily defeated Lancashire at Gravesend, Lancashire as easily defeated Kent at Old Trafford, so there was victorious "blow for blow" given in those two contests. As to the matches with Nottinghamshire, the Lancashire men winning the first by six wickets, and so nearly winning the return, went far in confirming opinions frequently expressed at the commencement of the season – "That if full strength was played Lancashire could hold their own with any County."

Lancashire bowling in 1876 was mainly entrusted to William McIntyre and Watson, who between them captured 140 of the 174 wickets that fell to the Shire's bowling; McIntyre having 89 (52 caught out), and Watson 51 (31 bowled). Mr Appleby bowled 232 overs (115 maidens) for 297 runs, and twenty wickets (nine bowled).

Lancashire batting in 1876 resulted in Mr Hornby being well ahead of the others in the three important average columns, he and Barlow scoring more runs than any other seven men. Both played up to their well-known form of brilliant hitting and rapid scoring by the one and stolid defence and slow scoring by the other; and perhaps their distinctively peculiar forms were never more aptly illustrated than when in Lancashire's first innings against Nottinghamshire, at Nottingham, the first wicket (Mr Hornby's) fell with the score as follows:

Mr A. N. Hornby c Selby b Oscroft	44
Barlow not out	0
B 1	1
(1 wkt)	45

LANCASHIRE v GLOUCESTERSHIRE

Played at Old Trafford, July 25, 26, 27, 1878

This was the first Lancashire v Gloucestershire match played, and the public interest created in Lancashire by this first visit of the famous West Country team to Old Trafford was so great, that on the third day (a Saturday) it resulted in the largest attendance ever seen at a cricket match on the Old Trafford ground. One who ought to know all about it stated, "Quite 16,000 were present on the Saturday; they were obliged to have four entrances that day, and the people came in such shoals that passing through the turnstiles was difficult; even with the four entrances they could not be admitted fast enough, and it is supposed that quite 2,000 went round, and got over the boards on to the ground without payment". It was estimated that more than 28,000 people witnessed the match. Anyhow the receipts for those three days were:

On Thursday,	On Friday,	On Saturday,
£88 7s. 0d.	£269 5s. 0d.	£400 5s. 0d.

On the first day the weather was dull, heavy, and threatening, and the wickets dead through heavy rain that had fallen during the night. At 12.30 Mr Hornby and Barlow started the Lancashire batting to the bowling of Mr W. Grace and Mr Miles. With the score at 5 Mr Hornby was had at wicket; and at 13 the two Steels were out. When 18 runs had been made a thunderstorm stayed play for two hours. On resuming Barlow and Mr Royle increased the score to 36, when Mr Royle was out for 19. The others did but little, and – after another stoppage to the play through rain – "time" was up with nine Lancashire wickets down, 88 runs scored, and Barlow (first man in), not out 40.

On the second day the weather was splendid and the attendance great. Play was resumed at 12.10. Mr Miles bowled a wide, and then Barlow was had at mid-off, and so the innings finished for 89 runs, made from 82 overs, Barlow first man in and last out. At 12.45 the Gloucestershire batting was commenced by Mr W. Grace and Mr Gilbert, to the bowling of Mr Appleby and Mr A. G. Steel. When only 2 runs had been made Mr Gilbert was had at slip. Mr W. Grace and Midwinter then hit the score to 42, when Midwinter had to leave for 22. At 60 a good catch at slip settled Mr W. Grace for 32; and at 80 Dr Grace was stumped for 21. The others made so ineffective a stand to the bowling of Mr A. G. Steel and McIntyre, that before half-past four they were all out for 116, or 27 on, those 116 runs having been made from 84 overs (less one ball). At five o'clock Mr Hornby and Barlow commenced Lancashire's second innings, but notwithstanding Mr W. Grace, Mr Miles, Mr Haynes, Mr Wright, Midwinter, Mr Gilbert and Dr Grace bowled, no wicket fell, and when play ceased that evening the score stood in this shape:

Mr A. N. Hornby not out	68
Barlow not out	15
Extras	7
(no wkt)	90

On the third day the weather was favourable and the attendance enormously large, so much so that at times the people so inconveniently crowded on the fielding ground as to stop the play. At twelve prompt, the not outs resumed their innings; they quickly made the score 100 (no wicket down); but at 108 Barlow was caught and bowled for 26; but the score was up to 156 when Mr Hornby was out from a catch at mid-off for 100. Just fancy, one man making 100 out of 156! Mr Royle left for 19 before another run was made. At 162 Mr A. G. Steel was out, and at 195 his brother "Mr D. Q." was done for by the Doctor, who also bowled Mr Appleby at 215. Mr Rowley was bowled at 224; and at 251 Mr Wright bowled Mr Patterson for 50 – a carefully played innings that was early stopped to admit of a discussion respecting a disputed boundary hit, which dispute is explained by one present as follows:

"Mr Patterson drove a ball to the boundary; the umpire not seeing if it went there, did not call 'four', but some of the spectators did, so the batters stopped running, and before he got home Mr Patterson's wicket was put down, the umpire giving him (run) out. An objection was raised, the game stopped, and two captains held a long consultation, but the matter was not settled until Dr Grace went to where the ball was hit to, and questioned those who saw it, when they all satisfactorily stated that the ball passed beyond the bounds, so Mr Patterson resumed his innings." The Lancashire innings was over at ten past four for 262 runs. At a quarter to five Mr G. F. Grace and Mr Wright commenced Gloucestershire's second innings; when the score was at 7 only, Mr Wright played on, at 14 Mr G. F. Grace was stumped, at 43 Midwinter was out, at 52 Dr Grace was bowled. and at 56 Mr Haynes was bowled, but from then Mr W. G. Grace and Mr Gilbert played up to time, when the match was drawn, the score at 125, Mr W. Grace not out 58, Mr Gilbert not out 10, Gloucestershire having five wickets to fall, and wanting 111 runs to win.

Lancashire

A. N. Hornby Esq. c J. A. Bush b W. Grace	5	– c Cranston b W. Grace	100
R. G. Barlow c W. Grace b Miles	40	– c and b Gilbert	26
A. G. Steel Esq. c Gilbert b Miles	0	– c W. Grace b Gilbert	6
D. Q. Steel Esq. c W. Grace b Miles	0	– b E. M. Grace	22
V. K. Royle Esq. c Cranston b Miles	19	– c J. A. Bush b Gilbert	19
W. S. Patterson Esq. c Gilbert b Miles	0	– b Wright	50
A. Appleby Esq. c Gilbert b Miles	1	– b E. M. Grace	7
E. B. Rowley Esq. b W. Grace	8	– b F. Grace	0
A. Watson c E. M. Grace b Miles	3	– not out	10
William McIntyre b W. Grace	6	– b E. M. Grace	8
R. Pilling not out	0	– c J. A. Bush b E. M. Grace	0
B 1, w 6	7	B 5, l-b 3, w 6	14
	89		262

Gloucestershire

W. G. Grace Esq. c Watson b W. McIntyre	32	– not out	58
W. Gilbert Esq. c Watson b A. G. Steel	1	– not out	10
W. Midwinter lbw b A. G. Steel	22	– c Pilling b A. G. Steel	25
Dr E. M. Grace st Pilling b A. G. Steel	21	– b Appleby	4
G. F. Grace Esq. c Watson b W. McIntyre	7	– st Pilling b A. G. Steel	6
J. Cranston Esq. b W. McIntyre	3		
C. E. Haynes Esq. run out	7	– b A. G. Steel	12
E. F. Wright Esq. st Pilling b A. G. Steel	4	– b A. G. Steel	5
J. A. Bush Esq. not out	15		
A. Robinson Esq. c Watson b W. McIntyre	0		
R. F. Miles Esq. c Appleby b A. G. Steel	3		
B 1	1	B 4, l-b 1	5
	116		125

Gloucestershire Bowling

	Overs	Mdns	Runs	Wkts	Overs	Mdns	Runs	Wkts
Mr W. Grace	41	19	44	3	27	6	65	1
Mr Miles	40.2	22	38	7	23	16	16	—
Mr Gilbert					26	5	63	3
Dr E. M. Grace					23	15	19	4
Mr F. Grace					15	—	32	1
Mr Wright					13	—	26	1
Midwinter					6	4	10	—
Mr Haynes					5	1	17	—

Lancashire Bowling

	Overs	Mdns	Runs	Wkts	Overs	Mdns	Runs	Wkts
Mr A. G. Steel	41.3	14	59	5	21	5	55	4
W. McIntyre	30	16	44	4	14	2	40	—
Mr Appleby	12	5	12	—	14	8	13	1
Watson					7	3	12	—

Umpires: Storer and C. K. Pullin.

LANCASHIRE v YORKSHIRE

Played at Old Trafford, August 5, 6, 7, 1880

Mr Hornby and Barlow commenced the first innings of Lancashire, in the style usual to them. When the luncheon interval arrived, Mr Hornby had made 28 and Barlow 1, and when the famous amateur was out at 45, 42 were credited to him. In the slashing innings of 44 by Emmett, there were five 4s. When Lockwood's capital innings of 41 was concluded, wickets fell with amazing rapidity, Nash taking six wickets for 32 runs; but this feat was completely eclipsed by the later performance of Peate, who, in the second innings of Lancashire, bowled 31 overs (20 maidens) for 24 runs and eight wickets. Rain interfered so seriously with the game on the third day that, like the previous one between these two counties, the match had to be abandoned, and thus an almost certain victory was snatched from Yorkshire.

Lancashire

A. N. Hornby Esq. lbw b Bosomworth	42	st Pinder b Peate	4
R. G. Barlow c Bates b Ulyett	14	not out	10
V. K. Royle Esq. c Lockwood b Peate	11	c Grimshaw b Peate	0
W. Robinson c Hudson b Bosomworth	7	b Bates	0
O. P. Lancashire Esq. c Peate b Ulyett	18	b Peate	0
J. E. Kershaw Esq. lbw b Peate	15	b Peate	5
R. Pilling b Peate	6	c Grimshaw b Bates	3
R. Briggs st Pinder b Peate	5	b Peate	4
S. Palmer Esq. c Hudson b Peate	4	c Bates b Peate	3
A. Watson not out	4	lbw b Peate	0
G. Nash b Peate	4	c Emmett b Peate	6
L-b 1, n-b 1	2	B 4	4
	132		47

Yorkshire

G. Ulyett c Hornby b Watson	16	not out	1
T. Emmett c Pilling b Nash	44	not out	3
E. Lockwood c Lancashire b Nash	41		
L. Hall b Barlow	5		
W. Bates c Briggs b Nash	7		
M. Burrows c and b Nash	1		
I. Grimshaw c Pilling b Nash	0		
B. Hudson b Barlow	1		
W. E. Bosomworth b Barlow	0		
G. Pinder c Pilling b Nash	2		
E. Peate not out	3		
B 4, l-b 1	5		
	125		4

Yorkshire Bowling

	Overs	Mdns	Runs	Wkts	Overs	Mdns	Runs	Wkts
Bates	20	6	36	—	37	27	19	2
Peate	36.1	15	56	6	38	20	24	8
Bosomworth	14	7	15	2				
Ulyett	15	4	23	2				

Lancashire Bowling

	Overs	Mdns	Runs	Wkts	Overs	Mdns	Runs	Wkts
Watson	32	16	40	1	7	4	3	—
Nash	42.3	26	32	6	7	6	1	—
Briggs	6	2	9	—				
Mr Hornby	2	2	—	—				
Barlow	19	10	39	3				

Umpires: Smith and Martin.

LANCASHIRE v CAMBRIDGE UNIVERSITY

Played at Liverpool, June 13, 14, 1881

This match will be memorable for several reasons. It was the opening match of the splendid new ground of the Liverpool Club at Aigburth. It was the match in which the Lancashire eleven suffered their one defeat in 1881; the only match in 1881 in which they had to follow their innings; and the match in which the lowest number were totalled for an innings by the county team in 1881. And it will be memorable as the match in which Mr G. B. Studd, on a soft and somewhat treacherous wicket, scored his highest and most meritorious innings in a first-class contest in 1881.

In considering the result of this match, the fact must not be overlooked that in Mr Steel the Lancastrians were not only deprived of the services of one of the most brilliant batsmen and finest bowlers in the county team, but that that distinguished cricketer's efforts were directed against them, and it is not too much to say that the University eleven were as much indebted for their victory to Mr Steel's bowling as to Mr G. B. Studd's batting. In the first innings of Lancashire the success of Mr Steel's bowling was simply marvellous.

Mr G. B. Studd was at the wickets three hours and ten minutes for his magnificent innings of 106 not out, and his principal hits were fourteen 4s, nine 3s and five 2s.

In the first innings of Lancashire, shortly after Mr Hornby was out, Mr Napier, who is a very fast bowler, had the misfortune to strain the muscles of his right arm, an accident which necessitated his retirement from the contest.

The match ended at 5.25 on the second day, in a victory for the University by seven wickets.

Cambridge University

G. B. Studd not out	106		
J. E. K. Studd Esq. b Watson	1	– c and b Watson	0
C. T. Studd Esq. b Barlow	18	– c Pilling b Watson	16
A. G. Steel Esq. c Pilling b Watson	11	– not out	9
H. Whitfeld Esq. b Watson	1	– st Pilling b Watson	9
O. P. Lancashire Esq. run out	4		
F. C. C. Rowe Esq. c and b Barlow	19		
R. Spencer Esq. b Miller	1		
C. P. Wilson Esq. b Wood	2	– not out	0
J. R. Napier Esq. c Briggs b Wood	10		
N. Hone Esq. lbw b Watson	1		
B 12, l-b 1	13	B 4	4
	187		38

Lancashire

A. N. Hornby Esq. c Hone b Napier	7 – c G. B. Studd b Steel	33
R. G. Barlow st Hone b Steel	11 – c Spencer b Steel	20
F. Taylor Esq. c Hone b Steel	10 – b C. T. Studd	5
W. Robinson c sub b Steel	17 – c Spencer b Steel	16
J. Briggs b Steel	11 – c Whitfield b C. T. Studd	8
R. Wood Esq. c and b Steel	0 – run out	9
E. Roper Esq. b Spencer	4 – c Lancashire b Spencer	20
H. Miller Esq. c Steel b Spencer	0 – c sub b Wilson	19
R. Pilling c and b Spencer	2 – c Wilson b Steel	8
A. Watson not out	1 – not out	3
G. Nash c Rowe b Steel	6 – c C. T. Studd b Steel	3
L-b 1, w 1	2 B 9	9
	71	153

Lancashire Bowling

	Overs	Mdns	Runs	Wkts	Overs	Mdns	Runs	Wkts
Watson	44.3	25	56	4	22	14	20	3
Nash	10	1	27	—				
Barlow	42	23	60	2	21.1	15	14	—
Mr Miller	18	10	22	—				
Mr Wood	10	5	9	2				

Cambridge Bowling

	Overs	Mdns	Runs	Wkts	Overs	Mdns	Runs	Wkts
Mr Steel	23.1	14	22	6	52.3	23	69	5
Mr Napier	6	4	20	1				
Mr Spencer	17	5	27	3	3	2	8	1
Mr C. T. Studd					46	20	62	2
Mr Wilson					3	1	5	1

LANCASHIRE IN 1882

President – Sir Humphrey de Trafford, Bart.

Vice-Presidents – The Earl of Derby, The Earl of Ellesmere, The Earl of Lathom, The Earl of Sefton, Sir R. A. Cross, R. N. Phillips Esq. MP, J. A. Bannerman Esq., J. Makinson Esq. and A. B. Rowley Esq.

Captain – A. N. Hornby Esq. *Treasurer* – James MacLaren Esq.

Hon. Sec. – S. H. Swire Esq.

Assistant Secretary and Collector – Mr F. Reynolds, Stretford, Lancashire

Thirteen Gentlemen of the County formed the Committee

Which was the Champion County in 1882? Lancashire or Nottinghamshire? That was a subject much debated at the conclusion of the cricket season. In County v County matches each Shire had lost but one game, and elaborate statistics were published to prove the post of honour belonged to Lancashire. But the claimants for Nottinghamshire had one very strong argument in their favour, and that was that Nottinghamshire had defeated Lancashire, but Lancashire had not defeated Nottinghamshire.

Leaving the sympathisers with each County to enjoy their own opinions on the subject, the compiler adopts the method always practised in *Wisden's* of including all matches played by the County eleven, and the result sets the vexed question at rest so far as the entire programme of the respective Counties is concerned. Lancashire lost four matches and Nottinghamshire only two, and the laurels of the year were therefore won by the latter County.

But the season was nevertheless a splendidly successful one for Lancashire, as of the four defeats the County suffered only one could be termed decisive – that by the MCC by eight wickets. The match v the Australians was lost by four wickets, the one v Nottinghamshire by 37 runs, and that v Cambridge University by only 14 runs; while on the other hand four of the twelve victories were won by a single innings, one by ten wickets, one by 204 runs, two by nine wickets, one by eight wickets, and one by seven wickets; and of the four drawn matches one was altogether in favour of Lancashire, while in the case of the other three, there was no certainty of defeat for the County Palatine had the games been played out.

The great strength of Lancashire lay in the bowling, and a glance at the bowling analysis will show that Barlow, Crossland, Nash, Watson and Mr Steel between them did nearly all the ball work, and that the first four met with wonderful success. No County eleven possessed a couple of bowlers who did so much work at so little cost as Barlow and Crossland, or whose proportion of wickets bowled down was so large. Barlow took more than twice as many wickets as in the previous year, and at almost exactly the same cost. Crossland captured more than seven times as many in '82 as in '81, and considering the number of wickets he obtained, his bowling must be considered as successful as that of Barlow's. Nash took ten more wickets than in the previous year, and at precisely the same cost. The largest share of the trundling fell to Watson, but he failed to obtain so many wickets as in '81, and his bowling was a trifle more expensive. Mr Steel, whose analysis in the previous year was a very fine one, fell off considerably, and his thirty-four wickets cost 16.14 in place of 11.2.

The widespread opinion that Crossland's delivery is not above the suspicion of being unfair culminated in a most unseemly exhibition of feeling in the Surrey v Lancashire match at The Oval. Certainly no first-class county bowler of the present day has so frequently been charged with throwing, but his great success may have had much to do with increasing the hostile criticism he has met with from the supporters of his opponents' cricket, and it seems impossible that so thorough a cricketer as Mr Hornby would countenance a style of bowling which he was not convinced was fair. Many independent critics, however, condemn Crossland's style, and take occasion to point out that the present unsatisfactory manner in which umpires are appointed is the real cause of the continuance of questionable bowling. May the coming season see these matters righted.

LANCASHIRE v LEICESTERSHIRE

Played at Manchester, June 12, 13, 1884

Lancashire won this match by an innings with 43 runs to spare. They had the advantage of going in first, but their start was not promising, as only 35 runs had been scored when the fourth wicket fell. Barlow and Mr Lancashire added 32, but seven wickets were down for 87. Watson then joined Mr Hornby, and the bowling was mastered, no fewer than 80 runs being put on before the Lancashire captain was caught at long-off. Mr Hornby ought to have been caught when he had made 27, but Watson made no mistake, and was the last man out. On Leicestershire going in Crossland performed the remarkable feat of taking seven wickets for 14 runs. The fifth, sixth and seventh wickets all fell at 28, and the whole side were out for 33 after fifty minutes'play. In following on the visitors lost three wickets for 37, and when stumps were drawn for the day had scored 65 for four. On the Friday the remaining batsmen were dismissed for an addition of 66 runs, and Lancashire won as before stated.

Lancashire

R. G. Barlow c Bottomore b Rylott	27
W. Robinson c Parnham b Rylott	9
E. Roper Esq. b Rylott	0
E. Leese Esq. c Wheeler b Rylott	8
J. Briggs b Rylott	9
O. P. Lancashire Esq. c Bottomore b Rylott	20
A. N. Hornby Esq. c Stone b Rylott	65
J. Burns b Bottomore	2
A. Watson c Rylott b Parnham	45
R. Pilling run out	6
J. Crossland not out	7
B 7, l-b 2	9
	207

Leicestershire

J. Wheeler b Crossland	2	c Pilling b Crossland	4
T. Warren b Crossland	10	c Hornby b Watson	3
W. H. Whittle b Crossland	5	run out	2
C. Marriott Esq. c Pilling b Crossland	0	b Crossland	20
C. C. Stone Esq. run out	9	c and b Barlow	17
F. Turner Esq. b Crossland	0	not out	38
C. L. Gardiner Esq. b Crossland	0	c Leese b Watson	3
W. Bottomore b Crossland	0	b Crossland	2
J. Parnham c Barlow b Watson	2	c Leese b Watson	12
E. Smith b Watson	0	b Watson	0
A. Rylott not out	0	b Crossland	10
B 5	5	B 14, l-b 6	20
	33		131

Leicestershire Bowling

	Overs	Mdns	Runs	Wkts
Rylott	54	20	102	7
Parnham	29	10	53	1
Bottomore	9	—	20	—
Smith	16	7	23	—

Lancashire Bowling

	Overs	Mdns	Runs	Wkts	Overs	Mdns	Runs	Wkts
Crossland	13.3	6	14	7	32.1	12	47	4
Watson	13	8	14	2	44	21	50	4
Burns					3	1	6	—
Barlow					10	7	8	1

Umpires: J. Rowbotham and J. Jackson.

LANCASHIRE v OXFORD UNIVERSITY

Played at Manchester, June 16, 17, 1884

For their five wickets' victory in this match the University were mainly indebted to the brilliant batting of Mr T. C. O'Brien, who, with innings of 91, not out, and 57, scored 148 out of 326 from the bat made by the winning side. Lancashire won choice of innings, and going in first lost three wickets for 35 runs. Mr Taylor and Mr Lancashire then made a good stand, and put on 50 runs before the latter was bowled. At luncheon the score was 131 for seven wickets, but on resuming the last three fell for a single run. The only noteworthy feature of the first innings of the University was the batting of Mr O'Brien, who went in first wicket down, with the total at 2, and carried his bat out for 91 out of 145 scored from the bat while he was at the wickets. The brilliancy of his hitting may be judged by his figures – fifteen 4s, one 3, two 2s and twenty-four singles. In their second innings Lancashire scored 42 for the loss of two wickets, and play then ceased for the day.

Barlow not out, 21, and Mr Lancashire, not out, 1, went on with the innings on the Tuesday, and were not parted until the total reached 100, when the professional, who had scored with much greater freedom than usual with him, was out for a good innings of 48. Briggs was bowled at 139, and at 172 the fifth wicket went down, Mr Lancashire being bowled for a remarkably well-played 65, which included nine 4s. The last five wickets fell for 48 runs, but the Oxonians had the by no means easy task set them of scoring 193 to win. Mr Brain was bowled at 17, but an excellent resistance was offered to the Lancashire bowling when Mr O'Brien joined Mr Hine-Haycock, the total being hit up to 91 before a separation was effected. Mr O'Brien was out at 123 for another brilliant display, and before Messrs Kemp and Page were got rid of the success of the University was practically assured.

Lancashire

R. G. Barlow b Bastard	0	– b Buckland	48
W. Robinson c Kemp b Whitby	12	– b Nicholls	20
E. Roper Esq. c Nichols b Page	12	– c Whitby b Nicholls	6
F. Taylor Esq. b Whitby	41	– c Kemp b Bastard	23
O. P. Lancashire Esq. b Whitby	21	– b Bastard	65
J. Briggs c O'Brien b Page	30	– b Nicholls	25
S. Haggas run out	8	– b Whitby	13
F. Ward b Whitby	0	– b Whitby	5
A. Watson c Page b Whitby	0	– c Kemp b Buckland	11
J. Crossland b Page	1	– not out	5
R. Pilling run out	0	– c Bastard b Whitby	0
B 5, l-b 2	7	B 5	5
	132		220

Oxford University

J. H. Brain Esq. b Watson	2	– b Crossland	8
T. H. Hine-Haycock Esq. b Crossland	0	– c Pilling b Briggs	31
T. C. O'Brien Esq. not out	91	– c Robinson b Watson	57
H. V. Page Esq. b Crossland	1	– b Crossland	24
M. C. Kemp Esq. b Watson	3	– c Robinson b Ward	35
A. R. Cobb Esq. b Crossland	17	– not out	15
K J. Key Esq. c and b Crossland	16	– not out	6
E. H. Buckland Esq. b Crossland	10		
B. E. Nicholls Esq. b Watson	0		
H. O. Whitby Esq. st Pilling b Watson	7		
E. W. Bastard Esq. b Crossland	0		
B 9, l-b 4	13	B 13, l-b 3	16
	160		195

Oxford Bowling

	Overs	Mdns	Runs	Wkts	Overs	Mdns	Runs	Wkts
Mr Bastard	12	3	34	1	25	8	44	2
Mr Whitby	22	7	40	5	27	7	72	3
Mr Page	21.3	12	32	3	17	5	40	—
Mr Nicholls	7	2	18	—	11	3	20	3
Mr Buckland	4	3	1	—	17	6	39	2

Lancashire Bowling

	Overs	Mdns	Runs	Wkts	Overs	Mdns	Runs	Wkts
Watson	27	12	47	4	29.2	11	58	1
Crossland	31.2	9	81	6	33	11	54	2
Barlow	13	7	19	—	18	8	30	—
Briggs					9	4	18	1
Ward					4	—	19	1

Umpires: V. A. Titchmarsh and J. Ricketts.

LANCASHIRE v GLOUCESTERSHIRE

Played at Manchester, July 24, 25, 1884

Owing to rain only three quarters of an hour's play took place before luncheon, and during that time Gloucestershire, who went in first, lost three wickets for 25 runs. On resuming two more went down by the time the total reached 34. Dr W. G. Grace, who went in late in consequence of an injury to one of his fingers, then came to the rescue of his side, and by seven 4s, one 3, four 2s and singles scored 53 out of 80 runs made while he was in. The Gloucestershire captain narrowly escaped being caught when he had scored 20, but that was the only fault in his innings. On Lancashire going in Barlow was bowled without scoring, but Mr Hornby and Mr Taylor made a capital stand for the second wicket. By dashing, if not faultless cricket, Mr Hornby made 46 out of the first 57 runs, and when he was dismissed Mr Taylor and Briggs carried the score to 79. At this total three wickets fell, and when time was called six wickets were down for 104 runs.

Three-quarters of an hour's play sufficed to finish off the Lancashire innings on the Friday, and Gloucestershire went in for the second time 22 runs to the bad. They had twelve minutes' batting before luncheon, and upon resuming Dr E. M. Grace was splendidly caught at mid-off, and his brother had just succeeded him when a telegram was received announcing the death of Mrs Grace, the mother of Drs E. M. and W. G. Grace. A short consultation was held, and it was decided to at once abandon the match.

Gloucestershire

Dr E. M. Grace lbw b Watson	12	c Whittaker b Barlow	14
W. R. Gilbert Esq. b Barlow	2	not out	8
E. J. Painter b Watson	8		
F. Townsend Esq. b Watson	3		
W. W. F. Pullen Esq. c Pilling b Barlow	5		
Dr W. G. Grace b Barlow	53	not out	1
J. H. Brain Esq. b Watson	12		
H. V. Page Esq. b Barlow	7		
E. J. Taylor Esq. c Watson b Barlow	0		
H. J. Boughton Esq. run out	5		
W. A. Woof not out	1		
B 8, l-b 3	11	B 2	2
	119		25

Lancashire

R. G. Barlow c E. M. Grace b W. G. Grace	0
A. N. Hornby Esq. c Painter b Page	46
F. Taylor Esq. c W. G. Grace b Woof	16
J. Briggs b Page	13
O. P. Lancashire Esq. b Page	0
W. Robinson c Brain b W. G. Grace	9
W. Wood Esq. lbw b Woof	22
D. Whittaker c and b Gilbert	13
A. Watson c W. G. Grace b Woof	11
R. Pilling not out	0
J. Crossland c Pullen b Woof	0
B 6, l-b 5, w 1	12
	142

Lancashire Bowling

	Overs	Mdns	Runs	Wkts	Overs	Mdns	Runs	Wkts
Barlow	37	19	49	5	10	4	16	1
Watson	34	17	39	4	9	6	7	—
Crossland	6	3	10	—				
Briggs	9	6	10	—				

Gloucestershire Bowling

	Overs	Mdns	Runs	Wkts
Dr W. G. Grace	26	10	54	2
Woof	26.3	12	48	4
Mr Page	20	10	25	3
Painter	2	—	3	—
Mr Gilbert	4	4	—	1

Umpires: W. Rigley and H. Holmes.

LANCASHIRE IN 1885

President – Sir Humphrey de Trafford, Bart.

Vice-Presidents – The Earl of Derby, The Earl of Ellesmere, The Earl of Lathom, The Earl of Sefton, Sir R. A. Cross, R. N. Phillips Esq., MP J. A. Bannerman Esq., J. Makinson Esq. and A. B. Rowley Esq.

Captain – A. N. Hornby Esq. *Treasurer* – James McLaren Esq.

Hon. Secretary – S. H. Swire Esq.

Assistant Secretary and Collector – Mr F. Reynolds, Stretford, Lancashire

Sixteen Gentlemen of the County formed the Committee

The following correspondence, extracted from the sporting papers, tells the history of a lamentable dispute which occurred during the Lancashire season of 1885, and which formed a sequel to the unfortunate difference between Nottinghamshire and Lancashire which resulted in the abandonment, for two seasons, of the matches usually played between those counties:

Huntingfield, Faversham,
June 1, 1885.

"Gentlemen, – I have the honour to beg your attention on a subject which has engaged the attention of the cricketing public of late years, and which has now, in my humble opinion, arrived owing to the action of your club, at a point requiring incisive treatment.

The subject is that of unfair bowling.

It is unnecessary to remind you that a very strong opinion has gained ground of late years that an unfair style of bowling has become too common, and that measures should be taken to check its increase.

In consequence, at a meeting of county secretaries, held at Lord's on December 11, 1883, it was proposed by Mr I. D. Walker and seconded by Mr C. W. Alcock, 'That the undermentioned counties agree among themselves not to employ any bowler whose action is at all doubtful,' and this was signed by the representatives of Yorkshire, Kent, Middlesex, Derbyshire, Nottinghamshire and Surrey.

Your representatives declined to agree to the resolution, contending, I presume, that the public feeling on the subject was groundless, that there were no unfair bowling actions, and that there was no necessity for any steps being taken in the matter; and with you, in not signing the agreement, were the representatives of Sussex and Gloucestershire.

Early in the following summer, however – and here, for the first time publicly permit me to observe I find it necessary to mention individuals by name, and only now, because otherwise I could not state my case – I found that, of those bowlers whose action had been particularly objectionable, Nash had disappeared from his county eleven; another, Crossland, was still in it, and, in my opinion, bowling as unfairly as in the previous season; but, personally, I was content to rest for the time being with the point I believed I had gained. I hoped that you meant, of your own free will, and without agreement with other counties, to place your eleven in an irreproachable position, and my hopes were justified by finding later on in the season that Crossland was also left out.

It was therefore with the greatest regret that, on arriving at Old Trafford on Thursday last, I found that both Crossland and Nash were to play. I acted as I thought best under the circumstances. I asked for an interview with your committee or its representatives, and I told Mr McLaren and Mr Hornby then, before the match began, that I held myself free to take what action I thought necessary. It was impossible for me to do anything more then. For all that I knew, both bowlers might have changed their deliveries; or again, if they had not, the umpires might 'no-ball' them. In my opinion, and in that of others, after watching them carefully this year, the delivery of neither bowler is consistently fair; the umpires did not 'no-ball' them; and it remains therefore for me – pledged, as I consider myself to be, to do everything in my power to discourage unfair bowling – to take the steps I told your representatives I thought it might be necessary for me to take.

First let me say that I consider your contention unanswerable – i.e., that the umpires, the sole judges, by the laws of cricket, of fair and unfair play, never have objected to the action of either of the bowlers above mentioned. I admit that it is unanswerable; and that being so, and still maintaining my opinion, in which I believe myself to be supported by a very large number of cricketers, that the action of neither bowler is consistently fair, and bearing in mind that your club has declined to pledge itself 'not to employ any bowler whose action is at all doubtful', I conceive, after careful consideration, that there is only one course open for me to adopt, and that is, to advise the committee of the Kent County Cricket Club to decline any further engagement with your club – certainly for this year, and until a more satisfactory state of things obtain.

Our clubs are engaged to play the return match at Tunbridge in August. What I shall suggest to my committee is to allow you, without appearance on the ground, to take the match by our default, or, if you prefer to go by the strict letter of the law and to send your team there, to take care that there be wickets pitched, someone to toss for choice of innings, and, on our declining to go to the wickets, umpires to give you the match. Of course, it is quite possible that my committee may decline to support me. In that case, I promise you no one shall ever hear another word from me on the subject of unfair bowling. I shall consider that I have taken the last step possible, and that I may fairly leave it to some other enthusiast, with more energy, and his cricket career to look forward to rather than back upon, to take up the cudgels.

Before I conclude, let me add a few words of personal interest, certainly to myself, I think to the Kent Eleven, and perhaps to your club.

I told your representatives before the match began, and I was but repeating what I have frequently said, that if there was one county in England against which I should have a disinclination to move, that county would be Lancashire. It is fourteen years since I first played on Old Trafford for Kent v Lancashire, and I think this makes the eleventh consecutive year that I have come up as captain of the Kent eleven. During all that time the relations between the two clubs, so far as I know, have been of the most cordial character. We always rejoiced when Lancashire was champion county. Kentish and Lancashire professionals have always been on the most friendly terms, the same amongst the amateurs; and if Mr Hornby will forgive me for mentioning him last, or indeed at all, entirely divergent as are his opinions and mine, strong as they are on the question of the deliveries of these two bowlers, we have never allowed those opinions to interfere with our personal friendship, and, indeed, I believe each has no better friend on the cricket field, perhaps in a wider sphere than the other; and, lastly, I had the gratification on Thursday last of meeting with such a reception from the enormous company present at Old Trafford as I have never received on any cricket ground, in or out of England, in my life – only surpassed by the still more complimentary manifestation at my summary dismissal.

Appreciating, then, at their highest worth, that cordial reception and these friendly relations, I ask you, gentlemen, and the Lancashire cricket-loving public, to believe that, in acting as I propose to do, I am actuated solely by my anxiety to see the noble game pursued in what I conceive to be the fairest way, by no petty or jealous feelings, and with infinite regret that my action should have to be directed against two professional cricketers and against the Lancashire County Cricket Club.

I remain, gentlemen, faithfully yours,

Harris"

June 8, 1885.

"My Lord, – I beg to acknowledge the receipt of your letter of the 1st inst. My committee instruct me to say that, unless your suggestions are adopted by the Kent executive, they decline to answer your letter in detail. Should however, such executive consent to your proposed course of procedure, my committee are prepared to consider the whole question, and decide in the interests of Lancashire and cricket generally.

I am, my lord, yours truly,

S. H. Swire, Hon. Secretary"

To The Right Hon. Lord Harris.

59, St. George's Street, Canterbury,
June 22, 1885.

"Sir, – I am directed by the managing committee of the Kent County Cricket Club to inform you that, having every confidence in the judgment and impartiality of the gentlemen who have played, and do play for the County Eleven, and having been informed by them that your club is in the habit of employing bowlers whose action is not consistently fair, the committee has decided to decline to play a return match with your club this year. The committee will be glad to know whether you would prefer to claim the match by default without appearance on the ground, oı to adopt the alternative course suggested by Lord Harris in his letter.

I am, Sir, yours faithfully,

Arthur J. Lancaster,
Secretary, *pro tem.*
Kent County Cricket Club."

To S. H. Swire, Esq., Hon. Secretary,
The Lancaster County and Manchester Cricket Club.

Lancashire County Offices,
Barton-arcade, Manchester,
June 29, 1885.

"Dear Sir, – Your letter of the 22nd inst. came duly to hand. My committee can only regret that Lord Harris has been able so far to influence your executive as to induce them to break an engagement made in all honour and good faith, without any reservations whatever as to who should or should not take part in the matches arranged for this season between our respective counties. My committee beg to remind you that since the bowling question was discussed at Lord's in 1883, when the umpires were specially instructed to carry out strictly Rule 18, the bowlers to whom you refer have appeared at Lord's and frequently elsewhere in first-class matches without having their fairness challenged by any of the most competent umpires in the country. It would appear, therefore, that you have no confidence in the body of experienced and carefully-selected men on the list of umpires of the MCC, or even in the MCC committee, but you are determined to set up a standard of your own in regard to what should be considered fair bowling, and to require cricketers throughout the country to conform to it. My committee desire to refer to the amendment our representative proposed to Lord Harris's resolution at the meeting already alluded to – viz., 'That the whole question of unfair bowling be left for decision in the hands of the MCC committee.' My committee leave your executive to bear the responsibility of the action they have adopted. For our part, so long as there is a recognised authority we decline to join any particular counties in the endeavour to override cricket rules, or to make laws for themselves. But any decision of the MCC would unhesitatingly be accepted as final by the Lancashire executive.

My committee have quite as much amount of confidence in Mr Hornby and other members of our clubs as you state you possess in the gentlemen of your county team, so under the circumstances are quite willing to accept your ultimatum as to the return match. In regard to the character of Crossland's bowling, we may remark that he was selected by the MCC committee, and played last year in the match North v South, at Lord's, and that the only reason why he did not play in the Kent and other matches at the close of last season was that he had injured his shoulder at Leicester, and was therefore unfit to bowl.

In these matches Nash was omitted because the hard state of the ground was not suited to his bowling.

A copy of the correspondence has been forwarded to the MCC committee, with a request that they will pursue such a course in regard thereto as they may consider best for the future interests and welfare of cricket.

I am, Sir, yours truly,

S. H. Swire, Hon. Secretary"

To Mr Arthur J. Lancaster,
Secretary, Kent County Cricket Club.

In the same edition of the paper from whence this last letter was taken there appeared the following paragraph:

"Crossland's Qualification for Lancashire. – The Committee of the Marylebone Club has passed the following resolution: 'That it having been established to the satisfaction of the committee that Crossland has resided in his native county, Nottinghamshire, from October, 1884, until April, 1885, this Committee is of opinion that he no longer possesses a residential qualification for Lancashire.' This question came before the MCC Committee on the objection made by the Nottinghamshire Committee to Crossland playing for Lancashire, on the ground that he, being a Nottinghamshire-born man, did not reside in Lancashire regularly and continuously."

Thus, by a side issue, the cricketer whose style of bowling had been the principal cause of the dispute between the two counties, was prevented for a lengthened period from taking part in the county matches of Lancashire; and though the date fixed for the commencement of the return match with Kent was over six weeks subsequent to Crossland's disqualification, the decision to abandon the contest was persisted in.

LANCASHIRE v KENT

Played at Old Trafford, Manchester, May 28, 29, 30, 1885

Lancashire had decidedly the worst of the match when stumps were drawn on the opening day, but some brilliant batting on the part of Briggs and Mr Hornby, on the Friday, entirely changed the aspect of the game; and though Kent played up most pluckily on the Saturday, they were ultimately defeated by 42 runs. The contest may be regarded as marking a chapter in the history of cricket, inasmuch as it was the presence of Crossland and Nash in the Lancashire team that induced Lord Harris, and afterwards the Kent executive, to take the decisive steps on the question of unfair bowling which brought about an estrangement between the counties for the remainder of the season, and induced the Kent County Cricket Club to decline to play the return match arranged to commence on the 20th of August at Tonbridge.

Fresh from their victory over Yorkshire, and strengthened by the presence of Lord Harris and Mr Mackinnon, Kent were seen to considerable advantage on the opening day. They were not fortunate enough to win the toss, but succeeded in dismissing their opponents for the poor total of 108, Briggs and Crossland alone offering any resistance to the Kent bowlers. Four Lancashire wickets had fallen for only five runs when Briggs went in. After being missed at slip by Lord Harris from the first ball he received, the little professional hit with power and freedom, his 56 including no fewer than nine 4s. Crossland rendered him useful assistance towards the close of the innings, and the two put on 35 runs for the ninth wicket. The Kent batting was of a far more even character, six of the team scoring double figures. Messrs Patterson, Jones, Mackinnon and Frank Hearne all batted in capital style, and when play ceased for the day Lancashire had lost a wicket (Mr Lancashire's) in their second innings, and were still 14 runs to the bad.

The feature of Friday's play was the splendid innings of 115 played by Briggs. The young professional went in when three wickets had fallen in the second innings of Lancashire for 65 runs, and was out fifth with the total at 245. He scored 115 out of 180 made during his stay. His batting was of the most brilliant description, and, except that he might have been run out just before his dismissal, he gave no chance whatever. He was at the wickets for two hours and twenty-five minutes, and the spirited character of his hitting will be judged from the following figures: a 5, thirteen 4s, four 3s and nine 2s. Coming as it did after his capital innings on the first day, his performance was all the more creditable. He received valuable support from Mr Hornby, Barlow, Robinson and Mr Roper. Barlow and Robinson put on 65 runs for the second wicket, and Mr Roper stayed with Briggs while 95 runs were added to the score. Mr Hornby and Briggs put on 85 runs during their partnership. The Lancashire captain, except for a few bad strokes at starting, played a dashing innings of 61, included in which were nine 4s, a 3 and three 2s. The last Lancashire wicket fell at 288, leaving Kent 256 runs to get to win. A heavy shower fell after the Lancashire innings, and was followed by some hot sunshine, so that the Kentish batsmen were placed at a disadvantage. Before the call of time three wickets fell for 69, Barlow bowling Mr Mackinnon and Frank and George Hearne. Mr Patterson, with 12, and Mr Jones, with 15, were the not out men.

On the Saturday Kent went on with their task of scoring 187 runs to win, with seven wickets to fall, and when only 14 runs had been slowly added to the overnight score Mr Patteson was bowled. Lord Harris then became Mr Jones' partner, and it was felt that upon these two batsmen depended any chance Kent might have of victory. For some little time everything went well, Lord Harris playing with freedom and vigour, while Mr Jones contented himself with a defensive game. The 100 was up at a quarter to one, but with the total at 125 Lord Harris was caught low down at mid-on. Wootton and Mr Christopherson were both out to Watson's bowling, the score when the seventh wicket fell being 141. Alec Hearne was Mr Jones' next partner, and at the luncheon interval the total was 158, Mr Jones being not out 54. Alec Hearne was bowled at 167, and Herbert Hearne took his place. The score was steadily increased to 186, and then, in attempting a fourth run for a hit of his partner's, Mr Jones unfortunately lost his wicket. His innings of 60 was in every way a capital display of batting, and the two chances he gave occurred after he had made 35. With nine wickets down for 186, the match appeared as good as over, but Pentecost and Herbert Hearne made so obstinate a stand that, between them, they carried the total to 213. Then Crossland went on to bowl, and at once dismissed Hearne, the innings closing at a quarter to four.

Lancashire

R. G. Barlow lbw b A. Hearne	3 – c Christopherson b H. Hearne	35
A. N. Hornby Esq. b Christopherson	2 – b Wootton	61
E. Roper Esq. b Christopherson	0 – b Christopherson	27
O. P. Lancashire Esq. c Jones b Christopherson	3 – b A. Hearne	0
W. Robinson c H. Hearne b Christopherson	0 – c Pentecost b Wootton	27
J. Briggs c and b Wootton	58 – run out	115
J. E. Kershaw Esq. b Christopherson	10 – b Wootton	0
A. Watson b Wootton	0 – not out	18
R. Pilling b Christopherson	2 – c Pentecost b A. Hearne	1
J. Crossland c Christopherson b A. Hearne	22 – c Harris b Wootton	0
G. Nash not out	0 – c Harris b Wootton	0
B 8	8 B 1, l-b 2, n-b 1	4
	108	288

Kent

F. A. Mackinnon Esq. c Kershaw b Crossland	26 – b Barlow	0
F. Hearne b Crossland	22 – b Barlow	22
G. G. Hearne b Crossland	11 – b Barlow	9
W. H. Patterson Esq. c Pilling b Barlow	31 – b Watson	13
R. S. Jones Esq. st Pilling b Barlow	21 – run out	60
Lord Harris b Crossland	0 – c Roper b Crossland	33
J. Wootton run out	2 – c and b Watson	9
S. Christopherson Esq. b Barlow	13 – b Watson	0
A. Hearne not out	1 – b Crossland	11
H. Hearne b Watson	1 – b Crossland	24
J. Pentecost b Barlow	5 – not out	13
B 3, l-b 3, w 2	8 B 11, l-b 8	19
	141	213

Kent Bowling

	Overs	Mdns	Runs	Wkts	Overs	Mdns	Runs	Wkts
Mr Christopherson	27	13	41	6	26	3	78	1
A. Hearne	11.3	2	27	2	41	10	90	2
Wootton	17	7	32	2	30.2	11	60	5
H. Hearne					13	1	46	1
G. G. Hearne					10	5	10	—

Lancashire Bowling

	Overs	Mdns	Runs	Wkts	Overs	Mdns	Runs	Wkts
Watson	35	23	37	1	77	38	82	3
Nash	9	4	6	—				
Barlow	33.2	25	18	4	85	54	58	3
Crossland	29	9	52	4	20.1	3	51	3
Briggs	21	11	20	—	4	2	3	—

LANCASHIRE v CHESHIRE

Played at Old Trafford, August 7, 8, 1885

The remarkable bowling of Briggs was emphatically the feature of the match, which Lancashire won by an innings with 141 runs to spare. Lancashire had first innings, and thanks to the excellent batting of Yates, Robinson, Mr Hornby and Mr Biddolph, succeeded in amassing the capital total of 284. Then Briggs and Watson got rid of the

Cheshire eleven for 35, the smallest innings played against Lancashire during the season. Briggs' analysis, it will be seen, was extraordinary. Cheshire had to follow their innings in a minority of 249, and when the days' play came to a close they had lost one wicket for 27.

When play commenced on the Saturday the visitors were 222 runs behind, and had nine wickets to fall. A far better resistance was offered than in the first innings, but Briggs again bowled with great success, and the innings closed for a total of 108, leaving Lancashire the victors as above stated.

Lancashire

A. N. Hornby Esq. c McLachlan b Wright	51
R. G. Barlow lbw b Bretherton	11
W. H. Bower b Bretherton	4
J. Briggs c Hollins b Bretherton	25
W. Robinson b Wotherspoon	44
C. Yates b Bretherton	76
G. H. Biddolph Esq. c and b Crosfield	50
L. D. Hildyard Esq. c Davenport b Crosfield	3
A. Watson c Fullalove b Crosfield	7
J. Burns lbw b Bretherton	0
G. W. Littlewood not out	0
B 10, l-b 3	13
	284

Cheshire

T. Whatmough b Briggs	0	c and b Briggs	4
S. M. Crosfield Esq. c Littlewood b Watson	4	b Briggs	22
J. O. Fullalove Esq. c Burns b Briggs	7	b Watson	15
G. Davenport st Littlewood b Briggs	0	c Robinson b Briggs	0
T. Burrows c Burns b Briggs	9	b Briggs	11
H. Thornber Esq. c Hildyard b Briggs	0	c Burns b Briggs	23
J. Wright lbw b Briggs	0	c Burns b Briggs	5
S. Hollins Esq. st Littlewood b Briggs	2	c Littlewood b Briggs	24
A. McLachlan Esq. not out	5	c and b Briggs	0
J. Bretherton Esq. st Littlewood b Watson	6	c Watson b Barlow	1
W. Wotherspoon c Bower b Watson	1	not out	0
B 1	1	B 2, l-b 1	3
	35		108

Cheshire Bowling

	Overs	Mdns	Runs	Wkts
Mr Bretherton	35	8	75	5
Wotherspoon	18	4	50	1
Wright	9	—	31	1
Mr Fullalove	17	3	46	—
Mr McLachlan	7	1	35	—
Mr Crosfield	13.2	4	34	3

Lancashire Bowling

	Overs	Mdns	Runs	Wkts	Overs	Mdns	Runs	Wkts
Watson	16.3	6	24	3	30	16	43	1
Briggs	16	11	10	7	36	17	47	8
Burns					3	—	10	—
Barlow					3.2	1	5	1

LANCASHIRE v SURREY

Played at Manchester, June 16, 17, 18, 1887

Up to the time of this match neither Surrey nor Lancashire had met with a single reverse, and this fact was of course sufficient to cause a lot of interest to be taken in the meeting of the two elevens, but the interest was further enhanced by the remembrance of how well Lancashire had acquitted themselves against Surrey at Liverpool in 1885 and 1886. In the former year rain alone saved Surrey from a crushing defeat, and in 1886 the Southern county, after having shown brilliant form for the first two months of the season, met with a single-innings' defeat. The prospects of Lancashire were further improved by the presence of Mr A. G. Steel in the eleven, this being the only occasion on which the famous Cantab was seen in county cricket during the summer. Mr Key being in residence at Oxford, Henderson was included in the Surrey eleven, but with this exception the two counties were as strongly represented as possible. The weather on the opening day was very pleasant, and an enormous crowd of people passed through the gates of Old Trafford. It was a piece of great fortune for Lancashire to win the toss, but the home side made comparatively poor use of their opportunity. Before luncheon, however, the batting was so good that 108 runs were obtained for the loss of only two wickets, those of Mr Hornby and Mr A. G. Steel. The latter shaped extremely well, and was well set when dismissed by a smart catch in the slips. After the interval Mr Shuter put on Bowley and Beaumont to bowl short and fast, and placed a lot of men in the slips, a course which answered so well that five wickets went down for the addition of 50 runs, and the innings was all over for 205. Barlow played a capital 43, and of the others Mr Jowett's 33 and Robinson's 25 not out were the most useful innings. On Surrey going in to bat Abel was cheaply disposed of, but then Mr Roller and Mr Shuter kept together until the last over, when the Surrey captain, who had eleven 4s, four 3s and three 2s in his brilliant 70, was out to a piece of very bad cricket. At the drawing of stumps Surrey, with eight wickets to fall, were 101 runs behind, Mr Roller being not out 15.

Friday's cricket produced one of the most remarkable performances of the season, Surrey losing only three wickets during the course of the day, and scoring 418 runs. The great share of this performance belonged to Mr Walter Read and Mr Roller, who became partners about eight minutes past twelve, and were not separated until ten minutes past five, the two amateurs adding 305 runs during this period. Allowing for intervals, they were together for just four hours, and so admirably did they play that only one chance was offered by each batsman. Mr Roller might have been caught in the slips when he had made 100, and Mr Read was let off in the long field with his total at 82. Mr Roller left at 409, his splendid innings of 120 including ten 4s, five 3s and twelve 2s. Mr Walter Read continued to score most brilliantly from all the Lancashire bowlers brought against him, and had succeeded when he was out at 490 in putting together no fewer than 247 – the largest score he had ever made in a big match. While the famous Surrey batsman made runs in all directions, the great feature of his innings – probably the best as well as the highest he had ever played – was the splendid off-driving. His enormous total was made up by a 5 (4 for an overthrow), thirty-five 4s, nine 3s, twenty 2s and thirty-five singles. Maurice Read, who had been waiting to go in more than five hours, failed to get a run, but Lohmann punished the worn-out bowling with great severity, and at the drawing of stumps was not out 50, the total being 522 for five wickets. The Lancashire team bore the trying day's cricket extremely well, for, while the wicket was so good that their bowlers could do little or nothing, the fielding of the eleven remained smart right up to the finish.

On the third day Surrey succeeded in gaining a most brilliant victory by 134 runs and an innings to spare. Of course they had made quite enough runs to win, and the great fear of their supporters was that they would stay in too long to allow of the match being played out. While at Nottingham during Whit week the Surrey men had undisguisedly thrown away their wickets, on the occasion under notice it was stated that the Southern batsmen all tried to make runs. It was curious, however, that five wickets should have gone down for the addition of 35 runs. Lohmann increased his score to 68, but his four partners were all out quickly bowled, the last wicket falling for the enormous total of 557. Lancashire, who had nothing to play for but a draw, began their second innings when four and a half hours remained for actual cricket. The ground was still in such excellent condition that the chances certainly inclined towards the home team averting a defeat. Of course runs were of no value, but Mr Hornby ran out Barlow from the first ball.

Mr Jowett and Mr Eccles were both got rid of by Bowley, and three wickets were down for 18 runs. Furthermore, Mr Hornby strained himself, and had to retire from the game. After this disastrous start Mr A. G. Steel was joined by Briggs, and these two very nearly succeeded in robbing Surrey of a victory. The amateur always plays a great game to save his side, and Briggs, after a rather rash commencement, played with much judgment. Together they added 103 runs before Briggs was bowled by a lob for a most valuable 51. Mr H. B. Steel hit up 27, and even when Robinson left at 194 there was a prospect of the game being left unfinished, as Mr Steel was still playing all the Surrey bowlers with great confidence and skill. The Cantab completed his 100 when less than an hour was left for play, but after scoring five more runs he was given out leg before wicket. Altogether he was at the wickets three hours and forty minutes, and the chief hits of his 105 were eleven 4s, five 3s and eight 2s. Considering that Mr Steel had had no first-class practice during the season his batting was really marvellous, and there was little doubt in the minds of those who saw the game that had he not been got rid of Surrey would not have secured a victory. After he left, however, the innings was quickly finished off, and half an hour before time Surrey had won a famous victory.

Lancashire

Mr A. N. Hornby b Beaumont	17	– retired hurt	1
R. G. Barlow c Lohmann b Beaumont	43	– run out	0
Mr A. G. Steel c Abel b Bowley	32	– lbw b Beaumont	105
Mr G. Jowett c Shuter b Bowley	33	– b Bowley	3
Mr J. Eccles c W. W. Read b Bowley	2	– c Abel b Bowley	4
J. Briggs c Abel b Bowley	16	– b W. W. Read	51
Mr H. B. Steel c Wood b Beaumont	4	– b Jones	27
W. Robinson not out	25	– b Beaumont	7
G. Yates lbw b Beaumont	9	– not out	8
A. Watson c Wood b Lohmann	11	– b Beaumont	0
R. Pilling c M. Read b Abel	1	– c Jones b Lohmann	5
B 8, l-b 4	12	B 5, l-b 2	7
	205		218

Surrey

R. Abel c Pilling b Yates	6
Mr J. Shuter st Pilling b A. G. Steel	70
Mr W. E. Roller c Pilling b Watson	120
Mr W. W. Read c Eccles b Watson	247
Maurice Reed c Pilling b Watson	0
G. Lohmann st Pilling b Briggs	68
R. Henderson b Briggs	9
H. Wood b Briggs	7
G. Jones b Watson	6
T. Bowley b Briggs	0
J. Beaumont not out	1
B 15, l-b 7, w 1	23
	557

Lancashire Bowling

	Overs	Mdns	Runs	Wkts
Watson	100	57	130	4
Briggs	68.2	35	106	4
Yates	31	6	90	1
Barlow	41	19	77	—
Mr A. G. Steel	45	11	101	1
Mr Eccles	5	2	10	—
Robinson	6	1	20	—

Surrey Bowling

	Overs	Mdns	Runs	Wkts	Overs	Mdns	Runs	Wkts
Bowley	44	17	66	4	31	17	45	2
Lohmann	30	11	48	1	45.2	20	62	1
Beaumont	33	13	64	4	30	8	56	3
Jones	4	1	11	—	19	9	23	1
Abel	3.3	1	4	1				
Mr Roller					7	3	13	—
Mr W. W. Read					2	—	12	1

LANCASHIRE v GLOUCESTERSHIRE

Played at Manchester, July 21, 22, 23, 1887

For the first match of their northern tour Gloucestershire had a representative team, Mr F. Townsend and Woof being for the first time available. Of course the new bowler, Roberts, had not then been discovered. The appearance of Gloucestershire at the Old Trafford ground is always a great attraction, and the attendances on the first two days were more than up to the average. The wicket was in splendid condition, and fine weather prevailed throughout the whole of the match. On the opening day Gloucestershire did remarkably well, and they certainly looked to have a great chance of success. The brothers Grace put on 73 runs for the first wicket, and later on Mr Townsend played a beautiful innings of 56. After Mr Townsend's departure only Mr Francis did anything of mention, and the whole side were out for 248. Mr E. M. Grace seldom played a better innings than his 84, and during his stay of three hours and a quarter he scarcely made a mistake, and though he did not hit with the vigour of his early days he played capital cricket throughout. His chief hits were eleven 4s, a 3 and five 2s. Before the drawing of stumps Lancashire scored 44 for the loss of one wicket, Barlow being bowled just on the call of time.

On the second day the character of the game changed, and Lancashire had matters all their own way. A complete mastery was obtained over the weak Gloucestershire bowling, and throughout the day runs came at a great pace, 400 being scored for the loss of nine wickets. Only one member of the team failed to reach double figures, and it was not until just before the close of the day that the innings terminated for 444. Mr Hornby hit most brilliantly for his 97, but was lucky, giving two palpable chances both at mid-off. His chief hits were a 5 (4 for an overthrow), thirteen 4s and six 2s. Briggs batted with tremendous vigour, making his 65 in fifty-five minutes by eleven 4s, seven 2s and seven singles. Mr Eccles's 49 was not at all a good innings, but Mr Jowett and Yates both hit freely and well. Late in the afternoon a most painful incident occurred. Mr A. C. M. Croome, who was fielding at long-on, ran to try to catch a ball hit by Yates, and not noticing the railings, which at that time surrounded the enclosed portion of the ground, he came with great severity against them, and one of the points ran into his neck. He at once cried out for assistance, and was carried to the pavilion, it being for some time extremely doubtful whether or not the injury would prove fatal. Fortunately, however, the point of the railing did not enter a vital part, so after a somewhat severe illness, Mr Croome thoroughly recovered his health. The affair created a most unpleasant feeling amongst the players and the spectators, and it was at one time suggested to adjourn the game for the day, but Mr Grace wisely thought the spectators would be less anxious if the game proceeded. Immediately after the match the Lancashire committee decided to protect the points of the railings, and there is therefore little chance of a repetition of such an unusual and regrettable accident.

On the concluding day the cricket was devoid of interest. Gloucestershire were in a minority of 196, and though they of course had no chance of making anything better than a draw of it, it was certainly thought they would have played a better uphill game than they did. The wicket was still in good condition, but one after another the Gloucestershire batsmen failed before the bowling of Watson and Briggs. Mr W. G. Grace, who is seldom lucky at Old Trafford, was dismissed for 23, and of the others Mr Radcliffe with 30 was the only man to show any form. Just after three o'clock the innings was all over for 98, and Lancashire were left with a most decisive victory by an innings and 98 runs. Mr Croome was of course unable to go in to bat. Watson's performance of taking six wickets for 58 runs was an excellent one, considering that the ground had borne the wear and tear very well.

Gloucestershire

Mr W. G. Grace c Hornby b Barlow	41	– c Watson b Briggs	23
Mr E. M. Grace c Watson b Barlow	84	– c Pilling b Watson	10
Mr J. H. Brain c Hornby b Briggs	12	– run out	0
Mr O. G. Radcliffe b Yates	4	– c Baker b Briggs	30
Mr F. Townsend b Barlow	56	– c Yates b Watson	4
Mr W. W. F. Pullen b Briggs	0	– b Watson	10
Mr H. Hale c Baker b Barlow	8	– b Watson	2
Mr G. Francis b Watson	31	– b Watson	0
Mr A. C. M. Croome not out	1	– absent hurt	0
Mr F. L. Cole b Barlow	0	– c Pilling b Watson	8
W. A. Woof c Pilling b Barlow	3	– not out	7
B 6, l-b 2	8	B 4	4
	248		98

Lancashire

Mr A. N. Hornby b W. G. Grace	97
R. G. Barlow b Radcliffe	16
F. H. Sugg lbw b W. G. Grace	29
Mr O. P. Lancashire c Cole b Francis	19
Mr J. Eccles b W. G. Grace	49
J. Briggs c Pullen b W. G. Grace	65
Mr G. Jowett b W. G. Grace	39
Baker b E. M. Grace	15
G. Yates not out	57
A. Watson c W. G. Grace b Brain	9
R. Pilling c Townsend b W. G. Grace	22
B 19, l-b 6, w 2	27
	444

Gloucestershire Bowling

	Overs	Mdns	Runs	Wkts
Woof	49	22	89	—
Mr W. G. Grace	64.1	21	138	6
Mr Hales	9	5	16	—
Mr E. M. Grace	19	5	48	1
Mr Radcliffe	9	3	25	1
Mr Croome	33	5	45	—
Mr Francis	3	—	16	1
Mr Brain	11	—	40	1

Lancashire Bowling

	Overs	Mdns	Runs	Wkts	Overs	Mdns	Runs	Wkts
Watson	52	30	58	1	44	24	53	6
Briggs	61	28	94	2	44	31	36	2
Yates	16	5	31	1				
Barlow	37.2	20	56	6				

Umpires: Rowbotham and Jupp.

LANCASHIRE v SUSSEX

Played at Manchester, May 31, June 1, 2, 1888

Thanks to a superb innings of 128 by Mr Newham and to the support he received from Mr McCormick and Humphreys, Sussex did extremely well in the opening of their first fixture with Lancashire. The fact that Sussex put together an innings of 280 was the more meritorious as Tester and Quaife were got rid of before a run had been scored. Messrs Newham and McCormick, however, scored 87 for the third wicket, and the former, with Humphreys for a partner, added 131 runs for the fifth partnership. Mr Newham's fine innings lasted four hours, and was without fault, his chief hits being eleven 4s, six 3s and sixteen 2s. During the second stage the Lancashire men were seen to great advantage in their uphill task, for, though they were got rid of a first time for 150, they followed on, and scored 228 for the loss of seven wickets, which left the match in a very interesting state. Unfortunately, rain fell from an early hour on Saturday, and a game that had promised to furnish an exciting finish was abandoned as a draw. The feature of Friday's cricket was the brilliant hitting of Briggs, who made sixteen 4s.

Sussex

W. Tester b Briggs	0
W. Quaife b Barlow	0
Mr W. Newham c Ward b Briggs	128
Mr E. J. McCormick c Whiteside b Briggs	64
J. Hide b Briggs	14
W. Humphreys not out	52
Mr C. A. Smith c Whiteside b Briggs	0
Mr G. Brann st Whiteside b Briggs	13
F. W. Tate lbw b Briggs	2
A. Hide b Briggs	0
H. Phillips c Kemp b Briggs	0
B 4, l-b 3	7
	280

Lancashire

Mr S. M. Crosfield c A. Hide b Smith	44	– c A. Hide b Smith	2
R. G. Barlow c Tate b Smith	29	– lbw b J. Hide	36
Mr J. Eccles b Smith	18	– lbw b Smith	3
Mr G. Kemp c Tate b Smith	14	– b Smith	1
J. Briggs c Phillips b Smith	1	– not out	126
W. Robinson c A. Hide b Smith	23	– b A. Hide	5
Mr C. L. Jones run out	2	– not out	20
Hudson c McCormick b J. Hide	10	– c Brann b J. Hide	12
F. Ward not out	4	– c A. Hide b McCormick	6
A. Watson c and b Smith	0		
Whiteside b J. Hide	0		
B 2, l-b 3	5	B 15, l-b 2	17
	150		228

Lancashire Bowling

	Overs	Mdns	Runs	Wkts
Briggs	60.3	27	88	9
Barlow	53	25	73	1
Watson	39	21	53	—
Ward	22	9	28	—
Hudson	9	2	22	—
Mr Crosfield	5	2	9	—

Sussex Bowling

	Overs	Mdns	Runs	Wkts	Overs	Mdns	Runs	Wkts
Mr Smith	43	21	59	7	27	13	41	3
A. Hide	25	12	32	—	14	1	38	1
Humphreys	10	3	16	—	8	—	18	—
J. Hide	28	11	38	2	36	11	53	2
Tate					14	7	20	—
Tester					10	2	24	—
Mr McCormick					4	1	17	1

Umpires: Panter and Jupp.

LANCASHIRE v DERBYSHIRE

Played at Manchester, July 23, 24, 1888

The Derbyshire men were outplayed at all points in this encounter, and were in the end beaten with ridiculous ease by an innings with 78 runs to spare. A lot of rain fell during the first day and considerably interfered with what cricket took place, which, by the way, went all against the Midland team. Derbyshire went in first, and put together a first innings of 87, Briggs taking seven of the wickets for 35 runs. When Lancashire went in, in turn, they lost one batsman, Mr Eccles, cheaply, but Barlow and Sugg then got together, and were still in at the call of time, when curiously enough the Lancashire total exactly equalled the Derbyshire innings. Tuesday's play furnished one of the most remarkable batting failures, and at the same time one of the most brilliant bowling achievements of the year. Lancashire, on going on with their innings, finished it off for 182, and then Briggs and Watson dismissed Derbyshire in an hour and ten minutes for 17 runs. In the match Briggs took thirteen wickets for 39 runs; while in the second innings his six wickets cost less than a run apiece. Admitting the weakness of the batting and the difficulty of the ground this will rank as one of the best things ever done by the popular Lancashire professional.

Derbyshire

Mr L. G. Wright c Barlow b Briggs	8	– b Briggs	0
J. Ratcliffe st Pilling b Briggs	1	– c and b Watson	0
W. Cropper b Watson	8	– c and b Briggs	1
W. Chatterton b Briggs	3	– c Barlow b Briggs	0
G. Davidson b Briggs	12	– b Briggs	1
Mr G. G. Walker c Baker b Briggs	11	– c Hornby b Watson	0
Mr W. E. Pedley b Briggs	16	– c Baker b Watson	4
Mr J. H. Shaw c Pilling b Watson	1	– b Briggs	1
Storer c Sugg b Barlow	13	– b Watson	2
J. Hulme b Briggs	4	– c Yates b Briggs	2
J. Disney not out	7	– not out	3
B 1, l-b 2	3	B 2, l-b 1	3
	87		17

Lancashire

Mr J. Eccles c Disney b Walker	7	G. Yates c Davidson b Hulme	15
R. G. Barlow b Hulme	27	R. Pilling b Chatterton	7
F. H. Sugg lbw b Hulme	60	Mr R. W. Kentfield b Hulme	0
Mr S. M. Crosfield c Chatterton b Hulme	22	A. Watson not out	0
J. Briggs c Disney b Hulme	13	B 2, l-b 3	5
G. Baker b Walker	0		
Mr A. N. Hornby c Storer b Hulme	26		182

Lancashire Bowling

	Overs	Mdns	Runs	Wkts	Overs	Mdns	Runs	Wkts
Briggs	41.3	27	35	7	19	16	4	6
Watson	28	14	35	2	18.1	11	10	4
Mr Kentfield	4	2	5	—				
Barlow	9	4	9	1				

Derbyshire Bowling

	Overs	Mdns	Runs	Wkts
Davidson	7	2	12	—
Mr Walker	25	6	57	2
Hulme	46.3	23	62	7
Cropper	4	—	18	—
Chatterton	24	13	28	1

Umpires: Hill and Jupp.

LANCASHIRE v GLOUCESTERSHIRE

Played at Liverpool, July 26, 27, 1888

Lancashire gained so great an advantage at Aigburth during the first stage of this encounter that all the interest was gone on the second and concluding day. After making 108 the home team got rid of Gloucestershire for 33, and then scored 89 more in their second innings for the loss of six wickets. The last four Lancashire wickets fell on Friday for an addition of 8 runs, but the ground was in a difficult condition, and Gloucestershire, who never looked like having a chance, lost easily by 116 runs. The remarkable bowling of Briggs, who took twelve wickets for 45 runs, of Barlow, who obtained six for 42, and of Woof, who got nine for 76, were the chief incidents of an otherwise uninteresting game.

Lancashire

First innings		Second innings	
Mr A. N. Hornby b Woof	7	lbw b W. G. Grace	16
R. G. Barlow lbw b Roberts	5	lbw b W. G. Grace	0
F. H. Sugg c Painter b Woof	8	b Radcliffe	23
Mr J. Eccles c W. G. Grace b Roberts	10	b Radcliffe	25
J. Briggs b W. G. Grace	35	c W. G. Grace b Woof	13
Mr S. M. Crosfield c E. M. Grace b Roberts	5	lbw b Radcliffe	1
G. Baker b Woof	8	c Page b Woof	6
Mr C. L. Jones c E. M. Grace b Woof	5	b Woof	3
G. Yates c E. M. Grace b Roberts	0	c E. M. Grace b Woof	1
R. Pilling c Pullen b W. G. Grace	10	not out	4
A. Watson not out	3	c Pullen b Woof	0
B 8, l-b 4	12	B 4, l-b 1	5
	108		97

Gloucestershire

First innings		Second innings	
Mr W. G. Grace b Barlow	4	b Barlow	16
Mr E. M. Grace c Watson b Barlow	8	c Sugg b Barlow	8
Mr W. W. F. Pullen b Briggs	12	c Hornby b Briggs	9
Mr O. G. Radcliffe run out	5	c Barlow b Briggs	10
Mr W. Troup st Pilling b Briggs	0	lbw b Briggs	0
J. Painter b Briggs	0	st Pilling b Briggs	0
Mr F. Townsend b Briggs	2	c Sugg b Briggs	0
Mr H. V. Page c Hornby b Briggs	0	b Briggs	7
W. A. Woof c Eccles b Briggs	0	run out	3
Mr J. A. Bush c Eccles b Barlow	0	not out	1
F. G. Roberts not out	2	c and b Barlow	0
		B 2	2
	33		56

Gloucesteshire Bowling

	Overs	Mdns	Runs	Wkts	Overs	Mdns	Runs	Wkts
Woof	39	21	41	4	32.2	15	35	5
Roberts	36	16	48	4	4	2	5	—
Mr W. G. Grace	3	—	7	2	22	8	31	2
Mr Radcliffe					6	—	21	3

Lancashire Bowling

	Overs	Mdns	Runs	Wkts	Overs	Mdns	Runs	Wkts
Briggs	15	9	13	6	23	9	32	6
Barlow	14.3	6	20	3	22.1	13	22	3

Umpires: Hill and Panter.

LANCASHIRE v LEICESTERSHIRE

Played at Manchester, August 20, 1889

For the second year in succession a county match at Old Trafford was commenced and finished in one day, but, whereas in 1888 Lancashire went down before Surrey, the home county on this occasion defeated Leicestershire in a single innings with 69 runs to spare. Briggs was the chief cause of the game being finished off in such a startlingly rapid fashion – the time occupied was only four hours and a quarter – and, admitting that the ground gave him any amount of assistance, he certainly bowled in wonderful form. As will be seen below, he took in all fifteen wickets at a cost of only 35 runs. Watson also bowled remarkably well, and in neither innings was there any need for a change. Pougher worked hard for his side, taking eight wickets for 54 runs, but the failure of the Leicestershire batting frustrated all his efforts.

Leicestershire

Mr C. E. de Trafford lbw b Briggs	0	– b Watson	6
T. Warren st Pilling b Briggs	2	– b Briggs	0
J. Tomlin b Briggs	0	– b Watson	4
Mr C. C. Stone b Briggs	10	– b Watson	1
A. D Pougher b Watson	2	– b Briggs	0
Mr J. M'Robie lbw b Briggs	1	– c Ward b Briggs	2
Hollands c Hornby b Briggs	0	– st Pilling b Briggs	4
Mr A. W. Crofts not out	6	– b Briggs	0
Atkins b Watson	1	– lbw b Briggs	1
J. Warren b Briggs	1	– b Briggs	8
Woodcock b Briggs	0	– not out	1
		B 4, etc	4
	23		31

Lancashire

Mr A. N. Hornby c de Trafford b Pougher	13	A. Paul run out	4
R. G. Barlow lbw b M'Robie	35	G. R. Baker b Pougher	4
R. Pilling b Pougher	6	A. Watson st Croft b Pougher	12
F. H. Sugg b Pougher	0	A. Mold not out	3
A. Ward b Pougher	0	B 14, etc	14
J. Briggs b Pougher	16		
Mr S. M. Crossfield b Pougher	16		123

Lancashire Bowling

	Overs	Mdns	Runs	Wkts	Overs	Mdns	Runs	Wkts
Watson	10	5	9	2	11	7	6	3
Briggs	9.4	4	14	8	10.4	3	21	7

Leicestershire Bowling

	Overs	Mdns	Runs	Wkts
Pougher	35	14	54	8
Atkins	8	1	16	—
J. Warren	6	3	6	—
Woodcock	5	1	9	—
T. Warren	6	2	9	—
Mr J. M'Robie	9	4	15	1

Umpires: Platts and Veitch.

LANCASHIRE v SURREY

Played at Manchester, June 9, 10, 1890

Several remarkable performances have been done in matches between Lancashire and Surrey, and the contest under notice fully maintained the tradition of exciting cricket. So treacherous was the ground on the opening day that twenty-nine wickets went down for 222 runs, Lohmann and Sharpe for the one side, and Briggs and Watson for the other, carrying off the honours. On the second morning Surrey finished their innings in ten minutes, and Lancashire went in with 112 to get to win. On the difficult wicket against the splendid bowling of Lohmann and Sharpe the home side never looked like getting the runs, and, the innings being finished off in an hour and a half for 50, Surrey gained a well-deserved victory by 61 runs. Lohmann had the remarkable record for the match of thirteen wickets for 54 runs, a performance almost equal to that which he achieved on the same ground two years before, when Surrey defeated Lancashire in the course of a single day's cricket.

Surrey

Mr J. Shuter c Sugg b Watson	6	– c Sugg b Briggs	0
R. Abel b Briggs	0	– st Kemble b Briggs	23
Watts lbw b Briggs	0	– c and b Watson	1
Mr W. W. Read b Watson	30	– c F. Ward b Briggs	6
M. Read b Briggs	2	– b Watson	23
R. Henderson c Paul b Briggs	1	– b Briggs	1
G. A. Lohmann b Watson	5	– b Watson	18
H. Wood c Watson b Briggs	9	– not out	24
W. Brockwell run out	9	– c Tinsley b Briggs	1
J. W. Sharpe c and b Watson	0	– lbw b Watson	0
T. Bowley not out	7	– b Briggs	5
		B 1	1
	69		103

Lancashire

Mr A. N. Hornby b Lohmann	0	– b Lohmann	4
R. G. Barlow b Lohmann	19	– b Lohmann	4
F. H. Sugg c Henderson b Lohmann	0	– b Lohmann	0
A. Ward c and b Lohmann	5	– b Lohmann	8
A. Paul c M. Read b Lohmann	7	– b Sharpe	6
J. Briggs b Sharpe	4	– b Sharpe	4
F. Ward b Sharpe	0	– b Lohmann	0
A. Tinsley b Sharpe	6	– b Lohmann	8
Mr A. T. Kemble b Sharpe	18	– b Lohmann	10
A. Watson not out	0	– b Sharpe	0
A. Mold c Abel b Lohmann	1	– not out	0
B 1	1	B 6	6
	61		50

Lancashire Bowling

	Overs	Mdns	Runs	Wkts	Overs	Mdns	Runs	Wkts
Watson	29	19	17	4	32	17	36	4
Briggs	28.1	10	52	5	28.1	8	60	6
Barlow					3	2	6	—

Surrey Bowling

	Overs	Mdns	Runs	Wkts	Overs	Mdns	Runs	Wkts
Lohmann	20.2	8	33	6	20.1	12	21	7
Sharpe	20	9	27	4	20	10	23	3

Umpires: T. Mycroft and A. Smith.

LANCASHIRE v SUSSEX

Played at Manchester, June 30, July 1, 2, 1890

Owing to heavy rain no cricket was possible on the first day, and it was not until nearly two o'clock that play was begun on the second. Then Lancashire, having the good fortune to win the toss, went in to bat, and after two wickets had fallen for 31, Briggs and Albert Ward became partners, and put on 215 runs without further loss. Ward batted with skill and judgment, and Briggs hit very brilliantly, making his hundred runs in as many minutes, whilst his full score included seventeen 4s, nine 3s and nine 2s. On the Wednesday it was found impossible to make a start until after luncheon. Mr Hornby, however, at once declared the Lancashire innings at an end. On the treacherous wicket Briggs and Watson bowled with such extraordinary effect that the first innings of Sussex only lasted from ten minutes to three until half-past four, and the second just an hour, Lancashire winning the match in a single innings with 187 runs to spare, thirty-five minutes before time. Watson actually took nine wickets for 13 runs, whilst Briggs had ten for 41 runs. It is worthy of note that, although Lancashire won so easily, only four of their team went in to bat. It is only fair to the Southern eleven to say that they had extraordinarily bad luck in the condition of the ground, which was wet and easy whilst the Lancashire batsmen were making the runs, and slow and treacherous when it came to the turn of the Sussex men to go to the wickets.

Lancashire

R. G. Barlow b Smith	13
F. H. Sugg	13
A. Ward not out	77
J. Briggs not out	129
B 13, l-b 1	14
	(2 wkts dec.) 246

A. Paul, G. R. Baker, R. Ward, G. Yates, Mr A. T. Kemble, A. Watson and A. Mold did not bat.

Sussex

W. Quaife b Briggs	4	– c Barlow b Briggs	5
G. Bean c Barlow b Watson	7	– c Baker b Watson	1
Mr F. Thomas st Kemble b Briggs	8	– run out	8
Mr W. Newham b Watson	5	– c Barlow b Watson	0
H. Tebay c and b Briggs	0	– b Watson	5
Mr C. A. Smith c Kemble b Briggs	0	– not out	0
W. Humphreys lbw b Briggs	3	– lbw b Briggs	0
T. C. Brown b Watson	5	– b Briggs	0
Shoubridge c Kemble b Watson	0	– c Barlow b Briggs	0
H. Butt b Watson	0	– b Briggs	0
Gibb not out	0	– b Watson	3
B 2, l-b 1	3	B 2	2
	35		24

Sussex Bowling

	Overs	Mdns	Runs	Wkts
Bean	30	13	50	—
Mr Smith	28	13	55	2
Gibb	21	8	37	—
Shoubridge	13	1	25	—
Brown	7	1	31	—
Humphreys	6	—	34	—

Lancashire Bowling

	Overs	Mdns	Runs	Wkts	Overs	Mdns	Runs	Wkts
Watson	27	21	7	5	19.4	16	6	4
Briggs	27	18	25	5	19	11	16	5

Umpires: J. Rowbotham and R. Carpenter.

LANCASHIRE v MIDDLESEX

Played at Manchester, July 16, 17, 1891

An exceptionally brilliant display of batting on the part of Mr A. E. Stoddart, who, going in first for Middlesex, carried his bat right through the innings, rendered this return engagement particularly noteworthy in the great county matches of the season. The Middlesex amateur may fairly be said to have on this occasion surpassed all his previous efforts, for not only was his score of 215 not out the highest innings played in first-class cricket last summer, but it was, by a considerable number of runs, the biggest score ever obtained in a good match by Mr Stoddart his previous best having been 151 for England against the Marylebone Club at Lord's in 1887. His innings of 215 lasted five hours, and except for two chances, one at slip when he had made 86 and another at the wicket when his total had reached 109, it was quite free from fault. His hitting at times was remarkably fine, whilst the accuracy with which he got Mold's bowling on to the middle of his bat all the time gave the performance additional value. The score was made up by twenty-five 4s, nine 3s, twenty-two 2s and forty-four singles. Mr Stoddart's innings was of course the achievement of the match, but there was other capital batting for Middlesex and some first-class bowling by J. T. Hearne. Early in the Middlesex innings Mr O'Brien hit in superb style scoring 51 in fifty minutes; indeed the old Oxonian while at the wickets quite eclipsed Mr Stoddart. Despite the play of the two batsmen mentioned. Mold's bowling presented difficulties which several of the Middlesex batsmen proved unable to overcome, and seven wickets were down for 158. This was a very moderate score considering the excellent condition of the turf, but every one of the last three batsmen rendered Mr Stoddart invaluable assistance, and thanks to their joint efforts the last three wickets actually realised 214 runs. West stayed while 101 runs were put on; Hearne assisted in adding 66; and Phillips helped to increase the score by 47 runs. Mold took seven of the ten wickets, but at a cost of 140 runs, a considerable proportion of which were hit from him late in the innings. Lancashire had a few minutes' batting after the Middlesex innings closed at six o'clock for 372, and scored 9 runs without loss.

As the weather continued very bright on the Friday and the ground remained in excellent condition, there was a general expectation that Lancashire, who had recently gained handsome victories over both Somersetshire and Gloucestershire, would reply to the Middlesex total of 372 with at least a score of 250, and great was the disappointment among the thousands of people present when, in the course of the day, the home team were twice got rid of for an aggregate of 303. The first innings, which amounted to 163, lasted about three hours, and opened so well that at one time 71 runs had been obtained with only one man out. Barlow was at the wickets an hour and forty minutes for a very careful 31, and Sugg batted in nice style, but of the last seven men on the side Mr Kemble alone showed himself able to contend against the Middlesex bowling. The main cause of this comparatively cheap dismissal of Lancashire was the admirable bowling of J. T. Hearne, who in the season in which he made his fame accomplished no greater performance than this at Old Trafford. Lancashire found themselves in a minority of 209 runs, and began their second innings so disastrously that all hope of their making a fight of it was soon dissipated. Four wickets went down for 27 runs, and though Yates and Briggs, hitting hard and pluckily, added 48 runs in half an hour, no one else, with the exception perhaps of Mr Hornby, gave much trouble, and the innings closed in two hours and a half for 140. Middlesex thus gained a victory by an innings and 69 runs, the cricket shown by the team being probably some of the best of the whole season. Of course Mr Stoddart's extraordinary score will stand out as the great feature of the match, but while that gentleman is entitled to all honour for his grand display of batting, the performance of Middlesex on the second day, inasmuch as the fine cricket shown was shared in by the whole of the eleven, was almost a more gratifying achievement. Better bowling than that of J. T. Hearne, who with the turf in capital order took ten wickets for 83 runs, was certainly not seen all through the season. Rawling and Mr Nepean – the former of whom dismissed three batsmen in each innings – rendered Hearne useful aid, while for the most part the fielding of the visitors was smart and accurate. It is a fact well worthy of mention that in each of the victories which Middlesex gained over Lancashire last summer Mr Stoddart and J. T. Hearne had an enormous share. At Lord's the young Middlesex professional took eleven wickets for 47 runs, and at Manchester ten for 83, giving him the extraordinary record for the two matches of twenty-one wickets for 130 runs. Mr Stoddart, too, in addition to his remarkable innings of 215 not out at Manchester, scored at Lord's 37 and 87, or 124 runs in the match. Lancashire's totals on that occasion were 63 and 67, of which six were extras, so that the Middlesex batsman himself made as many runs in the course of the game as the whole Lancashire eleven. The match of which the score is appended furnished the last instance during the season of Lancashire meeting with defeat, and although their batting on the Friday was far from good, the annoyance of the reverse was to some extent lessened by the reflection that the result had been brought about by some of the best cricket shown during the whole summer.

Middlesex

Mr A. E. Stoddart not out	215
Mr A. J. Webbe b Mold	2
Mr S. W. Scott c Watson b Mold	5
Mr T. C. O'Brien c Kemble b Watson	51
Mr E. A. Nepean b Mold	8
J. T. Rawlin b Mold	1
Mr E. M. Hadow c Kemble b Mold	4
Mr P. J. T. Kenery b Mold	6
J. E. West c Kemble b Baker	30
J. T. Hearne b Watson	19
J. Phillips b Mold	20
B 2, l-b 8, n-b 1	11
	372

Lancashire

R. G. Barlow b Hearne	31	– c West b Hearne	4
A. Ward run out	27	– lbw b Rawlin	9
A. Smith b Hearne	11	– c Hearne b Rawlin	7
F. H. Sugg c West b Hearne	30	– b Hearne	5
G. Yates b Hearne	5	– c Hearne b Nepean	33
J. Briggs c Webbe b Rawlin	8	– c West b Rawlin	26
G. R. Baker c and b Hearne	2	– c Rawlin b Nepean	10
Mr A. N. Hornby b Rawlin	8	– b Hearne	22
Mr A. T. Kemble not out	25	– c Rawlin b Nepean	7
A. Watson c Hadow b Hearne	3	– b Hearne	12
A. Mold c O'Brien b Rawlin	2	– not out	0
B 8, l-b 3	11	B 4, l-b 1	5
	163		140

Lancashire Bowling

	Overs	Mdns	Runs	Wkts
Mold	52.4	8	140	7
Briggs	26	5	84	—
Smith	12	5	28	—
Watson	43	16	82	2
Barlow	1	—	1	—
Baker	10	3	26	1

Middlesex Bowling

	Overs	Mdns	Runs	Wkts	Overs	Mdns	Runs	Wkts
Hearne	37	17	50	6	18	11	33	4
Mr Nepean	15	5	23	—	13	—	34	3
Phillips	17	7	42	—	3	1	12	—
Rawlin	15.3	4	37	3	25	6	56	3

Umpires: Holmes and Panter.

LANCASHIRE v ESSEX

Played at Manchester, August 3, 4, 5, 1891

Rain sadly interfered with the progress of this match, less than two hours' cricket being possible on the opening day, whilst on the Tuesday no play was practicable until after three o'clock. Essex, losing five wickets for 79 on the Monday, were all out for 118 on the following afternoon, and then Lancashire scored 97 for the loss of seven wickets, Frank Ward contributing an invaluable innings of 47. In their second innings Essex started well, putting on 61 for two wickets, but after the interval eight batsmen were dismissed for 38 runs. Lancashire had 75 to get to win, and although Albert Ward was out in the first over the runs were hit off without further loss, Lancashire winning the match by nine wickets. Briggs, it will be noticed, took fourteen wickets in the match for less than nine runs apiece.

Essex

Carpenter c and b Briggs	23	– b Briggs	16
Mr H. G. Owen b Briggs	7	– c Crosfield b Watson	31
J. Burns b Briggs	5	– c Crosfield b Briggs	9
Mr G. B. Gosling st Pilling b Briggs	27	– b Watson	4
Mr C. D. Buxton c Smith b Briggs	5	– b Watson	0
Mr F. E. Rowe b Briggs	21	– b Watson	8
Mr J. C. Bevington b Briggs	2	– st Pilling b Briggs	12
Rev. H. J. E. Burrell b Briggs	8	– c Pilling b Briggs	0
Mead c Baker b Watson	5	– c Yates b Briggs	0
H. Pickett c Crosfield b Watson	6	– c Sugg b Briggs	14
Mr F. A. Bishop not out	3	– not out	1
B 6	6	B 3, l-b 1	4
	118		99

Lancashire

A. Ward b Pickett	2	– b Pickett	0
F. H. Sugg c Rowe b Pickett	17	– not out	40
A. Smith c Mead b Bishop	13		
J. Briggs b Pickett	4		
G. Yates b Mead	7		
Heaton b Mead	0	– not out	29
G. R. Baker c Bishop b Pickett	2		
F. Ward b Mead	47		
Mr S. M. Crosfield not out	27		
A. Watson c Bevington b Owen	17		
W. Pilling run out	0		
B 4, l-b 3	7	B 8, l-b 1	9
	143		78

Lancashire Bowling

	Overs	Mdns	Runs	Wkts	Overs	Mdns	Runs	Wkts
Briggs	52	18	75	8	36.1	15	50	6
Watson	45	29	32	2	35	22	33	4
Smith	6	3	5	—	3	—	12	—
Baker					2	2	—	—

Essex Bowling

	Overs	Mdns	Runs	Wkts	Overs	Mdns	Runs	Wkts
Mead	34	16	67	3	6	—	29	—
Pickett	34	17	45	4	7	3	12	1
Mr Bishop	12.3	9	11	1	4	1	19	—
Mr Owen	8	4	13	1	2	1	1	—
Burns					2	—	4	—
Mr Buxton					0.1	—	4	—

Umpires: Henty and Carpenter.

LANCASHIRE v MIDDLESEX

Played at Manchester, July 14, 15, 16, 1892

It was in this match that G. MacGregor, the famous wicket-keeper, made his first appearance for Middlesex. Play on the opening day went all in favour of the bowlers, twenty-four wickets going down for 250 runs. Hearne and Rawlin for the one side, and Mold and Briggs for the other carried all before them. Next day Briggs batted in brilliant form, making 98 out of 156 by twelve 4s, four 3s, ten 2s and singles, and the total reached 243. Middlesex, wanting 227 to win, did very well for a time, but then, in a bad light, the batting broke down completely before the fast bowling of Mold, and at the close eight men were out for 102. The finish of the match was rather ludicrous. The players waited until a quarter to six before cricket was possible on Saturday, and then Lancashire, failing to get the last Middlesex wicket down, had to be content with a draw.

Lancashire

A. Ward b Rawlin	33	– c MacGregor b Rawlin	8
F. H. Sugg b Hearne	0	– b Rawlin	9
Mr A. C. MacLaren b Hearne	0	– b Rawlin	0
A. Smith c Scott b Hearne	8	– b Rawlin	6
J. Briggs b Rawlin	2	– c and b Phillips	98
G. R. Baker c Henery b Hearne	25	– c MacGregor b Rawlin	24
Mr T. R. Hubback c Stoddart b Hearne	7	– b Hearne	33
Mr S. M. Crosfield b Hearne	4	– c Greatorex b Stoddart	38
Mr A. T. Kemble c Webbe b Hearne	8	– c Stoddart b Hearne	22
A. Watson b Rawlin	0	– c Webbe b Hearne	4
A. Mold not out	0	– not out	0
B 4, l-b 1	5	L-b 1	1
	92		243

Middlesex

Mr A. E. Stoddart b Briggs	9	– b Mold	3
Mr T. C. O'Brien c Kemble b Mold	4	– b Mold	0
Mr S. W. Scott b Mold	4	– st Kemble b Briggs	29
Mr M. R. Jardine b Mold	20	– b Mold	4
Mr A. J. Webbe b Mold	8	– c Kemble b Mold	51
J. T. Rawlin run out	11	– b Mold	4
Rev. T. Greatorex b Mold	10	– b Mold	3
Mr P. J. T. Henery c Smith b Briggs	30	– c Smith b Mold	0
Mr G. MacGregor b Briggs	4	– b Mold	0
J Phillips not out	4	– not out	4
J. T. Hearne st Kemble b Briggs	5	– not out	4
		B 8, l-b 2	10
	109		112

Middlesex Bowling

	Overs	Mdns	Runs	Wkts	Overs	Mdns	Runs	Wkts
Hearne	20	7	42	7	45.2	7	122	3
Phillips	5	—	25	—	13	5	33	1
Rawlin	14.2	7	20	3	51	26	62	5
Mr Stoddart					9	3	25	1

Lancashire Bowling

	Overs	Mdns	Runs	Wkts	Overs	Mdns	Runs	Wkts
Mold	27	6	73	5	36	15	50	8
Briggs	26.2	11	36	4	35	16	38	1
Watson					23	18	14	—
Mr Crosfield	1	1	—	—				

Umpires: R. Carpenter and A. F. Smith.

LANCASHIRE v YORKSHIRE

Played at Manchester, August, 1, 2, 3, 1892

In the course of this game, at Old Trafford, on Bank Holiday, the Lancashire eleven accomplished undoubtedly the most brilliant performance of their season. Indeed, so admirable was their play at all points during the three days over which the game extended that it was difficult to understand how it was that Lancashire did not take a higher position in the struggle for the county championship. The match was the return to that at Bramall Lane in Whit week, when, after a most keen and exciting struggle, Yorkshire proved successful by four wickets. Both sides were very strongly represented, except for the notable absence of F. S. Jackson from the Yorkshire team. Though the weather was dull and rain often threatened, there was an enormous attendance, estimated at over 20,000, and of course the great batting triumph of the Lancashire cricketers was enthusiastically received. As we have said, the opening day's play furnished a big success for the home county, who, going in first, put together in five hours and a half a score of no fewer than 437 for the loss of only four wickets. Two batsmen made over a hundred and another scored 80. The greatest success achieved was that of Albert Ward, who, going in first, hit up 180 in four hours and a quarter. He was fourth out at 331, and hit twenty-eight 4s, a 3 and eighteen 2s, his play, so far as could be seen, being free from a single chance. He found an admirable partner in Smith, who, joining him with the score at 24 for one wicket, remained with him until the total reached 213, the partnership thus producing 189 runs. Smith – generally a very cautious batsman – hit far more freely than usual, and made his 80 in two hours and a half, 56 of his runs being obtained in 4s. Briggs and Ward afterwards added 113 runs, and during the last seventy minutes Briggs and Baker, hitting the worn-out bowling all over the field, obtained 106 more. There was a marked change on the second day, for, some rain having fallen, the ground played treacherously when the Lancashire innings was continued, and Peel and Wainwright bowled with such marked effect that in fifteen overs the Lancashire innings was brought to a close for 471, the six remaining wickets thus producing only 34 runs. Briggs brought his total to 115, a brilliant display of hitting, which extended over two hours and a half and included sixteen 4s, two 3s and six 2s. His partnership with Baker realised 109 runs, and furnished the third instance during the innings of more than a hundred runs being added for a wicket. In going in against the enormous score of 471 Yorkshire had, or course, nothing to play for beyond a draw, but they showed very creditable cricket, their first innings, which lasted three hours and a half, amounting to 209. The light was always defective, and for the first hour the state of the ground certainly gave the bowlers some assistance. Eight out of the eleven reached double figures, the finest display being that of Ernest Smith, who scored 57 in an hour and a half without a mistake. Tunnicliffe signalised his reappearance in the team by carrying out his bat for 32. When Yorkshire followed on, 262 to the bad, Lord Hawke took Tunnicliffe in with him, and 66 runs were put on for the first wicket, the score being 74 for the loss of one batsman at the call of time. The attendance did not reach the tremendous figures of the opening day, but there were probably quite ten thousand people on the ground. Briggs, it is to be noted, followed up his innings of 115 by taking eight wickets for 14 runs apiece. After the second day's play there was of course very little chance of Yorkshire saving the game, as with one wicket down in their second innings they were still 188 runs behind. Unfortunately for the visitors, several showers fell on Tuesday night and on the Wednesday morning, and though the turf was never really treacherous, the ball got up sufficiently now and then to place the bastmen at a considerable disadvantage. Seeing how well they had struggled on the previous day, it must be admitted that the form of the Yorkshiremen as a whole was rather disappointing in the concluding stage of the contest, for the nine outstanding wickets went down in about two hours and ten minutes for the addition of only 105 runs. The one batsman who really distinguished himself was Tunnicliffe, who increased his not out score of 32 to 50, an innings which lasted altogether an hour and forty minutes and included eight 4s, three 3s and two 2s. Altogether he made 82 runs in the match for once out, the performance naturally regaining him his place in the Yorkshire eleven. It is worthy of note that the same player had a great share in the victory which Yorkshire gained over Lancashire at Bramall Lane at Whitsuntide. Briggs again bowled with considerable effect, and it was largely due to him that Lancashire obtained their success, for he took thirteen wickets in the match for 209 runs and scored over a hundred. In the second innings Watson had the better analysis, taking five wickets for 55 runs. To Briggs, Albert Ward, and Smith Lancashire mainly owed their easy victory by an innings and 83 runs.

Lancashire

F. H. Sugg c Wardall b Smith	9
A. Ward c Hunter b Moorhouse	180
A. Smith c Wainwright b Wardell	80
Mr A. C. MacLaren b Peel	1
J. Briggs b Wainwright	115
G. R. Baker c Wainwright b Peel	49
Mr S. M. Crosfield b Peel	15
G. Yates b Wainwright	5
Mr A. T. Kemble b Peel	0
A. Watson not out	0
A. Mold b Wainwright	4
B 8, l-b 4, w 1	13
	471

Yorkshire

Lord Hawke b Briggs	12	– b Watson	35
T. Wardell b Briggs	3	– c Crosfield b Briggs	7
Mr E. Smith c and b Briggs	57	– c MacLaren b Watson	17
Mr A. Sellers c Kemble b Briggs	14	– b Watson	11
G. Ulyett c Ward b Briggs	21	– b Watson	1
E. Wainwright b Mold	17	– lbw b Briggs	18
R. Peel c Baker b Briggs	24	– c MacLaren b Watson	14
J. Tunnicliffe not out	32	– c Kemble b Briggs	50
J. Mounsey b Briggs	0	– not out	4
R. Moorhouse b Watson	21	– c Smith b Briggs	8
D. Hunter c and b Briggs	1	– c Sugg b Briggs	11
B 5, l-b 2	7	B 3	3
	209		179

Yorkshire Bowling

	Overs	Mdns	Runs	Wkts	Overs	Mdns	Runs	Wkts
Mr Smith	34	5	128	1				
Peel	55	29	79	4				
Wainwright	30	9	82	3				
Wardall	30	15	48	1				
Moorhouse	13	2	38	1				
Mounsey	6	1	26	—				
Mr Sellers	9	1	19	—				
Ulyett	11	2	38	—				

Lancashire Bowling

	Overs	Mdns	Runs	Wkts	Overs	Mdns	Runs	Wkts
Mold	35	14	67	1	7	2	15	—
Briggs	48.4	10	113	8	44	17	96	5
Watson	14	6	22	1	42	26	55	5
Smith					5	2	10	—

Umpires: Tuck and J. Street.

LANCASHIRE v KENT

Played at Manchester, May 22, 23, 24, 1893

Thanks to the really superb bowling of Walter Hearne and some admirable batting by Mr W. H. Patterson and Mr Marchant, Kent beat Lancashire by 80 runs, this being their first victory at Old Trafford since the season of 1888. The loss to Kent involved in Walter Hearne's subsequent accident and illness may be judged from his performance in this match, when he took in all fifteen wickets at a cost of only 114 runs. On no previous occasion in first-class cricket had he been seen to such conspicuous advantage. Patterson on the first day stayed in three hours and twenty minutes for his 82 not out, an innings which, though marred by a couple of chances of stumping, was a splendid display of patient and correct cricket. Very different in character was Marchant's brilliant 76 in the second innings.

Kent

A. Hearne b Briggs	5	– c Smith b Briggs	20
Mr F. Marchant b Mold	35	– c Baker b Mold	76
Mr W. H. Patterson not out	82	– run out	7
Mr W. L. Knowles b Briggs	4	– c MacLaren b Baker	0
Mr L. Wilson c MacLaren b Briggs	25	– c and b Smith	16
Mr C. J. M. Fox c Sugg b Briggs	17	– b Ellis	11
G. G. Hearne b Baker	7	– b Mold	9
Mr A. R. Layman c MacLaren b Briggs	1	– lbw b Mold	0
F. Martin c Sugg b Briggs	7	– not out	8
W. Wright c Sugg b Briggs	0	– b Mold	0
W. Hearne b Briggs	4	– b Mold	10
B 4	4	B 4, l-b 8	12
	191		169

Lancashire

Mr A. N. Hornby b W. Hearne	7	– c A. Hearne b W. Hearne	28
A. Ward c Layman b W. Hearne	10	– b A. Hearne	2
F. H. Sugg b W. Hearne	16	– c A. Hearne b W. Hearne	11
A. Smith b W. Hearne	8	– b W. Hearne	2
Mr A. C. MacLaren b W. Hearne	2	– b W. Hearne	6
J. Briggs c Wright b A. Hearne	66	– b W. Hearne	0
A. Tinsley b W. Hearne	17	– b W. Hearne	17
G. R. Baker c Marchant b A. Hearne	5	– b W. Hearne	2
Ellis b A. Hearne	0	– not out	26
Mr A. T. Kemble b W. Hearne	9	– c G. G. Hearne b W. Hearne	4
A. Mold not out	4	– c G. G. Hearne b A. Hearne	10
B 18, l-b 4	22	B 2, l-b 4	6
	166		114

Lancashire Bowling

	Overs	Mdns	Runs	Wkts	Overs	Mdns	Runs	Wkts
Briggs	59.2	25	87	8	29	13	34	1
Mold	42	22	73	1	33.4	11	74	5
Ellis	6	1	12	—	10	2	17	1
Baker	11	7	15	1	13	6	18	1
Smith					9	4	14	1

Kent Bowling

	Overs	Mdns	Runs	Wkts	Overs	Mdns	Runs	Wkt
W. Hearne	38	18	74	7	27	12	40	8
Martin	25	13	37	—	3	—	10	—
Wright	4	1	19	—				
A. Hearne	8	1	14	3	23.2	6	58	2

Umpires: A. F. Smith and J. Potter.

LANCASHIRE v YORKSHIRE

Played at Manchester, August 7, 8, 1893

At the time set apart for the return match between these famous Northern counties, t take place at Old Trafford, they occupied the two leading positions in the competition fo the championship – Yorkshire being in front, with Lancashire second – so it will be readil understood how keen was the interest evinced in the meeting. It may be said at once tha the interest, which merged into excitement as the game went on, was fully justified by th cricket displayed on both sides, and few of the vast crowd that witnessed it will ever forge the scene at the finish, when Lancashire gained a sensational victory by 5 runs. The matc opened on Bank Holiday, and despite a threatening morning following rain, there wer fully 10,000 present at midday, while though a heavy storm delayed the game from on o'clock until after luncheon, the crowd subsequently increased until it was estimated tha there were over 25,000 present – the actual number that paid at the turnstiles was 22,55 – which is an aggregate attendance far in advance of any previous record at Manchester Both sides were thoroughly representative. As the wicket was slow and difficult, and no likely to improve, it was felt that Mr Crosfield gained a big advantage for the home count by winning the toss, but, as will be seen, the batsmen made very little use of thei opportunities. It is true that the Yorkshiremen bowled and fielded magnificently, and tha runs were always difficult to obtain, but a little more hitting and a little less caution woul probably have improved the total considerably. To start with, four wickets fell for 2 before the rain referred to stopped play, and another batsman was dismissed directly afte the resumption without addition to the figures. Ward, who was batting nearly two hour for 19, and Baker infused some life into the proceedings by raising the score to 56, bu when the last wicket fell, though the innings had occupied two hours and a quarter, th total was only 64. Peel and Mr Smith bore off the bowling honours, the amateur havin the better of two remarkable analyses. The ground was becoming more difficult whe Yorkshire went in, but the spectators were certainly not prepared to see them fail a completely as the others had done. They did, however, for Brown, Tunnicliffe and Pee alone made double figures, and the whole side were dismissed by Briggs and Mold in a hour and fifty minutes for 58, while in the last quarter of an hour Lancashire scored 7 i their second innings without loss, and so left off with 13 runs in hand. Altogether pla lasted four hours and twenty minutes, during which time twenty wickets fell for a aggregate of 129 runs. Slow, however, as was the batting, it was more than atoned for b the excellence reached in the other departments. The even character of the first stag promised a second day of more than ordinary interest, and though the match was abrupth finished soon after luncheon, no fewer than 9,599 paid gate on Tuesday. Some shower had fallen, and as the sun came out the pitch was more difficult than ever. Just for a whil it seemed possible that Lancashire might do fairly well, for Ward and MacLaren score freely from Ernest Smith, who was unwisely put on first with Peel, but the profession was out at 18, and his dismissal was rapidly succeeded by others. The turning point wa when Wainwright was put on, for from that time the batsmen were outplayed, and th innings terminated for 50 after lasting an hour and a half. Then came the most sensational part of this remarkable match. Left with but 57 to make, Jackson and Sellers commenced Yorkshire's task just after one o'clock with so much resolution that 24 runs were obtained in sixteen minutes, and everything suggested an easy triumph for the visitors. Then Oakley was put on in place of Mold, and in his first over Jackson was out in the most unfortunate fashion. The ball hit his pad and glanced away, and Oakley appealed for leg before. Jackson ran half way up the pitch, but Sellers, under the impression that Potter had given his colleague out instead of not out, did not move, and so the Cantab lost his wicket. Sellers, evidently upset by this incident, was bowled at 25; Brown played on at 26, and Wainwright was leg before at 29. Thus a radical change took place in a few minutes. With Smith and Tunnicliffe together, the former hit out vigorously and made the next 12 runs, which appeared to give Yorkshire the advantage once more, but when everything seemed going well Smith hit a ball to cover-point, which Crosfield took close to the ground, with the result that the umpire, on appeal, gave the batsman out. It was a near thing, and Smith, with a large proportion of the spectators, did not think the catch had been made. Still he had to go, and the decision proved and important factor in Lancashire's ultimate victory. At luncheon six men were out for 42, while in twenty-five minutes afterwards the last four were dismissed for an additional 9 runs, which left the home side winners as stated above. Some little feeling was exhibited over the result, but in such a finish it was only to be expected. Briggs bowled with wonderful judgment, and took in all eleven wickets for 60 runs. His audacity in pitching a ball up for Ulyett to hit when only 6 runs were wanted was almost as much talked about afterwards as was the way in which Jackson and Smith lost their wickets. His efforts were admirably seconded by Mold and Oakley, and by the entire field. On the other hand, the absolutely best performance in the match was accomplished by Peel, who took ten wickets for 39 runs.

Lancashire

Mr A. C. MacLaren c Hirst b Peel	1	– c Hunter b Peel	16
A. Ward c Ulyett b Smith	19	– c Hunter b Peel	12
F. H. Sugg c Tunnicliffe b Hirst	3	– c Tunnicliffe b Peel	0
J. Briggs lbw b Hirst	0	– c Tunnicliffe b Peel	9
Mr S. M. Crosfield run out	10	– c Hunter b Wainwright	6
A. Tinsley c Tunnicliffe b Peel	0	– c Tunnicliffe b Peel	3
G. R. Baker b Peel	21	– st Hunter b Wainwright	0
G. Yates c Hunter b Smith	2	– b Wainwright	0
Mr A. T. Kemble b Smith	4	– b Wainwright	0
W. Oakley not out	0	– not out	3
A. Mold b Peel	1	– c Tunnicliffe b Peel	1
L-b 3	3		
	64		50

Yorkshire

Mr A. Sellers b Briggs	0	– b Oakley	13
Mr F. S. Jackson c and b Briggs	1	– run out	12
Mr E. Smith c Ward b Briggs	4	– c Crosfield b Briggs	12
J. Brown b Briggs	17	– b Oakley	0
J. Tunnicliffe c Ward b Briggs	11	– c Oakley b Mold	2
E. Wainwright b Mold	4	– lbw b Briggs	3
R. Peel b Mold	12	– lbw b Mold	1
R. Moorhouse c Tinsley b Mold	4	– st Kemble b Briggs	0
G. Ulyett c Baker b Briggs	0	– c Ward b Briggs	7
G. H. Hirst b Mold	1	– c Baker b Briggs	0
D. Hunter not out	1	– not out	1
B 2, l-b 1	3		
	58		51

Yorkshire Bowling

	Overs	Mdns	Runs	Wkts	Overs	Mdns	Runs	Wkts
Hirst	24	11	36	2	4	2	4	—
Peel	29.3	20	15	4	19.3	9	24	6
Smith	6	2	10	3	8	4	14	—
Wainwright					7	2	8	4

Lancashire Bowling

	Overs	Mdns	Runs	Wkts	Overs	Mdns	Runs	Wkts
Briggs	22	8	35	6	14.2	3	25	5
Mold	21.3	10	20	4	9	5	13	2
Oakley					5	1	13	2

Umpires: A. Smith and J. Potter.

LANCASHIRE v SUSSEX

Played at Manchester, May 31 and June 1, 1894

It was in this match that Alfred Shaw, the veteran Nottinghamshire bowler, reappeared in first-class cricket after an absence of seven years, playing for Sussex under the residential qualification. Although, of course, not so active as a young man, Shaw showed that he had lost nothing of his exceptional accuracy of pitch, and on a batsman's wicket, and handicapped by some faulty fielding, he took four wickets at a moderate cost. Lancashire going in first lost three wickets for 52 runs, but Baker played a great game in conjunction with Albert Ward, these two men staying together for an hour and forty minutes and putting on 142 runs. Briggs and Tinsley added 97 in an hour, but the Sussex men made many mistakes. Next day, with one notable exception, the Sussex batting broke down in a most deplorable fashion before the wonderful bowling of Mold, who, in the second innings of the visitors, actually took seven wickets in thirteen overs and four balls for 17 runs. The fast bowler maintained a remarkable pitch and pace, and occasionally whipped back in a manner which the visiting batsmen were quite unable to withstand. Newham in the first innings gave a wonderful display, going in first and carrying his bat right through the innings for 110 – a remarkable combination of resolute hitting and skilful defence.

Lancashire

A. Ward c Murdoch b Humphreys	69
Mr A. C. MacLaren b Killick	0
F. H. Sugg b Shaw	14
W. Brown b Shaw	7
G. R. Baker c Newham b Humphreys	96
J. Briggs st Butt b Shaw	65
A. Tinsley c Newham b Lowe	53
Mr W. H. Houldsworth b Shaw	21
G. H. Wharmby b Lowe	0
Mr A. T. Kemble not out	7
A. Mold c Bean b Lowe	0
B 8, l-b 12, w 2	22
	354

Sussex

G. Bean c Ward b Briggs	0	– c Kemble b Mold	1
Mr W. Newham not out	110	– b Mold	9
J. Lowe b Mold	5	– b Mold	4
Mr W. L. Murdoch b Mold	7	– b Briggs	3
Mr C. A. Smith c Kemble b Wharmby	3	– b Mold	10
W. Humphreys b Mold	1	– c Brown b Briggs	0
F. Guttridge b Wharmby	6	– b Mold	8
Killick lbw b Wharmby	0	– b Mold	3
H. Butt c Tinsley b Mold	6	– c Sugg b Mold	0
Mr G. Brann b Briggs	4	– absent hurt	6
A. Shaw b Briggs	16	– not out	0
B 15, l-b 1	16		
	174		38

Sussex Bowling

	Overs	Mdns	Runs	Wkts
Shaw	52	25	73	4
Killick	21	5	67	1
Guttridge	22	9	50	0
Lowe	15.3	6	41	3
Smith	13	1	38	0
Humphreys	20	6	64	2

Lancashire Bowling

	Overs	Mdns	Runs	Wkts	Overs	Mdns	Runs	Wkts
Mold	39	17	63	4	13.4	4	17	7
Briggs	30.2	4	42	3	14	4	21	2
Wharmby	18	6	35	3				
Brown	3	0	12	0				
Baker	3	0	6	0				

Umpires: A. F. Smith and Clarke.

LANCASHIRE v SOMERSET

Played at Manchester, July 16, 17, 1894

Some extraordinary cricket was witnessed in this game, in which no start could be made on the Monday. The second day's cricket, however, made full amends, for on a difficult wicket the play proved so sensational that the game was commenced and finished between twenty minutes to twelve and a quart-past six. Curiously enough, only two years before Lancashire had similarly beaten Somerset in the course of one day's cricket. The triumph for the northern county in the match under notice was mainly the work of Frank Sugg and Mold. The fast bowler did the "hat trick" in the first innings of the western team, who were all out in fifty minutes for 31. Three wickets fell at 19, and four others at 21, Mold narrowly missing the "hat trick" for the second time in the innings, and actually obtaining seven wickets for 10 runs. Up to this point Sugg had done scarcely anything worthy of his reputation, but he came out on the slow wicket in his finest form, and hit up an innings of 105 by one 5, nineteen 4s, a 3, five 2s and eleven singles. Smith helped him to put on 133 runs in sixty-five minutes for the second wicket. In the second innings of the visitors Lionel Palairet played a great game for his side, and scored a splendid innings of 69 in eighty minutes, but no one except Fowler gave him much assistance, and before time Somerset were beaten by an innings and 68 runs.

Somerset

Mr L. C. H. Palairet b Mold	8	– c and b Bardswell	69
Mr P. T. Ebden b Mold	7	– b Mold	0
Mr V. T. Hill c Sugg b Briggs	1	– b Mold	0
Mr R. C. N. Palairet b Mold	0	– c MacLaren b Mold	10
Mr W. C. Hedley b Mold	0	– b Mold	4
Mr G. Fowler b Briggs	0	– c Thomas b Briggs	31
Mr S. M. J. Woods c Bardswell b Briggs	7	– c MacLaren b Mold	0
G. C. Nichols b Mold	0	– b Mold	9
Mr D. L. Evans b Mold	0	– c MacLaren b Briggs	0
E. J. Tyler b Mold	0	– lbw b Briggs	0
Rev. A. P. Wickham not out	3	– not out	0
B 4, l-b 1	5	B 4, l-b 5	9
	31		132

Lancashire

Mr A. C. MacLaren b Woods	8	A. Tinsley not out	0
F. Sugg lbw b Tyler	105	Mr G. R. Bardswell c Hill b Hedley	4
A. Smith c Hedley b Woods	50	Thomas b Nichols	0
A. Ward c Fowler b Woods	0	A. Mold run out	2
J. Briggs c Fowler b Woods	6	L-b 5	5
G. R. Baker c Wickham b Hedley	37		
Mr S. M. Tindall b Nichols	14		231

Lancashire Bowling

	Overs	Mdns	Runs	Wkts	Overs	Mdns	Runs	Wkts
Briggs	9.4	3	16	3	11	2	50	3
Mold	9	7	10	7	18.2	4	50	6
Bardswell					10	4	23	1

Somerset Bowling

	Overs	Mdns	Runs	Wkts
Tyler	23	4	83	1
Woods	29	6	100	4
Hedley	10	4	20	2
Nichols	14	7	23	2

Umpires: Panter and Talboys.

THROWING IN FIRST-CLASS CRICKET (1894)

In conversation with several first-class cricketers during the past season I heard such serious complaints as to the unfairness of certain bowlers that I thought it advisable, on the principle that has several times before this been followed in *Wisden's Almanack* when a question has been ripe for discussion, to write to a number of the best-known amateurs asking them for an opinion on the subject. The questions referred to them were two: first "Do you think there was much throwing in first-class cricket last season"? and, secondly "Can you make any suggestion as to how the evil may be remedied"? It was not argued by any of the cricketers I met in the summer that the evil had assumed anything like the same proportions as when Lord Harris, some years ago, took such strong action in the matter, but there seemed a strong feeling that the mischief was certainly cropping up again, and that, as a prudent medical officer endeavours to grapple with an outbreak of disease while it is still confined to a small area, it was well that something should be done before things became worse than they were in 1894. Lest it should be thought that I am dealing merely with generalities, and, as it were, fighting the air, I may state that the bowlers of whom I heard the most serious complaints were Mold, Captain Hedley, Mr C. B. Fry, and Hardstaff. In dealing with a question so delicate, I did not write to any professional players, feeling that it would be placing them in a very false position to ask them to express an opinion. Moreover, in asking for the suggestion of a remedy, I went on the assumption that after fifteen years' experience it was altogether hopeless to look for any action from professional umpires. On the whole I have no reason to feel dissatisfied with the answers to my enquiries. As might have been expected, the experts who have favoured me with their views have abstained from naming individual offenders, but it will be seen that many of the writers are agreed in thinking that there was a certain amount of throwing last season in first-class matches. The letters may be left to speak for themselves, but perhaps I may be allowed to say, that, personally, I am strongly in favour of the suggestion made in different ways by Mr R. A. H. Mitchell, Mr Kemp, and Lord Hawke. I agree with Lord Hawke in thinking that there would be no utility in watching a suspected bowler if he knew he was under supervision. It would only be human nature for him under such circumstances to bowl with perfect fairness. There being no likelihood of an unfair bowler ever being no-balled by a professional umpire, I think that the captain of a side having reason to complain of throwing would be fully justified in reporting the offence to the committee of the Marylebone Club. As we all know, the umpires, according to the rules of cricket, are the sole judges of fair or unfair play; but for reasons readily to be understood they have in this particular instance so persistently shirked their duty that if English bowling is once and for all to be cleared from the stigma of unfairness some steps will have to be taken by those in authority. The committee of the Marylebone Club are clearly capable of acting in such a matter, and we may be quite sure that before barring a bowler from appearing at Lord's Ground, they would thoroughly satisfy themselves that the evidence against him was sufficient to justify so strong a measure. I have no doubt that a good many people will argue that while the laws of cricket fail to define what a throw is, it is illogical to attempt to punish a bowler for breaking the law; but to this contention I do not myself attach serious weight. I do not think there is any competent umpire who would experience a difficulty in distinguishing a throw from a fairly-bowled ball. In conclusion I think with Lord Hawke and Mr L. C. H. Palairet that much may be done by the County Captains.

S. H. P.

Mr E. M. Grace says: – "In answer to question No. 1, I do not think there was much throwing this year; but certainly there was some. Question No. 2. To My mind the rule about 'no-ball' is perfect as it is. All it wants is to be acted up to by all umpires fairly and honestly, and then we should have no throwers. If they acted according to the rule, they must 'no-ball' every thrower. At the same time it is possible they might 'no-ball' a man who did not throw, but the thrower would be certain to be no-balled. The rule, I think, says, if the umpire has any suspicion about the fairness of the delivery. Now no man can stand umpire and not be suspicious of some bowlers' delivery. He may not be certain, but the rule gives him every latitude, but they will not act up to it, they are afraid to do so, although they would be certain to be supported not only by the MCC, but by all right-thinking players. I have purposely avoided mentioning names, because I do not think that is what you want. Some umpires I have asked 'Why do not you no-ball So and so'? The usual answer is, 'No one else does' ".

Mr R. A. H. Mitchell writes: – "I see no first-class cricket to speak of now, and therefore can express no opinion as to whether there has been much throwing or not. It is a difficult question, and it is, perhaps, rather hard to expect professional umpires to no-ball a doubtful action, although the law commands them to do so. It might perhaps be possible to ask captains of sides in first-class matches to name any bowler to the committee of the MCC whose action they considered unfair. The MCC might perhaps then appoint a special umpire (gentleman or player) to watch a bowler of the kind and report to them. If the report was unfavourable, the MCC ought to have power to prevent him playing. This, of course, could not be done unless the committee agreed to it. I daresay there will be many objections, perhaps fatal ones, raised to this proposal, but I have no better suggestion to make. Apart from this, I consider that the umpire at the bowler's end is not in a good position to see whether the bowler throws or not. He has to watch foot and arm at the same time, and his position is not a good one for seeing the arm work. I would suggest that the duty of no-balling a bowler for throwing should fall on the umpire at the batsman's end. I think he can see much better than the other umpire, and he would have nothing but the arm to watch at the moment".

Mr W. G. Grace writes: – "I shall very likely write some notes on the past season, and if I do I intend mentioning the growing throwing nuisance; but how it is to be remedied is another question altogether. Old umpires won't 'no ball' them, and young ones ditto".

Mr V. E. Walker writes: – "I really see but comparatively little of first-class cricket now – at Lord's almost wholly – so that I feel I am not in a position to judge. I have myself not seen any unfair bowling lately, though I hear it talked of, but not so much as a few years since. In a well-proved and established case I should advise the MCC not to employ in any way either the offender or umpire again for one or two years".

Mr I. D. Walker says: – "I should not like to say I saw much throwing last season, but I certainly thought the deliveries of more than one bowler were very doubtful. Law 48a says: 'Unless the umpire is satisfied of the absolute fairness of the delivery he shall call "no-ball"'. This is comparatively a new law, and I believe that some of the umpires who officiate in county matches are not aware of its existence, or at any rate agree to ignore it. This law no doubt was made with the intention of putting a check on all doubtful deliveries. With regard to a remedy, I see none except the appointment of amateur umpires in the more important matches, and this is a contingency hardly likely to occur; for, irrespective of the amount of time required for the duty, it would not be an exactly pleasant task to 'no-ball' a Surrey man at The Oval, a Yorkshireman at Sheffield, or, perhaps hardest of all, a Derbyshire man at Derby".

Lord Hawke, dealing with the matter more boldly than most of my correspondents, writes: – "I am much obliged for yours of November 8th and am pleased to learn that you intend to ventilate the subject of 'Throwing' in the forthcoming edition of *Wisden*. You ask me two questions, and in answer to the first, I say without hesitation that there was much throwing in first-class cricket last season, and unless it is seriously taken notice of, it will go on increasing, and no one, not even the MCC, will be able to stop it. Your second question: 'Can I propose a remedy'? – certainly, If any captain of a first-class county is dissatisfied with the bowling of an opponent, and he can get two other county captains of his opinion, let them forward their complaint to Lord's, and I am sure the committee will make a move in the matter, appointing impartial judges to watch that bowler on occassions away from Lord's. It is no use bringing a man up to Lord's, asking him to bowl, and telling him you are especially going to watch his action – that has been tried and failed, I may say, ignominiously. A bowler must be watched without his having any knowledge of it whatsoever, and when one or two have been disqualified, it will be a lesson to the remainder. I know it is said it is hard to take the bread out of a professional's mouth, but there are amateurs who throw just as badly, and they must be watched in the same manner. The rule is very plain, the words 'absolute fairness' being used, so if it is worth printing, it is worth carrying into effect. One word more, I believe much can be done by a meeting of county captains, and I hope before next season to have the pleasure of asking them to meet me to discuss 'Throwing and Umpiring' ".

Mr W. L. Murdoch, who is known to feel very strongly on the subject of unfair bowling, writes: – "The subject you have tackled is a very serious one, and if others will be candid and say what they really think, I will be only too glad to express my opinion upon the first of your questions. To my mind the remedy for throwing is very simple; the rule says: 'If the umpire be not satisfied of the absolute fairness of the delivery of any ball he shall call "no-ball"'. Now if the MCC were to instruct all umpires that it was absolutely necessary to carry out this rule without respect to persons, I think it would have the desired effect".

Mr S. M. J. Woods says: – "The MCC are the proper body to deal with unfair bowling. I don't think there are more than half a dozen throwers playing in first-class cricket".

Mr M. C. Kemp writes: – "Compared with the years 1880 to 1886, I do not think there was as much unfair bowling during the last season. There is no bowler now, in my opinion, whose delivery is considered more than doubtful by the majority of cricketers, every ball he delivers, as was the case with several bowlers from 1880 to 1886. The evil of unfair bowling has assumed now a more disguised form, and it would not be difficult to mention bowlers who, when light and ground are favourable, are tempted to 'put in a chuck or two', and that this is true is the firm belief not only of those who have been playing against such bowlers, but has often been privately acknowledged by those who have been playing on the bowler's side. The remedy for this evil will ultimately be in the hands of the umpires. but it seems to me the committees of the County Clubs and the committee of the MCC could speedily check the evil. It is perfectly well known who the bowlers are whose fairness is occasionally doubted, and if county committees refused, as they ought to do, and as to my knowledge one county has done, to play bowlers with doubtful deliveries, the offenders would soon find honesty to be always the best policy. Failing this, why should not the committee of MCC receive evidence about bowlers, and when satisfied that there is reasonable ground of complaint, communicate with the county that employs the bowler complained of, and also with the umpires who may be standing in the matches where the doubtful bowler will be playing. Many complaints are now made on very insufficient grounds, but if complaints have to be formally made and substantiated before an impartial committee, they will, I feel sure, not be made recklessly, and will be few and far between. The mere fact that complaints can be formally lodged will deter bowlers from unfair practices".

Mr Ernest Smith writes: – "I am very pleased to see you are taking up the subject of throwing in first-class matches – it is quite time something was done about it. I don't think there is much throwing, but there are two or three distinct cases – one of them a very important case, as the bowling averages show – and these seem to me quite sufficient cause for agitation. There may be more throwing than I have come across, as I can play little first-class cricket now, and therefore only see a limited number of players. As to the remedy, it seems very difficult. The umpires will never stop it, I'm quite sure. It seems to me that the only way is for counties to refuse to play matches with any county whose team contains a bowler whose action is in any way doubtful, until that bowler has changed his doubtful action, or is left out of the team – the latter for choice – because I think a bowler who throws ought to be treated in much the same way as sharpers, who are warned off the Turf. In the case of professionals, there should be no scruples on the score of depriving a man of his means of livelihood, because unless he plays the game fairly he certainly does not deserve to make money by it. He seems to come under the head of one obtaining money by false pretences! I wish you every success in your endeavour to do away with this evil".

Mr C. W. Wright states: – "I only noticed isolated cases of throwing last season; a certain amateur, not Somersetshire, was the worst. I have long thought that the only way to stop it is to have amateur umpires, and that the short-leg umpire be allowed to judge of the fairness of the bowler's delivery, as the bowler's umpire certainly cannot look at his hands and feet both at the same time. The rule says 'The umpire shall call "no-ball" if he has any doubt of the fairness of delivery'. But no professional umpire will ever call 'no-ball' upon a mere doubt"!

A very well-known cricketer, who does not wish his name to appear writes: – "It is rather a difficult matter, and I personally got such a real sickener from the performance of the committee of the MCC in allowing Fry to bowl in the 'Varsity match of 1892 that I there and then made up my mind that throwing must not be allowed. If there had been forty times as much throwing last season in first-class matches as there was I should put it all down to that 'feeble committee'. I do not personally think there was much throwing last year; but I am not going to give myself away, and this must be anonymous. I think there are only three throwers in England (by a thrower I mean a man who deliberately throws a ball now and then) – one amateur and two professionals. I do not feel disposed to mention names, and I dare say in consequence you would rather I kept what I am writing to myself. In my opinion the best judge by a very long way as to whether a bowler throws or not is the 'batsman', because he can both watch the delivery and also notice the way in which the ball comes off the pitch. Against all these three throwers I have been fortunate enough to play long innings (over 100 against one and 80 against the others), so I ought to be able to judge from my own point of view. It is not for the man who is bowled by a thrower for 0 to say he throws, but the man who makes 99 before he is bowled. Now, to find a remedy, that is the question. A suggestion from a committee composed of, say, two reliable authorities on the game and absolutely unbiassed (this as far as possible) and eight first-class batsmen, all of whom have played innings of 50 and upwards against the men suspected, and let them discuss and vote by ballot upon the question of alteration of action or suspension altogether. Of course by this you deprive the umpires of their greatest responsibility, but they themselves are not apparently capable of holding this responsibility, and therefore they ought to be deprived of it. All the talk about amateur umpires I dismiss as monsense. It is impossible. There is another suggestion; the batsman to be allowed to appeal to the other umpire as to the fairness of delivery. This because unless a man is wall-eyed he cannot watch both feet and arms. I should like an opinion from you".

Mr Gregor MacGregor says: – "In answer to your letter of the 25th October I fear that I cannot take a very decided view on the question of throwing, as it seems to me that fair bowling and throwing can be assimilated in a bowler's action by practice to such an extent that it is almost impossible to detect the precise ball which is the throw".

Mr W. H. Patterson writes: – "I cannot say much about last season, as I was only able to play so very little, but speaking generally, after a considerable experience in first-class cricket, I am of opinion that there is very little throwing. A man may occasionally throw a ball, but I do not think there are many who do".

Mr Richard Daft, taking the part of all our present-day bowlers, states: – "I saw most of the first-class bowlers last season, and although occasionally there might be a ball that was the least bit suspicious, upon the whole I could not, if I had been umpire, have 'no-balled' it. I do not think there is anything to complain of regarding our first-class bowlers".

Mr J. A. Dixon says: – "In answer to questions (1) I do not consider there has been much throwing in first-class cricket in the season of 1894. (2) The suggestion I favour is that of transferring the duty of 'no-balling' unfair deliveries from the umpire at the bowler's end to the umpire at the batsman's end.

The Hon. R. H. Lyttelton writes: – "I have seen for the last two years so little first-class cricket, that my views on the question you ask will not be worth much. I've heard it stated that Mold and Richardson throw occasionally. Personally I have never seen Mold throw; Richardson I have never seen bowl. From the little cricket I've seen I should say that at the present time there is no unfair bowling. Nearly all the cricket I see is at Lord's, and I feel sure that no unfair bowling is practised there. If it ever becomes prevalent the MCC must take action, not through professional umpires, but through pressure on county committees'.

Mr H. W. Bainbridge writes: – "In reply to the two questions in your letter, (1) I think that some of the best fast bowlers send down occasionally balls that are not fairly delivered. (2) I do not believe that there is any remedy for this, and I do not think any interference is necessary. I have no sympathy with unfair bowling, but believe that its prevalence exists principally in the imagination of those who don't like fast bowling of any kind".

Mr George Marsham, of the Kent County Club, writes: – "In reply to your queries I may say: 1. I saw no throwing in first-class cricket this season, and 'doubtful delivery' was the exception rather than the rule. 2. The committee of the MCC should be powerful enough to stop any bowler with a doubtful delivery. It is useless and unfair to expect the professional umpire to decide the question".

Mr A. P. Lucas preferred, as he had seen so little first-class cricket during the last few seasons, to express no personal opinion, but said he thought that ventilating the question would do good.

Mr L. C. H. Palairet writes: – "In reply to yours I certainly think there was a great deal of throwing in first-class cricket last season, and that it is yearly becoming more common and more thinly veiled. With regard to a remedy I quite agree that it is hopeless to look to professional umpires, and I do not think the umpire at the bowler's end can be expected to no-ball the bowler, especially as now-a-days so many bowlers not only go near either the bowling or return crease, but unless very closely watched will bowl with their foot on one or other all the day. The umpire cannot be expected to watch a man's hand and foot exactly at the same time, and I am of opinion that the only people to stop throwing are the captains of the first-class counties. They succeeded in settling the classification question to the satisfaction of most cricketers, and the sooner they take up this new question and settle it the better for cricket. Many will say the MCC Committee should weed out the throwers, but I doubt if that would be satisfactory, for so many of them hardly ever see a first class match, except at Lord's, and is it not a well-known fact – any-way among cricketers themselves – that very few of the throwers will throw at Lord's now? Is it likely, then, that they will throw there, when they know they are being eagerly watched, and that their future career may be ruined"?

LANCASHIRE v KENT

Played at Manchester, June 6, 7, 8, 1895

More than twenty thousand people were present on the first day, when Lancashire obtained such a mastery over the Kent bowling that they put together a score of 341 for four wickets. Ward, who with Tinsley put on 96 runs for the first wicket, brought a remarkable fortnight's work to a close with an admirable 76, and Paul followed up his successes against Leicestershire and Yorkshire by scoring 122 not out. Sugg helped to add 83 runs, and Baker stayed while 122 more were made. Paul was soon out next day, his fine innings having lasted more than four hours and a half. The Lancashire total of 487 was up to this time the highest the county had ever obtained. After the triumph of the Lancashire batsmen Mold bowled so grandly that in three hours fourteen Kent wickets went down for 115 runs, and altogether Kent were twice dismissed for 196, Lancashire winning most decisively by an innings and 291 runs. Mold achieved a marvellous record, taking sixteen wickets out of the nineteen for 111 runs. This was the first occasion on which Kent had lost to Lancashire since 1892, and they were greatly handicapped by the absence of Walter Hearne. An accident marred the enjoyment of the match, F. H. Huish, the young Kent wicket-keeper, breaking his collar-bone.

Lancashire

A. Ward c Marchant b Martin	76	C. Smith b Hearne	30
A. Tinsley run out	35	A. Hallam c and b Hearne	4
A. Paul c Hearne b Wright	140	A. Lancaster not out	23
F. Sugg b Martin	39	A. Mold c Mason b Hearne	0
G. R. Baker b Mason	58	B 7, l-b 3, n-b 1	11
J. Briggs c Hearne b Mason	47		
Mr S. M. Tindall b Mason	24		487

Kent

A. Hearne b Briggs	2	– b Mold	3
Mr J. R. Mason c Smith b Mold	9	– b Mold	7
J. Easby b Mold	5	– b Mold	0
Mr W. H. Patterson c Smith b Mold	13	– not out	57
Mr W. L. Knowles b Mold	3	– b Mold	2
Mr G. J. V. Weigall c Smith b Mold	13	– c Smith b Mold	0
Mr F. Marchant run out	20	– b Mold	19
Mr J. Tonge b Mold	5	– b Mold	2
F. Martin b Mold	0	– c Smith b Mold	9
W. Wright not out	0	– b Mold	19
F. H. Huish run out	0	– absent hurt	0
L-b 1	1	B 6, w 1	7
	71		125

Kent Bowling

	Overs	Mdns	Runs	Wkts
Martin	77	34	106	2
Wright	47	19	73	1
Hearne	68.2	24	123	3
Mason	37	5	95	3
Tonge	5	1	23	0
Patterson	9	1	34	0
Easby	3	0	18	0
Marchant	2	1	4	0

Lancashire Bowling

	Overs	Mdns	Runs	Wkts	Overs	Mdns	Runs	Wkts
Briggs	25	14	21	1	22	10	40	0
Mold	24.1	6	49	7	29.4	9	62	9
Lancaster					7	1	13	0
Hallam					1	0	3	0

Umpires: Hay and Wheeler.

LANCASHIRE v GLOUCESTERSHIRE

Played at Manchester, July 22, 23, 24, 1895

Although play on the opening day did not commence until a quarter past one the ground was so exceedingly treacherous that an innings on each side was completed before the drawing of stumps. Grace and Wrathall scored 54 without loss before lunch, but all ten wickets fell afterwards for 45 more runs, Briggs dismissing eight batsmen for 21 runs after the interval. Lancashire began well, their total reaching 90 with only three men out, but Sugg left at this point, and the other six wickets fell in half an hour for 17 runs. Next day the ground recovered in surprising fashion, but Grace for the first time during the season was out for a single figure. A fair total was reached, but Lancashire batted so well they they left off wanting only 45 to win, and having five wickets in hand. Unfortunately such torrents of rain fell on Tuesday night that the wicket was rendered unfit for further cricket, and the game had to be abandoned as a draw. Grace offered to play out the game on a fresh pitch, but MacLaren declined.

Gloucestershire

	First innings		Second innings	
Mr W. G. Grace c Baker b Mold	42	–	c Smith b Briggs	5
H. Wrathall c Benton b Briggs	26	–	c Sugg, b Briggs	27
Mr W. M'G. Hemingway c Paul b Briggs	12	–	b Mold	3
Mr R. W. Rice c and b Briggs	0	–	c Ward b Briggs	37
Mr C. L. Townsend b Mold	7	–	b Mold	14
Mr G. L. Jessop c Paul b Briggs	4	–	st Smith b Hallam	32
Mr J. J. Ferris b Briggs	0	–	c Paul b Mold	49
Captain A. H. Luard st Smith b Briggs	0	–	absent	0
Mr S. De Winton c Mold b Briggs	5	–	b Baker	18
J. H. Board not out	2	–	c Sugg b Mold	1
F. G. Roberts st Smith b Briggs	0	–	not out	0
			B 13, l-b 1	14
	99			200

Lancashire

	First innings		Second innings	
Mr A. C. MacLaren c Grace b Townsend	25			
A. Ward b Jessop	13	–	c Board b Ferris	50
A. Paul c Jessop b Townsend	2	–	b Roberts	11
F. H. Sugg b Jessop	39	–	c Jessop b Townsend	7
G. R. Baker st Board b Townsend	3	–	b Jessop	31
J. H. Tyldesley c Wrathall b Townsend	13	–	not out	33
J. Briggs b Jessop	1			
Mr C. H. Benton st Board b Townsend	3	–	lbw b Jessop	8
C. Smith b Jessop	0			
A. Hallam b Jessop	0			
A. Mold not out	0			
B 6, l-b 1, n-b 1	8		B 2, l-b 3, n-b 3	8
	107			148

Lancashire Bowling

	Overs	Mdns	Runs	Wkts	Overs	Mdns	Runs	Wkts
Briggs	24	5	49	8	39	9	72	3
Mold	20	9	37	2	37	19	62	4
Hallam	7	0	13	0	18	8	33	1
Baker					9	2	19	1

Gloucestershire Bowling

	Overs	Mdns	Runs	Wkts	Overs	Mdns	Runs	Wkts
Townsend	23.3	8	47	5	21	4	64	1
Roberts	3	0	15	0	14	8	23	1
Ferris	9	1	24	0	6	3	9	1
Jessop	11	4	13	5	14.4	1	44	2

Umpires: G. Hay and L. Hall.

LANCASHIRE v GLOUCESTERSHIRE

Played at Manchester, July 30, 31, 1896

Gloucestershire brought down a very good team for this match, but the luck went all against them, for after fielding out an innings of 313 they lost three batsman in the failing light for 14 runs and then rain during the night so affected the ground that the west countrymen were always playing a losing game. Lancashire, however deserved their victory, the batting – which on a wicket somewhat affected by rain produced the total of 313 – being worthy of great praise. There were two curious incidents in the game. MacLaren, when only two, trod on his wicket, and the umpire when appealed to for hit wicket decided that the batsman had completed his stroke and was starting to run, and accordingly gave him not out. From the last ball of the match, Sugg was caught, but the umpire having previously called no-ball, the game ended in favour of Lancashire by ten wickets. Board met with an injury while keeping wicket, and Wrathall who took his place let an extraordinary number of byes.

Lancashire

Mr A. C. MacLaren c Jessop b Roberts	56		
Mr E. Rowley run out	17		
A. Ward c Board b Roberts	42		
J. H. Tyldesley lbw b Roberts	52	– not out	10
A. Paul b Jessop	19		
F. H. Sugg b Jessop	12	– not out	17
G. R. Baker c Grace b Roberts	10		
J. Briggs lbw b Brown	29		
C. Smith not out	16		
A. Hallam c Board b Roberts	3		
A. Mold c Jessop b Roberts	8		
B 31, l-b 11, n-b 3, w 4	49	B 2, n-b 1	3
	313		30

Gloucestershire

H. Wrathall b Briggs	0	– c Smith b Hallam	13
Mr R. W. Rice b Briggs	7	– b Hallam	10
Mr C. L. Townsend c Smith b Hallam	14	– b Mold	8
Mr W. S. A. Brown b Mold	0	– c Briggs b Mold	13
Mr W. G. Grace c Tyldesley b Briggs	9	– c Hallam b Mold	42
Mr W. M'G. Hemingway c MacLaren b Briggs	22	– b Baker	7
Mr C. O. H. Sewell c Tyldesley b Briggs	27	– c and b Hallam	3
Mr S. A. P. Kitcat c MacLaren b Briggs	2	– c Mold b Hallam	15
Mr G. L. Jessop not out	29	– b Baker	81
J. H. Board b Mold	4	– c MacLaren b Mold	10
F. G. Roberts c Paul b Briggs	1	– not out	10
B 7	7	B 8	8
	122		220

Gloucestershire Bowling

	Overs	Mdns	Runs	Wkts	Overs	Mdns	Runs	Wkts
Townsend	25	3	64	0				
Roberts	41	14	89	6	2.4	1	11	0
Jessop	20	5	58	2	2	0	16	0
Brown	17	8	32	1				
Grace	8	0	21	0				

Lancashire Bowling

	Overs	Mdns	Runs	Wkts	Overs	Mdns	Runs	Wkts
Briggs	26.2	9	59	7	11	1	59	0
Mold	8	5	8	2	20.3	4	67	4
Hallam	18	5	48	1	25	5	59	4
Baker					15	6	27	2

Umpires: G. Hay and W. Shrewsbury.

LANCASHIRE v DERBYSHIRE

Played at Manchester, August 10, 11, 12, 1896

Lancashire had to take the field in this match without either MacLaren or Mold, both of whom were at Kennington Oval for the third test match. Mold returned to Manchester to play, but during his absence Frank Ward, his substitute, had been put on to bowl, and so of course the fast bowler could take no part in the game. Derbyshire lost two wickets for 26, and then some superb cricket by Chatterton and Davidson added 208 runs in less than three hours, while at the drawing of stumps the score was 381 for three wickets, Davidson not out 185, and Storer not out 56. Rain prevented play until after one o'clock next day, but the two batsmen playing with strangely unnecessary care stayed together two hours and a quarter more, and put on 161 runs. The fourth wicket fell at 542, the partnership which was the longest ever recorded at Old Trafford producing 308 runs. Davidson's 274 was the highest innings he had ever played, and the third best score of the season. Storer also reached three figures, his 116 being his fifth hundred during the summer. For Lancashire, Sugg played a vigorous and invaluable 96, and Rowley and Paul did well, but when the end came Lancashire with seven wickets to fall were still 236 behind.

Derbyshire

Mr L. G. Wright c Sugg b Hallam	3
H. Bagshaw b Briggs	13
W. Chatterton b Hallam	104
G. Davidson c Sugg b Briggs	274
W. Storer c Paul b Briggs	116
W. Sugg c Paul b Briggs	11
J. Hulme c Tyldesley b Hallam	5
Mr G. A. Marsden st Smith b Briggs	4
Mr H. G. Curgenven c Sugg b Hallam	13
Mr W. B. Delacombe not out	2
G. Porter b Briggs	0
N 22, l-b 6, w 4	32
	577

Lancashire

Mr E. Rowley b Davidson	50	– c Curgenven b Chatterteon	14
A. Ward b Davidson	8		
A. Paul b Porter	50	– c Curgenven b Chatterton	0
J. H. Tyldesley c and b Hulme	1	– not out	20
F. H. Sugg st Wright b Storer	96	– not out	26
F. Ward b Davidson	10		
G. R. Baker c and b Hulme	30		
J. Briggs lbw b Hulme	18		
A. Lancaster c Curgenven b Hulme	7		
C. Smith not out	1	– c Wright b Curgenven	3
A. Hallam b Hulme	4		
B 1, l-b 1, w 1	3		
	278		63

Lancashire Bowling

	Overs	Mdns	Runs	Wkts
Briggs	90	32	185	6
Hallam	73	31	127	4
Baker	20	8	45	0
Lancaster	46	18	97	0
F. Ward	20	9	39	0
Paul	11	2	28	0
A. Ward	4	1	11	0
Tyldesley	3	1	6	0
Sugg	4	2	7	0

Derbyshire Bowling

	Overs	Mdns	Runs	Wkts	Overs	Mdns	Runs	Wkts
Davidson	57	34	75	3				
Hulme	48.3	19	94	5				
Porter	29	10	57	1				
Curgenven	7	1	16	0	15	4	31	1
Storer	15	3	33	1				
Chatterton					12	4	16	2
Bagshaw					4	0	16	0

Umpires: W. A. Woof and A. Chester.

LANCASHIRE v MIDDLESEX

Played at Manchester, June 27, 28, 29, 1898

Although weakened by the absence of both Cuttell and Mold, Lancashire, after an interesting game, beat Middlesex by 44 runs. No play was possible until after three o'clock on the opening day, but before the drawing of stumps some admirable batting by Ward and Tyldesley placed the home side in a favourable position. Out of 202 runs made for three wickets, the two professionals had put on 145 while together. Next day the pitch was extremely treacherous and 26 wickets went down for 306 runs. Hearne was quite the hero of the day, dismissing six batsmen for 16 runs in the morning, while when Lancashire went in a second time, he obtained six of the nine wickets that fell. Briggs also bowled with fine effect for Lancashire. The seven outstanding Lancashire wickets went down for 26 runs. For Middlesex Stoddart and Ford played skilfully, and Foley and MacGregor added 43 for the last wicket. Middlesex on the third day had 225 to get to win. Hayman and Warner made 61 for the first wicket, but afterwards Lancaster bowled with startling success and Middlesex were all our for 180.

Lancashire

A. Ward c Ford b Hearne	53	– b Hearne	4
Mr C. R. Hartley b Hearne	9	– b Webb	24
J. T. Tyldesley c and b Hearne	96	– b Hearne	2
G. R. Baker c and b Hearne	29	– b Hearne	15
Mr W.B. Stoddart b Hearne	16	– b Trott	8
F. H. Sugg c Hayman b Rawlin	5	– b Hearne	25
Mr S. M. Tindall c Hayman b Hearne	4	– b Hearne	7
J. Briggs not out	0	– not out	15
Lancaster b Hearne	5	– lbw b Hearne	2
Taylor b Hearne	0	– c Ford b Trott	6
L. Radcliffe b Hearne	0	– c Rawlin b Hearne	8
B 11	11	B 20, l-b 7	27
	228		143

Middlesex

Mr H. B. Hayman b Briggs	9	– st Radcliffe b Stoddart	33
Mr P. F. Warner b Briggs	19	– st Radcliffe b Stoddart	31
Mr A. E. Stoddart st Radcliffe b Briggs	36	– b Lancaster	19
J. T. Rawlin b Briggs	0	– b Baker	2
Mr F. G. J. Ford b Briggs	22	– c Baker b Lancaster	35
A. E. Trott c Ward b Briggs	0	– st Radcliffe b Lancaster	2
Mr A. J. Webbe b Lancaster	1	– b Lancaster	27
Mr C. P. Foley not out	28	– not out	20
J. T. Hearne c Radcliffe b Briggs	0	– b Lancaster	0
S. Webb st Radcliffe b Briggs	0	– st Radcliffe b Lancaster	0
Mr G. MacGregor c Tyldesley b Taylor	23	– lbw b Lancaster	0
B 9	9	B 7, l-b 3, w 1	11
	147		180

Middlesex Bowling

	Overs	Mdns	Runs	Wkts	Overs	Mdns	Runs	Wkts
Rawlin	43	19	53	1	4	2	4	0
Hearne	41	19	68	9	27.1	11	46	7
Webb	14	3	41	0	11	1	39	1
Trott	9	3	33	0	12	4	27	2
A. E. Stoddart	7	1	22	0				

Lancashire Bowling

	Overs	Mdns	Runs	Wkts	Overs	Mdns	Runs	Wkts
Briggs	34	9	63	8	17	6	33	0
Taylor	16.3	7	25	1	15	8	28	0
W. B. Stoddart	4	0	18	0	20	3	46	2
Lancaster	17	8	28	1	25	11	25	7
Baker	2	0	4	0	19	7	37	1

Umpires: J. Yeadon and C. E. Richardson.

LANCASHIRE v ESSEX

Played at Manchester, July 14, 15, 16, 1898

Interesting from start to finish this contest was rendered memorable by the unprecedented achievement – so far as county cricket is concerned – of Essex in their last innings. A splendid stand by Tyldesley and Sugg was the feature of the Lancashire's batting on the opening day, these two adding 169 runs for the third wicket. Sugg, who was in splendid form just at this period, made the large proportion of 104. Bull and Kortright subsequently bowled in great form, the last seven wickets falling for 48 runs. Essex commenced well, but had four wickets down for 93 when play was adjourned and next day there was a narrow escape from following on. In the second innings of the home side Tyldesley, Hartley, and Sugg were all seen to marked advantage, the first-named completing his thousand runs. Essex were set the tremendous task of making 336 to win, and on Friday evening had made 34 without loss. Owen and Carpenter raised the total to 88, but the Essex triumph was only obtained through some grand batting by McGahey and Perrin, who put on 191 runs. Essex won by four wickets.

Lancashire

Mr C. R. Hartley st Russell b Bull	29	– b Turner	61
A. Ward c Russell b Kortright	1	– lbw b Bull	12
J. T. Tyldesley c Russell b Bull	85	– c Owen b Bull	61
F. H. Sugg c McGahey b Lucas	104	– c McGahey b Kortright	70
Mr A. Eccles c Russell b Kortright	8	– b Kortright	1
G. R. Baker st Russell b Bull	7	– c Mead b Bull	4
W. R. Cuttell st Russell b Bull	2	– c Kortright b Turner	21
J. Briggs b Kortright	8	– lbw b Turner	9
J. Ellis b Kortright	0	– b Kortright	2
A. Mold c Lucas b Bull	12	– c Turner b Kortright	2
L. Radcliffe not out	0	– not out	1
B 5, l-b 2	7	B 5, l-b 1	6
	254		250

Essex

Mr H. G. Owen c Briggs b Mold	13	– b Cuttell	44
H. Carpenter c Tyldesley b Cuttell	38	– b Briggs	34
Mr P. Perrin b Mold	7	– b Cuttell	61
Mr C. McGahey c Tyldesley b Cuttell	48	– c Sugg b Ellis	145
Mr A. J. Turner b Mold	5	– c Radcliffe b Cuttell	0
Mr A. P. Lucas b Mold	15	– not out	23
Mr F. L. Fane b Cuttell	4	– b Cuttell	4
T. M. Russell b Cuttell	0	– not out	4
Mr C. J. Kortright c Tyldesley b Mold	7		
W. Mead c Briggs b Cuttell	19		
Mr F. G. Bull not out	12		
L-b 1	1	B 15, l-b 9	24
	169		339

Essex Bowling

	Overs	Mdns	Runs	Wkts	Overs	Mdns	Runs	Wkts
Kortright	28	8	74	4	26	10	56	4
Bull	30.1	3	88	5	35	6	91	3
Mead	19	9	19	0	15	2	50	0
Turner	3	1	5	0	11	1	47	3
Carpenter	4	0	16	0				
Perrin	9	2	28	0				
Lucas	2	0	17	1				

Lancashire Bowling

	Overs	Mdns	Runs	Wkts	Overs	Mdns	Runs	Wkts
Cuttell	24.4	4	92	5	44	16	69	4
Mold	28	7	75	5	42	13	81	0
Briggs	5	5	0	0	32	7	70	1
Ellis	1	0	1	0	11.4	2	47	1
Baker					9	0	39	0
Sugg					2	0	9	0

Umpires: A. Shaw and J. Wheeler.

LEICESTERSHIRE

LEICESTERSHIRE IN 1886

President – The Right Hon. Viscount Curzon, MP

Vice-Presidents – Mr C. Marriott, The Mayor of Leicester

Hon. Secretary – Mr T. Burdett *Treasurer* – Mr W. Billings

Leicestershire obtained considerable renown last season by gaining a brilliant victory over Surrey by ten wickets, and their record in the seven matches played of three won, one lost, and three drawn, was a very satisfactory one. The other successes were against Warwickshire. Curiously enough the highest and lowest innings hit against Leicestershire were both made by Surrey, the totals being 415 and 26 respectively. The county eleven were dismissed for 43 by Cheshire, and in their match with a strong MCC team they scored 164 for the loss of five wickets. In several of their contests Leicestershire lacked the services of Messrs W. H. Hay and J. A. Turner, but they had a most successful season nevertheless.

The one special feature in the averages given below is the extraordinary bowling of Pougher, who obtained 66 wickets at a cost of just under 8½ runs each. The veteran Rylott also met with considerable success, taking 35 wickets for 13.32 runs each. In batting Wheeler comes out at the top with an average of 23.7, but he owes his position to a not-out innings of 82 played against the MCC. Warren and Colver follow next with very good averages, and the remainder of the figures will speak for themselves.

LEICESTERSHIRE v SURREY

Played at Leicester, July 8, 9, 1886

This proved to be one of the most sensational matches of the season, and some extraordinary cricket was witnessed on the first day. Surrey, who were playing without Mr Shuter, Mr Roller, and Beaumont, won the toss and went in first, but so feeble was the batting on a fiery ground that the whole side was actually dismissed by Pougher and Rylott for 26 runs. A wicket fell to the first ball in the innings, two wickets were down for one run, three for 4, five for 8, and six for 11. Then Mr Bowden managed to score 10 runs, so that between them ten members of the Surrey team contributed 16 runs. Pougher and Rylott, the bowlers, deserve every credit for their remarkable performance, the former taking six wickets for 10 runs and the latter three for 16. In the Leicestershire innings there were also several failures, but thanks to a somewhat lucky 52 by Warren and a useful not-out 20 by Colver, the side put together the very respectable total of 107. Surrey commenced their second innings with a balance of 81 runs against them, and lost four of their batsmen for 45 before the call of time.

On the second day the match came to an early termination, the last six wickets of Surrey falling for the addition of 38 runs. Pougher and Rylott again met with great success. Altogether Pougher obtained thirteen wickets at a cost of only 54 runs, and

Rylott six for 55. It was, of course, due to their effective bowling and Warren's batting that Leicestershire won with great ease by ten wickets. It will be noticed that the home county did not give an extra in either innings.

Surrey

Mr K. J. Key c sub. b Pougher	0	– c Wheeler b Pougher	14
Abel b Rylott	0	– b Rylott	8
Diver c Pougher b Rylott	1	– b Pougher	1
Mr W. W. Read c Wheeler b Pougher	3	– c Pougher b Rylott	3
M. Read c Wheeler b Pougher	4	– c Turner b Pougher	29
Mr M. P. Bowden run out	10	– lbw b Pougher	0
Brackwell c Pougher b Rylott	0	– b Pougher	0
Lohmann c Hill b Pougher	3	– c Rylott b Pougher	9
Wood b Pougher	0	– b Rylott	2
Jones b Pougher	2	– b Pougher	5
Bowley not out	3	– not out	12
	26		83

Leicestershire

Wheeler b Bowley	1	– not out	4
Mr E. Hill b Lohmann	8		
Warren b Jones	52	– not out	0
M. J. A. Turner b Bowley	3		
Turner c Diver b Bowley	4		
Mr C. C. Stone b Lohmann	4		
Parnham c Wood b Lohmann	5		
Pougher b Lohmann	0		
Mr H. T. Arnall-Thompson c Wood b Bowley	6		
Colver not out	20		
Rylott c M. Read b Jones	0		
B 4	4		
	107		4

Leicestershire Bowling

	Overs	Mdns	Runs	Wkts	Overs	Mdns	Runs	Wkts
Pougher	11.1	6	10	6	35	18	44	7
Rylott	11	5	16	3	34	17	39	3

Surrey Bowling

	Overs	Mdns	Runs	Wkts	Overs	Mdns	Runs	Wkts
Bowley	44	21	49	4	1	0	4	0
Lohmann	43	23	44	4	1	1	0	0
Jones	7.3	3	10	2				

LEICESTERSHIRE v SURREY

Played at Leicester, August 10, 11, 1893

The opening day's cricket was of a startling character, a thunderstorm overnight having so seriously affected the ground that thirty-one wickets went down for 149 runs. Leicestershire at the drawing of stumps had nine wickets to fall and wanted 48 runs to win. For a little while on the second morning the result was in doubt, as half the side were out for 27 runs. At that point, however, Pougher and Hillyard became partners, and the former, playing very finely, Leicestershire won the game by five wickets. For their highly creditable victory the home side were largely indebted to Pougher's all-round cricket. In the whole match he took eleven wickets for 38 runs and scored 34 for once out. For Surrey, Richardson had a similar bowling record, taking eleven wickets for 35 runs. This was the first occasion since 1888 that Leicestershire had beaten Surrey on the Aylestone Road ground.

Surrey

R. Abel c Stocks b Woodcock	8	– c Lorrimer b Woodcock	10
T. Hayward c Whiteside b Pougher	3	– b Woodcock	0
A.Street c Pougher b Woodcock	0	– b Pougher	4
C. Baldwin c Whiteside b Woodcock	5	– c Lorrimer b Pougher	12
R. Henderson b Pougher	5	– b Pougher	7
W. Brockwell b Woodcock	9	– c Lorrimer b Woodcock	0
G. W. Ayres c Hillyard b Pougher	1	– c and b Pougher	14
H. Wood c Woodcock b Pougher	2	– c Whiteside b Pougher	4
J. W. Sharpe c Stocks b Woodcock	0	– run out	1
F. Smith c Finney b Pougher	0	– not out	4
T. Richardson not out	0	– c Tomlin b Pougher	0
B 1	1	B 7, w 1	8
	34		64

Leicestershire

J. Holland c Ayres b Richardson	10	– c Baldwin b Richardson	4
Finney c Smith b Sharpe	5		
Chapman b Sharpe	1	– c Brockwell b Richardson	4
W. Tomlin c and b Richardson	0	– c Brockwell b Richardson	13
A. D. Pougher b Richardson	10	– not out	24
Mr D. Lorrimer b Sharpe	0	– c Hayward b Richardson	0
Mr G. W. Hillyard c Abel b Richardson	0	– not out	9
Mr C. Marriott b Richardson	8	– b Richardson	1
A. Woodcock c Smith b Richardson	1		
Mr F. W. Stocks c Smith b Sharpe	2		
J. P. Whiteside not out	0		
B 2, l-b 4	6	W 1	1
	48		56

Leicestershire Bowling

	Overs	Mdns	Runs	Wkts	Overs	Mdns	Runs	Wkts
Woodcock	12	7	18	5	19	7	33	3
Pougher	12	6	15	5	19.4	11	23	6
Hillyard					1	1	0	0

Surrey Bowling

	Overs	Mdns	Runs	Wkts	Overs	Mdns	Runs	Wkts
Richardson	11	6	18	6	11	5	17	5
Sharpe	11	3	19	4	9	2	35	0
Brockwell					1.2	0	3	0

LEICESTERSHIRE v YORKSHIRE

Played at Leicester, May 17, 18, 1894

With their leading amateurs away, Yorkshire were not fully represented. The state of the ground gave the bowlers an advantage, and up to a certain point the batting successes were few and far between, though de Trafford and Tomlin on one side, and Moorhouse on the other, did themselves justice. On the second day, when the wicket was worse than before, de Trafford hit out in a style that was beyond praise, scoring 92 out of a total of 131. Yorkshire were left with 122 to make, but Pougher and Hillyard followed up their captain's dashing batting with some wonderfully effective bowling, and Leicestershire were left with a well-deserved victory by 47 runs.

Leicestershire

Mr C. E. de Trafford c Brown b Peel	32	– c and b Hirst	92
T. H. Warren b Peel	10	– b Hirst	4
J. Holland c Moorhouse b Whitehead	7	– c Wainwright b Hirst	1
A. D. Pougher b Wainwright	10	– b Peel	3
Chapman c Hirst b Wainwright	0	– c Moorhouse b Hirst	7
W. Tomlin not out	43	– c Hunter b Moorhouse	0
Hassall b Wainwright	20	– b Moorhouse	3
Mr G. W. Hillyard b Wainwright	3	– b Hirst	1
Finney b Hirst	9	– c Wainwright b Moorhouse	6
Mr F. W. Stocks b Hirst	0	– not out	0
J. P. Whiteside c Woodhead b Whitehead	1	– c Hunter b Hirst	4
L-b 1	1	B 6, l-b 4	10
	136		131

Yorkshire

J. Tunnicliffe c Warren b Hillyard	18	– b Hillyard	8
J. Mounsey c Warren b Hillyard	19	– b Pougher	8
J. T. Brown c Whiteside b Pougher	1	– c Stocks b Hillyard	0
E. Wainwright b Hillyard	9	– b Hillyard	22
R. Peel c Pougher b Hillyard	8	– c Whiteside b Pougher	0
R. Moorhouse c Whiteside b Pougher	47	– b Pougher	5
Mr F. E. Woodhead c Whiteside b Pougher	8	– c Hillyard b Pougher	0
G. H. Hirst c Warren b Hillyard	9	– c Stocks b Hillyard	3
Lees Whitehead b Hillyard	3	– c Warren b Pougher	5
T. W. Foster not out	10	– b Pougher	17
D. Hunter b Pougher	10	– not out	4
B 4	4	L-b 2	2
	146		74

Yorkshire Bowling

	Overs	Mdns	Runs	Wkts	Overs	Mdns	Runs	Wkts
Peel	29	10	50	2	15	4	38	1
Hirst	19	7	29	2	23.4	12	44	6
Wainwright	29	17	29	4	2	1	2	0
Whitehead	10.4	3	19	2	5	0	10	0
Foster	2	1	8	0				
Moorhouse					15	4	27	3

Leicestershire Bowling

	Overs	Mdns	Runs	Wkts	Overs	Mdns	Runs	Wkts
Hillyard	31	8	74	6	17	4	44	4
Pougher	30.4	12	60	4	16.4	8	28	6
Finney	1	0	8	0				

Umpires: Clements and Talboys.

LEICESTERSHIRE v NOTTINGHAMSHIRE

Played at Leicester, July 30, 31, August 1, 1894

Up to a certain point the game went slightly in favour of Nottinghamshire, who scored 133 for eight wickets against the home county's total of 122. On Tuesday, however, Leicestershire played better all-round cricket than their opponents, Woodcock as a bowler and de Trafford and the Lorrimers as batsmen helping to place their side in a very favourable position. Notts. required 177 to win and had seven wickets to fall when the final stage was entered upon, but they never looked like averting defeat, and in the end Leicestershire won by the handsome majority of 106 runs. Woodcock took fifteen wickets for 136 runs.

Leicestershire

Mr C. E. de Trafford c Wright b Attewell	12	– c Mee b Wilkinson	89
J. Holland b Mee	4	– c Gunn b Flowers	18
Mr A. Lorrimer c and b Mee	9	– b Attewell	87
W. Tomlin b Attewell	30	– c and b Flowers	22
A. D. Pougher c Barnes b Mee	12	– absent (hurt)	0
T. H. Warren b Wilkinson	8	– c Howitt b Gunn	21
Mr D. Lorrimer b Mee	13	– c Wright b Gunn	46
Mr G. W. Hillyard c Bagguley b Attewell	0	– c Pike b Gunn	0
Mr G. E. Rudd c Mee b Attewell	10	– not out	12
A. Woodcock c Wright b Flowers	6	– c Wilkinson b Gunn	10
J. P. Whiteside not out	5	– c Wilkinson b Flowers	0
B 5, l-b 7, n-b 1	13	B 6, l-b 2	8
	122		263

Nottinghamshire

Mr R. H. Howitt b Woodcock	8	– c A. Lorrimer b Woodcock	6
W. Gunn lbw b Woodcock	12	– c Whiteside b Woodcock	5
H. B. Daft b Woodcock	0	– lbw b Woodcock	0
W. Flowers b Woodcock	50	– c Whiteside b Tomlin	38
W. Barnes b Woodcock	0	– b Woodcock	4
Mr C. W. Wright c Whiteside b Hillyard	6	– c and b Hillyard	27
W. Attewell c Rudd b Tomlin	30	– c Whiteside b Woodcock	6
R. Bagguley b Woodcock	1	– c Whiteside b Woodcock	4
A. Pike b Woodcock	12	– not out	19
A. Wilkinson c and b Woodcock	6	– run out	17
R. J. Mee not out	0	– c sub. b Woodcock	11
B 8, l-b 6	14	B 3	3
	139		140

Nottinghamshire Bowling

	Overs	Mdns	Runs	Wkts	Overs	Mdns	Runs	Wkts
Mee	24	4	57	4	24	1	79	0
Attewell	27.2	15	24	4	28	4	65	1
Wilkinson	7	2	16	1	12	4	25	1
Flowers	3	0	12	1	13	2	41	3
Howitt					1	0	8	0
Bagguley					7	3	10	0
Gunn					8	2	27	4

Leicestershire Bowling

	Overs	Mdns	Runs	Wkts	Overs	Mdns	Runs	Wkts
Hillyard	27	12	45	1	31	15	62	1
Woodcock	25	6	67	8	28	6	69	7
Rudd	2	0	12	0				
Tomlin	2	1	1	1	2	0	6	1

Umpires: Coward and Atkinson.

LEICESTERSHIRE v SURREY

Played at Leicester, June 20, 21, 1895

When Surrey lost five wickets for 55 runs, and had seven men out for 123, Leicestershire looked to have none the worst of the opening of this engagement; but a remarkable batting display by young Street, assisted by Wood and Smith, helped the champions to leave off, when time was called, with only eight wickets down for 368, Street being not out 156. Street ultimately carried out his bat for a dashing if slightly fortunate 161 – made in three hours and a half, and containing twenty-four 4s – Surrey's innings terminating for 385. When it came to the home county's turn to bat, Richardson worthily followed up his comrade's admirable batting with some sterling bowling, and Leicestershire, got rid of twice before time expired for 165 and 129 respectively, were easily beaten by an innings and 91 runs. Richardson obtained twelve wickets for 165 runs. Hayward had a curious analysis, only delivering three balls in each innings, but taking three wickets without having a run hit from him.

Surrey

R. Abel b Woodcock	69
M. Read c Pougher b Woodcock	7
T. Hayward b Hillyard	7
F. C. Holland c Holland b Hillyard	0
Mr W. W. Read c Holland b Pougher	2
W. Brockwell c Whiteside b Hillyard	1
R. Henderson b Hillyard	17
A. Street not out	161
H. Wood c and b Hillyard	56
F. Smith c Pougher b Hillyard	45
T. Richardson c Hillyard b Pougher	12
B 5, l-b 2, w 1	8
	385

Leicestershire

Mr C. E. de Trafford c Street b Smith	11	– b Smith	12
J. Holland c Abel b Brockwell	37	– c Brockwell b Richardson	20
A. D. Pougher b Richardson	4	– b Richardson	4
Knight c Abel b Richardson	0	– b Richardson	4
Mr J. Powers run out	24	– b Richardson	2
M. Chapman c Abel b Richardson	16	– c Abel b Richardson	0
Mr G. W. Hillyard c Abel b Richardson	7	– c Brockwell b Smith	19
W. Tomlin not out	33	– b Richardson	31
F. Geeson b Richardson	0	– not out	12
A. Woodcock b Richardson	18	– b Hayward	16
J. P. Whiteside c Holland b Hayward	7	– c Wood b Hayward	0
B 8	8	B 8, l-b 1	9
	165		129

Leicestershire Bowling

	Overs	Mdns	Runs	Wkts
Pougher	52	22	90	2
Woodcock	26	3	97	2
Hillyard	39	7	125	6
Geeson	14	5	31	0
Tomlin	7	0	34	0

Surrey Bowling

	Overs	Mdns	Runs	Wkts	Overs	Mdns	Runs	Wkts
Richardson	32	10	91	6	22	4	74	6
Smith	15	5	32	1	21	7	46	2
Brockwell	18	8	34	1				
Hayward	0.3	0	0	1	0.3	0	0	2

Umpires: Goodyear and Clark.

LEICESTERSHIRE v WARWICKSHIRE

Played at Leicester, May 28, 29, 30, 1896

The chief credit of the very remarkable and altogether unexpected victory which Leicestershire gained over Warwickshire by the narrowest possible margin of a single wicket, was due to Pougher, who scored 162 in the match for once out. The game was always interesting from the constant, and at times almost startling changes it underwent. To begin with, Warwickshire in making 321 – towards which W. G. Quaife and Welford each contributed a hundred – hardly looked like being beaten, but Leicestershire in response put together 211, saving the follow on, and then dismissed their opponents for 156. This left the home side 267 to get, and although 47 were needed when the last pair became partners, Woodcock and Whiteside proved equal to the occasion, and fairly snatched the match out of the fire.

Warwickshire

Walter Quaife c Whiteside b Woodcock	1	– c de Trafford b Pougher	0
W. G. Quaife c Knight b Woodcock	105	– c Tomlin b Woodcock	2
Mr H. W. Bainbridge c Wright b Woodcock	15	– c Whiteside b Woodcock	3
A. Law c Whiteside b Woodcock	6	– b Woodcock	81
A. Lilley c Holland b Wright	28	– b Woodcock	6
E. J. Diver b Woodcock	2	– b Coe	47
J. W. Welford b Pougher	118	– c Pougher b Woodcock	3
H. J. Pallett lbw b Pougher	18	– b Woodcock	0
S. J. Santall b Wright	9	– b Wright	0
T. Forester c Whiteside b Wright	0	– b Wright	5
W. Ward not out	2	– not out	0
B 14, l-b 3	17	B 2, l-b 3, w 4	9
	321		156

Leicestershire

F. Brown c Lilley b Santall	0	– b Forester	0
J. P. Whiteside b Santall	5	– not out	5
C. Wood c Forester b Pallett	5	– run out	17
J. Holland c Forester b Santall	0	– c Lilley b Santall	3
A. D. Pougher not out	102	– c Forester b Ward	60
A. E. Knight c Law b Santall	16	– c Forester b Welford	25
Mr C. E. de Trafford b Santall	2	– c Diver b Pallett	33
W. Tomlin b Forester	25	– c Lilley b Pallett	11
Mr F. Wright run out	17	– b Ward	15
S. Coe b Santall	25	– b Ward	39
A. Woodcock b Santall	0	– not out	46
B 13, l-b 1	14	B 10, w 3	13
	211		267

Leicestershire Bowling

	Overs	Mdns	Runs	Wkts	Overs	Mdns	Runs	Wkts
Woodcock	37	8	95	5	21.1	6	46	6
Pougher	33.4	10	75	2	6	2	14	1
Wright	19	5	48	3	10	3	38	2
Coe	13	1	52	0	13	4	25	1
Wood	6	1	28	0	4	0	24	0
Tomlin	1	0	6	0				

Warwickshire Bowling

	Overs	Mdns	Runs	Wkts	Overs	Mdns	Runs	Wkts
Santall	45	19	68	7	36	11	92	1
Welford	6	1	27	0	8	0	36	1
Pallett	29	11	58	1	30	9	56	2
Forester	12	2	42	1	14	2	33	1
Ward	3	1	2	0	20	9	37	3

Umpires: W. Hearn and A.Chester.

LEICESTERSHIRE v YORKSHIRE

Played at Leicester, June 18, 19, 20, 1896

In this engagement, which followed in the same week the comparatively small scoring match with Surrey, Yorkshire put together an innings of 660, an aggregate altogether without parallel on the Leicester ground. Most of the batsmen – favoured by a good deal of luck in the field – went in for brilliant hitting, and the huge total was the outcome of about eight hours' cricket. Brown and Hirst each obtained over 100, and every member of the team reached double figures, Tunnicliffe, who made 79, playing perhaps the best innings. Disheartened by their disastrous experiences, Leicestershire made a comparatively poor show, and being twice dismissed, for 165 and 193 respectively, suffered a crushing defeat by an innings and 302 runs. Tomlin in each innings, and Knight and Pougher at the second attempt alone redeemed the batting from failure.

Yorkshire

J. T. Borwn c Tomlin b Pougher	131
J. Tunnicliffe c Holland b Geeson	79
Mr F. S. Jackson c Tomlin b Geeson	77
D. Denton b Coe	73
R. Moorhouse c de Trafford b Woodcock	19
E. Wainwright b Woodcock	23
G. H. Hirst c Coe b de Trafford	107
Mr F. W. Milligan c Pougher b de Trafford	48
J. Mounsey c Whiteside b Pougher	21
S. Haigh not out	32
D. Hunter c sub. b Pougher	31
B 15, l-b 3, n-b 1	19
	660

Leicestershire

Mr C. E. de Trafford b Haigh	24	– b Jackson	18
J. Holland c Denton b Hirst	9	– c Hunter b Jackson	10
A. E. Knight c Tunnicliffe b Hirst	16	– not out	45
A. D. Pougher c Wainwright b Hirst	4	– b Moorhouse	39
C. Wood c Hunter b Hirst	2	– lbw b Brown	10
S. Coe b Jackson	16	– c Haigh b Jackson	13
W. Tomlin b Milligan	62	– c Milligan b Hirst	37
L. Brown c Tunnicliffe b Hirst	0	– st Hunter b Brown	8
F. Geeson c Tunnicliffe b Jackson	13	– run out	4
A. Woodcock c Tunnicliffe b Jackson	2	– st Hunter b Brown	1
J. P. Whiteside not out	10	– run out	0
B 6, w 1	7	B 7, n-b 1	8
	165		193

Leicestershire Bowling

	Overs	Mdns	Runs	Wkts
Pougher	63.2	22	135	3
Woodcock	51	4	147	2
Geeson	46	12	160	2
Coe	22	3	114	1
Tomlin	2	0	5	0
Wood	2	0	19	0
de Trafford	7	0	47	2
Holland	2	0	14	0

Yorkshire Bowling

	Overs	Mdns	Runs	Wkts	Overs	Mdns	Runs	Wkts
Hirst	23	10	67	5	19	5	46	1
Haigh	17	4	40	1	10	4	17	0
Jackson	14	2	27	3	19	2	49	3
Wainwright	5	0	23	0				
Milligan	2.4	1	1	1	10	2	37	0
Moorhouse					4	2	9	1
Brown					7.4	0	20	3
Mounsey					4	2	7	0

Umpires: J. Lillywhite and J. Platts.

LEICESTERSHIRE v SURREY

Played at Leicester, June 10, 1897

In meeting Surrey on the Aylestone Ground, Leicestershire fared no better than they had done at the Oval, the famous southern eleven winning for the second time in an innings with runs to spare. The match, which was played on a treacherous pitch after rain, was commenced and finished in one day, Leicestershire being out twice and Surrey once in the course of four hours and three quarters. It is not too much to say that while the conditions were equally bad for both, Surrey were able to suit themselves to the difficulties in vastly superior fashion and Leicestershire were simply outplayed. The home side went in first and were got rid of for 35. Against this Surrey made 164, and then, curiously enough, Richardson and Hayward, bowling unchanged as in the first innings dismissed Leicestershire a second time for precisely the same total as before – 35. Hayward bowled finely and took seven wickets for 43 runs, but, exceptional as was his success, it was quite overshadowed by that of Richardson, who sent back five batsmen for six runs in the early part of the day, and seven others for 14 towards the finish, securing in all 12 wickets for 20 runs. There is little doubt that this was one of the best bowling performances of the season. It should be stated that the Surrey men, having seen their opponents fail while adopting cautious methods, went in for hitting, and the policy met with admirable results.

Leicestershire

Mr C. J. B. Wood c Brockwell b Hayward	10	– lbw b Richardson	5
A. E. Knight b Richardson	1	– b Richardson	9
Mr G. E. Rudd b Hayward	0	– run out	4
W. Tomlin b Richardson	0	– c and b Hayward	4
Mr C. E. de Trafford b Richardson	2	– c Wood b Richardson	4
S. Coe b Richardson	0	– b Richardson	6
L. F. Brown c Brockwell b Hayward	2	– c Key b Hayward	1
Cobley b Richardson	1	– b Richardson	1
F. Geeson b Hayward	11	– b Richardson	0
A. Woodcock not out	2	– c Hayward b Richardson	0
J. P. Whiteside b Hayward	0	– not out	0
B 2, l-b 2, n-b 2	6	N-b 1	1
	35		35

Surrey

W. Brockwell c Woodcock b Geeson	9
R. Abel c Cobley b Geeson	19
Mr H. B. Chinnery c Knight b Coe	8
Mr H. D. G. Leveson-Gower c and b Coe	7
T. Hayward c Whiteside b Woodcock	26
C. Baldwin b Coe	17
Mr W. W. Read b Woodcock	17
Mr K. J. Key c Cobley b Woodcock	25
W. Nice c Knight b Coe	13
H. Wood st Whiteside b Cobley	13
T. Richardson not out	3
B 5, l-b 2	7
	164

Surrey Bowling

	Overs	Mdns	Runs	Wkts	Overs	Mdns	Runs	Wkts
Hayward	12.4	3	23	5	12	2	20	2
Richardson	12	8	6	5	12	6	14	7

Leicestershire Bowling

	Overs	Mdns	Runs	Wkts
Geeson	19	2	66	2
Coe	24.1	9	47	4
Woodcock	11	2	35	3
Cobley	6	3	9	1

Umpires: M. Sherwin and W. Draper.

LEICESTERSHIRE v ESSEX

Played at Leicester, August 7, 8, 9, 1899

The home team made poor use of the opportunity of batting first, the form shown being so uncertain, after Wood and Knight had put on 74 for the first wicket that the whole side were out for 194. Before the close of the first day Essex got within 51 of their opponents total for the loss of Carpenter, and on the Tuesday they ran up a score of 673 – the highest ever hit on the Aylestone Ground. Fane and Perrin added no fewer than 235 and neither gave a chance. Perrin had sixteen 4s in his 132, and Fane a 5, and twenty-seven 4s in his grandly-played 207. McGahey who helped to add 189, hit hard, and Street and Ayres severely punished the bowling – weakened by the absence of Stocks. In face of a majority of 479 Leicestershire required to bat more than a day to save the game and they quite failed in this endeavour. Indeed half the side were out for 73, and it was only the skilful play of Knight which saved the honour of the side. In first, Knight was the last out after batting quite faultlessly for nearly three hours and a quarter. His 111 was deserving of the highest praise, but his splendid effort was unavailing, Essex gaining an overwhelming victory by an innings and 223 runs.

Leicestershire

Mr C. J. B. Wood lbw b Ayres	39	– c Mead b Bull	17
A. E. Knight b Mead	37	– c Russell b Mead	111
Mr H. H. Marriott b Young	7	– c Young b Mead	7
A. D. Pougher b Mead	4	– b Mead	8
Mr G. H. Fowke b Young	4	– b Mead	0
Mr R. Joyce b Mead	0	– b Young	1
Mr C. E. de Trafford c Street b Ball	37	– b Mead	12
F. Geeson b Bull	16	– b McGahey	39
S. Coe c Street b Bull	22	– c Owen b Young	16
Agar not out	12	– not out	25
J. P. Whiteside b Mead	9	– c and b Mead	6
B 2, l-b 4, n-b 1	7	B 12, l-b 1, w 1	14
	194		256

Essex

H. Carpenter b Geeson 17
Mr F. L. Fane c and b Agar 207
Mr P. Perrin c Whiteside b Fowke 132
Mr C. McGahey b Fowke 99
Mr F. Street c Geeson b Pougher 76
G. Ayres c Agar b Geeson 83
Mr H. G. Owen c Marriott b Pougher 6
T. M. Russell c de Trafford b Pougher 8
H. Young c Pougher b Geeson 10
Mr F. G. Bull b Geeson 6
W. Mead not out 5
B 9, l-b 9, n-b 4, w 2 24

673

Essex Bowling

	Overs	Mdns	Runs	Wkts	Overs	Mdns	Runs	Wkts
Mead	28.2	5	64	4	40.1	10	91	6
Young	28	5	57	2	21	2	52	2
Bull	23	5	62	3	25	11	50	1
Ayres	4	3	4	1	5	1	17	0
McGahey					6	0	17	1
Carpenter					6	2	8	0
Perrin					4	1	7	0

Leicestershire Bowling

	Overs	Mdns	Runs	Wkts
Geeson	43.4	13	131	4
Coe	35	6	117	0
Agar	44	8	137	1
Wood	21	3	71	0
Fowke	14	1	76	2
Pougher	23	2	81	3
Marriott	5	1	19	0
Joyce	3	0	17	0

Umpires: A. F. Smith and J. Moss.

MIDDLESEX

MIDDLESEX IN 1870

Middlesex played two matches last season, both v Surrey, and both on The Oval. The first match Middlesex won by four wickets; the return Surrey won by three wickets (a record of these matches will be found under the head of "Surrey cricket"). Whether the Middlesex County Club would be carried on in 1871 was a matter of uncertainty and doubt when this book was compiled; if that Club should collapse, the principal reasons why will be – want of funds, want of a suitable ground, and want of general support from the County. It will be a matter for regret should the Club be broken up mainly for the want of what the County is so rich in – the sinews of war; and it will be especially regrettable should the Club die out at a period when County cricket (the very best of all cricket) is so manifestly increasing in popularity in other parts of the country. But if the cricketers of Middlesex really do desire a County Club, and a County ground, they must be more liberal in their support – monetary and otherwise – than they have hitherto been.

IMMENSE SCORING

MIDDLESEX v OXFORD UNIVERSITY

At Prince's, June 19, 20, 21, 1876

In this match 551 overs were bowled; Mr I. D. Walker, Mr W. H. Game, and Burghes hit scores of more than 100 runs. The Elevens made innings of 612, 439 and 166 runs (for four wickets only); consequently so many as 1217 runs were made, and so few as 24 wickets fell. The time they were at wickets each day was from 12.15 until (luncheon intervening) seven o'clock. The result of each day's hitting being as follows:–

THE FIRST DAY	THE SECOND DAY	THE THIRD DAY
394 runs for the loss of eight wickets.	373 runs for the loss of seven wickets.	450 runs for the loss of nine wickets.

To detail in this little book three days of such large hitting as this is out of the question; so the following record of the principal items in this match of monster scores must be deemed sufficient.

Mr C. J. Ottaway and Mr I. D. Walker commenced the hitting. They had made over half a century of runs when Mr Ottaway was bowled; Mr Thornton, Mr Green, and Mr Nepean had also gone when 121 had been scored; and when 196 had been made Mr I. D. Walker was caught out at long field for 110, stated to have been made without a chance. Mr Walker's hits were twenty singles, nine 2s, five 3s, thirteen 4s, and a 5 – one of the 4s, a 2, and the 5 (a leg-hit) being made from one over of Mr Heath's. Mr Montagu Turner and Mr H. Ross then increased the score to 254, when Mr Ross was out; but Mr Turner and Burghes hit the score to 329, when Mr Turner was bowled for 82 – a fine hitting display that included five 4s. At 389 a capital c and b by Mr Game settled Mr Cottrell, and "time" was called that day with the score at 394 for 8 wickets – Burghes not out 77.

On the Tuesday Burghes and Mr E. Rutter went at it again a quarter of an hour after noon. With the score at 438 Burghes was caught out at leg for 104 – termed "a free-hitting innings with two lives". His hits included five 4s and six 3s. Then when one more run only had been made the innings was done with, the wickets having fallen as follows:

1/54 2/76 3/88 4/121 5/196 6/254 7/329 8/389 9/438 10/439

At ten minutes past one Oxford's huge innings was commenced by Mr H. R. Webbe and Mr Campbell. The latter was lost at 55; but Mr Webbe and Mr Heath tried the

Middlesex bowling so severely that they put 152 runs on ere the second wicket fell by Mr Webbe being caught out for 98 – an innings reported to have been "made in his best form by steady cricket". Mr Webbe's hits included five 4s and fifteen 3s. Mr Heath was out at 216 for 71, made by five 4s, four 3s, etc. At 239 Mr Dury was had at point, and at 257 Mr Pearson was bowled. Then Mr Game went to wickets. He hit hard and scored fast – so fast that when "time" was called Oxford had scored 328 for 5 wickets, Mr Briggs (patience) not out 41; Mr Game (pace) not out 40!

On the Wednesday it was hot all round; the weather was hot (glass at 148), the hitting on both sides was hot; consequently it was hot alike for bowlers, fielders, scorers, and chroniclers. The promenade "Under the Elms" was crowded; and on "Turf Terrace" and the public seats there was a large expectant throng of people who had gone to Prince's to witness big hitting, and it is to be hoped they had their fill of it. The two not outs went on with their hitting at 12.15. At five minutes to two they had made the score 400; but at 422 Mr Briggs was caught out at point for 71, made by nine 4s, two 3s, eight 2s, etc. Mr Game worked on until the 500 was passed, but at 506 he was caught out at short leg for 141 – the largest score made in this large-scoring match. 249 runs were booked during Mr Game's stay at wickets; his hits were 26 singles, seven 2s, five 3s, twenty 4s, and a 6. *Bell's Life* stated: "Mr Game did not give a fair change; his 141 was a fine hitting innings". Mr Royle and Mr Lewis then increased the score to 562, when Mr Lewis was out for 24, whereupon the last man, Mr H. G. Tylecote, went in, and doubtless the Middlesex men hoped he would soon go out; but "there is no rest for the weary", and it was not until those last men had made the big score bigger by 50 runs that the innings was over; then, at a quarter to five, Mr Tylecote was out for 26, and Mr Royle took his bat out for 67. The wickets in this vast innings fell in the following order:–

1/55 2/207 3/216 4/239 5/257 6/422 7/469 8/506 9/562 10/612

(Those 612 runs were made from 278 overs.)

At ten minutes past five Mr C. I. Thornton and Mr C. E. Green commenced Middlesex's second innings. Mr Green stood not on the order of his hitting, but hit at once, though Mr Thornton bided a while ere he let out, and when 29 runs had been scored only two singles had been hit by Mr Thornton, who, however, then launched out in his old form, for, recorded *Bell's Life* – "Mr Thornton made 15 from five successive balls – nine in one over. He also made 10 in another over, and three 4s in a third, the third 4 being hit clear over the new roadway by the Hans Place entrance". Mr Green and Mr Thornton had made 80 runs in 40 minutes! the 100 in 48 minutes!! and 120 in the hour!!! Then Mr Thornton was c and b for 79, made in 69 minutes by two 5s, eleven 4s, eight 2s, and nine singles. With the score at 124 Mr Green was bowled for 43 – six 4s his principal hits. But little was done afterwards; and, with the books showing individual scores of 141, 110, 104, 98, 82, 79, 71, 71, 67 not out, 43, etc., "time" was called on that third evening with this wonderful hitting match in the following extraordinary form:

Middlesex

I. D. Walker Esq. c A. J. Webbe b Royle	110		
C. J. Ottaway Esq. b Heath	19		
C. I. Thornton Esq. c and b Heath	14	– c and b Heath	79
C. E. Green Esq. b Dury	3	– b Dury	43
A. A. Nepean Esq. b Buckland	11	– not out	11
M. Turner Esq. b Heath	82	– c Briggs b Dury	7
H. Ross Esq. b H. G. Tylecote	35	– c and b Buckland	1
A. Burghes c Game b Buckland	104		
C. E. Cottrell Esq. c and b Game	23	– not out	23
E. Rutter Esq. not out	17		
R. Henderson Esq. b Buckland	0		
B 8, l-b 11, w 2	21	L-b 2	2
	439		166

Oxford University

A. J. Webbe Esq. c Cottrell b Henderson	98
D. Campbell Esq. c Henderson b Rutter	24
A. H. Heath Esq. c Turner b Henderson	71
T. S. Dury Esq. c Cottrell b Henderson	14
R. Briggs Esq. c Cottrell b Green	71
A. W. Pearson Esq. b Henderson	10
W. H. Game Esq. c I. D. Walker b Cottrell	141
F. M. Buckland Esq. b Rutter	22
V. K. Royle Esq. not out	67
C. P. Lewis Esq. c Turner b Rutter	24
H. G. Tylecote Esq. st Turner b I. D. Walker	26
B 30, l-b 12, w 2	44
	612

Oxford Bowling

	Overs	Mdns	Runs	Wkts	Overs	Mdns	Runs	Wkts
Mr Buckland	73.2	27	104	3	21	7	47	1
Mr Lewis	44	10	104	0				
Mr Heath	25	5	67	3	8	2	17	1
Mr Dury	19	5	28	1	18	4	38	2
Mr Pearson	15	7	23	0	7	1	34	0
Mr Tylecote	13	4	27	1				
Mr Game	12	2	40	1				
Mr Royle	11	3	18	1	4	0	28	0
Mr Campbell	3	0	7	0				

Middlesex Bowling

	Overs	Mdns	Runs	Wkts
Mr Henderson	95	29	185	4
Mr Cottrell	63	26	118	1
Mr Rutter	40	8	104	3
Burghes	33	13	49	0
Mr Nepean	21	9	29	0
Mr I. D. Walker	16	2	63	1
Mr Green	10	4	20	1

Umpires: E. Willsher and R. Thoms.

MIDDLESEX v NOTTINGHAMSHIRE

At Prince's, July 10, 11, 12, 1876

This Match will long be remembered with a saddening interest, from its connection with the awfully sudden death of poor Tom Box, who literally died in harness, the match being in full play on the third day when Box – engaged on his duties at the score board – fell from his seat and died almost instantaneously. As a Sussex County Player; as one of The Players of England against The Gentlemen; as a South v North Cricketer; as a member of Clarke's All England Eleven; as a Ground Proprietor, and in other capacities, Box had passed a long and honourable life time on the Cricket Grounds of England, taking – and holding, for a long career – front rank as a wicket-keeper and batsman. *Scores and Biographies* tells us Box commenced cricketing when a boy. We all know he continued cricketing until he was an old man, and was "playing his part" when Death, with such fearful suddenness, cut him down.

MIDDLESEX v GLOUCESTERSHIRE

Played at Lord's, June 13, 14, 1881

This match produced some very remarkable cricket. Gloucestershire, winning the toss, elected to bat, and on the brothers Grace going to the wickets, some surprising hitting, by Dr E. M., was soon witnessed. He early had a life at the hands of Mr Law, and encouraged by this, batted with astounding vigour. Off Clarke's bowling, he scored five 4s, and before he was caught at cover-point, had made 47 runs while Dr W. G. put on 12. Mr L. M. Day filled the vacancy, and the Gloucestershire captain then batted with greater freedom, and the score was raised to 117 before a separation was effected by Mr Day being lbw to Burton. During the partnership, Dr W. G. compiled 39 while Mr Day made 19. At this point of the game, Burton's bowling became so exceedingly destructive, that the remaining eight wickets were disposed of for an addition of only 43 runs. Dr W. G. Grace's excellent innings of 64 consisted of one 5, three 4s, two 3s, eleven 2s, and singles. On a good run-getting wicket the chances of Middlesex improving on the Gloucester performance seemed highly probable, but something under an hour and a half proved sufficient to bring the first innings of the home team to a conclusion for the very meagre total of 77, the only remarkable feature of which was the highly successful bowling of Dr W. G. Grace. In the follow on which resulted, Mr Walker and Mr Webbe played in dashing style, putting on 49 in less than half an hour, when the latter was caught, and the day's play ceased with the score at 86 for four wickets, Mr Walker, not out 30.

The interest of the play on the second day centred in the extraordinary and brilliant hitting of Mr Vernon. He and Mr Walker went on with the second innings of Middlesex, but with two runs added Mr Walker had to leave, and at 93 Mr Ford succumbed to a splendid catch by Mr Gribble. Burton came in, and it was then at Mr Vernon's remarkable hitting commenced. A ball from Midwinter was driven for 5, and from one over of Woof's he scored 12 runs by three drives of 4 each. Then from the other wicket he drove Midwinter for a 5, losing Burton shortly afterwards, and his successor, Mr O'Brien, and eight wickets were down for 134. With Mr Robertson as a partner, Mr Vernon, principally by 4s, raised the score to 150. Mr Vernon's next important hit was off Woof, through the open door of the Tennis Court, and as a light had to be obtained to find the ball, "lost ball" was called and 6 scored. A bowling change got rid of Mr Robertson, and 9 wickets were down for 159. Clarke, the last man, came in, and Mr Vernon continued his extraordinary hitting. He drove Mr Grace for 5, and shortly afterwards scored eleven runs – by a 2, a 2, a 4, and a 3 – from one over from the same hand. At 195, however, Midwinter bowled him for a magnificent innings of 88, made up of a 6, three 5s, nine 4s, four 3s, four 2s, and eleven singles. For this brilliant and almost unrivalled performance, it need scarcely be said, Mr Vernon was most enthusiastically cheered. Towards the 113 required by Gloucestershire to win Dr E. M. Grace scored 35 out of 47 while he was at wickets; Midwinter played a good innings of 25, and Mr Cranston another of 35, and in the end the visitors won by six wickets.

Gloucestershire

Dr W. G. Grace b Burton	64	– c and b Burton	4
Dr E. M. Grace c Law b Robertson	47	– lbw b Ford	35
L. M. Day Esq. lbw b Burton	19	– c Clarke b Ford	0
W. Midwinter run out	2	– b Clarke	25
W. R. Gilbert Esq. c Ford b Clarke	8	– not out	12
J. Cranston Esq. b Burton	1	– not out	35
A. D. Greene Esq. run out	2		
H. W. R. Gribble Esq. b Burton	0		
J. Painter b Burton	0		
J. A. Bush Esq. not out	6		
W. A. Woof c O'Brien b Burton	8		
B 1, l-b 2	3	L-b 3	3
	160		114

Middlesex

A. J. Webbe Esq. b W. G. Grace	4	– c Woof b Midwinter	25
I. D. Walker Esq. c Gilbert b Woof	2	– c Painter b Woof	30
G. Law Esq. c Greene b W. G. Grace	19	– lbw b Midwinter	7
T. S. Pearson Esq. lbw b W. G. Grace	5	– c Woof b Midwinter	13
G. F. Vernon Esq. b W. G. Grace	14	– b Midwinter	88
A. F. J. Ford Esq. b Woof	0	– c Gribble b Midwinter	1
T. C. O'Brien Esq. b Woof	0	– c Bush b Woof	0
J. Robertson Esq. b W. G. Grace	14	– b W. G. Grace	5
C. Robson Esq. b W. G. Grace	5	– run out	6
G. Burton not out	6	– b Midwinter	7
W. Clarke b W. G. Grace	0	– not out	6
B 5, l-b 3	8	B 3, l-b 3, n-b 1	7
	77		195

Middlesex Bowling

	Overs	Mdns	Runs	Wkts	Overs	Mdns	Runs	Wkts
Burton	33	11	45	6	20	8	41	1
Clarke	42	16	69	1	23	10	35	1
Mr Robertson	17	3	26	1	8	4	11	0
Mr Ford	7	2	17	0	11	4	21	2

Gloucestershire Bowling

	Overs	Mdns	Runs	Wkts	Overs	Mdns	Runs	Wkts
Woof	23	9	39	3	18	3	59	2
Dr W. G. Grace	22.1	10	30	7	11	1	57	1
Midwinter					32.1	16	53	6
Mr Gilbert					18	9	22	0

Umpires: G. Howitt and C. K. Pullin.

MIDDLESEX v NOTTINGHAMSHIRE

Played at Lord's, July 16, 17, 18, 1885

This match, which Notts. won by an innings and 154 runs, will be best remembered for the superb batting of Arthur Shrewsbury, who succeeded in scoring the highest individual innings made in a first-class match during the season of 1885. He went in first for Notts. at about ten minutes to four on the Thursday afternoon, and took out his bat at between ten minutes and a quarter-past five on the Friday, for the magnificent score of 224. Deducting all intervals, he was at the wickets for seven hours and fifty minutes, and except that he gave a very hard chance to point in the third over on the Thursday, when he had only scored two, his play was faultless, while for sustained excellence his innings could not have been improved upon. The bowlers could never tempt him to hit when it was unsafe to hit, but when a loose ball was sent down to him he rarely failed to punish it. His figures were twenty-two 4s, fifteen 3s, nineteen 2s, and fifty-three singles. The Middlesex bowling, as a whole, was not so difficult as to seriously tax his defence, but a good deal of it was very straight and good, and Burton, who had rarely bowled better, certainly wanted playing with a great deal of patience and judgment. Shrewsbury's innings was the highest that had been played at Lord's in a match of first-class importance since Mr Ward's famous 278 in 1820, beating, as it did, by seven runs, Mr Hadow's 217 for Middlesex against the MCC in 1871. Shrewsbury has, therefore, played three innings of over 200 for his county. The first was his 207 against Surrey, at the Oval, in 1882, and the second his 209 against Sussex, at Brighton, in 1884. Despite the long time he had been before the public, Shrewsbury was only a little over 29 years of age at the time the match under notice was played.

The match opened in a quiet and uneventful fashion, the weather being pleasantly fine, and the wicket apparently in good order. Middlesex won the toss and went in, the innings lasting from about ten minutes past twelve till twenty-five past three, and the total reached 128. Two wickets were lost before a run had been scored, and the total was only 15 when Mr O'Brien hit a ball on to the wicket. After this disastrous beginning some really admirable batting was shown by Mr Stanley Scott and Mr Webbe, who remained together for a long time and took the total up to 81, Walter Wright and Alfred Shaw, who started the bowling, having in the meantime given place to Attewell and Flowers. When at last Mr Webbe was dismissed, he was out to a catch at long-slip, which no one in the Nottingham eleven, except Gunn, could have reached. At lunch-time six wickets were down for 97, and after the interval Mr Scott could get no one to stay long with him, the last four wickets only adding 31 runs. Mr Scott, who went in first wicket down, took out his bat for a patiently-played, and in every way excellent innings of 46, his figures being a 4, five 3s, six 2s, and fifteen singles. At ten minutes to four Shrewsbury and Scotton opposed Nottingham's innings, to the bowling of Burton and Mr Cottrell. In the third over Shrewsbury cut a ball very hard to Mr O'Brien at point, but though the fieldsman touched it with his right hand, it went past him for two. This was the only mistake that Shrewsbury made, his batting afterwards being up to his best standard. He and Scotton made a most determined stand, and in the course of an hour and ten minutes the total reached 52. Then a fine piece of fielding by Mr Webbe ran out Scotton. After this, though Shrewsbury continued to play admirable cricket, matters went very badly with Nottingham for the rest of the day. Barnes was stumped at 73, Gunn was caught at mid-off at 94, Flowers was caught in the long-field at 99, Mr Wright stumped at 104, and Selby caught by the wicket-keeper standing back at 113. Then, with six wickets down, Attewell went in, and he and Shrewsbury remained together until the call of time, when the score was 139 for six wickets. Nottinghamshire being 11 runs to the good with four wickets to fall. Out of 135 runs from the bat, Shrewsbury had made 86 – an extraordinary proportion for so patient and careful a batsman.

Upon resumption of play next morning, Attewell, who had scored 13 overnight, was not dismissed until the total reached 290, the partnership adding the extraordinary number of 177 runs for the seventh wicket. Attewell's 89 – a very fine innings, and the highest he had ever played in a first-class match – included ten 4s, five 3s, and six 2s. Alfred Shaw went in when eight wickets were down for 317, and while he was in with Shrewsbury the score was increased to 411 – or 94 runs for the ninth wicket. With 287 runs wanted to save a single innings defeat, Middlesex went in for the second time at 5.35, but though Mr Webbe again played very fine cricket, four wickets were down at the drawing of stumps for 72 runs.

An hour and a quarter's play proved sufficient on the Saturday to bring the match to a conclusion. The first ball was bowled at 11.35, and at 12.50 the game was all over. When play began Middlesex had six wickets to fall, and wanted 215 runs to avert a single innings defeat. Mr Webbe, who had made 42 overnight, only added 4 to his score, but he stayed till the previous total of 72 had been increased to 107. He was the seventh man out, his admirable innings of 46 including four 4s, three 3s, and four 2s. West hit a couple of 4s in making 11, but the only batsman on Saturday who gave any serious trouble was Mr Cottrell. That gentleman went in with the total at 95 for six wickets, and was the last man out. Of the 38 runs scored while he was at the wickets, he made no fewer than 29. Walter Wright bowled in capital form all through the innings, and took eight wickets for 74 runs – a very fine average on hard ground.

Middlesex

S. C. Newton Esq. b W. Wright	0	– c Sherwin b W. Wright	12
E. M. Hadow Esq. c C. W. Wright b Shaw	0	– c Flowers b W. Wright	1
S. W. Scott Esq. not out	46	– b W. Wright	11
T. C. O'Brien Esq. b W. Wright	9	– b W. Wright	7
A. J. Webbe Esq. c Gunn b Attewell	40	– c C. W. Wright b Barnes	46
G. F. Vernon Esq. c Gunn b Flowers	5	– c Shaw b W. Wright	6
J. West run out	1	– c Sherwin b W. Wright	11
C. E. Cottrell Esq. b Flowers	10	– b W. Wright	29
J. Robertson Esq. c Flowers b Attewell	0	– c Scotton b Barnes	2
W. Williams Esq. c Shaw b Flowers	0	– c Scotton b W. Wright	4
G. Burton c Scotton b Flowers	6	– not out	2
B 10, l-b 1	11	L-b 2	2
	128		133

Nottinghamshire

A. Shrewsbury not out	224	W. Attewell c Robertson b Burton	89
W. H. Scotton run out	16	W. Wright b Burton	4
W. Barnes st Williams b Burton	5	A. Shaw c Vernon b Burton	52
W. Gunn c Webbe b Cottrell	8	M. Sherwin c Vernon b Burton	0
W. Flowers c Scott b Burton	4	B 6, l-b 4	10
C. W. Wright Esq. st Williams b Burton	1		
J. Selby c Williams b Cottrell	2		415

Nottinghamshire Bowling

	Overs	Mdns	Runs	Wkts	Overs	Mdns	Runs	Wkts
Shaw	22	13	25	1				
W. Wright	15	7	23	2	46.3	15	74	8
Attewell	33	15	53	2				
Flowers	27.3	18	16	4	22	13	21	0
Barnes					26	14	36	2

Middlesex Bowling

	Overs	Mdns	Runs	Wkts
Burton	112	68	96	7
Mr Cottrell	71	34	91	2
Mr Robertson	43	15	56	0
West	16	3	43	0
Mr Hadow	21	6	53	0
Mr Webbe	22	10	25	0
Mr O'Brien	2	1	13	0
Mr Scott	4	0	18	0
Mr Williams	3	0	10	0

MIDDLESEX v GLOUCESTERSHIRE

Played at Lord's, June 2, 3, 4, 1887

Middlesex had again the good fortune to put a representative side into the field, but Gloucestershire, as is usually the case with the London engagement at the beginning of the season, was very weak, Mr Townsend, Mr Brain, Mr Page, Mr Pullen, and Woof being all away. The opening day's cricket was chiefly remarkable for the fine play of Mr W. G. Grace, who obtained the first of his five hundreds for his county. In starting the ground bumped a good deal, and Mr Grace was several times beaten by the ball, but after the luncheon interval, and on a rapidly improving wicket, he hit in his finest style. He went in first soon after twelve o'clock, and was the ninth man out, the total when he left being 193, of which number 174 had been scored from the bat. He hit fifteen 4s, five 3s, eleven 2s, and 16 singles, and was at the wickets three hours and a quarter. It was only through Mr Newnham's assistance that he was able to get his 100, that gentleman playing very good cricket and helping to put on 84 runs for the ninth wicket. The Gloucestershire innings ended at a quarter-past four, and rain sadly interfered with play during the remainder of the day, stopping the game for forty minutes soon after five o'clock, and causing stumps to be drawn at half-past six. Two Middlesex wickets fell and 57 runs were scored, Mr Webbe being not out 24 and Mr J. G. Walker not out 7.

Persistent rain on Friday morning put cricket quite out of the question, and at half-past one it was decided to postpone the game until Saturday. On that day a start could not be made until a quarter to one, between which time and seven o'clock twenty-two wickets went down for 224 runs. The ground was fairly easy before luncheon, but, with the sun shining brightly, it became worse and worse as the afternoon wore on, and was very bad indeed before the finish. It is unnecessary to follow the game in any close detail, but something must be said for Mr Webbe, Mr Walker, Mr Vernon, and West. Mr Webbe's 47 was in every way an excellent innings, and Mr Vernon and West added 49 runs during their partnership in about half an hour. Gloucestershire's second innings only lasted an hour and forty minutes, Mr Robertson and Burton bowling with great success on the slow ground. When stumps were pulled up and the game left drawn, Middlesex had six wickets to fall, and wanted 85 runs to win. With the ground in the condition it was, and Messrs Stoddart, Webbe, Scott, and O'Brien out, it was not at all likely that this number would have been obtained, the draw being clearly in favour of the weaker team.

Gloucestershire

Mr E. M. Grace b Dunkley	6	– c O'Brien b Burton	15
Mr W. G. Grace lbw b Webbe	113	– b Robertson	9
Mr C. G. Radcliffe c Dunkley b Burton	9	– lbw b Burton	0
J. Painter b Dunkley	3	– b Robertson	10
Mr G. Francis b Dunkley	2	– b Robertson	18
Mr A. Lewis c Walker b Burton	7	– c Robertson b Burton	0
Mr E. L. Griffiths c Welman b Dunkley	13	– c Stoddart b Robertson	0
Mr J. Bloor c Walker b Dunkley	0	– b Burton	9
Mr F. L. Cole b Dunkley	0	– b Robertson	1
Mr A. Newnham not out	25	– b Robertson	20
Mr J. A. Bush c and b Robertson	1	– not out	0
B 12, l-b 6	18	B 2	2
	197		84

Middlesex

Mr A. E. Stoddart run out	6	– c E. M. Grace b W. G. Grace	0
Mr A. J. Webbe c Bloor b Newnham	47	– b W. G. Grace	1
Mr S. W. Scott b Newnham	15	– b Newnham	1
Mr J. G. Walker c Francis b W. G. Grace	25	– not out	19
Mr T. C. O'Brien c Bush b Newnham	0	– b W. G. Grace	0
Mr G. F. Vernon b W. G. Grace	33	– not out	3
J. E. West c E. M. Grace b W. G. Grace	23		
G. Burton not out	12		
Mr J. Robertson b Newnham	4		
Dunkley b W. G. Grace	0		
Mr F. T. Welman c Bush b W. G. Grace	2		
B 5	5	L-b 1	1
	172		25

Middlesex Bowling

	Overs	Mdns	Runs	Wkts	Overs	Mdns	Runs	Wkts
Burton	54	31	60	2	29	13	31	4
Dunkley	40	17	75	6	2	0	10	0
West	16	9	19	0				
Mr Robertson	10.1	4	18	1	26	10	41	6
Mr Webbe	6	3	7	1				

Gloucestershire Bowling

	Overs	Mdns	Runs	Wkts	Overs	Mdns	Runs	Wkts
Mr W. G. Grace	44.2	17	78	5	15	8	16	3
Mr Newnham	45	20	69	4	16	11	8	1
Mr Lewis	13	7	12	0				
Mr Painter	6	3	8	0				

Umpires: Coward and Payne.

MIDDLESEX v KENT

Played at Lord's, June 20, 21, 22, 1887

Middlesex was represented in the match against Kent by perhaps the strongest side the county had at command, the only prominent cricketers qualified to play who were absent being the Hon. Alfred Lyttelton and Mr G. F. Vernon. Kent, on the other hand, in the absence of several of the crack amateurs, had a poor side indeed. The weather was delightfully fine all through the match. Weak as the Kentish batting was, it was a wretched performance to go in first on a fast wicket on Monday and be dismissed in an hour and three-quarters for the very poor total of 98. George and Frank Hearne and Mr Ireland were the only batsmen who looked like getting runs at any time during the innings. When Middlesex went in after luncheon some batting of a very different character was shown. Messrs Webbe and Stoddart, who started the innings, not only passed the Kentish total before they were parted, but actually hit the score to 129, Mr Webbe then being bowled. Mr Stoddart was dismissed at 133 for a finely hit 78, but it was not one of his best efforts. Mr A. P. Lucas played in fine form for 47 – a display in quite his old characteristic style. Mr Scott and Mr T. C. O'Brien made runs rapidly, and when play ceased for the day Middlesex had scored 255 for the loss of seven wickets.

On Tuesday, owing to the festivities in connection with the celebration of the Queen's Jubilee, the game was not continued until three o'clock in the afternoon, and then in fifty-five minutes the three other batsmen added 72 runs, the innings closing just before four o'clock for 327, giving Middlesex the enormous majority of 229 runs over the visitors. The Kentish men did very much better at the second time of asking, George and Frank Hearne again showing the best batting, and receiving some valuable assistance from Mr Tonge, Mr Wilson, and, later on, Mr Ireland. When stumps were pulled up for the day they had made 195 for seven wickets, so with three wickets to fall they still wanted 34 runs to avoid being beaten in an innings.

On Wednesday the game was continued at twenty minutes past eleven, and, thanks to the continued free hitting of Mr Ireland, the score quickly reached 236. Middlesex were, therefore, left with eight runs to get, and these cost them one wicket, the Metropolitan county thus winning with nine wickets in hand. Mr Ireland, who made his appearance in this match for the Kentish eleven after an interval of ten years, hit most brilliantly for his 87, which included twelve 4s, five 3s, and eight 2s. It was not quite faultless, for he was missed when 33, but he batted quite well enough to entitle him to a further trial.

Kent

Mr J. N. Tonge b Dunkley	0	– lbw b Robertson	22
F. Hearne c Burton b Dunkley	17	– c O'Brien b Webbe	37
G. G. Hearne c Welman b Robertson	27	– c West b Robertson	26
Mr L. Wilson b West	2	– b Dunkley	26
Mr A. W. Fulcher b Robertson	6	– c Welman b West	4
Mr F. S. Ireland b West	15	– c Burton b Robertson	87
A. Hearne lbw b Burton	11	– b Webbe	11
E. Martin b West	2	– b Webbe	0
J. Wootton run out	8	– b Webbe	5
J. Pentecost lbw b Robertson	0	– lbw b Webbe	0
W. Hearne not out	8	– not out	9
B 2	2	B 6, l-b 3	9
	98		236

Middlesex

Mr A. E. Stoddart c Pentecost b G. Hearne	78		
Mr A. J. Webbe b Wootton	49	– not out	1
Mr A. P. Lucas b W. Hearne	47	– not out	3
Mr S. W. Scott c Wootton b W. Hearne	27		
Mr J. G. Walker b Martin	2		
Mr T. C. O'Brien c Pentecost b A. Hearne	34		
G. Burton c and b Tonge	11		
J. E. West c Pentecost b Wootton	27	– c W. Hearne b Wilson	0
Mr J. Robertson not out	29		
Mr F. T. Welman b Wootton	0		
Dunkley c Wilson b A. Hearne	11		
B 5, l-b 7	12	B 4	4
	327		8

Middlesex Bowling

	Overs	Mdns	Runs	Wkts	Overs	Mdns	Runs	Wkts
Burton	8	2	14	1	30	17	36	0
Dunkley	14	5	28	2	16	5	42	1
West	22	8	39	3	25	10	52	1
Mr Robertson	15	10	15	3	40.3	19	74	3
Mr Webbe					26	16	23	5

Kent Bowling

	Overs	Mdns	Runs	Wkts	Overs	Mdns	Runs	Wkts
Wootton	56	19	106	3	4	3	1	0
A. Hearne	26	14	29	2				
Martin	32	18	33	1				
W. Hearne	48	20	85	2				
Mr F. S. Ireland	5	2	10	0				
G. G. Hearne	16	4	33	1				
Mr J. N. Tonge	13	5	19	1				
Mr Wilson					4.3	2	3	1

Umpires: J. Chatterton and Jupp.

MIDDLESEX v OXFORD UNIVERSITY

Played at Chiswick Park, June 23, 24, 25, 1887

The match between Middlesex and Oxford University produced the most remarkable batting of the season, Messrs K. J. Key and H. Philipson making the largest number for a partnership that has ever been recorded in first-class cricket. The two gentlemen became partners at twenty minutes to three on the first day, when the Oxford University score stood at 104 for six wickets, and they were not separated until early on the Friday morning, when they had carried the total up to 444. They had thus scored no fewer than 340 runs while they were together. Previous to this performance the highest stands in first-class matches were 330 by Barnes and Gunn for MCC against Yorkshire at Lord's in 1885; 324 by Mr I. D. Walker and the Hon. Alfred Lyttelton for Middlesex against Gloucestershire at Clifton in 1883; and 305 by Messrs W. W. Read and W. E. Roller for Surrey against Lancashire at Manchester a week previous to the match under notice. In the match between the MCC and Leicestershire at Lord's at the beginning of June in 1882, Barnes and Midwinter put on no fewer than 454 runs while they were together, but this did not rank as a first-class contest. Throughout his brilliant career, Mr Key has never done anything so good as this 281, which stood as the highest individual score in important matches for the season. He was at the wickets as nearly as possible six hours, and the figures of his wonderful innings were thirty-eight 4s, eleven 3s, twenty-four 2s, and forty-eight singles. He gave one very easy chance to Birch at third man when he had scored only 10, but apart from this and one possible chance in the slips, he scarcely made a mistake. Mr Philipson, who through ill-health was kept out of cricket in 1886, played a surprisingly good innings of 150 – a long way the best thing he has ever done. He was batting for three hours and three-quarters, and his chief hits were fifteen 4s, sixteen 3s, and nine 2s. The only faults that could be urged against his performance were a hard chance to Burton at short slip when he had made 24, and a moderately easy one to Mr Welman at the wicket when his total was 104. His success for his University was extremely popular. As may be easily imagined, this extraordinary batting dwarfed everything else in the match, and left Oxford University with the prospect of certain victory. On the first day, Oxford winning the toss and going in on a good wicket, scored 435 for the loss of only six wickets, Mr Key being then not out 214, and Mr Philipson not out 150.

On the Friday only nine more runs were added before Mr Philipson was caught in the long field without adding to his overnight score. Mr Key was the last man out, and the total reached 555. At their first attempt the Middlesex batsmen, with the exception of Mr A. J. Webbe, could do little or nothing with the excellent bowling of Mr Whitby, who seemed to have come back to quite his old form. The innings was all over for 119, and Mr Webbe, who had gone in first, carried out his bat for 63 – an admirable innings – which included eight 4s, three 3s, and five 2s. Mr Whitby's average comes out as five wickets for 43, but in reality he took his five wickets for only 8 runs, as up to when he was put on for the third time at 104 he had not taken a wicket. His five wickets were obtained in five overs, two of which were maidens. Following their innings against the enormous majority of 436, the Middlesex men before the call of time scored 112 for the loss of five wickets. Mr Scott played extremely well, and was not out 47.

On the third morning Mr Whitby was not on the ground, and the main feature of the cricket was a good stand by Messrs Welman and Robertson, who put on 60 runs for the last wicket. Mr Scott increased his overnight score of 47 to 64, and the Middlesex innings ultimately terminated for 207, and so left Oxford University with a most decisive victory by an innings and 229 runs. Mr Brain was not representing his University owing to the injury he had received in the match against Lancashire, and in his absence Mr Key captained the eleven.

Oxford University

Mr F. H. Gresson run out	9
Mr E. A. Nepean c Webbe b Burton	4
Mr W. Rashleigh c O'Brien b Burton	10
Mr K. J. Key c Burton b Soppitt	281
Mr E. H. Buckland c O'Brien b Soppitt	7
Mr G. W. Ricketts c Welman b Soppitt	19
Mr H. W. Forster b Soppitt	0
Mr H. Philipson c Johnston b Burton	150
Mr A. K. Watson c Welman b Soppitt	5
Mr C. Wreford-Brown c O'Brien b Robertson	26
Mr H. O. Whitby not out	17
B 26, l-b 1	27
	555

Middlesex

Mr A. J. Webbe not out	63 – b Forster	25
Mr A. E. Stoddart c Rashleigh b Forster	1 – b Whitby	10
Mr S. W. Scott c Forster b Nepean	21 – st Philipson b Forster	64
Mr T. C. O'Brien b Buckland	0 – b Forster	4
Mr A. S. Johnston c Forster b Buckland	0 – c and b Forster	10
Mr W. J. Soppitt c Philipson b Forster	5 – c Watson b Ricketts	10
G. Burton c Wreford-Brown b Whitby	10 – c sub. b Buckland	1
J. E. West c Gresson b Whitby	0 – st Philipson b Nepean	14
Mr J. Robertson b Whitby	0 – c Rashleigh b Buckland	19
Birch b Whitby	0 – b Forster	4
Mr F. T. Welman c Gresson b Whitby	3 – not out	41
B 4	4 B 4, l-b 1	5
	119	207

Middlesex Bowling

	Overs	Mdns	Runs	Wkts
Burton	61	24	112	3
Mr Soppitt	64	20	159	5
West	17	4	60	0
Birch	28	7	67	0
Mr Robertson	27	8	55	1
Mr Webbe	18	5	39	0
Mr Stoddart	10	4	36	0

Oxford University Bowling

	Overs	Mdns	Runs	Wkts	Overs	Mdns	Runs	Wkts
Mr Whitby	26.2	13	43	5	17	5	40	1
Mr Forster	26	17	16	2	35	8	76	5
Mr Nepean	7	3	20	1	18	6	23	1
Mr Buckland	15	6	20	2	12	6	12	2
Mr Ricketts	3	0	16	0	6	1	13	1
Mr Wreford-Brown					12	4	29	0
Mr Gresson					6	4	9	0

Umpires: T. Hearne and G. Webb.

MIDDLESEX v KENT

Played at Lord's, May 31, June 1, 1888

Several of the most prominent cricketers were absent from each of the counties on this occasion. Kent, thanks to a splendid batting performance by the brothers George and Frank Hearne, who put on 135 for the second partnership, made an excellent total of 271, against which Middlesex did so badly that when stumps were drawn seven wickets were down for 81. From this bad start the Middlesex men could not recover on the second day, for, although, after following on against 174, they managed to put together 226, Kent won by seven wickets. The feature of Friday's cricket was the brilliant batting of Mr Stanley Scott, who went in first wicket down at 3, and carried his bat out for 121. Mr Hedley took fourteen wickets.

Kent

Mr F. M. Atkins b Buckland	2	– c Burton b Buckland	8
F. Hearne lbw b Burton	78	– not out	2
G. G. Hearne b Webbe	57	– b Buckland	0
Mr J. N. Tonge c Scott b Webbe	29		
Mr L. Wilson b Webbe	3	– c and b Burton	15
Lord Harris run out	6	– not out	29
Mr F. Marchant b Webbe	21		
Mr W. C. Hedley c Webbe b Robertson	31		
J. Wootton c Dauglish b Webbe	0		
F. Martin b Buckland	17		
J. Pentecost not out	0		
B 21, l-b 5, w 1	27	B 1	1
	271		55

Middlesex

Mr E. H. Buckland b Martin	8	– c and b Hedley	1
Mr A. J. Webbe b Hedley	2	– b Hedley	10
Mr S. W. Scott c Wilson b Hedley	12	– not out	121
Mr J. G. Walker c Pentecost b Hedley	11	– b F. Hearne	14
Mr P. J. de Paravicini b Martin	3	– c Harris b Hedley	22
Mr E. M. Hadow c Atkins b Hedley	10	– b Martin	40
Mr J. Robertson b Hedley	4	– b Martin	1
G. Burton b Hedley	14	– c Pentecost b Hedley	2
Mr P. Northcote b Hedley	21	– b Martin	0
J. E. West not out	6	– b Hedley	1
Mr M. J. Dauglish b Hedley	0	– c Harris b Hedley	4
B 6	6	B 10	10
	97		226

Middlesex Bowling

	Overs	Mdns	Runs	Wkts	Overs	Mdns	Runs	Wkts
Burton	45	24	59	1	11	4	12	1
Mr Buckland	45	18	71	2	8	3	22	2
Mr Robertson	7.3	2	24	1				
Mr Webbe	33	16	43	5	4	2	9	0
Mr Northcote	19	9	36	0	1.3	0	11	0
West	6	2	10	0				
Mr de Paravicini	1	0	1	0				

Kent Bowling

	Overs	Mdns	Runs	Wkts	Overs	Mdns	Runs	Wkts
Mr Hedley	26.1	11	31	8	49	23	78	6
Martin	20	10	34	2	48	28	44	3
Wootton	11	3	17	0	31	16	38	0
F. Hearne	3	0	9	0	23	7	44	1
G. G. Hearne					8	4	12	0

Umpires: Rowbotham and Nicholas.

MIDDLESEX v YORKSHIRE

Played at Lord's, June 20, 21, 22, 1889

Perhaps the most remarkable match of the season, and one that will always be remembered for the marvellous batting display on the part of Mr T. C. O'Brien, which enabled Middlesex to win within ten minutes of time on the last day. The Yorkshire eleven had been going through a long course of trial contests with local teams in various parts of the county, and this was their first match against an important county. They therefore went into the field with every feeling of confidence, but they were doomed to disappointment, and the match proved to be the commencement of a long series of disasters. That they had extraordinarily bad luck in meeting Mr O'Brien in such wonderful form was abundantly proved by the fact that, though their totals amounted to 259 and 388, they still lost by four wickets. We should say there are very few instances in cricket history of a side making nearly 400 runs in the second innings and then losing the match. Everything was in favour of a genuine test of the merits of the two teams, and there has seldom been a more perfect wicket prepared on Lord's ground. Both sides were very powerfully represented, and most people were prepared for a heavy scoring match, well knowing how much stronger are the Middlesex amateurs on a hard and true wicket. The weather, too, kept charmingly fine on all three days, and there was a large attendance of the public, though many people remained away on the Saturday thinking the result would be a draw. Could the end have been anticipated, probably Lord's ground would have been hardly big enough to accommodate the spectators. However, the interest was not only confined to the finish, the cricket on the first two days being of the highest class.

Yorkshire had the good luck to win the toss, and their innings lasted from a few minutes past twelve until just after five. The total of 259 seemed to be a good one, and one that under ordinary circumstances would have rendered the team pretty safe from defeat, but the conditions this day were so extremely favourable that the Yorkshiremen considered that anything under 300 was only a moderate score. Hall and Lord Hawke carried off the batting honours, though, of course, their play presented a most striking contrast. Hall went in first, and carried his bat for 85, an innings that extended over four hours and five minutes. Before luncheon he took nearly two hours to score 27, but afterwards his play was characterised by much more freedom. Not a single mistake could be urged against him, and among his hits were six 4s, eight 3s, and nine 2s. Lord Hawke only made 44, but it is doubtful whether he ever played a more brilliant innings. He was only at the wickets for thirty-two minutes, and the vigour of his hitting will best be judged from the following figures – nine 4s, a 3, and five singles. Lee and Moorhouse showed to fair advantage, and mention should be made of a splendid left-handed catch at cover-point with which Mr Vernon dismissed Ulyett. Middlesex had about two hours and thirty-five minutes' batting on the Thursday evening, and made such good use of their time that before the close 116 runs were scored for the loss of only two wickets. Mr Stoddart played fine cricket, but Mr Scott should have been caught in the longfield by Lord Hawke.

At the commencement of the second day's play Middlesex were 143 runs behind with eight wickets to fall, so that if anything Yorkshire appeared to have a trifling advantage. The cricket proved far more remarkable than on the opening day, and the fortunes of the game varied frequently. A tremendous rate of scoring was kept up, 474 runs being obtained and only ten wickets going down. The overnight score of 116 for the loss of two batsmen was increased by Middlesex to 368, and the home county were thus left with a lead of 109 runs. Some wonderful hitting was seen during the partnership of Messrs O'Brien and Vernon, the two gentlemen obtaining a complete mastery over the Yorkshire bowling, and putting on no fewer than 112 runs in sixty-four minutes. Mr O'Brien made 92 and Mr Vernon 86, and, though neither innings was absolutely faultless, both players deserved immense credit, and it was mainly their efforts that gave Middlesex such a good lead on the first innings. Mr O'Brien's 92 was hit up in two hours, and included fourteen 4s, six 3s, and five 2s; while Mr Vernon's 86, which lasted only an hour and three-quarters, was made up of thirteen 4s, two 3s, eight 2s, and twelve singles. At the commencement of their second innings the Yorkshiremen seemed pretty sure to be beaten, as two of the best wickets on the side – those of Ulyett and Lee – fell for 8 runs. Thus when Peel joined Hall, Yorkshire were 101 runs behind, with eight wickets to fall, and it was at this point that the game underwent an extraordinary change. The two men became partners at four o'clock in the afternoon, and gave a display of batting that overshadowed even what had been done earlier in the day by Messrs O'Brien and Vernon. Playing steadily for a time they wore down the Middlesex bowling, and then hit about with merciless severity. They scored at the rate of about 70 runs an hour, and, despite all the efforts of the Middlesex team to separate them, were still together when the long day's cricket came to an end at seven o'clock. Then the total stood at 222 for the loss of only two wickets, Peel being not out 149, and Hall not out 59. The two men had put on 214 runs, and had turned the game round in favour of their county, having obtained for them a lead of 113 runs, while there were still eight wickets to go down. Hall played a similar game to that of Thursday, but at one time he astonished the spectators by hitting three 4s in a single over. Peel played thoroughly sound and correct cricket, and, like Hall, did not give a fair chance. Indeed, both batsmen fully deserved the enthusiastic cheers which greeted them on the return to the dressing-room.

On the concluding day there came the most remarkable cricket of all. The partnership of Hall and Peel did not last much longer, for when 15 more runs had been added Peel was dismissed by a very fine catch at mid-off. The two men put on 229 runs while they were together, and Peel's 158 was the highest and certainly the best innings he has ever played in a first-class match. Coming at the time it did the performance was all the more valuable, and it is indeed high praise to say that during the four hours and fifty minutes he was at the wickets he never made a serious mistake. Among his hits were twenty-two 4s, seven 3s, and nine 2s. There was nothing in the finish of the Yorkshire innings to call for special comment, but several of the men did well, and more than once it seemed probable that the new rule would be applied. Indeed, nothing appeared more completely out of the question than a victory for Middlesex. Hall left at 313, having made 86 out of that number in four hours and fifty minutes. The figures of his marvellously patient and good innings were one 5 (4 for an overthrow), nine 4s, seven 3s, four 2s, and sixteen singles. It was a few minutes after three o'clock when the last Yorkshire wicket went down for 388, and so Middlesex were left with 280 runs to get to win, and only three hours and thirty-five minutes remaining for play. Under any circumstances 280 in the last innings against a first-class team would have been a tremendous task, but its difficulties were, of course, very much increased when the runs had to be obtained at the rate of nearly 80 runs an hour. There was, too, a possibility of the Yorkshiremen getting their opponents out in time to win the match, though with the ground still as good as ever this did not seem at all probable. At first the Middlesex men appeared to have made up their minds not to attempt to force the game. Indeed, so slowly were runs put on at the outset that by half-past five o'clock the score was only 129, and there were four of the best men out. Then in the last hour and a half came a most fitting climax to the game, and Mr O'Brien, joining Mr Nepean, commenced his hitting. From the first he seemed able to do practically as he liked with the bowling, but it was a long time before the spectators began to realise that his efforts might bring about the success of his county. Mr Nepean had been playing a good sound game before Mr O'Brien came in, but he tried to follow his partner's example, and in attempting to force the hitting was caught at 182. This left Middlesex with 98 runs to win and five wickets to fall, fifty-five minutes only remaining for cricket. By this time the interest of the spectators had been thoroughly aroused, and the excitement increased every moment as the prospect of Mr O'Brien's endeavours being successful became more and more hopeful. Mr Hadow only stayed a few moments, being caught at the wicket at 197. It was a quarter-past six when Mr Vernon came in, and so 83 runs had to be made in three-quarters of an hour. By this time the people had ceased to think about a drawn game, the pace at which Mr O'Brien had been scoring having made it clear that a win was possible. Of course, the attempt to get 83 runs in the time that remained might have cost Middlesex the match, but the idea of losing apparently never entered Mr O'Brien's mind. He and his partner played with masterly determination, and runs came at a tremendous rate. Once Mr Vernon played a ball on to his wicket without removing the bails, and once Mr O'Brien hit a ball up in the long-field, which Hall might perhaps of caught, but, considering the desperate game the two men were playing, it was really extraordinary how the excellence of the batting was maintained. At twenty minutes to seven 32 runs were wanted, but nothing could stop the hitting, and at ten minutes to seven the winning hit was made. The scene of enthusiasm at the end was something to be remembered, and reminded one of the finish of some of the England and Australia matches. Mr O'Brien just made his 100 before the close, and his innings was ranked by many of the best judges at Lord's as one of the finest displays of hitting ever seen on the ground. In an hour and twenty minutes he scored 100, and it is no exaggeration to say that he is the only batsman in England who would have been equal to such a feat. Considering the terrific pace at which he was scoring, the safety of his hitting was not less remarkable than its brilliancy. It made no difference what bowlers went on against him, for he played them all with the same easy confidence, and hit them time after time to the ring. His effort was one that required brains as well as executive ability, and his achievement was one of which too much cannot be said. To get 100 in eighty minutes was in itself a great achievement, but to make the number without giving a real chance and hardly making a bad hit was truly marvellous. The figures of the innings were fourteen 4s, six 3s, five 2s, and sixteen singles. In the whole match Mr O'Brien made 192 runs for once out, and Hall for Yorkshire scored 171 runs, and was also only once got rid of, the styles of the two men, of course, being totally different. Mr Vernon deserved more credit than he received, his performance being overshadowed by that of Mr O'Brien, but still he had a large share in the victory of Middlesex.

In the whole match no fewer than 1,295 runs were scored for the loss of thirty-six wickets, this being a record aggregate in a first-class match in this country. It has once been beaten in Australia, in the famous inter-Colonial match at Sydney in 1882, when 1,411 runs were obtained for thirty wickets. Then, however, the game extended over five days. In the contest between Middlesex and Yorkshire, however, five balls were bowled to the over. Under the old rule 1,295 runs in three days would have been almost impossible.

Yorkshire

G. Ulyett c Vernon b Bacmeister	20	– c Hadow b Burton	0
L. Hall not out	85	– c Nepean b Webbe	86
F. Lee b Hadow	32	– c West b Burton	4
R. Peel c Scott b Hadow	3	– c Webbe b Bacmeister	158
E. Wainwright b Bacmeister	17	– c Vernon b Stoddart	29
Lord Hawke c O'Brien b Nepean	44	– b Stoddart	20
R. Moorhouse run out	28	– b Stoddart	21
S. Wade c Stoddart b Burton	18	– st West b Nepean	20
L. Whitehead b Stoddart	0	– b Stoddart	16
D. Hunter lbw b Burton	3	– not out	9
W. Middlebrook c West b Burton	0	– c West b Nepean	5
B 5, l-b 4	9	B 15, l-b 5	20
	259		388

Middlesex

Mr A. E. Stoddart c Middlebrook b Ulyett	46	– b Ulyett	18
Mr A. J. Webbe c Hall b Middlebrook	13	– c Hall b Ulyett	5
Mr S. W. Scott c Moorhouse b Ulyett	33	– lbw b Peel	36
Mr E. A. Nepean c Middlebrook b Ulyett	31	– c Lee b Middlebrook	62
Mr J. G. Walker st Hunter b Wainwright	30	– c Hunter b Ulyett	25
Mr T. C. O'Brien lbw b Wade	92	– not out	100
Mr E. M. Hadow c Hall b Wainwright	0	– c Hunter b Middlebrook	1
Mr G. F. Vernon c Lee b Middlebrook	86	– not out	30
J. E. West c Lee b Middlebrook	2		
G. Burton not out	15		
Mr L. H. Bacmeister c and b Whitehead	15		
B 1, l-b 2, w 2	5	B 1, l-b 1, w 1	3
	368		280

Middlesex Bowling

	Overs	Mdns	Runs	Wkts	Overs	Mdns	Runs	Wkts
Burton	48.3	26	50	3	43	18	70	2
Mr Bacmesiter	30	12	62	2	27	14	53	1
Mr Nepean	13	0	44	1	19.2	1	69	2
Mr Stoddart	14	4	43	1	33	17	79	4
Mr Hadow	13	2	40	2	27	13	38	0
Mr Webbe	9	5	11	0	22	13	29	1
West					8	1	21	0
Mr O'Brien					2	0	9	0

Yorkshire Bowling

	Overs	Mdns	Runs	Wkts	Overs	Mdns	Runs	Wkts
Peel	36	9	91	0	32	12	69	1
Middlebrook	25	1	70	3	22	6	57	2
Wainwright	13	3	45	2	18	5	55	0
Ulyett	21	5	67	3	21	2	69	3
Whitehead	15.3	8	22	1	7	2	27	0
Wade	27	9	68	1				

Umpires: W. Draper and C. K. Pullin.

MIDDLESEX v SURREY

Played at Lord's, August 14, 15, 1890

Surrey put a strong team into the field, and, having the good fortune to win the toss, a score of 425 was obtained. The great feature of the cricket was the batting of Abel; the Surrey professional, after a number of disappointing performances, playing in his finest form, and carrying his bat right through the innings for 151. His stay extended over five hours and fifty minutes, during which time he never gave the least chance. His chief hits were twelve 4s, ten 3s, and eighteen 2s. Against such a tremendous total Middlesex could hope for nothing better than to save the game, but in this endeavour they failed signally, and though some good batting was shown in the first innings by Messrs Stoddart, Scott, and O'Brien, the batsmen afterwards gave a feeble display, and Surrey were left with a decisive victory by an innings and 162 runs. Lohmann and Sharpe worthily followed up the success of the Surrey batsmen on the previous day, and took nine wickets each, Sharpe having rather the better average.

Surrey

R. Abel not out	151
Mr J. Shuter b Ford	22
G. A. Lohmann st Dauglish b Ford	52
Mr W. W. Read c Hearne b Burton	46
M. Read b Rawlin	9
Mr K. J. Key c Scott b Burton	4
W. Lockwood c Henery b Rawlin	52
R. Henderson c Dauglish b Rawlin	11
W. Brockwell lbw b Rawlin	32
J. W. Sharpe b Hearne	2
Mr A. F. Clarke b Rawlin	30
B 10, l-b 4	14
	425

Middlesex

Mr A. E. Stoddart c Henderson b Lohmann	48	– b Sharpe	2
Mr A. J. Webbe c Abel b Lohmann	8	– b Sharpe	26
Mr S. W. Scott st Clarke b Sharpe	40	– c Shuter b Lohmann	0
Mr T. C. O'Brien lbw b Sharpe	33	– b Lohmann	4
J. T. Rawlin run out	4	– b Sharpe	0
Mr H. J. Mordaunt b Sharpe	8	– c and b Lohmann	16
Mr F. G. J. Ford b Lohmann	10	– c M. Read b Lohmann	7
Mr P. J. T. Henery c W. W. Read b Lohmann	5	– not out	23
J. T. Hearne b Sharpe	0	– b Sharpe	14
Mr M. J. Dauglish c Henderson b Lohmann	0	– c Brockwell b Sharpe	0
G. Burton not out	2	– run out	5
B 4	4	B 4	4
	162		101

Middlesex Bowling

	Overs	Mdns	Runs	Wkts
Burton	39	10	105	2
Hearne	33	12	82	1
Mr Stoddart	22	4	57	0
Mr Ford	18	5	47	2
Rawlin	52.2	23	78	5
Mr Webbe	3	0	16	0
Mr Mordaunt	4	1	26	0

Surrey Bowling

	Overs	Mdns	Runs	Wkts	Overs	Mdns	Runs	Wkts
Lohmann	36	11	74	5	18.2	2	65	4
Sharpe	36.1	12	78	4	18	6	32	5
Abel	3	2	2	0				
Brockwell	4	3	4	0				

Umpires: G. Panter and H. Holmes.

MIDDLESEX v YORKSHIRE

Played at Lord's, June 4, 5, 6, 1891

This was another of the many matches during the unfortunate season of 1891 that were seriously interfered with by rain. No start could be made on the first day, and afterwards, on a soft and treacherous wicket, the Middlesex team offered a poor resistance to Yorkshire, and had the worst of the game all the way through. On winning the toss for Middlesex Mr Webbe adopted the risky policy of putting his opponents in to bat, and the course of action turned out very badly, for Yorkshire scored a first innings of 109, which proved to be the highest of the four played, and sufficient to ensure the Northerners a victory. On the opening day some remarkable bowling was accomplished by Hearne, Peel, and Harrison. Yorkshire won the match by 69 runs, and fully deserved their success, but certainly the greatest thing in the game was done by a Middlesex man, J. T. Hearne bowling in his finest form, and taking in the two innings fourteen wickets at a cost of only 65 runs.

Yorkshire

	First innings	Second innings	
G. Ulyett c O'Brien b Rawlin	0	b Hearne	3
L. Hall c Scott b Hearne	32	b Hearne	0
J. T. Brown b Hearne	29	b Hearne	13
Mr A. Sellers b Rawlin	22	b Hearne	0
R. Peel b Hearne	0	st West b Phillips	14
Lord Hawke lbw b Hearne	0	b Rawlin	5
E. Wainwright c O'Brien b Hearne	12	c O'Brien b Hearne	28
R. Moorhouse b Hearne	1	lbw b Hearne	4
L. Whitehead b Rawlin	0	c O'Brien b Rawlin	1
D. Hunter not out	8	c O'Brien b Hearne	1
G. P. Harrison c Phillips b Hearne	0	not out	1
B 4, l-b 1	5	B 6, l-b 1	7
	109		77

Middlesex

	First innings	Second innings	
Mr A. E. Stoddart c Wainwright b Peel	0	b Peel	0
Mr A. J. Webbe b Harrison	5	not out	12
Mr S. W. Scott b Harrison	2	b Wainwright	0
Mr E. A. Nepean b Harrison	0	b Wainwright	13
Mr T. C. O'Brien lbw b Peel	9	b Wainwright	0
Mr E. M. Hadow c Whitehead b Peel	7	c Brown b Peel	7
Mr G. F. Vernon b Harrison	13	c Wainwright b Peel	0
J. T. Rawlin run out	4	b Wainwright	0
J. T. Hearne c Moorhouse b Harrison	0	b Peel	0
J.E.West lbw b Peel	11	c and b Harrison	0
J. Phillips not out	4	c Wainwright b Peel	0
B 6, l-b 2	8	B 2	2
	63		54

Middlesex Bowling

	Overs	Mdns	Runs	Wkts	Overs	Mdns	Runs	Wkts
Phillips	10	4	22	0	6	2	10	1
Rawlin	20	9	27	3	19	8	32	2
Hearne	22.1	8	37	7	26	14	28	7
Mr Nepean	6	2	8	0				
Mr Hadow	3	0	10	0				

Yorkshire Bowling

	Overs	Mdns	Runs	Wkts	Overs	Mdns	Runs	Wkts
Peel	13.2	2	41	4	21	12	19	5
Harrison	13	7	14	5	18	6	24	1
Wainwright					11	7	9	4

Umpires: F. Coward and R. Carpenter.

MIDDLESEX v LANCASHIRE

Played at Lord's, June 11, 12, 1891

During the progress of this match the cricket underwent some startling changes, but the Middlesex team always had the best of it, their victory, which was ultimately gained by 132 runs, being brought about by some splendid batting on the part of Mr Stoddart, Mr Webbe and Mr Scott, and some remarkably fine bowling by Hearne and Phillips. For once there was a fast wicket, and the small scoring on the opening day was perhaps attributable to the fact that most of the batsmen had had so many slow grounds to play upon. The sun was shining brilliantly when Middlesex, having won the toss, went in to bat, and the chances seemed all in favour of a long score being obtained. Messrs Stoddart and Webbe made an excellent start, putting on 40 runs for the first wicket, but after they had been separated the batsmen failed one after another before the admirable bowling of Mold and Briggs, and a few minutes after luncheon the whole side were out for a total of 96, the last eight wickets actually falling for an addition of 34 runs. Mold and Briggs bowled with wonderful effect. The former, despite his great pace, was able to get a good deal of work on the ball, and none of the Middlesex team, save Mr Stoddart and Mr Webbe, could play him with any degree of confidence. As will be seen from the analysis Briggs and Mold remained unchanged throughout the innings, and divided the wickets between them, but the figures of the latter were the more remarkable, his five wickets being obtained at a cost of only 6 and a half runs each. Great, however, as had been the Lancashire man's performance it was completely overshadowed by J. T. Hearne's achievement when the Northerners went in the first time. The display of the Lancashire eleven must have been extremely disappointing to their many supporters, as no one could have expected that on a fast ground such a strong batting side would be dismissed in an hour and a quarter for the paltry total of 63. Of this number three men – Mr Hornby, Briggs and Sugg – scored between them no fewer than 42. Except for the three cricketers mentioned the Lancashire team could do absolutely nothing against Hearne, the majority of them being beaten by the great pace of the ground. The young Middlesex professional bowled in quite his best form, and actually dismissed eight men for 22 runs, hitting the wicket on each occasion. He narrowly missed the "hat trick," for in one over he took three wickets with the first, third and fifth balls respectively, and he bowled another batsman with the first ball of his following over. Middlesex, holding a lead of 33 runs, began their second innings at a quarter to five in the afternoon, and the cricket that followed was in surprising contrast to what had gone before, some batting of the finest description being exhibited by Messrs Stoddart and Webbe. These two gentlemen opened the innings, and, playing in a style that aroused the spectators to a high pitch of enthusiasm, scored 121 runs in an hour and fifty minutes during their partnership for the first wicket. Mr Webbe played rather a defensive game, but Mr Stoddart hit in determined fashion, and scored 87 without giving a chance, the chief figures of his magnificent display being eleven 4s, one 3 and eleven 2s. Added to his 37 in the first innings this made Mr Stoddart's aggregate for the match 124, so that he had a very large share in the success of his county. Just before the call of time Mr Webbe, after being in two hours and a quarter for 34 – an admirable innings – was got rid of, and at the drawing of stumps the total was 131 for two wickets. This left the home county with a tremendous advantage, as they were 164 runs ahead with only two wickets down.

When the game was resumed on the Friday morning the Middlesex batsmen failed to follow up the brilliant start that had been made by Messrs Stoddart and Webbe, and, as on the previous morning, Mold and Briggs carried everything before them. Mr Scott increased his not out score of 6 to 27, but the others could do nothing, and in the course of an hour and ten minutes cricket eight wickets actually went down for the addition of 35 runs, the Middlesex total thus reaching 166. During this portion of the innings Mold did a remarkable piece of bowling, his analysis being fifteen overs and four balls, eleven maidens, four runs and four wickets. In the whole match Mold and Briggs each took ten wickets, but while the former's ten cost only 62 runs, no fewer than 138 were hit off Briggs. When Lancashire went in with 200 to get to win, the ground had broken up in a few places, and scarcely anyone thought that the runs would be made. Sugg, who under the circumstances was perhaps the most dangerous man on the side, was bowled without scoring, but then came a stand by Albert Ward and Barlow. The bowling had been opened by Hearne and Mr Nepean, but while Barlow and Ward were together the old Oxonian was taken off in favour of Phillips, a change that was attended with triumphant success. Barlow was out at 31, and then in quick succession Phillips got rid of Mr Crosfield, Paul and Briggs, so that at the luncheon interval five men were out for 54 and Lancashire's chance of winning was practically at an end. When play was resumed, the match was brought to a startingly rapid conclusion, the last five wickets falling in twenty-five minutes for the addition of 13 runs. Hearne again bowled wonderfully well, but on this occasion his performance was eclipsed by that of Phillips, who took six wickets for 25 runs. In the whole match, however, Hearne came out with the magnificent record of eleven wickets for 47 runs.

Middlesex

Mr A. E. Stoddart c Kemble b Briggs	37	– b Mold	87
Mr A. J. Webbe b Mold	11	– lbw b Briggs	34
Mr S. W. Scott c Baker b Mold	9	– c Crosfield b Briggs	27
Mr E. A. Nepean b Mold	7	– c Barlow b Briggs	2
J. T. Rawlin c Baker b Briggs	12	– b Briggs	2
Mr E. M. Hadow c Kemble b Briggs	5	– c Sugg b Briggs	6
J. E. West b Briggs	4	– b Mold	0
Mr F. Bryan b Mold	0	– b Mold	0
Mr J. Robertson c Kemble b Mold	4	– b Mold	0
J. T. Hearne c and b Briggs	0	– not out	0
J. Phillips not out	0	– b Mold	0
B 1, l-b 6	7	B 2, l-b 3	5
	96		166

Lancashire

R. G. Barlow b Hearne	9	– lbw b Hearne	17
F. H. Sugg b Hearne	11	– b Hearne	0
A. Ward b Nepean	4	– c Robertson b Phillips	33
Mr S. M. Crosfield b Hearne	0	– b Phillips	1
A. Paul b Hearne	0	– c West b Phillips	0
J. Briggs b Hearne	14	– c Scott b Phillips	2
G. Yates b Hearne	3	– run out	5
G. R. Baker b Hearne	2	– b Hearne	0
Mr A. N. Hornby not out	17	– b Phillips	3
Mr A. T. Kemble c Stoddart b Nepean	1	– b Phillips	2
A. Mold b Hearne	0	– not out	0
B 2	2	L-b 4	4
	63		67

Lancashire Bowling

	Overs	Mdns	Runs	Wkts	Overs	Mdns	Runs	Wkts
Briggs	27	8	56	5	44	17	82	5
Mold	26.2	11	33	5	34.4	18	29	5
Baker					11	5	19	—
Mr Crosfield					3	1	12	—
Barlow					9	2	19	—

Middlesex Bowling

	Overs	Mdns	Runs	Wkts	Overs	Mdns	Runs	Wkts
Hearne	12.1	4	22	8	18	7	25	3
Mr Nepean	11	3	35	2	6	2	13	—
Phillips	1	—	4	—	11	2	25	6

Umpires: J. Street and G. Panter.

MIDDLESEX v GLOUCESTERSHIRE

Played at Lord's, June 9, 10, 11, 1892

Being seen to advantage at all points of the game, Middlesex gained a most brilliant victory over Gloucestershire in a single innings, with 102 runs to spare. The match will always be remembered for a magnificent display of batting on the part of Mr Stanley Scott. This gentleman eclipsed all his previous performances in first-class cricket by scoring an innings of 224, going in first wicket down at twenty minutes to six on Thursday afternoon, and being the last man out at six o'clock on Friday. Deducting all intervals, he made his runs in six hours and forty minutes, the figures of his wonderful innings being twenty-seven 4s, four 3s, fifteen 2s and seventy-four singles. He sustained his form throughout in splendid fashion, and during all his long stay only two mistakes could be urged against him. He gave an easy chance to Roberts at mid-on when he had made 47, and was let off by the same fieldsman in the same position when his score stood at 136. On the concluding day Mr W. G. Grace played a very fine innings of 72 not out.

Gloucestershire

	First innings		Second innings	
Mr W. G. Grace c West b Nepean	47	–	not out	72
Mr E. M. Grace c West b Hearne	0	–	b Rawlin	28
Mr O. G. Radcliffe b Rawlin	82	–	c Hearne b Nepean	2
J. Painter c Hearne b Rawlin	19	–	b Phillips	10
Mr S. A. P. Kitcat b Nepean	14	–	c West b Hearne	8
Mr E. Sainsbury lbw b Nepean	16	–	b Hearne	5
Capt. A. H. Luard c O'Brien b Nepean	7	–	b Phillips	0
H. W. Murch c O'Brien b Hearne	25	–	b Phillips	26
W. A. Woof b Hearne	0	–	b Phillips	3
F. G. Roberts not out	9	–	lbw b Nepean	17
J. H. Board c West b Hearne	6	–	c Rawlin b Phillips	0
B 15, l-b 3, n-b 1	19		L-b 6	6
	244			177

Middlesex

Mr A. E. Stoddart lbw b Murch	24
Mr A. J. Webbe c Painter b Murch	19
Mr S. W. Scott b Woof	224
Mr E. A. Nepean c Board b Murch	44
Mr T. C. O'Brien c Kitcat b Woof	13
J. T. Rawlin b Woof	64
Mr P. J. T. Henery c E. M. Grace b Roberts	33
J. Phillips c Murch b E. M. Grace	52
Mr R. S. Lucas b Woof	9
J. E. West c Painter b E. M. Grace	22
J. T. Hearne not out	12
B 8, l-b 5, w 1, n-b 2	16
	523

Middlesex Bowling

	Overs	Mdns	Runs	Wkts	Overs	Mdns	Runs	Wkts
Mr Nepean	36	11	93	4	25	3	57	2
Hearne	33.3	16	51	4	28	13	41	2
Rawlin	29	12	58	2	23	9	39	1
Mr Stoddart	4	1	11	—	1	—	1	—
Phillips	15	9	12	—	24	7	33	5

Gloucestershire Bowling

	Overs	Mdns	Runs	Wkts
Roberts	27	7	51	1
Murch	41	15	95	3
Woof	81.3	24	188	4
Mr W. G. Grace	25	8	62	—
Mr E. M. Grace	26	5	83	2
Mr Radcliffe	2	—	13	—
Painter	6	2	15	—

Umpires: F. Coward and J. Lillywhite.

MIDDLESEX v NOTTINGHAMSHIRE

Played at Lord's, June 20, 21, 22, 1892

The match between Middlesex and Nottinghamshire will always be remembered for its remarkable finish, the result only being arrived at within four minutes of the call of time on the Wednesday evening, and the great change in the game being brought about by the unexpected success that attended the bowling of Sherwin. On the opening day rain caused three stoppages, but from a quarter to four until seven o'clock the game went on without interruption. For the whole of the time that play was in progress the Nottinghamshire team occupied the wickets, and left off for the day with the capital score of 256 for the loss of five batsmen. The early, play, however, gave no suggestion of such a performance, as three wickets – including those of Gunn and Barnes – went down for 38, and the fourth man left at 95. At this point Shrewsbury, who from the first had shown an easy mastery over the Middlesex bowling, was joined by Robinson, and from ten minutes past four until just upon seven o'clock the two stayed together. During all this long time the play was of much the same character. Shrewsbury made many fine hits, and his placing was as perfect as ever, but at no point in his innings did he run any risks, and, with Robinson almost equally cautious, the batting, good as it was, was at times open to the charge of monotony. Shrewsbury made no mistake, but Robinson gave a difficult chance to Hearne at short slip, when he had scored 21, and an easy one to O'Brien at point when he had made 39. The fifth wicket went down just before the call of time, the partnership having yielded no fewer than 161 runs.

On the Tuesday the remainder of the Nottinghamshire innings lasted from twenty minutes to twelve until a quarter to five, the total reaching 466. At times the scoring was painfully slow, and altogether the Nottinghamshire innings lasted within a minute or two of nine hours. Shrewsbury gave a most characteristic display of batting, showing all his old mastery in placing the ball, and, as on the previous day, never running the slightest risk. He remained at the wickets until ten minutes past four, being the eighth man out at 445, his share of that number being 212. He was batting altogether for just under eight hours and a-half, his hits being seventeen 4s, eight 3s, twenty 2s and eighty singles. Owing, perhaps, to a not unnatural feeling of fatigue, he became even more cautious after completing his 200, his last six runs – which included a hit for 4 – taking him half-an-hour to obtain. During his long stay at the wickets the only real chance he gave was one to Hearne at slip when he had made 158. This was Shrewsbury's second score of over 200 at Lord's ground, the previous one being his 224 not out – also against Middlesex – in the season of 1885. Two batsmen helped him to master the bowling, Attewell staying with him while the score was increased from 256 to 369, and Shacklock assisting him to put on 64 runs for the seventh wicket. After their long and trying time in the field Middlesex made a very bad start, losing three of their best wickets for 27 runs, but then Scott and Nepean caused matters to look very much better for their side, and at the drawing of stumps the score stood at 89 for three wickets.

On the concluding day Middlesex were in a thankless position, as they had no possibility of winning, their only hope being to remain in for the whole day and draw the game. Their first innings was finished off for 195, and just before the luncheon interval they had to follow on against a majority of 271.The wicket, which had worn wonderfully well, was still in excellent condition, and Middlesex, to save the match, had to resist the Nottingham bowlers for about four hours and a quarter. At the outset matters went badly, and four wickets were soon obtained. With six wickets to fall, three hours and ten minutes still remained for play, so that the victory of Nottinghamshire seemed almost assured, but at this point a great change came over the game, Stoddart and O'Brien, by splendid cricket, remaining together for sixty-five minutes, and carrying the score from 55 to 152. Webbe then became Stoddart's partner, and the two gentlemen played so well that it seemed almost certain they would save their side from defeat. At half-past six they were still together, and the score had reached 244. It did not appear possible for five wickets to fall in half an hour, but there came one of those turns of fortune that make the charm of cricket. The regular bowlers having been mastered, a trial was given to Sherwin, and this change was attended with extraordinary success. The Nottinghamshire wicket-keeper clean bowled Webbe at 247, and, with the score unaltered, Stoddart was out leg before wicket. Thus the whole position had changed, twenty-five minutes remaining for play, and there being three wickets to go down. Amidst tremendous excitement Thesiger was bowled at 250, and Rawlin at 252, while at 257 Hearne was caught by the wicket-keeper, the ball only being held at the second attempt, and Nottinghamshire won the match within four minutes of time by an innings and 14 runs. Stoddart's magnificent 130 included fourteen 4s, eight 3s and nine 2s.

Nottinghamshire

Batsman	Runs
Mr A. O. Jones c West b Hearne	7
A. Shrewsbury c Phillips b Rawlin	212
W. Gunn c Hearne b Nepean	1
W. Barnes c Stoddart b Nepean	14
W. Flowers b Hearne	27
Mr J. S. Robinson c Rawlin b Hearne	72
W. Attewell b Hearne	59
F. Shacklock b Nepean	36
H. B. Daft not out	13
W. Wilkinson b Rawlin	3
M. Sherwin c Thesiger b Nepean	10
B 10, l-b 1, n-b 1	12
	466

Middlesex

First innings		Second innings	
Mr A. E. Stoddart b Attewell	2	lbw b Attewell	130
Mr A. J. Webbe c Robinson b Shacklock	11	b Sherwin	32
Mr S. W. Scott c Shrewsbury b Shacklock	55	b Flowers	13
Mr T. C. O'Brien c Sherwin b Attewell	1	c Sherwin b Flowers	57
Mr E. A. Nepean b Shacklock	61	c Sherwin b Attewell	0
J. T. Rawlin c Robinson b Shacklock	4	b Attewell	1
Hon. F. J. N. Thesiger b Barnes	3	b Sherwin	3
J. T. Hearne b Barnes	3	c Robinson b Attewell	0
J. Phillips b Barnes	17	b Shacklock	4
Mr R. S. Lucas c Sherwin b Shacklock	2	not out	4
J. E. West not out	32	b Shacklock	4
B 4	4	B 5, l-b 4	9
	195		257

Middlesex Bowling

	Overs	Mdns	Runs	Wkts
Hearne	77	35	117	4
Mr Nepean	63.3	19	133	4
Rawlin	58	31	67	2
Phillips	39	10	93	—
Mr Stoddart	15	6	28	—
Mr Webbe	6	2	11	—
Mr O'Brien	1	—	5	—

Nottinghamshire Bowling

	Overs	Mdns	Runs	Wkts	Overs	Mdns	Runs	Wkts
Attewell	36	17	47	2	32.1	17	38	4
Shacklock	48	16	103	5	24	8	69	2
Flowers	9	4	14	—	28	11	46	2
Barnes	21.1	7	27	3	21	7	52	—
Wilkinson					7	2	26	—
Daft					5	1	8	—
Sherwin					7	4	9	2

Umpires: C. K. Pullin and A. F. Smith.

MIDDLESEX v NOTTINGHAMSHIRE

Played at Lord's, June 5, 6, 7, 1893

By reason of Stoddart's magnificent batting the first of the two meetings between Middlesex and Nottinghamshire stood out among the remarkable contests of the season. In matches between the MCC and Sussex, the MCC and the Australians, Middlesex and Gloucestershire, and Middlesex and Yorkshire, Stoddart had already given proof of being in splendid form, but his previous efforts in 1893 were completely thrown into the shade on this particular occasion when he scored 195 not out and 124. By obtaining two separate hundreds in the same game he accomplished a feat which previously had only been performed in first-class matches by W. G. Grace and George Brann, and his 195 not out proved, so far as important cricket was concerned, to be the highest individual innings of the year. In making his two long scores he showed some wonderful cricket, playing throughout both innings in his finest and most attractive style. On the Monday he went in first and took out his bat, his innings of 195, which extended over three hours and thirty-five minutes, comprising one 5, twenty-eight 4s, eight 3s, fourteen 2s and twenty-six singles. Before he had scored 50 he gave a couple of very sharp chances in the slips from Mee's fast bowling, but, so far as we are aware, these were his only mistakes. So uniform was his rate of scoring that he made 101 in an hour and fifty minutes before lunch, and 91 in an hour and three-quarters afterwards. Up to a certain time, though he played so well, it did not seem as if he would have a chance of doing anything out of the common, Mee's bowling proving so effective that on a perfect wicket Middlesex had six men out for 115. Then, however, came the turning point of the game, Ford giving such valuable support to Stoddart that the partnership of the two batsmen produced 112 runs in barely an hour. During the first forty minutes they were together they actually put on 85 runs. Eight wickets were down for 242, but MacGregor stayed with Stoddart, and in three-quarters of an hour 79 runs were added for the ninth wicket. Everyone hoped that Stoddart would crown his performance by making 200, but he was still five short of the coveted number when J. T. Hearne, his last partner, was bowled. On the first innings there was a difference of only 26 runs in favour of Middlesex, and at ten minutes past four on Tuesday afternoon Stoddart went in for the second time, He played, if possible in even more remarkable form than before, and at the drawing of stumps was not out 94, Middlesex's score standing at 184 for two wickets. Some heavy rain fell during the night, and on the game being resumed a little anxiety was felt as to whether the famous batsman would succeed in making his second hundred. In the course of ten minutes' cricket, however, he obtained the six runs he wanted, and having done this he was evidently satisfied, for he did not attempt afterwards to play anything like a strict game. He gave a couple of chances – one in the long field and the other to the bowler – and was out at 239, his being the sixth wicket to fall. His great innings of 124 lasted three hours and a quarter, and was composed of thirteen 4s, seven 3s, nine 2s and thirty-three singles. For once out he had the extraordinary record in the match of 319 runs, a performance which was not approached during the whole of the summer. Middlesex were out at twenty minutes past one for 304, and Nottinghamshire, who had just over four hours left for play, had 331 to get. The accomplishment of this task involved scoring at the rate of 80 an hour for the rest of the afternoon, but the wicket had so thoroughly recovered from the effects of the rain that victory, though improbable, was by no means out of the question. Up to a certain point Nottinghamshire did very well, Gunn and Shrewsbury in less than an hour making 74 runs. Then, however, an error of judgment on Shrewsbury's part cost Gunn his wicket, and matters afterwards went so badly with Nottinghamshire that five men were out for 116. With two hours and a half still remaining there did not seem much doubt about the result, but C. W. Wright played a splendid game for his side, and Attewell, after a couple of very lucky escapes, hit so well that in three-quarters of an hour the seventh wicket put on 56 runs. After Attewell's dismissal, Wright and Shacklock scored 48 together in twenty-five minutes, but in the end the innings closed for 273, Middlesex winning the match, with only ten minutes to spare, by 57 runs. Mee was out in a most foolish way, getting off his ground, after an appeal for lbw had been answered in his favour, and having his wicket very cleverly thrown down from point by O'Brien. In the first innings of Nottinghamshire Gunn played superbly for 120, going in first and being out seventh at 269. He was at the wickets as nearly as possible four hours and a half, and hit fifteen 4s, three 3s, eleven 2s and twenty-nine singles, his only mistake being a chance at the wicket when he had made 51. In the course of the three days 1,205 runs were scored for the loss of forty wickets, the smallest of the four totals being 273.

Middlesex

	First innings	Second innings	
Mr A. E. Stoddart not out	195	c Flowers b Mee	124
Mr A. J. Webbe b Mee	19	c Sherwin b Attewell	1
Mr S. W. Scott c Daft b Mee	10	b Shacklock	11
Mr C. P. Foley b Mee	0	c Wright b Attewell	68
Mr P. J. T. Henery c and b Mee	8	c Flowers b Mee	14
Mr T. C. O'Brien b Mee	1	c Shacklock b Attewell	19
J. Phillips lbw b Attewell	4	c Dixon b Attewell	8
Mr F. G. J. Ford b Attewell	45	c Attewell b Flowers	36
Mr H. J. Mordaunt c Shacklock b Mee	7	c Mee b Flowers	1
Mr G. MacGregor c Shacklock b Dixon	31	b Flowers	0
J. T. Hearne b Dixon	4	not out	2
B 2, l-b 1	3	B 15, l-b 6, w 1, n-b 1	25
	327		304

Nottinghamshire

	First innings	Second innings	
A. Shrewsbury c Scott b Hearne	18	b Phillips	41
W. Gunn c Hearne b Ford	120	run out	46
W. Barnes c MacGregor b Mordaunt	36	b Hearne	0
W. Flowers b Stoddart	34	c Mordaunt b Hearne	39
H. B. Daft c O'Brien b Mordaunt	14	lbw b Hearne	5
Mr J. A. Dixon b Phillips	9	lbw b Phillips	0
Mr C. W. Wright c Phillips b Hearne	18	c Stoddart b Phillips	61
W. Attewell b Hearne	10	b Hearne	36
F. Shacklock c MacGregor b Hearne	25	not out	23
P. J. Mee not out	3	run out	2
M. Sherwin b Ford	0	b Hearne	4
B 13, n-b 1	14	B 18, w 1	19
	301		273

Nottinghamshire Bowling

	Overs	Mdns	Runs	Wkts	Overs	Mdns	Runs	Wkts
Shacklock	12	1	74	—	8	1	32	1
Mee	19	7	120	6	38	9	104	2
Attewell	28	8	63	2	42	11	100	4
Flowers	8	—	31	—	11.2	3	26	3
Barnes	4	—	16	—	2	—	7	—
Dixon	5.4	2	7	2	5	1	12	—
Daft	4	—	13	—				

Middlesex Bowling

	Overs	Mdns	Runs	Wkts	Overs	Mdns	Runs	Wkts
Hearne	54	25	93	4	48.3	20	98	5
Ford	20.2	5	55	2	8	2	26	—
Phillips	32	9	70	1	34	7	84	3
Stoddart	15	4	37	1	11	2	33	—
Mordaunt	16	3	32	2	9	3	13	—

Umpires: F. Coward and A. F. Smith.

MIDDLESEX v SURREY

Played at Lord's June 22, 23, 24, 1893

No match during the eventful season of 1893 was more remarkable than the return between Middlesex and Surrey, for in it Middlesex accomplished a really extraordinary performance, following on against a majority of 179 and winning in the end by 79 runs. Seldom has a game undergone a greater change, as up to the time of an innings being completed on each side everything pointed to a very easy victory for Surrey. Then matters were made to assume a totally different aspect by the wonderful batting of Stoddart and O'Brien, the two men hitting off the arrears without being separated, and actually carrying the score to 228 before the first wicket fell. Despite the fact that there had been a lot of important cricket in London just previously, the match attracted a large amount of attention, and Lord's Ground was extremely well attended on all three days of the contest, the full number paying for admission being 18,039. Both sides were very strongly represented, though, owing to an injured hand. A. J. Webbe was unable to captain Middlesex. Though Surrey had lost the first match by seven wickets, everyone looked forward to a keen struggle, and anticipation was thoroughly borne out. Going in first on a capital wicket. Surrey were batting for the greater part of the opening day, their total reaching 287. Maurice Read, Abel and Key were all seen to advantage, but the Middlesex fielding was decidedly faulty, several bad blunders being made. Middlesex had thirty-five minutes' batting and scored 35 for the loss of two wickets. Their position on commencing play on the second day was far from hopeful, as they were 252 behind, with eight wickets to go down, and at the outset their batting was so feeble that it seemed almost certain they must be badly beaten. Certainly the conditions for a time were unfavourable, as rain overnight had made the wicket treacherous, but the ground recovered itself surprisingly after the close of the first innings of Middlesex. For an hour or two the bowlers were able to do pretty much as they liked, and despite some good hitting by Rawlin and Ford, the total of the Middlesex innings only amounted to 108 or 179 behind. At the beginning of the second innings of Middlesex occurred the wonderful achievement by Stoddart and O'Brien, to which reference has already been made. The two men set about their task with the utmost vigour and determination, and quickly obtained a complete mastery over the Surrey bowling. In the course of two hours and a half they put on no fewer than 228 runs, and apart from the remarkable nature of the performance, it possessed additional merit from the brilliant and skilful manner in which the batsmen obtained their runs. Despite the fact that they were always scoring at a great pace, the batting was practically without fault, as during all the time the runs were being made only one palpable chance was given. Just when the arrears had been hit off, a curious point arose, it being contended that O'Brien on turning round to hit a lob to leg had kicked off one of the bails. However, one umpire could not give a decision, and the umpire standing at short leg gave the batsman not out. Stoddart, who was the first to leave, hit eleven 4s, six 3s and eighteen 2s in his magnificent 125, while O'Brien, who was fourth out at 254, made eighteen 4s, four 3s and five 2s in his 113, which occupied him just three hours. This was far and away the best thing in batting that O'Brien did last season. At the time of his departure, Middlesex, with four wickets down, were only 75 runs ahead, but Ford came to the rescue of his side and gave a wonderful display of hitting. In the course of fifty-five minutes he actually hit up 74 out of 91, his figures being ten 4s, two 3s, ten 2s and eight singles. At the close of the day the Middlesex score was 353 for five wickets, or 174 ahead with half the wickets to go down. Though they had found run-getting so easy on the previous evening, the Middlesex batsmen failed badly at the start of the third day's play, and in fifty-five mintues the last five wickets went down for 24 runs, the total thus reaching 377. This left Surrey with 199 to get to win, and though the task was rather a formidable one, there seemed a reasonable prospect of the runs being obtained, as the ground was still in fairly good condition. From the first the struggle was contested in the keenest manner, the Middlesex bowling and fielding being admirable, and MacGregor at the wicket putting in some of his finest work. Four of the best Surrey wickets went down for 37, and though Key, Ayres and Brockwell made a desperate attempt to put a better appearance on the game, their efforts came too late, and Middlesex gained a remarkable victory by 79 runs.

Surrey

R. Abel run out	45	– c MacGregor b Hearne	12
W. Lockwood lbw b Rawlin	4	– b Rawlin	11
M. Read b Hearne	75	– run out	5
Mr W. W. Read c Stoddart b Ford	6	– b Hearne	0
Mr K. J. Key lbw b Stoddart	53	– b Hearne	15
R. Henderson c MacGregor b Hearne	0	– b Rawlin	17
G. Ayres b Hearne	2	– c MacGregor b Rawlin	20
Mr J. Shuter b Stoddart	19	– b Rawlin	1
W. Brockwell b Ford	26	– b Hearne	23
H. Wood c Phillips b Stoddart	17	– c Scott b Rawlin	7
T. Richardson not out	9	– not out	0
B 27, l-b 2, w 2	31	B 8	8
	287		119

Middlesex

Mr A. E. Stoddart c Henderson b Richardson	31	– c Brockwell b Lockwood	125
Mr T. C. O'Brien b Abel	8	– c Wood b Brockwell	113
Mr S. W. Scott st Wood b Abel	10	– c Henderson b Brockwell	1
Mr C. P. Foley c M. Read b Richardson	0	– c Wood b Brockwell	0
J. T. Rawlin b Brockwell	24	– c Wood b Lockwood	32
Mr F. G. J. Ford b Brockwell	29	– b Brockwell	74
Mr G. MacGregor c M. Read b Richardson	4	– b Richardson	8
Mr W. S. Hale c Brockwell b Lockwood	1	– not out	4
Mr P. J. T. Henery c Ayres b Lockwood	0	– c Henderson b Lockwood	4
J. Phillips not out	0	– b Lockwood	5
J. T. Hearne c W. W. Read b Brockwell	0	– b Richardson	0
L-b 1	1	B 4, l-b 6, w 1	11
	108		377

Middlesex Bowling

	Overs	Mdns	Runs	Wkts	Overs	Mdns	Runs	Wkts
Rawlin	33	12	61	1	31.2	13	47	5
Hearne	41	13	93	3	33	12	64	4
Ford	27.1	7	52	2	2	2	—	—
Stoddart	21	5	45	3				
Phillips	5	2	5	—				

Surrey Bowling

	Overs	Mdns	Runs	Wkts	Overs	Mdns	Runs	Wkts
Lockwood	13	4	33	2	35	13	89	4
Richardson	19	4	44	3	26.2	8	83	2
Abel	15	6	18	2	8	3	29	—
Brockwell	8.4	5	12	3	29	6	76	4
Henderson					11	2	22	—
M. Read					7	—	25	—
W. W. Read					4	—	23	—
Ayres					4	1	19	—

Umpires: F. Coward and A. F. Smith.

MIDDLESEX v YORKSHIRE

Played at Lord's May 21, 22, 23, 1896

Few more remarkable matches were seen during the season of 1896. Stoddart and Hayman opened the game by putting on 218 runs for the first Middlesex wicket, and at the close of the second day's play everything pointed to a draw, Yorkshire being within 35 runs of their opponents and having still five wickets to fall. Some heavy rain in the night, however, brought about a remarkable change in the conditions, and Yorkshire, though they were three runs behind in their first innings, gained a wonderful victory by ten wickets. Peel's fine bowling helped to dismiss Middlesex for 142, and then – the ground having practically recovered itself – Brown and Tunnicliffe hit off the requisite 146 without being separated. The match was a triumph for Brown, who scored 284 runs for once out.

Middlesex

Mr A. E. Stoddart c Brown b Peel	100	– c Wainwright b Hirst	24
Mr H. B. Hayman c Peel b Hirst	152	– b Wainwright	4
Mr R. S. Lucas c Smith b Peel	19	– st Hunter b Peel	30
J. T. Rawlin c Tunnicliffe b Peel	2	– c Brown b Peel	2
Mr G. MacGregor c and b Smith	50	– b Wainwright	3
Sir T. C. O'Brien b Peel	20	– c Wainwright b Peel	57
Mr A. J. Webbe b Milligan	5	– c and b Hirst	0
Mr F. W. Maude b Milligan	0	– c and b Peel	12
J. Phillips lbw b Smith	18	– c Tunnicliffe b Peel	5
Mr H. R. Bromley-Davenport b Smith	6	– c Brown b Peel	0
J. T. Hearne not out	3	– not out	2
B 3, l-b 5, w 1	9	B 3	3
	384		142

Yorkshire

J. Tunnicliffe c O'Brien b Hearne	62	– not out	63
J. T. Brown c Lucas b Rawlin	203	– not out	81
R. Moorhouse c Stoddart b Rawlin	13		
E. Wainwright lbw b Hearne	3		
R. Peel b Hearne	11		
G. H. Hirst c Rawlin b Hearne	13		
Mr E. Smith b Hearne	42		
Lord Hawke c Lucas b Hearne	5		
J. Mounsey c Lucas b Rawlin	0		
Mr F. W. Milligan not out	2		
D. Hunter c Rawlin b Hearne	14		
L-b 9, w 3, n-b 1	13	B 3	3
	381		147

Yorkshire Bowling

	Overs	Mdns	Runs	Wkts	Overs	Mdns	Runs	Wkts
Milligan	21	5	77	2				
Hirst	27	5	69	1	14	4	52	2
Peel	49	14	99	4	27	14	28	6
Smith	18.4	4	62	3				
Wainwright	13	1	52	—	14	4	59	2
Moorhouse	6	2	10	—				
Mounsey	2	1	6	—				

Middlesex Bowling

	Overs	Mdns	Runs	Wkts	Overs	Mdns	Runs	Wkts
Hearne	53.1	19	104	7	12	2	47	—
Rawlin	40	9	110	3	6	2	20	—
Phillips	16	2	65	—	11	1	22	—
Bromley-Davenport	14	4	51	—	2	—	13	—
Stoddart	7	3	20	—	7	—	32	—
Maude	4	1	18	—				
Lucas					0.3	0	10	—

Umpires: W. F. Collishaw and A. Chester.

MIDDLESEX v GLOUCESTERSHIRE

Played at Lord's June 2, 3, 4, 1898

It was not until Friday that a commencement could be made with this match, three days in succession having passed without a ball being bowled at Lord's. Naturally, after so much rain the wicket was seriously affected, but admitting the disadvantages under which they laboured the Middlesex batsmen, apart from Warner who played with marked skill, did nothing worthy of their reputation. The team were all out in an hour and a half for 75. Townsend taking nine wickets for 48 runs – his best performance since the season of 1895. Gloucestershire for a time fared no better than their opponents, six men being dismissed for 46 runs. Board and some of his colleagues, however, batted pluckily and the visitors gained a lead of 39. At their second attempt, Middlesex again began badly but Stoddart and Rawlin improved matters. On the Saturday, Stoddart batted in his finest form on the difficult wicket, but could get no one to stay with him. Gloucestershire wanting 126 runs to win obtained them at the cost of two wickets, but the task against some skilful bowling occupied nearly three hours. Townsend's bowling clearly won the match.

Middlesex

Mr P. F. Warner not out	46	– c Hale b Townsend	18
Mr H. B. Hayman b Townsend	0	– c Wrathall b Roberts	19
Mr A. E. Stoddart b Townsend	0	– not out	70
Mr J. R. Head c Roberts b Townsend	13	– c Brown b Townsend	0
J. T. Rawlin c Townsend b Roberts	0	– c and b Townsend	40
Mr F. G. J. Ford c Board b Townsend	0	– c Sewell b Townsend	1
Dr G. Thornton c and b Townsend	0	– lbw b Murch	4
Mr H. R. Bromley-Davenport c and b Townsend	4	– b Murch	1
Mr H. Philipson b Townsend	5	– b Townsend	3
J. T. Hearne b Townsend	2	– b Townsend	0
S. Webb b Townsend	2	– c Board b Murch	1
B 1, l-b 1, w 1	3	B 1, l-b 3, 3	7
	75		164

Gloucestershire

Mr W. G. Grace c Ford b Hearne	5	– not out	39
H. Wrathall c Hearne b Rawlin	23	– c Ford b Hearne	0
Mr W. Troup b Hearne	3	– not out	27
Mr C. O. H. Sewell b Hearne	3		
Mr C. L. Townsend c Thornton b Rawlin	1		
J. H. Board c Ford b Hearne	34		
W. H. Hale b Hearne	0		
Mr W. S. A. Brown c Philipson b Webb	13		
Mr S. de Winton not out	15	– c Stoddart b Webb	38
H. W. Murch b Hearne	0		
F. G. Roberts c Warner b Hearne	13		
B 2, l-b 2	4	B 8, l-b 9, w 5	22
	114		126

Gloucestershire Bowling

	Overs	Mdns	Runs	Wkts	Overs	Mdns	Runs	Wkts
Townsend	19.3	3	48	9	34	9	86	6
Brown	11	5	15	—	5	1	8	—
Roberts	8	4	9	1	19	7	36	1
Murch					9.1	2	27	3

Middlesex Bowling

	Overs	Mdns	Runs	Wkts	Overs	Mdns	Runs	Wkts
Hearne	26	11	50	7	32	18	26	1
Rawlin	17	5	34	2	19	9	19	—
Webb	8	1	26	1	18	9	30	1
Stoddart					7	3	7	—
Bromley-Davenport					11	6	8	—
Thornton					7.3	3	14	—

Umpires: J. Street and W. Richards.

MIDDLESEX v SUSSEX

Played at Lord's, July 14, 15, 16, 1898

Sussex were unable to place their full strength in the field, and after having the worst of the game all through, were beaten by 235 runs. Some capital all round cricket was shown on the opening day, when Middlesex after completing an innings of 251 dismissed four of the Sussex batsmen for 117. Fry increased his not out innings of 56 to 104, and moreover carried his bat right through the innings. He batted splendidly but met with poor support. Trott finished off the innings by taking five wickets for 18 runs. Several of the Middlesex batsmen were seen to great advantage at the second attempt, and on Saturday morning Stoddart declared. Fry was bowled first ball in the visitors' second innings and with his dismissal went all chance of saving the game. Trott again bowled with marked success. On the Friday afternoon Fry was no-balled for throwing.

Middlesex

Mr P. F. Warner run out	38	– b Bland	7
Mr H. B. Hayman b Bland	20	– c Fox b Bland	59
Mr A. E. Stoddart c Fox b Bland	60	– c Bean b Killick	25
Mr F. G. J. Ford b Bland	5	– b Bean	78
J. T. Rawlin b Bland	45	– run out	56
Sir T. C. O'Brien b Bland	8	– b Brann	62
A. E. Trott b Bland	13	– c and b Tate	14
Mr R. W. Nicholls c Killick b Bland	19	– b Tate	4
Mr F. H. E. Cunliffe st Fox b Killick	8	– not out	14
Mr E. H. Bray c Tate b Killick	22	– c Killick b Brann	23
J. T. Hearne not out	0		
B 16, l-b 4	20	B 15, l-b 17, n-b 3	35
	258	(9 wkts dec.)	377

Sussex

Mr G. Brann c Stoddart b Rawlin	1	– c Stoddart b Cunliffe	27
Mr C. B. Fry not out	104	– b Trott	0
Mr W. I. Murdoch c O'Brien b Rawlin	9	– b Hearne	42
F. W. Marlow b Cunliffe	11	– b Trott	45
E. H. Killick lbw b Cunliffe	20	– b Hearne	17
J. Vine b Hearne	18	– c Nicholls b Trott	11
J. Bean c Stoddart b Trott	10	– b Trott	18
G. Cox lbw b Trott	0	– c and b Trott	6
F. W. Tate b Trott	3	– c Bray b Trott	3
C. H. G. Bland b Trott	0	– b Hearne	0
Mr R. W. Fox b Trott	0	– not out	0
B 18, l-b 2, n-b 1	21	B 30, l-b 1, n-b 3	34
	197		203

Sussex Bowling

	Overs	Mdns	Runs	Wkts	Overs	Mdns	Runs	Wkts
Tate	19	7	44	—	34	7	117	2
Killick	25.2	7	62	2	12	—	50	1
Cox	19	18	32	—	13	3	26	—
Bland	34	5	100	7	26	4	72	2
Fry					5	—	24	—
Bean					13	2	44	1
Brann					5.2	2	9	2

Middlesex Bowling

	Overs	Mdns	Runs	Wkts	Overs	Mdns	Runs	Wkts
Hearne	27	8	62	1	28	1	56	3
Rawlin	10	2	31	2				
Cunliffe	17	3	47	2	28	8	41	1
Trott	11.3	3	36	5	36	7	72	6

Umpires: W. Hearn and M. Sherwin.

MIDDLESEX v SOMERSET

(For W. Flower's Benefit)

Played at Lord's, May 22, 23, 1899

By arrangement between Middlesex and the Marylebone Club the Whit-Monday match was allotted to Wilfrid Flowers for his benefit, the Nottinghamshire cricketer having been a member of the ground staff at Lord's since 1878. Unfortunately, as a benefit, the match was ruined by the weather. Not a ball could be bowled on the Bank Holiday, and so difficult was the wicket on the following day that in the course of little more than three hours' actual play the game was begun and finished, Middlesex winning by an innings and seven runs. With the ground as it was Albert Trott and J. T. Hearne proved quite irresistible, and in neither innings of Somerset was a change found necessary. In the first innings eight wickets fell in four overs for eight runs, and it seemed quite possible that Somerset would be out for the smallest score on record in first-class matches. This, however, was averted by Woods and Newton. Middlesex could not do very much on the difficult wicket, but inasmuch as the first two batsmen scored 24 before they were separated, the home team were always sure of being well ahead on the first innings. When Somerset went in for the second time with a balance of 54 runs against them five wickets were lost for five runs and eight were down with the score at 18. After that Nichols and Newton played up with great pluck, but they did not succeed in averting the single innings defeat.

Somerset

Mr F. A. Phillips b Hearne	1	b Trott	0
E. Robson b Hearne	2	– b Hearne	2
Mr R. C. N. Palairet run out	0	– b Trott	0
Mr W. N. Roe b Trott	0	– b Trott	0
Mr S. M. J. Woods lbw b Hearne	20	– c Rawlin b Hearne	6
Mr W. Trask b Hearne	0	– lbw b Trott	0
Mr H. T. Stanley b Hearne	0	– b Trott	5
G. B. Nichols b Trott	0	– c Roche b Hearne	18
E. J. Tyler c Hearne b Trott	0	– c Stogdon b Trott	0
Mr A. E. Newton b Trott	7	– lbw b Trott	12
G. Gill not out	2	– not out	0
B 2, l-b 1	3	B 1	1
	35		44

Middlesex

Mr H. B. Hayman c Stanley b Tyler	13
Mr P. F. Warner c and b Tyler	14
Mr H. H. Cobb b Robson	2
Mr F. G. J. Ford b Tyler	2
J. T. Rawlin c Stanley b Tyler	11
A. E. Trott st Newton b Tyler	0
Mr C. P. Foley c Phillips b Tyler	20
Mr J. H. Stogdon c Newton b Robson	2
Mr G. MacGregor c and b Tyler	3
J. T. Hearne not out	15
W. Roche c Woods b Tyler	0
B 2, w 2	4
	86

Middlesex Bowling

	Overs	Mdns	Runs	Wkts	Overs	Mdns	Runs	Wkts
Hearne	8	3	14	5	8.3	1	30	3
Trott	7	1	18	4	8	4	13	7

Somerset Bowling

	Overs	Mdns	Runs	Wkts
Gill	2	—	5	—
Robson	19	7	35	2
Tyler	17.2	3	42	8

Umpires: R. G. Barlow and W. Richards.

MIDDLESEX v GLOUCESTERSHIRE

Played at Lord's May 25, 26, 1899

This match is likely to have an historical interest inasmuch as it was the last in which Mr W. G. Grace played for Gloucestershire before breaking finally with the county committee. The wicket had by no means recovered from the drenching rain at the beginning of the week and runs proved very hard to get. Gloucestershire practically lost the game at the start being all out in an hour and ten minutes for 52 runs. From this disastrous beginning they could not, despite all their efforts, recover themselves. Grace finished up his county career with a very patient innings, staying in an hour and twenty minutes on the difficult wicket. At the end of the day Middlesex were left with only 70 wanted to win, and on a greatly improved pitch they won easily on the Friday morning by seven wickets.

Gloucestershire

Mr W. G. Grace c Foley b Hearne	11	– c Cobb b Hearne	33
Mr W. Troup b Hearne	5	– c MacGregor b Trott	6
Mr W. S. A. Brown b Trott	0	– c Cobb b Trott	24
H. Wrathall b Trott	9	– c Trott b Roche	1
Mr C. L. Townsend c MacGregor b Trott	1	– run out	13
Mr W. McG. Hemingway b Trott	6	– c Hayman b Roche	0
W. H. Hale c Warner b Hearne	0	– b Roche	6
J. H. Board b Hearne	8	– b Roche	0
Mr G. H. Beloe c MacGregor b Trott	6	– b Roche	9
Mr E. L. Thomas b Hearne	3	– b Roche	0
A. Paish not out	1	– not out	4
B 2	2	B 13, l-b 4	17
	52		113

Middlesex

Mr H. B. Hayman c Hale b Grace	23	– c Grace b Brown	33
Mr P. F. Warner c Wrathall b Paish	2	– b Paish	14
Mr H. H. Cobb c Thomas b Paish	1	– not out	14
Mr F. G. J. Ford b Paish	10	– c and b Brown	4
J. T. Rawlin b Paish	34		
Mr C. P. Foley b Paish	0	– not out	4
A. E. Trott b Paish	3		
Mr R. S. Lucas b Townsend	5		
Mr G. MacGregor not out	1		
J. T. Hearne c and b Paish	1		
W. Roche c and b Townsend	0		
B 1, l-b 1, w 1, n-b 3	6	N-b 1	1
	96		70

Middlesex Bowling

	Overs	Mdns	Runs	Wkts	Overs	Mdns	Runs	Wkts
Hearne	11.3	4	28	5	18	7	29	1
Trott	11	4	22	5	26	13	39	2
Roche					18.1	9	28	6

Gloucestershire Bowling

	Overs	Mdns	Runs	Wkts	Overs	Mdns	Runs	Wkts
Paish	17	5	49	7	13.4	4	29	1
Townsend	11.2	2	18	2	7	2	21	—
Brown	3	—	13	—	6	1	19	2
Grace	4	1	10	1				

Umpires: J. Wheeler and W. Richards.

MIDDLESEX v SUSSEX

Played at Lord's June 8, 9, 10, 1899

Continuing their successful career Middlesex beat Sussex by five wickets – a brilliant victory indeed in face of a total of 387 in the first innings. There was some wonderful batting for both counties and Fry, Brann and Ranjitsinhji may well have thought themselves unlucky to do so much and yet be on the losing side. In each innings Fry and Brann sent up the hundred for the first wicket – 135 in the first innings and 148 in the second. Ford scored his brilliant 160 in less than three hours, and Trott also hit finely but was very lucky after he passed 80. Inasmuch as he scored 123 and took a dozen wickets Trott had the chief share in the victory.

Sussex

Batsman	1st inns		2nd inns	
Mr C. B. Fry c Trott b Hearne	72	–	c Chinnery b Hearne	94
Mr G. Brann b Trott	58	–	c Rawlin b Stoddart	58
K. S. Ranjitsinhji c Rawlin b Hearne	120	–	b Trott	9
E. H. Killick b Trott	44	–	b Trott	2
Mr W. Newham lbw b Rawlin	4	–	b Trott	3
Mr W. L. Murdoch c Roche b Trott	0	–	st MacGregor b Trotter	1
Mr A. Collins not out	23	–	c Rawlin b Hearne	5
G. Cox st MacGregor b Trott	6	–	c Ford b Hearne	1
H. R. Butt c sub. b Trott	13	–	lbw b Trott	19
F. W. Tate c MacGregor b Trott	8	–	not out	10
C. H. G. Bland c Trott b Roche	9	–	b Trott	0
B 9, l-b 21	30		B 4, l-b 5, w 1	10
	387			212

Middlesex

Batsman	1st inns		2nd inns	
Mr H. B. Hayman b Bland	6	–	c Cox b Tate	1
Mr P. F. Warner c Butt b Bland	16	–	b Tate	33
Mr H. B. Chinnery c Butt b Tate	46	–	c Cox b Tate	13
Mr F. G. J. Ford c Fry b Tate	160	–	b Tate	19
J. T. Rawlin b Bland	30	–	b Cox	26
Mr A. E. Stoddart b Killick	0			
A. E. Trott run out	123	–	not out	35
Mr H. H. Cobb b Bland	18	–	not out	3
Mr G. MacGregor c Newham b Bland	11			
J. T. Hearne st Butt b Ranjitsinhji	22			
W. Roche not out	10			
B 16, l-b 8, n-b 5	29		B 4, l-b 1, w 1	6
	466			136

Middlesex Bowling

	Overs	Mdns	Runs	Wkts	Overs	Mdns	Runs	Wkts
Hearne	49	16	103	2	34	13	64	3
Trott	59	17	132	6	25.1	7	68	6
Roche	17.1	4	50	1	16	6	44	—
Rawlin	25	9	52	1	7	1	14	—
Ford	7	2	20	—				
Stoddart					6	3	12	1

Sussex Bowling

	Overs	Mdns	Runs	Wkts	Overs	Mdns	Runs	Wkts
Tate	28	8	98	2	18	5	40	4
Bland	47	11	138	5	18	4	65	—
Cox	8	—	24	—	3	—	5	1
Killick	17	2	62	1	3	1	20	—
Ranjitsinhji	14.4	1	70	1				
Brann	8	—	23	—				
Collins	4	—	22	—				

Umpires: J. J. Tuck and T. Milward.

MIDDLESEX v KENT

Played at Lord's, June 12, 13, 14, 1899

This match will always be remembered for the extraordinary performance of R. W. Nichols and Roche, who by putting on 230 for the last wicket for Middlesex beat a record in first-class cricket that had stood for fourteen years. The two batsmen were together for two hours and a half, Nicholls, who hit splendidly but with a good deal of luck, making a very large proportion of the runs. This extraordinary stand retrieved an otherwise disastrous first innings. Middlesex, always having something in hand for the rest of the game, won at half-past one on the third day by 118 runs.

Middlesex

Mr P. F. Warner c Mason b Bradley	0	– c Weigall b Martin	63
Mr H. B. Hayman b Bradley	14	– c Hearne b Bradley	17
Mr H. B. Chinnery c Huish b Mason	5	– c Huish b Bradley	4
Mr F. G. J. Ford c Huish b Mason	4	– b Bradley	0
J. T. Rawlin b Bradley	14	– b Bradley	25
A. E. Trott b Mason	1	– c Weigall b Martin	53
Mr H. H. Cobb b Mason	0	– b Martin	1
Mr G. MacGregor c Mason b Bradley	6	– run out	4
Mr R. V. Nicholls c Bradley b Stewart	154	– c Weigall b Mason	10
J. T. Hearne b Bradley	0	– not out	9
W. Roche not out	74	– b Martin	5
B 8, l-b 3, n-b 2	13		
	285		191

Kent

Mr C. J. Burnup c MacGregor b Trott	1	– c Trott b Hearne	17
A. Hearne c Trott b Rawlin	53	– run out	32
Mr H. C. Stewart b Hearne	17	– c MacGregor b Hearne	26
Mr L. J. LeFleming b Hearne	9	– b Trott	8
Mr G. J. V. Weigall b Trott	6	– b Trott	6
Mr J. R. Mason c and b Rawlin	50	– b Hearne	7
Mr H. M. Braybrooke c and b Trott	8	– b Hearne	22
F. Martin b Trott	12	– b Trott	6
F. H. Huish b Rawlin	14	– b Hearne	10
Mr H. M. Lawrence lbw b Trott	1	– not out	2
Mr W. M. Bradley not out	6	– b Hearne	8
B 10, l-b 7	17	B 13, l-b 7	20
	194		164

Kent Bowling

	Overs	Mdns	Runs	Wkts	Overs	Mdns	Runs	Wkts
Bradley	34	10	76	5	20	1	65	4
Mason	33	10	78	4	12	5	32	1
Martin	10	1	30	—	16.4	3	50	4
Lawrence	8	1	32	—	6	3	16	—
A. Hearne	9	—	38	—	6	1	28	—
Burnup	2	—	16	—				
Stewart	0.2	0	2	1				

Middlesex Bowling

	Overs	Mdns	Runs	Wkts	Overs	Mdns	Runs	Wkts
J. T. Hearne	29	9	52	2	35.3	14	63	6
Trott	35	12	61	5	38	16	72	3
Rawlin	16	7	31	3	4	1	9	—
Roche	11	1	33	—				

Umpires: J. Street and R. Clayton.

MIDDLESEX v LEICESTERSHIRE

Played at Lord's, June 19, 20, 1899

Thanks mainly to the remarkable bowling of Albert Trott, Middlesex had an easy task against Leicestershire and by a quarter to five on the second afternoon they won the game by ten wickets. At one point there seemed every prospect of a good fight, Leicestershire hitting off the arrears on the first innings with only two men out, but after that, on a drying pitch, Trott bowled irresistibly and placed the result beyond doubt. After lunch he sent down five overs and three balls for ten runs and five wickets.

Leicestershire

A. E. Knight b Trott	8	– c MacGregor b Trott	34
L. Brown c Rawlin b Trott	12	– c MacGregor b Hearne	23
A. D. Pougher c MacGregor b Hearne	12	– b Trott	0
Mr C. E. de Trafford b Trott	2	– b Rawlin	45
J. H. King b Trott	1	– c MacGregor b Trott	16
Mr C. J. B. Wood lbw b Roche	23	– c and b Hearne	10
H. Whitehead c Rawlin b Trott	17	– b Trott	16
J. King b Roche	9	– lbw b Trott	0
F. Geeson lbw b Trott	34	– lbw b Trott	0
Grewcock c Ford b Roche	1	– b Trott	1
J. P. Whiteside not out	0	– not out	0
B 13	13	B 8, l-b 5	13
	132		158

Middlesex

	First innings		Second innings
Mr P. F. Warner b Grewcock	19	– not out	32
Mr H. B. Hayman c Whiteside b Geeson	8	– not out	31
Mr H. B. Chinnery c Whitehead b Grewcock	24		
Mr F. G. J. Ford c Brown b Grewcock	12		
J. T. Rawlin run out	17		
A. E. Trott c Whitehead b Wood	23		
Mr R. W. Nicholls b Grewcock	6		
Dr G. Thornton b J. H. King	18		
Mr G. MacGregor not out	57		
W. Roche b Wood	22		
J. T. Hearne c Pougher b Geeson	7		
B 8, l-b 7, n-b 1	16	L-b 1, n-b 1	2
	229		65

Middlesex Bowling

	Overs	Mdns	Runs	Wkts	Overs	Mdns	Runs	Wkts
J. T. Hearne	21	10	25	1	24	8	58	2
Trott	29.1	6	80	6	27.3	10	45	7
Roche	11	5	14	3	12	4	28	—
Rawlin					5	—	14	1

Leicestershire Bowling

	Overs	Mdns	Runs	Wkts	Overs	Mdns	Runs	Wkts
Geeson	10.8	2	31	2	8	2	17	—
Grewcock	27	2	93	4	4	2	12	—
Wood	16	2	41	2	3	2	8	—
J. H. King	14	5	30	1	4	2	6	—
J. King	3	—	18	—				
Pougher					3	—	20	—

Umpires: H. Holmes and A. Chester.

NOTTINGHAMSHIRE

THE NOTTINGHAMSHIRE BATSMAN of 1869

RICHARD DAFT

Daft's two great not out innings for his county, and the marvellously patient and scientific defence he therein displayed, form "one of" the prominent batting features of the London Cricketing Season 1869. – At Lord's his defence was astonishing; on The Oval his patience was wonderful: both innings being great displays of rare judgment, backed up by scientific defence, resulting in large not out innings for himself, great success for his county, and one of the highest county averages yet made. It should be borne in mind that his 103 not out v MCC and Ground was played on one of the most difficult run-getting grounds in the country – a ground, however, whereon Daft had previously great innings, to wit his 78 for The North v The South in 1865, and his 118 for The North v The South in 1862, the latter innings being characterised by *The Bell's Life* of the period as – "One of the finest innings ever played at Lord's, or any other ground; not one chance did he give, and every ball bowled to him was played correctly". The following are Daft's

INNINGS PLAYED FOR NOTTINGHAMSHIRE IN 1869

Where played	Match	1st Inns	2nd Inns
Nottingham	Nottinghamshire v Yorkshire	39*	38
Lord's	Nottinghamshire v MCC and Ground	1	103*
Nottingham	Nottinghamshire v Surrey	56	—
Tunbridge	Nottinghamshire v Kent	9	—
The Oval	Nottinghamshire v Surrey	93*	9
Sheffield	Nottinghamshire v Yorkshire	50	31*
Nottingham	Nottinghamshire v Kent	42	—

* *Signifies not out.*

Results – 7 matches played, 11 innings commenced, not out 4 times (266 runs); total runs scored, 471. Average – 67 per innings and 2 over.

115 not out for All England Eleven v Twenty-Two of Bestwood, and 101 not out in a village match, were also scored by Daft in 1869.

NOTTINGHAMSHIRE v GLOUCESTERSHIRE

Played at Nottingham, August 21, 22, 23, 1871

This was Mr W. G. Grace's first match on the Trent Bridge Ground. His anticipated appearance there had put cricket-loving Nottinghamshire into an extraordinary state of excitement, and the weather being fine the famous old ground at the foot of the Bridge was thronged on the Monday and Tuesday to an extent it had never before been thronged at a cricket match. On the Monday 8,000 visitors passed on to the ground in excitable expectation of witnessing the great batsman play one of his great innings; but the Nottinghamshire men won choice of innings, and by some of the old true and good Nottinghamshire cricket they kept possession of the wickets the whole day, and then only five of their men were out; so being disappointed of witnessing the batting of the Crack on Monday; most of the visitors decided to come again on the Tuesday, on which day they crowded the ground in such increased numbers that it was computed there were 12,000 present in the afternoon; and when the takings at the gate that day had been cast up it was found the large sum of £236 had been paid for admission to the ground that day; and, notwithstanding the attendance on the Wednesday fell far short of either of the preceding days, fully 25,000 visitors must have passed through the entrance gate during the three days of Mr W. G. Grace's first match on The Trent Bridge Ground.

At 12.30 on the Monday the match was – on rare wickets – commenced by Bignall and Wyld opening the Nottinghamshire innings to the bowling of Dr Grace and Mr Miles, the wicket being kept by Mr W. G. Grace. When 14 runs only had been made Wyld was thrown out by a substitute (Furley); then Mr Royle and Bignall got hold the West Countrie bowling; Dr Grace, Mr Miles, Mr W. G. Grace, Mr Strachan, Mr F. Grace and Mr Carter all bowled, and bowled in vain, until the score had been hit from 14 to 120, when Mr Royle was "c and b" for 45; "he batted in rare style" was the verdict awarded to Mr Royle's cricket. When Mr Royle left, "dinner" was called. At 3.10 Bignall and Daft renewed the innings, and so effectively did they renew it that, despite five more bowling changes, they increased the score from 120 to 176, when Bignall was had at long-leg for 96 – the highest Nottinghamshire score, made by 27 singles, nine 2s, five 3s and nine 4s. From 176 for three wickets, Daft and Mr Williams hit the score to 221, when Mr Williams was out for 27, and at 224 Selby ran himself out; thereupon Mr Tolley faced Daft, and another stubborn stand was made for old Nottinghamshire; both batsmen were in good form – Daft in his best – and despite the Gloucestershire men tried nearly all their bowlers, they could not part the batsmen, as when "time" was called at 6.30 the result of the first day's cricket was as under:

Nottinghamshire 1st innings, 5 wickets down, 278 runs scored.

R. Daft not out 69; Mr R. Tolley not out 24.

On Tuesday play was resumed at a quarter to twelve, and ere the day's play was over the immense assemblage had the gratification of witnessing Mr W. G. Grace play an innings of 79 runs, and J. C. Shaw achieve the great bowling feat of securing nine wickets – four "bowled" – in one innings. Daft and Mr Tolley renewed their innings to the bowling of Mr Miles and Captain Wallace; they had increased the score to 316, when a clever catch at mid-off, by Mr W. G. Grace, ended Daft's innings for 84. So many as 196 runs had been made during Daft's stay at the stumps; his innings included four 4s and as many 3s. When the score was at 337, Mr Tolley was run out, by the wicket-keeper for 54, and at twenty minutes to two the Nottinghamshire innings was over for 364 runs, 180 of which had been made by Bignall and Daft. The wickets in that great innings fell as follows:

1/14 2/120 3/176 4/221 5/224 6/316 7/337 8/348 9/356 10/364

At ten minutes to three a loud cheer greeted Mr W. G. Grace's walk to the wickets to commence (with Mr Matthews) the Gloucestershire innings. The two Shaws started the bowling; they were in form, and being backed up by good fielding, the West Countrie innings was a comparative brief one. When 12 runs had been scored Mr Matthews was bowled by J. C. Shaw, who, at 16, also bowled Dr Grace. The younger Mr Grace then went to his brother's aid, and despite the good bowling and fielding of Nottinghamshire, they brought on McIntyre at A. Shaw's end, and had increased the score from 16 to 74 when three wickets went – Mr G. F. Grace being caught out at point. Mr Townsend bowled the next ball, and Captain Wallace "c and b", the 4th, 5th and 6th wickets all going with the figures at 74. From then, Mr W. Grace mainly increased the score to 112, when Mr Strachan was caught out by Wyld, who shortly after also caught out Mr W. Grace. First man in, Mr Grace was seventh man out with the score at 125; of these runs he had made – against good bowling and fielding – 79 by four 4s, seven 3s, three 2s and 36 singles; that the great batsman should have made nearly half his 79 by singles is a convincing testimony of the excellence of the Nottinghamshire bowling and fielding. Mr Grace was loudly cheered, and so – when the innings terminated at six o'clock – was

J. C. Shaw, for obtaining nine out of the ten wickets with his bowling. The second innings of Gloucestershire was duly commenced that evening by Captain Wallace and Mr Carter. When 4 runs had been made, Captain Wallace was stumped, whereupon the second day's cricket closed.

At noon on Wednesday Mr Carter and Dr Grace renewed their innings. With the score at 8 Mr Carter was bowled, and at 19 Mr Matthews was had at cover-point. Then Mr W. G. Grace went in, and although Mr Townsend made 30, and Mr Bush 26, the interest of that innings of Gloucestershire was centred in the great score made by Mr W. Grace. In with the score at 19 for three wickets, Mr Grace got fairly and well hold of the Nottinghamshire bowling; he hit finely and witnessed the downfall of the 4th, 5th, 6th and 7th wickets, then – being cleverly caught out at wicket – he was 8th man out with the score at 182. Of the 163 runs made whilst he was at wickets Mr Grace had actually made 116 – an innings that was chronicled as being "a fine, correctly played, and chanceless one". He was again loudly cheered, and deservedly so, for he had made more than half the runs in each innings played by his County, as out of the 350 runs scored (from the bat) in the match by Gloucestershire, 195 had been contributed by Mr W. Grace, whose 116 included ten 4s and nineteen singles. The innings closed at 5.15 for 217 runs, and as Gloucestershire's two innings exactly tied Nottinghamshire's one, the latter had to start a second innings to obtain the winning run; this was made by Mr Williams from the second ball bowled, and so – after three days play – the Nottinghamshire Eleven won by ten wickets the first match ever played on Trent Bridge Ground by Nottinghamshire and Gloucestershire.

Nottinghamshire

Bignall c Wallace b F. Grace	96	– not out	[illegible]
Wyld run out	8		
G. M. Royle Esq. c and b Carter	45		
Richard Daft c W. G. Grace b Townsend	84		
W. Williams Esq. c F. Grace b Miles	27	– not out	1
Selby run out	2		
R. Tolley Esq. run out	54		
Alfred Shaw c Strachan b W. G. Grace	16		
William McIntyre c Wallace b W. G. Grace	5		
Biddulph not out	13		
J. C. Shaw c Pontifex b Townsend	0		
B 6, l-b 7, n-b 1	14		
	364		1

Gloucestershire

W. G. Grace Esq. c Wyld b J. C. Shaw	79	– c Biddulph b Wyld	116
T. G. Matthews Esq. b J. C. Shaw	3	– c Selby b J. C. Shaw	[illegible]
Dr E. M. Grace b J. C. Shaw	2	– b Alfred Shaw	10
G. F. Grace Esq. c Daft b J. C. Shaw	24	– c and b J. C. Shaw	[illegible]
F. Townsend Esq. b J. C. Shaw	0	– b Wyld	30
Capt. Wallace c and b J. C. Shaw	0	– st Biddulph b J. C. Shaw	[illegible]
G. Strachan Esq. c Wyld b J. C. Shaw	7	– c and b Wyld	[illegible]
J. A. Bush Esq. c Tolley b J. C. Shaw	6	– b Wyld	26
Rev. A. Pontifex c Bignall b Alfred Shaw	6	– not out	[illegible]
F. A. Carter Esq. not out	13	– b Alfred Shaw	[illegible]
R. F. Miles Esq. b J. C. Shaw	0	– c McIntyre b J. C. Shaw	[illegible]
B 1, l-b 5, w 1	7	B 4, l-b 1, w 2	[illegible]
	147		217

Gloucestershire Bowling

	Overs	Mdns	Runs	Wkts	Overs	Mdns	Runs	Wkts
Mr F. Grace	49	31	47	1				
Mr Townsend	48.2	20	55	2	0.2	—	1	—
Mr Miles	41	13	69	1				
Mr W. Grace	39	17	79	2				
Dr E. Grace	36	12	51	—				
Mr Strachan	14	3	26	—				
Mr Carter	6	1	17	1				
Captain Wallace ...	4	—	6	—				

Nottinghamshire Bowling

	Overs	Mdns	Runs	Wkts	Overs	Mdns	Runs	Wkts
J. C. Shaw	53.2	19	86	9	46.1	18	77	4
W. McIntyre	30	12	34	—	16	6	39	—
A. Shaw	23	12	20	1	62	40	53	2
Wyld					24	13	33	4
Mr Williams					4	1	8	—

Umpires: W. Luck and Pullen.

NOTTINGHAMSHIRE v SURREY

Played at Nottingham, July 11, 12, 1872

On the Friday, play was resumed at twelve o'clock, the not outs going on with their innings to the bowling of Southerton and Mr Strachan; so excellent a stand was made by Oscroft and Wyld, that notwithstanding Southerton, Street, Martin, Mr Strachan, Jupp (slow), and Mr Chenery all took a turn at bowling, so many as 95 were added to the 59 runs made on Thursday ere they were parted by Mr Chenery bowling Oscroft for 68, a three hours' display of especially fine batting, that included seven 4s, brought him loud and deserved applause and an appreciable "reward of merit". Daft was unwell, and was clean bowled for 0, the score at 156, Wyld not out 55. They then retired to dinner, and in due time returned to cricket, Wyld and Selby batting to the bowling of Mr Strachan and Southerton. The light was bad and gradually grew worse, a storm evidently brewing all round, but they played on until the score reached 180 runs; then (3.30) play was stopped by one of the most terrific outbursts of lightning, thunder, hail, rain and wind witnessed for many years in the Midlands. One account stated: "In two minutes after the storm commenced every tent but the Printers' was blown down, the water lay in pools all over the ground, the flag pole was broken in twain, and many trees were dismantled." Another account recorded: "That four tents were blown down, the trees struck with lightning, and a greater portion of the ground submerged in water . . . The storm was truly alarming, and will make this match a remarkable event in cricket annals."

A third local account thought it: "The most violent storm ever witnessed in the district. To say it rained would be ridiculous; it poured in torrents, and not only flooded the ground, but, with the assistance of the wind and lightning, tore down the refreshment and ladies' booths as though they were mere shreds of paper." Of course there was no more play on the stormy Friday, and as rain set in again at 11 a.m. on the Saturday and continued to fall until one o'clock "the match was quashed", all that had been done therein being the following:

Nottinghamshire

Bignall b Strachan	29
Wm Oscroft b Chenery	68
Wyld not out	62
Richard Daft b Southerton	0
J. Selby not out	17
L-b 1, w 3	4
	180

Alfred Shaw, Martin McIntyre, H. Reynolds, T. Barnes, J. C. Shaw and Morley did not bat.

Surrey

C. J. Chenery Esq., G. Strachan Esq., Jupp, Richard Humphrey, Thomas Humphrey, Marten, Palmer, Pooley, Southerton, James Street and Carter.

Surrey Bowling

	Overs	Mdns	Runs	Wkts		Overs	Mdns	Runs	Wkts
Southerton	58	33	52	1	Street	5	1	15	—
Mr Strachan	32	9	49	1	Mr Chenery	5	—	11	1
Marten	11	2	33	—	Jupp	4	—	16	—

Umpires: T. Plumb and W. Luck.

HOW ALFRED SHAW FINISHED OFF HIS BOWLING FOR 1875

1st Innings, Alfred's bowling had eight wickets, and he caught out another.

2nd Innings, Alfred's bowling had nine wickets, and he threw out the other.

NORTH OF NOTTINGHAMSHIRE v SOUTH OF NOTTINGHAMSHIRE

Played at Kirkby-in-Ashfield, October 25, 26, 1875

Alfred Shaw's memorable ball season of 1875 was characteristically wound up in this eleven-a-side match, wherein his bowling had seventeen wickets, and his fielding settled two more, thus rivalling Alfred's celebrated bowling feat of 1870, when in a match played at Lord Petre's seat, Thorndon Hall, Essex (MCC and Ground v Thorndon Hall), Alfred Shaw's bowling had nine wickets in each innings, taking the nine wickets in the second innings for 19 runs, or 2 per wicket! The following is the score, etc., of the North v South of Nottinghamshire match, played on heavy wickets. (The bowling does not tally with the totals, but it is "as reported".)

North of Nottinghamshire

Mr Hodgkinson b Alfred Shaw	5	– c Taylor b Alfred Shaw	0
F. Wyld c Hogg b Alfred Shaw	6	– run out	11
W. Barnes c Alfred Shaw b Selby	3	– b Alfred Shaw	6
Martin McIntyre b Alfred Shaw	1	– b Alfred Shaw	6
W. Clark c J. Banks b Alfred Shaw	0	– b Alfred Shaw	0
J. C. Shaw c Bowman b Alfred Shaw	7	– b Alfred Shaw	3
F. Morley b Alfred Shaw	2	– c and b Alfred Shaw	0
W. Heath c Clamp b Selby	7	– b Alfred Shaw	1
W. Huffen b Alfred Shaw	1	– not out	4
J. Kesteven not out	0	– c and b Alfred Shaw	14
H. Brooks c Scotton b Alfred Shaw	0	– c Selby b Alfred Shaw	0
		Extras	3
	32		48

South of Nottinghamshire

J. Selby c and b W. Huffen	54	J. Banks b W. Huffen	0
Alfred Shaw c Clark b J. C. Shaw	2	C. Taylor c Barnes b W. Huffen	1
W. Scotton b Morley	2	H. Hays not out	1
J. Clamp b Clark	24	Mr Otter b Clark	6
J. H. Hogg b Morley	0	Extras	8
J. Huffen b J. C. Shaw	18		
W. H. Bowman c Barnes b Wyld	29		145

South Bowling

	Overs	Mdns	Runs	Wkts	Overs	Mdns	Runs	Wkts
A. Shaw	17.1	4	13	8	18	7	21	9
Selby	17	8	19	2	17	5	27	—

North Bowling

	Overs	Mdns	Runs	Wkts		Overs	Mdns	Runs	Wkts
J. C. Shaw	20	3	44	2	W. Huffen	9	7	8	3
Clark	15	7	14	2	Morley	9	—	30	2
McIntyre	15	7	19	—	Barnes	3	—	8	—
Wyld	11	3	20	1					

NOTTINGHAMSHIRE v DERBYSHIRE

Played at Nottingham, July 10, 11, 1879

Morley's marvellous bowling in both innings prevented Derbyshire standing much chance against their rivals. Although in the early part of the day the wickets were dead they improved towards noon, and Daft, who had won the toss, decided on batting. Selby shone far more brilliantly than any of his fellows. Going in first wicket down, he was the seventh to leave, having been batting three hours for his well-played 53. All the Nottinghamshire men scored, with a solitary exception, and the last retired for 159.

Derbyshire commenced in a disastrous manner, and continued so to the end. Before a run had been scored Rigley and Cook were both caught at cover-point; Mr Smith returned the ball at 3, Platts was stumped at 4, and at 11 Mr Wallroth was caught at long-field. Now came a complete collapse. At 16 the last four wickets fell for nothing – Osborne was clean bowled, Hay was caught at cover-point, Mycroft at wicket, and the Rev. E. Forman clean bowled. Of course the visitors followed on, and at the close of the day had lost two wickets for nothing.

On Friday the weather was better. The only double-figure score made for Derbyshire was by Foster. Of the remainder little need be said, as in the double innings they only obtained 60 runs, and were thus defeated by an innings and 99 runs.

Nottinghamshire

Richard Daft c W. Mycroft b Hay	9
William Oscroft lbw b W. Mycroft	18
J. Selby b W. Mycroft	53
Arthur Shrewsbury c A. Smith b Platts	12
F. Wyld c A. Smith b Platts	0
W. Barnes run out	11
W. Flowers b W. Mycroft	5
G. S. Foljambe Esq. c Wallroth b Platts	14
Alfred Shaw st A. Smith b Platts	12
W. Scotton not out	7
F. Morley c Rigley b W. Mycroft	10
B 6, l-b 2	8
	159

Derbyshire

R. P. Smith Esq. c and b Morley	2	– lbw b Alfred Shaw	0
W. Rigley c Oscroft b Morley	0	– c Oscroft b Morley	0
E. Cook c Oscroft b Morley	0	– b Alfred Shaw	0
T. Foster b Alfred Shaw	7	– c Shrewsbury b Morley	19
J. Platts st Wyld b Alfred Shaw	0	– c Selby b Alfred Shaw	0
C. A. Wallroth Esq. c Scotton b Morley	2	– b Morley	9
G. Osborne b Morley	5	– c Wyld b Morley	2
Rev. A. E. Forman b Morley	0	– c Barnes b Morley	6
G. Hay c Foljambe b Morley	0	– not out	8
William Mycroft c Wyld b Alfred Shaw	0	– c Scotton b Alfred Shaw	0
A. Smith not out	0	– c Barnes b Alfred Shaw	0
	16		44

Derbyshire Bowling

	Overs	Mdns	Runs	Wkts
W. Mycroft	75.3	43	71	4
Hay	40	24	35	1
Platts	33	13	45	4

Nottinghamshire Bowling

	Overs	Mdns	Runs	Wkts	Overs	Mdns	Runs	Wkts
A. Shaw	11	7	9	3	24	14	16	5
Morley	10.2	7	7	7	23	11	28	5

Umpires: Robert Carpenter and J. Rowbotham.

NOTTINGHAMSHIRE IN 1881

President – His Grace the Duke of Portland

Vice-President – Colonel Seely, MP

Captain – W. Oscroft. *Hon. Sec. and Treasurer* – Capt. Holden

Assistant Secretary – Mr E. Browne

The Committee was formed of Twelve Gentlemen of the County

No good purpose would be served by entering into the details of a dispute which caused Nottinghamshire to take a back seat among the cricketing counties in 1881. The subject has been worn threadbare, and however individual opinions may differ, one feeling is common and paramount with all lovers of the noble game – a feeling of deep regret that by any possibility a dispute could have arisen to bring about such deplorable results.

The quarrel brought one gratifying fact to light, and that was that the county possessed a splendid reserve of young cricketers giving promise of great excellence in the future. Wright, Attewell, E. Mills, and Shore would, in their present form, be welcome additions to many a first-class county team, and in course of time may be found foremost in upholding the cricketing fame of Nottinghamshire.

J. C. SHAW'S MATCH

NOTTINGHAMSHIRE v YORKSHIRE

Played at Nottingham, July 17, 18, 19, 1884

The seven wickets' victory Nottinghamshire gained in this match must be accounted that shire's most remarkable performance during the season. To score 181 in the last innings for the loss of only three wickets after the whole side had been dismissed in their first attempt for 114 would be a very creditable achievement under any circumstances, but to do so against a county so strong in bowling as Yorkshire, is a specially meritorious deed. The opening day was showery and the wickets slow from the effects of previous heavy rain. Consequently scoring was difficult and the bowlers carried off the honours. Flowers, with five wickets for 23 runs, and Attewell, with five for 44, divided the wickets, while Shaw had an extraordinary analysis though no batsman was dismissed off his bowling. Only 141 runs were totalled during the day, and at the call of time Yorkshire had played an innings, and Nottinghamshire had lost four of their best wickets for 46 runs, Scotton being not out 13, and Selby not out 8.

Bates' most brilliant batting was the feature of the second day's play. Thanks to some capital hitting by Selby, Nottinghamshire succeeded in heading their opponents by 19 runs on the first innings. On Yorkshire going in for the second time these arrears were knocked off just before the first wicket fell, which happened with the total at 20. It was at this point that a truly wonderful batting performance commenced.

Bates scored 116 out of 137 runs in two hours and thirty-five minutes,

an achievement which has certainly never been surpassed by the celebrated Yorkshireman, and which, all things considered, has few parallels in the history of the game. Bates gave one chance at mid-on when he had made 69, but otherwise his innings was faultless, and his 116 included fifteen 4s, seven 3s and seven 2s. Beyond Bates' grand hitting, and the admirable defensive play of Rawlin, there was nothing noteworthy in the innings, the conclusion of which brought the day's cricket to a close.

Nottinghamshire, on the last day, were set the task of scoring 181 to win, and though many might have considered its accomplishment as far from improbable, not one could have anticipated a victory at the cost of only three wickets. The ground, which had gone on improving from the commencement, played remarkably well, or it would have been impossible to have brought about such a result. The game was resumed at 12.10 and concluded at 4.50. Shrewsbury and Scotton began, and defied the efforts of the bowlers for two hours and a quarter. Six were tried, but 90 runs were scored before Scotton was dismissed for a most patient and excellent 33. Barnes was caught at the wicket before a run was added, but on Flowers joining Shrewsbury another stand was made. Shrewsbury now changed his tactics and played a defensive game, while Flowers hit with great freedom. By these means the total was raised to 130 before Shrewsbury was caught for a really admirable innings of 61, made with one chance in rather more than three hours, and including seven 4s and four 3s. Gunn and Flowers, by some brilliant batting, then hit off the remaining 51 runs in three-quarters of an hour, Flowers scoring six 4s, four 3s and two 2s in his finely-hit 53 not out. Not the least remarkable feature fo the match was the fact that Nottinghamshire did not give away a single extra in either innings.

It is gratifying to record that J. C. Shaw received a substantial reward for the brilliant services he rendered during the nine or ten seasons he played for Nottinghamshire. In his best days Shaw had no superior as a left-handed fast bowler.

Yorkshire

G. Ulyett c Wright b Attewell	18	– c Barnes b Attewell	17
L. Hall b Flowers	25	– c Wright b Attewell	3
W. Bates c Gunn b Attewell	1	– c Scotton b Attewell	116
I. Grimshaw c Sherwin b Flowers	24	– c Barnes b Shaw	6
J. T. Rawlin b Flowers	0	– run out	14
Hon. M. B. Hawke c Shaw b Attewell	5	– b Attewell	12
J. Hunter c Shrewsbury b Flowers	11	– not out	0
G. R. Baker c Sherwin b Flowers	7	– b Flowers	1
T. Emmett b Attewell	4	– run out	4
R. Peel not out	0	– lbw b Attewell	11
E. Peate c and b Attewell	0	– c Gunn b Flowers	15
	95		199

Nottinghamshire

	First innings		Second innings	
A. Shewsbury c Ulyett b Bates	14	–	c Bates b Emmett	61
W. H. Scotton b Peel	17	–	b Rawlin	33
W. Barnes c Hall b Bates	1	–	c Hunter b Rawlin	0
W. Flowers c Rawlin b Peate	4	–	not out	53
W. Gunn b Bates	1	–	not out	24
J. Selby b Emmett	38			
W. Attewell b Peel	10			
W. Wright c Hunter b Emmett	2			
E. Mills not out	8			
A. Shaw c Emmett b Peel	8			
M. Sherwin run out	0			
B 11	11		B 6, l-b 3, w 1	10
	114			181

Nottinghamshire Bowling

	Overs	Mdns	Runs	Wkts	Overs	Mdns	Runs	Wkts
Wright	5	1	14	—	6	2	16	—
Shaw	23	20	6	—	23	14	18	1
Attewell	49.3	35	44	5	36	14	55	5
Barnes	9	5	8	—	14	5	23	—
Flowers	22	10	23	5	39	16	67	2
Mills					5	—	15	—
Gunn					5	3	5	—

Yorkshire Bowling

	Overs	Mdns	Runs	Wkts	Overs	Mdns	Runs	Wkts
Peate	42	31	22	1	37	24	31	—
Bates	39	24	30	3	21	10	32	—
Ulyett	7.1	4	10	—	18	12	20	—
Peel	15	5	20	3	22	12	33	—
Emmett	11	4	21	2	21	9	36	1
Rawlin					13.1	7	19	2

Umpires: C. Coward and James Lillywhite.

NOTTINGHAMSHIRE v MIDDLESEX

Played at Nottingham, August 14, 15, 16, 1884

Nottinghamshire wound up their season, so far as county matches were concerned, by scoring a splendid victory over Middlesex by an innings and 91 runs. The feature of the opening day's play was a brilliant innings of 80 hit by Mr I. D. Walker, who was first in and seventh out, his fine display being marred by only one chance, and that not until he had made 57. His hits were a 5, six 4s, nine 3s, five 2s and fourteen singles. Mr Ridley was with him while 65 runs were put on, and Mr Paravicini added a useful 29. Nottinghamshire had an hours' batting before stumps were drawn for the day, and lost one wicket for 35 runs.

Scotton and Barnes were not separated on the Friday until their partnership had added 73 runs to the total, when the last-named was out for an excellent 47. At the luncheon interval, Flowers and Mr C. W. Wright had both been dismissed, and the total stood at 155. Just before this Scotton was credited with five runs under very uncommon circumstances. Mr Walker's hat slipped from his head whilst bowling, and Scotton driving the ball back the hat intercepted it. After lunch 30 runs were put on and then Scotton received a nasty knock on the hand, and was caught at the wicket directly after for a very fine defensive innings of 66, which had taken him three and three-quarter hours to compile, and included the 5 alluded to, three 4s, four 3s and nine 2s. Selby quickly made 20, and was out at 224. It was at this point that Attewell joined Gunn, and a thorough mastery was obtained over the Middlesex bowling. Eight of the team were tried, but it was not until 159 runs had been put on that Attewell was at last dismissed just before the call of time for a finely-hit innings of 84, made with one chance when he had scored 52, and consisting of twelve 4s, two 3s, five 2s and singles. Gunn, who was loudly cheered when he had made his hundred, was the not out man with 124 to his credit.

On the third day of the match the Nottinghamshire innings was finished off for an addition of 24 runs. Gunn played a ball into his wicket with the total at 400. His splendid innings of 138, certainly one of the best he has ever made, consisted of sixteen 4s, eleven 3s, five 2s and thirty-one singles. Middlesex required 196 runs to avert a single innings' defeat, and began batting at 12.35. The wicket had become much worn and helped the bowlers so materially that run getting was a matter of the greatest difficulty. Messrs Walker and Webbe were a long time scoring 20, at which total the former was out. With one run added Mr Webbe left, and then the Hon. Alfred Lyttelton and Mr Ridley made the only stand of the innings. Both batsmen began carefully, but afterwards hit with freedom. Several changes of bowling were found necessary, and at last, with the score at 80, Mr Ridley was bowled by a "yorker" which broke a stump. After this only Mr Pearson offered any resistance to the bowling of Shaw and Flowers, and by 4.45 the game was over.

Middlesex

I. D. Walker Esq. b Attewell	80	– c Gunn b W. Wright	11
A. J. Webbe Esq. c Shaw b Attewell	4	– c Sherwin b W. Wright	9
Hon. A. Lyttelton hit wkt b Attewell	6	– c Selby b Flowers	29
A. W. Ridley Esq. c Sherwin b Flowers	24	– b Shaw	29
T. C. O'Brien Esq. b W. Wright	14	– b Shaw	5
T. S. Pearson Esq. st Sherwin b Attewell	9	– not out	16
G. F. Vernon Esq. c W. W. Wright b Barnes	4	– c Shrewsbury b Flowers	0
P. J. de Paravicini Esq. lbw b Shaw	29	– b Shaw	1
J. Robertson Esq. b Shaw	0	– b Shaw	1
G. Burton c Sherwin b Barnes	14	– b Shaw	0
W. Clarke not out	12	– lbw b Flowers	0
B 11, l-b 4	15	B 4	4
	211		105

Nottinghamshire

A. Shrewsbury c Vernon b Robertson	8
W. H. Scotton c Lyttelton b Robertson	66
W. Barnes c Lyttelton b Clarke	46
W. Flowers c Pearson b Robertson	19
C. W. Wright Esq. c Burton b Robertson	1
W. Gunn b Robertson	138
J. Selby lbw b Burton	20
W. Attewell c Walker b Burton	84
W. Wright c Robertson b Burton	2
A. Shaw not out	3
M. Sherwin c Clarke b Burton	4
B 5, l-b 6, n-b 5	16
	407

Nottinghamshire Bowling

	Overs	Mdns	Runs	Wkts	Overs	Mdns	Runs	Wkts
Shaw	38	23	35	2	50	38	23	5
Attewell	64	33	75	4	16	12	14	—
Barnes	21.3	10	36	2	12	3	25	—
W. Wright	18	8	31	1	23	11	22	2
Flowers	8	2	19	1	23	11	17	3

Middlesex Bowling

	Overs	Mdns	Runs	Wkts
Burton	71.2	38	88	4
Mr Robertson	74	29	127	5
Mr Walker	23	11	36	—
Clarke	39	21	51	1
Mr Webbe	2	2	—	—
Mr O'Brien	16	9	21	—
Hon. A. Lyttelton	7	3	10	—
Mr Paravicini	9	6	13	—
Mr Ridley	11	1	45	—

Umpires: C. Coward and W. Rigley.

NOTTINGHAMSHIRE v SURREY

Played at Nottingham, May 30, 31, June 1, 1887

No county match of recent years had been anticipated with greater interest than this, the first meeting of the season between Nottinghamshire and Surrey. The Southern team had shown such greatly improved form that people felt certain a very bold bid for victory would be made against the champion county of 1886. A large crowd visited the Trent Bridge ground on the first two days, and indeed there was a greater number of people present than at any subsequent home match played by Nottinghamshire during the season. Nottinghamshire tried a rather bold experiment in playing Mee, a fast bowler, who had appeared with success against the Australians at Skegness in the autumn of 1886, and who had had a good opinion formed of him by the Nottinghamshire Committee. They also left out Selby, and played F. Butler, who in 1881 had a good trial in the county eleven. The captaincy was offered to Shrewsbury, but for some reason or other he did not care about the office, and so the choice fell upon Sherwin, who gave such satisfaction that he was made captain of the county team for the season. Surrey had their absolutely best eleven. Mr K. J. Key coming over from Oxford on purpose to assist his side.

The opening day was bitterly cold and cheerless, and the wicket was slow and somewhat difficult. Surrey won the toss and decided to go in, but the start was most disastrous, and it certainly seemed that Mee had justified his selection in the Nottinghamshire team, for in the course of a few overs he clean bowled Messrs Roller, W. W. Read, and Shuter. Mr Key, Abel, and Lohmann gave little trouble, and six wickets were down for 27 runs, so that the chances of Surrey seemed very small. However, a most valuable stand was made by Maurice Read and Wood, who together added 53 runs for the seventh wicket. Read batted very finely, and his 48 included two 4s, three 3s and six 2s. The innings eventually closed for 115. Attewell took five wickets for 36 runs, but Mee after his first few overs proved very expensive. Nottinghamshire had nearly two hours' batting, but so good was the Surrey bowling that in this time only 48 runs were scored for the loss of two good wickets – those of Shrewsbury and Barnes. Shrewsbury and Scotton were together for quite an hour and a half, and put on 36 runs for the first wicket. The result of the first day's play left Nottinghamshire with certainly the best of the game, as with only two wickets down the home side were within 69 runs of their opponents.

On the Tuesday, however, the condition of the game was completely reversed, and the cricket was of a much more interesting character than before. The weather was again cold, but there were between seven and eight thousand people on the ground. Lohmann and Bowley bowled so finely for Surrey that the innings of Nottinghamshire came to a most unexpectedly rapid conclusion, and the last wicket fell for 89, eight wickets going down for the addition of 43 runs. This left Surrey with a lead of 26 runs on the first innings. The visiting team followed up the brilliant dismissal of their opponents by some exceptionally good batting, Mr Key and Abel opened the innings, and it was in a large measure to their care and judgment that Surrey were indebted for their ultimate success. Mr Key made 42 out of 56 before being bowled by Shacklock, and then a determined stand was made by Mr Roller and Abel. The amateur was missed by Mee in the long field – a mistake which caused Nottinghamshire a lot of trouble. The score was up to 130 before Abel was run out for an admirable innings of 44, which had occupied him three hours and forty minutes. At 155 Mr Roller was clean bowled, and at the call of time the score was 157 for the loss of three wickets, so that Surrey were 183 runs ahead with seven wickets to go down.

The last day's play was awaited with keen interest all over the country. Surrey were, of course, in such a position that they could not very well lose the match, and it was a matter of great doubt if they would have time or not to win. The attendance was smaller than on either of the two previous days, but those present witnessed a curious and most interesting day's cricket. At the start of the day Mr Read and Maurice Read both played splendidly, the amateur hitting with great freedom. The 250 went up on the board with only three wickets down, so that the Nottinghamshire men looked forward to an almost certain drawn game. It was then, however, that Mr Shuter adopted the course which provoked so much discussion in the newspapers. He saw that his side had no possibility of being defeated, while if the wickets were thrown away there would be a good chance of winning the match. He therefore gave his men instructions to get out as quickly as possible, and this course they adopted, though in a terribly clumsy fashion. Mr W. W. Read, who was trying to get his hundred, was caught in the long field when he had made 92 – an admirable display of batting, which included nine 4s, nine 3s and six 2s. The last six wickets went down for 25 runs, and the innings was all over for 289. Nottinghamshire had to go in just before luncheon, and as 316 runs were required to win, they had therefore only one thing to do – to stay in for the remainder of the day, and so make a draw of the match. The wicket had gone on improving as the match progressed, so that the supporters of the home side felt hopeful of their own men averting defeat. The afternoon's cricket was watched with the closest attention, and the interest never flagged from the first ball to the last. For a time everything went in Surrey's favour, Lohmann and Bowley bowling very finely, and four of the best Nottinghamshire wickets going down for 38. On Mr Daft joining Gunn, however, there was a marked improvement, and the professional played a great game to save his side. The two men were well set when at 76 a brilliant catch disposed of Mr Daft. Butler stayed till 103, and was then run out through a piece of bad judgment by Gunn, which was a most serious mistake for Nottinghamshire. At a quarter to six the score was 133 with four wickets to go down, so that there was still a doubt as to whether Surrey would have time to win. Just at this point, however, an appeal for leg before wicket was answered against Gunn, who retired with a magnificent innings of 72, made up by four 4s, ten 3s and six 2s. With Gunn's departure all hope of Nottinghamshire was gone, and by a quarter past six the innings was over for 158, Surrey winning a remarkable game by 157 runs. The victory, which was earned by thoroughly good cricket, was hailed with great delight by all cricketers in the South of England, more especially as Surrey had not beaten Nottinghamshire on the Trent Bridge ground since 1870. Too much praise cannot be afforded to George Lohmann, who thoroughly kept up what is now almost a tradition, that Surrey seldom gain an exceptional victory without he has a large share in obtaining it. He bowled with great determination from the first, kept a beautiful length, and got a lot of work on the ball from both sides.

Surrey

Mr K. J. Key lbw b Attewell	4 – b Shacklock	42
R. Abel c Barnes b Attewell	0 – run out	44
Mr W. E. Roller b Mee	4 – b Flowers	53
Mr W. W. Read b Mee	7 – c Butler b Flowers	92
Maurice Read c Daft b Attewell	48 – b Mee	28
Mr J. Shuter b Mee	0 – hit wkt b Mee	10
G. Lohmann c Sherwin b Attewell	1 – c Attewell b Flowers	6
H. Wood c Sherwin b Shacklock	36 – st Sherwin b Mee	3
G. Jones c Sherwin b Attewell	5 – hit wkt b Flowers	2
J. Beaumont not out	7 – st Sherwin b Flowers	4
T. Bowley c Gunn b Flowers	0 – not out	0
B 3	3 B 1, l-b 4	5
	115	289

Nottinghamshire

W. Scotton b Lohmann	20 – b Lohmann	12
A. Shrewsbury c Abel b Bowley	17 – c and b Bowley	5
W. Barnes b Bowley	1 – b Lohmann	15
W. Gunn c Roller b Bowley	8 – lbw b Lohmann	72
W. Flowers b Bowley	6 – b Lohmann	3
Mr H. B. Daft b Lohmann	6 – c Abel b Jones	12
F. Butler b Lohmann	0 – run out	5
W. Attewell b Lohmann	6 – b Beaumont	12
F. Shacklock b Lohmann	8 – c sub b Roller	1
M. Sherwin run out	12 – c Wood b Lohmann	13
R. Mee not out	0 – not out	0
B 2, l-b 3	5 B 5, l-b 3	8
	89	158

Nottinghamshire Bowling

	Overs	Mdns	Runs	Wkts	Overs	Mdns	Runs	Wkts
Attewell	37	27	36	5	46	29	45	—
Mee	51	27	52	3	25	9	41	3
Shacklock	13	8	17	1	50	26	51	1
Flowers	11.3	6	7	1	41	23	55	5
Barnes					40	15	64	—
Gunn					4	—	8	—
Scotton					7	2	13	—
Mr H. B. Daft					11	6	7	—

Surrey Bowling

	Overs	Mdns	Runs	Wkts	Overs	Mdns	Runs	Wkts
Lohmann	47.2	27	39	5	60	31	66	5
Beaumont	12	10	4	—	22	13	28	1
Bowley	51	41	25	4	36	21	36	1
Mr Roller	6	2	14	—	3	2	1	1
Jones	10	9	2	—	10	6	12	1
Abel					3	1	7	—

NOTTINGHAMSHIRE v KENT

Played at Nottingham, June 25, 26, 27, 1888

A capital performance on the part of the Kent team, but on all three days the rate of scoring was extremely slow, and the game, therefore, lost a great amount of its interest.

Some idea of the cricket will be gathered from the analysis. Gunn played two very fine innings for Nottinghamshire. Kent won by six wickets.

Nottinghamshire

Mr J. A. Dixon c A. Hearne b Wootton	3 – hit wkt b Wright	5
W. Scotton c G. Hearne b Wootton	9 – b Wootton	14
W. Gunn c Wootton b Fox	73 – c Marchant b Fox	56
W. Barnes b Wright	12 – c and b Wright	2
Mr C. W. Wright lbw b Wright	2 – b Wootton	1
Mr H. B. Daft b A. Hearne	26 – lbw b Wright	11
W. Attewell c Streatfield-Moore b G. Hearne	50 – c Thornton b Wootton	5
W. Flowers b G. Hearne	5 – c F. Hearne b Wright	9
F. Shacklock run out	13 – not out	6
H. Richardson not out	3 – c and b Wootton	1
M. Sherwin b Fox	4 – c Wilson b Wootton	0
N-b 1	1 B 1, l-b 1	2
	201	112

Kent

Mr L. Wilson b Attewell	24 – b Barnes	10
F. Hearne b Barnes	21 – not out	8
Mr F. Marchant c Sherwin b Barnes	6 – b Barnes	2
G. G. Hearne b Shacklock	29 – not out	3
Rev. R. T. Thornton c Sherwin b Flowers	8 – b Barnes	9
Mr C. J. M. Fox c Sherwin b Daft	42	
W. Wright b Daft	37	
A. Hearne not out	18	
Mr A. M. Streatfield-Moore c Sherwin b Shacklock	36 – c and b Barnes	0
J. Wootton lbw b Sherwin	8	
J. Pentecost c and b Sherwin	31	
B 20, l-b 3	23	
	283	32

Kent Bowling

	Overs	Mdns	Runs	Wkts	Overs	Mdns	Runs	Wkts
Wright	55	21	76	2	54	35	30	4
Wootton	41	20	52	2	60.3	28	52	5
A. Hearne	29	13	28	1	8	6	7	—
F. Hearne	7	2	12	—				
Mr Fox	11.3	4	16	2	9	6	8	1
G. G. Hearne	17	9	16	2	11	4	13	—

Nottinghamshire Bowling

	Overs	Mdns	Runs	Wkts	Overs	Mdns	Runs	Wkts
Attewell	89	62	46	1	15	10	9	—
Barnes	75	44	86	2	14.3	6	23	4
Mr Dixon	27	16	24	—				
Flowers	40	21	45	1				
Shacklock	17	9	18	2				
Richardson	24	16	12	—				
Scotton	7	6	1	—				
Mr Daft	18	11	18	2				
Gunn	8	5	3	—				
Sherwin	11.1	6	7	2				

Umpires: Coward and Rowbotham.

NOTTINGHAMSHIRE v SUSSEX

Played at Nottingham, May 15, 16, 17, 1890

This, the first of Nottinghamshire's county engagements, was rendered memorable by an extraordinary performance on the part of Shrewsbury and Gunn, the two great batsmen putting on no fewer than 398 runs for the second wicket while they were together. This is a record partnership in first-class cricket, the previous best having been the 340 by Messrs Key and Philipson for Oxford University against Middlesex at Chiswick Park in the season of 1887. Shrewsbury and Gunn got together on the opening day with the score at 26 for one wicket, and at the drawing of stumps the total had been carried, without further loss, to 341, Shrewsbury being then not out 164 and Gunn not out 152. On the second morning they added 83 runs before being separated. Gunn at last being caught at mid-off. The Sussex bowling was not of a character to tax the defence of either player, but the batting was a model of care and skill. Nottinghamshire won by an innings and 266 runs.

Nottinghamshire

A. Shrewsbury c Butt b Humphreys	267	F. Shacklock c Butt b Humphreys	3
Mr J. A. Dixon c Butt b Bean	13	H. Richardson b Gibb	2
W. Gunn c Gibb b Humphreys	196	M. Sherwin b Quaife	14
W. Barnes lbw b Humphreys	4	W. Scotton not out	5
W. Flowers b Smith	46	B 12, l-b 3	15
F. Butler c Butt b Bean	15		
W. Attewell b Bean	10		590

Sussex

H. Tebay b Shacklock	3	– b Barnes	9
W. Quaife b Shacklock	10	– run out	0
Mr W. Newham c Shrewsbury b Shacklock	36	– hit wkt b Barnes	19
G. Bean c Barnes b Flowers	50	– c sub. b Barnes	10
J. Hide c Dixon b Shacklock	37	– c Scotton b Barnes	44
H. Butt lbw b Attewell	6	– lbw b Attewell	1
Mr E. J. McCormick b Flowers	17	– c Attewell b Barnes	9
Mr C. A. Smith c Shrewsbury b Shacklock	14	– c and b Attewell	32
Charlwood c Shrewsbury b Barnes	3	– b Barnes	6
W. Humphreys not out	3	– b Attewell	2
Gibb c Gunn b Shacklock	0	– not out	4
B 2, l-b 5	7	B 2	2
	186		138

Sussex Bowling

	Overs	Mdns	Runs	Wkts
J. Hide	65	22	135	—
Mr Smith	61	17	130	1
Bean	45	14	77	3
Gibb	51	16	101	1
Humphreys	31	1	72	4
Mr McCormick	9	4	10	—
Mr Newham	8	2	16	—
Quaife	14.4	1	34	1

Nottinghamshire Bowling

	Overs	Mdns	Runs	Wkts	Overs	Mdns	Runs	Wkts
Attewell	45	23	45	1	35	20	18	3
Shacklock	35.4	8	87	6	15	5	42	—
Richardson	8	2	18	—	7	3	4	—
Flowers	12	—	25	2	10	6	11	—
Barnes	6	3	4	1	28.4	—	60	6
Mr Dixon					2	1	1	—

Umpires: F. Silcock and R. Humphrey.

NOTTINGHAMSHIRE v SUSSEX

Played at Nottingham, July 16, 17, 18, 1891

This was certainly one of the most remarkable matches of the season, and it produced the altogether unusual circumstance of a side being defeated after scoring over 300 runs in their first innings. On the first two days there was some extremely good batting on the part of both counties, and when stumps were pulled up on the Friday evening, everything pointed to a draw, but the concluding day's cricket proved of a surprising and sensational character, and aroused the spectators to a high pitch of enthusiasm. Both counties were strongly represented, and the wicket was in excellent condition. Mr Newham had the good fortune to win the toss for Sussex, and his team made admirable use of their opportunity, remaining in for the whole of the first day, and scoring 283 runs for the loss of eight wickets. In previous years the Sussex men have usually given a poor account of themselves on the Trent Bridge ground, and it was a very novel experience for the Nottinghamshire team to have to field for a whole afternoon. The batting was singularly good and even, the highest score being Mr Newham's 61, and there being only two single figures on the side. The Sussex captain played with far more caution than usual, and was actually at the wickets for three hours and a quarter, during which time he only made two boundary hits. The eighth wicket went down at 220, but then came an excellent and unexpected stand by Butt and Humphreys, the two men remaining together until the call of time.

On the second morning Butt and Humphreys added 43, their partnership for the ninth wicket producing altogether 106 runs. Butt made his 77 in two hours, by eight 4s, four 3s, ten 2s, and singles, while Humphreys, who had gone in with the score at 177 for seven wickets, took out his bat for an extremely patient and well-played 43. The Sussex total in the end reached 332, the innings lasting as nearly as possible six hours. Against such a formidable score the prospects of the Nottinghamshire team looked anything but favourable, and probably no one on the ground considered it possible that the home side would be able to score a victory. Their innings started indifferently, as three good wickets – those of Mr Robinson, Gunn, and Mr Dixon – fell for 65 runs, but from this point matters went very much better with Nottinghamshire, and once again Arthur Shrewsbury gave evidence of his enormous value to the side. He played a masterly game from start to finish, going in first and being the seventh man out at 179. Of this number his share was 75, his innings being certainly the feature of the second day's cricket. He was batting three hours and forty minutes, and among his hits were a 5 (4 for an overthrow), four 4s, five 3s and eleven 2s. When time was called on the Friday the Nottinghamshire score was 239 for nine wickets, or 15 to save the follow on with one wicket to fall. The Sussex men had bowled and fielded extremely well, but they were greatly handicapped, as Butt, owing to a severe injury to his left hand, was unable to keep wicket after lunch. This accident kept him out of first-class cricket for two or three weeks.

As two whole days had been occupied in getting rid of nineteen batsmen, nothing seemed more unlikely than that a definite conclusion would be arrived at, and in the early part of the third day people seemed to have quite made up their minds that there would be a long and uninteresting afternoon's cricket with a draw a practical certainty. As it turned out, however, there came one of those extraordinary surprises which add so largely to the charm of cricket. When the news of the Sussex breakdown in the second innings got about, a large number of people came up to the ground, and in the afternoon there was a scene of excitement and enthusiasm seldom witnessed nowadays at Trent Bridge. Shacklock and Sherwin succeeded in saving the follow on, and the Nottinghamshire total reached 264. Sussex therefore commenced their second innings with a lead of 68 runs, and had they made anything like a reasonable score there would not have been time for them to have been beaten, but as it was they failed in a most remarkable manner before the admirable bowling of Attewell and Shacklock, and were dismissed in an hour and a quarter for the miserable total of 38, not one man on the side reaching double figures. The wicket certainly showed signs of wear, and the bowlers were able to make the ball get up awkwardly, but the difficulties of the ground offered by no means a sufficient excuse for that ignominious collapse. The home side wanted 107 to win, but as the Sussex men had found run-getting such a difficult matter the supporters of Nottinghamshire were by no means sanguine. As it turned out the last stage of the game proved remarkably interesting, and the issue hung in the balance up to within five or ten minutes of the finish. At the outset all went well with Nottinghamshire, and the score was up to 67 when the fourth wicket fell, but the Sussex eleven kept to their work manfully, and their efforts were rewarded with such success that with seven men out 20 runs were still wanted. At this point, however, Attewell played with great coolness, and thanks mainly to his exertions Nottinghamshire gained a memorable victory by three wickets.

Sussex

G. Bean c Bagguley b Attewell	18	– c Robinson b Attewell	8
Marlow c Dixon b Shacklock	7	– c Gunn b Shacklock	4
Mr G. L. Wilson c Shrewsbury b Shacklock	55	– run out	9
Mr W. Newham c Sherwin b Shacklock	61	– c Dixon b Attewell	0
J. Hide c and b Attewell	21	– st Sherwin b Attewell	4
S. Hollands b Bagguley	11	– c Sherwin b Shacklock	0
Mr W. H. Andrews run out	3	– b Shacklock	4
Mr C. A. Smith c Sherwin b Shacklock	25	– b Shacklock	2
W. Humphreys not out	43	– not out	2
H. Butt lbw b Bagguley	77	– absent hurt	0
F. W. Tate c Sherwin b Bagguley	5	– c Bagguley b Attewell	0
B 2, l-b 4	6	L-b 5	5
	332		38

Nottinghamshire

Mr J. S. Robinson b Tate	20	– not out	7
A. Shrewsbury b Tate	75	– c Humphreys b Smith	2
W. Gunn c Bean b Tate	22	– c Newham b Wilson	25
Mr J. A. Dixon c Hollands b Tate	2	– b Smith	19
Mr C. W. Wright c Hollands b Tate	26	– c Hide b Wilson	3
W. Flowers b Smith	14	– c Hollands b Smith	4
Mr H. B. Daft b Smith	5	– b Wilson	10
W. Attewell c Hide b Tate	28	– not out	18
F. Shacklock not out	40	– c sub. b Smith	17
R. Bagguley c Tate b Smith	7		
M. Sherwin b Smith	12		
B 6, l-b 7	13	B 6, l-b 1	7
	264		112

Nottinghamshire Bowling

	Overs	Mdns	Runs	Wkts	Overs	Mdns	Runs	Wkts
Shacklock	49	19	117	4	14	5	27	4
Attewell	58	31	62	2	14	12	6	4
Flowers	31	10	59	—				
Bagguley	31.1	17	43	3				
Daft	11	1	22	—				
Dixon	4	—	22	—				

Sussex Bowling

	Overs	Mdns	Runs	Wkts	Overs	Mdns	Runs	Wkts
Tate	61	33	87	6	13.2	6	42	—
Smith	37.1	17	73	4	20	9	34	4
Wilson	17	9	34	—	7	1	29	3
Humphreys	8	3	22	—				
Hide	7	3	18	—				
Bean	9	4	17	—				

Umpires: Hill and Draper.

NOTTINGHAMSHIRE v SOMERSET

Played at Nottingham, June 23, 24, 25, 1892

Peculiar interest attached to this match, as it was the first ever played between the two counties. The first day was almost a blank, play being only to progress from five minutes past one till two o'clock. Nottinghamshire won the game by six wickets, but they had to work hard for their victory, which was mainly due to Attewell's bowling and Mr Dixon's admirable not-out innings of 74. The Somerset eleven played up in capital style, and the good fight they made was all the more creditable to them, as they had to go into the field without L. C. H. Palairet and V. T. Hill. Hewett played an extraordinary second innings, hitting on a bad wicket with a brilliancy that roused the spectators at Trent Bridge to real enthusiasm. He scored his 73 runs in eighty minutes.

Somerset

Mr H. T. Hewett c Shacklock b Attewell	8	– b Attewell	73
Mr G. Fowler c Jones b Attewell	1	– b Attewell	34
Mr J. B. Challen c Sherwin b Attewell	19	– c Wright b Shacklock	4
Mr W. C. Hedley c Barnes b Attewell	2	– b Attewell	18
G. B. Nichols c Sherwin b Flowers	0	– b Attewell	3
Mr S. M. J. Woods c Shacklock b Attewell	6	– b Flowers	3
W. H. Hale c Shrewsbury b Flowers	17	– c Sherwin b Attewell	6
Mr C. E. Winter c Shrewsbury b Attewell	12	– b Attewell	7
E. J. Tyler c Dixon b Flowers	3	– c Dixon b Flowers	6
Mr C. J. Robinson c Gunn b Flowers	9	– c Flowers b Attewell	0
Rev. A. P. Wickham not out	0	– not out	2
		B 1, l-b 2	3
	77		159

Nottinghamshire

A. Shrewsbury b Nichols	23	– st Wickham b Tyler	10
W. Flowers c Woods b Tyler	2	– not out	34
W. Gunn c Challen b Hedley	27	– b Tyler	3
W. Barnes c and b Woods	5	– b Nichols	17
W. Attewell st Wickham b Tyler	20		
F. Shacklock c Hedley b Woods	0		
Mr J. A. Dixon b Woods	0	– not out	74
Mr C. W. Wright c and b Tyler	2	– b Nichols	7
Mr J. S. Robinson st Wickham b Tyler	2		
Mr A. O. Jones b Nichols	9		
M. Sherwin not out	0		
B 2	2		
	92		145

Nottinghamshire Bowling

	Overs	Mdns	Runs	Wkts	Overs	Mdns	Runs	Wkts
Shacklock	9	3	19	0	13	2	45	1
Attewell	24	11	28	6	24.3	6	57	7
Flowers	15.2	5	30	4	13	4	37	2
Barnes					2	0	17	0

Somerset Bowling

	Overs	Mdns	Runs	Wkts	Overs	Mdns	Runs	Wkts
Mr Woods	12	4	29	3	15	7	28	0
Tyler	18	4	38	4	33	9	61	2
Mr Hedley	7	3	14	1	2	0	12	0
Nichols	5.3	1	9	2	20	6	40	2
Hale					4	0	4	0

Umpires: Silcock and Henty.

NOTTINGHAMSHIRE v SURREY

Played at Nottingham, May 22, 23, 24, 1893

The Whit-Monday match with Surrey had all its old charm for the Nottingham public, 9,744 people paying for admission at Trent Bridge on the first day, and over six thousand on the second. The result was a heavy reverse for the home county, Surrey winning on the third morning by seven wickets. The victory was brought about by the amazingly effective fast bowling of Richardson, who took in all fourteen wickets for 145 runs. This was an extraordinary performance, but we are bound to add that several of the Nottinghamshire players – not, we think, without good reason – questioned the fairness of the very fast ball with which he obtained most of his wickets. Surrey's first innings was a remarkable one, a score of 238 being made after five of the best wickets had fallen before luncheon for 68.

Surrey

R. Abel c Daft b Shacklock	0	
Mr J. Shuter b Shacklock	12	– c Mee, b Shacklock 15
T. Hayward b Shacklock	8	– c Sherwin b Shacklock 16
Mr W. W. Read c Sherwin b Attewell	32	– not out 16
R. Henderson b Mee	7	
C. Baldwin c and b Flowers	20	– b Shacklock 1
W. Lockwood c Dixon b Attewell	63	
Mr K. J. Key c Attewell b Shacklock	43	– not out 20
W. Brockwell c Daft b Mee	16	
C. Marshall c Sherwin b Attewell	19	
T. Richardson not out	9	
B 5, l-b 4	9	B 4, l-b 1 5
	238	73

Nottinghamshire

A. Shrewsbury c Abel b Richardson	5	– b Richardson 10
Mr J. A. Dixon c Brockwell b Richardson	16	– c Marshall b Richardson 53
W. Gunn b Richardson	6	– c Henderson b Richardson 29
H. B. Daft c and b Lockwood	6	– c Henderson b Richardson 20
R. J. Mee b Lockwood	4	– b Richardson 10
W. Barnes b Richardson	7	– b Lockwood 16
W. Flowers not out	50	– b Richardson 8
W. Attewell b Richardson	0	– c Brockwell b Hayward 19
Mr C. W. Wright b Richardson	0	– not out 3
F. Shacklock c Henderson b Lockwood	14	– c Read b Lockwood 19
M. Sherwin b Richardson	2	– b Richardson 0
B 4, n-b 1	5	B 5, l-b 2, n-b 1, w 1 9
	114	196

Nottinghamshire Bowling

	Overs	Mdns	Runs	Wkts	Overs	Mdns	Runs	Wkts
Shacklock	38.4	19	65	4	17	7	36	3
Attewell	44	16	81	3	20	9	22	0
Mee	20	9	51	2	3.2	1	10	0
Flowers	18	4	32	1				

Surrey Bowling

	Overs	Mdns	Runs	Wkts	Overs	Mdns	Runs	Wkts
Lockwood	21	8	49	3	23	5	60	2
Richardson	21.3	8	60	7	26.2	6	85	7
Abel					9	1	27	0
Brockwell					5	1	11	0
Hayward					5	3	4	1

Umpires: G. Atkinson and J. Wheeler.

NOTTINGHAMSHIRE v SOMERSET

Played at Nottingham, June 1, 2, 3, 1893

With the brothers Palairet, J. B. Challen, W. C. Hedley, and V. T. Hill all away, it was not to be expected that Somerset would be able to beat Nottinghamshire, and after making a very creditable fight up to a certain point on the second day, the western county lost the match by the heavy margin of 255 runs. Flowers in the first innings, and Gunn and Attewell in the second, batted very finely for Nottinghamshire, but beyond everything else the feature of the game was the sensational bowling on the third morning of Shacklock, who took four wickets in four balls. With the second ball of an over he bowled Spurway; the third Newton played on to the wicket, and the fourth and fifth bowled Trask and Gibbs.

Nottinghamshire

A. Shrewsbury b Tyler	5	– c Spencer b Tyler	3
W. Gunn c Newton b Nichols	26	– c Newton b Nichols	71
W. Barnes c Newton b Nichols	33	– run out	6
W. Flowers c and b Woods	57	– c Spencer b Tyler	7
Mr J. A. Dixon b Tyler	36	– b Woods	23
H. B. Daft not out	16	– b Nichols	32
Wharmby b Woods	0	– b Woods	0
W. Attewell c Spencer b Tyler	15	– c Poynton b Tyler	78
F. Shacklock b Woods	8	– lbw b Fowler	15
R. J. Mee b Nichols	5	– c Newton b Nichols	14
M. Sherwin b Nichols	0	– not out	15
B 1	1	B 9, l-b 5	14
	202		278

Somerset

Mr H. T. Hewett c Mee b Shacklock	30	– b Shacklock	12
Mr G. Fowler c Dixon b Mee	8	– c Shacklock b Mee	11
Mr F. J. Poynton b Mee	28	– b Mee	0
Mr R. P. Spurway b Mee	30	– b Shacklock	12
Mr S. M. J. Woods c Wharmby b Attewell	1	– c Wharmby b Shacklock	27
G. B. Nichols b Mee	31	– not out	20
Mr A. E. Newton b Mee	0	– b Shacklock	0
Mr W. Trask b Attewell	22	– b Shacklock	0
Mr J. A. Gibbs c Sherwin b Attewell	5	– b Shacklock	0
E. J. Tyler b Mee	0	– c Attewell b Shacklock	4
Mr T. Spencer not out	0	– c Attewell b Shacklock	8
B 1, l-b 4	5	B 1	1
	160		95

Somerset Bowling

	Overs	Mdns	Runs	Wkts	Overs	Mdns	Runs	Wkts
Tyler	39	12	84	3	38	12	84	3
Woods	23	8	63	3	22	3	82	2
Nichols	19.2	5	50	4	26	7	73	3
Fowler	3	0	4	0	9	1	25	1

Nottinghamshire Bowling

	Overs	Mdns	Runs	Wkts	Overs	Mdns	Runs	Wkts
Mee	33	11	70	6	13	3	36	2
Shacklock	16	7	29	1	23.3	11	46	8
Attewell	31.2	18	28	3	11	8	12	0
Flowers	11	7	11	0				
Wharmby	4	0	17	0				

Umpires: J. Wheeler and J. Potter.

NOTTINGHAMSHIRE v MIDDLESEX

Played at Nottingham, August 17, 18, 19, 1893

This was the last county match of the season at Trent Bridge, and it proved a somewhat humiliating one for the Nottinghamshire team, who lost by 160 runs, after having had a lead of 67 on the first innings. They had largely to thank themselves for their defeat, their fielding during the second innings of Middlesex being very faulty. Still, Middlesex deserved high praise for the up-hill game they played, the batting of Ford and MacGregor, and the splendid bowling of J. T. Hearne – who took in all fifteen wickets for 154 runs – having most to do with the result. J. A. Dixon made his third successive hundred at Trent Bridge, and though he was twice badly missed, his innings was a fine one.

Middlesex

Mr A. E. Stoddart b Mee	0	– c Hardy b Attewell	39
Mr A. J. Webbe c Shrewsbury b Mee	50	– b Attewell	7
Mr C. P. Foley b Mee	1	– c Sherwin b Mee	0
Mr T. C. O'Brien b Flowers	21	– c Attewell b Flowers	12
J. T. Rawlin c Jones b Mee	19	– c Dixon b Attewell	42
Mr F. G. J. Ford c Shrewsbury b Mee	0	– b Dixon	86
Mr G. MacGregor c Dixon b Daft	51	– c Dixon b Flowers	52
Mr R. S. Lucas st Sherwin b Mee	15	– b Attewell	2
Mr H. B. Hayman not out	9	– c Sherwin b Hardy	27
Mr P. J. T. Henery b Mee	0	– b Daft	33
J. T. Hearne c Attewell b Daft	7	– not out	5
B 9, l-b 2	11	B 9, l-b 5	14
	184		319

Nottinghamshire

Mr J. A. Dixon c MacGregor b Hearne	133	– st MacGregor b Hearne	9
A. Shrewsbury c O'Brien b Rawlin	1	– c Stoddart b Hearne	31
W. Gunn c Stoddart b Hearne	7	– c Stoddart b Hearne	8
W. Barnes c Stoddart b Hearne	11	– c Stoddart b Hearne	1
W. Flowers c MacGregor b Stoddart	10	– b Hearne	5
H. B. Daft c O'Brien b Hearne	14	– lbw b Hearne	12
Mr A. O. Jones b Hearne	0	– c O'Brien b Hearne	5
W. Attewell c Lucas b Hearne	59	– c O'Brien b Stoddart	5
S. Hardy not out	12	– b Stoddart	6
R. J. Mee c Rawlin b Hearne	0	– c Rawlin b Hearne	4
M. Sherwin b Rawlin	0	– not out	0
B 2, w 2	4	B 6	6
	251		92

Nottinghamshire Bowling

	Overs	Mdns	Runs	Wkts	Overs	Mdns	Runs	Wkts
Mee	27	8	51	7	32	5	111	1
Attewell	20	5	46	0	49	20	72	4
Hardy	12	3	29	0	10	4	21	1
Flowers	15	7	27	1	14	2	41	2
Daft	10	3	20	2	9	1	29	1
Barnes					9	0	27	0
Dixon					2	0	4	1

Middlesex Bowling

	Overs	Mdns	Runs	Wkts	Overs	Mdns	Runs	Wkts
Hearne	49	19	99	7	28	10	55	8
Rawlin	38.4	15	63	2	20	9	26	0
Stoddart	15	5	31	1	7.2	5	5	2
Ford	8	0	28	0				
Lucas	2	0	14	0				
Webbe	7	4	12	0				

Umpires: J. Wheeler and F. Coward.

NOTTINGHAMSHIRE v SUSSEX

Played at Nottingham, May 16, 17, 18 1895

By scoring 726 – a total which beat the previous record in county cricket – and winning the game with 378 runs to spare, the Nottinghamshire eleven started their county matches in remarkable style. Their long innings, which did not end till nearly half-past three on the second afternoon, lasted altogether eight hours and a half. Far and away the finest cricket was shown by Gunn, who in a few minutes under five hours scored 219 in superb form, his only mistake, so far as could be seen, being a skyer to mid-on when he had made 35, which Murdoch, running under the ball, failed to reach. He hit twenty-six 4s, ten 3s and twenty 2s. His partnership with Daft produced 115 for the second wicket, and Flowers helped him to put on 103 for the third. In the latter part of the innings Howitt and Bagguley added no fewer than 201 runs for the seventh wicket, each scoring over 100 for the first time in county cricket. In face of such a total as 726, Sussex had a thankless task and apart from a well played, though by no means faultless 75 not out by Newham, their batting did not rise above the common place. The weather was bitterly cold during the match, and on the last day the wicket was slightly affected by rain.

Nottinghamshire

Mr A. O. Jones b Tate	3
H. B. Daft b Brann	46
W. Gunn lbw b Butcher	219
W. Flowers b Shaw	64
Mr J. A. Dixon b Bean	35
W. Attewell c Butt b Bean	4
Mr R. H. Howitt c Newham b Butcher	119
R. Bagguley c Bean b Shaw	110
A. Wilkinson c Marlow b Shaw	62
A. Pike not out	23
A. Handford c Marlow b Shaw	24
B 12, w 5	17
	726

Sussex

G. Bean b Attewell	30 – c Daft b Attewell	2
F. W. Marlow c Dixon b Attewell	34 – c Dixon b Wilkinson	6
Mr W. L. Murdoch c and b Wilkinson	3 – c and b Dixon	15
K. S. Ranjitsinhji run out	29 – c and b Attewell	27
Mr W. Newham c Jones b Flowers	9 – not out	75
Mr G. Brann not out	39 – c Pike b Dixon	10
A. Butcher b Wilkinson	5 – b Flowers	0
H. Butt lbw b Wilkinson	7 – c Daft b Attewell	17
F. Parris b Wilkinson	5 – c Handford b Attewell	15
F. W. Tate b Wilkinson	0 – c Gunn b Attewell	5
A. Shaw c Bagguley b Attewell	4 – c Jones b Flowers	1
B 5	5 B 2, l-b 1, w 2	5
	170	178

Sussex Bowling

	Overs	Mdns	Runs	Wkts
Shaw	100.1	31	168	4
Tate	36	8	99	1
Butcher	38	12	108	2
Parris	32	4	98	0
Brann	18	5	71	1
Ranjitsinhji	14	0	94	0
Bean	29	6	71	2

Nottinghamshire Bowling

	Overs	Mdns	Runs	Wkts	Overs	Mdns	Runs	Wkts
Handford	12	4	38	0	7	1	22	0
Attewell	29.1	9	57	3	34	17	36	5
Wilkinson	21	5	56	5	20	4	48	1
Flowers	6	1	14	1	19.3	3	39	2
Dixon					12	3	28	2

NOTTINGHAMSHIRE v LANCASHIRE

Played at Nottingham, June 17, 18, 1895

Unfortunately for Flowers, the Lancashire match, which had been given to him for his benefit, was abruptly finished off on the second day, Lancashire winning by an innings and 188 runs. By scoring 315 for seven wickets on the first afternoon the Northern team soon made themselves secure against defeat, but with the ground in excellent order they had no reason to expect such an easy victory. The result was brought about by the wonderful bowling of Mold, who has never done anything more startling. In all he took fifteen wickets – eight for 20 runs and seven for 65. The way he made the ball break back on the hard ground was quite marvellous. In Nottinghamshire's first innings the first five wickets went down for 6 runs, and the total of 35 proved the smallest of the season in county matches. It should be mentioned that Mold was suffering from an injured finger, and that only on the second morning of the match did Mr Hornby resolve to let him play. In their different ways Albert Ward, Frank Sugg, and Tinsley batted admirably.

Lancashire

Mr A. N. Hornby b Attewell	6
A. Ward b Howitt	116
A. Tinsley st Wright b Gunn	65
A. Paul st Wright b Gunn	9
F. H. Sugg b Howitt	91
G. R. Baker c Wright b Attewell	7
J. Briggs b Attewell	5
C. Smith b Attewell	18
A. Lancaster c Wright b Attewell	6
A. Hallam c Gunn b Attewell	4
A. Mold not out	0
B 15, l-b 3	18
	345

Nottinghamshire

A. Shrewsbury b Mold	1	– b Mold	10
Mr A. O. Jones b Mold	5	– b Mold	0
W. Gunn lbw b Mold	5	– b Mold	4
H. B. Daft b Mold	0	– c Smith b Mold	8
Mr J. A. Dixon b Mold	0	– b Mold	4
Mr C. W. Wright c Smith b Mold	0	– lbw b Briggs	4
W. Attewell c Smith b Mold	11	– b Mold	19
R. Bagguley not out	6	– run out	17
Mr R. H. Howitt b Briggs	0	– c Tinsley b Briggs	10
A. Wilkinson c Smith b Mold	0	– c and b Mold	24
A. Handford c Sugg b Briggs	5	– not out	14
B 2	2	B 8	8
	35		122

Nottinghamshire Bowling

	Overs	Mdns	Runs	Wkts
Attewell	56.4	21	76	6
Handford	23	4	63	0
Wilkinson	23	7	33	0
Daft	13	5	21	0
Dixon	7	1	12	0
Howitt	17	7	25	2
Bagguley	18	3	44	0
Gunn	15	4	53	2

Lancashire Bowling

	Overs	Mdns	Runs	Wkts	Overs	Mdns	Runs	Wkts
Mold	9	4	20	8	27	6	65	7
Briggs	8.3	1	13	2	26	12	49	2

Umpires: G. Ulyett and Wheeler.

NOTTINGHAMSHIRE v GLOUCESTERSHIRE

Played at Nottingham, July 25, 26, 27, 1895

With Shrewsbury kept away by an injured hand, the Nottinghamshire eleven were fairly outplayed on a slow wicket, and before half-past three on the third afternoon Gloucestershire won the match in the easiest fashion by 135 runs. This decisive result was clearly brought about by Townsend, who actually took sixteen wickets (eight in each innings) at a cost of only 122 runs. On the slow ground he had the Nottinghamshire batsmen at his mercy, Gunn in particular being quite at fault in trying to play him. Townsend, Hemingway, and Wrathall all batted well on the second day, but the best innings in the match was Jessop's 55, a brilliant display which lasted just thirty-five minutes. Only 61 runs were scored while he was in.

Gloucestershire

Mr W. G. Grace c Gregory b Attewell	4	– c and b Attewell	14
Mr R. W. Rice b Gregory	1	– c Flowers b Attewell	6
Mr W. McG. Hemingway b Flowers	23	– b Daft	45
Mr J. J. Ferris c sub b Flowers	13	– c Bagguley b Attewell	2
H. Wrathall b Gregory	15	– c Bagguley b Flowers	41
Mr C. L. Townsend ht wkt b Flowers	6	– c Lowe b Attewell	41
Mr G. L. Jessop c Gunn b Attewell	55	– c and b Flowers	1
J. H. Board c and b Attewell	21	– lbw b Gregory	16
Mr S. De Winton c Wilkinson b Gregory	24	– c Wilkinson b Flowers	5
Mr F. C. Bracher c Sub b Gregory	3	– b Attewell	13
F. G. Roberts not out	2	– not out	2
B 3, l-b 3	6	B 2	2
	173		188

Nottinghamshire

W. Flowers ht wkt b Townsend	2	– b Ferris	24
R. Bagguley b Townsend	27	– b Townsend	11
W. Gunn c Grace b Townsend	5	– c Wrathall b Townsend	10
Mr J. A. Dixon b Roberts	19	– c Grace b Townsend	16
Mr C. W. Wright st Board b Townsend	7	– c Board b Townsend	2
Mr A. C. Jones c Jessop b Townsend	13	– b Townsend	0
W. Attewell c Ferris b Townsend	1	– c Wrathall b Ferris	11
H. B. Daft c Board b Townsend	1	– st Board b Townsend	2
Mr W. H. G. Lowe not out	15	– b Townsend	14
A. Wilkinson st Board b Townsend	12	– not out	11
D. Gregory b Jessop	0	– b Townsend	0
B 11, n-b 7	18	B 3, n-b 2	5
	120		106

Nottinghamshire Bowling

	Overs	Mdns	Runs	Wkts	Overs	Mdns	Runs	Wkts
Attewell	40	18	71	3	13.2	11	63	5
Gregory	15.3	30	48	4	21	3	41	1
Flowers	24	5	48	3	18	2	56	3
Daft					11	4	22	1
Dixon					2	1	1	0
Wilkinson					1	0	3	0

Gloucestershire Bowling

	Overs	Mdns	Runs	Wkts	Overs	Mdns	Runs	Wkts
Townsend	37	12	52	8	21.1	2	70	8
Jessop	14	6	22	1	7	5	6	0
Ferris	4	1	9	0	12	2	25	2
Roberts	19	9	19	1				

Umpires: Hay and Collishaw.

NOTTINGHAMSHIRE v YORKSHIRE

Played at Nottingham, June 1, 2, 3, 1896

Nottinghamshire did not win their match against Yorkshire, but the draw they secured in face of their opponents' total of 450 did them as much credit as any of their victories last season. When on the third afternoon, with over three hours left for play, they were 31 behind, with only four wickets to fall in their second innings, defeat seemed certain, but

C. W. Wright and Attewell put on 131 runs while they were together, and practically saved the game. So delighted were the spectators with Attewell's fine hitting, that a sum of ten guineas was collected and presented to him. He scored his 96 in an hour and twenty minutes, whereas C. W. Wright, who played with admirable patience and judgment, was at the wickets nearly three hours and a half for his 69. Gunn batted finely in both innings. At this period of the season the Yorkshiremen were batting in wonderful form, and in scoring their 450, they showed some very brilliant cricket; Brown, who lost his wicket in foolishly hitting back-handed at a lob, taking the chief honours.

Yorkshire

J. T. Brown b Gunn	107	Lord Hawke b Daft	11
Mr F. S. Jackson b Hardstaff	38	G. H. Hirst not out	67
J. Tunnicliffe c and b Attewell	65	Mr F. W. Milligan c Pike b Attewell	0
D. Denton b Mee	3	D. Hunter b Attewell	2
R. Moorhouse b Attewell	23	B 9, l-b 7, n-b 1	17
E. Wainwright c Pike b Hardstaff	30		
R. Peel b Hardstaff	87		450

Nottinghamshire

Mr A. O. Jones b Hirst	13	c Wainwright b Hirst	27
A. Shrewsbury c Peel b Wainwright	49	c Hirst b Jackson	4
W. Gunn c Tunnicliffe b Jackson	64	c Brown b Jackson	56
W. Flowers c Hawke b Jackson	4	b Jackson	5
Mr J. A. Dixon b Hirst	14	b Jackson	0
Mr C. W. Wright run out	28	c Peel b Denton	69
H. B. Daft lbw b Jackson	24	c and b Wainwright	16
W. Attewell c Hunter b Peel	38	c Jackson b Wainwright	96
A. Pike b Wainwright	20	c Tunnicliffe b Wainwright	21
R. J. Mee not out	6	not out	20
R. G. Hardstaff b Wainwright	3	b Peel	3
B 8, l-b 6, w 1, n-b 1	16	B 5, l-b 5, w 1	11
	279		328

Nottinghamshire Bowling

	Overs	Mdns	Runs	Wkts
Mee	34	4	107	1
Attewell	48.3	20	78	4
Jones	17	2	77	0
Hardstaff	38	12	93	3
Dixon	9	2	16	0
Gunn	11	1	33	1
Flowers	3	1	11	0
Daft	7	3	18	1

Yorkshire Bowling

	Overs	Mdns	Runs	Wkts	Overs	Mdns	Runs	Wkts
Hirst	29	8	77	2	21	6	46	1
Peel	23	10	53	1	21.2	6	37	1
Milligan	11	3	19	0	13	1	32	0
Wainwright	20.2	6	34	3	24	7	52	3
Jackson	35	11	56	3	45	16	87	4
Brown	9	4	24	0	3	0	15	0
Moorhouse					5	0	19	0
Denton					5	0	19	1
Tunnicliffe					3	1	10	0

Umpires: H. Draper and G. Remnant.

NOTTINGHAMSHIRE v KENT

Played at Nottingham, June 26, 27, 28, 1899

Having won two matches in the previous week, Nottinghamshire entered with a good deal of confidence upon their match with Kent, but as it turned out they fared very badly and in the end suffered defeat by 365 runs. Kent had a substantial lead on the first innings and when they went in for the second time some extraordinary batting was shown by Alec Hearne and Mason, the Kent innings being declared closed on the Wednesday morning. Up to this time Mason had been less successful than any first-class batsman in the county, and his return to form gave extreme satisfaction. Bradley as bowler and Huish as wicket-keeper had much to do with Kent's decisive victory.

Kent

Mr C. J. Burnup c Bottom b J. Gunn	0	– lbw b Wass	0
A. Hearne b J. Gunn	15	– not out	162
Mr F. D. Brown c Oates b Wass	3		
Mr R. O'H. Lovesay b Wass	53	– b Jones	47
Mr J. R. Mason c Dixon b J. Gunn	1	– not out	181
Mr A. H. Du Boulay c Attewell b J. Gunn	58		
Mr G. J. V. Weigall c Dixon b Wass	8		
F. H. Huish b J. Gunn	23		
F. Martin not out	15		
Mr J. Murrell c W. Gunn b Bottom	9		
Mr W. M. Bradley b J. Gunn	1		
B 5, l-b 1, w 1	7	B 13, l-b 7, w 1	21
	193	(2 wkts dec.)	411

Nottinghamshire

Mr A. O. Jones c Martin b Hearne	32	– c Mason b Bradley	3
A. Shrewsbury c Huish b Bradley	2	– b Martin	26
W. Gunn b Bradley	35	– c Huish b Bradley	0
F. H. Guttridge c Huish b Hearne	0	– c Bradley b Martin	17
P. Mason b Bradley	1	– c Huish b Bradley	6
Mr J. A. Dixon c Huish b Hearne	11	– b Hearne	20
W. Attewell c Huish b Mason	9	– b Bradley	0
J. Gunn c Murrell b Bradley	10	– c Hearne b Bradley	7
Bottom c Huish b Bradley	6	– c Huish b Bradley	7
T. Oates b Bradley	0	– not out	19
T. Wass not out	6	– c Livesay b Martin	16
B 2, w 1	3	B 2, w 1	3
	115		124

Nottinghamshire Bowling

	Overs	Mdns	Runs	Wkts	Overs	Mdns	Runs	Wkts
Wass	27	6	74	3	22	2	86	1
J. Gunn	32.2	13	58	6	36	13	58	0
Attewell	10	6	8	0	24	11	46	0
Bottom	9	4	23	1	22	5	65	0
Guttridge	2	0	11	0	5	0	21	0
Jones	2	0	12	0	17	2	65	1
Mason					4	2	4	0
Dixon					8	2	20	0
W. Gunn					6	1	25	0

Kent Bowling

	Overs	Mdns	Runs	Wkts	Overs	Mdns	Runs	Wkts
Bradley	27.1	12	41	6	51	34	42	6
Martin	10	1	19	0	17.3	11	17	3
Hearne	17	9	27	3	25	18	19	1
Mason	8	5	12	1	25	17	27	0
Du Boulay	6	3	13	0	7	5	9	0
Murrell					3	3	4	0
Burnup					3	1	3	0

Umpires: J. Wheeler and T. Mycroft.

NOTTINGHAMSHIRE v GLOUCESTERSHIRE

Played at Nottingham, July 20, 21, 22, 1899

Rain prevented a ball being bowled on the third day and a very interesting match had consequently to be abandoned. At the finish Nottinghamshire were 43 runs ahead with seven wickets to fall in their second innings, some admirable batting being shown, more particularly by Shrewsbury, when the team followed on. In the first innings of Nottinghamshire the last five wickets fell for 20 runs, Paish bowling with extraordinary success. For Gloucestershire, Townsend scored his 114 in two hours and a half, and Jessop 126 in an hour and a half. Up to a certain point Jessop played with amazing brilliancy, actually reaching his hundred in an hour.

Gloucestershire

Mr W. Troup b J Gunn	0
H. Wrathall lbw b Jones	31
Mr C. L. Townsend c sub b Dench	114
Mr S. A. P. Kitcat c Oates b J. Gunn	23
Mr G. L. Jessop c Dench b Attewell	126
Mr W. S. A. Brown c J. Gunn b Dench	37
J. H. Board lbw b Dench	18
Mr G. Romans st Oates b Jones	6
Mr J. N. B. Champain c Oates b Jones	2
A. Paish b Jones	0
F. G. Roberts not out	6
B 3, l-b 6	9
	372

Nottinghamshire

A. Shrewsbury c Jessop b Paish	11	– not out	89
P. Mason c Wrathall b Jessop	6		
Mr J. A. Dixon c Kitcat b Paish	13	– not out	0
Mr A. O. Jones c Board b Paish	87	– b Wrathall	20
C. E. Dench c Board b Paish	3		
W. Gunn c and b Paish	52	– c Champain b Townsend	54
Mr W. B. Goodacre c Brown b Paish	0	– c Brown b Paish	57
W. Attewell c Champain b Paish	1		
J. Gunn not out	9		
T. Oates st Board b Paish	0		
T. Wass b Brown	1		
B 2, l-b 1, n-b 4	7	B 2, l-b 3	5
	190		225

Nottinghamshire Bowling

	Overs	Mdns	Runs	Wkts
Wass	14	3	54	0
J. Gunn	24	6	92	2
Dench	23.4	5	71	3
Attewell	27	15	48	1
Jones	17	2	64	4
Dixon	4	0	34	0

Gloucestershire Bowling

	Overs	Mdns	Runs	Wkts	Overs	Mdns	Runs	Wkts
Jessop	18	9	39	1	9	0	30	0
Paish	33	6	77	8	24	6	79	1
Roberts	13	5	29	0	10	4	39	0
Townsend	3	0	13	0	12	4	28	1
Brown	7.1	1	25	1	12	3	33	0
Wrathall					5	1	11	1

Umpires: J. Wheeler and A. Chester.

NOTTINGHAMSHIRE v MIDDLESEX

Played at Nottingham, August 24, 25, 26, 1899

The closing match of the season at Trent Bridge was a bitter disappointment to the Nottinghamshire eleven who suffered a ten wickets defeat after having started the game by scoring 223 with only three men out. Middlesex owed their sensational victory to the all-round cricket of C. M. Wells who played an innings of 244 and took nine wickets. He was batting for five hours and three quarters and, so far as could be seen, gave only one chance – a high and very hard return to Dixon when 54. His 244 is the highest score ever made against Nottinghamshire. Shrewsbury could not play.

Nottinghamshire

Mr A. O. Jones b Trott	117	– st McGregor b Wells	42
Mr J. A. Dixon lbw b Trott	18	– b Ford	2
W. Gunn lbw b Ford	72	– c Roche b Ford	28
Mr W. B. Goodacre c R. Douglas b Wells	38	– b Wells	6
C. E. Dench b Trott	1	– lbw b Wells	1
Mr G. J. Groves c MacGregor b Trott	13	– b Wells	51
J. Carlin c Hearn b Trott	8	– c Wells b Trott	43
W. Attewell b Wells	1	– c and b Wells	0
F. H. Guttridge b Wells	8	– st MacGregor b Trott	1
J. Gunn c MacGregor b Trott	8	– not out	13
T. Wass not out	0	– b Wells	1
B 6, w 1, n-b 1	8	B 7, l-b 1, w 3	11
	292		199

Middlesex

Mr P. F. Warner c Jones b Wass	16	– not out	7
Mr J. Douglas c W. Gunn b Wass	0	– not out	10
Mr L. J. Moon c Carlin b Wass	8		
Mr C. M. Wells c Dench b Dixon	244		
Mr R. N. Douglas c Attewell b Wass	77		
J. T. Rawlin c Dench b J. Gunn	45		
Mr F. G. J. Ford c Groves b Dixon	52		
A. E. Trott not out	12		
Mr G. MacGregor not out	0		
B 8, l-b 5, w 1, n-b 7	21		
(7 wkts dec.)	475		17

W. Roche and J. T. Hearne did not bat.

Middlesex Bowling

	Overs	Mdns	Runs	Wkts	Overs	Mdns	Runs	Wkts
Trott	47.3	13	123	6	17	10	20	2
Hearne	25	7	47	0	14	6	45	0
Rawlin	4	1	12	0	2	0	12	0
Wells	18	3	50	3	24.3	19	61	6
Roche	8	2	18	0	8	3	12	0
Ford	11	1	34	1	16	5	38	2

Nottinghamshire Bowling

	Overs	Mdns	Runs	Wkts	Overs	Mdns	Runs	Wkts
Wass	51	20	123	4				
J. Gunn	38	13	86	1	1	0	2	0
Jones	24	7	78	0	1.4	0	15	0
Dench	10	2	37	0				
Attewell	12	4	30	0				
Dixon	10	2	32	2				
Guttridge	5	1	13	0				
Goodacre	6	0	34	0				
Groves	2	0	6	0				
W. Gunn	3	0	15	0				

Umpires: A. F. Smith and G. Porter.

SOMERSET

SOMERSET v MIDDLESEX

Played at Taunton, August 21, 22, 1890

This match had been looked forward to with an immense amount of interest from the fact that Somerset had beaten Middlesex at Lord's in Whit week, and had since then won all their engagements. The ground was affected by heavy rain, and bowlers had matters pretty much their own way. The first day's play was of a singularly even character, there being only a difference of one run when an innings had been completed by each team. Afterwards Somerset lost one wicket for 4 runs, and on the Friday they increased their score to 127, leaving Middlesex exactly that number to get to win. Mr A. J. Webbe played such a great game for his side that when he was fifth out at 114 only 13 runs were required to win. Then, however, came a collapse, two runs being still wanted when Mr Dauglish the last man, came in. He scored a single, and in trying a second run lost his wicket, and a most remarkable match ended in a tie. Such a result is rare in county cricket, and the only instances of a similar kind that we remember were the two games between Middlesex and Surrey in 1868 and 1876 respectively.

Somerset

Mr H. T. Hewett c Burton b Hearne	1	– b Rawlin	34
Mr L. C. H. Palairet c Dauglish b Hearne	5	– b Hearne	4
Mr J. B. Challen b Hearne	49	– run out	1
G. B. Nicholls lbw b Hearne	1	– b Rawlin	9
Mr W. N. Roe b Hearne	0	– c Dauglish b Webbe	33
Mr J. E. Trask b Hearne	3	– c Hearne b Burton	9
E. J. Tyler lbw b Burton	4	– b Stoddart	1
Mr R. C. N. Palairet c Dauglish b Burton	16	– b Stoddart	16
Mr S. M. J. Woods c Henery b Hearne	12	– b Hearne	7
Mr A. E. Newton c Dauglish b Hearne	11	– not out	5
Mr W. A. R. Young not out	0	– c Ford b Hearne	0
B 2, l-b 3	5	B 5, l-b 2, w 1	8
	107		127

Middlesex

Mr A. J. Webbe c Newton b Tyler	43	– c Newton b Woods	57
Mr A. E. Stoddard c L. Palairet b Woods	6	– c Newton b Woods	11
Mr M. R. Jardine b Tyler	4	– b Tyler	1
J. T. Rawlin c Roe b Tyler	3	– b Woods	16
Mr T. C. O'Brien b Woods	1	– b Tyler	3
Mr H. J. Mordaunt c Newton b Woods	0	– b Tyler	4
Mr F. G. J. Ford b Tyler	0	– b Nicholls	17
Mr P. J. T. Henery b Nicholls	21	– c Nicholls b Woods	3
J. T. Hearne c Young b Tyler	0	– not out	3
G. Burton not out	16	– c and b Woods	0
Mr M. J. Dauglish c Trask b Woods	12	– run out	1
B 1, n-b 1	2	B 10	10
	108		126

Middlesex Bowling

	Overs	Mdns	Runs	Wkts	Overs	Mdns	Runs	Wkts
Burton	33	11	42	2	24	12	30	1
Hearne	33.2	17	55	8	26	13	44	3
Mr Stoddart	7	5	5	0	6.1	1	5	2
Rawlin					15	6	27	2
Mr Webbe					4	3	4	1

Somerset Bowling

	Overs	Mdns	Runs	Wkts	Overs	Mdns	Runs	Wkts
Tyler	22	4	64	5	17	4	43	3
Mr Woods	14.2	4	34	1	22.4	2	61	5
Nicholls	7	4	8	1	10	7	4	1
Mr Roe					8	4	8	0

Umpires: Allen Hill and C. K. Pullin.

SOMERSET v LANCASHIRE

Played at Taunton, July 9, 10, 1891

The Somerset men gave a poor display of batting in this game, and were badly beaten by nine wickets. The main factor in Lancashire's success was the superb bowling of Mold, who in all obtained fifteen wickets for 131 runs – a remarkable achievement on a fast, run-getting ground. A long stand in Lancashire's first innings was made by Smith and Briggs, who put on 105 runs for the fifth wicket. Both batted finely in their different styles, Briggs hitting brilliantly, while his partner played a more cautious game. Mr Lionel Palairet and Mr Woods were the only batsmen on the home side to play Mold's bowling with confidence, and the former curiously enough had the best analysis in the match, taking four wickets for 18 runs.

Lancashire

R. G. Barlow b Woods	0 –	b L. Palairet	12
A. Ward b Nichols	19 –	not out	35
A. Smith c Wickham b Woods	50 –	not out	4
F. H. Sugg run out	0		
G. Yates b Nichols	0		
J. Briggs st Wickham b Tyler	68		
G. R. Baker c Woods b L. Palairet	29		
Mr A. N. Hornby b L. Palairet	32		
Mr A. T. Kemble st Wickham b L. Palairet	0		
A. Watson b Nichols	1		
A. Mold not out	0		
B 2	2		
	210		51

Somerset

Mr H. T. Hewett run out	0 –	b Mold	13
Mr L. C. H. Palairet c Kemble b Mold	37 –	b Watson	8
Mr R. C. N. Palairet b Mold	6 –	c Kemble b Mold	9
Mr G. Fowler run out	20 –	c Hornby b Mold	5
G. B. Nichols b Mold	25 –	c Kemble b Mold	12
E. J. Tyler b Mold	13 –	b Watson	17
Mr E. J. Lock b Mold	0 –	c and b Mold	10
Mr S. M. J. Woods b Mold	10 –	not out	38
Mr J. A. Gibbs b Watson	6 –	c and b Mold	6
Mr C. J. Robinson c Baker b Mold	0 –	b Mold	0
Rev. A. P. Wickham not out	0 –	b Mold	4
B 4, l-b 7	11	B 8, l-b 2	10
	128		132

Somerset Bowling

	Overs	Mdns	Runs	Wkts	Overs	Mdns	Runs	Wkts
Mr Woods	28	8	76	2	7	2	20	0
Tyler	34	9	80	1	8	1	19	0
Nichols	18	9	39	3	5	2	7	0
Mr L. Palairet	2	0	13	3	3.2	1	5	1

Lancashire Bowling

	Overs	Mdns	Runs	Wkts	Overs	Mdns	Runs	Wkts
Watson	24	11	36	1	30	14	50	2
Mold	22.1	3	59	7	29.2	5	72	8
Briggs	9	3	22	0				

Umpires: Pullin and Lillywhite.

SOMERSET v NOTTINGHAMSHIRE

Played at Taunton, August 18, 19, 1892

The first visit of the famous Nottinghamshire eleven to Taunton had been looked forward to with considerable interest, but, despite the fact that Somerset had accomplished several very fine performances, no one anticipated that they would check the successful career of the Midland side. The uncertainty of cricket was fully exemplified in the game, and the Somerset men, completely out-playing their opponents at all points, gained a remarkable victory in a single innings with 122 runs to spare. The match unfortunately was not played under even conditions, Nottinghamshire having the worst of the wicket, but there was not sufficient difference to account for such a crushing defeat. Up to this point Nottinghamshire had not lost a county match, and, as may be imagined, their disaster created a great sensation in cricket circles. It may be mentioned as some excuse for their severe reverse that the Nottinghamshire men had been in the field the whole of the previous day at Cheltenham, trying in vain to beat Gloucestershire, and were probably somewhat stale after their exertions. The main factors in Somerset's success were the admirable batting of Messrs Hewett, Challen, and Hill and the splendid bowling of Tyler. The left-hander fairly eclipsed all his previous achievements for his county in an important match, and in the two innings of Nottinghamshire obtained fifteen wickets for 96 runs.

On Thursday morning the weather was threatening, and shortely before noon rain came on, and lasted about an hour. There was a further brief shower afterwards, and then the weather improved, and the afternoon turned out fine. The winning of the toss was an important matter, and considerable satisfaction was experienced among the spectators when it became known that Mr Hewett had been successful. The game commenced at five minutes past three, and having a time to bowl and field with a wet ball the Nottinghamshire men were placed at a great disadvantage. Hewett and Palairet opened the home county's innings, and, making free use of their opportunity, made a splendid start. The ground was bad, and the ball travelled slowly, but despite this fact runs were put on at the rate of a run a minute. Palairet played a defensive game, but the captain hit with his customary daring and brilliancy. The two gentlemen were partners for seventy minutes, and in that time scored 73 runs. Palairet was the first to leave, and Hewett was second out at 81, having made 60 of that number. Though, as usual, running great risks, Hewett gave no chance, and he obtained his runs in an hour and a quarter. Afterwards Challen, who went in first wicket down, and for the first half hour was in some difficulties, batted admirably, and was in while 95 runs were put on. Hill hit with vigour, and at six o'clock, when stumps were drawn, was not out 27, while the score stood at 181 for six wickets.

On the second morning the remaining Somerset batsmen followed up their advantage in brilliant style, and in an hour and thirty-five minutes added 125 runs, the total – the highest hit against the Nottinghamshire bowlers during the season – thus reaching 309. As the wicket was by no means easy this was a meritorious performance, the credit belonging to Hill and Fowler, who added 96 runs in seventy minutes, their partnership for the seventh wicket producing altogether 112 runs. Fowler batted with sound judgment, while his partner hit in the most determined fashion and increased his score to 93. The first thing in the morning Hill gave a difficult chance to Gunn in the long field, but this was the only serious blemish in a singularly brilliant innings. The young Oxonian, was only batting two hours, hit twelve 4s, his innings being the highest he has played for his county.

With the wicket becoming more difficult as the day advanced Nottinghamshire were placed in a most unfortunate position, and it soon became evident that their chances of escaping defeat were rather remote. Before lunch they lost a wicket for 7 runs, and after the interval the game went all against them, most of the batsmen being greatly puzzled by Tyler's slow bowling. Shrewsbury was dismissed at 25, and Barnes was out at 30. Realising that the only chance was to knock off Tyler, Flowers hit with grim determination and made 31 in a quarter of an hour, but his example was not followed by the others. Though in frequent difficulties Gunn managed to stay in an hour and twenty minutes for 25, but after he left the innings was rapidly finished off, the whole side being dismissed in a little over two hours for 118, or no fewer than 191 behind. It was naturally thought that at their second attempt the Nottinghamshire men would make a big effort to retrieve their position, more especially as Woods, who had strained himself while bowling in the first innings, was unable to go into the field. This expectation was not realised, and with the exception of Daft and Dixon the visitors completely failed. In rather less than an hour and a quarter they were put out a second time for the paltry score of 69, and Somerset were left with a wonderful triumph. Bowling with admirable judgment, and making the ball break both ways, Tyler was the absolute master of the batsmen, and had the extraordinary analysis of nine wickets for 33 runs. The ground helped him considerably, but his record in the match of 15 wickets for 96 runs was quite exceptional for a slow bowler. An appeal on his behalf to the spectators, who numbered about 4,000, was responded to in generous fashion, £44 being quickly collected.

Somerset

Mr H. T. Hewett c Gunn b Flowers	60
Mr L. C. H. Palairet c and b Attewell	18
Mr J. B. Challen c Attewell b Barnes	47
Mr W. C. Hedley run out	16
Mr A. E Newton c Sherwin b Flowers	10
Mr V. T. Hill c Sherwin b Daft	93
Mr S. M. J. Woods lbw b Barnes	0
Mr G. Fowler c Flowers b Daft	39
G. B. Nichols c Shrewsbury jun. b Flowers	5
Mr C. J. Robinson c Gunn b Attewell	16
E. J. Tyler not out	0
B 2, l-b 3	5
	309

Nottinghamshire

Mr J. A. Dixon c Challen b Tyler	4	– b Tyler	10
A. Shrewsbury c Palairet b Woods	25	– b Tyler	0
W. Gunn lbw b Tyler	25	– lbw b Tyler	5
W. Barnes st Newton b Tyler	1	– c Newton b Tyler	0
W. Flowers b Tyler	31	– c Newton b Tyler	3
H. B. Daft lbw b Tyler	6	– b Hedley	25
F. Shacklock c and b Hedley	7	– c Nichols b Tyler	5
Mr A. O. Jones c Newton b Tyler	4	– c Fowler b Tyler	8
W. Attewell c Newton b Hedley	15	– b Tyler	0
A. Shrewsbury jun. run out	0	– c Palairet b Tyler	0
M. Sherwin not out	2	– not out	1
B 4, l-b 1	5	B 2, l-b 3	5
	118		69

Nottinghamshire Bowling

	Overs	Mdns	Runs	Wkts
Attewell	44.1	18	76	2
Shacklock	16	6	48	0
Barnes	16	1	61	2
Flowers	32	5	88	3
Mr Dixon	3	0	12	0
Daft	4	1	19	2

Somerset Bowling

	Overs	Mdns	Runs	Wkts	Overs	Mdns	Runs	Wkts
Mr Woods	19	5	44	1				
Tyler	24	8	63	6	14	2	33	9
M. Hedley	5	2	6	2	10	5	20	1
Nichols					3	0	11	0

Umpires: T. Whatmough and T. Veitch.

SOMERSET v YORKSHIRE

Played at Taunton, August 25, 26, 27, 1892

Though Somerset have only for two years been reckoned among the first-class counties, they have done many things to render themselves famous in the cricket world. Among all their achievements, however, nothing has been more extraordinary or has caused such a vast amount of excitement as what was done in this match against Yorkshire, when there was a performance of altogether exceptional merit by H. T. Hewett and L. C. H. Palairet, the two gentlemen establishing a new record for a first-wicket partnership, and putting into the shade that of W. G. Grace and B. B. Cooper, which had stood unbeaten for more than twenty-five years. The opening day's cricket was of a bright and varied character, but it was quite eclipsed by the sensational batting on the Friday. Yorkshire were without the services of Lord Hawke and Hunter, but Somerset were represented by their full strength, the one thing against them being that, owing to the strain he had suffered in the match against Nottinghamshire, Woods was unable to bowl in anything like his best form. Yorkshire were fortunate enough to win the toss, and on an exceedingly good wicket they remained in for the greater part of the time that play was in progress, the batting being wonderfully consistent, and the total in the end reaching 299. Smith and Jackson set the side a capital example, putting on 83 runs in fifty-five minutes for the first wicket, and later on some excellent form was shown by Peel and Wainwright. One of the chief features of the day was the success that attended the slow bowling of Tyler, the Somerset left-hander taking seven wickets at a cose of 111 runs – a capital performance on such a good pitch. Newton, who was suffering from sore hands, relinquished the post of wicketkeeper after luncheon to Palairet, who filled an unaccustomed position in creditable fashion. After spending four hours and a quarter in the field, it would not have been surprising if the home eleven had in the three-quarters of an hour that remained for play lost two or three wickets, but no such disaster befell them, Hewett and Palairet giving an admirable display of batting, and scoring 78 runs without being separated. When he had made 28 Palairet was palpably missed at the wicket, and, as it turned out, this was a blunder for which the Yorkshiremen had to pay a terribly expensive price.

As no rain fell during the night, it was expected that the Somerset men would make a lot of runs, but the extraordinary success which attended their efforts far exceeded all anticipation. As Hewett and Palairet actually scored 346 runs during their partnership for the first wicket, and created a tremendous sensation throughout the cricket world, it is necessary to put on record some details of their wonderful stand, which was remarkable not only for the excellence of the form shown by both men, but for the pace at which runs were obtained from first to last. The two men were always forcing the hitting, but considering the rate at which they scored it was really wonderful how few mistakes there were and how few bad strokes were made. Usually in performances of this character one sees a great many lucky snicks behind the wicket, but no such fault could be urged against the play of Hewett and Palairet. The batsmen sent the ball to the boundary time after time, and treated all the bowlers with scant respect, but most of the hits were clean, hard drives in front of the wicket, the ball going yards away from any fieldsman. The first hundred went up at twenty-five minutes to twelve, the runs having taken sixty-five minutes to obtain, and the next hundred was hit up in exactly an hour. Just previous to this Hewett had completed his hundred, a number which took him exactly two hours. Holding a complete mastery over the bowling, the batsmen did practically as they liked and the spectators vigorously applauded every hit. The 250 went up at five minutes past one, and though the Yorkshire captain tried all sorts of experiments in changing his bowling, his efforts were fruitless, Hewett and Palairet crowning their success by passing the 283, which was the record established by W. G. Grace and B. B. Cooper at The Oval in 1869 for the Gentlemen of the South against the Players of the South. When the 300 went up and the Yorkshire total was headed without loss there was a scene of enthusiasm, which will always live in the memory of those who were fortunate enough to be present. At the luncheon interval the telegraph board presented a peculiar spectacle, the score standing at 301, with no wicket down, Hewett being not out 168, and Palairet not out 123. This being the first time in important cricket that 300 had been put on the board without a wicket down, a special photograph was taken of the figures. The partnership came to an end at ten minutes to three, Hewett being clean bowled in attempting to pull a ball from Peel. The 346 had been obtained in just three hours and a half, Hewett's magnificent innings – which is far and away his best achievement in first-class cricket – including thirty 4s, three 3s, and fifteen 2s. During all his long stay the only mistake that could be urged against him was a chance at forward square leg when he had scored 189. This was the first three-figure score Hewett had ever made for Somerset as a first-class county. Challen was bowled at 358, and at 372 Palairet was brilliantly caught at short slip, low down with the right hand. His innings of 146, which lasted three hours and fifty-five minutes, cannot be praised too highly. He played in a style that was absolutely a model to young cricketers, and his only mistake was the chance at the wicket which he gave on Thursday evening, when he had made 28. Among his hits were a splendid drive out of the ground for 6, nineteen 4s, five 3s, and six 2s. Like Hewett, he was enthusiastically applauded. By this time, of course, all the sting had been taken out of the bowling, but it must be admitted that the Yorkshiremen never relaxed their efforts, which fielding all through the long, and to them weary afternoon, being maintained at a high pitch of excellence. The bowling, of course looked quite harmless, but Peel stuck to his work in a style quite worthy of his reputation. Taking full advantage of the opportunity afforded him, Hedley, played a very free game, and succeeded in scoring 102, his first innings of over a hundred for the county. Of course his performance was overshadowed by the great doings of Hewett and Palairet, but it was nevertheless a fine display of batting. He made his 102 in two hours and a half, without giving a chance, by ten 4s, four 3s, seven 2s, and singles. The fifth hundred went up on the board at ten minutes to five, the runs having been scored in six hours and a half, and ultimately the total reached 592, which was the highest aggregate scored in first-class county cricket during the season. In such a long innings Peel's performance of taking seven wickets for 133 runs was more than creditable. Some idea of the character of Somerset's hitting may be gathered from the fact that in an innings of 592 only 173 overs and three balls were delivered. Stumps were drawn at the close of Somerset's innings, the Yorkshiremen being left with 293 runs required to avert a single innings defeat – a most strange position for an eleven to find themselves in after having played a first innings of just on 300. Before dismissing the day's play, it should be stated that not only is this 346 a record for the first wicket, but with one exception, it is the most productive partnership, in a first-class match, being only inferior to the 398 scored by Shrewsbury and Gunn for the second wicket in the contest between Nottinghamshire and Sussex at the Trent Bridge ground, Nottingham, in May, 1890.

Everyone was looking forward to an interesting day's cricket to finish off the match, and it was, of course, hoped that the Somerset team would crown their brilliant display of batting with a victory; but, unfortunately, the weather played them a very bad turn, rain preventing a ball being bowled. There never seemed much prospect of cricket, but the captains were so reluctant to give up the idea of finishing the match that it was not until half-past four in the afternoon that it was agreed to abandon the contest as a draw. This was, a piece of extremely bad luck for Somerset, as the draw was enormously in their favour.

Yorkshire

Mr E. Smith b Tyler	45
Mr F. S. Jackson run out	55
J. Tunnicliffe lbw b Tyler	30
Mr A. Sellers c Hewett b Tyler	29
G. Ulyett b Hedley	6
R. Peel c Nichols b Tyler	47
E. Wainwright st Palairet b Tyler	43
T. Wardall c Hill b Tyler	14
J. T. Brown not out	12
R. Moorhouse c Woods b Tyler	11
Ellis b Nichols	0
B 7	7
	299

Somerset

Mr L. C. H Palairet c Sellers b Jackson	146
Mr H. T. Hewett b Peel	201
Mr J. B. Challen b Peel	6
Mr W. C. Hedley c Wardall b Peel	102
Mr A. E. Newton c Sellers b Jackson	4
Mr V. T. Hill c Brown b Peel	39
Mr S. M. J. Woods c Wardall b Wainwright	31
Mr G. Fowler not out	32
G. B. Nichols c Sellers b Peel	7
Mr C. J. Robinson st Ellis b Peel	2
E. J. Tyler b Peel	1
B 19, l-b 2	21
	592

Somerset Bowling

	Overs	Mdns	Runs	Wkts
Tyler	50	13	111	7
Nichols	22.4	7	62	1
Mr Hedley	28	6	67	1
Mr Woods	19	7	52	0

Yorkshire Bowling

	Overs	Mdns	Runs	Wkts		Overs	Mdns	Runs	Wkts
Mr Jackson	39	8	148	2	Wardall	9	1	35	0
Peel	59.3	15	133	7	Brown	2	0	8	0
Wainwright	33	6	117	1	Uylett	3	0	12	0
Mr Smith	23	1	97	0	Moorhouse	5	0	21	0

Umpires: C. K. Pullin and J. Lillywhite.

SOMERSET v SUSSEX

Played at Taunton, August 10, 11, 12, 1893

Somerset experienced terribly bad luck in this match, rain causing the game to be drawn when Sussex, with only one wicket to fall, wanted 149 runs to win. The cricket was full of contrasts in the earlier stages, and the best performances were those of Humphreys, who took fifteen wickets for 193 runs, and Mr Challen, who hit up 108 in two hours by seventeen 4s, three 3s, four 2s, and singles. L. C. H. Palairet's 73 was rather a lucky innings, but Murdoch's 62 not out was an excellent display. Sussex were without Bean, who was suffering from an injured hand.

Somerset

Mr W. C. Hedley st Butt b Humphreys	43	b Humphreys	38
Mr L. C. H. Palairet c Hide b Lowe	73	b Humphreys	25
Mr J. B. Challen c Humphreys b Lowe	25	c Marlow b Humphreys	108
Mr H. T. Hewett b Humphreys	9	b Lowe	10
Mr R. C. N. Palairet c and b Humphreys	10	b Humphreys	5
Mr V. T. Hill c and b Humphreys	9	c Hide b Humphreys	11
Mr A. E. Newton st Butt b Humphreys	6	c Lowe b Humphreys	14
Mr S. M. J. Woods b Lowe	2	c Murdoch b Wilson	34
Mr C. E. Dunlop b Humphreys	2	b Humphreys	9
E. J. Tyler not out	1	b Humphreys	1
G. B. Nichols st Butt b Humphreys	1	not out	2
B 1, l-b 1	2	B 2, l-b 1, w 4	7
	183		264

Sussex

F. W. Marlow c Woods b Tyler	44	c L. Palairet b Woods	6
Mr G. L. Wilson c Dunlop b Tyler	19	c R. Palairet b Woods	13
Mr W. L. Murdoch not out	62	c R. Palairet b Woods	13
Mr G. Brann b Tyler	2	not out	29
Mr W. Newham run out	30	b Tyler	23
J. Hide b Woods	0	b Woods	6
F. Guttridge c L. Palariet b Hedley	3	c Dunlop b Hedley	15
H. Butt b Woods	0	b Woods	4
J. Lowe lbw b Tyler	9	b Hedley	0
F. W. Tate b Tyler	7	c Newton b Woods	0
W. Humphreys b Tyler	4	not out	8
B 2	2		
	182		117

Sussex Bowling

	Overs	Mdns	Runs	Wkts	Overs	Mdns	Runs	Wkts
Lowe	22	7	48	3	20	8	44	1
Guttridge	5	0	18	0	5	0	21	0
Tate	4	0	21	0	17	7	40	0
Humphreys	25.4	4	72	7	27.4	3	121	8
Wilson	7	0	22	0	10	2	21	1

Somerset Bowling

	Overs	Mdns	Runs	Wkts	Overs	Mdns	Runs	Wkts
Tyler	32.4	11	55	6	13	6	32	1
Woods	27	5	80	2	27	4	68	6
Hedley	22	7	39	1	8	2	17	2
Nichols	5	3	6	0				

Umpires: R. Carpenter and A. F. Smith.

SOMERSET v LANCASHIRE

Played at Taunton, July 15, 16, 17, 1895

Severe as had been their beating in the previous match, Somerset fared even worse in this engagement, Lancashire defeating them by an innings and 452 runs – one of the most decisive wins on record. The match was made memorable for all time by the wonderful innings of 424 by A. C. MacLaren, who thus surpassed all previous individual scores in first-class matches. The previous highest was, of course, W. G. Grace's 344 in 1876. Only once had MacLaren's score been beaten in any kind of cricket, A. E. Stoddart making 485 for the Hamstead Club in 1886. MacLaren, who went in first and was seventh out at 792, was batting for seven hours and fifty minutes, and only gave two chances, the first at 262. His score comprised one 6, sixty-two 4s, eleven 3s, thirty seven 2s, and sixty three singles. Paul, who played a fine innings of 177, assisted MacLaren to put on 363 runs in three hours and ten minutes for the second wicket – a partnership which has only been surpassed in first-class cricket by the 398 by Shrewsbury and Gunn for Nottinghamshire against Sussex in 1890. Lancashire's innings only lasted eight hours, the total of 801 being the highest ever obtained in a county match.

Lancashire

Mr A. C. MacLaren c Fowler b Gamlin	424
A. Ward c R. Palairet b Tyler	64
A. Paul c Gamlin b L. Palairet	177
A. Hallam c Fowler b L. Palairet	6
Mr C. H. Benton c and b Fowler	43
F. H. Sugg c Wickham b Woods	41
A. Tinsley c Gamlin b Woods	0
G. R. Baker st Wickham b L. Palairet	23
J. Briggs not out	9
C. Smith c Trask b L. Palairet	0
A. Mold c R. Palairet b Gamlin	0
B 9, l-b 4, w 1	14
	801

Somerset

Mr L. C. H. Palairet b Briggs	30	– b Mold	4
Mr G. Fowler c sub b Hallam	39	– c MacLaren b Mold	46
Mr R. C. N. Palairet c Hallam b Mold	2	– st Smith b Briggs	7
Mr H. T. Stanley c Smith b Briggs	8	– c Smith b Mold	12
Mr R. B. Porch run out	18	– c MacLaren b Mold	1
Mr S. M. J. Woods c Smith b Mold	11	– b Briggs	55
Dr J. E. Trask c Ward b Mold	11	– c and b Mold	26
Rev. A. P. Wickham b Mold	3	– not out	0
E. J. Tyler not out	15	– b Briggs	41
Mr E. W. Bartlett b Briggs	4	– c Mold b Briggs	6
Gamlin st Smith b Briggs	0	– hit wkt b Briggs	0
L-b 2	2	L-b 8	8
	143		206

Somerset Bowling

	Overs	Mdns	Runs	Wkts
Tyler	59	5	212	1
Woods	46	5	163	2
L. Palairet	44	10	133	4
Gamlin	26	8	100	2
Fowler	23	5	97	1
R. Palairet	11	3	41	0
Trask	2	0	9	0
Porch	5	3	16	0
Bartlett	6	0	16	0

Lancashire Bowling

	Overs	Mdns	Runs	Wkts	Overs	Mdns	Runs	Wkts
Briggs	37.3	15	59	4	37	17	78	5
Mold	35	15	75	4	33	11	76	5
Hallam	2	1	7	1	8	2	19	0
Baker					5	8	25	0

Umpires: J. Lillywhite and E. Goodyear.

SOMERSET v SUSSEX

Played at Taunton, August 8, 9, 1895

This return match produced some remarkable cricket. On the opening day Lionel Palairet, on a wicket that was soft at starting and subsequently became difficult, played with such skill as to score 91 out of 180 in two hours and three-quarters. Only one difficult chance marred this fine achievement. With a wicket to his liking, Tyler bowled with astonishing success on the Friday. In an hour and fifty minutes Sussex were put out for 97, and following on in a minority of 123 lost seven wickets for 31. Then came some brilliant batting by Fry, who had gone in first. After completing his 50 in seventy minutes he added 40 more in as many minutes. Butt helped him to put on 75 for the ninth wicket, but Somerset, with only 21 to get, won by ten wickets. Though giving three chances, Fry's 90 was a great innings. Tyler's record of fifteen wickets for 95 runs was one of the most brilliant of the season.

Somerset

Mr. L. C. H. Palairet st Butt b Hartley	91		
Mr G. Fowler c Butt b Tate	4		
Mr V. T. Hill b Tate	15	– not out	8
Mr W. N. Roe c Brann b Hartley	25		
Mr R. C. N. Palairet c Butt b Parris	14		
Mr S. M. J. Woods c Tate b Hartley	28		
Mr C. E. Dunlop c Marlow b Fry	1		
G. B. Nichols b Fry	6		
Capt. W. C. Hedley not out	13	– not out	13
Mr A. E. Newton c Butt b Hartley	3		
E. J. Tyler c Butt b Tate	15		
B 5	5	W 1	1
	220		22

Sussex

Mr C. B. Fry c Hill b Nichols	7	– c Hedley b Tyler	90
F. W. Marlow st Newton b Tyler	3	– b Nichols	1
K. S. Ranjitsinhji c L. Palairet b Tyler	1	– st Newton b Tyler	7
Mr W. L. Murdoch st Newton b Tyler	32	– st Newton b Tyler	0
Mr W. Newham c Hill b Tyler	5	– c Nichols b Tyler	5
Mr G. Brann st Newton b Tyler	9	– lbw b Tyler	0
G. Bean b Tyler	30	– c Newton b Nichols	0
F. Parris lbw b Tyler	0	– b Tyler	0
Mr J. C. Hartley c Woods b Tyler	7	– b Tyler	6
H. Butt b Nichols	0	– not out	28
F. W. Tate not out	0	– b Woods	6
L-b 1, n-b 1, w 1	3		
	97		143

Sussex Bowling

	Overs	Mdns	Runs	Wkts	Overs	Mdns	Runs	Wkts
Tate	28.3	6	88	3	3	1	5	0
Parris	17	6	39	1				
Fry	16	4	42	2	2	0	13	0
Hartley	24	7	46	4	1	0	3	0

Somerset Bowling

	Overs	Mdns	Runs	Wkts	Overs	Mdns	Runs	Wkts
Tyler	22.2	4	51	8	27	6	44	7
Woods	6	3	14	0	4.4	0	20	1
Nichols	13	6	25	2	18	5	43	2
Hedley	3	1	4	0	2	0	14	0

Umpires: T. Veitch and J. Wickens.

SOMERSET v SURREY

Played at Taunton, August 22, 23, 24, 1895

In this return match the Somerset men gained a great triumph, outplaying the champions in the later stages of the game, and winning by 53 runs. The match was rendered memorable by Tyler in Surrey's first innings taking all ten wickets, one of the rarest of feats in first-class cricket. A collection made on the ground on his behalf realised over £35. Lionel Palairet, who was in great form during August, played a beautiful innings of 64 on the first day, and Fowler was also seen to advantage on both occasions, his second score of 44 being particularly serviceable. Though several of the Surrey men reached double figures their batting fell considerably below its usual standard, and Richardson's bowling – admirable though it was – could not compensate for the batting failures.

Somerset

Mr L. C. H. Palairet c Marshall b Lockwood	64	– c Marshall b Richardson	26
Mr G. Fowler b Richardson	20	– b Richardson	44
Mr W. N. Roe c W. W. Read b Richardson	0	– b Lohmann	6
Mr C. E. Dunlop c Lockwood b Lohmann	7	– c Lohmann b Richardson	33
Mr W. C. Hedley b Lohmann	1	– lbw b Lohmann	8
Mr S. M. J. Woods c Marshall b Richardson	26	– c Marshall b Richardson	2
W. Smith b Lockwood	7	– b Richardson	1
G. B. Nichols b Richardson	15	– c Lohmann b Richardson	4
Mr A. E. Newton b Richardson	14	– c Richardson b Lohmann	1
Westcott c Marshall b Richardson	0	– not out	2
E. J. Tyler not out	5	– c and b Richardson	13
B 5, l-b 4	9	B 1	1
	168		141

Surrey

R. Abel c Hedley b Tyler	34 – run out	16
M. Read c Hedley b Tyler	21 – c Newton b Woods	15
T. Hayward c Palairet b Tyler	34 – b Hedley	12
W. Brockwell b Tyler	4 – c Palairet b Tyler	27
F. Holland c Dunlop b Tyler	13 – lbw b Tyler	11
Mr W. W. Read b Tyler	8 – run out	1
W. Lockwood not out	11 – c Woods b Tyler	7
Mr H. D. G. Leveson-Gower lbw b Tyler	0 – run out	3
G. Lohmann c and b Tyler	0 – not out	5
C. Marshall c Newton b Tyler	6 – c and b Hedley	10
T. Richardson b Tyler	4 – b Hedley	10
B 4	4	
	139	117

Surrey Bowling

	Overs	Mdns	Runs	Wkts	Overs	Mdns	Runs	Wkts
Lohmann	15	3	46	2	23	6	52	3
Richardson	25.4	4	85	6	29	8	67	7
Lockwood	11	4	28	2	5	1	21	—

Somerset Bowling

	Overs	Mdns	Runs	Wkts	Overs	Mdns	Runs	Wkts
Woods	13	7	44	—	10	1	32	1
Tyler	34.3	15	49	10	32	15	42	3
Nichols	14	4	28	—				
Hedley	3	1	14	—	22.2	6	43	3

Umpires: J. Wickens and W. J. Collishaw.

SOMERSET v SURREY

Played at Taunton, August 27, 28, 1896

After a remarkable match, Somerset gained a brilliant victory by nine wickets. Such a result seemed highly improbable on Thursday evening, as on a slow pitch Somerset were in a serious position – 100 runs behind with eight wickets down. On the second morning, however, Hill and Tyler hit with splendid resolution and fairly pulled the game round, their partnership for the ninth wicket producing 127 runs. It was unfortunate for Surrey, that, owing to an attack of rheumatism, Richardson was unable to bowl on Friday, the loss of his services being severely felt. Under the influence of sunshine, the wicket had become treacherous when Surrey went in a second time. The visitors made a disappointing show, Hedley bowling with marked success. Somerset only required 60 runs to win, and thanks to the forcing tactics of L. Palairet and Hedley, the task was accomplished for the loss of one wicket.

Surrey

R. Abel c Nichols b Tyler	13	– c and b Hedley	3
W. Brockwell c Newton b Hedley	12	– c and b Hedley	6
T. Hayward c Woods b Robson	16	– c Challen b Woods	8
C. Baldwin c Hill b Robson	22	– c Nichols b Hedley	0
E. G. Hayes c and b Woods	0	– not out	29
Mr K. J. Key c Woods b Robson	9	– c Challen b Woods	1
Mr W. W. Read c and b Tyler	54	– b Woods	0
R. Henderson c Hill b Robson	2	– b Hedley	4
G. A. Lohmann c Woods b Robson	1	– c Hill b Robson	10
H. Wood st Newton b Tyler	27	– b Hedley	1
T. Richardson not out	5	– b Hedley	0
B 9, l-b 2	11	B 4, l-b 2, w 1	7
	172		69

Somerset

Mr L. C. H. Palairet b Hayward	20	– b Hayes	36
Capt. W. C. Hedley c Wood b Richardson	1	– not out	24
Mr R. C. N. Palairet b Richardson	10	– not out	0
Mr W. N. Roe b Hayward	3		
G. Robson b Hayward	6		
Mr S. M. J. Woods c Brockwell b Hayward	0		
Mr J. B. Challen b Richardson	2		
Mr V. T. Hill b Hayward	61		
G. B. Nichols b Hayward	6		
E. J. Tyler b Lohmann	66		
Mr A. E. Newton not out	0		
B 5, l-b 2	7		
	182		60

Somerset Bowling

	Overs	Mdns	Runs	Wkts	Overs	Mdns	Runs	Wkts
Tyler	15.3	2	47	3				
Hedley	16	4	39	1	17.2	8	26	6
Robson	28	10	47	5	7	3	17	1
Woods	19	11	26	1	10	3	19	3
Nichols	2	1	2	—				

Surrey Bowling

	Overs	Mdns	Runs	Wkts	Overs	Mdns	Runs	Wkts
Richardson	13	5	23	3				
Hayward	27.3	10	70	6	5	1	17	—
Lohmann	9	—	39	1	6	—	27	—
Abel	3	—	29	—	2	—	12	—
Brockwell	4	1	14	—				
Hayes					1	1	—	1
Read					0.1	—	4	—

Umpires: W. A. Woof and W. Shrewsbury.

SOMERSET v LANCASHIRE

Played at Taunton, June 20, 21, 22, 1898

After gaining a good lead on the first innings. Lancashire set Somerset 540 to get to win. The home eleven made a creditable effort, but were beaten by 260 runs. Some fine batting was witnessed, the chief honours being carried off by Tyldesley on Monday, Ward and Sugg on Tuesday, and Woods on the third afternoon. Ward and Sugg put on 278 runs in three hours, Sugg making 169 of the number. Sugg hit a six and twenty-three 4s. Ward was batting for four hours and fifty minutes. Woods gave a characteristic display, hitting up his 85 out of 114, in less than an hour. At the finish of the match Tyler and Wickham between them scored 65 in thirty-five minutes.

Lancashire

Mr C. R. Hartley c R. Palairet b Fowler	4	c Woods b Tyler	32
A. Ward b Fowler	11	c Wickham b Tyler	135
J. T. Tyldesley c L. Palairet b Tyler	90	c Fowler b Tyler	2
G. R. Baker b Tyler	0	not out	50
W. R. Cuttell c Robson b Tyler	1	c Wickham b Gill	19
F. H. Sugg c Daniell b Tyler	6	lbw b Tyler	169
J. Hallows b Fowler	43	absent ill	0
Mr S. M. Tindall b Tyler	13	b Tyler	21
J. Briggs c Woods b Tyler	19	c and b Tyler	2
A. Mold not out	16	b Woods	1
L. Radcliffe st Wickham b Tyler	4	c R. Palairet b Tyler	15
B 4, l-b 5	9	B 6, l-b 4, n-b 2	12
	216		458

Somerset

Mr L. C. H. Palairet b Baker	59	b Cuttell	1
Mr J. L. Daniell c Mold b Cuttell	4	b Mold	1
Mr R. C. N. Palairet c Radcliffe b Baker	23	b Mold	56
E. Robson b Cuttell	4	c Mold b Briggs	2
Mr H. T. Stanley c Radcliffe b Baker	16	c Radcliffe b Mold	22
Mr S. M. J. Woods b Baker	1	c Baker b Mold	85
G. B. Nichols c Mold b Cuttell	0	c Radcliffe b Mold	0
Mr G. Fowler c Sugg b Briggs	16	b Mold	26
G. Gill b Baker	11	c Tyldesley b Baker	4
E. J. Tyler b Briggs	0	b Cuttell	59
Rev. A. P. Wickham not out	0	not out	18
L-b 1	1	B 1, l-b 4	5
	135		279

Somerset Bowling

	Overs	Mdns	Runs	Wkts	Overs	Mdns	Runs	Wkts
Fowler	27	10	76	3	21	6	57	—
Tyler	34	7	93	7	49.3	8	142	7
Robson	2	2	—	—	13	3	48	—
Gill	8	2	23	—	22	7	84	1
Woods	3	1	15	—	15	3	68	1
L. Palairet	2	2	—	—	15	5	35	—
Nichols					6	2	10	—
R. Palairet					2	1	2	—

Lancashire Bowling

	Overs	Mdns	Runs	Wkts	Overs	Mdns	Runs	Wkts
Cuttell	28	6	56	3	25.4	8	58	2
Briggs	22	10	33	2	27	14	54	1
Hallows	2	—	9	—				
Baker	20.1	8	36	5	12	2	45	1
Mold					27	4	117	6

Umpires: A. Hide and T. Westell.

SOMERSET v HAMPSHIRE

Played at Taunton, July 20, 21, 22, 1899

Hampshire won by an innings and 151 runs, their victory being the more remarkable as on Thursday night they had four wickets down for 63. Friday's cricket brought about an astonishing change in the state of affairs. Soar stayed with Poore while 196 runs were added for the fifth wicket, and then Poore and Wynyard put on 411 runs in four hours and twenty minutes. Poore, who was missed at the wicket when only four and gave two other chances, was batting six hours and fifty minutes and hit forty-five fours. Wynyard was also let off three times, but he had scored nearly 150 before he made his first mistake. His score included two fives and thirty-six fours. Soar hit fifteen 4s. Some capital batting was shown by the Somerset eleven on the first day, but on Saturday the home county only made a moderate effort to draw the match. Hampshire adopted the closure first thing on Saturday and won in brilliant style.

Somerset

Mr H. T. Stanley b Soar	28	– c Steele b Heseltine	9
Mr C. A. Bernard c Robson b Heseltine	42	– c Steele b Baldwin	7
E. Robson b Soar	74	– run out	19
Mr R. C. N. Palairet c Robson b Soar	29	– run out	27
Mr J. Daniell c Robson b Baldwin	0	– c Lee b Baldwin	57
G. B. Nichols b Baldwin	64	– c Lee b Wynyard	13
G. Gill c Steele b Heseltine	8	– c Webb b Wynyard	6
Mr A. E. Newton c Robson b Wynyard	46	– c Steele b Baldwin	33
E. J. Tyler not out	15	– c English b Baldwin	10
Rev. A. P. Wickham b Wynyard	1	– not out	0
B. Cranfield absent	0	– b Wynyard	3
L-b 7, n-b 1	8	B 19, l-b 1, w 2	22
	315		206

Hampshire

Mr C. Robson c and b Tyler	15
V. Barton lbw b Tyler	12
Major R. M. Poore st Wickham b Tyler	304
Mr E. A. English b Gill	0
Mr E. C. Lee c Nichols b Cranfield	11
T. Soar c Cranfield b Gill	95
Capt. E. G. Wynyard c Bernard b Tyler	225
H. Baldwin not out	1
A. Webb not out	2
L-b 3, w 4	7
(7 wkts dec.)	672

Mr C. Heseltine and Mr D. A. Steele did not bat.

Hampshire Bowling

	Overs	Mdns	Runs	Wkts	Overs	Mdns	Runs	Wkts
Heseltine	26	4	80	2	19	2	58	1
Baldwin	39	13	84	2	25.4	13	53	4
Lee	6	1	15	—	3	1	10	—
Steele	7	1	34	—	4	—	14	—
Soar	19	4	74	3	15	5	31	—
Wynyard	11.3	3	20	2	10	3	18	3

Somerset Bowling

	Overs	Mdns	Runs	Wkts
Gill	44	8	127	2
Tyler	63	6	201	4
Cranfield	22	3	113	1
Robson	22	4	75	—
Nichols	21	2	104	—
Stanley	3	—	26	—
Daniell	4	—	19	—

Umpires: G. Burton and H. Pickett.

SOMERSET v SUSSEX

Played at Taunton, August 10, 11, 12, 1899

Some remarkable scoring occurred in this match, 1,293 runs being obtained for 26 wickets, and the game was left drawn. The batting honours were carried off by Phillips, Woods, Hedley and Bernard for Somerset, and Fry, Killick, Ranjitsinhji and Latham for Sussex. On the perfect wicket the bowlers were helpless and there was never any chance of a definite conclusion being arrived at. Bernard and Phillips put on 171 runs while together, Latham and Killick added 126, and in Sussex's second innings Latham and Fry together scored 195. In a match of so many batting successes it was a little curious that Vine should be twice dismissed without scoring. At the close, Sussex with three wickets in hand were 188 runs on.

Somerset

Mr V. T. Hill b Tate	22
Mr C. A. Bernard c Ranjitsinhji b Brann	85
E. Robson c Killick b Brann	28
Mr F. A. Phillips c Ranjitsinhji b Killick	163
Mr S. M. J. Woods c Latham b Ranjitsinhji	109
Mr J. Daniell c Newham b Killick	5
Mr J. B. Challen c Fry b Killick	2
Capt. W. C. Hedley c and b Ranjitsinhji	93
Rev. A. F. Wickham not out	0
G. Gill run out	15
E. J. Tyler c Fry b Tate	5
B 18, l-b 7, w 2	27
	554

Sussex

Mr C. B. Fry lbw b Woods	49	– c Gill b Challen	162
Mr G. Brann c Wickham b Robson	45	– c Robson b Tyler	30
E. H. Killick c Phillips b Gill	117	– c Woods b Tyler	18
Mr P. H. Latham c Tyler b Hedley	25	– st Wickham b Challen	85
Mr A. Collins c Johnson b Tyler	3	– not out	16
K. S. Ranjitsinhji not out	86	– c Woods b Robson	42
J. Vine c Hedley b Tyler	0	– lbw b Challen	0
Mr C. L. A. Smith st Wickham b Woods	3	– c Hill b Challen	13
F. W. Tate c Bernard b Woods	10		
H. R. Butt b Gill	5		
Mr W. Newham absent hurt	0		
B 8, l-b 6, w 3, n-b 1	18	B 8, l-b 6, n-b 1	15
	361		381

Sussex Bowling

	Overs	Mdns	Runs	Wkts
Tate	40	5	134	2
Vine	19	4	67	—
Killick	32	4	128	3
Brann	25	5	78	2
Smith	3	—	9	—
Ranjitsinhji	22.1	5	67	2
Fry	2	—	15	—
Latham	3	—	29	—

Somerset Bowling

	Overs	Mdns	Runs	Wkts	Overs	Mdns	Runs	Wkts
Gill	23.2	6	79	2	14	5	38	—
Tyler	35	5	93	2	21	3	58	2
Hedley	15	5	48	1	10	2	30	—
Hill	9	3	22	—	6	—	28	—
Woods	23	8	34	3	13	2	60	—
Robson	17	6	51	1	23	8	60	1
Bernard	2	—	16	—				
Daniell					4	—	22	—
Challen					16.1	3	43	4
Phillips					6	1	24	—
Wickham					2	—	3	—

Umpires: R. G. Barlow and H. Pickett.

SURREY

SURREY v THE WORLD

Played at The Oval, August 28, 1867

The World

E. M. Grace Esq. st Lockyer b Southerton	115
T. Hearne st Jupp b Lockyer	47
C. Payne c Jupp b Griffith	11
James Lillywhite c Pooley b Southerton	4
H. Charlwood not out	55
T. A. Mantle st Lockyer b Southerton	6
E. Willsher st Lockyer b Southerton	0
G. Bennett c Pooley b Miller	33
F. Silcock not out	0
B 2, l-b 1	3
	(7 wkts) 274

J. Payne and W. G. Grace did not bat.

Surrey

Rev. C. G. Lane, F. Burbidge, Esq., F. P. Miller Esq., Julius Cæsar, G. Griffith, T. Humphrey, H. Jupp, T. Lockyer, Mortlock, E. Pooley, J. Southerton.

Umpires: John Lillywhite and T. Sewell.

SURREY v MCC AND GROUND

Played at The Oval, July 1, 2, 1869

"Mr Grace was the only one in it", critically exclaimed a professional when this match was over; and inasmuch as Mr Grace was first man in and took his bat out for 138 (out of a total of 215); as his innings exceeded the total runs in either innings played by the Surrey Eleven; as his bowling had eight wickets and he caught out another, the critical pro. was about right in his criticism. From one over of Street's, Mr Grace hit a 4 and a 5, and from another over two 4s and a 2, or 19 runs from two overs. His hits comprise two 5s, twelve 4s, five 3s and sixteen 2s. Mr Thornton hit a 4, a 6, and a 3 from the first three balls of an over of Southerton's, and Mr Dale hit a 4 from the fourth ball, making 17 runs hit from that one over. Mr Thornton hit his 26 runs in thirteen minutes. Mr Potter played the good MCC bowling steadily and well; he saw five wickets go whilst making his 27. H. H. Stephenson's 35 included some remarkably well timed, hard, and fine leg-hitting; and in Humphrey's 32 there was some as clean, hard, and brilliant cutting as T. H. ever made. Street hit 22 of his 31 runs in twenty minutes, and Jupp played well for his 14 and 25. MCC won by nine wickets.

MCC and Ground

W. G. Grace Esq. not out	138		
E. G. Sutton Esq. hit wkt b Street	19		
T. Hearne b Southerton	6		
J. W. Dale Esq. b Street	0	– not out	6
Walter Price c Griffith b Street	20		
C. I. Thornton Esq. st Pooley b Street	0	– lbw b Southerton	26
Capt. F. Watson c Pooley b Street	0	– not out	3
W. J. Maitland Esq. c Griffith b Southerton	11		
Biddulph lbw b Southerton	7		
Wootton c Street b Southerton	0		
Marten st Pooley b Southerton	11		
B 1, l-b 1, w 1	3		
	215		35

Surrey

Griffith c Thornton b Grace	4 – b Grace	0
S. R. Akroyd Esq. b Grace	2 – c Biddulph b Price	0
H. H. Stephenson run out	0 – b Hearne	35
Jupp c Wootton b Grace	14 – c Wootton b Price	25
Pooley c Grace b Wootton	19 – c Sutton b Price	3
T. Humphrey b Grace	10 – c Thornton b Wootton	32
C. W. Potter Esq. not out	27 – lbw b Wootton	11
Southerton b Wootton	1 – not out	0
Bristow b Grace	0 – c Watson b Wootton	11
Buckle b Grace	8 – c and b Grace	4
James Street c Dale b Price	31 – b Price	4
B 1, l-b 1	2 B 1, l-b 4	5
	118	130

Surrey Bowling

	Overs	Mdns	Runs	Wkts	Overs	Mdns	Runs	Wkts
Southerton	42	10	90	5	6	2	26	1
Street	33	5	104	5	5	1	9	—
Griffith	9	3	18	—				

MCC Bowling

	Overs	Mdns	Runs	Wkts	Overs	Mdns	Runs	Wkts
Mr Grace	38	14	70	6	31.3	17	48	2
Wootton	34	22	35	2	31	20	30	3
Marten	6	4	5	—				
Price	4	—	6	1	30	19	19	4
Hearne					31	17	28	1

Umpires: Willsher and George Street.

(The MCC professionals bowled (all told) 136 overs (82 maidens) for 125 runs.)

GENTLEMEN OF THE SOUTH v PLAYERS OF THE SOUTH

Played at The Oval, July 15, 16, 17, 1869

In this match 1136 runs were scored – the greatest number of runs ever scored in a cricket match. 1000 runs were made before the match was half played out, 1028 had been made when the match was half played out, and 1136 scored for the loss of only twenty-one wickets – giving an average of 54 runs per wicket.

The first day's cricket ended with seven players' wickets down for 406 runs.

The second day's cricket ended with the score in this form:

The Players (1st innings) 475
The Gentlemen (2 wkts down) 306

The third day's cricket ended with 2164 balls having been bowled in the match, twenty-one wickets gone (only two "bowled"), and 1136 runs scored.

How the wickets fell

Players' 1st innings

1/142 2/160 3/191 4/210 5/222 6/305 7/317 8/454 9/457 10/475

Gentlemen's 1st innings

1/283 2/293 3/345 4/402 5/478 6/481 7/496 8/504 9/508 10/553

Players' 2nd innings – 1 for 66.

Jupp and Pooley were the Players who in both innings scored the runs for the Professionals' first wickets, and Mr W. G. Grace and Mr B. B. Cooper were the Gentlemen who made the 283. The 283 was indeed an extraordinary affair. The innings was commenced at a quarter past two, at a quarter past four the 100 was up, at ten minutes to five the 150 was hoisted, at twenty-five past five the 200 was scored, and at twenty minutes to seven the 283 runs were made and no wicket down. Then Mantle bowled for the first time. From the third ball of his first over he "c and b" Mr Cooper, and from the second ball of his second over he "c and b" Mr Grace. Thus, in six balls, did Mantle get rid of those two great batsmen who had previously successfully defended their wickets and made 283 runs from the bowling of Silcock, Southerton, Lillywhite, Willsher, Bennett and Griffith.

As many as 142 runs were made during Pooley's innings of 78; whilst Jupp was playing his 76 there were 160 runs scored; 185 whilst Mr I. D. Walker was in for his 90; as many as 232 whilst Charlwood was hitting his 155; 283 during Mr Cooper's stay at the wickets, and 293 whilst Mr W. Grace was in.

In "the match" seven 6s, fifteen 5s, fifty-five 4s and fifty 3s were hit, or 487 runs from 127 hits. Mr W. Grace hit two of the 6s, Mr Cooper one, Charlwood one, Pooley one, Mr Yardley one, and Lillywhite the other.

The weather was bright and burning hot, and the wickets throughout the match were in splendid form for batting. Match unfinished.

The Players

Pooley c Richardson b W. Grace	78	– c Richardson b Fryer	50
Jupp c and b V. E. Walker	76	– not out	43
Frank Silcock c Fryer b W. Grace	11	– not out	12
James Lillywhite lbw b G. F. Grace	27		
T. Humphrey c W. Grace b I. D. Walker	40		
Griffith c V. E. Walker b G. F. Grace	7		
H. Charlwood b G. F. Grace	155		
T. A. Mantle st Richardson b I. D. Walker	2		
Willsher not out	57		
Bennett st Richardson b I. D. Walker	3		
Southerton c W. Grace b I. D. Walker	5		
B 3, l-b 9, w 2	14	B 1, l-b 1, w 1	3
	475		108

The Gentlemen

W. G. Grace Esq. c and b Mantle	180	G. F. Grace Esq. c Pooley b Silcock	6
B. B. Cooper Esq. c and b Mantle	101	H. A. Richardson Esq. c and b Bennett	1
B. Pauncefote Esq. b Lillywhite	31	V. E. Walker Esq. not out	21
I. D. Walker Esq. c Willsher b Bennett	90	F. Baker Esq. c Pooley b Southerton	18
W. Yardley Esq. lbw b Southerton	25	B 16, l-b 12, w 1	29
F. E. R. Fryer Esq. c Mantle b Bennett	49		
C. I. Thornton Esq. b Bennett	2		553

The Gentlemen's Bowling

	Overs	Mdns	Runs	Wkts	Overs	Mdns	Runs	Wkts
Mr W. G. Grace	63	19	129	2	15	11	12	—
Mr G. F. Grace	58	19	83	3	13	4	24	—
Mr I. D. Walker	32	12	53	4	8	1	32	—
Mr V. E. Walker	27	6	52	1				
Mr Fryer	25	4	52	—	20	7	37	1
Mr Yardley	14	2	43	—				
Mr Pauncefote	13	2	38	—				
Mr Richardson	1	—	11	—				

The Players' Bowling

	Overs	Mdns	Runs	Wkts
Silcock	65	27	113	1
Lillywhite	57	13	124	1
Bennett	42	12	82	4
Southerton	38	8	91	2
Willsher	24	7	49	—
Mantle	18	8	44	2
Griffith	8	—	21	—

Umpires: Mortlock and George Street.

SURREY v YORKSHIRE

Played at The Oval, August 5, 6, 7, 1869

On Friday rain prevented play until ten minutes to four, and the match was not finished until ten to seven on Saturday ("Time" again floored). Young Ephraim Lockwood and Rowbotham scored 166 before the first Yorkshire wicket (Rowbotham's) fell. These two and Freeman made 318 out of the 353 runs "from the bat"; and of the 345 runs "from the bat" scored by Surrey, 208 were made by Jupp and Humphrey. Jupp went in one wicket down, the score at 20; he was last man out, the score 187. Lockwood was first man in and fifth out, the score 275. Humphrey went in two down with the score 15, and was eighth out at 158. Southerton at one time bowled thirty-five successive balls without a run being made from him, and Freeman bowled thirteen overs for 6 runs; West bowled well and effectively. Yorkshire won by seven wickets. (Lockwood and Rowbotham were each presented with a handsome silver jug.)

Surrey

Pooley c Iddison b Atkinson	25	– b Freeman	6
C. W. Potter Esq. b Freeman	9	– run out	5
Jupp run out	96	– c Stephenson b Freeman	16
S. R. Akroyd Esq. b Atkinson	2	– c Freeman b Iddison	12
T. Humphrey b West	8	– c Iddison b West	88
W. B. Money Esq. b Emmett	19	– b Iddison	18
Griffith b Freeman	3	– b Emmett	1
H. Mayo Esq. b West	11	– c Ullathorne b Iddison	3
Collett c Ullathorne b West	0	– c Atkinson b Freeman	9
James Street run out	5	– b Emmett	9
Southerton not out	0	– not out	0
B 6, l-b 2, n-b 1	9	B 3, l-b 2, w 2, n-b 2	9
	187		176

Yorkshire

E. Lockwood st Pooley b Southerton	103	– not out	34
Rowbotham c Mayo b Griffith	101	– c Mayo b Southerton	18
E. B. Rawlinson b Southerton	9	– lbw b Southerton	6
Roger Iddison b Southerton	0	– not out	11
Freeman c and b Mayo	53	– c Potter b Street	9
E. Stephenson b Southerton	5		
Ullathorne b Southerton	0		
Mr Firth c Pooley b Mayo	4		
Emmett b Southerton	0		
West run out	0		
Atkinson not out	0		
B 6, l-b 2, w 1	9	B 3	3
	284		81

Yorkshire Bowling

	Overs	Mdns	Runs	Wkts	Overs	Mdns	Runs	Wkts
Freeman	37	19	57	2	48	25	64	3
Emmett	37	19	38	1	33	15	36	2
West	22	9	31	3	9	4	11	1
Atkinson	18	7	36	2	15	8	17	—
Iddison	3	—	16	—	31	12	39	3

Surrey Bowling

	Overs	Mdns	Runs	Wkts	Overs	Mdns	Runs	Wkts
Southerton	46	13	88	6	25.2	12	26	2
Griffith	43	17	63	1				
Mr Money	22	3	67	—				
Street	14	4	32	—	20	7	36	1
Mr Mayo	14	8	13	2	5	1	16	—
Humphrey	3	—	12	—				

Umpires: G. Chatterton and Willsher.

SURREY v MIDDLESEX

Played at The Oval, August 16, 17, 18, 1869

A wonderful match this, that Middlesex pluck and Middlesex skill nearly pulled off, although at one time it was quite 100 to 1 against them. Wickets dead but otherwise good. Middlesex (ten men only) was out in one hour and a half for a first innings of 76. Surrey at a quarter-past two commenced an innings that was finished at ten past four the second day for 353 runs; Pooley 88 (out of 124) and Jupp 106 not out the top scorers. Jupp commenced at five to five on the Monday; eight wickets went and 269 runs were made during his stay up to ten past four on the Tuesday. At twenty-five minutes to five Mr R. D. Walker and Mr Rutter commenced the second innings of Middlesex. At twenty minutes to two on Wednesday Mr R. D. Walker was fifth out, the score 247, of which Mr R. D. had made 92. 102 runs were made whilst Messrs. R. D. and I. D. Walker were together. At twenty to four Surrey had 37 to win. Mr R. D. Walker and Howitt bowled. Splendid fielding and some great bowling by Howitt crumpled up the Surrey wickets thus:

1/0 2/15 3/16 4/16 5/16 6/18 7/26 8/31

Then a 4 and a single by Pooley made "the tie", and a bye won the match. Howitt commenced with three maiden overs; a 2 and a single were made from his fourth over, and a 3 from his fifth; the following nine overs were all maidens, with four wickets. Surrey won by two wickets; but although "the victory" is Surrey's, "the honours" of this great up-hill cricket fight belong to Middlesex.

Middlesex

R. D. Walker Esq. c Pooley b Bristow	5	c and b Street	92
T. Hearne c Pooley b Street	14	not out	39
B. Pauncefote Esq. b Bristow	11	b Street	14
I. D. Walker Esq. st Pooley b Street	13	b Humphrey	56
G. Nixon Esq. b Street	2	c Pooley b Bristow	54
V. E. Walker Esq. c Stephenson b Bristow	1	c and b Humphrey	13
E. Rutter Esq. b Bristow	0	run out	7
R. Bissett Esq. b Street	4	c Griffith b Humphrey	9
T. Ratliff Esq. b Bristow	18	c Pooley b Humphrey	2
Howitt not out	4	b Street	7
No. 11 was absent	—	(—Tebbutt Esq.) b Humphrey	3
B 3, l-b 1	4	B 10, l-b 7	17
	76		313

Surrey

Pooley run out	88 – not out	14
C. W. Potter Esq. c substitute b R. D. Walker	12 – run out	0
H. H. Stephenson b I. D. Walker	9 – c Hearne b R. D. Walker	0
Jupp not out	106 – c I. D. Walker b Howitt	14
Mortlock run out	17 – b Howitt	0
T. Humphrey c Pauncefote b Howitt	8 – st Bissett b R. D. Walker	4
S. R. Akroyd Esq. c Howitt b Hearne	11 – b Howitt	1
W. J. Collyer Esq. run out	8 – b Howitt	0
Griffith c Pauncefote b R. D. Walker	42 – c I. D. Walker b R. D. Walker	0
Bristow run out	28 – not out	0
James Street st Bissett b R. D. Walker	7	
B 8, l-b 8, w 1	17 B 3, l-b 1	4
	353	37

Surrey Bowling

	Overs	Mdns	Runs	Wkts	Overs	Mdns	Runs	Wkts
Street	25	7	43	4	50.3	11	114	3
Bristow	24.1	11	29	5	23	6	55	1
Humphrey					26	5	65	5
Stephenson					11	3	21	—
Griffith					11	5	22	—
Mortlock					4	—	19	—

Middlesex Bowling

	Overs	Mdns	Runs	Wkts	Overs	Mdns	Runs	Wkts
Howitt	55	28	79	1	14.1	12	6	4
Mr R. D. Walker	52.2	18	93	3	14	6	27	3
Hearne	50	30	49	1				
Mr Rutter	49	19	81	—				
Mr I. D. Walker	14	4	23	1				
Mr Pauncefote	3	—	11	—				

Umpires: Julius Cæsar and Willsher.

SURREY v KENT

Played at The Oval, August 23, 24, 25, 1869

This good old county match – first played in 1773 – terminated the Surrey season, 1869. Surrey played an amateur colt in Mr L. S. Howell, a very fine hitter and a good field; and Kent played a professional colt in Croxford, who, if the opportunities are allowed him, bids fair to work on to a useful "all round" hand. Willsher was too unwell to play in the after part of the match, but his little bit of bowling in Surrey's first innings was of his old very fine form, as out of the sixteen overs he bowled thirteen were maidens (eleven of the thirteen being successive maidens), and the only runs scored from him were a 4, a 1 and a 2; a marvellously good bit of bowling this, especially so on Surrey wickets. Kent began the batting; the first hit was by Mr Thornton, who drove the ball so far that it pitched outside the seated visitors. Bennett went in fifth wicket down, the score at 38; he was last man out, the score 152. Only 99 had been made when Marten (No. 11) went in; so he and Bennett put 53 runs on for the last wicket. Pooley and Mr Potter made 50 before the first Surrey wicket fell, when the steady young player was had at wicket for 18. Mr Howell began with a clean, hard, and good square-leg hit for 5 from the first ball bowled to him; he also made three 4s and two 3s – 23 in 6 hits. Humphrey's off hitting was as good as ever; he made five 4s in his 34; and in Pooley's 48 there was a 7 (overthrow for 4), a 5, four 4s and three 3s. The innings over left Surrey 72 runs to the good, and with an excellent chance of winning – a chance however that was rapidly hit away by Mr Thornton, who with Payne, at five past five, began the second innings of Kent. Mr Thornton began with a 4 from the first ball bowled; he then drove one from Southerton so high and so very far that it struck (near) "the top" of the black wooden partition of the Racket Court. 6 was run for this truly grand hit – a hit that on Parker's Piece or Woolwich Common would have been 8. Soon after this Mr Thornton drove one from Street for 5, the ball flying far away over the seated visitors' heads; and when time was up that day Kent had scored 87, no wicket down, Payne 28 not out, and Mr Thornton 55 not out. Next day Payne was out with the score at 95, Bennett at 98, and Mr Kelson at 99. Mr Norton and Mr Thornton then made the score 154, when Mr Thornton was bowled for 110 (out of 147 from the bat), his principal hits being six 4s, two 5s and two 6s – or 46 in ten hits. The innings ended at ten minutes past five for 284, or 212 on. There was then but fifty-five minutes left for play, but in that time Surrey made 77 for one wicket. Pooley left with the score at 20, of which runs Pooley had made 19 in ten minutes, by a 5, a 4, three 3s and a single. Mr Howell then went in, and in three-quarters of an hour scored 32, by two 7s, a 4, a 3, two 2s, etc.; one 7 was a square-leg hit for 5, made 7 by an overthrow for 2, but the other 7 was a splendid on drive – a clean, hard, far, well kept down, and truly magnificent hit. Mr Potter again played carefully and well, and this, the last County match on The Oval in '69, ended in "a draw".

Kent

C. I. Thornton Esq. run out	11	– b Griffith	110
Charles Payne c Stephenson b Street	0	– c Pooley b Griffith	29
E. A. White Esq. c Jupp b Southerton	13	– c Pooley b Griffith	32
G. M. Kelson Esq. st Pooley b Southerton	17	– b Griffith	0
W. S. Norton Esq. c Bristow b Southerton	2	– b Southerton	45
L. A. White Esq. b Southerton	0	– b Griffith	17
Bennett b Bristow	50	– b Southerton	0
Henty c Bristow b Southerton	8	– c Jupp b Griffith	6
Willsher c Pooley b Southerton	11	– (unwell) did not bat	0
Croxford c Howell b Southerton	7	– c Southerton b Griffith	23
Marten not out	27	– not out	9
B 4, l-b 2	6	B 3, l-b 8, n-b 2	13
	152		284

Surrey

Pooley c Payne b Croxford	48	– run out	19
C. W. Potter Esq. c Henty b Croxford	18	– not out	23
L. S. Howell Esq. b Marten	35	– not out	32
Jupp st Henty b Bennett	16		
T. Humphrey c Thornton b Bennett	34		
H. H. Stephenson b Marten	16		
James Street c E. White b Bennett	23		
S. R. Akroyd Esq. b Marten	3		
Griffith b Bennett	5		
Bristow b Marten	13		
Southerton not out	4		
B 3, l-b 5, w 1	9	B 2, w 1	3
	224		77

Surrey Bowling

	Overs	Mdns	Runs	Wkts	Overs	Mdns	Runs	Wkts
Southerton	48	21	64	7	54	16	122	2
Street	43	15	72	1	16	4	33	—
Bristow	6.2	3	10	1	17	7	29	—
Griffith	2	2	—	—	50.2	23	71	7
Humphrey					10	4	16	—

Kent Bowling

	Overs	Mdns	Runs	Wkts	Overs	Mdns	Runs	Wkts
Marten	52.3	30	54	4	9	4	19	—
Bennett	42	12	85	4	7	—	23	—
Croxford	28	12	45	2	6	1	17	—
Willsher	16	13	7	—				
Mr Kelson	10	5	24	—	2	—	3	—
Mr Thornton					2	—	12	—

Umpires: Julius Cæsar and Luck.

SURREY v OXFORD UNIVERSITY

Played at The Oval, June 30, July 1, 2, 1870

891 runs (exactly the same number as were scored in the Surrey v Cambridge match) were made in this match, which was finished in exciting form by Mr Pauncefote, whose great hitting on the Saturday evening not only defeated Surrey, but beat time; twenty minutes' late commencement each morning, and inexcusable waste of time at luncheons having much endangered the probability of playing the match out. Mr Nepean kept wicket for the University; and Mr Bray (Westminster School and Cambridge) played for the first time in the County Eleven. Some very fine hitting (on side) by Mr Howell for 49, and a display of first-class batting by Mr Ottaway were the prominent items in the two first innings which closed with the University having a majority of 7 runs only. Mr Hadow and Mr Ottaway increased the score from 2 runs for one wicket, to 121 for two in the "Varsity's" first innings. The second day's cricket (interrupted by rain) closed with Surrey's second innings at 117 for two wickets (R. Humphrey's and Mr Potter's). Mr Howell not out 68. On the Saturday Mr Howell in half an hour increased his score to 96, a display of fine, free, and punishing hitting that included two 5s and nine 4s (two of the 4s and a 2 being hit from one over of Mr Belcher's); Mr Howell's was third wicket down the score at 156. Jupp played with great care, and was out from the ball bounding from his hand on to the wicket; his 18 included an 8 made so by an overthrow for 3. Griffith hit 18 runs in fifteen minutes; he hit two 4s and a 3 from one over of Mr Fortescue's. Mr Bray was absent, and when the nine Surrey wickets were down 218 runs were up, Pooley (hands much damaged) not out 24. At 3.15 the second innings of Oxford commenced, and when Mr Fortescue was splendidly stumped by Pooley, and Mr Ottaway bowled by Griffith (both out with the score 15 only) the cheering for Surrey was indeed loud. At 45 Vince bowled Mr Hadow, who was seventy minutes scoring 19 runs, so true had been the Surrey bowling, and so close and good their fielding. Then at 4.30 Mr Pauncefote commenced his memorable two hour's hitting; with the score 71 he lost Mr Francis, and at 93 Mr Bray (in his second over) clean bowled Mr Tylecote, five wickets then being down. Mr Hill thereupon faced Mr Pauncefote, and these two by great hitting had made

the score 142, when a really splendid bit of fielding by Vince run out Mr Hill. Mr Nepean then went in, and Mr Pauncefote continued his hitting in so fine a form that when at twenty-three minutes past six Mr Nepean was out for three singles the score was 172, or 40 to win. Mr Marriott took the vacated wicket, and in seventeen minutes the required 40 runs were made; at 6.30 the score was 180; Mr Pauncefote then drove one from Griffith past "the tree" for 7, he then hit a 4, a 2 and a 4 from one over of Vince's, and this 10 from one over characteristically finished Mr Pauncefote's great hitting, as immediately after a 4 by Mr Marriott made the required 212 runs, and at twenty to seven Oxford had won by three wickets. Mr Pauncefote's not out 116, hit in two hours and ten minutes by one 7, one 5, twelve 4s, two 3s, fourteen 2s and twenty-two singles. The pavilion seats were crowded and there were about 3000 visitors on the ground; everybody was cheering, so the energetic applause that greeted Mr Pauncefote's return to the pavilion can be readily imagined.

Surrey

R. Humphrey b Francis	24	st Nepean b Hadow	40
L. S. Howell Esq. b Fortescue	49	c Nepean b Fortescue	96
Griffith c Belcher b Fortescue	33	c Pauncefote b Belcher	18
Jupp c Francis b Fortescue	6	b Francis	18
Pooley b Belcher	17	not out	24
T. Humphrey c Pauncefote b Belcher	9	b Francis	5
C. W. Potter Esq. c Belcher b Hill	22	run out	2
James Street c Ottaway b Hadow	16	b Francis	4
E. Bray Esq. b Hill	9	absent	0
Buckle not out	20	hit wkt b Francis	1
Vince c Nepean b Hadow	9	b Francis	2
B 2, l-b 9, w 2	13	B 2, l-b 4, w 2	8
	227		218

Oxford University

A. T. Fortescue Esq. b Street	2	st Pooley b Griffith	11
W. H. Hadow Esq. lbw b T. Humphrey	58	b Vince	19
C. J. Ottaway Esq. c and b Griffith	67	b Griffith	0
B. Pauncefote Esq. b Griffith	7	not out	116
E. F. S. Tylecote Esq. c T. Humphrey b Street	27	b Bray	8
F. H. Hill Esq. c Pooley b T. Humphrey	6	run out	18
C. E. B. Nepean Esq. run out	0	c Griffith b Street	3
C. Marriott Esq. c Street b Vince	0	not out	7
W. Townshend Esq. b Street	8		
C. K. Francis Esq. c Pooley c Griffith	30	b Griffith	23
T. H. Belcher Esq. not out	13		
B 1, l-b 4, w 2	7	B 3, l-b 4	7
	234		212

Oxford University Bowling

	Overs	Mdns	Runs	Wkts	Overs	Mdns	Runs	Wkts
Mr Fortescue	36	19	39	3	17	7	40	1
Mr Francis	30	16	47	1	43.2	19	66	5
Mr Belcher	28	10	43	2	33	15	52	1
Mr Hill	22	6	52	2	8	3	17	—
Mr Hadow	13.1	6	17	2	14	6	22	1
Mr Marriott	5	1	16	—				
Mr Pauncefote					3	—	13	—

Surrey Bowling

	Overs	Mdns	Runs	Wkts	Overs	Mdns	Runs	Wkts
Street	47	13	74	3	29	7	61	1
Griffith	37	11	73	3	51	23	71	3
Vince	18	5	27	1	19.2	4	57	1
T. Humphrey	13	5	22	2	5	2	8	1
Mr Bray	13	3	16	—	5	—	8	1
Buckle	8	5	15	—				

Umpires: Julius Cæsar and Mortlock.

THE GENTLEMEN v THE PLAYERS OF ENGLAND

Played at The Oval, July 14, 15, 16, 1870

The 513 scored by the Gentlemen, and the 215 by Mr W. Grace in this match are respectively the two largest innings yet played in a Gentlemen v Players of England match. The 16,000 visitors that during the three days visited The Oval evidenced the contest had lost none of its old attraction, and that it is still the match of the Surrey season. The Gentlemen played very strong, and scored 711 runs in their two innings. The Players played weak, and left off in a minority of 454 runs with six wickets to fall. An injured leg prevented Charlwood playing; and on the morning of the match the Eleven was incomplete until Price had been sent for from Lord's. To mend matters for the Players Wootton shortly after commencement of play injured his hand and had to cease bowling, he then having shown good form by bowling fourteen overs (ten maidens) for 10 runs and a wicket. The Gentlemen began the batting; they lost Mr Dale with the score at 3, and Mr W. Grace at 11. Mr Money then went in, and by batting of high-class stayed until the score was 147, when he was seventh out, his 70 including a 5 and four 4s. Mr Green hit hard for 39 not out, and the innings ended for 198 runs. In the Players' first innings Daft was one hour and twenty-five minutes at wickets for 27 runs, but Wootton made his 27 in twenty-six minutes, and at 2 o'clock on the second day the innings ended for 148, or 50 runs short of the Gentlemen's first. The Gentlemen were admirably placed and fielded in excellent form; their bowling sums up 115 overs (58 maidens) for 145 runs from the bat. It was twenty-three minutes past two when Mr W. Grace and Mr Dale commenced the Gentlemen's second innings, and in the third over bowled Mr Grace was "nearly" had at short slip by Willsher. After dinner the two batsmen got well set; at 4 o'clock 60 was scored (Mr Grace 40), and at quarter to five the 100 was up (the Players fielding very indifferently); at five minutes past five the score was 130, and it rapidly rose to 160 (when Mr Grace had made his 100). But shortly after Alfred Shaw bowled Mr Dale for 55, and thus at twenty-five minutes to six the first wicket went with the score 164. Mr Ottaway took the vacant wicket and another great stand was made, the Oxonian playing cautiously, and Mr Grace hitting brilliantly, driving one ball from Wootton so grandly past the Racket Court that 8 was run – 7 for the hit and one for an overthrow. The cheers that rang out at this superb hit were almost deafening, and were repeated when the 200 was hoisted on the boards; Mr Grace then having made 131, and so he went on hitting in his finest form till "time" was called, the second day's cricket closing with the Gentlemen having made 264 runs for one wicket – Mr Ottaway not out 26, Mr W. Grace not out 175. On resuming play on Saturday the fourth ball delivered bowled Mr Ottaway for the steady and well played 26 he had made the proceding day. Then with the score at 264 for two wickets Mr Money commenced his great innings. By 12.30 Mr W. Grace and Mr Money had increased the score to 301, Mr Grace then having made his 200 exact, but when he had made 15 more runs he was bowled by Alfred Shaw. First man in at twenty-three minutes to two on the Friday Mr Grace was third man out at five minutes past one on Saturday, the score then at 329. Mr Grace's 215 was made by one 8, three 5s, fourteen 4s, nine 3s, twenty-seven 2s and fifty-five singles. Of brilliant hitting this 215 was a grand display, and for judicious and successful "placing" the ball the innings was a marvel. Being played on The Oval it can be well imagined how vociferously Mr Grace was "ovated". Mr Money then had Mr Pauncefote for a partner, and so ably was the batting fame of the Universities maintained by the two captains, that by ten minutes past two they had increased the score from 329 to 400. Dinner was called at 2.30, with the score at 428 for three wickets. After dinner it was further increased to 445, when Willsher bowled Mr Pauncefote for 48. At 488 Mr Walker was caught out at mid off; before another run was scored Mr Green was wondrously well caught out by T. Humphrey at deep square leg (hit and catch alike very fine); and at 489 Pooley stumped Mr F. Grace. Mr Absolom was next man in, and at twelve minutes to five a rattling, ringing cheer greeted the hoisting the 500 on the board (seven wickets down), Mr Money then having made his 100 exact. The remaining three wickets did but little, as at three minutes past five the innings finished for 513 runs. Mr Money not out 109. The wickets fell as follows:

1/164 2/264 3/329 4/445 5/488 6/488 7/489 8/504 9/511 10/513

So it will be seen each of the first four wickets averaged considerably more than 100 runs per wicket, but the last five wickets added but 25 runs to the score. Mr Money's 109 not out was a superb display on defence and hit, he was greatly cheered; the occupants of the pavilion seats "rose at him" to a man, and gave him such a welcome as will not readily be forgotten. Mr Money went to the wickets with the score 264 for two wickets; his hits included two 5s, five 4s and eight 3s. It was twenty-five minutes past five when Jupp and T. Humphrey began the Players' second innings; they hit 40 runs in twenty-three minutes; at 46 Jupp was out for 20, and at 90 Humphrey was superbly "c and b" by Mr F. Grace for 48, brilliantly hit in one hour, by four 5s, two 4s, one 3, six 2s and five singles. Silcock was third man out, the score 98; his 34 included so many as six 4s, and when Pooley had played the ball hard on to his wicket, time was up and the match drawn, there having been 968 runs made, thirty-four wickets fallen, and 2217 balls bowled in the three days. The wickets were wonders for truthful playing, and appeared to play as well on the third day as on the first.

The Gentlemen

W. G. Grace Esq. c Pooley b Southerton	6	– b Alfred Shaw	215
J. W. Dale Esq. b Wootton	3	– b Alfred Shaw	55
C. J. Ottaway Esq. c Pooley b Silcock	24	– b Wootton	26
W. B. Money Esq. b Alfred Shaw	70	– not out	109
I. D. Walker Esq. c Willsher b Southerton	6	– c Price b Alfred Shaw	26
B. Pauncefote Esq. c Southerton b Wootton	20	– b Willsher	48
G. F. Grace Esq. c and b Silcock	0	– st Pooley b Alfred Shaw	0
C. E. Green Esq. not out	39	– c Humphrey b Alfred Shaw	0
C. Absolom Esq. b Alfred Shaw	0	– c Jupp b Southerton	9
A. Appleby Esq. run out	11	– run out	1
R. Bissett Esq. b Alfred Shaw	16	– c Southerton b Alfred Shaw	2
B 1, l-b 1, w 1	3	B 9, l-b 13	22
	198		513

The Players

T. Humphrey c Absolom b Appleby	7 – c and b G. F. Grace	48
Jupp c and b Absolom	10 – c Bissett b Appleby	20
F. Silcock c Money b G. F. Grace	21 – c Appleby b G. F. Grace	34
Pooley b Absolom	11 – b G. F. Grace	2
Richard Daft c Bissett b Absolom	27 – not out	2
Alfred Shaw st Bissett b G. F. Grace	8	
Griffith c Pauncefote b G. F. Grace	6	
Walter Price b Absolom	4	
Willsher not out	22	
Wootton c Dale b G. F. Grace	27	
Southerton b G. F. Grace	2	
L-b 1, w 2	3	B 2, l-b 1 3
	148	109

The Players' Bowling

	Overs	Mdns	Runs	Wkts	Overs	Mdns	Runs	Wkts
Southerton	46	15	73	2	52	12	134	1
A. Shaw	35.2	16	48	3	62.3	17	99	6
Wootton	22	13	25	2	23	6	52	1
Silcock	21	8	30	2	11	1	32	—
Willsher	11	5	19	—	39	12	76	1
Price					22	10	31	—
Griffith					32	15	41	—
Daft					7	—	26	—

Gentlemen's Bowling

	Overs	Mdns	Runs	Wkts	Overs	Mdns	Runs	Wkts
Mr Absolom	52	25	68	4	16	6	38	—
Mr G. F. Grace	31.2	13	38	5	15.2	11	9	3
Mr Appleby	31	20	37	1	9	5	12	1
Mr Money	1	—	2	—	6	1	19	—
Mr W. Grace					8	1	28	—

Umpires: H. H. Stephenson and Mortlock.

SURREY v GLOUCESTERSHIRE

Played at The Oval, June 3, 4, 1872

This was the first great match of the Surrey season of 1872. It attracted numerous audiences both days; was excitingly contested; and, by a bit of bad Gloucestershire fielding and good luck for Surrey, terminated in favour of the home eleven by one wicket. Gloucestershire was not aided by the celebrated hard hitting, fine pointing Doctor, whose slow potions so physicked the Surrey Eleven in the '71 match; but they introduced a new bowler in Mr Brice, whose fast bowling successfully worked up to the following result:

Overs	Mdns	Runs	Wkts
66.3	37	69	12 – 6 bowled

The Surrey Eleven included Caffyn, "the veteran", and Palmer, Hall and Chester, "the Colts"; and that County team found Mr G. Strachan playing against them, and who not only made the highest score but one on the Gloucestershire side, but had a couple of Surrey's best wickets with his bowling. The Shire-men commenced the batting with Mr W. Grace and Mr Matthews. With the score at 11 Mr Matthews was out, at 16 Mr Gordon was out, and at 26 Southerton clean bowled down the off stump of Mr W. Grace's wicket. Mr F. Grace and Mr Strachan then made the score 86, when a good catch at long-field by Freeman settled Mr F. Grace for a freely hit and rapidly scored 40, the highest score made in the match for the Shire. Mr Strachan stayed until 106 were scored, when Marten bowled him for 35, including a hard drive for 5 from Caffyn. Then a capital catch at slip by Southerton ("who rolled over in securing the catch"), ended Mr Filgate's innings soon after it commenced, and after interruptions from rain, and in a queer light for batting, the innings was closed up for 153 runs. Jupp and Richard Humphrey commenced batting for Surrey to the slow bowling of Mr Miles and fast by Mr Brice; they started hitting so hopefully for the old County that 66 runs were made before they were parted by a catch at wicket that settled R. Humphrey for a very finely hit (in one hour) 42, that included a couple of 4s and one 8, made so by an overthrow for 4. Then down fell four Surrey wickets like wheat before a reaper's sickle – Palmer was cyphered at 67, Thomas Humphrey bowled at 69, and before another run was scored, Jupp was had at wicket for 18, so steadily played as to have occupied over seventy minutes. Freeman was then bowled, and the day's cricket closed with the Surrey score at 75 for five wickets down – Pooley not out 2, Caffyn not out 1.

On Tuesday the remaining five Surrey wickets added but 40 runs to the score, the lot being out for 115. Mr W. Grace and Mr Filgate commenced the Shire's second innings in fine hitting form. They had rapidly made 43 when Mr Filgate was bowled off his leg, and at 49 Southerton (again) enjoyed the pleasure of clean bowling Mr W. G. Grace. Mr Filgate's 16 included a hard drive from Marten for 5 and a 4, and in Mr Grace's 25 there was a splendid drive for 5 also from Marten's bowling. But little was done for Gloucestershire after the collapse of the crack. Mr Gordon was out at 53 for 10, made by a 2 and two 4s; a very clever c and b – low down – by Marten settled Mr Strachan at 63; and before 4 o'clock struck the eleven were out for 71, Marten having at one time bowled ten consecutive maiden overs, taking three wickets in those ten maiden overs. Southerton bowled throughout the innings so successfully that he averaged only a shade beyond one run per over, and five wickets at a cost of only a trifle over 6 runs per wicket. At 4.30 the Surrey men commenced their second innings, having 110 runs to score to win. They started with Freeman and Chester, but lost a wicket (Freeman's) before a run was scored, and another (Hall's) when only 5 had been booked. Chester had made 10 when a fine catch at slip settled him; thereupon Jupp and young Humphrey were together, and by capital cricket they increased the score to 74, when Humphrey was had at slip for another 42, an innings loudly and worthily applauded, for without it Surrey would have had to stand out in the cold of defeat in this their first County match of the season. Pooley was stumped at 78 and Jupp c and b at 80. Caffyn and Thos. Humphrey made it 86, when in one over Mr Brice bowled both Caffyn and Palmer. There were then two wickets to fall and 24 runs to win, when Marten went to T. Humphrey's aid, and amid much excitement, those two increased the score to 108, or two to win, when the fast bowler bowled Humphrey; thereupon Southerton went in – the score one to tie, one wicket to fall – and the hands of old Kennington Church clock pointing to five minutes to "time". Mr W. Grace then bowled to Marten, who played the ball to mid-on, thereby giving an easy chance to Mr Miles, who, however, dropped it, and thus victory – which had been literally in the grasp of Gloucestershire (whose eleven should have won by one run) – was immediately after secured by Surrey, whose men won the match by one wicket. The excitement at this close termination, both as to time and otherwise, was one of those things beyond description.

Gloucestershire

W. G. Grace Esq. b Southerton	13	– b Southerton	25
T. G. Matthews Esq. st Pooley b Southerton	5	– c Marten b Southerton	0
C. Gordon Esq. b Marten	2	– c T. Humphrey b Caffyn	10
G. F. Grace Esq. c Freeman b Caffyn	40	– c T. Humphrey b Marten	7
G. Strachan Esq. b Marten	35	– c and b Marten	4
J. A. Bush Esq. b Southerton	13	– c Pooley b Southerton	0
C. R. Filgate Esq. c Southerton b Marten	4	– b Caffyn	16
E. A. Brice Esq. b Marten	13	– c Caffyn b Southerton	0
R. F. Miles Esq. b Southerton	10	– b Marten	1
E. K. Browne Esq. st Pooley b Southerton	7	– not out	3
H. S. Cobden Esq. not out	5	– c Jupp b Southerton	2
B 4, l-b 1, w 1	6	B 1, l-b 2	3
	153		71

Surrey

H. Jupp c Bush b Brice	18	– c and b Brice	19
Richard Humphrey c Bush b Brice	42	– c Filgate b Strachan	42
T. Palmer c and b W. Grace	0	– b Brice	0
Thomas Humphrey b W. Grace	2	– b Brice	8
Pooley c Matthews b Brice	8	– st Bush b Strachan	3
Freeman b Brice	1	– b Brice	0
W. Caffyn st Bush b W. Grace	5	– b Brice	8
A. Chester c Matthews b W. Grace	4	– c Filgate b Brice	10
C. Hall not out	9	– c Browne b W. Grace	3
W. Marten b Brice	9	– not out	9
Southerton c Matthews b Brice	6	– not out	0
B 3, l-b 3, w 5	11	B 4, l-b 1, w 1, n-b 2	8
	115		110

Surrey Bowling

	Overs	Mdns	Runs	Wkts	Overs	Mdns	Runs	Wkts
Southerton	42.2	13	71	5	28.3	15	32	5
Marten	35	12	55	4	17	12	21	3
Caffyn	7	—	21	1	11	4	15	2

Gloucestershire Bowling

	Overs	Mdns	Runs	Wkts	Overs	Mdns	Runs	Wkts
Mr W. Grace	33	14	37	4	23	9	38	1
Mr Brice	30.2	18	35	6	36.1	19	34	6
Mr F. Grace	8	1	17	—	10	4	13	—
Mr Miles	6	2	15	5				
Mr Strachan					13	7	17	2

Umpires: Griffith and Pullen.

SURREY v NOTTINGHAMSHIRE

Played at The Oval, August 12, 13, 14, 1872

They had three days of fine weather for this match, wherein illness prevented Alfred Shaw playing for Nottinghamshire, and a Sussex match being on, lost Surrey the aid of Southerton. It was a curiously fluctuating match, unquestionably lost for Nottinghamshire by bad fielding, and all but won for Surrey by good fielding. Nottinghamshire won choice of in or out, and at 12.30 they commenced the batting. When the score was at 19, a well judged catch at square leg by Mr Chenery settled Oscroft, and at 21, a capital bit of fielding between Street (at short leg) and Pooley ran out Bignall; then it was Daft went to the wickets, and for three and a half hours played cautious, scientific, and successful cricket, such as but few other batsmen can play. The bowling and fielding of Surrey just then was excellent; slowly had the score risen to 31, when a clever c and b (right hand low down) by Mr Strachan settled Wyld, and at 33, Street, with successive balls, bowled Selby and Reynolds, half the Nottinghamshire wickets being then down for 33 runs, made from 31 overs; Barnes was stumped at 42, and when Seaton had been bowled by Street, the score stood at 55 for seven wickets, Daft having then been sixty-nine minutes at wickets for 12 runs. Then Martin McIntyre went in, and at luncheon call – 2.30 – the Nottinghamshire score was at 80 for seven wickets, Daft not out 23, McIntyre not out 14. On resuming play at 3.20, runs came at a greatly increased pace, McIntyre hit freely and scored fast, and the bowling underwent various changes. Mr Boult succeeded Street, Mr Bray relieved Mr Strachan, Street went on again v Mr Boult, Mr Chenery v Street, Mr Strachan v Mr Bray, and subsequently Mr Bray v Mr Strachan, and from the second ball of this last change Daft was stumped, the score having been increased from 80 to 202 since the previous wicket fell. Then Morley was cleverly caught out at point, and J. C. S. bowled, and so the innings ended for 209 runs – 207 from the bat, 186 of which had been made by Daft and Martin McIntyre.

Daft went in at seven minutes to one, the score at 28 for two wickets; at ten minutes past five, he was eighth out, the score 202; when he had been fifteen minutes at wickets he had scored only four runs, when he had been sixty-nine minutes there he had made but 12 runs, and when he had been at wickets ninety-seven minutes he had scored 23 only; his 78 included four 4s and thirty-three singles.

McIntyre went to the wickets at 1.50, the score at 55 for seven wickets; when the innings was over at 5.25 for 209 runs, Mc. was the not out man, having made 88 by one 5 (drive from Street), seven 4s, etc., etc.

The Surrey innings was brief and curious; it was commenced at a quarter to six by Richard Humphrey and Jupp, to the bowling of J. C. Shaw and McIntyre. The left hand bowler led off with 5 successive maiden overs, and McIntyre started by bowling both Jupp and Thos. Humphrey in his second over before a run had been scored; in fact Mc. was so irresistible with the ball that evening that when time was called at 6.30 there were five Surrey wickets down and only 17 runs scored, McIntyre having then bowled eleven overs (eight maidens) for 4 runs (singles) and five wickets all bowled. The innings was resumed next morning at five minutes past twelve, and ended at five minutes to one for 60 runs. Richard Humphrey – first man in – being the not out man for 30, a truly fine innings that included masterly defence, and three hits for 4 each. In that innings the two Nottinghamshire men bowled 50 overs (less one ball) for 52 runs from the bat, McIntyre having nine of the ten wickets, seven of the nine being bowled. But although not fortunate in obtaining wickets, J. C. Shaw's bowling was exceedingly fine. On the Monday evening his first five overs were maidens, and on the Tuesday he led off with nine successive maiden overs.

Surrey followed on with Richard Humphrey and Mr B. Akroyd to the same bowlers as in their first innings, 21 runs having been made from the first twenty overs bowled; Morley and Seaton took a turn at bowling, the result being Mr Akroyd was lbw at 33, and Jupp run out at 35. Richard Humphrey made a cut for 4 and another for 5 from one over of Seaton's, and the score had been rapidly hit to 107, when Mr Chenery was clean bowled for 38, and when only two more runs had been made, Humphrey hit the ball on and was out for 52, an innings that included a 5 and four 4s, the 5 and three of the 4s being capital cuts. Pooley was bowled at 139, but T. Humphrey and Mr Strachan put 50 more runs on ere the next wicket fell by Mr Strachan going for 28, his principal hits being a couple of 4s and a splendid drive to the Racket Court for 5. Mr Cumberlege left with the score at 199, and T. Humphrey at 200, his 35 included three 4s, two of them fine drivers from one over of Morley's, the good cricket played by T. H. eliciting hearty applause from the Surrey people. The second day's play closed with the Surrey score at 208 for eight wickets. On the third day, Mr Boult and Mr Bray rapidly and effectively increased the score; both hit well, especially Mr Boult, but the fielding of some of the Nottinghamshire men was loose and ineffective, the wicket keeper missing several chances of running out, and so the two amateurs rapidly ran up the score to 292, when Daft bowled Mr Bray. The rise from 292 to 315 was quickly effected by Mr Boult and Street; then an easy catch at point settled Mr Boult for 65, a freely hit innings that included nine 3s and an exceedingly fine off drive for 5 from Shaw. At a quarter to four, Nottinghamshire's second innings was started by Oscroft and Bignall to the bowling of Street and Mr Strachan. Street was in rare form; he started with six successive maiden overs; with the score at 23 he bowled Bignall, and at 51, he bowled Wyld, there then having been fifty overs bowled. McIntyre and Oscroft brought the score to 79 and Mr Bray on to bowl, and from the second ball bowled by that gentleman Oscroft was stumped for 40, a capital bit of batting. Daft had made three singles only when he was caught out at mid-on by Buckle (sub.), the fourth wicket going at 87, and at 95, a well judged catch at deep long on by Mr Boult settled McIntyre's innings for 27. At 98 three wickets went down, the middle stump of Barnes' wicket being bowled by Street; Reynolds being grandly run out by Pooley, and Seaton clean bowled by Street; Reynolds' run out was a superb bit of fielding – Pooley took the ball leg side and swept down the wicket in one action. Soon after this, time was up and the match ended "a draw". Mr B. Akroyd fielded pluckily and splendidly at point, and so did Mr Chenery at leg and cover point, in fact the Surrey fielding in that second innings of Nottinghamshire was quite up to the old Surrey form.

Nottinghamshire

Bignall run out	8	– b Street	12
Wm. Oscroft c Chenery b Strachan	12	– st Pooley b Bray	40
Wyld c and b Strachan	7	– b Street	8
Richard Daft st Pooley b Bray	78	– c Buckle (for Cumberlege) b Bray	3
J. Selby b Street	1	– not out	7
H. Reynolds b Street	0	– run out	0
Thos. Barnes st Pooley b Strachan	7	– b Street	1
John Seaton b Street	6	– b Street	0
Martin McIntyre not out	88	– c Boult b Street	27
F. Morley c Akroyd b Street	0	– not out	6
J. C. Shaw b Street	0		
B 1, l-b 1	2	B 1, l-b 2	3
	209		107

Surrey

Richard Humphrey not out	30	– b J. C. Shaw	52
Jupp c McIntyre	0	– run out	0
Thomas Humphrey b McIntyre	0	– c Oscroft b McIntyre	35
C. J. Chenery Esq. b McIntyre	1	– b Morley	38
Pooley c and b McIntyre	0	– b McIntyre	17
G. Strachan Esq. b McIntyre	4	– c J. C. Shaw b McIntyre	28
B. N. Akroyd Esq. b J. C. Shaw	2	– lbw b Seaton	13
F. H. Boult Esq. b McIntyre	2	– c Oscroft b J. C. Shaw	65
C. F. Cumberlege Esq. b McIntyre	3	– c J. C. Shaw b Daft	1
E. Bray Esq. b McIntyre	6	– b Daft	32
James Street c Seaton b McIntyre	4	– not out	14
B 8	8	B 8, l-b 11, n-b 1	20
	60		315

Surrey Bowling

	Overs	Mdns	Runs	Wkts	Overs	Mdns	Runs	Wkts
Street	50	27	92	5	46	24	45	5
Mr Bray	14	4	28	1	15	8	13	2
Mr Strachan	52	19	62	3	31	13	46	—
Mr Boult	6	—	17	—				
Mr Chenery	4	2	8	—				

Nottinghamshire Bowling

	Overs	Mdns	Runs	Wkts	Overs	Mdns	Runs	Wkts
J. C. Shaw	25	19	19	1	63.2	30	91	2
McIntyre	24.3	10	33	9	65	35	66	3
Morley					39	19	63	1
Daft					19	4	41	2
Oscroft					10	2	22	—
Scaton					5	2	12	1

Umpires: Thos Hearne sen. and W. Luck.

(Martin McIntyre's 88 not out and 27, with the bat; and 90 overs (less one ball) for 99 runs and twelve wickets – eight bowled – with the ball, was indeed a great performance.)

SURREY IN 1873

Patron – HRH The Prince of Wales

President – Lieut-Col F. Marshall

Vice-President – The Hon. F. Ponsonby (from 1844)

Treasurer – H. Mortimer Esq.

Secretary – C. W. Alcock Esq.

Committee – F. Burbidge, J. Cressingham, E. Garland, F. Gale, W. Holt, J. Jackson, T. Lambert, C. J. Martyn, W. T. Morrison, F. P. Miller, A. Roberts, H. T. Smith, H. Scott, J. F. Verrall, John Walker, V. E. Walker, E. Winterflood, Mark Cattley, W. Burrup, G. Strachan, R. James, J. Ansted, Esqrs., and Dr E. B. Jones.

Professional Bowlers engaged on The Oval in 1873 – Southerton (Superintendent), Crowden, Freeman, Higgs, and Roberts.

Size of Ground – (playing portion) $10\frac{3}{4}$ acres

Ground keeper – Geo. Street

The annual general meeting of the Surrey County Club was held on Thursday the 1st of May, 1873, at the Bridge House Hotel. The whole of the officers of 1872 were re-elected. The balance-sheet, read by the Secretary, told that despite unfavourable weather in 1872, and that £250 had been expended in improvements, and another £250 paid for the first time as Secretary's salary, there was a balance in hand of £380. The takings at the gate in 1872 (including admission to the football matches) amounted to £1032 19s; and the ground expenses (including £26 15s as gratuities to players) amounted to £729 12s 1d. The committee were empowered to expend £100 in the erection of a Committee room, and £50 in providing additional seats for the public. The annual meeting over, The Anniversary Dinner was held the same evening, the President, Col F. Marshall, presided and the Secretary was Vice-Chairman. The attendance was "limited", but among those present were three of the County's members: – Sir R. Baggallay, W. Peek, Esq., and Jas Watney, Esq., each of whom warmly advocated support to the County Cricket Club, Mr

Peek winning a hearty cheer by his assurance that "the County members had every desire to make their appearance at the dinner of the Surrey Club an annual event". In acknowledging the toast of "The Army, The Navy, and The Reserve Forces", Col Marshall said, "from his experience in Her Majesty's service, he had no hesitation in stating that men who excelled in sports – especially Cricketers – always proved to be the best soldiers". The toast of the evening, "Prosperity to the Surrey Club", was enthusiastically received; Mr F. Burbidge, in responding, contended – as he had frequently before contended – "that it was from the gentlemen players that Surrey must in a great measure look for its regeneration; Surrey had in its ranks some of the best amateurs and finest professionals in England, and he anticipated the time was near at hand when Surrey would be able to meet England as in the days of old".

SURREY CLUB AND GROUND v MCC AND GROUND

Played at The Oval, July 31 and August 1, 1873

Two mis-catches when the match was at a tie, and the last of the MCC men had gone in, enabled MCC to win this match by one wicket. The first day's cricket ended with each side having played an innings, MCC having 99 runs in hand. The prominent items of that day's play were: a top-class innings played by Jupp; "an awful break-back" settling Mr G. F. Grace; "a good ball" bowling Mr Kelson; a score made in promising form by Mr Cole; nine runs made from the first over bowled by Southerton; fourteen runs from one over bowled by Mr G. F. Grace, and a free and hard hit 52, quickly rattled up by Mr Tomkinson.

The second day's cricket was a remarkable one. A fierce thunder and rain-storm preceded the play. Surrey's second innings totalled 153 runs, a finely hit and rapidly scored 60 by Mr F. Grace materially working up that total. Then, at 5.20, the MCC men commenced their apparently easy task of scoring 55 runs to win. They started with Mr Duncan and Rylott, who made 17 runs, when Rylott was run out; at 26 Mr F. Grace in one over bowled Mr Duncan and Capt. Young; at 39 Mr Udal, Mr Herbert, Alfred Shaw, and Mr Tomkinson were all four settled; at 41 Mr Anstruther was had at mid-off, and at 46 Biddulph was bowled; so there were then nine wickets down, and 9 runs required to win. Mr W. G. Grace (who did not go in until the sixth wicket had fallen) was then faced by last man Clayton; they added 8 runs, and had thereby brought the match to a tie, when in one over of Southerton's Clayton was missed (a hot chance) at mid-off by Mr Howell, and from the following ball he was missed at long field by Mr F. Grace, so, as the required run was made from that last hit, MCC won by one wicket, just escaping "tieing the tie match" played in 1868 on The Oval by the same clubs.

Surrey Club and Ground

H. Jupp b Alfred Shaw	29	– lbw b Alfred Shaw	11
Richard Humphrey b Alfred Shaw	6	– c Tomkinson b Rylott	26
A. Freeman b Rylott	16	– c Udal b Rylott	4
G. F. Grace Esq. b Rylott	4	– st Biddulph b W. Grace	60
J. Swann c and b Alfred Shaw	0	– c and b Alfred Shaw	7
L. S. Howell Esq. b Rylott	0	– st Biddulph b Alfred Shaw	5
T. G. Cole Esq. c Duncan b Alfred Shaw	20	– b Alfred Shaw	0
G. M. Kelson Esq. b Rylott	1	– c Tomkinson b W. Grace	2
A. Chandler Esq. c Biddulph b Alfred Shaw	23	– not out	27
Southerton run out	4	– c Tomkinson b W. Grace	0
James Street not out	0	– st Biddulph b Alfred Shaw	8
L-b 2	2	B 1, l-b 2	3
	105		153

MCC and Ground

W. G. Grace Esq. c Swann b Southerton	24 – not out	5
A. S. Duncan Esq. b Street	19 – b F. Grace	6
A. W. Anstruther Esq. run out	21 – c Humphrey b F. Grace	0
A. W. Herbert Esq. b Southerton	9 – c Street b F. Grace	23
J. S. Udal Esq. c Jupp b Southerton	16 – c Howell b Southerton	1
R. E. Tomkinson Esq. c Swann b Southerton	52 – c Chandler b Southerton	0
Capt. Young c Street b Southerton	11 – b F. Grace	0
Alfred Shaw b Freeman	16 – c Kelson b F. Grace	0
Rylott b Freeman	21 – run out	7
R. Clayton c Humphrey b Freeman	10 – not out	6
Biddulph not out	0 – b Southerton	4
B 3, l-b 2	5 B 2, w 1	3
	204	55

MCC Bowling

	Overs	Mdns	Runs	Wkts	Overs	Mdns	Runs	Wkts
A. Shaw	33	14	61	5	42.2	17	74	5
Rylott	25	11	37	4	25	10	52	2
Mr W. Grace	7	3	5	—	17	8	24	3

Surrey Bowling

	Overs	Mdns	Runs	Wkts	Overs	Mdns	Runs	Wkts
Southerton	50	16	98	5	19	6	28	3
Street	26	14	29	1				
Mr F. Grace	16	7	44	—	19	8	24	5
Mr Kelson	13	8	8	—				
Freeman	7	3	20	3				

Umpires: Thomas Humphrey and Mortlock.

THE TIE MATCH

SURREY v MIDDLESEX

Played at The Oval, August 10, 11, 12, 1876

Notwithstanding the Middlesex men were 77 runs wrong on the first innings, they succeeded in bringing this match of 920 runs to a tie, Mr R. D. Walker's 104 and two capital catches by William Lambert being the main reasons why of that glorious result, although an easy catch at cover-point by Burghes actually made the tie, at a time, too, when – according to *The Sportsman* – "it was imagined that Surrey had lost by one run".

On "excellent wickets" and in enjoyably fine weather, Middlesex commenced the batting at 12.15. Burghes and Mr Turner stayed and increased the score from 54 for six wickets to 113 for seven, when Mr Turner was run out for 30. Burghes stayed until 123 up, when he was finely had at wicket by Pooley for 44, in scoring which runs Burghes made a great drive for 5 from Street. The innings ended at 3.50 for 138 runs, Pooley having caught out four of the ten wickets.

At 4.10 Jupp and Mr Avory (fresh hand) started Surrey's scoring; but at 18 both Jupp and his successor Elliott, were out; and when 53 runs had been scored, Mr Avory was out for 31, a 5, a 4, and four 3s proving he could hit a bit. When the score was at 105 for six wickets Barratt went to Mr Read's aid. They hit freely, Barratt making a 5 and Mr Read a 6 from successive balls of an over by Flanagan; and when "time" came, the Surrey score was at 158 for six wickets, Mr Read not out 68, Barratt not out 31.

Friday was bright and very hot. In one hour the Surrey innings was over. Barratt went at 160, but Mr Read stayed until 214 was booked, when Mr Henderson bowled him; then Mr V. E. Walker summarily settled Street, and the innings was up for 215, Southerton not out 24. Mr Read went to wickets with the score at 18 for two down; he was ninth man out, 196 runs having been made while he was playing his patient and excellent 94, which included a superb drive for 6 from Flanagan, five 4s, six 3s, eleven 2s and twenty-eight singles.

Middlesex's second was commenced at twenty to two by Mr I. D. Walker and Mr A. J. Webbe. When 9 runs only had been scored, Mr Webbe was out; then it was Mr R. D. Walker commenced his three-figure innings. The two brothers had made the score 58 when the little lad from Mitcham – Jones – made a capital one-hand catch at slip, and thereby ended Mr I. D. Walker's innings for 25. "Mr R. D." and Mr Buller then laid on to the Surrey bowling so effectively that 25 runs were made from three overs bowled by Barratt, and in all 64 runs from twenty-two overs, when Swann caught out Mr Buller for 32, the score at 122 for three wickets. Another stand was then made by "Mr R. D." and Mr H. R. Webbe. They made 25 runs from four overs bowled by Mr Read, and defied all bowling until the score was hit (from 122) to 208; then Southerton bowled (with successive balls) Mr H. R. Webbe and Burghes. Mr Webbe's 52, included a fine cut from Street for 5, and two 4s. Lambert made no sign; but "Mr R. D." and Mr Turner made the score 263, and then a catch at long-field by Jupp ended Mr R. D. Walker's score for 104. Mr Walker commenced with the score at 9 for one man out; he was seventh out, the score at 263, his 104 being made by two 5s, five 4s, six 3s, twelve 2s, and thirty-two singles. Mr Henderson was thrown out by Pooley, and the day's play ended with Middlesex having scored 271 runs for eight wickets, Mr M. Turner not out 27.

The third day – "the tie day" – was of brilliant weather, and a large company looked on and enjoyed the end of this remarkable match. Mr Turner and Mr V. E. Walker resumed the innings at 12.15. The score was raised to 304, when a catch at wicket ended Mr V. E. Walker's inning for 23 runs. Eighteen more had been made when Mr Lindsay, from cover-point, splendidly threw out Flanagan for 14; and so the innings ended, Mr M. Turner not out 41.

Wanting 246 to win, Jupp and Mr Avory commenced Surrey's second at twenty-five to two. They lunched at 2 o'clock, when 58 runs had been scored and no wicket down. On resuming, they made the figures 74, when Mr Avory was c and b for 42. Elliott was again unfortunate; but Jupp and Mr Read made the score 119, when Flanagan bowled Jupp for 43. At 128 Pooley was lbw, and at 133 Flanagan bowled Mr Lindsay. Then Barratt went in and "all but" won the match for Surrey. He lost Mr Read at 145, and seven men being then out, the match loomed promisingly for Middlesex; but Jones stayed, and both men hit, the score getting to 191, when Lambert, at long-on, caught out Jones, leaving two wickets to fall and 55 runs to score to win. Southerton went in; he and Barratt got well hold; the bowling was changed, but runs came until only six were wanted to win. Then William Lambert, at square-leg, caught out Southerton, and the last man – Street – went to Barratt's aid, the excitement extensive. Barrat made a single from R. D. Walker, and a 3 from Mr Henderson. Street backed that up with a single, and the match looked safe for Surrey; but then Barratt was easily caught at cover-point; and so, at ten minutes to six, the innings ended for 245 – A Tie.

Middlesex

Batsman	1st innings	2nd innings	
A. J. Webbe Esq. b Southerton	16	c Read b Street	6
I. D. Walker Esq. c E. Pooley b Southerton	4	c Jones b Southerton	25
R. D. Walker Esq. c Jupp b Southerton	0	c Jupp b Street	104
C. F. Buller Esq. b Street	6	c Swann b Jones	32
H. R. Webbe Esq. c E. Pooley b Street	7	b Southerton	52
A. Burghes c E. Pooley b Southerton	44	b Southerton	0
William Lambert lbw b Street	8	b Street	0
M. Turner Esq. run out	30	not out	41
V. E. Walker Esq. c E. Pooley b Southerton	1	c E. Pooley b Jones	23
R. Henderson Esq. c Swann b Street	18	run out	6
Flanagan not out	2	run out	14
B 2	2	B 7, l-b 12	19
	138		322

Surrey

Batsman	1st innings	2nd innings	
H. Jupp c I. D. Walker b Henderson	4	b Flanagan	43
H. K. Avory Esq. c A. J. Webbe b V. E. Walker	31	c and b R. D. Walker	42
George Elliott b Henderson	0	run out	0
W. W. Read Esq. b Henderson	94	st Turner b Henderson	41
J. Swann b Henderson	1	b Flanagan	1
E. Pooley c Turner b V. E. Walker	8	lbw b Henderson	3
W. Lindsay Esq. b Henderson	10	b Flanagan	5
E. Barratt c sub. b Henderson	31	c Burghes b Henderson	67
G. Jones b R. D. Walker	0	c Lambert b V. E. Walker	16
Southerton not out	24	c Lambert b R. D. Walker	12
James Street c and b V. E. Walker	0	not out	1
B 9, l-b 3	13	B 6, l-b 8	14
	215		245

Surrey Bowling

	Overs	Mdns	Runs	Wkts	Overs	Mdns	Runs	Wkts
Southerton	39	21	38	5	65.3	29	88	3
Street	38.2	10	69	4	52	14	104	3
Jones	10	5	9	—	25	6	47	2
Barratt	10	4	20	—	3	—	25	—
Elliott					11	5	14	—
Mr Read					4	1	25	—

Middlesex Bowling

	Overs	Mdns	Runs	Wkts	Overs	Mdns	Runs	Wkts
Mr Henderson	46	18	66	6	40	15	78	3
Mr V. E. Walker	33	7	66	3	12	1	51	1
Mr R. D. Walker	14	3	37	1	18	2	41	2
Flanagan	7	—	34	—	23	7	46	3
Burghes					5	2	15	—

Umpires: Thomas Humphrey and George Howitt.

Surrey cricket history is comparatively rich in tie matches, as in 1831 the East Surrey Club played "a tie" at Chislehurst against the West Kent Club. In 1834 the East Surrey Club played a "tie" at Camberwell v MCC and Ground. In 1847 Surrey played "a tie" on the Oval against Kent, the eighth, ninth, and tenth wickets all going down at "the tie." In 1868 Surrey County played "a tie" on The Oval against MCC and Ground, a catch by a Surrey man, W. Tanner, fielding as sub. for Mr Buller, settling poor little Tom Sewell ending that match in "a tie". In 1868, also, Surrey played "a tie" on The Oval v Middlesex when the last Surrey man in, a much pitied colt, walked up to the wicket to be forthwith shot down by old Tom Hearne, who bowled the poor colt "all over his wicket", and so brought that match to "a tie"; and now, in 1876, the above, another Surrey v Middlesex match on The Oval, was brought to "a tie".

SURREY v CAMBRIDGE UNIVERSITY

Played at The Oval, June 14, 15, 16, 1877

Mr D. Q. Steel's 158, including as it did his 17 runs from one over! was the feature of this match, wherein 839 runs were scored for thirty-five wickets. Both sides played full strength, excepting Surrey wanted their wicket-keeper, who had not then returned from Australia. The weather was splendid, and the attendances large each day; and as the Oxford v Cambridge match was set for ten days later on some idea may be formed of the interest created by Mr Steel's splendid hitting, especially at Lord's, where Oxford v Middlesex was being played, and when on the Friday as telegram after telegram arrived telling of the increasing greatness of Mr Steel's score the interest therein became very lively.

Surrey commenced the batting, and all present at the match who retained pleasant recollections of other days, were gratified at witnessing Jupp and Humphrey well to the front again for the old county, Jupp scoring 38 and 52, and Richard Humphrey 51 and 19, the latter making a dead heat for second Surrey position with Mr W. Lindsay, who scored 20 and 50.

Mr Steel commenced his famous innings when the University score was at 37 for three wickets, the Hon. A. Lyttelton having made 30 of those 37 runs. That evening, however, play ceased with the Cambridge innings at 69 for five wickets, Mr Steel, not out, 18; Mr Jarvis, not out, 4. About noon on the Friday the not outs went on with their innings, and with such effect, that when Mr Jarvis was out for 36, the score stood at 147, so many as 85 runs having been put on since the fall of the preceding wicket. Mr R. Jones was next man in, and not only was another big stand made, but Mr Steel gave such frightful punishment to one over as to call for special record in *Wisden's*. Luncheon time was then handy, and in order to part the hitters before they left for refreshment, Mr Wyatt was put on to bowl, but he only bowled one over, and that over was punished by Mr Steel for 17 runs! Thus:

> The first ball Mr Steel cut past slip for 4;
>
> The second ball he grandly drove down Vauxhall way for 6;
>
> The third ball he hit away for 2, and
>
> The fourth ball he finely drove for 5.

The applause at this marvellous hitting was tremendous, but the scoring went on, and when they left for luncheon the figures were 242, Mr Steel, not out, 121. On resuming they hit away again until 278 were scored, when Mr Jones was had at wicket for 28, and when 295 had been booked time was up with Mr Steel, who was then caught out at mid-off for 158 – a superb display of hitting, made by thirty-three singles, fifteen 2s, five 3s, eleven 4s, six 5s and the aforesaid 6; the last-named three lots telling of 80 runs having been made in eighteen hits! At 3.35 the University innings was over for 297 runs, hit from 144 overs, Mr Steel having made 158 of the 258 runs scored whilst he was batting. About four o'clock Jupp and Humphrey commenced Surrey's second, and when time stayed play for that day Humphrey, Elliott, Jupp, and Barratt were out, and the County innings stood at 151 – or 52 on, – Mr Wyatt, by resolute hitting, having made 48 not out.

On the Saturday Mr Wyatt and Mr Lindsay increased the Surrey score to 170, when a cool and clever right hand catch at short slip settled Mr Wyatt for 57 – the highest score on his side – and one that included a hit for 5, and three 4s; but Mr Lindsay stayed and hit away until he had made 50, his vigorous hitting including two 4s, two 5s (drives), and a great on-drive for 6; the others did but little, and at 1.30 the innings was over for 221 runs, setting the University 123 to win. The Hon. E. Lyttelton and Mr Mellor commenced; they had made 18 runs in ten minutes, when the luncheon bell rang. On resuming, both left with the score at 49, Mr E. Lyttelton for 22, by two on-drives for 5 each, etc.; and Mr Mellor for 27 by a square leg hit for 5, two 4s, etc. Mr Patterson's 12 included a leg hit for 5, and a 4; and shortly after the Captain left the match was won for the University by five wickets, Hon. A. Lyttelton, not out, 24, Mr Jarvis, not out, 16.

Surrey

H. Jupp b Schultz	38	c and b Patterson	52
M. C. Clarke Esq. b Patterson	0	b Patterson	1
G. N. Wyatt Esq. b Luddington	1	c E. Lyttelton b Patterson	57
L. A. Shuter Esq. b Luddington	21	b Schultz	4
Geo. Elliott run out	20	c Lucas b Luddington	21
W. S. Trollope Esq. b Schultz	0	c Bury b Schultz	0
Barratt b Patterson	15	b Bury	6
Richard Humphrey b Schultz	51	b Jarvis	19
W. Lindsay, Esq. run out	20	c A. Lyttelton b Bury	50
Southerton b Patterson	5	not out	5
Geo. Jones not out	0	c R. Jones b Schultz	0
B 18, l-b 5, w 3, n-b 1	27	B 4, l-b 2	6
	198		221

The University

Hon. A. Lyttelton c Jupp b Southerton	30	not out	24
A. P. Lucas Esq. b Barratt	4		
W. S. Patterson Esq. lbw b Barratt	1	b Jones	11
Hon. E. Lyttelton b Barratt	6	b Trollope	22
D. Q. Steel Esq. c Clarke b Southerton	158		
F. H. Mellor Esq. b Jones	1	b Barratt	27
L. K. Jarvis Esq. b Trollope	36	not out	16
R. Jones Esq. c Jupp b Southerton	28	b Barratt	6
S. S. Schultz Esq. lbw b Barratt	2		
L. Bury Esq. not out	1	b Southerton	16
H. T. Luddington Esq. c Jupp b Southerton	0		
B 16, l-b 14	30	L-b 1	1
	297		123

University Bowling

	Overs	Mdns	Runs	Wkts	Overs	Mdns	Runs	Wkts
Mr Patterson	44.1	26	52	3	50	26	63	3
Mr Luddington	27	16	38	2	28	13	50	1
Mr Schultz	26	15	41	3	32	12	62	3
Mr Jarvis	10	8	4	—	8	6	7	1
Mr Bury	8	1	25	—	13.3	3	20	2
Mr Lucas	7	5	11	—	10	2	13	—

Surrey Bowling

	Overs	Mdns	Runs	Wkts	Overs	Mdns	Runs	Wkts
Southerton	60	27	84	4	20	8	38	1
Barratt	59	23	101	4	24.1	8	39	2
Jones	20	4	54	1	10	2	30	1
Mr Trollope	4	—	11	1	6	1	15	1
Mr Wyatt	1	—	17	—				

Umpires: James Street and M. Sherwin.

SURREY v NOTTINGHAMSHIRE

Played at The Oval, August 7, 8, 9, 1882

This match will be ever memorable for the extraordinary batting of Shrewsbury and Barnes, which produced the longest partnership on record in a county contest – a partnership second only in point of number of runs scored to that of Messrs A. H. Trevor and G. F. Vernon in their wonderful batting display against Rickling Green, and exceeding that of Messrs G. F. Grace and I. D. Walker, at Beeston, in 1870, by one run, and that of Messrs W. G. Grace and B. B. Cooper, at Kennington Oval, in 1869, by six runs.

The opening day was Bank Holiday, and a very large crowd attended. Nottinghamshire won the toss and sent in Oscroft and Shrewsbury, soon after twelve o'clock, the wicket being fast and easy. Oscroft was caught at 26, and on Barnes coming in the most sensational batting in the annals of County cricket commenced. Barnes seemed rather unsteady at starting, and was let off at slip soon after he went in, and Shrewsbury was badly missed at extra mid-off when he had made 30. These, however, were the only blemishes in either batsman's innings. At the luncheon interval the score had reached 100; at twenty minutes past four the 200 was hoisted; and at a quarter to six 300 appeared on the telegraph board, and Shrewsbury and Barnes were still together, nine of the Surrey team having been put on to bowl. With 15 runs added, however, a catch at short-leg got rid of the latter, and it was then seen that

BARNES and SHREWSBURY had put on 289 runs!

Barnes was at the wickets as nearly as possible four hours and a-half, and his splendid innings of 130 consisted of seventeen 4s, six 3s, eight 2s, and twenty-eight singles. Selby came in, and he and Shrewsbury played out time, the score then standing as under:

W. Oscroft c Abel b Jones	15
A. Shrewsbury not out	182
W. Barnes c Jones b Key	130
J. Selby not out	11
B 9, l-b 5	14
	(2 wkts) 352

Resuming next morning, Shrewsbury added 25 to his overnight total and was then bowled, his magnificent innings (the highest scored by an English batsman in a first-class match in 1882) having taken him, altogether, six hours and thirty-five minutes to compile – the figures of his remarkable innings being one 5, twenty-four 4s, twelve 3s, nineteen 2s, and thirty-two singles. Flowers hit very finely, seven 4s figuring in his 59, and Mr Wright carried out his bat for a spirited and well-played 26, the innings closing at ten minutes past three for 501 – the second highest score made by a first-class County in 1882, but not nearly so large a total as might have been expected after such an extraordinary success as that which attended the start.

On Surrey going in the first wicket realised 39, but the eighth fell for 86, Flowers bowling in very fine form. Then, thanks to Jones and Johnson, the last two wickets put on 35 runs; but Surrey had to follow their innings with a dead weight of 380 runs. They had ten minutes batting before the drawing of stumps, and in that short space of time lost two wickets for only three runs. The continuation of the innings on the Wednesday was alone remarkable for the free and fine batting of Messrs Game and W. W. Read, who scored between them 128 out of 188 made that day. Mr Game gave a couple of chances in making his 84, the chief hits of which were nine 4s and three 3s; but Mr Read's score was compiled without a mistake. At thirty-five minutes past four Nottinghamshire gained a most decisive victory by an innings and 189 runs.

Nottinghamshire

W. Oscroft c Abel b Jones	15	F. Butler c Pooley b Barratt	0
A. Shrewsbury b Game	207	A. Shaw st Pooley b Barratt	4
W. Barnes c Jones b Key	130	M. Sherwin c Key b Barratt	3
J. Selby c Key b Barratt	17	F. Morley b Jones	1
W. Flowers c W. W. Read b Key	59	B 11, l-b 13	24
W. Scotton c Abel b Barratt	15		
C. W. Wright Esq. not out	26		501

Surrey

J. Shuter Esq. c Selby b Flowers	24	– b Flowers	1
Mr Read c Oscroft b Shaw	18	– c Flowers b Shaw	12
W. W. Read Esq. b Shaw	2	– c Shrewsbury b Flowers	44
E. O. Powell Esq. b Flowers	5	– hit wkt b Shaw	3
W. H. Game Esq. lbw b Shaw	10	– not out	84
G. Jones b Flowers	27	– b Shaw	17
K. J. Key Esq. b Shaw	0	– hit wkt b Shaw	7
E. Pooley c Morley b Flowers	3	– c Butler b Flowers	4
R. Abel c Shaw b Flowers	0	– run out	8
F. Johnson b Shaw	18	– b Flowers	5
E. Barratt not out	5	– b Flowers	0
B 9	9	B 6	6
	121		191

Surrey Bowling

	Overs	Mdns	Runs	Wkts
Barratt	91	43	124	5
Jones	93.1	57	110	2
Mr Game	33	11	65	1
Johnson	27	12	58	—
Mr Key	24	9	36	2
M. Read	11	3	37	—
Abel	12	6	16	—
Mr W. W. Read	4	—	14	—
Mr Shuter	4	—	17	—

Nottinghamshire Bowling

	Overs	Mdns	Runs	Wkts	Overs	Mdns	Runs	Wkts
Shaw	48	24	59	5	62	34	63	4
Morley	11	3	22	—	13.1	8	13	—
Flowers	36.3	26	31	5	60	31	80	5
Barnes					10	3	29	—

Umpires: R. Carpenter and R. Humphrey.

SURREY v LANCASHIRE

Played at The Oval, August 23, 24, 25, 1883

This match was productive of some very remarkable cricket, and Crossland's success with the ball in the first innings of Surrey gave rise to another disgraceful exhibition of feeling similar to that displayed in the corresponding match of the previous year. Lancashire had first innings, and after losing five wickets for 24 runs were all out to the bowling of Mr Horner and Barratt in an hour and a quarter for 75. Surrey then went in, and at one time it seemed probable that their total would not reach that of their opponents, but Abel stood up to the fast bowling in capital style and Mr Horner hit most pluckily, with the result that the home team had an advantage of 7 runs on the first innings. Crossland took seven wickets, all bowled, for only 34 runs. "Well thrown", and "take him off", was shouted from all parts of the ground during the innings, and at its conclusion a large number of the spectators rushed on the ground, and as Crossland walked quietly to the players' room he was greeted with hissing and hooting, mingled – it is pleasing to record – with a fair amount of cheering. This demonstration nearly resulted in the abandonment of the match, but after an interval of about half-an-hour Barlow and Mr Taylor appeared to commence the second innings of Lancashire, to the bowling of Mr Horner and Barratt. Both batted in splendid form, and obtained so complete a mastery over the Surrey bowling that when time was called 96 runs had been scored without the loss of a wicket, Mr Taylor having made 55 and Barlow 40.

The not outs resumed their innings at 12.5 on the Friday, and it was not until the total had been hit up to 128 that Mr Taylor was caught at point for a brilliant and faultless innings of 83, which included nine 4s, five 3s, and four 2s. Then wickets fell so fast that at lunch time six more were down for an addition of 70 runs. On continuing the game Crossland joined Barlow, and rapidly hit up 24, and the score eventually reached 240 at 3.20, Barlow being the last man dismissed for an invaluable innings of 88. He had been at the wickets four and a quarter hours without giving a chance, and his figures were six 4s, two 3s, nine 2s, and forty singles. Surrey had 234 to get to win, and began with Messrs Shuter and Diver. With the score at 13 the former was bowled middle stump. Abel was out at 20, and then Messrs W. W. Read and Diver, by capital cricket, carried the score to 67 before the latter was bowled for a good 34. Maurice Read was clean bowled at 89, and Henderson came in. At 107 Mr Read, who had been hit several times on the hands and legs by Crossland, was given out leg before wicket for an exceedingly well-played 43, which included five 4s. Mr Roller became Henderson's partner, but at 112 the latter was caught at the wicket, and Mr Bowden, who succeeded, was bowled at 122. Seven wickets were then down, and 112 runs were wanted to win. The game now seemed as good as over, but on Mr Key joining Mr Roller, a most obstinate resistance was offered, and by good defence and very hard hitting half the required runs were hit off before time was called. Mr Roller had then made 35 and Mr Key 32, the former batting with the disadvantage of an injury to his hand, sustained in the first innings.

Punctually at noon on the Saturday morning Messrs Roller and Key, after diligent practice at the nets, set about their task of getting 56 runs to win. Both batted with coolness and confidence and made some brilliant hits, neither being credited with the slightest mistake. Crossland, Watson, Barlow, Nash and Briggs all tried but without effect, and amid the greatest excitement and enthusiasm, Mr Roller made the winning hit at ten minutes to one, and Surrey scored a most unexpected victory by three wickets. Mr Key's 60 included eight 4s, three 3s, and six 2s, and Mr Roller's 55 four 4s, three 3s, and nine 2s. Mr Key hit with power and freedom, while Mr Roller showed great judgment in running, and the cheers which greeted their splendid performance were of the most enthusiastic description.

Lancashire

A. N. Hornby Esq. c Henderson b Barratt	0	– c J. M. Read b Barratt	2
R. G. Barlow b Barratt	12	– c Abel b Horner	88
F. Taylor Esq. b Horner	5	– c Diver b Barratt	83
J. Briggs c Henderson b Horner	7	– b Henderson	11
W. Robinson b Horner	2	– c Abel b Barratt	9
Rev. V. F. Royle b Horner	0	– lbw b Barratt	5
J. H. Payne Esq. c W. W. Read b Horner	23	– b Henderson	3
A. Watson c J. M. Read b Barratt	1	– c J. M. Read b Barratt	0
J. Crossland c J. M. Read b Horner	11	– c Shuter b J. M. Read	24
R. Pilling not out	7	– lbw b Horner	0
G. Nash c Roller b Barratt	0	– not out	2
B 4, l-b 3	7	B 9, l-b 3, n-b 1	13
	75		240

Surrey

M. P. Bowden Esq. b Crossland	4	– b Watson	0
R. Henderson b Watson	6	– c Pilling b Watson	8
W. E. Roller Esq. b Watson	5	– not out	55
W. W. Read Esq. b Crossland	14	– lbw b Watson	43
J. M. Read b Crossland	3	– b Crossland	10
J. Shuter Esq. b Crossland	0	– b Crossland	7
E. J. Diver Esq. st Pilling b Watson	15	– b Nash	34
R. Abel not out	10	– b Watson	0
K. J. Key Esq. b Crossland	2	– not out	60
E. Barratt b Crossland	4		
C. E. Horner Esq. b Crossland	13		
B 5, l-b 1	6	B 13, l-b 3, w 1	17
	82		234

Surrey Bowling

	Overs	Mdns	Runs	Wkts	Overs	Mdns	Runs	Wkts
Barratt	19.3	9	32	4	58	26	92	5
Mr Horner	19	9	36	6	27	19	48	2
J. M. Read					18	9	28	1
Abel					4	—	8	—
Henderson					41	20	42	2
Mr Key					6	2	9	—

Lancashire Bowling

	Overs	Mdns	Runs	Wkts	Overs	Mdns	Runs	Wkts
Crossland	30.1	19	34	7	41	9	108	2
Watson	31	16	42	3	36	22	44	4
Barlow					41	28	32	—
Nash					12	3	31	1
Briggs					1.2	1	2	—

Umpires: F. H. Farrands and H. Holmes.

SURREY v HAMPSHIRE

Played at The Oval, May 14, 15, 1884

Surrey won the match by an innings and 280 runs, and some curious cricket was witnessed on the opening day. Hampshire were all got rid of in an hour for a total of 32, and then Surrey made 464 for the loss of six wickets. The only excuse offered for the Hampshire men was that they had been playing on heavy wickets, and therefore found the ground too fast for them. Not one of them seemed able to offer a resistance to Lohmann's bowling, and though the first wicket put on 12 runs, there were nine wickets down for 23. Lohmann at one time took four wickets in seven balls, and altogether, as will be seen below, he obtained seven wickets at a cost of only 13 runs. Surrey went in to bat at a little over a quarter-past one, and so fast was the scoring that the 404 runs were made in as nearly as possible four hours and a half. The Hampshire bowling was mastered from the start, the ball being sent to all parts of the field. It should be mentioned that, as the wickets were pitched considerably to the right of the pavilion, the boundaries on one side were easier than usual. Mr Shuter played a brilliant innings of 135, in which were one 5, twenty 4s, five 3s and seven 2s. He went in first and was the fourth man out, the total when he left being 260. Abel and Mr Diver gave their captain valuable help, 86 being scored by the first wicket and 123 by the second. Mr Diver's finely-hit 67 included ten 4s. In the latter part of the afternoon Mr Roller punished the worn-out bowling with great severity. Wood joined him with the total at 334, and at the call of time the two batsmen were still together, Mr Roller having made 81, and Wood 26.

Upon resuming the game on the Friday, the innings was finished off in rather less than three-quarters of an hour for 464. Mr Roller only made 11 more runs, and then played a ball on to his wicket, his finely-hit innings including twelve 4s, six 3s and six 2s. While he and Wood were together, Surrey's score was increased from 334 to 423. When Hampshire went in for the second time a good start was made, Messrs Bonham-Carter, Armstrong and Lacey doing so well that the 100 was put up with only three wickets down. Then came a rapid change. Three wickets fell at 104, and though Mr Pember and Mr Currie played pluckily, the innings was all over for 149. Mr Walkinshaw had injured his hand, and did not bat. Lohmann again bowled exceedingly well, his five wickets costing 16 runs. Altogether he had taken nineteen wickets for Surrey during the week, and only 62 runs had been hit from him.

Hampshire

L. G. Bonham-Carter Esq. b Barratt	10	– c Abel b Lohmann	40
H. H. Armstrong Esq. b Lohmann	6	– b Bowley	20
E. O. Powell Esq. b Lohmann	1	– b Lohmann	4
F. E. Lacey Esq. c Abel b Barratt	4	– c Roller b Barratt	19
F. W. Pember Esq. c Wood b Lohmann	6	– b Bowley	30
F. Walkinshaw Esq. b Lohmann	0	– (absent hurt)	0
E. Sheldrake Esq. b Lohmann	0	– b Lohmann	0
W. Dible b Lohmann	0	– c Roller b Lohmann	0
C. Young c Roller b Barratt	0	– c and b Lohmann	5
C. E. Currie Esq. b Lohmann	0	– not out	14
E. Barratt Esq. not out	3	– b Bowley	5
L-b 2	2	L-b 12	12
	32		149

Surrey

J. Shuter Esq. b Lacey	135
R. Abel c Pember b Young	34
E. J. Diver Esq. c Barratt b Young	67
W. W. Read Esq. c Bonham-Carter b Dible	12
G. A. Lohmann run out	28
W. E. Roller Esq. b Lacey	92
M. P. Bowden Esq. c Walkinshaw b Lacey	1
H. Wood c Pember b Young	38
T. Bowley b Lacey	9
E. Barratt b Lacey	17
C. E. Horner Esq. not out	2
B 14, l-b 8, w 4	26
	464

Surrey Bowling

	Overs	Mdns	Runs	Wkts	Overs	Mdns	Runs	Wkts
Barratt	14	5	17	3	27	12	49	1
Lohmann	13.3	9	13	7	18	10	16	5
Bowley					24	8	47	3
Mr Horner					13	5	16	—
Mr Roller					7	4	9	—

Hampshire Bowling

	Overs	Mdns	Runs	Wkts
Dible	33	10	71	1
Mr Armstrong	28	10	67	—
Young	44	11	119	3
Mr Currie	15	2	59	—
Mr Lacey	32	9	70	5
Mr Barratt	9	1	36	—
Mr Sheldrake	4	1	13	—

SURREY v LEICESTERSHIRE

Played at The Oval, May 26, 27, 1884

Thanks to a splendid not out innings of 162 by Mr W. W. Read, and to the invaluable assistance that batsman received from Barratt, Surrey won this match by seven wickets. Surrey won choice of innings, and going in first lost Mr Shuter at 4 and Lohmann at 22. Mr W. W. Read then commenced his remarkable innings. He was missed at slip before he had scored, and gave three chances subsequently. None of his partners stayed very long until he was joined by Barratt at 212. Then, for the second time during the season, the Surrey bowler stayed while over 100 runs were added for the last wicket. Mr Read hit in splendid style, and at 3.30 a round of applause announced the fact that he had scored his century. Barratt made some capital hits, but at last fell to a catch in the slip and the innings terminated. Mr Read was at the wickets while 295 runs were scored, and hit one 5, twenty-three 4s, six 3s and twelve 2s. On Leicestershire going in six wickets were down at 47, but the batting then improved, and when time was called the score stood at 109 for eight wickets.

Next day Bottomore, who had made 22 over night, succeeded in carrying his bat for a well-played 41. Being 171 runs to the bad, Leicestershire had to follow on, and mainly by the praiseworthy batting of Mr W. H. Hay a single-innings defeat was averted. Mr Hay went in first and carried his bat for a patiently-played 69, an innings which occupied nearly four hours in compilation, but was marred by two or three chances. Surrey, who only wanted 16 to win, lost three wickets before that number was obtained.

Surrey

J. Shuter Esq. b Rylott	0		
G. Lohmann c Marriott b Parnham	12	– b Bottomore	0
J. M. Read b Rylott	32		
W. W. Read Esq. not out	162	– not out	1
E. J. Diver Esq. b Rylott	17		
R. Henderson c Crofts b Bottomore	8	– b Rylott	9
R. Abel c Stone b Rylott	14	– not out	6
M. P. Bowden Esq. c Crofts b Bottomore	9	– b Rylott	0
G. Jones c Hay b Rylott	16		
H. Wood c Hay b Rylott	1		
E. Barratt c Bottomore b Rylott	38		
B 2, l-b 6	8		
	317		16

Leicestershire

J. Wheeler b Jones	15	– b Lohmann	8
W. H. Hay Esq. run out	7	– not out	69
T. Warren b Jones	9	– c Wood b Abel	8
C. Marriott Esq. run out	6	– b Abel	14
C. C. Stone Esq. b Jones	4	– c W. W. Read b Abel	4
G. Panter c Lohmann b Barratt	6	– c W. W. Read b Lohmann	18
A. W. Crofts Esq. c Shuter b Barratt	25	– b Abel	2
J. Parnham b Jones	11	– c Diver b Barratt	23
W. Bottomore not out	41	– b Barratt	20
E. Richardson b Abel	17	– b Abel	9
A. Rylott c Lohmann b Barratt	5	– c Abel b J. M. Read	6
		L-b 3, w 2	5
	146		186

Leicestershire Bowling

	Overs	Mdns	Runs	Wkts	Overs	Mdns	Runs	Wkts
Rylott	56.1	20	96	7	6	3	3	2
Parnham	31	6	107	1				
Bottomore	38	14	88	2	5.2	2	13	1
Richardson	2	—	18	—				

Surrey Bowling

	Overs	Mdns	Runs	Wkts	Overs	Mdns	Runs	Wkts
Barratt	34.1	9	76	3	30	12	38	2
Jones	43	25	39	4	36	17	64	—
Lohmann	9	2	19	—	15	6	28	2
Abel	6	1	12	1	30	15	34	5
J. M. Read	1	1	—	—	4	—	17	1

Umpires: James Lillywhite and R. Carpenter.

SURREY v SUSSEX

Played at The Oval, September 8, 9, 10, 1884

Surrey won their final match of the season by four wickets after one of the most extraordinary and exciting finishes of the year. Rain considerably interfered with play on the opening day, and in a little over three hours and a quarter during which cricket was possible thirteen wickets fell for only 101 runs. Mr Shuter won the toss for Surrey, but the wicket being slow and treacherous, he sent Sussex in to bat. From the first, runs were difficult to obtain, Mr Whitfield being at the wickets an hour for his 10. Both Mr McCormick and Jesse Hide played on, and when six wickets were down only 33 runs had been scored. Tester and Mr Blackman then improved the aspect of the game somewhat by adding 28 before the latter was bowled. At the luncheon interval the total was 71 for nine wickets, and owing to rain the game could not be resumed until 3.35, when the innings was finished off for the addition of 3 runs, Abel, who was the last bowler tried, taking two wickets for two runs. More rain then fell, and Surrey could not commence batting until 4.15. In the bad light, Mr Blackman and Jesse Hide, the fast bowlers of the Sussex team, managed to secure three wickets between them for 27 runs, and then for the third time rain caused a cessation of play. This was at five minutes to five, and a chance of continuing the match that day seeming hopeless stumps were drawn about a quarter of an hour afterwards.

Mr W. W. Read, not out, 11, and Mr Shuter, not out 3, went on with the innings on the Tuesday. Mr Read, who had given a chance overnight, was again missed when 8 runs had been added to the total, and after this piece of luck the score mounted at a fair pace until Mr Blackman succeeded in bowling Mr Shuter at 52. When Mr Bowden came in the bowling was very good, and runs came slowly. During this partnership the Sussex total was passed, and Mr Read had another life, giving an easy chance to Humphreys at point. Mr Bowden played on at 84, and when Mr Roller came in Mr Read scored so freely that when he was at last clean bowled, it was seen the two had put on 57 runs, of which number Mr Roller had only contributed 6. Mr Read had been at the wickets while 134 runs had been scored, and the chief hits in his innings of 83 were seven 4s, five 3s and fourteen 2s. The Surrey innings closed about 3.20, and twenty minutes later Sussex went in for the second time, 80 runs to the bad. Tester and Mr McCormick were soon out, but Mr Whitfield and Humphreys, by stubborn defence, defied the Surrey bowlers for nearly an hour, when the professional was bowled off his legs at 35. Mr Wyatt, Jesse Hide and Mr Newham were rapidly got rid of, but on Mr Blackman joining Mr Whitfield the single innings defeat was averted just before play ceased for the day, when the total stood at 84 for six wickets, Mr Whitfield, not out 37, and Mr Blackman, not out, 20.

Mr Blackman did not add to his overnight score when the game was resumed on the morning of the third day, but mainly by a useful 14 by H. Phillips, the total ultimately reached 109. Mr Whitfield succeeded in carrying his bat through the innings for 41, a splendid display of sound defensive cricket. His stay at the wickets extended over three hours and a quarter, and his principal hits were two 4s, two 3s and seven 2s. To get 30 runs to win appeared far from a difficult task for Surrey, but as matters turned out it seemed probable that had a few more been required the home team would have been unable to make them. Maurice Read and Abel were the first pair of batsmen, and with only two runs scored the former was caught at the wicket. Mr Diver joined Abel and without further loss the total was raised to 22, or only 8 to win. Then came the most remarkable cricket witnessed during the match. Mr Blackman and Jesse Hide proved so destructive on the soddened ground that five of the best Surrey wickets fell before those eight runs were scored. "'Tis only fair to add", remarks Robert Thoms, one of the umpires in this match, "that Read, Shuter and other Surrey cracks came in to hit only, and as is often the case, failed when not playing strict cricket".

Sussex

H. Whitfield Esq. b Lohmann	10	– not out	41
E. J. McCormick Esq. b Barratt	5	– b Abel	0
J. Hide b Lohmann	12	– c J. M. Read b Lohmann	0
W. Humphreys c Wood b Roller	3	– b Horner	15
G. N. Wyatt Esq. c Abel b Lohmann	2	– b Lohmann	4
W. Newham Esq. c Barratt b Roller	0	– b Lohmann	0
W. Tester not out	17	– b Lohmann	3
W. Blackman Esq. b Barratt	13	– c Roller b Lohmann	20
H. Phillips b Lohmann	7	– st Wood b Barratt	14
A. Hide b Abel	1	– st Wood b Barratt	0
J. Juniper b Abel	2	– b Roller	1
L-b 2	2	B 11	11
	74		109

Surrey

J. M. Read b Blackman	2	– c Phillips b Blackman	2
E. J. Diver Esq. c Humphreys b J. Hide	1	– c Tester b Blackman	8
R. Abel b Blackman	7	– c Juniper b J. Hide	14
W. W. Read Esq. b Newham	83	– b Blackman	0
J. Shuter Esq. b Blackman	20	– c McCormick b Blackman	1
M. P. Bowden Esq. b A. Hide	16	– c Humphreys b J. Hide	1
W. E. Roller Esq. st Phillips b Juniper	9	– not out	1
G. Lohmann st Phillips b Juniper	1	– not out	4
H. Wood c Tester b Juniper	7		
E. Barratt b Tester	2		
C. E. Horner Esq. not out	0		
B 5, l-b 1	6	N-b 1	1
	154		32

Surrey Bowling

	Overs	Mdns	Runs	Wkts	Overs	Mdns	Runs	Wkts
Mr Horner	20	14	12	—	39	29	15	1
Barratt	22	8	17	2	6	2	11	2
Mr Roller	26	19	18	2	23.3	17	11	1
Lohmann	19	11	23	4	37	21	35	5
Abel	3	2	2	2	21	12	22	1
J. M. Read					5	2	4	—

Sussex Bowling

	Overs	Mdns	Runs	Wkts	Overs	Mdns	Runs	Wkts
Mr Blackman	40	20	44	3	14	8	11	4
J. Hide	26	16	26	1	9.1	6	11	2
Juniper	34.1	16	40	3	4	1	9	—
Tester	6	2	9	1				
A. Hide	4	—	12	1				
Humphreys	5	2	8	—				
Mr McCormick	2	1	2	—				
Mr Newman	6	3	7	1				

Umpires: R. Thoms and W. Clarke.

SURREY v MIDDLESEX

Played at The Oval, May 21, 24, 1885

This was the fourth match in succession which Surrey won with an innings to spare, and the total of 25 made by Middlesex at their first attempt was the smallest completed innings scored by any first-class county during the season. Middlesex tried three new men – Mr Williams, West and Mr Haycraft. Mr Williams was played for his wicket-keeping, and took part in all but one of the subsequent matches. Mr Haycraft and West were tried on the strength of their good batting the previous week for the Colts of Middlesex against the MCC, but Mr Haycraft was not seen again in the County ranks during the season. West, however, though he failed to score in either innings, took part in every match, and proved a very useful addition to the team, both as batsman and bowler. The opening day's cricket will rank among the curiosities of the season, from the fact that the Middlesex Eleven were got rid of in a little over an hour for the ridiculously small score of 25. The heavy rains of the two previous days had made the ground very soft and slow; but, though the wicket became more difficult as the afternoon advanced, its condition did not in any way excuse such a complete collapse as this. The batsmen seemed utterly unable to contend against the bowling of Beaumont and Lohmann. Beaumont had never bowled for Surrey before, and of his many successes for his adopted County, none equalled his performance in this innings. As will be seen below, he took six wickets at a cost of only 11 runs; while Lohmann took three wickets for nine runs. Surrey's innings, which lasted from twenty minutes past twelve until shortly after four, was chiefly noticeable for the capital hitting of Maurice Read, who went in with the score at 29 for three wickets, and was the seventh man out, the total when he left being 135. He was badly missed at long-on when he had made 55; but, apart from this blemish, there was little fault to find with his batting. He and Mr Roller raised the score from 29 to 80, and during his partnership with Beaumont the total was increased from 80 to 133, the fifth and sixth wickets putting on 104. Beaumont played fairly well, but he was missed being caught and bowled by Burton when he had made 4. The collapse of Middlesex practically destroyed the interest of the game. Having to follow on against a majority of 141, the visitors lost two wickets for 33 runs, and then stumps were drawn for the day.

Rain prevented any cricket on the Friday, and owing to a heavy shower about mid-day on the Saturday, play did not begin until 2.45. By 4.20 Surrey had won the match by an innings and 64 runs. Middlesex wanted 108 runs to avert a single innings defeat and had eight wickets to fall when the day's play began, but there never appeared any likelihood of these runs being obtained, owing to the batsmen, with only two exceptions, being utterly unable to play Beaumont's bowling on the soft wicket. Mr Paravicini went in at the fall of the fifth wicket, and took out his bat for 17, but he ought to have been caught at long-on by Mr Diver when he had made 10. Mr Scott made a couple of 4s in his 15, but no one else reached double figures. Beaumont took six wickets for 37 runs, and in the whole match was credited with twelve wickets for 48 runs – a remarkable performance.

Surrey

J. Shuter Esq. lbw b West	8	G. A. Lohmann b Robertson	8
R. Abel c Pearson b Burton	4	H. Wood c Scott b Robertson	10
E. J. Diver Esq. c Williams b Burton	9	E. Barratt not out	7
W. W. Read Esq. b Cottrell	8	C. E. Horner Esq. b Robertson	4
J. M. Read b Ridley	69	B 6, n-b 2	5
W. E. Roller Esq. b West	14		
J. Beaumont b Robertson	20		166

Middlesex

J. S. Haycraft Esq. b Lohmann	0	– b Lohmann	5
A. J. Webbe Esq. b Beaumont	7	– c Wood b Horner	20
S. W. Scott Esq. b Beaumont	3	– c Horner b Beaumont	15
A. W. Ridley Esq. b Beaumont	0	– run out	0
T. S. Pearson Esq. c Abel b Lohmann	0	– b Beaumont	2
J. West c Shuter b Lohmann	0	– b Beaumont	0
P. J. de Paravicini Esq. c Wood b Beaumont	3	– not out	17
C. E. Cottrell Esq. c J. M. Read b Beaumont	0	– b Lohmann	1
J. Robertson Esq. run out	0	– b Beaumont	6
W. Williams Esq. lbw b Beaumont	4	– b Beaumont	1
G. Burton not out	3	– c and b Beaumont	0
B 3, l-b 2	5	B 7, l-b 3	10
	25		77

Middlesex Bowling

	Overs	Mdns	Runs	Wkts
Burton	35	16	52	2
West	20	5	44	2
Mr Cottrell	26	15	25	1
Mr Robertson	17.2	8	23	4
Mr Ridley	6	2	17	1

Surrey Bowling

	Overs	Mdns	Runs	Wkts	Overs	Mdns	Runs	Wkts
Beaumont	16	12	11	6	37	21	37	6
Lohmann	15	9	9	3	40	29	28	2
Mr Horner					5	3	2	1
Mr Roller					1	1	—	—

SURREY v ESSEX

Played at Leyton, June 15, 16, 1885

Hitherto the Essex home matches had been played at Brentwood, but the encounter under notice took place on the new ground at Leyton, the property of Lord Lyttelton and Mr Crawley, and was alone remarkable for the very brilliant batting of Mr W. W. Read, who scored the largest innings played by him for Surrey during the season. Mr Read went in with the total at 10, and at the close of the innings for the formidable score of 355 he was not out for 214, having been batting for just under five hours. So far as could be seen he did not give a single chance that came to hand, but as was only natural in so long a display, he made several risky strokes. The vigorous nature of his batting may be judged from the fact that he hit twenty-five 4s, twelve 3s, nineteen 2s and forty singles. But for the Reigate amateur's splendid contribution, the Surrey total would have been by no means a great one, and as it was Mr Read, Maurice Read and Beaumont between them contributed 303 runs. The fourth wicket, while the Reads were together, put on 107 runs, and the seventh, while Mr Read and Beaumont were in, added 147 runs. With the fall of the last Surrey wicket play ceased for the day.

The wicket had suffered from the wear and tear consequent on the long innings of Surrey, and when the Essex men began batting on the Tuesday the ground gave the bowlers considerable assistance. In the first innings of the home team Bowley and Mr Horner bowled unchanged, and dismissed the side in a little over an hour and a half for 67, which necessitated a follow on against a majority of 288 runs. The second attempt was slightly more successful, thanks to the confident and dashing innings of 44 played by Mr Stevens, and the steady defence of Mr Francis; but in the end the total only amounted to 114, and the home county were defeated by an innings with 174 runs to spare.

Surrey

Mr P. Bowden Esq. b McEwen b Bishop	0
F. Abel b Bishop	21
E. J. Diver Esq. b Bishop	5
W. W. Read Esq. not out	214
J. M. Read run out	41
G. A. Lohmann b Bishop	1
H. Wood c Pickett b Silcock	4
J. Beaumont c Sewell b Bishop	48
E. Mills st McEwen b Silcock	12
T. Bowley b Silcock	0
C. E. Horner Esq. lbw b Pickett	0
B 5, l-b 3, n-b 1	9
	355

Essex

H. G. Owen Esq. c Wood b Bowley	0 – b Bowley	4
C. E. Green Esq. c Read b Bowley	21 – b Beaumont	8
J. Jones c Diver b Bowley	21 – b Mills	9
F. Silcock c Diver b Horner	0 – run out	0
W. Francis Esq. b Bowley	3 – c Bowden b Lohmann	14
F. H. Stevens Esq. c Abel b Bowley	0 – c Bowley b Beaumont	44
D. Wormersley Esq. b Bowley	1 – b Beaumont	4
R. P. Sewell Esq. b Horner	0 – b Bowley	3
H. Pickett not out	15 – b Bowley	12
G. McEwen Esq. c W. W. Read b Horner	0 – b Beaumont	3
F. A. Bishop Esq. c Diver b Horner	6 – not out	0
	B 13	13
	67	114

Essex Bowling

	Overs	Mdns	Runs	Wkts
Mr Bishop	70	27	136	5
Silcock	63	24	105	3
Pickett	35.3	16	47	1
Jones	7	1	23	—
Mr Owen	4	1	14	—
Mr Sewell	8	1	21	—

Surrey Bowling

	Overs	Mdns	Runs	Wkts	Overs	Mdns	Runs	Wkts
Mr Horner	28.3	9	43	4				
Bowley	28	19	24	6	18.3	9	28	3
Mills					17	11	14	1
Abel					8	3	11	—
Beaumont					23	13	27	4
Lohmann					14	6	21	1

A RECORD

SURREY v SUSSEX

Played at The Oval, June 29, 30, July 1, 1885

The innings of 631 played by Surrey in this match was the highest ever made in a contest between county teams of first-class rank, and in absolutely first-class matches in England had only been beaten on one occasion, viz., by the Australians at Brighton in 1882, when the colonial team scored 643 against Sussex. Surrey had first innings, and when play came to an end on the opening day the home team had scored 462, and had still three wickets to fall, the batting throughout the greater part of the afternoon being of the most brilliant description. Mr Shuter made 27 out of 31 scored for the first wicket; 22 were added before Mr Diver was bowled; and then Mr W. W. Read and Abel put on 36 for the third. So far the batting had been good, but not remarkable. When, however, Maurice Read joined Mr W. W. Read a complete mastery was obtained over the Sussex bowling, and 78 runs were scored before the batsmen were parted, while the succeeding partnership, that of Messrs Read and Roller, added no fewer than 144. Messrs Roller and Bowden increased the total by 94, and finally Mr Roller and Wood put together 57 before the latter was caught a minute or two before time. Mr Read scored 163 out of 258 put on while he was in, and Mr Roller was seen to almost equal advantage in making 131, not out, out of 295. Mr Read's hitting was of a much more dashing character throughout than Mr Roller's, although the latter batted very freely towards the close. The former occupied but three hours and ten minutes, while Mr Roller was batting for forty minutes longer. Mr Read's score was made up of twenty-one 4s, five 3s, seventeen 2s and thirty singles. At the commencement of the game the weather was very gloomy, but after luncheon it became bright and fine.

The last Surrey wicket was not obtained until three-quarters of an hour after luncheon on the Tuesday, occupying in all eight hours and three-quarters in compiling. Mr Roller, who had made 131 on the Monday, was the ninth man out with the total at 585, having been in while 418 runs were put on. Like Mr Read, he made his long and splendid score apparently without a mistake, and the figures of his 204 – the highest innings scored by him during the season – were seventeen 4s, seventeen 3s, twenty-seven 2s and thirty-one singles. The wickets in Surrey's historical innings fell as under:

1/31 2/53 3/89 4/167 5/311 6/405 7/462 8/523 9/585 10/631

Sussex, whose bowling and fielding had been thoroughly worn out, started their batting at 3.55, and were dismissed in just over three hours for 168, their last wicket falling within a few minutes of time. The first two or three batsmen did fairly well, and indeed 130 went up with only four out, but then came a series of disasters. Mr Roller was put on to bowl, and after being hit for several overs he performed the "hat trick" by getting J. Hide caught at point from the last ball of one over and bowling Humphreys and Mr Brann with the first two balls of his following over.

The weather had been bright and summerlike throughout the second day, but the light was very bad when Wednesday's play commenced, and Sussex wickets fell fast when the county started their second innings in a minority of 463. Six were down for 62 when Mr Brann went in to Mr Newham's assistance, the latter up to that time being the only batsman who had shown any ability to cope with the bowling. The two Ardingly cricketers, however, made a stand, and were not separated until after luncheon, having added 55 runs. Mr Brann then left, but before Mr Newham was bowled the record was up to 131. The latter, who had been in while 115 runs were put together, had scored 62 without a mistake, his principal hits being a 5, four 4s, five 3s and seven 2s. After he left came the surprising part of the cricket. The brothers Phillips became partners, and both hitting out with the greatest pluck and determination they put on no fewer than 107 runs for the eighth wicket. Neither of them gave a chance, and they were both loudly cheered on retiring. Finally, the innings closed just after five o'clock, and this match of 1,041 runs resulted in a victory for Surrey by an innings and 221 runs.

Surrey

R. Abel b Tester	24
J. Shuter Esq. b J. Hide	27
E. J. Diver Esq. b J. Hide	8
W. W. Read Esq. c H. Phillips b Newham	163
J. M. Read b A. Hide	40
W. E. Roller Esq. c and b Newham	204
M. P. Bowden Esq. b Tester	37
H. Wood c J. Phillips b Tester	23
G. A. Lohmann b Newham	28
J. Beaumont c Newham b J. Hide	29
C. E. Horner Esq. not out	31
B 14, l-b 3	17
	631

Sussex

G. N. Wyatt Esq. c Abel b Lohmann	28	– b Beaumont	4
W. A. Tester c Wood b Horner	15	– b Lohmann	11
W. Newham Esq. st Wood b Lohmann	22	– b Lohmann	62
R. T. Ellis Esq. b Beaumont	13	– c Shuter b Lohmann	4
W. Humphreys b Roller	25	– c W. W. Read b Beaumont	8
J. Hide c W. W. Read b Roller	27	– b Horner	7
W. Quaife c Diver b Roller	8	– b Horner	0
G. Brann Esq. b Roller	0	– c W. W. Read b Beaumont	22
J. Phillips not out	11	– c Diver b Roller	56
H. Phillips c W. W. Read b Abel	7	– not out	55
A. Hide b Beaumont	1	– c Horner b Roller	0
B 5, l-b 6	11	B 10, l-b 3	13
	168		242

Sussex Bowling

	Overs	Mdns	Runs	Wkts
J. Hide	79	38	132	3
A. Hide	87	36	131	1
Tester	79	21	169	3
Humphreys	24	2	79	—
Mr Newham	35	18	57	3
Mr Brann	9	2	31	—
Mr Wyatt	8	4	15	—

Surrey Bowling

	Overs	Mdns	Runs	Wkts	Overs	Mdns	Runs	Wkts
Beaumont	32	10	57	2	49	18	78	3
Mr Horner	29	17	36	1	26	13	28	2
Lohmann	23	11	36	2	37	15	62	3
Mr Roller	16	6	28	4	16	8	16	2
Abel	3	3	—	1	10	3	17	—
Mr W. W. Read					7	3	12	—
J. M. Read					5	1	16	—

SURREY v CAMBRIDGE UNIVERSITY

Played at The Oval, June 20, 21, 22, 1887

Except that Mr M. P. Bowden was playing in the absence of Mr Key, Surrey put their very best eleven into the field, and there was at no time any probability of the University being successful. The Cambridge side differed in one instance from the eleven which afterwards went down before Oxford at Lord's, Mr Kemp playing and Mr Eustace Crawley standing out. It was, we believe, his indifferent performance, both with the bat and in the field, in this match, that led to Mr Kemp being eventually left out of the University contest. Fresh from their great performance against Lancashire at the beginning of the week, at Old Trafford, the Surrey men won the toss, and going in first on a hard fast ground had scored 454 at the call of time for the loss of only six wickets. Abel made 92 and Maurice Read 68, the two batsmen putting on 109 runs for the second wicket, but the great feature of the day was the hitting of Mr W. W. Read, who, at the drawing of stumps, was not out 200.

On the Tuesday (Jubilee Day) the game was continued, and an immense crowd of people visited Kennington Oval, about 11,000 paying for admission at the turnstiles. Surrey's innings was finished off in fifty minutes, but in that time no fewer than 89 runs were added, the total thus reaching 543. Mr W. W. Read took out his bat for 244, and so complete a mastery had he obtained over the University bowling that there is no saying how many he might have made had there been partners to stop with him. He has on occasions played finer cricket, but the moderate quality of the University bowling on a good wicket tempted him to a risky game. On the whole, however, his display was an extraordinarily fine one, and he scarcely made a real mistake, except when, with his score at 157, he was nearly caught by Mr Buxton with one hand at third man. His innings comprised thirty 4s, ten 3s, twenty-three 2s and forty-eight singles. We may add that we have no recollection of any other instance of a batsman in first-class matches playing two successive innings of over 200 as Mr Read did at Manchester and in the match under notice. When the Cambridge men went in they scored very rapidly from the Surrey bowling, but their total of 251 would have been considerably reduced had the Surrey fielding been up to its best mark. Mr Bowden, who kept wicket in Wood's place owing to the latter having a bad finger, was sadly at fault, and Lohmann, Abel and Bowley all made mistakes. Play during the day lasted from twenty-five minutes to twelve until seven o'clock, and no fewer than 445 runs were scored for the loss of fifteen wickets. Mr Sutthery's 72 was an admirable display of both hitting and defence, and included six 4s, two 3s and eleven 2s. Cambridge had to follow on against a majority of 292, and at seven o'clock had made 105 for one wicket, Mr Marchant being not out 67, and Mr Thomas not out 14.

On Wednesday the Cambridge batting by no means maintained its former standard, and in rather less than two hours the match was concluded, Surrey winning by an innings and 67 runs. Mr Marchant had some luck, but his 72, which included ten 4s, four 3s and four 2s, was an admirably hit innings. Jones's bowling on the hard ground deserves special mention, inasmuch as he took four wickets for 19 runs and three for 40. The Cambridge eleven did not make a good impression on the London public, as though it was evident there were plenty of good batsmen in the team, the bowling was far from formidable, and the fielding slovenly and below the average.

Surrey

R. Abel c Martineau b Sutthery	92	Mr M. P. Bowden c Topping b Ford	1
Mr J. Shuter c Sutthery b Martineau	3	J. Beaumont c Ford b Sutthery	10
M. Read c Ford b Hale	68	T. Bowley b Martineau	11
Mr W. W. Read not out	244	G. Jones b Toppin	0
Mr W. E. Roller c Orford b Toppin	28	B 40, l-b 3, w 3	46
G. Lohmann c Marchant b Ford	14		
H. Wood c Marchant b Ford	26		543

Cambridge University

Mr C. D. Buxton c W. W. Read b Bowley	23	– b Jones	22
Mr F. Marchant c Bowley b Lohmann	41	– c and b Lohmann	72
Mr F. Thomas c Bowden b Bowley	32	– c Bowden b Roller	22
Mr G. Kemp c Jones b Lohmann	12	– b Lohmann	2
Mr A. M. Sutthery b Jones	72	– run out	2
Mr F. G. J. Ford c Abel b Beaumont	27	– b Jones	21
Mr W. C. Bridgeman b Abel	13	– b Jones	6
Mr L. Martineau c W. W. Read b Jones	2	– b Lohmann	5
Mr L. Orford b Jones	5	– not out	30
Mr H. Hale not out	2	– b Roller	17
Mr C. Toppin b Jones	2	– c Bowden b Roller	0
B 13, l-b 7	20	B 13, l-b 13	26
	251		225

Cambridge Bowling

	Overs	Mdns	Runs	Wkts
Mr L. Martineau	45	17	97	2
Mr A. Sutthery	48	13	120	2
Mr C. Toppin	37	8	78	2
Mr H. Hale	17	7	21	1
Mr F. G. J. Ford	43	10	110	3
Mr C. Buxton	25	4	54	—
Mr F. Marchant	6	2	17	—

Surrey Bowling

	Overs	Mdns	Runs	Wkts	Overs	Mdns	Runs	Wkts
Bowley	36	15	70	2	14	3	48	—
Beaumont	30	15	48	1	7	3	30	—
Lohmann	32	12	56	2	28	13	50	3
Jones	22	14	19	4	24	13	40	3
Mr Roller	8	4	13	—	20.2	4	39	3
Abel	8	2	25	1	4	1	13	—

Umpires: Burke and Barratt.

SURREY v KENT

Played at The Oval, August 22, 23, 24, 1887

This was one of the few occasions on which Kent was able to put a strong team in the field, and, while no definite result was arrived at after three full days' cricket, the visitors played an excellent game throughout. There was little of interest in the opening day, Surrey, who won the toss, being dismissed in about three hours and a half for 136. There was no collapse, but at no time did Surrey look like making a good score. At the start Maurice Read and Mr Shuter hit hard, and later on Abel and Henderson batted very steadily for 33 and 20 not out respectively. Wootton, who took seven wickets for 57 runs, did the best piece of cricket. The Kent eleven had fielded extremely well, and on going in to bat scored 87 runs in two hours for the loss of only one wicket (Frank Hearne). Messrs Rashleigh and Patterson batted in capital form, and at the call of time they were both not out, the former having made 31 and the latter 26.

The two Oxonians added 27 runs on the second morning, having taken the Kent score from 38 to 108. After five wickets had fallen for 124, Lord Harris and Mr Marchant played a very hard punishing game, and put on 71 runs in fifty minutes, the Kent captain, despite his want of practice, batting in a manner quite worthy of his great reputation. The innings closed from the first ball after lunch for 256. In arrears of 120, Surrey went in at three o'clock, and at twenty minutes past six, when play ceased for the day, they had scored 253 for the loss of two wickets, the home team being then 133 on with eight wickets to fall. For this favourable position Surrey had to thank Mr W. W. Read and Mr K. J. Key, who achieved one of the most brilliant performances of the season. Mr Shuter was dismissed with the score at 12, but then Messrs Read and Key obtained a thorough mastery over the bowling, and put on no fewer than 241 runs. Nine members of the Kent eleven went on to bowl, and although there were several of them in no way deadly, the fielding maintained a high degree of excellence. Mr Read had just succeeded in reaching his 100 when he was caught and bowled for a faultless innings, in which were nine 4s, seven 3s and sixteen 2s. This fine display of batting by Mr Read, after a run of ill-luck, was highly appreciated by the Surrey crowd. Mr Key also gave no chance, and he hit with even greater vigour than Mr Read, the Oxonian at the close of the day being 139 not out. It may be mentioned that whereas the first 108 occupied an hour and forty minutes, 133 more were put on in an hour and a quarter.

On the third day Maurice Read was soon out, but Abel rendered Mr Key some assistance, the figures 300 going up with only three wickets down. Sixteen runs later Abel was out, and then so complete a collapse ensued that the other six wickets fell for 27 runs, the innings closing for 343. Mr Key, who had gone in first wicket down, was fifth out with the total at 324, having been at the wicket four hours and a half. As a display of brilliant and powerful hitting, Mr Key's 179 was scarcely surpassed during the season. It was by far the biggest thing he had ever done for Surrey, and it included a 6 to square leg, out of the ground, nineteen 4s, five 3s and twenty-two 2s. With the failure of the last few Surrey batsmen the home side were by no means safe from defeat, when Kent, with 224 to win, and three hours and three-quarters left for play, commenced their second innings. At the start matters went very badly with the visitors, Mr Rashleigh, Mr Patterson and Mr Thornton being all out for 20 runs. But Lord Harris and Frank Hearne were together for more than an hour and a half, and defied the Surrey bowling. They added 91 runs, and a victory for Kent was quite possible, when at 111 the Kent captain was dismissed for a capital 51. Frank Hearne and his brother Alec, however, did not attempt to force the game; though they put on 50 runs, the rate of scoring was far too slow for any chance of victory. Frank Hearne stayed until 161, having played a perfect innings of 56, which lasted three hours and a half. When stumps were finally pulled up, Kent, with four wickets to fall, wanted 56 runs to win, so that neither side could claim any real advantage. A most unusual incident occurred in the second innings of Kent. Mr Patterson having played a ball to point made no attempt to run, but stepped out of his ground under the idea that the fieldsman would return the ball to the bowler. But instead of so doing, Mr Read, the cricketer in question, threw the ball to the wicket-keeper, who removed the bails. Mr Patterson was fairly out, but it was very unsatisfactory to see so good a batsman got rid of in such a way.

Surrey

M. Read c Marchant b Christopherson	14	– b Wootton	6
Mr J. Shuter b Wootton	23	– c Thornton b Christopherson	8
Mr K. J. Key b Wootton	2	– c Patterson b Wootton	179
Mr W. W. Read b Wootton	15	– c and b Patterson	100
R. Abel b Wootton	33	– c Patterson b Martin	15
G. Lohmann b Wootton	4	– lbw b Wootton	5
Mr W. G. Wyld c Kemp b Wootton	7	– b Martin	3
R. Henderson not out	24	– c and b Wootton	5
H. Wood run out	2	– st Kemp b Wootton	4
T. Bowley lbw b Wootton	8	– st Kemp b Martin	0
E. Mills c Patterson b A. Hearne	1	– not out	6
B 3	3	B 10, l-b 2	12
	136		343

Kent

Mr W. Rashleigh b Lohmann	37	– b Lohmann	0
F. Hearne c W. W. Read b Abel	20	– b Lohmann	56
Mr W. H. Patterson lbw b Mills	46	– run out	16
Rev. R. T. Thornton c Wyld b Lohmann	3	– b Lohmann	0
Lord Harris c Abel b Lohmann	44	– c W. W. Read b Lohmann	51
A. Hearne c Wood b Lohmann	4	– run out	21
Mr F. Marchant c Bowley b Lohmann	37	– not out	6
Mr M. C. Kemp c Mills b Lohmann	21		
Mr S. Christopherson c Shuter b Lohmann	15		
F. Martin c Henderson b M. Read	0		
J. Wootton not out	8		
B 14, l-b 6, w 1	21	B 14, l-b 4	18
	256		168

Kent Bowling

	Overs	Mdns	Runs	Wkts	Overs	Mdns	Runs	Wkts
Wootton	61	35	57	7	73	31	109	5
Mr Christopherson	19	3	39	1	18	3	63	1
Martin	21	14	14	—	71	35	91	3
Alec Hearne	27.3	18	23	1	12	4	16	—
Frank Hearne					9	4	15	—
Mr Marchant					8	2	16	—
Lord Harris					5	2	14	—
Mr Patterson					4	2	7	1
Mr Rashleigh					1	1	—	—

Surrey Bowling

	Overs	Mdns	Runs	Wkts	Overs	Mdns	Runs	Wkts
Lohmann	65.1	28	102	7	60	36	50	4
Mills	52	31	55	1	18	8	24	—
Abel	20	8	30	1	24.2	13	20	—
Bowley	22	10	37	—	27	14	43	—
M. Read	7	4	11	1	4	—	13	—

Umpires: Rowbottom and Hill.

SURREY v SUSSEX

Played at The Oval, August 29, 30, 31, 1887

Mr Roller, Jones, and Beaumont were still kept out of the Surrey team by ill-health, while the absence of the brothers Lucas and Mr Thomas from Sussex prevented that side from being fully representative. The first day's cricket was decidedly disappointing, especially from a Surrey point of view. During the day each county completed an innings, Surrey, who went in first, for 118, and Sussex for 163. Lohmann's 31 for the home eleven was the highest individual score of the day, but the best features of the cricket were the bowling performances of Mr C. A. Smith (five wickets for 40 runs) and Humphreys (four for 18 runs) for Sussex, and of Lohmann (six wickets for 63 runs) for Surrey.

On Tuesday Surrey opened their second innings in much better form, for after Mr Shuter and Henderson had been dismissed for 28 runs, Maurice Read and Abel made a splendid stand, the total at the luncheon adjournment being 125 for two wickets, with the pair still together. Read was not out 63 and Abel not out 28. Just before the usual time for resumption rain began to fall, and before the game could be continued, the interval had extended to twenty-five minutes to six. Half an hour previously the players had gone out, but had been driven for shelter before a ball was bowled. On continuing Read played on, without adding to the score, his 63 being an excellent contribution, containing four 4s, five 3s and six 2s. Subsequently Abel was dismissed at 143, but Messrs Read and Key played out time together, the former being not out 24 and the Oxonian not out 16, with the full score at 174 for four wickets.

On Wednesday the wet and easy ground gave the Surrey batsmen an immense advantage in the early part of the day. Messrs Read and Key kept together until the total reached 248, having put on 105 runs for the fifth wicket, and then Mr Read was out for a capital 58, in which he had made three 4s, three 3s and ten 2s. Mr Key continued to bat splendidly until within one of his hundred, when he was out leg before wicket. His 99 was a faultless display, containing ten 4s, five 3s and eleven 2s. He was eighth out at 310. Then came some curious-looking cricket. The last two or three Surrey men had been told to hit and get out quickly, but Bowley kept running up the pitch and endeavoured in such a palpable manner to get stumped that Mr Dudney did not try to put down the wicket. The ground at this point was playing most treacherously, and as by keeping their opponents in the Sussex men lessened their own chance of defeat, the play for a while became absolutely farcical. Bean in one over bowled no fewer than eight "no-balls" in order to prolong the innings, while Bowley continued for awhile his curious tactics. Why he did not do at first what he eventually did – tread his wicket down – must always be a matter for wonderment. The Surrey innings closed at last for 362 at a quarter to five, and when their opponents went in only an hour and twenty-five minutes were left for play. The wicket, however, was so bad and the light so treacherous that it seemed at one time that Sussex would not save the game after all. Lohmann made the fullest use of the advantage afforded him by the ground, and got rid of batsman after batsman until seven were out for 61. When time was called and the match was left drawn, Lohmann had secured all the wickets that had fallen at a cost of but 34 runs; and in the match he had taken thirteen wickets for 97 runs.

Surrey

M. Read c and b Smith	0	– b A. Hide	63
Mr J. Shuter c Dudney b Smith	19	– c Bean b Smith	15
Mr K. J. Key c Dudney b Smith	5	– lbw b Bean	99
Mr W. W. Read c Gresson b Smith	4	– b Smith	58
G. Lohmann b Humphreys	31	– b Smith	1
R. Abel c Newham b J. Hide	0	– c Gresson b Smith	36
Mr M. P. Bowden c Bean b Humphreys	8	– c J. Hide b A. Hide	16
R. Henderson not out	22	– lbw b J. Hide	8
H. Wood c Dudney b Smith	9	– c Newham b A. Hide	14
T. Bowley c Gresson b Humphreys	11	– hit wkt b A. Hide	22
E. Mills b Humphreys	2	– not out	11
B 7	7	B 13, l-b 2, n-b 4	19
	118		362

Sussex

W. Quaife st Wood b Lohmann	29	– b Lohmann	20
W. Tester b Bowley	0	– c Abel b Lohmann	10
Mr W. Newham b Bowley	4	– b Lohmann	9
Mr F. H. Gresson c Bowley b Lohmann	30	– c W. W. Read b Lohmann	4
W. Humphreys st Wood b Lohmann	13	– b Lohmann	0
J. Hide b Lohmann	1	– b Lohmann	0
G. Bean c Shuter b Lohmann	14	– c Wood b Lohmann	15
Mr C. A. Smith b Lohmann	4	– not out	2
Mr W. H. Dudney c Wood b Mills	22	– not out	0
Mr G. Brann lbw b M. Read	22		
A. Hide not out	15		
B 7, l-b 5	12	L-b 1	1
	163		61

Sussex Bowling

	Overs	Mdns	Runs	Wkts	Overs	Mdns	Runs	Wkts
A. Hide	13	5	27	—	46.2	15	79	4
Mr C. A. Smith	26	11	40	5	56	21	85	4
J. Hide	14	8	19	1	36	17	49	1
Bean	9	5	7	—	28	15	53	1
Humphreys	8.2	2	18	4	8	1	15	—
Mr Gresson					7	2	21	—
Tester					20	7	26	—
Quaife					10	6	15	—

Surrey Bowling

	Overs	Mdns	Runs	Wkts	Overs	Mdns	Runs	Wkts
Lohmann	39	16	63	6	27	15	34	7
Bowley	30	18	34	2	10	7	6	0
Abel	11	4	22	0	5	3	8	0
Mills	18	9	20	1	9	6	12	0
Mr W. W. Read	3	0	9	0				
M. Read	1.2	0	3	1				

Umpires: Pullin and Panter.

SURREY v OXFORD UNIVERSITY

Played at The Oval, June 25, 26, 27, 1888

One of the most remarkable matches of the year, inasmuch as it produced the second highest individual score ever obtained in a contest of first-class importance. Mr W. W. Read made 338 for Surrey, and thus fell short by only 6 runs of Mr W. G. Grace's record-innings in first-class matches – 344 for the MCC against Kent in the Canterbury week of 1876. Mr Read went in shortly before half-past one on the first day with the total at 96 for two wickets, was not out 235 at the drawing of stumps, and ended his innings on the Tuesday afternoon, rain preventing any cricket on the second day until after luncheon. He was batting altogether for six hours and a half, the figures of his phenomenal score being one 5, forty-six 4s, fourteen 3s, twenty-nine 2s and forty-nine singles. He gave two very hard chances of being caught and bowled when his score stood at 55 and 76 respectively, but his innings was a wonderful display of hard and brilliant hitting. Mr W. G. Grace, who has performed the feat twice, Mr W. L. Murdoch, and Mr W. W. Read are the only batsmen who have played an innings of over 300 in a first-class match. Abel's 97 was a masterly innings. Surrey's total of 650 was, up to this time, the highest total ever obtained in England in a first-class match. Rain only admitted of fifty-five minutes' cricket on the Wednesday, and Messrs Simpson and Gresson were batting two hours and a quarter.

Surrey

R. Abel b Forster 97
Mr J. Shuter c Philipson b Brown 24
Mr K. J. Key c Thesiger b Forster 35
Mr W. W. Read c Forster b Gresson 338
M. Read c Forster b Gresson 41
G. A. Lohmann c Scott b Brown 7
R. Henderson c Croome b Watson 36
H. Wood c Simpson b Brown 25
Mr M. P. Bowden c Cochrane b Forster ... 21
J. Beaumont not out 10
T. Bowley c Gresson b Forster 4
B 5, l-b 7 12

650

Oxford University

Mr E. T. B. Simpson not out	15
Mr F. H. Gresson not out	30
B 2	2
	47

Mr A. K. Watson, Mr W. Rashleigh, Hon. F. J. N. Thesiger, Lord G. Scott, Mr H. W. Forster, Mr C. Wreford-Brown, Mr A. C. M. Croome, Mr H. Philipson, Mr A. H. J. Cochrane did not bat.

Oxford Bowling

	Overs	Mdns	Runs	Wkts
Mr Cochrane	49	16	92	—
Mr Croome	59	18	120	—
Mr Forster	71.1	26	169	4
Mr Wreford-Brown	66	29	124	3
Mr Gresson	20	7	41	2
Lord G. Scott	6	3	12	—
Hon. F. Thesiger	18	3	42	—
Mr Watson	23	10	38	1

Surrey Bowling

	Overs	Mdns	Runs	Wkts
Lohmann	40	28	26	—
Beaumont	26	23	3	—
Abel	18	15	7	—
Bowley	9	7	5	—
Mr W. W. Read	4	2	4	—

Umpires: Voss and Webb.

SURREY v MIDDLESEX

Played at The Oval, July 19, 20, 21, 1888

A singularly even match, which was brought to a definite issue on the third day after a draw had seemed almost inevitable. Surrey won by three wickets, but the 52 runs required in the last innings cost considerable trouble to get on a very treacherous pitch. In the early stages of the game the ground had not dried sufficiently after drenching rains to be really difficult. Burton accomplished the great feat – very rare in a first-class match – of taking all the ten wickets in an innings, and Lohmann's fine bowling on the Saturday went far to make Surrey's victory possible. Jones was played for Surrey, but did little to justify his place, and had evidently not recovered his form.

Middlesex

Mr J. G. Walker run out	43	– b Lohmann	2
Mr A. J. Webbe c Abel b Beaumont	2	– b Lohmann	0
Mr S. W. Scott st Wood b Jones	60	– lbw b Lohmann	0
Mr T. C. O'Brien c Jones b Lohmann	37	– run out	12
Mr E. M. Hadow b Lohmann	7	– b Lohmann	22
Mr G. F. Vernon b Beaumont	0	– b Jones	9
Mr P. J. de Paravicini b Beaumont	3	– st Wood b Lohmann	3
Mr F. G. J. Ford st Wood b Beaumont	3	– st Wood b Lohmann	2
Mr J. Robertson run out	0	– st Wood b Jones	1
G. Burton not out	0	– b Lohmann	0
Mr H. W. Bryant c Abel b Lohmann	2	– not out	0
B 3, l-b 1	4	B 1, l-b 1	2
	161		53

Surrey

R. Abel c Vernon b Burton	0	– c Hadow b Burton	13
Mr J. Shuter b Burton	17	– b Robertson	10
M. Read c Robertson b Burton	29	– b Robertson	0
Mr W. W. Read c Robertson b Burton	3	– c Walker b Burton	9
Mr K. J. Key c Hadow b Burton	51	– run out	6
H. Wood c Robertson b Burton	0	– not out	4
Mr M. P. Bowden c Robertson b Burton	21	– st Bryant b Burton	2
G. A. Lohmann c O'Brien b Burton	5	– c Burton b Robertson	2
Mr C. A. Trouncer c Hadow b Burton	26	– not out	2
J. Beaumont not out	7		
G. Jones c Walker b Burton	0		
B 3, l-b 1	4	B 4	4
	163		52

Surrey Bowling

	Overs	Mdns	Runs	Wkts	Overs	Mdns	Runs	Wkts
Lohmann	52.1	25	67	3	24	11	32	7
Beaumont	38	22	31	4	18	10	16	—
Jones	22	7	31	1	8.1	6	3	2
Abel	8	4	6	—				
Mr Trouncer	4	1	13	—				
M. Read	5	1	9	—				

Middlesex Bowling

	Overs	Mdns	Runs	Wkts	Overs	Mdns	Runs	Wkts
Burton	52.3	25	59	10	20.1	11	19	3
Mr Ford	15	9	27	—				
Mr Robertson	23	13	34	—	20	9	29	3
Mr Hadow	6	3	9	—				
Mr Webbe	12	6	16	—				
Mr Scott	3	—	14	—				

Umpires: Payne and Pullin.

SURREY v SUSSEX

Played at The Oval, August 9, 10, 11, 1888

By the time this match commenced on the Thursday of the Bank Holiday week The Oval had completely recovered itself, and the wicket was indeed in the best possible condition. The Surrey Eleven, on winning the toss, took the fullest advantage of an exceptional opportunity, and, by beating their total of 650 against Oxford University, established a new record in English cricket. Their 698 is absolutely the highest score ever obtained in this country in a match of first-rate importance. This memorable innings commenced at five minutes past twelve on the Thursday, and ended at about ten minutes past three on

Friday, its actual duration being eight hours and fifty minutes. The Sussex bowling was far from formidable on the easy wicket, and from the start it was thoroughly mastered. Abel and Mr Shuter went in first, and made perhaps the longest of their many stands together in 1888, scoring before they were separated 161. It was a curious thing that, after staying in for two hours and twenty minutes, they should both have been dismissed at the same total. Before lunch they scored 126 in an hour and fifty-five minutes. Abel was out first – easily caught at slip – and Mr Shuter was directly afterwards bowled leg stump. Abel played fairly well without being seen at anything like his best, his 59 comprising five 4s, four 3s and four 2s. Mr Shuter had some luck in the early part of his innings, giving a chance to Mr Brann at cover-slip when he had scored 11, and playing a ball on to his wicket without removing the bails when his total was 13, but after that his batting was most brilliant. He hit in his 95 thirteen 4s, three 3s and two 2s, his cutting being especially fine. Lohmann was out at 206, and then came a stand which, though it lasted a shorter time than that of Mr Shuter and Abel, was even more productive in the matter of runs. Becoming partners with the total at 206 for three wickets, Messrs W. W. Read and Key stayed together for two hours and ten minutes, and in that time carried the score to 399. Mr Key was the first out, playing a ball hard on to his wicket. Included in his admirable innings of 84 were ten 4s, six 3s and ten 2s. When time was called the score stood at 424 for five wickets, Mr W. W. Read being not out 128 and Mr Bowden not out 6.

On the Friday the Sussex bowling was even more mercilessly punished than before, and, as already stated, the innings did not end until about ten minutes past three for 698. Mr Read increased his overnight score of 128 to 171, and was out at last to a catch at the wicket. He was batting altogether for five hours and thirty-five minutes, and no finer display of hitting, at once safe and brilliant, was seen on The Oval during the season. The batsman seemed delighted to again have a dry true wicket to play on, and was at his best from the start to the finish of his long innings. He hit one 5, nineteen 4s, ten 3s, twelve 2s and thirty-six singles. Even with his departure the Sussex men were by no means at the end of their troubles, for Mr Bowden and Henderson put on 116 runs together for the seventh wicket. Mr Bowden made the highest score of the innings, and, though the bowling was worn out long before he had done with it, his hitting was of a kind to demand more than passing mention. Indeed, he had never before been seen to such advantage in a first-class match, or made such a long score. He was batting for only three hours and a half, and hit one 5, twenty-five 4s, six 3s, seventeen 2s and thirty-two singles. Every member of the Sussex eleven went on to bowl during the Surrey innings, and as a matter of record we give the falls of the wickets:

1/161 2/161 3/206 4/399 5/414 6/541 7/657 8/659 9/678 10/698

There is no need to dwell at length on the Sussex batting. Tired by their tremendous outing the batsmen offered a very feeble resistance. Their first innings was all over in two hours and a half, and at the drawing of stumps on Friday they had lost one wicket at their second attempt for 31 runs.

On Saturday morning an hour and twenty minutes proved sufficient to bring the match to a close, Surrey winning by an innings and the enormous margin of 485 runs. Lohmann bowled very finely, and took in the two innings twelve wickets for 78 runs – a remarkable record on a hard ground. It was the general opinion that a mistake was made in giving Mr Cotterill out caught and bowled in his second innings.

Surrey

R. Abel c A. Hide b J. Hide	59	R. Henderson c A. Hide b Gresson	33
Mr J. Shuter b A. Hide	95	H. Wood b Gresson	1
G. A. Lohmann st Phillips b Humphreys	24	J. Beaumont b Smith	5
Mr W. W. Read c Phillips b A. Hide	171	T. Bowley b Smith	7
Mr K. J. Key b Newham	84	B 13, l-b 5	18
M. Read c and b Humphreys	12		
Mr M. P. Bowden not out	189		698

Sussex

Mr F. H. Gresson c Abel b Lohmann	2	– b Beaumont	2
W. Quaife b Bowley	10	– c Bowden b Lohmann	0
Mr W. Newham c Lohmann b Beaumont	4	– c and b Beaumont	24
Mr J. M. Cotterill b Lohmann	14	– c and b Lohmann	2
J. Hide c Wood b Bowley	15	– c and b Lohmann	0
W. Humphreys c and b Lohmann	9	– not out	8
Mr G. Brann c Shuter b Lohmann	5	– c W. Read b Beaumont	4
Mr C. A. Smith b W. Read	29	– b Lohmann	37
A. Hide not out	21	– b Bowley	18
H. Phillips b Lohmann	1	– c Beaumont b Lohmann	0
F. W. Tate c Abel b Lohmann	3	– c W. Read b Lohmann	0
B 1	1	B 4	4
	114		99

Sussex Bowling

	Overs	Mdns	Runs	Wkts
A. Hide	73	30	118	2
J. Hide	57	21	105	1
Tate	30	9	79	—
Mr C. A. Smith	36.1	11	95	2
Humphreys	37	5	94	2
Mr Gresson	23	3	68	2
Mr Newham	12	2	51	1
Quaife	6	1	22	—
Mr Brann	6	2	7	—
Mr Cotterill	5	2	20	—
Phillips	5	1	21	—

Surrey Bowling

	Overs	Mdns	Runs	Wkts	Overs	Mdns	Runs	Wkts
Lohmann	34	15	56	6	18	8	22	6
Beaumont	9	6	10	1	27	12	44	3
Bowley	18	8	31	2	13	6	29	1
Mr W. W. Read	6	—	16	1	3	3	—	—

Umpires: Breedon and Henty.

SURREY v OXFORD UNIVERSITY

Played at The Oval, June 24, 25, 26, 1889

Nothing in the previous performances of the Oxford eleven suggested their being able to make any fight against Surrey, but the actual result of the match exceeded all expectation, the county winning by an innings and the enormous number of 367 runs. In one respect the game furnished a curious parallel to the match between the same teams in 1888, Surrey for the second year in succession scoring an innings of over 600. On the first occasion, however, bad weather saved Oxford from defeat. The Surrey total then was 650, whereas in the match now being described it was 614. Going in on Monday on a good hard wicket, the county scored 463 for five wickets before the drawing of stumps, and it was not until about twenty minutes to two on the second day that the innings terminated. Abel hit twelve 4s, six 3s and twelve 2s in his 138, and was at the wickets for rather more than three hours and three-quarters. Maurice Read's brilliantly hit 136 included sixteen 4s, seven 3s and nine 2s. This 614 was Surrey's sixth total of over 600 at The Oval – all within seven seasons.

Surrey

R. Abel c and b Jardine	138
Mr J. Shuter c Croome b Fowler	40
Mr F. Fielding c Gresson b Jardine	75
Mr W. W. Read c Philipson b Jardine	91
Mr K. J. Key c Philipson b Jardine	0
M. Read c Croome b Jardine	136
G. A. Lohmann c Croome b Bassett	28
R. Henderson b Moss	0
W. Lockwood not out	53
J. W. Sharpe run out	0
T. Bowley c Croome b Fowler	27
B 18, l-b 7, w 1	26
	614

Oxford University

Mr A. C. M. Croome b Bowley	1	b Lohmann	0
Mr H. Bassett st Fielding b Lohmann	0	run out	9
Mr W. Rashleigh b Lohmann	50	not out	8
Mr A. K. Watson b Bowley	24	c Lockwood b Lohmann	5
Lord G. Scott b Lohmann	5	c Fielding b Lockwood	4
Mr M. R. Jardine b Lohmann	9	c W. Read b Lohmann	13
Mr F. H. Gresson lbw b Lohmann	6	c Lohmann b Lockwood	22
Hon. F. J. N. Thesiger c M. Read b Lohmann	46	run out	0
Mr H. Philipson not out	17	c Fielding b Lockwood	1
Mr G. Fowler b Lockwood	7	b Lohmann	0
Mr R. H. Moss b Lockwood	0	b Lohmann	0
B 14, l-b 1	15	B 4, l-b 1	5
	180		67

Oxford University Bowling

	Overs	Mdns	Runs	Wkts
Bassett	56	24	100	1
Moss	60	23	133	1
Croome	53	10	133	—
Fowler	34	5	108	2
Gresson	13	4	36	—
Jardine	33	7	78	5

Surrey Bowling

	Overs	Mdns	Runs	Wkts	Overs	Mdns	Runs	Wkts
Lohmann	50	19	70	6	25	13	25	5
Bowley	29	17	36	2				
Sharpe	15	3	40	0				
Lockwood	5.2	3	7	2	25	14	37	3

Umpires: Barratt and Webb.

SURREY v YORKSHIRE

Played at The Oval, August 26, 27, 1889

The return match with Yorkshire was the last fixture of first-rate importance at The Oval, and a very remarkable match it proved, the finish being one of the closest and best that was seen during the whole of the summer. Both counties were fully represented, but in the course of the game the strength of each side was reduced by an accident. Maurice Read injured one of his fingers so badly in making a catch at long-on that he had to go in last and bat with one hand, while Lord Hawke had his right hand so severely knocked about that, after his first innings, he took no further part in the contest. Heavy rain in the previous week had considerably affected the ground, but the wicket steadily improved, and was in much better order on the second day than the first. Uneventful up to a certain point, the game grew in interest, till at the close the spectators were roused to the highest pitch of excitement. How, in the end, after the chances had seemed all against them, Surrey won by two wickets, will presently be described.

Yorkshire won the toss, and commenced with Ulyett and Hall to the bowling of Lohmann and Beaumont. So good a start was made by the two batsmen that for some little time it seemed likely, despite the condition of the ground, that a good score would be obtained. Thirty went up without a wicket being lost, but then came so great a change that, with seven men out the total was only 71. The cause of this rapid downfall was the admirable bowling of Beaumont, whose analysis at one point of the innings showed five wickets for 24 runs. With the game in a very bad state for Yorkshire, Moorhouse joined Wade, and by some brilliant hitting the total was increased to 130 during the partnership. At lunch time the score was 93, and after the interval Surrey's bowling was so freely knocked out that thirty-seven runs were put on in twenty-three minutes. Wade was at last bowled by Sharpe, who quickly dismissed the last two men, and finished off the innings by about a quarter-past three for a total of 138. Moorhouse took out his bat for 47, and it may safely be said that the innings was one of the best he has ever played for his county.

Surrey's innings was by no means a brilliant display. It commenced at twenty minutes to four, and by a quarter to six it was all over, the total being only 114, or 24 runs to the bad. The fact of Maurice Read having to go in last was, of course, a great disadvantage, but admitting that, and giving all due credit to Peel and Whitehead for their excellent bowling, the performance was certainly unworthy of the Surrey eleven. But for some mistakes in the field, the score would have been even smaller than it was. Hunter missed one chance, but otherwise his wicket-keeping was superb. Whitehead's bowling will repay perusal. At the close of the day Yorkshire had ten minutes' batting in their second innings, and scored half a dozen runs without the loss of a wicket.

On play being continued on the second morning two wickets fell for 29 runs, but Hall and Lee played capitally together, and raised the score to 75 before they were parted. With a lead of 99 runs, and only three wickets down, Yorkshire looked to have much the best of the match, and when their innings closed for 141 the chances still seemed in their favour, 166 being a good many for Surrey to get on a wicket that had never been easy. The early play did not give much hope of the task being accomplished, Abel, Mr Shuter and Mr W. W. Read being all out by the time the score had reached 25. Lohmann left at 43, but with Mr Key and Henderson together the batting improved, and by steady degrees the total was hit up to 77. Then a great misfortune happened to Surrey, Mr Key – well set and playing his best – losing his wicket in attempting a second run for a hit of his own. Lockwood shaped badly, and was bowled at 97, and then indeed Surrey's chance seemed gone. With only four wickets to fall, and one batsman disabled, no fewer than 60 runs were wanted to win. This was bad enough, but things looked still worse when at 105 Wood was bowled. The remaining portion of the match can never be forgotten by those who were present. Henderson batted magnificently, but all his efforts would have been fruitless if Sharpe and Beaumont had not been able to assist him. Thirty runs were required when Beaumont went in, and four of them had been obtained when the question arose as to playing the game out that night or leaving the finish over till the next morning. The time for drawing stumps was a quarter-past six, and it was arranged to go on till a quarter to seven. Everyone thought that before that time the match would be won by Yorkshire, but when it came Henderson and Beaumont were still together, and only 8 runs were wanted. The light was now very bad, and Mr Shuter being allowed a free choice, put it to the two batsmen whether or not they would go on. They elected to finish, and the result bore out their judgment, a cut for 4 by Henderson winning the game for Surrey by two wickets. Henderson's innings of 59 not out lasted two hours and three-quarters, and included four 4s, six 3s and seven 2s.

Yorkshire

G. Ulyett c Shuter b Beaumont	22	– b Lohmann	2
L. Hall b Beaumont	14	– b Lohmann	33
F. Lee b Beaumont	12	– b Lockwood	32
R. Peel c Henderson b Beaumont	2	– b Lohmann	22
E. Wainwright b Beaumont	7	– b Lohmann	5
Lord Hawke c M. Read b Lohmann	7	– absent hurt	0
J. T. Brown c Wood b Beaumont	3	– c Wood b Beaumont	10
S. Wade b Sharpe	23	– c W. W. Read b Sharpe	3
H. Moorhouse not out	47	– c Wood b Beaumont	17
L. Whitehead b Sharpe	0	– b Lohmann	2
D. Hunter b Sharpe	0	– not out	1
L-b 1	1	B 12, l-b 1, n-b 1	14
	138		141

Surrey

R. Abel c Whitehead b Peel	5	– c Wainwright b Peel	4
Mr J. Shuter b Wainwright	24	– b Peel	11
Mr K. J. Key c Lee b Peel	6	– run out	33
Mr W. W. Read st Hunter b Peel	14	– b Wainwright	4
G. A. Lohmann st Hunter b Peel	6	– b Wainwright	1
R. Henderson b Whitehead	14	– not out	59
W. Lockwood st Hunter b Peel	13	– b Wainwright	7
H. Wood c Wainwright b Whitehead	21	– b Wainwright	8
J. W. Sharpe b Whitehead	0	– b Ulyett	14
J. Beaumont c Hunter b Whitehead	2	– not out	8
M. Read not out	4		
B 3, l-b 2	5	B 14, l-b 3	17
	114		166

Surrey Bowling

	Overs	Mdns	Runs	Wkts	Overs	Mdns	Runs	Wkts
Beaumont	30	15	46	6	22.2	15	25	2
Lohmann	29	8	68	1	33	14	53	5
Sharpe	4.3	2	7	3	17	8	28	1
Mr Read	1	0	4	0	3	0	9	0
Abel	2	0	12	0				
Lockwood					15	9	12	1

Yorkshire Bowling

	Overs	Mdns	Runs	Wkts	Overs	Mdns	Runs	Wkts
Peel	29	11	50	5	42	16	51	2
Wainwright	20	6	46	1	26	15	43	4
Whitehead	8.3	3	13	4	14	6	27	0
Wade					15	8	13	0
Ulyett					9.3	4	15	1

Umpires: Thoms and Carpenter.

SURREY v LEICESTERSHIRE

Played at The Oval, May 12, 1890

The peculiarity of this match was the fact of its being finished off in one day. At half-past six, the time at which it had been arranged to draw stumps, the Leicestershire eleven were in a hopeless position, and the captain very properly agreed to go on and play out the game rather than bring the Surrey team up for a few minutes' cricket on the following morning. At every point the Surrey men completely outplayed their opponents, and the match was utterly uninteresting. We believe this is the first instance at The Oval of a match of any public importance being finished in one day. Lohmann and Sharpe bowled in irresistible form on a wicket that had been damaged by rain, and in the second innings of Leicestershire the latter took nine of the ten wickets. In the second innings Lohmann was not put on. Some excellent batting was shown for Surrey by Abel and Mr Key, the former being at the wickets an hour and three-quarters.

Leicestershire

J. Wheeler b Beaumont	0	– b Sharpe	10
T. H. Warren b Lohmann	14	– lbw b Sharpe	0
Tomlin b Lohmann	1	– b Sharpe	0
S. Holland b Lohmann	2	– b Sharpe	0
Mr C. E. de Trafford b Lohmann	26	– b Lockwood	2
Mr S. R. Wright c Lohmann b Sharpe	5	– b Sharpe	12
A. D. Pougher b Lohmann	0	– not out	17
Nash c and b Lohmann	1	– b Sharpe	7
Hallam not out	0	– c and b Sharpe	0
Marshall b Sharpe	0	– b Sharpe	0
A. Rylott c Henderson b Sharpe	0	– b Sharpe	0
B 2, l-b 4	6		
	55		48

Surrey

R. Abel c Warren b Pougher	49	W. Lockwood c Tomlin b Pougher	4
Mr J. Shuter b Pougher	14	H. Wood st Marshall b Rylott	20
M. Read b Hallam	8	J. Beaumont b Pougher	3
Mr W. W. Read b Pougher	9	J. W. Sharpe not out	4
Mr K. J. Key c Rylott b Nash	37	B 17, l-b 4	21
G. A. Lohmann b Nash	14		
R. Henderson b Pougher	0		183

Surrey Bowling

	Overs	Mdns	Runs	Wkts	Overs	Mdns	Runs	Wkts
Lohmann	22	11	20	6				
Beaumont	10	4	18	1				
Sharpe	11.2	7	11	3	12.3	4	24	9
Lockwood					12	3	25	1

Leicestershire Bowling

	Overs	Mdns	Runs	Wkts
Pougher	34	14	50	6
Rylott	10.4	2	40	1
Hallam	14	6	27	1
Mr Wright	7	2	18	0
Nash	13	6	27	2

Umpires: Thoms and Pullin.

SURREY v YORKSHIRE

Played at The Oval, August 21, 22, 23, 1890

Except perhaps the meeting of Middlesex and Lancashire at Lord's, no county match during the season furnished so surprising and unexpected a result as the return contest between Surrey and Yorkshire at The Oval. At lunch time on the third day the Surrey men seemed to have the game in their hands, and yet in the end they were beaten by 15 runs. How this remarkable state of things was brought about may be briefly told. Nominally both sides had their full strength at command, but unfortunately for Surrey neither Wood nor Henderson was really fit to play, both having badly injured hands. Wood was only able to keep wicket for a short time during the first innings of Yorkshire, and Henderson, after getting three runs on the first day, found his hand so painful that he could not go on with his innings, and had to have a substitute to field for him. Just at the finish of the match, when Surrey wanted 17 to win with a wicket to fall, he went in, but was only able to hold the bat with his left hand. While giving the Yorkshire eleven every credit for a remarkable achievement, it is quite necessary to bear these facts in mind.

On the opening day the Surrey men were batting till ten minutes past five, when rain came on and stopped the game for the rest of the day. The cricket shown during the time available for play was of a curious character, the home side losing four of their best wickets for 50 runs, and yet running up a total of 284 for seven wickets before the game was suspended. The two batsmen who brought about this extraordinary change were Mr Key and Lockwood, who, though seven bowlers went on against them – three or four of them more than once – stayed together for two hours and a half, and in that time put on 189 runs. Both played a fine forcing game on a slow wicket, the certainty with which they took balls from the middle and off stumps and hit them round to square leg being little less than astonishing. Finely as he played, however, Mr Key was very lucky, Peel missing him palpably at cover slip when he had made two, and again in the same spot, when his score had reached 13. These two blunders cost Yorkshire a tremendous lot of trouble, for Mr Key afterwards obtained a mastery over the bowling, and did practically what he liked with it. Included in his 98 were one 5, nine 4s, five 3s, and thirteen 2s. Lockwood's 102 comprised fourteen 4s, one 3, and eleven 2s: and, so far as we know, the professional batsman's only mistake up to the time he had scored 98 was a chance to Wainwright at extra mid-off. With his total at 98 he was badly missed being caught and bowled; but this, as it happened, made very little difference. Towards the close of his innings Lockwood was much handicapped by an attack of cramp in the leg, and for a few overs he was obliged to have a man to run for him. On the second morning Surrey's innings closed for 293, and for the rest of the day the Yorkshiremen were engaged in a very up-hill task. Just before four o'clock they had to follow their innings against a majority of 156 runs, and it is not probable that at this point any member of the team had an idea of winning the match. Ulyett played a magnificent innings of 90, which, lasting only two hours and a quarter, included eleven 4s, six 3s, three 2s, and twenty-two singles, and received such useful support from Brown and Lord Hawke that at the call of time the score had reached 188 for five wickets, or 32 runs to the good with five wickets to go down. A feature of Friday's cricket was the effective bowling of Mr Streatfeild, who finished off Yorkshire's first innings by taking four wickets in four overs at a cost of 3 runs. On the Saturday morning several heavy showers fell, and it was not until a quarter past one that the match could be proceeded with. The Yorkshiremen carried their overnight score to 247, but in doing this they were greatly favoured by luck, Moorhouse being badly missed by Sharpe at mid-off, and Hunter, with his score at six, having a still easier escape at the hands of Maurice Read at third man. These two blunders, like those committed by Peel for Yorkshire on the opening day, had far-reaching results. Lohmann bowled finely in this last stage of the innings, and made a marvellous catch at cover slip. Surrey had 92 to get, and, though the ground was drying quickly, it was certainly not thought that they would fail in so light a task. For a little while all went well with them, Mr Shuter hitting so hard that 23 runs were scored in twenty minutes before the fall of the first wicket. Then, however, came such an astonishing change that with six wickets down the total was only 49. The Yorkshiremen played up in the most brilliant fashion, Peel and Harrison bowling their best, and the fielding being only marred by one mistake. Do what they would the Surrey men never after this looked like saving the game, and in the end they were beaten by 15 runs. Previous to this match Yorkshire had not beaten Surrey since 1885.

Surrey

Mr J Shuter b Wainwright	1	– c Moorhouse b Wainwright	20
R. Abel c and b Wainwright	40	– c Moorhouse b Harrison	14
G. A. Lohmann run out	1	– c Peel b Harrison	11
Mr W. W. Read b Harrison	14	– b Harrison	7
M. Read b Harrison	5	– c Whitwell b Harrison	0
Mr K. J. Key b Tinsley	98	– c Hunter b Peel	3
W. Lockwood c Hunter b Harrison	102	– c and b Peel	2
R. Henderson retired hurt	3	– b Harrison	0
Mr E. C. Streatfeild b Harrison	16	– st Hunter b Peel	11
H. Wood c Wainwright b Harrison	0	– not out	2
J. W. Sharpe not out	3	– lbw b Peel	5
B 7, l-b 3	10	L-b 1	1
	293		76

Yorkshire

G. Ulyett b Lohmann	19	– b Sharpe	90
L. Hall c Lockwood b Lohmann	56	– b Streatfeild	2
J. T. Brown c sub. b Lohmann	2	– lbw b Abel	29
Lord Hawke c Streatfeild b Lohmann	5	– b M. Reid	36
R. Peel c M. Read b Abel	7	– c Lockwood b Lohmann	12
H. Tinsley c Lohmann b Sharpe	0	– c M. Read c Sharpe	4
R. Moorhouse b Streatfeild	28	– c M. Reid b Lohmann	30
E. Wainwright b Streatfeild	0	– b Lohmann	7
Mr W. F. Whitwell b Streatfeild	0	– c W. W. Read b Lohmann	0
G. P. Harrison not out	1	– c Lohmann b Sharpe	0
D. Hunter b Streatfeild	0	– not out	22
B 17, l-b 2	19	B 13, l-b 2	15
	137		247

Yorkshire Bowling

	Overs	Mdns	Runs	Wkts	Overs	Mdns	Runs	Wkts
Peel	32	13	58	0	24	14	25	4
Wainwright	27	10	51	2	6	1	22	1
Harrison	38.2	14	72	5	17.1	6	28	5
Mr Whitwell	11	2	32	0				
Ulyett	7	3	28	0				
Brown	8	2	24	0				
Tinsley	4	1	18	1				

Surrey Bowling

	Overs	Mdns	Runs	Wkts	Overs	Mdns	Runs	Wkts
Lohmann	37	16	65	4	32.2	13	73	4
Sharpe	24	9	34	1	24	8	60	3
Mr Streatfeild	16	9	16	4	21	5	45	1
Abel	3	3	0	1	7	1	16	1
Mr. W. Read	1	0	3	0				
Lockwood					4	0	17	0
M. Read					6	0	21	1

Umpires: Tuck and F. Silcock.

SURREY v KENT

Played at The Oval, August 28, 29, 1890

This fixture brought Surrey's first-class engagements to a very inglorious conclusion. Kent played by far the better cricket all through the game, and at twenty minutes to five on the second afternoon won very easily by eight wickets. Admirable bowling and some consistently good batting were the main elements of success, and the victory was all the more welcome as Kent had not previously beaten Surrey since the season of 1884. A painful incident marred the pleasure of the second day's play, Walter Wright, in trying to stop a very hard return by George Lohmann, suffering a compound dislocation of his left thumb. The accident was an extremely severe one, and Wright was assisted off the field and conveyed to St. Thomas's Hospital, where he remained as an in-patient for five weeks.

Surrey

R. Abel b Martin	29	– c A. Hearne b Wright	4
Mr W. W. Read c and b Wright	8	– c G. Hearne b A. Hearne	27
G. A. Lohmann c Marchant b Wright	11	– st Kemp b A. Hearne	4
M. Read c Wilson b Martin	0	– b Wright	0
Mr K. J. Key b Martin	0	– c Kemp b A. Hearne	13
W. Lockwood b Wright	21	– b A. Hearne	7
Mr J. Shuter c G. Hearne b Wright	21	– b A. Hearne	20
Mr E. C. Streatfeild b Wright	4	– b A. Hearne	15
W. Brockwell c and b Wright	5	– b Martin	30
Watts b Wright	0	– b A. Hearne	11
J. W. Sharpe not out	0	– not out	3
B 1, l-b 1	3	B 4, l-b 1	5
	101		139

Kent

Mr L. A. Hamilton c Watts b Streatfeild	25	– c and b Lohmann	1
A. Hearne b Lohmann	13		
Mr W. H. Patterson b Brockwell	24	– not out	13
Mr L. Wilson lbw b Lohmann	11	– not out	9
Mr C. J. M. Fox b Lohmann	33		
Mr M. C. Kemp c Streatfeild b Sharpe	13		
G. G. Hearne c W. Read b Lohmann	30		
Mr A. Duffen c Watts b Streatfeild	12		
Mr F. Marchant b Lohmann	4	– b Sharpe	5
W. Wright b Streatfeild	5		
F. Martin not out	4		
B 20, l-b 2, w 1	23	B 7	7
	206		35

Kent Bowling

	Overs	Mdns	Runs	Wkts	Overs	Mdns	Runs	Wkts
Martin	21	4	50	3	40.1	14	74	1
Wright	20.2	3	49	7	6.3	4	4	2
A. Hearne					33	11	56	7

Surrey Innings

	Overs	Mdns	Runs	Wkts	Overs	Mdns	Runs	Wkts
Lohmann	49	20	79	5	10.1	2	16	1
Sharpe	16	8	32	1	10	2	16	1
Mr Streatfeild	31	18	30	3				
Brockwell	6	1	16	1				
Watts	11	3	21	0				
Abel	4	1	5	0				

Umpires: J. Lillywhite and R. Carpenter.

SURREY v CAMBRIDGE UNIVERSITY

Played at The Oval, June 11, 12, 1891

The annual match between Surrey and Cambridge University in 1891 was remarkable for the fact that it was the first in which the champion county suffered defeat, a hard-fought game ending on the second afternoon in a victory for the University by 19 runs. The Cambridge men, though they had shown a lot of good cricket, had been very unsuccessful in their home matches, and their triumph – as great as it was unexpected – caused a genuine sensation. Owing in a considerable measure to the cold winds of the early spring, The Oval was by no means in its ordinary condition, the ball getting up in a style to which batsmen are certainly not accustomed on the Surrey ground, but the wicket was just the same for one side as the other, and the Surrey men did not attempt to make any excuse for their defeat. The county had the same team as in the great majority of their engagements during the season, but the Cambridge side differed in three instances from the eleven which afterwards beat Oxford, the places of Messrs N. C. Cooper, H. M. Braybrooke, and the Hon. M. G. Tollemache being filled at Lord's by Mr C. P. Foley, Mr W. I. Rowell, and Mr G. J. V. Weigall. The match attracted a large company each day, and the victory of the Cambridge men was received in the most cordial fashion. The University team played a thoroughly good game, but their victory was mainly brought about by the extraordinarily fine bowling of Mr Woods, who was unchanged at the Gasworks end throughout the two innings of Surrey, and who took in all fourteen wickets for 154 runs – seven for 91 in the first innings, and seven for 63 in the second. His average, fine as it was, ought to have been still better, two or three chances being missed off his bowling in the first innings. He took the fullest advantage of the opportunity afforded him by the condition of the ground, and on the whole perhaps never bowled better.

As it was term time at Cambridge the match could not be commenced on the Thursday till half-past twelve, so that the opening day's play was shorter by half an hour than it otherwise would have been. Cambridge went in first – this being the first time during the season that Surrey had lost the toss – and the innings lasted till just upon four o'clock, the total reaching 179. Douglas and Cooper, playing very well together, scored 45 for the first wicket, but with four men out the total was only 67. At this point McGregor was joined by Jackson, and during their partnership the two batsmen put on 50 runs, this being the best stand in the innings. McGregor was bowled at 117, and then with Jackson and Streatfeild together runs came at a tremendous pace, no fewer than 40 being scored in twenty minutes. With 160 on the board and only five wickets down Cambridge seemed certain of making considerably over 200, but Lockwood, who had gone at 143, took the last four wickets at a cost of only 15 runs, and finished off the innings for 179. His analysis was a remarkable one, for of the 15 runs hit from him 12 were scored in his first over. Jackson's innings of 62 was, perhaps, the best he has ever played for his University. He hit nine 4s, six 3s, a 2, and six singles, and was only at the wickets for an hour and twenty minutes. So successful was he in "pulling" the bowling that the Surrey captain found it necessary to have three men on the on side for him. When Surrey went in Abel played very finely, but he lost Lockwood at 31 and Maurice Read at 39. Then W. W. Read joined him, and despite Woods' splendid bowling on the fiery ground the score had reached 82 before a catch at mid-off brought Abel's admirable innings to a close. After this three more wickets soon fell, the total with six men out being only 109. Shuter, who then went in, ought to have been caught at mid-off at the same total, but Jephson missed him, and he hit away in such brilliant style that in the end Surrey's score reached 190, or 11 runs to the good, stumps being drawn for the day at the fall of the last wicket. Shuter had a second escape when he had made 23, but his 51 was nevertheless a good display of vigorous hitting.

On the Friday the second innings of Cambridge lasted from twenty-five minutes to twelve till close upon two o'clock for a total of 133, the batting being fairly good, but in no way exceptional. McGregor played an invaluable innings of 25, and Woods hit with great spirit. Lohmann was not tried till the score stood at 69, but when at last he was put on he took five wickets for 28 runs. Surrey wanted 123 to win, and though it was felt that

Woods would be very hard to play, most people seemed to think the task would be accomplished. With four men out the score was only 52, but so long as Lohmann and Maurice Read stayed together the chances looked in Surrey's favour. The score was raised to 76, and then Read was finely caught at extra mid-off. Henderson was bowled first ball at 76, and with the total unaltered Shuter pulled a ball on to his wicket. Lohmann left at 87, but Lockwood and Wood played well together, and had carried the total to 98 when a misjudged run cost Lockwood his innings. After that the end soon came, Woods bowling down Sharpe's leg stump and winning the match for Cambridge by 19 runs.

Cambridge University

Mr R. N. Douglas b Sharpe	24	– c Brockwell b Lockwood	15
Mr N. C. Cooper b Lohmann	25	– b Sharpe	7
Mr C. M. Wells c Wood b Sharpe	0	– c W. W. Read b Sharpe	3
Mr A. J. L. Hill c and b Sharpe	9	– b Lohmann	11
Mr G. McGregor b Sharpe	19	– b Abel	25
Mr F. S. Jackson c Brockwell b Sharpe	62	– b Sharpe	12
Mr E. C. Streatfeild b Lockwood	22	– c Wood b Lohmann	7
Mr D. L. A. Jephson b Lockwood	0	– c Key b Lohmann	9
Hon. M. G. Tollemache b Lockwood	1	– c Abel b Lohmann	1
Mr S. M. J. Woods not out	9	– c Read b Lohmann	27
Mr H. M. Braybrooke c Wood b Lockwood	0	– not out	4
B 8	8	B 11, l-b 1	12
	179		133

Surrey

R. Abel c Tollemache b Woods	43	– b Hill	6
W. Lockwood c Tollemache b Woods	8	– run out	4
M. Read b Woods	6	– c Tollemache b Woods	10
Mr W. W. Read b Woods	28	– c Streatfeild b Hill	9
G. A. Lohmann c Woods b Wells	14	– c McGregor b Woods	27
Mr K. J. Key b Woods	6	– b Woods	14
R. Henderson run out	23	– b Woods	0
Mr J. Shuter b Woods	51	– b Woods	0
W. Brockwell b Woods	0	– c Wells b Woods	23
H. Wood b Hill	0	– not out	8
J. W. Sharpe not out	3	– b Woods	2
B 7, 2 1	8		
	190		103

Surrey Bowling

	Overs	Mdns	Runs	Wkts	Overs	Mdns	Runs	Wkts
Lohmann	34	15	61	1	16.3	6	28	5
Sharpe	39	16	94	5	26	9	56	3
Lockwood	5.2	3	15	4	15	8	26	1
Abel	1	0	1	0	5	2	11	1

Cambridge University Bowling

	Overs	Mdns	Runs	Wkts	Overs	Mdns	Runs	Wkts
Mr Woods	38	8	91	7	19.4	2	63	7
Mr Hill	9	4	16	1	19	5	40	2
Mr Streatfeild	15	5	28	0				
Mr Jackson	9	1	29	0				
Mr Wells	4	0	18	1				

Umpires: Beaumont and Carpenter.

SURREY v MIDDLESEX

Played at The Oval, June 15, 16, 1891

This match added another to Surrey's list of victories, the home county winning the game at ten minutes past one on the second day by an innings and three runs. If, however, they had fielded moderately well, and accepted the palpable chances that were offered them, the Middlesex eleven would certainly have made a much better fight. There ought not to have been any great difference between the two sides on the first innings, but, thanks in a considerable degree to the good fortune they enjoyed, the Surrey men got a lead of nearly 150 runs. It was the misfortune of Middlesex that they had to go into the field without a proper wicket-keeper. In the unavoidable absence of West, Mr J. P. Rogers was tried, but whether through nervousness or want of skill he proved quite unequal to his position, his mistakes being many and grievous. Sharpe bowled wonderfully well, taking nine wickets for 47 runs and five for 50. The wicket was rather bumpy on the first day and deluged with rain the second, but for all that Sharpe's performance was a remarkable one. Probably the best display of batting in the match was given by Mr T. C. O'Brien, who, at this period of the season, was playing under the name of J. E. Johnston.

Middlesex

Mr A. E. Stoddart c Henderson b Sharpe	14	– b Sharpe	2
Mr A. J. Webbe c Abel b Sharpe	4	– c Lohmann b Sharpe	38
Mr S. W. Scott c Abel b Sharpe	16	– c M. Read b Lohmann	0
Mr E. A. Nepean c Wood b Sharpe	19	– b Sharpe	13
Mr T. C. O'Brien c Abel b Sharpe	1	– b Sharpe	49
J. T. Rawlin c Abel b Lohmann	6	– b Sharpe	0
Mr E. M. Hadow b Sharpe	2	– c W. W. Read b Lohmann	8
Mr G. F. Vernon c Henderson b Sharpe	6	– c sub. b Lohmann	10
Mr J. P. Rogers not out	7	– c W. W. Read b Lohmann	0
J. T. Hearne c Lohmann b Sharpe	2	– c W. W. Read b Lockwood	10
J. Phillips c Wood b Sharpe	0	– not out	9
B 8, l-b 1	9	B 2, l-b 2, w 1	5
	86		144

Surrey

R. Abel c Rogers b Hearne	11	W. Lockwood b Hearne	7
Mr J. Shuter b Nepean	2	W. Brockwell c Rawlin b Phillips	33
M. Read c Rawlin b Phillips	49	H. Wood b Hearne	33
Mr W. W. Read b Nepean	4	J. Sharpe not out	20
G. A. Lohmann c Stoddart b Phillips	43	B 10, l-b 4	14
Mr K. J. Key b Hearne	7		
R. Henderson c Hearne b Nepean	10		233

Surrey Bowling

	Overs	Mdns	Runs	Wkts	Overs	Mdns	Runs	Wkts
Lohmann	19	11	30	1	28	7	67	4
Sharpe	18.3	4	47	9	28.1	12	50	5
Lockwood					9	2	20	1
Abel					1	0	2	0

Middlesex Bowling

	Overs	Mdns	Runs	Wkts
Hearne	28.2	7	67	4
Mr Nepean	23	5	63	3
Rawlin	11	2	31	0
Phillips	15	3	58	3

Umpires: Rowbotham and Draper.

SURREY v WARWICKSHIRE

Played at The Oval, August 24, 25, 1891

For this match Surrey put a weak eleven into the field, Mr Shuter, Mr W. W. Read, Lohmann and Wood taking a rest, but nevertheless the champion county gained an easy victory on the second afternoon by ten wickets. Though otherwise uneventful, the match will always be remembered for the bowling of Lockwood, who, in the first innings of Warwickshire, accomplished the extraordinary feat of taking four wickets in four balls – the last ball of one over and the first three balls of the next. His fast "yorkers" were altogether too much for the Warwickshire batsmen. Another gratifying feature of the game was the batting of Mr Key, who had not for some time shown so much of his old power. He and Brockwell put on 91 runs together for Surrey's sixth wicket.

Surrey

R. Abel c Bryan b West	34		
M. Read c West b Pallett	40		
W. Lockwood b West	10		
Mr C. B. Fry b West	3	– not out	0
R. Henderson b West	0		
Mr K. J. Key b Pallett	45		
W. Brockwell c Bainbridge b Pallett	52	– not out	5
Ayres c Collishaw b Shilton	1		
Watts b Pallett	0		
J. W. Sharpe c West b Shilton	0		
Osman not out	0		
	185		5

Warwickshire

Mr H. W. Bainbridge c Watts b Lockwood	1	– b Lockwood	1
Mr E. J. Hill c Lockwood b Sharpe	24	– not out	16
J. E. Shilton b Lockwood	4	– c Abel b Lockwood	4
Mr A. F. Bryan c Brockwell b Lockwood	2	– retired hurt	0
West b Sharpe	0	– c Brockwell b Lockwood	32
W. Richards b Sharpe	13	– b Sharpe	7
H. J. Pallett b Sharpe	0	– run out	0
Devey not out	0	– b Osman	2
W. F. Collishaw b Lockwood	0	– st Watts b Sharpe	38
Bates b Lockwood	0	– c Brockwell b Abel	17
Leake b Lockwood	0	– c Watts b Sharpe	6
B 9, l-b 1	10	B 8, l-b 2, n-b 2	12
	54		135

Warwickshire Bowling

	Overs	Mdns	Runs	Wkts	Overs	Mdns	Runs	Wkts
Shilton	26	8	42	2	1.1	0	2	0
Pallett	29.3	7	72	4	1	0	3	0
Leake	13	4	40	0				
West	16	6	31	4				

Surrey Bowling

	Overs	Mdns	Runs	Wkts	Overs	Mdns	Runs	Wkts
Sharpe	17	10	20	4	24.1	12	27	3
Lockwood	16.3	7	24	6	30	9	49	3
Osman					21	7	25	1
Brockwell					5	2	15	0
Abel					5	2	7	1

Umpires: Lillywhite and Clayton.

SURREY v ESSEX

Played at The Oval, June 18, 19, 20, 1894

Having regard to the respective strength of the sides, there was nothing surprising in the fact of Surrey beating Essex, but it was scarcely to be expected that they would win by such an enormous margin as an innings and 261 runs. The Surrey men gave a remarkable display of batting, but beyond everying else the feature of the game was the bowling of Richardson, who, in the first innings of Essex, took all ten wickets, a feat that had not been performed in first-class matches since 1890, when Mr S. M. J. Woods took all the wickets for Cambridge University against Mr Thornton's England eleven. But for the recognition, however, of the Warwickshire, Derbyshire, Leicestershire and Essex matches as first-class, Richardson's performance would have obtained less than the credit due to it. All through the game the fast bowler was quite irresistible, fifteen wickets falling to him at a total cost of only 95 runs. For the second time Brockwell made over a hundred for Surrey, beating by a single run his score of 107 against Gloucestershire in May. So far as could be seen his innings was quite free from fault. He completed his hundred in an hour and fifty minutes, but it took him another half-hour to make his last eight runs. Jephson took out his bat for a capital 94 – his highest score for Surrey.

Essex

Burns c Marshall b Richardson	9	– b Smith	6
H. Carpenter b Richardson	0	– b Richardson	25
Mr H. G. Owen b Richardson	5	– st Marshall b Smith	4
Mr H. Hailey b Richardson	3	– absent ill	0
Mr R. J. Burrell b Richardson	31	– b Richardson	1
Russell b Richardson	0	– run out	12
Mr C. McGahey b Richardson	1	– b Jephson	16
Mr A. P. Lucas b Richardson	5	– b Richardson	3
Mr C. J. Kortright c Hayward b Richardson	5	– c Read b Richardson	34
H. Mead b Richardson	11	– b Richardson	1
H. Pickett not out	1	– not out	0
L-b 1	1	B 3	3
	72		105

Surrey

R. Abel c Pickett b Mead	65	G. W. Ayres b Kortright	16
M. Read b Burns	59	F. Smith c Lucas b Kortright	4
T. Hayward b Owen	35	C. Marshall b Owen	22
W. Brockwell hit wkt b Burns	108	T. Richardson c and b Mead	6
Mr D. L. A. Jephson not out	94	B 13, l-b 4, n-b 1	18
R. Henderson c Burns b Mead	1		
A. Street b Mead	10		438

Surrey Bowling

	Overs	Mdns	Runs	Wkts	Overs	Mdns	Runs	Wkts
Richardson	15.3	3	45	10	16.3	5	50	5
Smith	13	4	22	0	14	4	27	2
Street	2	0	4	0				
Jephson					5	1	17	1
Brockwell					3	1	8	0

Essex Bowling

	Overs	Mdns	Runs	Wkts
Kortright	38	10	96	2
Mead	48.3	11	139	4
Burns	47	12	104	2
Pickett	14	2	28	0
Owen	13	2	37	2
Carpenter	4	0	16	0

Umpires: R. Thoms and J. Lillywhite.

SURREY v LANCASHIRE

Played at The Oval, August 16, 17, 18, 1894

This was the sensational match of the London season, the result being a tie. Owing to bad weather not a ball could be bowled on the opening day, but the interest in the game did not suffer. When stumps were drawn on Friday, Surrey were nine runs behind with four wickets down in their second innings, but on the third morning they played up remarkably well, and set Lancashire 75 to get. At first it looked as though Surrey would win in the easiest way, five of Lancashire's best wickets going down for 9 runs, and the total with seven men out being only 26. Tinsley and C. Smith, however, put on 39 in thirty-five minutes, only 10 being wanted to win when Smith left. With 2 runs still required, Bardswell was caught by the wicket-keeper standing back, and with the score at a tie Mold was out in the same way and the match was over. Nothing like the excitement of the last half hour was experienced on any London ground during the season.

Surrey

R. Abel c Paul b Briggs	5	– b Mold	13
W. Lockwood c Bardswell b Briggs	7	– c Paul b Mold	13
T. Hayward c Bardswell b Briggs	16	– c Bardswell b Briggs	0
W. Brockwell b Briggs	1	– c Bardswell b Briggs	5
Mr W. W. Read c Ward b Briggs	8	– not out	33
A. Street b Mold	48	– c Baker b Mold	12
G. W. Ayres st C. Smith b Briggs	2	– c MacLaren b Bardswell	23
Mr K. J. Key c Smith b Mold	1	– st Smith b Briggs	7
F. Smith c Mold b Briggs	0	– b Briggs	0
T. Richardson b Mold	6	– c and b Briggs	2
H. Wood not out	2	– c Bardswell b Briggs	10
L-b 1	1	B 2, l-b 4	6
	97		124

Lancashire

Mr A. C. MacLaren c Wood b Richardson	10	– c Abel b Lockwood	6
A. Ward b Lockwood	15	– b Lockwood	0
F. Sugg c W. Read b Richardson	8	– b Lockwood	0
A. Paul c Wood b Richardson	5	– b Richardson	3
J. Briggs c Wood b Lockwood	4	– b Lockwood	1
G. R. Baker b Lockwood	0	– b Richardson	0
Mr S. M. Tindall c and b Hayward	49	– c Abel b Lockwood	11
A. Tinsley st Wood b Smith	19	– not out	19
C. Smith c Wood b Richardson	20	– c Smith b Hayward	21
Mr G. R. Bardswell c Ayres b Richardson	12	– c Wood b Richardson	4
A. Mold not out	0	– c Wood b Lockwood	0
L-b 5	5	B 4, l-b 5	9
	147		74

Lancashire Bowling

	Overs	Mdns	Runs	Wkts	Overs	Mdns	Runs	Wkts
Briggs	34	16	46	7	28.4	11	47	6
Mold	24.1	14	34	3	22	8	61	3
Bardswell	9	5	16	0	6	3	10	1

Surrey Bowling

	Overs	Mdns	Runs	Wkts	Overs	Mdns	Runs	Wkts
Richardson	22.3	9	52	5	13	3	26	3
Lockwood	17	3	48	3	14	4	30	6
Smith	4	1	11	1				
Abel	2	0	15	0				
Hayward	5	1	16	1	1	0	9	1

Umpires: Henty and Draper.

SURREY v HAMPSHIRE

Played at The Oval, September 2, 3, 1895

As the result of their three defeats at the hands of Yorkshire, Lancashire and Somerset, the Surrey eleven, despite all their splendid performances, were in a very critical position at the end of the season, and in the improbable event of their being beaten by Hampshire, in this their last fixture, they would have lost the championship. The game excited widespread interest, the Hampshire eleven having never before drawn such crowds to The Oval. The Surrey men did not cause their numberless supporters any anxiety, and on the second afternoon gained a single innings victory with 20 runs to spare. For this highly satisfactory result they were mainly indebted to Richardson and Maurice Read. With nothing in the condition of the ground to help him, the great fast bowler finished up his season's work for Surrey with a very fine performance, taking fifteen wickets at a cost of 155 runs. Maurice Read, exceeding the hundred for the first time during the season in a big match, played in quite his best form. A. J. L. Hill and Barton batted finely for Hampshire, and the old Kent player, Wootton, punished Richardson's bowling severely. Surrey gave a trial for the first time to Nice, a promising bowler – right-hand medium pace.

Hampshire

Mr H. F. Ward b Lockwood	4	– c Marshall b Brockwell	34
V. Barton c Read b Richardson	23	– c sub. b Richardson	57
Capt. E. G. Wynyard c M. Read b Richardson	21	– c Street b Richardson	1
Capt. F. D. Quinton b Richardson	1	– c Marshall b Richardson	11
Mr A. J. L. Hill b Nice	59	– b Richardson	9
F. E. Bacon b Richardson	0	– b Richardson	6
Mr C. J. Richards b Richardson	43	– b Richardson	5
Mr C. Robson b Nice	0	– b Richardson	1
T. Soar b Nice	6	– c Marshall b Richardson	4
H. Baldwin b Richardson	8	– not out	6
J. Wootton not out	4	– b Richardson	37
B 5, l-b 7, n-b 1	13	B 1	1
	182		172

Surrey

R. Abel c Quinton b Baldwin	24
M. Read b Hill	131
T. Hayward c and b Wootton	19
W. Brockwell b Baldwin	28
F. C. Holland c Quinton b Hill	25
W. Lockwood b Hill	13
Mr W. W. Read run out	43
A. Street c Hill b Wootton	46
Nice not out	1
C. Marshall c Hill b Baldwin	9
T. Richardson b Wootton	3
B 16, l-b 7, w 1, n-b 8	32
	374

Surrey Bowling

	Overs	Mdns	Runs	Wkts	Overs	Mdns	Runs	Wkts
Richardson	34.2	9	85	6	29.2	7	70	9
Lockwood	15	3	38	1				
Nice	19	5	46	3	10	4	17	0
Hayward					6	0	34	0
Abel					4	0	11	0
Brockwell					16	6	39	1

Hampshire Bowling

	Overs	Mdns	Runs	Wkts
Baldwin	39	10	83	3
Soar	26	4	80	0
Wootton	29.1	8	74	3
Hill	22	6	77	3
Wynyard	2	0	6	0
Ward	6	1	22	0

Umpires: R. Thoms and J. Lillywhite.

SURREY v LEICESTERSHIRE

Played at The Oval, May 7, 8, 1896

Easily as Surrey had beaten Warwickshire at the beginning of the week, they gained a still more decisive victory over Leicestershire, winning before half-past four on the second afternoon by an innings and 259 runs. For this overwhelming victory they were indebted in the first place to the batting of Abel and Holland, and secondly to the remarkable bowling of Richardson. Abel and Holland, in the course of only two hours and a quarter, put on 220 runs, carrying the score from 56 to 276. Never has Abel played with greater vigour. Going in first at twelve o'clock, he actually completed his 100 before luncheon – a thing he had probably never done before in a first-class match. He gave a chance at slip when he had made 36, but his innings of 152, which included a 5 and twenty 4s, was a superb display. Holland in his 110 hit twenty 4s, but on the whole his innings could not bear comparison with Abel's. Of the Leicestershire batsmen, de Trafford alone showed any real capacity to deal with Richardson's bowling. In the second innings he scored, in an hour and a half, 72 out of 96. Richardson, who did the hat-trick on the second day, had the remarkable record for the match of fifteen wickets for 113 runs.

Surrey

Mr W. W. Read b Geeson	15
R. Abel c de Trafford b Woodcock	152
F. C. Holland st Whiteside b Pougher	110
G. W. Ayres c Whiteside b Pougher	25
L. C. Braund c and b Pougher	19
W. H. Lockwood b Coe	17
A. E. Street b Geeson	0
Mr K. J. Key not out	62
H. Wood c de Trafford b Coe	0
F. E. Smith b Coe	5
T. Richardson lbw b Pougher	21
B 11, l-b 4, n-b 2	17
	443

Leicestershire

Mr C. E. de Trafford b Richardson	12 – c Wood b Richardson	72
J. Holland b Richardson	0 – b Richardson	3
W. Tomlin b Lockwood	1 – b Smith	1
Knight b Lockwood	3 – b Smith	15
A. D. Pougher b Lockwood	2 – b Richardson	6
Wood b Richardson	1 – b Richardson	14
Brown not out	15 – c Holland b Richardson	3
F. Geeson b Richardson	19 – b Richardson	0
Coe c Wood b Richardson	0 – b Richardson	0
A. Woodcock b Richardson	1 – b Richardson	4
J. P. Whiteside b Richardson	0 – not out	7
N-b 1	1 B 4	4
	55	129

Leicestershire Bowling

	Overs	Mdns	Runs	Wkts
Pougher	48.2	15	156	4
Woodcock	29	3	102	1
Geeson	30	9	67	2
Coe	21	4	76	2
Wood	8	0	25	0

Surrey Bowling

	Overs	Mdns	Runs	Wkts	Overs	Mdns	Runs	Wkts
Richardson	20.1	11	31	7	28.3	8	82	8
Lockwood	14	7	21	3				
Abel	6	5	2	0				
Smith					28	12	43	2

Umpires: J. Lillywhite and V. A. Titchmarsh.

SURREY v GLOUCESTERSHIRE

Played at The Oval, May 31, June 1, 2, 1897

In this match, Surrey suffered the first check in their victorious career, Gloucestershire after a splendid struggle winning on the third morning by five wickets. A heavy thunderstorm on the Sunday evening had damaged the wicket, and Mr Grace on winning the toss put Surrey in to bat. The pitch did not prove so difficult as might have been expected. but by getting five of Surrey's wickets down in three-quarters of an hour for 30 runs Gloucestershire secured an advantage that they never wholly lost. With runs hard to get, the cricket formed a striking contrast to that seen in previous matches at The Oval. Gloucestershire deserved their victory which, as they had not beaten Surrey at The Oval since 1885, was a memorable one. With the game to win on the third morning, Jessop treated Richardson as if he had been a medium-pace bowler.

Surrey

	First innings		Second innings	
W. Brockwell c and b Jessop	9	–	c Board b Jessop	1
R. Abel c Wrathall b Roberts	4	–	c Jessop b Townsend	25
T. Hayward b Townsend	34	–	c and b Townsend	31
Mr H. G. D. Leveson-Gower b Jessop	0	–	c and b Townsend	8
Mr H. B. Chinnery b Jessop	2	–	c Kitcat b Jessop	24
Mr W. W. Read c Murch b Roberts	7	–	c Grace b Townsend	0
Mr K. J. Key c Grace b Jessop	16	–	c Roberts b Jessop	1
C. Baldwin not out	30	–	c Murch b Townsend	2
W. Lees b Jessop	0	–	run out	3
C. Marshall b Jessop	9	–	c Hale b Jessop	7
T. Richardson c sub. b Townsend	32	–	not out	0
B 9, l-b 1, n-b 4	14		B 4, n-b 3	7
	157			109

Gloucestershire

	First innings		Second innings	
Mr W. G. Grace b Lees	29	–	not out	23
H. Wrathall c Marshall b Richardson	0	–	c and b Hayward	0
Mr S. A. P. Kitcat c Marshall b Richardson	54			
Mr C. L. Townsend c Marshall b Lees	4			
J. H. Board c and b Richardson	4			
Mr F. B. Champain b Lees	8	–	not out	9
Mr G. L. Jessop c Key b Richardson	1	–	c and b Richardson	26
Mr S. de Winton run out	29	–	c Hayward b Richardson	1
W. H. Hale c Marshall b Hayward	38	–	c Abel b Hayward	11
H. W. Murch not out	7	–	run out	3
F. G. Roberts c Chinnery b Lees	4			
B 6, l-b 3, n-b 1	10		B 1, l-b 4, n-b 1	6
	188			79

Gloucestershire Bowling

	Overs	Mdns	Runs	Wkts	Overs	Mdns	Runs	Wkts
Jessop	26	7	74	6	17.1	6	33	4
Roberts	21	5	46	2	4	0	14	0
Townsend	4.4	0	23	2	17	2	55	5

Surrey Bowling

	Overs	Mdns	Runs	Wkts	Overs	Mdns	Runs	Wkts
Brockwell	14	3	40	0	1	0	4	0
Richardson	25	10	47	4	14	2	38	2
Hayward	15	6	34	1	14	8	30	2
Lees	21.4	11	47	4	0.4	0	1	0
Chinnery	2	0	10	0				

Umpires: R. G. Barlow and V. A. Titchmarsh.

SURREY v MIDDLESEX

Played at The Oval, June 28, 29, 1897

This was one of the most remarkable matches seen at The Oval during the season. Drenching rain on the Sunday had more or less ruined the wicket, and on both days runs were hard to make. The finish of the game was magnificent. Middlesex only went in to get 98, but so wonderfully well did Richardson, Lees and Hayward bowl, that the innings was finished off for 88, Surrey winning amid great excitement by nine runs. Stoddart's 28 was as good as an ordinary hundred, and the fact that it took Webbe three quarters of an hour to score six runs – four of them in one hit – will give a fair idea of what the bowling was like. Hayward played a remarkable innings when the wicket was at its worst, but had something more than his fair share of luck.

Surrey

W. Brockwell c Ford b Rawlin	12	– run out	0
R. Abel b Hearne	47	– st MacGregor b Stoddart	30
T. Hayward c Stoddart b Rawlin	12	– b Hearne	77
C. Baldwin c MacGregor b Rawlin	16	– b Hearne	5
Mr H. G. Leveson-Gower st MacGregor b Rawlin	0	– c O'Brien b Rawlin	10
Mr H. B. Chinnery run out	0	– b Rawlin	0
Mr W. W. Read lbw b Stoddart	0	– b Rawlin	0
Mr K. J. Key b Hearne	1	– st MacGregor b Hearne	33
W. Lees c Warner b Rawlin	16	– c MacGregor b Rawlin	5
H. Wood not out	1	– b Hearne	4
T. Richardson b Hearne	2	– not out	0
B 4, l-b 1	5		
	112		164

Middlesex

Mr H. B. Hayman b Richardson	0	– b Richardson	13
Mr P. F. Warner c Wood b Lees	29	– b Richardson	5
Mr A. E. Stoddart c Hayward b Richardson	12	– c Brockwell b Hayward	28
J. T. Rawlin c Brockwell b Richardson	1	– b Hayward	3
Mr F. G. J. Ford b Lees	11	– c Lees b Richardson	0
Sir T. C. O'Brien b Richardson	22	– b Lees	0
Dr G. Thornton b Lees	46	– c Wood b Richardson	12
Mr A. J. Webbe b Richardson	1	– c Baldwin b Lees	6
Mr G. MacGregor c Wood b Lees	40	– b Lees	13
J. T. Hearne not out	8	– c Wood b Richardson	0
J. Phillips b Richardson	0	– not out	0
B 4, l-b 5	9	B 4, l-b 4	8
	179		88

Middlesex Bowling

	Overs	Mdns	Runs	Wkts	Overs	Mdns	Runs	Wkts
J. T. Hearne	24.3	10	34	3	34.4	17	60	4
Rawlin	30	12	61	5	34	11	61	4
Stoddart	6	4	12	1	7	4	19	1
Phillips					7	2	24	0

Surrey Bowling

	Overs	Mdns	Runs	Wkts	Overs	Mdns	Runs	Wkts
Richardson	25.4	8	86	6	20.4	5	38	5
Hayward	10	1	41	0	8	2	16	2
Lees	17	8	27	4	13	5	26	3
Brockwell	5	0	16	0				

Umpires: W. Draper and T. Mycroft.

SURREY v HAMPSHIRE

Played at The Oval, August 9, 10, 11, 1897

Just at this time the Surrey eleven were in their greatest form, and a sad exhibition they made of Hampshire, winning the match, on the third morning, in the easiest fashion by an innings and 303 runs. The game is already historical, Brockwell and Abel scoring 379 together, and thereby establishing a record for the first wicket in first-class cricket. They only beat, however, by a single run the partnership of Brown and Tunnicliffe, for Yorkshire against Sussex at Sheffield in July. Brockwell, with a score of 225, beat all his previous performances. He had never before, in a match of importance, played an innings of 200. It will be noticed that every member of the Hampshire eleven went on to bowl.

Surrey

R. Abel st Steele b Wynyard	173	Mr K. J. Key c Barton b Soar	29
W. Brockwell b Soar	225	W. Lees c Kitchener b Soar	3
T. Hayward run out	0	H. Wood not out	0
Mr N. F. Druce b Soar	32	T. Richardson c Steele b Kitchener	0
C. Baldwin c Steele b Kitchener	16	B 18, l-b 2, w 1, n-b 2	23
Mr H. D. G. Leveson-Gower b Kitchener	29		
Mr D. L. A. Jephson c Baldwin b Soar	49		579

Hampshire

Mr C. G. Ward c Abel b Richardson	25	– b Richardson	6
V. Barton run out	7	– c Hayward b Richardson	51
Captain E. G. Wynyard b Lees	3	– c Wood b Hayward	4
A. Webb c Druce b Lees	8	– c and b Jephson	1
Mr E. C. Lee b Richardson	5	– b Richardson	3
Mr D. A. Steele run out	29	– c Druce b Lees	1
H. Baldwin b Richardson	19	– b Lees	4
T. Soar c Leveson-Gower b Lees	0	– not out	31
Light b Richardson	1	– c Wood b Richardson	1
Mr C. Robson not out	30	– c Wood b Hayward	1
F. Kitchener c Wood b Abel	16	– c Baldwin b Richardson	4
B 5, l-b 1	6	B 6, l-b 4	10
	149		127

Hampshire Bowling

	Overs	Mdns	Runs	Wkts
Soar	55	16	127	5
Baldwin	50	17	106	0
Light	23	5	76	0
Steele	9	4	20	0
Lee	14	6	29	0
Wynyard	21	3	75	1
Ward	6	1	13	0
Webb	4	0	19	0
Robson	6	0	25	0
Barton	3	0	12	0
Kitchener	15	3	54	3

Surrey Bowling

	Overs	Mdns	Runs	Wkts	Overs	Mdns	Runs	Wkts
Richardson	24	3	85	4	15.2	4	35	5
Lees	24	6	55	3	9	3	23	2
Hayward	1	0	3	0	9	4	24	2
Abel	4	0	0	1				
Brockwell					9	4	16	0
Jephson					6	0	19	1

Umpires: R. Thoms and J. H. Holmes.

SURREY v NOTTINGHAMSHIRE

Played at The Oval, August 1, 2, 3, 1898

On a splendid pitch Surrey at one time had 250 on the board with only four men out, several members of the team playing capital cricket, but the last five wickets went down for 75 runs. Nottinghamshire lost Dixon before time, and next morning their batsmen failed so badly, that the innings was all over for 157. In the follow-on Shrewsbury was quickly dismissed, and despite good work by Jones and Gunn, Nottinghamshire with three wickets down, were still 64 behind. Guttridge, having succeeded in the first innings, was then sent in, and with such satisfactory results to the visitors that 95 runs were added without further loss. On the Wednesday Nottinghamshire saved the match in wonderful style, keeping Surrey in the field for the whole of the day, and leaving off 376 runs ahead with a wicket to fall. William Gunn batted superbly to save his side, and in the end carried out his bat for 236, the highest score he has ever made. He was at the wickets eight hours and accomplished a great feat of physical endurance. Dixon, even when he could with safety have declared, did not put the closure in force and a draw being inevitable, the last part of the match was robbed of all interest.

Surrey

R. Abel c Shrewsbury b Jones 28
W. Brockwell b J. Gunn 71
F. C. Holland b Jones 46
W. H. Lockwood b Daft 74
T. Hayward c Oates b Jones 0
Mr D. L. A. Jephson c W. Gunn b Attewell . 54
C. Baldwin c Oates b Attewell 13
Mr K. J. Key run out 12
Mr V. F. S. Crawford run out 7
H. Wood not out 13
T. Richardson c and b Henson 5
B 2, l-b 3, w 1 6

329

Nottinghamshire

Mr J. A. Dixon b Lockwood	2 – b Brockwell	11
C. E. Dench b Richardson	4 – c Baldwin b Hayward	49
J. Gunn b Jephson	14 – c Crawford b Hayward	47
A. Shrewsbury c Wood b Lockwood	30 – b Richardson	1
W. Gunn c Holland b Richardson	4 – not out	236
Mr A. O. Jones b Lockwood	16 – c Wood b Brockwell	52
W. Attewell c Abel b Lockwood	0 – b Brockwell	16
H. B. Daft lbw b Lockwood	16 – b Brockwell	7
F. H. Guttridge not out	43 – c Jephson b Lockwood	79
T. Oates st Wood b Jephson	18 – lbw b Hayward	0
W. Henson c and b Jephson	3 – not out	35
B 2, n-b 5	7 B 7, l-b 4, n-b 4	15
	157	548

Nottinghamshire Bowling

	Overs	Mdns	Runs	Wkts
Attewell	46	19	87	2
J. Gunn	19	5	42	1
Jones	25	5	73	3
Henson	13.2	4	36	1
Guttridge	5	0	25	0
Daft	25	7	60	1

Surrey Bowling

	Overs	Mdns	Runs	Wkts	Overs	Mdns	Runs	Wkts
Lockwood	30	13	51	5	37	8	110	1
Richardson	27	9	57	2	38	6	120	1
Jephson	12.3	2	32	3	23	3	68	0
Brockwell	5	3	10	0	28	7	66	4
Hayward					31	5	88	3
Crawford					11	4	22	0
Holland					6	3	14	0
Baldwin					14	1	44	0
Key					2	1	1	0

Umpires: W. A. Woof and E. Goodyear.

SURREY v LANCASHIRE

Played at The Oval, August 18, 19, 20, 1898

For the fifth time during the month Key won the toss and Surrey made over 300 runs. Three wickets fell for 81, but after Holland's dismissal at 133, Jephson helped Hayward to put on 175, the score at the close being 361 for five wickets, Hayward not out 163. On the following day Hayward had the satisfaction of carrying out his bat for 315, the highest individual score of the season, and with one exception the highest ever hit for Surrey. He batted for six hours and three-quarters and hit two 5s, thirty-seven 4s, seven 3s, twenty-nine 2s, and seventy-eight singles. He had some luck but his driving on the off side was exceptionally fine. It was not until half-past three that the innings closed for 634 – the highest of all their scores – the delay in finishing the innings probably costing Surrey a victory. Lancashire lost four wickets for 39 runs, but Baker and Eccles carried the score to 116, and on Saturday the visitors had not much difficulty in saving the game. In the follow-on they had to keep up their wickets for four hours and as Ward and Hallows, the first pair of batsmen, withstood the bowling for an hour and three-quarters there was never much likelihood of the game being played out.

Surrey

R. Abel c and b Cuttell	10
W. Brockwell lbw b Baker	43
F. C. Holland c Hartley b Hallows	45
W. H. Lockwood c Radcliffe b Baker	5
T. Hayward not out	315
Mr D. L. A. Jephson b Cuttell	54
Mr K. J. Key b Lancaster	31
E. G. Hayes run out	22
L. C. Braund c Eccles b Briggs	85
H. Wood c Ward b Briggs	6
T. Richardson b Briggs	0
B 13, l-b 4, w 1	18
	634

Lancashire

Mr C. R. Hartley c Wood b Lockwood	0 – b Braund	32
A. Ward b Richardson	10 – not out	63
J. T. Tyldesley b Richardson	21 – c Jephson b Brockwell	44
Mr A. C. MacLaren b Richardson	3 – c Brockwell b Abel	15
G. R. Baker b Lockwood	42	
Mr A. Eccles b Richardson	51	
W. R. Cuttell c Holland b Lockwood	5	
J. Briggs b Brockwell	18	
J. Hallows not out	19 – c Abel b Hayward	51
Lancaster c and b Brockwell	0	
L. Radcliffe c Holland b Lockwood	0	
B 4	4	B 4, n-b 1 5
	173	210

Lancashire Bowling

	Overs	Mdns	Runs	Wkts
Lancaster	45	13	126	1
Cuttell	54	15	121	2
Briggs	56	8	142	3
Baker	28	7	75	2
Hallows	29	8	68	1
Ward	13	5	38	0
Hartley	10	1	42	0
MacLaren	1	0	4	0

Surrey Bowling

	Overs	Mdns	Runs	Wkts	Overs	Mdns	Runs	Wkts
Richardson	32	13	62	4	25	12	59	0
Lockwood	28.2	4	77	4	21	9	40	0
Hayes	4	0	9	0	9	5	10	0
Brockwell	7	4	12	2	19	7	41	1
Jephson	4	1	5	0	9	4	12	0
Braund	2	1	4	0	1.3	0	12	1
Hayward					9	2	21	1
Abel					4	2	10	1

Umpires: W. Draper and J. J. Tuck.

SURREY v WARWICKSHIRE

Played at The Oval, September 1, 2, 3, 1898

Surrey finished up their season in most brilliant style, beating Warwickshire by an innings and 357 runs. With Key, as well as Lockwood absent, Jephson won the toss and at the close of the first day 361 runs had been made for two wickets. Abel and Brockwell surpassed all their previous fine partnerships for the first wicket during the season, putting on no fewer than 265 before they were separated. Each man played very finely and made over a hundred, Abel for once scoring faster than his colleague. On the following day Hayward showed splendid form, and Wood hit vigorously for 74 not out. Warwickshire, having to face the tremendous total of 609, lost, despite some careful cricket by W. G. Quaife, six batsmen for 132. Richardson performed the "hat trick" in getting rid of Santall, Dickens, and Lilley, the innings being finished off for the addition of only six runs. In the follow on Warwickshire lost four wickets for 35 and one of these being W. G. Quaife's, all chance of saving the game disappeared. Lilley, despite a damaged finger, played extremely well, but his colleagues could do nothing with Richardson who took fifteen wickets in the match for 83 runs.

Surrey

R. Abel c W. G. Quaife b Hopkins	135
W. Brockwell st W. G. Quaife b Lilley	152
F. C. Holland b Santall	42
Mr D. L. A. Jephson b Field	16
T. Hayward b Manton	94
Mr V. F. S. Crawford b Dickens	7
L. C. Braund b Dickens	11
E. G. Hayes b Dickens	0
H. Wood not out	74
F. E. Smith c Field b Santall	3
T. Richardson c Santall b Field	28
B 26, l-b 15, w 5, n-b 1	47
	609

Warwickshire

W. Quaife c Smith b Brockwell	29	– c and b Richardson	4
Kinneir b Richardson	5	– b Richardson	12
Mr J. Manton b Richardson	0	– b Richardson	5
W. G. Quaife c Wood b Brockwell	65	– c Wood b Richardson	3
Mr F. R. Loveitt c and b Hayes	23	– c Crawford b Braund	5
S. Santall b Richardson	3	– b Richardson	7
A. A. Lilley b Richardson	0	– b Brockwell	57
Charlesworth c Crawford b Richardson	0	– not out	9
Dickens b Richardson	0	– b Richardson	2
Field b Richardson	2	– c Brockwell b Richardson	0
F. J. Hopkins not out	3	– b Richardson	0
B 7, l-b 1	8	B 10	10
	138		114

Warwickshire Bowling

	Overs	Mdns	Runs	Wkts
Santall	64	12	181	2
Field	46.4	11	130	2
Dickens	27	7	71	3
Charlesworth	7	0	21	0
Manton	22	7	51	1
Hopkins	16	5	62	1
Kinneir	5	3	9	0
W. G. Quaife	4	1	10	0
Lilley	5	0	27	1

Surrey Bowling

	Overs	Mdns	Runs	Wkts	Overs	Mdns	Runs	Wkts
Richardson	27	4	55	7	19	8	28	8
Smith	10	7	11	0	7	3	22	0
Jephson	7	1	17	0	6	1	19	0
Brockwell	11.3	5	17	2	14	7	20	1
Braund	8	6	13	0	9	4	15	1
Hayes	6	1	17	1				

Umpires: T. Mycroft and R. Thoms.

SURREY v DERBYSHIRE

Played at The Oval, May 4, 5, 6, 1899

A few dry days had done wonders for The Oval, and the cricket proved quite different in character to that seen earlier in the week in the match against Leicestershire. Winning the toss Surrey began batting in a temperature that would have been cold for March, and ran up a total of 375, their innings lasting until ten minutes to five. Brockwell and Lockwood played most brilliant cricket together, putting on for the third wicket 133 runs in an hour and a quarter. At one point fifty runs were hit in a quarter of an hour, thirty of them from four overs bowled by F. Wright. Brockwell actually made his hundred before luncheon, a feat which one can only remember having been previously performed at the Oval by Abel and Mr G. F. Vernon. Derbyshire, for whom Storer played very finely in both innings, batted pluckily after following on, but never had the least chance of escaping a bad beating, and in the end Surrey won by ten wickets there being only half-an-hour's play on the third day. In both these early matches T. Richardson did not play.

Surrey

R. Abel c L. G. Wright b Hulme	6	– not out	19
W. Brockwell lbw b Storer	102	– not out	31
F. C. Holland b Hulme	0		
W. Lockwood c Hulme b Bestwick	77		
T. Hayward b Hulme	55		
Mr D. L. A. Jephson c Storer b Bestwick	33		
Mr H. B. Richardson not out	45		
Mr V. F. S. Crawford c Storer b Bestwick	5		
Mr K. J. Key b Hancock	24		
E. G. Hayes c Storer b Higson	4		
H. Wood c L. G. Wright b Hancock	1		
B 13, l-b 10	23		
	375		50

Derbyshire

Mr L. G. Wright b Brockwell	34	– c and b Hayward	60
H. Bagshaw b Brockwell	3	– b Hayes	24
W. Chatterton b Lockwood	26	– c Crawford b Brockwell	42
F. Wright b Lockwood	4	– b Jephson	0
W. Storer not out	77	– c Wood b Jephson	40
J. Hulme c Abel b Lockwood	0	– b Lockwood	4
Mr T. A. Higson run out	7	– c Jephson b Brockwell	11
J. Hancock b Jephson	2	– b Jephson	28
Mr W. B. Delacombe c Holland b Jephson	3	– not out	20
W. Bestwick c Crawford b Brockwell	0	– st Wood b Jephson	8
Steeples c Hayes b Jephson	2	– b Jephson	16
L-b 2	2	B 10	10
	160		263

Derbyshire Bowling

	Overs	Mdns	Runs	Wkts	Overs	Mdns	Runs	Wkts
Hulme	36	7	97	3	13	5	19	0
Bestwick	29	5	96	3	9	2	20	0
Hancock	11.1	0	52	2	3.4	1	11	0
Storer	9	3	26	1				
Wright F.	4	0	37	0				
Steeples	6	0	21	0				
Higson	7	1	23	1				

Surrey Bowling

	Overs	Mdns	Runs	Wkts	Overs	Mdns	Runs	Wkts
Lockwood	23	5	53	3	22	5	59	1
Brockwell	22	10	53	3	22	6	68	2
Hayes	7	1	23	0	13	4	38	1
Jephson	7.3	1	29	3	15.2	4	51	5
Hayward					12	2	37	1

Umpires: M. Sherwin and A. F. Smith.

SURREY v SOMERSET

Played at The Oval, May 29, 30, 31, 1899

For two reasons the Surrey and Somerset match will always be remembered. Surrey scored 811, the highest total ever hit on The Oval, and Abel carried his bat right through the innings for 357 the second best individual score ever obtained in a first-class match. On the opening day, Surrey scored 495 for five wickets, and altogether their innings lasted just over eight hours and a half. As a matter of record it may be stated that Abel hit one six, seven 5s, thirty-eight 4s, eleven 3s, and twenty-three 2s. He was from the start completely master of the weak Somerset bowling, and so far as could be seen his only mistakes were two chances of stumping, the first at 224 and the second at 237. A collection on his behalf resulted in £33 3s being subscribed. Surrey won the match before half-past four on the third day by an innings and 379 runs. Though naturally overshadowed by Abel, Hayward and Crawford hit in brilliant style, Crawford making his first hundred in a big match.

Surrey

R. Abel not out 357
W. Brockwell c Newton b Gill 11
E. G. Hayes c Daniell b Hedley 56
Mr D. L. A. Jephson b Hedley 18
T. Hayward c Hedley b Cranfield 158
Mr H. B. Richardson c Daniell b Cranfield . 1
Mr V. F. S. Crawford c Daniell b Stanley ..129
Mr K. J. Key c Cranfield b Hedley 43
W. Lees c and b Gill 20
C. Marshall b Gill 0
T. Richardson b Gill 2
B 8, l-b 6, n-b 2 16

811

Somerset

	1st inns		2nd inns
Mr H. T. Stanley b T. Richardson	8	– c Marshall b T. Richardson	33
Capt. W. C. Hedley b Lees	1	– c Crawford b Brockwell	7
E. Robson b T. Richardson	5	– c Marshall b T. Richardson	23
Mr W. Trask c Brockwell b Lees	70	– lbw b T. Richardson	0
Mr S. M. J. Woods b Hayward	49	– b Brockwell	53
G. B. Nichols b Hayward	0	– b T. Richardson	9
G. Gill b Brockwell	3	– b Jephson	36
Mr J. Daniell c H. B. Richardson b Brockwell	50	– c Crawford b Brockwell	0
Lieut C. S. Hickley b T. Richardson	4	– b Brockwell	8
Mr A. E. Newton c Brockwell b T. Richardson	0	– not out	20
B. Cranfield not out	27	– b Brockwell	0
B 12, l-b 5	17	B 5, l-b 4	9
	234		198

Somerset Bowling

	Overs	Mdns	Runs	Wkts
Gill	43.2	6	170	4
Cranfield	56	5	180	2
Robson	23	6	87	0
Hedley	48	16	105	3
Woods	16	1	73	0
Daniell	4	1	20	0
Nichols	14	1	76	0
Trask	6	0	24	0
Stanley	12	0	60	1

Surrey Bowling

	Overs	Mdns	Runs	Wkts	Overs	Mdns	Runs	Wkts
Richardson	28	5	77	4	21	3	59	4
Lees	23	6	52	2	9	2	33	0
Hayward	19	6	47	2				
Brockwell	12.4	6	25	2	24.3	7	76	5
Abel	7	2	14	0				
Jephson	3	1	2	0	7	2	21	1

Umpires: R. Thoms and A. A. White.

SURREY v SUSSEX

Played at The Oval, August 10, 11, 12, 1899

This was in every way an extraordinary match. Surrey led off in wonderful style and when on the second afternoon they finished their innings 329 runs ahead, their victory seemed absolutely certain. From this point, however, the game underwent an astonishing change, George Brann and Ranjitsinhji in the second innings of Sussex putting on 325 runs in abour four hours and ten minutes for the second wicket. Ranjitsinhji, far surpassing anything he had ever done at The Oval, played a magnificent innings, but Brann, though he also showed excellent cricket, was missed three times – first at 53 and afterwards at 109 and 128. Despite all that the two batsmen did, there seemed little chance of Sussex saving the game for with six wickets down and three hours and ten minutes left for play, the team were only 65 runs to the good. At this critical point however, C. L. A. Smith and Vine stayed together for two hours and made a draw inevitable. Richardson's bowling on the first day equalled anything he did during the whole summer.

Sussex

Mr G. Brann b T. Richardson	12	– c Wood b Lockwood	157
Mr C. B. Fry b T. Richardson	7	– c Wood b Lockwood	20
K. S. Ranjitsinhji b Brockwell	40	– c and b Abel	197
E. H. Killick b Lees	4	– c Wood b T. Richardson	5
F. W. Marlow c Jephson b T. Richardson	21	– b Lockwood	0
Mr A. Collins c Hayward b Brockwell	0	– b Lockwood	4
Mr C. L. A. Smith c Wood b T. Richardson	7	– b Brockwell	51
J. Vine c Hayward b T. Richardson	9	– b Hayward	39
F. W. Tate not out	21	– b Brockwell	52
H. R. Butt run out	0	– c Leveson-Gower b Brockwell	7
C. H. G. Bland c Leveson-Gower b T. Richardson	7	– not out	6
		B 11, l-b 8, w 1, n-b 3	23
	128		561

Surrey

Mr D. L. A. Jephson c Brann b Bland	28	Mr K. J. Key c Butt b Brann	53
W. Brockwell b Killick	24	W. Lees c Marlow b Brann	36
T. Hayward b Killick	21	H. Wood not out	30
Mr H. D. G. Leveson-Gower c Butt b Tate	25	T. Richardson c Bland b Brann	20
R. Abel c Butt b Brann	88	B 6, l-b 4, w 1, n-b 2	13
W. H. Lockwood b Brann	88		—
Mr H. B. Richardson c Butt b Tate	31		457

Surrey Bowling

	Overs	Mdns	Runs	Wkts	Overs	Mdns	Runs	Wkts
T. Richardson	25.4	5	60	6	47	16	105	1
Lees	15	5	36	1	19	6	50	0
Brockwell	14	9	14	2	27.1	9	75	3
Abel	2	0	8	0	16	5	36	1
Jephson	4	3	10	0	14	2	53	0
Lockwood					41	8	120	4
Hayward					26	7	82	—
Leveson-Gower					8	1	17	—

Sussex Bowling

	Overs	Mdns	Runs	Wkts
Bland	31	3	103	1
Tate	40	15	111	2
Killick	29	11	72	2
Vine	5	1	15	0
Ranjitsinhji	5	1	16	0
Fry	13	2	48	0
Brann	19.2	6	73	5
Collins	2	0	6	0

Umpires: W. Hearn and J. J. Tuck.

SURREY v YORKSHIRE

Played at The Oval, August 10, 11, 12, 1899

This was beyond question the most sensational of all the matches played at The Oval during the season, 1,255 runs being scored for the loss of only seventeen wickets. The Oval has been the scene of many wonderful things in the way of run-getting, but nothing we fancy quite so startling as this. On each side there was an astonishingly successful partnership, Wainwright and Hirst putting on in three hours and a half 340 runs for Yorkshire's fifth wicket, and Abel and Hayward, with nothing but a draw to play for, staying together for six hours and a half, and in that time adding no fewer than 448 runs for Surrey's fourth wicket. Never before we should think in a first-class match have four such individual scores been made at 228, 186, 193, and 273. The batting, it need hardly be said was wonderfully good and the wicket perfect. A curious incident occurred on the second afternoon, the Yorkshiremen contending that Hayward was bowled out by a ball from Haigh before he had made seventy. The umpire, however, thinking the ball had come back off the wicket-keeper's pads decided in the batsman's favour. It may be mentioned that Yorkshire's 704 is the highest total ever hit against Surrey, and that Wainwright and Hirst have never scored so heavily in a big match.

Yorkshire

Mr F. S. Jackson c Richardson b Brockwell	18	S. Haigh not out	24
J. Tunnicliffe c Hayes b Richardson	50	Lord Hawke b Richardson	18
D. Denton c Pretty b Brockwell	47	W. Rhodes b Richardson	8
Mr F. Mitchell b Jephson	87	D. Hunter b Richardson	0
E. Wainwright c Hayward b Lockwood	228	B 25, l-b 7, w 2, n-b 1	35
G. H. Hirst b Richardson	186		
Mr E. Smith c Jephson b Lockwood	8		704

Surrey

W. Brockwell c Mitchell b Smith	29	W. H. Lockwood c sub. b Jackson	4
Mr H. C. Pretty hit wkt b Smith	15	Mr K. J. Key not out	4
E. G. Hayes c Mitchell b Smith	6		
R. Abel c Smith b Jackson	193	W 2, n-b 2	4
T. Hayward c Hunter b Jackson	273		
Mr D. L. A. Jephson c Tunnicliffe b Jackson	23		551

Mr H. D. G. Leveson-Gower, T. Richardson and A. Stedman did not bat.

Surrey Bowling

	Overs	Mdns	Runs	Wkts
Lockwood	39	9	146	2
Richardson	53.1	15	152	5
Brockwell	49	12	144	2
Hayward	14	4	56	0
Jephson	25	1	97	1
Abel	10	2	42	0
Pretty	4	1	15	0
Hayes	4	0	17	0

Yorkshire Bowling

	Overs	Mdns	Runs	Wkts
Rhodes	28	11	51	0
Smith	55	16	141	3
Jackson	47.2	15	101	4
Hirst	22	5	63	0
Wainwright	31	7	100	0
Haigh	31	8	61	0
Denton	6	0	25	0
Tunnicliffe	2	0	5	0

Umpires: V. A. Titchmarsh and A. A. White.

SURREY v LANCASHIRE

(For T. Richardson's Benefit)

Played at The Oval, August 24, 25, 26, 1899

There is no disguising the fact that in taking his benefit last season Richardson was a good deal affected by his falling off as a bowler. In the course of the autumn it was officially announced that the benefit would produce about £1,000, but though, of course, this is in itself a handsome sum, there is no doubt that Richardson would have received a great deal more if earlier in the summer he had bowled with his old success for Surrey and taken part in the Test matches between England and Australia. Considering all he had done for Surrey since 1892, it was hard luck for him to suffer both in gate money and subscriptions, but the fact remains that the public were far less enthusiastic about the match than they would have been even a twelve-month before. Surrey gave a splendid display of all round cricket and at twenty minutes to five on the third day gained an easy victory by an innings and 121 runs. Surrey's batting after a poor start was extraordinarily good, Abel and Lockwood putting on 287 in four hours and a quarter for the fifth wicket. Abel's 178, apart from a palpable chance at forward short leg when he had made 84, was free from fault until just before he was out when he gave a second chance at cover-point. Lockwood, though a little slow for him, played finely, and Jephson for the only time during the season made a hundred. His hitting was most brilliant.

Surrey

Batsman	Runs
R. Abel c Eccles b Barnes	178
W. Brockwell b Mold	8
E. G. Hayes run out	3
Mr H. C. Pretty b Ward	21
T. Hayward b Ward	11
W. H. Lockwood c Cuttell	131
Mr D. L. A. Jephson b Barnes	100
W. Lees c Mold b Baker	38
Mr K. J. Key b Barnes	28
H. Wood b Ward	2
T. Richardson not out	2
B 26, l-b 7, w 1	34
	556

Lancashire

Batsman	First innings	Second innings	
Mr R. H. Spooner b Richardson	1	– b Lees	17
A. Ward b Jephson	12	– c Wood b Richardson	1
J. T. Tyldesley c Key b Jephson	9	– c Wood b Brockwell	71
Mr A. C. MacLaren b Brockwell	27	– b Jephson	5
Mr A. Eccles b Brockwell	43	– b Lockwood	44
Mr C. R. Hartley b Richardson	49	– b Brockwell	24
G. R. Baker st Wood b Jephson	26	– b Richardson	33
W. R. Cuttell not out	12	– not out	30
Barnes b Richardson	5	– c Wood b Lockwood	2
C. Smith c Wood b Brockwell	9	– run out	0
A. Mold b Richardson	1	– b Lockwood	6
B 4, l-b 1	5	B 2, w 1	3
	199		236

Lancashire Bowling

	Overs	Mdns	Runs	Wkts
Mold	33	3	98	1
Ward	64	13	171	3
Barnes	44	15	99	3
Spooner	6	2	18	0
Baker	17	3	48	1
Cuttell	34	8	88	1

Surrey Bowling

	Overs	Mdns	Runs	Wkts	Overs	Mdns	Runs	Wkts
Richardson	33.3	16	75	4	20	9	49	2
Jephson	28	8	57	3	13	1	27	1
Brockwell	20	8	49	3	25	7	73	2
Lees	7	3	13	0	7	1	36	1
Lockwood					16.2	5	48	3

Umpires: M. Sherwin and R. Daft.

SUSSEX

THE SUSSEX BATSMEN OF 1869

"You play too many old hands to be successful", was the friendly argument used to Sussex men ere the season 1869 commenced. During the season the County played Mr Winslow, the Rev. Mr Cotterill, Mr Green, C. Charlwood, Dummer, Humphreys, Shoesmith, and other fresh hands; in fact as many as 23 different cricketers played for Sussex in the 7 matches chronicled in this book, so it was not for the want of trying fresh blood that when last season was over Sussex had gone through bad times.

Mr Smith, the Hon. Sec., commenced well with his 77 and 21 against Surrey, but accident subsequently compelled him to "ware hand" when batting, and so he fell off from his true form. Mr Winslow scored each time he went to the wickets for Sussex; he averaged excellently well for a Colt, and there can be no doubt but this young gentleman's free and good style, hard hitting, and efficient fielding will make him a useful member of the County Eleven. Mr Green scored 67 in the only match he played, and Mr Cotterill 64 in the only match he played for Sussex last season. If these gentlemen are enabled to play more frequently for the County next season why so much more the probable will be Sussex's chances of success.

Killick is highest average man, and his 78 is (by one run) the largest innings hit for Sussex in 1869; his 10 innings of 29, 15, 46, 5, 20, 29, 0, 34, 6, and 78 runs tell better than words can what a useful scorer Killick is for his county. Reed is second highest average man for Sussex in 1869; his freely, hard, and at times finely-hit 70 not out finished off his season's batting in winning form, and (aided by his 30 not out at the Crystal Palace) places him second highest on the Sussex average poll for 1869. H. Charlwood scored more runs for Sussex than any other man in '69, and, although on some occasions he failed to make double figures, they were all well squared up by innings of 23, 36, 37, 38, 48, 51, and 60 not out, the innings of 60 runs being emphatically commended by all who witnessed its being played for the truthful and excellent cricket shown; in fact, when Charlwood gets well in his cricket is of the A1 order. (Charlwood's great innings of 155 in The Gentlemen v The Players of the South match at The Oval enabled him to average 30 runs per innings in the first-class eleven a-side matches of 1869.) Humphreys is a promising Colt both with the bat and the gloves, and Dummer's average of 15 per innings is a fairly good one for a young hand's first season for his County. John Lillywhite played for Sussex so far back as 1850, and the compiler of this annual recollects Wells helping Sussex to defeat MCC and Ground at Lord's in 1854, and yet we find John Lillywhite scoring an innings of 28 and Wells one of 33 runs for Sussex in 1869.

THE NEW SUSSEX COUNTY GROUND

(*Courteously communicated*)

The new Sussex County Ground is a little nearer to Brighton than the old one, and about as far to the north of the Cliftonville road as the other was to the south. Its length from N. to S. is 238 yards, and from E. to W. 181 yards. At the south extremity there is a slip 121 yards by 36 which will be separated from the cricket ground and set apart for archery and croquet. The Tavern will be built outside the ground, at the S.W. corner, and the Pavilion will be nearly in the middle of the W. side. The ground is surrounded by a concrete wall 7 feet high. Inside this will be planted a double row of trees, and inside these a roadway 20 feet wide runs all round the ground. The whole has been carefully levelled, but more work had to be done than was expected owing to the fact that the fall from N. to S. was found to be 18 feet. Mr Fane Bennett Stanford and the Trustees of the Estate generously gave the Committee of the County Club the whole of the turf off the old Brunswick, so that it is hoped that in a couple of years the turf will "play" nearly as well as it did in its old quarters.

P.S. – In round numbers the cricket ground is all but 9 acres, and the croquet ground all but one.

SUSSEX v NOTTINGHAMSHIRE

Played at Brighton, August 14 and 15, 1873

231 overs (less 1 ball) and 231 runs were all the scorers had to book in this remarkably small County contest. The feature of this little cricket go was an innings of 19 runs played by the 10 Sussex men; that innings was commenced at 12.35 and concluded at 1.20, therefore was of exactly three-quarters-of-an-hour's duration. One man made 9 runs by two 3s and 3 singles; another man took his bat out for 8, made by two 2s and 4 singles; two others scored 1 run each, but the rest of the crew were cyphered. There were just 20 overs and 2 balls bowled in that small affair, wherein the wickets were summarily tumbled down as follows:–

1/5 2/8 3/10 4/10 5/10 6/11 7/11 8/12 9/19

Sussex's second innings contained five times as many runs. Mr G. Cotterill made 17; Killick knocked off 20; and James Lillywhite secured Sussex from a one innings defeat by a carefully played 34 not out. In Nottinghamshire's innings, William Oscroft was highest scorer with 23; four others made double figures; but little Phillips was "up to his work"; he had four wickets; and the innings ended for 101. The 15 runs required by Nottinghamshire to win were quickly knocked off by Wyld, who made the whole 15, and Nottinghamshire won by ten wickets. (A singular bit of retributive cricket was played a fortnight later on, when nearly the same Nottinghamshire Eleven, who here got the Sussex men out for 19 runs, were themselves got out by 16 of Derbyshire for an innings of 14 runs!)

Sussex

H. Killick c Morley b Alfred Shaw	0	– b Alfred Shaw	20
F. J. Greenfield Esq. b Alfred Shaw	9	– c Oscroft b Alfred Shaw	2
Rev G. Cotterill b Morley	0	– c Daft b Alfred Shaw	17
H. Charlwood c Alfred Shaw b Morley	1	– c Clifton b Morley	5
Fillery c Wyld b Morley	0	– b Morley	0
J. M. Cotterill Esq. b Alfred Shaw	0	– b Morley	4
G. E. Jeffery Esq. not out	8	– b Morley	1
C. H. Smith Esq. b Alfred Shaw	0	– b Alfred Shaw	4
Jas. Lillywhite st Biddulph b Alfred Shaw	1	– not out	34
H. Phillips, had not arrived – missed the train		– lbw b Alfred Shaw	2
H. Stubberfield b Alfred Shaw	0	– c Bignall b Alfred Shaw	7
	19		96

Nottinghamshire

Bignall c J. Cotterill b Lillywhite	7	– not out	0
Wyld run out	14	– not out	15
William Oscroft b Lillywhite	23		
Richard Daft c Phillips b Lillywhite	1		
C. Clifton c Phillips b Lillywhite	14		
Martin McIntyre c Greenfield b Lillywhite	5		
J. Selby b Fillery	1		
Alfred Shaw c Stubberfield b Lillywhite	6		
Biddulph c Phillips b Fillery	14		
Morley c Phillips b Lillywhite	14		
J. C. Shaw not out	0		
B 2	2		
	101		15

Nottinghamshire Bowling

	Overs	Mdns	Runs	Wkts	Overs	Mdns	Runs	Wkts
A. Shaw	10.2	5	8	6	50	29	38	6
Morley	10	5	11	3	44	26	49	4
McIntyre					5	2	9	0

Sussex Bowling

	Overs	Mdns	Runs	Wkts	Overs	Mdns	Runs	Wkts
Fillery	54.1	35	43	2	2	1	8	0
Lillywhite	54	27	56	7	1	0	7	0

Umpires: W. H. Luck and Thos. Humphrey.

SUSSEX v GLOUCESTERSHIRE

Played at Brighton, June 11, 12, 1874

Splendid weather and large attendances favoured this match. The wickets were, like the weather, "splendid"; and as there was a lack of first-class bowling on both sides, the scoring was expected to be like the attendance, "large"; and so it was, for when the two days' play had worked off the match, it was found one man had hit an innings of 179 runs; another one of 87; and that so many as 760 runs had been made for the 30 wickets down.

Mr W. Grace won choice, and with Mr Matthews commenced the batting to the bowling of Fillery and Lillywhite. Mr Grace started with a capital cut for 4; then he lifted one that – "owing to a misunderstanding" – neither mid-off nor cover point secured, and then, as is his wont on such occasions, Mr Grace laid on to the bowling with great severity, and eventually brought off one of his famous and fine three figure innings; he lost Mr Matthews with the score at 23, Mr Gordon at 51, and Mr G. F. Grace at 77. Then "Mr W. G." and Mr Crooke thoroughly mastered the bowling, and had brought the score to 147 (Mr Grace not out 92), when the luncheon bell sounded. On resuming play the score increased to 161, when Mr Crooke was lbw for 27. On Mr Knapp facing his captain the bowling again suffered, so much so that the score was raised from 161 to 220, when a catch at point settled Mr Knapp for 24. Mr Monkland was next man in, and once again was the work bad for bowlers and busy for fielders; both batsmen hit freely; from one over of Skinner's Mr Grace made two 4s (drives) and "a magnificent leg hit for 6"; and by such hitting was the score enlarged by 79 runs, when the big bat was at last done with by "lbw" for 179, and so – reported *Bell's Life* – "one of the finest innings ever played by Mr Grace was brought to a close". Mr Grace was first man in and sixth out, the score at 299; his 179 was made by 48 singles, seven 2s, five 3s, nineteen 4s, four 5s, and the aforesaid leg hit for 6. For the rest, Mr Monkland, Mr Miles, and Mr Ford hit and scored well; and at a quarter past six the innings was over for 381 runs.

Sussex lost two wickets – Geo. Humphreys' and Mr Mare's – that evening; and "time" was called with Sussex 14, two men gone, and Fillery and James Phillips not out. Next noon these two went at it again in excellent form, Phillips for defence, Fillery for batting; Mr W. Grace, Mr F. Grace, Mr Gordon, Mr Halford, and Mr F. Grace (again) bowled, but despite all that the score had increased to 92, when Phillips was stumped for 24; and when Fillery and Charlwood had made the figures 135, a Yorker bowled Fillery for 87, an excellent sample of "Fill's" best hitting, made by 9 singles, seven 2s, eight 3s, and ten 4s, or nearly half of his innings by fourers. Then Charlwood, W. Humphreys, and Lillywhite did most of the work in increasing the score to 231, when the innings was over, and Sussex had to "follow on." The two Phillips made their mark on the bowling, Henry P. driving one from Mr W. Grace into the Pavilion, but nine wickets had gone down when but 116 runs had been scored, and then Hall (the Colt) faced Charlwood, with 35 runs wanting to save the one-innings defeat; the Colt "playing the game"; he made a 4 from each of the Grace's; Charlwood backed this up in good form, and they hit the score to 148, or 3 to save the innings, when cover point captured the Colt; so Gloucestershire won by an innings and 2 runs, Charlwood not out 31, reported "a very fine innings".

Gloucestershire

W. G. Grace Esq. lbw b Lillywhite	179
T. G. Matthews Esq. st H. Phillips b Lillywhite	6
C. Gordon Esq. c Fillery b Lillywhite	19
G. F. Grace Esq. c Hall b Lillywhite	9
F. J. Crooke Esq. lbw b Lillywhite	27
E. M. Knapp Esq. c Fillery b Hall	24
F. G. Monkland Esq. c Mare b Fillery	24
G. H. Halford Esq. b Fillery	0
C. E. B. Ford Esq. not out	32
R. F. Miles Esq. b Lillywhite	38
G. E. R. Brown Esq. c Skinner b Fillery	8
B 9, l-b 6	15
	381

Sussex

Geo. Humphreys run out	2 – c and b W. Grace	2
James Phillips st Ford b W. Grace	24 – b F. Grace	25
J. M. Mare Esq. c Ford b W. Grace	0 – c and b W. Grace	12
Fillery b Knapp	87 – b W. Grace	0
H. Charlwood c F. Grace b Knapp	20 – not out	31
Walter Humphreys not out	35 – run out	12
James Lillywhite c and b F. Grace	38 – c and b F. Grace	14
Geo. Knight b F. Grace	11 – c Halford b W. Grace	3
Henry Phillips c F. Grace b W. Grace	5 – c Matthews b W. Grace	26
J. Skinner b W. Grace	0 – c Halford b W. Grace	0
W. Hall b W. Grace	1 – c Miles b W. Grace	18
B 5, l-b 2, n-b 1	8 B 3, l-b 2	5
	231	148

Sussex Bowling

	Overs	Mdns	Runs	Wkts
Lillywhite	59	22	113	6
Fillery	55	15	118	3
Hall	25	2	57	1
Skinner	15	3	44	0
Knight	6	0	18	0
W. Humphreys	5	0	16	0

Gloucestershire Bowling

	Overs	Mdns	Runs	Wkts	Overs	Mdns	Runs	Wkts
Mr W. Grace	60	31	76	5	44	15	82	7
Mr F. Grace	47.1	18	87	2	43.3	18	61	2
Mr Knapp	10	4	27	2				
Mr Gordon	9	5	21	0				
Mr Halford	3	1	12	0				

Umpires: H. Killick and Pullin.

SUSSEX v KENT

Played at Brighton, July 3, 4, 5, 1884

This was the second match of over 1000 runs played by Sussex during the season, and resulted in a draw altogether in favour of the home eleven. Sussex had the good fortune to win the toss and were batting from 12.15 until 5.20. Mr Newham batted very finely for his 76, and never gave the semblance of a chance. He hit eleven 4s, two 3s, six 2s, and 14 singles, and during his partnership with Tester 75 runs were added to the score, 45 more being put on while he was in with Mr Whitfeld. The Sussex captain's 44 included six 4s and three 3s, and was a capital innings of two and a half hours' duration. Towards the close of the innings the Kent bowling was freely punished by Jesse Hide and Mr W. Blackman. Kent scored 53 for the loss of one wicket, and stumps were then drawn for the day.

The continuation of the Kent innings on the Friday was alone remarkable for the splendid batting of Lord Harris. The Kent captain went in when two wickets had fallen for 58 runs, and was the last man out. He was at the wickets for two hours and 35 minutes, and scored the very large proportion of 101 out of 161 runs put on during his stay, his figures being fifteen 4s, a 3, five 2s and singles. Sussex had an advantage of 51 runs when they began their second innings, and when the day's play came to an end they had only lost two wickets for 176. Mr Ellis was dismissed for 18, and Mr Newham for a faultless 48, Tester and Jesse Hide being the not out men with 72 and 26 respectively.

On resumption of play on the last day Tester ran himself out after adding 8 runs to his overnight score. He had gone in first on the previous day, and was out at 214. He batted very patiently, but his innings of 80 contained some lucky hits, and he might have been caught when he had made 68. His chief hits were eight 4s, five 3s, and seven 2s. Hide batted in brilliant style, and scored 112 out of 180 put on while he was in, his figures being fourteen 4s, two 3s, and thirteen 2s. He made a couple of mistakes, but his innings was nevertheless a very fine one, and the highest he scored for Sussex during the season. Some exceedingly rapid hitting was done when Mr Blackman and Mr Wyatt came together, 109 runs being actually scored in 50 minutes. Mr Wyatt was out at 423, but Mr Blackman carried his bat out, his dashing innings of 77 being his best effort for his county during the year. The last 150 runs in the innings were scored in 72 minutes. Only two hours and 20 minutes remained for play when Kent went in for the second time against the enormous total of 515. They made 54 runs for the first two wickets, but six were down at 103. Lord Harris and Mr Christopherson then made the stand which saved Kent from defeat, the latter being stumped off the last ball bowled. The Kent captain offered to continue the game for another fifteen minutes to finish, but this sportsmanlike offer was not accepted by Mr Whitfeld. It will be seen that 1,083 runs were scored in the match for the loss of 37 wickets, an average of over 29, and that in the second innings of Sussex the whole of the Kent eleven went on to bowl.

Sussex

R. T. Ellis Esq b Wootton	8 – c Harris b Christopherson	18
W. Tester c Pentecost b C. Wilson	22 – run out	80
W. Newham Esq. b Christopherson	76 – lbw b Wootton	48
H. Whitfeld Esq. b H. Hearne	44 – c H. Hearne b Wootton	13
W. Humphreys c Harris b Christopherson	14 – b Christopherson	22
G. N. Wyatt Esq. b Wootton	0 – b Pentecost	45
J. Hide b H. Hearne	39 – hit w b H. Hearne	112
H. Phillips c G. G. Hearne b Wootton	13 – c Pentecost b Harris	7
W. Blackman Esq. not out	32 – not out	77
A. Hide lbw b Wootton	11 – b Harris	9
J. Juniper st Pentecost b Wootton	0 – c L. Wilson b Harris	7
B 6, l-b 3, w 2	11 B 20, l-b 5, w 1	26
	270	464

Kent

C. Wilson Esq. c Phillips b Blackman	15 – st Phillips b Humphreys	24
F. Hearne b Blackman	21 – c Phillips b A. Hide	22
G. G. Hearne b Blackman	16 – b Tester	6
Lord Harris st Phillips b Humphreys	101 – not out	40
S. Christopherson Esq. b A. Hide	7 – st Phillips b Humphreys	16
J. Wootton c Whitfeld b A. Hide	4 – b Humphreys	0
L. Wilson Esq. b Blackman	15 – c Whitfeld b Juniper	7
F. Marchant Esq. c Phillips b Tester	5 – st Phillips b Humphreys	7
A. C. Gibson Esq. b J. Hide	6	
J. Pentecost st Phillips b Humphreys	10	
H. Hearne not out	5	
B 8, l-b 4, n-b 2	14 B 7, n-b 1	8
	219	130

Kent Bowling

	Overs	Mdns	Runs	Wkts	Overs	Mdns	Runs	Wkts
Wootton	62.1	30	94	5	50	25	88	2
Mr Christopherson	43	18	63	2	44	20	71	2
G. G. Hearne	14	7	20	0	44	24	55	0
H. Hearne	34	21	34	2	44	19	74	1
Mr C. Wilson	7	1	33	1	16	3	36	0
Mr Gibson	6	1	15	0	7	1	20	0
Lord Harris					11.1	3	28	3
Mr Marchant					4	2	5	0
Mr L. Wilson					4	0	24	0
F. Hearne					4	0	18	0
Pentecost					6	1	19	1

Sussex Bowling

	Overs	Mdns	Runs	Wkts	Overs	Mdns	Runs	Wkts
A. Hide	28	16	40	2	16	11	11	1
J. Hide	31	10	5	1	4	3	6	0
Mr Blackman	32	13	49	4	15	9	8	0
Humphreys	4	0	13	2	30.2	12	66	4
Juniper	11	3	27	0	11	4	13	1
Tester	15	9	25	1	9	3	18	1

Umpires: J. Street and R. Thoms.

SUSSEX v SURREY

Played at Brighton, July 13, 14, 15, 1885

For the second time during the season Surrey made a very long score against Sussex, and defeated them in a single innings. Surrey, having the good fortune to win the toss, remained in for the whole of the afternoon. At the call of time they had still two wickets to fall, and their total stood at the enormous figure of 457. A fortnight previously Surrey made 631 against Sussex, and by a strange coincidence the two batsmen who were most successful in that match were also the top scorers in this. At The Oval Mr W. E. Roller made 204 and Mr W. W. Read 163, while in the match under notice Mr Roller scored 144 and Mr Read 101. For two members of an eleven to get two hundreds each against the same county in the same season is certainly a cricket curiosity of the most extraordinary kind. When Mr Read and Mr Roller became partners Surrey's score was only 44 for three wickets, but when they were separated it had been increased to 213, the two gentlemen thus putting on 169 runs while they were together. Mr Read only took two hours to get his 101, and his innings was a superb one – free from anything like a mistake. His figures were nineteen 4s, a 3, six 2s, and ten singles. Mr Roller stayed in till the total had reached 350, and was the sixth man out. Like Mr Read he gave no chance that came to hand, but he ought to have been run out when he had made 77. He was three hours and twenty-five minutes at the wickets, the hits of his splendid innings being twenty-three 4s, two 3s, nine 2s, and 28 singles. Though overshadowed by their brilliant companions, Messrs Diver and Key also played capital cricket, and Mr Key was 61, not out, when play ceased for the day.

The Surrey innings was completed on the Tuesday for 501, Mr Key increasing his overnight score to 82, and taking out his bat. His brilliantly-hit innings included no fewer than thirteen 4s. The Sussex men, in face of their opponents' enormous total, had of course no possibility of winning the match, and only a very remote chance of saving it. Their first innings, which amounted to 209, was rendered remarkable by the splendid batting of Mr Newham. That gentleman went in first wicket down with the score at 7, and of 187 runs put on during his stay, made no fewer than 115. He was batting for two hours and 55 minutes, and though he made one or two bad strokes, he gave no chance. The figures of his innings were twelve 4s, four 3s, sixteen 2s, and 23 singles. Being 292 behind in the first innings, Sussex had as a matter of course, to follow on, and during the remaining time that play lasted, 92 runs were scored for the loss of three wickets, Mr Wyatt and Humphreys being the not out men, with 49 and 8 respectively.

On the resumption of play on the Wednesday the home side, with seven wickets to go down, still wanted 200 runs to avert a single innings defeat. This proved a task altogether beyond their powers, for in the absence of Mr Newham, who had sprained his hand while batting on the Tuesday, the remaining batsmen were got rid of in an hour and twenty minutes for an addition of 76, the innings closing for 168. Mr Wyatt increased his score to 65, an innings of the greatest merit, and made without a mistake. In all the Sussex captain was batting for two hours and a quarter, having gone in first, and being dismissed at 120; his hits were five 4s, four 3s, and eight 2s. Jesse Hide made some good hits in his 32, and Mr Smith stayed in some time, but the others offered a very poor resistance to the bowling of Mr Horner and Lohmann, and in the end were defeated by an innings with 129 runs to spare.

Surrey

R. Abel b Smith	9
J. Shuter Esq. c Ellis b J. Hide	27
M. P. Bowden Esq. b J. Hide	1
W. W. Read Esq. c Newham b Tester	101
W. E. Roller Esq. b Tester	144
E. J. Diver Esq. b Newham	51
K. J. Key Esq. not out	82
G. A. Lohmann c and b Humphreys	21
J. Beaumont b H. Phillips	12
T. Bowley c Tester b J. Hide	39
C. E. Horner Esq. b J. Hide	0
B 14	14
	501

Sussex

W. A. Tester b Lohmann	14	– b Lohmann	16
H. Phillips c Lohmann b Beaumont	0	– not out	4
W. Newham Esq. c and b Lohmann	115	– absent (hurt)	
R. T. Ellis Esq. c Diver b Lohmann	8	– b Lohmann	5
W. Humphreys c Abel b Lohmann	6	– b Lohmann	13
J. Hide b Lohmann	0	– c Bowden b Horner	32
G. N. Wyatt Esq. c Shuter b Horner	33	– c Bowden b Beaumont	65
G. Brann Esq. c Bowley b Horner	6	– c Key b Lohmann	7
J. Phillips c Bowley b Horner	2	– c Bowden b Horner	0
C. A. Smith Esq. not out	2	– b Horner	16
A. Hide c Shuter b Horner	6	– c Key b Lohmann	0
B 13, l-b 4	17	B 6, l-b 2, w 2	10
	209		168

Sussex Bowling

	Overs	Mdns	Runs	Wkts
Mr Smith	64	27	126	1
A. Hide	21	8	53	0
J. Hide	52	28	79	4
Mr Newham	30	13	33	1
Humphreys	30	10	78	1
Tester	27	8	74	2
Mr Wyatt	5	2	8	0
Mr Brann	3	0	17	0
H. Phillips	7	3	19	1

Surrey Bowling

	Overs	Mdns	Runs	Wkts	Overs	Mdns	Runs	Wkts
Beaumont	31	11	54	1	44	19	67	1
Lohmann	45	17	84	5	43.3	18	62	5
Mr Horner	21.3	8	25	4	18	8	25	3
Bowley	12	4	21	0	2	1	3	0
Abel	8	3	8	0	5	4	1	0

SUSSEX v HAMPSHIRE

Played at Brighton, June 14, 15, 1886

Sussex for their first match against Hampshire had again a good side, and the game produced some highly sensational cricket. On the first day Hampshire, winning the toss, remained in for the greater part of the afternoon, and scored 198, Mr F. E. Lacey (59 not out) and Mr Powell (41) playing capitally. Then, in a rather bad light, Sussex lost three wickets for 85, Mr F. M. Lucas being not out 15, and Mr Brann not out 31, at the call of time.

On the second day Mr Lucas and Mr Brann made an extraordinary stand, and at one time scored 100 runs within the hour. Mr Brann, who was batting altogether three hours and forty minutes, made 219, and the exceptional character of his cricket may be gathered from the fact that he hit no fewer than thirty-five 4s. Mr Lucas hit a 5 and fourteen 4s in a very finely played 109, his only chance being a very sharp one to Dible. The total of the innings was 420, and of this number the two batsmen scored between them 328. Going in to bat after a long outing, the Hampshire men failed ignominiously against Arthur Hide's bowling, and were quickly got rid of for 68, Sussex winning the match by an innings and 154 runs. Arthur Hide in Hampshire's second innings delivered thirty-nine overs, twenty-five maidens, and took nine wickets for 25 runs – a remarkable analysis on any ground, and certainly an extraordinary one at Brighton.

Hampshire

Mr B. de B. Carey b A. Hide	9	– b A. Hide	0
Parsons b J. Hide	2	– c Newham b A. Hide	3
Dible b Bean	24	– c Quaife b A. Hide	0
Mr E. O. Powell c Phillips b A. Hide	41	– c Phillips b A. Hide	28
Mr F. E. Lacey not out	59	– b A. Hide	0
Mr C. R. Seymour c Phillips b A. Hide	12	– b A. Hide	7
Young c and b J. Hide	18	– c Budgen b Humphreys	10
Mr C. E. Currie b J. Hide	11	– b A. Hide	2
Colonel Fellowes b Bean	5	– c Tester b A. Hide	1
Shrimpton run out	1	– c Newham b A. Hide	9
Willoughby b J. Hide	0	– not out	8
B 14, l-b 2	16		
	198		68

Sussex

J. Hide b Currie	17
Tester b Dible	9
Mr W. Newham lbw b Dible	6
Mr F. M. Lucas c Lacey b Currie	109
Mr G. Brann b Parsons	219
Bean b Currie	11
W. Humphreys not out	21
Quaife c Young b Currie	1
Budgen c Shrimpton b Young	8
Phillips c Young b Currie	2
A. Hide b Currie	2
B 9, l-b 5, w 1	15
	420

Sussex Bowling

	Overs	Mdns	Runs	Wkts	Overs	Mdns	Runs	Wkts
J. Hide	44.2	16	66	4	31	18	31	0
A. Hide	45	23	56	3	39	25	25	9
Bean	15	4	20	2				
Tester	5	3	9	0				
Humphreys	5	2	18	0	7	1	12	1
Mr Newham	5	1	13	0				

Hampshire Bowling

	Overs	Mdns	Runs	Wkts
Dible	44	18	64	2
Willoughby	28	11	54	0
Mr Currie	43	17	94	6
Young	19	4	53	1
Colonel Fellowes	26	13	40	0
Mr Carey	4	0	21	0
Mr Lacey	15	4	46	0
Parsons	10	2	33	1

SUSSEX v KENT

Played at Brighton, July 8, 9, 10, 1886

A perfect wicket was provided at Brighton for the first meeting of Sussex and Kent, and the batsmen on both sides showed such appreciation of it that in the course of the contest no fewer than 1,063 runs were scored. It is not often that three days of busier cricket are seen, and it was not until ten minutes past six on the Saturday that the end was reached. Neither county had its best eleven, Mr Newham and Mr Brann being absent from the

Sussex side, while Kent was without Mr W. H. Patterson, Mr C. Wilson, Mr Rashleigh, and Mr M. C. Kemp. On the opening day, when rain caused a stoppage for a little over an hour, Sussex played a first innings of 161, and Kent lost four wickets for 187, Lord Harris hitting up a brilliant 73, which included eight 4s and six 2s. In the Sussex innings Wootton accomplished one of his best bowling performances of the season, getting rid of eight batsmen in 40 overs and a ball at a cost of 55 runs.

On the second day Kent went on hitting with great success, Rev. R. T. Thornton and Alec Hearne actually adding 84 runs for the last wicket, and the total of the innings reaching 319. With 158 runs wanted to save a single innings defeat, Sussex went in for the second time, and played so finely that when stumps were drawn the score stood at 302 for seven wickets, Jesse Hide being not out 124.

On the Saturday morning Jesse Hide continued hitting, and was not got rid of until he had scored 173 – the highest and perhaps the best innings he has ever played in a first-class match. He hit splendidly all through, and made a straight drive out of the ground for 6, twenty-one 4s, one 3, and sixteen 2s. Kent had 213 runs to win, and four hours and a half to get them in, and the task seemed by no means a certainty. However, a capital stand by George and Frank Hearne mastered the Sussex bowling, and in the end Kent gained a creditable victory by four wickets.

Sussex

First innings		Second innings	
Mr E. J. McCormick run out	20	b Wootton	3
Tester b Wootton	10	b Wootton	29
J. Hide b Wootton	0	c Hickmott b G. G. Hearne	173
Mr F. M. Lucas b Wootton	14	c Hickmott b Christopherson	49
Humphreys c F. Hearne b Wootton	43	c G. G. Hearne b A. J. Thornton	51
Mr W. Mitchell b Wootton	3	b Wootton	0
Quaife st Hickmott b Wootton	46	st Hickmott b Wootton	9
Bean c Hickmott b Wootton	5	lbw b Wootton	0
Budgen b G. G. Hearne	2	c A. Hearne b G. G. Hearne	32
H. Phillips not out	6	not out	5
A. Hide c A. J. Thornton b Wootton	5	c R. T. Thornton b Wootton	1
B 5, l-b 2	7	B 4, l-b 14	18
	161		370

Kent

First innings		Second innings	
Mr A. J. Thornton c Phillips b J. Hide	7	not out	11
F. Hearne c Lucas b J. Hide	34	st Phillips b Humphreys	59
G. G. Hearne b J. Hide	42	b Humphreys	71
Lord Harris c Lucas b J. Hide	73	b J. Hide	1
Mr L. Wilson run out	40	hit wicket b Tester	18
Captain Friend c Bean b Tester	22	b Humphreys	16
Rev R. T. Thornton c Phillips b J. Hide	64	not out	30
Wootton c Humphreys b Tester	0	c McCormick b Tester	6
Hickmott c Phillips b A. Hide	0		
Mr S. Christopherson c and b Tester	6		
A. Hearne not out	27		
B 2, l-b 2	4	B 1	1
	319		213

Kent Bowling

	Overs	Mdns	Runs	Wkts	Overs	Mdns	Runs	Wkts
Wootton	40.1	19	55	8	58	22	107	6
Mr A. J. Thornton	20	2	43	0	36	11	72	1
A. Hearne	12	5	31	0	23	9	47	0
Mr Christopherson	3	0	8	0	37	11	69	1
G. G. Hearne	11	3	17	1	21	7	27	2
Lord Harris					12	4	30	0

Sussex Bowling

	Overs	Mdns	Runs	Wkts	Overs	Mdns	Runs	Wkts
A. Hide	56	23	83	1	21	11	23	0
J. Hide	51.2	18	86	5	26	12	36	1
Tester	40	11	70	3	47.2	24	50	2
Humphreys	17	2	53	0	26	2	75	3
Bean	15	6	23	0	26	18	28	0

SUSSEX v LANCASHIRE

Played at Brighton, August 9, 10, 11, 1886

Sussex was fully represented for the return match with Lancashire, Messrs F. M. Lucas, Newham, Thomas, and Brann being all available, and a place for the first time being given to Mr G. H. Cotterill, son of the Rev. G. E. Cotterill, and nephew of the famous batsman Mr J. M. Cotterill. Lancashire won the toss, and staying in on a good wicket from a quarter past twelve until half-past four, ran up a total of 211. Robinson's freely-hit but not especially good innings of 54 included nine 4s, a 3, and three 2s. Mr Hornby and Barlow both played well and scored 51 for the first wicket. Walter Humphreys bowled his lobs with conspicuous success, taking four wickets in nine overs and two balls for 26 runs, and Harry Phillips kept wicket in his very best style, catching three batsmen and stumping another. Sussex had an hour and forty minutes' batting at the end of the afternoon, and made 98 runs for three wickets, Tester being not out 39, and Mr Thomas not out 17 at the drawing of stumps.

On the second morning each batsman increased his score to 58, and curiously enough each hit seven 4s. Mr Thomas gave a chance at the wicket on the Monday evening before he had made a run, but otherwise played capitally. Tester's innings, except for a chance at slip, was also a good one. There was a good deal of rain on the Tuesday morning, and when Lancashire went in for the second time the wicket had become decidedly difficult. Its condition, however, did not excuse the complete failure of the northern team, who were all out in an hour and a half for 60 runs. Tester and Jesse Hide bowled uncommonly well, and Walter Humphreys, going on at the end of the innings, took two wickets in six balls without a run being hit from him.

On the Wednesday morning the Lancashire men bowled and fielded so well that at one time the result of the game seemed in doubt, Sussex wanting 24 to win with only four wickets to go down. At this point, when the partisans of Sussex were getting decidedly nervous, Jesse Hide hit five 4s in quick succession and won the match for Sussex at twelve minutes past one by four wickets.

Lancashire

Mr A. N. Hornby c Smith b Tester	37	– c Lucas b Tester	7
Barlow c Phillips b J. Hide	30	– run out	1
Mr P. Dobell c Phillips b Tester	0	– run out	8
Briggs c Newham b Tester	8	– lbw b J. Hide	3
Mr J. Eccles c Phillips b A. Hide	34	– b Tester	1
Robinson c J. Hide b A. Hide	54	– c Tester b J. Hide	0
Mr O. P. Lancashire b Humphreys	24	– c Smith b Tester	21
Yates not out	15	– c Cotterill b J. Hide	1
Mr A. Teggin st Phillips b Humphreys	0	– c Tester b Humphreys	9
Watson c Lucas b Humphreys	9	– c Lucas b Humphreys	6
Pilling lbw b Humphreys	0	– not out	2
		L-b 1	1
	211		60

Sussex

J. Hide c Pilling b Barlow	4	– not out	21
Tester c Watson b Briggs	58	– b Barlow	8
Mr G. H. Cotterill b Barlow	0	– b Briggs	1
Mr W. Newham lbw b Watson	37	– c Pilling b Barlow	25
Mr F. Thomas run out	58	– b Watson	0
Mr F. M. Lucas c Pilling b Barlow	23	– c Hornby b Watson	4
Mr G. Brann lbw b Barlow	3	– not out	3
Humphreys not out	11	– b Barlow	4
Mr C. A. Smith c Pilling b Barlow	0		
H. Phillips b Barlow	0		
A. Hide b Briggs	1		
B 2, l-b 3	5	B 1, l-b 6	7
	200		73

Sussex Bowling

	Overs	Mdns	Runs	Wkts	Overs	Mdns	Runs	Wkts
J. Hide	45	19	75	1	25	13	27	3
A. Hide	32	11	61	2				
Tester	28	16	36	3	24	11	32	3
Humphreys	9.2	2	26	4	1.2	1	0	2
Mr Smith	6	2	13	0				

Lancashire Bowling

	Overs	Mdns	Runs	Wkts	Overs	Mdns	Runs	Wkts
Barlow	50	30	54	6	35	17	43	3
Briggs	61.3	27	79	2	12	10	8	1
Mr Teggin	5	2	7	0				
Watson	26	10	43	1	24	19	15	2
Yates	4	0	12	0				

SUSSEX v GLOUCESTERSHIRE

Played at Brighton, May 21, 22, 23, 1888

In a season, distinguished perhaps above all its predecessors for bad weather and small scoring, the engagement between these old opponents stood out as a brilliant example of cricket of the happier and more enjoyable, if not actually the better, kind. Big scoring was certainly pretty frequent about this time in May, and we had not yet suffered the bitter experiences of June and July, but among the 70s, 80s, and 90s recorded contemporaneously with the contest we are about to describe, the innings of Mr Grace stood out prominently as a thing of itself. When afterwards Jesse Hide, Mr C. A. Smith, and Mr Newham all made their fine scores, and it was found after three full days and an aggregate total of 1,117 runs, that the match was actually left drawn in favour of Sussex, admirers of south country cricket became enthusiastic. Gloucestershire won the toss, and at the end of the first day Mr Grace was 188 not out. He had received admirable assistance from Mr Troup, Mr O. G. Radcliffe, and Painter, and, except for one chance to Tester at mid-off when he had made 26, his batting was altogether free from fault. The Gloucestershire score was 361 for six wickets, and nine of the Sussex bowlers had been tried. There was a large crowd on the ground, the weather being beautifully fine, and the wicket was in that almost perfect condition in which we generally see the turf at Hove.

On the second day Gloucestershire continued their hitting until the score was 428. Mr Grace was ninth out for 215, hitting his wicket in playing at a lob. The champion was in for very nearly seven hours, and only gave the one chance we have mentioned. He hit twenty 4s, three 3s, twenty-six 2s, and 74 singles, and his innings of 215 was the largest score in first-class county matches in 1888. It was remarkable for the power and freedom of its all round hitting, and for the unerring judgment and masterful ease with which all kinds of bowling were met. Sussex, on going in, lost three of their best wickets for 16 runs. The next two men did better, and when Jesse Hide was joined by Mr Smith, the total was 104 for five wickets. These two then obtained a thorough mastery over the bowling, and hit with really remarkable freedom. They put on 161 runs in an hour and forty minutes, and completely altered the aspect of the game. Jesse Hide gave a chance to Painter in the long field when he had scored 78, but there was not much else to find fault with in his excellent innings, the figures of which were twenty-two 4s, two 3s, nine 2s, and 18 singles. Mr Smith gave two chances, at 38 and 51, but he nevertheless deserves great praise for his 85, in which were eleven 4s, three 3s, and eight 2s. At the close of the day nine Sussex wickets were down for 334, or one wicket to fall, and 15 runs wanted to save the follow-on. Up to this time nineteen wickets had fallen for 762 runs, and, although it was Whit week and there was a great deal of important cricket going on all over the country, the Brighton match was certainly the thing of the hour.

On the third morning Phillips and Arthur Hide played up capitally and saved the follow on. Gloucestershire went in for their second innings with 74 runs in hand, but, except for the partnership for the fourth wicket of Messrs Radcliffe and Pullen, the batting failed before Mr Smith and Arthur Hide, and the total of the innings was only 174. Mr Radcliffe's 68 was a capital display of batting, marred by a chance to Humphreys at point when he had scored only 6. Sussex, with two hours and a half left, had to go in for 249. There was, of course, no chance of winning, but a possibility of losing, and when Quaife, Tester, and Arthur Hide were out for 33, defeat seemed not improbable. Messrs Newham and McCormick, however, soon made the game safe, and like their rivals earlier in the day scored 88 runs while they were together. Jesse Hide and Mr Newham then played out time, Sussex, with six wickets to fall, being 88 runs short of victory, so that for the third time in the day that combination of figures is to be noticed. Mr Newham's principal hits were eight 4s, four 3s, and nine 2s. He gave a chance at 37, and might afterward have been run out, but his batting nevertheless was of a high order.

Gloucestershire

Mr W. G. Grace hit wkt b Humphreys	215	– c and b A. Hide	5
Mr E. M. Grace c Quaife b J. Hide	5	– c Smith b A. Hide	6
Mr W. Troup c Humphreys b J. Hide	32	– b A. Hide	5
Mr W. W. F. Pullen b Smith	22	– b Tate	33
Mr O. G. Radcliffe b McCormick	44	– c Brann b Smith	68
Mr J. H. Brain b McCormick	0	– b Smith	4
J. Painter b Humphreys	64	– c Newham b Smith	2
Mr A. Newnham c Brann b A. Hide	13	– lbw b Tate	0
Mr G. Francis b A. Hide	0	– not out	21
Mr J. A. Bush not out	26	– b Smith	16
F. G. Roberts st Phillips b Humphreys	0	– c J. Hide b Smith	5
B 5, l-b 2	7	B 7, l-b 2	9
	428		174

Sussex

W. Quaife lbw b Newnham	10 – c Radcliffe b W. G. Grace	8
W. Tester b Newnham	3 – c Pullen b Radcliffe	2
Mr W. Newham b Roberts	1 – not out	81
J. Hide c and b Radcliffe	130 – not out	19
Mr E. J. McCormick run out	22 – b Radcliffe	34
W. Humphreys c Troup b W. G. Grace	22	
Mr C. A. Smith c Roberts b Newnham	85	
Mr G. Brann b Newnham	15	
F. W. Tate c W. G. Grace b Newnham	4	
H. Phillips c Bush b W. G. Grace	31	
A. Hide not out	19 – b Radcliffe	9
B 8, w 1, n-b 3	12 B 4, l-b 3, n-b 1	8
	354	161

Sussex Bowling

	Overs	Mdns	Runs	Wkts	Overs	Mdns	Runs	Wkts
A. Hide	73	26	101	2	23	14	22	3
J. Hide	63	29	78	2	20	7	31	0
Mr C. A. Smith	41	21	58	1	24	11	49	5
Humphreys	21.3	2	71	3	4	2	5	0
Tate	16	4	34	0	21	5	42	2
Tester	18	9	27	0	8	6	8	0
Mr McCormick	16	6	36	2	4	9	8	0
Mr Brann	6	1	10	0				
Quaife	6	2	6	0				

Gloucestershire Bowling

	Overs	Mdns	Runs	Wkts	Overs	Mdns	Runs	Wkts
Roberts	34	15	61	1	10	5	18	0
Mr W. G. Grace	42.2	12	91	2	44	22	53	1
Mr Newnham	39	15	77	5	5	0	15	0
Mr Radcliffe	41	13	75	1	24	7	52	3
Mr E. M. Grace	15	6	23	0	6	0	15	0
Painter	5	0	15	0				

SUSSEX IN 1889

The almost complete failure of the Sussex eleven was the more remarkable as of the first four county matches played one ended in victory, another was drawn by pluck and determination, and the two defeats were at the hands of admittedly stronger sides, Nottinghamshire and Lancashire. From that point, however – June 26 – the Southern team only played two good matches. Nottinghamshire thrashed them at Brighton; Kent scored a big innings against them and won anyhow at Gravesend; Surrey beat them by three wickets after a capital fight at Brighton, and then, to make up for this comparatively close game, won in a single innings with 84 runs to spare at the Oval. Then followed three single innings' defeats by Gloucestershire, Lancashire, and Kent respectively, the season finishing up with the return against Yorkshire, which the northern eleven won by 68 runs. We believe that Ellis, the Yorkshire wicket-keeper, who was tried some time ago, is now qualifying for Sussex, but a great deal more than this must be done if the team are to keep their place in the cricket world. That place has now been at the bottom of the first-class counties for two seasons, and, unless some recruits are found, home grown or imported, even this position will soon be untenable. The men who do most of the work for Sussex are not likely to improve, but are, on the other hand, getting past their best. Mr Newham's batting ability is handicapped by the cares and anxieties of his position as captain; Humphreys, one of the most individual of the cricketers, is, as a player, an old man, the brothers Hide, though they do their work steadily and conscientiously, can never hope to do much better than they have done, and for the rest the amateurs are either too much engaged in business or too lukewarm in the cause to be of real service, and the professionals, except Quaife and Bean, are players of distinctly inferior ability.

We have thought it well to state clearly and uncompromisingly the unfortunate position of Sussex, and we should say that the best remedy is to import some young professionals from Nottinghamshire or Yorkshire. We do not think that anything will excuse one county club endeavouring to take away from another men who are actually employed and wanted in their own county. Further than that, before importation is resorted to long and earnest efforts should be made to find native players. Sussex have tried for years, and in the nett result have failed. The courses now open are either to adopt importation as a settled policy or to be content to gradually sink to the position of their neighbour Hampshire. The present writer has on several occasions, while thoroughly opposing anything like the offering of unfair inducements to a professional to leave a club that is employing his talent, spoken in favour of taking full and legitimate advantage of the residential law. It is notorious that in Nottinghamshire and in Yorkshire there are scores of cricketers who will in all probability never be wanted for their own counties, but who would certainly strengthen less powerful elevens. The strict birth qualification is a beautiful thing in theory, but in practice it goes for very little. County cricket to-day owes an enormous share of its importance to the wise adoption of the residential law by Surrey, Lancashire, and others, and those who will look at the facts fairly and squarely and free their minds from sentiment and prejudice must admit that residents are quite as loyal and quite as contented as the majority of those men who were born in the counties for which they play. We by no means wish to see English professionals become mere mercenaries, as American base-ball players confessedly are, but we do not believe there is any danger of such a condition of things coming about so long as the present restrictions are in force and committees exercise their powers with judgment and good feeling. But, as we have said, the alternatives present to the Sussex committee to-day are, that either they must slide down the hill and drop out of important cricket – they are the possessors of perhaps the finest bit of playing turf in the country – or else find the money and summon up the energy to recruit their eleven fairly and openly from the good but unemployed material ready to their hands in the villages of the great cricketing counties of the north.

SUSSEX v SURREY

Played at Brighton, July 15, 16, 17, 1889

On their own ground the Sussex eleven generally make a good fight against Surrey, and this match proved no exception to the rule. The wicket was difficult, and some sensational cricket was witnessed before the game ended in favour of Surrey by three wickets. On the opening day the home team, thanks to a fine batting performance by Jesse Hide, scored 180, the professional taking out his bat for an invaluable 75. Afterwards Surrey lost two wickets for 15 runs, and on Tuesday they looked like being in a big minority. However, Mr Key and Henderson put on 48 runs, and Sharpe and Beaumont added 43 for the last wicket. Sussex started their second innings badly, losing five wickets for 43 runs. Messrs Newham and Brann then raised the score to 81, and at this total the last five wickets went down in nine balls without the addition of a single run. In the match Lohmann had the extraordinary record of fifteen wickets for 98 runs. Surrey went in on the third day with 81 to get, but seven wickets were lost before the necessary runs were obtained. Arthur Hide took six of those wickets for 29 runs.

Sussex

Mr F. H. Gresson c M. Read b Lohmann	6	– lbw b Beaumont	8
J. Major b Beaumont	19	– b Lohmann	0
Mr W. Newham c Abel b Lohmann	14	– b Sharpe	25
W. Quaife c Henderson b Lohmann	13	– b Lohmann	0
J. Hide not out	75	– b Lohmann	9
W. Humphreys b Lohmann	4	– b Lohmann	7
Mr G. Brann b Lohmann	37	– c M. Read b Abel	32
G. Bean b Lohmann	0	– c M. Read b Lohmann	0
A. Hide b Lohmann	4	– b Lohmann	0
T. Mayes b Lohmann	0	– run out	0
F. W. Tate b Lohmann	0	– not out	0
B 7, l-b 1	8		
	180		81

Surrey

Mr J. Shuter c Humphreys b A. Hide	0	– c Humphreys b Tate	1
R. Abel b Tate	15	– c and b A. Hide	0
M. Read b A. Hide	5	– c and b A. Hide	17
Mr W. W. Read b Tate	1	– b A. Hide	0
Mr K. J. Key run out	33	– b A. Hide	19
R. Henderson b J. Hide	47	– c Gresson b A. Hide	20
W. Lockwood b Bean	13	– not out	8
G. A. Lohmann c A. Hide b Bean	13	– c Newham b A. Hide	0
H. Wood c Mayes b J. Hide	2	– not out	7
J. W. Sharpe not out	22		
J. Beaumont st Brann b Humphreys	20		
B 9, l-b 1	10	B 9, l-b 1	10
	181		82

Surrey Bowling

	Overs	Mdns	Runs	Wkts	Overs	Mdns	Runs	Wkts
Lohmann	44.4	13	67	9	21.3	9	31	6
Sharpe	24	11	54	0	6	2	15	1
Beaumont	20	15	16	1	16	9	27	1
Lockwood	9	2	21	0				
Abel	7	2	14	0	1	0	8	1

Sussex Bowling

	Overs	Mdns	Runs	Wkts	Overs	Mdns	Runs	Wkts
A. Hide	233	6	54	2	20.1	9	29	6
Tate	33	10	69	2	11	2	23	1
J. Hide	10	3	14	2	5	1	7	0
Bean	18	5	28	2	4	0	13	0
Humphreys	2.4	1	6	1				

Umpires: Draper and Tuck.

SUSSEX v CAMBRIDGE UNIVERSITY

Played at Brighton, June 19, 20, 21, 1890

The Cambridge University eleven had been showing such capital form at all points of the game that their appearance on the Brighton ground, where previous Light Blue teams had in recent years distinguished themselves, was looked forward to with a large amount of interest. Expectation was more than realised, as the University eleven accomplished a remarkable performance, and succeeded in beating the record score for a first-class match in England, after which they followed up their successful batting with a victory that reflected upon them the highest credit. On the form that the county had been displaying it was perhaps nothing very remarkable that Cambridge should have obtained a success, but the way in which the victory was brought about was certainly altogether out of the common. On the opening day the cricket of the Light Blue team was somewhat disappointing. They had the advantage of going in first on a hard and true wicket, but, except that Douglas and McGregor played extremely well, the batting presented no features of interest, and the whole side were out for 179. Douglas made his 84 in an hour and ten minutes, and hit ten 4s. Sussex made an excellent start, and Quaife, Bean, Mr Newham, Mr Cotterill, and Mr Smith all scored with the utmost freedom from the Cambridge bowling, the score at the call of time being 246 for the loss of six wickets, or 67 to the good with four wickets to go down.

On the second day the game underwent a complete change, and the batting of the Cambridge team was of a character to delight their many supporters. The innings of Sussex was quickly finished off for 270, which left the county with a lead of 91 runs, and Cambridge, going in a second time at twenty-five minutes past twelve, obtained such a complete mastery over the Sussex bowling that they remained in till the call of time, and made no fewer than 494 for the loss of seven wickets, a tremendously rapid rate of scoring being kept up throughout. At the start of the innings Douglas played in beautiful style, fully justifying the many good things that had been said of him, but his innings of 62 was completely put into the shade by the hitting that followed. McGregor, who went in second down with the score at 47, remained in till it had reached 301, his faultless innings, which extended over three hours and three-quarters, including one 6, eleven 4s, a 3, and nineteen 2s. Foley helped McGregor to put on no fewer than 214 runs, but he was twice let off from successive balls when he had scored 39, and just when he had reached his hundred he was missed at third man. Despite these blemishes, however, his innings of 117 was admirably played, and deserved all credit. It lasted two hours and fifty minutes, and included twelve 4s, two 3s, and ten 2s. Later in the day Ford and Hale punished the worn-out bowling with merciless severity, and the former at the call of time was not out 117.

The third day's cricket was perhaps the most remarkable of all. Woods was of course anxious to win the match, but he was also desirous that, if possible, his team should establish a record score in English first-class cricket, and the hitting in the morning was most brilliant. In the first hour and a half the Sussex bowling was punished to such a tremendous extent that no fewer than 209 runs were added to the overnight score, and the total reached 703. Directly Surrey's previous record of 698 – made against Sussex at The Oval in 1888 – had been beaten, Woods declared the Cambridge innings at an end, and made an attempt to win the match. Ford increased his overnight score to 191 before being caught at point, and the vigour of his hitting will best be judged from the fact that he was only at the wickets two hours and three-quarters, and that he scored twenty-five 4s, eighteen 2s, and fifty-five singles. His only mistake was that he should have been stumped when he had made 54. Jackson also played good cricket, and he and Ford put on 132 runs in an hour. Sussex were placed in the unenviable position of having nothing to play for but a draw, as they wanted no fewer than 613 to win. They entered upon their uphill task at half-past one, and though they made a very plucky attempt – Mr Newham and Tebay playing exceedingly well – the side were all out by twenty-five minutes past five for 187. In the whole match no fewer than 1339 runs were scored, this being the highest aggregate ever obtained in a first-class match in England, the previous best having been 1295 in the memorable game between Middlesex and Yorkshire at Lord's in the previous year. After this match Mr Woods decided to depend upon the same team against Oxford at Lord's.

Cambridge University

	First innings		Second innings	
Mr F. G. Ford b Bean	0	–	c Humphreys b Bean	191
Mr R. N. Douglas c Butt b Parris	84	–	b Gibb	62
Mr C. P. Foley b Smith	6	–	c Gibb b Smith	117
Mr G. McGregor b Smith	35	–	b Cotterill	131
Mr A. J. L. Hill lbw b Bean	19	–	b Humphreys	2
Mr F. S. Jackson c Butt b Bean	7	–	c Humphreys b Cotterill	60
Mr S. M. J. Woods lbw b Smith	4	–	not out	33
Mr R. C. Gosling c Butt b Smith	2	–	c Cotterill b Bean	15
Mr D. L. A. Jephson c Tebay b Smith	5	–	lbw b Gibb	7
Mr H. Hale c and b Bean	11	–	hit wkt b Humphreys	34
Mr E. C. Streatfeild not out	0	–	not out	42
B 5, l-b 1	6		B 1, l-b 7, n-b 1	9
	179		(9 wkts dec.)	703

Sussex

	First innings		Second innings	
W. Quaife st McGregor b Ford	58	–	c Hill b Woods	8
H. Tebay b Streatfeild	6	–	c Gosling b Jackson	43
G. Bean b Ford	46	–	c Goslin b Woods	15
Mr W. Newham lbw b Hill	46	–	b Streatfeild	56
Mr G. H. Cotterill c Hill b Streatfeild	26	–	b Jackson	4
Mr C. A. Smith c Streatfeild b Woods	33	–	c Foley b Hill	14
W. Humphreys c Streatfeild b Woods	21	–	c Woods b Jackson	20
T. C. Brown c Hill b Woods	17	–	lbw b Hale	0
Parris b Woods	4	–	not out	7
H. Butt b Woods	0	–	c Douglas b Hale	4
Gibb not out	1	–	b Jephson	0
B 9, l-b 3	12		B 11, l-b 4, w 1	16
	270			187

Sussex Bowling

	Overs	Mdns	Runs	Wkts	Overs	Mdns	Runs	Wkts
Bean	23	6	42	4	38	3	145	2
Mr Smith	20.2	3	57	5	30	3	117	1
Gibb	5	0	21	0	47	9	140	2
Brown	5	2	18	0				
Parris	6	0	13	1	15	0	60	0
Humphreys	4	0	22	0	35	3	137	2
Quaife					8	1	16	0
Mr Newham					5	1	20	0
Mr Cotterill					11	1	59	2

Cambridge University Bowling

	Overs	Mdns	Runs	Wkts	Overs	Mdns	Runs	Wkts
Mr Woods	21	5	61	5	17	6	41	2
Mr Streatfeild	35	17	62	2	16	5	44	1
Mr Jackson	12	6	23	0	23	12	31	3
Mr Hill	14	3	41	1	15	3	31	1
Mr Ford	17	7	33	2				
Mr Jephson	8	2	25	0	9.3	4	11	1
Mr Hale	6	1	13	0	9	2	13	2

Umpires: Carpenter and Payne.

SUSSEX v LANCASHIRE

Played at Brighton, August 14, 15, 16, 1890

Sussex were unable to break their spell of ill-luck, and suffered a crushing defeat at the hands of Lancashire in a single innings with 62 runs to spare, being quite outplayed from the start of the game to the finish. The wicket was hardly up to the usual standard obtained at Brighton, and Mold's fast bowling kicked up a good deal, but still it was a poor performance on the part of Sussex to be dismissed as they were in their first innings for 86. The innings of Lancashire was mainly remarkable for the astounding success of Mr A. C. MacLaren, the Harrow captain, who made his first appearance in the county team, and scored 108 in splendid style. It was probably quite without parallel for a schoolboy to make over a hundred in his first important county match, and he more than justified the high opinions that had been formed of him in the contest between Eton and Harrow. He made his 108 in two hours and ten minutes, without giving a single chance, and hitting nine 4s, six 3s, and fifteen 2s. Going in a second time the Sussex team again fared very badly, and only Mr Smith, the captain, played with any degree of confidence. Mold in the whole match took ten wickets for 111 runs and Watson eight wickets for 64 runs.

Sussex

W. Quaife run out	13	– c Kemble b Watson	7
W. Humphreys b Mold	3	– retired hurt	0
Mr W. Newham c MacLaren b Mold	4	– b Mold	15
G. Bean b Mold	7	– b Watson	10
J. Hide b Mold	25	– b Mold	13
Mr C. A. Smith b Mold	5	– b Mold	39
Mr G. L. Wilson b Watson	11	– b Watson	0
Mr C. J. M. Godfrey b Mold	11	– c Briggs b Mold	0
A. Hide b Watson	0	– b Watson	4
H. Butt not out	2	– not out	1
Mr W. O. Holloway b Watson	1	– b Watson	10
B 4	4	B 1	1
	86		100

Lancashire

R. G. Barlow b Godfrey	3
F. H. Sugg b Godfrey	1
A. Ward c Godfrey b A. Hide	19
Mr A. C. MacLaren c Holloway b Humphreys	108
J. Briggs b Wilson	54
A. Paul lbw b Wilson	0
G. R. Baker c Butt b Wilson	17
Mr A. N. Hornby c Butt b Humphreys	14
Mr A. T. Kemble b Humphreys	17
A. Watson c Godfrey b Wilson	7
A. Mold not out	0
B 6, l-b 1, n-b 1	8
	248

Lancashire Bowling

	Overs	Mdns	Runs	Wkts	Overs	Mdns	Runs	Wkts
Watson	27.4	15	23	3	26.2	11	41	5
Mold	27	5	59	6	22	9	52	4
Briggs					4	1	6	0

Sussex Bowling

	Overs	Mdns	Runs	Wkts
A. Hide	16	6	23	1
Godfrey	12	3	54	2
Mr Smith	7	1	24	0
J. Hide	4	0	10	0
Bean	7	0	28	0
Mr Holloway	4	1	12	0
Mr Wilson	14	2	47	4
Humphreys	10	1	42	3

Umpires: W. Clarke and R. Carpenter.

SUSSEX v HAMPSHIRE

Played at Brighton, May 18, 19, 1891

At this early period of the season the Hampshire executive were unable to put their full strength into the field, and the match with Sussex was from the first entirely one-sided. In very unsettled weather on the opening day Sussex headed their opponents' score of 99 with only four men out, and on the second afternoon they won the game in the easiest fashion by ten wickets. Quite the feature of the match was the bowling of Tate, who, in the second innings of Hampshire, took nine out of the ten wickets at a cost of only 24 runs. The batting honours of the match rested wtih Mr Newham for the winners and Mr Russell Bencraft for Hampshire, the latter gentleman carrying his bat right through the first innings, and hitting in his 57 not out four 4s, seven 3s, and five 2s.

Hampshire

Mr A. Russell b Smith	7	– b Tate	22
Mr R. Bencraft not out	57	– b Tate	1
Batchelor run out	7	– b Hilton	2
Mr F. E. Lacey b Smith	3	– b Tate	0
Mr L. H. Gay st Butt b Hilton	12	– b Tate	12
Baldwin b Bean	0	– c Humphreys b Tate	0
Rev. A. L. Porter b Hilton	0	– b Tate	3
Mr E. Sheldrake b Hilton	6	– c Bean b tate	0
Smith b Hilton	0	– not out	11
Mr C. Heseltine b Hilton	0	– b Tate	0
Soar st Butt b Tate	4	– b Tate	1
B 2, l-b 1	3	B 8	8
	99		60

Sussex

W. Quaife st Gay b Soar	14		
F. W. Marlow c Gay b Baldwin	26		
G. Bean b Soar	0		
Mr W. Newham c Batchelor b Soar	53		
Mr C. A. Smith b Soar	8		
W. G. Quaife c Bencraft b Baldwin	11	– not out	1
Mr W. H. Dudney b Baldwin	23		
W. Humphreys not out	19	– not out	0
H. Butt c Russell b Soar	0		
F. W. Tate b Baldwin	0		
Hilton st Gay b Baldwin	0		
B 3	3	L-b 2	2
	157		3

Sussex Bowling

	Overs	Mdns	Runs	Wkts	Overs	Mdns	Runs	Wkts
Tate	14.3	3	27	1	18	8	24	9
Mr Smith	17	8	28	2	5	2	12	0
Hilton	21	14	20	5	12	3	16	1
Bean	12	7	21	1				

Hampshire Bowling

	Overs	Mdns	Runs	Wkts	Overs	Mdns	Runs	Wkts
Baldwin	45.4	24	71	5	1.1	0	1	0
Soar	36	16	51	5	1	1	0	0
Heseltine	10	0	32	0				

SUSSEX v CAMBRIDGE UNIVERSITY

Played at Brighton, June 18, 19, 20, 1891

Of all the matches played last season that between Sussex and Cambridge University at Brighton stood out beyond dispute as the finest struggle which the summer produced. The Light Blues derived such advantage as is gained by batting first on a perfect wicket, and in four hours and forty minutes put together a total of 359. The scoring, however, was far from being even, Messrs Streatfeild, Hill, Douglas and McGregor making between them 282 out of 349 runs hit from the bat. All four played extremely well in their different styles, but the most sensational achievement was that of Mr Streatfeild, who going in with the score at 237 for six wickets, hit up 98 out of the last 122 in seventy minutes. Early in the day Mr Douglas played sound and stylish cricket for 61, and Mr Hill put together an excellent 75, being at the wickets three hours. The start of the Sussex innings gave little promise of the fine score which was eventually obtained, for in twenty minutes three wickets went down for 40 runs, but at the drawing of stumps the total had been raised to 83 without further loss.

Mr Newham and Mr Andrews, who had played uncommonly well on Thursday evening hit very brilliantly next morning and put on 135 for the fourth wicket. After the fall of the fifth wicket, Mr Brann went in and hit so finely that had he been better supported Sussex might easily have been ahead on the first innings. As it was the last wicket fell for 314 or 45 behind, Mr Brann carrying out his bat for a splendid 88. During the rest of the afternoon the Cambridge men remained at the wickets, scoring 240 for the loss of seven batsmen.

When play began on Saturday Cambridge, with three wickets in hand, were 285 runs to the good, and so splendidly did the last few batsmen play up that in an hour and twenty minutes the score of the Light Blues was increased to 366, Messrs Woods and Jephson adding 99 runs in an hour for the last wicket. Four hours and fifty minutes remained for cricket when Sussex entered upon the enormous task of trying to make the 412 runs necessary to win, and heavy and rapid as the scoring had been during the previous stages of the match, there seemed, of course, no likelihood whatever of the number being obtained. Not only had the county 412 runs to get in the last innings – in itself a stupendous task for any side – but they had also to keep up a rate of scoring of 85 runs an hour. For a little while an overwhelming defeat seemed in store for the county, as three wickets fell for 68. Then, however, came a complete change. Messrs Newham and Brann in eighty minutes put on 102 runs for the fourth wicket, and Humphreys stayed with Mr Brann whilst 60 runs were added in forty minutes for the fifth. This batting notwithstanding, there was so far no probability of success, but on Mr Andrews joining Mr Brann, these two batsmen hit away in such astonishing and powerful fashion that when six o'clock came a victory for Sussex was quite possible. An hour was left for play, the two batsmen were well set and scoring fast, and with five wickets to fall only 87 runs were wanted to win. For another twenty minutes Messrs Brann and Andrews stayed together, but then in one over they were both out, and the end came so quickly afterwards that twenty minutes before time Cambridge won an extraordinary match by 48 runs. Messrs Brann and Andrews, to whom the chief credit of the fine performance of Sussex belonged, scored 120 runs in seventy minutes. The former batsman, who in the first innings had scored 88 not out, put together in the second the splendid total of 161.

Altogether the match may be described as one of the most remarkable in the history of cricket. On the first day 442 runs were obtained for the loss of thirteen wickets; on the second day 471 for twelve wickets; and on the third day 489 for thirteen wickets, giving a grand aggregate of 1,402 runs for the three days. This number of runs is the highest ever made in a first-class match in England, beating the previous record of 1,339, which curiously enough was established in the Sussex v Cambridge match of 1890, by 63 runs, and it is within nine of the Australian record of 1,411, the scoring of which it must not be forgotten occupied five days. In connection with the game we may also notice that while only one individual innings of over a hundred was played, five batsmen made more than a hundred runs in the match, Mr Brann scoring 249 for once out, Mr Newham 146, Mr Hill 136, Mr Streatfeild 133, and Mr Andrews 102. Five other batsmen made 50 or more runs in the course of the game, and there were thirty double-figure innings. Four times were 100 runs or more put on for a single partnership, while each of the four innings produced more than 300 runs. Altogether 1,360 runs were hit from 513 overs and a ball, the aggregate of 1,402 being made in seventeen hours and ten minutes.

Cambridge University

Mr R. N. Douglas b Tate	61	– b Tate	26
Mr N. C. Cooper lbw b Humphreys	13	– b Tate	3
Mr G. J. V. Weigall b Humphreys	9	– b Humphreys	41
Mr A. J. L. Hill st Butt b Humphreys	75	– c Hilton b Bean	61
Mr F. S. Jackson c Newham b Mitchell	4	– b Tate	42
Mr G. McGregor c Hilton b Mitchell	48	– c Hilton b Bean	5
Mr C. M. Wells c Butt b Humphreys	19	– c Brann b Tate	29
Mr E. C. Streatfeild b Mitchell	98	– c Butt b Mitchell	35
Mr S. M. J. Woods run out	12	– c Andrews b Tate	62
Mr H. M. Braybrooke st Butt b Humphreys	0	– c Butt b Humphreys	13
Mr D. L. A. Jephson not out	10	– not out	36
B 7, l-b 3	10	B 9, l-b 4	13
	359		366

Sussex

W. Quaife c Streatfeild b Jackson	13	– c Jephson b Jackson	13
F. W. Marlow b Jackson	1	– b Jackson	13
G. Bean b Jackson	21	– c Braybrooke b Jackson	34
Mr W. Newham c Weigall b Wells	95	– b Woods	51
Mr W. H. Andrews c McGregor b Wells	46	– c Hill b Streatfeild	56
W. Humphreys c Streatfeild b Jackson	9	– c Streatfeild b Woods	12
Mr G. Brann not out	88	– c Douglas b Streatfeild	161
Mitchell c McGregor b Jackson	6	– c Jackson b Streatfeild	9
F. W. Tate b Woods	6	– b Hill	0
H. Butt c Streatfeild b Woods	16	– c Jackson b Hill	2
Hilton c Cooper b Streatfeild	4	– not out	2
B 9	9	B 4, w 6	10
	314		363

Sussex Bowling

	Overs	Mdns	Runs	Wkts	Overs	Mdns	Runs	Wkts
Tate	29	6	97	1	47.4	13	120	5
Hilton	35	5	67	0	17	7	37	0
Humphreys	38	3	105	5	29	2	94	2
Mitchell	22.1	2	42	3	22	6	40	1
Bean	16	5	24	0	21	4	55	2
Mr Brann	11	6	14	0	3	0	7	0

Cambridge Bowling

	Overs	Mdns	Runs	Wkts	Overs	Mdns	Runs	Wkts
Mr Woods	34	5	99	2	15	2	38	2
Mr Jackson	36	6	102	5	38	4	118	3
Mr Wells	16	3	53	2	19	5	58	0
Mr Hill	7	2	22	0	24	7	68	2
Mr Streatfeild	8.3	1	29	1	20.3	7	52	3
Mr Jephson					4	0	19	0

Umpires: Carpenter and Lillywhite.

SUSSEX v KENT

Played at Brighton, August 10, 11, 12, 1891

Three weeks after their victory against Middlesex the Sussex men played their return match with Kent, and again they proved successful, winning by 84 runs. Drenching rain during the Tuesday night entirely altered the character of the game. Tate's bowling in the second innings of Kent was extremely difficult, and on each side there was a remarkable display of batting, Bean's innings being as worthy of praise as Mr Patterson's. In the last innings, Mr Fox, who was not out at two o'clock, left the ground to lunch with some friends, and returned too late to resume his batting.

Sussex

G. Bean c Wilson b A. Hearne	102 – c A. Hearne b Martin	13
F. W. Marlow c Wilson b Daffen	41 – b Martin	0
J. Hide b Wright	3 – c Wright b Martin	14
Mr G. Brann lbw b G. Hearne	36 – b Wright	7
Mr G. L. Wilson c Wilson b G. Hearne	29 – c G. Hearne b Martin	1
Mr W. Newham run out	9 – c Patterson b Wright	13
Mr C. A. Smith not out	50 – b Martin	9
W. Humphreys b Martin	4 – c Marchant b Martin	10
Mr W. H. Andrews c A. Hearne b Daffen	15 – c Daffen b Wright	0
Mr W. H. Dudney b A. Hearne	24 – b Martin	5
F. W. Tate c Wilson b A. Hearne	3 – not out	0
B 10, l-b 2	12 B 5	5
	328	77

Kent

Mr W. Rashleigh b Humphreys	28	– c Brann b Hide	9
A. Hearne c Dudney b Humphreys	25	– lbw b Tate	0
Mr F. Marchant b Humphreys	27	– b Hide	21
Mr W. H. Patterson c and b Tate	120	– b Tate	3
Mr C. J. M. Fox c Dudney b Smith	5	– absent	0
Mr L. Wilson run out	6	– b Tate	0
Mr A. Daffen run out	24	– b Hide	0
Mr F. M. Atkins c Humphreys b Wilson	1	– b Tate	0
G. G. Hearne c Andrews b Humphreys	4	– not out	1
W. Wright b Tate	14	– b Tate	9
F. Martin not out	4	– b Tate	0
B 3, l-b 6	9	B 7, l-b 4	11
	267		54

Kent Bowling

	Overs	Mdns	Runs	Wkts	Overs	Mdns	Runs	Wkts
Martin	52	21	84	1	27.3	14	27	7
Wright	37	15	53	1	27	11	45	3
A. Hearne	33.2	9	72	3				
G. G. Hearne	22	6	40	2				
Mr Daffen	20	6	46	2				
Mr Patterson	6	2	21	0				

Sussex Bowling

	Overs	Mdns	Runs	Wkts	Overs	Mdns	Runs	Wkts
Tate	19.4	8	37	2	12.3	6	23	6
Mr Smith	22	4	56	1				
Hide	15	6	21	0	12	5	20	3
Humphreys	28	7	97	4				
Bean	8	3	10	0				
Mr Wilson	16	5	37	1				

Umpires: Tuck and Allen Hill.

SUSSEX v LANCASHIRE

Played at Brighton, August 15, 16, 1892

In few of their engagements were the Sussex eleven more completely overmatched than in this return fixture. Lancashire showed marked superiority at every point, and on the second afternoon won the game by an innings and 125 runs. The victory was practically secured on the opening day, A. C. MacLaren and Arthur Smith, during a partnership which lasted three hours and twenty minutes, putting on no fewer than 208 runs. MacLaren played a magnificent innings, staying at the wickets three hours and three-quarters and giving no chance until after he had reached three figures. Even then his only real mistake was a sharp chance in the slips. He hit twenty 4s, three 3s, and ten 2s. It is a fact worth recalling that MacLaren made his first appearance for Lancashire at Brighton in the season of 1890, scoring on that occasion 108. Smith batted with admirable steadiness for four hours and a half, but his play was certainly not so attractive as MacLaren's. But for the sun being in the fieldsman's eyes he would have been easily caught at short leg with his score at 56, and he afterwards gave one or two chances at the wicket. On the second day, after Lancashire's innings had closed for 356, the Sussex men gave a most inglorious display, being twice dismissed for an aggregate score of 231 runs. Mold and Watson bowled unchanged, the former taking fourteen wickets for 159 runs. A severe sore throat kept Briggs out of the Lancashire team.

Lancashire

A. Ward c Tate b Guttridge	16	Mr T. R. Hubback b Tate	2
Mr A. C. MacLaren c Humphreys b Bean	132	Mr A. T. Kemble c Marlow b Humphreys	7
F. Sugg b Guttridge	0	A. Watson not out	22
A. Smith st Butt b Humphreys	111	A. Mold c Bean b Humphreys	22
G. R. Baker b Humphreys	15	B 2, l-b 8	10
Mr S. M. Crosfield b Humphreys	13		
G. Yates b Humphreys	6		356

Sussex

G. Bean c Yates b Watson	20 – c Kemble b Watson	18
F. W. Marlow b Mold	4 – b Mold	16
S. Hollands b Watson	12 – run out	9
Mr W. Newman c Hubback b Mold	16 – run out	2
Mr G. Brann c Baker b Mold	10 – c Baker b Mold	0
F. Guttridge b Mold	17 – b Mold	31
J. Hide b Mold	6 – b Mold	22
Mr W. H. Andrews not out	15 – b Mold	2
W. Humphreys b Mold	0 – not out	14
H. Butt c Baker b Mold	1 – c Ward b Mold	8
F. W. Tate b Watson	0 – b Mold	3
B 4	4 B 1	1
	105	126

Sussex Bowling

	Overs	Mdns	Runs	Wkts
Tate	56	26	87	1
Guttridge	45	14	114	2
Humphreys	37.3	4	80	6
Mr Brann	16	7	31	0
Hide	5	3	6	0
Bean	16	7	28	1

Lancashire Bowling

	Overs	Mdns	Runs	Wkts	Overs	Mdns	Runs	Wkts
Mold	24	8	72	7	29.3	7	87	7
Watson	23.1	8	29	3	29	15	38	1

Umpires: E. Goodyear and T. Foster.

SUSSEX v KENT

Played at Brighton, August 22, 23, 24, 1892

The return match with Kent was marked by one of the most brilliant things that has ever been done for Sussex, Mr George Brann playing two innings of over a hundred, and thus accomplishing a feat which previous to last season had only been performed in modern first-class cricket by Mr W. G. Grace. In his first innings Mr Brann went in fourth wicket down with the total at 68, and was the last man out. Having regard, however, to the position of the game, his second display was even more remarkable as during the whole time he was in Sussex were engaged in a hard fight to save the match. Again he went in fourth wicket down, and when he left – eighth man out – there was no fear of his side being beaten, the single innings defeat having been averted with only a quarter of an hour left for cricket. When he had made 76 he cut a ball straight into George Hearne's hands at point, the blunder probably robbing Kent of a victory. Towards Kent's great score of 422 Mr Le Fleming contributed a splendid 134.

Kent

A. Hearne c Butt b Guttridge	7	Mr M. C. Kemp b Tate	12
Mr H. C. Stewart c Marlow b Brann	50	W. Wright not out	70
Mr G. J. V. Weigall b Humphreys	5	F. Martin c Heasman b Somerset	34
Mr W. H. Patterson b Guttridge	66	W. Hearne lbw b Tate	5
Mr J. Le Fleming c Butt b Tate	134	B 6, l-b 7	13
G. G. Hearne c Bean b Humphreys	22		
Mr F. de L. Solbe c Butt b Somerset	4		422

Sussex

G. Bean b W. Hearne	3	– c Patterson b A. Hearne	13
F. W. Marlow b Martin	14	– c and b W. Hearne	2
Mr W. G. Heasman b Wright	48	– st Kemp b Wright	29
Hollands c and b W. Hearne	19	– st Kemp b A. Hearne	2
Mr W. Newham lbw b W. Hearne	10	– st Kemp b A. Hearne	32
Mr G. Brann c Patterson b Wright	105	– b W. Hearne	101
Mr A. F. Somerset b W. Hearne	12	– b G. G. Hearne	0
F. Guttridge b W. Hearne	0	– lbw b Wright	30
W. Humphreys c Kemp b W. Hearne	7	– not out	0
H. Butt c A. Hearne b Wright	0	– b W. Hearne	6
F. W. Tate not out	1	– not out	2
B 6, l-b 4	10	B 5, l-b 1	6
	229		223

Sussex Bowling

	Overs	Mdns	Runs	Wkts
Tate	47.2	18	70	3
Guttridge	43	14	83	2
Humphreys	29	3	120	2
Bean	22	7	40	0
Mr Brann	16	6	32	1
Mr Somerset	18	2	37	2
Mr Heasman	15	9	14	0
Marlow	4	1	13	0

Kent Bowling

	Overs	Mdns	Runs	Wkts	Overs	Mdns	Runs	Wkts
W. Hearne	46	20	70	6	36	13	68	3
Martin	40	16	68	1	20	5	41	0
A. Hearne	14	4	38	0	32	16	38	3
Wright	25.1	11	43	3	38	22	47	2
G. G. Hearne					7	2	17	1
Mr Le Fleming					4	2	6	0

Umpires: G. Panter and J. Street.

SUSSEX v GLOUCESTERSHIRE

Played at Brighton, May 22, 23, 24, 1893

Many contests between Sussex and Gloucestershire have produced very interesting struggles, but none so close and exciting as the one under notice. During the earlier stages of the match Gloucestershire succeeded in obtaining a considerable advantage, but the Sussex men played up in a surprising manner, and, thanks mainly to the brilliant batting of Bean and G. L. Wilson, and the effective bowling of Humphreys, they gained a remarkable success by the narrow margin of three runs. The weather throughout was of the most favourable description, and the attendance of the public highly satisfactory, being in advance of that at any previous match. The home team won the toss – a decided advantage, as the wicket was in splendid order – but very moderate use was made of the opportunity, and in three hours and ten minutes they were dismissed for a total of 202. Eight members of the side reached double figures, but the only batting worthy of special mention was that shown by C. A. Smith and W. Newham, who, between them, scored 104 runs out of 192 obtained from the bat. There was a marked contrast in their styles, Newham playing with extreme caution, while Smith hit with great brilliancy. In fourth wicket down at 75, Smith was ninth out at 194, the chief hits in his admirable though not faultless innings being twelve 4s, a 3, and five 2s. When Gloucestershire went in, an hour and fifty minutes remained for play, and good use was made of the time. Three wickets went down for 61, and then Ferris, who had played exceedingly well, was joined by Kitcat, the two men taking the score to 133.

On the second day Gloucestershire increased their total to 297, and Ferris had the satisfaction of making his first innings of three figures in first-class cricket, raising his score from 58 to 106. He was seventh out at 243, and only made one real mistake, his chief hits being fifteen 4s, three 3s, and ten 2s. In a minority of 95, Sussex went in a second time, and Wilson and Bean treated the spectators to a marvellous display of batting. Both men hit with equal brilliancy and freedom, and in two hours and twenty minutes they actually scored 217 runs for the first partnership. Though runs came at this rapid rate, the cricket was singularly free from blemish, the only real fault that could be urged against either of the batsmen being a difficult chance by Wilson when he had made 63. When the separation was effected, Wilson was 105 and Bean not out 107. Included in Wilson's dashing innings were nineteen 4s, a 3, and seventeen 2s. Sussex lost the second wicket without another run being scored, and thus at the drawing of stumps the total stood at 217, or 122 runs on with eight wickets in hand.

Sussex now had certainly the best of the match, and as the wicket still wore well it was expected that they would run up a big score, but this anticipation was not realised, the remaining batsmen failing to follow up the splendid start that had been made. So poor, indeed, was the resistance offered to Murch and Roberts that in an hour and twenty minutes the last eight wickets went down for the addition of 77 runs, the total thus reaching only 294. Bean increased his score to 120, and was the seventh man out at 254. Altogether he was at the wickets about three hours without making any real mistake, the chief hits of his fine display being nineteen 4s, two 3s, and seven 2s. It seemed as though the poor batting of the Sussex men in the morning would cost them the match, for Gloucestershire were only set 200 runs to win, a task that appeared fairly easy to accomplish on the capital wicket. At the outset of the Gloucestershire innings Sussex received no little encouragement, as both Radcliffe and W. G. Grace were got rid of for 23 runs. Then, however, came a marked change in the character of the cricket, Ferris and Painter playing so well together that a victory for the Western team seemed tolerably certain. In sixty-five minutes the two men raised the score to 127, their partnership thus producing 104 runs. This stand appeared to have won the match for Gloucestershire, but another rapid change took place, Humphreys, who had been put on to bowl with the score at 114, meeting with astonishing success. In five overs he actually got rid of four batsmen for 11 runs. Thus, while 120 was on the board with only two men out, the score was but 148 when the sixth wicket fell. The result was quite open, and the spectators, realising that Sussex after all had a chance, displayed renewed interest in the contest. At this critical point E. M. Grace and De Winton played with great nerve and skill, and once again Gloucestershire looked to be winning. The two men had added 35 runs, when De Winton was stumped. Only 17 runs were wanted, and seven of these had been obtained when E. M. Grace was bowled by a lob. Three runs later Murch, rushing out to drive, was easily stumped, and with three more added Smith clean bowled Board, Sussex winning an extraordinary match by three runs amid a scene of great excitement. Humphreys, whose lob bowling turned the scale, was the hero of the hour, and he was carried shoulder-high to the dressing room.

Sussex

G. Bean c Rice b Murch	12 – c Board b Murch	120
Mr G. L. Wilson c Rice b Murch	18 – c E. M. Grace b Roberts	105
Mr W. L. Murdoch b Ferris	18 – c W. G. Grace b Roberts	9
Mr W. Newham c E. M. Grace b Roberts	34 – not out	24
Mr G. Brann b Ferris	11 – b Murch	5
Mr C. A. Smith c Painter b Murch	70 – c Murch b Roberts	0
F. Guttridge st Board b W. G. Grace	13 – c De Winton b Murch	6
W. Humphreys c Board b Murch	11 – c Murch b Roberts	4
F. W. Tate lbw b W. G. Grace	0 – c De Winton b Roberts	0
H. Butt not out	0 – b W. G. Grace	12
Hilton c Painter b Murch	5 – lbw b W. G. Grace	4
B 5,l-b 5	10 B 5	5
	202	294

Gloucestershire

Mr W. G. Grace c Guttridge b Tate	17 – b Tate	16
Mr J. J. Ferris c Tate b Guttridge	106 – st Butt b Humphreys	47
J. Painter c Smith b Hilton	4 – b Humphreys	51
Mr R. W. Rice lbw b Humphreys	22 – b Humphreys	2
Mr S. A. P. Kitcat st Butt b Smith	52 – c and b Humphreys	14
Mr O. G. Radcliffe c Butt b Smith	0 – c Bean b Tate	7
Mr E. M. Grace lbw b Humphreys	16 – b Humphreys	26
Mr G. S. De Winton b Humphreys	22 – st Butt b Humphreys	15
H. W. Murch not out	38 – st Butt b Humphreys	5
F. G. Roberts b Tate	7 – not out	2
J. H. Board c and b Tate	4 – b Smith	3
B 4,l-b 5	9 B 7,l-b 1	8
	297	196

Gloucestershire Bowling

	Overs	Mdns	Runs	Wkts	Overs	Mdns	Runs	Wkts
Roberts	25	13	47	1	33	8	97	5
Murch	20	5	50	5	27	7	82	3
Ferris	22	4	61	2	10	4	17	0
W. G. Grace	17	6	34	2	10.4	3	32	2
Radcliffe					8	1	32	0
Kitcat					7	1	15	0
E. M. Grace					5	2	14	0

Sussex Bowling

	Overs	Mdns	Runs	Wkts	Overs	Mdns	Runs	Wkts
Hilton	27	6	80	1	3	0	14	0
Tate	11.2	4	25	3	21	7	49	2
Humphreys	19	4	59	3	17	5	30	7
Guttridge	21	4	58	1	12	1	49	0
Bean	20	11	27	0	3	0	7	0
Smith	15	6	39	2	15.3	3	39	1

Umpires: C. Clements and W. Goodyear.

SUSSEX v NOTTINGHAMSHIRE

Played at Brighton, June 8, 9, 10, 1893

The Nottinghamshire batsmen again found the Sussex bowling much to their liking, and ran up the tremendous score of 674, which is, with one exception, the highest total ever made in a first-class county match, being only inferior to the 698 obtained by Surrey against Sussex, at The Oval, in 1888. Altogether the innings lasted nine hours, the score at the fall of the sixth wicket averaging 100 runs a wicket. Shrewsbury, Gunn, and Barnes all played magnificent cricket, but the later batsmen would have been better advised had they made fewer runs, as by staying in so long they prejudiced their chance of winning. When Sussex went in on the Friday only an hour and a half remained for cricket, but though four wickets fell for 20 runs, the home team rendered a very much better account of themselves on the Saturday, and – thanks to some admirable batting by Murdoch, Bean, Newham and Guttridge – succeeded in making the game a draw.

Nottinghamshire

A. Shrewsbury c Humphreys b Hilton	164
Wharmby c Butt b Humphreys	6
W. Gunn b Tate	156
W. Barnes b Guttridge	102
W. Flowers c Wilson b Humphreys	38
W. Attewell c Guttridge b Tate	89
Mr C. W. Wright b Tate	54
H. B. Daft c Hilton b Humphreys	32
F. Shacklock st Butt b Humphreys	6
R. J. Mee c Newham b Humphreys	0
M. Sherwin not out	10
B 14, l-b 1, n-b 2	17
	674

Sussex

G. Bean b Mee	21	– b Gunn	69
Mr G. L. Wilson b Mee	0	– c Attewell b Mee	18
Mr W. L. Murdoch b Shacklock	75	– b Wharmby	61
Mr W. Newham b Mee	9	– b Mee	52
Mr G. Brann b Shacklock	9	– not out	34
Mr C. A. Smith b Shacklock	19	– b Mee	9
F. Guttridge c and b Attewell	50	– c Daft b Flowers	0
W. Humphreys b Attewell	0	– not out	10
H. Butt c Shrewsbury b Daft	21		
F. W. Tate not out	0		
Hilton b Shacklock	0		
B 13, l-b 2, n-b 2	17	B 5, l-b 5, n-b 1	11
	221		264

Sussex Bowling

	Overs	Mdns	Runs	Wkts
Guttridge	42	10	107	1
Humphreys	48.4	12	141	5
Hilton	45	11	106	1
Tate	43	16	97	3
Bean	39	11	90	0
Wilson	26	8	76	0
Smith	4	0	18	0
Brann	7	1	22	0

Nottinghamshire Bowling

	Overs	Mdns	Runs	Wkts	Overs	Mdns	Runs	Wkts
Mee	41	17	84	3	25	10	58	3
Attewell	29	12	60	2	21	9	31	0
Shacklock	22	12	38	4	11	3	47	0
Flowers	8	3	20	0	8	2	22	1
Daft	3	2	2	1				
Gunn					17	1	56	1
Wharmby					9	0	39	1

Umpires: A. F. Smith and J. Potter.

SUSSEX v LANCASHIRE

Played at Brighton, August 13, 14, 1894

For the third time during the season on the Brighton ground the side winning the toss and putting their opponents in to bat proved successful, MacLaren adopting this course and Lancashire winning the match by six wickets. The game on the first day underwent some surprising changes. Sussex seemed to have lost all their chances by being dismissed for 75, but on going in against a majority of 66 they recovered all their lost ground, Marlow and Bean playing so finely that 83 runs were scored without the loss of a wicket. Being 17 runs ahead there seemed every prospect of Sussex making a splendid fight of it, but the hopes held out were by no means fulfilled. When once Bean and Marlow had been separated the Sussex batting broke down completely before the wonderful bowling of Mold, and the whole side were out for 160. Mold had an enormous share in the success of his county, taking in the two innings fifteen wickets for 87 runs.

Sussex

G. Bean c MacLaren b Mold	14	– b Mold	32
F. W. Marlow b Briggs	4	– b Mold	62
Mr W. L. Murdoch b Briggs	0	– b Briggs	4
Mr W. Newham c Baker b Mold	2	– lbw b Mold	14
Mr G. Brann b Mold	0	– b Mold	4
Mr C. B. Fry b Mold	7	– lbw b Mold	5
F. Guttridge st C. Smith b Briggs	1	– b Mold	22
H. Butt b Mold	0	– b Mold	2
F. Parris b Mold	28	– b Mold	0
W. Humphreys not out	9	– not out	4
Hilton b Mold	8	– c MacLaren b Briggs	0
L-b 2	2	B 10, l-b 1	11
	75		160

Lancashire

A. Ward c Guttridge b Parris	42	– c Butt b Guttridge	9
F. H. Sugg b Parris	7	– b Hilton	4
A. Smith b Parris	0		
Mr A. C. MacLaren b Parris	0	– run out	4
J. Briggs b Parris	17	– b Humphreys	16
G. R. Baker c Butt b Humphreys	8	– not out	8
Mr S. M. Tindall b Bean	26		
A. Paul run out	17	– not out	47
C. Smith not out	18		
Mr G. R. Bardswell c Butt b Hilton	0		
A. Mold c Newham b Parris	3		
B 1, l-b 2	3	L-b 8	8
	141		96

Lancashire Bowling

	Overs	Mdns	Runs	Wkts	Overs	Mdns	Runs	Wkts
Briggs	16	3	50	3	34.3	11	62	2
Mold	17.2	9	20	7	34	10	67	8
Bardswell	2	1	3	0	5	0	13	0
Baker					3	2	7	0

Sussex Bowling

	Overs	Mdns	Runs	Wkts	Overs	Mdns	Runs	Wkts
Parris	28.3	8	64	6	19	10	26	0
Hilton	17	8	24	1	16	4	31	1
Humphreys	9	0	32	1	5	0	16	1
Bean	5	3	10	1				
Guttridge	7	3	8	0	5	2	8	1
Fry					2.4	1	7	0

Umpires: J. Street and W. F. Collishaw.

SUSSEX v OXFORD UNIVERSITY

Played at Brighton, June 24, 25, 26, 1895

This was the fourth contest in succession on the Brighton ground in which over a thousand runs were scored. In the whole game 1,410 runs were made for the loss of only twenty-eight wickets, this being a record aggregate in first-class cricket in England, beating the 1,402 obtained in the Sussex and Cambridge University match – also on the Brighton ground – in 1891. An extraordinary start was made, G. L. Wilson and Marlow putting on 303 runs in two hours and fifty minutes during their partnership for the first Sussex wicket, this number being second only to the memorable 346 obtained by Hewett and L. C. H. Palairet for the first Somerset wicket against Yorkshire at Taunton in 1892. Oxford had to face a total of 487, but accomplished a superb performance by scoring 651, and so gaining a lead of 164. Mordaunt, the captain, played a wonderful innings of 264 not out, being in four hours and a half, and hardly making a mistake. There were no fewer than five separate innings of over a hundred in the match.

Sussex

Mr G. L. Wilson c Cunliffe b Leveson-Gower	174	– c Hartley b Cunliffe	37
F. W. Marlow c Phillips b Leveson-Gower	130	– c Lewis b Cunliffe	11
K. S. Ranjitsinhji c Lewis b Leveson-Gower	38	– not out	137
Mr W. L. Murdoch c Fry b Cunliffe	32	– c Foster b Hartley	31
Mr W. Newham c Foster b Leveson-Gower	11	– c Leveson-Gower b Cunliffe	22
Mr G. Braunn c Foster b Cunliffe	38	– c Mordaunt b Hartley	9
G. Bean c and b Fry	0	– c Phillips b Cunliffe	1
Mr A. Collins c Lewis b Arkwright	7	– c Phillips b Cunliffe	2
F. Parris b Cunliffe	39	– b Cunliffe	0
H. Butt c Smith b Cunliffe	0	– not out	6
W. Humphreys not out	3		
B 12, l-b 2, w 1	15	B 9, l-b 3, w 1, n-b 3	16
	487		272

Oxford University

Mr C. B. Fry c Bean b Brann	125
Mr P. F. Warner c Parris b Humphreys	46
Mr H. K. Foster c Brann b Bean	79
Mr G. J. Mordaunt not out	264
Mr H. D. G. Leveson-Gower b Parris	17
Mr F. A. Phillips b Brann	38
Mr G. O. Smith c Butt b Parris	15
Mr H. A. Arkwright c Bean b Parris	15
Mr F. H. E. Cunliffe c Butt b Parris	13
Mr J. C. Hartley c Butt b Brann	25
Mr R. P. Lewis b Brann	0
B 12, l-b 2	14
	651

Oxford University Bowling

	Overs	Mdns	Runs	Wkts	Overs	Mdns	Runs	Wkts
Cunliffe	50	9	121	4	36	17	62	6
Arkwright	32	7	111	1	14	2	39	0
Fry	31	8	89	1	12	4	39	0
Hartley	16	3	58	0	24	2	105	2
Warner	3	0	18	0				
Leveson-Gower	23	4	75	4	4	0	11	0

Sussex Bowling

	Overs	Mdns	Runs	Wkts
Collins	37	9	120	0
Parris	64	13	183	4
Humphreys	49	12	143	1
Wilson	19	5	72	0
Bean	22	6	62	1
Brann	15.2	4	57	4

Umpires: J. Lillywhite and D. Eastwood.

SUSSEX v GLOUCESTERSHIRE

Played at Brighton, May 25, 26, 27, 1896

In many ways one of the most sensational matches of the season, Sussex playing a magnificent game and only just failing to snatch a victory. The early stages of the contest were rendered remarkable by the wonderful batting of W. G. Grace, who went right through the Gloucestershire innings and scored 243. Sussex, following on against a majority of over 200, looked to have a thankless task, but in their second innings was witnessed some of the best batting seen at Brighton last summer. Ranjitsinhji, Bean and Marlow each scored over 100, and when the innings was declared closed, Gloucestershire were left with an hour and a quarter in which to make 204, on a wicket that was beginning to crumble. Tate and Collins bowled very finely, and it was only after considerable excitement that Gloucestershire succeeded in making the game a draw.

Gloucestershire

Mr W. G. Grace not out	243	– b Collins	3
H. Wrathall c Bean b Parris	43	– st Butt b Tate	13
Mr W. McG. Hemingway c Murdoch b Collins	1	– c Marlow b Collins	12
J. H. Board c Ranjitsinhji b Collins	3	– c and b Collins	4
Mr C. L. Townsend b Parris	11	– not out	8
Mr H. S. Goodwin b Collins	10		
Mr C. O. H. Sewell b Tate	19	– b Tate	37
Mr E. L. Thomas b Tate	109	– b Tate	0
Mr S. de Winton c Collins b Tate	10	– b Killick	3
H. W. Murch b Tate	4		
F. G. Roberts c Bean b Collins	8		
L-b 2	2	B 7, l-b 1	8
	463		88

Sussex

G. Bean c Hemingway b Grace	2 – c Board b Murch	113
F. W. Marlow c Murch b Townsend	61 – c Grace b Townsend	108
K. S. Ranjitsinhji c Wrathall b Roberts	7 – not out	114
Mr W. L. Murdoch b Murch	47 – c Roberts b Murch	23
Mr W. Newham b Murch	1 – not out	57
Mr G. Brann b Townsend	26	
Mr A. Collins c Roberts b Murch	21	
F. Parris c Board b Townsend	10	
E. H. Killick b Murch	25	
H. R. Butt not out	34	
F. W. Tate lbw b Murch	11	
B 1	1	B 2,l-b 3 5
	246	(3 wkts dec.) 420

Sussex Bowling

	Overs	Mdns	Runs	Wkts	Overs	Mdns	Runs	Wkts
Tate	49	10	102	4	17	11	26	3
Killick	25	4	86	0	1	1	0	1
Collins	43.4	8	113	4	15	3	54	3
Parris	20	4	58	2				
Brann	19	2	56	0				
Bean	21	3	46	0				

Gloucestershire Bowling

	Overs	Mdns	Runs	Wkts	Overs	Mdns	Runs	Wkts
Grace	16	3	51	1				
Roberts	17	3	37	1	49	17	114	0
Townsend	27	3	95	3	42	4	149	1
Murch	23.2	8	62	5	65	23	133	2
Wrathall					3	0	19	0

Umpires: J. J. Tuck and H. Draper.

SUSSEX v OXFORD UNIVERSITY

Played at Brighton, June 25, 26, 27, 1896

As in the matches against Gloucestershire and Somerset, Sussex played a wonderful uphill game, and only just failed to gain a remarkable victory. The Oxford captain declared his innings at an end when he considered his position safe, Sussex having to make 339 runs in three hours and a half, but so extraordinary was the hitting of Ranjitsinhji, Bean, and Killick, that when time was called and the match left drawn, Sussex were within ten of the required number, and had four wickets to go down. As Leveson-Gower stated at the Ranjitsinhji banquet at Cambridge in September, he had been caused, by the young Indian batsman, the most uncomfortable quarter of an hour he ever experienced at cricket.

Oxford University

Mr G. J. Mordaunt c Tate b Killick	28 – c Tate b Killick	10
Mr P. F. Warner c Arlington b Parris	22 – b Killick	77
Mr H. K. Foster b Killick	17 – c Ranjitsinhji b Killick	15
Mr F. G. H. Clayton c Butt b Killick	0 – c Ranjitsinhji b Parris	3
Mr C. C. Pilkington c Killick b Parris	5 – c Parris b Marlow	67
Mr H. D. G. Leveson-Gower st Butt b Killick	78 – not out	40
Mr G. R. Bardswell c Arlington b Parris	59 – st Arlington b Tate	13
Mr P. S. Waddy b Killick	5 – run out	9
Mr G. B. Raikes not out	24 – lbw b Tate	41
Mr F. H. E. Cunliffe c Butt b Parris	1 – c Arlington b Killick	0
Mr E. D. Compton c Butt b Parris	4 – not out	5
B 1	1 B 12	12
	244	(9 wkts dec.) 292

Sussex

F. W. Marlow c Bardswell b Cunliffe	9 – c Bardswell b Waddy	2
G. Bean c Compton b Cunliffe	22 – c and b Cunliffe	67
K. S. Ranjitsinhji c Bardswell b Cunliffe	4 – not out	171
Mr W. L. Murdoch c Foster b Cunliffe	53 – b Cunliffe	8
Mr W. Newham b Pilkington	21 – c Mordaunt b Cunliffe	3
Mr G. Brann b Cunliffe	32 – c Mordaunt b Cunliffe	10
Mr G. H. Arlington c Bardswell b Waddy	4 – b Clayton	6
E. H. Killick not out	27 – not out	44
F. Parris c Raikes b Cunliffe	4	
H. R. Butt c Cunliffe b Raikes	15	
F. W. Tate c Bardswell b Raikes	3	
N-b 4	4 B 13, n-b 5	18
	198	329

Sussex Bowling

	Overs	Mdns	Runs	Wkts	Overs	Mdns	Runs	Wkts
Tate	18	2	58	0	33	12	63	2
Parris	46.3	17	85	5	50	12	87	1
Killick	41	17	67	5	39	11	81	4
Arlington	3	0	11	0				
Ranjitsinhji	6	1	22	0	5	1	13	0
Brann					13	4	23	0
Marlow					3	0	13	1

Oxford University Bowling

	Overs	Mdns	Runs	Wkts	Overs	Mdns	Runs	Wkts
Cunliffe	38	14	92	6	36	6	109	4
Waddy	36	13	42	1	17	2	76	1
Raikes	18	9	34	2	8	1	37	0
Pilkington	9	3	18	1	14	3	52	0
Clayton	3	2	8	0	14	3	37	1

Umpires: J. Lillywhite and D. Eastwood.

SUSSEX v YORKSHIRE

Played at Brighton, August 20, 21, 22, 1896

Ranjitsinhji, in this engagement, surpassed all his previous performances for the year, scoring two innings of a hundred in the same match. His doings were the more remarkable, as when he went in Sussex looked to be in serious danger of defeat, but his brilliancy and determination enabled the county to escape honourably from their position, the game being left drawn. Ranjitsinhji's batting was more extraordinary than that of the other famous players who have done a similar thing, as his two hundreds were not only made in the same match, but on the same day. As may be supposed, his marvellous exhibition caused the wildest excitement among the spectators at Brighton. It is not often that the Yorkshire bowlers have been treated with so little respect. As a matter of record it should be stated that Ranjitsinhji went in on the second day, but had not scored a run when rain caused stumps to be pulled up. For Yorkshire, there was some excellent batting, F. S. Jackson and Peel both exceeding the 100, and Tunnicliffe only missing a three-figure innings by a single run. The performance of Ranjitsinhji, of course, overshadowed all the other Sussex batting.

Yorkshire

Mr F. S. Jackson b Killick	102
J. Tunnicliffe c Newham b Parris	99
J. T. Brown st Butt b Hartley	31
D. Denton c Butt b Tate	3
G. H. Hirst b Tate	6
R. Peel run out	106
R. Moorhouse b Killick	20
E. Wainwright c Parris b Hartley	21
Mr E. Smith b Parris	9
Lord Hawke c Tate b Hartley	1
A. L. Bairstow not out	0
B 3, l-b 2, w 4	9
	407

Sussex

Mr C. B. Fry c Bairstow b Wainwright	14	– c Bairstow b Brown	42
E. H. Killick b Hirst	9	– not out	53
K. S. Ranjitsinhji c Jackson b Smith	100	– not out	125
Mr W. L. Murdoch c Jackson b Hirst	0		
Mr W. Newham c Jackson b Smith	37		
F. W. Marlow c Bairstow b Hirst	1	– c Bairstow b Peel	30
G. Bean c Bairstow b Smith	5		
Mr J. C. Hartley b Smith	0		
F. Parris b Hirst	0		
H. R. Butt not out	16		
F. W. Tate hit wkt b Smith	5		
L-b 4	4	B 6, l-b 4	10
	191		260

Sussex Bowling

	Overs	Mdns	Runs	Wkts
Killick	30	7	76	2
Parris	56.4	15	109	2
Hartley	36	7	110	3
Fry	5	1	17	0
Tate	40	16	79	2
Bean	3	0	6	0
Ranjitsinhji	3	2	1	0

Yorkshire Bowling

	Overs	Mdns	Runs	Wkts	Overs	Mdns	Runs	Wkts
Hirst	25	10	49	4	13	2	27	0
Wainwright	10	4	27	1	8	2	15	0
Peel	17	7	33	0	18	10	21	1
Jackson	10	3	36	0	11	3	39	0
Smith	15.4	4	42	5	17	8	34	0
Brown					17	4	65	1
Denton					6	0	30	0
Moorhouse					4	1	19	0

Umpires: W. Hearn and M. Sherwin.

SUSSEX v LANCASHIRE

Played at Brighton, August 16, 17, 18, 1897

Playing very finely at all points, Lancashire gained a decisive victory over Sussex by an innings and 186 runs, but it must be confessed that the luck was all on their side. They had to bat on a wicket up to the best Brighton standard, while when their opponents went in, the ground had been seriously damaged by rain. Further than that, Sussex were most unfortunate in losing the services of their fast bowler Bland, and the match will be remembered for a very unusual circumstance. Before being taken ill, Bland sent down three overs for 13 runs and consequently got his name on the score sheet, but Mr MacLaren, the Lancashire Captain, allowed another man to play in his place. It was, of course, a sportsmanlike action, but set up a very dangerous precedent, and was generally disapproved of at the time. In Lancashire's first innings, some splendid cricket was shown by Baker, MacLaren, Ward, Tindall and Cuttell. Baker's 186 was the biggest score he had ever obtained in a first class match.

Lancashire

Albert Ward b Ranjitsinhji	54
Mr A. C. MacLaren c Butt b Hartley	76
F. H. Sugg c Fry b Hartley	0
J. T. Tyldesley b Ranjitsinhji	1
G. R. Baker c Fry b Tate	186
Mr S. M. Tindall c Brann b Ranjitsinhji	86
J. Briggs st Butt b Hartley	2
W. R. Cuttell b Tate	47
A. Hallam c Bean b Hartley	10
A. Mold st Butt b Hartley	10
L. Radcliffe not out	4
B 4, l-b 4, w 2, n-b 2	12
	488

Sussex

Mr G. Brann lbw b Mold	25	– c Hallam b Briggs 0
F. W. Marlow c Radcliffe b Briggs	13	– not out 9
K. S. Ranjitsinhji c Radcliffe b Mold	11	– run out 58
Mr W. L. Murdoch b Cuttell	42	– c Baker b Briggs 19
Mr C. B. Fry c Hallam b Briggs	0	– b Cuttell 1
Mr W. Newham b Cuttell	17	– c Radcliffe b Briggs 0
G. Bean c Tyldesley b Briggs	3	– c MacLaren b Briggs 12
E. H. Killick not out	5	– c Briggs b Hallam 18
Mr J. C. Hartley lbw b Briggs	0	– c Tindall b Cuttell 8
H. R. Butt b Cuttell	8	– c MacLaren b Cuttell 23
F. W. Tate b Cuttell	6	– b Cuttell 8
L-b 1	1	B 14, l-b 1 15
	131	171

Sussex Bowling

	Overs	Mdns	Runs	Wkts
Tate	40.1	12	98	2
Bland (retired ill)	3	0	13	0
Fry	20	6	63	0
Hartley	47	8	138	5
Ranjitsinhji	38	8	102	3
Killick	24	9	51	0
Brann	2	0	11	0

Lancashire Bowling

	Overs	Mdns	Runs	Wkts	Overs	Mdns	Runs	Wkts
Briggs	33	10	60	4	28	9	66	4
Mold	26	7	62	2				
Cuttell	6.4	3	8	4	34.4	16	72	4
Hallam					16	10	18	1

Umpires: W. A. Woof and G. Hay.

SUSSEX v SOMERSET

Played at Eastbourne, June 2, 3, 4, 1898

There was a sensational finish to this match, Somerset gaining an unexpected victory by 108 runs. Sussex were set 219 to get to win and with only an hour and fifty minutes left for play a draw seemed inevitable. However, Somerset won with ten minutes to spare. The honours of this triumph rested largely with Woods. On the third morning he took three of the last five Sussex wickets for 10 runs. His batting was wonderfully brilliant and he made his runs out of 173 put on while he was in. Brann played an admirable innings, being in for three hours and scoring 118 out of 190. Owing to wet weather the game was not commenced until the second day and Somerset gained a doubtful advantage in taking first innings.

Somerset

Mr S. M. J. Woods b Parris	28	– c and b Bland	143
Mr V. T. Hill b Bland	5	– b Bland	28
Mr H. T. Stanley run out	9	– run out	17
Mr W. Trask b Bland	0	– c Butt b Bland	28
G. B. Nichols not out	40	– run out	25
E. Robson b Parris	0	– b Bland	3
Captain R. P. Spurway b Bland	0	– b Parris	0
Mr G. Fowler b Bland	5	– b Parris	0
G. Gill b Bland	4	– b Parris	1
E. G. Tyler b Killick	27	– not out	26
Mr E. W. Ebdon run out	4	– c Murdoch b Bland	5
B 8, l-b 2, n-b 1	11	B 6, l-b 3, n-b 2	11
	133		287

Sussex

Mr G. Brann b Gill	118	– c Fowler b Tyler	25
F. W. Marlow b Woods	29	– b Fowler	5
Mr W. L. Murdoch b Gill	9	– c and b Gill	0
Mr W. Newham st Ebdon b Tyler	1	– b Tyler	36
E. H. Killick b Robson	5	– b Tyler	8
J. Vine b Tyler	10	– c and b Tyler	0
G. Bean c Woods b Tyler	2	– b Woods	12
F. Parris c Fowler b Gill	5	– not out	14
G. Cox not out	5	– b Woods	0
H. R. Butt lbw b Tyler	2	– b Woods	0
C. H. G. Bland c Gill b Tyler	0	– st Ebdon b Tyler	0
B 9, l-b 5, w 1, n-b 1	16	B 3, l-b 7	10
	202		110

Sussex Bowling

	Overs	Mdns	Runs	Wkts	Overs	Mdns	Runs	Wkts
Bland	25	6	63	5	37.3	12	87	5
Parris	22	6	47	2	32	11	84	3
Killick	2.4	0	12	1	9	2	30	0
Cox					21	5	60	0
Vine					3	0	15	0

Somerset Bowling

	Overs	Mdns	Runs	Wkts	Overs	Mdns	Runs	Wkts
Tyler	22.1	5	67	5	14.1	5	41	5
Gill	21	13	29	3	13	5	32	1
Woods	9	2	30	1	5	3	10	3
Fowler	13	5	25	0	6	2	9	1
Robson	15	6	31	1	2	1	8	0
Nichols	5	3	4	0				

Umpires: R. Thoms and A. Chester.

SUSSEX v MIDDLESEX

Played at Brighton, July 25, 26, 27, 1898

Far and away the most important feature of this match was the batting of C. B. Fry, who accomplished the feat of scoring two separate innings of over a hundred. In the first innings he made 108 out of 177 in three hours, and in the second 123 not out in a total of 224 in less than three hours and a half. Perhaps the most remarkable fact in connection with Fry's performance was that in neither innings did he give a chance that went to hand, his play apart from two or three faulty hits being irreproachable. In their first innings the Middlesex batsmen were handicapped by a sea mist which became so thick that once the players left the field for twenty minutes. Sussex made a fine effort to win, but Middlesex, aided by a shower which delayed the game for twenty minutes, succeeded in making a draw of it.

Sussex

Mr C. D. Fisher lbw b Trott	6	– c Ford b Webb	2
Mr C. B. Fry c Rawlin b Ford	108	– not out	123
Mr W. L. Murdoch c and b Trott	43	– b Trott	38
Mr G. H. A. Arlington c Trott b Ford	18	– c Rawlin b Webb	0
E. H. Killick not out	76	– b Trott	11
J. Bean b Hearne	2	– b Trott	0
F. Parris b Webb	7	– not out	19
H. R. Butt c Ford b Haerne	52	– c Rawlin b Webb	14
F. W. Tate b Webb	14	– b Webb	0
C. H. G. Bland b Webb	8		
W. Humphreys jun. lbw b Trott	1		
B 18, l-b 3, w 1	22	B 9, l-b 7, n-b 1	17
	357		(7 wkts dec.) 224

Middlesex

Mr P. F. Warner c Butt b Parris	37	– c Bean b Tate	18
Mr H. B. Hayman c Bean b Tate	66	– b Tate	0
Mr A. E. Stoddart b Tate	69	– c Butt b Bland	42
Mr F. G. J. Ford c Bean b Parris	0	– c Butt b Humphreys	36
J. T. Rawlin c Butt b Parris	19	– not out	17
Sir T. C. O'Brien c and b Tate	0	– b Bland	3
A. E. Trott b Parris	6	– c and b Humphreys	1
Mr R. W. Nicholls c Butt b Humphreys	14	– b Humphreys	20
Mr E. H. Bray c and b Humphreys	19	– not out	2
J. T. Hearne not out	29		
S. Webb b Bland	17		
B 4, l-b 3	7	B 8, l-b 2, n-b 1	11
	283		150

Middlesex Bowling

	Overs	Mdns	Runs	Wkts	Overs	Mdns	Runs	Wkts
Hearne	50	22	89	2	34	14	56	0
Rawlin	17	7	23	0				
Trott	39.4	13	119	3	20	5	64	3
Webb	26	8	58	3	30	8	76	4
Ford	19	5	46	2				
Stoddart					4	1	11	0

Sussex Bowling

	Overs	Mdns	Runs	Wkts	Overs	Mdns	Runs	Wkts
Bland	21.2	8	58	1	20	9	35	2
Humphreys	32	7	88	2	21	5	42	3
Parris	36	11	88	4	5	0	22	0
Tate	25	10	42	3	33	10	40	2

Umpires: W. A. J. West and G. H. Remnant.

SUSSEX v HAMPSHIRE

Played at Brighton, August 8, 9, 10, 1898

In beating Hampshire by 134 runs the Sussex eleven gained their first win of the season. Their victory was very largely brought about by the brilliant batting of Fry and the successful bowling of Tate and Bland. Fry was within an ace of repeating his great triumph against Middlesex, and his double success was all the more remarkable as there was only one other individual score of over fifty. The match was played throughout on a more or less treacherous wicket, but Fry overcame all difficulties, his cricket in both innings being of a highly skilful order. No other Sussex batsman could fairly cope with the bowling of Baldwin, who obtained no fewer than fifteen wickets.

Sussex

Mr C. B. Fry b Baldwin	99	– c Studd b Baldwin	131
Mr W. L. Murdoch b Steele	13	– b Lee	3
E. H. Killick b Lee	20	– lbw b Baldwin	24
F. W. Marlow b Baldwin	6	– b Baldwin	0
Mr W. Newham b Baldwin	4	– b Baldwin	10
Mr C. D. Fisher st Bennett b Tate	26	– b Baldwin	0
Mr C. L. A. Smith b Baldwin	17	– b Tate	0
F. Parris c Lee b Baldwin	0	– lbw b Baldwin	11
H. R. Butt c Poore b Baldwin	0	– c Studd b Baldwin	9
F. W. Tate not out	4	– st Bennett b Baldwin	9
C. H. G. Bland c Barrett b Baldwin	8	– not out	0
B 2, l-b 2, w 1, n-b 1	6	B 9	9
	203		206

Hampshire

Mr E. I. M. Barrett b Tate	8	– lbw b Bland	55
Mr R. A. Bennett b Tate	16	– b Tate	0
A. Webb b Tate	3	– run out	0
Major R. M. Poore run out	0	– c Butt b Bland	26
V. Barton b Parris	28	– c Marlow b Killick	12
Mr H. W. Studd lbw b Tate	25	– c Butt b Killick	8
Mr E. C. Lee b Tate	0	– b Bland	20
Mr D. A. Steele b Tate	16	– c Fry b Bland	24
H. Baldwin b Tate	12	– b Bland	9
E. Light b Bland	0	– not out	1
E. Tate not out	0	– c Killick b Bland	1
B 3, l-b 2	5	B 6	6
	113		162

Hampshire Bowling

	Overs	Mdns	Runs	Wkts	Overs	Mdns	Runs	Wkts
Baldwin	46.4	14	68	7	32.4	10	74	8
Light	8	3	28	0				
Tate	35	17	49	1	11	2	36	1
Steele	13	6	27	1	17	3	41	0
Lee	13	4	25	1	6	2	13	1
Barton					4	1	7	0
Studd					4	1	13	0
Webb					4	0	13	0

Sussex Bowling

	Overs	Mdns	Runs	Wkts	Overs	Mdns	Runs	Wkts
Bland	17	6	39	1	25	4	73	6
Tate	24.3	10	48	7	11	5	27	1
Parris	7	2	21	1	4	0	15	0
Killick					18	4	41	2

Umpires: R. Clayton and W. A. J. West.

FORMATION OF A COUNTY CRICKET COUNCIL

THE FIRST MEETING AT LORD'S

On Tuesday morning, July 12th, 1887, a meeting of county delegates was held at the Lord's Cricket Ground to receive the report of the sub-committee appointed at the county secretaries' meeting in the previous December to consider the advisability of forming a County Cricket Council. In their report, while suggesting the advisability of forming such a Council, the sub-committee recommended that the Council should have no power to deal with the laws of cricket or the rules of county qualification, but that the MCC should remain as heretofore the arbiter in such matters. Thirteen counties were represented at the meeting, viz.:– Nottingham, Mr W. H. C. Oates and Captain Holden; Yorkshire, Mr M. J. Ellison and Mr J. B. Wostinholm; Lancashire, Mr S. H. Swire and Mr J. McLaren; Surrey, Mr C. W. Alcock; Middlesex, Mr A. J. Webbe; Sussex, Mr Montagu Turner; Kent, Mr George Marsham and Lord Harris; Cheshire, Mr J. Horner; Hampshire, Mr R. Bencraft; Warwickshire, Mr W. Ansell; Leicestershire, Mr T. Burdett, Northamptonshire, Mr T. H. Vials; and Somersetshire, Mr H. Murray-Anderdon.

Of the more important counties it will be noticed that Gloucestershire and Derbyshire were absentees, but Mr W. G. Grace, who usually represents the Western shire, was engaged in the match, Gentlemen v Players, which was proceeding while the meeting was sitting.

Lord Harris, having been voted to the chair, remarked that what the meeting had to do was to decide whether a County Cricket Council should be formed, and in order to raise that question he moved that the report of the sub-committee be received.

Captain Holden seconded the motion, which, after a brief discussion, was carried unanimously.

Mr Ellison then moved, and Mr Alcock seconded, the following motion: "That a County Cricket Council be formed."

Captain Holden asked whether it would not be well to first of all know what the duties of this Council would be. If it was going to interfere with the powers of the Marylebone Club, then he should object to it.

Mr Ellison pointed out that the report distinctly recommended that the Council should not interfere with the Marylebone Club.

The Chairman also observed that the report clearly laid down that the duties of the Council should not extend to any interference with the laws of cricket. But what the Council could do would be to discuss suggested alterations in the law, and to make such recommendations as were deemed advisable to the MCC.

Mr Ansell said that his impression as regards the laws of the game was that the MCC were the best judges, and in cases of dispute on the subject of county qualification the MCC would be the best arbiters.

Captain Holden observed that the laws of county cricket were made by the counties, and the MCC adopted the rules of county qualification laid down by them.

Mr Alcock said it seemed to him that as the counties made the rules of county qualification it was quite competent for them to suggest alterations.

The Chairman: Leaving it to the Marylebone Club to be the arbiter.

Mr Alcock: Distinctly.

Captain Holden said it would be within the recollection of those present that this question was discussed at the general meeting, when the Chairman (Lord Harris) proposed some alteration, which was negatived by a large majority.

The Chairman said there was no question of alteration, but whether the Council should have the power to make any alteration. He suggested that the simplest course would be to put Mr Ellison's motion, and if it were adopted it would then be open for the meeting to limit its own powers. It was important that the meeting should proceed formally and gradually, and that the powers of the Council should be clearly defined.

Captain Holden was opposed to the idea of forming a Council in which the smaller counties would be on an equality with those that supplied half the players of England. If such a Council were formed, the county qualification would soon be done away with, and they might have a case, as he once remembered, of a gentleman playing for three counties in one year.

Mr Webbe thought it ought to be left to the first-class counties to frame the county qualification.

Mr Burdett said Leicestershire did not consider itself below some of the first-class counties.

Mr Webbe suggested that the matter might be left to the counties who originally framed the rules.

Mr Ansell was opposed to such a suggestion, as circumstances had altered. When the rules were framed the first-class counties were the only counties; but things had changed, and it would be absurd to shut out the more recently formed county clubs.

The Chairman said he would now take the liberty of making an appeal to them on behalf of the game, whether it was worth while for them to extend a difference of opinion which undoubtedly had arisen between what were called first-class and second-class counties. Was it worth while to extend that difference at a moment when it was possible to establish what he believed would be a most valuable Council – one which would have the power of improving cricket in several ways, and putting it within the power of second-class counties – if they would allow him to use the misnomer – of getting up into the first rank? At present there was a great difficulty in the way of their so doing, but he thought that difficulty might be settled by the Council. Mr Ellison had moved that this Council should be formed, and if they went into the question of first and second-class counties there would be such a difference of opinion that it would very likely be impossible to carry the motion. He should regret that, for the sub-committee took a great deal of trouble over the question, and were unanimous that the Council should be formed; and they further pointed out that, once formed, then would be the time to raise the question of county status. He thought the raising of the question of what were first and what were second-class counties before they came to the motion upon the formation of the Council might result in those old feelings being revived, and that the first-class counties would vote that the rules of county qualification should only be altered by them, while the second-class counties would vote the other way, and there would be a great danger of the whole scheme falling to the ground. He appealed to them first to carry Mr Ellison's motion and then leave it to the Council to deal with the vexed question of county qualification. If they carried Mr Ellison's motion they would have no reason to regret it.

Mr Alcock pointed out that two years ago he proposed there should be no difference in the status of the counties. That motion was carried, and it seemed rather strange to introduce the question again.

Captain Holden said that if a Cricket Council were formed for all the counties, he felt perfectly certain there would be an attempt to alter the county qualification, and that he strongly objected to. That qualification had been settled and carried on for years, and he was opposed to a council interfering with it.

Mr Burdett observed that, so far as Leicestershire was concerned, Captain Holden was quite in error. That county was in favour of the term for residential qualification being extended from two years to three.

Mr Ansell objected to the conclusion that those counties who in 1870 were so fortunate as to possess a county club, should be deemed to constitute the cricket wisdom of England for the rest of time. County clubs were springing up all over the country, and it would be absurd to shut them out now.

Mr Ellison's motion was then put and carried *nem. con.*, all the counties voting except Middlesex.

The Chairman then moved, and Mr Ansell seconded, the following resolution:– "That as regards the laws of cricket, the Council shall have no executive powers."

The motion was carried unanimously.

Captain Holden then raised the question as to whether the Council should have power to deal with the subject of county qualification, and a long discussion took place upon the point.

The Chairman observed that it was an open question whether at some future time the counties which considered themselves the chief counties might not alter the rules if they pleased. He would beg to point out that the question was never raised when he made his motion last autumn at the meeting of county secretaries, proposing an alteration of the county qualification. The question as to whether that secretaries' meeting had the power to alter the rules never arose, it being seemingly assumed that it could do so, and had there been sufficient in agreement with him (Lord Harris) his motion would have come into force immediately. That being so, he was inclined to think that, the Council having been formed, it would have the power to make alterations.

Mr Alcock suggested that the Council should have control over all matters connected with county cricket, but none over the laws of the game itself. He thought it was absurd that the counties should have no power over their own affairs.

Mr Webbe asked whether the Council would decide the vexed question of the qualification.

The Chairman thought it would be in the power of the Council. The counties should lay down what the rules were, leaving the MCC to be arbiters.

Mr Oates objected to any alteration as regarded the MCC being arbiters, and moved, "That upon all questions raised under the rules of County Cricket Qualification the Committee of the MCC shall adjudicate."

Mr Swire seconded the motion, which, after some little discussion, was carried unanimously.

Mr Alcock proposed, "That it shall be competent for the Council to alter or amend the rules of County Cricket Qualification."

Mr Horner seconded the motion, which was also carried *nem. con.*, Nottinghamshire being the only county which did not vote.

The Chairman said the next business of the meeting would be to consider the composition of the Council. He was anxious to afford equal justice to the so-called second-class counties, but they must be careful themselves that no county should be admitted that could not be looked upon as playing real county matches. His own impression as to the definition of what constituted a cricketing county was that it should have an established club and should play matches extending over three days. It might be very difficult to come to a decision upon this point, as he understood that in some cases of second-class playing first-class counties the latter had refused to play three-day matches. He submitted it would be possible to lay down the definition, and he first suggested that no county should be qualified to send a representative to the Council that did not possess a county cricket club.

Some little discussion took place on the subject, and eventually, on the proposition of Mr Marsham, seconded by Mr Ellison, the following motion was unanimously agreed to:– "That the Council consist of one representative each from those counties assembled at the meeting held at Lord's in December, 1886." It may be mentioned that the counties represented at that meeting were:– Nottinghamshire, Yorkshire, Surrey, Kent, Lancashire, Sussex, Gloucestershire, Middlesex, Derbyshire, Essex, Warwickshire, Norfolk, Leicestershire, Staffordshire, Somersetshire, Northamptonshire, Hampshire, Durham, Hertfordshire, and Cheshire.

Some little difficulty was then experienced in selecting a sub-committee to frame by-laws, and to decide upon subscriptions, time and place of meeting, and other details, but the meeting at length agreed to the following motion, proposed by Mr Oates, and seconded by Mr Vials:– "That a committee of five representatives from the counties of Middlesex, Kent, Surrey, Sussex, and Gloucestershire be appointed to frame by-laws, and to report to the Council before the end of the year." This motion, it may be stated, practically amounted to the reappointment of the sub-committee, whose report had formed the subject of the day's discussion.

A vote of thanks was then proposed to Lord Harris for presiding, and the proceedings came to a close.

A MEETING AT LORD'S

December 5, 1893

The Classification of Counties

Mr Ellison (Yorkshire) introduced the subject of the classification of counties, and moved the following resolution:– "That for the purposes of classification there should be no distinction drawn between counties who play out and home three-day matches with not less than six other counties." He thought such a motion, if adopted, would do away with that very invidious distinction which had existed for some years, and would also abolish that hated word "championship", which he thought the whole of the cricket world would be glad to get rid of.

Mr Wilson (Derbyshire), in seconding the resolution, remarked that his county had suffered from the curious classification that existed. He thought this resolution met the case, and would act as a salve to the so-called second-class counties. At one time Derbyshire were regarded as first-class, but they went down the hill and were degraded. Under the system that now existed there was not the smallest chance of Derbyshire regaining their lost position; but this motion would probably secure for them the opportunity.

Mr Oates (Nottinghamshire) asked Mr Ellison if he intended his resolution to come into force next year.

Mr Ellison thought it had better take effect next year. Perhaps, however, such a motion would hardly be in order, as no notice had been given. He did not know whether there were any special rules to guide the meeting, or whether he should give notice of his motion.

The Chairman remarked that the resolution was quite in order. It did not affect the rules or jurisdiction of cricket, but was merely a matter of detail. It was quite open to that meeting to say which should be reckoned as first-class averages and which should not.

Mr Oates thought some notice of the motion should have been given, so that the county Committees might have been consulted. It was a subject of such importance that even if he were in favour of it, he should not vote without having had an opportunity of consulting with his Committee.

Mr Alcock (Surrey) took a similar view. In being asked to vote on such an important question without instructions from their Committees, the delegates were placed in an awkward position.

This view of the situation seemed pretty general, and the Chairman observed that after such an expression of opinion it would be advisable to adjourn the subject to some future date. He asked Mr Ellison what he proposed to do.

Mr Ellison preferred to stand or fall by the decision of the meeting that day.

Mr Alcock asked as a point of order whether, apart from the arrangement of fixtures, any sort of business should be produced and decided at that meeting. He thought it inadvisable that any business should be considered save the arrangements of fixtures. He was so bold as to suggest that the County Cricket Council was the proper authority to deal with such matters, and that it should be revived.

Mr Ellison did not know why the meeting of the Cricket Council was not called as usual last year.

This remark caused some little amusement, as most of those present no doubt remembered that Mr Ellison at the last meeting of the Council gave his casting vote in favour of an adjournment *sine die*. A delegate called out, "You voted against it"; but Mr Ellison replied, "No, certainly not." Another delegate reminded Mr Ellison that he voted in favour of *sine die*; but the Yorkshire president's memory was still at fault.

Mr Alcock certainly thought that a proposal to resuscitate the Council might well come from Mr Ellison. If it was agreed that the Council was defunct, they might perhaps agree on its reconstruction on a different basis.

Mr Wostinholm (Yorkshire) could not see how the Council was defunct, as its funds were still in existence. Until the money had been divided the Council could not be dead; it was in abeyance.

The Chairman, interposing, observed that matters were now altogether out of order. He had nothing to do with the Cricket Council, was not a member of it, and never had been. If its resuscitation was desired it must be done in the proper manner. With regard to Mr Ellison's motion he thought it desirable that the matter should go before the county Committees, who could either send their votes to the Marylebone Club or hold another meeting; after what had been said it would be useless to take the opinion of that meeting.

The subject then dropped, but after lunch Mr Ellison revived it. He said that though his resolution was withdrawn from the consideration of that meeting the Yorkshire Committee would at once take steps to obtain the opinion of the counties now playing three-day matches. When that opinion had been ascertained they would propose to hold another meeting at Lord's early in January of the secretaries of each of these counties, and one representative from each county in addition, and then his resolution could be adopted or rejected as was deemed advisable. At that time it was possible that some question might be raised in regard to the appointment of umpires, a subject of vital importance in county cricket. He hoped this proceeding would be acceptable to the representatives of the counties concerned, and that they would attend the next meeting prepared to determine the question of classification. In reply to a question, Mr Ellison remarked that he desired the change to take place next year – that was the object of calling the meeting in January.

A MEETING AT LORD'S

December 11, 1894

The Appointment of Umpires

Lord Hawke (Yorkshire), in introducing the subject of umpires and their appointment, remarked that a good deal of dissatisfaction had been expressed during the last two or three seasons with regard to umpiring. (Hear, hear.) He thought he could suggest a solution of that difficulty. He desired that each county should nominate as many umpires as they liked, and forward the names to the MCC by the 1st of February. After that date and before the season commenced he hoped to call a meeting of the county captains, who, with their elevens, were the people most interested in the matter of good and bad decisions. At that meeting they could talk over the subject of umpiring, and they might arrive at some proposals to put before their committees. They might, for instance, ask that the fee of umpires should be raised from £5 to £6. (Hear, hear.) That was a small item when so much money was taken at the gates. He believed there were many good men who could not umpire because they were not allowed to stand in matches in which their own county was engaged. He believed it was the wish of the captains that they should be allowed to do so. What he thought the captains might do would be to choose the best umpires they could, and at the end of the season strike out those who gave bad decisions.

Mr Denison (Nottinghamshire) understood Lord Hawke to suggest that a county might recommend any good men whom they considered fit, and that the captains would make a selection.

Mr Onslow (Surrey), as an old cricketer, objected to the captains being allowed to lay down hard and fast rules with regard to umpires. He was also opposed to permitting men to stand in matches in which the county for which they had played was engaged. That would be a mischievous thing to do, and opening as it would the door to temptation might bring about an undesirable state of affairs. He presumed that the decision of the captains would not be final: that must rest with the MCC.

Lord Hawke observed that the captains would place their views before the MCC. He did not propose that they should constitute themselves a governing body, but they were the persons mostly concerned. There were several good umpires whom captains would not object to standing in matches where their own county was playing.

Mr Denison: There are a good many people who would not object to George Ulyett.

Mr Webbe (Middlesex) said it was not so much a question of a man umpiring for his own county, but under the present system counties suffered from nominating good umpires. An umpire was not allowed to stand for the county nominating him. He would be delighted to nominate Ulyett, but he would be defeating his own object, for Ulyett could not then stand in a Middlesex match. That was the difficulty they wanted to get over.

Lord Hawke (to Mr Webbe): If you nominate Ulyett he could stand in the Middlesex and Surrey match.

Mr Webbe: No, no.

Mr Denison remarked that so far as Middlesex was concerned there was no necessity for them to nominate Ulyett; Yorkshire would do that. A county might possess six or eight good umpires, and they should be able to nominate them.

Mr Grace understood that what was desired was to do away with the nomination of umpires by different counties, but that umpires should be nominated by all the counties. It was not desirable that a man should stand for the county with which he had played.

Mr Denison thought that what was needed was to allow a county to send in a list – not a nomination – of umpires, and the captains would select a sufficient number.

Mr Ellison (Yorkshire) remarked that it was understood that no man would be allowed to stand for the county for which he had played.

Mr Ansell (Warwickshire): Let the captains meet at the end of the year and strike out the inefficient men.

Mr Ellison: That is too invidious.

Mr Ansell, continuing, said that they could not get away from the fact that if a man umpired for the county nominating him he would be liable to the suggestion of favouring that county. He thought the list of umpires should be revised annually and the men who were known to be inefficient struck out.

Mr Murdoch (Sussex) did not think that the captains should have this onerous duty thrust upon them. The captains, however, might go through the list, and having selected the best men, forward their views to the MCC. That was the proper authority to deal with the question. He had a strong opinion – he spoke from experience and suggested the matter for the consideration of the counties – that it was desirable to provide a room for umpires. At present they went into the players' room and were subjected to all sorts of remarks and sometimes abuse; and no matter how honest an umpire might be – and he believed they were all honest – they could hardly fail to be affected. If umpires were kept apart from the cricketers a great deal of good would be done. He had no objection to umpires standing for counties nominating them. With regard to Ulyett he should have every confidence in him umpiring in a Yorkshire and Sussex match, and he thought if more confidence were shown, umpires would be benefited and encouraged to be as honest as possible. It would be a step in the right direction for the list of umpires to be gone through by the captains, and they would forward any suggestions they had to make to the MCC, who would act.

The Chairman remarked that all Lord Hawke was asking for was that counties would send a list of umpires before February 1, and that so far as that meeting was concerned the matter was at an end.

The discussion then terminated.

WARWICKSHIRE

WARWICKSHIRE v YORKSHIRE

Played at Birmingham, May 7, 8, 9, 1896

A match that will always be remembered from the fact that Yorkshire scored the huge total of 887 and put into the shade all previous records in first-class cricket. By making so many runs Yorkshire robbed themselves of the chance of victory, but, of course, it was a great thing to have accomplished such a memorable performance. As may be supposed the wicket was in almost perfect condition, but for all that the Yorkshiremen deserve the highest praise for the manner in which they seized their opportunity. Yorkshire had the honour of lowering another record, this being the first time in an important match that four separate scores of over a hundred had been obtained in the same innings. Jackson played splendid cricket, while the Warwickshire bowling was at its best, and late in the innings Lord Hawke and Peel put on 240 runs during their partnership. Every member of the Warwickshire team, with the exception of Law went on to bowl. Yorkshire's innings occupied the whole of the two first days.

Yorkshire

Mr F. S. Jackson c Law b Ward	117
J. Tunnicliffe c Pallett b Glover	28
J. T. Brown c Hill b Pallett	23
D. Denton c W. G. Quaife b Santall	6
R. Moorhouse b Ward	72
E. Wainwright run out	126
R. Peel not out	210
Mr F. W. Milligan b Pallett	34
Lord Hawke b Pallett	166
G. H. Hirst c Glover b Santall	85
D. Hunter b Pallett	5
B 5, l-b 6, w 4	15
	887

Warwickshire

Mr H. W. Bainbridge c Hunter b Hirst	5	– b Wainwright 29
Walter Quaife b Hirst	0	– not out 18
W. G. Quaife not out	92	
A. Law c Jackson b Hirst	7	
A. Lilley b Hirst	0	
Mr J. E. Hill b Hirst	4	
E. J. Diver b Peel	27	
H. J. Pallett c Wainwright b Jackson	25	
S. J. Santall b Hirst	29	
Mr A. C. S. Glover b Hirst	1	
W. Ward b Hirst	3	
B 4, l-b 3, w 1, n-b 2	10	N-b 1 1
	203	48

Warwickshire Bowling

	Overs	Mdns	Runs	Wkts		Overs	Mdns	Runs	Wkts
Santall	65	9	223	2	Bainbridge	6	1	17	—
Ward	62	11	175	2	Hill	3	—	14	—
Glover	30	1	154	1	Lilley	6	1	13	—
Pallett	75.3	14	184	4	W. Quaife	9	1	18	—
W. G. Quaife	8	1	33	—	Diver	10	1	41	—

Yorkshire Bowling

	Overs	Mdns	Runs	Wkts	Overs	Mdns	Runs	Wkts
Hirst	40.1	16	59	8				
Peel	31	21	27	1	2	2	4	—
Jackson	18	9	23	1				
Wainwright	16	7	35	—	2.1	1	4	1
Milligan	13	5	14	—	5	1	15	—
Brown	4	—	24	—				
Moorhouse	4	1	11	—	4	—	24	—

Umpires: W. A. J. West and R. G. Barlow.

WARWICKSHIRE v LANCASHIRE

For H. J. Pallett's Benefit

Played at Birmingham, July 5, 6, 7, 1897

This was another the many games played at Birmingham last season in which, through heavy scoring, it was impossible to arrive at a definite issue. In the course of the three days, 1,027 runs were obtained for the loss of 32 wickets – a striking testimony to the excellence of the Edgbaston ground. More than anything else, the match will be remembered for the fact that Tyldesley achieved the rare distinction of making two separate hundreds in a game of first class importance, sharing the honour with W. G. Grace, Stoddart, Brann, Storer, Ranjitsinhji and MacLaren. About this time Tyldesley was playing in remarkable form, but subsequently his cricket was disappointing. Warwickshire did well to exceed by 13 runs their opponents' total of 292, much credit due to Diver, Glover, Bainbridge, Lilley and Byrne. For once in a way, William Quaife was quite a failure.

Lancashire

A. Ward run out	23	– c Lilley b Santall	19
Mr C. R. Hartley c Field b Pallett	23	– b Santall	18
F. H. Sugg c and b Lilley	51	– c W. G. Quaife b Byrne	27
G. R. Baker b Field	1	– run out	10
J. T. Tyldesley c Bainbridge b W. Quaife	106	– not out	100
J. Briggs c and b Field	13	– c and b W. Quaife	7
C. Smith b Field	11	– c Diver b Pallett	2
W. R. Cuttell c Byrne b W. Quaife	33	– c Byrne b Santall	43
Mr A. N. Hornby b Byrne	11	– lbw b W. Quaife	10
A. Hallam c Pallett b Byrne	3	– c Byrne b Pallett	24
A. Mold not out	3		
B 7, l-b 5, w 2	14	L-b 11, w 5	16
	292	(9 wkts dec.)	276

Warwickshire

Walter Quaife c Hallam b Mold	33	– b Cuttell	5
Mr H. W. Bainbridge c Smith b Hallam	45	– c Sugg b Baker	60
Mr J. F. Byrne b Hallam	13	– lbw b Baker	58
A. A. Lilley b Hallam	42	– not out	19
W. G. Quaife b Hallam	2		
E. J. Diver c Smith b Briggs	59		
Mr T. S. Fishwick c Smith b Cuttell	15		
Mr A. C. S. Glover c Cuttell b Baker	55		
S. J. Santall b Mold	7		
H. J. Pallett not out	20		
Field b Cuttell	0		
B 10, l-b 4	14	B 8, l-b 3, w 1	12
	305		154

Warwickshire Bowling

	Overs	Mdns	Runs	Wkts	Overs	Mdns	Runs	Wkts
Pallett	29	6	72	1	34	12	72	2
Santall	24	7	58	—	37	7	92	3
Field	26	10	51	3	22	5	62	—
W. G. Quaife	8	1	26	—				
Lilley	7	1	33	1				
Byrne	10.1	2	31	2	7	2	12	1
W. Quaife	4	1	7	2	20	8	22	2

Lancashire Bowling

	Overs	Mdns	Runs	Wkts	Overs	Mdns	Runs	Wkts
Mold	33	6	95	2	3	2	9	—
Cuttell	46.2	21	73	2	26	9	61	1
Hallam	46	21	86	4	22	11	26	—
Briggs	19	7	33	1	8	2	23	—
Baker	3	2	4	1	6.4	1	23	2

Umpires: M. Sherwin and T. Mycroft.

WARWICKSHIRE v YORKSHIRE

Played at Birmingham, August 2, 3, 4, 1897

Although they made a very plucky up-hill fight on going in a second time, the Warwickshire cricketers never recovered from their bad start when they were dismissed for 172 and an interesting match ended in favour of Yorkshire by nine wickets. Denton played remarkably well for 141 not out and so consistent was the Yorkshire batting that only three members of the side failed to reach double figures. In Warwickshire's second innings, Glover hit most vigorously for 93 and Bainbridge, Pallett and Forester all struggled desperately hard to improve the position for their side. A most unusual thing occurred when that experienced cricketer, Lilley was out for hitting the ball twice.

Warwickshire

W. Quaife c Tunnicliffe b Hirst	4	– b Jackson	15
Mr H. W. Bainbridge b Hirst	52	– b Hirst	62
Mr J. F. Byrne c Milligan b Hirst	0	– c Brown b Haigh	19
A. A. Lilley b Smith	11	– hit ball twice	13
W. G. Quaife c Bairstow b Milligan	11	– b Brown	1
E. J. Diver c Brown b Denton	53	– c Bairstow b Brown	14
S. J. Santall b Denton	26	– b Hirst	1
Mr A. C. S. Glover lbw b Jackson	4	– b Hirst	93
H. J. Pallett b Jackson	0	– c and b Brown	34
T. Forester not out	0	– run out	38
Lord b Denton	3	– not out	5
B 3, l-b 5	8	B 3, l-b 6, w 1	10
	172		305

Yorkshire

Mr F. S. Jackson b Lord	30 – run out	11
J. Tunnicliffe c Bainbridge b Forester	27 – not out	36
J. T. Brown c W. Quaife b Forester	47 – not out	54
D. Denton not out	141	
R. Moorhouse c Lilley b Forester	18	
G. H. Hirst lbw b Byrne	31	
Mr F. W. Milligan c Forester b Lord	27	
Lord Hawke b Forester	10	
Mr Ernest Smith b Lord	1	
S. Haigh b Lilley	30	
A. L. Bairstow lbw b Lilley	0	
B 7, l-b 2, w 3	12	L-b 1, w 2 3
	374	104

Yorkshire Bowling

	Overs	Mdns	Runs	Wkts	Overs	Mdns	Runs	Wkts
Smith	19	5	38	1	20	6	41	—
Hirst	24	9	37	3	36	14	54	3
Jackson	15	2	34	2	28	9	35	1
Haigh	4	2	12	—	11	5	20	1
Milligan	11	3	29	1	21	9	30	—
Brown	3	—	10	—	18	3	60	3
Denton	3.3	2	4	3	22	8	35	—

Warwickshire Bowling

	Overs	Mdns	Runs	Wkts	Overs	Mdns	Runs	Wkts
Santall	36	8	81	—	3	—	16	—
Lord	39	9	113	3	5	1	22	—
Forester	34	11	70	4	9	1	29	—
Pallett	14	1	49	—	3	—	7	—
Byrne	12	5	25	1	2	—	8	—
W. Quaife	8	1	17	—	6	—	19	—
Lilley	2.2	—	7	2				

Umpires: J. Wheeler and J. H. Holmes.

WARWICKSHIRE v LEICESTERSHIRE

Played at Birmingham, May 8, 9, 10, 1899

The match between these midland counties was made memorable by a wonderful innings by Diver, who, contributing 184 out of 260 in two hours and a half, put together the highest score of his career. He hit twenty-eight 4s, eight 3s and ten 2s, and his brilliant display was only marred by three chances – all of a difficult character. It was entirely owing to him that Warwickshire gained so considerable an advantage on the opening day. Leicestershire at the drawing of stumps were 136 runs behind, six wickets having fallen for 140. However, rain on Tuesday prevented more than an hour's cricket – during which the visitors' innings was finished off – and on Wednesday when a late start was compulsory, time did not permit of a definite conclusion being reached. The draw was all in favour of Warwickshire.

Warwickshire

W. G. Quaife b Agar	2	– not out	35
Mr T. S. Fishwick c Agar b Pougher	35	– st Whiteside b Pougher	20
E. J. Diver b Geeson	184	– c Pougher b Geeson	12
J. Devey run out	18		
A. A. Lilley c and b Geeson	18	– c Geeson b Agar	40
Mr A. C. S. Glover b King	0		
A. Law c Agar b Geeson	10		
C. Charlesworth c Whiteside b Geeson	0		
S. Santall not out	9		
F. E. Field b King	0		
F. Dickins absent	0		
	276	(3 wkts dec.)	107

Leicestershire

A. E. Knight run out	22	– c Devey b Quaife	18
L. Brown lbw b Dickins	10	– c Lilley b Quaife	11
Mr C. J. B. Wood c Lilley b Santall	20	– c Law b Quaife	0
A. D. Pougher b Charlesworth	90	– not out	10
King b Field	10	– not out	5
Mr C. E. de Trafford b Field	12		
S. Coe c Glover b Dickins	14		
H. Whitehead b Charlesworth	14		
F. Geeson c Field b Quaife	0		
Agar run out	2		
J. P. Whiteside not out	0		
L-b 1	1	B 4, l-b 1	5
	195		49

Leicestershire Bowling

	Overs	Mdns	Runs	Wkts	Overs	Mdns	Runs	Wkts
Coe	6	2	12	—	7	2	11	—
Agar	20	4	73	1	10.4	3	29	1
King	23.3	3	78	2	13	6	12	—
Geeson	15	2	47	4	8	—	24	1
Pougher	10	3	34	1	18	4	31	1
Wood	9	—	32	—				

Warwickshire Bowling

	Overs	Mdns	Runs	Wkts	Overs	Mdns	Runs	Wkts
Field	26	7	56	2	5	5	—	—
Dickins	28	5	62	2	9	9	—	—
Santall	23	9	45	1	21	15	17	—
Charlesworth	6	3	16	2	15	8	20	—
Devey	1	—	2	—				
Quaife	6	1	13	1	13	8	7	3

Umpires: J. Lillywhite and M. Sherwin.

WARWICKSHIRE v ESSEX

Played at Birmingham, June 19, 20, 21, 1899

For their capital innings of 324 Warwickshire were largely indebted to W. G. Quaife and Bainbridge, who fairly divided the honours of the day. Unfortunately for Essex rain during the night spoilt the wicket on the second day, and but for the brothers Turner, they would have fared badly indeed. The Turners, however, fairly pulled the game round, the elder brother scored a matchless 124 in the face of great difficulties. Cricket was curtailed by more wet on Tuesday and although there was a broken wicket on the Wednesday, time did not permit the game to be played out. Young's bowling was superb.

Warwickshire

W. G. Quaife c Perrin b Young	115	– b Young	11
W. Quaife b Mead	0	– c Bull b Young	18
E. J. Diver c Carpenter b Young	13	– c Russell b Young	0
A. Law c Lucas b Young	4	– c Lucas b Young	11
A. A. Lilley c W. Turner b Carpenter	18	– c and b Young	18
Mr H. W. Bainbridge c Bull b Young	80	– c Young b Bull	13
Mr A. C. S. Glover c and b Young	19	– b Young	4
C. Charlesworth hit wkt b Bull	22	– b Young	2
S. Santall b Young	9	– c Owen b Young	4
J. Cresswell b Young	16	– not out	9
A. Lord not out	1	– not out	3
B 22, l-b 4, w 1	27	L-b 9	9
	324	(9 wkts dec.)	102

Essex

Mr F. G. Bull lbw b Lord	29		
H. Young c Cresswell b Charlesworth	18		
H. Carpenter b Santall	6	– b Charlesworth	15
Mr P. Perrin c Cresswell b Charlesworth	10	– c Law b Santall	23
Mr C. McGahey st Lilley b W. G. Quaife	18	– b Charlesworth	13
Mr A. J. Turner c and b Lord	124	– c Lilley b Santall	1
Mr A. P. Lucas c Cresswell b Santall	3	– not out	13
Mr W. M. Turner c Diver b Charlesworth	28	– c W. G. Quaife b Charlesworth	11
Mr H. G. Owen b Charlesworth	34	– not out	0
T. M. Russell b Lord	0	– b Charlesworth	0
W. Mead not out	14		
B 6, l-b 5, n-b 3	14	B 1, l-b 2, n-b 1	4
	298		80

Essex Bowling

	Overs	Mdns	Runs	Wkts	Overs	Mdns	Runs	Wkts
Mead	39	12	80	1	9	4	19	—
Young	51	18	100	7	26	9	54	8
Bull	40	21	68	1	18	9	20	1
Carpenter	10	4	18	1				
A. J. Turner	6	3	11	—				
W. M. Turner	4	1	14	—				
McGahey	4	2	6	—				

Warwickshire Bowling

	Overs	Mdns	Runs	Wkts	Overs	Mdns	Runs	Wkts
Lord	13	—	39	3				
Cresswell	11	4	23	—				
Santall	43	17	96	2	19	5	48	2
Charlesworth	43.1	13	88	4	18	10	28	4
W. G. Quaife	9	3	15	1				
Lilley	3	—	14	—				
W. Quaife	3	1	9	—				

Umpires: A. Shaw and C. E. Richardson.

WARWICKSHIRE v HAMPSHIRE

Played at Birmingham, July 24, 25, 26, 1899

Heavy scoring during the first two days, together with the rain which caused a curtailment on the third, prevented the match from being played out. Hampshire started by completing an innings of 425, in which the feature was A. J. L. Hill's superb 168. Warwickshire, after scoring 6 without loss in the last few minutes on Monday, raised their figures to 419 for six wickets on the Tuesday, and on Wednesday declared their innings at 657 for six wickets. All the home side batted well, but the chief honours were borne off by W. G. Quaife, Fishwick and Glover. The first two made 186 runs together, and then Quaife with Glover, added 194 more without being parted. Quaife and Glover each did better than ever before in first-class cricket, and the grand total of 657 was the highest ever hit by Warwickshire. Quaife was batting six hours and a half. He hit eighteen 4s and fifteen 3s, and did not give a chance. Hampshire after their big first innings were put in to make 232 to avert a single innings defeat, but after they had scored 76 for one wicket, rain necessitated the game being abandoned.

Hampshire

Mr C. Robson b Dickins	9		
Mr A. J. L. Hill c Dickins b Devey	168	– b Santall	37
Major R. M. Poore st Lilley b W. G. Quaife	36	– not out	0
Capt. F. W. D. Quinton c Lilley b W. G. Quaife	0		
Capt. E. G. Wynyard c Devey b Santall	89	– not out	28
V. Barton b Santall	2		
T. Soar c Santall b Dickins	70		
Mr C. Heseltine b Santall	0		
Mr R. A. Bennett st Lilley b Santall	2		
Mr D. A. Steele c Quaife b Dickins	33		
H. Baldwin not out	1		
B 7, l-b 7, w 1	15	B 11	11
	425		76

Warwickshire

J. Devey c Bennett b Hill	21
S. P. Kinnier c Wynyard b Baldwin	51
E. J. Diver b Heseltine	25
Mr T. S. Fishwick c Robson b Baldwin	109
W. G. Quaife not out	207
A. A. Lilley b Hill	29
Mr H. W. Bainbridge c Baldwin b Hill	72
Mr A. C. S. Glover not out	119
B 14, l-b 3, w 7	24
(6 wkts dec.)	657

F. E. Field, F. Dickins and S. Santall did not bat.

Warwickshire Bowling

	Overs	Mdns	Runs	Wkts	Overs	Mdns	Runs	Wkts
Field	27	7	91	—	10	4	18	—
Dickins	22.4	4	66	3	5	1	15	—
Santall	39	6	139	4	14	3	32	1
Quaife	21	5	79	2				
Kinnier	7	1	28	—				
Devey	4	1	7	1				

Hampshire Bowling

	Overs	Mdns	Runs	Wkts
Heseltine	39	7	116	1
Baldwin	42	19	90	2
Quinton	12	2	29	—
Soar	8	1	43	—
Hill	54	17	148	3
Steele	18	2	54	—
Wynyard	42	6	124	—
Barton	10	1	29	—

Umpires: C. E. Richardson and A. Shaw.

WORCESTERSHIRE

WORCESTERSHIRE v HAMPSHIRE

Played at Worcester, July 27, 28, 29, 1899

The first of the two engagements with Hampshire had to be left drawn, but it will always take a distinguished place in the history of cricket, for it was marked by a feat quite without precedent, two Worcestershire batsmen playing two innings each of over a hundred. On the first day the honours were easily carried off by W. L. and R. E. Foster, who, between them, put on 161 runs in an hour and a half. W. L. Foster was batting just over three hours and hit sixteen 4s, while his brother sent the ball fifteen times to the boundary during his stay of two hours and three-quarters. Major Poore played a faultless innings.

Worcestershire

Mr W. L. Foster c Webb b Baldwin	140	– not out	172
Mr G. Bromley-Martin b Steele	33	– b Heseltine	21
Mr H. K. Foster c Bennett b Baldwin	16	– c Tate b Heseltine	10
Mr R. E. Foster lbw b Steele	134	– not out	101
E. Arnold b Hill	14		
F. Wheldon b Hill	0		
Mr G. H. Simpson-Hayward lbw b Hill	8		
A. Bird lbw b Quinton	10		
R. Burrows c Hill b Steele	35		
T. Straw not out	10		
G. Wilson c Hill b Quinton	12		
B 11, l-b 3, w 1, n-b 1	16	B 1, l-b 3	4
	428	(2 wkts dec.)	308

Hampshire

Mr A. J. L. Hill c Burrows b Wilson	0	– b Burrows	19
V. Barton c R. E. Foster b Burrows	62	– b Arnold	36
Major R. M. Poore c H. K. Foster b Burrows	122	– lbw b Arnold	17
A. Webb c and b Burrows	33	– c R. Foster b Bird	20
Capt. F. W. D. Quinton c H. K. Foster b Arnold	40	– b Wilson	7
Mr R. A. Bennett lbw b Burrows	0	– b Simpson-Hayward	17
Mr C. Heseltine b Wilson	26	– b Simpson-Hayward	31
Mr E. C. Lee b Arnold	31	– not out	3
Mr D. A. Steele not out	10		
H. Baldwin run out	9		
E. Tate b Arnold	4		
B 2, l-b 13, w 1	16	B 7	7
	353		157

Hampshire Bowling

	Overs	Mdns	Runs	Wkts	Overs	Mdns	Runs	Wkts
Heseltine	16	1	66	—	32	4	100	2
Baldwin	34	10	80	2	18	3	50	—
Hill	27	4	80	3	15	1	50	—
Tate	30	7	66	—	11	1	37	—
Steele	22	2	62	3	8	1	41	—
Lee	1	—	16	—				
Quinton	9.2	—	32	2				
Webb	3	—	10	—				
Barton					5	—	26	—

Worcestershire Bowling

	Overs	Mdns	Runs	Wkts	Overs	Mdns	Runs	Wkts
Wilson	30	11	101	2	26	10	54	1
Burrows	29	7	73	4	10	4	22	1
Bird	33	11	79	—	16	6	27	1
Arnold	16.4	1	56	3	24	9	46	2
Simpson-Hayward . .	9	—	28	—	2.1	1	1	2

Umpires: J. Moss and W. Shrewsbury.

THE DEVELOPMENT OF CRICKET

By Hon. R. H. Lyttelton

Some old-fashioned critics, every cricketer knows them well, will say on reading the heading of this article that cricket has developed only in the sense of becoming worse, that, leaving W. G. Grace out of the question, Shrewsbury is no better than Joe Guy, not Gunn than Fuller Pilch, that the bowling altogether is not so good, and the fielding distinctly much inferior. Why are the old fogies at all games apt to become a little tiresome, or what ill-natured people would call bores? We venture to assert that it is partly owing to a lack of proportion; they do not recognise that in their youthful days everything they saw was seen when the mind was enthusiastic and unable, from its simple joyousness, to notice the ugly and bad side of anything. The bowling might not have been so straight, but if it was well hit, the youth remembered the hit, but forgot the crooked ball.

The grounds were rougher than they are now, and fine gallery bits of wicket-keeping were perhaps commoner; but how does our venerable friend account for the fact that, even with a long-stop, extras were far more numerous than they are in these days with only a wicket-keeper? Boys will always be impressed by the one fine stroke; the man weighs and balances, and sees a very trifling inaccuracy; in other words, he becomes the critic, while the boy is only the charmed spectator; he does not yet know enough to be critical, though his faculty of enjoyment is intense. Hence it is that an accurate and attentive perusal of scores is apt to irritate the veteran; it recalls facts that should be forgotten; he is bewildered, he cannot remember such things, and the reason is obvious – he remembers what is good and forgets what is amiss, and who can blame him?

Of all inventions that ever worked a revolution in cricket, nothing had more effect than the heavy roller and the mowing machine. The old scythe, however deftly wielded, left a tuft of grass here and there; you can see it rather exaggerated in your newly-mown meadow. But watch the mowing machine – it shaves to a perfectly uniform length or shortness, the wicket becomes a billiard table, while, if the weather is dry, only a ponderous modern roller can have any effect on a clay soil; so in former days, in addition to the tufts of grass you had little lumps of clay. With such a wicket as this you wanted a fast bowler, who would keep short in the sense that he never would bowl half-volleys, and the ground would do the rest. Of course, in circumstances like these, there were any amount of bowlers who could get wickets at small cost, and speaking of the years from 1858 to 1868, one cannot fail to be struck with the fact that the number of fast or fastish bowlers was enormous, while the real slow round-arm bowler was very rarely found.

You may take the representative matches at random, and you will find that the leading bowlers were men who kept a fairish length, and were straight and fast, and in cricket, as in all other things in life, the predominant style is predominant because it answers its purpose – in other words, because it succeeds. Modern opinion, in judging of the merits of strictly fast and slow head-bowling, judges that on hard true wickets the straight fast bowler is easy as compared to slow bowlers, or bowlers who, at any rate, are more slow than fast, and if we look at the years 1861 to 1864 inclusive, we can find some corroboration of this. There were in those days two grounds almost, if not quite, as easy and as true as the modern grounds. There were very likely more, but these two – Kennington Oval and the University Ground at Cambridge – are taken as samples. A comparison of the scores of the period just mentioned and the present day will not show an average excess of runs now as compared to the former time.

The four Gentlemen and Players' matches, 1861 to 1864, show the average number of runs per wicket to be 24. The same matches for the four years ending 1891 show an average of 21. In the famous Surrey v Cambridgeshire match at the Oval in 1861, the average number of runs per wicket was 27, and there were three individual innings of over 100. In the corresponding match at Cambridge on Fenner's, only twenty-one wickets were lowered, Caffyn and Tom Hayward each got 100, and the average number of runs per wicket was 31. Even in the years when W. G. Grace was in his prime – when, on going in first, he so demoralized the bowling and fielding that his side, at any rate, nearly always made a big score – we shall find the same story. W. G.'s average for the four years, 1871, 1872, 1873 and 1874 was 78, 57, 71 and 53. And let us look at Gentlemen and Players' matches at the Oval during these years. The average number of runs per wicket for these years amounts to 22 against 24 from 1861 to 1864.

Our object in quoting these figures is to show that on the same level wickets there is not much difference in the number of runs scored thirty years ago and now, but that, in consequence of the far more numerous good grounds that now exist, owing to the invention of the mowing-machine and the greater expenditure of time and money on their making and preservation, there are more good bats now than then, and the runs have not increased, because the bowling is better.

We can see our venerable friend's face as this opinion is stated, and three of his white hairs drop off. Lohmann, Briggs, Attewell and Mold better than Willsher, Wootton, Jackson, and Caffyn; the idea is preposterous! We are talking of English bowlers only. We do not say anything of Spofforth, Palmer, Giffen, and Turner; that marvellous batch of bowlers, whose deeds and feats, considering whom they opposed, have never been equalled.

Wherein does the greater merit of the modern bowler lie? Simply in the fact that, in these days of greater batting science and perfect wickets, the mere accuracy and pace are of no avail – you must use your head. The excellence of grounds and the consequent facilities afforded to batsmen have worked the revolution. Bowlers have found out that it is no good pounding away on good wickets, for you will only tire yourself out. You must bowl every variety of good length. You must even, on purpose, bowl one or two balls to be hit for four, to raise the batsman's hopes and tempt him to hit at the next ball – a little shorter and a tiny bit slower – with the prospect of seeing him mistime it and send it up.

On Lord's Ground thirty years ago Jackson, Willsher, and Tarrant had merely to bowl their fastest and straightest, and the batsman might any ball expect either a dead shooter or a body blow. No wonder, under these circumstances, that it did not pay to bowl anything except fast and straight. Who can deny that the higher form of art is that of the modern bowler, where accuracy has to be assisted by craft, cuteness, and artifice of every description? What the rougher wickets in old days did to get batsmen out has to be done now by generalship in bowlers, indifference to being hit and longheadedness. To see Lohmann bowl on an Oval wicket is an intellectual delight. "To a right-hand batsman he bowls on or just outside the off-stump, and breaks back very quickly, but now and then he puts in a very fast one with a break from leg. Should a left-hand batsman follow, especially if he can hit well on the leg side, he pitches everything on the wicket or off-stump, varying it with a faster one, breaking slightly from the off-to leg. But the ball he has been as successful with as any is a simple, straight, good length one, without any break. The batsman expects something exceptional from him every ball, and never thinks that he will treat him with such an easy one; and so, while he is looking for the break, his wicket is bowled down". So writes W. G. Grace of Lohmann, and this description shows what a vast amount of head and skill is required to become a successful bowler on modern wickets.

The improvement of grounds is, perhaps, the chief cause of the development of bowling, but the batting of W. G. Grace and the bowling of the Australians of 1878, 1880 and 1882, are two other factors to be considered. W. G. Grace began his first-class cricket on the old-fashioned wickets to the old-fashioned bowling. As the wickets gradually improved, all fast bowling became to him child's play. Cricketers of that time will tell you that if you wanted to get him out on a good wicket, you stood a better chance of doing so with two inferior slow bowlers than with Freeman and Martin McIntyre. Slow bowling, largely owing to this cause, came in, and about 1877 there were a host of slow bowlers – Shaw, Lockwood, Barratt, Watson, Southerton, Midwinter, Strachan, Grace, W. S. Patterson, F. M. Buckland, A. P. Lucas, and many others – playing in first-class cricket. They were not all good; some were almost bad, but, bad as they were, they succeeded better than good fast bowlers did, and at this time English bowling was at a low ebb.

In the following year, 1878, the Australians first came to England, and Spofforth and Boyle began a new and glorious era. Spectators rubbed their eyes at what they saw. They saw two bowlers of consummate skill adopting a quite new method. On the hard dry wickets at Sydney and Melbourne, these bowlers had found out what English bowlers had not yet discovered, that to get batsmen out on modern wickets it was no good trusting to any assistance from the ground, but to your own head. They bowled differently, and they placed the field differently. They dispensed altogether with a long-stop, they bowled many balls off the wicket, and no two consecutive balls were bowled with similar paces. The famous MCC match, when Spofforth and Boyle got rid of a strong MCC eleven for 33 and 19, may well be taken as a starting point in the new era of cricket.

From this time, slowly, perhaps, but surely, the English learnt from the Colonists, and now they have beaten them on their own ground. From 1860 to 1870 bowling was mainly fast; from 1870 to 1878 it became mainly slow; from 1878 to 1891 it cannot be accurately classified under either of these heads. Lohmann, Peel, and Attewell, are not slow or fast. They never bowl a raking fast ball, but a mistake of the wicket-keep to Attewell or Peel on Woolwich Common would mean five byes. The bowling of the present day is of infinite variety of pace, length, and direction, and the change is owing to the improvement of grounds, which made fast bowling easy. W. G. Grace's skill first brought this fact powerfully to the cricketer's mind, and the example of Spofforth, Boyle, and Palmer, who inaugurated the new order of bowlers, completed the tale.

What we have said hitherto refers chiefly to the development of bowling, which so largely influences batting that the two act and re-act on each other. It is quite as difficult to judge of the respective merits of the batting giants of twenty-five or thirty years ago as compared with those of to-day, as it is in the case of bowlers. As difficult wickets make batsmen weak and bowlers strong, so easy wickets make batsmen strong and bowlers weak. It is quite safe to assume that Hayward, Carpenter, Parr, Mitchell, and Daft, for instance, would have been great bats in any age and under any circumstances, as Shrewsbury, Gunn, O'Brien, and Steel would. The great bats of any particular time would be great under any conditions. In one sense, however, we admit that the batsmen of twenty-five years ago excelled those of to-day, and we say, judging from a purely æsthetic standard, the play of first-class bats now is infinitely less graceful than it used to be. We are not prepared to admit that this fact is owing to the fault of the batsmen themselves; on the contrary, we think it is the fault of the bowlers for the following reason.

There can be no question that bowling is far more accurate now than formerly, for fast bowling must, of necessity, afford greater facilities to the hitter than the slow and medium. The bowling is now so accurate, and the field so carefully placed, that the batsman, in order to get runs, must resort to what our venerable friend would call unorthodox hitting. If Attewell is bowling nine out of ten balls on the off-stump, or outside the off-stump, of a beautiful length, and with eight fields on the off-side, what are you to do to score? You must obviously hit where fields do not stand, and this is only on the on-side; in other words, you must pull, and if the pull comes on, you score four runs. Now a pull is ugly, brutal, and effective, and is a product of modern accuracy in attack, and if you want to see it in full development, go to the Oval and watch W. W. Read and K. J. Key.

Take another hit that modern bowling has completely wiped out of first-class cricket – the leg hit. Look at the accounts of the players of thirty years ago, and you will find So-and-so described as a fine leg hitter. Who can be so described now, and how can anyone be, when there are no leg balls bowled to hit? You will see more leg hitting in one public school match to-day than you will in any four first-class matches you may choose. A striking testimony, no doubt, to the splendid science of the modern bowler: but, shade of Parr, we should like to see Parr at one end and R. A. H. Mitchell at the other for an hour, and each get a leg ball every four overs. To hit a leg ball square over the ropes at Lord's is the greatest and most supreme delight that can fall to the lot of a batsman, and next, perhaps, to the perfect cut, there is nothing in cricket more enjoyable to watch, from the spectators' point of view. We heard an old cricketer remark, at this year's Eton and Harrow match, when Brewis made a fine hit to square leg, "That is the first genuine leg hit I have seen this year".

So many modern bowlers bowl for catches – that is, they place the fields and bowl accordingly – that the batsmen, knowing and understanding the tactics, hesitate to hit, and that is another reason why play is less graceful – it has to be more careful. Broadly speaking, we assert that if hitting has declined in form and style, accurate defence has developed in a wonderful degree, but defence, however good, cannot be so fascinating as graceful and vigorous hitting.

Fielding is easier now than it used to be, for the grounds are smoother, but it ought to be better than it is, and the same remark, we suspect, would have applied thirty years ago. There is not much fault to be found with the ground fielding, but far too many catches are dropped, breaking the hearts of bowlers and creating unspeakable feelings in the minds of partisans. Why so many catches are dropped, it is difficult to understand. We are not discussing catches that are not easy, but the feasible two-hand catches that go straight into the hands and promptly drop out again; and it is a shocking sight to see young cricketers, amateur and professional, equally blameable as the veteran.

There is one development of fielding that is the outcome of the smooth grounds and accurate bowling, and that is the astonishing precision of the wicket-keeping. There is nothing so awe-inspiring in cricket at the present day as to see Woods bowling on a hard wicket, and McGregor calmly standing up to the wicket with no long-stop. This state of things never existed in the wildest imagination of anybody thirty years ago, and from it we learn the facts, that even the fast amateur bowlers practically never bowl a leg ball, and that the modern wickets are so good that the old-fashioned shooter is nearly as extinct as the dodo. It was Blackham, the great Australian, who first set this fashion, and we cannot close this article in any more graceful way than by rendering our tribute to the Australians, that, while they taught us little, or perhaps nothing, in batting, to Blackham we owe the dispensing with a long-stop, and that in Spofforth, Boyle, Palmer, Giffen, and Turner, we have glorious examples of the infinite resource, intelligence, and accuracy that, together blended, make the great bowlers of this year of grace, 1891.

YORKSHIRE

YORKSHIRE v ALL ENGLAND ELEVEN

At Sheffield, July 17, 18, 19, 1865

All England Eleven

W. Oscroft hit wkt b Hodgson	54
J. Smith c Holgate b A. Walker	32
T. Bignall c Holgate b Dawes	27
T. Hayward c Smith b Hodgson	112
R. Carpenter c Smith b Hodgson	134
E. Whittaker Esq. c Smith b Hodgson	13
G. Parr b Darnton	78
J. Jackson c Smith b Hodgson	15
G. Wootton b Darnton	14
S. Biddulph not out	16
R. C. Tinley c Greenwood b Darnton	12
B 9, l-b 7, n-b 1	17
	524

Yorkshire

T. Darnton c Parr b Jackson	14	not out	81
W. Smith c Hayward b Tinley	0	b Wootton	0
J. Thewlis st Biddulph b Tinley	34	b Wootton	21
G. Holgate lbw b Jackson	0	b Wootton	5
A. Walker Esq. run out	2	b Wootton	6
L. Greenwood c Hayward b Tinley	0	c and b Wootton	3
W. Cuttle c Biddulph b Tinley	25	b Wootton	0
J. Dawes c Whittaker b Jackson	10	b Wootton	2
John Berry c and b Wootton	18	c Carpenter b Wootton	4
C. Appleton Esq. not out	14	c Hayward b Wootton	18
I. Hodgson run out	2	c Oscroft b Wootton	0
B 3, l-b 2, w 1	6	B 4	4
	125		144

All England Eleven winning in one innings and 255 runs.

Umpires: H. Wright and W. Slinn.

YORKSHIRE v CAMBRIDGESHIRE

Played at Hunslet (near Leeds), July 12, 13, 1869

This was Cambridgeshire's only match in 1869; its result was decisively unfortunate to them. Illness deprived them of Tarrant's aid (a great bowling loss this). Not one of their famed trio of batsmen got set. Their general fielding was queer, and their form all round appeared to be all wrong. The bowling of Yorkshire's two – Freeman and Emmett – was of their best form. Freeman bowled (all told) thirty-six overs (twenty-four maidens) for 31 runs and four wickets; and Emmett had sixteen wickets out of the twenty, taking nine out of the ten (he caught out the tenth) in the second innings of Cambridgeshire. In addition to this great work with the ball, Emmett played a not out innings of 47 runs. Roger Iddison was nearly five hours and a half at the wickets; and his fine hitting in his innings of 112 runs brought him a present of £5, and loud, hearty cheering from the thousands present. The two celebrated Yorkshire bowlers bowled (all told) seventy-one overs (forty-five maidens) for 69 runs and twenty wickets – fourteen "bowled". Yorkshire won by an innings and 226 runs.

Yorkshire

E. Lockwood b G. Smith	3	Anderson c Fordham b Mason	17
Pinder c J. Smith b G. Smith	33	Atkinson run out	10
Rowbotham b G. Smith	31	Luke Greenwood c G. Smith b T. Hayward	0
Roger Iddison c Watts b Mason	112	Emmett not out	47
G. Savile Esq. b Fordham	24	B 7, l-b 3, w 1	11
E. B. Rawlinson c Carpenter b T. Hayward	34		—
Freeman c Fordham b Mason	30		352

Cambridgeshire

John Smith b Emmett	1	– c Emmett b Freeman	12
Pryor b Freeman	10	– c and b Emmett	6
H. J. Browne Esq. b Emmett	0	– b Emmett	4
T. Hayward b Emmett	0	– b Emmett	7
R. Carpenter b Emmett	6	– c Rowbotham b Emmett	2
D. Hayward b Emmett	4	– b Emmett	0
Mason b Freeman	0	– b Iddison b Emmett	0
Fordham b Freeman	3	– lbw b Emmett	1
Newman not out	6	– b Emmett	3
G. Smith c and b Emmett	1	– not out	3
Watts b Emmett	0	– b Emmett	0
B 4, l-b 4, w 1	9	B 6, l-b 2	8
	—		—
	40		46

Yorkshire Bowling

	Overs	Mdns	Runs	Wkts	Overs	Mdns	Runs	Wkts
Freeman	17	10	16	3	19	14	15	1
Emmett	17	11	15	7	18.2	10	23	9

Cambridgeshire Bowling

	Overs	Mdns	Runs	Wkts
T. Hayward	71	31	99	2
G. Smith	71	18	141	3
Mason	28	9	48	3
Watts	14	—	42	—
Fordham	5	2	11	1

Umpires: Dakin and Duthoit.

ROGER IDDISON'S MATCH

YORKSHIRE v GLOUCESTERSHIRE

Played on The Bramall Lane Ground, Sheffield, July 29, 30, 31, 1872

Yorkshire v Gloucestershire was a judiciously selected match to play in compliment to Roger Iddison, who had served his Shire so long and so ably in the cricket field; for it was the first match ever played by those counties, and it ensured the first appearance of Mr W. G. Grace on the Country ground at Sheffield, the centre of as ardent, keen, thorough, and numerous a body of admirers of our national game as any county can boast of, and who flocked on to the ground in such numbers that nearly 17,000 were present during Iddison's three days; and although no reliable information could be gathered respecting the actual monetary result, there can be no doubt but that when the subscription lists are sent in and settled the benefit to Iddison will have been one worthy the man, the match, and the county. The thousands that thronged the ground on the Monday went there full of hope of witnessing some big batting by Mr W. G. Grace; how those hopes must have been more than realised, and what a wonderful commencement of the match was made by Mr W. G. Grace and Mr Matthew, the following brief record of the play will tell.

On Monday, the first day, the weather was fine up to noon; then rain fell heavily; but at 1.15 they commenced the match and played (barring the interval for dinner) up to 5.10, when a storm put a stop to further cricket on that day. The friends of Iddison mustered so strongly that it was cumputed there were nearly 8,000 at one time on the ground, and those thousands witnessed one of the most extraordinary day's cricket over played, for when the storm ended the play there had been 208 runs scored and, no wicket down, the score books showing the following unique bit of batting as the result of that two hours and fifty minutes cricket:

Mr W. G. Grace not out	132
Mr T. G. Matthews not out	69
B 2, l-b 5	7
	208

The bowlers that afternoon were Freeman, Lockwood, Hill, Iddison, Clayton, Freeman again, Lockwood again, and Luke Greenwood. When we record that Mr Grace twice hit the ball out of the ground for 6, made three 4s from one over of Freeman's, and (by a 2, a 6, and a 4) 12 runs from an over of Luke Greenwood's, some estimate can be formed of the exciting afternoon with Mr Grace the 8,000 Yorkshiremen enjoyed on that memorable 29th of July.

On Tuesday, the second day, the weather was cool, dull and dark, nevertheless those experienced in that kind of thing estimated there were quite 6,500 visitors on the ground. It was a quarter past twelve when the not outs resumed their innings to the bowling of Luke Greenwood and Freeman, and in such true and good form was Freeman that his first eight overs were bowled for 2 runs, and when 30 had been added to the monster score made on Monday, Mr Grace was easily had at mid off by Andrew Greenwood. Mr Grace had been about three and a-half hours at the wickets, and of the 238 runs scored when he was out he had made 150 by thirty-three singles, sixteen 2s, eight 3s, eleven 4s, one 5, and two 6s – both grand hits to leg out of the ground, one from Clayton, the other from Luke Greenwood. Lusty and long was the cheering that greeted the great batsmen on his return from the wicket, and for many a season to come one of the most prolific sources of cricket gossip among Yorkshiremen will be the 150 made by Mr W. G. Grace at Roger Iddison's benefit match in 1872. Only 6 more runs had been added to the 238, when Mr Matthews was caught out at wicket for 85, an innings that comprised a chance or two, and 20 singles, ten 2s, eleven 3s, and three 4s. The two stickers having been done for, the other 7 wickets (one absent) were easily got rid of, the innings exemplifying the glorious etc. etc. of the game by the two first men making 235 runs, the other seven only 49. The wickets fell as follows:

1/238 2/244 3/251 4/255 5/272 6/277 7/284 8/289 9/294

The bowling of Freeman and Luke Greenwood was very fine on the Tuesday.

Allen Hill and Rawlinson commenced the Yorkshire batting at 4.30; they had made 24 when Hill was had at point and his successor, Andrew Greenwood, at leg. At 30 Lockwood was bowled, at 32 Freeman was stumped, and at 33 Rawlinson fell a victim to square leg. Then Iddison went in, and the loud hearty cheers that greeted burly Roger's walk to the wickets told that his long and successful work for his Shire was gratefully remembered by Yorkshiremen. He lost Rowbotham with the score at 52, and before another run was scored Lumb, the Colt, was pointed. At 66 first Luke Greenwood and then Pinder were settled, and before the score could be altered a splendid left hand c and b – hand high up – by Mr W. G. used up Iddison and ended the innings; thereupon play ceased for that day.

On Wednesday, the third day, a bright pleasant morning gave way to a dull, dark afternoon, and it was supposed the numbers present that day did not exceed 2,000. The

Yorkshiremen followed on, Luke Greenwood and Freeman starting. Luke was had at point before a run was booked, and Freeman at mid wicket when 3 only had been scored. Iddison and Lockwood then made a bit of a stand, but with the score at 25, catches at slip settled Lockwood and Greenwood, and when 35 had been scored, Rowbotham was had at wicket. Then Iddison (in good form) and Rawlinson stayed until 113 had been made, when Iddison ran Rawlinson out for the top Yorkshire score, a somewhat lucky 47. Only three more runs had been made when three more wickets went – Lumb being pointed again, Iddison stumped, and Pinder had at mid wicket; and so the innings and the match ended at four o'clock, Gloucestershire the winner by an innings and 112 runs. Iddison went in with the score at 3 for two wickets; he was ninth man out with the score 116; his 34 was a carefully played and good defensive innings, made by eighteen singles, six 2s, and one 4.

Gloucestershire

W. G. Grace Esq. c A. Greenwood b L. Greenwood	150
T. G. Matthews Esq. c Pinder b Freeman	85
D. E. M. Grace st Pinder b Freeman	11
F. Townsend Esq. b Freeman	3
G. F. Grace Esq. b Freeman	3
G. Strachan Esq. b L. Greenwood	12
F. R. Price Esq. not out	10
F. A. Carter Esq. run out	3
R. F. Miles Esq. c Clayton b L. Greenwood	3
H. S. Cobden Esq. b Freeman	4
J. A. Bush Esq. absent (unwell)	—
B 2, l-b 8	10
	294

Yorkshire

E. B. Rawlinson c Miles b W. Grace	19	– run out	47
Allen Hill c E. Grace b W. Grace	3	– b W. Grace	1
Andrew Greenwood c Townsend b W. Grace	0	– c F. Grace b W. Grace	0
Ephraim Lockwood b W. Grace	6	– c F. Grace b W. Grace	15
Freeman st Price b W. Grace	1	– c Strachan b W. Grace	0
Rowbotham c E. Grace b W. Grace	14	– c Price b W. Grace	10
Roger Iddison c and b W. Grace	4	– st Price b Miles	34
L. Lumb c E. Grace b W. Grace	0	– c W. Grace b Miles	0
Luke Greenwood c W. Grace b E. Grace	12	– c E. Grace b W. Grace	0
Pinder b E. Grace	0	– c Carter b W. Grace	0
Clayton not out	0	– not out	0
B 1, l-b 1, w 5	7	B 7, l-b 1, w 1	9
	66		116

Yorkshire Bowling

	Overs	Mdns	Runs	Wkts
Freeman	72.3	32	97	5
L. Greenwood	52	21	83	3
Hill	18	5	45	—
Lockwood	10	1	31	—
Clayton	7	3	19	—
Iddison	2	—	9	—

Gloucestershire Bowling

Mr W. Grace	24	12	33	8	36.1	17	46	7
Dr Grace	23	9	26	2	5	3	5	—
Mr F. Grace					17	2	35	—
Mr Miles					14	5	21	2

Umpires: Reynolds and Palin.

To play time out, Mr W. Grace and other Gloucestershire gentlemen batted, but the only feature of interest that cropped up was Mr W. Grace being caught out at mid wicket by Lumb for 2.

LUKE GREENWOOD'S MATCH

YORKSHIRE v GLOUCESTERSHIRE

Played at Sheffield, July 27, 28, 29, 1874

Although the weather was not wholly favourable, and despite the cricket was over before two o'clock on the third day, Greenwood's friends were gratified at finding his match a success. The following are the official returns of the numbers who paid to enter the ground, and the cash receipts each day:

1st Day.	2nd Day.	3rd Day.
6,753 paid.	3,745 paid.	1,054 paid
Receipts, £212 17s. 7d.	Receipts, £124 17s. 0d.	Receipts, £35 8s. 9d.

The early conclusion of the match on the Wednesday explains the small cash receipts that day, but subscriptions and gate-takings combined were sufficient to ensure a balance of about £300 in Greenwood's favour, for which "he feels very grateful to all".

Mr W. G. Grace and Mr Knapp commenced the hitting on "splendid wickets", and to the intense gratification of the thousands of Yorkshiremen present, Mr W. G. Grace stayed and hit one of his familiarly fine three figure innings. Mr W. Grace started at twenty-five minutes to one, to the bowling of Hill and Clayton; with the figures at 22 Clayton bowled Mr Knapp, and Ullathorne at long leg made a splendid one hand catch that settled Mr Monkland. Mr G. F. Grace then went in, and the brothers hit fully up to their form and fame; Hill (owing to illness) had to cease bowling; Ulyett took his place, but the hitting was severe, and the score was rapidly hit and ran up to 84, when Mr G. F. Grace was bowled (off his pad) for 30, two-thirds of those runs having been made by five 4s. On Mr Townsend batting a great stand was made; at luncheon 146 runs had been scored; and after luncheon, notwithstanding several bowling changes, the score was hit to 229, when Ulyett bowled Mr Townsend, so many as 145 runs having been put on by this gentleman and Mr W. Grace between the falls of the third and fourth wickets; Mr Townsend's 66 included eight 4s. Mr Crooke was bowled at 233; Mr Quentin at 301, and then, at 303, Mr W. G. Grace lifted one to long-on, whereat Mr Monkland (fielding for Hill) waited and watched for the ball in capital form, and making a clever catch, Mr W. Grace was out for 167; Mr Grace was first man in and seventh out; he was about four hours at wickets; his 167 runs were made by fifty-six singles, twelve 2s, one 3, and twenty-one 4s, or half his score by 4s. The remaining wickets fell so quickly that at ten minutes past six all were out for 314; thereupon the first day's play ceased.

On the Tuesday it rained hard at noon, and the Yorkshiremen commenced batting on soft wickets. Lockwood was lost before a run was scored; and when Ullathorne and Andrew Greenwood were settled, only 15 runs had been booked for Yorkshire; Rowbotham, Ulyett, and Pinder then hit a bit, and the score had been increased to 72 for eight wickets, when (as Hill was unable to play) Luke Greenwood was last man in; he and Pinder increased the score to 117, when Mr Townsend, at long field, splendidly caught out Pinder for 28; and so, at 4.30, the innings was ended, Luke not out 20. They followed on, and had lost three wickets and scored 52 runs when "time" stopped play for that day. The next day they went at it again about noon, but none stayed long; Pinder and Luke Greenwood increased the score from 63 to 94, when Greenwood was out for 12; and when Pinder had made another 28, he played the ball on, and the innings ended shortly after one o'clock for 103. So Gloucestershire won by an innings and 94 runs.

Gloucestershire

W. G. Grace Esq. c sub. b Clayton	167
E. M. Knapp Esq. b Clayton	8
F. G. Monkland Esq. c Ullathorne b Clayton	0
G. F. Grace Esq. b Ulyett	30
F. Townsend Esq. b Ulyett	66
F. J. Crooke, Esq. b Ulyett	0
G. A. Quentin Esq. b Ulyett	22
E. C. B. Ford Esq. not out	2
R. F. Miles Esq. c Byrom b Clayton	4
A. Collings Esq. b Ulyett	1
J. A. Bush Esq. b Clayton	4
B 5, l-b 5	10
	314

Yorkshire

Ephraim Lockwood b W. Grace	0	c Bush b W. Grace	16
Ullathorne c Bush b F. Grace	1	c and b W. Grace	0
Andrew Greenwood b F. Grace	11	c Bush b W. Grace	9
J. L. Byrom Esq. run out	8	c W. Grace b F. Grace	0
Rowbotham b F. Grace	21	c Bush b W. Grace	19
G. Ulyett c F. Grace b W. Grace	20	b W. Grace	17
R. Clayton c F. Grace b W. Grace	2	c Townsend b W. Grace	0
Pinder c Townsend b W. Grace	28	b W. Grace	28
W. Oates c and b F. Grace	0	not out	0
Luke Greenwood not out	20	c sub. b F. Grace	12
Allen Hill unwell – did not bat	–	unwell – did not bat	
B 3, l-b 1, w 2	6	L-b 1, w 1	2
	117		103

Yorkshire Bowling

	Overs	Mdns	Runs	Wkts
Ulyett	56	15	126	5
Clayton	46.3	17	91	5
Lockwood	17	2	39	—
Hill	16	5	27	—
L. Greenwood	10	5	21	—

Gloucestershire Bowling

	Overs	Mdns	Runs	Wkts	Overs	Mdns	Runs	Wkts
Mr W. Grace	45	30	57	4	32.3	16	44	7
Mr F. Grace	42	20	53	4	25	9	43	2
Mr Townsend	3	2	1	—	7	2	14	—

Umpires: John Thewlis, sen., and Pullen.

YORKSHIRE v NOTTINGHAMSHIRE

Played at Sheffield, May 31 and June 1, 1875

Pleasant Cricketing weather favoured this match, wherein 274 overs were bowled for 360 runs from the bat, and nineteen of the thirty-four wickets down were bowled. The first half of the match was played out with curious equality, thus: the Yorkshiremen played a first innings of 89 runs, their highest scorer being Ulyett with 26; then Nottinghamshire played a first of 84 runs, their highest scorer being young Shrewsbury with 26. In the Yorkshiremen's innings six wickets were bowled down. In the Nottinghamshiremen's innings five wickets were bowled down; and when the first day's play ceased each side had played out one innings, the high bowling fame of each Shire having been ably maintained; the result of that day's ball work being 140 overs for 151 runs from the bat. Ulyett's 26 was chronicled as "made without giving a chance", and included three 4s, two of them fine on-drives from McIntyre; Arthur Shrewsbury's 26 included five 4s, and was reported "a fine innings".

The second day's play resulted in some good bowling by Shaw and Morley; an innings of 27 runs by Rowbotham; another 26 by young Shrewsbury; a splendidly hit innings of 61 runs by Wyld, and a very unpleasant incident. Yorkshire had played a second innings of 107 runs, setting Nottinghamshire 113 to score to win. Wyld and William Oscroft commenced to the bowling of Emmett and Hill; they had made 10 runs when the following took place as reported word for word in *Bell's Life*:

> "Wyld played one of Hill's to Ullathorne at mid-off. That fielder immediately returned the ball to Pinder, the wicket keeper, who at once transferred it to Hill, the bowler. The latter seeing that Oscroft had not regained his crease, out of which he had been in the act of making ground, put down the wicket and the decision of Coward was against the batsman. Wyld accompanied Oscroft off the ground, and the Yorkshire team, after waiting some time, also made their way to the Pavilion. A delay of half-an-hour occurred during which the spectators got on the ground and gave vent to expressions indicative of a wish for the continuation of play. Of course the whole thing hangs on whether the ball was finally settled in the wicket keeper's hands or not. The Yorkshiremen aver that Pinder received a signal from Hill to shy it over, and he threw the ball with the intention of running him out. However Coward was the only one to judge, and his decision, right or wrong, should have been respected."

Old "Bell" is right, "Umpires decisions should in every case be strictly obeyed", and the two Nottinghamshire batsmen leaving the ground displayed bad taste, bad cricket, and a bad example. However, in thirty minutes Shrewsbury accompanied Wyld back to wickets, and the two hit finely; so finely that they had increased the score from 10 to 85 when Shrewsbury was smartly had at wicket for 26 another good innings. Wyld and Selby then made the score 104 when Hill bowled Wyld for 61, the largest score in the match, and a sample of free, fine, and heavy hitting that included nine 4s (six cuts). Anthony was bowled at 106, and shortly after Nottinghamshire had won by six wickets.

Yorkshire

First innings		Second innings	
J. Hicks c and b Alfred Shaw	3	b Alfred Shaw	1
T. Armitage c Alfred Shaw b McIntyre	12	c Daft b Alfred Shaw	11
Andrew Greenwood lbw b McIntyre	1	c Morley b McIntyre	1
Ephraim Lockwood b McIntyre	10	b Alfred Shaw	21
George Ulyett c Selby b Alfred Shaw	26	c Alfred Shaw b McIntyre	2
Emmett b McIntyre	0	c Clark b Alfred Shaw	8
R. Clayton b McIntyre	3	b Morley	8
C. Ullathorne b Alfred Shaw	14	hit wkt b Morley	1
Rowbotham b Alfred Shaw	8	b Morley	27
Allen Hill not out	3	b Morley	0
Pinder b Alfred Shaw	0	not out	15
B 6, l-b 2, w 1	9	B 5, l-b 3, w 1	9
	89		107

Nottinghamshire

William Oscroft c Pinder b Hill	9 – run out	9
F. Wyld b Emmett	3 – b Hill	61
Arthur Shrewsbury b Hill	26 – b Hill	26
Richard Daft lbw b Hill	6	
Martin McIntyre b Emmett	1 – not out	9
J. Selby c Lockwood b Armitage	8 – not out	6
H. Reynolds b Armitage	0	
Alfred Shaw c Pinder b Clayton	18	
W. Clark run out	0	
A. Anthony b Hill	0 – b Hill	0
Morley not out	0	
B 6, l-b 7	13 B 3, n-b 1	4
	84	115

Nottinghamshire Bowling

	Overs	Mdns	Runs	Wkts	Overs	Mdns	Runs	Wkts
A. Shaw	39	23	33	5	36	24	34	4
M. McIntyre	31	14	44	5	10	2	23	2
Morley	7	6	3	—	34.3	18	40	4
Oscroft					3	2	1	—

Yorkshire Bowling

	Overs	Mdns	Runs	Wkts	Overs	Mdns	Runs	Wkts
Hill	31.1	18	29	4	24	8	45	3
Emmett	20	12	19	2	13.1	4	21	—
Clayton	8	6	5	1	4	1	11	—
Armitage	4	—	18	2	2	—	9	—
Lockwood					5	—	12	—
Ulyett					2	—	13	—

Umpires: C. Coward and W. H. Luck.

THOMAS EMMETT'S MATCH

YORKSHIRE v GLOUCESTERSHIRE

Played at Sheffield, July 29, 30, 31, 1878

"We shall play a benefit match at Sheffield next year for Emmett, and we think it will be a great success," pleasantly said one of the Sheffield Committee to the compiler of this book on The Oval in 1877. That match has now been played, and "the great success" accomplished; so there cannot be a more fitting page than this to record "Mr Tom's" thankfulness for that match and its "great success", with the following extract from a letter sent to the writer of this by Emmett on the 27th of last September:

> "With regard to my benefit match, I have not yet got it squared up, but my friend is confident I shall clear £600 over it. I wish you would thank the Gentlemen Cricketers of England and the public for me, for the prompt and substantial manner they have supported me."

Such a success is most gratifying to record, because it has fallen to one of the heartiest, cheeriest, most earnest, hard working, and best all round professionals that ever played the game.

The morning of the first day of the match was discouraging, but the mid-day, afternoon, and evening were all right, and, chronicled *The Sportsman*, "The company augmented into something like 10,000". Ulyett and Hall began the Yorkshire batting; they had made 35 runs when Ulyett was out for 29; but Hall stayed and saw Lockwood, Mr Hirst, Bates, Haggas and Emmett come and go, and the scored increased to 130 when – after having been near upon three hours at wickets for 45 runs – he was had at slip. Mr Bottomley, the amateur Colt, made 29; but at ten past five, the Yorkshire innings closed for 158 runs, made from 118 Gloucestershire overs, backed up by some very fine Gloucestershire fielding. At 5.30 Mr F. Grace and Mr Gilbert started the West Countrymen's innings, to the bowling of Bates and Mr Bottomley. At 14 Bates bowled Mr Gilbert; and 27 Bates bowled Mr F. Grace; at 52 Bates bowled Mr Haynes; and at 59 Emmett (who had relieved Mr Bottomley) bowled Midwinter; whereupon the first day's cricket ceased, the Glucestershire score at 59, Mr Moline 19 not out.

On the Tuesday at noon Mr Moline and Mr W. G. Grace went on with the West Country innings, the attendance being thus early very large. The bowling was commenced by Bates and Emmett. The score rose to 87 when Mr Moline was bowled for 28. Dr Grace had made 16 when he was bowled by Ulyett, who, with the following ball, bowled Mr Cranston; and when he had made 62 Mr W. Grace fell to a splendid one hand catch by Emmett, the hitter and the catcher being loudly applauded. Mr Grace was missed by Mr Hirst at slip when he had made 49. Mr Robinson and Mr Miles put on 33 runs for the last wicket, the innings closing for 201 runs, made from 110 overs (less one ball), nine of the ten wickets being bowled down, four by Bates, three by Ulyett, one by Hill and one by Emmett, who also got the great wicket. After luncheon Ulyett and Hall commenced Yorkshire's second innings. Hall was steady, Ulyett full of hitting, and fortunate in escapes; his hitting materially and rapidly increased the score to 80, when Hall was out for 13! Lockwood was next man in; he played grandly, and Ulyett hit so fiercely that, by a 6, a 4 and a 6, he actually made 16 runs from one over of Mr Miles'; but shortly after Midwinter bowled Ulyett for 109 – an innings that included eleven 4s and two 6s, or 56 runs in thirteen hits. Lockwood brought out repeated cheers by his splendid and successful batting, "time" stopping play for that day with the Yorkshire second innings in this form:

George Ulyett b Midwinter	109
Louis Hall c Robinson b Midwinter	13
Ephraim Lockwood not out	73
T. Armitage c Bush b W. Grace	8
Mr Hirst not out	0
Extras	18
(3 wkts)	221

On the third day at noon the innings was resumed. The Yorkshire score was increased to 276 when Mr Hirst was had at wicket for 23; and at 288 Lockwood was finely caught out at long field for 107 – an innings that was without a chance until he had made 87, and an innings that was praised by all the critics for its skill and great excellence. Lockwood's hitting included ten 4s. There were then five wickets down and 288 runs made, two of those five men out having made over 100 runs. A remarkable item of County batting this! After this all seemed tame, Bates took his bat out for 38, and the innings finished just before luncheon for 360 runs, made from 179 overs, Mr F. Grace having bowled

Eleven overs (seven maidens) for 7 runs and four wickets – all bowled.

It was 3.20 when the second innings of Gloucestershire was commenced, all present anticipating a full day's cricket, none dreaming of defeat for the Gloucestershire men; but so it turned out; none could made any stand but Dr Grace (who made 21) and Mr W. Grace, who took his bat out for 38, the other nine men making only 14 runs between them, the innings being played out in one hour and thirty-five minutes for 73 runs, made from forty overs (less one ball) bowled by Bates and Ulyett; and so it turned out that, at five minutes to five on the third day, Emmett's match had been (appropriately) won by

Yorkshire by 244 runs, fourteen of the twenty Gloucestershire wickets having been bowled down, seven by Bates, five by Ulyett, one by Hill and one by Emmett. (There were 18 wide balls bowled in this match.)

Yorkshire

Louis Hall c Gilbert b Miles	45	– c Robinson b Midwinter	13
George Ulyett c J. A. Bush b Miles	29	– b Midwinter	109
Ephraim Lockwood b Miles	11	– c Gilbert b W. Grace	107
E. T. Hirst Esq. c W. Grace b Gilbert	3	– c J. A. Bush b W. Grace	23
W. Bates run out	3	– not out	38
S. Haggas b Gilbert	0	– b F. Grace	11
T. Emmett c Midwinter b Gilbert	15	– b F. Grace	18
I. H. Bottomley Esq. c W. Grace b Miles	29	– st J. A. Bush b W. Grace	10
T. Armitage not out	11	– c J. A. Bush b W. Grace	8
Allen Hill b W. Grace	0	– b F. Grace	0
J. Hunter c Miles b W. Grace	2	– b F. Grace	0
B 3, l-b 1, w 6	10	B 11, l-b 2, w 10	23
	158		360

Gloucestershire

G. F. Grace Esq. b Bates	8	– c and b Bates	6
W. Gilbert Esq. b Bates	10	– b Bates	0
C. E. Haynes Esq. b Bates	19	– b Bates	0
E. R. Moline Esq. b Bates	28	– b Ulyett	0
W. Midwinter b Emmett	0	– c and b Bates	2
W. G. Grace Esq. c and b Emmett	62	– b Bates	35
Dr E. M. Grace b Ulyett	16	– lbw b Ulyett	21
J. Cranston Esq. b Ulyett	0	– b Ulyett	1
J. A. Bush Esq. b Hill	4	– c Hirst b Bates	2
A. Robinson Esq. not out	34	– not out	2
R. F. Miles Esq. b Ulyett	9	– c E. Lockwood b Bates	1
B 6, l-b 3, w 2	11	B 1, l-b 2	3
	201		73

Gloucestershire Bowling

	Overs	Mdns	Runs	Wkts	Overs	Mdns	Runs	Wkts
Mr W. Grace	44	21	48	2	57	18	128	4
Mr Miles	31	13	42	4	40	16	86	—
Mr Gilbert	31	19	37	3	23	10	35	—
Dr E. M. Grace	12	4	21	—	5	1	17	—
Midwinter					32	13	51	2
Mr F. Grace					11	7	7	4
Mr Haynes					11	5	13	—

Yorkshire Bowling

	Overs	Mdns	Runs	Wkts	Overs	Mdns	Runs	Wkts
Bates	38	13	68	4	19.3	6	38	7
Emmett	26	14	41	2				
Ulyett	20.3	10	27	3	20	4	32	3
Hill	11	3	21	1				
Mr Bottomley	8	2	19	—				
Hall	6	1	14	—				

Umpires: George Pinder and C. K. Pullin.

YORKSHIRE v SURREY

Played at Huddersfield, June 2, 3, 1881

The Yorkshiremen were fortunate enough to win the toss, and elected to go in. The wicket was in splendid condition, and there was a large attendance on both days. Ulyett and Hall took the score from 27 to 161, when Hall was caught. Ulyett played with great freedom, and was not out until he had made 112, his chief hits including nine 4s, ten 3s and seven 2s. Lockwood was at the wickets whilst 206 were scored, and was then caught for a remarkably good innings of 109, made chiefly by one 5, nine 4s, six 3s and eleven 2s. Bates and Emmett both played well for 55 and 41 respectively; Peate was absent, and the innings closed for 388. It is remarkable that not a single extra was given in this long innings. None of the Surrey men, with the exception of Mr Lucas, could do anything with the bowling of Hill and Peate. Mr Lucas played a grand innings of 62, and the total reached 110. Being in a minority of 278, the southerners followed on, but could only total 61. Yorkshire thus won by an innings and 217 runs. Peate's bowling throughout the match is worthy of note – 62 overs and 2 balls (27 maidens) for 77 runs and fourteen wickets.

Yorkshire

G. Ulyett c Lucas b Potter	112
L. Hall c Lucas b Barratt	47
J. H. Wood Esq. b Barratt	14
E. Lockwood c Shuter b Potter	109
W. Bates b W. W. Read	55
T. Emmett c and b Potter	41
A. Thornton c Lucas b Potter	6
I. Grimshaw c W. W. Read b Barratt	2
A. Hill c Jones b Barratt	1
J. Hunter not out	1
E. Peate absent	
	388

Surrey

J. Shuter Esq. c Peate	0	b Peate	13
H. Jupp c Hill b Peate	8	c Emmett b Peate	6
A. P. Lucas Esq. b Hill	62	c Hill b Peate	12
W. W. Read Esq. b Hill	11	b Hill	7
M. Read b Hill	0	b Peate	1
R. Humphrey b Peate	5	b Peate	6
Cafferey c Lockwood b Peate	6	b Peate	0
F. Johnson c Emmett b Peate	0	b Peate	0
J. Potter b Hill	8	b Hill	4
E. Barratt not out	2	lbw b Peate	8
G. Jones c Thornton b Peate	2	not out	1
B 3, l-b 3	6	B 3	3
	110		61

Surrey Bowling

	Overs	Mdns	Runs	Wkts
Barratt	51	5	158	4
Jones	16	1	46	—
Potter	43	17	79	4
Johnson	14	3	27	—
Mr Lucas	7	1	23	—
Cafferey	5	—	19	—
Mr Shuter	2	—	16	—
Mr W. W. Read	6	1	20	1

Yorkshire Bowling

	Overs	Mdns	Runs	Wkts	Overs	Mdns	Runs	Wkts
Hill	39	17	57	4	24	14	28	2
Peate	38.3	19	47	6	28.3	9	30	8

YORKSHIRE v KENT

Played at Bramall Lane, June 12, 13, 1882

There was some extraordinary cricket in this match, which the Yorkshiremen won in a single innings with 20 runs to spare. Kent batted first, and their first wicket (Mr Mackinnon's) went at 20. Then George Hearne joined Lord Harris, and a most determined stand was made. At luncheon both were still in, and the score 91. Resuming after a storm of rain, Hearne was stumped at 98, and ten runs later Lord Harris was easily caught for a faultless innings of 62, which contained only one hit for 4. Then the sensational part of the innings occurred, for

the remaining seven wickets fell for 5 runs!

Peate bowled with great success. Mr Wilson went in three wickets down, and carried out his bat for 8! Yorkshire went in at 5.30, and when stumps were drawn, Hall was not out with 12, and Ulyett out with 63! Ulyett hit at everything, and had made 31 before Hall had scored; and his first 50 were made in half-an-hour. When Hall's innings was completed next morning it was found that he had taken three hours and a half to score 29! Kent went in the second time wanting 59 runs to save the single innings' defeat; but Bates took six wickets at an average cost of two runs, and Peate three for 25, and the Kent eleven were all disposed of for 29. Peate in that innings performed the "hat trick", getting rid of Lord Harris, O'Shaughnessy and Lord Throwley with successive balls.

Kent

Lord Harris c Ulyett b Bates	62	– lbw b Peate	7
F. A. Mackinnon Esq. b Peate	9	– c Hunter b Bates	4
G. G. Hearne st Hunter b Peate	26	– st Hunter b Bates	10
C. Wilson Esq. not out	8	– run out	1
F. Pentecost b Peate	2	– c Lockwood b Bates	2
E. O'Shaughnessy b Peate	0	– c Ulyett b Peate	0
Lord Throwley lbw b Peate	0	– b Peate	0
F. M. Atkins Esq. b Bates	0	– st Hunter b Bates	5
F. Hearne hit wkt b Bates	0	– b Bates	8
F. Lipscombe Esq. b Peate	0	– c Sidgwick b Bates	0
J. Wootton b Peate	0	– not out	0
B 3, w 3	6	B 2	2
	113		39

Yorkshire

G. Ulyett c O'Shaughnessy b Harris	63
L. Hall c Atkins b F. Hearne	29
W. Bates c Wootton b Harris	4
E. Lockwood c Pentecost b F. Hearne	8
R. Sidgwick Esq. c Lipscombe	17
T. Emmett b Lipscombe	3
J. Padgett b Lipscombe	2
I. Grimshaw c Lipscombe b Wootton	1
A. Hill c Throwley b F. Hearne	18
E. Peate c and b Harris	13
J. Hunter not out	2
B 10, l-b 2	12
	172

Yorkshire Bowling

	Overs	Mdns	Runs	Wkts	Overs	Mdns	Runs	Wkts
Bates	53	29	47	3	18.3	12	12	6
Peate	47.3	25	31	7	18	6	25	3
Ulyett	11	5	12	—				
Emmett	11	6	11	—				
Hill	6	4	6	—				

Kent Bowling

	Overs	Mdns	Runs	Wkts
G. G. Hearne	16	8	25	—
Mr Lipscombe	18	8	25	3
F. Hearne	30	15	31	3
Wootton	52	16	51	1
Lord Harris	22	7	28	3

Umpires: T. Brownhill and W. Goodhew.

YORKSHIRE v NOTTINGHAMSHIRE

Played at Bramhall Lane, Sheffield, June 24, 25, 26, 1883

Wet weather greatly interfered with this match on the first and second days, and caused it to result in a draw on the third, continuous rain putting an end to play at 3.30. About 10,000 persons witnessed the game on the opening day, and were spectators of some extraordinary cricket. Yorkshire batted first on a fairly good wicket, and 69 runs were scored when the fifth wicket fell, but the last six batsmen failed so completely that their efforts only added 12 runs to the total. When Nottinghamshire went in, Shrewsbury was dismissed after he had scored 5, and when Barnes and Scotton had carried the total to 24, rain stopped play. On resumption only six overs were bowled before time expired, but in those six overs five wickets fell for only 2 runs, the third, fourth, and sixth going at 25.

Scotton, not out 5, and Gunn, not out 1, continued the innings on the Tuesday, and the bowlers and fieldsmen being heavily handicapped by a thoroughly saturated wicket, the Nottinghamshire total was only three short of their opponents' when the innings closed. Gunn batted in free and vigorous style, and contributed just over half the runs from the bat made by his side. Bates dismissed the last three batsmen for 8 runs. When Yorkshire went in a second time four wickets fell for 23 runs. Then Ulyett and Grimshaw put on 23 runs before the latter was caught. Emmett came in, and he and Ulyett played out time, the score standing at 64 for five wickets, Ulyett, not out 36; Emmett, not out 2.

Ulyett added four runs to his overnight total when the game was resumed on the Wednesday, and was then caught. He had played with greater care than usual and his excellent innings of 40 included four 4s, a 3 and seven 2s. Sugg was the only other Yorkshireman who batted well in this innings, and it is a curious fact that in this match, in which the bowlers had matters so very much their own way, the 28 by Grimshaw and the 13 not out by Sugg, were the highest scores these two batsmen made during the season in the first-class matches of Yorkshire. Nottinghamshire lost six wickets in their second innings for 45, and then rain finally stopped the game, the visitors wanting 54 runs to win with four wickets to fall.

Yorkshire

G. Ulyett st Sherwin b Shaw	8	– c Scotton b Wright	40
L. Hall c Sherwin b Shaw	17	– c Gunn b Wright	1
E. Lockwood b Shaw	14	– b Shaw	2
W. Bates b Barnes	7	– b Wright	7
I. Grimshaw lbw b Wright	28	– c Shaw b Flowers	14
T. Emmett b Wright	0	– b Wright	3
W. H. Bowers b Shaw	5	– c Shaw b Barnes	5
F. H. Sugg lbw b Shaw	4	– not out	13
R. Peel c Attewell b Shaw	2	– run out	0
E. Peate not out	1	– c Gunn b Wright	0
G. P. Harrison b Wright	0	– c Scotton b Shaw	7
B 1, l-b 3	4	B 3	3
	90		95

Nottinghamshire

A. Shrewsbury lbw b Peate	5 – b Bates	13
W. Scotton b Peate	12 – not out	6
W. Barnes b Peate	13 – b Peate	1
W. Flowers b Harrison	1 – c Hall b Peate	7
J. Selby b Harrison	0 – not out	13
A. Shaw run out	0	
F. Butler b Harrison	0 – c Lockwood b Peate	0
W. Gunn not out	42 – b Peate	3
W. Attewell c Sugg b Bates	7 – c Emmett b Peate	0
W. Wright c and b Bates	3	
M. Sherwin b Bates	0	
B 1, l-b 3	4 B 2	2
	87	45

Nottinghamshire Bowling

	Overs	Mdns	Runs	Wkts	Overs	Mdns	Runs	Wkts
Shaw	53	39	27	6	29.3	15	22	2
Wright	35.1	19	35	3	36	20	49	5
Barnes	20	10	24	1	11	7	14	1
Attewell	3	3	—	—				
Flowers					18	15	7	1

Yorkshire Bowling

	Overs	Mdns	Runs	Wkts	Overs	Mdns	Runs	Wkts
Peate	33	17	25	3	18	8	17	5
Harrison	25	12	37	3	2	1	2	—
Peel	7	3	13	—	1	1	—	—
Bates	7.1	5	8	3	18	8	24	1

Umpires: C. Coward and G. Panter.

YORKSHIRE v SURREY

Played on the Holbeck Ground, Leeds, July 23, 24, 1883

Yorkshire won this match by an innings and three runs, and Peate's success in the first innings of Surrey was the most remarkable bowling performance of the year in a first-class match. Heavy rain on the previous Saturday and Sunday rendered the ground in a condition to materially help the bowlers. Yorkshire had first innings, and towards their total of 116 Bates contributed a finely-hit and excellent 55, which comprised six 4s, seven 2s and seventeen singles; Ulyett made 21 out of 35; and Hall scored a carefully-played 22. Surrey went in to bat at 3.30, and in sixty-five minutes were all out for the miserable total of 31, Peate taking eight wickets in 16 overs for only 5 runs, no fewer than seven of the Surrey team failing to make a run. Being 85 runs to the bad Surrey followed their innings, and at the call of time had lost five wickets for 33 runs, Henderson, the not out man, having made 18.

The game was resumed at 12.15 on the second day, and concluded at 1.50, rain in the meantime having caused a delay of half-an-hour. The only noteworthy feature of the day's play was the batting of Henderson, who scored 41 in admirable form – a highly meritorious performance, considering the extremely difficult wicket. His hits included five 4s and seven 2s. It will be seen that Mr W. W. Read was twice dismissed without scoring.

Yorkshire

G. Ulyett c L. A. Shuter b Barratt	21	T. Emmett c L. A. Shuter b Horner	2
L. Hall c W. W. Read b Horner	22	J. Hunter c Henderson b Horner	1
E. Lumb Esq. run out	1	E. Peate not out	2
E. Lockwood b Roller	2	G. P. Harrison c Chester b Henderson	2
W. Bates b Henderson	55	B 3, l-b 1	4
Hon. M. B. Hawke c W. W. Read b Barratt	0		
E. T. Hirst Esq. c J. Shuter b Barratt	4		116

Surrey

J. M. Read st Hunter b Peate	12	– b Harrison	1
L. A. Shuter Esq. c and b Peate	1	– b Harrison	9
R. Henderson c and b Peate	0	– b Emmett	41
W. W. Read Esq. c Emmett b Peate	0	– b Harrison	0
J. Shuter Esq. c Hall b Bates	0	– c and b Harrison	4
W. E. Roller Esq. st Hunter b Peate	0	– lbw b Peate	11
E. J. Diver Esq. not out	11	– b Peate	0
R. Abel c Hirst b Bates	2	– c Ulyett b Emmett	5
A. Chester c Lumb b Peate	0	– b Peate	0
C. E. Horner Esq. b Peate	0	– not out	2
E. Barratt b Peate	0	– b Harrison	4
B 5	5	B 1, l-b 4	5
	31		82

Surrey Bowling

	Overs	Mdns	Runs	Wkts
Barratt	28	8	60	3
Mr Roller	18	8	20	1
Mr Horner	15	6	21	3
Henderson	6.3	3	11	2

Yorkshire Bowling

	Overs	Mdns	Runs	Wkts	Overs	Mdns	Runs	Wkts
Peate	16	11	5	8	30	19	25	3
Bates	16	7	21	2	27	19	12	—
Emmett					19	12	17	2
Harrison					17.2	11	23	5

Umpires: G. Wootton and C. Coward.

YORKSHIRE v KENT

Played at Sheffield, May 25, 26, 1885

A magnificent bowling performance by young Alec Hearne enabled Kent to score a brilliant victory by eight wickets. The pitch was soft and spongy owing to heavy rains during the previous week, and Yorkshire, who began batting at 12.20, were all out five minutes before luncheon time for the very poor total of 86, Alec Hearne taking five wickets at a cost of only 13 runs. When Kent went in to bat the cricket was extremely slow for some considerable time, only five runs being scored after nearly half-an-hour's play. Mr Jones and George Hearne were out after scoring a couple each, but matters improved very considerably for Kent when Mr Patterson and Frank Hearne became partners. Both played sterling cricket, and numerous changes of bowling were made before the professional was at last caught at the wicket for a finely-played innings of 37. Mr Patterson soon after shared the same fate as Frank Hearne, and when he retired at 74 for a faultless innings of 29, nothing of a stand was afterwards made. O'Shaughnessy and Wootton were together for a short time, and the former dispatched Peel splendidly to the off for 5. The innings was brought to a close for 105, and play then ceased for the day.

Play on the Tuesday began with the second innings of Yorkshire, and Alec Hearne again bowled with extraordinary success. The only man on the side who played him well was Hall, who went in first and carried his bat through the innings without giving a chance. Kent were only left with 63 runs to get to win, and though they lost F. Hearne immediately, the result was never in doubt, George Hearne and the two old Blues knocking off the required runs.

Yorkshire

G. Ulyett c G. G. Hearne b Christopherson	4	– c Christopherson b A. Hearne	0
L. Hall c Collins b Wootton	10	– not out	32
W. Bates c A. Hearne b Christopherson	0	– st Pentecost b A. Hearne	4
H. Lee c Pentecost b Christopherson	3	– b A. Hearne	0
W. H. Woodhouse Esq. run out	13	– c Pentecost b A. Hearne	3
I. Grimshaw c Patterson b A. Hearne	21	– c and b Christopherson	5
R. Peel lbw b A. Hearne	9	– st Pentecost b A. Hearne	12
J. T. Rawlin c F. Hearne b A. Hearne	3	– c Pentecost b A. Hearne	16
T. Emmett b A. Hearne	0	– b A. Hearne	0
E. Peate c Wootton b A. Hearne	18	– b A. Hearne	0
J. Hunter not out	0	– c and b Wootton	4
B 1, l-b 4	5	L-b 5	5
	86		81

Kent

R. S. Jones Esq. b Peel	2	– b Emmett	18
F. Hearne c Hunter b Peel	37	– run out	0
G. G. Hearne c Rawlin b Peate	2	– not out	30
W. H. Patterson Esq. c Hunter b Peel	29	– not out	14
E. O'Shaughnessy b Bates	10		
S. Christopherson Esq. b Peel	0		
C. Collins b Peel	0		
J. Wootton b Peel	13		
A. Hearne lbw b Peate	3		
H. Hearne not out	1		
J. Pentecost st Hunter b Peel	0		
B 5, l-b 3	8	B 1	1
	105		63

Kent Bowling

	Overs	Mdns	Runs	Wkts	Overs	Mdns	Runs	Wkts
Mr Christopherson	34	22	41	3	21	14	22	1
Wootton	20	9	26	1	6.1	4	4	1
A. Hearne	14.2	8	13	5	42	24	35	8
G. G. Hearne	1	—	1	—				
H. Hearne					15	9	15	—

Yorkshire Bowling

	Overs	Mdns	Runs	Wkts	Overs	Mdns	Runs	Wkts
Peel	51	27	51	7	20	12	14	—
Peate	30	22	17	2	26	19	17	—
Bates	18	12	12	1	11	7	9	—
Ulyett	5	2	7	—	7	4	5	—
Emmett	15	10	10	—	16	12	10	1
Rawlin					8	5	7	—

YORKSHIRE v DERBYSHIRE

Played at Leeds, August 26, 27, 28, 1886

This was the last match of the Yorkshire inter-county season, and was played at Holbeck, a ground notorious in previous years for the advantages it afforded to bowlers. The first day's cricket consisted of the success of one man – Bates – who made no fewer than 106 out of 142 runs hit from the bat while he was at the wickets. He gave a chance to long-on at 62, another to mid-off at 99, and a third in the slips at 105, but not one of these was easy. He hit twelve 4s, five 3s and thirteen 2s. Nine of the eleven made only 30 runs between them, so that the team generally could not claim any credit. Derbyshire lost two wickets for 21 runs, but Mr Docker and W. Chatterton, playing in excellent form, raised the total to 91 before the drawing of stumps, when the amateur was not out 38 and the professional 26.

On the second day Chatterton again played extremely well; indeed his batting was probably the most perfect in the match. Like Bates, however, he received very poor assistance, and although he scored 82 not out, including two 6s, five 4s, two 3s and fifteen 2s, the visitors could only claim an advantage of 21 runs on the first innings. Even this slight lead, however, looked like seriously prejudicing the chances of Yorkshire, as in the second innings of the home county Bates, Hall, Mr Hawke and Preston were out for 34 runs, or only 13 runs on. From this point, however, the batting improved in most remarkable fashion. Ulyett and Wade added 57 runs, and later on Peel and Grimshaw, getting together, completely mastered the Derbyshire bowling. At the call of time Grimshaw was not out 59 and Peel not out 33, the pair having already put on 94 runs out of a total of 193 for six wickets.

There was a capital finish on the third day, Yorkshire gaining a thoroughly well-earned victory by 121 runs. Peel was dismissed for 55, but Grimshaw not only reached his hundred, but carried out his bat for 122 – his best performance during the season. As far as could be seen, he gave no fair chance, and he hit twelve 4s, three 3s and fifteen 2s, scoring 122 out of 187 during his stay. Derbyshire had 266 runs to get to win the match, but only three hours and a half remained before time. The attempt to draw the game proved unsuccessful, for though Chatterton again showed good form, and Cropper and Coupe tried their best, the innings was all over for 144, Yorkshire winning as stated above.

Yorkshire

Bates b Cropper	106	– st Disney b Cropper	14
Hall b Walker	0	– b Cropper	11
Ulyett c Disney b Walker	9	– b Davidson	34
Hon. M. B. Hawke c Coupe b Walker	18	– b Davidson	0
Preston c Disney b Cropper	9	– b Davidson	0
Ward st Disney b Davidson	2	– run out	26
Peel b Cropper	3	– b Doughty	55
Grimshaw b Davidson	3	– not out	122
Wade not out	2	– b J. Chatterton	0
Emmett run out	1	– c Sugg b Doughty	1
Mr G. A. B. Leatham run out	1	– b Doughty	3
B 5, l-b 1, n-b 1	7	B 13, l-b 6, n-b 1	20
	161		286

Derbyshire

F. Sugg b Emmett	16 – c Ulyett b Bates	4
Coupe b Emmett	0 – lbw b Preston	33
Mr L. C. Docker c Leatham b Emmett	44 – b Bates	8
W. Chatterton not out	82 – b Wade	23
Cropper b Bates	9 – b Wade	36
Mr E. A. J. Maynard b Bates	4 – c Grimshaw b Bates	2
Davidson run out	2 – c Leatham b Ulyett	8
J. Chatterton c Grimshaw b Bates	1 – b Bates	4
Doughty c Bates b Emmett	8 – b Bates	0
Mr G. G. Walker c Preston b Bates	0 – c Leatham b Ulyett	10
Disney c Grimshaw b Bates	0 – not out	0
B 12, l-b 3, w 1	16 B 13, l-b 2, w 1	16
	182	144

Derbyshire Bowling

	Overs	Mdns	Runs	Wkts	Overs	Mdns	Runs	Wkts
Davidson	25	8	42	2	46	24	52	3
Mr Walker	20	6	61	3	27	12	35	0
Cropper	27	15	37	3	40	11	75	2
W. Chatterton	12	7	7	0	25	9	48	0
Doughty	3	1	3	0	14.2	4	28	3
J. Chatterton	2	1	4	0	19	6	28	1
Mr Docker					1	1	0	0

Yorkshire Bowling

	Overs	Mdns	Runs	Wkts	Overs	Mdns	Runs	Wkts
Wade	18	8	34	0	17	12	9	2
Emmett	48	24	52	4	26	10	38	0
Preston	16	5	26	0	7	3	12	1
Bates	21.3	16	30	5	32	13	45	5
Peel	19	13	22	0	8	4	16	0
Ulyett	2	1	2	0	8.3	6	8	2

YORKSHIRE v MIDDLESEX

Played at Huddersfield, August 11, 12, 13, 1887

The wicket at Huddersfield, where Yorkshire played their return match with Middlesex, suffered much by comparison with that on which the game between Yorkshire and Lancashire had taken place at the beginning of the same week. It kicked a good deal on the first day, and the bowling of Preston for Yorkshire and West for Middlesex proved most effective. During the first day 22 wickets fell for 357 runs. The Hon. Alfred Lyttelton, for the first and only time in the season, appeared in the Middlesex eleven. Yorkshire played the same team as at Bradford, Mr J. Wilson, the lob bowler, who was to have appeared in place of Denton, being prevented from playing, at the last moment, by a slight accident. Middlesex won the toss, but at the start of the innings could do next to nothing with the fast bowling of Preston, who kept a beautiful length and got up at times very awkwardly. Eight wickets went down for 64 runs, but the last three batsmen played up so pluckily that the score ultimately reached 130. Preston obtained seven wickets for 55 runs, and had he bowled with a little more judgment towards the close of the Middlesex innings, the total might not have reached 100. The main feature of the Yorkshire batting was the brilliant hitting of Mr Hawke and Ulyett, the former scoring 64 in his best form by twelve 4s, four 2s and singles, and the latter 57 in an hour and ten minutes by nine 4s, seven 2s, and singles. When Yorkshire looked to have an immense advantage, the last few batsmen did very little, and the innings was all over for 181, so that Yorkshire could only claim a lead of 51 runs on the first innings. Going in a second time, Middlesex started badly and lost two wickets, those of Mr Stoddart and Mr Walker for 46 runs. Mr Webbe was not out with 18, and Mr Lyttelton with 6. Thus the game seemed all in favour of Yorkshire, Middlesex, with two good wickets down, being 5 runs behind.

On the second day, however, a most remarkable change came over the game, and Mr A. J. Webbe accomplished one of the most notable performances of the season. The wicket certainly played better than on the opening day, but still the ball every now and then got up in a very awkward manner. The Middlesex batsmen, however, following the excellent example set them by their captain, hit out in a brilliant manner, and fairly wore down the Yorkshire bowling, which after a time certainly became loose and erratic. Mr Lyttelton played in beautiful form in the early morning, but it was the partnership of Messrs Webbe and O'Brien that really turned the game. These two gentlemen while they were together put on 163 runs, and both hit in fine style. Mr O'Brien gave one chance, but on the whole there was little fault to find with his excellent innings of 78, which included twelve 4s and six 2s. When five wickets had fallen, Mr Ford in company with his captain added 113 runs, and the young Cantab in his 58 made nine 4s, four 3s and two 2s. In the end the Middlesex total reached the tremendous number of 527, and the visitors deserved all the congratulations they received on a remarkable batting triumph. Of course the chief honours lay with Mr Webbe, who went in first and carried out his bat for 243. This is the highest innings the famous old Oxonian has ever played in a first-class match, though he once made 299 in a college engagement. His performance was by no means without fault, as he gave an easy chance to Wade at slip when he had made 63, and might afterwards have been caught on two or three occasions. In addition to this, many of his hits through the slips just went out of the reach of the fieldsmen. In saying this, however, it must be remembered that the wicket was never a very easy one, though it was one on which runs could be made at a great pace. Mr Webbe was batting for six hours and ten minutes, and the figures of his memorable innings were forty-one 4s, nine 3s, eleven 2s and thirty singles. Yorkshire were set no fewer than 477 runs to win, so that their chance of success was of course very remote. Only a quarter of an hour remained for cricket, and the usual order of batting was altered. This policy, however, was by no means successful, as two wickets, those of Emmett and Hunter, fell before the call of time for 13 runs, and Yorkshire thus wanted 464 runs to win, with eight wickets to fall.

Unluckily for Middlesex rain fell heavily on the Friday night, and continued with brief intervals all day on Saturday. There was no chance of making a start, and so the game had to be abandoned early as a draw, Middlesex being robbed of what in all probability would have been a brilliant victory.

Middlesex

Mr A. J. Webbe c Hunter b Preston	17	– not out	243
Mr A. E. Stoddart c Bates b Emmett	13	– c Hunter b Preston	20
Mr J. G. Walker c Hunter b Preston	20	– c Hunter b Preston	0
Mr T. C. O'Brien c Lee b Preston	0	– c Lee b Preston	78
Mr G. F. Vernon c Hunter b Emmett	4	– c Hall b Ulyett	20
Hon. A. Lyttelton c Ulyett b Preston	5	– c Lee b Emmett	40
Mr F. G. J. Ford c Lee b Preston	0	– lbw b Emmett	58
G. Burton c Bates b Preston	0	– b Peel	2
Mr P. J. de Paravicini c Bates b Peel	20	– c Bates b Peel	15
J. E. West not out	18	– c Hall b Emmett	19
Mr J. Robertson c Wade b Preston	24	– c Bates b Preston	8
B 7, l-b 1, w 1	9	B 11, l-b 7, w 6	24
	130		527

Yorkshire

G. Ulyett c Paravicini b Burton	57		
L. Hall c O'Brien b West	0		
F. Lee c Stoddart b West	12		
Hon. M. B. Hawke run out	64		
W. Bates c Lyttelton b West	18		
S. Wade c Paravicini b Ford	13		
R. Peel c Ford b West	4		
J. M. Preston c Burton b Ford	4		
J. Denton c Paravicini b Ford	0	– not out	4
T. Emmett not out	4	– c Vernon b West	4
J. Hunter b Ford	0	– lbw b Ford	1
B 3, l-b 2	5	B 4	4
	181		13

Yorkshire Bowling

	Overs	Mdns	Runs	Wkts	Overs	Mdns	Runs	Wkts
Ulyett	4	2	9	0	13	3	38	1
Emmett	21	9	40	2	34	7	102	3
Preston	23.1	10	55	7	55.1	18	153	4
Peel	6	1	17	1	38	17	65	2
Wade					19	5	50	0
Bates					31	10	72	0
Hall					5	0	23	0

Middlesex Bowling

	Overs	Mdns	Runs	Wkts	Overs	Mdns	Runs	Wkts
West	29	8	74	4	2	0	6	1
Burton	14	3	53	1				
Mr Robertson	8	4	15	0				
Mr Webbe	2	0	17	0				
Mr Ford	13	8	17	4	1.1	0	3	1

Umpires: Coward and Platts.

YORKSHIRE v NOTTINGHAMSHIRE

Played at Sheffield, July 23, 24, 1888

When there is anything like fine weather the match between these counties at Bramall Lane always attracts a large company, and on the opening day this time, notwithstanding that there was rain shortly before noon, some 8,000 spectators were present. The teams included two or three new men on each side. For instance, Mr G. Beves, T. Brown and Joe Briggs were included in the visitors' side, while for Yorkshire, Middlebrook appeared again, and Ellis kept wicket. About half-past eleven a heavy shower of rain fell on the already soft ground, and though it cleared off about twelve o'clock it was not until twenty minutes later that a start took place in what proved to be a most curious day's cricket. Sherwin beat Hall in the toss, and, acting upon the perfectly justifiable surmise that the wicket would be easier then with the wet freshly upon it, decided to take first innings. Accordingly Gunn and Scotton began the Nottinghamshire batting at 12.20, to the bowling of Peel and Wainwright. Gunn got a 2 from the first ball bowled in consequence of Wainwright misfielding it at cover-point, but this little mistake was the only piece of bad cricket shown on the Yorkshire side during the innings. The Nottinghamshire batting, on the other hand, was of the most feeble character throughout. The score was only 3 when Scotton was out to a fine left-handed catch at short-slip, and at 4 Gunn got his leg in front to Peel. Then Barnes and Mr Daft got together, and played carefully for some time. In the first forty minutes 15 runs were scored, and then Barnes in hitting out was caught at extra cover-point. Mr Beves followed, but just after one o'clock, when the record was 18 for three wickets, a brief storm of rain broke over the ground and stopped play for about ten minutes. On resuming Peel and Wainwright again shared the bowling, and this time carried all before them. Wainwright with his first ball dismissed Mr Beves, and with his third bowled Attewell, while, as Peel in his first over bowled Mr Daft with a break back, with the total unaltered, the fourth, fifth and sixth wickets all fell at 18. Brown and Flowers were next together, but a catch at short-slip by Middlebrook soon got rid of Flowers, and, as Briggs was bowled in Peel's next over, the seventh and eighth wickets fell at 22. Afterwards, at 24, Peel bowled Richardson and Sherwin with successive balls, and the innings closed at 1.40 for the smallest total of the season thus far in a first-class match. Peel was heartily cheered. The Yorkshiremen went in before luncheon for five minutes, and Ulyett and Hall scored 4 runs from Attewell and Richardson before the interval. Subsequently the Nottinghamshire bowlers did extremely well, and as Ulyett was bowled at 4, Hall caught at "silly point" at 6, Lee bowled at 14, and Mr Hill caught at cover-point at 16, it did not look as though Yorkshire would make many. However, Peel and Wainwright made a brief stand and added 21 runs before Peel was bowled at 37 for the only double-figure score in either side's first innings. Then once more the bowlers had matters all their own way. At 41 Wainwright was bowled, and at 43 Moorhouse and Preston were smartly stumped, and Middlebrook caught and bowled. Wade was caught from a skier at mid-on at 46, and the innings closed for that score at four o'clock, having lasted an hour and twenty minutes, against an hour and ten minutes that Nottinghamshire had occupied. The wicket, though a trifle easier than in the early part of the day, was still very difficult, and it was generally expected that the 22 runs Nottinghamshire were behind would place them at an immense disadvantage. At a quarter past four Scotton and Gunn again went in, and Peel and Wainwright again bowled. Gunn was stumped at 5, and Barnes came in. Scotton was twice let off, Ellis missing him at the wicket and Peel in the slips, but later the left-hander batted patiently and well. Barnes after a while hit two 4s from Peel, but at 24, or just after the arrears had been hit off, Peel bowled him. On Mr Daft coming in a stand was made, and at 33 the first bowling change took place, Middlebrook going on for Peel, while at 38 Wade displaced Wainwright. As the fast bowler was freely hit Peel resumed at 42, and no further change was necessary. Mr Daft was at once caught at point, and Mr Beves joined Scotton. The 50 went up with only three wickets down, but then, as in the first innings, the batting completely broke down. At 53 Wade dismissed Mr Beves and Attewell in one over, while at 55 he got Brown stumped. At 56 Peel bowled Flowers and Briggs, and at 58 he sent back Richardson and Sherwin, the innings closing at 6.15 and stumps being drawn for the day. The day's cricket had been a most remarkable one, the thirty wickets having only earned an aggregate of 128 runs. Peel had an extraordinary analysis, having taken fourteen wickets for 33 runs. Next to Peel's, Richardon's was the best bowling achievement, his six Yorkshire wickets costing but two runs each.

On the Tuesday morning rain fell for three hours, and it was not until past three o'clock that the game could be continued. If there had been no more wet, Yorkshire might have found the necessary 37 runs difficult to get, but as it was Ulyett and Hall hit them off in forty minutes – a somewhat tame finish to an otherwise sensational game. Yorkshire thus won by ten wickets.

Nottinghamshire

W. Gunn lbw b Peel	2	– st Ellis b Wainwright	1
W. Scotton c Middlebrook b Peel	1	– not out	17
W. Barnes c Preston b Peel	1	– b Peel	14
Mr H. B. Daft b Peel	5	– c Middlebrook b Peel	12
Mr G. Beves b Wainwright	1	– b Wade	4
W. Attewell b Wainwright	0	– b Wade	0
Brown not out	2	– st Ellis b Wade	0
W. Flowers c Middlebrook b Peel	1	– b Peel	1
Joseph Briggs b Peel	0	– b Peel	0
H. Richardson b Peel	0	– b Peel	0
M. Sherwin b Peel	0	– lbw b Peel	0
B 4, l-b 1	5	B 8, l-b 1	9
	24		58

Yorkshire

G. Ulyett b Richardson	1	– not out	26
L. Hall c Gunn b Attewell	5	– not out	11
F. Lee b Richardson	3		
Mr H. Hill c Flowers b Attewell	6		
R. Peel b Richardson	13		
E. Wainwright st Sherwin b Briggs	8		
J. M. Preston st Sherwin b Richardson	4		
H. Moorhouse st Sherwin b Briggs	1		
S. Wade c Beves b Richardson	3		
W. Middlebrook c and b Richardson	0		
J. E. Ellis not out	0		
L-b 2	2		
	46		37

Yorkshire Bowling

	Overs	Mdns	Runs	Wkts	Overs	Mdns	Runs	Wkts
Peel	20.2	13	12	8	33.3	24	21	6
Wainwright	20	16	7	2	19	14	10	1
Middlebrook					4	1	9	0
Wade					13	9	9	3

Nottinghamshire Bowling

	Overs	Mdns	Runs	Wkts	Overs	Mdns	Runs	Wkts
Attewell	14	6	19	2	3	0	7	0
Richardson	19.1	12	12	6	12.3	9	11	0
Briggs	6	0	13	2				
Flowers					4	2	8	0
Brown					5	1	11	0

Umpires: Whatmough and Coward.

YORKSHIRE v MIDDLESEX

Played at Sheffield, August 6, 7, 8, 1888

The first day's cricket in this contest drew the usual Bank Holiday crowd to Bramall Lane on Monday, but the cricket was somewhat tame, fourteen wickets falling for 174 runs before rain caused stumps to be drawn at about five o'clock. On Tuesday the play was much more interesting, the bowlers on both sides being seen to great advantage. The Middlesex innings closed for 98, and then Yorkshire were dismissed a second time for 122. Middlesex wanted 138 to win, and scored 84 before play ceased, for the loss of three wickets. On Wednesday Middlesex won by six wickets, thanks chiefly to Burton and Mr O'Brien.

Yorkshire

G. Ulyett c Hadow b Ford	40	– b Ford	23
L. Hall b Hadow	11	– st Bryant b Burton	0
F. Lee c Walker b Burton	1	– c Robertson b Burton	58
Mr E. T. Hirst c Paravicini b Burton	10	– b Robertson	8
R. Peel c Bryant b Burton	19	– c Vernon b Burton	5
Lord Hawke c O'Brien b Burton	15	– b Burton	2
E. Wainwright c Scott b Burton	0	– c and b Burton	0
Mr J. Wilson not out	13	– c Robertson b Burton	4
J. M. Preston c Walker b Burton	0	– c Ford b Burton	8
S. Wade b Burton	2	– not out	3
J. E. Ellis c Hadow b Burton	0	– c Webbe b Burton	3
B 1, l-b 1	2	B 5, l-b 1, n-b 2	8
	113		122

Middlesex

Mr A. J. Webbe c Ulyett b Peel	8	– b Wainwright	6
Mr J. G. Walker b Wainwright	1	– b Preston	1
Mr T. C. O'Brien b Preston	27	– not out	79
Lord George Scott b Peel	0	– c and b Wilson	4
Mr E. M. Hadow b Wade	16	– b Wainwright	34
Mr G. F. Vernon run out	30	– not out	7
Mr P. J. de Paravicini c Lee b Preston	0		
Mr F. G. J. Ford c Preston b Wainwright	11		
Mr J. Robertson b Wainwright	2		
G. Burton c Wainwright b Preston	0		
Mr H. W. Bryant not out	2		
L-b 1	1	B 5, l-b 1, n-b 1	7
	98		138

Middlesex Bowling

	Overs	Mdns	Runs	Wkts	Overs	Mdns	Runs	Wkts
Burton	50.1	28	48	8	44.2	15	66	8
Mr Robertson	16	10	15	0	27	16	25	1
Mr Hadow	24	14	35	1	17	13	8	0
Mr Ford	10	4	13	1	6	1	11	1
Mr Webbe					1	0	1	0
Mr O'Brien					1	0	3	0

Yorkshire Bowling

	Overs	Mdns	Runs	Wkts	Overs	Mdns	Runs	Wkts
Peel	24	12	37	2	29	14	37	0
Wainwright	14	4	24	3	16	5	25	2
Wade	7	1	24	1	4.1	0	16	0
Preston	15.3	8	12	3	14	5	36	1
Mr Wilson					3	0	10	1
Ulyett					1	0	7	0

Umpires: Platts and Holmes.

YORKSHIRE v LANCASHIRE

Played at Huddersfield, July 18, 19, 1889

This was one of the most remarkable matches of the season, inasmuch as Yorkshire, having so far lost all their first-class county fixtures, looked to have no chance whatever at the start, and yet at the end of the first day seemed to have the game in hand. Then, in the second stage, they threw away their chances in the most extraordinary manner, and in the end were beaten by 3 runs. Both teams were strongly represented, though Barlow was still absent from the visitors' side, and the Fartown ground was exceedingly well attended when play commenced on the first day. Having won the toss, Mr Hornby went in with Mr Eccles to open the Lancashire batting, and Peel began the bowling, while Lord Hawke, rightly judging that the wicket would prove a bumpy one, put on Ulyett at the other end. As it happened, this pair of bowlers proved fully equal to the task set them, for, in the course of an hour and forty minutes, they dismissed the eleven for 81 runs. From the outset the batsmen could make no stand against the bowling, and half the wickets fell for 21 runs. Then Briggs came to the rescue of his county, and rapidly hit up 25, this plucky hitting improving the aspect of the innings to such an extent that the total was 60 before the ninth batsmen was out, while subsequently Watson hit out also, and in the end the innings closed for 81. Ulyett, who bumped the ball down at a great pace, took seven wickets for 50 runs, while Peel kept a good length from the other end, and secured the remaining wickets for 10 runs each. This innings had lasted until nearly luncheon time, and after the interval the home county began their batting to the bowling of Mold and Briggs. Mold bowled from the same end as Ulyett had done, and, like the Yorkshireman, he was eminently successful. Two or three of the batsmen, however, played in a very different style to that adopted by the Lancashire men, and Lee, Lord Hawke, and Moorhouse managed to score 114 out of the 160 runs put together by the side in a little over two hours and a half. Lee hit brilliantly, and made 42 out of 80 while he was batting. He went in first wicket down, with a single scored, and was fifth out at 81, his innings being made in fifteen hits by eight 4s, a 3, a 2, and five singles. Lord Hawke, who went in at the fall of the fourth wicket at 67, batted with great brilliancy, though he should have been caught at slip when he had scored 4. He was let off, however, and afterwards carried out his bat for the highest individual score in the match – 52. In this he made a fine square-leg-hit out of the ground for 6, nine 4s, three 2s and four singles. Yorkshire's total of 160 gave a lead of 79 runs on the first attempt, and, on Lancashire going in against this, they did so badly that before stumps were drawn they had lost four wickets for 22 runs. Ulyett bowled from his old end, and was even more difficult than before, for he dismissed the two amateurs and Frank Sugg and Albert Ward for 17 runs, while, in addition, he had Frank Ward badly missed in the slips from him before play closed for the day. Up to that time Ulyett had taken in the match eleven wickets for 58 runs.

Everything pointed to an easy triumph for Yorkshire when the second day's cricket commenced, as the visitors, with six wickets to fall, still wanted 57 runs to avert a single-innings defeat. The game, however, underwent a complete and extraordinary change. Frank Ward and Mold were the not-outs, but Mold was got rid of at 27, and Briggs came in. Ward was then missed by Wainwright in the slips from an easy catch, and, as it turned out, the blunder cost Yorkshire the match. Ward batted wretchedly, but he kept in while Briggs made runs in his usual dashing style. The pair nearly hit off the arrears before they were parted, and in all added 51 runs for the sixth wicket. This stand seemed to put heart into the remaining batsmen, and Baker, Paul and Watson all made runs, Yorkshire were eventually put in to get 75 to win. Mold and Watson were put on to bowl, and the former met with such success, and was backed up by such admirable fielding, that in the course of eight overs he dismissed Wade, Lee, Hall and Ulyett when only 9 runs had been scored. Peel made a stand, and though he lost Lord Hawke and Moorhouse at 24, he batted with great pluck and determination, and with Wainwright made a capital attempt to save the game. Unluckily he lost his wicket through slipping down when out of his ground, and was out at 38. Wainwright, after Peel left, hit well, and while he stayed at the wicket the hopes of the Yorkshiremen rose again, but he was at length caught from a miss-hit at 63, when, with two wickets in hand, 12 runs were wanted to win. Eight of these were obtained, but then both Whitehead and Middlebrook were dismissed, and the match ended in a victory for Lancashire by 3 runs. The victory was undoubtedly due to the batting of Briggs and the bowling of Mold, the latter's thirteen wickets costing only 111 runs.

Lancashire

Mr J. Eccles c Lee b Ulyett	0	– c Lee b Ulyett	5
Mr A. N. Hornby lbw b Peel	8	– c Wainwright c Ulyett	1
F. Sugg c Lee b Ulyett	1	– c Middlebrook b Ulyett	3
A. Ward b Peel	7	– c Hall b Ulyett	7
F. Ward c Hunter b Ulyett	4	– c Lee b Middlebrook	22
J. Briggs c Wainwright b Ulyett	25	– c Hunter b Middlebrook	41
A. Paul b Ulyett	4	– b Peel	16
G. R. Baker b Ulyett	5	– b Peel	29
A. Watson not out	16	– not out	16
A. Mold b Peel	4	– c Wade b Ulyett	5
R. Pilling c Hunter b Ulyett	6	– c Lee b Peel	2
L-b 1	1	B 6	6
	81		153

Yorkshire

L. Hall b Mold	1	– b Mold	2
S. Wade c Baker b Mold	7	– b Mold	3
F. Lee c Baker b mold	42	– c Pilling b Mold	0
R. Peel c and b Briggs	14	– run out	18
G. Ulyett b Watson	7	– b Mold	2
Lord Hawke not out	52	– b Watson	3
H. Moorhouse c Watson b Mold	20	– b Watson	0
E. Wainwright b Mold	0	– c F. Ward b Mold	27
L. Whitehead b Mold	12	– b Mold	5
D. Hunter lbw b Briggs	3	– not out	7
W. Middlebrook c Pilling b Briggs	0	– c Hornby b Mold	0
B 2	2	B 4	4
	160		71

Yorkshire Bowling

	Overs	Mdns	Runs	Wkts	Overs	Mdns	Runs	Wkts
Peel	22	7	30	3	29.2	4	55	2
Ulyett	21.2	9	50	7	23	9	52	5
Middlebrook					11	2	25	2
Wainwright					5	1	15	0

Lancashire Bowling

	Overs	Mdns	Runs	Wkts	Overs	Mdns	Runs	Wkts
Mold	35	16	76	6	25.4	14	35	7
Watson	9	4	24	1	25	17	32	2
Briggs	26	7	58	3				

Umpires: Holmes and Panter.

YORKSHIRE v KENT

Played at York, June 9, 10, 1890

Owing to the non-arrival of three of the Kent team in sufficient time to take their innings, the chances of the Southern eleven were severely prejudiced, and in a terribly bad light the seven wickets were got down by Peel and Ulyett in an hour for 46. The ground also favoured the bowlers, and Yorkshire, although they gained a useful lead, found run-getting very difficult against Martin and Wright. Kent in their second innings lost three wickets for 70, and in the course of the day twenty wickets went down for 230 runs. On the second day Kent set the Yorkshiremen 100 runs to get to win, and, though Ulyett and Lee were dismissed by the time the score was up to 35, Lord Hawke and Hall hit off the remainder without further loss, Yorkshire winning by eight wickets. Up to this point of the season Yorkshire were the only team that had not lost a first-class county match. It is worthy of note that in the three victories the eleven had obtained, Yorkshire had always had to play the last innings, and that in each instance Hall had been at the wickets when the success was actually achieved.

Kent

G. G. Hearne b Ulyett	0	– c Hunter b Wainwright	22
A. Hearne b Peel	14	– b Peel	39
Mr C. J. M. Fox b Peel	1	– c Hawke b Ulyett	6
Mr F. Marchant c Whitehead b Ulyett	3	– b Peel	11
Mr L. Wilson b Peel	10	– b Peel	20
J. Pentecost c Brown b Ulyett	6	– b Ulyett	1
W. Wright not out	2	– c Hunter b Peel	3
F. Martin c and b Peel	0	– c Whitehead b Wainwright	1
W. Hearne absent	0	– b Peel	12
Mr S. Christopherson absent	0	– not out	3
Mr W. H. Spottiswoode absent	0	– b Wainwright	37
B 10	10	B 12	12
	46		167

Yorkshire

L. Hall c A. Hearne b Martin	5	– not out	33
G. Ulyett b Wright	29	– b Wright	15
F. Lee c Marchant b Wright	4	– b Wright	12
Lord Hawke c A. Hearne b Martin	10	– not out	28
R. Peel c A. Hearne b Wright	24		
E. Wainwright c A. Hearne b Martin	2		
J. T. Brown b Martin	2		
R. Moorhouse b Martin	9		
Mr W. F. Whitwell c and b Martin	0		
L. Whitehead b Wright	14		
D. Hunter not out	5		
B 10	10	B 12	12
	114		100

Yorkshire Bowling

	Overs	Mdns	Runs	Wkts	Overs	Mdns	Runs	Wkts
Peel	14.4	5	21	4	34	20	27	5
Ulyett	14	8	15	3	26	11	68	2
Mr Whitwell					11	5	13	0
Wainwright					16.2	7	30	3
Whitehead					8	4	11	0
Brown					2	0	6	0

Kent Bowling

	Overs	Mdns	Runs	Wkts	Overs	Mdns	Runs	Wkts
Wright	34	12	56	4	17	4	31	2
Martin	33	16	48	6	12	2	30	0
Mr Christopherson .					5	1	27	0

Umpires: G. Panter and J. Lillywhite.

YORKSHIRE v LANCASHIRE

Played at Huddersfield, July 17, 18, 19, 1890

Mold's fast bowling proved far too good for the Yorkshiremen in this match, and thanks mainly to the efforts of the professional, who took thirteen wickets in the match for 76 runs – nine of them in the first innings for 41 runs – Lancashire gained a single innings victory with 28 runs to spare. No play at all was possible on the opening day, but on the Friday, on a bumpy wicket, the Yorkshiremen were dismissed in two hours and ten minutes for 90, Mold sending down his last eight overs and a ball for 13 runs and 8 wickets. Ulyett's admirable innings was the one noteworthy feature in the Yorkshire batting. The Lancashire innings lasted no longer than that of Yorkshire, but so much more effective was the batting that a lead of 85 runs was obtained. There were six wickets down for 63, but Baker and Mr Kemble put on 52, both batsmen hitting very hard. Rain prevented any more cricket that day, but Yorkshire's second innings, against Mold and Watson, proved even more disastrous than the first. It is worthy of remark that not one of the last seven Yorkshire batsmen made double figures in either innings.

Yorkshire

G. Ulyett b Mold	45	– c Hornby b Watson	13
L. Hall c Barlow b Mold	5	– c Watson b Mold	23
H. Tinsley b Watson	0	– c Mold b Watson	0
Mr E. Smith b Mold	16	– c Paul b Watson	5
R. Peel c Sugg b Mold	6	– c Sugg b Mold	4
Mr F. S. Jackson b Mold	2	– c Baker b Watson	0
Mr A. Sellars b Mold	6	– c and b Mold	2
E. Wainwright c Kemble b Mold	0	– run out	4
R. Moorhouse not out	8	– c and b Watson	1
J. T. Brown c Sugg b Mold	0	– not out	2
D. Hunter c Barlow b Mold	0	– c Barlow b Mold	0
B 2	2	B 1, l-b 2	3
	90		57

Lancashire

F. H. Sugg c Hunter b Peel	30
R. G. Barlow c Sellars b Jackson	3
A. Ward c Hunter b Peel	11
A. Paul b Peel	0
G. Yates c Hunter b Jackson	7
G. R. Baker c and b Smith	51
Mr A. N. Hornby lbw b Peel	1
Mr A. T. Kemble c and b Peel	35
Hewitson st Hunter b Peel	8
A. Watson b Smith	15
A. Mold not out	0
B 11, l-b 2, n-b 1	14
	175

Lancashire Bowling

	Overs	Mdns	Runs	Wkts	Overs	Mdns	Runs	Wkts
Watson	32	15	47	1	28	16	19	5
Mold	31.1	19	41	9	27.1	14	35	4

Yorkshire Bowling

	Overs	Mdns	Runs	Wkts
Peel	24	12	43	6
Ulyett	6	0	33	0
Mr Jackson	12	1	50	2
Mr Smith	5.4	3	13	2
Tinsley	3	1	16	0
Wainwright	3	1	6	0

Umpires: G. Henty and J. Platts.

YORKSHIRE v GLOUCESTERSHIRE

Played at Dewsbury, July 28, 29, 30, 1890

This was one of the most interesting matches of the whole season, the Gloucestershire eleven, after they had apparently lost the game on the opening day, playing up so finely that on the Wednesday their efforts were rewarded with a victory by 84 runs. At the end of the previous week rain had presumably robbed the western county team of a victory over Lancashire, and the visitors thus appeared to have an excellent prospect of holding their own with Yorkshire. On the opening day, however, Gloucestershire, on a wicket which although hard enabled the bowlers to get some work on the ball, were all dismissed in two hours for the wretched total of 72. The chief element in this cheap dismissal of the Gloucestershire batsmen was the bowling of Peel, who, making the ball break back a little at a good pace, succeeded in taking seven wickets at the exceptionally low cost of 27 runs. Mr Bolton, the Hull amateur, had the distinction of dismissing both Mr W. G. Grace and Mr Cranston, the two batsmen who later on completely altered the aspect of the match. When Yorkshire went in to bat Peel again carried off the honours, hitting most brilliantly for 51, an innings which lasted only fifty-five minutes. Hall was batting two hours, making half his runs in the first thirty minutes. In direct contrast to the Gloucestershire batsmen, nine of the Yorkshiremen reached double figures, the last wicket falling shortly before time for 209, a score which gave the home side an advantage of 137 runs. Next morning Gloucestershire, on commencing their second innings, lost Mr Radcliffe, Mr E. M. Grace, and Mr Pullen by the time the score reached 19. At this point, the visitors, with three good wickets down, were still 118 runs behind, and everything pointed to an easy victory for the home side. On Mr Cranston joining Mr W. G. Grace, however, some grand batting was witnessed. The two Gloucestershire amateurs both hit with power and freedom, and though numerous changes of bowlers were tried, 50 runs were made in three-quarters of an hour and 100 in eighty-five minutes. At one time 120 runs were scored in sixty-five minutes, and though the pace slackened afterwards the batsmen were still together at lunch time with the total at 174. Afterwards the score was hit up to 207, when Mr Grace, wanting only two for his hundred, was out on an appeal for lbw. He and Mr Cranston had put on 188 runs in two hours and twenty minutes, and what rendered their performance almost phenomenal was the fact that neither batsman gave any chance. Mr Grace made his splendid 98 in two hours and forty minutes by means of fifteen 4s, three 3s, six 2s, and singles, hitting at times with all the freedom of youth. With Painter in, Mr Cranston completed his hundred in two hours and a half, and was not dismissed until the total reached 302. The famous left-hander played perfect cricket for nearly three hours and a half, and in his score of 152 – the highest he had ever made in a first-class match – were twenty 4s, four 3s, and seventeen 2s. It is worthy of note that in each of the Gloucestershire matches with Yorkshire, Mr Cranston should have played an innings of over a hundred. Gloucestershire were all out for 341, Yorkshire being set 205 to get to win. Mr Smith played dashing cricket, but despite his efforts there were four men out at the call of time for 65, Yorkshire then being left with 140 runs to get and having six wickets to fall. This task proved far too severe for the remaining Yorkshire batsmen on the Wednesday morning, the six outstanding wickets in the second innings only carrying the score from 65 to 120. Woof bowled very finely, taking six wickets for only 27 runs, and at no time did the home side look like getting the number they required; indeed the match was finished off in sixty-five minutes. The result was, of course, disappointing to the Yorkshire spectators, but it would be hardly possible to overpraise the victory of the Gloucestershire team, who, after being 137 runs behind on the first innings, lost three more wickets for 19 runs, and then gained a decisive triumph.

Gloucestershire

Mr W. G. Grace c Hunter b Bolton	5	– lbw b Peel	98
Mr E. M. Grace c sub. b Peel	0	– c Hall b Bolton	1
Mr W. W. F. Pullen c Bolton b Peel	7	– c Peel b Bolton	1
Mr O. G. Radcliffe b Peel	3	– c Wainwright b Bolton	3
Mr J. Cranston c Ulyett b Bolton	11	– c Hill b Smith	152
J. Painter b Bolton	0	– b Smith	17
Mr F. Townsend b Peel	9	– b Smith	9
Mr C. F. Belcher st Hunter b Peel	19	– b Peel	18
W. A. Woof b Peel	2	– c Hill b Smith	13
F. G. Roberts st Hunter b Peel	12	– not out	6
Mr J. A. Bush not out	1	– c Moorhouse b Bolton	5
L-b 3	3	B 14, l-b 4	18
	72		341

Yorkshire

G. Ulyett b Roberts	19	– c and b Woof	7
L. Hall st Bush b Woof	49	– b Woof	22
Mr E. Smith b Radcliffe	10	– c Bush b W. G. Grace	33
R. Peel c Pullen b W. G. Grace	51	– b Roberts	9
R. Moorhouse c Pullen b W. G. Grace	11	– c Painter b W. G. Grace	4
E. Wainwright c W. G. Grace b Roberts	19	– b Woof	1
Mr H. Hill run out	10	– b Roberts	0
J. T. Brown c Painter b W. G. Grace	2	– lbw b Woof	22
L. Whitehead c and b W. G. Grace	12	– not out	7
Mr B. C. Bolton c Bush b Roberts	6	– c Belcher b Woof	11
D. Hunter not out	13	– b Woof	0
B 6, n-b 1	7	L-b 4	4
	209		120

Yorkshire Bowling

	Overs	Mdns	Runs	Wkts	Overs	Mdns	Runs	Wkts
Mr Bolton	29	14	42	3	27.2	13	63	4
Peel	29.2	18	27	7	50	20	76	2
Wainwright	1	1	0	0	14	4	40	0
Whitehead					16	5	38	0
Mr Smith					18	3	66	4
Ulyett					6	0	34	0
Brown					3	2	6	0

Gloucestershire Bowling

	Overs	Mdns	Runs	Wkts	Overs	Mdns	Runs	Wkts
Roberts	22.1	13	43	3	20	7	60	2
Woof	24	13	42	1	27	17	27	6
Mr W. G. Grace	23	3	74	4	7	1	29	2
Mr Radcliffe	8	3	12	1				
Mr Townsend	2	0	18	0				
Mr Belcher	3	0	13	0				

Umpires: G. Panter and R. Humphrey.

YORKSHIRE v STAFFORDSHIRE

Played at Sheffield, August 4, 5, 1890

An achievement on the part of Wainwright, who succeeded in taking all ten Staffordshire wickets at a cost of only 31 runs, was the feature of the opening day's cricket in this return match. Six of the batsmen were bowled, three caught, and one was leg before. Yorkshire batted first, and, though three wickets were down for 45, a total of 268 was reached. Tinsley played excellent cricket for 96, in which were a 6, fifteen 4s, two 3s, and nine 2s, and after nine wickets had fallen, Hunter assisted Peel to put on no fewer than 92 runs before the innings had closed. Ulyett and Peel went in respectively eighth and ninth. Staffordshire were dismissed in an hour and thirty-five minutes, and next day they were not much more successful. The ten wickets were got down in an hour and fifty minutes for 88, Yorkshire being left with a victory by an innings and 113 runs. Brown and Tinsley both bowled with considerable success.

Yorkshire

Batsman	Runs
L. Hall c Burroughs b Brown	5
R. Moorhouse c Burrows b Alcock	8
J. Redfearn hit wkt b Brown	19
H. Tinsley c Durban b Brown	96
Mr J. Mounsey b Crutchley	5
J. T. Brown lbw b Brown	30
E. Wainwright lbw b Alcock	2
G. Ulyett c sub. b Alcock	1
R. Peel not out	41
L. Whitehead b Brown	1
D. Hunter b Brown	52
B 4, l-b 4	8
	268

Staffordshire

Batsman	First innings		Second innings	
Burrows	b Wainwright	25	b Wainwright	0
Durban	c Whitehead b Wainwright	2	c Wainwright b Whitehead	1
Marlow	b Wainwright	15	st Hunter b Tinsley	26
Mr H. Vaughton	b Wainwright	3	st Hunter b Brown	15
Mr E. R. Coe	b Wainwright	0	st Hunter b Brown	1
Mr W. Calkin	c Hunter b Wainwright	0	b Brown	6
Mr C. H. Alcock	b Wainwright	0	c Moorhouse b Brown	4
Brown	not out	3	b Tinsley	3
Hawkins	c Mounsey b Wainwright	5	b Tinsley	13
Johnson	lbw b Wainwright	10	not out	0
Crutchley	b Wainwright	0	b Tinsley	4
	B 4	4	B 12, l-b 2, n-b 1	15
		67		88

Staffordshire Bowling

	Overs	Mdns	Runs	Wkts
Brown	35.2	14	87	6
Alcock	23	5	65	3
Mr Calkin	17	4	36	0
Marlow	7	1	25	0
Crutchley	10	3	34	1
Johnson	2	0	13	0

Yorkshire Bowling

	Overs	Mdns	Runs	Wkts	Overs	Mdns	Runs	Wkts
Wainwright	22.4	6	31	10	12	5	18	1
Whitehead	9	3	17	0	11	5	18	1
Peel	11	9	5	0				
Tinsley	2	1	10	0	14	6	19	4
Brown					14	4	18	4

Umpires: Reaney and Downing.

YORKSHIRE v SURREY

Played at Leeds, June 20, 21, 22, 1892

Up to the day of this match at Headingley, Yorkshire had won nine matches off the reel, and notwithstanding the formidable team opposed to them it may fairly be said that the prospects of the Northern County holding their own with Surrey had not been so favourable for several years. Naturally the contest was looked forward to with immense interest, but, much to the disappointment of thousands of people, the weather was so wet on the Monday that the start of the game had to be deferred until the following day. Lord Hawke was too unwell to lead the home team, and his place was given to Hayley, a local cricketer of considerable reputation. A day's play lost through rain very often robs a game of nearly all interest, but this was far from being the case in the match under notice, for on the Tuesday a crowd, estimated at fully 15,000, visited the Headingley ground. After so much rain the wicket was of course terribly soft, and though rather wet at starting it became exceptionally difficult as the day wore on. Under these circumstances winning the toss was naturally a great advantage, and the spin of the coin went in favour of the Surrey captain. Accordingly Surrey went in to bat, but so finely did Peel bowl on the soft wicket that half the side were out for 62 runs. So far there was little reason to expect that Surrey would reap an advantage from their luck in going in first, but Henderson proved a valuable partner to Maurice Read, the latter forcing the game in brilliant style, a thing which he can perhaps do on a soft wicket as well as anybody in England. Altogether these batsmen put on 42 runs, Read's 45 being the highest innings of the match. Later on, however, Key and Brockwell made a very useful stand for the eighth wicket, adding no fewer than 44 runs before they were separated. In the end the total reached 151, the last five wickets having put on 89 runs. Peel bowled with exceptional skill, getting rid of seven batsmen at a cost of 43 runs, but unfortunately for Yorkshire Wainwright for once was both expensive and ineffective. Yorkshire, on going in to bat, were all dismissed in two hours for 87, or 64 runs to the bad. They never looked like reaching the Surrey total; indeed, for a while there seemed small prospect of the score amounting to as many as it did. So destructive was Lohmann that half the wickets were down for 30. Moorhouse and Tunnicliffe, however, hit away pluckily, adding 31 runs, and Hayley showed very fair form. But for these players Yorkshire would undoubtedly have had to follow no, but as it was they had little chance after finishing 64 runs behind on the first innings. Lohmann obtained six wickets for 37 runs, and Abel, going on late in the innings, actually dismissed three batsmen for 3 runs. With half an hour left for play, Surrey entered upon their second innings, but could make so little of the bowling of Wainwright and Peel that at the drawing of stumps three of the best wickets were down for 20, the visitors at the close being 84 runs ahead with seven wickets to fall. There was a sensational finish on the Wednesday, for, owing to more rain during the night, the game could not be proceeded with until after the luncheon interval. Then Surrey lost two more wickets for the addition of eight runs, but Shuter being favoured with some luck, he and Henderson added 39 runs, the latter coming off in each innings. With seven men out for 81, Shuter, running a slight risk of being beaten in order not to miss a victory, declared the innings at an end. Yorkshire were set 146 runs to get to win, whilst to save the game they had to keep up their wickets for two hours and five minutes. With the ground so difficult it would have been an extraordinary performance for the runs to have been obtained against such first-class bowling, whilst it would also have been a highly creditable achievement to have stayed in for two hours on the treacherous wicket. For a time Surrey looked like winning easily, four of Yorkshire's best wickets going down for 21 runs. Moorhouse, however, stayed, whilst, thanks to the capital batting of Wainwright, the score was taken up to 51, and then 23 more runs were put on before Wainwright's finely hit innings of 44 was brought to a close by a clever running catch. Even now Surrey looked to have the match well in hand, for with three-quarters of an hour left for cricket they had got down six of the Yorkshire wickets. Hayley and Tunnicliffe, however, offered a stubborn resistance, and raised the total to 97, and subsequently Hayley and Fletcher kept together until within ten minutes of time. The last man came in with five minutes left for play, and then Fletcher was dismissed, and a most exciting struggle ended in favour of Surrey by seventeen runs. Lohmann again bowled very finely, and for the whole match had the splendid record of fourteen wickets for 107 runs. This, it may be mentioned, was the first reverse which Yorkshire sustained in a county match during the season, and certainly the defeat carried with it no disgrace.

Surrey

R. Abel c Hunter b Peel	11	– c Hirst b Wainwright	4
Mr W. W. Read c and b Peel	20	– b Wainwright	5
G. A. Lohmann b Wainwright	1	– c Hayley b Hirst	2
M. Read b Hirst	45	– b Hirst	0
Mr J. Shuter c Fletcher b Peel	6	– b Wainwright	27
W. Lockwood c Sellers b Peel	6	– not out	7
R. Henderson b Mounsey	14	– b Wainwright	21
Mr K. J. Key c Ulyett b Peel	30	– b Peel	3
W. Brockwell c Ulyett b Peel	13	– not out	6
J. W. Sharpe not out	0		
Mr A. F. Clarke c Ulyett b Peel	0		
B 5	5	B 6	6
	151	(7 wkts dec.)	81

Yorkshire

G. Ulyett b Lohmann	0	– c Lockwood b Lohmann	7
J. Mounsey c Lohmann b Lockwood	14	– c Sharpe b Lohmann	6
R. Peel st Clarke b Lohmann	5	– b Lohmann	0
Mr A. Sellers st Clarke b Lohmann	2	– lbw b Lohmann	0
E. Wainwright c and b Lohmann	2	– c M. Read b Lohmann	44
R. Moorhouse b Lohmann	26	– c Sharpe b Lohmann	5
J. Tunnicliffe c Brockwell b Abel	10	– b Lockwood	23
H. Hayley b Abel	17	– b Lohmann	24
A. Fletcher b Lohmann	0	– c Shuter b Sharpe	12
G. H. Hirst b Abel	2	– lbw b Lohmann	4
D. Hunter not out	0	– not out	0
B 8, l-b 1	9	B 2, l-b 1	3
	87		128

Yorkshire Bowling

	Overs	Mdns	Runs	Wkts	Overs	Mdns	Runs	Wkts
Peel	33.3	14	43	7	22	8	31	1
Wainwright	25	7	71	1	22	5	27	4
Hirst	14	7	17	1	11	6	17	2
Mounsey	9	2	15	1				

Surrey Bowling

	Overs	Mdns	Runs	Wkts	Overs	Mdns	Runs	Wkts
Lohmann	21	4	37	6	24	5	70	8
Lockwood	16	6	25	1	9	4	16	1
Sharpe	5	2	13	0	13.2	5	29	1
Abel	3.1	2	3	3	2	0	10	0

Umpires: T. Foster and F. Silcock.

YORKSHIRE v SUSSEX

Played at Dewsbury, June 7, 8, 1894

At this period of the season the weather was far too wet for cricket, and match after match was either ruined or largely affected by the condition of the ground. Yorkshire practically won the game on the opening day, when they batted first, on a very treacherous wicket. Hawke and Jackson made 33 before they were separated. Seven wickets were down for 57, both Alfred Shaw and Parris bowling with marked effect, Yorkshire eventually put together a highly creditable total, and Wainwright and Peel then dismissed Sussex in an hour and twenty minutes for 55, the visitors only just escaping a follow on. Before the drawing of stumps Yorkshire scored 57 for four wickets, and next morning Sussex were set 218 to win. Again the Sussex batsmen were almost powerless against Wainwright and Peel, and the home team gained an easy victory by 166 runs. Wainwright finished the match in a most sensational way, taking the last five wickets in seven balls. He did the "hat trick", and in all obtained thirteen wickets at the marvellously small cost of 38 runs.

Yorkshire

Lord Hawke c Killick b Parris	18	– lbw b Shaw	0
Mr F. S. Jackson c Murdoch b Shaw	22	– b Killick	10
J. Tunnicliffe c Lowe b Shaw	5	– b Killick	0
Mr A. Sellers b Parris	3	– run out	41
J. T. Brown b Shaw	0	– b Parris	23
R. Peel st Butt b Parris	0	– b Shaw	5
J. Mounsey b Parris	14	– c Butt b Lowe	21
E. Wainwright b Shaw	6	– b Lowe	13
R. Moorhouse not out	25	– not out	10
G. H. Hirst b Shaw	24	– c Butt b Lowe	0
D. Hunter b Killick	7	– b Shaw	8
B 7, l-b 2	9	B 6, l-b 2	8
	133		139

Sussex

G. Bean c Jackson b Wainwright	14	– b Wainwright	19
Mr G. H. Arlington b Wainwright	3	– st Hunter b Wainwright	9
Mr W. L. Murdoch b Peel	7	– b Peel	6
Mr W. Newham st Hunter b Peel	9	– c Jackson b Peel	0
Mr C. A. Smith b Peel	0	– b Peel	8
F. Guttridge b Wainwright	3	– b Wainwright	1
F. Parris b Wainwright	3	– c and b Wainwright	7
Killick b Wainwright	4	– b Wainwright	0
H. Butt c Tunnicliffe b Peel	0	– b Wainwright	0
J. Lowe not out	5	– not out	0
A. Shaw c and b Wainwright	0	– b Wainwright	0
B 5, l-b 2	7	B 1	1
	55		51

Sussex Bowling

	Overs	Mdns	Runs	Wkts	Overs	Mdns	Runs	Wkts
Shaw	43	20	58	5	49	19	54	3
Parris	36	11	57	4	11	3	20	1
Lowe	6	3	9	0	11	5	12	3
Killick	0.3	0	0	1	26	8	45	2

Yorkshire Bowling

	Overs	Mdns	Runs	Wkts	Overs	Mdns	Runs	Wkts
Wainwright	16	9	18	6	15.2	8	20	7
Peel	16	4	30	4	15	2	30	3

Umpires: F. Coward and Clements.

YORKSHIRE v SOMERSET

Played at Leeds, July 22, 23, 1895

Heavy rain had fallen on the three previous days, and the ground was so soft and difficult that on the opening day twenty-one wickets went down for 176 runs. With the exception of Tunnicliffe the Yorkshiremen failed badly before the bowling of Hedley, who, making his first appearance during the season, dismissed after lunch six batsmen for 9 runs. Somerset, facing a total of 73, were only 27 behind when the third wicket fell; but Peel then bowled magnificently, taking in all nine wickets for 22 runs. Yorkshire on the second day ran up a fine score, the chief honours being borne off by Denton, who was seen to exceptional advantage. Hedley again bowled with great effect, and had a record of fourteen wickets for 70 runs. Peel did even better, taking fifteen wickets in the match for 50, and it was largely due to him that Yorkshire won by 103 runs.

Yorkshire

Mr F. S. Jackson c Wood b Hedley	12	– b Hedley	21
Mr F. Mitchell b Tyler	2	– c Wood b Tyler	26
J. Tunnicliffe c Hill b Hedley	32	– c Hill b Tyler	1
J. T. Brown c Palairet b Hedley	3	– c sub. b Tyler	1
D. Denton c Hedley b Tyler	3	– c Palairet b Tyler	60
R. Peel c Palairet b Hedley	3	– b Hedley	5
E. Wainwright lbw b Hedley	0	– c Porch b Hedley	8
R. Moorhouse not out	4	– not out	15
Lord Hawke b Hedley	1	– b Hedley	8
G. H. Hirst c Compton b Hedley	9	– b Hedley	3
Wood b Hedley	0	– c Woods b Hedley	2
B 4	4	B 7, l-b 6	13
	73		163

Somerset

Mr S. M. J. Woods c Wainwright b Peel	3	– b Peel	5
Mr V. T. Hill b Peel	20	– st Wood b Peel	16
Mr R. C. N. Palairet lbw b Peel	5	– c Hawke b Peel	2
Mr G. Fowler b Hirst	15	– c and b Peel	11
Mr R. B. Porch c Hirst b Peel	3	– b Jackson	4
Mr W. C. Hedley c Moorhouse b Peel	0	– b Jackson	7
Mr J. E. Trask b Peel	8	– b Peel	8
Mr E. D. Compton c Brown b Peel	0	– not out	2
G. B. Nichols b Peel	7	– b Jackson	0
Westcott not out	4	– b Jackson	0
E. J. Tyler b Peel	1	– b Peel	6
B 2, l-b 1	3	B 3	3
	69		64

Somerset Bowling

	Overs	Mdns	Runs	Wkts	Overs	Mdns	Runs	Wkts
Tyler	22	4	51	2	22	2	66	4
Hedley	21.4	13	18	8	26.3	9	52	6
Woods					6	2	21	0
Nichols					2	0	11	0

Yorkshire Bowling

	Overs	Mdns	Runs	Wkts	Overs	Mdns	Runs	Wkts
Peel	21.3	10	22	9	15	5	28	6
Wainwright	11	3	26	0	9	3	20	0
Hirst	10	4	18	1				
Jackson					6	0	13	4

Umpires: Collishaw and Lowe.

YORKSHIRE v AN ENGLAND ELEVEN

Played at Scarborough, September 5, 6, 1895

It had been intended that the concluding fixture of the Scarborough Festival should be between elevens of Yorkshire and Lancashire, but the first match at Hastings, by taking some of the Lancashire men away, rendered the arrangement impossible. As an alternative an England team was got together to oppose Yorkshire, and though by no means representative it proved quite strong enough for the task in hand, the county suffering a severe defeat by nine wickets. A very disagreeable incident marred the pleasure of a game that presented few features of interest. Owing to the state of the ground a start could not be made at the ordinary time on the first day, and a section of the crowd indulged in a most unseemly demonstration, such insulting remarks being addressed to Mr H. T. Hewett that that gentleman – who was to have captained the England team – retired from the match after fielding till the luncheon interval. We think he acted unwisely, but he was much provoked.

Yorkshire

Mr F. S. Jackson lbw b Mead	9	– b Spofforth	8
J. T. Brown b Mead	1	– c Mead b Spofforth	6
J. W. Tunnicliffe c Jones b Hearne	35	– c Tyler b Mead	3
R. Moorhouse b Hearne	8	– b Mead	9
E. Wainwright c and b Mead	6	– c Spofforth b Mead	0
R. Peel b Hearne	1	– c Woodcock b Spofforth	0
Lord Hawke c Tyler b Mead	5	– c and b Mead	4
J. Mounsey run out	0	– b Mead	13
G. H. Hirst b Mead	4	– c Baker b Mead	9
Haigh c MacLaren b Hearne	0	– c Tyler b Spofforth	18
D. Hunter not out	0	– not out	7
B 11	11	B 4, l-b 1	5
	80		82

An England Eleven

Mr A. C. MacLaren c and b Haigh	24		
Mr A. O. Jones c Tunnicliffe b Peel	2	– not out	32
A. Hearne c Peel b Jackson	44		
W. G. Quaife c and b Jackson	19	– not out	6
Mr G. L. Jessop st Hunter b Jackson	4		
G. R. Baker c Tunnicliffe b Jackson	0	– run out	5
Mr F. R. Spofforth c Tunnicliffe b Jackson	1		
W. Mead c Hunter b Wainwright	10		
E. J. Tyler c Mounsey b Jackson	1		
Woodcock c Tunnicliffe b Wainwright	0		
J. H. Board not out	3		
B 13	13	B 1, l-b 1	2
	121		45

An England Eleven Bowling

	Overs	Mdns	Runs	Wkts	Overs	Mdns	Runs	Wkts
Mead	15.3	3	29	5	16	1	38	6
Tyler	10	0	12	0				
Hearne	13	2	28	4				
Spofforth					17	5	39	4

Yorkshire Bowling

	Overs	Mdns	Runs	Wkts	Overs	Mdns	Runs	Wkts
Peel	10	2	21	1				
Haigh	5	0	29	1	3	0	15	0
Jackson	18.1	9	24	6	6.2	2	20	0
Wainwright	15	3	34	2	3	1	3	0

Umpires: Ulyett and Whatmough.

YORKSHIRE v ESSEX

Played at Bradford, June 11, 12, 1896

After the rain which had interfered so materially with the Surrey match, the ground at Bradford was very difficult, and on the opening day twenty-seven wickets went down for 237 runs. Yorkshire had nothing like their full strength – Jackson, Peel, Moorhouse, and Hunter being all away, and except for a fine piece of hitting by Tunnicliffe, the northern batsmen could do nothing with the bowling of the Essex amateur, F. G. Bull. At the start of the Essex second innings, Wainwright proved so destructive that six wickets fell for 20 runs, and there were seven men out for 48 at the close of the day. Yorkshire had only 85 to get to win, but considerable anxiety was felt as to the result. Fortunately for the home side Tunnicliffe again hit in rare form, and Yorkshire in the end won with seven wickets to spare. The credit of the win belonged almost entirely to Tunnicliffe and Wainwright – the former scoring 102 runs for once out, and the latter taking 14 wickets for 77 runs.

Essex

H. Carpenter b Shaw	3	– b Wainwright	0
Mr C. G. Littlehales b Shaw	2	– c Earnshaw b Shaw	1
Mr P. Perrin lbw b Wainwright	40	– b Wainwright	0
Mr C. McGahey c Denton b Hirst	12	– b Wainwright	2
Mr H. G. Owen b Wainwright	7	– b Wainwright	0
Mr C. J. Kortright c Hirst b Milligan	17	– run out	17
Mr J. W. Bonner b Wainwright	1	– c Shaw b Wainwright	9
T. M. Russell c and b Wainwright	5	– b Wainwright	18
Mr F. G. Bull c Hirst b Wainwright	1	– b Wainwright	2
W. Mead c Denton b Wainwright	14	– lbw b Wainwright	2
H. Pickett not out	1	– not out	3
B 5, l-b 1	6	L-b 1	1
	109		55

Yorkshire

J. T. Brown b Bull	11	– st Russell b Mead	10
J. Tunnicliffe c Owen b Bull	47	– not out	55
D. Denton b Bull	0	– b Mead	6
Lord Hawke c and b Bull	1	– c and b Bull	12
E. Wainwright c Russell b Bull	0	– not out	1
G. H. Hirst c Perrin b Mead	9		
Kilburn b Mead	8		
Mr F. W. Milligan b Bull	0		
J. Mounsey b Bull	0		
Shaw b Bull	1		
W. Earnshaw not out	1		
B 1, l-b 1	2	B 1	1
	80		85

Yorkshire Bowling

	Overs	Mdns	Runs	Wkts	Overs	Mdns	Runs	Wkts
Wainwright	30.1	11	43	6	15	4	34	8
Shaw	34	15	42	2	14	7	20	1
Hirst	7	4	6	1				
Milligan	3	1	12	1				

Essex Bowling

	Overs	Mdns	Runs	Wkts	Overs	Mdns	Runs	Wkts
Mead	16	3	34	2	10	2	42	2
Bull	15.4	4	44	8	9	1	28	1
Kortright					2	0	14	0

Umpires: Young and M. Sherwin.

YORKSHIRE v SURREY

Played at Leeds, June 21, 22, 23, 1897

Immense interest was taken in this contest all over the country, and while over 20,000 people were present on the opening day, the attendance amounted to 30,000 on the Tuesday. This was the largest company ever seen at a cricket match in Yorkshire, the Leeds people celebrating the Queen's Jubilee by attending the match. A splendid struggle took place at a certain point, but Yorkshire batted so well in the second innings, that they set Surrey 272 to get to win, and on the third day, won the match by exactly a hundred runs. Richardson and Haigh for their respective sides, bowled wonderfully well on Monday, when not only was an innings completed on each side, but Yorkshire going in again, gained the upper hand in scoring 70 runs for one wicket.

Yorkshire

Mr F. S. Jackson c Abel b Richardson	0	– c and b Hayward	92
J. Tunnicliffe b Hayward	4	– b Richardson	20
J. T. Browne c Lees b Richardson	11	– b Hayward	22
D. Denton b Richardson	22	– c and b Richardson	77
Mr E. Smith c Brockwell b Richardson	15	– c Hayward b Richardson	2
R. Moorhouse b Richardson	5	– b Richardson	1
E. Wainwright c Richardson b Hayward	6	– b Richardson	21
G. H. Hirst c Brockwell b Hayward	14	– b Richardson	5
R. Peel b Richardson	10	– b Richardson	1
S. Haigh not out	0	– b Richardson	3
D. Hunter b Richardson	0	– not out	1
L-b 1, n-b 2	3	B 6, l-b 1, w 1, n-b 3	11
	90		256

Surrey

	First innings		Second innings	
R. Abel b Wainwright	8	– c and b Wainwright	17
W. Brockwell b Wainwright	2	– c Haigh b Wainwright	12
T. Hayward b Haigh	16	– b Haigh	9
C. Baldwin b Haigh	4	– b Hirst	17
Mr H. D. G. Leveson-Gower b Haigh	9	– c Tunnicliffe b Peel	6
Mr H. B. Chinnery b Haigh	0	– b Wainwright	11
Mr W. W. Read not out	24	– b Wainwright	29
Mr K. J. Key b Haigh	0	– b Hirst	1
W. Lees b Haigh	8	– c Hunter b Hiagh	44
H. Wood b Haigh	0	– c Haigh b Peel	6
T. Richardson b Hirst	3	– not out	4
L-b 1	1	B 13, l-b 1, w 1	15
	75		171

Surrey Bowling

	Overs	Mdns	Runs	Wkts	Overs	Mdns	Runs	Wkts
Richardson	21.3	5	55	7	42	13	99	8
Hayward	21	9	32	3	31	8	57	2
Lees					11	3	32	0
Brockwell					12	4	30	0
Chinnery					4	0	18	0
Abel					5	1	9	0

Yorkshire Bowling

	Overs	Mdns	Runs	Wkts	Overs	Mdns	Runs	Wkts
Peel	10	6	13	0	13.2	2	26	2
Wainwright	10	6	44	2	22	10	43	4
Haigh	12	5	17	7	23	3	56	2
Hirst	2.2	2	0	1	17	7	26	2
Jackson					4	3	5	0

Umpires: G. Hay and R. G. Barlow.

YORKSHIRE v SUSSEX

Played at Sheffield, July 12, 13, 14, 1897

This was the memorable match in which Brown and Tunnicliffe established a new record for the first wicket, putting on 378 runs before they were separated. Sussex were dismissed for 164, and at the close of the first day the Yorkshire total was 216 for no wicket. Tunnicliffe put together his highest innings for the county; but his achievement was put into the shade by that of Brown, who when he was fourth man out at 519, had made 311. Brown batted about six hours and a quarter, and had the distinction, not only of scoring the highest innings of the season, but the highest ever played for Yorkshire. Although he scored so rapidly, his only mistake was a chance in the slips at 170, and his wonderful innings was made up by forty-five 4s, nineteen 3s, eleven 2s and fifty-two singles. Sussex were beaten by an innings and 307 runs.

Sussex

Mr G. Brann c Mounsey b Haigh	57	– c Tunnicliffe b Milligan	1
F. W. Marlow c Mitchell b Haigh	11	– c Mitchell b Milligan	13
Mr W. L. Murdoch c Tunnicliffe b Peel	2	– b Milligan	0
J. Vine c Tunnicliffe b Milligan	33	– c Milligan b Brown	20
Mr W. Newham c Wainwright b Milligan	6	– c Haigh b Brown	42
G. Bean c Hunter b Milligan	15	– c Mitchell b Milligan	39
F. Parris b Milligan	6	– not out	52
E. H. Killick not out	6	– b Milligan	4
H. R. Butt c Hunter b Milligan	15	– c Denton b Milligan	3
C. Bland b Haigh	0	– c Denton b Wainwright	13
F. W. Tate c Wainwright b Hiagh	2	– b Milligan	5
B 8, l-b 3	11	B 17, l-b 1	18
	164		210

Yorkshire

J. T. Brown c Parris b Killick	311	Mr F. Mitchell run out	35
J. Tunnicliffe c Parris b Vine	147	R. Peel not out	39
D. Denton c Killick b Bland	11	B 18, l-b 5, w 2	25
R. Moorhouse lbw b Parris	9		
E. Wainwright not out	104	(5 wkts dec.)	681

Mr F. W. Milligan, J. Mounsey, S. Haigh and D. Hunter did not bat.

Yorkshire Bowling

	Overs	Mdns	Runs	Wkts	Overs	Mdns	Runs	Wkts
Peel	19	4	33	1	5	2	7	0
Haigh	30	12	47	4	14	4	34	0
Wainwright	7	1	28	0	18	4	44	1
Milligan	18	6	45	5	24.3	5	65	7
Brown					9	0	35	2
Mounsey					7	3	7	0

Sussex Bowling

	Overs	Mdns	Runs	Wkts
Bland	52	15	165	1
Tate	57	19	107	0
Killick	26	6	74	1
Parris	45	10	117	1
Brann	23	10	51	0
Marlow	6	1	14	0
Bean	5	2	20	0
Vine	22	3	79	1
Newham	8	1	29	0

Umpires: A. Young and W. Shrewsbury.

YORKSHIRE v GLOUCESTERSHIRE

Played at Harrogate, July 29, 30, 31, 1897

G. L. Jessop was quite the hero of this match, giving one of the most wonderful displays of hitting ever witnessed. In the course of twenty minutes before the interval, he made 43 out of 54, and afterwards in eight overs he obtained 58 out of 64, making in all 101 out of 118 in the course of forty minutes. Although he scored at such a tremendous pace, he gave no chance. Gloucestershire won by 140 runs.

Gloucestershire

Mr W. G. Grace c Tunnicliffe b Wilson	22 – c Wainwright b Milligan	33
Mr R. M. Rice c Milligan b Hirst	9 – b Jackson	22
Mr F. H. B. Champain c Tunnicliffe b Jackson	44 – b Wainwright	26
H. Wrathall b Jackson	17 – c Wainwright b Wilson	34
Mr G. L. Jessop b Jackson	101 – c Denton b Wainwright	0
Mr C. L. Townsend c Milligan b Wilson	109 – run out	1
Mr W. McG. Hemingway c Milligan b Jackson	0 – c Jackson b Milligan	27
J. H. Board run out	43 – b Milligan	69
Mr H. S. Goodwin c Wainwright b Jackson	11 – c Hirst b Milligan	26
Mr W. S. A. Brown b Milligan	10 – not out	12
F. G. Roberts not out	1	
L-b 2, w 1	3 B 21	21
	370	(9 wkts dec.) 271

Yorkshire

Mr F. S. Jackson b Jessop	7 – b Jessop	4
J. Tunnicliffe c and b Jessop	24 – c Board b Jessop	25
J. T. Brown c Townsend b Roberts	80 – b Jessop	49
D. Denton c Board b Jessop	10 – c Townsend b Brown	55
E. Wainwright c Board b Roberts	1 – c Board b Jessop	9
Mr C. E. M. Wilson c Goodwin b Roberts	0 – b Jessop	22
G. H. Hirst c and b Jessop	55 – c Wrathall b Brown	35
Mr F. W. Milligan c and b Roberts	15 – c Townsend b Brown	2
Mr R. W. Collinson c Wrathall b Roberts	34 – c Townsend b Brown	2
Lord Hawke c Hemingway b Roberts	38 – not out	9
D. Hunter not out	1 – c Champain b Roberts	5
L-b 7, n-b 4	11 B 5, l-b 2, w 1	8
	276	225

Yorkshire Bowling

	Overs	Mdns	Runs	Wkts	Overs	Mdns	Runs	Wkts
Hirst	27	7	86	1	17	8	44	0
Wainwright	27	14	43	0	24	7	83	2
Wilson	19	5	54	2	15	7	16	1
Jackson	35	13	73	5	17	6	40	1
Milligan	19.1	2	96	1	19.4	5	67	4
Brown	5	1	15	0				

Gloucestershire Bowling

	Overs	Mdns	Runs	Wkts	Overs	Mdns	Runs	Wkts
Townsend	8	1	28	0	9	2	24	0
Jessop	37	10	106	4	34	10	71	5
Roberts	33.3	10	84	6	33	12	91	1
Wrathall	3	1	4	0				
Brown	3	0	12	0	8	2	14	4
Grace	9	1	31	0	6	0	17	0

Umpires: J. Potter and W. Shrewsbury.

YORKSHIRE v DERBYSHIRE

Played at Bradford, August 19, 20, 21, 1897

Heavy rain had fallen on the previous day, and bowlers had matters all their own way in the opening stages of this game. Derbyshire began extremely well, and at one point had 120 on the board with onloy four men out. Then came an astonishing piece of work by

Haigh, who, in two overs, sent back five batsmen without a run being scored off him, dismissing the last three with successive balls and thus performing the "hat trick". He had done nothing so good since the match with Surrey at Leeds in June. The Yorkshiremen could do nothing against Davidson and Walker, and although 31 runs were added for the last wicket, the total only reached 83. Next day when the weather was very showery, Derbyshire again began well, but fell off badly, and on the Saturday, twenty-five minutes of actual cricket sufficed to give Yorkshire a creditable victory by five wickets.

Derbyshire

Mr L. G. Wright run out	7	– c and b Haigh	18
Mr S. H. Evershed b Wainwright	36	– c and b Haigh	0
W. Chatterton b Haigh	10	– c Brown b Haigh	43
H. Bagshaw c Wainwright b Milligan	12	– c Denton b Haigh	14
G. Davidson c Milligan b Wainwright	29	– b Wainwright	4
W. Storer lbw b Haigh	25	– c Tunnicliffe b Wainwright	16
W. Sugg b Haigh	0	– c Tunnicliffe b Wainwright	0
Mr E. M. Ashcroft b Haigh	0	– c Hirst b Wainwright	15
Mr G. G. Walker b Haigh	0	– c Mounsey b Haigh	8
Gould b Haigh	0	– c Brown b Wainwright	1
Hancock not out	0	– not out	0
B 5, l-b 4	9	W 1	1
	128		120

Yorkshire

J. Tunnicliffe b Davidson	1	– c Chatterton b Davidson	0
J. T. Brown c Storer b Davidson	13	– b Walker	11
D. Denton c Chatterton b Davidson	6	– run out	11
E. Wainwright c and b Walker	0	– c Sugg b Hancock	33
G. H. Hirst b Walker	0	– not out	63
Mr F. W. Milligan b Davidson	1	– c Chatterton b Bagshaw	32
R. Moorhouse c Chatterton b Davidson	8	– not out	7
Lord Hawke b Walker	11		
J. Mounsey not out	8		
S. Haigh c Davidson b Walker	0		
D. Hunter c Gould b Davidson	19		
B 16	16	B 8, n-b 1	9
	83		166

Yorkshire Bowling

	Overs	Mdns	Runs	Wkts	Overs	Mdns	Runs	Wkts
Wainwright	22	8	44	2	16.1	5	39	5
Hirst	22	13	39	0	3	1	11	0
Haigh	13	7	18	6	17	3	62	5
Milligan	7	3	17	1	3	0	7	0
Denton	1	0	1	0				

Derbyshire Bowling

	Overs	Mdns	Runs	Wkts	Overs	Mdns	Runs	Wkts
Davidson	19.1	12	23	6	28	12	51	1
Walker	19	4	44	4	15	3	46	1
Chatterton					1	0	7	0
Hancock					5	0	19	1
Bagshaw					9.3	1	34	1

Umpires: H. Richardson and J. Tuck.

YORKSHIRE v SURREY

Played at Bradford, June 6, 7, 8, 1898

In some respects this was one of the most remarkable matches of the season, the extraordinary collapse of the Surrey team in their second innings being by far the worst performance of the southern county all through the summer. No play was possible on the first day, but there was some interesting and even cricket on the Tuesday, Yorkshire scoring 142 for eight wickets, against Surrey's total of 139. Wednesday's play was truly phenomenal. Hirst and Haigh added 155 runs before they were separated, their partnership in all producing 192. Certainly the Surrey bowling, apart from that of Lockwood, was poor, but the performance of the two Yorkshire professionals deserved great praise. Hirst's 130 not out, was his one great batting success last summer. Haigh had never before made so many runs for his county. Wanting 158 to escape an innings defeat, Surrey, had, of course, a thankless task, but a good fight was expected from them. Their batsmen, however, failed utterly before Rhodes and Wainwright, losing nine wickets for 23 and being all out in an hour and a half for 37. Wainwright took the first three wickets and Rhodes the last seven, the latter being splendidly helped by David Hunter at the wicket. Yorkshire won by an innings and 121 runs.

Surrey

R. Abel st Hunter b Wainwright	51	– c Jackson b Rhodes	6
W. Brockwell b Wainwright	19	– lbw b Wainwright	5
T. Hayward st Hunter b Rhodes	1	– b Wainwright	2
C. Baldwin c and b Wainwright	3	– b Wainwright	0
Mr D. L. A. Jephson c and b Wainwright	4	– c Brown b Rhodes	0
Mr K. J. Key c Jackson b Rhodes	32	– not out	8
A. E. Street c Tunnicliffe b Rhodes	0	– st Hunter b Rhodes	4
W. H. Lockwood st Hunter b Rhodes	2	– c Hunter b Rhodes	0
W. Lees b Wainwright	18	– st Hunter b Rhodes	0
H. Wood not out	8	– st Hunter b Rhodes	0
T. Richardson c Denton b Rhodes	0	– c Hunter b Rhodes	9
L-b 1	1	B 3	3
	139		37

Yorkshire

J. T. Brown b Lockwood	0
J. Tunnicliffe run out	21
Mr F. S. Jackson c Wood b Lockwood	3
D. Denton b Lockwood	11
E. Wainwright lbw b Richardson	5
G. H. Hirst not out	130
R. Moorhouse c Hayward b Lockwood	12
Lord Hawke b Lees	5
W. Rhodes c Jephson b Richardson	13
S. Haigh c Abel b Brockwell	85
B 4, l-b 2, w 2, n-b 4	12
(9 wkts dec.)	297

D. Hunter did not bat.

Yorkshire Bowling

	Overs	Mdns	Runs	Wkts	Overs	Mdns	Runs	Wkts
Rhodes	30.3	12	46	6	19.1	9	24	7
Wainwright	27	14	43	5	20	14	10	3
Haigh	13	3	28	0				
Jackson	16	6	21	0				

Surrey Bowling

	Overs	Mdns	Runs	Wkts
Lockwood	41	18	74	4
Hayward	13	3	36	0
Richardson	29	7	64	2
Lees	18	8	41	1
Jephson	8	0	30	0
Brockwell	6.2	1	18	1
Abel	4	1	8	0
Street	5	0	14	0

Umpires: A. Young and C. E. Richardson.

YORKSHIRE v HAMPSHIRE

Played at Huddersfield, June 9, 10, 1898

Journeying on, after their triumph over Surrey, to Huddersfield, Yorkshire had a very easy task against Hampshire. Only a fortnight previously they had beaten the southern county at Southampton in one day, and the return game did not last up to lunch time on the second day, Yorkshire winning by an innings and 98 runs. Hampshire had not their full strength, and to further handicap them they lost the toss. Brown and Tunnicliffe put on 85 runs for the first Yorkshire wicket, and this stand, coupled with the splendid bowling Yorkshire possessed, practically decided the match. Tunnicliffe played splendid cricket, and Brown hit very brilliantly. Going in against a total of 226, Hampshire were all dismissed by Wainwright and Rhodes in an hour and a half for 45, this being the third time running that the southern team had been got rid of by Yorkshire for less than fifty. Following on, Hampshire scored 10, without loss, before the drawing of stumps, but next day the end was speedily reached. Wainwright damaged his hand, but Haigh and Rhodes were always masters of the Hampshire batsmen. Rhodes had a wonderful week, taking twenty wickets for 125 runs.

Yorkshire

J. T. Brown c Heseltine b Tate	88	W. Rhodes b Hill	6
J. Tunnicliffe st Robson b Tate	50	Lord Hawke c Steele b Tate	23
Mr F. S. Jackson st Robson b Tate	3	S. Haigh not out	4
D. Denton c Steele b Tate	6	D. Hunter b Hill	0
E. Wainwright lbw b Light	6	B 4, l-b 2	6
G. H. Hirst b Hill	17		
R. Moorhouse c Poore b Hill	17		226

Hampshire

V. Barton lbw b Wainwright	4	– c Moorhouse b Haigh	12
Major R. M. Poore lbw b Rhodes	7	– c Tunnicliffe b Wainwright	0
A. Webb b Wainwright	10	– lbw b Rhodes	3
Dr W. C. Russell b Wainwright	2	– c Tunnicliffe b Rhodes	5
Mr A. J. L. Hill b Rhodes	8	– b Haigh	14
Mr D. A. Steele b Wainwright	4	– b Haigh	13
Mr C. Heseltine b Wainwright	0	– c Denton b Rhodes	6
Mr C. Robson c Hawke b Wainwright	6	– c Hirst b Wainwright	14
E. Tate b Rhodes	3	– not out	1
E. Light not out	0	– b Haigh	6
L-b 1	1		
	45		83

Hampshire Bowling

	Overs	Mdns	Runs	Wkts
Baldwin	13	3	31	0
Hill	21.4	6	46	4
Light	24	9	56	1
Tate	30	7	83	5
Steele	7	5	4	0
Barton	1	1	0	0

Yorkshire Bowling

	Overs	Mdns	Runs	Wkts	Overs	Mdns	Runs	Wkts
Wainwright	22	12	24	7	12	5	17	2
Rhodes	21	13	20	3	18	7	35	4
Hirst					3	0	10	0
Haigh					10	3	21	4

Umpires: R. Daft and A. Young.

YORKSHIRE v GLOUCESTERSHIRE

Played at Sheffield, July 25, 26, 1898

Gloucestershire had been playing so well previous to this contest, that it was generally expected Yorkshire would have a hard task to beat the western county. Unfortunately W. G. Grace, suffering from a bruised heel, found himself unable to play, and as the game went Gloucestershire quite failed to realise expectations. Yorkshire practically placed themselves safe from defeat on the opening day when they put together a score of 331 – a remarkable total considering that the wicket was so soft that Hawke hesitated before taking first innings. The batting honours were again carried off by Jackson, who in an innings of 160 – his fifth hundred for Yorkshire – quite excelled himself. In the course of the second day the game terminated in a single innings victory for Yorkshire with twelve runs to spare. Yorkshire bowled exceedingly well, and the light was at times defective, but the cricket was a great blow to the reputation of Gloucestershire. Two good performances, however, were accomplished, Champain and W. Hemingway hitting up 95 in an hour in the morning; while in the follow-on Sewell played superbly, carrying his bat right through the innings and scoring 88 out of 127. The contrast between his mastery over the Yorkshire bowling and the failure of his colleagues was quite remarkable.

Yorkshire

J. T. Brown c Board b Roberts	25
J. Tunnicliffe st Board b Townsend	15
Mr F. S. Jackson c Sewell b Jessop	160
D. Denton c Jessop b Brown	9
E. Wainwright c Sewell b Roberts	29
G. H. Hirst b Roberts	6
Mr F. W. Milligan lbw b Townsend	18
Lord Hawke c G. Hemingway b Townsend	36
S. Haigh c Board b Jessop	13
W. Rhodes c Brown b Jessop	1
D. Hunter not out	0
B 12, l-b 4, n-b 3	19
	331

Gloucestershire

Mr C. O. H. Sewell st Hunter b Rhodes	6 – not out	88
Mr W. Troup b Wainwright	26 – run out	6
Mr F. H. B. Champain c Tunnicliffe b Rhodes	57 – b Haigh	0
Mr C. L. Townsend c Hawke b Wainwright	0 – b Haigh	1
Mr G. L. Jessop st Hunter b Rhodes	9 – c Tunnicliffe b Rhodes	0
Mr W. McG. Hemingway c Denton b Rhodes	49 – b Haigh	8
H. Wrathall not out	29 – c Wainwright b Rhodes	8
Mr G. Hemingway b Haigh	0 – b Jackson	0
J. H. Board c Jackson b Rhodes	2 – c Denton b Wainwright	2
Mr W. S. A. Brown lbw b Haigh	1 – b Wainwright	11
F. G. Roberts st Hunter b Rhodes	6 – b Jackson	0
B 6, n-b 1	7 B 1, n-b 2	3
	192	127

Gloucestershire Bowling

	Overs	Mdns	Runs	Wkts
Townsend	43	4	123	3
Brown	20	5	32	1
Roberts	34	6	105	3
Jessop	26.1	8	42	3
Sewell	4	0	10	0

Yorkshire Bowling

	Overs	Mdns	Runs	Wkts	Overs	Mdns	Runs	Wkts
Haigh	10	1	27	2	16	4	45	3
Rhodes	30	8	71	6	17	6	42	2
Wainwright	13	3	38	2	6	0	23	2
Milligan	1	0	2	0				
Jackson	8	3	19	0	6.3	1	14	2
Hirst	8	2	28	0				

Umpires: W. Richards and A. A. White.

YORKSHIRE v MIDDLESEX

Played at Leeds, August 15, 16, 1898

Strong as Middlesex had begun to show themselves by this time, it was generally held that they would be most formidable on a hard wicket, and with the ground slow the prospects of Yorkshire seemed to be decidedly hopeful. Yorkshire, however, were all out for 142 – a total which would have been considerably reduced had not Middlesex made three blunders in the field. For the visitors, Warner and Stoddart batted skilfully, but half the side were out for 108. With rain during the night, followed by bright sunshine, there came some sensational cricket on Tuesday, fifteen wickets actually falling before lunch for 65 runs. Jackson bowled so finely that the five outstanding Middlesex wickets realised only 20 runs, but a bigger sensation was in store, the Yorkshiremen – apart from Tunnicliffe – being at their second attempt so helpless against Albert Trott, that they were all out in eighty minutes for 45. Tunnicliffe stayed for more than an hour, but the other ten members of the team scored only a dozen runs between them. Trott actually dismissed seven batsmen for 13 runs, but Hearne bowled nearly as well. Middlesex made very light of the task of scoring the 60 wanted to win, and gained a memorable victory by eight wickets. James Douglas and Warner made a capital start and Ford hit brilliantly.

Yorkshire

J. Tunnicliffe c Bray b Trott	8 – run out	31
J. T. Brown c Trott b Hearne	30 – c Bray b Trott	5
Mr F. S. Jackson b Hearne	3 – c Ford b Trott	1
D. Denton b Hearne	22 – c and b Hearne	1
Mr E. Smith c Ford b Trott	16 – b Trott	3
Mr F. W. Milligan c Warner b Cunliffe	1 – c Bray b Trott	0
W. Rhodes c Trott b Cunliffe	20 – b Trott	0
Lord Hawke b Hearne	24 – b Trott	0
S. Haigh c and b Trott	6 – c Bray b Hearne	0
G. H. Hirst lbw b Trott	1 – not out	2
D. Hunter not out	0 – b Trott	0
B 6, l-b 5	11 B 1, l-b 1	2
	142	45

Middlesex

Mr J. Douglas b Smith	7 – b Jackson	13
Mr P. F. Warner lbw b Jackson	24 – c Brown b Rhodes	13
Mr A. E. Stoddart c and b Jackson	26 – not out	7
Mr F. G. J. Ford b Haigh	1 – not out	29
J. T. Rawlin b Jackson	27	
Mr R. N. Douglas c Hunter b Jackson	9	
Mr C. M. Wells c Hirst b Rhodes	15	
A. E. Trott lbw b Jackson	0	
Mr F. H. E. Cunliffe not out	9	
Mr E. H. Bray b Jackson	0	
J. T. Hearne b Jackson	5	
B 3, l-b 2	5	
	128	62

Middlesex Bowling

	Overs	Mdns	Runs	Wkts	Overs	Mdns	Runs	Wkts
Hearne	33.3	16	43	4	15	5	30	2
Trott	30	12	70	4	14.1	8	13	7
Cunliffe	9	4	18	2				

Yorkshire

	Overs	Mdns	Runs	Wkts	Overs	Mdns	Runs	Wkts
Rhodes	23	3	52	1	7.4	2	24	1
Smith	10	5	12	1	3	0	12	0
Jackson	24.3	11	42	7	9	2	19	1
Haigh	12	4	17	1	2	0	7	0

Umpires: A. Young and R. Daft.

THE AUSTRALIANS AND OTHERS IN ENGLAND

To understand the nature of the achievements of cricketers visiting Victorian England, it is helpful to pause for a moment in contemplation of the logistics governing their lives. In fact, the ideal arrangement might perhaps have been to append a list of departure and arrival times of the various shipping lines sailing between the outposts of Empire. In the days covered by this volume, when the sea voyage to and from Australia took eight weeks, it was considered an impressive feat to survive the trip at all, let alone be in a fit state to play cricket on arrival, a fact which demonstrates the gladiatorial nature of G. J. Bonnor's performance in stepping off the boat in England in 1882 and winning a bet by throwing a cricket ball 119 yards. To underline the spirit of adventure which must have pervaded tours of this kind, in the same year of Bonnor's feat an English side set sail for Australia, with consequences alarming enough to bring home the pioneering aspect of the touring cricketer's life:

> Of the twelve players eight were amateurs, and in a collision with another ship on the voyage out, Morley, the one fast bowler, suffered an injury to his ribs which crippled him for most of the tour, and ultimately led to his untimely death.

There were other dangers, more subtle but no less deadly. When D. W. Gregory's side arrived in England in 1878 to cause the greatest sensation in the history of Anglo-Australian cricket, it had not been so very long since the Mother Country stopped regarding Australia as a dumping ground for criminals. As late as 1849 the government of Lord John Russell had most generously sent, absolutely free of charge, a boatload of convicts to Melbourne, whose inhabitants, insisting that a civilised township was no place to dump felons, and thereby implying that civilised townships can usually be relied upon to have plenty of felons of their own, had the whole consignment moved on to Brisbane, an action which most unkindly suggested that Brisbane was not a civilised township.

No doubt as late as 1878 there must have existed many Englishmen who firmly believed that the Australians, all direct descendents of Bill Sikes, were accustomed to whiling away the long Pacific summers by slaughtering, dismembering and digesting each other. Dickens was still not long dead, and the popular image of an Australian may have had less to do with Spofforth than with Magwitch in *Great Expectations*, of whom Pip remarks at one point, "the abhorrence in which I held the man, the dread I had of him, the repugnance with which I shrank from him, could not have been exceeded if he had been some terrible beast." It may seem fanciful to suggest that to the English Gentleman batsman facing him for the first time, Spofforth might have seemed like the very embodiment of Magwitch's malevolence on the Kentish marshes, but H. S. Altham has testified that before the arrival of Gregory's men in England, the president of the Cambridge University Cricket Club was under the impression that the visitors were all black-skinned, a conviction presumably based on the assumption that the Australian sub-continent supported no other kind of wild life.

Even the more enlightened regarded the Australians as some sort of exotic species from the far side of the planet, which indeed they were, and after

Gregory's men had won their famous victory over the MCC at Lord's, Altham says that "crowds came flocking to the Tavistock Hotel in Covent Garden to look on the men who had thus flung open a new era in the history of the game." This rarity value soon evaporated with the frequency of visits by Australian touring sides, (David Gregory's nephew Sydney enjoyed no fewer than eight tours of Britain with successive Australian sides between 1890 and 1912), but the subconscious belief that a match against Australians at either test or county, or occasionally even club level, constituted a special event is one which has never quite disappeared. The other two visiting nationals whose deeds echo through these pages, represent the two contrasting fates which lie before any emergent cricketing nation. The South Africans were just beginning to develop into an authentic international power, but the Philadelphians who came to England in the 1890s proved to be the last of a dying breed, cricketers struggling to survive in an environment already hopelessly corrupted by the barbarism of Baseball.

The fortunes of the various Australian touring sides and the opponents who met them will sound familiar enough to the student of cricket history. There are the usual wails of despair at the decadence of the English game; the predictable accusations of sharp practice (witness W. G. Grace's running out of an Australian batsman in a Test match in 1882), the customary occasional echoes of bad feeling as described in the report of the Gloucestershire v Australians match of August, 1886; the age-old discontent of the professionals at the size of their wage-packets. (In referring to the mutiny of leading professionals before the Oval Test in 1896. Wisden defines the malcontents with a masterly ambiguity of phrase as "the revolting players".) Scrupulousness of observation of a rather different kind is apparent in the almanack's report of the tourists' match against Middlesex at Lord's in 1899; in explaining the style of the barracking indulged in by a crowd displeased with the scoring rate, Wisden says that the choral effects included a rendition of "Dead March in Saul", leaving nothing to the reader's imagination except perhaps the tempo at which the performance proceeded.

Some of the other remarkable incidents could only have taken place in the context of an emergent sport. At Birmingham, for instance, the crowd carries W. G. Grace round the ground; at the opening of the 1888 season, the Surrey v Australians fixture coincides with the opening of the Press Box; two years before, the same fixture is the occasion of a visit to the ground by the club's landlord, the Prince of Wales; in 1884, again at The Oval, England tries all eleven members of the side as bowlers; in the Lords match of 1886 we read of the sad death of a respected spectator, after which a gold watch is presented to one of the Australian players, the two events having no apparent connection; when a Leicestershire player bowls out the tourists singlehanded, the size of his bonus, £8, reflects dramatically the inflationary distance separating his epoch from our own. It prompts the reader to wonder what, in monetary terms, was the value of the famous deed of another Leicestershire hero, A. D. Pougher, who, at Lord's in 1896, returned some of the most extraordinary bowling figures in cricket history, and whose fame has proved so enduring that seventy years later the match-card celebrating his great day was exhibited under glass in the entrance lobby of the St Marylebone Public Library, where its contents were digested by visitors who bore themselves as if confronted by a document of unfathomable antiquity.

Inevitably there have occurred moments in cricket history when the phenomenal nature of events has not altogether been apparent to the eye-witness, so that the Wisden report tends to play down the wondrous aspects of the day's play. In rectifying one such oversight, I hope I am at a single stroke stressing the difficulties facing the compiler of on-the-spot accounts, who by the very nature of his predicament cannot possibly have access to those extraneous facts which create most of the melodrama, and also conveying the extent to which a match between England and Australia has always been considered the most prestigious of all cricketing events. The reader coming across the particulars of the Test match at The Oval in 1882, will be told that at one point, as the game was approaching its absurdly tense denouement, a long succession of maiden overs was bowled. That is the bald fact of the matter. The poetic truth is that, while the game was delicately balanced in this way, an Epsom stockbroker called Arthur Courcy witnessed those successive maiden overs with so intense a degree of absorption that he chewed off the handle of his brother-in-law's umbrella. If there was in this world such a thing as poetic justice, which most decidedly there is not, then the name of Arthur Courcy would surely be engraved on the tablets of the game, below that of Pougher and the Gregorys. But not too far below.

THE AUSTRALIANS AT PRINCE'S

Prince's is the only ground whereon the Australians measured their cricketing skill and strength against The Gentlemen of England *and* The Players of England. Both contests will ever retain a prominent interest in the wonderfully busy and successful tour of this remarkable Eleven, not only on account of their decisive defeat by the Gentlemen, and their virtual victory over the Players, but because there cannot possibly be given more convincing evidence of the vast improvement made in their batting by the Australians since they first played on English grounds, than their match at Prince's against The Gentlemen, in June; and their match at Prince's against The Players, in September, scoring as they did but 138 runs in two innings against The Gentlemen's bowling on wet wickets; and 236 in one innings against The Players bowling on easier playing, but still somewhat dead wickets.

THE AUSTRALIANS v THE GENTLEMEN OF ENGLAND

Played at Prince's, June 17, 18, 1878

This match created wide-spread and intense excitement among our cricketing community; and as The Australians had just previously defeated MCC and Ground by 9 wickets, Yorkshire by 6 wickets, and Surrey by 5 wickets, Englishmen became anxiously jealous that the old country's team should be fully representative, and when the original list of the Gentlemen's Eleven was published, minus the name of A. G. Steel, public opinion in favour of that gentleman playing was so strongly expressed, that that very young and exceedingly popular bowler was forthwith enrolled as one of the team; and albeit a good old English growl or two was chronicled about one or two others set down to play, the B.P. soon felt satisfied that the "improved" Eleven would do full justice to the cricketing fame of Old England. The admission charge was 1s. each day; and, notwithstanding rain fell on both days, the attendances were computed by the chroniclers at – "about" – 11,000 on the first day and 6,000 on the second. The arrangements on the ground created great and general dissatisfaction; the first row of seats were stated to have been placed only 65 yards distant from each wicket. The want of sufficient sitting accommodation for the large number present on the first day, led to a successful raid being made on the reserved extra price chairs, upon some of which the, at times, umbrella-covered visitors stood in front of the little hut allotted to the Gentlemen of the Press, who subsequently penned strong complaints of the discomforting difficulties they encountered in the performance of their duties at so important a match. The wickets had been carefully prepared and tended, but heavy rains had made them play slow and deceptive, putting big hitting and large scoring out of the question, and making it a thorough bowlers' and fieldsmen's match, as 30 wickets for 277 runs eventually proved; and that, too, notwithstanding the Australians played their full force, including Midwinter, and the English Eleven comprised several of the old Country's very finest batsmen.

The Australians commenced the batting at noon with Charles Bannerman and Midwinter, to the bowling of W. Grace and A. G. Steel. Slowly was the score played up to 20, when a clever catch at point, by Dr Grace, settled Midwinter for 6. At 32 W. Grace bowled Horan for 7, close upon one hour having then been played away. Murdoch was next man in, and E. M. Grace bowled v A. G. Steel; and when the score had reached 44 a splendid one-hand catch, at deep cover-point, by Strachan, finished Charles Bannerman's innings for 28 – the largest score made in the match. Rain fell as A. Bannerman walked to the wickets, and the hundreds of upraised opened umbrellas around the ground was not only a curious sight, but those put up in front of the little press hut shut out all view of the play from the reporters, and all that could thenceforth be noted was that at a few minutes past four the Australians' innings closed for 75 runs, made from 103 overs, only one of the Eleven having been bowled. At twenty-five past four W. Grace and W. Gilbert commenced England's batting to the bowling of Spofforth and Allen. The Englishmen made runs at a faster pace than had the Australians, and when 30 had been scored Boyle bowled v Allen; and at 37 Midwinter was tried v Spofforth; but still the score rose, and many hoped the Englishmen would equal, and pass, the Australians' total without losing a wicket; but not so, for at 43 a loud shout greeted Boyle clean bowling W. Grace for 25 – the largest English score made. Then the wickets went down fast; at 54 Gilbert was caught out at wicket for 20; at 61 Hornby was had at mid-on; at 74 Boyle c and b Lucas; at 77 F. Grace was out; and at 82 the Doctor was caught out at wicket. The two Cantabs – A. Lyttelton and A. G. Steel – then played up to "time", the stumps being drawn with the English score at 86 for 5 wickets; A. Lyttelton, not out, 5; Steel, not out, 1.

On the Tuesday play commenced at ten past twelve, to the bowling of Spofforth and Boyle; at 89 Spofforth bowled Steel, and at 90 Boyle bowled E. Lyttelton. Then A. Lyttelton and Strachan played (rain falling fast) the score up to 106, when one of Gregory's now famous smart catches at slip settled A. Lyttelton for 16; and when the last man, Bush, walked to the wickets but few more runs were expected; nevertheless the Australians found Strachan and Bush hard to part, as those two Englishmen hit away until ten minutes past one, when the innings ended for 139, or 64 on, so many as 33 runs having been put on for that last wicket, Bush being then had at point for 16, Strachan taking his bat out for 21. Those 139 runs of England's were made from 107 overs and 2 balls of Australian bowling. At 1.30 the Colonials commenced their second innings with Horan and Midwinter, to the bowling of W. Grace and Steel. When 4 runs only had been made, Midwinter was missed by Lucas, but at 5 a catch by Strachan got rid of Horan for one run. At 7 smart fielding by E. Lyttelton and Steel ran out A. Bannerman, and at 14 Charles Bannerman was bowled by Steel; then they luncheoned. Play was resumed at five past three, Spofforth then being Midwinter's mate, but with the score at 25 Spofforth was out for 8. Murdoch next faced Midwinter, who was then well set and hitting in good form, when his career was ended by a grand catch at long-field by Hornby, who caught the ball as it was flying over the seated visitors' heads, and thereby evoked roars of lusty cheers that rang out again, again, and still again; and many a time since then has the compiler of this little book heard admiring reminders of Hornby's great catch that settled Midwinter in the Australians' match against the Gentlemen at Prince's. The score was at 38 for five wickets when Midwinter left for 26. Then Murdoch and Garrett hit hard, the latter making three drives for 4 each out of his total of 15, when he was settled at long-off with the score at 57. At 62 Murdoch was had at wicket for 7; a bye was then run, leaving only 2 more runs to be made to save the one innings' defeat, but those 2 runs the Australians failed to score, as at the 63 Blackham, Gregory, and Allan were all three got out, and so it was that at 4.15 on the second day the Gentlemen of England won this match by an innings and a run.

The Australians

Charles Bannerman c Strachan b E. M. Grace	28	– b A. G. Steel	0
W. Midwinter c E. M. Grace b W. Grace	6	– c Hornby b W. Grace	26
T. Horan b W. Grace	7	– c Strachan b A. G. Steel	1
W. L. Murdoch c Hornby b A. G. Steel	1	– c J. A. Bush b A. G. Steel	7
A. Bannerman c and b A. G. Steel	13	– run out	0
F. E. Spofforth c J. A. Bush b W. Grace	6	– c A. Lyttelton b W. Grace	8
T. W. Garrett run out	0	– c F. Grace b A. G. Steel	15
F. E. Allan c E. M. Grace b A. G. Steel	0	– b A. G. Steel	0
D. Gregory c Hornby b W. Grace	1	– c E. Lyttelton b A. G. Steel	0
J. M. Blackham not out	6	– c W. Grace b A. G. Steel	5
H. F. Boyle c E. M. Grace b A. G. Steel	3	– not out	0
B 1, l-b 3	4	B 1	1
	75		63

Gentlemen of England

W. G. Grace b Boyle	25	Hon. E. Lyttelton b Boyle	1
W. Gilbert c Blackham b Boyle	20	A. G. Steel b Spofforth	5
A. N. Hornby c Spofforth b Boyle	9	G. Strachan not out	21
A. P. Lucas c and b Boyle	6	J. A. Bush c Murdoch b Midwinter	16
G. F. Grace c Spofforth b Boyle	11	B 6, l-b 2	8
E. M. Grace c Blackham b Boyle	1		
Hon. A. Lyttelton c Gregory b Spofforth	16		139

England Bowling

	Overs	Mdns	Runs	Wkts	Overs	Mdns	Runs	Wkts
W. G. Grace	52	38	25	4	27	14	27	2
A. G. Steel	32.1	17	37	4	26.3	8	35	7
E. M. Grace	19	12	9	1				

Australian Bowling

	Overs	Mdns	Runs	Wkts
Boyle	35	11	48	7
Spofforth	35	13	53	2
Allan	20	14	11	—
Midwinter	14.2	6	15	1
Garratt	3	1	4	—

THE AUSTRALIANS v THE PLAYERS OF ENGLAND

Played at Prince's, September 11, 12, 1878

This two days' match was hastily got up, was played on excellent wickets, barring being a bit dead through rain, was favoured with fairly fine weather, was attended by about 5,000 visitors each day at 1s. admission, and was but half played out, the second day's cricket ending with each side having played an innings, to the Colonials' advantage of 76 runs. It was reported in *Bell's Life* and *The Sportsman* that the Australian Eleven received £400, or at the rate of £36 per man, from the Messrs Prince, for playing that two days' cricket, though it is but fair to record that the Australians, on the day previous to the commencement of this match, sent a subscription of £100 to The Mansion House Fund, formed for the relief of the sorrowing sufferers through the unfortunate steamer collision on the Thames, that resulted in the awfully sudden loss of nearly 700 lives. It will be perceived that the Players had not the aid of Emmett, Richard Daft, Jupp, Morley, Pooley, William Oscroft, Barlow, Wyld, Barnes, or Allen Hill, consequently they did not play full strength; on the other hand, an accident in the match deprived the Australians of the brilliant wicket-keeping services of Blackham, a loss this to the team beyond all calculation.

At 12.20 on the St Leger Day the brothers Bannerman commenced the Australian hitting, to the bowling of Alfred Shaw and Ulyett; 9 runs had been made from 10 overs, when Shaw c and b A. Bannerman for one run. Horan was next man in; both he and Charles Bannerman played steady good cricket, and when 27 overs had been bowled for 29 runs, Barratt bowled v. Ulyett; but Barratt's bowling being punished for 16 runs from 7 overs, he was put on one side for McIntyre, in whose ninth over Horan was had at wicket for 16, the score then standing at 58 for two wickets, the result of 90 minutes' cricket. Spofforth then went to wickets and stayed up to luncheon call, 2 o'clock, when the score stood at two wickets down, 61 runs scored, 65 overs bowled, Charles Bannerman, not out 39, Spofforth, not out 3, Alfred Shaw then having bowled 33 overs (26 maidens) for 11 runs and a wicket. Luncheon over, play was resumed with advantage to the Australians, as Shaw was hit a bit and gave up the ball to Blamires, from whose bowling Charles Bannerman was not only missed being stumped, but he played the ball on to his wicket without moving a bail; however, in time, the young left-hand bowler (a good one) had Spofforth caught out at cover-point for 33, the score then standing at 107 for three wickets. Gregory then helped Charles Bannerman, who at 116 was superbly caught, left-hand high up, by Ulyett, the grand catch deservedly bringing out two distinct peals of rattling cheers, and Charles Bannerman also gained hearty applause, his 61 being the result of 165 minutes of careful and more scientific cricket than any he had previously played in London. Gregory was then missed by Flowers, at long-on, who got well to the ball but failed to hold it, and Gregory played an unconquered game for the remainder of that day; he lost Garrett, Murdoch, and Bailey, the latter leaving with the score at 170 for seven wickets, and, although the bowling was changed at both ends, no other wicket fell that day, the stumps being drawn at six o'clock with the score at 187 for seven wickets, Gregory (greatly applauded), not out, 30, and Blackham, not out, 14, the English players having fielded queerly, and the 5,000 or so lookers on having witnessed that day's play in a form nearly as meekly and mute as a Quaker's meeting.

On the Thursday, at 11.45, under dark and rain-threatening clouds, the not outs renewed their innings to the bowling of Barratt and McIntyre, who bowled 11 overs before a run was scored, the scoring being then started by Blackham pulling a ball from Barratt round to leg for 3; but when 20 overs had been bowled for 9 runs Ulyett bowled in the place of Barratt, and when McIntyre had sent in 14 overs for one run (made in his eighth over) he also was shunted; then the score rose, a shout greeting the hoisting of the 200. Blackham was then hurt, and shortly after had his thumb split open by a ball bowled by Blamires; this completely knocked up Blackham, who played no more in the match. Boyle took Blackham's place, but, at 228, he was caught at wicket, and, at 1.45, the innings was finished for 236 runs by Gregory being had at square-leg for a well played innings of 57 runs, that, however, included two escapes, one at long-on as aforesaid, and one at point just prior to his capture. The Australians' 236 runs were made from 244 overs (less one ball) of English bowling, which was not, as a rule, backed up by either smart or even good English fielding, the wicket-keeping of H. Phillips being really far below Players of England form.

A furious rain storm of nearly an hour's duration fell whilst the men were luncheoning; then, at a quarter to three, the English batting was commenced by Ulyett and Rigley (Derbyshire), to the bowling of Spofforth and Garrett, the wicket being kept by Murdoch, and an Australian sub. fielding in the place of Blackham. Runs were freely made from Spofforth's bowling, but Garrett was so difficult to score from that he had bowled 8 overs for three singles when he was taken off and succeeded by Allan, who, however, shortly gave up the ball to Boyle, but both failing, and 65 runs having been scored, the Captain again tried Garrett, who, with the first ball he delivered, hit Rigley hard on the hand, and, with the second ball, bowled him for a patiently, well played, and deservedly applauded 27. Then came a series of disasters to the Players, for, at 72, Ulyett slipped down on his hinder parts and Selby was thereby run out, and, at 84, Shrewsbury was caught out marvellously low down at point, a decision that did not at all please the young Nottinghamshire man. Lockwood was next man in; he made a dozen runs and then skied one that the Captain collared with ease, and four wickets were down for 122 runs. Flowers was next man in; he began with a drive for 4 from Spofforth, and the score was progressing more hopefully for Old England when a splendid sparkler from Spofforth clean bowled Ulyett, who left heartily cheered all round, the Australians swelling the applause with real good will, and properly so, for Ulyett had played a long way the best innings in the match, his fine, forward, defensive play, clean and well timed leg-hitting, and free, manly, powerful driving powers were never more scientifically displayed than in building up this 79 against the Australians; commencing the Players innings at 2.45, Ulyett was fifth man out at 5.17, the score at 143; his principal hits were three 3s (leg, cut, and drive) and seven 4s (four to leg and 3 drives). Barratt hit a 3 to leg from Spofforth and was then caught out, close to the ground, at mid-on by A. Bannerman, and so went the sixth wicket, the score at 150; and, at 153, Flowers was had at point for 18. Then all went rapidly to the bad for the Players; Alfred Shaw was magnificently had at very short slip, the score still 153; at 155 McIntyre was c and b by Garrett, who, at 160, also easily c and b Phillips, and so, at a quarter to six, ended the Players' innings and the match, the engagement of the Australians extending to two days only, the half played out match being 76 runs in favour of the Colonials, a result greatly due to their fine smart fielding and improved batting, but also partly accountable to the, at times, very inferior fielding of some of the English professionals.

The Australians

Charles Bannerman c Ulyett b Blamires	61
A. Bannerman c and b Alfred Shaw	1
T. Horan c H. Phillips b W. McIntyre	16
F. E. Spofforth c Ulyett b Blamires	33
D. W. Gregory c A. Shrewsbury b E. Lockwood	57
T. W. Garrett b Barratt	12
W. L. Murdoch c Alfred Shaw b Barratt	14
G. H. Bailey c E. Lockwood b Barratt	2
J. M. Blackham retired hurt	25
H. F. Boyle c H. Phillips b Alfred Shaw	6
F. E. Allan not out	5
B 1, l-b 3	4
	236

Players of England

George Ulyett b Spofforth	79
W. Rigley b Garrett	27
J. Selby run out	3
Arthur Shrewsbury c C. Bannerman b Spofforth	8
Ephraim Lockwood c Gregory b Garrett	12
W. Flowers c C. Bannerman b Garrett	18
Barratt c A. Bannerman b Garrett	3
Henry Phillips c and b Garrett	4
Alfred Shaw c Gregory b Garrett	0
William McIntyre c and b Garrett	0
Blamires not out	3
B 3	3
	160

English Bowling

	Overs	Mdns	Runs	Wkts
A. Shaw	75	52	47	2
McIntyre	54	37	31	1
Barratt	47	21	54	3
Blamires	36	17	45	2
Ulyett	26	7	47	1
E. Lockwood	5.3	2	8	1

Australian Bowling

	Overs	Mdns	Runs	Wkts
Spofforth	39	4	86	2
Garrett	30.2	13	41	7
Allan	10	3	12	—
Boyle	5	—	18	—

Umpires: E. Willsher and E. Henty.

MIDDLESEX v THE AUSTRALIANS

Played at Lord's, June 20, 21, 22, 1878

The Australians' second appearance at Lord's was favoured with glorious cricketing weather of true English summer form, bright and burning hot, weather that was the more welcome because, up to that time, it had been so rare. The MCC authorities most praiseworthily kept the daily admission charge down to the old fashioned 6d., and the official returns as to the numbers who paid for admission were 5,788 on the first day, 6,191 on the second day, and 774 on the third day – when it was expected there would be but little cricket wanting to finish off the match, but that little comprised some of the very finest hitting displayed by any man in '78, and those few visitors who had the good fortune to be present from start to finish of the cricket at Lord's on that hot Saturday morning, will long remember with pleasure how, in 74 minutes, the Hon. E. Lyttelton brilliantly hit his score from 37 to 113 from the Australian bowling.

Midwinter was to have played for the Australians, and just before noon on the first day he was duly flannelled and practising at Lord's ready for play, but shortly after W. G. Grace arrived in hot haste from Kennington, claiming and obtaining Midwinter to play for Gloucestershire v Surrey, which match was commenced that day on The Oval. It was rumoured W. G. Grace acted on a prior made agreement; be that as it may Midwinter played that day for Gloucestershire, and never again played for the Australians.

The Australians lost choice of innings, and were put in to bat on carefully tended but dead wickets. At fourteen minutes past twelve a hearty cheer welcomed the brothers Bannerman's walk to wickets, and the Australian batting forthwith commenced to the slow round bowling of Henderson and W. H. Hadow. Charles Bannerman characteristically started the hitting with a 4 to leg, and his brother followed up with a 2; then a very fine left-hand catch at point settled Charles for his one hit innings. With the score at 12 A. Bannerman skied one that fell into the hands of cover-point, and at 13 long-on settled Horan. Then Gregory and Garrett played steadily and well, but found it difficult to get the ball away for runs against the smart, close, and capital fielding of the well placed Middlesex men; however, soon after Garrett made two 4s (drive, and very fine cut up the ground), and Hadow gave up the ball to Robertson, whose fast bowling forthwith paid, as with the third ball he delivered he bowled Garrett for 19, and with the seventh ball he bowled Spofforth for two 3s. The score was at 39 when Garrett was out, at 43 when Spofforth was out, and at 46 when an easy catch at point got rid of Murdoch for 0. Bailey then played; he and Gregory stayed up to lunch call, two o'clock, when Gregory had made 22, Bailey 18, and the score was at 82 for 6 wickets. On resuming play, at 2.45, the not outs went at it again to the bowling of Hadow and I. D. Walker. At three o'clock the 100 was hoisted, but at 3.20 Bailey was easily had at point for 39, the score at 124; and at 125 a catch at short-slip settled Gregory, who had been two hours and five minutes making his 42, a carefully and well played score that included three fine drives for 4 each. Boyle then faced Blackham, but at 136 smart fielding ran out Boyle for 5, and Allan, the last man in, stayed with Blackham until 29 more runs were made, when, at ten minutes past four, Allan was bowled for 15, and the innings ended for 165 runs, made from 116 English overs, Mr W. H. Hadow having had a hand in the downfall of five of the ten Australian wickets.

Middlesex batting was commenced at 4.30 by A. J. Webbe and I. D. Walker; they started so well that, despite the bowling of Spofforth, Boyle, Allan, and Garrett, they made 46 runs before a wicket fell by I. D. Walker being had at short-leg for 24 – an innings that included a 4 to leg from Spofforth, and a cut for 4 from Garrett, who at 48 bowled Hadow for 2. Then A. Lyttelton faced A. J. Webbe, and the cricket all round was truly fine, and deservedly applauded, the Australian bowling and fielding and the Middlesex batting alike impartially receiving earnest English cheers; and so the score rose to 107, when Allan bowled A. J. Webbe for 50 – a fine and a fortunate innings, insomuch as it included six 4s and a miss at short-leg when he had made 11. Then disasters set in so seriously for Middlesex that at 111 A. Lyttelton played on for 25, and H. R. Webbe played on for 0; at 113 Scott was smartly stumped for 2, and E. Lyttelton bowled for 4; at 120 both Henderson and Salmon were bowled, and at 122 Studd was also bowled; and so, at two minutes to seven, the Middlesex innings was finished for 122, and cricket ceased for that day, Middlesex's 122 runs having been made from 91 Australian overs.

On the Friday, a grand summer day, the two Bannermans commenced the Australians' second innings at ten past twelve, to the bowling of Henderson and Hadow. When 15 overs had been bowled for 11 runs, A. Bannerman was had at cover-point for 3, and when 18 only had been made, Horan was had at wicket for 2. A hearty cheer then greeted Gregory's walk to wicket, and steady play increased the score to 35, when Henderson clean bowled Charles Bannerman for 23, a well played innings of nearly one hour's duration, and that included two 4s (one a splendid drive that sent the ball over the seated visitors' heads). Gregory and Garrett then made so good a stand, that the score, despite lots of bowling changes, was hit from 35 to 93, when a fine hit was splendidly conquered at long-on by a fine catch by Studd, and so Garrett was out for 34; whereupon Spofforth faced Gregory, who, however, at 109, was had at slip for another 42, an innings that included 5 very fine on-drives for 4 each, and an innings that deserved, and received, a heap of hearty applause. Murdoch was next man in, and next man out, Scott bowling him for 13, when the score was at 159. Then Bailey and Spofforth increased the runs to 197, when Salmon, the wicket-keeper, settled Spofforth for 56, not only the highest Australian score in the match, but the highest Australian score then hit in England. Spofforth (an especial favourite with the British public) was loudly cheered. Bailey and Blackham then made a stand, and, in defiance of all bowling changes, hit the score to 240, when Robertson wound up the innings clean off the reel, as with an over, that stands in the score book this wise – w w . w, successively bowling Bailey, Boyle, and Allan, and so, at seven minutes past five, did Robertson excitingly finish off the innings at 240, loud cheers of "well bowled," "well bowled, Sir," "well bowled," ringing out again, and again, in compliment to so marvellously successful an over.

Wanting 284 runs to win, the Middlesex men commenced their second innings at 5.30, with Studd and A. Lyttelton, to the bowling of Allan and Garrett. Five runs and a wide ball had been scored when A. Lyttelton was had at wicket for 3, Garratt then having bowled 4 overs (all maidens) for that wicket. Then four Englishmen were rapidly got out, as, when the score was at 14 only, Studd was bowled, A. J. Webbe played on, Scott settled at point, and Hadow bowled, all four wickets being captured with the score at 14. Here, at a quarter past six, E. Lyttelton went to the rescue, and began an innings that will live fresh in cricket history so long as the Australians' visit to the old Country is talked about. I. D. Walker and E. Lyttelton brilliantly and rapidly hit the score up to 71, when Walker was bowled for 23, an innings that included two 3s and three 4s. Seven more runs were then added, when time stopped play for that day, Middlesex's second innings standing at 79 for six wickets,

E. Lyttelton, not out, 37. H. R. Webbe, not out, 5.

On the Saturday they began play in weather so hot that the glass then stood at 105 in the sun; under that hot sun the not outs resumed their innings, at four past twelve, to the bowling of Allan and Garrett. After scoring a single, E. Lyttelton hit so brilliantly and scored so rapidly, that, by a 4, a 2, and a 4 he made 10 runs from one over of Allan's; by a 4, a 2, a 4, and a 2 he made 12 runs from one over of Spofforth's; he made 31 runs in 14 minutes! (a fact), and when, at a quarter to one, Spofforth bowled H. R. Webbe for 17, the score stood at 148, so many as 69 runs having been put on in 41 minutes that morning, 12 of those runs by H. R. Webbe, and 57 by E. Lyttelton, who went on hitting in really superb style until 18 minutes past one, when he was last man out, a catch at slip by Gregory ending his innings for 113 runs, made by nineteen singles, thirteen 2s, four 3s, and fourteen 4s, his 76 runs that morning having been made in 74 minutes. Very few people were present at the earlier portion of E. Lyttelton's hitting that day, when he was punishing the bowling in his most brilliant form, but when he was out for 113, all present applauded him most lustily, the Australians joining heartily in complimenting him on the, unquestionably, very finest hitting display made in 1878. The Australians won the match by 98 runs.

The Australians

	1st innings		2nd innings	
Charles Bannerman c W. H. Hadow b Henderson	4	–	b Henderson	23
A. Bannerman c Henderson b W. H. Hadow	8	–	c Scott b W. H. Hadow	3
T. Horan c A. Lyttelton b W. H. Hadow	1	–	c Salmon b Henderson	2
D. Gregory c E. Lyttelton b Henderson	42	–	c W. H. Hadow b Henderson	42
T. W. Garrett b Robertson	19	–	c J. E. K. Studd b Henderson	34
F. E. Spofforth b Robertson	6	–	c Salmon b Henderson	56
W. L. Murdoch c W. H. Hadow b Henderson	0	–	b Scott	13
G. H. Bailey c W. H. Hadow b Henderson	39	–	b Robertson	32
J. M. Blackham not out	20	–	not out	21
H. F. Boyle run out	5	–	b Robertson	0
F. E. Allan b Robertson	15	–	b Robertson	0
B 4, l-b 2	6		B 10, l-b 3, w 1	14
	165			240

Middlesex

	1st innings		2nd innings	
A. J. Webbe b Allan	50	–	b Allan	0
I. D. Walker c C. Bannerman b Garrett	24	–	b Boyle	23
W. H. Hadow b Garrett	2	–	b Allan	0
Hon. A. Lyttelton b Garrett	25	–	c Blackham b Garrett	3
Hon. E. Lyttelton b Allan	4	–	c Gregory b Allan	113
H. R. Webbe b Garrett	0	–	b Allan	17
Stanley-Scott st Blackham b Garrett	2	–	c Murdoch b Garrett	3
J. E. K. Studd b Allan	2	–	b Allan	7
R. Henderson b Garrett	5	–	b Garrett	7
E. H. Salmon b Garrett	0	–	not out	5
J. Robertson not out	2	–	b Allan	4
B 5, l-b 1	6		L-b 2, w 1	3
	122			185

Middlesex Bowling

	Overs	Mdns	Runs	Wkts	Overs	Mdns	Runs	Wkts
Henderson	48	20	60	4	52	18	96	5
Hadow	35	14	47	2	42	19	56	1
Robertson	20.3	10	31	3	21	6	35	3
I. D. Walker	7	1	18	—	8	2	14	—
Scott	5	3	3	—	8	3	15	1
E. Lyttelton					6	2	6	—
A. J. Webbe					6	2	4	—

Australian Bowling

	Overs	Mdns	Runs	Wkts	Overs	Mdns	Runs	Wkts
Garrett	30	15	38	7	29	14	44	3
Allan	24	12	27	3	41.3	16	76	6
Spofforth	22	13	29	—	14	3	34	—
Boyle	14	7	16	—	6	—	15	1
Horan	1	—	6	—	3	—	13	—

Umpires: Robert Thoms and Nixon (*Cambs.*)

THE AUSTRALIANS v LEICESTERSHIRE

Played at Leicester, July 15, 16, 17, 1878

The Field of July 20th, in an especially interesting report of this match, stated "It is not perhaps generally known that the Leicestershire Club were the first to make an engagement with the Australians, and the only one to pay them a lump sum for playing." And here it may be as well to acknowledge that it is to the ably written and elaborate report in *The Field* that the Compiler is indebted for all that follows respecting this match.

The weather was exceptionably favourable, and the attendances extremely large, play on the first day being resumed after luncheon in the presence of about 12,000 spectators, and on the other days the assemblages were also great.

The Leicestershire cricket was remarkable for John Wheeler and A. Sankey scoring 113 runs before the first wicket fell, Sankey playing finely for 70, and Wheeler (the MCC pro.) scoring 60, and backing that up with a second of 65 – two innings that won him great praise from the critics and the thousands of Leicestershire men who witnessed them played. Another feature in the County cricket was, that when the second day's play closed Leicestershire had lost four wickets only of their second innings for 129 runs; but on the Wednesday, the remaining six wickets were so rapidly shut up that the innings ended for 145, Bishop taking his bat out for 10.

The Australian cricket was wound up in sensational form by Charles Bannerman. At one o'clock on the third day Charles Bannerman and Murdoch began the Australians' second innings, 209 being the number of runs required to win. Bannerman began in ominously successful form by making three 4s from the first over bowled. At 2 o'clock they left for luncheon, Charles Bannerman having then made 58, not out. At 3 o'clock they went at it again, Bannerman characteristically resuming his innings with two 4s and a 2. When 93 runs had been scored the first Australian wicket fell by Murdoch being bowled (off his pad) for 24. Then Horan went in, and he and Charles Bannerman all but won the match. At seven minutes past four Bannerman had made his 100 (and mightly was he cheered thereon); and when, at a quarter to five, the score stood at 201, Bannerman was thrown out for 133 – an innings described in *The Field* as "made in a masterly style, and it would be difficult to imagine more faultless play, or in which tremendous hitting was accompanied by so large an amount of scientific cricket."

This 133 by Charles Bannerman was the first three figure innings hit in England by an Australian batsman; his hits were nine singles, nine 2s, three 3s, twenty-three 4s – (92 by fourers!) – and one 5. At five minutes to five the Australians had won this extraordinary match by 8 wickets, T. Horan, not out, 40.

Leicestershire

John Wheeler (of Lord's) c Boyle b Spofforth	60	– c Blackham b Spofforth	65
A. Sankey b Garrett	70	– retired hurt	0
Panter c Gregory b Garrett	20	– b Bailey	32
G. S. Marriott c Horan b Garrett	7	– b Blackham	18
Collier not out	20	– lbw b Boyle	6
Parnham c Garrett b Spofforth	0	– c Gregory b Garrett	0
Rodwell b Garrett	4	– c Bailey b Spofforth	6
Walter c Allan b Spofforth	2	– c Boyle b Spofforth	0
Rylott run out	4	– b Garrett	0
F. Randon b Spofforth	2	– lbw b Spofforth	0
Bishop b Spofforth	0	– not out	10
L-b 4	4	B 5, l-b 3	8
	193		145

The Australians

Charles Bannerman c Bishop b Rylott	15 – run out	133
W. L. Murdoch b Rylott	16 – b Parnham	24
T. Horan run out	1 – not out	40
D. Gregory c Bishop b Parnham	23 – not out	3
T. W. Garrett b F. Randon	7	
F. E. Spofforth c Marriott b F. Randon	7	
G. H. Bailey c Panter b F. Randon	0	
F. E. Allan c Rodwell b Parnham	5	
J. M. Blackham not out	24	
Conway c Bishop b Parnham	12	
H. F. Boyle b Rylott	8	
B 8, l-b 4	12	B 8, n-b 2 10
	130	210

Australian Bowling

	Overs	Mdns	Runs	Wkts	Overs	Mdns	Runs	Wkts
Spofforth	27	4	60	5	8.1	2	26	4
Allan	24	9	44	—	11	4	23	—
Garrett	22	10	30	4	8	3	28	2
Boyle	18	8	27	—	16	8	21	1
Bailey	10	6	13	—	11	3	19	1
Horan	6	1	15	—	6	2	16	—
Blackham					3	1	4	1

Leicestershire Bowling

	Overs	Mdns	Runs	Wkts	Overs	Mdns	Runs	Wkts
Rylott	42.3	25	45	3	30	11	66	—
F. Randon	27	14	39	3	12	4	30	—
Parnham	15	3	34	3	19	6	40	1
Bishop					6.2	3	12	—
Collier					4	1	6	—
Wheeler					4	—	26	—
Panter					3	—	20	—

THE AUSTRALIANS v ELEVEN ENGLISH PROFESSIONALS

Played on The Oval, September 2, 3, 1878

The match originally set down to be played on those days on The Oval was "The Australians v The Players of England," of course meaning the very best eleven professionals of England available, and for that match the Committee of the Surrey CCC had, with praiseworthy courtesy, placed the free use of their ground at the service of The Australians, with whom rested all arrangements, liabilities, and the profits of the match. Unfortunately, owing to some very much debated, but never clearly explained, misunderstanding as to remuneration, many of the very best professionals of England did not play. It is impossible to give space in this little book to a full, and, consequently, fair expression of the published Why's and Wherefore's of this misunderstanding, and so the compiler passes it by with the expression of a regret that it ever occurred, and with a further regret that it was not amicably arranged.

The weather was as fine and warm as English weather could be expected to be in September, and the two days' attendances were so very large that the cricket critic of *The Sportsman* computed them at about 10,000 on the Monday, and about 12,000 on the Tuesday, and, inasmuch as the admission charge was 1s. each day, the result must have been highly remunerative to the Australians, and amply warranted them in generously increasing their originally agreed payment of £10 to each English player to £20, and of, furthermore, giving Barratt a bonus of £5, in compliment to the great success of his bowling in obtaining all the ten wickets in Australia's first innings.

The Australians, at 12.35, commenced the batting on soft wickets, with the brothers Bannerman, to the bowling of Barratt and Watson. When the score was at 12, A. Bannerman was easily caught out at mid-on; at 14, Horan was had at slip; and, at 16, Murdoch was stumped. Then Spofforth faced Charles Bannerman, and so much of a stand was made that the score was increased to 50, when there occurred an awful smash up of Australian wickets, Spofforth being stumped for 14, and (in one over) Bailey had at mid-off, Gregory caught out at cover-point, and Blackham stumped, all four wickets going down at 50, Barratt then having bowled 17 overs for 24 runs and the 7 wickets down. Charles Bannerman stayed until the last man came in; then he was had at point for 51 (out of 77), an innings that won great praise for its clever timing and good hitting on such slow playing wickets. Charles Bannerman's hits included four 3s and three 4s. In that innings

Barratt's bowling captured all 10 wickets – 3 stumped, 7 caught out.

The Englishmen's innings was commenced at 3.20 by Rigley and Barlow, to the bowling of Spofforth and Garrett. The bowling had to be changed frequently before a wicket fell, and the score was hit to 23 when Rigley was well caught and bowled – hand high up, catch hot – by Allan for 18. Barlow and James Phillips made the score 44, when Barlow was stumped for 16. James Phillips and young Hearne then increased the runs to 59, when Spofforth had four wickets clean off the reel, as, before another run was made, he bowled Hearne, got Charlwood caught out at mid-on, bowled Wheeler first ball, and caused Watson to play the ball on, all four English wickets falling to Spofforth's bowling with the score at 59. H. Phillips, Lillywhite, and Barratt merely walked to the wickets and walked back again, and, when the ninth man was out, there had actually been six 0s in succession scored. William McIntyre (the last man in) then hit a bit, and, as he and James Phillips increased the score from 63 to upside the Australians' total, and then to pass that total by 5 runs, the cheering was hearty indeed, and quite as hearty for the Australians when a catch at wicket finished off the innings for 82 (only 71 from the bat). Time was then up, that day's cricket having consisted of 131 overs and 2 balls bowled, 148 runs from the bat and 11 extras scored, so many as thirteen 0s being attached to the 20 wickets then down.

On the Tuesday the Australians began their second innings at 12.25; they went to wickets in the same order as on the preceding day; but the Bannermans this time made 44 runs before a wicket was lost; then Charles played on for 15, and in that same over McIntyre bowled Horan. Murdoch was quickly out, and A. Bannerman c and b for 25 – the largest innings made that day; and although Gregory and Garrett increased the score by 19 runs for the last wicket, they were all out by 3.35 for 89, leaving the Englishmen 85 runs to score to win.

At five minutes to four Rigley and Barlow began the second innings of the Englishmen, to the bowling of Spofforth and Allan. Steadily was the score worked up to 13 when Spofforth bowled Barlow, and at 22 Allan bowled Rigley. James Phillips and Hearne then brought out British cheers by increasing the British score to 39, when a middle stump ball from Spofforth settled Hearne for a 12, that included a square-leg crack for 5 from the fast bowler. James Phillips and Charlwood stayed and made the score 56, when Charlwood was also bowled by Spofforth for 12; and at 60 James Phillips was c and b by Boyle for 14 – the highest score hit in that innings. At 67 Spofforth bowled Watson, the Englishmen then having four wickets to fall, and 18 runs to score to win, against frequently changed good bowling, backed up by some of the finest fielding all round by a team ever seen in this glorious old cricketing country of ours. John Wheeler and Harry Phillips then made the score 71, when a fair chance for English success was excitingly discounted by Phillips being run out, and Wheeler bowled. Two more runs only had been made when Garrett bowled Lillywhite, and there were then only McIntyre and Barrett left to make the dozen runs wanted to win. Old Mc made 3 of those runs, but then Spofforth sent in a sparkler that hit the middle stump of Barrett's wicket, and so the Australians won this closely contested match by 8 runs, whereupon the thousands on the ground rushed to the front of the Pavilion and there stood cheering the Australians so lustily, loud, and long, that the principal members of the team had to appear and bow their acknowledgments, and Conway addressed the B.P. in a brief speech.

The Australians

Charles Bannerman c Barlow b Barratt	51	– b W. McIntyre	15
A. Bannerman c W. McIntyre b Barratt	4	– c and b Barlow	25
T. Horan c Watson b Barratt	0	– b W. McIntyre	4
W. Murdoch st H. Phillips b Barratt	0	– c G. Hearne jun. b W. McIntyre	0
F. E. Spofforth st H. Phillips b Barratt	14	– b W. McIntyre	0
G. H. Bailey c Lillywhite b Barratt	0	– b Barlow	12
D. Gregory c J. Phillips b Barratt	0	– not out	9
J. M. Blackham st H. Phillips b Barratt	0	– b Barlow	0
H. F. Boyle c J. Phillips b Barratt	8	– c and b W. McIntyre	4
T. Garrett c Watson b Barratt	0	– c G. Hearne jun. b Barratt	10
F. Allan not out	0	– b W. McIntyre	4
		B 3, l-b 3	6
	77		89

English Professionals

W. Rigley c and b Allan	18	– b Allan	10
R. G. Barlow st Murdoch b Allan	16	– b Spofforth	8
James Phillips not out	19	– c and b Boyle	14
G. G. Hearne jun. (son of George), b Spofforth	8	– b Garrett	12
H. Charlwood c Boyle b Spofforth	0	– b Spofforth	12
John Wheeler b Spofforth	0	– b Spofforth	4
A. Watson b Spofforth	0	– b Spofforth	7
Henry Phillips c Boyle b Spofforth	0	– run out	2
James Lillywhite c Allan b Boyle	0	– b Garrett	2
E. Barratt b Spofforth	0	– b Spofforth	0
William McIntyre c Murdoch b Spofforth	10	– not out	3
B 4, l-b 7	11	B 2	2
	82		76

English Bowling

	Overs	Mdns	Runs	Wkts	Overs	Mdns	Runs	Wkts
Barratt	29	11	43	10	11.1	2	15	1
Watson	14	4	23	—				
Lillywhite	8	4	9	—				
G. Hearne jun.	6	4	2	—	9	4	15	—
W. McIntyre					29	21	24	6
Barlow					28	18	29	3

Australian Bowling

	Overs	Mdns	Runs	Wkts	Overs	Mdns	Runs	Wkts
Spofforth	34.2	18	37	7	27	11	38	5
Allan	20	13	18	2	15	8	16	1
Garrett	12	8	8	—	13	8	13	2
Boyle	8	5	8	1	8	4	7	1

Umpires: W. Caffyn and Potter.

On the 3rd of September, 1878, about two hours after the termination of the above match, a fearful calamity occurred on the River Thames, that overwhelmed England with sorrow. Two steamers came into collision; one ("The Princess Alice," a pleasure boat) was cut in twain and over 700 lives – then in the fulness of joy and pleasure – were sacrificed with awful suddenness, and very many families sadly and seriously bereaved.

By one who was deeply impressed by the magnitude of this calamity, and the painful and wide-spread distress that must be suffered thereby, a proposition was publicly made (with the two-fold object of Cricketers doing something to mitigate this distress, and to heal up a disruption of friendship that never should have been severed) that The Australians and the very best Eleven Players of England should play a match on The Oval, the proceeds to be equally divided between "The Thames Calamity Fund," The Australians, and The Players. This proposition appeared to be favoured by general approval, but it was not adopted; why was never clearly understood, because, although it was stated The Australians could not find vacant days for the match, such a match – i.e., The Australians v The Players of England – was actually played at Prince's on the 11th and 12th of September, six days subsequent to the above proposition being made; but although that match was not played on behalf of The Fund, it is but fair to repeat here that The Australians subscribed £100 in aid of that sorely needed help to the bereaved.

THE THAMES CALAMITY FUND MATCH

NORTH v SOUTH

Played at The Oval, September 17, 18, 19, 1878

Robert Thoms, the umpire, upon the non-success of the above mentioned proposition, feelingly suggested a North v South match should be played in behalf of "The Thames Fatality Fund". This idea met with the ready and earnest support of most of the influential English Cricketers, Gentlemen and Professionals, and the Surrey Club, and their Secretary backing up the suggestion with prompt and generous energy in the offering the free use of their ground, etc., the match was quickly shaped into playing form; two really splendid sides were selected, willing and ready to play for so praiseworthy an object, and albeit the season was old for cricket, London was out of town, the weather was uncomfortably cold for lookers on, and the batting of one side collapsed in curiously brief form, there were fairly large attendances of spectators on the first two days, and the satisfactory end was attained of £258 being sent in aid of "The Thames Calamity Fund".

Those who know who's who in the cricketing world, and will cast their eyes over the names forming those two fine Elevens, will be surprised to find that not only did the South Eleven (fairly worth 200 runs at any time) go out for two innings of 64 and 116 runs in the match, but in playing a third innings in a fill up of the time match on the Saturday, they were (one man short it is true) actually settled for 58; in fact, in the match, there was only one Southerner who batted up to known form; he was:–

Mr. F. Grace, who scored 22, not out, and 54, not out.

And when the dead wickets and the really splendid bowling and fielding of the Northmen is duly considered, it cannot be doubted but that Mr. F. Grace's batting in this match was equal to the very best Grace form ever played. Alfred Shaw and Morley's bowling was of such splendid excellence that they took 18 of the 20 South wickets at the cost of 134 runs, Morley 8 for 55 runs, and Shaw 10 for 79. As for the North fielding, that was really splendid, notably so three catches, i.e., one by Emmett at deep long-on, who judged and waited for the ball in fine form from a monster hit, high and far, by Mr Thornton; a splendid one hand catch, hand high up, by Bates that settled Barratt; and a very remarkable catch by Shrewsbury that got out Mr Thornton in the second innings. Shrewsbury was fielding deep long-on in front of the people by the tavern; Mr Thornton let out powerfully at one from Morley; Shrewsbury ran to the front of the pavilion, and there, with back hard up against the paling, he caught the ball and tumbled over – head first, heels in the air form – into the lap of some old member, cosily enjoying the cricket on a front seat; but Shrewsbury held the ball all the while, and came up smiling and tossing the ball up in the usual neat form that Shrewsbury displays in all his cricket. The North batting was commenced with such ominous success by Ulyett and Lockwood that they made 97 runs before a wicket fell, when Ulyett was had at mid-off for 71 (71 out of 97!), made by five 4s – one a big drive on to the "Stand". At 110 Lockwood was out for a patiently played 36. Selby and Shrewsbury then hit the score to 162, when Shrewsbury was out for 41. Selby and Daft increased the figures to 189, when Daft hit wicket, and Oscroft was bowled by a ball that was stated to have "run clean round his bat". Selby and Emmett then hit the score to 259, whereupon the first day's play finished; Selby 64, not out; Emmett, 28, not out.

Next day Emmett was out for 45, the score at 285. At 288 Bates was out, and at 293 an easy catch at mid-off finished Selby's innings for 76 – the highest and the finest played score on his side. Selby went in at 110 for two wickets, so 183 runs were made and five wickets fell during his stay. The North innings ended at twenty minutes to one that day for 303 runs, and at a quarter to two on the Saturday the North had won the match by an innings and 123 runs.

The North

Geo. Ulyett c Ridley b G. Hearne jun.	71	W. Bates c and b F. Grace	1
Ephraim Lockwood b Barratt	36	Alfred Shaw c and b F. Grace	2
Arthur Shrewsbury c Shuter b F. Grace	41	George Pinder b F. Grace	6
J. Selby c Ridley b G. Hearne jun.	76	F. Morley not out	3
Richard Daft hit wkt b Barratt	13	B 9	9
William Oscroft b Barratt	0		
T. Emmett c Ridley b G. Hearne jun.	45		303

The South

C. I. Thornton Esq. c Emmett b Alfred Shaw	1	– c Shrewsbury b Morley	0
J. Shuter Esq. b Alfred Shaw	2	– b Alfred Shaw	8
A. P. Lucas Esq. c Selby b Morley	17	– c Emmett b Alfred Shaw	3
A. W. Ridley Esq. b Alfred Shaw	6	– b Emmett	3
G. F. Grace Esq. not out	22	– not out	54
G. G. Hearne jun. (son of George), c W. Oscroft b Alfred Shaw	0	– c Pinder b Alfred Shaw	9
F. Penn Esq. b Morley	3	– c Bates b Alfred Shaw	2
Lord Harris c Pinder b Morley	0	– c Pinder b Emmett	1
E. Pooley c W. Oscroft b Morley	7	– c Alfred Shaw b Morley	11
I. D. Walker Esq. c E. Lockwood b Morley	3	– b Morley	10
E. Barratt c W. Oscroft b Alfred Shaw	1	– c Bates b Alfred Shaw	3
B 1, l-b 1	2	B 7, l-b 1, w 4	12
	64		116

South Bowling

	Overs	Mdns	Runs	Wkts
G. Hearne jun.	56	25	80	3
Barratt	50	12	106	3
Mr F. Grace	37	19	33	4
Mr Lucas	25	10	34	—
Mr Ridley	15	6	22	—
Mr Thornton	5	1	8	—
Lord Harris	5	—	9	—
Mr F. Penn	4	2	2	—

North Bowling

	Overs	Mdns	Runs	Wkts	Overs	Mdns	Runs	Wkts
A. Shaw	37	16	33	5	47	25	46	5
Morley	36	25	29	5	17	7	26	3
Emmett					10	4	16	2
Bates					7	3	9	—
Ulyett					3	1	7	—

Umpires: James Southerton and Robert Thoms.

Another North v South match was commenced to pass away the Saturday afternoon. The South first batted (only 10), but they were all got out for 58 – Emmett's bowling having taken 8 wickets – 4 bowled, 3 c and b – for 32 runs, one of Mr Tom's c and b's being so hot and truly fine a catch as to elicit shouts of "Bravo!" "Well done!" "Well done, old 'un!" The North's turn at batting proceeded up to "time," when they were 10 runs ahead, and had seven wickets to the good, thus:

The South (only 10 men batted), 58. The North (only 3 men out), 68.

So ended the three days' cricket played to benefit The "Thames Calamity Fund", the following being a copy of the officially published Dr. and Cr. account:

Receipts	£	s.	d.
Sept. 19 – Gate and Stand .	139	15	0
20 – Gate and Stand .	122	14	6
21 – Gate and Stand .	47	9	0
Tickets per Mr Strachan	8	4	6
Tickets per Mr W. Burrup ...	2	2	0
Tickets per Mr H. T. Smith ..	7	16	0
Tickets sold at Gate	8	18	6
Total	£336	19	6

Expenditure	£	s.	d.
The North Eleven, at £5 per man	55	0	0
The 3 South Players, at £3 per man	9	0	0
Umpires, £1 each	2	0	0
Commissionaires	1	19	0
Scorers	2	0	0
Gatekeepers and Check-takers	5	0	0
Police	3	6	0
Bill-stickers, 5s, bill-poster, 8s	0	13	0
	78	18	0
Balance sent to the Mansion House Fund	258	1	6
Total	£336	19	6

ENGLAND v AUSTRALIA

Played at The Oval, September 6, 7, 8, 1880

The compiler much regrets that the limited space allotted to the Australians' matches in this book precludes the possibility of giving a lengthened account of this famous contest. He must therefore rest content to put on record the following anent the match: That in the history of the game no contest has created such world-wide interest; that the attendances on the first and second days were the largest ever seen at a cricket match; that 20,814 persons passed through the turnstiles on the Monday, 19,863 on the Tuesday, and 3,751 on the Wednesday; that fine weather favoured the match from start to finish; that the wickets were faultless; that Mr Murdoch's magnificent innings of 153 not out was made without a chance, and contained one 5, eighteen 4s, three 3s, thirteen 2s and forty-one singles; that Mr W. G. Grace's equally grand innings was made with only one hard chance, and comprised twelve 4s, ten 3s, fourteen 2s and forty-six singles; that superb batting was also shown by Mr Lucas, Lord Harris, Mr McDonnell and Mr Steel; that the fielding and wicket-keeping on both sides was splendid; that a marvellous change in the aspect of the game was effected on the last day; that universal regret was felt at the unavoidable absence of Mr Spofforth; and that England won the match by five wickets.

England

Dr W. G. Grace b Palmer	152	– not out	9
Dr E. M. Grace c Alexander b Bannerman	36	– b Boyle	0
A. P. Lucas b Bannerman	55	– c Blackham b Palmer	2
W. Barnes b Alexander	28	– c Moule b Boyle	5
Lord Harris c Bonnor b Alexander	52		
F. Penn b Bannerman	23	– not out	27
A. G. Steel c Boyle b Moule	42		
Hon. A. Lyttelton not out	11	– b Palmer	13
G. F. Grace c Bannerman b Moule	0	– b Palmer	0
A. Shaw b Moule	0		
F. Morley run out	2		
B 8, l-b 11	19	N-b 1	1
	420		57

Australia

W. L. Murdoch c Barnes b Steel	0	– not out	153
A. C. Bannerman b Morley	32	– c Lucas b Shaw	8
T. U. Groube b Steel	11	– c Shaw b Morley	0
P. S. McDonnell c Barnes b Morley	27	– lbw b W. G. Grace	43
J. Slight c G. F. Grace b Morley	11	– c Harris b W. G. Grace	0
J. M. Blackham c and b Morley	0	– c E. M. Grace b Morley	19
G. J. Bonnor c G. F. Grace b Shaw	2	– b Steel	16
H. F. Boyle not out	36	– run out	3
G. E. Palmer b Morley	6	– c and b Steel	4
G. Alexander c W. G. Grace b Steel	6	– c Shaw b Morley	33
W. H. Moule c Morley b W. G. Grace	6	– b Barnes	34
B 9, l-b 3	12	B 7, l-b 7	14
	149		327

Australia Bowling

	Overs	Mdns	Runs	Wkts	Overs	Mdns	Runs	Wkts
Boyle	41	15	71	—	17	7	21	2
Palmer	70	27	116	1	16.3	5	35	3
Alexander	32	10	69	2				
Bannerman	50	12	111	3				
McDonnell	2	—	11	—				
Moule	12.3	4	23	3				

England Bowling

	Overs	Mdns	Runs	Wkts	Overs	Mdns	Runs	Wkts
Morley	32	9	56	5	61	30	90	3
Mr Steel	39	9	58	3	31	6	73	2
Shaw	13	5	21	1	33	18	42	1
Mr W. G. Grace	1.1	—	2	1	28	10	66	2
Barnes					8.3	3	17	1
Mr Lucas					12	7	23	—
Mr Penn					3	1	2	—

Umpires: H. H. Stephenson and R. Thoms.

THE AUSTRALIANS IN ENGLAND, 1882

The third Team of Cricketers from Australia sailed from Melbourne for England in the Peninsular and Oriental Company's steamer Assam on March 16, 1882, and after a very pleasant though not particularly speedy voyage, the vessel anchored at Plymouth at 10.30 on the morning of Wednesday, May 3. The manager of the team, Mr C. W. Beal, of the South Wales Cricket Association, accompanied by Messrs Murdoch, Bonnor and Garrett, left the ship and proceeded by train to London. On arriving at Paddington they at once drove to the quarters secured for them at the Tavistock Hotel, Covent Garden, by Mr Henry Perkins, Secretary of the Marylebone Cricket Club, who had been acting as their agent. The other members of the team came round to London in the steamer, and joined their companions about twelve hours after. Mr McDonnell had had to be carried on board the vessel at Melbourne, suffering from a severe sunstroke, but he, as well as every member of the team, appeared in excellent health and spirits on landing on the shores of the Old Country. Bonnor, it may be mentioned, shortly after landing, threw a cricket ball 119 yards, 5 inches, and thereby won a bet made by one of the passengers that he would not, without practice, throw 115 yards.

Seven of the Team hailed from New South Wales, viz: Murdoch, Bannerman, Garrett, Massie, Bonnor, Spofforth, and Jones. Victoria furnished five – Boyle, Blackham, Palmer, Horan and McDonnell, while South Australia contributed only one – Giffen.

The following table, which has been compiled from the editions of *Wisden's* for the years 1879, 1881 and 1883, will shew the composition of each of the three Teams which have visited England; how the members of these teams acquitted themselves with the bat, and what success the principal trundlers had with the ball.

THE THREE AUSTRALIAN TEAMS, AND THEIR BATTING AVERAGES IN ELEVEN-A-SIDE MATCHES

1878		1880		1882	
W. L. Murdoch	14.18	W. L. Murdoch	25.15	W. L. Murdoch	30.31
A. C. Bannerman	13.13	A. C Bannerman	17.19	A. C. Bannerman	22.8
J. McC. Blackham	18.9	J. McC. Blackham	13.10	J. McC. Blackham	17
H. F. Boyle	6.14	H. F. Boyle	15	H. F. Boyle	9.9
F. R. Spofforth	13.19	F. R. Spofforth	21.1	F. R. Spofforth	8.10
T. Horan	14.8	A. H. Jarvis	16.7	T. Horan	25
T. W. Garrett	14.27	G. Alexander	14.8	T. W. Garrett	11.34
C. Bannerman	24.2	P S. McDonnell	23.4	P. S. McDonnell	17.16
W. Midwinter	15.4	G. J. Bonnor	9.1	G. J. Bonnor	20.15
G. Bailey	14	G. E. Palmer	14.3	G. E. Palmer	11.2
D. Gregory	11.7	T. U. Groube	13.2	H. H. Massie	24.35
F. Allan	10.11	W. H. Moule	12.3	G. Giffen	18.9
		J. Slight	6.5	S. P. Jones	12.3

BOWLING AVERAGES OF THE FOUR PRINCIPAL BOWLERS IN EACH OF THE THREE TEAMS IN ELEVEN-A-SIDE MATCHES

1878		1880		1882	
F. R. Spofforth	11.46	F. R. Spofforth	8.28	F. R. Spofforth	12.24
H. F. Boyle	10.26	H. F. Boyle	15.31	H. F. Boyle	11.96
T. W. Garrett	10.17	G. Alexander	33.5	T. W. Garrett	13.95
F. Allan	18.26	G. E. Palmer	11.10	G. E. Palmer	12.75

The Team soon got to work, as on the Saturday following their arrival Murdoch, Massie and Garrett played for the Orleans Club against Bexley, at Twickenham, but as they scored only 3 runs between them, and were all bowled by Mr C. E. Horner, their batting display was not indicative of their real merits. Garrett, however, captured four wickets and Massie three. Giffen and Jones on the same day played for the City Ramblers against Addiscombe, the former making 37 and the latter 6, while Giffen took four wickets for 16 runs, and Jones five for 18.

On the following Monday, at Mitcham, ten of the team had their first day's hard practice, Spofforth, Bonnor and Horan being the absent members. On the following day all the team, except Bonnor and Spofforth, went in for more practice, and on the Wednesday, Murdoch, Massie, McDonnell and Spofforth had some practice at Lord's, while all the others except Bonnor, who was suffering with a bad hand, had about three hours cricket at Mitcham. On Friday, May 12, the Australians were entertained at a Luncheon in the City, and next day Murdoch, Massie and Spofforth played for the Orleans Club against Richmond, and Giffen, Jones and Blackham for the City Ramblers v Erith. Murdoch scored 21 and 23, Massie 22 and 1, and Spofforth 17 and 6, the three Colonists scoring 90 runs out of 151 made from the bat in the two innings of the Orleans Club. Spofforth took four wickets, but at considerable cost. Jones played an innings of 70; Giffen scored only 5, but took seven wickets at a trifle over 8 runs apiece, and Blackham made 33 and took two wickets for 17 runs.

This was the last day's practice, and on the following day (Sunday) the majority of the team journeyed to Oxford to play their first match.

THE AUSTRALIANS v OXFORD UNIVERSITY

Played on the Christ Church Ground, Oxford, May 15, 16, 17, 1882

Monday. Sky overcast but no rain. East wind bitterly cold. Murdoch won the toss and chose first innings. Massie scored his highest innings in England, and his batting display will take rank as one of the most brilliant performances ever witnessed in the cricket field. He gave a difficult chance when he had made 12, and another when he had scored his first century. At the luncheon interval he had scored 100 out of 145, and had seen five batsmen dismissed. At 257 Massie had made 200 in three hours and five minutes, and with an addition of 8 runs to the score a good catch at the boundary terminated his innings for 206, comprising twenty-four 4s, fifteen 3s, fifteen 2s and thirty-five singles. Jones and Garrett played cautiously, and the innings was concluded at 5.25. The University had ten minutes' batting, and in that short space of time lost two wickets with the score at 5 only. In the evening the Australians were entertained at dinner by the Oxford University Cricket Club, in the Hall of Corpus Christi College.

Tuesday. A welcome change in the weather, the sun shining brightly during the afternoon. Shaw, not out overnight with 2, carried his bat for 78 – a first class innings, conspicuous for good defence and clean hitting. He received valuable assistance from Robinson, who helped him to put on 57 for the last wicket. In the follow on Leslie played an innings of 56 worthy of his high reputation, and at the call of time the University had lost four wickets for 119 runs.

Wednesday. Weather delightful. Whiting, who had made 15 the previous evening, was not out until he had made 55 in admirable style, without giving a chance. Hamilton played an excellent innings of 37, and Harrison a useful 25, and in the end the capital total of 234 left the Colonists 62 to get to win. In trying to obtain these, Bannerman was bowled before a run was scored, but Massie, after being badly missed when he had made 12, again played most brilliant cricket, and by six 4s, two 3s, three 2s and ten singles, scored 46 while Murdoch made 15, and won the match for Australia by nine wickets.

The Australians

H. H. Massie Esq. c Hamilton b Peake	206	– not out	46
A. C. Bannerman b Robinson	14	– b Robinson	0
W. L. Murdoch Esq. b Robinson	0	– not out	15
P. S. McDonnell Esq. b Harrison	0		
G. Giffen Esq. b Peake	19		
J. McC. Blackham Esq. b Godfrey b Shaw	7		
S. P. Jones Esq. c Whiting b Harrison	39		
T. W. Garrett Esq. b Godfrey	41		
G. E. Palmer Esq. b Peake	18		
H. F. Boyle Esq. b Godfrey	0		
F. P. Spofforth Esq. not out	14		
B 2, l-b 2	4	L-b 2, w 1	3
	362		64

Oxford University

E. D. Shaw Esq. not out	78	– c Jones b Palmer	9
E. Peake Esq. c Bannerman b Palmer	2	– b Giffen	28
A. O. Whiting Esq. b Palmer	0	– b Boyle	55
M. C. Kemp Esq. b Boyle	23	– b Giffen	0
C. F. H. Leslie Esq. c Murdoch b Boyle	13	– c and b Giffen	56
J. G. Walker Esq. c Blackham b Garrett	17	– b Giffen	1
W. A. Thornton Esq. b Garrett	2	– c Jones b Giffen	13
W. D. Hamilton Esq. c Giffen b Spofforth	5	– c Jones b Giffen	37
G. C. Harrison Esq. c Giffen b Spofforth	7	– b Palmer	25
C. J. M. Godfrey Esq. run out	2	– b Giffen	1
G. E. Robinson Esq. b Palmer	28	– not out	0
B 9, l-b 2, n-b 1	12	B 2, l-b 7	9
	189		234

Oxford Bowling

	Overs	Mdns	Runs	Wkts	Overs	Mdns	Runs	Wkts
Mr Robinson	34	13	78	2	11	3	18	1
Mr Harrison	40	11	98	2	9	5	17	—
Mr Godfrey	21	3	65	2	2	1	7	—
Mr Peake	40	14	82	3	4.2	1	19	—
Mr Shaw	13	6	26	1				
Mr Thornton	9	4	9	—				

Australian Bowling

	Overs	Mdns	Runs	Wkts	Overs	Mdns	Runs	Wkts
Mr Spofforth	29	10	39	2	12	2	28	—
Mr Palmer	25.3	9	36	3	27.3	12	42	2
Mr Boyle	25	5	66	2	23	8	30	1
Mr Garrett	20	4	35	2	11	1	27	—
Mr Jones	1	—	1	—	10	3	20	—
Mr Giffen					36	14	78	7

Umpires: L. Greenwood and V. A. Titchmarsh.

THE AUSTRALIANS v LEICESTERSHIRE

Played at Leicester, June 29, 30, 1882

Thursday. Parnham accomplished a bowling feat unequalled by any bowler against the Colonials during their tour, taking nine of the Australians' wickets for 68, despite the fact that four chances were missed off his bowling. His success so delighted the spectators that they subscribed £8 for him on the ground. On the Leicestershire men going in Spofforth and Palmer obtained five wickets each at a less cost per wicket than those of Parnham, but the home team was very weak in batting, and their performance in no way detracted from the merit of the Leicestershire bowler's feat. The Colonists went in a second time for ten minutes' batting and lost one wicket (Bannerman's) for 8 runs.

Friday. Parnham scored another success, though not so great as that on the previous day, and Wheeler played the highest innings in the match, and that a splendid one too. A second rate county lost the match by 74 runs, but they were far from disgraced by the defeat.

The Australians

H. H. Massie Esq. c Bottomore b Parnham	22	– c Curzon b Bottomore	8
A. C. Bannerman c Crofts b Parnham	17	– c Warren b Parnham	3
W. L. Murdoch Esq. c Rylott b Parnham	6	– c Crofts b Parnham	18
P. S. McDonnell Esq. c Wheeler b Parnham	4	– c Parnham b Bottomore	25
T. Horan Esq. b Parnham	8	– b Parnham	21
G. J. Bonnor Esq. c Curzon b Parnham	2	– c Thompson b Parnham	2
J. McC. Blackham Esq. not out	20	– c Turner b Parnham	0
G. Giffen Esq. c and b Parnham	8	– run out	8
G. E. Palmer Esq. b Rylott	1	– not out	9
F. R. Spofforth Esq. st Crofts b Parnham	16	– c G. S. Marriott b Parnham	2
T. W. Garrett Esq. c Rylott b Parnham	1	– run out	8
B 1	1	B 3, l-b 2	5
	106		116

Leicestershire

Lord Curzon b Spofforth	2	– b Palmer	0
A. W. Crofts Esq. c sub. b Palmer	8	– c Blackham b Spofforth	6
J. Wheeler b Spofforth	3	– c Giffen b Spofforth	38
C. Marriott Esq. c Palmer b Spofforth	17	– c Bonnor b Spofforth	14
G. S. Marriott Esq. b Palmer	0	– b Palmer	4
F. Turner b Palmer	0	– b Spofforth	13
J. Parnham c Massie b Spofforth	4	– c Bannerman b Spofforth	5
Warren st Blackham b Palmer	0	– c Murdoch b Palmer	0
Thompson b Palmer	0	– c Massie b Spofforth	5
A. Rylott c Bannerman b Spofforth	5	– c sub b Spofforth	3
W. Bottomore not out	0	– not out	10
B 3, l-b 1	4	B 5, n-b 2	7
	43		105

Leicestershire Bowling

	Overs	Mdns	Runs	Wkts	Overs	Mdns	Runs	Wkts
Parnham	43.3	16	68	9	37	12	61	6
Rylott	43	21	37	1	17.1	5	32	—
Bottomore					19	11	18	2

Australian Bowling

	Overs	Mdns	Runs	Wkts	Overs	Mdns	Runs	Wkts
Mr Spofforth	18	9	24	5	33.2	11	54	7
Mr Palmer	17	10	15	5	28	14	32	3
Mr Giffen					5	1	12	—

Umpires: Mr H. F. Boyle and Mr M. A. Cook.

AUSTRALIA v ENGLAND

Played at The Oval, August 28, 29, 1882

Before entering into any of the details of the play in this match, the compiler desires to place before the readers of *Wisden's* the names of the rival teams and their Batting and Bowling Averages in First-class Matches from the commencement of the season to the time they engaged in this memorable struggle.

The averages of the Australian team have been compiled from the twenty-five first-class matches played by the Colonials from the commencement of their tour until they entered the cricket field to contest All England. The matches omitted in the calculation are those the Colonists played against Leicestershire, Northamptonshire, Northumberland and Gentlemen of Scotland.

The averages of the England Eleven have been compiled from the whole of the First-class Matches in which each member of the side participated from the beginning of the season up to the time they met the Colonists in the grand contest at The Oval, including, of course, the batting and bowling of each member of the team against the Australians themselves. The batting and bowling of Barlow, Ulyett and Peate in the matches they played in Australia in the early months of 1882 are not, of course, included. The full scores and bowling summaries of all the first-class matches played in England in 1882 appear in this book, and as the full scores of only two minor contests (beyond those played by the Australians), viz., MCC and Ground v Leicestershire, and Orleans Club v Rickling Green, are printed in this annual, there can be no mistake as to what are generally accepted as first-class encounters.

The following averages, which may be relied upon for accuracy, have been compiled at considerable sacrifice of time by Mr Henry Luff, to whose zeal and untiring exertions the compiler is in a great measure indebted for the correctness which will be found to characterise the bowling analyses and averages in this edition of *Wisden's Almanack*.

BATTING AVERAGES IN FIRST-CLASS MATCHES FROM THE COMMENCEMENT OF THE SEASON TO DATE

Australia		England	
Mr W. L. Murdoch	36.22	Mr A. P. Lucas	38.3
Mr T. Horan	31.16	Hon. A. Lyttelton	35.1
Mr H. H. Massie	27.31	Mr C. T. Studd	34.12
A. Bannerman	23.21	W. Barnes	30.36
Mr J. McC. Blackham	21.19	G. Ulyett	30.22
Mr G. Giffen	21.6	R. G. Barlow	29.25
Mr G. J. Bonnor	19.21	Mr A. G. Steel	29.18
Mr S. P. Jones	15.12	Mr A. N. Hornby	29.9
Mr H. F. Boyle	11.7	Dr W. G. Grace	24.1
Mr T. W. Garrett	9.20	M. Read	24
Mr F. R. Spofforth	9.20	E. Peate	11.18

BOWLING AVERAGES IN FIRST-CLASS MATCHES FROM THE COMMENCEMENT OF THE SEASON TO DATE

Australia		England	
Mr H. F. Boyle	12.77	R. G. Barlow	11.53
Mr F. R. Spofforth	13.87	E. Peate	11.12
Mr T. W. Garrett	27.2	G. Ulyett	14.23
		Mr C. T. Studd	16.9
		Mr A. G. Steel	20.4
		W. Barnes	35

It will be observed that in every instance the batting averages of each member of the Australian team is lower than that of the English batsman placed opposite him, and that the bowling averages of the two men who had the largest share of the trundling for England are both better than either of those of the two bowlers who sent down the largest number of overs for Australia.

A perusal of these statistics must in the first place create a feeling of surprise that when the two elevens met there was the slightest probability of the English one being defeated. Secondly, no sensation but one of the highest admiration of the achievement of the Australian team can be felt when the result of the match is considered; and thirdly the figures prove, if figures prove anything, that the inevitable result of a series of encounters between the two elevens would be victory for the Englishmen in a very large proportion of the matches; and they further offer the strongest protest to the oft-raised cry of the decadence of English cricket.

With these few remarks the compiler proceeds to give a short account of the contest, leaving the reader to attribute the Australian victory to the fact that the Colonists won the toss and thereby had the best of the cricket; to the fact that the English had to play the last innings; to the brilliant batting of Massie; to the superb bowling of Spofforth; to the nervousness of some of the England side; to the "glorious uncertainty of the noble game"; or to whatever he or she thinks the true reason.

Monday. Murdoch beat Hornby in the toss and deputed Bannerman and Massie to commence the innings. Massie was clean bowled by a yorker on the leg-stump at 6. At 21 Murdoch played a ball from Peate on to his wicket, and, after adding a single, Bonnor was clean bowled middle stump. Horan came in, and then, at 26, Bannerman was splendidly caught by Grace at point, left hand, low down, having been in an hour and five minutes for 9 runs. Horan was bowled, leg-stump, at 30. Blackham joined Giffen, and, with the total unchanged, was bowled with the second ball he received. Garrett was the new batsman, and a double change of bowling was found necessary before the newcomer was well caught at long-off just after luncheon. At 50 a splendid ball from Barlow just took the top of Boyle's wicket. Jones came in and rain fell for a few minutes. At 59 Blackham skied a ball and was caught, and Spofforth, the last man, joined Jones. The "Demon" hit a 4, and then Jones was caught at third man, the innings closing for 63. At 3.30 Grace and Barlow started the first innings of England. Spofforth bowled Grace at 13, and Barlow was caught at forward point at 18. With Lucas and Ulyett together, the score was raised to 50 after half-an-hour's play, but at 56 the latter ran out to drive Spofforth and was easily stumped. At 59 Lucas was snapped at the wicket, and one run later Studd was bowled with a bailer without scoring, and half the wickets were down for 60. Read joined Lyttelton, and just when the score reached the total of the Australian innings the latter was caught at the wicket. Barnes came in and scored a single and a 4 and was then bowled by a breaking ball. Steel became Read's partner and 26 runs were added before Steel pulled a ball into his wicket. Eight wickets were down for 96 when Hornby came in. Read made a cut for 3 and Hornby scored a single, bringing up the 100. With only one run added, however, Hornby's leg stump fell, and the innings closed about five minutes before the call of time.

Tuesday. Massie and Bannerman commenced the Australians' second innings at 12.10, the Colonists being 38 to the bad. 30 went up after about twenty-eight minutes' play, two bowling changes having been tried. At 12.45 the balance of 38 runs was knocked off. Barnes relieved Studd at 47, and from his first ball Lucas badly missed Massie at long-off, the batsman then having made 38. 50 was hoisted after forty minutes' play. It was not until the score reached 66 that loud applause greeted the dismissal of the great hitter, bowled leg stump by Steel. Massie had made 55 out of 66 in fifty-five minutes, and his hits consisted of nine 4s, two 3s, three 2s and seven singles. Bonnor took the vacant wicket, but at 70 his middle stump was knocked clean out of the ground, and Murdoch came in, but immediately lost Bannerman, caught at extra mid-off, with the total unchanged. Bannerman had played with great patience for an hour and ten minutes for his 13. Horan joined Murdoch, and the bowling was changed, with the result that the incomer was easily caught. Giffen, who took his place, was out in the same way, and the fourth and fifth wickets were down at 79. Blackham came in, and when the score had been hit up to 99 rain fell, and luncheon was taken.

Resuming at 2.45, after another shower, Blackham was well caught at the wicket without any addition to the score. Jones filled the vacancy and a single by Murdoch sent up the 100. At 114 Jones was run out in a way which gave great dissatisfaction to Murdoch and other Australians. "Murdoch played a ball to leg, for which Lyttelton ran. The ball was returned, and Jones having completed the first run, and thinking wrongly, but very naturally, that the ball was dead, went out of his ground." Grace put his wicket down, and the umpire gave him out. Several of the team spoke angrily of Grace's action, but the compiler was informed that after the excitement had cooled down a prominent member of the Australian Eleven admitted that he should have done the same thing had he been in Grace's place. There was a good deal of truth in what a gentleman in the pavilion remarked, amidst some laughter, that "Jones ought to thank the champion for teaching him something". Spofforth partnered Murdoch, but was bowled middle stump at 117. Garrett came in, and very shortly after, a very smart piece of fielding on the part of Hornby, Studd and Lyttelton caused Murdoch to be run out at 122 for a very careful and good innings of 29. Boyle was last man in, but failed to score, and the tenth wicket fell at the same total at 3.25.

England, wanting 85 runs to win, commenced their second innings at 3.45 with Grace and Hornby. Spofforth bowled Hornby's off stump at 15, made in about as many minutes. Barlow joined Grace, but was bowled first ball at the same total. Ulyett came in, and some brilliant hitting by both batsmen brought the score to 51, when a very fine catch at the wicket dismissed Ulyett. 34 runs were then wanted, with seven wickets to fall. Lucas joined Grace, but when the latter had scored a 2 he was easily taken at mid-off. Lyttelton became Lucas' partner, and the former did all the hitting. Then the game was slow for a time, and twelve successive maiden overs were bowled, both batsmen playing carefully and coolly. Lyttelton scored a single, and then four maiden overs were followed by the dismissal of that batsman – bowled, the score being 66. Only 19 runs were then wanted to win, and there were five wickets to fall. Steel came in, and when Lucas had scored a 4, Steel was easily caught and bowled. Read joined Lucas, but amid intense excitement he was clean bowled without a run being added. Barnes took Read's place and scored a 2, and 3 byes made the total 75, or 10 to win. After being in a long time for 5 Lucas played the next ball into his wicket, and directly Studd joined Barnes the latter was easily caught off his glove without the total being altered. Peate, the last man, came in, but after hitting Boyle to square-leg for 2 he was bowled, and Australia had defeated England by 7 runs.

BOWLING IN THE SECOND INNINGS OF ENGLAND

(Copied from the Australian Score Book)

Spofforth	. . . .	1 1 . .	. . . 1	. 2 4 .	w . 1 w	2 . . .	3 . 4 .	. . . .
	. . . 2	. . . 1	1 2 4 1	2 1 1 .	. . . w	. 3 1 .	. . . .	. . . .
	. . . 4	. . . .	. . . .	. . . .	. . . .	. . . .	. . . .	. . . .
	. . . .	. . . w	w 2 w .	. w . .	Spofforth bowled a no ball.			

So Spofforth's last eleven overs (ten maidens) were bowled for 2 runs and four wickets!

Garrett	1 1 . .	. . . .	1 1 . .	1 . . .	. 3 . .	. . . .	. 1 . 1	
Boyle	. . . 1	. 4 . 1	. . . 1	. . . .	w . 2 .	. . . .	. 2 . .	1 . . .
	. . . .	. . . .	. . . .	. . . .	. . . .	. . . .	. . . 1	. . . .
	. . . .	. . 4 .	. . . .	. w w 2				

Australia

A. C. Bannerman c Grace b Peate	9	– c Studd b Barnes	13
H. H. Massie Esq. b Ulyett	1	– b Steel	55
W. L. Murdoch Esq. b Peate	13	– run out	29
G. J. Bonnor Esq. b Barlow	1	– b Ulyett	2
T. Horan Esq. b Barlow	3	– c Grace b Peate	2
G. Giffen Esq. b Peate	2	– c Grace b Peate	0
J. McC. Blackham Esq. c Grace b Barlow	17	– c Lyttelton b Peate	7
T. W. Garrett Esq. c Read b Peate	10	– not out	2
H. F. Boyle Esq. b Barlow	2	– b Steel	0
S. P. Jones Esq. c Barnes b Barlow	0	– run out	6
F. R. Spofforth Esq. not out	4	– b Peate	0
B 1	1	B 6	6
1/6 2/21 3/22 4/26 5/30 6/30 7/48 8/50 9/59	63	1/66 2/70 3/70 4/79 5/79 6/99 7/114 8/117 9/122	122

England

R. G. Barlow c Bannerman b Spofforth	11	– b Spofforth	0
Dr W. G. Grace b Spofforth	4	– c Bannerman b Boyle	32
G. Ulyett st Blackham b Spofforth	26	– c Blackham b Spofforth	11
A. P. Lucas Esq. c Blackham b Boyle	9	– b Spofforth	5
Hon. A. Lyttelton c Blackham b Spofforth	2	– b Spofforth	12
C. T. Studd Esq. b Spofforth	0	– not out	0
M. Read not out	19	– b Spofforth	0
W. Barnes b Boyle	5	– c Murdoch b Boyle	2
A. G. Steel Esq. b Garrett	14	– c and b Spofforth	0
A. N. Hornby Esq. b Spofforth	2	– b Spofforth	9
E. Peate c Boyle b Spofforth	0	– b Boyle	2
B 6, l-b 2, n-b 1	9	B 3, n-b 1	4
1/13 2/18 3/56 4/59 5/60 6/63 7/70 8/96 9/101	101	1/15 2/15 3/51 4/53 5/66 6/70 7/70 8/75 9/75	77

England Bowling

	Overs	Mdns	Runs	Wkts	Overs	Mdns	Runs	Wkts
Peate	38	24	31	4	21	9	40	4
Ulyett	9	5	11	1	6	2	10	1
Barlow	31	22	19	5	13	5	27	—
Mr Steel	2	1	1	—	7		15	2
Barnes					11	5	15	1
Mr Studd					4	1	9	—

Australian Bowling

	Overs	Mdns	Runs	Wkts	Overs	Mdns	Runs	Wkts
Mr Spofforth	36.3	18	46	7	28	15	44	7
Mr Garrett	16	7	22	1	7	2	10	—
Mr Boyle	19	7	24	2	20	11	19	3

Umpires: R. Thoms and L. Greenwood.

THE AUSTRALIANS v AN ELEVEN OF ENGLAND

Played at Birmingham, May 26, 1884

This contest was one of the most remarkable played during the year, and though the Australians won it by four wickets, it was not a victory of which they could feel proud considering the composition of their opponents' team. The match was played out in four hours of actual cricket, thirty-six wickets falling for 197 runs from the bat, of which 80 were made by three batsmen. It was to Spofforth's phenomenal bowling in the second essay of the Englishmen, and McDonnell's dashing play in both innings that the Australians owed their victory. Spofforth's extraordinary success is chronicled in the score book as under:

. w2 . . . . w . . . . w . w1 . ww . . . . w

The wicket on which this match was played was almost bare of grass, and was said to have been freely watered on the previous evening. Whether that was so or not it is certain that the extremely low scoring was alone due to the badness of it.

Eleven of England

R. G. Barlow b Palmer	8	– b Spofforth	2
J. G. Walker Esq. b Spofforth	18	– b Boyle	0
F. H. Sugg b Spofforth	5	– st Blackham b Boyle	0
L. C. Docker Esq. b Spofforth	19	– b Spofforth	5
J. Briggs c McDonnell b Spofforth	0	– b Boyle	2
A. H. Heath Esq. b Boyle	2	– b Spofforth	4
W. Robinson c and b Boyle	7	– c Boyle b Spofforth	1
A. Watson b Spofforth	2	– not out	7
S. Christopherson Esq. not out	8	– b Spofforth	0
R. Pilling b Spofforth	0	– c Palmer b Spofforth	0
H. Rotherham Esq. st Blackham b Spofforth	8	– b Spofforth	1
B 3, l-b 2	5	B 4	4
	82		26

The Australians

A. C. Bannerman b Barlow	1	– c Docker b Christopherson	7
P. S. McDonnell b Barlow	21	– b Christopherson	17
W. L. Murdoch c and b Rotherham	7	– b Barlow	1
G. Giffen b Barlow	9	– b Barlow	1
J. McC. Blackham b Rotherham	3	– b Christopherson	0
G. J. Bonnor b Barlow	0	– not out	1
H. J. H. Scott c Watson b Rotherham	3	– not out	5
F. R. Spofforth b Barlow	9	– b Christopherson	0
G. Alexander b Barlow	5		
G. E. Palmer c Docker b Barlow	4		
H. F. Boyle not out	4		
B 9, l-b 1	10	L-b 1	1
	76		33

Australian Bowling

	Overs	Mdns	Runs	Wkts	Overs	Mdns	Runs	Wkts
Spofforth	15.3	3	34	7	8.3	6	3	7
Palmer	7	1	30	1				
Boyle	8	2	13	2	8	2	19	3

Eleven of England Bowling

	Overs	Mdns	Runs	Wkts	Overs	Mdns	Runs	Wkts
Mr Rotherham	17	4	35	3	2	—	9	—
Barlow	17	9	31	7	12	6	13	2
Mr Christopherson					9.1	4	10	4

THE AUSTRALIANS v YORKSHIRE

Played at Bradford, June 9, 10, 1884

The wicket was in a spongy and treacherous condition, owing to two days' heavy rain, and the bowlers carried off all the honours of a match which the Australians finally won by three wickets. An injury to one of his fingers kept Murdoch out of the match. Bates scored the highest innings, making 24 out of 36 put on while he was in. In the match Palmer took eleven wickets for 54 runs, Peate ten for 62, Spofforth nine for 61, and Emmett six for 40.

Yorkshire

G. Ulyett c Bonnor b Palmer	5	– c Midwinter b Palmer	8
L. Hall lbw b Spofforth	6	– c Boyle b Palmer	0
G. R. Baker b Palmer	0	– c Bonnor b Palmer	3
E. Lockwood c Blackham b Spofforth	0	– c Giffen b Spofforth	1
W. Bates c Bonnor b Spofforth	24	– c Giffen b Spofforth	8
F. Lee c Spofforth b Palmer	2	– c Bonnor b Palmer	5
I. Grimshaw c McDonnell b Spofforth	2	– b Spofforth	0
R. Peel b Palmer	4	– b Palmer	1
T. Emmett b Spofforth	3	– b Palmer	16
E. Peate b Palmer	3	– not out	12
J. Hunter not out	5	– c Giffen b Spofforth	7
B 1	1	B 5, l-b 5, n-b 1	11
	55		72

The Australians

	First innings		Second innings	
P. S. McDonnell c Lockwood b Emmett	0	– c and b Peate		4
A. C. Bannerman c Baker b Emmett	8	– lbw b Peate		14
W. Midwinter c Lee b Emmett	18	– c Hunter b Peel		17
G. Giffen c Baker b Emmett	2	– b Peate		5
H. J. H. Scott c Ulyett b Peate	1	– c Ulyett b Peate		0
G. J. Bonnor c Peate b Emmett	2	– c Grimshaw b Peate		5
J. M'C. Blackham b Peate	3	– c Lockwood b Peate		10
G. E. Palmer c Bates b Peate	5	– not out		7
F. R. Spofforth c Bates b Peate	7	– not out		5
G. Alexander not out	10			
H. F. Boyle c Baker b Emmett	0			
B 4	4	L-b 1		1
	60			68

Australian Bowling

	Overs	Mdns	Runs	Wkts	Overs	Mdns	Runs	Wkts
Spofforth	19	9	29	5	23	11	32	4
Palmer	19	8	25	3	22	11	29	6

Yorkshire Bowling

	Overs	Mdns	Runs	Wkts	Overs	Mdns	Runs	Wkts
Peate	27	11	29	4	27	12	33	6
Emmett	27	14	27	6	12	6	13	—
Ulyett					2	—	7	—
Peel					12	6	14	1

Umpires: Luke Greenwood and Allen Hill.

THE AUSTRALIANS v LIVERPOOL AND DISTRICT

Played at Liverpool, June 23, 24, 1884

No match throughout the tour of the Australians resulted in so close and exciting a finish as this, the scratch team being beaten by one wicket, after a splendidly contested game. The home team went in first, and after D. Q. Steel had been dismissed with only one run scored, Barlow and A. G. Steel put on 66 for the second wicket, and later on Price and Leach added precisely the same number, both batting in excellent form. A. G. Steel hit most brilliantly for his 72, but was lucky in being twice missed. He made five 4s, six 3s and ten 2s, and was at the wickets only about an hour and a half scoring his runs. Spofforth's plucky hitting saved the Australians from the necessity of following their innings, and when Liverpool went in again Boyle and Palmer bowled with remarkable success, A. G. Steel alone offering any resistance. When the Australians went in again, wanting 128 to win, they lost five wickets for only 23 runs, and a victory for Liverpool seemed assured. But the association of Murdoch and Blackham greatly changed the aspect of the game, for before they were parted they had increased the total by 69 runs.

When Boyle, the last man, went in four runs were wanted to win. Murdoch hit a 3, and a bye won the match. Crossland's bowling in the second innings of the Australians was remarkably successful, and appears in the score book as under:

w . . .	. . . .	. . . w	. . . .	. . . .	. . . .	3 . . .	w 1 . 2
. . . w	. w . .	. . . .	. . 3 .	. . . .	. . . .	. . . .	. . . .
. . . .	. . 1 .	. . . .	4 . 1 .	. . . .	3 . . 2	. . w .	

So his first ten overs were bowled for 6 runs and five wickets.

Liverpool and District

R. G. Barlow c Bannerman b Palmer	24	– c Bonnor b Palmer	9
D. Q. Steel Esq. c Giffen b Spofforth	0	– c and b Boyle	0
A. G. Steel Esq. c Bannerman b Boyle	72	– b Palmer	29
G. R. Cox Esq. b Giffen	0	– b Palmer	0
J. Briggs b Spofforth	23	– c Scott b Boyle	2
H. B. Steel Esq. c Murdoch b Boyle	4	– b Palmer	0
A. Watson b Boyle	19	– b Palmer	5
H. Leach Esq. not out	22	– c Spofforth b Boyle	0
A. Price c and b Scott	37	– c Scott b Boyle	1
R. Wood Esq. c Palmer b Boyle	1	– not out	7
J. Crossland c Bannerman b Boyle	0	– c Bannerman b Boyle	0
B 9, l-b 2	11	L-b 1	1
	213		54

Australians

P. S. McDonnell c H. B. Steel b Wood	11	– c A. G. Steel b Crossland	0
A. C. Bannerman b Watson	23	– b Crossland	10
W. L. Murdoch b Crossland	8	– not out	38
G. Giffen c Price b Barlow	36	– b Crossland	12
G. E. Palmer b Crossland	4	– c A. G. Steel b Crossland	0
J. McC. Blackham b Crossland	6	– lbw b Wood	28
G. J. Bonnor b Crossland	4	– b Crossland	0
H. J. H. Scott st D. Q. Steel b Barlow	11	– b Wood	14
W. Midwinter b Crossland	0	– b Crossland	1
F. R. Spofforth b A. G. Steel	19	– c Barlow b Wood	3
H. F. Boyle not out	0	– not out	0
B 16, l-b 2	18	B 21, l-b 1	22
	140		128

Australian Bowling

	Overs	Mdns	Runs	Wkts	Overs	Mdns	Runs	Wkts
Spofforth	31	11	66	2				
Palmer	32	12	54	1	20	8	29	5
Giffen	15	3	39	1				
Boyle	21	10	33	5	20	9	24	5
Scott	6	1	10	1				

Liverpool and District Bowling

	Overs	Mdns	Runs	Wkts	Overs	Mdns	Runs	Wkts
Crossland	22	6	50	5	23.1	17	20	6
Mr Wood	10	6	17	1	10	5	19	3
Barlow	27	15	28	2	15	8	24	—
Watson	12	4	18	1	15	7	24	—
Mr A. G. Steel	3.1	1	9	1	7	4	7	—
Briggs					7	2	12	—

THE AUSTRALIANS v MIDDLESEX

Played at Lord's, July 17, 18, 1884

It was to Spofforth's superb bowling that the Australians chiefly owed the easy victory they gained in this match. In all he obtained twelve wickets for 43 runs, and his feat of taking seven for 16 in the first innings of Middlesex is chronicled in the score book as follows:

. . . . 4 . 1 . . . . . . 2 . . . w 1 1 . . . . w . . . .
. . w . . w . . 3 . . . . 1 . . . w 1
. w . . . . 1 . . w

After the Australians had lost two wickets for four runs Murdoch and Giffen put on 50 for the third wicket, and Bonnor and Murdoch 67 more for the fourth. Bonnor's 43 included a drive on to the pavilion roof, and another over the heads of the spectators by the side of the pavilion. Murdoch's 64 not out, was an admirably steady innings, and consisted of seven 4s, two 3s, eleven 2s and eight singles. Both Lucas and O'Brien played well in their second inings, the former being badly run out. The Australians won by an innings with 29 runs to spare.

Middlesex

I. D. Walker Esq. c McDonnell b Spofforth	4	– c Bonnor b Palmer	6
A. P. Lucas Esq. b Spofforth	5	– run out	26
Hon. A. Lyttelton b Spofforth	4	– c Murdoch b Spofforth	0
A. W. Ridley Esq. b Spofforth	0	– b Spofforth	7
T. C. O'Brien Esq. c Murdoch b Spofforth	0	– b Palmer	26
T. S. Pearson Esq. b Palmer	8	– b Palmer	0
G. F. Vernon Esq. c Giffen b Palmer	13	– c and b Spofforth	4
P. J. de Paravicini Esq. b Spofforth	0	– b Palmer	2
C. E. Cottrell Esq. b Spofforth	0	– b Spofforth	10
J. Robertson Esq. c Murdoch b Palmer	0	– not out	0
G. Burton not out	0	– st Murdoch b Spofforth	0
B 12, l-b 7	19	B 20, l-b 5	25
	53		106

The Australians

P. S. McDonnell b Cottrell	4
A. C. Bannerman c Lucas b Burton	0
W. L. Murdoch not out	64
G. Giffen b Cottrell	32
G. J. Bonnor c Robertson b Burton	43
W. Midwinter b Burton	8
J. McC. Blackham b Cottrell	5
H. J. H. Scott b Cottrell	0
G. E. Palmer c Walker b Cottrell	0
F. R. Spofforth b Robertson	21
H. F. Boyle c Lucas b Burton	4
B 4, l-b 3	7
	188

Australian Bowling

	Overs	Mdns	Runs	Wkts	Overs	Mdns	Runs	Wkts
Spofforth	18.2	10	16	7	20	8	27	5
Palmer	18	10	18	3	19	4	54	4

Middlesex Bowling

	Overs	Mdns	Runs	Wkts
Burton	39.3	16	75	4
Mr Cottrell	45	18	68	5
Mr Walker	3	—	18	—
Mr Robertson	10	6	18	1
Mr Paravicini	1	1	—	—
Mr Lucas	2	1	2	—

Umpires: F. H. Farrands and C. K. Pullen.

THE AUSTRALIANS v THE PLAYERS OF ENGLAND

Played at The Oval, July 31, August 1, 1884

Nottinghamshire having an engagement with Gloucestershire on the days set apart for this match, the committee of the former county declined to spare any of their eleven, and the Players' team, without a Nottinghamshire man in it, was therefore no more a representative one than that which suffered defeat at the hands of the Australians a month previously at Sheffield. The score will show that the hardest hitters engaged in the match made the most runs, and that Spofforth bowled splendidly, taking fourteen wickets at a cost of only 96 runs. Ulyett scored 22 and 33, McDonnell 26 and 9 not out, and Bonnor 68 and 12, the latter's first innings being the feature of the match. Bonnor went in with the score at 73 for four wickets, and was eighth out with the total at 149, and therefore made the extraordinary proportion of 68 out of 76 runs put on while he was in. He scored ten 4s, two 3s, eight 2s and six singles, and made several splendid drives, one going clean over the pavilion. The Australians won the match by nine wickets.

Players

L. Hall c Murdoch b Boyle	10	– b Spofforth	4
G. Ulyett c Bonnor b Spofforth	22	– c Bannerman b Spofforth	33
J. M. Read c McDonnell b Spofforth	7	– run out	4
W. Bates b Spofforth	2	– b Midwinter	0
J. Briggs c Palmer b Boyle	7	– b Midwinter	2
J. Hide b Spofforth	3	– c Palmer b Midwinter	3
G. G. Hearne b Spofforth	12	– b Spofforth	1
W. Humphreys b Spofforth	18	– b Spofforth	0
T. Emmett b Spofforth	8	– c Bonnor b Spofforth	0
E. Peate b Spofforth	4	– b Spofforth	19
J. Hunter not out	9	– not out	0
B 5	5	B 5	5
	107		71

The Australians

A. C. Bannerman b Peate	0		
P. S. McDonnell st Hunter b Humphreys	26	– not out	9
W. L. Murdoch b Ulyett	19	– not out	6
G. Giffen st Hunter b Peate	12		
H. J. H. Scott st Hunter b Peate	9		
G. J. Bonnor run out	68	– b Peate	12
W. Midwinter b hide	6		
J. M'C. Blackham lbw b Peate	1		
G. E. Palmer b Peate	0		
F. R. Spofforth b Hide	0		
H. F. Boyle not out	2		
B 4, l-b 3, w 1	8	L-b 1	1
	151		28

Australian Bowling

	Overs	Mdns	Runs	Wkts	Overs	Mdns	Runs	Wkts
Spofforth	38.1	12	62	8	22	10	34	6
Boyle	29	16	33	2				
Palmer	9	6	7	—	4	2	3	—
Midwinter					17	8	29	3

Players' Bowling

	Overs	Mdns	Runs	Wkts	Overs	Mdns	Runs	Wkts
Peate	31	11	55	5	7	4	10	1
Emmett	14	8	29	—				
Ulyett	12	5	17	1				
Humphreys	5	—	25	1				
Hide	9.3	5	17	2	7	1	17	—

Umpires: C. K. Pullin and F. H. Farrands.

AUSTRALIA v ENGLAND

Played at The Oval, August 11, 12, 13, 1884

The third and last of the three great matches arranged to be played against the full strength of England resulted in a draw, England wanting 120 runs to avert a single innings defeat, with eight wickets to go down. The fact that three individual scores of over 100 runs each were scored on the first day rendered the match unique in the annals of the game. When stumps were drawn on the first day, the score stood as under:

Australia

A. C. Bannerman c Read b Peate	4
P. S. McDonnell c Ulyett b Peate	103
W. L. Murdoch not out	145
H. J. H. Scott not out	101
B 4, l-b 6	10
(2 wkts)	363

Bannerman was out with the score at 15, and McDonnell at 158, but 205 more runs were added that day without further loss. On the Tuesday Scott was caught at the wicket after adding a single to his overnight score, but Murdoch was not dismissed until he had compiled 211, being the sixth batsman out with the total at 494. The remainder of the innings was alone remarkable for the success which attended Lyttelton's lobs. He went on for the second time when six wickets were down for 532, and took the last four wickets in eight overs for only 8 runs. The wickets fell in the following order:

1/15 2/158 3/365 4/432 5/454 6/494 7/532 8/545 9/549 10/551

McDonnell's very brilliantly-hit 103 consisted of fourteen 4s, two 3s, nine 2s and twenty-three singles, and was made while 158 runs were scored. Scott was batting three hours and a half for his 102, out of 207 put on while he was in, and he only gave one real chance in his splendid innings, and that was when he made 60. His figures were one 5 (4 for an overthrow), fifteen 4s, three 3s, seven 2s and fourteen singles. Murdoch's magnificent innings of 211 consisted of twenty-four 4s, nine 3s, twenty-two 2s and forty-four singles, and the celebrated batsman was at the wickets a little over eight hours, while 479 runs were scored. He gave three chances, all off Ulyett's bowling, when his individual score reached 46, 171 and 205 respectively.

The only innings on the England side calling for special notice were those played by Scotton and Read. The two batsmen became partners when eight wickets had fallen for 181 runs, of which number Scotton had scored 53, 21 of them having been made on the previous evening. They were not separated until they put on 151 runs for the ninth wicket. Scotton was the first to leave, having been at the wickets five hours and three-quarters, while 332 runs were made. He never gave the slightest chance, and it is not too much to say that his splendid display of defensive cricket was the cause of England saving the match. The figures of his innings were nine 4s, five 3s, nine 2s and twenty-one singles. Read's 117 was a superb display of hard and rapid hitting of two hours and a quarter's duration, his hits being twenty 4s, one 3, twelve 2s and ten singles. One difficult chance to Spofforth was the only blemish in his innings.

Australia

A. C. Bannerman c Read b Peate	4
P. S. McDonnell c Ulyett b Peate	103
W. L. Murdoch c Peate b Barnes	211
H. J. H. Scott c Lyttelton b Barnes	102
G. Giffen c Steel b Ulyett	32
G. J. Bonnor c Read b Grace	8
W. Midwinter c Grace b Lyttelton	30
J. McC. Blackham lbw b Lyttelton	31
G. E. Palmer not out	8
F. R. Spofforth b Lyttelton	4
H. F. Boyle c Harris b Lyttelton	1
B 7, l-b 10	17
	551

England

Dr W. G. Grace run out	19		
W. H. Scotton c Scott b Giffen	90		
W. Barnes c Midwinter b Spofforth	19		
A. Shrewsbury c Blackham b Midwinter	10	– c Scott b Giffen	37
A. G. Steel Esq. lbw b Palmer	31		
G. Ulyett c Bannerman b Palmer	10		
R. G. Barlow c Murdoch b Palmer	0	– not out	21
Lord Harris lbw b Palmer	14	– not out	6
Hon. A. Lyttelton b Spofforth	8	– b Boyle	17
W. W. Read Esq. b Boyle	117		
E. Peate not out	4		
B 8, l-b 7, w 6, n-b 3	24	B 3, l-b 1	4
	346		85

England Bowling

	Overs	Mdns	Runs	Wkts
Peate	63	25	99	2
Ulyett	56	24	96	1
Mr A. G. Steel	34	7	71	—
Barnes	52	25	81	2
Barlow	50	22	72	—
Dr W. G. Grace	24	14	23	1
Mr W. W. Read	7	—	36	—
Scotton	5	1	20	—
Lord Harris	5	1	15	—
Hon. A. Lyttelton	12	3	19	4
Shrewsbury	3	2	2	—

Australia Bowling

	Overs	Mdns	Runs	Wkts	Overs	Mdns	Runs	Wkts
Bonnor	13	4	33	—				
Palmer	54	19	99	4	2	1	2	—
Spofforth	58	31	81	2	6	2	14	—
Boyle	13	7	24	1	8	1	32	1
Midwinter	31	16	41	1	3	—	15	—
Giffen	26	13	36	1	7	1	18	1
Scott	3	—	17	—				

Umpires: C. K. Pullin and F. H. Farrands.

THE AUSTRALIANS v NORTH OF ENGLAND

Played at Nottingham, September 1, 2, 3, 1884

The North of England won this match by 170 runs, and the victory was the triumph of three men. Barlow scored 111 for once out, and took ten wickets for 48 runs. Flowers scored 116 in his two innings, and Attewell was credited with nine wickets for 48 runs. The score book records the bowling of Attewell and Barlow, in the first innings of the North as follows:

Attewell	. . 1 .	. . . .	w . . 1	. . . .	. . . 1	. 1 2 .	. . . .	. . . .
	. . w .	. . . .	w w 1 .	. . . .	. 1 . .	. . 3 .	1 4 . .	. . . .
	. . . .	. . w 1	. . . .	. . . .	. . . .	. . . .	. 1 . .	
Barlow	. . . .	1 w . .	. . w .	. . 1 .	. . . .	. w w 4		

In the second innings of the North of England the first five wickets fell for only 53. Then Barlow and Flowers obtained a complete mastery over the Australian bowling. Change after change was tried, and after all the regular bowlers had been knocked off Bonnor and Bannerman were put on. At last, when the total had reached 211, Flowers was caught off Bonnor. His splendid innings of 90 consisted of six 4s, six 3s, sixteen 2s, and singles, and was made with one chance of stumping when he had scored 56. His partnership with Barlow had yielded 158 runs. Barlow as the last man out for a faultless 101, having been at the wickets four hours and twenty-five minutes, while the score was taken from 11 to 255. His innings was made up of five 4s, ten 3s, fifteen 2s and twenty-one singles.

North of England

W. Shrewsbury b Spofforth	2	– c Palmer b Boyle	1
W. H. Scotton c Blackham b Boyle	17	– b Boyle	4
W. Barnes b Spofforth	10	– c Scott b Spofforth	17
W. Gunn lbw b Spofforth	2	– b Boyle	11
R. G. Barlow not out	10	– b Bannerman	101
W. Bates c Bonnor b Boyle	7	– c Palmer b Spofforth	4
W. Flowers c McDonnell b Boyle	26	– c Spofforth b Bonnor	90
W. Attewell b Spofforth	3	– c Bannerman b Bonnor	9
M. Sherwin c Murdoch b Boyle	1	– c Blackham b Bannerman	7
J. Selby hit wkt b Boyle	2	– c Blackham b Bonnor	2
E. Peate c Murdoch b Spofforth	6	– not out	0
L-b 4, n-b 1	5	B 7, n-b 2	9
	91		255

Australians

P. S. McDonnell b Peate	23	– b Attewell	5
A. C. Bannerman c Peate b Attewell	0	– c Peate b Attewell	4
W. L. Murdoch c Selby b Attewell	1	– b Barlow	3
H. J. H. Scott lbw b Attewell	7	– c Shrewsbury b Barlow	4
G. Giffen b Barlow	20	– st Sherwin b Attewell	6
W. Midwinter b Attewell	0	– c Bates b Attewell	17
G. J. Bonnor b Attewell	38	– c Barnes b Barlow	0
J. McC. Blackham b Barlow	3	– c Gunn b Barlow	15
F. R. Spofforth c Selby b Barlow	0	– b Barlow	7
G. E. Palmer not out	1	– c Gunn b Barlow	8
H. F. Boyle b Barlow	4	– not out	3
B 3	3	B 2, l-b 1, w 1	4
	100		76

Australian Bowling

	Overs	Mdns	Runs	Wkts	Overs	Mdns	Runs	Wkts
Spofforth	35.1	18	40	5	32	12	56	2
Palmer	9	4	14	—	15	7	23	—
Boyle	26	12	32	5	34	15	53	3
Giffen					17	7	34	—
Midwinter					10	5	18	—
Scott					3	—	13	—
Bonnor					18	7	34	3
Bannerman					17	9	15	2

North of England Bowling

	Overs	Mdns	Runs	Wkts	Overs	Mdns	Runs	Wkts
Peate	15	3	45	1				
Attewell	23	13	18	5	28	17	30	4
Flowers	3	—	28	—				
Barlow	6	3	6	4	27	13	42	6

Umpires: R. Carpenter and F. H. Farrands.

THE AUSTRALIANS v I ZINGARI

Played at Scarborough, September 4, 5, 6, 1884

The Australians beat I Zingari by eight wickets. With the exception of Whitfield all the eleven got into double figures in one or both innings, and the feature of the I Zingari's batting was the 80 hit by Forbes. Though seldom seen in first class company now Forbes hit the Australians' bowling to all parts of the ground, in very brilliant fashion. He gave a chance to Midwinter when he had scored 23, but his innings was nevertheless a splendid one. He was at wickets while 151 runs were put on, and his chief hits were a 6 off Spofforth, clean out of the ground, nine 4s, four 3s and five 2s.

In their first innings the Australians lost eight wickets for 140 runs, and then a fine display of hard, determined hitting by Blackham and Spofforth resulted in an addition of 91 to the score before the latter was finally caught. When the Australians went in to get 137 to win, the runs were hit off in an hour and thirty-five minutes. McDonnell hit brilliantly, and after Bannerman had been dismissed at 62, he and Murdoch scored runs at a great rate. McDonnell was out at 110, of which number he had made 67, an innings which included two drives out of the ground for 6 off Steel. Only 27 were wanted when he left and these were very soon obtained.

I Zingari

H. Whitfield Esq. b Spofforth	1	– b Spofforth	6
W. H. Patterson Esq. b Spofforth	10	– b Palmer	26
Lord Harris b Spofforth	24	– c Scott b Spofforth	3
A. G. Steel Esq. c McDonnell b Spofforth	15	– c Boyle b Midwinter	20
Hon. A. Lyttelton c McDonnell b Spofforth	37	– run out	1
G. B. Studd Esq. b Spofforth	3	– b Spofforth	28
W. F. Forbes Esq. st Blackham b Midwinter	80	– b Spofforth	10
H. W. Hadow Esq. b Bonnor	25	– c Blackham b Spofforth	7
P. J. de Paravicini Esq. b Spofforth	3	– not out	15
C. E. Cottrell Esq. b Midwinter	15	– b Spofforth	0
S. Christopherson Esq. not out	0	– c Scott b Spofforth	14
B 5, l-b 7, w 4	16	B 5, l-b 3, n-b 2	10
	229		140

Australians

P. S. McDonnell c Patterson by Cottrell	20 – c Christopherson b Steel	67
A. C. Bannerman b Steel	10 – c Lyttelton b Forbes	10
W. L. Murdoch b Cottrell	14 – not out	36
H. J. H. Scott b Cottrell	7 – not out	15
G. Giffen c Christopherson b Cottrell	34	
G. J. Bonnor c and b Steel	21	
J. McC. Blackham b Steel	8	
W. Midwinter not out	49	
G. E. Palmer c Forbes b Steel	4	
F. R. Spofforth c Whitfield b Steel	49	
H. F. Boyle c Steel b Cottrell	2	
B 9, l-b 6	15	B 7, l-b 2, w 1, n-b 1 11
	233	139

Australian Bowling

	Overs	Mdns	Runs	Wkts	Overs	Mdns	Runs	Wkts
Spofforth	57	22	114	7	47.2	22	71	7
Boyle	30	14	47	—				
Palmer	11	4	17	—	15	4	30	1
Midwinter	6.2	3	10	2	33	21	29	1
Giffen	3	—	13	—	1	1	—	—
Bonnor	4	1	12	1				

I Zingari Bowling

	Overs	Mdns	Runs	Wkts	Overs	Mdns	Runs	Wkts
Mr Cottrell	41	20	72	5	16	4	46	—
Mr Forbes	32	17	28	—	6	4	13	1
Mr Christopherson	9	3	22	—	6	3	9	—
Mr Steel	37	13	76	5	13	4	35	1
Hon. A. Lyttelton	3	—	8	—	2	—	8	—
Mr Hadow	3	1	12	—				
Mr Whitfield					5	1	17	—

Umpires: C. K. Pullin and F. H. Farrands.

THE AUSTRALIANS v SOUTH OF ENGLAND

Played at The Oval, September 11, 12, 1884

With the very moderate total of 163, the Australians won their last match by an innings with five runs to spare. Spofforth bowled throughout both innings of the South, and, altogether, took twelve wickets for 77 runs, thus finishing the tour in splendid form. In the second innings of the South he accomplished the "hat trick", clean bowling Grace, Maurice Read and Painter with successive balls. Palmer took five wickets in the first innings of the South for only 5 runs, thus:

. . . . 1 . . . . 3 . . . . . 2 . . . . . .
. . . . 1 . . . w . w . . . . . . w . . . . .
1 2 . . ww

Grace made the whole of the first 24 runs scored in that innings, and in the second helped Whitfield to put on 50 for the first wicket. Bannerman and Murdoch scored 53 for the second Australian wicket, and Giffen and Bonnor added 51 more during their partnership.

Horner was the most successful bowler against the Australians, and his analysis in the score book reads thus:

1 . . . . 1 . . 1 . . . . 2 . . .
4 . . . . 1 . . . . . 1 . . . . 1 . . 2 . w . 1 . .
. . 2 . . . . . w . w . . . . . 2 . . . . w

South of England

Dr W. G. Grace c McDonnell b Spofforth	24 – b Spofforth	26
H. Whitfield Esq. c McDonnell b Spofforth	0 – c Palmer b Boyle	21
T. C. O'Brien Esq. c McDonnell b Spofforth	15 – c Palmer b Boyle	7
W. W. Read Esq. b Spofforth	6 – c Scott b Boyle	14
E. J. Painter c and b Spofforth	0 – b Spofforth	0
J. M. Read b Palmer	0 – b Spofforth	0
A. F. J. Ford Esq. b Palmer	0 – b Spofforth	2
H. Wood not out	8 – b Spofforth	19
J. Wootton b Palmer	0 – c and b Spofforth	0
W. A. Woof c Bannerman b Palmer	2 – c and b Spofforth	0
C. E. Horner Esq. b Palmer	0 – not out	1
N-b 1	1 B 11, n-b 1	12
	56	102

Australians

P. S. McDonnell b Ford	6	J. McC. Blackham lbw b Wootton	4
A. C. Bannerman c Painter b Ford	35	G. E. Palmer not out	3
W. L. Murdoch b Ford	23	F. R. Spofforth c Painter b Horner	0
H. J. H. Scott b Ford	11	H. F. Boyle b Horner	1
G. Giffen c Wood b Horner	38	B 12, l-b 3	15
G. J. Bonnor c Wootton b Horner	27		
W. Midwinter c and b Wootton	0		163

Australian Bowling

	Overs	Mdns	Runs	Wkts	Overs	Mdns	Runs	Wkts
Spofforth	25	19	34	5	40	24	43	7
Boyle	7	2	11	—	23	11	20	3
Palmer	17.2	12	10	5	16	5	27	—

South of England Bowling

	Overs	Mdns	Runs	Wkts
Woof	26	12	43	—
Mr Ford	41	27	38	4
Mr Horner	21.2	9	19	4
Wootton	21	10	35	2
Dr Grace	7	2	13	—

Umpires: R. Thoms and F. H. Farrands.

AUSTRALIANS v SURREY

Played at The Oval, May 20, 21, 22, 1886

The meeting of the Australian team with the county of Surrey caused very much more excitement than it would have done a few years before, as on all hands it was admitted that the Surrey eleven had made immense improvement, and would have stood a good chance against almost any team against whom they could have been pitted. The first day was rendered additionally important by the visit of the Prince of Wales to the ground. This was the first time that His Royal Highness, who is the ground landlord of The Oval, had attended a cricket match on the ground, and the Australians naturally considered it a great compliment that he should make his visit on the occasion of their first appearance in London. The team had the honour of being presented to the Prince, as did the leading officials of the Surrey Club and the amateurs of the side. The weather was again most unfavourable for cricket, rain stopping the game at one time for an hour and a half, and the remainder of the day being dull and miserable. Spofforth, owing to slight indisposition, stood out from the Australian team, and the other absentee was McIlwraith. Winning the toss, Surrey went in first and put together the respectable score of 171. So even was the play that no fewer than eight batsmen reached double figures. The honours, however, distinctly rested with the young professional, George Lohmann, who went in with the score at 110 for six wickets, and took out his bat for 43 – an innings which was as well played as it was freely and vigorously hit. The performance was the more remarkable as Lohmann had never previously played against Australian bowling. Six bowlers were tried, Evans being about the most successful. The Australians had twenty-five minutes' batting, and altered their usual order of going in, with the result that two wickets fell before the call of time for 12 runs.

The second day's cricket was of a thoroughly interesting character, and the Australians were engaged nearly all the time in playing an uphill game. The weather was much more favourable, and there was an immense attendance, about 12,000 persons visiting the ground. The actual number that paid for admission was 10,305. Play lasted from five minutes to twelve to half-past six, and during the whole time the attention of the spectators never relaxed, every point of the game being eagerly followed. The Australians continuing their first innings fared very badly against the admirable bowling and fielding of the Surrey men. Jarvis made 19 and Jones 14, but the others did little, and the whole side were out for 82, or 89 runs to the bad. Lohmann followed up his batting success of the first day by taking six wickets at the cost of only 36 runs, while Bowley obtained three wickets for 24 runs. Going in a second time the Australians made a splendid effort to retrieve their fallen fortunes, and thanks mainly to the fine defensive cricket of Giffen, the free, vigorous hitting of Blackham, and a capital 34 by Bonnor, the total was 171 for nine wickets when time was called for the day. Thus the Australians were 82 runs to the good, with one wicket to fall. Considering that they were in the field for the entire day, the Surrey men deserve great praise for their performance.

Under ordinary circumstances Surrey would no doubt have gained a very easy victory, but a heavy thunderstorm, which broke over London on the Saturday morning, put quite a different aspect on the game, and those who visited The Oval were rewarded by witnessing a splendid finish. Naturally all this rain made Surrey's task very much more formidable than it would otherwise have been. The Australian innings closed for 172, Giffen taking out his bat for a superb 54. Surrey commenced their task at a little after half-past twelve, and from that time to the completion of the match the interest of the spectators never for a moment declined. From the outset it was evident that run-getting on the difficult wicket was by no means an easy matter, and for some time it seemed after all as if the Australians would snatch the game out of the fire. Three of the best wickets on the side went down for 19 runs, and when the luncheon interval took place six wickets still had to go down, and 46 runs were required to win. With the total at 50, Abel, who had been batting an hour and three-quarters for 13, was caught at short-slip, and with half the wickets down 32 runs were still wanted. Mr Roller scored an invaluable innings of 19, and the score was 69 when he was bowled by Evans. The concluding portion of the match was watched amid tremendous excitement, and it was in no small measure due to the coolness of Lohmann and Jones that Surrey in the end were enabled to score a remarkable victory by three wickets. On all hands the Australians were highly complimented for the admirable manner in which they played their uphill game, and the result of the match put additional interest into the return game, which took place at the end of July.

Surrey

Abel run out	24 – c Jones b Garrett	13
Mr J. Shuter c Jones b Evans	5 – c Giffen b Evans	11
Diver c Bonnor b Giffen	13 – c Jones b Garrett	2
Mr W. W. Read b Palmer	14 – c Bruce b Garrett	0
Read b Evans	27 – b Evans	14
Mr W. E. Roller b Garrett	14 – b Evans	19
Wood run out	14 – lbw b Giffen	8
Lohmann not out	43 – not out	8
Jones c Blackham b Bruce	12 – not out	4
Bowley c Giffen b Garrett	2	
Beaumont c Palmer b Evans	0	
B 1, l-b 1, n-b 1	3 B 5, l-b 3	8
	171	87

Australians

J. W. Trumble b Lohmann	13 – c Wood b Beaumont	1
G. E. Palmer lbw b Lohmann	2 – b Beaumont	1
E. Evans b Lohmann	0 – c Wood b Jones	6
G. J. Bonnor b Bowley	5 – b Bowley	34
S. P. Jones b Bowley	14 – b Jones	6
H. J. H. Scott b Lohmann	5 – st Wood b Lohmann	0
G. Giffen b Lohmann	4 – not out	54
T. W. Garrett b Bowley	0 – c Roller b Jones	3
A. H. Jarvis b Beaumont	19 – b Jones	1
J. McC. Blackham b Lohmann	7 – c Jones b Beaumont	43
W. Bruce not out	4 – b Jones	7
B 8, l-b 1	9 B 12, l-b 4	16
	82	172

Surrey Bowling

	Overs	Mdns	Runs	Wkts	Overs	Mdns	Runs	Wkts
Lohmann	36	17	36	6	27	13	26	1
Beaumont	14	9	13	1	30	17	39	3
Bowley	24	14	24	3	22	11	41	1
Jones	3	3	0	0	27.2	14	34	5
Abel					3	0	16	0

Australian Bowling

	Overs	Mdns	Runs	Wkts	Overs	Mdns	Runs	Wkts
Evans	40.1	18	53	3	41.2	23	31	3
Giffen	22	6	41	1	3	1	3	1
Garrett	28	12	32	2	33	15	39	3
Palmer	22	9	29	1	5	2	6	0
Trumble	4	2	3	0				
Bruce	5	2	10	1				

AUSTRALIANS v OXFORD UNIVERSITY

Played at Oxford, May 27, 28, 1886

Heavy rain just before the day of the match had rendered the wicket at the Christ Church Ground very treacherous indeed, and batsmen were seriously handicapped. Twenty-two wickets fell on the opening day for 123 runs, or something less than 6 runs apiece. His Royal Highness Prince Christian was amongst the company, which was above the average. Bruce and Trumble stood out of the Australian team. Play did not begin until nearly one o'clock, when the Australians went in to bat, and a slight rain kept the wicket fairly easy for about half an hour. In this time Jones and Blackham batted creditably, but the latter was run out at 20. Jones and Scott took the score up to 49, and then came a complete collapse before the bowling of Cochrane and Whitby. Jones, who was in an hour for 28, left at 55, and then down went the wickets one after another, until the whole side were out for 70. The condition of the ground was even worse when the University went in to bat, and the innings lasted only sixty-five minutes. Spofforth, of course, with every advantage that a bowler could wish for, proved irresistable, and dismissed nine of the Dark Blues, his analysis reading – fifteen overs, two balls, seven maidens, 18 runs, nine wickets. Being 25 runs ahead, the Australians commenced their second innings, and at the call of time had lost Blackham and Scott for 8 runs, the not-outs being Jones 4 and Garrett 0.

Remarkable as had been the success of the bowlers on the Thursday, batsmen fared even more disastrously when the game was continued, and the other eighteen wickets went down for 68 runs. Whitby and Cochrane were again the successful Oxford bowlers, and except that Jones scored 10, no one reached double figures, and the innings came to an end for the paltry total of 38. Whitby dismissed McIlwraith, Palmer and Spofforth in one over, and the innings, which had lasted only an hour and a half, ended as stated above for 38, the smallest score for which any Australian team had ever been dismissed in England. Whitby and Cochrane divided the wickets between them, and accomplished a sensational performance. The 64 runs required by the University to win proved far too heavy a task against Spofforth and Garrett. Twenty-three runs had been made for three wickets at lunch time, but when the game was resumed no stand whatever was made, and the last wicket fell for exactly the same total as that put together by the Australians, who thus gained a victory by 25 runs. In all Spofforth took fifteen wickets for 36 runs, eleven of them being clean bowled. The Dark Blues had something the worst of the luck, and although defeated, were not by any means disgraced.

Australians

S. P. Jones c Rashleigh b Whitby	28	– c Buckland b Cochrane	10
J. McC. Blackham run out	15	– c Hildyard b Whitby	1
H. J. H. Scott st Cobb b Buckland	8	– b Cochrane	2
G. Giffen c Arnall-Thompson b Cochrane	9	– c and b Whitby	1
G. J. Bonnor b Whitby	0	– b Cochrane	8
J. McIlwraith b Whitby	0	– b Whitby	1
A. H. Jarvis c Cobb b Cochrane	0	– c and b Cochrane	4
G. E. Palmer lbw b Cochrane	0	– c Buckland b Whitby	0
T. W. Garrett run out	1	– c Glennie b Cochrane	8
F. R. Spofforth c Hildyard b Whitby	1	– b Whitby	0
E. Evans not out	1	– not out	0
B 3, l-b 2, n-b 2	7	B 2, l-b 1	3
	70		38

Oxford University

Mr J. H. Brain b Spofforth	0	– b Spofforth	10
Mr R. G. Glennie b Spofforth	1	– b Spofforth	2
Mr W. W. Rashleigh b Spofforth	0	– b Garrett	5
Mr K. J. Key b Spofforth	3	– b Garrett	7
Mr A. R. Cobb b Spofforth	0	– b Garrett	0
Mr H. V. Page lbw b Garrett	10	– lbw b Spofforth	0
Mr E. H. Buckland b Spofforth	0	– b Spofforth	5
Mr L. D. Hildyard c Palmer b Spofforth	12	– c Jones b Spofforth	2
Mr A. H. J. Cochrane c Jarvis b Spofforth	2	– not out	0
Mr H. T. Arnall-Thompson not out	11	– c Evans b Garrett	0
Mr H. O. Whitby b Spofforth	0	– b Spofforth	0
L-b 4, n-b 2	6	B 7	7
	45		38

Oxford Bowling

	Overs	Mdns	Runs	Wkts	Overs	Mdns	Runs	Wkts
Mr Cochrane	22.1	12	22	3	20	8	19	5
Mr Anall-Thompson	4	0	12	0				
Mr Buckland	12	6	10	1				
Mr Whitby	23	15	19	4	20	13	16	5

Australian Bowling

	Overs	Mdns	Runs	Wkts	Overs	Mdns	Runs	Wkts
Spofforth	15.2	7	18	9	17	9	18	6
Garrett	15	6	21	1	16	11	13	4

AUSTRALIANS v NORTH OF ENGLAND

Played at Manchester, May 31, 1886

Just at the time of this important engagement, the country was being indulged with an extraordinary amount of wet weather, and the one day's cricket that was practicable at Old Trafford was certainly a curiosity, 31 wickets falling, and only 137 runs being scored. The Australians left out Trumble and McIlwraith, neither of whom had up to this time done anything to justify his Colonial reputation, and the North, despite the absence of Mr A. G. Steel and the fact of the fixture clashing with a Nottinghamshire match, had a very strong team, comprising five men from Lancashire, two from Nottinghamshire, and four from Yorkshire. The Nottinghamshire committee had been asked for two men, and generously let off Shrewsbury and Gunn. About 10,000 persons visited the ground on the Monday, and the fluctuations of the game were watched with the keenest interest. As in the course of the whole afternoon only three batsmen succeeded in getting into double figures, it is unnecessary to go into any description of the play. The fielding on each side was almost perfect, and the bowling of the highest quality, but still it was generally considered that the condition of the wicket was not so bad as to account for such a miserably weak display of batting by both sides. Peate, who had twice before during his career done big things for the North of England against Australia, took eight wickets for 23 runs, and four for 27, while Watson, after only obtaining one wicket for 22 in the Colonial team's first innings, did an extraordinary piece of bowling in their second essay, delivering twenty-seven overs, eighteen maidens, for 12 runs and six wickets. The North's first innings was actually finished off in twenty-eight overs and three balls, Spofforth taking seven wickets for 19 runs, and Palmer three for 9 runs. At the close the Englishmen, with nine wickets to fall in their second innings, wanted only 40 runs to get to win, and the chances of course looked immensely in their favour.

As ill-luck would have it, however, Manchester was visited with such torrents of rain, that after the first day no further progress was made with the game, which on the Wednesday afternoon was abandoned as a draw. Even though only one day's cricket was practicable, the match stands out as one of the curiosities of the season of 1886.

Australians

S. P. Jones b Peate	15 – c Shrewsbury b Watson	2
J. McC. Blackham c Shrewsbury b Peate	1 – c Pilling b Watson	0
H. J. H. Scott b Peate	9 – c Barlow b Peate	4
G. Giffen st Pilling b Peate	2 – st Pilling b Peate	9
G. J. Bonnor c Briggs b Peate	2 – c Preston b Peate	0
A. H. Jarvis b Peate	0 – not out	10
W. Bruce c and b Watson	4 – c Pilling b Watson	4
T. W. Garrett b Peate	0 – c Shrewsbury b Watson	10
G. E. Palmer st Pilling b Peate	3 – b Peate	0
E. Evans run out	4 – c Pilling b Watson	0
F. R. Spofforth not out	5 – c Gunn b Watson	0
	B 2, l-b 2	4
	45	43

North of England

Barlow b Spofforth	0 – not out	2
Mr A. N. Hornby c Garrett b Palmer	0 – b Palmer	2
Shrewsbury c Evans b Spofforth	4 – not out	9
Ulyett c Palmer b Spofforth	0	
Bates c Bruce b Palmer	7	
Briggs b Spofforth	0	
Gunn b Palmer	5	
Preston b Spofforth	1	
Watson b Spofforth	2	
Pilling c Blackham b Spofforth	1	
Peate not out	8	
B 1, l-b 4, n-b 1	6 L-b 2	2
	34	15

North of England Bowling

	Overs	Mdns	Runs	Wkts	Overs	Mdns	Runs	Wkts
Peate	22	11	23	8	27	13	27	4
Watson	21.3	12	22	1	27	18	12	6

Australian Bowling

	Overs	Mdns	Runs	Wkts	Overs	Mdns	Runs	Wkts
Spofforth	14.3	8	19	7	10	9	1	0
Palmer	14	11	9	3	9	3	12	1

AUSTRALIANS v GENTLEMEN OF ENGLAND

Played at Lord's, June 3, 4, 1886

On the opening day of this contest, Spofforth, in attempting to stop a ball hit hard back to him by Lord Harris, dislocated the third finger of his bowling hand. The great Australian had immediately to leave the field, and he did not appear again until the match at Chichester, on June 28. He afterwards continually complained of the weakness of the finger that had been injured, and the difficulty he found in imparting anything like the old spin to the ball. This was the first of the two matches between the Australians and the Gentlemen, and the home side was distinctly less powerful than previous elevens that had represented the Gentlemen of England. Mr Steel had only just been married, and had therefore perfectly legitimate excuse for being absent. There were, of course, several famous men in the team, but the composition of the eleven, and also of the team that afterwards played at The Oval, showed the cricket public perhaps more clearly than anything else could have done the comparative weakness of the amateur element last season. The opening day's cricket was dull and uninteresting. Scott won the toss, and considering that the wicket was dead and heavy from recent rain, he put the Englishmen in. In just under two hours and a half the team were dismissed for 99, no one showing any particular form after the failure of W. G. Grace and Walter Read. Perhaps the most remarkable thing of the innings was the long stand made by C. W. Rock, who was in an hour and twenty minutes for his 9 runs. The Colonists went in at half-past three, and directly after their last wicket fell play ceased for the day, the total being 150, or 51 to the good. Jones played very carefully for his 8 runs, and was in nearly an hour, but the best batting was shown by Bonnor and Scott, both of whom were seen to considerable advantage. The 100 went up with only three wickets down, but the remainder of the batsmen did very little. Rock's figures, five wickets for 51 runs, were exceedingly good.

On the second afternoon, at five o'clock, the match was finished, Australia winning by seven wickets. This was the first great victory the Colonists had gained, and it was a thoroughly well-deserved success, as they were seen to greater advantage than their opponents in all points of the game. The performance was the more honourable to them, as it was accomplished without Spofforth's aid after the first hour and a half. Several of our great batsmen again failed, and G. B. Studd, G. F. Vernon and M. C. Kemp were the only men who played a forcing and suitable game. Giffen's bowling was expensive but very effective. Jones and Blackham opened the second innings of Australia so well that of the 86 wanted to win they made 47 before they were separated. Of course this left the match a certainty, and, as we have said, it was all over by five in the afternoon.

Gentlemen

Mr W. G. Grace b Spofforth	7	– b Giffen	11
Mr C. W. Rock b Garrett	9	– c Jarvis b Garrett	19
Mr W. W. Read b Palmer	13	– c Giffen b Garrett	4
Mr W. E. Roller b Palmer	2	– c Scott b Giffen	4
Mr G. F. Vernon c Bonnor b Spofforth	15	– c and b Giffen	27
Lord Harris c Jarvis b Garrett	9	– b Palmer	8
Mr S. W. Scott c Bonnor b Garrett	16	– b Giffen	7
Mr G. B. Studd b Palmer	15	– c Blackham b Giffen	29
Mr M. C. Kemp not out	0	– not out	17
Mr S. Christopherson b Palmer	0	– b Garrett	1
Mr G. G. Walker c Palmer b Garrett	3	– st Blackham b Giffen	1
B 6, l-b 4	10	B 8	8
	99		136

Australians

J. McC. Blackham b Rock	20	– lbw b Walker	32
S. P. Jones c Kemp b Rock	8	– c Kemp b Roller	36
H. J. H. Scott lbw b Grace	27	– b Roller	1
G. Giffen c and b Rock	5	– not out	3
G. J. Bonnor c Read b Roller	39	– not out	13
A. H. Jarvis b Rock	14		
J. W. Trumble c and b Grace	2		
W. Bruce c and b Rock	7		
T. W. Garrett b Christopherson	9		
G. E. Palmer not out	11		
F. R. Spofforth retired hurt	0		
B 8	8	L-b 1	1
	150		86

Australian Bowling

	Overs	Mdns	Runs	Wkts	Overs	Mdns	Runs	Wkts
Spofforth	29.3	13	30	2				
Palmer	34	18	37	4	18	7	26	1
Garrett	21.1	10	16	4	38	23	31	3
Giffen	2	0	6	0	47.1	25	71	6

Gentlemen Bowling

	Overs	Mdns	Runs	Wkts	Overs	Mdns	Runs	Wkts
Mr C. W. Rock	44	22	51	5	14	4	19	0
Mr G. G. Walker	8	1	19	0	8	2	18	1
Mr W. G. Grace	19	6	32	2	6	1	13	0
Mr Christopherson	19.3	11	14	1	7	2	18	0
Mr W. E. Roller	15	5	26	0	8.3	3	17	2

AUSTRALIANS v DERBYSHIRE

Played at Derby, June 7, 8, 1886

Spofforth having been disabled at Lord's on the previous Thursday, was, of course, unable to play against Derbyshire, and the other man to stand out of the Colonial Eleven was Evans. Derbyshire had got together a representative side, but outside Derby itself the match did not arouse much interest, the result being regarded as a foregone conclusion. As it turned out, however, the home side made a better fight than could have been expected, and had every reason to feel satisfied with their performance. On the first day the Australians had everything their own way, dismissing the County Eleven on a hard wicket for the meagre total of 95, and then scoring themselves 163 for seven wickets. Giffen, who about this time was bowling in irresistible form, took seven Derbyshire wickets at the cost of only 41 runs, the majority of the batsmen being quite at fault with his break. McIlwraith, for the Australians, was seen to advantage for the first time in England, going in first and scoring 39. He and Jones put on 83 runs for the second wicket. Bonnor, for once in 1886, played his true game, and in his innings of 46 made three big drives over the ring for 6 each, from Cochrane's bowling.

On the second day the Australians finished off their innings for 191, or an advantage of 96 runs. When the County went in for the second time, five wickets fell for 55 runs, and a single-innings defeat seemed almost certain. Chatterton, Davidson and Mr Eadie, however, played up remarkably well, and the total reached 144. Chatterton's innings of 41 – a good performance under any circumstances – was really remarkable, considering that he was suffering from a badly injured hand. The Australians had only 49 to get to win, but on a rather dusty wicket they did not find the task such an easy one as it looked, four good wickets falling to Cropper's bowling before the runs were obtained. The match was all over at half-past six on the second day, the Australians winning by six wickets. Even in fine weather the Derby ground helps the bowlers, and in this particular match there were two extraordinary performances. Giffen took in all sixteen Derbyshire wickets for 101 runs, while Cropper, who ought to have been put on earlier in the first innings, obtained eight Australian wickets for 43 runs.

Derbyshire

Cropper b Giffen	7	– b Giffen	8
Coupe st Blackham b Giffen	20	– c Blackham b Giffen	0
Mr W. S. Eadie c Blackham b Giffen	10	– b Giffen	13
Mr L. C. Docker b Giffen	0	– b Giffen	10
Chatterton c Jones b Garrett	16	– b Giffen	41
Sugg lbw b Giffen	3	– b Giffen	23
Mr E. A. J. Maynard not out	8	– st Blackham b Giffen	0
Davidson b Garrett	0	– not out	33
Mr A. H. J. Cochrane b Giffen	9	– b Giffen	6
Mr G. G. Walker c Bruce b Garrett	12	– run out	2
Disney b Giffen	0	– st Blackham b Giffen	5
B 9, l-b 1	10	B 2, l-b 1	3
	95		144

Australians

J. McC. Blackham b Cochrane	3	– lbw b Cropper	7
J. McIlwraith c Maynard b Cropper	39	– b Cropper	3
S. P. Jones b Cropper	41	– b Cropper	13
H. J. H. Scott b Walker	2	– b Cropper	4
G. Giffen c Docker b Cochrane	4	– not out	16
G. J. Bonnor c Chatterton b Walker	46	– not out	1
A. H. Jarvis c Chatterton b Walker	8		
J. W. Trumble b Walker	1		
W. Bruce b Cropper	2		
G. E. Palmer c Chatterton b Cochrane	8		
T. W. Garrett not out	15		
B 17, l-b 5	22	B 3, l-b 2	5
	191		49

Australian Bowling

	Overs	Mdns	Runs	Wkts	Overs	Mdns	Runs	Wkts
Giffen	35.2	19	41	7	35	12	60	9
Palmer	7	2	13	0	3	1	15	0
Garrett	28	16	31	3	16	5	32	0
Bruce					9	2	16	0
Trumble					6	2	13	0
Jones					2	0	5	0

Derbyshire Bowling

	Overs	Mdns	Runs	Wkts	Overs	Mdns	Runs	Wkts
Mr A. H. Cochrane	19.1	3	28	3				
Davidson	14	4	25	0				
Chatterton	11	2	24	0				
Mr G. G. Walker	32	13	62	3	23.3	13	30	0
Cropper	26	13	29	4	24	16	14	4

AUSTRALIANS v LANCASHIRE

Played at Manchester, June 14, 15, 16, 1886

Weather in the North of England on Whit Monday was very wet, and Manchester like other places suffered considerably in this respect. A big crowd of people assembled on the Old Trafford, but, much to their disappointment, they only witnessed an hour's cricket. At this part of the season the Lancashire eleven were in very poor form, and it was a great piece of luck for the Australians to win the toss, as the wicket was wet and easy. During the sixty minutes that the game was proceeded with, Jones and Scott for the Australians scored exactly a run a minute. Scott was seen to considerable advantage, and though Jones's play was not quite so good, they were both together when the rain came on and prevented any more play, Jones being not out 34 and Scott not out 20.

On the Tuesday the wicket, as was only to be expected, was all in favour of the bowling, and during the day twenty wickets went down for 160 runs. The good start made by the Colonists on the previous day served them considerably, for, against the bowling of Watson and Barlow, the ten wickets outstanding went down for the addition of 85 runs, the last nine wickets indeed falling for 59 runs. Scott left at 86, and then, until Garrett hit with some vigour, there was no real stand made against the bowling. The innings closed for 145 at half-past three, and then, in just over an hour and a half, the county eleven were dismissed for the paltry total of 46. A more feeble display of batting against Giffen was scarcely seen during the summer, even making every allowance for the ground. The small total of Lancashire might have been still further reduced had the Australians fielded up to form. Mr Hornby gave a couple of chances, but made very poor use of his good luck, and except Messrs H. B. Steel and O. P. Lancashire, who made 30 out of the 43 runs from the bat, no one offered any resistance to the bowling. The South Australian's eight wickets, it will be noticed, cost him only 23 runs. When Lancashire followed on with 99 runs in arrears, Mr Hornby and Barlow did so much better than before that at the call of time 29 had been made without loss of a wicket, the amateur being not out 9 and Barlow not out 14.

There was another complete collapse on the part of the county eleven on the third day, and the second innings, which had given promise of amounting to a respectable total, was finished off in less than an hour and a half for the addition of 58 runs. Mr H. B. Steel again played pluckily and well, being chief scorer in each innings, but he received no support, and again the wickets went down in quick succession before the bowling of Giffen, the match ending very early in a decisive victory for the Australians by an innings and 12 runs. It must not be forgotten that winning the toss and batting for an hour on the first day was a tremendous help to the Colonists, but admitting this, Giffen's performance in the match was probably his best bit of bowling during the whole of the tour. In all he took sixteen wickets (eleven of them clean bowled) for 65 runs. In the three matches at Derby, Cambridge and Manchester, the South Australian secured forty wickets in five consecutive innings at the cost of 222 runs, or an average of just over 5½ runs per wicket.

Australians

S. P. Jones c Briggs b Barlow	54	J. McC. Blackham c Pilling b Briggs	10
H. J. H. Scott lbw b Watson	28	T. W. Garrett c Yates b Watson	22
G. Giffen b Barlow	3	J. McIlwraith b Watson	4
W. Bruce b Barlow	0	E. Evans not out	2
G. J. Bonnor c Lancashire b Barlow	2	B 6, l-b 3	9
A. H. Jarvis b Watson	0		
J. W. Trumble b Watson	11		145

Lancashire

Mr A. N. Hornby c Scott b Garrett	9	– c Trumble b Garrett	11
Barlow b Giffen	0	– b Giffen	16
Mr H. B. Steel c and b Giffen	21	– b Giffen	24
Briggs b Giffen	0	– b Giffen	4
Mr P. Dobell b Giffen	0	– c Scott b Giffen	5
Mr F. Taylor b Giffen	0	– c and b Giffen	2
Mr O. P. Lancashire not out	9	– b Giffen	0
Mr H. Eccles c Giffen b Garrett	2	– b Giffen	7
Yates c Blackham b Giffen	1	– b Giffen	10
Watson b Giffen	0	– b Evans	1
Pilling c Trumble b Giffen	1	– not out	0
B 1, l-b 2	3	B 6, w 1	7
	46		87

Australian Bowling

	Overs	Mdns	Runs	Wkts	Overs	Mdns	Runs	Wkts
Giffen	26.3	10	23	8	40.1	22	42	8
Garrett	26	16	20	2	31	16	35	1
Bruce					3	2	1	0
Evans					6	5	2	1

Lancashire Bowling

	Overs	Mdns	Runs	Wkts
Watson	66.2	38	54	5
Barlow	46	21	61	4
Yates	6	2	12	0
Briggs	15	11	9	1

AUSTRALIANS v MIDDLESEX

Played at Lord's, June 24, 25, 26, 1886

The play on the opening day was thoroughly good and enjoyable. Middlesex scored a very respectable first innings, Spillman and J. G. Walker being by far the most prominent of the batsmen; and then the Australians, in an hour and a quarter, put on 96 runs without losing a wicket, Jones being not out 52, and Scott not out 42, at the close of play. The ground was in splendid condition, and the company was very large. It must be mentioned here as a matter of record that Captain Hyde, a retired captain of the Peninsular and Oriental Company's service, died suddenly on the ground during the game. The deceased gentleman was a well-known frequenter of Lord's Ground, and his face and figure were doubtless familiar to hundreds of people.

On the second day the wicket was still in grand order for run-getting, and the Australians increased their score to 155 before the first wicket fell, when Jones was caught for an altogether admirable 76. Giffen came in, and after he was missed by Spillman at the wicket, runs came at a great pace, the total at lunch-time being 237 for one wicket, Scott 115 not out. During the interval Jones was presented, in the committee-room of the pavilion, with a gold watch and chain, subscribed for him at the Gentlemen's match in the previous week. The Hon. W. Wilson, of Victoria, made the presentation on behalf of the Australian friends of the team, to whom the subscription was restricted. On the resumption of the game, the County total was soon left behind, and the score was up to 272 before the second wicket fell. Scott was then lbw for 123, a splendid display of batting, lasting four hours and twenty minutes and including sixteen 4s, six 3s and ten 2s. After this the Australians went out one after another in the most extraordinary way, and the whole side were out for only 354, or 95 to the good, after it had seemed as if they were set for a 500 innings. The Middlesex eleven fielded up very well, and Burton deserves a special word of praise for his excellent bowling. When the County went in for the second time they scored 83 for one wicket, A. J. Webbe being not out 33, and S. W. Scott not out 30, at the call of time. They were thus only 12 runs behind, with nine wickets to fall – one of the most extraordinary changes from lunch-time to the finish which we ever remember to have seen in a first-class match in fine weather. Cricketers and the public are familiar enough with sensational incidents on treacherous wickets, but here there was nothing to account for the fluctuations which passed over the game.

On the Saturday Webbe and Scott both played capitally, and increased the total to 129 before the second wicket fell. Then, except for G. F. Vernon's 37, no stand was made against Palmer's destructive bowling, the famous Victorian taking seven wickets for 84 runs, and bowling quite as well as ever he did in the tour. He got on his leg-break with wonderful success, and some of the batsmen could hardly look at him. The Colonists had 123 to get to win, and the 100 went up with only three wickets down. Four runs later Giffen, who had played superb cricket for 52, struck a ball into his wicket, and then followed a "rot" which is difficult to understand or excuse. One after another the Australians went out from sheer bad cricket, and 8 runs were wanted to win with only one wicket to fall. Blackham and Pope were the last two in, and the veteran played with the utmost coolness. Burton, who had been bowling with excellent judgment and great success, was perhaps unwise to tempt Blackham to hit when matters got to the very finish, but, however that may be, he pitched a slow ball up, which the Australian jumped at and drove to the boundary, this winning the game, amidst the greatest excitement, by one wicket. English cricketers have often been blamed for exhibiting a lack of nerve at the pinch of a game, but here the Australians, with a very easy task before them, got into a condition that was much like panic. Burton's bowling in this match, fourteen wickets for 192 runs, was one of the features of the season at Lord's. It may be as well to mention here, for the purposes of permanent record, that Giffen's 52 was the last of four great innings in succession. He scored, in the week which ended with this match, 72, 78, 77 and 52.

Middlesex

Mr A. E. Stoddart lbw b Palmer	3	– b Palmer	16
Mr A. J. Webbe c Jones b Palmer	13	– c Scott b Palmer	61
Mr S. W. Scott c Blackham b Garrett	29	– c sub b Giffen	68
Mr J. G. Walker b Evans	67	– b Palmer	0
Spillman c and b Evans	87	– st Blackham b Palmer	6
Mr T. C. O'Brien c Evans b Garrett	16	– b Palmer	0
Mr G. B. Studd b Evans	1	– st Blackham b Palmer	3
Mr G. F. Vernon c Bruce b Palmer	23	– c Giffen b Palmer	37
West b Evans	2	– c Pope b Giffen	0
Burton b Evans	5	– c Bruce b Giffen	1
Mr J. Robertson not out	2	– not out	4
B 3, l-b 7, n-b 1	11	B 14, l-b 7	21
	259		217

Australians

S. P. Jones c Webbe b Burton	76	– c Webbe b Burton	22
H. J. H. Scott lbw b Robertson	123	– st Spillman b Burton	4
G. Giffen c Studd b Burton	77	– b Burton	52
A. H. Jarvis c Stoddart b Burton	6	– c Spillman b Burton	19
W. Bruce c Walker b Burton	3	– c Burton b West	1
J. W. Trumble c and b Burton	3	– c Webbe b Burton	4
E. Evans lbw b Robertson	3	– c Walker b West	1
J. McC. Blackham c and b Burton	0	– not out	6
T. W. Garrett c Scott b Burton	29	– c Spillman b West	7
G. E. Palmer c Webbe b Burton	8	– c Robertson b Burton	5
R. J. Pope not out	11	– not out	0
B 9, l-b 5, n-b 1	15	L-b 2	2
	354		123

Australian Bowling

	Overs	Mdns	Runs	Wkts	Overs	Mdns	Runs	Wkts
Giffen	19	7	33	0	51	20	89	3
Palmer	43	10	72	3	48.1	21	84	7
Garrett	23	3	63	2	7	3	13	0
Bruce	3	1	5	0				
Trumble	20	7	35	0	4	1	5	0
Jones	3	2	4	0				
Evans	36	18	36	5	9	6	5	0

Middlesex Bowling

	Overs	Mdns	Runs	Wkts	Overs	Mdns	Runs	Wkts
Burton	72.2	24	136	8	32	13	56	6
Mr Robertson	65	28	88	2	19	7	40	0
West	33	17	62	0	13	7	25	3
Mr Webbe	14	5	29	0				
Mr Stoddart	3	1	11	0				
Mr S. W. Scott	9	5	7	0				
Mr O'Brien	1	0	6	0				

AUSTRALIA v ENGLAND

Played at Manchester, July 5, 6, 7, 1886

The first of the three great contests between England and Australia had been looked forward to with an immense amount of interest, and the composition of the English team had caused a good deal of controversy. In the original team Mr Hornby was to have been captain, and Barnes was selected; but owing to an injury to his leg the popular Lancashire captain had to stand out, while Barnes was prevented from playing by a strain he received in his side when representing the Players against the Australians a fortnight before. Barlow and Briggs were the two men chosen to fill the vacancies, and the Australians left out Evans and McIlwraith. Fully 10,000 persons witnessed the first day's play, which was good and interesting throughout. The weather, although dull and overcast in the morning, turned out beautifully fine in the afternoon, and the wicket afforded the bowlers very little assistance. Having the good fortune to win the toss the Australians went in first, and at the start of their innings fared remarkably well. Jones played superb cricket, and Jarvis hit with great brilliancy for 45. The score was 181 when the fifth wicket fell, and there seemed every prospect of a long total, but afterwards there came such a collapse that the last five wickets went down for 24 runs, and the innings closed for 205. Jones, who went in first, was out lbw at 134, his faultless 87, the result of two hours and fifty minutes' cricket, being made up of six 4s, ten 3s, five 2s, and singles. Jarvis hit six 4s, a 3 and four 2s. It will be noticed that out of 204 runs from the bat, Jones, Jarvis, Trumble and Scott made no fewer than 177. The English fielding was exceedingly smart and accurate, and Pilling kept wicket to perfection. The two crack bowlers on the English side, however, Lohmann and Peate, only took one wicket between them. A little less than an hour remained for play when the Englishmen commenced their innings, and the score was only 9 when Mr W. G. Grace was very cleverly caught at slip. Shrewsbury, who followed, was let off from a sharp chance in the same position from the first ball he received, but afterwards batted well, and he and Scotton were together at the call of time, when the score stood at 36 for one wicket.

On the second day the interest in the match was thoroughly sustained throughout. The Australians bowled and fielded admirably, and the Englishmen, who scarcely seemed to play in their best form, scored with difficulty. Shrewsbury, after making 31, was bowled by a yorker, and Scotton, after exhibiting great patience, was caught at point at 80. Mr W. W. Read batted in splendid style for 51 – the highest score on the side – and was out to a very good catch at third man at 131. The chief hits of his 51 were seven 4s, three 3s and two 2s. When the luncheon interval took place the score was 140 for five wickets, and afterwards Ulyett and Briggs were speedily disposed of, the score, with seven men out, being only 160. Then, when it seemed most probable that the Australians would lead on the first innings, Lohmann and Barlow made an invaluable stand, and quite altered the aspect of affairs. When he scored only a single, however, Lohmann was badly missed from an easy chance by Palmer at long-on, and for this mistake the Australians had to pay very dearly. Lohmann hit with great nerve and judgment, while Barlow played his usual sound and steady game. The score was up to 206 before Lohmann was bowled, 46 having been added during the partnership. In the end the total reached 223, or 18 runs to the good, Barlow taking out his bat for an invaluable 38. Spofforth took the most wickets for the Australians, but Palmer came out with the best analysis. With an hour and twenty minutes remaining for play, the Australians went in a second time at ten minutes past five, and though Jones and Scott put on 37 runs for the first wicket, matters went so badly with the Colonists afterwards that before the call of time four wickets had fallen for 55 runs. Giffen and Jarvis were both out to Barlow's bowling, and Bonnor, who exhibited very bad judgment, was caught from a very tame stroke on the off side within five minutes of time. The close of the second day's play left the Australians 36 to the good, with six wickets to fall in their second innings.

On the concluding day the Australians thoroughly kept up their reputation for playing an uphill game, and though they were defeated at the finish, they made a splendid fight of it, and the interest in the match never for a moment ceased. Thanks mainly to the capital batting of Scott, and the plucky hitting later on by Garrett and Spofforth, the Australians' total reached 123. Included in Scott's 47 were four 4s, two 3s and eight 2s. As the Englishmen were only left with 106 runs to get to win, it looked as if they would gain a very easy victory but so disastrous was the start that perhaps the three best batsmen in England, Grace, Read and Shrewsbury, were dismissed for a total of only 24. It must be stated, however, that the wicket was beginning to crumble a little, and was by no means so easy as it had been on either of the two previous days. The Australians now began to realise that they had a chance, and they bowled and fielded with remarkable keenness. It was at this point, when three wickets were down for 24, that Barlow became Scotton's partner, and the two men, displaying the most praiseworthy care and judgment, wore down the splendid bowling of the Australians, and again turned the scale in favour of England. The partnership altogether lasted an hour, and yielded 41 runs, the score being thus 65 when the fourth wicket fell. Later on, Mr Steel played in moderate form, but he was missed from an easy chance by Bonnor at short slip, and had this come off the Englishmen would probably have had to fight very hard for their victory. At 90 Barlow's long and extremely good innings of 30 was brought to a close by a clever catch close in, and when the game was a tie Ulyett hit out recklessly, and was caught in the long field. Briggs made the winning stroke at twenty minutes to six, and the English were left winners of a remarkable match by four wickets. Special praise must be awarded to Barlow, who took seven wickets at a cost of 44 runs in the second innings of the Australians, made three catches, and scored 68 runs in the match for once out.

Australians

S. P. Jones lbw b Grace	87	– c Ulyett b Steel	12
H. J. H. Scott c Barlow b Ulyett	21	– b Barlow	47
G. Giffen b Steel	3	– c Shrewsbury b Barlow	1
A. H. Jarvis c Scotton b Ulyett	45	– c Lohmann b Barlow	2
G. J. Bonnor c Lohmann b Barlow	4	– c Barlow b Peate	2
J. W. Trumble c Scotton b Steel	24	– c Ulyett b Barlow	4
W. Bruce run out	2	– c Grace b Barlow	0
T. W. Garrett c Pilling b Lohmann	5	– c Grace b Ulyett	22
J. McC. Blackham not out	7	– lbw b Barlow	2
G. E. Palmer c Lohmann b Ulyett	4	– c Pilling b Barlow	8
F. R. Spofforth c Barlow b Ulyett	2	– not out	20
W 1	1	B 3	3
	205		123

England

Scotton c Trumble b Garrett	21 – b Palmer	20
Mr W. G. Grace c Bonnor b Spofforth	8 – c Palmer b Giffen	4
Shrewsbury b Spofforth	31 – c and b Giffen	4
Mr W. W. Read c Scott b Garrett	51 – c Jones b Spofforth	9
Mr A. G. Steel c Jarvis b Palmer	12 – not out	19
Barlow not out	38 – c Palmer b Spofforth	30
Ulyett b Spofforth	17 – c Scott b Garrett	8
Briggs c Garrett b Spofforth	1 – not out	2
Lohmann b Giffen	32	
Peate st Jarvis b Palmer	6	
Pilling c Bruce b Palmer	2	
Extras	4	Extras 11
	223	107

England Bowling

	Overs	Mdns	Runs	Wkts	Overs	Mdns	Runs	Wkts
Peate	19	7	30	0	46	35	45	1
Lohmann	23	9	41	1	5	3	14	0
Mr A. G. Steel	27	5	47	2	8	3	9	1
Ulyett	36.1	20	46	4	6.3	3	7	1
Barlow	23	15	19	1	52	24	44	7
Mr W. G. Grace	9	3	21	1	1	0	1	0

Australian Bowling

	Overs	Mdns	Runs	Wkts	Overs	Mdns	Runs	Wkts
Spofforth	53	22	82	4	29.2	13	40	2
Giffen	32	15	44	1	24	9	31	2
Garrett	45	23	43	2	17	9	14	1
Bruce	9	6	9	0				
Palmer	17.2	4	41	3	7	3	11	1

AUSTRALIANS v YORKSHIRE

Played at Sheffield, July 12, 13, 14, 1886

There was an immense attendance of spectators at Bramall Lane to welcome the Australians, the number paying for admission on the first day being 10,209. The visitors, who won the toss, lost six of their best men for 81, and then the game changed so remarkably that the last four batsmen increased the score by 194 runs. Of this number G. E. Palmer, who had been out of form with the bat for several weeks, scored 94 in really superb fashion. He made no mistake, and was in for two hours and a half, his hits being ten 4s, six 3s, nine 2s, and singles. Trumble and Spofforth helped him considerably, the seventh wicket putting on 98 runs, and the last 61 runs. Hall and Bates scored 42 without being separated before play ceased for the day.

On the Tuesday there was another big gate, and the Yorkshiremen, after coming to grief in their first innings, played up well in their second. Bates, who had been very unfortunate for some time, scored 57 and 44 by some really brilliant cricket, and Preston, Ulyett, Peel, Hall and Lee all did themselves justice. Palmer's bowling in the first innings of Yorkshire was remarkable for the way he got on his leg break. At the drawing of stumps Yorkshire, with three wickets to go down, were 114 runs to the good.

The third day produced some sensational cricket. The County only added 18 runs to their score, and left the Australians 133 to get to win, and this number they made for the loss of only four wickets. The extraordinary part of the day's play was in the last over, when Wade, a colt who afterwards bowled with great success for his county, was opposed to Scott. The Australian captain had been playing exceedingly well and hitting hard, and when this memorable over commenced 19 runs were wanted to win. Wade bowled very slowly with a big break from the off, and Scott stood back and waited for the first ball, hitting it tremendously hard in front of square leg for 6. The second ball, a very similar one, was sent in the same quarter of the ground for 4, and then for the third time Scott waited for the break to take effect, and lashed out, hitting the ball clean over the seats for another 6. There was some little delay as several of the fieldsmen changed places in the belief the over was finished. When the umpire had set them right, Wade unwisely again bowled a very slow ball with a big break, and Scott, opening his shoulders at this, hit it also clean out of the ground for the third 6, or 22 runs in one over. This was, perhaps, the most startling finish witnessed during the season, and certainly the achievement has not often been approached in first-class matches, Bonnor's 20 in an over – two 6s and two 4s, at Scarborough, in 1882, being the nearest parallel that we can recall. Scott was loudly cheered at the finish, and his innings of 67 was one of his most valuable contributions of the season. We should add that the weather changed on the Wednesday morning, and the Yorkshiremen had the disadvantage of bowling with a wet ball and fielding on slippery turf.

Australians

S. P. Jones b Emmett	26	– b Peate	2
H. J. H. Scott b Bates	2	– not out	67
G. Giffen c Emmett b Peate	11	– lbw b Emmett	30
A. H. Jarvis b Bates	20	– c Preston b Peate	18
J. McIlwraith run out	5		
J. W. Trumble b Preston	45	– not out	0
T. W. Garrett b Preston	0		
G. E. Palmer run out	94	– c Preston b Wade	15
W. Bruce b Preston	5		
E. Evans b Emmett	11		
F. R. Spofforth not out	37		
B 12, l-b 3, w 4	19	B 2, l-b 2	4
	275		136

Yorkshire

Hall st Jarvis b Garrett	8	– c Bruce b Giffen	30
Bates c Giffen b Garrett	57	– b Evans	44
Ulyett c Palmer b Garrett	30	– b Trumble	31
Hon. M. B. Hawke b Palmer	14	– b Evans	11
Preston lbw b Palmer	11	– b Trumble	37
Peel b Garrett	9	– b Spofforth	28
Wade b Palmer	0	– not out	16
Lee b Garrett	4	– c McIlwraith b Trumble	29
Emmett not out	3	– c and b Spofforth	0
Peate c McIlwraith b Garrett	1	– c Giffen b Spofforth	7
Hunter b Palmer	0	– b Garrett	3
B 13, l-b 6, n-b 2	21	B 9, l-b 4	13
	158		249

Yorkshire Bowling

	Overs	Mdns	Runs	Wkts	Overs	Mdns	Runs	Wkts
Bates	51	27	60	2	16	5	27	0
Emmett	33	13	56	2	5	1	23	1
Peate	15	9	19	1	28	13	34	2
Preston	31.1	17	46	3	9	4	14	0
Peel	8	2	30	0				
Ulyett	9	4	22	0	5	2	8	0
Wade	6	1	23	0	3	1	26	1

Australian Bowling

	Overs	Mdns	Runs	Wkts	Overs	Mdns	Runs	Wkts
Spofforth	21	10	37	0	24	9	27	3
Giffen	5	0	21	0	14	2	49	1
Garrett	32	16	46	6	22.3	10	38	1
Palmer	17.3	5	33	4	22	6	56	0
Evans					18	5	34	2
Trumble					20	7	32	3

AUSTRALIANS v SURREY

Played at The Oval, July 29, 30, 31, 1886

The return match between Surrey and the Australians had been looked forward to with a very large amount of interest, as it was thought that the Colonists would be certain to make a great effort to reverse the result that had been arrived at at the first meeting of the two sides, when Surrey after an interesting struggle won by three wickets. As it turned out, however, so far from that result being reversed, the Surrey men gained a most remarkable and brilliant triumph, beating the Australians with consummate ease, and accomplishing one of the finest batting performances of the season. The Australian team differed in two instances from that which opposed Surrey in the previous match, Spofforth and McIlwraith replacing Evans and Bonnor. The first day's cricket proved by far the most uneventful of the three, and though the Australians won the toss and went in first on a good wicket, their total only amounted to 185, this number taking as nearly as possible four hours and a half to obtain. The Surrey men bowled and fielded admirably, and Bowley's figures came out extremely well. Surrey had about three quarters of an hour's batting, and in that time lost one wicket (Mr Shuter) for 39 runs, so that the County had a slight advantage.

The second day's play produced a performance which has never been equalled against Australian bowling in England, and during the whole day the Australians only got down two of the Surrey wickets. As may be supposed, the condition of the ground gave the bowlers no assistance whatever, but every praise is due to the Surrey batsmen for their most admirable display. During the six hours that play lasted 388 runs were scored for the loss of two batsmen. Diver was bowled at 51, and then Abel and Mr Walter Read added 135 runs during their partnership. The amateur's finely played 80 included nine 4s, five 3s and ten 2s, and the score was 186 for three wickets, or one run ahead of the Australian total, with seven wickets to fall. Then came the remarkable part of the cricket. Maurice Read became Abel's partner, and the two batsmen obtained such a complete mastery over the bowling, and treated it with such merciless severity, that they were still together when stumps were drawn for the day, and had then put on 241 runs. The batting of the two men was in strong contrast, for Read, although he was not out 156 at the call of time, did not go in until Abel's score was 67, and the latter professional at the close had only made 144. Hardly a real fault could be urged against either man, and the Surrey crowd were of course most enthusiastic in their praise. A collection was made on the ground for Abel and Maurice Read, which amounted to £68 4s.

On the concluding day the brilliant batting was followed up by some equally good bowling, and the Surrey men were enabled to score a splendid victory. Abel did not add a run to his overnight score of 144, and he was on all hands congratulated for certainly the biggest thing he had ever accomplished in the cricket-field. He was batting for six hours and fifty minutes, and included in his innings were fourteen 4s, seven 3s and twenty 2s. Read continued his hitting until 469, when he was dismissed by a very fine catch, close in, at mid-on. Read's 186 – the highest innings played in this country against Australian bowling, beating Shrewsbury's 164 at Lord's by 22 runs – was one of the best displays of clean and vigorous hitting that has ever been seen. His chief hits were twenty-three 4s, twelve 3s and ten 2s. The Surrey innings ultimately closed for 501 – the first score of 500 ever made against Australian bowling in England. The Australians went in for their second innings at a quarter past one, and, deducting the luncheon interval, they had to remain in four hours and a half to save the game. Although the wicket was not nearly so good as on the previous day, heavy rain having fallen on the Friday night, the batting of the Australians was very disappointing, and another blow was dealt at the reputation Colonial cricketers had gained for up-hill play. Giffen certainly made a noble effort to save his side, and Scott and McIlwraith batted fairly well, but the others were completely beaten by the superb bowling of Lohmann, and by a quarter past five the innings was all over for the paltry total of 107, Surrey being left with a remarkable victory by an innings and 209 runs. The result was received with much enthusiasm. Certainly the chances of the Australians making a draw were much discounted by the rain of Friday night.

Australians

H. J. H. Scott b Bowley	8	– lbw b Jones	18
S. P. Jones c Wood b Bowley	25	– b Jones	9
G. Giffen b Jones	59	– b Beaumont	39
G. E. Palmer c W. Read b Bowley	13	– b Lohmann	1
J. McIlwraith c Roller b Lohmann	21	– c Jones b Lohmann	12
J. W. Trumble b Lohmann	12	– c Roller b Lohmann	0
A. H. Jarvis not out	21	– b Lohmann	4
J. McC. Blackham b Bowley	7	– not out	10
W. Bruce c Lohmann b Bowley	0	– b Lohmann	0
T. W. Garrett c Wood b Bowley	11	– c Read b Lohmann	2
F. R. Spofforth b Bowley	0	– c Jones b Beaumont	7
B 4, l-b 4	8	L-b 2, n-b 3	5
	185		107

Surrey

Mr J. Shuter b Spofforth	13
Abel c Palmer b Giffen	144
Diver b Palmer	14
Mr W. W. Read b Trumble	80
M. Read c Palmer b Giffen	186
Mr W. E. Roller c Scott b Giffen	0
Lohmann not out	31
Jones c Scott b Garrett	2
Wood b Giffen	8
Bowley b Giffen	0
Beaumont b Giffen	2
B 11, l-b 5, w 2, n-b 3	21
	501

Surrey Bowling

	Overs	Mdns	Runs	Wkts	Overs	Mdns	Runs	Wkts
Bowley	57	31	64	7	19	11	21	0
Lohmann	55	31	60	2	44	19	58	6
Abel	11	4	10	0				
Beaumont	18	6	25	0	10.2	9	4	2
Jones	16	11	14	1	19	13	12	2
Mr Roller	8	5	4	0	6	4	7	0

Australian Bowling

	Overs	Mdns	Runs	Wkts
Spofforth	50	21	102	1
Palmer	51	27	80	1
Giffen	54.1	22	106	6
Garrett	46	20	74	1
Bruce	15	2	29	0
Trumble	29	12	43	1
Jones	15	8	19	0
Blackham	16	8	27	0

AUSTRALIANS v GLOUCESTERSHIRE

Played at Cheltenham, August 16, 17, 18, 1886

The second meeting between Gloucestershire and the Australians, which formed the first match of the Cheltenham week, had been looked forward to with a great deal of interest, owing to the good show made by the western county in the first contest at Clifton. Jarvis's foot was too bad to admit of his playing for the Australians, and Giffen stood out owing to a domestic bereavement, news having been received of the death in Australia of his elder brother. Bonnor was telegraphed for, but never got to Cheltenham, and consequently Jarvis went in to bat on the second day. The first day's play proved of a very ordinary character, and as rain had seriously affected the condition of the ground, the bowlers had a considerable advantage. Winning the toss, the Australians put together a total of 119, out of which number four batsmen between them made no fewer than 84. Gloucestershire started very badly, losing three wickets before the call of time for 23 runs, Spofforth clean bowling Messrs Grace, Radcliffe and Townsend. Rain caused two brief interruptions during the afternoon.

On the Tuesday the attendance was the largest ever known on the Cheltenham ground, and the cricket was far more interesting than on the previous day. Bowlers were still favoured by the condition of the ground, and the Gloucestershire innings was quickly finished off for 74, or 45 runs to the bad. At the commencement of their second innings the Australians fared worse than before, and five wickets went down for 41 runs. Blackham and Bruce then became partners, and put an entirely different appearance on the game. Bruce, however, was badly missed at slip before he had made a run, and Blackham, when he had scored 2, should have been easily stumped. For these blunders Gloucestershire had to pay dearly, as the two batsmen put on 69 runs for the sixth wicket. Woof took the last four wickets in fourteen balls without a run being scored off him, and the Australians were all out for 114. It will be seen that Woof's analysis was an exceptionally good one. Wanting 160 runs to win, Gloucestershire went in a second time at ten minutes to five. When stumps were drawn they had scored 58 for the loss of three wickets, Mr E. M. Grace being not out 31 and Mr Moberly not out 1.

On the concluding day Gloucestershire required 102 runs to win with seven wickets to fall, but on the slow and rather difficult wicket this task proved too heavy. The brothers Grace batted very well, and made a plucky effort to score a victory for their side, but they received little support, and the innings closed for 133, leaving the Australians winners of a close and exciting game by 26 runs. Spofforth accomplished a remarkable bowling performance, taking in the whole match ten wickets for 106 runs.

It was during this match that the Australian manager, Major Wardill, abandoned, in compliance with instructions received from the Melbourne Club, the idea of taking out an English team to the Colonies at the conclusion of the season. We shall say very little about this matter, because there was a good deal of ill-feeling displayed at the time, and as that feeling passed away, it is unnecessary to more than briefly record the fact that it was the intention of the Melbourne Club to take out an English side of gentlemen and players to Australia, and that this intention was persevered in for some time after it became known that Shaw and Shrewsbury were going out with a powerful professional eleven. The Melbourne Club wisely decided to make terms with Shaw and Shrewsbury, who by their agent agreed to play the Melbourne matches upon the club's ground. It would have been simply deplorable if two English teams had competed with each other for the favour and countenance of the Australian public.

Australians

S. P. Jones b Page	17	– c Brain b W. G. Grace	0
G. E. Palmer lbw b Woof	20	– c Radcliffe b Woof	29
H. J. H. Scott c W. G. Grace b Page	2	– c Bush b Woof	9
J. W. Trumble c Brain b W. G. Grace	21	– lbw b Woof	0
J. McIlwraith c E. M. Grace b Woof	1	– b W. G. Grace	3
J. McC. Blackham b Page	3	– c E. M. Grace b Woof	37
W. Bruce b Page	0	– c Wood b Page	30
T. W. Garrett b W. G. Grace	26	– c Bush b Woof	0
G. J. Bonnor absent	0	– (A. H. Jarvis) c Brain b Woof	0
E. Evans not out	9	– c Page b Woof	0
F. R. Spofforth c Brain b W. G. Grace	8	– not out	0
B 6, l-b 4, w 2	12	B 2, l-b 4	6
	119		114

Gloucestershire

Mr W. G. Grace b Spofforth	5	– c Jones b Spofforth	30
Mr O. G. Radcliffe b Spofforth	1	– b Spofforth	3
Painter run out	10	– b Palmer	14
Mr F. Townsend b Spofforth	8	– c Palmer b Spofforth	6
Mr J. H. Brain c Trumble b Garrett	9	– c Blackham b Palmer	4
Dr E. M. Grace c Trumble b Garrett	2	– b Spofforth	50
Mr H. V. Page c Palmer b Spofforth	15	– b Trumble	2
Mr W. O. Moberly b Garrett	0	– c Jarvis b Spofforth	0
Mr H. Hale not out	11	– b Garrett	8
Woof b Garrett	6	– b Trumble	4
Mr J. A. Bush b Spofforth	5	– not out	0
N-b 2	2	B 4, l-b 7, n-b 1	12
	74		133

Gloucestershire Bowling

	Overs	Mdns	Runs	Wkts	Overs	Mdns	Runs	Wkts
Mr W. G. Grace	24	10	28	3	31	14	46	2
Woof	38	18	42	2	29	17	32	7
Mr Hale	2	1	4	0				
Mr Page	34	17	33	4	17.2	7	30	1

Australian Bowling

	Overs	Mdns	Runs	Wkts	Overs	Mdns	Runs	Wkts
Spofforth	25	10	37	5	48	22	69	5
Palmer	11	3	24	0	28	20	9	2
Garrett	13	7	11	4	25	8	37	1
Trumble					5.3	3	6	2

AUSTRALIANS v SURREY

Played at The Oval, May, 14, 15, 1888

There was a large crowd to see the first big match of the London season, 14,302 paying for admission on the two days, and although regret was plainly enough shown at the county's poor form, there could be no doubt as to the cordiality of the visitors' reception. It was pretty clear by this time that McDonnell and Bannerman, as in 1884 were the regular pair to start the batting, and in this particular game they started it wonderfully well. Lohmann and Maurice Read had only landed at Plymouth the day before, and the great bowler, besides being out of form, was lame through an injured nail, and had to give up the ball when 158 runs had been scored for five wickets. The chief feature of the first day was the superbly free hitting of Turner, who surprised cricketing England by his 103, an innings which included nineteen 4s, two 3s and four 2s. Turner and Ferris, as in the two previous games, bowled superbly, and the Australians won by an innings and 154 runs. The new press-box at The Oval was first used for this match. The Surrey Committee, acting on suggestions made by the Editor of this Annual, extended their pavilion, and, while the reporters were given a splendid view and greater accommodation than anywhere else in England, the card-sellers and telegraph clerks were housed just inside the gates.

Australians

P. S. McDonnell b Lohmann	56
A. C. Bannerman b W. Read	43
S. P. Jones b Bowley	16
G. J. Bonnor b Lohmann	3
H. Trott b Henderson	35
J. McC. Blackham c Key b Bowley	9
C. T. B. Turner c Wood b M. Read	103
J. Worrall b Bowley	16
J. J. Lyons b Bowley	5
J. J. Ferris not out	37
H. F. Boyle c Abel b Beaumont	22
B 13, l-b 4, n-b 1	18
	363

Surrey

R. Abel b Ferris	11	– b Ferris	8
Mr J. Shuter c and b Ferris	6	– b Turner	8
Mr K. J. Key b Ferris	24	– b Ferris	20
Mr W. W. Read lbw b Turner	15	– lbw b Turner	4
H. Brockwell b Turner	3	– c Trott b Jones	0
M. Read c sub b Ferris	12	– run out	28
R. Henderson b Turner	1	– b Jones	5
G. A. Lohmann lbw b Turner	0	– lbw b Trott	26
H. Wood c Boyle b Turner	12	– c Trott b Turner	7
T. Bowley c and b Turner	5	– not out	0
J. Beaumont not out	0	– b Jones	8
		B 6	6
	89		120

Surrey Bowling

	Overs	Mdns	Runs	Wkts
Lohmann	37	17	48	2
Bowley	39	10	77	4
Beaumont	23.1	6	60	1
Abel	19	8	43	0
Henderson	15	2	36	1
W. W. Read	13	5	27	1
Brockwell	14	6	32	0
M. Read	8	2	22	1

Australian Bowling

	Overs	Mdns	Runs	Wkts	Overs	Mdns	Runs	Wkts
Turner	30.1	13	44	6	32	11	57	3
Ferris	30	12	45	4	28	17	40	2
Trott					8	5	13	1
Jones					4.3	2	4	3

Umpires: Farrands and Carpenter.

AUSTRALIANS v ELEVEN OF ENGLAND

Played at Birmingham, June 18, 19, 20, 1888

A fairly strong mixed eleven won the toss and played a good game for a time against the Australians. Radcliffe played a brilliant innings of 71, including eleven 4s. McDonnell on the first day, and Bonnor, Trott and Worrall on the second, batted so well that the Colonial team had a great advantage. Turner and Ferris then rattled the other men out, and early on Wednesday the Australians won by ten wickets. Grace had a tremendous reception from the Birmingham crowd, who carried him round the ground.

Eleven of England

First innings		Second innings	
Mr W. G. Grace run out	18	c Bonnor b Ferris	4
G. Ulyett c McDonnell b Ferris	17	b Turner	5
J. Painter b Turner	4	b Turner	9
R. Peel c and b Trott	22	b Ferris	11
Mr O. G. Radcliffe c and b Turner	71	c Bonnor b Ferris	8
Mr H. W. Bainbridge b Trott	0	b Turner	10
Mr C. W. Wright c and b Boyle	26	b Turner	3
Mr L. C. Docker b Turner	0	b Ferris	23
Rev. R. T. Thornton b Turner	12	not out	16
Mr H. T. Hewitt c and b Boyle	12	c Jarvis b Turner	1
J. E. Shilton not out	1	b Ferris	0
B 14, l-b 7	21	B 7, l-b 2	9
	204		99

Australians

First innings		Second innings	
P. S. McDonnell b Shilton	67		
A. C. Bannerman c Thornton b Grace	27		
H. Trott c Ulyett b Grace	37		
G. J. Bonnor c Docker b Peel	73		
J. McC. Blackham c Grace b Peel	9		
C. T. B. Turner c Shilton b Grace	1		
A. H. Jarvis lbw b Grace	0		
J. D. Edwards lbw b Grace	13		
J. Worrall run out	46	not out	3
J. J. Ferris b Grace	3		
H. F. Boyle not out	13	not out	5
B 5, l-b 3	8		
	297		8

Australian Bowling

	Overs	Mdns	Runs	Wkts	Overs	Mdns	Runs	Wkts
Turner	45.2	24	60	4	32	18	44	5
Ferris	33	13	62	1	32.2	14	43	5
Trott	15	8	21	2				
Worrall	9	3	22	0				
Boyle	18	9	18	2				

England Bowling

	Overs	Mdns	Runs	Wkts	Overs	Mdns	Runs	Wkts
Grace	52	25	74	6	1.2	1	4	0
Shilton	32	12	45	1				
Peel	46	17	91	2	2	0	4	0
Ulyett	13	5	51	0				
Radcliffe	12	3	23	0				
Bainbridge	1	0	5	0				

Umpires: Farrands and Bates.

AUSTRALIANS v LEICESTERSHIRE

Played at Leicester, July 5, 6, 1888

This was one of the Sensational matches of the season. The Australians had won eleven and only lost three of their seventeen fixtures; but now, with a good deal the worst of a bad wicket, the Colonial eleven came to grief. Warren hit capitally, and the two Leicestershire bowlers, helped by some more rain on the Tuesday night, won a fine match for their county by 20 runs. The Australian bowling was as good as ever, but the batting failed on the wretched ground, and the fielding was faulty. Leicestershire deserved and received a great deal of praise for their achievement, and they certainly played with wonderful spirit all through.

Leicestershire

J. Wheeler c Trott b Turner	0	b Turner	11
T. H. Warren c Blackham b Trott	42	lbw b Turner	0
Tomlin c Jarvis b Trott	14	c Trott b Turner	2
Mr C. Marriott b Turner	5	c Worrall b Ferris	12
Mr C. E. de Trafford c Trott b Boyle	7	run out	1
Mr C. C. Stone c Blackham b Turner	8	c Trott b Ferris	0
A. D. Pougher c Worrall b Turner	18	c Lyons b Turner	11
Mr A. W. Crofts b Turner	0	b Turner	3
Mr J. Collier not out	11	b Ferris	1
Mr H. T. Arnall-Thompson b Turner	0	c and b Ferris	2
Atkins b Trott	9	not out	4
L-b 5	5	B 3	3
	119		50

Australians

A. C. Bannerman c Crofts b Pougher	2	c Crofts b Pougher	20
J. McC. Blackham c Crofts b Arnall-Thompson	2	lbw b Pougher	3
H. Trott c de Trafford b Arnall-Thompson	0	c Wheeler b Atkins	19
G. J. Bennor c and b Pougher	21	b Arnall-Thompson	0
A. H. Jarvis b Arnall-Thompson	16	c Stone b Pougher	8
P. S. McDonnell b Arnall-Thompson	1	c Arnall-Thompson b Pougher	12
C. T. B. Turner c Collier b Pougher	8	c Stone b Arnall-Thompson	3
J. J. Lyons c Pougher b Arnall-Thompson	0	c de Trafford b Pougher	9
J. Worrall b Pougher	0	c and b Pougher	0
J. J. Ferris c Warren b Arnall-Thompson	6	c Warren b Arnall-Thompson	7
H. F. Boyle not out	6	not out	0
		B 6	6
	62		87

Australian Bowling

	Overs	Mdns	Runs	Wkts	Overs	Mdns	Runs	Wkts
Turner	32	16	44	6	23	16	20	5
Worrall	6	3	6	0				
Ferris	9	5	11	0	22.3	12	27	4
Boyle	18	7	35	1				
Trott	16.3	7	18	3				

Leicestershire Bowling

	Overs	Mdns	Runs	Wkts	Overs	Mdns	Runs	Wkts
Pougher	23	11	31	4	33	13	40	6
Arnall-Thompson	22.1	11	31	6	24	10	34	3
Atkins					9	6	7	1

Umpires: Farrands and Bishop.

AUSTRALIANS v ELEVEN OF ENGLAND

Played at Stoke, July 12, 13, 1888

Mr A. H. Heath, the captain of the Staffordshire county team, had several disappointments in getting his scratch eleven together. The wicket was nearly under water in the early part of Thursday, and it was not expected that play would be possible at all on that day, but the rain held off, and, as Mr Heath thought it would be better to play than disappoint the spectators, the match was practically tossed for. McDonnell won, and on a sodden wicket, upon which the bowlers could hardly stand, the Colonists hit out at everything, and between three o'clock and the drawing of stumps, scored 201 for eight wickets. McDonnell and Blackham made 41 for the first wicket, and the former and Trott 24 for the second, while McDonnell was third out at 97 for a dashing 52. There was some good free hitting by Ferris and Worrall after eight wickets had fallen for 151, and when stumps were drawn the total, as we have said, was 201.

On the Friday the wicket played treacherously under the hot sun, and got worse and worse throughout the day. The Australian innings closed for 242, and then the Englishmen went in. Their first innings was a remarkable one, and was all over in about an hour and ten minutes for 28. Turner was simply unplayable, and he took nine of the ten wickets – the other being a run out – for 15 runs. Scotton carried his bat through for 9 runs. The second innings lasted two hours, and amounted to 79, which left the Australians a single innings victory with 135 runs to spare. Scotton again played better than anyone else, and was in an hour and twenty-five minutes for his 20. In the whole match Turner took thirteen wickets for 48 runs.

Australians

J. McC. Blackham b Pougher	23
P. S. McDonnell c Heath b Flowers	52
H. Trott c Heath b Flowers	6
G. J. Bonnor c Heath b Flowers	38
J. D. Edwards c McGregor b Pougher	10
C. T. B. Turner c Richardson b Flowers	0
A. H. Jarvis run out	18
H. F. Boyle c Heath b Pougher	0
J. Worrall st McGregor b Attewell	36
J. J. Ferris b Pougher	30
J. J. Lyons not out	20
B 9	9
	242

An England Eleven

Mr A. H. Heath b Turner	11 – b Turner	6
W. Scotton not out	9 – b Ferris	20
W. Chatterton b Turner	0 – c Turner b Ferris	2
Mr D. H. Brownfield run out	0 – b Ferris	4
J. Painter b Turner	4 – c Bonnor b Turner	5
W. Flowers lbw b Turner	2 – c Blackham b Ferris	5
Mr G. McGregor b Turner	0 – b Turner	1
W. Attewell b Turner	0 – c Bonnor b Turner	0
A. D. Pougher lbw b Turner	2 – c Blackham b Ferris	6
Mr H. T. Richardson b Turner	0 – b Ferris	15
Briscoe b Turner	0 – not out	4
	B 7, l-b 3, n-b 1	11
	28	79

English Bowling

	Overs	Mdns	Runs	Wkts
Attewell	24.2	8	54	1
Pougher	47	21	84	4
Briscoe	24	12	28	0
Flowers	28	10	52	4
Chatterton	4	0	15	0

Australian Bowling

	Overs	Mdns	Runs	Wkts	Overs	Mdns	Runs	Wkts
Turner	17.1	10	15	9	31	14	33	4
Ferris	17	12	13	0	30.2	11	35	6

ENGLAND v AUSTRALIA

Played at Lord's, July 16, 17, 1888

Although of course it was seen that the Australians were by no means equal on their merits to the best team in England, there was a considerable amount of anxiety as to the result of the first of the three great test matches. In dry weather and on a hard wicket, confidence in the strength of English batting would have been almost unlimited, but the weather for weeks had been so bad, and the Australian bowling had proved so destructive, with the condition of the turf favouring it, that many quite dispassionate judges thought the game would be so fluky, that victory would depend almost entirely upon success in the toss. It need scarcely be remarked that there had been only one previous Australian victory in this country over the full strength of England, and that that was accomplished in 1882 by a team which, by general consent, was the best that ever came here from

Australia. Our batting had probably become stronger so far as the professionals were concerned, but it certainly had not maintained its position among amateurs, there being many good Gentlemen batsmen, but no new ones who had any claim to be chosen in a strictly representative eleven. On the other hand, our bowling was probably stronger than ever, while the wicket-keeping and fielding of the selected team left nothing to be desired. Attewell had been chosen by the Marylebone Committee, and Mr Shuter, of whose innings for the Gentlemen we have already spoken, would also have played but for lameness. As it was, Abel, the most consistent scorer among the Players, had a place, and at the last moment the old Oxonian, T. C. O'Brien, was put in as a hitter. Good man as he is, O'Brien entirely failed in his mission, and Abel, of whom so much was expected by his friends, probably could not help his play being influenced by his sense of responsibility. The Australians left out Lyons and Boyle, and McDonnell, having won the toss, went in with Bannerman to commence a match about which every one's nerves were in a high state of tension, and at a time when it is not too much to say that all concerned, from batsmen, bowlers, and umpires down to the merest spectators, felt the importance of the issue, and how much was at stake. We ought, however, to say that to the best of our knowledge there was little or no betting of any consequence, and certainly, with all the eagerness and keenness of feeling, there was no bitterness or acrimony on either side. Winning the toss was known to be a much greater advantage than is usually the case, for there had been so much rain within a few hours of the start that it was impossible the ground should be in anything like condition for good cricket. It was for some hours uncertain whether there would be any play on Monday at all, and the gates were not opened until after lunch time. Some thousands of people had crowded in the St John's Wood Road, and there was a great crush to get in, but the people had obtained places, and formed a thick ring all round the ground when play began at five minutes past three. The game had been often described, and it is not our intention to follow the play in detail. It was one in which the Australians, starting with a distinctly inferior team, played with great courage and spirit, and achieved a performance for which they were fully entitled and for which they received a large amount of credit. The Australians played quite the right game, hitting out pluckily, and never attempting to show correct cricket. The Englishmen started well enough, getting rid of Bannerman and Trott for 3 runs, but then Bonnor and McDonnell were both missed. The total was only 82 when the ninth wicket fell, and, though this score was not a bad one under the conditions, it was not good enough to look like winning. Ferris, the last man, joined Edwards, who should have been easily run out, and then this pair, by some invaluable and fearless hitting, put on 30 runs before they were separated. The Englishmen went in in a bad light, and lost Abel, Barnes and Lohmann for 18 before stumps were drawn for the day.

On Tuesday morning play began at half-past eleven, and W. G. Grace did not add to the 10 he had made overnight. Wicket after wicket fell until eight men were out for 37, and it looked quite possible that England would have to follow on. Briggs and Peel averted this disaster, but the whole side were out before half-past twelve for 53, or 63 to the bad. The English bowling and fielding during the second innings of Australia were superb, and the ground was altogether against batsmen, so that it was no wonder the Australians were out for 60. Indeed, but for Ferris's capital hitting the total would not nearly have reached that number. But it was clear England was at a great disadvantage, and that the 124 wanted to win would be more than could be made. Mr Grace began really well, and 29 runs were made before the first wicket fell. At 34, however, the champion was out, and from that time Turner and Ferris carried everything before them. The Australians played a winning game with tremendous energy and unfailing skill, and at twenty-five minutes past four in the afternoon they were successful with 61 runs to spare. The vast crowd rushed across the ground directly the game was over, and thousands upon thousands of people formed a dense mass in front of the pavilion, and cheered with a spontaneous and genuine heartiness that could scarcely have been exceeded if the Englishmen had made the runs instead of being badly beaten. So ended a game that will never be forgotten in cricket history, and one which practically ensured the fame of the Australian team.

Australians

	1st inns	2nd inns	
A. C. Bannerman c Grace b Lohmann	0	b Peel	0
P. S. McDonnell c O'Brien b Peel	22	b Lohmann	1
H. Trott c Lohmann b Peel	0	b Lohmann	3
G. J. Bonnor b Lohmann	6	c Lohmann b Peel	8
J. McC. Blackham b Briggs	22	run out	1
S. M. J. Woods c Gunn b Briggs	18	c Grace b Peel	3
C. T. B. Turner c Lohmann b Peel	3	c Grace b Briggs	12
J. D. Edwards not out	21	c Sherwin b Lohmann	0
A. H. Jarvis c Lohmann b Peel	3	c Barnes b Peel	4
J. Worrall c Abel b Briggs	2	b Lohmann	4
J. J. Ferris c Sherwin b Steel	14	not out	20
B 5	5	B 3, l-b 1	4
	116		60

England

	1st inns	2nd inns	
Mr W. G. Grace c Woods b Ferris	10	c Bannerman b Ferris	24
R. Abel b Ferris	3	c Bonnor b Ferris	8
W. Barnes c Jarvis b Turner	3	st Blackham b Ferris	1
G. A. Lohmann lbw b Turner	2	st Blackham b Ferris	0
Mr W. W. Read st Blackham b Turner	4	b Turner	3
Mr T. C. O'Brien b Turner	0	b Turner	4
R. Peel run out	8	b Turner	4
Mr A. G. Steel st Blackham b Turner	3	not out	10
W. Gunn c Blackham b Ferris	2	b Ferris	8
J. Briggs b Woods	17	b Turner	0
M. Sherwin not out	0	c Ferris b Turner	0
L-b 1	1		
	53		62

English Bowling

	Overs	Mdns	Runs	Wkts	Overs	Mdns	Runs	Wkts
Lohmann	20	9	28	2	14	4	33	4
Peel	21	7	36	4	10.2	3	14	4
Briggs	21	8	26	3	4	1	9	1
Barnes	6	0	17	0				
Mr Steel	3.2	2	4	1	1	1	0	0

Australian Bowling

	Overs	Mdns	Runs	Wkts	Overs	Mdns	Runs	Wkts
Turner	25	9	27	5	24	8	36	5
Ferris	21	13	19	3	23	11	26	5
Woods	4	2	6	1				

Umpires: Farrands and Pullin.

AUSTRALIANS v PAST AND PRESENT OF CAMBRIDGE UNIVERSITY

Played at Leyton, July 23, 24, 25, 1888

The feature of the University innings was the admirable batting of A. P. Lucas, who in two hours and twenty minutes, without giving a chance, made 50 runs, in his old splendid form. The weakness of the Cambridge bowling was soon apparent when the Australians went in. Bonnor hit nine 4s, four 3s, and five 2s in his brilliant 78, which only occupied him an hour and fifty minutes. Bannerman carried his bat through the whole innings, and was in for six hours and ten minutes, his 93 consisting of eleven 4s, five 3s, seven 2s, and singles. It was a really remarkable display of patient defensive cricket. Rain prevented any play on the Wednesday, and the game was left drawn. Blackham was suffering from a chill, and did not go in to bat, while Woods, though he played for his University, had strained his side so badly that his bowling was of nothing like its usual value. Despite the attractive character of the match, there was not a large gate on the Essex county ground, people having by this time got rather tired of cricket in rain and mud.

Cambridge

Mr C. I. Thornton c Trott b Ferris	7	– not out	12
Mr A. P. Lucas b Turner	50		
Mr A. M. Sutthery b Turner	24		
Mr F. E. Lacey b Turner	4		
Mr C. D. Buxton c Blackham b Ferris	6		
Mr W. N. Roe c and b Ferris	1		
Mr S. M. J. Woods b Ferris	0		
Mr C. A. Smith b Turner	3		
Mr P. J. de Paravicini run out	18		
Mr G. McGregor not out	8	– not out	9
Mr F. G. J. Ford b Worrall	16		
		B 1	1
	137		22

Australians

A. C. Bannerman not out	93
P. S. McDonnell c and b Smith	16
H. Trott b Sutthery	18
G. J. Bonnor c Woods b Ford	78
A. H. Jarvis b Buxton	33
J. J. Ferris run out	10
C. T. B. Turner b Lacey	9
J. D. Edwards b Lucas	36
J. Worrall c Lacey b Lucas	2
H. F. Boyle b Woods	0
J. McC. Blackham absent ill	
B 19, l-b 5	24
	319

Australian Bowling

	Overs	Mdns	Runs	Wkts	Overs	Mdns	Runs	Wkts
Turner	49	24	56	4	6	2	8	0
Ferris	48	23	52	4				
Trott	8	2	15	0	5	1	13	0
Worrall	14.3	8	12	1				
Boyle	5	5	2	0				

Cambridge Bowling

	Overs	Mdns	Runs	Wkts
Ford	41	22	55	1
Smith	52	25	82	1
Roe	11	5	12	0
Buxton	35	21	47	1
Sutthery	12	6	21	1
Woods	32.1	16	42	1
Lacey	21	11	29	1
Lucas	5	2	7	2

Umpires: Thoms and Nicholas.

AUSTRALIANS v YORKSHIRE

Played at Huddersfield, July 26, 27, 28, 1888

Heavy rain prevented any play at Huddersfield on the Thursday, but on the Friday the sun came out, and there was a full day's curious cricket. The county won the toss, and, thanks to Ulyett and Hall, 53 runs were scored for the first wicket. Ulyett was out at 64 for an admirable 48, but some more good hitting by Lee took place, until he was bowled just before luncheon at 92, his being the fourth wicket that fell. Afterwards, however, Turner and Ferris got the remaining six wickets for 15 runs in twenty-five minutes, the innings closing for 107. The Australians made a disastrous start, for Peel dismissed Bonnor, Bannerman, and Woods for 3 runs. Trott and Blackham then stopped together, and put on 34 runs, but Blackham was out at 37, and later on Peel and Preston bowled with such effect that the innings was over in seventy minutes for the paltry total of 48. It should be stated that McDonnell was injured and could not bat. Peel did a splendid performance, taking six wickets for 19 runs, while Preston's three wickets cost but 5 runs. This innings was over by five minutes to five, and Yorkshire had an advantage of 59 runs on going in a second time. Their beginning was of a most sensational character. Ulyett was out before a run was scored, Lee was caught at the wicket at 1, Mr Hirst bowled at 2, Wade at 3, and Hall at 10. With five wickets thus down, the game looked bad for Yorkshire, but Peel and Wainwright did much better, and when stumps were pulled up the score was 49 for nine wickets, which gave Yorkshire a lead of 108 with a wicket to fall. Ferris and Turner's figures were remarkable. More rain fell overnight, and it was soon realised that further progress was impossible on the Saturday, when accordingly the match was abandoned as drawn quite early in the day.

Yorkshire

G. Ulyett c Bannerman b Worrall	48	– c Trott b Ferris	0
L. Hall c Jarvis b Worrall	11	– b Turner	6
F. Lee b Turner	25	– c Jarvis b Turner	0
Mr E. T. Hirst b Turner	6	– b Ferris	0
R. Peel lbw b Turner	2	– b Turner	14
Mr H. Hill b Turner	5	– b Turner	0
E. Wainwright b Turner	2	– c Trott b Ferris	16
J. M. Preston b Ferris	5	– b Ferris	5
R. Moorhouse b Ferris	1	– not out	4
S. Wade not out	1	– b Turner	0
J. E. Ellis c Trott b Ferris	0	– not out	0
B 1	1	B 4	4
	107		49

Australians

G. J. Bonnor b Peel	0	C. T. B. Turner b Preston	4
A. C. Bannerman c Ulyett b Peel	0	J. Worrall b Peel	2
H. Trott c Ellis b Peel	28	J. D. Edwards not out	2
S. M. J. Woods b Peel	2	P. S. McDonnell absent hurt	
J. McC. Blackham b Peel	7		
J. J. Ferris b Preston	3		
A. H. Jarvis b Preston	0		48

Australian Bowling

	Overs	Mdns	Runs	Wkts	Overs	Mdns	Runs	Wkts
Turner	31	19	23	5	17	8	23	5
Ferris	31.3	10	46	3	14	9	16	4
Woods	10	6	16	0	2	1	6	0
Worrall	11	6	21	2				

Yorkshire Bowling

	Overs	Mdns	Runs	Wkts
Peel	16	9	19	6
Wainwright	9	3	24	0
Preston	6	4	5	3

Umpires: Farrands and Reaney.

AUSTRALIANS v AN ELEVEN OF ENGLAND

Played at Hastings, August 2, 3, 4, 1888

More bad weather and wet wickets were experienced at Hastings, where no play was possible on the Thursday. On the Friday morning on slow and heavy turf the Australians batted first, and scored a really excellent innings. McDonnell, despite a couple of chances, hit well, and Lyons and Jarvis both played better cricket than they had done for some time. Lyons, indeed, played his first creditable innings in England. Peel had been wonderfully successful up to this match, but the ground did not "hold" enough to suit him. Turner, with the wicket rapidly drying, bowled superbly in the afternoon, and seldom have a good side been so helpless as the scratch eleven were against the famous Australian. The ball broke a lot and did it fast, and his eight wickets were taken for about a run and a half each. On the Saturday the Englishmen kept in a little longer, but Turner prevented them having any chance, and the Australians won in one innings with 27 runs to spare. Turner's seventeen wickets for 50 runs was the talk of the cricket public throughout England.

Australians

P. S. McDonnell c Wright b Wainwright	36
A. C. Bannerman c H. Pigg b Pougher	17
H. Trott c Hall b Wainwright	6
G. J. Bonnor b Wainwright	0
C. T. B. Turner c Mordaunt b C. Pigg	16
J. McC. Blackham b Pougher	7
A. H. Jarvis b Wright	23
J. D. Edwards run out	1
J. J. Lyons c Wright b Sutthery	32
J. J. Ferris c Sutthery b Peel	9
J. Worrall not out	16
B 3, l-b 2	5
	168

An England Eleven

L. Hall b Ferris	9	– b Turner	2
Mr J. Phillips lbw b Turner	3	– not out	24
Mr A. M. Sutthery b Turner	0	– b Turner	7
Mr H. J. Mordaunt b Turner	0	– b Turner	0
Mr H. Pigg b Turner	4	– b Worrall	16
R. Peel b Turner	13	– b Turner	4
E. Wainwright b Worrall	16	– lbw b Turner	3
Mr C. Pigg b Turner	0	– b Turner	3
Mr W. H. Dudney b Turner	3	– b Turner	7
A. D. Pougher b Turner	0	– b Turner	7
H. Wright not out	0	– st Blackham b Turner	4
B 4, l-b 1	5	B 7, l-b 2, n-b 2	11
	53		88

An Eleven of England Bowling

	Overs	Mdns	Runs	Wkts
Peel	31.2	12	44	1
Pougher	21	9	41	2
Wainwright	23	8	34	3
Mr C. Pigg	10	5	10	1
Mr Sutthery	13	5	24	1
Wright	8	4	10	1

Australian Bowling

	Overs	Mdns	Runs	Wkts	Overs	Mdns	Runs	Wkts
Turner	21.3	12	13	8	47.1	25	37	9
Ferris	18	9	26	1	25	16	14	0
Worrall	3	0	9	1	22	8	26	1

Umpires: Farrands and Bennett.

AUSTRALIANS v LORD LONDESBOROUGH'S ELEVEN

Played at Scarborough, September 6, 7, 8, 1888

The team selected by C. I. Thornton was so strong that it was almost entitled to be called England, and few people expected that the Australians would have much chance. The wicket was soft and a little easy to start with, but it got worse, and during the last innings of the Australians was extremely difficult. The visitors had slightly the best of the game on the first day, as only one wicket was down in their first innings for 53. After that, however, their batting broke down against the splendid bowling of Briggs and Peel, and, though Turner worked wonderfully well to try and save the game, Lord Londesborough's eleven won by 155 runs. Briggs's thirteen wickets for 40 runs was one of the greatest achievements of a sensational year.

Lord Londesborough's Eleven

Mr W. G. Grace c Worrall b Ferris	8	– c Worrall b Turner	35
Mr C. I. Thornton c Blackham b Turner	0	– b Turner	0
R. Abel b Turner	0	– b Turner	14
W. Barnes c McDonnell b Lyons	45	– b Lyons	1
W. Gunn c Worrall b Lyons	33	– b Turner	21
Lord Harris c Blackham b Turner	16	– b Turner	0
G. Ulyett b Lyons	10	– b Turner	13
G. A. Lohmann st Blackham b Ferris	7	– c Jones b Ferris	21
J. Briggs b Turner	23	– lbw b Turner	13
R. Peel b Ferris	3	– not out	7
R. Pilling not out	11	– b Turner	12
L-b 7	7	B 5, l-b 3	8
	163		145

Australians

P. S. McDonnell lbw b Peel	13	– b Briggs	9
A. C. Bannerman b Briggs	26	– b Briggs	0
H. Trott c Grace b Peel	25	– lbw b Peel	0
G. J. Bonnor c Lohmann b Briggs	21	– c Lohmann b Briggs	13
S. P. Jones c Barnes b Briggs	0	– st Pilling b Peel	0
J. J. Lyons c Lohmann b Briggs	0	– b Briggs	7
C. T. B. Turner lbw b Peel	0	– c Grace b Briggs	7
J. Worrall c Abel b Peel	5	– b Briggs	8
J. McC. Blackham c Grace b Briggs	0	– not out	2
J. D. Edwards b Briggs	0	– b Briggs	0
J. J. Ferris not out	1	– run out	9
B 4, l-b 1	5	– B 1, l-b 1	2
	96		57

Australian Bowling

	Overs	Mdns	Runs	Wkts	Overs	Mdns	Runs	Wkts
Turner	39.3	18	48	4	40.1	14	74	8
Ferris	52	24	63	3	36	19	44	1
Worrall	5	0	13	0				
Lyons	18	5	32	3	4	0	19	1

English Bowling

	Overs	Mdns	Runs	Wkts	Overs	Mdns	Runs	Wkts
Peel	42	30	37	4	20	7	33	2
Lohmann	16	5	36	0				
Briggs	25.1	18	18	6	19.3	10	22	7

Umpires: Sherwin and Farrands.

AUSTRALIANS v LORD SHEFFIELD'S ELEVEN

Played at Sheffield Park, May 8, 9, 10, 1890

The Australians could not have wished for a more successful commencement to their tour, as they succeeded in defeating in a single innings, with 34 runs to spare, one of the strongest elevens that England could produce. However, in gaining their victory, the Australians had tremendous luck in the matter of weather. They won the toss, and so having the advantage of batting first on a hard and true wicket, remained in for the whole of the first day, scoring 190 for the loss of eight wickets. Then the weather underwent a complete change, and rain fell so heavily on the Friday that not a ball could be bowled. On the Saturday the sun came out with great power, and made the wicket terribly difficult. The Australian innings finished for 191, and then Turner and Ferris accomplished a sensational performance, dismissing the English team for the paltry total of 27, of which number Mr W. G. Grace made 20. On going in a second time, the Englishmen fared much better than before, but despite a plucky attempt by Peel and Briggs, they were unable to save the game. Ferris took twelve wickets for 88 runs, and Turner six for 50. On the first day Murdoch played in quite his old style for 93, though he had some luck. He was at the wickets just over four hours, and his batting created a most favourable impression.

Australians

J. E. Barrett c and b Peel	12
J. J. Lyons c Sherwin b Attewell	15
W. L. Murdoch b Lohmann	93
H. Trott c Grace b Briggs	35
S. P. Jones c Briggs b Attewell	5
F. H. Walters c Sherwin b Briggs	26
C. T. B. Turner c and b Attewell	1
J. McC. Blackham st Sherwin b Briggs	1
S. E. Gregory c Lohmann b Briggs	3
P. C. Charlton b Lohmann	0
J. J. Ferris not out	0
	191

Lord Sheffield's Eleven

Mr W. G. Grace b Turner	20 – c Trott b Ferris	9
A. Shrewsbury c Charlton b Turner	2 – c Trott b Ferris	11
Mr W. Newham c Walters b Turner	0 – st Blackham b Ferris	2
Mr A. E. Stoddart b Ferris	1 – c Murdoch b Ferris	21
Mr W. W. Read c Turner b Ferris	0 – c Barrett b Ferris	12
R. Peel b Ferris	0 – not out	28
J. Briggs run out	0 – run out	35
G. A. Lohmann lbw b Turner	2 – st Blackham b Ferris	2
W. Humphreys st Blackham b Ferris	0 – b Turner	2
W. Attewell not out	0 – c Turner b Ferris	2
M. Sherwin b Ferris	2 – b Turner	0
	L-b 1, n-b 5	6
	27	130

Lord Sheffield's Eleven's Bowling

	Overs	Mdns	Runs	Wkts
Attewell	54	33	53	3
Briggs	37	21	47	4
Lohmann	24.2	8	48	2
Peel	13	9	17	1
Humphreys	6	3	13	0
Mr Grace	5	1	13	6

Australian Bowling

	Overs	Mdns	Runs	Wkts	Overs	Mdns	Runs	Wkts
Turner	14	9	9	4	28	13	41	2
Ferris	14	7	18	5	33	12	70	7
Charlton					6	1	13	0

Umpires: F. Farrands and R. Carpenter.

AUSTRALIANS v WARWICKSHIRE

Played at Birmingham, May 13, 14, 1890

Few people could have expected Warwickshire to have much chance of success against the Colonial team, but on the whole the county made a creditable fight, although beaten in the end by 132 runs. The county batsmen failed ignominiously before the bowling of Turner and Ferris, assisted as it was by the false and treacherous condition of the ground, but the two well-known Warwickshire bowlers, Pallett and Shilton, rendered an excellent account of themselves, and took in the whole match seventeen wickets between them. Pallett obtained eleven wickets for 92 runs and Shilton six for 100. For the Australians Turner and Ferris bowled unchanged throughout both innings, and worthily followed up the triumph they had achieved at Sheffield Park. This time Turner was the more successful, taking twelve wickets at a cost of only 34 runs, while Ferris's seven wickets were obtained for 42 runs. The condition of the ground will best be judged from the fact that the highest individual score in the match was 34.

Australians

S. P. Jones b Pallett	1	– b Cresswell	14
J. J. Lyons c Shilton b Pallett	25	– b Cresswell	34
W. L. Murdoch b Pallett	4	– c Cresswell b Pallett	1
H. Trott b Pallett	12	– c Docker b Creswell	8
J. E. Barrett b Pallett	6	– b Pallett	2
F. H. Walters b Shilton	12	– b Pallett	14
C. T. B. Turner b Pallett	0	– b Shilton	24
J. McC. Blackham st Lilley b Shilton	8	– b Shilton	6
S. E. Gregory not out	18	– c Richards b Shilton	10
J. J. Ferris b Pallett	1	– c Bainbridge b Pallett	13
H. Trumble b Shilton	0	– not out	0
B 2	2	B 2, l-b 2, w 1, n-b 1	6
	89		132

Warwickshire

Mr E. Wheeler st Blackham b Ferris	2	– lbw b Turner	0
A. Law c Walters b Ferris	11	– c Turner b Ferris	5
Richards b Turner	0	– st Blackham b Ferris	1
Mr L. C. Docker b Turner	0	– st Blackham b Ferris	20
Mr H. W. Bainbridge run out	12	– b Ferris	2
H. J. Pallett b Ferris	0	– b Turner	0
J. E. Shilton c Lyons b Turner	5	– b Turner	2
W. F. Collishaw c Trumble b Turner	2	– lbw b Turner	3
Cresswell b Turner	0	– b Turner	10
A. Bird b Turner	0	– not out	0
Lilley not out	1	– c Jones b Turner	0
B 4, n-b 1	5	B 4, l-b 2, n-b 2	8
	38		51

Warwickshire Bowling

	Overs	Mdns	Runs	Wkts	Overs	Mdns	Runs	Wkts
Shilton	31	11	49	3	18	4	51	3
Pallett	30	16	38	7	31	13	54	4
Cresswell					14	7	21	3

Australian Bowling

	Overs	Mdns	Runs	Wkts	Overs	Mdns	Runs	Wkts
Turner	22.2	11	17	6	20.3	10	17	6
Ferris	22	14	16	3	20	9	26	4

Umpires: J. Platts and Bates.

AUSTRALIANS v PLAYERS OF ENGLAND

Played at Lord's, June 19, 20, 21, 1890

In some respects this was the most remarkable match of the Australian tour. The fact that the Players scored 526 – the biggest total hit against the seventh Colonial team – would in itself have been sufficient to lend distinction to the fixture, but this performance on the part of the English Eleven was quite put into the shade by the personal achievement of Gunn, who played an innings of 228, which is the highest individual score ever obtained against Australian bowling in England. The Nottinghamshire batsman went in first for the Players at five minutes past twelve on the Thursday, and was not out till long after lunch on the second day, his being the ninth wicket to fall. Altogether he was at the wickets for rather more than nine hours and a half, and so correct was his play that during the whole of that time he did not give a chance. On the first day he scored 147 not out, these runs taking him something over five hours and a half to obtain, and on the second day he was batting four hours for 81 runs. It could certainly be urged against him that on the second day at least he played with undue caution, but he was no doubt pardonably anxious to beat the previous record score against Australian bowlers in England – Maurice Read's 186 for Surrey at The Oval in 1886 – and we at least shall not blame him. It is quite open to question whether so long an innings was ever played against first-class bowling with such complete freedom from mistakes. Moreover, in excuse for his slow scoring on the second day, it may be stated that he was fatigued by his previous exertions, and that the wicket, as it began to crumble a little, was not in the same perfect condition as in the opening stages of the match. The figures of his remarkable innings – a display indeed which will be talked of for a good many years to come – were seventeen 4s, seventeen 3s, twenty-six 2s, and fifty-seven singles. For finish and grace of style his batting was equal to anything we have seen. The support accorded him was wonderfully good, the only man on the Players' side who absolutely failed being Briggs. Barnes, Ulyett, Peel, Maurice Read, and Lohmann all did well, but emphatically the best cricket was shown by Barnes, who, for perhaps the only time during the summer, showed his true form. He played at the last moment as substitute for Shrewsbury, and assisted Gunn in carrying the score from 158 for three wickets to 295 for four. His splendid innings of 67 included seven 4s, four 3s, and seven 2s. All through the long innings of the Englishmen the Australians bowled and fielded with untiring perseverance, Ferris in particular doing splendid work. Even with 400 runs on the board, when most bowlers would have been quite disheartened, the left-hander varied his pace as well as if the innings had only just commenced, and the batsmen were never able to treat him lightly.

After their long outing the Australians went in to bat at ten minutes to five on the second day, and the innings started in such remarkable style that 77 runs were scored in the first fifty minutes. Of this number Lyons made no fewer than 50, his innings, which was a wonderful display of hard driving, being ended by a superb catch by Lohmann close to the ground at mid-off. After Lyons left the Australians fared very badly, and at the call of time five wickets were down for 96. On the Saturday, with the wicket considerably crumbled, the Australians could do very little against the admirable bowling of Briggs and Lohmann, and by five minutes to four the match was all over, the Players winning by an innings and 263 runs. It was a memorable victory, the bowling and fielding at the finish being quite worthy of comparison with the remarkable batting of the first two days. With an overwhelming defeat in prospect the Australians batted with less resolution than might have been expected, but it is only fair to them to say that Briggs was able to get a lot of work on the ball. The game excited great interest, 7,155 people paying for admission on Thursday and 9,095 on Friday. Except for the absence of Shrewsbury, who had met with some trifling accident, the Players' team was about as strong as it could have been at this period of the season, and comprised five representatives from Nottinghamshire, two each from Surrey and Yorkshire, and one each from Lancashire and Derbyshire. The weather all through the match was delightfully fine and, as may be imagined, the splendid all-round play of the English professionals gave the keenest satisfaction.

Players

G. Ulyett b Lyons	40	J. Briggs c Blackham b Trumble	1
W. Gunn b Lyons	228	G. A. Lohmann b Turner	34
M. Read c and b Turner	33	W. Attewell not out	20
W. Chatterton st Blackham b Ferris	16	M. Sherwin b Lyons	9
W. Barnes b Lyons	67	B 5, l-b 6, n-b 6	17
R. Peel c Blackham b Ferris	41		——
W. Flowers c Gregory b Ferris	20		526

Australians

J. J. Lyons c Lohmann b Peel	50	run out	24
J. McC. Blackham b Lohmann	4	b Briggs	4
W. L. Murdoch b Ulyett	23	b Briggs	7
H. Trott c Sherwin b Peel	0	c Gunn b Briggs	6
J. E. Barrett b Lohmann	29	b Briggs	0
S. P. Jones c Sherwin b Peel	1	c Gunn b Lohmann	34
F. H. Walters c Attewell b Lohmann	6	st Sherwin b Lohmann	0
S. E. Gregory lbw b Lohmann	7	st Sherwin b Briggs	13
C. T. B. Turner c Ulyett b Briggs	1	c Briggs b Lohmann	10
J. J. Ferris not out	27	c Briggs b Lohmann	2
H. Trumble c Gunn b Lohmann	8	not out	4
		B 3	3
	156		107

Australian Bowling

	Overs	Mdns	Runs	Wkts
Trott	4	0	21	0
Turner	70	33	116	2
Ferris	93	33	134	3
Lyons	43.3	7	123	4
Trumble	52	22	99	1
Jones	2	0	16	0

Players' Bowling

	Overs	Mdns	Runs	Wkts	Overs	Mdns	Runs	Wkts
Lohmann	37.3	15	61	5	20.3	3	53	4
Ulyett	10	7	10	1	1	1	0	0
Briggs	12	4	19	1	21	10	51	5
Attewell	24	9	48	0				
Peel	11	4	18	3				

Umpires: J. Lillywhite and F. Coward.

ENGLAND v AUSTRALIA

Played at Lord's, July 21, 22, 23, 1890

This was emphatically the great match of the Australian tour. No other game was looked forward to so eagerly, and to the result of no other game was so much importance attached. Victory on this special occasion would be a very large extent have made up to the Australians for all their previous defeats and disappointments, and given, as it were, a fresh start to the trip. As everyone interested in cricket is well aware, the result of the match was a victory for England by seven wickets but, repeating in other words what we have said a few pages back, we may state emphatically that scarcely any one of their thirty-eight engagements reflected so much credit on the Australians as this encounter with the representative England eleven. No side could well have given a better display of bowling and fielding, or striven harder to beat opponents manifestly superior to themselves. The Australians had meant to include Jones in their eleven, but the New South Wales cricketer was taken ill the day before the match, and the selection committee, leaving out Walters as a batsman little calculated to do himself justice on so great an occasion, gave the eleventh place to Burn. The England team was an immensely strong one, and yet not quite so powerful as that originally chosen by the MCC committee, the places intended for Mr Stoddart and Briggs being given to Maurice Read and Barnes. Mr Stoddart preferred playing for Middlesex against Kent at Tonbridge, and Briggs very properly resigned his place when he found that he had not sufficiently recovered from a strain to enable him to bowl. The eleven, if not quite the best in the country, still formed a splendid combination, and as it happened, Maurice Read's cricket at a critical point proved invaluable. The strength of the batting can best be judged from the fact that the three last men on the order were Lohmann, Mr McGregor, and Attewell. It was a great compliment to Mr McGregor to select him as wicket-keeper for England against Australia, but no one disputed that the distinction had been fairly earned by his achievements for Cambridge. It may be said at once that, though he missed one or two difficult chances, he kept wicket magnificently all through the match, fairly dividing honours with Blackham. In the whole course of the game neither wicket-keeper gave away a single bye. Before describing the cricket it may be stated that 12,345 people paid at the gates on the first day, 12,726 on the second day, and 5,208 on the third, making a total number for the match of 30,279.

An immense amount of rain had fallen in London on the Thursday and Friday before the match, but the ground recovered itself far more rapidly than any one expected, and the wicket – rather slow to begin with – got steadily better and better as the game went on, and was at its best on the concluding day. The Australians, who won the toss, were batting on the Monday from just after twelve o'clock till a quarter to four, for a total of 132. The one feature of the innings was the amazing hitting of Lyons, who in three-quarters of an hour scored 55 runs out of 66 before being bowled by a yorker on the middle stump. His innings comprised eight 4s, a 3, five 2s, and ten singles. When England went in the cricket was of the most sensational character, Grace, Shrewsbury, W. W. Read, and Gunn – unquestionably the four best bats on the side – being all got rid of for 20 runs. With things looking very black indeed for their side, Maurice Read and Ulyett then became partners, and in the course of an hour and a half, against superb bowling and fielding, put on 72 runs. The stand they made, coming when it did, was invaluable, and it would be difficult to praise them beyond their deserts. At the close of the day the score was 108 for five wickets, and on the Tuesday the innings finished at twenty minutes past one for a total of 173, or 41 runs to the good. The innings lasted four hours and a quarter, and not a single chance was missed. Ulyett's 74 was a splendid display, only marred by a little unsteadiness towards the close. Never before had the Yorkshire batsman met with anything like the same success in a match between England and Australia. Lyons bowled with great success on a wicket that was considerably firmer and faster than on the previous day, and had a remarkable analysis.

Going in for the second time at twenty minutes to two, the Australians were batting all the rest of the afternoon, and at the drawing of stumps had made 168 for nine wickets. Lyons again hit brilliantly, scoring 33 runs in twenty-five minutes, but the feature of the day was the wonderful defence of Barrett. On the third morning the Australian innings closed for 176, Barrett, who had gone in first, taking out his bat for 67. He was at the wickets for four hours and forty minutes. England had 136 to get to win, and with the wicket in capital order there was not much doubt about the task being accomplished. Shrewsbury was out at 27, but Grace and Gunn took the score to 101 and thus practically decided the match. Towards the finish Grace hit magnificently, and his not out innings of 75 was entirely worthy of his reputation.

Australians

J. J. Lyons b Barnes	55	– c Attewell b Peel	33
C. T. B. Turner b Attewell	24	– lbw b Peel	2
W. L. Murdoch c and b Attewell	9	– b Lohmann	19
J. E. Barrett c Grace b Ulyett	9	– not out	67
H. Trott run out	12	– b Peel	0
S. E. Gregory b Attewell	0	– c Lohmann b Barnes	9
P. C. Charlton st McGregor b Peel	6	– lbw b Grace	2
J. McC. Blackham b Peel	5	– c Barnes b Grace	10
J. J. Ferris b Attewell	8	– lbw b Lohmann	8
K. E. Burn st McGregor b Peel	0	– c McGregor b Attewell	19
H. Trumble not out	1	– c Barnes b Lohmann	5
L-b 3	3	L-b 2	2
	132		176

England

Mr W. G. Grace c and b Turner	0	– not out	75
A. Shrewsbury st Blackham b Ferris	4	– lbw b Ferris	13
W. Gunn run out	14	– c and b Ferris	34
Mr W. W. Read c and b Ferris	1	– b Trumble	13
M. Read b Lyons	34	– not out	2
G. Ulyett b Lyons	74		
R. Peel c and b Trumble	16		
W. Barnes b Lyons	9		
G. A. Lohmann c and b Lyons	19		
Mr G. McGregor b Lyons	0		
W. Attewell not out	0		
L-b 2	2		
	173		137

English Bowling

	Overs	Mdns	Runs	Wkts	Overs	Mdns	Runs	Wkts
Lohmann	21	10	43	0	29	19	28	3
Peel	24	11	28	3	43	23	59	3
Attewell	32	15	42	4	42.2	22	54	1
Barnes	6	2	16	1	6	3	10	1
Ulyett	3	3	0	1	6	2	11	0
Grace					14	10	12	2

Australian Bowling

	Overs	Mdns	Runs	Wkts	Overs	Mdns	Runs	Wkts
Turner	65	17	53	1	22	12	31	0
Ferris	40	17	55	2	25	11	42	2
Trott	3	0	16	0				
Lyons	20.1	7	30	5	20	6	43	0
Trumble	12	7	17	1	8	1	21	1

Umpires: A. Hill and C. K. Pullin.

AUSTRALIANS v CAMBRIDGE PAST AND PRESENT

Played at Leyton, August 7, 8, 9, 1890

The match at Leyton between the Australians and the Past and Present of Cambridge produced some very bad, as well as some very good cricket, but the game presented so many remarkable features, and its fortunes varied in such an extraordinary manner, that something more than a passing record is called for. On no occasion during their tour did the Colonial side play an up-hill game, for though they went in first against a total of 389, and followed their innings against the formidable majority of 171, another half-hour's play on the Saturday evening would have given them the victory. In view of the match against England at The Oval on the following Monday, the Australians gave a rest to both Turner and Ferris, and more than that only allowed Blackham who suffered from a bad hand, to keep wicket on the closing day. The Australians thus handicapped themselves considerably, but, on the other hand, it must be borne in mind that the Cambridge team, though a fairly strong one at all points, was not thoroughly representative, the most notable absentees being Mr A. G. Steel and Mr Douglas. A great misfortune for the University was the fact that a strained side reduced Mr Woods in the second innings of the Australians to the necessity of bowling lobs. Fine weather favoured the game all through, and a better wicket has never been prepared on the Leyton ground. Having the good fortune to win the toss, the Cambridge men were batting on the first day from a quarter past twelve until three minutes to six for a total of 389. At one time no such score seemed in the least degree probable, for, though Messrs Lucas and Owen scored 71 for the first wicket, there were six wickets down for 129. The astonishing change in the game was mainly brought about by Mr Streatfeild, who indulged the spectators with some of the most daring and vigorous hitting that was seen during the season of 1890. He began badly, giving a couple of chances to Pope, who was keeping wicket and standing five or six yards back, but after being let off his play was astonishing. He made 50 runs in thirty-seven minutes, 70 in forty-five minutes, completed his hundred within the hour, and scored in all 145 in an hour and fifty minutes, his hits being one 5 (two for an overthrow), eighteen 4s, six 3s, fourteen 2s and twenty-two singles. One of his drives was especially fine, the ball pitching on the highest point of the Pavilion roof. After the fall of the sixth wicket 260 runs were actually scored in less than two hours and a half. At the close of the afternoon the Australians had twelve minutes' batting, and lost one wicket for 7 runs. On the Friday the Australians were batting all through the day, their first innings ending at twenty minutes to five for a total of 218, and the score reaching 83 for two wickets when they followed on, Murdoch being not out 40 at the drawing of stumps, and Trott not out 39. The Saturday's cricket was quite sensational, Murdoch and Trott going on with their batting at ten minutes past twelve, and staying together till about twenty minutes to four. Their partnership, which practically saved their side from all risk of defeat, lasted altogether for just over three hours and a half, and produced 276 runs. Both played very finely, Trott's score of 186 being the highest he have ever made in England, but both were indebted to Mr McGregor, who has never in public kept wicket so indifferently, Apparently he was troubling himself less about the contest that was in progress than the England match, which was to be played on the following Monday at The Oval. Off Mr Woods's lobs he allowed a chance of stumping to escape him that he probably would not miss once in twenty times. Trott hit one 6 (two for an overthrow), twenty-four 4s, ten 3s and eleven 2s, and Murdoch ten 4s, eleven 3s and thirteen 2s. With six wickets down for 355, the Australians declared their innings at an end, and with no possibility of being beaten took the best chance of winning. Cambridge went in with an hour and twenty-five minutes left for play, and 185 runs wanted to win. The task was obviously impracticable, but the batsmen, instead of playing carefully for a draw, went in for reckless hitting, and had they been beaten they would have well deserved their defeat. As it was the call of time found them with two wickets still to fall. The bowling of Trumble and Charlton and the wicket-keeping of Blackham in this last innings were admirable.

Cambridge

Mr A. P. Lucas c Trumble b Charlton	37 – c Trumble b Charlton	12
Mr H. G. Owen b Trott	31 – c sub. b Trumble	1
Mr H. J. Mordaunt c Jones b Charlton	13 – b Trumble	2
Mr G. McGregor b Trott	19 – c Charlton b Trumble	7
Mr F. E. Rowe c Trumble b Trott	17 – not out	4
Mr H. Pigg c Murdoch b Trumble	37 – c Burn b Trumble	2
Mr J. A. Turner b Charlton	4 – b Trumble	1
Mr E. C. Streatfeild b Charlton	145 – c Pope b Charlton	20
Mr C. D. Buxton b Trumble	0	
Mr C. A. Smith not out	58	
Mr S. M. J. Woods c Burn b Lyons	23 – run out	18
B 2, l-b 3	5 B 8, l-b 3	11
	389	78

Australians

R. J. Pope b Streatfeild	0	
K. E. Burn c Smith b Streatfeild	13 – not out	10
J. J. Lyons c Rowe b Streatfeild	14 – c and b Smith	0
J. E. Barratt b Woods	9 – b Streatfeild	0
W. L. Murdoch run out	34 – c Buxton b Smith	129
H. Trott c Buxton b Lucas	38 – b Streatfeild	186
S. P. Jones c McGregor b Woods	0	
J. McC. Blackham not out	66 – c Buxton b Smith	0
P. C. Charlton c and b Streatfeild	24 – c Buxton b Streatfeild	6
S. E. Gregory c Buxton b Streatfeild	6	
H. Trumble b Smith	1	
B 13	13 B 20, l-b 1, w 3	24
	218	(6 wkts dec.) 355

Australian Bowling

	Overs	Mdns	Runs	Wkts	Overs	Mdns	Runs	Wkts
Lyons	18.4	1	53	1				
Trumble	28	9	88	2	20	9	38	5
Charlton	46	10	116	4	19	9	29	2
Trott	34	5	108	3				
Pope	2	0	19	0				

Cambridge Bowling

	Overs	Mdns	Runs	Wkts	Overs	Mdns	Runs	Wkts
Woods	42	20	81	2	10	1	41	0
Streatfeild	43	24	47	5	46.4	20	78	3
Smith	6.2	0	22	1	32	6	88	3
Pigg	14	5	24	0	17	3	47	0
Lucas	6	2	5	1	24	10	27	0
Turner	3	0	26	0				
Mordaunt					8	1	18	0
Owen					7	2	11	0
Buxton					7	2	24	0

Umpires: J. Wheeler and F. Silcock.

AUSTRALIANS v LORD LONDESBOROUGH'S ELEVEN

Played at Scarborough, September 4, 5, 6, 1890

Lord Londesborough secured a magnificent England eleven; but, unfortunately, the wicket had been ruined by rain before a ball was bowled. Play could not be commenced until after three o'clock on the opening day, and all through the match the ball had a manifest advantage over the bat. On the second morning Mr Grace thought it best not to have the wicket rolled, but there can be little doubt that he committed an error of judgment. The best part of the match came on the third day, Messrs Woods and McGregor making a splendid effort for the English team. When they became partners 33 runs were wanted to win with one wicket to fall, but they put on 24, and the Australians won a great game by 8 runs. This was one of the most notable achievements of the tour, and the Australians clearly owed their success to Turner, who took thirteen wickets for 57 runs, and made the two best scores in the match. Briggs also bowled marvellously well for the Englishmen.

The Australians

J. J. Lyons lbw b Briggs	2	– c Woods b Peel	3
C. T. B. Turner c Lohmann b Briggs	34	– c Stoddart b Briggs	21
W. L. Murdoch b Briggs	2	– c Grace b Lohmann	11
H. Trott c Lohmann b Briggs	8	– c Grace b Briggs	1
J. E. Barrett not out	8	– b Peel	4
J. McC. Blackham b Briggs	2	– lbw b Briggs	0
P. C. Charlton run out	5	– lbw b Briggs	7
J. J. Ferris st McGregor b Briggs	0	– st McGregor b Peel	2
K. E. Burn c Lohmann b Briggs	0	– lbw b Briggs	1
S. E. Gregory c Woods b Briggs	3	– not out	2
H. Trumble st McGregor b Briggs	11	– st McGregor b Briggs	8
L-b 2	2		
	77		60

Lord Londesborough's Eleven

G. Ulyett run out	2	– b Turner	15
Mr A. E. Stoddart b Turner	1	– c Gregory b Turner	5
Mr W. G. Grace b Turner	14	– b Turner	19
W. Gunn lbw b Turner	1	– b Turner	13
Mr W. W. Read st Blackham b Ferris	4	– lbw b Turner	0
Mr H. T. Hewett c Charlton b Turner	3	– b Ferris	0
G. A. Lohmann c Gregory b Turner	2	– b Ferris	0
R. Peel not out	5	– lbw b Ferris	5
J. Briggs b Ferris	0	– b Turner	6
Mr S. M. J. Woods c Burn b Ferris	2	– not out	9
Mr G. McGregor c and b Turner	2	– lbw b Turner	13
B 1, l-b 2	3	B 2, l-b 2, n-b 1	5
	39		90

Lord Londesborough's Eleven's Bowling

	Overs	Mdns	Runs	Wkts	Overs	Mdns	Runs	Wkts
Briggs	29.1	16	31	9	24.2	14	26	6
Lohmann	5	1	16	0	5	1	16	1
Peel	24	13	28	0	19	8	18	3

Australian Bowling

	Overs	Mdns	Runs	Wkts	Overs	Mdns	Runs	Wkts
Turner	16.3	9	11	6	24.3	7	46	7
Ferris	16	7	25	3	24	6	38	3
Charlton					1	0	1	0

Umpires: F. Farrands and F. Wild.

THE AUSTRALIANS IN ENGLAND, 1893

Had the eighth Australian team come to England with no more preliminary flourish than attended the visits of 1888 and 1890, their record of eighteen victories, ten defeats, and eight drawn games would not have been regarded as at all unsatisfactory. The team, however, came as an absolutely representative side, every player now before the Australian public, with the single exception of H. Moses, having been available for selection, and the combination had of necessity to bear comparison with the great elevens of 1882 and 1884 – elevens which, so far at least as this country is concerned, showed Australian cricket at its highest point of development. Judged from this high standard, it cannot be said that the band of players who toured here last summer under the leadership of Blackham came up to the sanguine expectations formed of them. Indeed, many writers in Australia have not scrupled to speak of the trip as a failure. In any general sense this would be a hard word to use, but taking into account the special circumstances of the case, it can scarcely be considered unjust. It was certainly thought by a large number of people in Australia – though a few good judges were less hopeful – that the side, including as it did most of the players who won the rubber against Lord Sheffield's team in the Australian season of 1891-92, would be quite equal to the task of holding its own against our representative elevens, and the general results of the tour have undoubtedly caused a great deal of disappointment. The point as to whether the promoters of the trip made the best possible selection is beside the question. They had a very wide field of choice, and as they preferred to dispense with the services of W. L. Murdoch and Dr. Barrett, they had necessarily to stand or fall by their own judgment. The exclusion of Murdoch, after he had thought that he would be a member of the eleven, gave rise to some correspondence in English papers that might very well have been avoided. One of the arguments used to account for Murdoch being left out was that the Australian public did not wish the team to include any players who had settled in England, and were therefore out of touch with Colonial cricket. This theory was all very well so far as it went, but we do not think the fact of Murdoch having lived for some little time in England would have weighed at all with English cricketers. That his presence would have been an element of strength, we have no doubt. He would have made the batting even more powerful than it was, and his judgment, tact, and strong will would have been invaluable in the management of the eleven, had he, as in 1880, 1882, 1884 and 1890, been captain.

AUSTRALIANS v GLOUCESTERSHIRE

Played at Bristol, May 15, 16, 17, 1893

In the two previous matches George Giffen had done little or nothing in batting in this game, but the famous South Australian gave a remarkable display. He went in to bat when Lyons had hit up 48 out of 60 in forty minutes, and at the close of the first day was 124 not out, with the total at 277 for two wickets. In all he made 180, being fifth out at 381 after a stay of five hours and three-quarters, hitting thirteen 4s, ten 3s and twenty-five 2s. His play, if not quite so brilliant as might have been expected on a good wicket, against bowling none too formidable at the start, and thoroughly worn out after a time, was characterised by marked skill and judgment, and scarcely ever during his long stay did he make a bad stroke. His success, however, did not end with his batting, for late on the second day, when Gloucestershire went in for an hour's batting, his bowling proved so puzzling that eight wickets fell for 36 runs, W. G. Grace keeping himself back with disastrous result. Next morning the innings was finished off for 41 runs. Giffen's seven wickets cost only 11 runs, so that he had an altogether extraordinary record for the match. Unfortunately for the Australians, rain prevented any more cricket, and the match had to be left drawn, Gloucestershire being 462 runs behind. Bannerman batted more than three hours and a half for his 39; Trott and Graham scored well and in good style, whilst late in the innings McLeod and Coningham made runs freely from the tired bowlers.

Australians

J. J. Lyons c and b W. G. Grace	48	S. E. Gregory c Painter b W. G. Grace	3
A. C. Bannerman b Murch	39	A. Coningham b Radcliffe	43
G. Giffen st Board b Ferris	180	H. Trumble not out	8
G. H. S. Trott c Roberts b Murch	68	J. McC. Blackham c Luard b Roberts	1
W. Bruce c E. M. Grace b Murch	0	B 7, l-b 10, n-b 1	18
H. Graham st Board b Ferris	59		
R. W. McLeod c Board b Radcliffe	36		503

Gloucestershire

Mr E. M. Grace c Graham b Trumble	3	Capt. A. H. Luard c and b Trumble	1
Mr O. G. Radcliffe c Trumble b Coningham	14	Mr J. J. Ferris c Coningham b Giffen	0
Mr R. W. Rice c Bruce b Giffen	5	Mr W. G. Grace not out	4
F. G. Roberts c Trumble b Giffen	0	J. H. Board c Trumble b Giffen	0
Mr S. A. P. Kitcat b Giffen	6	B 3, l-b 1	4
H. W. Murch b Giffen	4		
J. Painter b Giffen	0		41

Gloucestershire Bowling

	Overs	Mdns	Runs	Wkts
Roberts	38.4	9	100	1
Murch	53	14	124	3
W. G. Grace	57	22	137	2
Ferris	61	17	95	2
E. M. Grace	5	0	15	0
Radcliffe	7	1	14	2

Australian Bowling

	Overs	Mdns	Runs	Wkts
Coningham	6	2	12	1
Trumble	12	4	14	2
Giffen	6	3	11	7

Umpires: R. Carpenter and E. Goodyear.

AUSTRALIANS v MCC AND GROUND

Played at Lord's, May 18, 19, 20, 1893

This game proved one of the msot interesting of the whole tour, extending over three full days, and, though in the end the want of a few more minutes led to the contest being left drawn, it is not too much to say that the manner in which the Colonials acquitted themselves did more for their reputation than almost any one of the other thirty-five engagements. Blackham, after winning the toss, put the Englishmen in to bat – a course which turned out so disastrously that it was five o'clock in the afternoon before the MCC innings closed for 424. The best performance in the early portion of the game was that of Stoddart, who scored 58 out of 109. Gunn rendered him some assistance, but there were four men out for 145 when Flowers and Wilson came together. In twenty-five minutes before lunch Flowers hit so hard that 57 runs were added, and the total reached 204 before Wilson was out, 86 runs having been added in fifty minutes. Bright and attractive as the cricket had been, it became even more brilliant when Marchant joined Flowers. The two Englishmen gave a grand display, and in seventy minutes actually put on 152 runs. Flowers, who played one of the best innings of his career, scored his 130 in two hours without giving a chance, and hit nineteen 4s, six 3s and four 2s. Marchant and Attewell hit vigorously, and 400 went up with only six men out, but afterwards Trott's slow bowling met with marked success, and the innings was all over for 424. Marchant had given a fine exhibition of clean and powerful hitting, being at the wickets an hour and three-quarters, and his figures including eleven 4s, eight 3s and ten 2s. At the close of the day the Australians had four wickets down for 84.

Next morning there was some fine batting shown by the Colonials, Coningham playing plucky cricket for 46. Nine wickets were down for 183, but Blackham and Gregory made a rare stand before the innings closed and added 60 runs. It was when the Australians followed on that there was seen one of the most wonderful displays of hitting ever recorded. At a quarter-past three they went in with a balance of 181 runs against them, and in an hour and thirty-five minutes this number had actually been obtained without the loss of a wicket. Lyons and Bannerman were the batsmen, and the main share of the performance belonged to the South Australian, whose partner all through was quite content to keep up his wicket. Lyons, who gave an extraordinary exhibition of fast-footed forcing play, scored with almost equal freedom from all the bowlers brought against him. Fifty runs were made in about half an hour, and as time went on Lyon's hitting became even more brilliant, the hundred appearing at the end of fifty minutes' cricket. Still the South Australian in no way slackened his scoring, and completed his hundred in an hour, with the total at 124. There was, of course a loud cheer when the arrears were hit off with the first two batsmen still together, but from the next ball Lyons was out to a grand running catch at long-off. The hits of Lyons's wonderful innings were twenty-two 4s, three 3s, twenty 2s and twelve singles. The game greatly changed when Giffen joined Bannerman. Strangely enough, it was not until 215 that Hearne was put on to bowl at the Pavilion end, from which he had been very successful on Thursday, and again he proved effective, with the result that at the drawing of stumps four wickets were down for 247.

On Saturday morning Bannerman and Graham sent up 300 before they were separated. Bannerman altogether was at the wickets four hours and ten minutes for his 75, an innings in which his exceptional powers of defence were seen to unusual advantage. The last five wickets fell for 45 runs. Hearne bowled very well and met with all his success from the Pavilion end. Wanting 167 runs to win, Marylebone commenced batting at twenty minutes past three, and no reasonable doubt existed as to the ability of the Englishmen to obtain this number. A couple of showers interrupted play, but Grace and Stoddart scored for nearly an hour in a manner that promised an easy victory. At half-past four 72 runs had been made without the loss of a wicket, when a heavy shower delayed the game for half an hour. Afterwards the match underwent a great change. Stoddart was caught at slip at 80 for a splendid innings of 45; a catch at long-on disposed of Grace; while at 88 a slow full pitch took Gunn's wicket and Flowers played on. Wilson and Marchant sent up the hundred, but in quick succession Marchant, Nepean, and Wilson were all dismissed, and instead of having a winning game before them the Englishmen had to fight hard to avert defeat. Attewell and Shacklock, however, played with rare nerve and put on 21 runs, and with twenty minutes left for play Hearne joined Attewell. When the finish came at half-past six two wickets had to fall and 14 runs were required. Attewell played a great game, going in when the match looked to be lost and staying for nearly fifty minutes.

MCC and Ground

Mr W. G. Grace c Trumble b Coningham	13	– c Gregory b Giffen	33
Mr A. E. Stoddart c Trumble b Bruce	58	– c Trumble b McLeod	45
W. Gunn c Graham b Trumble	28	– b Giffen	3
Mr E. A. Nepean b Trumble	3	– b McLeod	2
Mr L. Wilson c Graham b Giffen	31	– c Graham b Giffen	10
W. Flowers c Trumble b Bruce	130	– b McLeod	1
Mr F. Marchant st Blackham b Trott	103	– c Trumble b McLeod	6
W. Attewell c Blackham b Trott	31	– not out	26
F. Shacklock c Lyons b Coningham	0	– c Gregory b McLeod	15
J. T. Hearne not out	0	– not out	6
M. Sherwin c Blackham b Trott	2		
B 18, l-b 5, w 2	25	B 2, l-b 3, w 1	6
	424		153

Australians

J. J. Lyons c Grace b Hearne	0 – c Wilson b Attewell	149
A. C. Bannerman c Flowers b Hearne	10 – b Shacklock	75
G. Giffen b Attewell	2 – c Sherwin b Hearne	28
G. H. S. Trott c and b Hearne	29 – b Hearne	6
W. Bruce c Sherwin b Nepean	37 – lbw b Hearne	7
H. Graham st Sherwin b Nepean	24 – c Sherwin b Hearne	29
A. Coningham lbw b Flowers	46 – b Shacklock	0
R. W. McLeod b Shacklock	15 – c Attewell b Hearne	7
S. E. Gregory not out	41 – b Hearne	31
H. Trumble b Flowers	0 – c Sherwin b Shacklock	4
J. McC. Blackham c Gunn b Hearne	31 – not out	1
B 1, l-b 7	8 L-b 9, n-b 1	10
	243	347

Australian Bowling

	Overs	Mdns	Runs	Wkts	Overs	Mdns	Runs	Wkts
Giffen	29	3	117	1	31	7	72	3
Trumble	18	4	70	2	3	0	7	0
Coningham	22	6	65	2	4	0	17	0
McLeod	7	0	41	0	19	9	29	5
Bruce	17	1	52	2	8	3	14	0
Trott	4.1	0	11	3	3	1	8	0
Lyons	4	0	20	0				
Gregory	5	0	23	0				

MCC Bowling

	Overs	Mdns	Runs	Wkts	Overs	Mdns	Runs	Wkts
Hearne	25.1	10	50	4	36.1	14	74	6
Attewell	21	3	51	1	41	16	91	1
Nepean	19	1	70	2	12	2	52	0
Shacklock	15	6	25	1	31	11	82	3
Flowers	9	2	30	2	5	1	18	0
Grace					13	7	20	0

Umpires: J. Wheeler and J. Lillywhite.

AUSTRALIANS v PLAYERS OF ENGLAND

Played at Lord's, June 19, 20, 1893

Although with Lancashire and Yorkshire playing, and Shrewsbury away, the Players' team was far from representative, the Australians deserved great praise for the handsome victory which their capital cricket gained them. The wicket was not quite up to the average of Lord's ground, but the condition of the turf detracted little from the achievement of the Australians. The success was mainly due to Hugh Trumble, who took fourteen wickets – seven in each innings – for 116 runs. Thanks to Gunn, the Players cleared off the runs they were in arrear for the loss of one batsman, but the last eight wickets fell for 63 runs. Going in to get 74 runs the Australians lost three batsmen for 23, but they won easily by six wickets. Tyler, it should be noted, bowled with conspicuous success for the English professionals.

Australians

J. J. Lyons c Bean b Attewell	30	– c Davidson b Tyler	3
A. C. Bannerman b Richardson	11	– c Davidson b Tyler	7
G. Giffen c Davidson b Richardson	0	– b Richardson	27
G. H. S. Trott st Sherwin b Tyler	48	– b Richardson	1
W. Bruce b Davidson	14	– not out	18
H. Graham c Sherwin b Tyler	15	– not out	18
S. E. Gregory b Tyler	7		
R. W. McLeod b Tyler	7		
C. T. B. Turner c Sherwin b Tyler	12		
H. Trumble b Tyler	7		
J. McC. Blackham not out	23		
B 11, l-b 4	15	B 1, l-b 1	2
	189		76

Players of England

W. Chatterton c and b Trumble	18	– c Blackham b Trumble	28
W. Gunn b Trumble	1	– c Trumble b Turner	43
G. Bean b Trumble	5	– c Graham b Trumble	30
W. Barnes lbw b McLeod	0	– lbw b Giffen	0
W. Flowers b Trumble	13	– c Giffen b Trumble	10
W. Lockwood c and b Trumble	15	– c Bruce b Trumble	26
W. Attewell b McLeod	13	– b Trumble	6
G. Davidson not out	5	– b Trumble	11
T. Richardson c and b Trumble	15	– b Trumble	5
E. J. Tyler c Gregory b Trumble	0	– b McLeod	0
M. Sherwin b McLeod	4	– not out	0
		B 11, l-b 3	14
	89		173

Players of England Bowling

	Overs	Mdns	Runs	Wkts	Overs	Mdns	Runs	Wkts
Richardson	27	8	72	2	18	5	32	2
Attewell	12	2	39	1	5	2	7	0
Lockwood	5	0	16	0	2	1	10	0
Davidson	8	3	14	1				
Tyler	17.3	6	33	6	9	3	25	2

Australian Bowling

	Overs	Mdns	Runs	Wkts	Overs	Mdns	Runs	Wkts
Trumble	21	11	31	7	28	10	85	7
McLeod	20.4	5	58	3	19	6	38	1
Turner					5	2	11	1
Giffen					11	4	16	1
Trott					3	0	9	0

Umpires: F. Coward and A. F. Smith.

AUSTRALIANS v SOMERSET

Played at Taunton, July 20, 21, 22, 1893

This was one of the few experiences which the 1893 team had of really bad weather. So wretched was the outlook in the morning that it was actually decided to defer play until the Friday, but late in the afternoon the players were gathered together and a start was made, with the result that Somerset completed a first innings for 119. No doubt it would have been very annoying for people who had come a long distance to see no cricket, but the precedent set by the Somerset authorities in overruling the umpires is one greatly to be regretted. Next day no play was possible, but the game was fought out to a definite issue on the third day. Woods bowled with so much success that the Australians failed to reach Somerset's total, but then the county, trying to play a forcing game, fared so disastrously against Turner that they were all dismissed, in a little over an hour, for 64. Giffen and Trott played capital cricket in the second innings of the Australians, who won the match with six wickets to spare.

Somerset

Mr H. T. Hewett c Trumble b Turner	12	– c Coningham b Turner	7
Mr L. C. H. Palairet c Gregory b Coningham	30	– c Gregory b Turner	2
Mr W. C. Hedley c Lyons b Coningham	10	– c Bruce b Trumble	7
Mr V. T. Hill c Gregory b Giffen	21	– b Turner	13
Mr S. M. J. Woods c and b Trumble	8	– c Bruce b Turner	5
Mr F. J. Poynton c Graham b Trumble	1	– b Turner	0
Mr G. Fowler c Bruce b Turner	10	– b Turner	17
G. B. Nichols lbw b Turner	6	– b Turner	2
Bolus run out	1	– c Trumble b Coningham	0
E. J. Tyler not out	3	– c Trott b Trumble	6
Rev. A. P. Wickham b Turner	4	– not out	1
B 10, l-b 3	13	B 4	4
	119		64

Australians

J. J. Lyons c Hill b Tyler	3	– b Woods	1
A. C. Bannerman b Hedley	21	– c Hill b Woods	4
G. Giffen b Woods	36	– b Woods	45
G. H. S. Trott b Woods	12	– b Nichols	20
W. Bruce b Woods	0	– not out	1
S. E. Gregory c Fowler b Woods	0	– not out	6
H. Graham c and b Woods	2		
C. T. B. Turner b Woods	10		
H. Trumble not out	15		
A. Coningham b Nichols	3		
J. McC. Blackham c and b Nichols	0		
B 4, l-b 1	5	B 1	1
	107		78

Australian Bowling

	Overs	Mdns	Runs	Wkts	Overs	Mdns	Runs	Wkts
Turner	12.4	4	43	4	13.3	3	26	7
Giffen	9	1	31	1				
Coningham	10	2	19	2	4	0	10	1
Trumble	7	1	13	2	10	2	24	2

Somerset Bowling

	Overs	Mdns	Runs	Wkts	Overs	Mdns	Runs	Wkts
Tyler	9	2	25	1	11	3	26	0
Nichols	9.4	3	22	2	2	0	6	1
Hedley	12	5	29	1	10	3	14	0
Woods	14	6	26	6	9.1	1	31	3

Umpires: J. Lillywhite and G. Atkinson.

AUSTRALIANS v OXFORD AND CAMBRIDGE PAST AND PRESENT

Played at Portsmouth, July 31, August, 1, 2, 1893

When this match opened there was every reason to expect that it would prove one of the least interesting of the whole tour, for the team of past and present University players which C. W. Wright had got together was so far from representative that over a dozen cricketers might be mentioned, any one of whom had better qualifications than those who took the field against the Colonials. The extreme weakness, however, of the Englishmen served to render the match memorable, for so completely did the Australians master the bowling of their opponents that, one after another, records which had stood for several years were all broken. The United Services ground was as firm and true as the proverbial billiard table, and when it became known that the Australians had won the toss everybody realised that the Englishmen had a long spell in the field before them. The commencement was to some extent suggestive of what subsequently took place, as Lyons, at once forcing the run-getting, hit up 61 out of 72 in the first three-quarters of an hour. Then Giffen obtained 43 out of 61 added for the second wicket and Trott 61 out of 88 put on for the third wicket in the next hour. All this time Bannerman had been playing wonderfully, and what to many people appeared absurdly, quiet cricket, showing a steadiness of defence which might, perhaps, have been necessary had the bowling been that of first-class professionals instead of moderate amateurs. However, he stayed in all day, and at the close 346 runs had been obtained for the loss of only four wickets, Bannerman being not out 102 and Graham, who had been twice badly missed, not out 61.

The extraordinary portion of the game took place on the following day, when the Australians were again at the wickets until the call of time, adding 450 runs for the loss of four more batsmen. Graham, who had helped Bannerman to add 110 runs, was soon out, his innings including some fine hits, but being spoiled by three easy chances. It was when Graham left that Bruce came in, and commenced his wonderful hitting. Bannerman stayed with him for an hour and a quarter while 97 runs were put on, and was then at 469 caught at the wicket for 133, an innings which lasted six hours, and included thirteen 4s, eight 3s and fourteen 2s. Undoubtedly the most brilliant portion of this phenomenal batting display was witnessed when Trumble became Bruce's partner, these two men in two hours and twenty minutes adding no fewer than 232 runs. The bowling was, of course, thoroughly worn out, and there was some slackness in the field, but all the same it was a wonderful performance. While they were together the previous record of an Australian eleven in England – 643 by the 1882 team against Sussex at Brighton – was headed, and before they were parted the total had been raised to 701 when they were both out. Bruce gave one chance at 111, and another at 185, but allowing for these blemishes his innings of 191 was an altogether exceptional piece of cricket, noticeable especially for powerful on-drives and well-timed square-leg hits. The figures of his remarkable innings, which lasted three hours and forty minutes, were twenty-three 4s, eight 3s, twenty-one 2s and thirty-three singles. Trumble, who in this match obtained his first hundred in England, made no mistake whatever, and his hitting on the off-side was of a description that any batsman might have been proud of. Play lasted fifty-five minutes afterwards, and in this time Turner and Walter Giffen added 104 more, the score at the close of the day being 805 for eight wickets. Two more records were broken during their partnership, the 703 made by Cambridge against Sussex at Brighton in 1890, which had stood as the best score made in a big match in England, and the world's record of 803 obtained by the Non-Smokers against the Smokers at Melbourne in March, 1887.

On Wednesday the match came to a tame conclusion, for by staying in so long the Australians threw away all chance of victory. The innings, which lasted ten hours, closed for 843. The falls of the wickets were as follows:–

1/2 2/133 3/221 4/236 5/372 6/469 7/701 8/701 9/822 10/843

The cricket was of little interest while the Englishmen were batting, and when stumps were finally pulled up and the game abandoned as a draw the Universities, with nine wickets to fall, were still 570 runs behind.

Australians

J. J. Lyons b Bainbridge	51	H. Trumble b Bainbridge	105
A. C. Bannerman c Forster b Hornsby	133	C. T. B. Turner c Forster b Arkwright	66
G. Giffen c Arkwright b Bainbridge	43	W. F. Giffen b Berkeley	62
G. H. S. Trott c Wilson b Arkwright	61	A. H. Jarvis not out	6
S. E. Gregory c Hornsby b Wilson	11	B 20, l-b 8, w 3	31
H. Graham c Wilson b Forster	83		
W. Bruce st Gay b Forster	191		843

Oxford and Cambridge

Mr H. W. Forster (*Oxford*) c and b Turner	43	– not out	6
Mr J. H. J. Hornsby (*Oxford*) c Trumble b Trott	13		
Mr H. W. Bainbridge (*Cambridge*) c Trumble b Turner	5	– not out	42
Mr G. L. Wilson (*Oxford*) b Turner	34		
Mr K. S. Ranjitsinhji (*Cambridge*) c Jarvis b Turner	44		
Mr W. N. Roe (*Cambridge*) b G. Giffen	17		
Mr T. Lindley (*Cambridge*) b G. Giffen	0	– c Jarvis b Gregory	33
Mr L. H. Gay (*Cambridge*) b G. Giffen	11		
Mr C. W. Wright (*Cambridge*) c Trumble b Turner	8		
Mr H. A. Arkwright (*Oxford*) b G. Giffen	8		
Mr G. F. H. Berkeley (*Oxford*) not out	2		
B 6	6	L-b 1	1
	191		82

Universities Bowling

	Overs	Mdns	Runs	Wkts
Wilson	35	5	126	1
Berkeley	60.2	15	165	1
Forster	51	9	162	2
Bainbridge	29	5	122	3
Arkwright	29	7	62	2
Hornsby	17	1	84	1
Roe	13	1	48	0
Ranjitsinhji	6	0	27	0
Lindley	3	0	9	0
Wright	1	0	7	0

Australian Bowling

	Overs	Mdns	Runs	Wkts	Overs	Mdns	Runs	Wkts
Trott	19	3	63	1	2	0	11	0
Turner	63	14	54	5				
G. Giffen	20	2	61	4				
Trumble	5	3	7	0				
Bruce					6	1	16	0
Lyons					6	2	15	0
Graham					4	0	22	0
Gregory					4	1	17	1

Umpires: J. Lillywhite and G. Hay.

AUSTRALIANS v ESSEX

Played at Leyton, August, 3, 4, 5, 1893

The attempt to get together a representative side of the Past and Present of Cambridge University having failed, the Essex executive decided to pit their own team against the Colonials. The great feature of the match was the bowling of Mead, who, although having to face a strong wind, actually took nine of the ten wickets in the first innings of the Australians. Next day rain prevented any cricket after lunch, and on Saturday, when the weather was again showery, the game had to be left drawn. Mead again bowled with remarkable skill, and for the innings had the extraordinary record of seventeen wickets for 295 runs.

Australians

J. J. Lyons c Taberer b Mead	7	– c and b Mead	29
A. C. Bannerman lbw b Mead	34	– c Russell b Mead	29
G. H. S. Trott c and b Mead	25	– c sub. b Mead	0
S. E. Gregory b Mead	26	– c Carpenter b Pickett	5
H. Graham c Taberer b Mead	35	– st Russell b Mead	7
W. Bruce c Russell b Mead	56	– b Mead	5
H. Trumble b Mead	28	– c Mead b Pickett	15
C. T. B. Turner c Lucas b Mead	27	– b Mead	18
W. F. Giffen not out	9	– b Mead	0
A. Coningham b Pickett	1	– not out	19
A. H. Jarvis b Mead	0	– b Mead	10
L-b 1, n-b 1	2	B 4	4
	250		141

Essex

Mr A. S. Johnston b Trumble	7	– not out	10
H. Carpenter c Jarvis b Coningham	42	– b Trott	7
Mr H. G. Owen b Coningham	36	– not out	2
Mr A. P. Lucas c and b Trumble	15		
Mr H. Hailey not out	38		
J. Burns b Trumble	7		
Russell c Gregory b Trumble	8		
Mr H. M. Taberer c Bruce b Trumble	8		
Mr C. J. Kortright lbw b Turner	23		
W. Mead c Giffen b Trumble	8		
H. Pickett st Jarvis b Bruce	25		
B 12, l-b 4, w 4	20	B 13	13
	237		32

Essex Bowling

	Overs	Mdns	Runs	Wkts	Overs	Mdns	Runs	Wkts
Kortright	17	0	60	0	3	0	18	0
Mead	41.4	6	136	9	31	11	69	8
Taberer	4	0	19	0				
Pickett	21	7	33	1	27	12	50	2

Australian Bowling

	Overs	Mdns	Runs	Wkts	Overs	Mdns	Runs	Wkts
Turner	41	19	81	1	5	2	8	0
Trumble	58	27	87	6				
Trott	6	3	17	0	5	0	11	1
Coningham	13	6	26	2				
Bruce	1.4	0	6	1	1	1	0	0

Umpires: W. Clarke and R. Clayton.

AUSTRALIANS v WEMBLEY PARK

Played at Wembley Park, June 8, 9, 1896

This was, perhaps, the only match during the Australian tour that ought not to have been played. The Wembley Park ground at its best is not yet sufficiently matured for first-class cricket, and to make matters worse than they otherwise would have been, rain on the Sunday night was followed by bright sunshine. The Australians always had the best of the game, and on the second afternoon they gained an easy victory by 135 runs. For the most part the batsmen on both sides did very badly, but Gregory triumphed over the difficulties of the wicket, his innings of 43 being a most skilful display. Trumble, Giffen and Trott bowled finely for the Australians, and for the English team Spofforth showed that he could still be deadly on a treacherous pitch.

Australians

J. Darling b Rawlin	0	– c and b Spofforth	2
H. Graham b Spofforth	8	– c Phillips b Rawlin	6
S. E. Gregory lbw b Spofforth	26	– c Maude b Phillips	43
G. Giffen c Nepean b Spofforth	13	– c Whitehead b Spofforth	11
C. Hill c Nepean b Spofforth	8	– b Spofforth	8
F. A. Iredale c Maude b Pickett	3	– b Spofforth	0
G. H. S. Trott b Pickett	8	– not out	2
H. Donnan b Spofforth	0	– c Whitehead b Rawlin	1
H. Trumble c Pickett b Spofforth	25	– b Spofforth	9
J. J. Kelly c and b Phillips	4	– c and b Pickett	21
E. Jones not out	6	– b Rawlin	4
B 3, l-b 1, n-b 1	5	B 17, l-b 5, n-b 2	24
	106		131

Wembley Park

Mr C. E. de Trafford c Darling b Trumble	13	– run out	1
Mr E. A. Nepean b Giffen	3	– b Trott	12
Mr C. McGahey c Gregory b Trumble	0	– c Trumble b Trott	4
Mr P. Perrin b Giffen	0	– c Kelly b Trott	1
J. T. Rawlin b Giffen	0	– c and b Trumble	2
J. Whitehead b Giffen	5	– st Kelly b Trott	6
Mr F. W. Maude b Trumble	0	– b Trumble	6
Mr F. R. Spofforth b Giffen	2	– b Trumble	1
J. Phillips not out	11	– run out	0
T. M. Russell c Iredale b Trumble	2	– run out	1
H. Pickett c Darling b Giffen	20	– not out	0
B 7, l-b 2	9	B 1, l-b 2	3
	65		37

Wembley Park Bowling

	Overs	Mdns	Runs	Wkts	Overs	Mdns	Runs	Wkts
Spofforth	24.4	11	49	6	26	7	51	5
Rawlin	10	2	19	1	15	9	11	3
Pickett	11	4	24	2	11	3	25	1
Phillips	3	1	9	1	3	0	3	1
Nepean					3	0	17	0

Australian Bowling

	Overs	Mdns	Runs	Wkts	Overs	Mdns	Runs	Wkts
Jones	3	0	8	0				
Trumble	15	5	28	4	13.1	5	16	3
Giffen	12.4	4	20	6				
Trott					14	3	18	4

Umpires: R. G. Barlow and W. A. J. West.

AUSTRALIANS v MCC AND GROUND

Played at Lord's, June 11, 12, 1896

So far the Australians had had a career of uninterrupted success, but in this match – perhaps the most sensational of the whole tour – they met with a rude check, the MCC beating them by an innings and 18 runs. The game is already a historical one, the Australians being got rid of in their first innings by J. T. Hearne and Pougher for 18, the smallest score for which an Australian team has ever been dismissed in this country. George Giffen's illness compelled them to bat one short, but though his absence of course made a difference, it is hardly likely he would have been able to save his side from disaster. By winning in such sensational style the MCC at last took their revenge for the never-to-be-forgotten defeat in 1878. J. T. Hearne and Pougher bowled with extraordinary averages. Pougher, who went on with the total at 18 for three wickets, took five wickets, and not another run was scored. Nearly twenty-four hours' rain had considerably affected the ground, and the MCC gained a decided advantage in winning the toss, but even allowing for this, and two or three missed catches, they did uncommonly well to score 219. On the second day Darling played a fine innings, and J. T. Hearne again bowled splendidly.

MCC and Ground

Mr W. G. Grace b Trumble	15
Mr A. E. Stoddart st Kelly b Trott	54
K. S. Ranjitsinhji b Trumble	7
Mr F. S. Jackson c and b Trumble	51
W. Gunn b McKibbin	39
Mr G. MacGregor b Trumble	0
G. Davidson b Trumble	0
Mr F. Marchant b McKibbin	20
A. D. Pougher not out	9
W. Attewell b Trumble	7
J. T. Hearne b McKibbin	1
B 13, l-b 2, n-b 1	16
	219

Australians

J. J. Kelly c and b Pougher	8	– b Hearne	0
H. Graham b Hearne	4	– b Hearne	5
G. H. S. Trott b Hearne	6	– c MacGregor b Hearne	14
S. E. Gregory b Hearne	0	– c MacGregor b Hearne	28
F. A. Iredale b Hearne	0	– b Hearne	0
C. Hill b Pougher	0	– b Hearne	4
H. Trumble b Pougher	0	– b Hearne	0
J. Darling not out	0	– c Stoddart b Hearne	76
C. J. Eady b Pougher	0	– c Grace b Hearne	42
T. R. McKibbin c Davidson b Pougher	0	– not out	3
G. Giffen absent ill	0	– absent	0
		B 11	11
	18		183

Australian Bowling

	Overs	Mdns	Runs	Wkts
Trumble	34	8	84	6
Giffen	9	0	22	0
McKibbin	19.2	2	51	3
Trott	13	1	35	1
Eady	8	2	11	0

MCC Bowling

	Overs	Mdns	Runs	Wkts	Overs	Mdns	Runs	Wkts
Hearne	11	9	4	4	50.3	22	73	9
Attewell	8	5	14	0	10	4	14	0
Pougher	3	3	0	5	28	15	33	0
Jackson					10	3	16	0
Davidson					7	3	15	0
Grace					8	1	21	0

Umpires: W. A. J. West and J. Phillips.

ENGLAND v AUSTRALIA

Played at Lord's, June 22, 23, 24, 1896

The first of the three test matches proved an enormous attraction, the official return showing that on the opening day no fewer than 25,414 people paid for admission. The full attendance was estimated at nearly 30,000, but while this great crowd was in itself a compliment to the Australians it had a grave disadvantage. The field of play was seriously encroached upon, and it is to be feared that a good many of the people saw very little of the cricket. Under the circumstances it would hardly be fair to criticise the conduct of those present, but there was certainly an absence of the quiet and decorum usually characteristic of Lord's ground. For two days the match was favoured with delightful weather, but the conditions changed on the third morning, when a most inopportune fall of rain rendered England's task in the last innings far more difficult than it otherwise would have been. The committee of the MCC took the utmost pains in choosing the England eleven, and leaving aside the question of whether they were right or wrong in not asking Ranjitsinhji, there was little fault to be found with their final selection. The Australian team differed in two instances from the side that afterwards appeared at Manchester and The Oval, Graham and Eady being chosen to the exclusion of Iredale and McKibbin. Iredale had in the previous week seemed quite out of form, and McKibbin had so far done nothing to uphold his Australian reputation. The match was the most sensational of the whole tour, its fortunes changing from time to time in a fashion that was quite bewildering. England won by six wickets, but before that gratifying end was reached some startling things happened. Trott had the good fortune to beat W. G. Grace in the toss for innings, and when the Australians went in to bat on a perfect wicket a score of at least 250 was confidently expected. To the amazement of everyone on the ground, however, the Australians failed in a fashion that has seldom been seen on a dry, true pitch, being all got rid of by Richardson and Lohmann in an hour and a quarter for 53 runs. The Surrey bowlers did wonders, but lack of nerve on the part of the Australians must have been largely answerable for such an astounding collapse.

With the match to all appearance in their hands, England went in to bat soon after half past one, and when time was called at the close of the afternoon, they had scored 286 for eight wickets. This was a very fair performance but at one time something much bigger seemed in prospect, 250 being on the board with only four men out. It must be admitted, however, that the Australian bowlers were far from fortunate in the support they received, Abel being palpably missed in the slips when he had scored nine, and W. G. Grace let off at long-on at 51. Abel, apart from his one chance, played a splendid innings, going in first wicket down at 38, and being out fifth at 256. He hit thirteen 4s, and was at the wickets three hours. Jackson, who in brilliant style scored 44 out of 69, palpably gave away his innings. The encroachment of the crowd prevented Darling catching him on the on-side, and he at once gave the fieldsman a second opportunity.

The attendance on the second day was only half as large as on Monday, a great many people evidently thinking the match was as good as over. Those who stayed away, however, had reason to regret their want of faith in the Australians, as they missed seeing some of the finest cricket of the whole season. England's innings was quickly finished off for 292, and then the Australians, with a balance of 239 against them, went in for the second time. The early play suggested a repetition of Monday's breakdown, Darling and Eady being got rid of for three runs. Giffen and Trott, however, stayed together at the critical time and carried the score to 62. Then on Giffen's dismissal, Gregory joined Trott, and a partnership commenced which as long as cricket is played will cause the match to be remembered. Getting together before one o'clock, the two batsmen resisted the England bowling for nearly two hours and three quarters, putting on in that time no fewer than 221 runs. Both played superbly, their cricket leaving no room whatever for adverse criticism. So far as could be seen, neither of them gave a chance, but the English players were positive that Trott, with his score at 61, was caught by Hayward in the slips. Gregory hit seventeen 4s in his 103, and Trott, who was batting nearly three hours and a half, twenty-four 4s in his 143. When Gregory left at 283 the Australians were 44 runs ahead with six wickets to fall, and the position of England was certainly an anxious one. Richardson and J. T. Hearne, however, bowled in splendid form, and by six o'clock the innings ended for 347, the last six wickets having gone down for 64 runs. Donnan batted practically with one hand.

England wanted only 109 to win, and at the call of time they had scored 16 for the loss of Abel's wicket. Had the ground remained firm and dry, the finish of the game on Wednesday morning would no doubt have been uneventful, but rain quite altered the condition of the pitch, and the Englishmen had a vastly more difficult task than they had expected. Thanks chiefly to Brown and Stoddart, they hit off the runs for the loss of four wickets, but it might have gone desperately hard with them if the Australians had accepted all the chances offered. Kelly, standing back to Jones's bowling, was especially at fault.

Australia

H. Donnan run out	1	– b Hearne	8
J. Darling b Richardson	22	– b Richardson	0
G. Giffen c Lilley b Lohmann	0	– b Richardson	32
G. H. S. Trott b Richardson	0	– c Hayward b Richardson	143
S. E. Gregory b Richardson	14	– c Lohmann b Hearne	103
H. Graham b Richardson	0	– b Richardson	10
C. Hill b Lohmann	1	– b Hearne	5
C. J. Eady not out	10	– c Lilley b Richardson	2
H. Trumble b Richardson	0	– c Lilley b Hearne	4
J. J. Kelly c Lilley b Lohmann	0	– not out	24
E. Jones b Richardson	4	– c Jackson b Hearne	4
B 1	1	B 7, l-b 4, w 1	12
	53		347

England

Mr W. G. Grace c Trumble b Giffen	66	– c Hill b Trumble	7
Mr A. E. Stoddart b Eady	17	– not out	30
R. Abel b Eady	94	– c sub b Jones	4
J. T. Brown b Jones	9	– c Kelly b Eady	36
W. Gunn c Kelly b Trumble	25	– not out	13
Mr F. S. Jackson c Darling b Giffen	44		
T. Hayward not out	12	– b Jones	13
A. Lilley b Eady	0		
G. A. Lohmann c sub b Giffen	1		
J. T. Hearne c Giffen b Trott	11		
T. Richardson c Hill b Trott	6		
B 5, l-b 2	7	B 3, l-b 4, w 1	8
	292		111

England Bowling

	Overs	Mdns	Runs	Wkts	Overs	Mdns	Runs	Wkts
Richardson	11.3	3	39	6	47	15	134	5
Lohmann	11	6	13	3	22	6	39	0
Hayward					11	3	44	0
Hearne					36	14	76	5
Jackson					11	5	28	0
Grace					6	1	14	0

Australian Bowling

	Overs	Mdns	Runs	Wkts	Overs	Mdns	Runs	Wkts
Jones	26	6	64	1	23	10	42	2
Giffen	26	5	95	3	1	0	9	0
Eady	29	12	58	3	3	0	11	1
Trott	7.4	2	13	2	0.1	0	4	0
Trumble	19	3	55	1	20	10	37	1

Umpires: W. A. J. West and J. Phillips.

AUSTRALIANS v LEICESTERSHIRE

Played at Leicester, July 13, 14, 15, 1896

In meeting a side so weak in batting as Leicestershire, the Australians had one of their easiest tasks, and if they had been content to finish off their innings a little earlier than they did, they would have won the match in the most decisive fashion. As it was, Leicestershire just contrived to save the game, the chief credit for avoiding defeat belonging to Geeson, with whom Whiteside stayed in during the last half hour's cricket. Darling had the distinction of scoring 194, the highest innings hit for the Australians during their tour. All through a stay of six hours and a half he played in characteristic style, his cricket being a skilful combination of watchful defence and hard driving. His hits included a 5, twenty-one 4s, twelve 3s, and fourteen 2s. Far more attractive to the spectators, however, was the batting of Gregory, who hit up his 102 in two hours and a half. In this match Giffen met with one of his greatest successes as a bowler, taking 14 wickets for 119 runs.

Australians

F. A. Iredale c Tomlin b Woodcock	0
J. Darling c Geeson b Pougher	194
G. Giffen c Woodcock b Pougher	67
H. Donnan run out	66
S. E. Gregory c Tomlin b Pougher	102
H. Graham b Woodcock	12
C. Hill b Coe	16
C. J. Eady c Pougher b Coe	19
H. Trumble not out	45
J. J. Kelly b Pougher	1
E. Jones b Pougher	34
B 11, l-b 13, w 3, n-b 1	28
	584

Leicestershire

Mr C. E. de Trafford c Iredale b Giffen	7 – lbw b Giffen	0
J. Holland b Giffen	41 – c Kelly b Trumble	10
W. Tomlin b Jones	6 – b Giffen	7
A. E. Knight c Darling b Giffen	5 – c and b Giffen	19
Mr H. H. Marriott c Eady b Giffen	0 – c Eady b Trumble	36
A. D. Pougher st Kelly b Giffen	14 – b Donnan	26
Mr S. R. Wright lbw b Giffen	0 – c Gregory b Giffen	1
S. Coe run out	0 – st Kelly b Giffen	10
F. Geeson b Giffen	5 – not out	53
A. Woodcock c Darling b Giffen	1 – b Giffen	5
J. P. Whiteside not out	8 – not out	1
	B 9, l-b 3	12
	87	180

Leicestershire Bowling

	Overs	Mdns	Runs	Wkts
Woodcock	48	10	159	2
Geeson	28	9	87	0
Pougher	49.1	18	114	5
Wright	27	7	75	0
Coe	27	8	59	2
Marriott	6	2	12	0
Tomlin	15	3	50	0

Australian Bowling

	Overs	Mdns	Runs	Wkts	Overs	Mdns	Runs	Wkts
Jones	11	3	16	1				
Eady	1	0	3	0	3	2	1	0
Trumble	26	16	21	0	19	7	35	2
Giffen	24.2	13	30	8	35	12	89	6
Donnan	8	3	17	0	13	2	43	1

Umpires: J. Phillips and W. Shrewsbury.

ENGLAND v AUSTRALIA

Played at Manchester, July 16, 17, 18, 1896

The second of the three great test matches, which ended in a well-earned victory for the Australians by three wickets, was in many ways one of the most remarkable contests of the season, for though the Englishmen were defeated at the finish, the two best performances in the game were accomplished for them, Ranjitsinhji playing perhaps the greatest innings of his career, and Richardson bowling in a style he has seldom approached. Though England had won at Lord's by six wickets, the issue of the game at Manchester was awaited with unusual interest, owing mainly to the fact that the Australians from the time of their defeat at Lord's had been showing vastly improved form. The composition of the England team aroused considerable discussion, a good deal of exception being taken to the inclusion of MacLaren, who had had scarcely any practice in first class matches during the season. Lohmann and Pougher were engaged to represent England, but the former, owing to slight indisposition on the first morning, did not care to play, and the selection committee left out Pougher. This had the effect of letting nearly all the work in bowling fall upon Richardson, J. T. Hearne, and Briggs, and it was generally admitted that a mistake was made in going into the field, in fine weather and on a beautiful wicket, without at least four first-class bowlers. Iredale had been making immense strides from the time of his being left out of the first test match, and the men whom the Australian selection committee decided to dispense with were Graham, Eady, and Johns. The match proved a great attraction on the first two days, and the attendance on the third only suffered from the fact that the Englishmen seemed in a hopeless position. As it turned out, however, the last day's cricket was the most remarkable of all, and those who had the good fortune to be present are never likely to forget it.

With the ground in such excellent condition for run-getting it was a fortunate circumstance for Trott to win the toss, and his team made admirable use of their opportunity. Richardson often puzzled the batsmen, and was many times unlucky in just failing to hit the wicket, but on the whole the English bowling looked anything but deadly, and the Australians started so well that they seemed, in the first three hours, to have rendered themselves practically secure against defeat. Following up his recent successes, Iredale played a beautiful innings of 108, and so excellent was the assistance afforded him by Giffen, Trott and Darling that at one time the score stood at 294 with only three men out. At this point the prospects of the Englishmen were particularly gloomy, but Richardson came with a fine effort, and before the call of time, eight Australian wickets were down for 366. On the following morning, thanks to a useful stand by Kelly and McKibbin, the Australian total was carried to 412. With the conditions still most favourable and the wicket practically as good as ever, it seemed quite possible that the Englishmen would get very near to their opponents' total, but with a few exceptions the batting was particularly feeble and the whole side were out for 231. Trott changed his bowling with remarkable skill and judgement, and it was quite a stroke of genius to go on first himself with Jones. He had the satisfaction of easily getting rid of Grace and Stoddart, thus giving his side the good start they so needed. Ranjitsinhji and Lilley played exceedingly well, but the other batting was certainly unworthy of the picked representatives of the old Country. Having slightly strained himself, Jones only bowled five overs and the best work was accomplished by McKibbin.

England had to follow on against a majority of 181, and the start of their second innings was disappointing, as despite some admirable batting by Stoddart and Ranjitsinhji, four of the best wickets on the side had fallen before the drawing of stumps for 109. At the close of the second day's play therefore, the Englishmen with six wickets to go down were still 72 runs behind, and nothing seemed less likely than that they would before the end of the game, hold practically a winning position. Such however proved to be the case, the Englishmen playing a wonderful uphill game and struggling hard, though without success, to atone for the shortcomings of the two previous afternoons. Much depended upon Ranjitsinhji, and the famous young Indian fairly rose to the occasion, playing an innings that could, without exaggeration, be fairly described as marvellous. He very quickly got set again, and punished the Australian bowlers in a style that, up to that period of the season, no other English batsman had approached. He repeatedly brought off his wonderful strokes on the leg side, and for a while had the Australian bowlers quite at his mercy. Could the other English batsmen have rendered him any material assistance, there is no saying to what extent the English total might have been increased, but as it was, there was no other score on the Saturday morning higher than nineteen. Ranjitsinhji's remarkable batting, and the prospect of the Englishmen after all running their opponents close, worked the spectators up to a high pitch of excitement, and the scene of enthusiasm was something to be remembered when the Indian cricketer completed the first hundred hit against the Australians last season. MacLaren, Lilley and Hearne all tried hard to keep up their wickets for Ranjitsinhji, but Briggs after making sixteen, could not resist the temptation of jumping out to try and drive a slow ball from McKibbin. The innings came to an end for 305, Ranjitsinhji carrying out his bat for 154. It is safe to say that a finer or more finished display has never been seen on a great occasion, for he never gave anything like a chance, and during his long stay the worst that could be urged against him was that he made a couple of lucky snicks. He was at the wickets for three hours ten minutes, and among his hits were twenty-three 4s, five 3s and nine 2s.

The Australians were left with 125 to get to win, and with the ground showing very few signs of wear, most people looked forward to seeing the number hit off for the loss of perhaps three or four batsmen. As it turned out, the Australians had many very anxious moments, Richardson making a magnificent effort in bowling, which was quite worthy of comparison with Ranjitsinhji's batting earlier in the day. Almost before one could realise what was happening, four of the best Australian wickets had fallen for 45, and with the prospect of a keenly exciting finish, the remainder of the game was watched with breathless interest. Another failure for the Colonials might have been attended with most serious results, but Gregory and Donnan played with splendid nerve at the critical time, and the score reached 79 before the former was caught at short leg for an invaluable 33. Still the match was far from over. Donnan was out at 95 and Hill at 100, the position being that the Australians with three wickets to fall, wanted 25 runs to win. With Richardson bowling in his finest form, and nearly all the best Australian batsmen gone, the Englishmen at this point seemed to have actually the best of the game, and the excitement was intense. Everything rested upon Trumble and Kelly, and it would be difficult to speak too highly of the manner in which they got through a terribly trying ordeal. The bowling was so good that they could only score at rare intervals, and generally by singles, but they surely and slowly placed their score on the high road to victory. When only nine runs were required to win, Lilley, who up to that time had kept wicket absolutely without a mistake, failed to take a chance offered him by Kelly. Had this come off, there is no saying what might have happened, but as it was, Trumble and Kelly hit off the remaining runs, and a splendid match ended in favour of Australia by three wickets. Some idea of the excellence of the bowling may be gathered from the fact that the last 25 runs took just an hour to obtain. There was a scene of great enthusiasm at the finish, the Australians being received with a heartiness that reflected immense credit on the Manchester public. Richardson, who bowled for three hours without sending down one really loose ball, took in the innings six wickets for 76 runs, and considering that the ground scarcely afforded him any assistance, it is safe to say he has never accomplished a finer performance. So great was the effort, that one could not help regretting it was not crowned by a victory for his side. Before giving the score of a game that will always be memorable in the history of cricket, it should be stated that Richardson in the whole match, bowled 110 overs and three balls, and took thirteen wickets at a cost of 244 runs. The Australians fairly beat the picked eleven of England, on a wicket that was firm and true throughout, and it would be hard to give them too much praise for their brilliantly earned success.

Australia

F. A Iredale b Briggs	108	– b Richardson	11
J. Darling c Lilley b Richardson	27	– c Lilley b Richardson	16
G. Giffen c and b Richardson	80	– c Ranjitsinhji b Richardson	6
G. H. S. Trott c Brown b Lilley	53	– c Lilley b Richardson	2
S. E. Gregory c Stoddart b Briggs	25	– c Ranjitsinhji b Briggs	33
H. Donnan b Richardson	12	– c Jackson b Richardson	15
C. Hill c Jackson b Richardson	9	– c Lilley b Richardson	14
H. Trumble b Richardson	24	– not out	17
J. J. Kelly c Lilley b Richardson	27	– not out	8
T. McKibbin not out	28		
E. Jones b Richardson	4		
B 6, l-b 8, w 1	15	L-b 3	3
	412		125

England

Mr W. G. Grace st Kelly b Trott	2	– c Trott b Jones	11
Mr A. E. Stoddart st Kelly b Trott	15	– b McKibbin	41
K. S. Ranjitsinhji c Trott b McKibbin	62	– not out	154
R. Abel c Trumble b McKibbin	26	– c McKibbin b Giffen	13
Mr F. S. Jackson run out	18	– c McKibbin b Giffen	1
J. T. Brown c Kelly b Trumble	22	– c Iredale b Jones	19
Mr A. C. MacLaren c Trumble b McKibbin	0	– c Jones b Trumble	15
A. Lilley not out	65	– c Trott b Giffen	19
J. Briggs b Trumble	0	– st Kelly b McKibbin	16
J. T. Hearne c Trumble b Giffen	18	– c Kelly b McKibbin	9
T. Richardson run out	2	– c Jones b Trumble	1
B 1	1	B 2, l-b 3, w 1	6
	231		305

English Bowling

	Overs	Mdns	Runs	Wkts	Overs	Mdns	Runs	Wkts
Richardson	68	23	168	7	42.3	16	76	6
Briggs	40	18	99	2	18	8	24	1
Jackson	16	6	34	0				
Hearne	28	11	53	0	24	13	22	0
Grace	7	3	11	0				
Stoddart	6	2	9	0				
Lilley	5	1	23	1				

Australian Bowling

	Overs	Mdns	Runs	Wkts	Overs	Mdns	Runs	Wkts
Jones	5	2	11	0	17	0	78	2
Trott	10	0	46	2	7	1	17	0
Giffen	19	3	48	1	16	1	65	3
Trumble	37	14	80	2	29.1	12	78	2
McKibbin	19	8	45	3	21	4	61	3

Umpires: J. Phillips and A. Chester.

AUSTRALIANS v DERBYSHIRE

Played at Derby, July 20, 21, 22, 1896

A superb wicket was prepared at Derby, and after three days' play the match was left drawn, no fewer than 978 runs being scored. The Australians, who won the toss, were batting until a quarter past five on the second day, their total of 625 being the highest during the tour. By remaining at the wickets so long, however, they practically destroyed their chance of victory as, with Jones and Trumble away, there was little likelihood of their getting Derbyshire out twice in the time left for cricket. It will be noticed that Trott, Donnan and Hill scored over 100 each, Donnan's 167 – his highest in England – lasting about six hours. He played very well, but considering that the Derbyshire bowling had been completely mastered, his cricket at times was needlessly slow and cautious. Trott played finely, and Hill, apart from one absurdly easy chance, gave an admirable display. A draw being certain, not one of the regular Australian bowlers was tried in Derbyshire's second innings.

Australians

F. A. Iredale c and b Davidson 73
J. Darling c Storer b Hulme 4
G. Fiffen c Wright b Storer 63
G. H. S. Trott b Hulme 141
S. E. Gregory b Hulme 8
H. Donnan b Sugg 167
C. Hill b Sugg 130
H. Graham b Sugg 0
C. J. Eady c Storer b Bagshaw 2
T. R. McKibbin c Evershed b Sugg 0
A. E. Johns not out 31
B 4, l-b 1, w 1 6

625

Derbyshire

Mr S. H. Evershed c Donnan b Giffen	10	– b Darling	4
Mr L. G. Wright c Donnan b McKibbin	81		
Mr G. A. Marsden c Iredale b Giffen	0	– c and b Graham	24
H. Bagshaw c Johns b Donnan	35	– not out	0
W. Chatterton c Eady b McKibbin	45		
G. Davidson c McKibbin b Giffen	60		
W. Storer lbw b Giffen	13		
W. Sugg b McKibbin	34	– not out	29
J. H. Purdy c Donnan b Giffen	6		
G. Porter not out	3		
J. Hulme absent hurt	0		
B 2, l-b 1, w 2	5	L-b 4	4
	292		61

Derbyshire Bowling

	Overs	Mdns	Runs	Wkts
Davidson	63	23	114	1
Hulme	55	19	115	3
Purdy	32	10	48	0
Porter	44	7	124	0
Storer	17	1	61	1
Bagshaw	18	2	49	1
Sugg	17	1	61	4
Chatterton	19	4	47	0
Evershed	1	1	0	0

Australian Bowling

	Overs	Mdns	Runs	Wkts	Overs	Mdns	Runs	Wkts
Giffen	32	7	123	5	1	0	11	0
Trott	11	2	50	0				
McKibbin	29.2	9	70	3				
Donnan	28	13	44	1				
Eady	1	1	0	0				
Iredale					5	0	18	0
Graham					4	2	19	1
Darling					3	2	5	1
Hill					2	0	4	0

Umpires: J. Wheeler and G. Littlewood.

ENGLAND v AUSTRALIA

Played at The Oval, August 10, 11, 12, 1896

The third and concluding test match was preceded by a regrettable incident, which for a time caused intense excitement in the cricket world. The Surrey committee, after much deliberation, chose nine cricketers as certainties for the England eleven, and four others from amongst whom the last two places were to be filled. Early in the week previous to the match, however – indeed almost as soon as the selection had been made known – they received a letter signed by Lohmann, Gunn, Abel, Richardson and Hayward, in which these players demanded £20 each for their services in the match. Ten pounds per man had been paid to the professionals in the test matches at Lord's and Manchester, and the Surrey committee, without going into the question of whether or not £20 was an excessive fee on an occasion of such importance, declined point blank to be dictated to. It is betraying no secret to say that they felt greatly aggrieved, on the eve of the most important match of the season, at being placed in a difficulty by four of their own professionals. However, they did not hesitate for a moment as to the course to be pursued, at once taking steps to secure the best possible substitutes for the revolting players. For two or three days the position remained unchanged, and as soon as the facts became known to the general public, nothing else in the way of cricket was talked about. Friendly counsels, however, were soon at work, and on the evening of Saturday, August 8th, a communication was received at The Oval from Abel, Hayward and Richardson, to the effect that they withdrew from the position they had taken up, and placed themselves without reserve in the hands of the Surrey committee. Much gratified at the turn which things had taken, the Surrey committee resolved on the Saturday evening to let the final selection of the England eleven stand over until the meeting of the match committee on Monday morning. At that meeting, Sir Richard Webster presided, and after a good deal of deliberation, it was determined that Abel, Richardson, and Hayward should play for England. Among leading cricketers, opinions were a good deal divided as to the wisdom of this policy, but in our judgment the match committee took a just, as well as a popular course of action. Lohmann did not act with the other professionals, but at a subsequent period, he wrote a letter of apology, and made his peace with the Surrey Club. Even when the question of the professionals had been settled, however, the match committee were by no means at the end of their difficulties. Statements in certain newspapers as to the allowance made for expenses to amateurs caused great irritation, and for a time there was much uncertainty as to how the England eleven would be finally constituted. In the end matters were smoothed over, but not till a definite statement – which will be found in another portion of this Almanack – had been made public as to the financial relations between Mr W. G. Grace and the Surrey Club.

Happily, the match, which had been preceded by all these storms and troubles, passed off in the pleasantest fashion, and proved a complete success. Played on a wicket ruined by rain, it produced some startling cricket, and was in the end won by England by 66 runs, the old Country thus securing the rubber. Rain on the first day delayed the start until five minutes to five, and with the ground by no means so difficult as it became on the following day, England profited to a considerable extent by having won the toss. They started well, and at the drawing of stumps at half-past six had scored 69 for one wicket. The second day was fine, and up to a certain point England did very well, but after having had 113 on the board with only three wickets down, the side were all out for 145. Trumble, after crossing over to the Pavilion end, bowled nine overs for ten runs and five wickets. Darling and Iredale made a wonderful start for the Australians, and when, with a little luck, the score reached 70 without the loss of a wicket, the Australians seemed to have more than made up for the disadvantage of losing the toss. However, a foolish attempt to get a fifth run for a hit of his partner's, cost Iredale his wicket at 75, and then, thanks chiefly to Hearne's fine bowling, such an astonishing change came over the game that the innings was finished off for 119, or 26 runs behind. England, on going in for the second time, had a terribly difficult pitch to bat on, and at the close of play, five wickets were down for 60 runs. It was anybody's game on the third morning, everything depending on the condition of the ground. It was freely predicted that the wicket would improve, but such was far from being the case, the pitch being perhaps more difficult than ever. England's innings was finished off for 84, the Australians being left with 111 to get to win. This task they commenced shortly before half-past twelve, the excitement being of course at a very high pitch. In the second over, before a run had been scored, Darling was bowled, and then the Australians went from bad to worse, the climax being reached when the seventh wicket fell at 14. All this time, Hearne and Peel had bowled in wonderful form, the latter having been put on in place of Richardson directly Darling was out. The ninth wicket was lost at 25, and the Englishmen had the game in their hands, but McKibbin, by some plucky hitting, delayed the end, the total having reached 44 when Abel caught him most brilliantly at slip with one hand. Thus amidst great enthusiasm, England won the match by 66 runs.

England

	First innings	Second innings	
Mr W. G. Grace c Trott b Giffin	24	b Trumble	9
Mr F. S. Jackson c McKibbin b Trumble	45	b Trumble	2
K. S. Ranjitsinhji b Giffen	8	st Kelly b McKibbin	11
R. Abel c and b Trumble	26	c Giffen b Trumble	21
Mr A. C. MacLaren b Trumble	20	b Jones	6
T. Hayward b Trumble	0	c Trott b Trumble	13
Captain Wynyard c Darling b McKibbin	10	c Kelly b McKibbin	3
R. Peel c Donnan b Trumble	0	b Trumble	0
A. Lilley c Ireland b Trumble	2	c McKibbin b Trumble	6
J. T. Hearne b McKibbin	8	b McKibbin	1
T. Richardson not out	1	not out	10
L-b 1	1	L-b 2	2
	145		84

Australia

	First innings	Second innings	
J. Darling c MacLaren b Hearne	47	b Hearne	0
F. A. Iredale run out	30	c Jackson b Hearne	3
G. Giffen b Hearne	0	b Hearne	1
G. H. S. Trott b Peel	5	c sub b Peel	3
S. E. Gregory b Hearne	1	c Richardson b Peel	6
C. Hill run out	1	b Peel	0
H. Donnan b Hearne	10	c Hayward b Peel	0
J. J. Kelly not out	10	lbw b Peel	3
H. Trumble b Hearne	3	not out	7
E. Jones c MacLaren b Peel	3	b Peel	3
T. R. McKibbin b Hearne	0	c Abel b Hearne	16
B 8, l-b 1	9	B 2	2
	119		44

Australian Bowling

	Overs	Mdns	Runs	Wkts	Overs	Mdns	Runs	Wkts
Giffen	32	12	64	2	1	0	4	0
Trumble	40	10	59	6	25	9	30	6
McKibbin	9.3	0	21	2	20	8	35	3
Jones					3	0	13	1

England Bowling

	Overs	Mdns	Runs	Wkts	Overs	Mdns	Runs	Wkts
Peel	20	9	30	2	12	5	23	6
Hearne	26.1	10	41	6	13	8	19	4
Richardson	5	0	22	0	1	1	0	0
Hayward	2	0	17	0				

Umpires: J. Phillips and W. Hearn.

1896

Nothing in connection with Cricket has for some years past caused so much excitement as the so-called strike of the professionals, on the eve of the England and Australian match at The Oval Happily the storm subsided almost as soon as it was raised, the players quickly withdrawing from the position which, without thoroughly weighing the consequences, they had taken up. I thought at the time, and I think still, that the players were right in principle, but that their action was ill-judged and inopportune. To my mind it was, to say the least, ungracious of the Surrey men to raise a difficulty with their own committee after accepting ten pounds each for the England matches at Lord's and Manchester. That they felt this themselves was made pretty clear by their speedy submission. Out of their revolt, however, I hope and believe that good will come. With England and Australia matches attracting such immense crowds of people, it is only right that the professionals should be liberally rewarded for their services, and I hope that when the Australians pay us their next visit, it will be agreed to pay every professional chosen for England in the test matches, a fee of twenty pounds. An arrangement to this effect, made at the annual meeting of county secretaries at Lord's, in December, would avoid all difficulties. In this connection, it is interesting to recall the fact that the Surrey Club, without, so far as I know, any pressure being brought to bear upon them, paid twenty pounds each to Alfred Shaw, Morley and Barnes, in 1880, on the occasion of the first England and Australia match in this country.

A subject which is just now exercising the minds of county committees is that of winter wages for professionals, Yorkshire's arrangement to pay two pounds a week, from September to April inclusive, to their ten regular players, having excited a feeling of anxiety, not to say alarm. It is clear that only clubs with a large amount of money – Yorkshire's experiment will cost roughly £600 – will be able to act with such liberality, and there is a fear that young players will drift away from their own counties to Yorkshire in the hope of participating in the benefit. Surely, however, this danger is more imaginary than real. There must always be a limit to the number of professionals for whom room can be found in one county eleven, and the law of supply and demand may be trusted to keep things tolerably straight. Moreover, the Yorkshire Committee are strongly averse to playing any but native-born men. All the same there is certainly a danger that the liberality of the Yorkshire executive will breed dissatisfaction in counties where such a winter wage as two pounds a week is out of the question. This matter of payment in the winter months is no new thing, however, the Surrey Club having for some time past, in a less public way, remunerated many of their professionals during the off season. The earnings of the players have certainly not risen in proportion to the immensely increased popularity of cricket during the last twenty years, but to represent the average professional as an ill-treated or down-trodden individual is, I think, a gross exaggeration. The field of his labours has widely extended, and as regards The Oval, Lord's, Manchester, and various Yorkshire grounds, the Benefit match, which is the special prize of a professional cricketer's life, is a much bigger thing than it was years ago. There is plenty of room for further improvement, but, taken all round, things are certainly far better than they were. Into the thorny question of amateurs' expenses I do not propose to enter, for the good and sufficient reason that I do not possess the necessary information. No doubt there are some abuses, but as a famous cricketer – a county captain and quite behind the scenes – has assured me that he does not know more than half-a-dozen men, playing as amateurs, who make anything out of the game, the evil would not seem to be very widespread. Mr W. G. Grace's position has for years, as everyone knows, been an anomalous one, but "nice customs curtsey to great kings" and the work he has done in popularising cricket outweighs a hundredfold every other consideration.

MR W. G. GRACE AND THE SURREY CLUB

Various rumours having gained currency as to the amount of money allowed to Mr Grace for expenses when playing for England at The Oval, the following official statement was made public on August 10 – the opening day of the third test match.

"The Committee of the Surrey County Cricket Club have observed paragraphs in the Press respecting amounts alleged to be paid, or promised to, Dr W. G. Grace for playing in the match England v Australia. The Committee desire to give the statements contained in the paragraphs the most unqualified contradiction. During many years, on the occasions of Dr W. G. Grace playing at The Oval, at the request of the Surrey County Committee, in the matches Gentlemen v Players and England v Australia, Dr Grace has received the sum of £10 a match to cover his expenses in coming to and remaining in London during the three days. Beyond this amount Dr Grace has not received, directly or indirectly, one farthing for playing in a match at The Oval.

Signed on behalf of the Committee,

August 10, 1896. C. W. ALCOCK."

AUSTRALIANS v GLOUCESTERSHIRE

Played at Cheltenham, August 20, 21, 22, 1896

In this, the second match of the Cheltenham week, the Australians beat Gloucestershire by an innings and 54 runs. The game was a memorable one, Gloucestershire in their second innings being dismissed for 17 – the smallest score ever made by an English team against Australian bowlers. The wicket, drying after drenching rain, was excessively difficult, but for all that Trumble and McKibbin bowled in marvellous form. It will be seen that Trumble took six wickets for eight runs and McKibbin four for seven. Though so badly beaten at the finish, Gloucestershire did very well up to a certain point, scoring 133 and getting six Australian wickets down for 54. Then, however, Gregory's splendid batting, and some mistakes in the field by the county, turned the fortunes of the game. On the second day the weather was so bad that only three overs could be bowled. In scoring his 71 Gregory was at the wickets an hour and fifty minutes, the way in which he overcame the difficulties of the pitch being beyond praise. Townsend bowled finely, and with better support in the field would have had an astonishing record. Even as it was he took eight wickets for just under ten runs each. At one point he got rid of four batsmen in three overs.

Gloucestershire

Mr W. G. Grace sen. st Johns b McKibbin	26	– b Trumble	9
Mr R. W. Rice b McKibbin	11	– c and b Trumble	1
Mr W. McG. Hemingway b Trumble	0	– b Trumble	0
Mr C. O. H. Sewell c Iredale b McKibbin	18	– b Trumble	0
Mr C. L. Townsend c Darling b Trumble	0	– c Graham b Trumble	0
Mr G. L. Jessop st Johns b McKibbin	30	– c Gregory b Trumble	0
Mr W. G. Grace jun. c Johns b Jones	22	– c Donnan b McKibbin	0
Mr F. H. B. Champain b McKibbin	2	– c Graham b McKibbin	3
Mr W. S. Brown run out	7	– not out	1
H. Wrathall not out	8	– st Johns b McKibbin	1
J. H. Board b McKibbin	1	– c Trott b McKibbin	0
B 7, l-b 1	8	B 2	2
	133		17

Australians

F. A. Iredale b Townsend	7	H. Trumble c Sewell b Townsend	28
J. Darling c Board b Jessop	26	E. Jones c Jessop b Townsend	2
G. H. S. Trott c Wrathall b Townsend	17	T. McKibbin lbw b Townsend	22
H. Donnan b Townsend	1	A. E. Johns c and b Jessop	10
C. Hill b Townsend	0	B 14, l-b 1, n-b 4	19
S. E. Gregory not out	71		
H. Graham st Board b Townsend	1		204

Australian Bowling

	Overs	Mdns	Runs	Wkts	Overs	Mdns	Runs	Wkts
Trumble	18	2	68	2	10	6	8	6
McKibbin	21.2	8	48	6	9.1	7	7	4
Jones	4	0	9	1				

Gloucestershire Bowling

	Overs	Mdns	Runs	Wkts
Jessop	21.3	3	55	2
Townsend	28	5	79	8
Brown	3	0	21	0
Grace, jun.	2	0	8	0
Grace, sen.	6	0	22	0

Umpires: G. Young and G. Remnant.

AUSTRALIANS v SOUTH OF ENGLAND

Played at Hastings, September 3, 4, 5, 1896

Up to a certain point the Australians did very well in the last match of their tour, but their batting broke down completely on the Saturday afternoon, and in the end they had all the worst of the draw, the South, with eight wickets to fall, wanting only 49 runs to win. In the Australians' second innings J. T. Hearne did a wonderful piece of bowling. He went on after luncheon with the score at 22 for one wicket, and took six wickets for eight runs. At one time his analysis read:– 13 overs and two balls, 12 maidens, two runs, and five wickets. On each side there was a capital display of batting, Clement Hill and W. G. Grace – the latter of whom strained his leg on the Friday and took no further part in the game – playing very finely. Rain delayed the start on the second day till after three o'clock.

Australians

F. A. Iredale lbw b Lohmann	17	– c Butt b Lohmann	6
H. Donnan b Lohmann	11	– b Hearne	16
G. Giffen b Richardson	17	– c and b Hearne	0
G. H. S. Trott b Lohmann	10	– b Lohmann	5
S. E. Gregory c Lohmann b Townsend	10	– c Butt b Hearne	6
C. Hill b Richardson	65	– b Hearne	11
H. Graham b Lohmann	4	– c Townsend b Hearne	0
J. J. Kelly b Hayward	16	– c and b Lohmann	5
H. Trumble not out	26	– not out	6
E. Jones b Richardson	26	– c Townsend b Hearne	4
T. R. McKibbin b Townsend	0	– c Stoddart b Lohmann	4
B 9, l-b 11	20		
	222		63

South of England

Mr W. G. Grace c Iredale b McKibbin	53		
Mr A. E. Stoddart b McKibbin	4	– c Kelly b McKibbin	10
R. Abel c Donnan b McKibbin	15	– c Trott b McKibbin	24
T. Hayward c Gregory b Giffen	21	– not out	11
Mr C. L. Townsend b McKibbin	1		
W. Brockwell st Kelly b McKibbin	14		
E. H. Killick c Kelly b Giffen	16		
G. A. Lohmann lbw b Giffen	11		
J. T. Hearne not out	29		
H. R. Butt b Giffen	5		
T. Richardson c Jones b McKibbin	15		
B 5, l-b 2, w 1, n-b 1	8		
	192		45

South of England Bowling

	Overs	Mdns	Runs	Wkts	Overs	Mdns	Runs	Wkts
Hearne	9	4	16	0	17	13	8	6
Townsend	14.2	1	54	2	7	1	10	0
Richardson	24	11	54	3				
Lohmann	25	7	63	4	23.4	6	45	4
Hayward	6	2	15	1				

Australian Bowling

	Overs	Mdns	Runs	Wkts	Overs	Mdns	Runs	Wkts
McKibbin	34.1	10	65	6	9	2	30	2
Trumble	13	2	36	0	9	3	15	0
Giffen	21	1	83	4				

Umpires: R. Thoms and J. Phillips.

THROWING

In reviewing in last year's *Wisden* the tour of the Australian team of 1896, I ventured to condemn as unfair the bowling of both Jones and McKibbin. I had no wish to say anything disagreeable, but while closely watching all the matches played in London by the team, I was so struck by the deplorable change that had come over the methods of Australian bowlers, that I did not see how the question could be ignored. The criticism has, I think, been more than justified by subsequent events. On the 26th of January, a letter condemning McKibbin's action in most uncompromising terms was addressed by Mr Spofforth to the *Sporting Life*, and at Adelaide at the end of October, in the first match played in Australia by Mr Stoddart's Team, Jones was no-balled by James Phillips for throwing. The significance of Mr Spofforth's letter, which is quoted in full further on, and of Phillips's action at Adelaide seems to me very great. It is certain that Mr Spofforth would not, unless he had felt very strongly indeed on the matter, have gone to the length of denouncing a brother Australian as an unfair bowler, and no one who knows James Phillips can think it possible that he would have no-balled Jones without adequate cause. From what Phillips has done nothing but good can come. If years ago any representative English umpire had shown the same courage many scandals would have been avoided. As regards both McKibbin and Jones the point to bear in mind is that the fault lies primarily with English bowlers and English umpires. Australian bowlers never threw in England till we had shown them over and over again that Law X. could be broken with impunity. The following is Mr Spofforth's letter:–

CONCERNING "THROWING" AND THE "FOLLOW-ON" RULE

TO THE EDITOR OF THE "SPORTING LIFE."

Sir, – The all-absorbing topic among cricketers seems to be altering of the "follow on" rule: but I scarcely think, no matter how this rule is changed, it will have much effect on the game, seeing that in the annals of first-class cricket it has only been "infringed" twice, and that by a body of cricketers anyone would have least expected it from.

In the first instance there may have been an excuse, but when a conservative body like the MCC thought it so serious as to alter the rule, it showed the worst possible taste to breathe it again.

But what I consider a far more serious consideration for the authorities is, Are they going to legalise throwing? There is scarcely a first class county which does not include a "thrower" amongst its cricketers, many of them men who would scorn to cheat an opponent out, and who, if a wicket-keeper were in the habit of kicking down the stumps or knocking off the bails with his hands and appealing for a bowl out, would not hesitate to bring him before his committee, or refuse to play with him again. Still, they will not only employ a man to throw, but will actually throw themselves, and acknowledge it, their only excuse being that "others do it," and they will name many.

This practice of throwing is growing rapidly, and many young cricketers are now adopting it who a year or so back were quite above suspicion.

Australia has now taken it up, and with the last eleven there was one who hardly ever delivered a "fair" ball, and although I am quite aware I may raise a "hornet's nest" about my head by mentioning names, I allude to McKibbin who, I shall always maintain, should never be allowed to play under the existing rule. Now, I think it is only fair I should mention an Englishman, and although I could name many I am anxious not to injure any one. So I will take Bobby Peel, one of England's best bowlers, and one who has no need to resort to throwing. I acknowledge he does not often take to it, still it is well known to cricketers that at times he does "shy." Again, there are many who, while not exactly throwing, do not bowl fairly according to the existing rule. They "put" the ball, which is they throw only from one point, mostly the elbow. The remedy for this unfair play is rather hard to find, especially as there is no umpire in England who dare no-ball a cricketer, while should a fair bowler even touch the bowler's crease when delivering a ball he is at once "called."

I am of opinion the best way to put down throwing is to form a committee of all the captains of the first class counties with Lord Harris as chairman, and on anyone being reported for throwing, a vote be taken, and if unfavourable the cricketer be suspended for a week, if brought up a second time fined and suspended, a third time he should be disqualified for the season. Both jockeys and footballers are suspended and fined for unfairness, and why should cricketers be exempt?

In conclusion, if nothing is done in the matter, the best way is to legalise throwing, and in one season it would bring about its own cure. – Yours. etc.,

January 25, 1897. Fred. R. Spofforth.

THE AUSTRALIANS IN ENGLAND, 1899

By common consent the tenth Australian team formed the strongest combination that had come from the Colonies since the great side captained by Mr W. L. Murdoch in 1882. Looking at their record as a whole, it might be argued that this is too high an estimate, but personally I regard it as not in any way beyond the truth. The prestige of the team suffered a good deal during August from the large number of unfinished matches, and forgetting the brilliant things that had been done during the first two months or so of the tour some good judges were inclined at the end of the season to rate the players at less than their true value. That at least was the impression left on my mind by comments that appeared in somewhat influential quarters. The strain of playing day after day for four months on hard wickets naturally produced some degree of staleness, and in gauging the real merit of the eleven I attach most weight to the cricket shown up to the third meeting with England at Manchester on the 17th of July. That match, though it ended in a draw, marked a very sharp change in the fortunes of the team. When they went into the field at Old Trafford, Darling and his colleagues had a truly wonderful record. They had played 20 matches of which they had won 12, lost only one and left seven unfinished. Even these figures, however, remarkable as they look, scarcely showed to the full extent what the team had accomplished, for in not one of the drawn matches had the Australians the worst of the position. Indeed, in every case except the Whit-Monday match with Yorkshire, in which the rain admitted of little progress being made, they would have won readily enough if another day had been available for cricket. After the match at Manchester the Australians only gained four victories, and, as during the same time they were twice beaten, their general record suffered very seriously. In all – playing two matches a week for 17 weeks, and finishing up in the first half of the Hastings Festival – they took part in 35 matches, of which they won 16, lost 3 and left 16 drawn. The number of defeats was smaller than in the case of any previous team from Australia, but on the other hand the number of drawn games had never been exceeded except during the tour of 1886. The fine weather and splendid wickets had, of course, much to do with matches being left unfinished, but another cause could be found in the methods of play adopted. While expressing my firm conviction that the team were stronger than any that had come to this country for 17 years, I have no intention of instituting a close comparison with the great eleven of 1882. The conditions during the two years were indeed so different as to render a fair comparison almost impossible. The summer of 1882 was one of unsettled weather and wet wickets, while that of 1899 had not, in the amount of sunshine, been equalled in England for just over 30 years. The two elevens were equally well suited to the conditions under which they had to play. Possessing in Massie, Percy McDonnell and Bonner, three of the most remarkable hitters that ever played on the same side, the team of 1882 were in proportion more formidable on a soft wicket than a hard one, whereas Darling's eleven included so many stubborn batsmen that the better the ground the more difficult became the task of beating them. Indeed, as the results of the tour prove, they could not within the space of three days be defeated on a perfect pitch. It has been contended by eye witnesses that there was nothing the matter with the wicket at Canterbury, but I cannot bring myself to believe this, for on the third day of the match the Kent eleven had to fight for their lives to get less than 140 runs and would assuredly have been beaten if the catches had been held. In the case of the other two matches lost by Darling's team the state of the ground had certainly much to do with the result. At Leyton the wicket, unsound to begin with, was seriously affected by heavy dews, and in the return match with Surrey at The Oval the pitch was quite soft on the opening day. In estimating the strength of the Australian eleven great allowance must be made for the disadvantages under which they laboured. Clement Hill was laid aside by illness after the end of June, and though he afterwards played in three matches, he was far too weak to again do himself justice, while Worrall, from the start of the tour to the finish, was hampered by a badly-damaged knee. Moreover, Frank Iredale was kept out of the team for more than a fortnight in June by a sharp attack of measles. Hill's illness would in itself have been sufficient to ruin the trip if the eleven had not been so exceptionally rich in run-getters. At the time he had to lay up he was playing in wonderful form, and was beyond question the best bat on the side. He had to undergo an operation for the removal of some growth in the nose, and the later consequences proved far more serious than had been expected. He lost weight and strength to an alarming extent, and was not himself again till the last matches being played.

The sixteen victories gained by the team comprised one against England, two against the MCC, one against the South of England (at Hastings), two against England Elevens at Eastbourne and Truro, one against Cambridge University, one against Oxford University Past and Present, one against the Midland Counties, and seven against county elevens – Surrey, Lancashire, Leicestershire, Derbyshire, Gloucestershire, Warwickshire and

Middlesex. The three defeats were suffered at the hands of Essex, Surrey and Kent, the record in this case being in curious contrast to that in 1896 of Trott's eleven who did not once go down before a county team. The victories when analysed do not make by any means an overwhelming show, and forming an opinion from them alone it would be difficult to prove how strong the team really were. More conclusive evidence of their great qualities could be found in the fact that they met England five times and did not once suffer defeat. I am personally of opinion that the plan adopted for the first time in this country of playing five test matches had a somewhat prejudicial effect upon the tour as a whole, the players, as was almost inevitable under the circumstances, saving themselves more than in former trips for the big events. The team were far too strong in batting to be in danger of being beaten by weak sides on hard wickets, and though I would not for a moment suggest that they were ever slack or careless in their cricket I think they took some of their smaller engagements rather lightly. Certain of their ability to make a lot of runs they went into the field without anxiety, and were not, as it seemed to me, greatly dissatisfied at playing for three days without arriving at a definite result. This criticism, however, only applies with any force to the latter part of the tour, when, no doubt, the men were becoming a little stale and weary. Probably if the exceptional nature of the summer could have been foreseen one or two dates would have been left blank in order to give the men a rest. Only at the last moment was it determined to bring over fourteen players, but Darling and Major Wardill must, when Hill's health gave way, have been glad indeed that the extra man was included in the side. With match after match played on hard wickets the resources of the team were severely taxed, and more than once Worrall went into the field far too lame to do himself justice.

As they won the only test match that was brought to a definite conclusion the honours of the season clearly rested with them. Up to a certain point they established a regular scare, thoroughly outplaying England at Trent Bridge and then gaining in the most brilliant fashion a ten-wickets victory at Lord's. The England side at Lord's was certainly not so well chosen as it might have been, a great mistake being made in allowing the fast bowling to depend entirely upon Jessop, but the match was won with so much to spare that those who took a pessimistic view of England's prospects in the remaining fixtures seemed to have ample cause for their despondency. As everyone knows, however, the subsequent play was such as to put English cricketers once more on excellent terms with themselves. Differing from the general opinion the Australians, I believe, thought they would have won at Leeds if, without the rain coming on, it had been possible to play the match out, but be this as it may the England eleven played a fine game, and with the least bit of luck to help them on the second afternoon would very likely have scored a victory without a third day being necessary. The Australians in their second innings had five wickets down for 39 and then for the best part of an hour they had literally to struggle for their runs against Young and J. T. Hearne's superb bowling. In the end they ran up a score of 224, but though their performance was a miracle of resolution they would not once in ten times under the same conditions have obtained such a total. I have never seen a bowler beat the bat to the extent that Young did and yet never have the good fortune to hit the wicket. In judging the Leeds match, too, it must be remembered that Briggs's sudden illness left England on the second day without a good slow bowler. It is useless to speculate as to what would have happened if rain had not prevented play on the Saturday, but the number left for England to get was smaller than the total obtained in any one of the three previous innings, so that, on paper at least, the draw was in England's favour. In the two subsequent matches, at Old Trafford and The Oval, English batting at last asserted itself, and on both occasions the Australians, with no prospect of victory, had to devote all their energies to the task of avoiding defeat. They showed great qualities in playing for a draw – Noble's defence at Manchester being the most remarkable thing of the sort I have ever seen – but for all that the chief honours of the two games were clearly with the Englishmen. Personally I do not think that in any one of the five matches we were so well armed as the Australians at every point – being always to my mind a bowler short – but, allowing for the loss to the Australians involved at Manchester and The Oval in Clement

Hill's absence, one is fairly entitled to say that there was no such disparity between Australian and English cricket in 1899 as the matches at Nottingham and Lord's had suggested. Even if nothing else had been done for England the magnificent score of 576 at The Oval – when more than half the batsmen played a false game to save time – would have gone far to sustain our prestige.

Unlike most of the previous teams the Australians were seen at their very best at Lord's. Playing there four times they gained four brilliant victories, defeating – in addition to England – the MCC in June and July, and Middlesex in August. The MCC were not so well represented as they ought to have been, but inasmuch as they won the toss on both occasions the crushing defeats they suffered were somewhat humiliating. In the return match the Australians were seen to extreme advantage, for though the first day's cricket went all against them they had the game in their hands when stumps were drawn on the second evening. Outside the England and MCC matches the Australians perhaps did nothing better than their wins against Surrey and Cambridge University, their draw with Yorkshire at Bradford, and the victory over the South of England at Hastings with which they brought their tour to a close. In the mere fact of their beating Cambridge there was nothing, but the way in which they won the game after the University had played a first innings of over 400 was astounding.

To my thinking the one weakness of the Australians was their inability on so many occasions to actually win within the space of three days against opponents far inferior to themselves. Leaving that one point aside they formed as fine a combination as one could wish to see got together for touring purposes. In picking the side not a single mistake had been committed, every man sooner or later during the trip proving worthy of his place. In saying this I might be tempted to leave out Johns, but, as a matter of fact, the Victorian wicket-keeper was afforded so few opportunities that it would be quite unfair to describe him as a failure. Inasmuch as he came here as a representative cricketer and by no means as a mere understudy for Kelly, I think he ought to have been played more often, though by reason alone of his great inferiority as a batsman he had no claim to be chosen in the Test matches. Except as regards the management of his wicket-keepers Darling proved himself one of the very best captains that ever took a team into the field. In following Harry Trott he was of necessity judged by the highest standard, and it is only the truth to say that he exceeded all anticipations. He placed the field with the nicest skill according to the peculiarities of different batsmen, and like Trott he showed a perfect genius for changing his bowling, always seeming to put the right bowler on at the right time and at the proper end. The way in which he utilised Jones's pace was in itself sufficient to prove him a great leader. Judged by general results the batting of the Australians was stronger than the bowling, but in this connection I think figures were to some extent fallacious. The bowlers, it is true, suffered a good deal in many of the smaller fixtures, but apart from the England matches at Manchester and The Oval they nearly always did wonderful work when any special effort was demanded of them. Perhaps by reason of old associations I cannot bring myself to believe that Jones, Trumble, Howell, Noble and McLeod were equal to the famous group of 1882 – Spofforth, Palmer, Boyle, Garratt and Giffen – but allowing for the enormous difference in the character of the seasons there may not have been very much to choose. It struck me that Jones bowled with a fairer action than in 1896, and though there were occasions – notably the opening fixture at the Crystal Palace and the England match at Manchester – when his delivery was far from satisfactory there can be no doubt, I think, that he strove to keep within the law. This being the case it was gratifying to find that he lost nothing either in pace or effectiveness. The team owed him far more than could be gleaned from his average, the four victories at Lord's being due in large measure to his efforts. Trumble bowled quite as well as in 1896, the falling off in his average being more than accounted for by the number of dry wickets on which he had to play. He never seemed easy to hit, and whenever the ground gave him the least advantage, as for example in the first match with Surrey and the opening stage of the return with that county, he was deadly, his off break, in combination with an accuracy of pitch that would have done credit to Alfred Shaw in his best day, being far too much for the majority of the batsmen. He was particularly skilful in bowling his slow, dropping ball, and with it had the satisfaction in the England matches of deceiving both Jackson and MacLaren, the result in each case being that the ball was played straight back into his hands. It is likely enough that if he had not been such a wonderful success as a batsman Noble would have done great things with the ball, but as it was he scarcely came up to expectation, proving comparatively ineffective in the latter half of the season and failing to secure his 100 wickets. On his good days, however, he always looked extremely difficult to play, notably in the England match at Leeds and the later part of the return match with the MCC at Lord's. I am bound to add – somewhat reluctantly – that the fairness of his delivery was often questioned by those who played against him. No one alleged that his action was habitually unfair, but that he threw now and then scarcely seemed to be disputed. In this connection I may mention that on the first morning the team practised at Lord's at the beginning of May I had not been on the ground ten minutes before three people – quite independent of one another – told me that Noble's action was questionable. Howell, without realising all the hopes raised by his wonderful performance against Surrey in May, proved himself a first-rate bowler, and seemed just as good at the end of the tour as he had been at the beginning. Taking one day with another, however, I do not think he did so much with the ball on hard wickets as had been expected. Still, he always looked to have plenty of spin, and for subtle variations of pace without apparent change of action it would be hard to find his superior. McLeod, by reason of his failures as a batsman, did not till the tour was nearly three parts over have much chance of bowling on big occasions, but in August he suddenly came out in first-rate form. In the Warwickshire match at Birmingham circumstances compelled him to bowl, contrary to his usual practice, round the wicket and he found the new method answer uncommonly well, the ball going away with his arm in a very puzzling fashion. Laver on occasions was a successful change bowler, his best work being done on the last day of the England match at Lord's when, with tempting half volleys pitched wide of the off stump, he got rid of Hayward, Tyldesley and Jessop in a few overs and destroyed England's last chance of avoiding defeat.

Of the Australian batting one might write columns and yet leave the subject unexhausted. Certainly no travelling team has ever possessed a band of more consistent run-getters. Having regard to the character of the summer not one of them came out with an astonishing record, but in a collective sense the strength was overwhelming. A side so difficult to get rid of on hard wickets has certainly never before been sent to England from the Colonies. Clement Hill, Noble, Darling, Worrall and Trumper formed in themselves a superb combination, and in addition the team included Gregory, Iredale, Trumble, Kelly, Laver and McLeod. No wonder, with the sun shining day after day, that the scoring was high. Personally, I think Hill was the best bat of the lot, but there can be very little to choose between him and Darling, judging the latter on his form in August. Up to a certain point the responsibilities of captaincy seemed to tell against Darling, but during the last weeks of the tour he played marvellous cricket. Except against Oxford and in the first match against the MCC he did not in the early part of the season do anything out of the common. Very few Australian batsmen coming to England for the first time have approached the form shown by Noble and Trumper. They were quite different in style and method, Noble developing an amount of caution for which his colleagues were in no way prepared, while Trumper by his free and attractive cricket made himself, for a time at least, the most popular member of the eleven. To Trumper fell the honour of making the highest score ever obtained by an Australian in England – 300 not out against Sussex at Brighton. It is possible that of the two Trumper may have the more brilliant future, but at present Noble, by reason of his finer defence and inexhaustible patience, is the greater personality on a side. I am, of course, speaking just now of batting alone, for as an all-round man Noble has had no equal in Australia except George Giffen. To Worrall's batting I have already referred incidentally. The veteran of the team, he alone preserved the old tradition of fearless fast-footed hitting, and it was wonderful that he should have done so well when so sadly handicapped by his injured knee. He did his best on the most important occasions, playing splendid cricket against England at Leeds, Manchester and

The Oval. Gregory, taking the whole summer through, was by no means the man he had been three years before, but he played a great innings against England at The Oval, and though he may be a little past his best there is evidently plenty of cricket left in him. Iredale wound up with a good average, but it would be idle to say that he added to the reputation he had gained in 1896. He is, and always has been, such an uncertain beginner that one hesitates to place him quite in the front rank of Australian batsmen. McLeod, when he at last ran into form, proved himself a capital batsman of the steady modern school, and Frank Laver, for all his ungainliness of style, made a good number of runs. Trumble, who alone in the team accomplished the double feat of scoring a thousand runs and taking a hundred wickets, played so consistently well as to make it clear that if he had not been a bowler he would have been a great batsman. Kelly as a bat has no graces of style but, like Blackham before him, he is by reason of his strong nerve the very man to face a crisis. It was said that he missed a good many catches when standing back to Jones's bowling, but considering the enormous amount of work he had to do he kept wicket wonderfully well. As a fielding side the Australians on their best days were unsurpassable. Jones at mid-off was better than anyone I have ever seen in the same position; Gregory at cover point seemed as good as ever, and two better points than Noble and Laver could not at the present time be found in any eleven in the world. Trumper, too, as an out-field reached the highest standard. All through their long tour the team worked admirably together both on and off the field, Major Wardill as manager having a far pleasanter task than when he was here in 1886.

S. H. P.

AUSTRALIAN RESULTS – ALL MATCHES

Played 35 – *Won 16, Lost 3, Drawn 16.*

TEST MATCHES

Played 5 – *Won 1, Drawn 4.*

AUSTRALIANS v ESSEX

Played at Leyton, May 11, 12, 13, 1899

In some respects this was the most sensational match of the whole tour. After the form they had shown at the Crystal Palace no one imagined the Australians would be defeated, but as it turned out Essex beat them on the third morning by 126 runs. The wicket – unsound to begin with, and much affected by heavy dews – was always difficult and as the game went on runs proved harder and harder to get. Early in their second innings Essex did not seem at all likely to win, three wickets being lost for eight runs, but McGahey and Turner – both favoured by luck just after they went in – played splendid cricket, putting on 93 runs together and quite turning the fortunes of their side. Young won the match for Essex on the Saturday morning and at the same time establishing his fame as a bowler. He was practically unplayable, pitching outside the off stump and turning in six or eight inches with his arm.

Essex

Mr H. G. Owen c Darling b Trumble	28 – c Iredale b Jones	6
H. Carpenter b McLeod	23 – c Kelly b Trumble	2
Mr P. Perrin lbw b Trumble	5 – c Iredale b Jones	0
Mr C. McGahey b Trumble	12 – b McLeod	39
Mr A. J. Turner b Trumble	0 – b Trumble	54
T. M. Russell b Trumble	22 – st Kelly b McLeod	14
Mr A. P. Lucas not out	46 – not out	8
Mr F. L. Fane b Trumble	0 – b Trumble	0
W. Mead c Darling b Trumble	4 – b McLeod	8
Mr F. G. Bull c Noble b Trumble	11 – c and b Trumble	2
H. Young b Jones	33 – c Jones b McLeod	0
B 4, l-b 11	15 B 8, l-b 2, n-b 1	11
	199	144

Australians

F. A. Iredale c Carpenter b Bull	4 – c Turner b Mead	0
J. Darling c Russell b Bull	5 – b Young	15
C. Hill c Fane b Young	36 – c Lucas b Young	4
S. E. Gregory c Russell b Young	21 – b Young	8
J. J. Kelly b Mead	16 – b Young	6
M. A. Noble run out	5 – b Mead	17
V. Trumper b Young	0 – b Young	3
F. Laver c and b Mead	9 – not out	0
C. E. McLeod not out	20 – b Young	6
H. Trumble b Mead	6 – b Mead	0
E. Jones b Young	6 – b Young	5
B 14, l-b 2	16 B 4, l-b 5	9
	144	73

Australian Bowling

	Overs	Mdns	Runs	Wkts	Overs	Mdns	Runs	Wkts
Jones	12.2	4	27	1	18	3	30	2
McLeod	21	11	45	1	15	6	32	4
Trumble	33	7	79	8	36	16	52	4
Noble	19	8	33	0	10	5	16	0
Laver					4	3	3	0

Essex Bowling

	Overs	Mdns	Runs	Wkts	Overs	Mdns	Runs	Wkts
Bull	10	2	30	2				
Mead	31	12	56	3	15	6	32	3
Young	27	11	42	4	14.4	6	32	7

Umpires: M. Sherwin and W. Hearn.

AUSTRALIANS v SURREY

Played at The Oval, May 15, 16, 17, 1899

On the Monday following their defeat at Leyton the Australians played their first match at The Oval and lost no time in reasserting themselves. Though they had the bad luck to lose the toss on a soft wicket they outplayed Surrey completely, winning the game by an innings and 71 runs. Howell, who had not played either at the Crystal Palace or Leyton, made a sensational first appearance in England, taking all ten wickets in Surrey's first innings and having a record for the whole game of fifteen wickets for 57 runs. Well as he often bowled later in the tour he never did anything to approach this extraordinary performance. Apart from Hayes's vigorously hit 43 in the second innings the Surrey eleven had nothing on which to congratulate themselves. With Lockwood prevented from playing by a bad leg, their bowling was very weak and the batting gave no suggestion of the great things afterwards done by the team on the same ground. The Australian batting on the other hand was very consistent, Kelly, who hit ten 4s, doing particularly well. On the second day rain restricted the cricket to forty minutes.

Surrey

R. Abel b Howell	22	– b Howell	0
W. Brockwell b Howell	29	– c Darling b Howell	7
E. G. Hayes b Howell	12	– c Darling b Howell	43
Mr D. L. A. Jephson c Darling b Howell	16	– lbw b Trumble	0
T. Hayward b Howell	16	– c Kelly b Howell	6
Mr H. B. Richardson b Howell	5	– c and b Trumble	1
F. C. Holland c and b Howell	2	– b Trumble	1
Mr K. J. Key not out	4	– b Trumble	0
Clode b Howell	0	– b Howell	3
T. Richardson b Howell	2	– b Trumble	2
C. Marshall b Howell	0	– not out	0
B 6	6	B 1	1
	114		64

Australians

J. Worrall b T. Richardson	22	C. E. McLeod c Key b Hayward	4
J. Darling b Clode	10	J. J. Kelly not out	50
C. Hill c T. Richardson b Hayes	29	H. Trumble b Hayes	11
S. E. Gregory b T. Richardson	36	W. Howell b Hayward	6
M. A. Noble c Holland b T. Richardson	16	B 1, l-b 3, n-b 1	5
F. A. Iredale c Abel b Clode	47		
V. Trumper b Hayward	13		249

Australian Bowling

	Overs	Mdns	Runs	Wkts	Overs	Mdns	Runs	Wkts
Noble	7	1	25	0				
Howell	23.2	14	28	10	15	6	29	5
Trumble	22	8	44	0	14.1	4	34	5
McLeod	8	4	11	0				

Surrey Bowling

	Overs	Mdns	Runs	Wkts
Richardson	29	9	62	3
Clode	26	7	68	2
Brockwell	12	4	23	0
Hayward	18	1	62	3
Hayes	7	1	26	2
Jephson	2	0	3	0

Umpires: J. Moss and V. A. Titchmarsh.

AUSTRALIANS v LANCASHIRE

Played at Manchester, May 25, 26, 1899

Lancashire have been curiously unsuccessful in their matches against the various Australian teams, never having won a match except in 1888. The game under notice resulted in a severe disaster to them, the Australians winning on the second afternoon by an innings and 84 runs. The victory was fairly earned by brilliant all-round cricket, but fortune was on the side of the winners, the wicket, though always helping the bowlers more or less, being far more difficult on the second day than on the first. All the same it was a capital performance on the part of the Australians to play a first innings of 267. Up to a certain point there was no suggestion of such a score being made, five of the best wickets going down before lunch time for 65 runs. Gregory played in a way so foreign to his ordinary style that it took him three-quarters of an hour to get four. After lunch the character of the batting entirely changed, the last four wickets putting on 202 runs. Trumper played superb cricket on the slow ground, his defence being most watchful and his pulling accurate to a degree. On the second day the Lancashire batsmen were for the most part helpless, but Tyldesley played wonderfully well, his fine cricket under difficulties going far to secure him his place in the England eleven a week later at Trent Bridge.

Australians

F. A. Iredale c Mold b Cuttell	21
J. J. Darling c Ward b Cuttell	16
C. Hill c Ainsworth b Cuttell	11
S. E. Gregory c Bardswell b Briggs	4
J. Worrall c Hartley b Briggs	12
M. A. Noble c Mold b Cuttell	0
V. Trumper b Baker	82
J. J. Kelly b Briggs	36
C. E. McLeod b Cuttell	1
H. Trumble b Cuttell	51
W. P. Howell not out	20
B 6, l-b 6, w 1	13
	267

Lancashire

G. R. Baker c Iredale b Howell	0	c Hill b Trumble	0
Mr G. R. Bardswell c and b Trumble	0	b Howell	0
L. Radcliffe b Trumble	6	not out	0
A. Mold b Howell	0	c Worrall b Trumble	1
A. Ward b McLeod	8	run out	6
J. T. Tyldesley c and b Noble	56	c and b Howell	42
Mr A. Eccles b Noble	5	b Howell	0
Mr C. R. Hartley c Trumble b Noble	5	c Kelly b Noble	1
W. R. Cuttell c Worrall b McLoed	11	b Trumble	4
J. Briggs b Noble	0	c and b Trumble	1
Mr J. L. Ainsworth not out	0	c Noble b Trumble	0
B 6, l-b 3, n-b 2	11	B 8, l-b 7, w 1	16
	102		81

Lancashire Bowling

	Overs	Mdns	Runs	Wkts
Cuttell	53	19	83	6
Ainsworth	32	15	74	0
Briggs	36	10	70	3
Mold	5	3	4	0
Baker	9	1	23	1

Australian Bowling

	Overs	Mdns	Runs	Wkts	Overs	Mdns	Runs	Wkts
Trumble	21	10	18	2	14	5	20	5
Howell	16	9	26	2	13.1	7	16	3
McLeod	19	6	29	2	7	2	12	0
Noble	15.3	4	18	4	8	4	17	1

Umpires: M. Sherwin and T. Mycroft.

AUSTRALIANS v CAMBRIDGE UNIVERSITY

Played at Cambridge, June 8, 9, 10, 1899

This was in many respects an extraordinary game, the Australians in face of a first innings of 436 by their opponents winning by ten wickets. At the start of play on the third morning a draw seemed certain, but the Australians, after carrying their overnight score of 331 for seven wickets to 436, got the University out in double quick time. They left themselves an hour and a half in which to get the 123 runs they required and won the game with just over a quarter of an hour to spare, Darling and Worrall scoring at the finish 74 runs in twenty-eight minutes. On perhaps no other occasion did the Australians show such dazzling cricket.

Cambridge University

Mr L. J. Moon c Noble b Howell	138	– c Iredale b Jones	18
Mr E. R. Wilson lbw b Noble	12	– b Howell	0
Mr J. H. Stogdon b Noble	43	– st Johns b Howell	3
Mr S. H. Day c Darling b Jones	17	– b Jones	0
Mr G. L. Jessop b Howell	13	– c Jones b Howell	11
Mr T. L. Taylor b Howell	110	– retired hurt	4
Mr G. E. Winter b Howell	16	– c Gregory b Howell	24
Mr R. N. R. Blaker c Howell b McLeod	26	– b Howell	0
Mr E. F. Penn lbw b Noble	21	– b McLeod	27
Mr A. E. Hind c Worrall b Noble	2	– lbw b Howell	14
Mr H. H. B. Hawkins not out	11	– not out	11
B 13, l-b 14	27	B 6, l-b 4	10
	436		122

Australians

J. Worrall c Wilson b Jessop	8	– not out	53
J. Darling b Hind	0	– not out	60
C. Hill c Hawkins b Jessop	160		
M. A. Noble c Taylor b Jessop	8		
S. E. Gregory c Moon b Wilson	102		
F. A. Iredale c Taylor b Jessop	40		
V. Trumper c Wilson b Jessop	3		
C. McLeod c Stogdon b Jessop	2		
E. Jones c Winter b Wilson	53		
W. P. Howell not out	49		
A. E Johns c Moon b Wilson	4		
B 3, n-b 4	7	B 6, l-b 3, n-b 2	11
	436		124

Australian Bowling

	Overs	Mdns	Runs	Wkts	Overs	Mdns	Runs	Wkts
Jones	43	7	124	1	23	8	48	2
Noble	29	3	105	4	1	0	1	0
McLeod	19	4	68	1	1.1	0	2	1
Howell	28.4	6	91	4	20	3	61	6
Worrall	6	1	15	0				
Gregory	1	0	6	0				

Cambridge University Bowling

	Overs	Mdns	Runs	Wkts	Overs	Mdns	Runs	Wkts
Jessop	35	3	142	6	11	1	33	0
Hind	22	3	60	1	11	1	55	0
Wilson	25.2	1	145	3				
Hawkins	9	0	34	0	2.1	0	9	0
Penn	7	1	24	0	2	0	16	0
Winter	3	0	24	0				

Umpires: M. Sherwin and A. A. White.

ENGLAND v AUSTRALIA

Played at Lord's, June 15, 16, 17, 1899

The second of the Test matches was the only one of the five brought to a definite conclusion, and its result was a heavy blow to English cricket, the Australians gaining a brilliant victory on the third afternoon by ten wickets. They played a winning game all the way through, fairly beating the Englishmen at every point. The match, indeed, furnished one of the most complete triumphs gained by Australian cricketers in England since Gregory's team came over and astonished us in 1878. Without in any way attempting to make excuses for an overwhelming defeat, it must be said that the committee in picking the England eleven laid themselves open to obvious criticism. They made no fewer than five changes from the side that had done duty at Trent Bridge a fortnight before, A. C. MacLaren, Townsend, G. L. Jessop, Lilley and Mead taking the places of W. G. Grace, William Gunn, Hirst, Storer and J. T. Hearne. As regards batting, they were probably right to leave out Grace and Gunn, but having done that they ought assuredly to have invited Shrewsbury to play. The Nottingham batsman had given conclusive evidence that he was in form, and with Grace standing down there would have been no difficulty about his fielding at point. A still more serious blunder, however, was committed in connection with the bowling. It was tempting providence to go into the field on a fine day at Lord's with no other fast bowler than Jessop, and it was a dangerous experiment – by no means justified by results – to give Walter Mead the preference over J. T. Hearne on the latter's favourite ground. There was, too, some risk in playing MacLaren, who had not so far taken part in any first-class cricket during the season. In this case, however, the committee had reason to congratulate themselves, MacLaren playing a magnificent second innings and making a great, though fruitless, effort to save the game.

The Englishmen really lost the match during the first hour or so on the opening day. They won the toss and when they went in to bat on a carefully-prepared wicket it was confidently expected they would stay for the whole of the afternoon. To the dismay of the crowd, however, six wickets went down for 66 runs – a deplorable start from which the team were never able to recover. Jackson and Jessop by putting on 95 runs together saved their side from complete collapse, but Jackson, who played a superb innings, might have been run out by several yards when England's score stood at 70. It was felt when the innings ended for 206 – Jones's terrific bowling being the chief cause of the breakdown – that the Australians had an immense advantage, and so it proved. For a little time there seemed some chance of an even game, Worrall, Darling and Gregory being got rid of for 59 runs, but thenceforward the Australians were always winning. The turning point of the game was the partnership of Clement Hill and Noble. The two batsmen had carried the score from 59 to 156 at the drawing of stumps, and on the following morning they took the total to 189 before Noble left. Then came another good partnership, Hill and Trumper putting Australia well in front with six wickets in hand, and increasing the score to 271. At this point Hill was brilliantly caught by Fry in the deep field. Later on Trumper found a valuable partner in Trumble, and it was not until after four o'clock that the Australian innings ended, the total reaching 421, or 215 runs ahead. In their different styles Hill and

Trumper, who curiously enough made exactly the same score, played magnificent cricket. Trumper's innings was by far the more brilliant of the two, but inasmuch as Hill went in while there was still a chance of an even game, and had to play the English bowling at its best, it is only right to say that the left-handed batsman had the greater share in the ultimate success of his side. Hill, who was missed at slip by Ranjitsinhji when he had made 119, was batting just over four hours, and hit seventeen 4s, seven 3s and eighteen 2s. Trumper, who so far as could be seen gave no chance whatever, hit twenty 4s, four 3s and six 2s, and was at the wickets for three hours and a quarter.

Going in for the second time against a balance of 215, the Englishmen had a very gloomy outlook, and their position was desperate when at 23 their third wicket went down, the batsmen out being Fry, Ranjitsinhji and Townsend. Hayward and Jackson made things look a little better, but just before the time for drawing stumps Jackson was easily caught and bowled in playing forward at Trumble, the total at the close being 94. Hayward batted well, but when he had made a single he was palpably missed by the wicket-keeper, standing back to Jones. On the third morning MacLaren joined Hayward, and so long as these two batsmen stayed together there was still a chance of England making something like a fight. Indeed, things were looking comparatively cheerful when 150 went up without further loss. However, on Laver being tried Hayward, Tyldesley and Jessop were caught in quick succession, and with seven wickets down for 170 the match was as good as over. MacLaren, who so long as Hayward stayed in had been steadiness itself, hit in wonderful form from the time that Lilley joined him, but despite his efforts England were all out for 240. Never has MacLaren played a greater innings. The Australians only required 26 runs – a trifling number, which after lunch Darling and Worrall obtained without being separated.

England

Mr C. B. Fry c Trumble b Jones	13	– b Jones	4
Mr A. C. MacLaren b Jones	4	– not out	88
K. S. Ranjitsinhji c and b Jones	8	– c Noble b Howell	0
Mr C. L. Townsend st Kelly b Howell	5	– b Jones	8
Mr F. S. Jackson b Jones	73	– c and b Trumble	37
T. Hayward b Noble	1	– c Trumble b Laver	77
J. T. Tyldesley c Darling b Jones	14	– c Gregory b Laver	4
Mr G. L. Jessop c Trumper b Trumble	51	– c Trumble b Laver	4
A. A. Lilley not out	19	– b Jones	12
W. Mead b Jones	7	– lbw b Noble	0
W. Rhodes b Jones	2	– c and b Noble	2
B 2, l-b 6, w 1	9	B 2, l-b 2	4
	206		240

Australia

J. Worrall c Hayward b Rhodes	18	– not out	11
J. Darling c Ranjitsinhji b Rhodes	9	– not out	17
C. Hill c Fry b Townsend	135		
S. E. Gregory c Lilley b Jessop	15		
M. A. Noble c Lilley b Rhodes	54		
V. Trumper not out	135		
J. J. Kelly c Lilley b Mead	9		
H. Trumble c Lilley b Jessop	24		
F. Laver b Townsend	0		
E. Jones c Mead b Townsend	17		
W. P. Howell b Jessop	0		
L-b 4, n-b 1	5		
	421		28

Australian Bowling

	Overs	Mdns	Runs	Wkts	Overs	Mdns	Runs	Wkts
Jones	36.1	11	88	7	36	15	76	3
Howell	14	4	43	1	31	12	67	1
Noble	15	7	39	1	19.4	8	37	2
Trumble	15	9	27	1	15	6	20	1
Laver					16	4	36	3

English Bowling

	Overs	Mdns	Runs	Wkts	Overs	Mdns	Runs	Wkts
Jessop	37.1	10	105	3	6	0	19	0
Mead	53	24	91	1				
Rhodes	39	14	108	3	5	1	9	0
Jackson	18	6	31	0				
Townsend	15	1	50	3				
Ranjitsinhji	2	0	6	0				
Hayward	6	0	25	0				

Umpires: T. Mycroft and W. A. J. West.

AUSTRALIANS v SUSSEX

Played at Brighton, July 27, 28, 29, 1899

This was a memorable match in which the Australians, although they did not win, covered themselves with distinction. Though they had to go in against a total of 414 they had all the best of the draw, and on the Saturday afternoon there seemed quite a possibility that they would gain a victory, Sussex, with two hours left for play, quickly losing three of their best wickets to Jones's bowling. Then, however, Killick and Collins saved the situation. Trumper, with his 300, not out, made a record score for an Australian batsman in England, beating the 286, not out, obtained on the same ground by W. L. Murdoch in 1882. Trumper was batting for six hours and twenty minutes, his play from first to last being of the most perfect character.

Sussex

Mr C. B. Fry c Trumble b McLeod	181	– c and b Jones	10
Mr G. Brann b McLeod	24	– b Jones	0
K. S. Ranjitsinhji b McLeod	5	– c Darling b Jones	15
E. H. Killick b McLeod	106	– b Hill	57
F. W. Marlow c Trumper b Trumble	34	– not out	20
Mr A. Collins not out	35	– not out	31
J. Vine b Trumble	4		
F. Parris c Noble b Jones	9		
F. W. Tate c Trumble b McLeod	1		
H. R. Butt c Kelly b Trumble	5		
C. H. G. Bland c Laver b Trumble	0		
L-b 10	10	B 6, l-b 4	10
	414		143

Australians

H. Trumble b Bland	26	J. Darling not out	56
J. Worrall c Brann b Killick	128		
V. Trumper not out	300	B 9, n-b 4	13
S. E. Gregory st Butt b Killick	73		
C. Hill c Butt b Brann	28	(4 wkts dec.)	624

M. A. Noble, F. Laver, J. J. Kelly, C. E. McLeod and E. Jones did not bat.

Australian Bowling

	Overs	Mdns	Runs	Wkts	Overs	Mdns	Runs	Wkts
Jones	44	9	147	1	17	4	30	3
Noble	21	9	31	0	3	1	11	0
Trumble	32.4	6	75	4	18	7	53	0
McLeod	48	20	91	5	6	3	7	0
Laver	5	0	26	0	1	1	0	0
Worrall	4	1	15	0				
Gregory	4	1	19	0				
Hill					5	0	16	1
Kelly					3	0	16	0

Sussex Bowling

	Overs	Mdns	Runs	Wkts
Tate	35	6	113	0
Bland	38	4	170	1
Parris	23	6	69	0
Ranjitsinhji	8	1	29	0
Killick	28	6	80	2
Brann	29	5	70	1
Vine	14	3	52	0
Collins	8	2	28	0

Umpires: V. A. Titchmarsh and W. Hearn.

AUSTRALIANS v HAMPSHIRE

Played at Southampton, August 3, 4, 5, 1899

This was not one of the most interesting of the Australian matches, for only at one point on the third day did there seem any likelihood of a definite result being arrived at. When danger threatened, however, Major Poore and Captain Wynyard stayed together for an hour and twenty minutes and made a draw practically certain. Quite the feature of the game was the all round play of Llewellyn, a young cricketer from South Africa who, though not qualified, was allowed by the courtesy of the Australians to appear for Hampshire. His bowling – left-hand, slow to medium pace – made a great impression, and as a batsman he proved himself a free and effective hitter. For the Australians, Trumble not only made the highest score, but showed the best cricket. Captain Bradford was no-balled by both umpires for throwing.

Hampshire

Mr A. J. L. Hill c Trumble b Jones	60	– b Trumble	37
Capt. E. G. Wynyard b Howell	79	– b Howell	51
Major R. M. Poore b Howell	29	– lbw b Howell	71
Capt. E. R. Bradford b Jones	0	– not out	6
V. Barton c Trumble b Noble	33	– c and b Trumble	9
Mr C. Robson c McLeod b Trumble	10	– b Trumble	9
Mr G. C. B. Llewellyn b McLeod	72	– c Jones b Howell	21
Mr C. Heseltine c Hill b McLeod	24		
Mr D. A. Steele lbw b Noble	31		
H. Baldwin c Howell b Jones	29		
Sutherland not out	15		
B 4, l-b 6, n-b 1	11	B 4, l-b 2, n-b 2	8
	393		(6 wkts dec.) 212

Australians

J. Worrall c Wynyard b Llewellyn	3	– run out	6
H. Trumble c Baldwin b Llewellyn	83	– b Baldwin	27
M. A. Noble b Llewellyn	20	– b Bradford	1
S. E. Gregory b Llewellyn	4	– not out	36
J. Darling c Barton b Llewellyn	48	– not out	17
C. Hill c Robson b Llewellyn	15		
F. A. Iredale b Bradford	69		
C. McLeod lbw b Sutherland	32		
J. J. Kelly not out	40		
W. P. Howell c Hill b Llewellyn	2		
E. Jones c Steele b Llewellyn	26		
B 9, l-b 7, w 1, n-b 1	18	B 4, n-b 1	5
	360		92

Australian Bowling

	Overs	Mdns	Runs	Wkts	Overs	Mdns	Runs	Wkts
Jones	24.1	10	56	3	16	4	48	0
Howell	34	8	87	2	22.1	9	52	3
Noble	22	3	85	2	7	2	14	0
Trumble	26	5	79	1	30	10	72	3
McLeod	18	2	75	2	5	2	18	0

Hampshire Bowling

	Overs	Mdns	Runs	Wkts	Overs	Mdns	Runs	Wkts
Heseltine	13	2	47	0				
Llewellyn	40	7	132	8	16	4	27	0
Sutherland	9	2	24	1	3	0	11	0
Baldwin	15	4	28	0	7	6	1	1
Hill	17	4	50	0	5	1	20	0
Steele	3	0	10	0	1	0	4	0
Wynyard	7	2	20	0	2	0	6	0
Bradford	11	2	31	1	10	4	18	0

Umpires: H. Pickett and A. A. White.

ENGLAND v AUSTRALIA

Played at The Oval, August 14, 15, 16, 1899

Though like the contests at Nottingham, Leeds, and Manchester, the Test match at the Oval – the fifth and last of the series – ended in a draw, it had one highly satisfactory result. So amazingly good was the batting on the opening day, that English cricketers were once more placed on good terms with themselves, the depression caused by the severe defeat at Lord's in June, being to a very large extent removed. Only once before in a Test match in this country, has a more remarkable display of batting been given on the first day. When stumps were drawn England's score stood at 435 for four wickets, these figures being only inferior to the 363 for two wickets obtained at The Oval by the Australians in 1884. The two performances, indeed, admitted of an even closer comparison than the totals would suggest. In 1884 the Australians played the strict game all the afternoon and gave nothing away, whereas, the Englishmen, last August in order to give themselves a chance of actually winning the game, began to force the pace soon after the score had reached 300 with only one wicket down. MacLaren asked a good deal of his side in instructing them to play false cricket on an occasion when success meant so much in the way of individual glory, but that he took the right course will scarcely be disputed. If by any chance England could have won the game, a full revenge for the defeat at Lord's would have been obtained, and the honours of the season equally divided. The well-meant effort failed, the wicket at The Oval being too good to admit of the Australians being got rid of twice in the time available, but the attempt to win was certainly worth making. MacLaren showed that he cared nothing for his own chances of distinction as distinct from the well-being of the side, for in hitting up his 49 he lifted the ball in a style quite foreign to his ordinary methods. It was a happy thought on MacLaren's part when he won the toss to begin the innings with Jackson and Hayward – the two batsmen who had played the best cricket for England in the previous matches – but the result must have far exceeded his wildest expectations. Such a wonderful start was made that 185 runs were scored for the first wicket, this number beating by fifteen, the fine stand by Mr W. G. Grace and the late William Scotton, for England on the same ground in 1886. Out of the 185 runs Jackson, who was the first to leave scored 118, his innings lasting two hours and fifty minutes. In many respects he played splendid cricket, his off-driving being especially fine, but he was a good deal at fault when facing McLeod, making several bad strokes off that bowler and giving a palpable chance to Trumble at slip when his score stood at 70. A second chance that he offered to Gregory at cover point – also from McLeod's bowling – did not affect the game as he was out before he had obtained another run. On the original batting order Townsend was to go in first wicket down, but by a good piece of generalship – the situation demanded brilliancy and not steady cricket – MacLaren changed his plans and sent Ranjitsinhji in to assist Hayward. Some splendid batting followed and when the innings had been in progress something over four hours 300 went up with only one man out. This was perhaps the happiest moment experienced by England in any of the Test matches last season, the only incident to compare with it being J. T. Hearne's "hat trick" at Leeds. Hayward and Ranjitsinhji put on 131 runs in less than an hour and a half. The former batsman was caught in the slips at 316, and just afterwards having beaten the score obtained at Lord's by Clement Hill and Trumper Hayward at 318 hit a ball into cover-point's hands. From an English point of view Hayward's play in the Test matches was the feature of the whole season. At The Oval for the first time in the five games he had the opportunity of starting his innings when the side were not in difficulties, and nothing could well have been finer than his batting. Risking nothing at the start of the match he took nearly two hours and a half to get his first fifty, doubled his score in an hour and twenty-five minutes, and wound up by making his last 37 runs in forty minutes. Above everything else his innings was remarkable for the perfection of his placing in front of short leg. Watching the game with the utmost closeness, he only made three strokes that could be described as dangerous. After Hayward was out, Fry and MacLaren put on 110 runs in sixty-five minutes, MacLaren being caught in the long-field at 428.

The Englishmen having on the first day made themselves safe against all possibility of defeat, the remainder of the match resolved itself into an effort on their part to snatch a victory in the time that remained and a struggle by the Australians to secure a draw. It cannot be said that there ever looked to be much hope of victory. England's innings ended at twenty minutes to one on Tuesday for 576, this being the largest total ever obtained in a Test in this country. The Australians naturally set themselves to play a steady game, and at the drawing of stumps their score stood at 220 for five wickets, Darling after playing most skilful cricket for two hours and forty minutes, being out in the last over of the day. On the Wednesday the Australians played up in splendid style and saved the match, with so much to spare that in the end they were 30 ahead with five wickets to fall in their second innings. Gregory, in carrying his overnight score of 37 to 117, played finer cricket than on other occasion during the tour. McLeod in both innings showed wonderful defence, and Noble at the end of the afternoon gave one of his best displays. Nothing, however, on this last day was quite so fine as Lockwood's bowling in the morning. By taking in an innings of 352, seven wickets for 71 runs, he showed what his absence had meant to England in the four previous matches. A collection made on Hayward's behalf on the first day resulted in a sum of £131 3s. 6d. being subscribed.

England

Mr F. S. Jackson b Jones	118
T. Hayward c Iredale b McLeod	137
K. S. Ranjitsinhji c Howell b Jones	54
Mr C. B. Fry c Worrall b Jones	60
Mr A. C. MacLaren c Trumper b Trumble	49
Mr C. L. Townsend b Jones	38
Mr W. M. Bradley run out	0
W. H. Lockwood b Trumble	24
Mr A. O. Jones b Noble	31
A. A. Lilley c Iredale b Noble	37
W. Rhodes not out	8
B 9, l-b 6, w 4, n-b 1	20
	576

Australians

H. Trumble c and b Jones	24	– not out	3
J. Worrall c Hayward b Lockwood	55	– c Lilley b Hayward	75
V. Trumper c Lilley b Jones	6	– c and b Rhodes	7
M. A. Noble b Lockwood	9	– not out	69
J. Darling c Fry b Lockwood	71	– run out	6
S. E. Gregory c Jones b Lockwood	117	– b Rhodes	2
F. A. Iredale b Lockwood	9		
J. J. Kelly lbw b Jones	4		
C. McLeod not out	31	– b Rhodes	77
E. Jones b Lockwood	4		
W. P. Howell b Lockwood	0		
B 5, l-b 10, n-b 6, w 1	22	B 7, n-b 4, w 4	15
	352		254

Australian Bowling

	Overs	Mdns	Runs	Wkts
Jones	53	12	164	4
Noble	35.4	12	96	2
Trumble	39	11	107	2
McLeod	43	15	131	1
Howell	15	3	43	0
Worrall	3	0	15	0

English Bowling

	Overs	Mdns	Runs	Wkts	Overs	Mdns	Runs	Wkts
Bradley	29	12	52	0	17	8	32	0
Lockwood	50.3	17	71	7	15	7	33	0
Townsend	5	0	16	0	8	4	9	0
Rhodes	25	2	79	0	22	8	27	3
Jones	30	12	73	3	12	2	43	0
Jackson	14	7	39	0	13	2	54	0
Hayward					11	3	38	1
Fry					2	1	3	0

Umpires: A. A. White and W. Richards.

AUSTRALIANS v MIDDLESEX

Played at Lord's, August 21, 22, 1899

By arrangement, part of the proceeds of this match were given to James Phillips – so well known for years past in connection with both Middlesex and Australian cricket. Invincible at Lord's, the Australians won the match in wonderful style by an innings and 230 runs, the game coming to an end on the second afternoon. Bowling in irresistible form on a wicket that was perhaps a trifle worn, Jones and McLeod were unchanged through both innings of Middlesex. On the first day the game was marred by an unseemly demonstration on the part of the spectators, happily without precedent at Lord's ground. Resenting the extreme caution with which Darling and Iredale were batting, a section of the crowd forgot their manners, cheering ironically when a run was obtained, and at one point whistling the "Dead March in Saul." That his play was monotonous may be judged from the fact that Darling took three hours to get his first 38 runs. His explanation of this extreme slowness was that he was suffering from a painfully bruised heel.

Australians

H. Trumble c MacGregor b Trott	10	J. J. Kelly c Ford b Hearne	10
C. E. McLeod run out	48	F. Laver not out	29
M. A. Noble c R. N. Douglas b Trott	14	E. Jones b Wells	8
S. E. Gregory c MacGregor b Trott	10	W. P. Howell c Wells b Hearne	10
V. Trumper c MacGregor b Trott	62	B 12, l-b 10	22
J. Darling lbw b Wells	111		
F. A. Iredale c Rawlin b Hearne	111		445

Middlesex

Mr P. F. Warner c Darling b McLeod	39	– b Jones	5
Mr J. Douglas b Jones	0	– c Kelly b McLeod	7
Mr L. J. Moon c Howell b McLeod	17	– c Kelly b Jones	0
Mr R. N. Douglas c Darling b McLeod	12	– b Jones	13
J. T. Rawlin c Trumble b McLeod	11	– b Jones	4
Mr F. G. J. Ford b McLeod	0	– c Kelly b Jones	0
A. E. Trott c Howell b McLeod	8	– c Noble b McLeod	43
Mr C. M. Wells b McLeod	7	– c Kelly b McLeod	30
Mr G. MacGregor (capt.) c Laver b Jones	1	– b Jones	4
W. Roche not out	5	– c Kelly b Jones	2
J. T. Hearne c Howell b Jones	1	– not out	0
B 4	4	L-b 1, n-b 1	2
	105		110

Middlesex Bowling

	Overs	Mdns	Runs	Wkts
Trott	49	15	107	4
Hearne	49.2	20	87	3
Ford	14	7	30	0
Rawlin	16	6	41	0
Wells	42	9	82	2
Roche	22	8	66	0
Warner	1	0	10	0

Australian Bowling

	Overs	Mdns	Runs	Wkts	Overs	Mdns	Runs	Wkts
Jones	20.2	5	44	3	20.1	5	40	7
McLeod	20	4	57	7	20	7	68	3

Umpires: A. Shaw and L. Hall.

AUSTRALIANS v MR C. I. THORNTON'S ENGLAND ELEVEN

Played at Scarborough, August 31, September 1, 2, 1899

A storm of rain on the third afternoon caused an eventful match to be left drawn, and in all probability robbed the Australians of a victory, the English eleven at the finish wanting 51 runs to win, with only three wickets to go down. Becoming partners at a very critical time Wainwright and Leveson-Gower put on 50 runs in half an hour and in all added about eighty to the score. Still more remarkable was the bowling of Rhodes, who had never met the Australians before on a treacherous pitch. His success was extraordinary, his analysis after he went on for the second time being four overs and four balls, two maidens, five runs and seven wickets. Three times in the innings he took two wickets with successive balls. Among the Australian bowlers Trumble, on the second day, and Jones on the third did splendid work.

The Australians

H. Trumble c Jones b Smith	60	– c Storer b Rhodes	29
C. E. McLeod c Jones b Smith	26	– b Wainwright	0
V. Trumper c Storer b Rhodes	14	– st Storer b Rhodes	12
M. A. Noble b Smith	23	– lbw b Rhodes	0
J. Darling c and b Wynyard	6	– b Rhodes	20
F. A. Iredale c Rhodes b Wynyard	49	– b Rhodes	0
S. E. Gregory b Hirst	1	– st Storer b Rhodes	0
F. Laver not out	21	– c Leveson-Gower b Rhodes	14
J. J. Kelly c Storer b Smith	4	– c Jackson b Rhodes	0
E. Jones b Wynyard	19	– c Mitchell b Rhodes	2
W. P. Howell c Gunn b Wynyard	0	– not out	6
B 9, l-b 1	10		
	233		83

Mr C. I. Thornton's Eleven

Mr A. O. Jones b Jones	17	– c Darling b McLeod	7
Mr F. S. Jackson b Howell	17	– run out	15
W. Gunn c Iredale b Jones	2	– b Jones	2
Mr F. Mitchell c Laver b Trumble	11	– b Jones	2
Capt. Wynyard c Darling b Trumble	10	– c Darling b Jones	1
W. Storer c Jones b Trumble	19	– c Laver b Jones	10
E. H. Wainwright not out	54	– c Laver b Jones	8
G. H. Hirst c and b Trumble	3	– not out	24
Mr A. D. Leveson-Gower c Noble b Trumble	36	– not out	11
Mr E. Smith b Howell	4		
W. Rhodes c and b Trumble	1		
B 9, l-b 1, w 1	11	W 1	1
	185		81

Mr C. I. Thornton's Eleven Bowling

	Overs	Mdns	Runs	Wkts	Overs	Mdns	Runs	Wkts
Hirst	18	9	28	1				
Rhodes	19	9	27	1	18.4	10	24	9
Wainwright	8	2	13	0	10	2	26	1
Jones	8	1	14	0				
Smith	26	4	94	4	6	2	24	0
Jackson	9	4	17	0	5	2	9	0
Wynyard	15.2	4	30	4				

Australian Bowling

	Overs	Mdns	Runs	Wkts	Overs	Mdns	Runs	Wkts
Jones	13	6	24	2	21	9	35	5
McLeod	17	6	33	0	17	8	27	1
Howell	18	8	31	2	4	1	18	0
Trumble	20	2	70	6				
Noble	5	3	14	0				
Laver	1	0	2	0				

Umpires: T. Emmett and L. Hall.

THE SOUTH AFRICANS IN ENGLAND

SOUTH AFRICANS v GLOUCESTERSHIRE

Played at Bristol, June 28, 29, 30, 1894

On the occasion of their meeting W. G. Grace for the second time, the South Africans received striking evidence of the great cricketer's powers, both with bat and ball. After taking nine wickets he played, as will be seen from the score below, a not-out innings of 129. In the second innings of the South Africans, Halliwell and Frank Hearne gave a fine display, but Gloucestershire won the match very comfortably by five wickets.

South Africans

Mr D. Davey c W. G. b E. M. Grace	49	– c Board b Ferris	3
Mr E. A. Halliwell lbw b W. G. Grace	8	– b Roberts	110
Mr C. O. H. Sewell c Wrathall b W. G. Grace	5	– b Ferris	0
Mr T. Routledge lbw b W. G. Grace	13	– b Ferris	1
F. Hearne b W. G. Grace	56	– b Roberts	104
Mr A. W. Seccull c Board b W. G. Grace	17	– c Brown b Roberts	2
Mr G. Cripps b W. G. Grace	13	– b Roberts	3
Mr H. H. Castens not out	20	– c Brown b W. G. Grace	0
Mr G. Glover lbw b W. G. Grace	0	– not out	17
Mr D. Parkin lbw b W. G. Grace	0	– lbw b W. G. Grace	8
Mr G. Rowe c and b W. G. Grace	0	– st Board b W. G. Grace	6
L-b 4	4	B 7, l-b 1	8
	185		262

Gloucestershire

Mr J. J. Ferris b Parkin	6	– not out	19
Mr R. W. Rice run out	0	– b Glover	35
Wrathall c Halliwell b Parkin	95		
Mr F. Henry b Parkin	0	– b Glover	33
Mr E. M. Grace c Hearne b Rowe	9	– c Seccull b Parkin	29
Mr W. G. Grace not out	129		
Mr W. G. Grace jun. c Hearne b Sewell	33	– not out	15
Mr R. W. Brown b Rowe	6	– b Glover	5
E. R. Murch b Rowe	0	– run out	10
E. G. Roberts c Parkin b Rowe	3		
A. B. Board lbw b Parkin	16		
B 1, l-b 3	4	B 1	1
	301		147

Gloucestershire Bowling

	Overs	Mdns	Runs	Wkts	Overs	Mdns	Runs	Wkts
Grace, jun.	4	0	21	0	5	1	18	0
Roberts	23	12	36	0	29	17	38	4
Grace, sen.	37.2	11	71	9	29.2	3	106	3
Brown	5	1	15	0	12	1	35	0
Murch	5	1	17	0	4	1	13	0
E. M. Grace	2	0	13	1	8	2	16	0
Ferris	9	6	8	0	23	8	28	3

South African Bowling

	Overs	Mdns	Runs	Wkts	Overs	Mdns	Runs	Wkts
Rowe	45	15	95	4	19	7	28	0
Parkin	40	13	108	4	22	8	63	1
Glover	12	2	32	0	16.3	8	24	3
Seccull	7	0	24	0	4	2	5	0
Cripps	2	0	6	0	7	2	15	0
Sewell	7	2	19	1	6	1	11	0
Hearne	4	0	13	0				

SOUTH AFRICANS v SUSSEX

Played at Brighton, July 2, 3, 1894

Meeting Walter Humphreys for the second time, the South Africans were scarcely more successful against the lob bowler than they had been at Sheffield Park, and Sussex won the match in the easiest fashion by nine wickets. The game failed entirely to attract the Brighton public.

Sussex

G. Bean c Halliwell b Kempis	54	– b Routledge	0
F. W. Marlow c Middleton b Glover	75	– not out	4
Mr G. Brann b Johnson	47	– not out	0
Mr W. Newham c Middleton b Glover	2		
Mr G. H. Arlington st Halliwell b Johnson	26		
Mr C. A. Smith b Johnson	0		
Mr A. F. Somerset b Middleton	28		
F. Guttridge b Middleton	20		
H. Butt c Middleton b Glover	4		
W. Humphreys not out	7		
A. Hilton c Middleton b Johnson	1		
B 3, l-b 10, w 1	14		
	278		4

South Africans

Mr T. Routledge c Butt b Guttridge	2	– st Butt b Humphreys	49
Mr C. L. Johnson b Humphreys	12	– st Butt b Humphreys	4
Mr C. O. H. Sewell c and b Humphreys	1	– c Butt b Guttridge	54
F. Hearne c Bean b Humphreys	8	– b Guttridge	4
Mr E. A. Halliwell run out	21	– not out	48
Mr A. W. Seccull c Arlington b Humphreys	9	– b Humphreys	2
Mr G. Cripps b Humphreys	1	– c Somerset b Humphreys	17
Mr H. H. Castens not out	7	– c Brann b Smith	1
Mr G. Glover c Butt b Humphreys	0	– c Marlow b Humphreys	3
Mr G. Kempis b Guttridge	4	– b Guttridge	16
G. Middleton b Guttridge	4	– b Guttridge	10
L-b 2	2	B 4	4
	71		210

South African Bowling

	Overs	Mdns	Runs	Wkts	Overs	Mdns	Runs	Wkts
Johnson	22.2	6	62	4				
Middleton	62	20	88	2				
Glover	32	9	72	3				
Kempis	24	9	42	1				
Routledge					1	1	0	1
Cripps					0.4	0	4	0

Sussex Bowling

	Overs	Mdns	Runs	Wkts	Overs	Mdns	Runs	Wkts
Guttridge	16.1	4	35	3	14.1	4	37	4
Humphreys	16	5	34	6	19	2	86	5
Hilton					13	1	45	0
Smith					7	1	20	1
Bean					6	0	18	0

THE GENTLEMEN OF PHILADELPHIA IN ENGLAND

GENTLEMEN OF PHILADELPHIA v GENTLEMEN OF GLOUCESTERSHIRE

Played at Cheltenham, June 30, July 1, 1884

The very fine bowling of Clark in one innings and of C. A. Newhall in the other, and the thoroughly good all-round play of the visitors throughout the two days, resulted in a most unexpectedly easy and meritorious victory over the Gentlemen of Gloucestershire by 168 runs. The match took place on the new and picturesque ground of the East Gloucestershire Club, and for the fourth time in succession the American captain won the toss. The Gentlemen of Philadelphia began batting in very unpromising form, as, with the score at 19 only, three wickets had fallen. R. S. Newhall, by hard and good hitting, and Morgan, by careful play, then carried the score to 52 before the latter was bowled, and this good stand appeared to inspire the remaining batsmen with confidence, for despite the disastrous start the respectable total of 162 was ultimately reached, MacNutt and C. A. Newhall batting especially well. In direct contrast to their opponents, the Gentlemen of Gloucestershire began well and ended badly. E. M. Grace and Gilbert put on 32 runs for the first wicket, and after Cranston had been dismissed, W. G. Grace and Gilbert made a good stand. When the latter was caught, however, Clark carried all before him, and the Gloucestershire captain could find no one to stay with him, the last seven batsmen on the list contributing only five runs between them. W. G. Grace was the last man out, and fell to a splendid catch at mid-off from a very hard hit which turned the fieldsman completely round. Grace showed his appreciation of this fine piece of fielding by making Thayer a present of his bat on the spot. Up to this point of the game the Grace family – the brothers E. M. and W. G. and Gilbert – had scored 84 runs out of 89 from the bat, and taken 8 out of the ten wickets lowered. In the three-quarters of an hour which remained for play, the visitors, in their second innings, made 65 by some very free hitting, for the loss of only one wicket – Brewster's, Thayer being 35 not out and Scott 23 not out.

Next morning Thayer, by first-class cricket, increased his score to 50. R. S. Newhall quickly made 29 in good form, and four other batsmen contributed double-figure scores. W. G. Grace bowled nearly all through the innings, and again took seven wickets with a good analysis. The total reaching 207, the home team had to go in wanting 276 to win. Except for an excellent innings of 44 by Cranston, but little resistance was offered to the capital bowling of C. A. Newhall, whose fast deliveries proved so difficult to score from that W. G. Grace was at the wickets twenty-one minutes before he made a run. Charles Newhall's five wickets (including the great batsman's) for 24 runs in this innings was the best performance of that bowler on British soil. With the dismissal of the Gloucestershire captain, all hope of saving the match was at an end, and though Leatham hit pluckily at the last, the game was over at 5.15, and the Gentlemen of Gloucestershire were defeated by 168 runs. MacNutt's catch, which got rid of Clowes, was a very fine one, the fieldsman running hard and capturing the ball from a hit to long-on.

Gentlemen of Philadelphia

J. A. Scott c E. M. Grace b W. G. Grace	0	c E. M. Grace b W. G. Grace	28
E. W. Clark b W. G. Grace	10	b W. G. Grace	21
J. B. Thayer b Pemberton	8	b Pemberton	50
R. S. Newhall b W. G. Grace	36	b Leatham	29
W. C. Morgan b W. G. Grace	7	c E. M. Grace b W. G. Grace	1
C. A. Newhall b E. M. Grace	25	c E. M. Grace b W. G. Grace	14
D. P. Stoever c Hattersley-Smith b W. G. Grace	19	b Leatham	4
F. E. Brewster c E. M. Grace b W. G. Grace	4	c Clowes b W. G. Grace	5
H. MacNutt b W. G. Grace	32	c Clowes b W. G. Grace	18
H. Brown b Pemberton	10	not out	14
W. C. Lowry not out	0	c Leatham b W. G. Grace	2
B 7, l-b 4	11	B 19, l-b 1, w 1	21
	162		207

Gentlemen of Gloucestershire

E. M. Grace c Brewster b C. A. Newhall	18	b C. A. Newhall	11
W. R. Gilbert c Clark b C. A. Newhall	25	b Clark	3
J. Cranston c Thayer b Clark	0	c Brown b C. A. Newhall	44
W. G. Grace c Thayer b Clark	41	c Clark b C. A. Newhall	6
G. Francis c Stoever b Clark	1	c Scott b MacNutt	0
Rev. P. Hattersley-Smith b Clark	0	b C. A. Newhall	10
F. L. Cole b Clark	2	c Brown b C. A. Newhall	7
H. Clowes b Clark	0	c MacNutt b Brewster	2
J. Hatton b Clark	0	c Brewster b Lowry	3
A. E. Leatham b C. A. Newhall	0	not out	14
P. Pemberton not out	2	c MacNutt b Lowry	0
B 2, l-b 3	5	B 3, l-b 3, w 1	7
	94		107

Bowling of the Gentlemen of Gloucestershire

	Overs	Mdns	Runs	Wkts	Overs	Mdns	Runs	Wkts
W. G. Grace	41.3	14	68	7	50.2	18	84	7
Pemberton	19	9	28	2	23	11	33	1
Gilbert	8	2	15	—	9	2	19	—
Leatham	7	3	10	—	19	6	38	2
E. M. Grace	7	1	30	1	3	1	12	—

Bowling of the Gentlemen of Philadelphia

	Overs	Mdns	Runs	Wkts	Overs	Mdns	Runs	Wkts
Lowry	9	2	15	—	10.1	6	11	2
C. A. Newhall	27	10	41	3	29	18	24	5
Clark	18.2	4	33	7	30	14	44	1
MacNutt					6	2	12	1
Brewster					5	2	9	1

Umpires: R. Carpenter and C. K. Pullin.

The *American Cricketer* contains the following paragraph with reference to the Gentlemen of Philadelphia:– "During their stay in Cheltenham the cricketers were most hospitably treated. They were made honorary members of the New Club, and were received there cordially on the occasions when use was made of the invitation."

GENTLEMEN OF PHILADELPHIA v LANSDOWN CLUB

Played at Lansdown, near Bath, July 2, 3, 1884

Heavy scoring on both sides caused the tenth match to end in a draw. The home team had first innings, and going in at noon remained at the wickets until just before six o'clock. Grace and Sainsbury made a splendid stand for the first wicket, eight bowlers being tried before a separation could be effected. At the luncheon interval the total stood at 109, and no wicket down, Grace having made 67 and Sainsbury 40. On resuming, the score was taken to 149 before the former was out for a hard-hit innings of 89, which included twelve 4s and six 3s, and was made with one difficult chance. Sainsbury continued batting for another hour, and, altogether, was at the wickets four hours and a quarter for a very finely-played 108, in which he did not make a bad hit. With the score at 60, however, he was, on his own admission, run out, but Wootton, the umpire, gave him in. His chief hits were eight 4s and seven 3s. Trask hit very hard for a somewhat lucky 57, and at the fall of the fifth wicket 290 runs had been totalled. The last five, however, only added 21. Before play concluded for the day Clark and C. A. Newhall were both dismissed, and the first innings of the visitors stood at 20 for two wickets.

Play began at eleven on the second day, and Morgan and Scott, by first-class cricket, carried the score to 135 before the latter ran himself out for a dashing and admirable innings of 80, out of 115 added while he was in. He hit thirteen 4s, three 3s, and five 2s. Morgan was seventh out for a very fine defensive innings of 59, made while 228 runs were put on. Like Sainsbury, he was lucky in being given in when he was unquestionably stumped. Brewster hit with much freedom, but enjoyed some luck, and was the last to leave. Considerable excitement was manifested when the Lansdown total was passed, and the Gentlemen of Philadelphia were heartily cheered on their return to the pavilion. Lansdown, in their second innings, lost one wicket for 18 runs, and then time was called. This was the only match in which Lowry did not play, and it is further noteworthy for the fact that Brewster's 70, Morgan's 59, and Fox's 24 were the highest scores they made during the tour.

Lansdown Club

E. M. Grace lbw b Law	89	– not out	13
E. Sainsbury c Clark b Fox	108		
P. K. Stothert c Stoever b Clark	6		
D. D. Pontifex lbw b Clark	0		
Rev. E. Graham c sub b Thayer	19	– c Fox b Stoever	5
J. E. Trask b Thayer	57		
E. C. B. Ford c Scott b C. A. Newhall	6		
G. T. Mirehouse b C. A. Newhall	6		
L. Porter c Morgan b C. A. Newhall	4		
P. Smith st Morgan b Fox	5		
E. Casson not out	0		
B 8, l-b 3	11		
	311		18

Gentlemen of Philadelphia

E. W. Clark c Sainsbury b Mirehouse	3
W. C. Morgan c Stothert b Mirehouse	59
C. A. Newhall lbw b Trask	6
J. A. Scott run out	80
J. B. Thayer c Stothert b Mirehouse	21
R. S. Newhall b Mirehouse	1
D. P. Stoever st Ford b Grace	1
F. E. Brewster c Trask b Grace	70
S. Law b Trask	19
J. M. Fox c Pontifex b Grace	24
H. MacNutt not out	7
B 13, l-b 10, w 4, n-b 1	28
	319

Bowling of the Gentlemen of Philadelphia

	Overs	Mdns	Runs	Wkts	Overs	Mdns	Runs	Wkts
C. A. Newhall	37	18	50	3				
MacNutt	23	9	46	—				
Clark	22	8	54	2				
Thayer	26	7	42	2	4	1	17	—
Fox	14.2	6	39	2				
Law	11	4	21	1				
Stoever	5	2	25	—	3.3	2	1	1
Brewster	11	4	23	—				

Bowling of the Lansdown Club

	Overs	Mdns	Runs	Wkts
Casson	13	4	49	—
Mirehouse	50	25	75	4
Trask	12	4	33	2
E. M. Grace	30	14	60	3
Smith	12	5	18	—
Sainsbury	26	8	53	—
Porter	2	—	3	—

Umpires: R. Carpenter and Wootton.

GENTLEMEN OF PHILADELPHIA v CASTLETON CLUB

Played at Sparth Bottom, Rochdale, July 4, 5, 1884

Scott, C. A. Newhall and MacNutt stood out of this match, and consequently the easy victory of the visitors by an innings and 16 runs was the more meritorious. The Gentlemen of Philadelphia accomplished a capital batting performance on the opening day, and this was followed up by some wonderfully effective bowling by Lowry, who, with one exception, was never seen to greater advantage throughout the tour. The visitors went in first, but the start was not promising, as two wickets were down at 16. Thayer and R. S. Newhall, however, soon put a different complexion on the game, and hit the bowling to all parts of the field. The batting of both was of the most vigorous description, and while they were together over 100 runs were scored in an hour. Both were out at the same total, and after Stoever and Fox had been dismissed in quick succession, Brewster and Brockie made a good stand. Brockie was the first to leave, and Brewster followed a few runs later for a well-played 45. With the association of Law and Brown, the bowling was for the third time collared, and the former succeeded in carrying out his bat for a capital 51. In the hour, or thereabouts, which remained for play, the Castleton Club lost three men – all caught off Lowry – for 39.

On the morning of the 5th, Lowry followed up his overnight success by taking six out of the seven remaining wickets, Taylor, with a well-played 31, being considerably the highest scorer in the innings. The Castleton Club had to follow-on in a minority of 214, but very vigorous hitting placed 120 on the score before the fourth wicket fell, and it seemed probable that the visitors would have to go in again. Chadwick played admirably for 60, an innings which included seven 4s and three 3s, but when he was beaten by a lob, the wickets fell rapidly, and the home eleven were 38 runs behind when the last man went in. Heavy rain then drove the players to shelter, and a drawn game seemed inevitable, but an opportunity of finishing the match presenting itself, the Castleton captain, with a sportsmanlike determination which greatly pleased the visitors, insisted on resuming play, with the result that Osborne lost his wicket, and the Americans won as before stated.

Gentlemen of Philadelphia

E. W. Clark b Butterworth	11
W. C. Morgan b Taylor	3
J. B. Thayer run out	53
R. S. Newhall c Sawyer b Taylor	64
F. E. Brewster c Taylor b Standring	45
D. P. Stoever b Butterworth	0
W. Brockie c Clegg b Leach	29
J. M. Fox lbw b Clegg	1
S. Law not out	51
H. Brown c Clegg b Taylor	21
W. C. Lowry c Molesworth b Taylor	1
B 9, l-b 5, w 4, n-b 1	19
	298

Castleton Club

R. R. Osborne c Brockie b Lowry	3	b Law	12
W. Standring c Stoever b Lowry	12	c Stoever b Lowry	10
F. Taylor b Lowry	31	c Brewster b Lowry	15
J. H. Clegg c Clark b Lowry	3	c Newhall b Fox	29
E. L. Chadwick c Stoever b Lowry	2	c Brown b Fox	60
A. H. Sawyer c Thayer b Lowry	2	run out	8
A. Molesworth b Law	4	b Lowry	18
J. Leach c Fox b Lowry	2	not out	10
P. Butterworth b Lowry	8	c Law b Lowry	9
E. Leach not out	4	c Fox b Lowry	0
J. Holt b Lowry	10	b Lowry	12
B 3	3	B 10, l-b 3, n-b 2	15
	84		198

Bowling of the Castleton Club

	Overs	Mdns	Runs	Wkts
Butterworth	31	6	70	2
Taylor	26	4	64	4
Leech	10	—	33	1
Clegg	10	2	43	1
Sawyer	9	—	27	—
Holt	7	2	12	—
Chadwick	4	—	17	—
Standring	3	—	13	1

Bowling of the Gentlemen of Philadelphia

	Overs	Mdns	Runs	Wkts	Overs	Mdns	Runs	Wkts
Stoever	20	14	19	—	2	1	4	—
Lowry	30.1	10	51	9	39	7	81	6
Law	10	5	11	1	6.3	4	5	1
Brockie					2	—	12	—
Thayer					2	—	8	—
Clark					8	1	25	—
Fox					24	6	48	2

Umpires: R. Carpenter and Barks.

The correspondent of the *American Cricketer* concluded his account of this match as follows:– "I wish, before I close, to say a few words about the manner in which the glorious Fourth was celebrated. After the conclusion of the first day's play we were entertained at dinner in the pavilion by the Castleton Club. Mr John Standing, one of the prominent men of the town, was in the chair. The Queen and the President were toasted, and the chairman in proposing these toasts did not let us forget what day it was we were celebrating, or what the feeling of Englishmen toward men of English descent, whether dependent or independent, in the old country or in the new England beyond the sea. And then Mr John William Mellor, in proposing the visitors, emphasized the words of the chairman. 'Mark Twain,' he said, 'wept at the tomb of Adam because his ancestors had never known him.' The same mistake was made a hundred years ago. It shall not be repeated. These tours, these matches, these entertainments, are small things in themselves, no doubt; but it is out of these small things that there grows up that feeling of intimacy and brotherhood which assures us of the future.

"Then we prevailed on our friend, Mr Bowen, to make a 'few remarks.' The captain followed with an admirable ten minutes' talk about cricket, thereby proving that on previous occasions, like some bowlers, he had not been 'tried enough.' There were more songs and more speeches; and finally, when the dinner came to an end, we were all well satisfied that there never had been a Fourth more appropriately celebrated.

"Nor were the ladies of our party neglected. There was tea in the scorer's tent on each afternoon, and the number of Rochdale ladies who attended could have been counted by the hundreds. Indeed the general attendance at the ground on both days exceeded our expectations. On the second there must have been between fifteen hundred and two thousand people present to anathematize the weather."

PHILADELPHIANS v GENTLEMEN OF SURREY

Played at The Oval, July 18, 19, 20, 1889

This was the first appearance of the Americans in the metropolis, and the match, which created considerable interest, was certainly productive of some noteworthy performances. The Surrey amateurs were a powerful batting side, including three regular members of the county team – W. W. Read, John Shuter, and K. J. Key – but they had very little bowling; and, with the Americans also presumedly far from strong in this department of the game, it was expected that there would be some very heavy scoring. The spectators were certainly not disappointed, for during the full three days over which the game extended no fewer than 1,150 runs were scored, and even then the match was unfinished, only thirty-three wickets having fallen when it was left drawn. The home side went in first, and, thanks chiefly to Walter Read's 105, scored 294, against which by the call of time on the first day the Philadelphians had made 70 for three wickets. On the Friday, Scott and Morgan scored 169 runs together for the fifth wicket, and in the end the visitors' innings amounted to the enormous total of 458. Of this number Scott contributed 142 without a chance, while Morgan just failed to get his hundred. The Surrey men had then to go in against a majority of 164, and though they lost a wicket that night for 46, and had to bat on Saturday in showery weather, they ultimately succeeded in saving the game. W. W. Read outdid his first achievement by making 130 runs, and as he was helped by J. Shuter's dashing score of 71, the innings reached 355 before it closed – about an hour before time. In this last hour the visitors lost three wickets in making 43 runs, so that the draw was perhaps slightly against them. Of course the most remarkable performance in the match was that of W. W. Read in scoring two individual innings of over 100, a feat that had only been previously accomplished by five players – W. G. Grace (three times), F. W. Maude, W. Townshend, D. G. Spiro, and (in 1817) W. Lambert.

Gentlemen of Surrey

	First innings		Second innings	
Mr W. W. Read c R. Brown b Clark	105	–	c Newhall b Clark	130
Mr L. A. Shuter b Sharp	17	–	c and b Scott	24
Mr C. L. Morgan c Stoever b Scott	32	–	c Patterson b Scott	8
Mr J. Shuter c H. Brown b Scott	3	–	b Scott	71
Mr K. J. Key b Scott	16	–	b Scott	17
Mr F. Fielding c Morgan b Clark	3	–	b Clark	26
Mr T. P. Harvey c R. Brown b Scott	5	–	not out	12
Mr F. W. Freeman b Scott	49	–	b Clark	44
Mr D. L. A. Jephson not out	32	–	st Morgan b Scott	0
Mr C. L. Hemmerde b Scott	15	–	b Clark	15
Mr C. E. Horner c Patterson b Scott	8	–	c Morgan b Clark	0
B 3, l-b 5, w 1	9		B 3, l-b 4, w 1	8
	294			355

Philadelphians

	First innings		Second innings	
Mr G. S. Patterson run out	6	–	not out	2
Mr R. D. Brown c Fielding b Horner	14	–	c Read b Horner	7
Mr W. Scott c Freeman b Jephson	142			
Mr D. P. Stoever st Fielding b Read	24			
Mr E. W. Clark c Morgan b Horner	40			
Mr W. C. Morgan c Key b Read	98			
Mr F. E. Brewster run out	39			
Mr N. Etting b Horner	17	–	c Hemmerde b Jephson	19
Mr D. S. Newhall b Hemmerde	47			
Mr H. I. Brown b Horner	4	–	c Fielding b Horner	14
Mr J. W. Sharp not out	0			
B 15, l-b 9, w 3	27		W 1	1
	458			43

Philadelphians' Bowling

	Overs	Mdns	Runs	Wkts	Overs	Mdns	Runs	Wkts
Clark	44	14	75	2	34	13	82	5
Patterson	19	6	29	0	18	1	50	0
Sharp	17	2	38	1	5	1	20	0
H. I. Brown	17	8	31	0	7	2	21	0
Thomson	4	1	21	0				
Scott	31.4	7	91	7	32	10	139	5
R. Brown					7	1	16	0
Newhall					3	0	19	0

Gentlemen of Surrey's Bowling

	Overs	Mdns	Runs	Wkts	Overs	Mdns	Runs	Wkts
Horner	60.3	31	99	4	13	8	9	2
Harvey	24	8	58	0	10	5	28	0
Read	32	8	82	2				
Jephson	35	16	68	1	2.3	1	5	1
Morgan	30	12	50	0				
Freeman	9	2	23	0				
Hemmerde	8	2	20	1				
L. Shuter	5	1	16	0				
Key	8	3	15	0				
J. Shuter	2	2	0	0				

Umpires: Wood and Carpenter.

THE PHILADELPHIANS IN ENGLAND, 1897

The tour undertaken by the Philadelphian cricketers was far more ambitious than had ever been attempted by them before and if the results were less satisfactory than had been anticipated by the promoters, the fact must be borne in mind that the campaign was arranged mainly for educational purposes and that probably few of those who formed the team expected to win a majority of the matches. When Americans on previous occasions visited this country the contests were always against amateur elevens, and the batsmen consequently were never opposed by English professional bowlers. However, those in authority considered the time had arrived when a move should be made into a higher class of cricket and with that idea, Mr C. W. Alcock was asked to arrange a programme against the leading counties, the two Universities, the Marylebone Club and one or two other sides. Doubtless what caused the Americans to have more belief in themselves was the fact that twice in about three years they had beaten an Australian eleven in Philadelphia. That in their English tour they over estimated their own abilities, is now a matter of cricket history, but what they learned here will probably be of great service and we may yet see an American team in England capable of holding their own against the best of our counties. Exception was taken to the statement that the Americans had aimed too high, but it must be borne in mind that only a few of the counties thought it worth while to put their best elevens into the field, showing the public very clearly what estimate they had formed of the merits of the Philadelphian team. From a social point of view the tour was a complete success, the men being popular wherever they went and Mr George S. Patterson proving himself one of the best and most sportsman-like of captains. Nothing could have been more to the liking of the English public than the manner in which he promptly refuted a charge made in one of the leading American papers that his team had been unfairly treated by our umpires. As a matter of record therefore, we reproduce the letter which he wrote to the *Field*:

Maidstone, July 26th.

Dear Sir, – My attention has been directed to a letter signed "W.S." in the *Field* of July 24th, enclosing a clipping from the *Philadelphia Public Ledger*, severely criticising the umpiring in the Philadelphian matches during our tour through England. I wish to state on behalf of the Philadelphia team that the sentiments expressed in the clipping are not those of the team, and that we emphatically repudiate any insinuation of unfair treatment. On the contrary, we have been received with the most unvarying courtesy and fairness both on and off the field. I wish to take this opportunity of making a public acknowledgement of our indebtedness to Mr Perkins, of the MCC, for the umpires assigned to us, and to testify, unnecessary though it be, to their ability and integrity.

I am, truly yours,

George Stuart Patterson,

Captain of the Philadelphia Team.

PHILADELPHIANS v SUSSEX

Played at Brighton, June 17, 18, 1897

This was far and away the most sensational achievement of the Philadelphians throughout the whole tour. Judged by what had happened against Oxford, Lancashire and Cambridge, the team appeared to have little chance against the full strength of Sussex, but as an example of how little public form can be trusted at cricket, they had the best of the match throughout and gained a highly creditable victory by eight wickets. It did not seem that anything exceptional had been done when the Americans completed their first innings for 216, but the cricket that followed took everyone by surprise, King and Cregar dismissing Sussex in less than an hour for the paltry total of 46. The ground was in excellent condition, the only thing to assist the bowlers being a strong side wind. Of this, King availed himself in magnificent fashion, making the ball swerve in the air, and taking seven wickets at a cost of only 13 runs. Sussex did very much better in their second attempt, Ranjitsinhji, Newham and Brann all playing well, but the disastrous start could never be atoned for. King, in the whole match, took 13 wickets for 115 runs, a wonderful performance on the Brighton ground.

Philadelphians

Mr G. S. Patterson c Butt b Bland	4	– b Bland	4
Mr A. M. Wood b Tate	10	– b Tate	42
Mr J. A. Lester b Tate	92	– not out	34
Mr L. Biddle c Butt b Tate	21	– not out	1
Mr J. B. King c Ranjitsinhji b Tate	58		
Mr C. Coates b Tate	4		
Mr F. W. Ralston b Tate	13		
Mr H. L. Clark lbw b Bland	1		
Mr H. P. Baily c Bean b Tate	9		
Mr E. M. Cregar c Butt b Bland	0		
Mr P. H. Clark not out	0		
L-b 4	4	B 2	2
	216		83

Sussex

F. W. Marlow c P. Clark b King	6	– b Baily	19
Mr W. L. Murdoch b King	3	– c sub b King	1
K. S. Ranjitsinhji b King	0	– c H. Clark b P. Clark	74
Mr G. Brann b King	10	– c Wood b King	41
Mr W. Newham c Biddle b Cregar	0	– b King	67
J. Vine b King	4	– c Patterson b Cregar	8
E. H. Killick c Ralston b Cregar	7	– c King b Cregar	4
G. Bean not out	8	– b King	29
H. R. Butt b King	4	– b King	1
F. W. Tate b King	0	– b King	2
C. Bland c Biddle b Cregar	1	– not out	0
B 1, w 2	3	B 1, l-b 4, w 1	6
	46		252

Sussex Bowling

	Overs	Mdns	Runs	Wkts	Overs	Mdns	Runs	Wkts
Bland	32	14	53	3	13	2	37	1
Tate	38	12	84	7	17	10	21	1
Killick	12	4	30	0	9	2	23	0
Ranjitsinhji	5	2	22	0				
Bean	7	2	23	0				

Philadelphian Bowling

	Overs	Mdns	Runs	Wkts	Overs	Mdns	Runs	Wkts
King	10	5	13	7	38.1	11	102	6
Cregar	10	2	30	3	13	2	41	2
Baily					17	6	37	1
P. Clark					16	1	53	1
Patterson					5	0	12	0
Coates					1	0	1	0

Umpires: J. Wheeler and R. Clayton.

OTHER MATCHES

Not the least of the manifestations of genius scattered across the lush water meadows of English cricket history is the imagination shown in concocting excuses for matches to be fought out in a fierce competitive spirit. Glancing through the pages which follow, it seems as though no division of society was so artificial, no qualification so arbitrary, no sub-group so exclusive, that it could not be used as the pretext for a game of cricket. The gradations from the grim to the flippant are of the subtlest kind, with the varsity matches clearly events of world-shattering import, and the Eton v Harrow contests the occasion for unseemly deportment by carriage-holders, and fixtures like Married v Single and Smokers v Non-Smokers quivering happily on the rim of pure farce. (It was reported that the Australian giant G. J. Bonnor once marched out to do battle for the Non-Smokers with a vast cigar clenched between his splendid antipodean teeth, thus substantiating what could have been Kipling's dictum that while an umpire is only an umpire, a good cigar is a smoke.) Somewhere between these extremes fall institutions like Gentlemen v Players, in which class distinctions were deployed as one more excuse for a contest, and occasions like North v South, supposedly of indispensable assistance to Test match selectors who already knew everyone's form backwards.

In these sternly utilitarian times, when a university career is assumed, especially by those who have never experienced one, to be tied to the substance or at least the ghost of academic ambition, the career of a cricketing Victorian sprig must seem delightfully improbable. There is no question that in those days, when a stint at one of the ancient universities was seen as the administering of the final lick of social polish, or perhaps as a kind of sabbatical before the harsh realities of life on the Stock Exchange or the Civil Service, many of the great cricketing champions of Oxford and Cambridge performed their finest cerebral feats out of doors. A contemporary reminiscence of Charlie Absolom, the great Cambridge blue of the 1860s, says that "it was an amusing speculation as to how he had managed to get through his Little-go, for he seemed to know nothing well except cricket", and there is a letter extant from the Cambridge captain Gilbert Jessop in which he writes, with more sincerity than syntax, that he has been "to infernally busy to write earlier".

But the occasional academic shortcoming was more than balanced by an athletic command of very much more than parochial proportions. The great university sportsmen were very often world leaders, as Charles Fry, himself a distinguished Oxonian academic, demonstrated when at the University Sports in the 1890s he performed a long jump of nearly twenty-four feet, establishing a world record which stood for the next twenty-one years. In cricket, too, the university men were of true international class, and it comes as no surprise to read in these pages of Oxford and Cambridge elevens extending and often actually defeating some of the strongest cricketing sides in the world; it is perfectly obvious that in the game between Cambridge and Yorkshire in 1899, the Yorkshire bowlers were as little children in the hands of Jessop, and that G. Kemp, in his innings for the university against the Gentlemen of England, was almost as dominant. In a game which took place in 1885 between the light blues and Yorkshire there were no fewer than 120 extras conceded, while in the following year it was suddenly discovered that the wickets were too far apart, which is almost as absurd as events in the 1886 Rugby v Marlborough game, where somebody managed to bowl two overs in succession.

The modulation from varsity to Public School is natural enough, for if we reverse it, we arrive at the process by which so many precocious schoolboys crossed the bridge into international status; there were even a few rare cases, notably that of C. L. Townsend, where the schoolboy and the international cricketer were virtually one. Most of the great Public Schools employed as coaches ageing professionals with international reputations, and, in the case of Shrewsbury School, even hired a callow professional of no reputation at all, who, being called Cardus, went on to distinguish himself in a more sedentary branch of the game. In any case, greatness at cricket almost always comes very early in a player's life, and certainly the cricket masters at the public schools of the Victorian age could usually spot a matchwinner when they saw one, just as half a century later it was apparent to all at Tonbridge that the thirteen-year-old Cowdrey might well develop into a useful adult.

Of the tours undertaken to foreign parts by representative English sides, no further comments are necessary as to the arduous nature of their travels, but it is worth mentioning that young E. M. Grace, taking with him to Australia in 1864 the dictum so well proven at Waterloo, that one Englishman was worth any number of foreigners, actually challenged any six of the locals to a contest; this was the tour after which E.M., the great batting champion of England, reversed the Byronic process by waking up to find his brother famous. Fifteen years later it was the experience of the compilers of the almanack to find that in giving an accurate account of events in the match between New South Wales and Lord Harris's side at Sydney, they had achieved a cross between a short story, a morality play and a most revealing fragment of colonial history. Just as remarkable in their way are the antics of the second of the two famous Captain Blighs in English maritime history, the Hon. Ivo Francis Walter Bligh, who so disregarded the onus of his responsibilities as commander as to participate too boisterously in a shipboard tug-o'-war and incapacitate himself. Then there are the mysteries, like the identity of the waterer of the pitch at Adelaide in 1887; sensations, like the gathering of the first pair of spectacles of his life by Arthur Shrewsbury at Sydney in 1887; astonishing individual feats, like Shaw's bowling figures against New South Wales in 1882; constitutional crises like the one at Sydney in 1892 when W. G. Grace bruised the umpire's delicate sensibilities. And, taking the broader view, there are some touching examples of how the touring cricketers could sometimes perform the vital function of showing the flag in the outposts of what was certainly the most far-flung empire in history. Concerning the arrival of Shaw's team at Suez en route for the 1884-5 tour of Australia, *Wisden* gives a brief but unforgettable account of the friendly match which the tourists played against British residents: "The scene of the contest was a plain of sand, in the centre of which a piece of coconut matting was tightly stretched."

The tour in which Grace insulted an umpire was subsidised by Henry North Holroyd, third Earl of Sheffield, Viscount Pevensey, Baron of Dunsmore, Meath, Baron Sheffield of Roscommon and of Sheffield, Yorkshire, who had once represented the Gentlemen of Sussex against the Gentlemen of Kent. To commemorate the success of the Grace tour, which his lordship had underwritten for the express purpose of giving the colonials a chance to see Grace's comprehensive cricketing technique, including, presumably, his browbeating of umpires, a further sum of money was donated for a trophy, to be called the Sheffield Shield, to be competed for by the Australian states. They are still competing to this very day, but in view of the origins of the trophy, it is perhaps poetic justice that the man who appears to have dominated the early contests for the shield should have been the cricketer known as the Australian W.G.; the amazing George Giffen. All-round feats of every kind have been documented in cricket's history, but one doubts if anybody ever monopolised a single game as George Giffen monopolised a game for South Australia against Victoria in which he scored a double century and took sixteen wickets. Those readers who take note of Giffen's bowling figures (particularly in the game against England at Adelaide at the end of March 1895) will soon be prepared to accept as gospel truth the famous story that after bowling for some hours, Giffen, captain of his side, was advised by the other players to change the bowling. "Certainly", the irrepressible Giffen is supposed to have replied, "what a good idea. I'll change ends."

Of the rest of the contents of this volume, let them speak for themselves. In any case, it is difficult to know what to say of a match in which the qualification for playing was to be over sixty years of age, or of a contest cryptically designated "One Arm v One Leg" without further hints as to whether the players were short of a limb or merely disqualified from using all they had. The modern mind simply boggles in the face of the fortitude, the ingenuity, the agility, the raw obsessional determination to get a game of cricket, which characterises the behaviour of those stalwarts of the great freeze-up of the winter of 1878-79 who defined an ice-floe as little more than a hard pitch slightly exaggerated. The test match between Canada and the United States of America might seem a parochial business until one remembers that it was these two outsider nations who played the first test match in recorded history. One's heart goes out, and also one's smiles, to the umpire who requested that he be laid to rest in his umpire's coat holding a cricket ball – free at last, one feels tempted to add, from the hectoring of Gloucestershire doctors. One mourns the brevity of Prince's career as a great metropolitan venue, its story going from grand opening to ignominious takeover in less than a decade; in view of the high hopes held for it as a centre of cricketing fashion, it may not be out of place to add to *Wisden's* strictly factual coverage of events, the romantic postscript recorded by F. S. Ashley-Cooper, who says that "its beautiful turf, obtained from Salisbury Plain, was carted to Battersea and sold for what it could fetch." On a happier and more convivial note, it is enlightening to learn that when Major Wharton's side went to South Africa in 1888-89, the sternest opposition they encountered was not from the local bowling but from the local hospitality.

I would regard it as a dereliction of editorial duty were I not to draw attention to three other tiny facts buried in this great ocean of cricketing data. The matches and personalities selected for inclusion have claims which are self-evident, but it would be a thousand pities if the reader were to overlook the possibilities of pleasure-by-hindsight and fail to notice that the tail-end batsman on that too-convivial tour of South Africa who scored a half-century in the first innings of one of the matches, was the same Smith who at a later stage of his life, finding himself too old for such important business, filled in his time with frivolities like the stage portrayal of Professor Henry Higgins opposite the Eliza Doolittle of Mrs Patrick Campbell, and a subsequent apotheosis as Hollywood's archetypal Englishman in such dramas as *Tarzan the Ape-Man*, *China Seas* and *The Prisoner of Zenda*. Smith, incidentally, remains the only cricketer of his generation to have a cricket ground named after him, a signal honour rendered only fractionally less signal by the fact that the ground in question happens to be in Los Angeles.

As to the inclusion of what appears to be an insignificant Public Schools match of

1899 between Tonbridge School and Dulwich College, a match in which no apparent statistics or incidents occur which would justify its inclusion, I can only beg the reader to scrutinise the scorecard a little more closely, in the hope that he will find there the germ of a great comic idea, which led to the best cricketing novel of the Edwardian epoch, and from there to the prolific activities of the most fecund comic writer in the history of English literature. I did say there were three tiny facts in danger of being submerged, and the third of them seems to me to be a real-life echo of the comic fictions of that Dulwich fast bowler who was never to forget his day of triumph against Tonbridge, recalling it in detail more than seventy years later. In the tales which the Dulwich cricketer later wove, the device of assumed identity was so commonplace that within their context a man might easily fall under suspicion for using his real name. Critics have sometimes questioned the degree of poetic license assumed in these tissues of pseudonymous moonshine, saying that in real life nobody would dare carry on in such a fashion. For those who obstinately cling to the realist lobby, I cannot too strongly recommend the brief but extraordinary remarks pertaining to the Surrey v Middlesex game of 1891 when Mr, later Sir, T. C. O'Brien, third Baronet, no doubt finding himself enmeshed in the coils of some Wodehousean dilemma of his own contriving, took the gentleman's way out. With Sir Timothy, who will appear in the second volume of this anthology in an Indian summer whose brevity is exceeded only by its comical ferocity, I have always felt a special affinity, perhaps for no more logical reason than that he died on the day I came of age. It therefore pleases my sense of the accidental fitness of things in general and cricket history in particular that he should have made so typically Wodehousean a mark on the affairs of his day.

Benny Green

OXFORD AND CAMBRIDGE UNIVERSITIES

CAMBRIDGE MATCHES

CAMBRIDGE UNIVERSITY v YORKSHIRE

Played at Cambridge, May 26, 27, 28, 1884

On the Thursday and Friday prior to the day on which this contest was commenced a team of the MCC and Ground accomplished the feat, hitherto unprecedented in a first-class match in England, of playing an innings in which three individual scores of over 100 runs were made, the club's opponents being the Australians. Yorkshire succeeded in repeating this extraordinary performance in the match under notice. Cambridge had first innings, and in three hours and ten minutes were dismissed for 114, Emmett taking six wickets for 34 runs in fifty-three overs, thirty-nine of which were maidens. Under any circumstances such an analysis would be remarkable, but on a ground in first-class order, and against so good an eleven, the feat was simply a splendid one. When stumps were drawn on the opening day the Yorkshire score stood as follows:

G. Ulyett b Topham	4
L. Hall not out	49
T. Wardall b Bainbridge	0
W. Bates not out	80
B 26, l-b 3, w 1	30
	(2 wkts) 163

Continuing the innings on the Tuesday Bates and Hall were not parted until the total reached 242, the two having put on no fewer than 219 runs while they were together. Bates was missed three times, but despite these blemishes his 133 was a brilliant display of hitting. He was batting for three hours and twenty-five minutes, and his hits included sixteen 4s, eight 3s and ten 2s. Grimshaw joined Hall, and after batting steadily for a time played dashing cricket. At the interval he had made 25, and Hall 91, the total being 303. With the score at 347 Hall's steadily-played and admirable innings was brought to a close. He made eleven 4s, six 3s, fourteen 2s and twenty-five singles without giving a chance, and was at wickets for nearly four hours and a quarter. The fourth wicket had put on 105 runs. By nine 4s, two 3s, five 2s and only five singles, Peel made 57 in an hour and was then bowled, Emmett sharing the same fate directly after. Grimshaw and Peate took the score to 517, adding 81 while they were together, and then the former was out for a faultless innings of 115, made up of fifteen 4s, six 3s, six 2s, and singles. Peate and Hunter were soon dismissed, and as Lockwood could not go in owing to an injury to his finger, the innings closed for 539. Mr Greatorex's analysis is a curiosity, and the fact that five Yorkshire batsmen made 461 runs, and the remainder only 10, is another. In the short time that remained after the conclusion of the Yorkshire innings, the University lost one wicket (Mr Milner's) for 19 runs.

Wanting 406 runs to avert a single innings' defeat, and with nine wickets to fall, Cambridge continued their second innings on the Wednesday. The eighth wicket fell when the score had only reached 100; but thanks to the batting of Messrs Turner, Marchant and Knatchbull-Huggessen, the last two wickets put on no fewer than 122 runs. Mr Turner's 63 not out was the highest he had scored for his University, and except for a chance when he had made 49, was a most excellent innings. Yorkshire won the match by an innings and 203 runs, and, if for nothing else, the game would be remarkable for the extraordinary number of extras scored, Cambridge giving away 68 and Yorkshire 52. Thus, out of a match of 875 runs no fewer than 120 extras were totalled.

Cambridge University

J. E. K. Studd Esq. c Bates b Harrison	1	– b Peate	9
C. W. Wright Esq. c Harrison b Emmett	22	– c Hunter b Bates	17
Hon. C. M. Knatchbull-Hugessen b Emmett	14	– lbw b Harrison	21
Hon. J. W. Mansfield c Hunter b Emmett	5	– c Wardall b Ulyett	0
P. J. de Paravicini Esq. c Hunter b Harrison	6	– c and b Bates	2
T. Greatorex Esq. b Emmett	4	– c sub. b Harrison	15
J. A. Turner Esq. b Harrison	2	– not out	63
F. Marchant Esq. b Emmett	10	– c Wardall b Ulyett	27
H. W. Bainbridge Esq. not out	18	– b Ulyett	29
M. H. Milner Esq. b Emmett	3	– c Hall b Emmett	1
H. G. Topham Esq. c Hunter b Harrison	3	– c Emmett b Peate	12
B 20, l-b 5, w 1	26	B 12, l-b 11, w 3	26
	114		222

Yorkshire

G. Ulyett b Topham	4
L. Hall b Paravicini	115
T. Wardall b Bainbridge	0
W. Bates b Topham	133
I. Grimshaw st Knatchbull-Hugessen b Greatorex	115
R. Peel b Bainbridge	57
T. Emmett b Bainbridge	1
E. Peate c Mansfield b Greatorex	40
J. Hunter c Topham b Greatorex	5
G. P. Harrison not out	0
E. Lockwood absent hurt	
B 57, l-b 6, w 5	68
	539

Yorkshire Bowling

	Overs	Mdns	Runs	Wkts	Overs	Mdns	Runs	Wkts
Harrison	37.3	19	44	4	20.3	3	47	2
Emmett	53	39	34	6	32	18	37	1
Ulyett	8	5	7	—	17	8	22	3
Peate	8	5	3	—	32	18	30	2
Bates					21	6	42	2
Peel					10	2	18	—

Cambridge University Bowling

	Overs	Mdns	Runs	Wkts
Mr Bainbridge	45	8	119	3
Mr Topham	30	12	60	2
Mr Turner	38	15	81	—
Mr Paravicini	22	5	61	1
Mr Milner	34	13	67	—
Mr Studd	14	3	39	—
Mr Marchant	8	4	23	—
Mr Mansfield	10	3	17	—
Mr Greatorex	4	1	4	3

Umpires: A. Cribden and T. Alley.

CAMBRIDGE UNIVERSITY v MR C. I. THORNTON'S ELEVEN

Played at Cambridge, May 18, 19, 20, 1885

Mr Thornton's team batted first, and when two batsmen had been dismissed it was discovered that the wickets were a yard and a quarter too wide apart. The match consequently had to be commenced over again. The game was four times interrupted by rain, and Mr Thornton's eleven were not all disposed of until ten minutes to six. Messrs Crawley and Quinton put on 57 runs for the fourth wicket, and Messrs Brutton and Cottrell 40 for the eighth. Before time was called the University had scored 22 runs for the loss of Mr Eaton's wicket, Mr Wright being not out 10, and Mr Toppin not out 9.

There was a full day's play on the Tuesday, and the cricket was of an interesting character, the University showing to advantage at all points of the game. The fifth Cambridge wicket fell at 56, but from this point an excellent resistance was offered to the bowling of Crossland and Wright. Mr Kemp helped Mr Bainbridge to take the score to 97 before he was bowled, and the partnership of Messrs Bainbridge and Lindley augmented the total by 62 runs. Mr Bainbridge left at 165, his sterling innings of 62 including four 4s, six 3s and eight 2s. Mr Marchant then hit with considerable freedom, and while he was associated with Mr Buxton 52 runs were added. Mr Marchant carried his bat for 50, five 4s, four 3s and four 2s being his chief hits. This was the highest innings he scored for the University during the season, and was made with one chance when he had scored 30. Mr Thornton and Walter Wright started the second innings of the visitors, and no fewer than 92 runs were scored before the former was bowled. His dashing innings of 56 included a hit for 6, the ball pitching over the wall into the Mortimer Road premises, eight 4s, two 3s and three 2s. After his dismissal eight wickets fell for an addition of only 38 runs, but Mr Studd and Crossland could not be parted, though the game was prolonged considerably beyond the usual time. While they were together 35 runs were scored from eleven overs.

On the third day rain fell so heavily that it was impossible to proceed with the match, and what promised to prove a very interesting contest had to be abandoned as a draw.

Mr C. I. Thornton's England Eleven

J. E. K. Studd Esq. c Lindley b Mirehouse	5	– not out	24
C. I. Thornton Esq. st Wright b Toppin	27	– b Toppin	56
W. Wright c Mirehouse b Toppin	18	– b Toppin	23
H. E. Crawley Esq. c Bainbridge b Lindley	39	– b Mirehouse	6
F. W. D. Quinton Esq. c Lindley b Bainbridge	31	– c Wright b Toppin	7
C. W. Burls Esq. b Toppin	22	– c Eaton b Mirehouse	10
S. S. Schultz Esq. b Lindley	11	– b Toppin	2
E. B. Brutton Esq. not out	18	– b Toppin	0
C. E. Cottrell Esq. c Hawke b Mirehouse	31	– b Mirehouse	0
R. Pilling c Hawke b Bainbridge	4	– c Hawke b Mirehouse	1
J. Crossland run out	5	– not out	13
B 18, l-b 4, w 2	24	B 18, l-b 2, w 2, n-b 1	23
	235		165

Cambridge University

C. W. Wright Esq. c Pilling b Crossland	22	T. O. Lindley Esq. b Crossland	27
H. Eaton Esq. b Crossland	0	F. Marchant Esq. not out	50
C. Toppin Esq. lbw b Crossland	15	C. D. Buxton Esq. c Crossland b Cottrell	14
Hon. M. B. Hawke b Crossland	15	G. T. Mirehouse Esq. b Cottrell	1
T. Greatorex Esq. b Crossland	0	B 5, l-b 3	8
H. W. Bainbridge Esq. c and b Wright	62		
G. M. Kemp Esq. b Crossland	17		231

Cambridge University Bowling

	Overs	Mdns	Runs	Wkts	Overs	Mdns	Runs	Wkts
Mr Buxton	15	1	45	—				
Mr Mirehouse	27	9	46	2	31	16	51	4
Mr Toppin	23	7	45	3	34	12	60	5
Mr Bainbridge	25	5	52	2	7	3	16	—
Mr Lindley	20	10	23	2	5	2	15	—

Mr Thornton's Eleven Bowling

	Overs	Mdns	Runs	Wkts
Crossland	71	27	117	7
Wright	62	32	86	1
Mr Brutton	1	—	8	—
Mr Cottrell	6.1	2	12	2

CAMBRIDGE UNIVERSITY v GENTLEMEN OF ENGLAND

Played at Cambridge, June 14, 15, 16, 1886

Another capital performance on the part of the Light Blues, and one which closed the season of home matches. Mr Thornton got up the amateur team, which was on the whole a very good one. Mr J. C. Mackinnon, who was engaged in the eleven, was himself an undergraduate at Cambridge, and only played as an emergency. The first day produced some most remarkable cricket. The Gentlemen won the toss, and though the ground was in capital order for run-getting, started so badly that six wickets went down for 21 runs. Then it was that Mr M. C. Kemp, the late Oxford captain, commenced an extraordinary innings. He received some capital assistance from Mr G. G. Walker, but the score was only 88 when the seventh wicket fell. Mr J. G. Walker only made 27 out of the 68 scored for the eighth wicket, and Mr Mackinnon only 8 out of the 51 for the ninth wicket. Mr Leatham also stayed while Mr Kemp hit. At the call of time the score 270 for nine wickets, of which number Mr Kemp had made the wonderful proportion of 164 (not out). Such a performance speaks for itself. He hit with a power and vigour not readily to be forgotten by those who had the good fortune to witness it.

Resuming play on the Tuesday, the Gentlemen's innings closed for 298, Mr Kemp being caught and bowled for 175. Against this brilliant achievement hardly a fault could be urged, as he never gave a chance that went to hand, and the character of his cricket may be best judged from the fact that he made twenty-one boundary hits, seven 3s and seventeen 2s. There was nothing sensational in the innings of the University, although the batting was consistently good. All the first eight batsmen reached double figures, but the best cricket was shown by Messrs Bainbridge and Buxton, who put on 95 runs for the first wicket. Later on some capital form was displayed by Messrs Turner and Rock, the latter of whom was at the wickets for an hour and a half for 26. The follow-on was averted by 10 runs, much to the delight of the spectators. Mr A. E. Leatham bowled with considerable success, taking seven wickets for 54 runs. The Gentlemen went in a second time, and lost one wicket, that of Mr Hine-Haycock, for 43 runs.

The chances now seemed certainly in favour of a draw, but the Light Blues bowled so well, and batted so brilliantly at their second attempt that they were once more able to score a victory. The batting of the Gentlemen fell very far below what had been expected after the performance on the opening day, and only Messrs Thornton and G. G. Walker offered any serious resistance to the admirble bowling of Messrs Rock, Toppin, Dorman and Buxton. When Cambridge went in three hours and a half remained for play, and there were 210 runs required to win. Of course, the condition of the ground was in favour of run-getting, but the task seemed a heavy one. Nevertheless it was accomplished with great ease. Messrs Buxton and Bainbridge made 70 in the first hour, and put on 105 runs before they were separated, both playing admirable cricket. Mr Buxton made seven 4's and seven 3s, and Mr Bainbridge six 4s and four 3s. Later on Messrs Thomas and Rock put on 86 runs during their partnership, and hit the amateur bowling to all parts of the field. The runs were hit off by six o'clock for the loss of only three wickets, and Cambridge were left with a victory by seven wickets. This was the third time that the Light Blues had pulled a game out of the fire.

Gentlemen of England

Mr E. J. C. Studd c Dorman b Rock	5	– c Turner b Rock	0
Mr C. I. Thornton c Turner b Toppin	3	– c Rock b Toppin	35
Mr G. B. Studd c Dorman b Rock	4	– c Knatchbull-Hugessen b Dorman	10
Mr T. R. Hine-Haycock b Rock	0	– b Buxton	18
Mr H. Hale b Toppin	2	– b Toppin	4
Mr A. E. Leatham lbw b Toppin	0	– not out	12
Mr M. C. Kemp c and b Toppin	175	– b Toppin	12
Mr G. G. Walker run out	39	– c Turner b Buxton	21
Mr J. G. Walker b Rock	27	– c Rock b Dorman	1
Mr J. C. Mackinnon c Toppin b Rock	8	– c Buxton b Rock	10
Mr G. A. B. Leatham not out	14	– c Thomas b Rock	1
B 16, l-b 4, n-b 1	21	B 14, l-b 1	15
	298		139

Cambridge University

Mr H. W. Bainbridge c Hine-Haycock b A. E. Leatham.	38	– c and b Mackinnon	47
Mr C. D. Buxton c J. G. Walker b A. E. Leatham	57	– c Hine-Haycock b Hale	63
Mr F. Thomas c G. B. Studd b A. E. Leatham	14	– not out	58
Mr J. A. Turner c G. B. Studd b G. G. Walker	36	– b Hale	1
Mr C. W. Rock c Hine-Haycock b A. E. Leatham	26	– not out	21
Mr A. M. Sutthery not out	15		
Mr T. Greatorex b G. G. Walker	12		
Mr F. Marchant c Hine-Haycock b G. G. Walker	11		
Mr C. Toppin c G. B. Studd b A. E. Leatham	0		
Hon. C. M. Knatchbull-Hugessen st G. A. Leatham b A. E. Leatham.	2		
Mr A. W. Dorman c and b A. E. Leatham	2		
B 10, l-b 1, w 4	15	B 19, w 1	20
	228		210

Cambridge University Bowling

	Overs	Mdns	Runs	Wkts	Overs	Mdns	Runs	Wkts
Mr Rock	60	25	92	5	55.1	24	55	3
Mr Toppin	31.1	7	82	4	17	7	28	3
Mr Dorman	13	2	33	0	30	23	21	2
Mr Buxton	10	2	28	0	16	11	20	2
Mr Marchant	3	0	14	0				
Mr Turner	7	1	24	0				
Mr Sutthery	1	0	4	0				

Gentlemen of England Bowling

	Overs	Mdns	Runs	Wkts	Overs	Mdns	Runs	Wkts
Mr Walker	51	17	102	3	26	12	53	0
Mr Mackinnon	13	7	16	0	28	11	50	1
Mr Hale	20	5	41	0	43	23	54	2
Mr A. E. Leatham	28.3	11	54	7	11	4	33	0

CAMBRIDGE MEMORIES, 1890

By A. G. Steel

I was sitting in the smoking-room of a country house one night last autumn, thoroughly tired out after a long day's shooting. I felt perfectly comfortable in my large armchair watching the smoke slowly ascend from my "briar". My companions, of whom there were several, were all lazily inclined, and beyond an occasional remark about some shooting incident of the day none seemed inclined to do much talking. I was dreamily thinking of some old Cambridge friends now scattered over various quarters of the globe, and as their names flashed through my mind each one brought happy recollections of well-fought matches at Fenner's, Lord's, and The Oval. I was far away, oblivious almost to the presence of others, and my thoughts in their hazy wanderings had fixed on one particular hit – never by me to be forgotten. Charley Bannerman was the strike, P. H. Morton the bowler, and the match Cambridge v Australians at Lord's, 1878. Half-asleep I seemed to see again that sturdy striker raise his massive shoulders and hit the ball a warrior's knock; the ball flew low, over the bowler's head, struck the iron-bound ground twenty yards in front of the outfield, and bounded right over the awning of Lord Londesborough's drag and struck the wall behind. Truly a mighty hit. I could almost hear the cheers and shouts that greeted it.

Alas! too soon was my pleasant reverie ended. A low voice sitting at my elbow recalled me to the smoking-room and its surroundings. The speaker was a young Cambridge undergraduate, and the words he was uttering were these: "I am not much of a cricketer myself, but the general opinion is that our eleven this year is the best we have had for twenty years at Cambridge." "What about 1878?" said I, quietly. "1878," said my young friend contemptuously. "That year had a good bat or two – A. P. Lucas, Alfred and Edward Lyttelton were not bad players – but what bowlers had it? There was none to be compared to Woods, the present captain."

It is hardly necessary to say that a long discussion followed, and afterwards it occurred to me that a few remarks in *Wisden* on Cambridge cricketers of the last dozen years or so by one who has played with most, if not all of them, might be interesting to University men and, perhaps, others.

As I was one of the unvanquished 1878 team I am naturally open to the charge of prejudice; I shall risk that, however, and say that in my opinion that was the best side that Cambridge has turned out in my recollection. It played eight matches, and won every one, including a defeat of Gregory's Australian team by an innings and 72 runs. As a batting side it was exceptionally strong. Alfred and Edward Lyttelton were then at their very best; in fact, the latter's success that one season was phenomenal. Always a good batsman, the office of captain had no sooner become his than he played as he never did before, or since. He went to the very top of the tree, and the close of the season's record showed his to be the highest amateur average – viz., 29.25, the champion running a very close second. Alfred Lyttelton was then, as always, a really great batsman. No first-class cricketer ever possessed the elegance of style that was his; no flourish, but the maximum of power with the minimum of exertion.

These two, with that perfect master of stylish defence, A. P. Lucas, made a really sound nucleus for the batting strength of the side. The last-named batsman, when the bowling was very accurate, was a slow scorer, but always a treat to watch. If the present generation of stone-wall cricketers, such as Scotton, Hall, Barlow, A. Bannerman, nay, even Shrewsbury, possessed such beautiful ease of style the tens of thousands that used to frequent the beautiful Australian grounds would still flock there, instead of the hundred or two patient gazers on feats of Job-like patience that now attend them. There were several lesser lights of the team who were far from useless with the bat – Ivo Bligh, Whitfeld, L. K. Jarvis, and A. G. Steel – as will be seen from the fact that the average of the whole eleven came to 219 runs per innings, and that in one of the very wettest seasons on record.

The bowling of the team was strong, though looking at it now, after a dozen years, one cannot help wondering at its success. P. H. Morton was during that season a really good fast bowler; not as good as Woods of today, certainly not; but at times he was very deadly. The "divilment" in his bowling was the great pace the ball left the pitch. Tallish, but of spare physique, he scarcely looked the stamp of man to bowl really fast, but he had most powerful muscles at the back of his shoulders, and it was to these that he owed his success. I owed my great success of taking seventy-five wickets for the University at a cost of 7.32 runs apiece to the novelty of my bowling. At that time no bowler in first-rate cricket broke from the leg-side, and for a short period many a first-class batsman made but sorry attempts to play the "curly" ones. A. F. J. Ford and A. P. Lucas were the only changes. With a good fielding side and a superb wicket-keeper the team was one that in 1878 would have taken a very high-class side to beat.

Alfred Lyttelton's year as captain, 1879, saw the Cambridge eleven again undefeated. This was a good side, but lacking Edward Lyttelton and A. P. Lucas it could not be considered equal to the preceding one. G. B. Studd first made his appearance, getting the last place by the mere skin of his teeth. It is a strange fact that two such fine cricketers as Ivo Bligh and G. B. Studd just managed to scrape as eleventh men into the team in their respective years. The rival of each for the last place was the same man, O. P. Lancashire – hard lines indeed just to miss his blue so narrowly two consecutive years. This year saw the last of the Lytteltons – doughty champions indeed for Cambridge cricket. During the five years, 1874 to 1879, the ranks of Cambridge cricket were being continually recruited by some of the very best boy players – D. Q. Steel, W. S. Patterson, A. P. Lucas, Edward and Alfred Lyttelton, A. G. Steel, Ivo Bligh, P. H. Morton and G. B. Studd were amongst the most prominent. It was hardly to be expected that the public schools could go on supplying such good men; but in 1880 Eton sent up C. T. Studd, who, in a very short time, took his place in quite the first flight of cricketers. He had a fine, upright, commanding style as a batsman, and was a very useful slow bowler, quick from the pitch, and on a hard ground getting up to an inconvenient height. In 1881 Cambridge suffered their first defeat by Oxford since the great collapse in 1877. The eleven was strong in batting, but sadly weak in bowling, especially on the hard fast ground on which the University match was played. A. H. Evans at last had his revenge; as hard working a cricketer as ever played for either University, his bowling for Oxford in the three preceding 'Varsity matches had been magnificent, and that against strong batting sides. Supported by very weak batting all his efforts had been unavailing till 1881, and then his bowling, backed up by a beautiful innings of over 100 by that finished player, W. H. Patterson, and a 70 (ever memorable for a strange stroll to the pavilion at its beginning) by C. F. H. Leslie, secured a well-earned and long-desired victory for Oxford.

The Australians fared but badly in their first three contests with the representatives of Cambridge. In 1878 the Australian management had found it impossible to give a date for a Cambridge fixture until after the University match at Lord's. I believe that this is the first occasion on which a University team has played as a University after the meeting at Lord's. However, keen for the fray, full of confidence after a most successful season, we reunited on July 22 to try conclusions with the eleven which early in the year had inflicted such a terrible defeat upon a good team of the MCC. It was glorious weather, and a perfect wicket. We won the toss, and despite the unavoidable absence of A. P. Lucas ran up a total of 285. The most noticeable feature of the innings was the woeful lack of judgment the Australians showed in placing their field. In the first two hours their bowling was collared, and away went the majority of the field to the boundary. I recollect well batting to Spofforth that day without any cover-point or third man. We have learnt a lot from the Australians in bowling; they have learnt a lot from us in batting and general knowledge of the game.

The Australians' two innings were 111 and 102. These small scores were entirely owing to P. H. Morton, whose bowling on that day was about the best fast bowling on a true wicket I ever saw. He got twelve wickets for 90 runs, and clean bowled nine, most of them with really fast breakbacks.

The next match between Cambridge and the Australians was in 1882 at Fenner's. Their team this year was undoubtedly the best they ever brought over, before or since, and Cambridge did a great performance in beating them by six wickets. The wicket was a fine one and the weather splendid, and the Australians won the toss, C. T. Studd and R. C. Ramsay bowled them out for 139. Cambridge retaliated with 266, the chief feature being a grand 118 by C. T. Studd. His off-driving of Spofforth and Palmer was perfection. The Australians making 291 in their second innings left the 'Varsity a big task – 165 to win on a well-used wicket. The weather, however, kept fine, the wicket played well, and the runs were got for four wickets. J. E. K. Studd played a fine innings of 66, and G. B. Studd 48. It will be a long time before I forget the face of the old President (Rev. A. Ward) when Cambridge had won. "Mr Steel," he said, "I never yet got a new hat, except for the University match: I shall order one tomorrow in honour of this victory."

The next match was at Portsmouth the same year, and was Australians v Past and Present Cambridge. This was a magnificent game, and the finish never to be forgotten by those who witnessed it. Cambridge won by 20 runs after many exciting incidents. The University went in first, and made 196. C. I. Thornton and A. P. Lucas, 45 and 42 respectively, were the highest scorers. The Australians made 141. Then Cambridge ran up 152, Alfred Lyttelton's 60 being the highest score, and left the Australians 208 to win. They began their task well – too well it seemed to the numerous partisans of the University. I have no record of how the wickets fell in this innings, but unless my memory plays me false I think that the Australians at the fall of the second wicket – Bonnor's – were about 90 or 100. This was not pleasant. Bonnor had made 66 in just half-an-hour. His hitting of C. T. Studd's bowling was appalling. The wicket seemed good and played well; but late in the innings I noticed that several balls that pitched on the middle and off stumps got up very uncomfortably for the batsmen. I happened to be bowling, and keeping the ball as well as I could on that spot, innocent of all break, and almost medium pace, I met with great success. The finish was exciting when the Australians wanted about 25 runs to win and two wickets to get them; horror of horrors, two catches were missed, one a very very easy one – imagine our feelings. However, all was well eventually, and amidst the very wildest excitement amongst the blue jackets we won. One of the Australians said to me afterwards: "After this third defeat, you've only to hold up a light-blue coat and we'll run." However, since 1882 the Australians have amply avenged themselves both against the University and Cambridge Past and Present.

Since 1882 many fairly good batsmen have appeared in the ranks of the Cambridge teams, and a few moderate bowlers, but the decade has been one remarkably deficient in any brilliant talent. We look in vain for any names that have taken such a high place as the old ones. Not one Cambridge batsman during this period has earned the distinction of representing England; and it was not till 1888 that two such first-class men in their respective spheres as Woods and McGregor appeared. Lord Hawke, C. W. Wright (for a short period), F. Marchant, F. Thomas, Mordaunt, Foley, G. Kemp, Hon. J. W. Mansfield, C. D. Buxton and F. G. J. Ford are amongst the best batsmen. There have been fewer bowlers than batsmen. Rock was a very steady, slow bowlers; Toppin at one time showed considerable promise, but never realised expectations. The young Australian, S. M. J. Woods, the present captain, is far away the finest fast bowler Cambridge has had for many years. Very fast, straight, with a good command over the ball both as regards pitch and change of pace, he is the *beau ideal* of a fine amateur bowler. He is a dangerous batsman too, one of those plucky, dashing players who appear to greater advantage the more things are going wrong for their side. What a pity we cannot keep this fine young cricketer at home; we could do very well with him in Gentlemen v Players matches for the next five or six years. We are told that Ferris has taken a house or cottage of some sort near Bristol in order to secure some so-called qualification for Gloucestershire, though from all accounts he himself is at present in Australia. I should like to hear Woods had done the same thing in any English city he pleased.

Wicket-keeping has been of late above the average. Orford, the predecessor of McGregor, was as good as any University team wants, and very much better than the ordinary run, but McGregor, another pupil of that best of old cricketers, H. H. Stephenson, has now reached the very top of the tree, as this last season he was deservedly chosen to keep wicket for England in preference to any of the professionals. He is a great wicket-keeper, and though I have not seen quite as much of him as I have of some other of the past stumpers, my own opinion is that he is the best amateur I ever saw. Firm and steady as a rock, without a whisper of a flourish, he takes the ball close to the stumps. Alfred Lyttelton was a great wicket-keeper; as a catcher at the wicket he was unsurpassed, for the very reason that made him a slow stumper, viz., he allowed the ball to pass the line of stumps a considerable distance before taking it. McGregor is a quick stumper and a fine catcher too, and his quiet and sure style reminds me of that prince of wicket-keepers, Richard Pilling.

With Woods and McGregor up again next season, and with the two promising youngsters, Streatfeild and Douglas, Cambridge should hold her own again at Lord's next year.

To old Cantabs the University pavilion is hardly the same now that our late President, "old" (as we used to call him) Ward, has passed away. Who that ever played at Cambridge in days gone by can forget his portly figure, his round and ruddy face? His jokes, some, alas, so oft-told yet always new to him, his laughter, his kindly genial sympathy as he greeting the discomfited batsman in the pavilion, will ever live in the memory of those who knew him. A cricketer's visit to Cambridge in the old President's days was never complete without an attack of the presidential "Bollinger", which according to its owner could only cheer but not inebriate – an idle tale as many a thirsty soul could prove.

CAMBRIDGE UNIVERSITY v MR C. I. THORNTON'S ELEVEN

Played at Cambridge, May 12, 13, 1890

This was the first of the important matches in the Cambridge programme, and an absolute triumph for the University eleven, who won the game by four wickets. Mr Thornton had a more than usually fine side at his command, though it is likely enough some of the batsmen were short of practice, and the strength of the bowling, with Briggs, Mold and Walter Wright available, was not to be questioned. All the more credit therefore to the Cambridge men for beating so powerful a combination. Beyond everything else, the feature of the match was the superb bowling of Mr Woods, who in all took fifteen wickets for 88 runs. In the second innings he achieved the distinction – a very rare one in first-class cricket – of getting the whole ten wickets, no fewer than seven of the ten being bowled down. Unfortunately for Cambridge, within a few days of this exceptional performance he strained his side most severely, and in his absence the University lost two matches.

Mr C. I. Thornton's Eleven

Batsman	1st inns		2nd inns	
Mr C. I. Thornton c McGregor b Streatfeild	5	–	b Woods	0
Mr A. J. Webbe c McGregor b Woods	11	–	b Woods	35
Mr C. J. M. Fox c Jephson b Woods	1	–	b Woods	0
Mr H. W. Forster c Hill b Streatfeild	16	–	b Woods	0
Mr T. C. O'Brien c McGregor b Woods	0	–	c McGregor b Woods	7
J. Briggs c Beresford b Streatfeild	3	–	b Woods	19
Mr G. F. Vernon c McGregor b Streatfeild	21	–	c Gosling b Woods	8
Mr P. J. de Paravicini b Streatfeild	0	–	c and b Woods	44
W. Wright b Woods	9	–	b Woods	0
J. Carlin c Gosling b Woods	0	–	not out	10
A. Mold not out	1	–	b Woods	2
B 1	1		B 6, l-b 1, n-b 1	8
	68			133

Cambridge University

Mr G. H. Cotterill st Carlin b Briggs	13 – run out	3
Mr R. N. Douglas b Mold	11 – b Wright	5
Mr R. C. Gosling c O'Brien b Briggs	3 – b Mold	0
Mr R. A. A. Beresford b Mold	20 – b Mold	22
Mr F. S. Jackson c Vernon b Briggs	17 – not out	19
Mr G. McGregor b Mold	36 – lbw b Wright	0
Mr H. Hale run out	11 – not out	5
Mr E. C. Streatfeild b Briggs	12	
Mr S. M. J. Woods st Carlin b Briggs	0 – c Webbe b Briggs	15
Mr A. J. L. Hill lbw b Mold	2	
Mr D. L. A. Jephson not out	0	
B 2, l-b 3	5 B 4	4
	130	73

Cambridge University Bowling

	Overs	Mdns	Runs	Wkts	Overs	Mdns	Runs	Wkts
Mr Streatfeild	20	9	41	5	20	7	32	0
Mr Woods	18.4	7	19	5	31	6	69	10
Mr Hill	1	0	7	0				
Mr Jephson					18	8	24	0

Mr C. I. Thornton's Eleven Bowling

	Overs	Mdns	Runs	Wkts	Overs	Mdns	Runs	Wkts
Wright	17	8	18	0	3	1	20	2
Briggs	35	12	63	5	9	1	22	1
Mold	24.1	6	44	4	16	7	27	2

Umpires: R. Carpenter and A. Millward.

CAMBRIDGE UNIVERSITY v SUSSEX

Played at Cambridge, May 24, 25, 26, 1897

In no match last year were the Light Blues seen to so little advantage. They had the opportunity of the first innings on a good wicket, but offered a most feeble resistance to the bowling of Bland and Tate, and from their wretchedly bad start they could never recover. Their bowling met with no more success than their batting had done and Sussex, playing in fine style at all points, won a one-sided game by an innings and 264 runs. Cambridge lacked the services of Druce, but otherwise had nearly all their best men available. Bland and Tate bowled unchanged throughout both innings at Cambridge, such a thing being probably without precedent in the annals of Sussex cricket. Bland had the splendid record of fourteen wickets for 72 runs. The batting honours fell to Brann, Murdoch, Bean and Marlow.

Cambridge University

Mr C. J. Burnup c Ranjitsinhji b Bland	28 – c Butt b Bland	7
Mr L. J. Moon c Tate b Bland	17 – c Parris b Bland	24
Mr H. H. Marriott b Bland	5 – c Butt b Bland	4
Mr C. E. M. Wilson b Bland	4 – b Bland	5
Mr J. H. Stogdon c Marlow b Bland	1 – b Bland	5
Mr E. H. Bray c Newham b Tate	23 – c Parris b Tate	4
Mr G. L. Jessop c Ranjitsinhji b Tate	4 – c Butt b Bland	36
Mr T. L. Taylor lbw b Bland	0 – c and b Tate	2
Mr H. W. De Zoete c Bean b Tate	0 – b Bland	9
Mr E. B. Shine b Bland	7 – c Bland b Tate	0
Mr A. E. Fernie not out	4 – not out	1
L-b 2, n-b 1	3 L-b 3	3
	91	100

Sussex

F. W. Marlow b Shine	60	F. Parris c Stogdon b Jessop	1
E. H. Killick c Bray b De Zoete	2	C. Bland b Jessop	1
K. S. Ranjitsinhji c Fernie b Shine	26	H. R. Butt not out	5
Mr W. L. Murdoch c Wilson b Fernie	105	F. W. Tate c Bray b De Zoete	1
Mr G. Brann c Bray b Jessop	126	B 16, l-b 2, w 3, n-b 2	23
Mr W. Newham c Wilson b De Zoete	28		
G. Bean c Shine b Jessop	77		455

Sussex Bowling

	Overs	Mdns	Runs	Wkts	Overs	Mdns	Runs	Wkts
Bland	22	7	40	7	26.1	15	32	7
Tate	21.1	7	48	3	26	8	65	3

Cambridge University Bowling

	Overs	Mdns	Runs	Wkts
Jessop	47	16	96	4
De Zoete	50.3	20	103	3
Shine	44	19	88	2
Fernie	36	11	70	1
Wilson	27	4	75	0

Umpires: R. Carpenter and G. Watts.

CAMBRIDGE UNIVERSITY v YORKSHIRE

Played at Cambridge, May 18, 19, 20, 1899

Despite a truly wonderful innings by Jessop on the opening day Cambridge found the task of playing Yorkshire considerably beyond their powers, and on the Saturday afternoon the match ended in a victory for the county by an innings and 83 runs. At one time it seemed likely that the weather would prevent Yorkshire winning, a storm of rain stopping play for some little time during Cambridge's second innings. However, Jackson and Rhodes by dint of some capital bowling, promptly settled the matter when cricket became practicable. Jessop's innings of 171 not out, was marred by a lofty chance at point when he had made 24, and later by a second chance in the deep field, but for all that it was an astonishing display. At the wickets for less than two hours, he hit twenty-seven 4s, six 3s and fourteen 2s. Sullivan, maintaining a capital defence, while his captain scored, was batting an hour and twenty minutes for 3 runs. For Yorkshire, J. T. Brown and Jackson played most brilliant cricket, their partnership for the second wicket putting on 194 runs. Except for a couple of chances at the wicket, the first at 93 and the second at 148, Brown played faultless cricket, and Jackson, though he also was twice missed, was seen to great advantage during a stay of three hours and fifty minutes.

Cambridge University

Mr L. J. Moon c Bairstow b Brown jun.	9	– b Rhodes	15
Mr A. M. Sullivan c Tunnicliffe b Rhodes	3	– b Jackson	19
Mr J. H. Stogdon run out	0	– st Bairstow b Rhodes	10
Mr E. R. Wilson b Rhodes	24	– b Jackson	12
Mr G. L. Jessop not out	171	– c Wainwright b Jackson	2
Mr T. L. Taylor b Hirst	14	– c Bairstow b Rhodes	3
Mr S. H. Day c Bairstow b Hirst	1	– c Bairstow b Jackson	4
Mr G. E. Winter b Hirst	8	– c Bairstow b Rhodes	22
Mr E. F. Penn c Tunnicliffe b Rhodes	3	– lbw b Jackson	11
Mr A. E. Hind c Bairstow b Hirst	0	– not out	0
Mr H. H. B. Hawkins b Jackson	6	– b Jackson	0
B 1, l-b 6	7	L-b 2	2
	246		100

Yorkshire

J. T. Brown sen. c Sullivan b Hawkins	168
J. Tunnicliffe b Hawkins	42
Mr F. S. Jackson c Moon b Wilson	133
Mr F. Mitchell c Hawkins b Penn	0
D. Denton c Sullivan b Penn	5
E. Wainwright c Stogdon b Penn	11
G. H. Hirst c Day b Wilson	10
Lord Hawke not out	38
W. Rhodes c Taylor b Wilson	1
J. T. Brown jun. b Jessop	0
A. L. Bairstow b Jessop	1
B 11, l-b 5, w 2, n-b 2	20
	429

Yorkshire Bowling

	Overs	Mdns	Runs	Wkts	Overs	Mdns	Runs	Wkts
Hirst	24	10	69	4	7	4	12	0
Brown jun.	12	4	33	1	7	3	17	0
Rhodes	20	6	80	3	15	5	18	4
Jackson	10.2	3	48	1	14.4	4	51	6
Brown sen.	2	1	9	0				

Cambridge University Bowling

	Overs	Mdns	Runs	Wkts
Hind	22	8	49	0
Penn	35	4	122	3
Jessop	18.4	3	57	2
Wilson	34	5	103	3
Hawkins	25	6	63	2
Winter	3	0	15	0

Umpires: R. Carpenter and G. Watts.

OXFORD MATCHES

OXFORD UNIVERSITY v GENTLEMEN OF ENGLAND

Played at Oxford, May 19, 20, 21, 1884

The composition of the University team was identical with that which gained so meritorious a victory over the Australian eleven on the previous Saturday, and as the Gentlemen's team, though strong in batting, included only a couple of really good bowlers, another success for the Oxonians was generally anticipated, this impression being strengthened when, at the close of the first day's play, the Gentlemen were in a minority of 72 on the first innings. Tuesday's play, however, entirely changed the aspect of the game. The University bowling was completely mastered when the visitors went in a second time, and the Gentlemen, after making 337 runs, succeeded in taking five of their opponents' best wickets for 73 before stumps were drawn for the day. On the third day the home team made a most plucky effort to save the match, but were not successful, the Gentlemen winning by 31 runs. The result was naturally a great disappointment to the Oxford men after their splendid victory over the Colonists. Their defeat was mainly attributable to the very fine bowling of Mr Rotherham, who, in this match of 923 runs, took no fewer than fourteen wickets at a cost of only 150 runs.

The Gentlemen of England batted first, and nine batsmen were dismissed for 130 runs at the interval. Messrs Studd and Christopherson put on 40 runs while they were together, but this was the only stand made against the bowling of Messrs Bastard and Whitby. On Oxford going in to bat a moderate score only seemed probable, as the first four wickets were down for 58 runs. Messrs Page and Key, however, offered a stubborn resistance, and by excellent cricket put on no fewer than 108 runs before the latter was out for a freely-hit 47. Mr Page was dismissed at 198, his 72 being a very fine innings, which included ten 4s, four 3s and seven 2s. The last five wickets fell for 46 runs, and at the conclusion of the innings stumps were drawn for the day. It will be seen that Mr Rotherham captured eight wickets at a cost of just over 7 runs each, but that despite this Oxford held an advantage of 72 runs on the first innings.

On the Tuesday the visitors commenced their second innings with Messrs Studd and J. G. Walker, and 80 runs were totalled before the former was caught at the wicket. Mr I. D. Walker filled the vacancy, and at the interval the score stood at 144 for one wicket, and it was increased to 183 before the Middlesex captain was bowled for an excellent innings of 55. Three runs later Mr J. G. Walker fell to a catch at the wicket, his splendid contribution of 92 including five 4s, nine 3s and fourteen 2s. Messrs Schultz and Pearson, by vigorous hitting, put on 70 runs during their partnership, the former being the last man out for an excellent innings of 63, made without a chance. The home team started their second innings in disastrous form, as Messrs O'Brien and Hine-Haycock were both dismissed before a run was scored, and Mr Cobb only made 8. Messrs Brain and Kemp carried the score to 51, before the former was bowled, and when the captain was stumped for a valuable 33, play ceased for the day, the University having five wickets to fall and wanting no fewer than 193 runs to win.

On the third day Mr Page, not out 8, was joined by Mr Key, and 27 runs were scored in the first quarter of an hour. Mr Page was bowled at 105, and Mr Key at 120. When Messrs Nicholls and Grant-Asher became associated the hitting was of the most vigorous description. So quickly did the score rise that the first 100 runs were made in sixty-five minutes. Mr Nicholls was caught at point at 190 for a finely-hit 44, no fewer than 70 runs having been put on for the eighth wicket. Mr Grant-Asher was bowled at 205 for an excellent 43. In the hope of finishing the match before the interval play was prolonged until 2.15, but as Messrs Whitby and Bastard could not be parted luncheon was then taken. Only two runs were added on resuming, and so the Oxonians suffered their only defeat in 1884 by 31 runs.

Gentlemen of England

I. D. Walker Esq. c Kemp b Whitby	5	– b Page	55
A. J. Webbe Esq. c Key b Bastard	8	– run out	17
J. G. Walker Esq. b Bastard	25	– c Brain b Page	92
G. F. Vernon Esq. b Bastard	11	– c Page b Bastard	4
T. S. Pearson Esq. c Nicholls b Whitby	10	– b Key	38
S. S. Schultz Esq. b Whitby	7	– c Brain b Nicholls	63
E. J. C. Studd Esq. c Kemp b Bastard	31	– c Brain b Page	31
W. E. Collins Esq. st Kempt b Whitby	7	– b Key	16
H. Rotherham Esq. c O'Brien b Whitby	0	– b Nicholls	4
S. Christopherson Esq. b Page	24	– c Hine-Haycock b Nicholls	6
G. A. B. Leatham Esq. not out	3	– not out	0
B 7, l-b 2	9	B 8, l-b 3	11
	140		337

Oxford University

T. C. O'Brien Esq. c Rotherham b Christopherson	13	– c Collins b Rotherham	0
T. R. Hine-Haycock Esq. b Rotherham	17	– b Christopherson	0
A. R. Cobb Esq. c Leatham b Rotherham	8	– b Christopherson	8
H. V. Page Esq. c Webbe b Rotherham	72	– b Rotherham	29
M. C. Kemp Esq. b Rotherham	8	– st Leatham b Pearson	33
K. J. Key Esq. c Schultz b Christopherson	47	– b Rotherham	19
A. G. Grant-Asher c Leatham b Rotherham	17	– b Rotherham	43
J. H. Brain Esq. b Rotherham	0	– b Rotherham	22
B. E. Nicholls Esq. c Christopherson b Rotherham	10	– c Studd b Christopherson	44
H. O. Whitby Esq. not out	2	– c Leatham b Rotherham	21
E. W. Bastard Esq. c and b Rotherham	0	– not out	11
B 16, l-b 1, w 1	18	B 4	4
	212		234

Oxford University Bowling

	Overs	Mdns	Runs	Wkts	Overs	Mdns	Runs	Wkts
Mr Bastard	24.1	9	54	4	38	15	65	1
Mr Whitby	24	4	67	5	25	1	84	—
Mr Page	4	3	2	1	36	9	80	3
Mr Nicholls	4	2	8	—	35.2	14	65	3
Mr Key					15	4	32	2

Gentlemen of England Bowling

	Overs	Mdns	Runs	Wkts	Overs	Mdns	Runs	Wkts
Mr Rotherham	36	16	57	8	41.1	12	93	6
Mr Christopherson	34	14	74	2	38	14	97	3
Mr I. D. Walker	6	1	31	—				
Mr Collins	8	3	22	—				
Mr Webbe	5	2	10	—	2	—	3	—
Mr Pearson					6	—	28	1
Mr Schultz					3	—	9	—

Umpires: G. Webb and V. A. Titchmarsh.

OXFORD UNIVERSITY v MCC AND GROUND

Played in the Parks at Oxford, June 21, 22, 1886

This, the last home match of the Oxford season, was rendered remarkable by the extraordinary performance of Mr W. G. Grace, who scored an innings of 104, and took the whole of the ten Oxford wickets, this being the only instance in first-class cricket in 1886 of all ten wickets being taken by the same bowler. The match was robbed of a great deal of its importance from the fact that a large number of the Oxford eleven were engaged in the schools and unable to appear in the team, and the weakness of the home team will readily be seen, when it is stated that there were only five men taking part who subsequently appeared against Cambridge. The eleven brought down by the MCC proved far too strong for the Dark Blues, who were outplayed from start to finish. Going in first Oxford scored 142, the best cricket being played by Mr H. V. Page, who made 49. Messrs W. G. Grace and E. J. C. Studd opened the Marylebone innings, and before the call of time scored 83 without the loss of a wicket, the Champion being not out 50, and Mr Studd not out 29.

On the following day Mr Grace increased his overnight score to 104, and the best hits of his innings were a 6 and fifteen 4s. The total of the MCC reached 260, or 118 runs to the good. In their second innings the Oxonians failed completely before the bowling of Mr Grace, and Mr Page was again the only man to offer any serious resistance. The whole side were out for 90, and the MCC won with great ease by an innings and 28 runs.

Oxford University

Mr J. H. Brain c Nepean b Wright	19	–	c Hine-Haycock b Grace	15
Mr P. Coles b Wright	14	–	c Attewell b Grace	1
Mr A. K. Watson c Grace b Attewell	9	–	b Grace	0
Mr H. V. Page b Attewell	49	–	st Kemp b Grace	26
Mr W. Rashleigh b Wright	2	–	b Grace	19
Mr C. Wreford-Brown c Kemp b Grace	4	–	c Attewell b Grace	13
Mr E. H. F. Bradby c Hine-Haycock b Grace	4	–	b Grace	0
Mr E. H. Buckland b Titchmarsh	20	–	b Grace	4
Mr A. R. Cobb b Wright	6	–	c Paravicini b Grace	0
Mr H. W. Forster c Grace b Attewell	8	–	not out	0
Mr J. H. Ware not out	4	–	lbw b Grace	10
B 2, l-b 1	3		L-b 2	2
	142			90

MCC and Ground

Mr W. G. Grace lbw b Page	104
Mr E. J. C. Studd c Wreford-Brown b Forster	36
Mr C. Booth c Buckland b Wreford-Brown	14
Mr T. R. Hine-Haycock c Forster b Wreford-Brown	0
Mr P. J. de Paravicini c Coles b Wreford-Brown	9
Mr M. C. Kemp c and b Forster	15
W. Wright c Wreford-Brown b Buckland	9
Attewell c Buckland b Wreford-Brown	22
Lord George Scott not out	25
Mr E. A. Nepean c and b Buckland	6
Titchmarsh st Cobb b Forster	10
B 8, l-b 2	10
	260

MCC Bowling

	Overs	Mdns	Runs	Wkts	Overs	Mdns	Runs	Wkts
Mr Grace	32	11	60	2	36.2	17	49	10
Wright	59	42	31	4	25	12	28	0
Attewell	38.1	22	39	3	11	7	11	0
Titchmarsh	11	7	9	1				

Oxford University Bowling

	Overs	Mdns	Runs	Wkts
Mr Buckland	44	23	55	2
Mr Forster	32.3	12	65	2
Mr Ware	14	2	43	0
Mr Page	15	1	45	1
Mr Wreford-Brown	23	8	42	4

OXFORD UNIVERSITY v SURREY

Played at Oxford, May 23, 24, 1889

The Oxonians were completely overmatched, and Surrey won in a single innings with 183 runs to spare. There were two remarkable performances which will render the game memorable. J. W. Sharpe, the young Surrey bowler, took five wickets in twenty-one overs and a ball (eighteen maidens) at a cost of only 5 runs, and Mr K. J. Key made 176 not out, which tied Mr Marchant's innings at Gravesend as being the highest individual score of the season. Sharpe's achievement was all the more remarkable, as the condition of the ground gave him no assistance whatever. Oxford's score at luncheon time was 90 for the loss of four batsmen, and then the last six wickets went down for the addition of only 8 runs, the bowling of Sharpe being, of course, the main cause of this breakdown in the batting. Mr Key made his 176 in three hours and a half, and, though he gave three clear chances after reaching his 100, his innings was a most brilliant one. He made every use of his opportunity, and punished the Oxford bowling with merciless severity. The vigour of his hitting will best be judged from the following figures – two 6s, eighteen 4s, nine 3s, twenty-one 2s and twenty-three singles. Mr Rashleigh played an extremely good innings of 54, and one the second day Lohmann bowled wonderfully well, taking seven wickets for 42 runs.

Oxford University

Mr F. H. Gresson c W. W. Read b Beaumont	33	– b Lohmann	0
Mr H. Philipson b Lohmann	4	– b Beaumont	18
Mr W. Rashleigh c Wood b Lohmann	0	– c Shuter b Lohmann	54
Mr A. K. Watson b Sharpe	16	– lbw b Lohmann	0
Mr M. R. Jardine b Sharpe	21	– c Abel b Beaumont	1
Mr F. J. N. Thesiger c and b Lohmann	10	– c Abel b Lohmann	4
Mr H. W. Forster c and b Lohmann	0	– b Lohmann	0
Mr A. C. M. Croome b Sharpe	0	– c Abel b Lohmann	17
Mr C. Wreford-Brown not out	2	– b Lohmann	0
Mr E. Smith b Sharpe	3	– not out	5
Mr H. Bassett b Sharpe	0	– c Wood b Sharpe	3
B 8, l-b 1	9	B 4	4
	98		106

Surrey

Mr J. Shuter b Smith	15
R. Abel c Forster b Smith	33
M. Read b Bassett	44
Mr W. W. Read b Croome	10
G. A. Lohmann b Croome	4
Mr K. J. Key not out	176
R. Henderson c Smith b Croome	51
J. W. Sharpe c Philipson b Forster	4
H. Wood c Wreford-Brown b Croome	4
J. Beaumont b Wreford-Brown	34
T. Bowley b Bassett	2
B 7, l-b 2, w 1	10
	387

Surrey Bowling

	Overs	Mdns	Runs	Wkts	Overs	Mdns	Runs	Wkts
Lohmann	27	14	31	4	31	14	42	7
Bowley	14	4	29	0				
Beaumont	10	4	24	1	22	8	49	2
Sharpe	21.1	18	5	5	9.2	5	11	1

Oxford University Bowling

	Overs	Mdns	Runs	Wkts
Mr Forster	19	6	59	1
Mr Smith	31	7	95	2
Mr Bassett	44.4	18	82	2
Mr Croome	37	9	94	4
Mr Wreford-Brown	17	4	47	1

Umpires: G. Webb and Henwood.

OXFORD UNIVERSITY v LANCASHIRE

Played at Oxford, May 26, 27, 1892

Few matches during the remarkable season of 1892 produced a keener struggle or created a greater surprise than this meeting between Oxford University and Lancashire, and it was the unexpected but well-earned victory of the Dark Blues that made people fancy that Oxford would have a much stronger eleven than had in the earlier part of the summer seemed probable. A good deal of rain had fallen, and it was, of course, a decided advantage to obtain first innings, but though this piece of luck fell to the Oxonians, scarcely anyone though that there was any hope of success against the powerful Lancashire eleven. However, the young team set about their work with vigour and determination, and their efforts were ultimately attended with success, Oxford gaining a victory on the second evening, amid a scene of great excitement and enthusiasm, by seven runs. On the strength of some good bowling in a College match J. B. Wood was given a place in the eleven, and it was his lob bowling that largely helped Oxford to win. The Lancashire men in their first innings played in a very tame and spiritless fashion, and were dismissed for a total of 88, which gave Oxford a lead of 45 runs. Palairet played extremely well in the second innings of Oxford, but, with the exception of Brain, the others failed completely before Briggs on a soft wicket. Lancashire were left with 150 runs to get to win, and up to a certain point seemed to have the match well in hand, the score being up to 123 when the sixth wicket fell, but from that point there came a series of disasters for Lancashire, two wickets being thrown away by bad judgment in running, and the whole side being out for 142. Admirable fielding had much to do with the result, Palairet setting his team an example that was brilliantly followed up.

Oxford University

Mr L. C. H. Palairet b Mold	0	– c Sugg b Briggs	57
Mr F. A. Phillips c MacLaren b Briggs	27	– c MacLaren b Briggs	2
Mr C. B. Fry c Sugg b Watson	50	– b Briggs	0
Mr V. T. Hill b Briggs	10	– b Mold	9
Mr T. S. B. Wilson c Crosfield b Briggs	6	– b Briggs	3
Mr T. B. Case b Briggs	5	– b Briggs	0
Mr R. T. Jones b Watson	2	– run out	5
Mr H. D. Watson b Watson	2	– c Kemble b Briggs	0
Mr J. B. Wood b Briggs	16	– not out	2
Mr W. H. Brain b Watson	6	– b Briggs	19
Mr G. F. H. Berkeley not out	4	– c and b Watson	0
B 4	4	B 5, l-b 3	8
	132		105

Lancashire

A. Ward c Wilson b Palairet	7	– c sub. b Berkeley	24
F. H. Sugg st Brain b Wood	30	– b Berkeley	0
Mr A. C. MacLaren c Brain b Palairet	7	– c Brain b Palairet	28
Mr G. Kemp b Wood	0	– c Hill b Palairet	18
J. Briggs c Brain b Wood	2	– c and b Berkeley	17
G. R. Baker c Palairet b Wood	8	– c Jones b Palairet	17
Mr S. M. Crosfield run out	4	– run out	15
Mr A. N. Hornby c Hill b Palairet	16	– run out	7
Mr A. T. Kemble c Hill b Wood	13	– b Berkeley	6
A. Watson not out	0	– c Wilson b Palairet	6
A. Mold b Palairet	0	– not out	0
B 1	1	B 1, l-b 3	4
	88		142

Lancashire Bowling

	Overs	Mdns	Runs	Wkts	Overs	Mdns	Runs	Wkts
Watson	22	9	42	4	13	3	42	1
Mold	8	3	20	1	16.2	6	23	1
Briggs	22	7	34	5	29	15	32	7
Baker	9	1	32	0				

Oxford University Bowling

	Overs	Mdns	Runs	Wkts	Overs	Mdns	Runs	Wkts
Mr Berkeley	7	3	27	0	25	11	38	4
Mr Palairet	14.4	3	27	4	24.2	8	52	4
Mr Wood	8	0	33	5	9	1	24	0
Mr Fry					8	1	24	0
Mr Wilson					3	3	0	0

Umpires: Hughes and F. Coward.

OXFORD UNIVERSITY v MCC AND GROUND

Played at Oxford, June 10, 11, 1897

After a thoroughly interesting game from start to finish, Oxford defeated a strong eleven of the MCC by 13 runs, there being considerable excitement towards the close. Up to a certain point, Oxford seemed to have the match well in hand, but a splendid effort by Vernon, Hearne and Roche nearly turned the scale in favour of the Marylebone Club. On winning the toss for the MCC, Mr Webbe put his opponents in to bat, but his course of action was far from being attended with successful results. J. T. Hearne bowled with surprising effect, taking fifteen wickets at a cost of 110 runs and no man could have tried harder for his side. In the second innings of the MCC, Sir T. C. O'Brien, owing to an injured foot, was unable to bat and his absence probably gave the match to Oxford.

Oxford University

Mr F. L. Fane b Crawley b Hearne	44	– run out	20
Mr F. H. B. Champain b Hearne	5	– b Hearne	31
Mr G. E. Bromley-Martin c Board b Hearne	48	– b Roche	0
Mr R. E. Foster b Hearne	27	– b Hearne	8
Mr A. Eccles c Roche b Hearne	8	– c Rawlin b Roche	2
Mr G. R. Bardswell b Hearne	19	– c Board b Hearne	3
Mr T. B. Henderson c Roche b Hearne	0	– c Board b Hearne	5
Mr E. C. Wright b Hearne	0	– b Roche	0
Mr F. H. E. Cunliffe c and b Attewell	5	– b Hearne	31
Mr F. W. Stocks not out	1	– c Board b Hearne	9
Mr H. W. Fox c Board b Hearne	4	– not out	2
B 6	6	B 6	6
	167		117

MCC and Ground

Mr A. J. Webbe c Cunliffe b Stocks	47	– b Henderson	15
J. H. Board c Wright b Cunliffe	2	– c Wright b Cunliffe	26
Mr G. Kemp b Cunliffe	15	– b Henderson	11
J. T. Rawlin b Wright	3	– b Wright	8
Mr A. S. Crawley b Wright	3	– c Bardswell b Henderson	2
Sir T. C. O'Brien c Henderson b Wright	2	– absent hurt	0
Mr G. F. Vernon c Bromley-Martin b Cunliffe	6	– not out	57
W. Attewell c Henderson b Cunliffe	3	– c Fox b Wright	6
Mr A. E. Leatham not out	8	– b Wright	0
J. T. Hearne c Wright b Stocks	0	– b Stocks	12
W. Roche c Bardswell b Stocks	0	– c Wright b Stocks	20
B 6, l-b 2, n-b 4	12	B 9, l-b 1, n-b 3	13
	101		170

MCC Bowling

	Overs	Mdns	Runs	Wkts	Overs	Mdns	Runs	Wkts
Hearne	31	14	54	9	26	11	56	6
Roche	13	3	48	0	17	6	30	3
Attewell	25	14	43	1	8	2	25	0
Rawlin	7	3	16	0				

Oxford University Bowling

	Overs	Mdns	Runs	Wkts	Overs	Mdns	Runs	Wkts
Cunliffe	21	5	55	4	13	3	30	1
Wright	19	11	19	3	22	3	58	3
Stocks	9.4	3	15	3	14.4	6	30	2
Henderson					13	4	39	3

Umpires: D. Eastwood and Glossop.

THE PUBLIC SCHOOLS

"THE TIMES" ON THE PUBLIC SCHOOLS MATCHES

"The subject, as we have already said, is not below the dignity of the present time. It is important to secure a race of young Englishmen who in days to come, when our bones have mouldered away, shall retain the grasp of England upon the world." – The Times, August, 1857.

RUGBY SCHOOL v MARLBOROUGH COLLEGE

Played at Lord's, June 23 and 24, 1869

Curious cricket incidents cropped up in this match. Rugby lost two wickets before a run was made, three wickets for 1 run, and seven for 24; then Mr Walker went in and took his bat out for 53, a busy, timely innings, that deserved all the applause it gained. At a quarter to two, the Marlborough innings commenced; at twenty minutes to four it was over for 51 runs – Mr Leach not out 25. In Rugby's second innings, Mr Pearson made 20 runs in eighteen minutes; but the feature of the match was the effective fast bowling of Mr Francis that, in twenty-four overs, took all the ten wickets in Marlborough's second innings. In his first, second, fourth and fifth overs Mr Francis had a wicket; he then bowled six successive maiden overs, having a wicket in his eleventh. In his eighteenth over he had two wickets, another in his twenty-first over, and with the second and third balls of his twenty-fourth over he had the other two, thus taking all ten wickets (nine "bowled"). Rugby won by 179 runs.

Rugby

T. S. Pearson Esq. b W. Leach	0	– hit wkt b Dawson	20
E. A. R. Benham Esq. b W. Leach	0	– b Dawson	0
G. R. Westfeldt Esq. b Dawson	1	– b Copleston	52
H. W. Gardner Esq. b Dawson	9	– b Kempe	14
W. O. Moberley Esq. b Dawson	6	– b Copleston	24
C. K. Francis Esq. c Woollcombe b Dawson	5	– c R. Leach b Copleston	4
S. K. Gwyer Esq. c Robinson b Inchbald	18	– b Copleston	6
E. H. Warner Esq. c Woollcombe b W. Leach	0	– b Dawson	0
J. R. Walker Esq. not out	53	– c R. Leach b Dawson	6
A. Gray Esq. b Dawson	10	– lbw b Dawson	9
H. Tubb Esq. b Kempe	11	– not out	0
B 5	5	B 3, l-b 3, w 6, n-b 1	13
	118		148

Marlborough

W. E. Leach Esq. c Moberley b Francis	9	– b Francis	7
C. P. Woollcombe Esq. b Tubb	2	– b Francis	0
J. A. Kempe Esq. b Francis	0	– b Francis	0
R. Leach Esq. not out	25	– b Francis	0
F. Kingsford Esq. c Gray b Tubb	2	– b Francis	2
H. B. Carlyon Esq. b Francis	2	– c Walker b Francis	12
A. C. G. Hervey Esq. b Francis	6	– b Francis	0
A. F. Robinson Esq. b Francis	0	– b Francis	9
F. S. Copleston Esq. b Francis	0	– not out	0
R. M. Inchbald Esq. c Gray b Tubb	1	– b Francis	0
W. A. Dawson Esq. b Francis	0	– b Francis	0
B 4	4	B 1, l-b 5	6
	51		36

Rugby Bowling

	Overs	Mdns	Runs	Wkts	Overs	Mdns	Runs	Wkts
Mr Francis	22	13	25	7	23.3	17	15	10
Mr Tubb	21	11	22	3	23	17	15	—

Marlborough Bowling

	Overs	Mdns	Runs	Wkts	Overs	Mdns	Runs	Wkts
Mr W. Leach	28	13	45	3	20	8	30	—
Mr Dawson	22	7	42	5	22.3	10	45	5
Mr Inchbaid	10	2	20	1	26	13	33	—
Mr Kempe	4	2	6	1	13	8	14	1
Mr Copleston					12	13	4	4

Umpires: Royston and Biddulph.

ETON v HARROW

Played at Lord's, July 13, 14, 1888

The Schools' match of 1888 resulted in a victory by Harrow by 156 runs and on the cricket shown at Lord's there can be no question whatever that the better side proved successful. We believe, however, that the most faithful supporters of Harrow cricket were surprised at the nature of the victory, and we shall probably not be far outside the truth in suggesting that, while the Harrow boys played above their form, the Etonians fell below what might reasonably have been expected of them. Up to a certain point it was a very even and interesting game, but before the drawing of stumps on the first day Harrow had gained such an advantage that little doubt could be felt as to the ultimate result. Before going into any details of the play it may be well to say that Eton had only three "old choices" available – Bromley-Davenport, the captain, Tollemache and Bathurst; while in the Harrow team there were five members of the side which had been beaten in 1887 – the two MacLarens, Watson, Ramsay, and Jackson.

Harrow's first innings commenced at five minutes past eleven on the Friday, the wicket being very slow and difficult from the effects of recent rains, and was all over by one o'clock for the paltry total of 80. Five wickets fell for 17 runs, and only some plucky play by Jackson, Gilroy, and Roffey averted a complete collapse. There was every excuse for failure, but the total was certainly discouraging. H. W. Studd – one of the youngest members of the famous family – bowled with great success. Bowling medium pace, with rather a slinging action, he seemed to have considerable command over the ball. Pechell, a very slow left-handed bowler, was on most of the time with him, and we may take this opportunity of saying that Eton was sadly handicapped by the fact that Bromley-Davenport had almost entirely lost the bowling of which so much was thought in the two previous seasons. There was nothing to account for his decline, but his arm was lower, and he had become quite ineffective. Eton went in at twenty minutes past one, and started so badly that three good wickets were lost for 9 runs. At lunch time the score was 22, and afterwards the team did sufficiently well to pass Harrow's total with six wickets down, Yate-Lee hitting in capital style for 37 – so far the best innings in the match. However, when the last wicket fell the total was only 106, or 26 runs to the good. Jackson (right-hand fast) bowled admirably.

When Harrow's second innings commenced at ten minutes to five the wicket had improved wonderfully, and the last two hours' cricket practically decided the match. Two wickets fell for 4 runs, and then the batting gained the upper hand. Hoare and Watson carried the score to 74 – an invaluable stand – and then Hoare and Jackson punished the bowling so severely that when seven o'clock came the total had been raised to 167, Hoare being not out 80, and Jackson not out 50. Both boys played admirably, and in the last three-quarters of an hour scored 67 runs, the fielding, as was not unnatural after such a long day, becoming rather loose towards the close. On the Saturday morning the innings was finished off in rather less than an hour and a half for a total of 234. Hoare and Jackson were parted at 188, having put on 114 for the fourth wicket. Hoare had the great distinction of scoring over 100, following among Harrow batsmen the late A. W. T. Daniel, A. K. Watson, and Eustace Crawley, and except that he was badly missed at point when he had scored 73, and gave a chance low down at mid-off with his total at 76, his innings, in respect both of hitting and defence, was a very fine one. He was at the wicket three hours and a quarter, and his 108 comprised ten 4s, nine 3s, ten 2s, and twenty-one singles. Jackson's capital 59 included seven 4s, a 3, and seven 2s.

Eton had 209 to get to win – a formidable task for a school eleven – and all doubts as to the result were soon at an end. In a bad light the batsmen seemed to lose all their nerve in playing Jackson's bowling, and so complete was the failure that four wickets fell for nine runs and eight for 17. Goad and Hodgson afterwards made something of a stand, but for a total of 52 the innings was all over, Harrow winning by 156 runs. Jackson and Hoare had an enormous share in gaining the victory, the former scoring 21 and 59, and taking eleven wickets for 68 runs, and Hoare, in addition to his innings of 108, taking five wickets for 58 runs. The only Etonian who could look back upon the match with any great amount of personal satisfaction was H. W. Studd, who worked very hard for his side, and took in all fourteen wickets. Jackson's performance for Harrow was all the more remarkable, as he had been ill a little time before the match.

Harrow

Mr A. C. MacLaren c Ward b Studd	0	– b Studd	4
Mr W. E. Greaves c Tollemache b Studd	4	– b Studd	0
Mr H. D. Watson c and b Pechell	1	– b Studd	26
Mr R. B. Hoare b Studd	4	– b Jones	108
Mr F. S. Jackson b Studd	21	– b Studd	59
Mr J. A. MacLaren (captain) st Hodgson b Pechell	2	– b Studd	0
Mr W. J. F. Giffard run out	3	– b Studd	2
Mr C. E. Gilroy b Bathurst	24	– c Goad b Studd	16
Mr G. W. Roffey b Studd	12	– c Bathurst b Studd	0
Mr R. D. Cheales not out	6	– b Jones	3
Mr N. Ramsay c and b Studd	0	– not out	5
L-b 3	3	B 8, l-b 2, w 1	11
	80		234

Eton

Hon. M. G. Tollemache c Roffey b Jackson	0	– b Jackson	1
Mr R. T. Jones b Hoare	1	– b Jackson	0
Mr W. S. Gosling lbw b Jackson	3	– b Jackson	9
Mr C. Yate-Lee c Gilroy b Jackson	37	– b Jackson	0
Mr H. W. Studd b Jackson	10	– b Hoare	1
Mr H. Bromley-Davenport (captain) lbw b J. MacLaren.	8	– c Jackson b Hoare	1
Hon. R. A. Ward c Roffey b Jackson	12	– b Jackson	0
Mr F. E. Goad b Jackson	11	– b Hoare	22
Mr F. R. H. Bathurst b Ramsay	6	– st Roffey b Hoare	0
Mr E. T. Hodgson lbw b Ramsay	7	– b Gilroy	14
Mr C. A. K. Pechell not out	10	– not out	2
B 1	1	B 1, l-b 1	2
	106		52

Eton Bowling

	Overs	Mdns	Runs	Wkts	Overs	Mdns	Runs	Wkts
Studd	27.2	15	27	6	45	17	72	8
Pechell	19	5	31	2	11	2	40	0
Bromley-Davenport	6	4	5	0	12	5	24	0
Jones	4	2	2	0	19	11	23	2
Bathurst	6	2	12	1	34	14	41	0
Ward					7	1	23	0

Harrow Bowling

	Overs	Mdns	Runs	Wkts	Overs	Mdns	Runs	Wkts
Hoare	25	12	37	1	23	12	21	4
Jackson	35	19	40	6	21	7	28	5
J. A. MacLaren	9	3	11	1				
Gilroy	6	2	11	0	2.3	2	0	1
Ramsay	7.1	4	6	2	1	0	1	0

Umpires: Wheeler and T. Mycroft.

HIGHBURY PARK SCHOOL v ISLINGTON HIGH SCHOOL

Played at Muswell Hill, June 12, 1897

The score of this match is published as a curiosity, the losers being dismissed without getting a run and second innings for five, a total of 21 proving sufficient to win the game by an innings and 16 runs. Wiggins took eleven wickets for two runs.

Highbury Park School

Innes b Jones	3
Haslett b Fairman	4
L. Jones b Fairman	3
Wiggins c Bartram b Fairman	2
C. Buckney c Taylor b Jones	4
Wright b Fairman	2
Masters run out	1
A. Vasey not out	0
Poulton b Fairman	0
Kirby b Fairman	1
W. Reid c Rilerosthy b Fairman	0
B 1	1
	21

Islington High School

Fairman c Haslett b Wiggins	0	– b Wiggins	0
Staley b Jones	0	– b Jones	0
Bull c Haslett b Jones	0	– b Jones	0
Bartram b Wiggins	0	– b Wiggins	0
Rilerosthy b Wiggins	0	– c Wiggins b Jones	0
Cook b Wiggins	0	– not out	0
Gardner b Jones	0	– c Innes b Wiggins	2
Taylor run out	0	– b Wiggins	2
C. Jones not out	0	– b Wiggins	0
Dunn b Wiggins	0	– c Haslett b Wiggins	1
	0		5

TONBRIDGE SCHOOL v DULWICH COLLEGE

Played at Dulwich, June 3, 1899

Tonbridge winning easily by 170 runs

Dulwich College

	First innings		Second innings	
C. F. Krabbe b Marriott	12	–	c K. Hutchings b Worthington	6
F. L. Nightingale run out	13	–	b Marriott	0
J. C. L. Farquharson c Hammill b Worthington	12	–	c K. Hutchings b Worthington	8
A. L. Inglis c Manser b F. V. Hutchings	11			
L. A. Whitely c Walford b F. V. Hutchings	0	–	c Worthington b Manser	35
G. F. Legg c Hammill b Worthington	17	–	not out	9
D. G. Hurlbatt b Worthington	0	–	b Manser	0
H. W. Ripley run out	4			
N. A. Knox b Worthington	0			
A. G. Skey not out	1	–	c Hammill b Manser	0
P. G. Wodehouse c Worthington b Walford	0			
B 5, n-b 2	7		B 1	1
	77			59

Tonbridge School

F. V. Hutchings b Wodehouse	74
R. M. Manser lbw b Whitely	0
R. H. Marriott lbw b Wodehouse	12
R. F. Worthington b Ripley	23
K. L. Hutchings c Skey b Wodehouse	60
A. Brown b Wodehouse	3
G. S. Cooper b Wodehouse	7
S. S. Hayne b Wodehouse	13
A. T. Millner c Farquharson b Wodehouse	1
A. Hammill b Knox	28
J. A. S. Walford not out	0
B 15, l-b 9, n-b 2	26
	247

ENGLAND IN AUSTRALIA

GRACE AND TARRANT v ELEVEN OF OTAGO

Played at Dunedin, February 15, 1864

The Two

E. M. Grace lbw b Wills	7	– b Wills	10
G. Tarrant c Murison b Wills	1	– lbw b Wills	6
	8		16

The Eleven

McDonald b Tarrant	0	Murison b Tarrant	1
Winter b Tarrant	0	Hamilton b Tarrant	0
Jacomb b Tarrant	0	Lamont b Tarrant	3
Redfern b Tarrant	0	Thomas b Tarrant	1
Wills c and b Tarrant	1		
Worthington b Tarrant	1		
Smith b Tarrant	0		7

The Eleven did not play their second innings.

After the Castlemaine match, 1864, the following Single Wicket Match was played, Tarrant fielding for the two. England won by 12 runs.

England

E. M. Grace c Smith b Crawshaw	13
J. Jackson b Crawshaw	0
N-b 1	1
	14

Castlemaine

Amos b Jackson	1	Smith b Jackson	0
Lewis b Jackson	0	Dow hit wkt b Jackson	1
Easton b Jackson	0	Bond b Jackson	0
Wilson b Jackson	0	B. Butterworth hit wkt b Jackson	0
Govett b Jackson	0		
Morris b Jackson	0		
Crawshaw b Jackson	0		2

TARRANT'S ELEVEN v PARR'S ELEVEN

Played at Maryborough, April 14, 15, 1864

Tarrant's Eleven

E. M. Grace run out	37	– c Lockyer b Hayward	14
Marshall c and b Hayward	23	– c and b Hayward	15
J. Cæsar b Hayward	3	– c Clarke b Caffyn	13
R. Carpenter c Caffyn b Freestone	18	– b Hayward	4
G. Tarrant b Hayward	35	– st Lockyer b Hayward	3
Garland run out	5	– b Hayward	6
R. C. Tinley st Lockyer b Caffyn	10	– c Clarke b Jackson	10
J. Freestone b Caffyn	16	– st Lockyer b Caffyn	1
Maher c and b Hayward	6	– b Jackson	0
Howliston b Caffyn	6	– not out	3
G. Anderson not out	0	– c Jackson (Cox sub.)	0
L-b 3, w 2	5	Extras	8
	164		74

Parr's Eleven

J. Jackson b Cæsar	45	– b Cæsar	2
Morres b Grace	2	– b Tinley	0
A. Clarke c J. Freestone b Tinley	4	– c Grace b Tinley	15
T. Hayward st Marshall b Cæsar	32	– b Cæsar	19
W. Caffyn c Cæsar b Tinley	6	– c J. Freestone b Cæsar	10
G. Parr st Marshall b Tinley	3	– b Cæsar	6
T. Lockyer c Tarrant b Tinley	0	– b Cæsar	5
A. Freestone c and b Tinley	2	– not out	0
Torriano c and b Tinley	4	– c Grace b Cæsar	4
W. Freestone b Cæsar	5	– run out	8
Barlow not out	1	– b Cæsar	1
B 5, l-b 1, w 2	8		
	112		70

Tarrant's Eleven winning by 56 runs.

At the conclusion of the grand match, a Single Wicket match was got up, Mr Grace challenging any six of the local players; and going first to the wickets, remained there the rest of the day, hitting away in brilliant style to the tune of 106, and carrying his bat out into the bargain. His play during this afternoon was eagerly watched, and some of his hits were enthusiastically cheered. The bowling was repeatedly changed, but the "great gun" was invulnerable.

THE ENGLISH ELEVEN v THE NEW SOUTH WALES ELEVEN

Played on the Association Ground, Sydney, February 7, 8, 10, 1879

The weather was splendid. On the first day it was recorded there were 4000 persons present, including Lady Robinson and party. On the second day, a Saturday, and the day of disturbance, it was reported there were fully 10,000 persons present; but on the third day (Monday) there were not more than 1,500 on the ground.

The Englishmen having won choice, commenced the batting on good wickets, with Hornby and Lucas, to the bowling of Spofforth and Evans. They made a truly great stand, for, notwithstanding several bowling changes, the score was hit to 125 before the first wicket fell by Spofforth bowling Lucas for 51 – chronicled in the *The Australasian* as "A fine exhibition of cricket, he did not give a chance all through". When but 7 more runs had been added, Spofforth also bowled Hornby for 61 – stated to have been "A fine innings, with only one possible chance". Ulyett and Lord Harris then made another good stand, as they increased the score from 132 to 217 ere they were separated by Ulyett being magnificently caught out for 55 by Evans close to the pavilion fence. Touching this catch, *The Australian* remarked, "Ulyett hit a ball from Spofforth towards the pavilion enclosure; Evans running at full speed made a kangaroo-like bound at the flying leather, and secured it with one hand. The performance of course brought down the house". With the score at 234 Evans bowled Lord Harris for "a fine innings of 41 runs". Then came a collapse, for the fifth wicket also fell at 234, the sixth at 235, the seventh at 247, the eighth at 255, the ninth at 262, and the tenth at 267. Soon after the third wicket fell Charles Bannerman had to retire from fielding, consequent on the reopening of a wound on his hand received in a previous match. It may here be stated that Hornby's 67 included seven 4s; Lucas's 51, four 4s; Ulyett's 55, seven 4s; Lord Harris's 41, four 4s; and Penn's 13, two 4s. The NSW innings was commenced by A. Bannerman and Murdoch to the bowling of Lucas and Schultz, who were subsequently relieved by Emmett and Ulyett, and in the latter's first over A. Bannerman was out for 16 (including three 4s), the score standing at 34 for that first wicket. At 37 Thompson was out, whereupon Massie faced Murdoch, and when (in a bad light) the stumps were drawn for that day the Sydney score stood at 53 for two wickets, Murdoch, not out, 28.

On the Saturday the not outs resumed their innings about noon, to the bowling of Lucas and Emmett, the former being subsequently succeeded by Ulyett, and he by Hornby, who, later on, clean bowled Massie for 38 – an innings that included four 4s. The score was at 130 when Massie was bowled. Then Emmett's bowling had a good time, inasmuch as it captured the remaining seven wickets, the innings closing for 177 runs, Murdoch having triumphantly played all through the innings, taking his bat out for 82 – described "a grand innings". Murdoch's hits were eleven 4s, three 3s, nine 2s and eleven singles. Emmett's bowling in that innings summed up 52 overs (less one ball) for 47 runs and eight wickets. Being in a minority of 90 runs, the NSW men, in due course, "followed on", Murdoch and A. Bannerman commencing their second innings, 19 runs had been made, 10 of them by Murdoch, when an appeal to Coulthard, the Umpire, resulted in Murdoch being run out, then arose

The Disturbance

that *The Australasian* remarked would "for ever make the match memorable in the annals of New South Wales cricket". It appears that on the decision being given Murdoch (like a true cricketer) retired; whereupon arose cries of "Not Out!" – "Go back, Murdoch!" – "Another Umpire!" and so on. The crowds rushed to the wickets, and, stated *The Australasian*, "rowdyism became rampant for the rest of the afternoon". The Eleven Englishmen were surrounded by a rough and excited mob, who prevented further cricket being played that day. Much was said and written on this deplorably disgraceful affair; but it is gratifying to record that all respectable portions of Australian society, and all the leading journals in the Colonies strongly condemned this outrage. *The South Australian Register* stated "The scene was a disgrace to the people", and "profound regret is expressed at the occurrence". *The Sydney Mail* remarked, "The English team soon found themselves in the centre of a surging, gesticulating, and shouting mob, and one rowdy struck Lord Harris across the body with a whip or stick". *The Australasian* stated "His Excellency, Lady Robinson, and party were present, and were pained witnesses of all that occurred", and "The disgraceful affair was the talk of the town"; furthermore, *The Australasian* headed a report with "What will they say in England!" *The South Australian Chronicle* chronicled the remark that "Such a scene had never before been witnessed on a cricket field". And in a subsequent edition, *The Australasian* added – "Before the game was resumed on the Monday, Mr R. Driver (President of the Cricket Association), Mr F. H. Dangar, and others, waited upon Lord Harris, and on behalf of the cricketers of Sydney expressed their extreme regret at the disgraceful scene that took place on the Saturday. The Captain of the English team, in reply, said, 'he did not place any blame on the Association, or the cricketers of Sydney, but it was an occurrence which it was impossible he could forget' ".

The Sydney Morning Herald of February 27, said: – "Our English readers will be glad to learn that steps have been taken to wipe out the disgrace of the discreditable attack on Lord Harris and his cricketers. William Rigney and John Richards were recently charged at the Water Police Court with having participated in the disorder arising in consequence of Murdoch being declared out by the Umpire for the English team. Both men expressed deep regret for what had occurred, and pleaded guilty, and it was in consideration of this rather tardy contrition, and the good character given them by the police that the Bench fined them 40s., and to pay 21s. professional costs, and 5s. costs of Court. Mr Driver, who appeared for the prosecution, stated that inmates of the pavilion who had initiated the disturbance, including a well-known book-maker of Victoria who was at the time ejected, had had their fees of membership returned to them, and they would never again be admitted to the ground. The Bench referring to the kindly hospitable treatment the Australian cricketers received in England, expressed deep regret that Lord Harris and his team should have met such a disagreeable experience".

On Monday, the third day, play was resumed at 12.20. In the interim the wickets had been softened by heavy rainfalls; none made a stand but A. Bannerman who (first man in) was ninth out, the score at 49, his 20 being made by three 4s, one 2 and six singles. The tenth wicket fell with the score unaltered, so the Englishmen won by an innings and 41 runs, Emmett's bowling having taken five wickets for 21 runs, and Ulyett's three for 13 runs.

The English Eleven

A. N. Hornby b Spofforth	67	V. Royle c and b Evans	6
A. P. Lucas b Spofforth	51	C. A. Absolom c and b Evans	6
George Ulyett c Evans b Spofforth	55	S. S. Schultz c and b Evans	5
Lord Harris b Evans	41	L. Hone not out	4
F. Penn c Massie b Spofforth	13	Extras	19
A. J. Webbe b Evans	0		
T. Emmett c Evans b Spofforth	0		267

The New South Wales Eleven

W. Murdoch not out	82	– run out	10
A. Bannerman c Royle b Ulyett	16	– c A. J. Webbe b Emmett	20
N. Thompson c Lucas b Emmett	3	– c F. Penn b Emmett	0
H. H. Massie b Hornby	38	– b Emmett	8
Charles Bannerman c F. Penn b Emmett	9	– c Hornby b Emmett	4
E. Evans b Emmett	5	– c Emmett b Ulyett	1
D. Gregory c Ulyett b Emmett	4	– c A. J. Webbe b Ulyett	0
E. Sheridan c Schultz b Emmett	0	– b Emmett	0
F. Spofforth b Emmett	0	– c A. J. Webbe b Ulyett	0
E. Powell c Hone b Emmett	5	– not out	0
E. Tindall lbw b Emmett	0	– c F. Penn b Emmett	0
Extras	15	Extras	6
	177		49

The New South Wales Bowling

	Overs	Mdns	Runs	Wkts
Spofforth	44	12	93	5
Evans	38	13	62	5
Tindall	27	6	79	—
Thompson	11	4	14	—

The English Bowling

	Overs	Mdns	Runs	Wkts	Overs	Mdns	Runs	Wkts
Emmett	51.3	27	47	8	28	13	21	6
Hornby	22	13	24	1	5	2	9	—
Ulyett	17	4	44	1	22	15	13	3
Lucas	12	4	20	—				
Schultz	15	5	27	—				

Umpires: Mr E. Barton for NSW and Coulthard for England.

Any notice of this match would be inexcusably incomplete that left out two important documents subsequently published, i.e., – Lord Harris's letter to a friend that appeared in the London newspapers early in April, and The New South Wales Cricket Association's reply to that letter, published in the London newspapers the last week of July. Space in this little book can ill be spared for these letters, but they are deemed of such import that the compiler has no choice but to chronicle them. Here follows a copy of

Lord Harris's Letter

"I am not certain whether you will be astonished or not at what I have to tell you, but I know you will be distressed that your friends, a party of gentlemen travelling through these Colonies for the purpose of playing a few friendly games of cricket, should have been insulted and subjected to indignities it distresses us to look back upon. We began the return match with the NSW Eleven on Friday, February 7, scored 267, and got our opponents out for 177 by 3.30 on the Saturday afternoon. Murdoch, who had carried his bat out in the first, and A. Bannerman went to the wickets to commence the second innings. At 19 on the telegraph the former was run out. Before he got back to the pavilion I heard shouts of "not out", "go back", etc., arise from that quarter, and saw the occupants of it rise almost *en masse*. I at once saw what was the matter, and instead of waiting for D. Gregory (the captain) to come out to me, perhaps unwisely walked to the pavilion to meet him at the gate. He, I found, in the name of the NSW Eleven, objected to Coulthard, the umpire. I must here diverge to explain certain facts connected with umpires in these Colonies which are not known or understood at home. Contrary to our custom, it is here the exception to employ professional umpires. This I was not told until after the disturbance. As you know, we brought no umpire, and on arrival at Adelaide I asked the representatives of the Melbourne CC if they could recommend anyone to us whom we could take about with us throughout our tour. They mentioned this man Coulthard, a professional on their ground, whom they had constantly tried and found competent, and added that if we *on trial* also considered him competent, the MCC would be very glad to give him leave of absence so long as we wanted his services. I considered him on trial a good and trustworthy umpire, and arranged with the MCC that he should accompany us to NSW. Had we known on our arrival that a feeling existed in these Colonies against the employment of professional umpires, it is possible we might have acted differently; but, understand, at the same time, that I have seen no reason as yet to change my opinion of Coulthard's qualities, or to regret his engagement, in which opinion I am joined by the whole team. To resume my account of the disturbance on the ground on the Saturday. I asked Gregory on what grounds the objection was raised, and he said at first general incompetence, but afterwards admitted that the objection was raised on account of the decision in Murdoch's case. I implored Gregory, as a friend, and for the sake of the NSW Cricket Association, which I warned him would be the sufferer by it, not to raise the objection, but he refused to take my view of the case. Looking back in the midst of this conversation, I found the ground had been rushed by the mob, and our team was being surrounded. I at once returned to the wickets, and in defending Coulthard from being attacked was struck by some 'larrikin' with a stick. Hornby immediately seized this fellow, and in taking him to the pavilion was struck in the face by a would-be deliverer of the 'larrikin', and had his shirt nearly torn off his back. He, however, conveyed his prisoner to the pavilion in triumph. For some thirty minutes or so I was surrounded by a howling mob, resisting the entreaties of partisans and friends to return to the pavilion until the field was cleared, on the grounds that if our side left the field the other eleven could claim the match. I don't suppose that they would have done so, but I determined to obey the laws of cricket, and may add that for one hour and a half I never left the ground, surrounded during the whole time, with two short intervals, by some hundreds of people. At about five o'clock the crowd was cleared off somehow. I then took the opinion of the Eleven as to changing the umpire, and it was decided *nem. con.* that there were no grounds for the objection, and that we should decline to change him. I informed Gregory of the decision, whereupon he said, 'Then the game is at end'. On Coulthard appearing from the pavilion groans arose from the crowd, and at the same moment it began to break the ring again. The two batsmen who had been standing at the wickets returned to the pavilion, re-called, I afterwards found, by Gregory, but at the time I thought possibly because of the threatened irruption of the crowd. I turned to Mr Barton, the NSW Eleven umpire, and asked if I could not claim the match according to the laws of cricket. His answer was, 'I shall give it you in two minutes' time if the batsmen do not return'. I said to him, 'I won't claim it yet. I'll give the other side every chance of reconsidering a decision arrived at, I believe, unadvisedly, and in a moment of passion. Please ask Gregory what he means to do." On returning Mr Barton informed me that Gregory would send two men to the wickets – a curiously sudden change of mind I think you will allow. However, before the batsmen could appear the crowd had covered the ground for the second time. After some twenty minutes it was cleared for the second time also. A. Bannerman and Thompson then took their places at the wickets, but before a ball could be bowled the crowd broke in for the third and last time. I remained on the ground until the time for drawing the stumps, surrounded as before. Beyond slyly kicking me once or twice the mob behaved very well, their one cry being, 'Change your umpire'. And now for the cause of this disturbance, not unexpected, I may say, by us, for we have heard accounts of former matches played by English teams. It was started and fomented by professional betting men in the pavilion, members of the association. The disgraceful part of the business is that other members of the association – one a member of the legislative assembly – aided and abetted the bookmakers in raising the cry. I blame the NSW eleven for not objecting to Coulthard before the match began, if they had reason to suppose him incompetent to fulfil his duties. I blame the members of the association (many, of course, must be excepted) for their discourtesy and uncricket like behaviour to their guests; and I blame the committee and others of the association for ever permitting betting, but this last does not, of course, apply to our match only. I am bound to say they did all in their power to quell the disturbance. I don't think any thing would have happened if A. Bannerman had been run out instead of Murdoch, but the latter, besides being a great favourite, deservedly I think, was the popular idol of the moment through having carried his bat out in the first innings. As a contrast to the reception the Australian Eleven met with after beating the MCC at Lord's, I may say that when we won the match on Monday, hardly a cheer was given us by the ring. The occupants of the pavilion acknowledged our victory. They are capital winners out here, but I am afraid I can't apply the same adjective to them as losers. To conclude, I cannot describe to you the horror we felt that such an insult should have been passed on us, and that the game we love so well, and wich to see honoured, supported, and played in an honest and manly way everywhere, should receive such desecration. I can use no milder word. The game was finished on Monday without interruption. Coulthard had made two mistakes in our first innings, one favouring us, the other the opposite. Murdoch's decision was considered by cover-point and point to be a good one, and I repeat that the NSW Eleven had no grounds whatever for raising an objection. We never expect to see such a scene of disorder again – we can never forget this one.

I remain, Yours sincerely,

February 11. HARRIS"

The New South Wales Cricket Association's Reply

(Contributed to *The Daily Telegraph* by Mr J. M. Gibson, the hon. secretary to the Association)

"A few days ago a letter from Lord Harris, published in your issue of April 1, appeared in the Colonial Press. That letter dilated upon a lamentable disturbance which occurred at Moore Park, near this city, during a match played between his lordship's eleven and an eleven of New South Wales, on February 7, 8, and 10 last. Upon the appearance of the letter in our newspapers a feeling of indignation was generally expressed, and within a few hours a requisition influentially signed was presented, calling on me to convene a special general meeting of the New South Wales Cricket Association for the purpose of considering the letter and comments made upon it in some of the London papers. A meeting was accordingly convened, and took place this evening. The President, Mr Richard Driver, MP, occupied the chair, in the presence of an unusually large attendance of members. The letter referred to having been read, and the President, Sir George Innes, MLC, Mr M. H. Stephen, QC, Mr G. H. Reid, and

Mr Richard Teece having addressed the meeting, it was unanimously resolved that I should ask you to publish the following statement, in correction of the account transmitted by Lord Harris, which, principally upon the following grounds, is universally regarded here as both inaccurate and ungenerous.

"When Lord Harris prepared his letter of February 11, he was fully aware of the following facts:

1. That on the previous day a deputation from the association, consisting of our president, some of the vice-presidents, officers, and members waited upon him, and expressed profound sorrow and regret for the conduct of the unruly portion of the crowd, and Lord Harris was pleased to assure the deputation that he did not hold the association in any way responsible for what had occurred.

2. That immediately after the disorder on the cricket ground the public and the press were loud in their indignation at the occurrence, and assured our visitors of their utmost sympathy; and the team received similar marks of good feeling from all quarters.

3. That betting on cricket matches is strictly prohibited by the trustees of the ground, so far as it can be so prohibited, and large placards to that effect have always been kept posted throughout the pavilion and its inclosures.

Lord Harris, by what we feel to be a most ungenerous suppression of these facts and others, has led the British public to suppose that in New South Wales, to quote his own words, 'a party of gentlemen travelling through these colonies for the purpose of playing a few friendly games of cricket should have been insulted and subjected to indignities', whilst the press and inhabitants of Sydney neither showed surprise, indignation, nor regret. We cannot allow a libel upon the people of New South Wales so utterly unfounded as this to pass without challenge. The country upon which such a reproach could be fastened would be unworthy of a place among civilised communities, and in the imputation is especially odious to Australians, who claim to have maintained the manly, generous, and hospitable characteristics of the British race.

Having shown that for what actually occurred the fullest acknowledgments were made, it is now right to point out that the misconduct of those who took possession of the wickets has been exaggerated. So popular amongst our people is the game of cricket that multitudes of all ages and classes flock to a great match. They watch these contests with an interest as intense as any felt in England over a great political question. Lord Harris is, we believe, the first English cricketer who failed to observe that they applaud good cricket on either side, and, so far from our crowds being the bad losers he represents, the English Elevens who have visited New South Wales were never made more of than when they defeated the local team. Previous decisions of the professional brought from Melbourne to act as umpire for the English Eleven had created real, though suppressed dissatisfaction, and one, giving Lord Harris a second 'life', was openly admitted by his lordship to be a mistake; and when Mr Murdoch, the hero of the hour, who had carried his bat through in the first innings, was at the crisis of the game given 'run out' by what a large proportion of the spectators, both in the pavilion and round the inclosure, as well as the batsman himself, whether rightly or wrongly, took to be a most unfair decision, the excitement and indignation of a section of the spectators, led by the juvenile element, unhappily broke through restraint. Only once before in New South Wales was a cricket ground rushed, and then, as in the present instance, the crowd was seized with a conviction of foul play. But the present demonstration was entirely against the umpire, whom Lord Harris still considers competent, whilst admitting 'he had made two mistakes in our innings'. It certainly was not against our gallant visitors. The only cry was 'Change your umpire!' and the mob voluntarily left the ground more than once in the hope that that would be done. The betting men to whom Lord Harris alludes, and of whom only one or two were present, were not members of this association at all, and it is completely unjust to assign the demonstration to any such agency. Bad as it was, it sprang from no mercenary motive.

Sydney, June 4th."

SHAW'S ELEVEN v ELEVEN OF NEW SOUTH WALES

Played at Sydney, December 9, 10, 12, 13, 1882

It was estimated that 7,000 spectators were on the ground on the opening day, while on the Saturday there was a company of 20,000, the largest number ever known to be present on the Association Ground. Shaw won the toss, and elected to bat first; it being arranged to change wickets after each innings. The New South Wales bowling was mastered at the start, and when stumps were drawn for the day only five of the Englishmen's wickets were down, and the score 235, Barlow being not out with 71. Ulyett scored 47 out of 71, and on Barlow coming in Jones so sprained his foot, in trying to stop one from Selby, that he was unable to take any further part in the match.

Resuming next day, the last five wickets put on only 37 runs. The start of the home team was almost exactly like that of the visitors, as the first wicket was not captured until 73 had been scored (out of which Massie had made 56), and at the call of time only three wickets were down and the total stood at 164. On continuing the innings on the Monday Peate and Bates bowled with such effect that the other seven wickets collapsed for 46, and the New South Wales men were 62 to the bad. The Englishmen were then got out for 162, Midwinter scoring an excellent 48; and though Massie made 76 in his second innings, the other nine men could only score 74 between them, and so Shaw's eleven won by 68 runs. Barlow's splendid defence and Pilling's wicket-keeping were greatly praised. Murdoch played very fine cricket, and Massie's brilliant batting gained him the prize for the highest aggregate. In the first innings of England, Evans, though he took but two wickets, bowled in admirable form, at one time sending down thirteen maiden overs in succession; but Shaw's trundling in the second innings of New South Wales – twenty-nine overs (twenty-five maidens) for 5 runs and three wickets – is one of the most extraordinary performances on record.

Shaw's Eleven

G. Ulyett b Jones	47	– b Evans	17
J. Selby c and b Hiddleston	56	– c Murdoch b Evans	24
W. Bates c and b Hiddleston	0	– c Murdoch b Evans	12
W. Midwinter c Bannerman b Hiddleston	10	– b Evans	48
R. G. Barlow c Davis b Garrett	75	– b Evans	23
A. Shrewsbury c Davis b Garrett	23	– b Garrett	12
W. Scotton b Garrett	25	– c C. Bannerman b A. Bannerman	7
T. Emmett b Evans	13	– b Evans	0
A. Shaw c Davis b Garrett	5	– c Murdoch b Evans	0
E. Peate c Garrett b Evans	2	– c Evans b A. Bannerman	6
R. Pilling not out	5	– not out	7
Extras	11	Extras	6
	272		162

New South Wales

C. Bannerman b Bates	23	– b Peate	11
H. H. Massie c Midwinter b Barlow	56	– c Pilling b Emmett	76
W. L. Murdoch b Peate	58	– b Emmett	21
A. C. Bannerman c Pilling b Bates	15	– not out	30
D. Gregory c Pilling b Bates	15	– b Shaw	0
H. Moses c and b Bates	5	– c Pilling b Peate	0
T. W. Garrett run out	6	– c Emmett b Midwinter	2
E. Evans c Emmett b Peate	2	– b Shaw	4
J. Davis not out	18	– c Midwinter b Peate	6
T. W. Hiddleston b Peate	3	– st Pilling b Shaw	0
S. P. Jones absent hurt	0	– absent	0
Extras	9	Extras	6
	210		156

New South Wales Bowling

	Overs	Mdns	Runs	Wkts	Overs	Mdns	Runs	Wkts
Evans	90.1	58	77	2	56	34	60	4
Garrett	78	40	86	4	41	13	65	1
Gregory	10	—	27	—				
Jones	15	7	21	1				
Hiddleston	27	12	39	3	9	3	19	—
A. Bannerman	7	4	8	—	11	5	12	3
Massie	8	6	3	—				

The Bowling of Shaw's Eleven

	Overs	Mdns	Runs	Wkts	Overs	Mdns	Runs	Wkts
Peate	66.1	33	64	3	43	14	36	3
Bates	57	36	51	4	13.1	4	25	—
Midwinter	22	10	33	—	8	3	23	1
Shaw	26	16	24	—	29	25	5	3
Barlow	12	3	19	1	9	—	31	—
Ulyett	5	—	10	—				
Emmett					17	6	20	2

THE HON. IVO BLIGH'S TWELVE in AUSTRALIA

THE HON. IVO BLIGH'S TEAM v FIFTEEN OF SOUTH AUSTRALIA

Played at Adelaide, November 10, 11, 1882

While taking part in the game called "Tug of War" on board the "Peshawur" – the steamship which carried the English Cricketers to the Antipoles – the Hon. Ivo Bligh severely injured his right hand, and this mishap prevented his playing in any of the first six matches. This accident was not, unfortunately, the least serious one to befall a member of the team. On Monday, October 16th, the "Peshawur" came into violent collision with the barque "Glenroy", a short distance from Colombo. One of the crew, a Lascar, had one of his legs fractured in two places, but it was believed that scratches and bruises represented the full extent of the damage suffered by any one else on board. It was subsequently ascertained, however, that Morley had sustained a severe injury to one of his ribs, and though, with admirable pluck, he bowled in several matches, the unfortunate accident compelled him to leave the field during the progress of the second game, and prevented his taking any part in the third, seventh, eighth, ninth, tenth, fourteenth, fifteenth and seventeenth contests.

Owing to the inability of the Hon. Ivo Bligh to play Mr Tylecote captained the team in the first match, and, winning the toss, chose first innings. There was not much fault to be found with the wicket, but the weather was cold, dull and frequently showery on the opening day. The game was started at 2.5, in the presence of about 1000 spectators, and the Colonial bowling was so successful at first that six of the best English wickets were down for 45. Tylecote then joined Barnes, and when, at 4.26, rain stopped play for the day, the former had made 8 and the latter 19.

Continuing the match on the Saturday, Barnes and Tylecote were not parted until the century was hoisted, and, as the score will show, it was entirely due to their capital batting that the respectable total of 153 was reached. Barnes' 42 was the highest score he made during the tour, and he batted in the best form of any of the team. The South Australians scored 128 for the loss of seven wickets, and the match was then abandoned as a draw.

The home team included A. H. Jarvis, who visited England in 1880; W. Giffen, brother of G. Giffen, a member of Murdoch's team who came to the old country in 1882; and Jesse Hide, ground-man at Adelaide, and formerly of the Sussex County eleven.

The Hon. Ivo Bligh's Team

R. G. Barlow c King b Quilty	1
G. B. Studd Esq. c Pateman b Quilty	19
W. W. Read Esq. c Gordon b Quilty	5
C. T. Studd Esq. b Quilty	9
A. G. Steel Esq. b Jones	4
W. Bates b Jones	0
W. Barnes c Jarvis b Noel	42
E. F. S. Tylecote Esq. (Capt.) c Giffen b Quilty	59
C. F. H. Leslie Esq. c and b Noel	5
G. F. Vernon Esq. not out	2
F. Morley b Quilty	1
Extras	6
	153

English Bowling

	Overs	Mdns	Runs	Wkts
Mr Steel	17	6	38	—
Barnes	18	11	12	2
Morley	19	12	17	3
Bates	10	6	16	—
Mr C. T. Studd	17	6	30	1
Barlow	15	11	13	1

South Australia, 128 for seven wickets; Noel, 37, W. Giffen, 33, Waldron, 17 not out, W. Slight, 16 not out.

THE HON. IVO BLIGH'S TEAM v MR MURDOCH'S ELEVEN

Played at Melbourne, January, 19, 20, 22, 1883

The splendid bowling of Bates was the chief factor in the reverse the home team experienced in this contest, though the defeat would undoubtedly have been less severe had the easy chance Bates gave before he had scored been accepted. The eighth wicket would then have fallen at 199, whereas the mistake allowed the Yorkshireman to compile 55, and, with Read, to carry the total to 287. Bates' wonderful analysis in the Australians' first innings was even better than it reads, as four of the runs debited to him were the result of an overthrow. His great services in the match were rewarded by a present of £31, the result of a collection at the conclusion of the game.

The English captain won the toss, and at twelve o'clock, on a splendid wicket, C. T. Studd and Barlow faced the bowling of Spofforth and Palmer. At 28 Studd was bowled middle stump by Palmer, and at 35 Barlow's wicket fell to the same bowler. Though Leslie and Steel were both suffering from the enervating influences of the Australian climate, they succeeded in making a long stand, both playing excellent cricket, though batting with less vigour than usual. At the interval (1.30) Leslie had made 31 and Steel 8, and on resuming at 2.15 the score was taken to 106 before the two were parted by a splendid piece of fielding on the part of Spofforth. The Oxonian played a ball hard to the off and started for a run. The ball went to Spofforth who, standing forward cover-point, very smartly threw down the wicket, and Leslie was run out for an almost faultless innings of 54, his only mistake being a hard return to Palmer when he had made 48. Read filled the vacancy, but at 131 lost Steel, easily caught for a well-played 39, made without a chance. Barnes joined Read, and but for a very bad throw-in by Horan, would have been run out before he had made many runs. This let-off resulted in 64 runs being added while the two were together. Barnes was bowled at 195, and half the wickets were down. With only four runs added Tylecote was clean bowled, and without any further addition to the score Bligh's wicket fell to a shooter. Bates became Read's next partner, and experienced a great piece of good luck directly he came in. He gave a very hot return to Giffen which was not accepted, and was then badly missed by Horan, two mistakes for which the Australians paid dearly. When play was adjourned for the day at six o'clock both batsmen were still in, and the score 248 for seven wickets.

On the game being continued on the Saturday at noon, a separation was not effected until 39 more runs had been added to the overnight total, Bates being then caught for an exceedingly well-played innings, despite the chances he gave at the commencement. The score stood at 287 when he was dismissed, he and Read having put on 88 runs. The innings was then quickly finished off. At 293 Read was caught and bowled for a masterly contribution of 75, in which he had given only one chance, and that a hard one, when he had compiled 64, his fine score being made up of eight 4s, a 3, eight 2s and twenty-four singles. G. B. Studd, the last man, added a single and was then bowled, and when the wicket had been rolled Massie and Bannerman went in to commence the first innings of the Australians. At the luncheon interval Massie had made 26, Bannerman none, and four byes had been scored. Massie was clean bowled at 56 for à brilliant 43, and when Murdoch joined Bannerman the play became so exceedingly slow that half an hour was consumed in scoring ten runs. Bannerman was clean bowled at 72, and at 75 Horan was finely caught – right hand very high up. Then at 78 Bates accomplished the "hat trick", dismissing McDonnell, Giffen and Bonnor with successive balls. Blackham was bowled at 85, and Garrett shared the same fate at 104. With an addition of ten runs a yorker got rid of Palmer, and without any increase to the total Spofforth was bowled and the innings terminated at 5.15 for 114, Murdoch carrying his bat for 19, the result of a two and a half hours stay at the wickets. Being in a minority of 180 the Australians had to follow their innings. Murdoch and Bannerman began, and when 21 runs had been scored in ten minutes the first-named was bowled. Blackham came in, and seven runs were added before the call of time, Bannerman being then 5, not out, and Blackham 6, not out.

The game was resumed at five minutes after noon on the Monday, and Blackham was clean bowled before any addition had been made to the overnight total. Bonnor filled the vacancy and at once commenced to hit grandly. The first 26 runs scored that day were all made by him, and included in the 34 he contributed before he was finely caught by Morley at 66 were three hits out of the ground for 5 each. Bannerman was caught at 72, and Horan and McDonnell carried the score rapidly to 93, when another good catch by Morley got rid of the former, and half the wickets were disposed of. Massie was splendidly caught at 104, and McDonnell clean bowled at 113. Luncheon was then taken with the total at 122, and upon resumption of play ten runs were added and then Giffen was caught. The remaining two wickets were accounted for in a similar way, Garrett being caught at 139, and Palmer at 153. The Englishmen thus gained a decisive victory by an innings and 27 runs.

The Hon. Ivo Bligh's Team

C. T. Studd Esq. b Palmer	14
R. G. Barlow b Palmer	14
C. F. H. Leslie Esq. run out	54
A. G. Steel Esq. c McDonnell b Giffen	39
W. Barnes b Giffen	32
E. F. S. Tylecote Esq. b Giffen	0
Hon. Ivo Bligh (Capt.) b Giffen	0
W. Bates c Horan b Palmer	55
W. W. Read Esq. c and b Palmer	75
G. B. Studd Esq. b Palmer	1
F. Morley not out	0
B 3, l-b 3, n-b 4	10
	294

Mr Murdoch's Eleven

H. H. Massie b Barlow	43	– c C. T. Studd b Barlow	10
A. C. Bannerman b Bates	14	– c Bligh b Bates	14
W. L. Murdoch (Capt.) not out	19	– b Bates	17
T. Hogan c and b Barnes	3	– c Morley b Bates	15
P. S. McDonnell b Bates	3	– b Bates	13
G. Giffen c and b Bates	0	– c Bligh b Bates	19
G. J. Bonnor c Read b Bates	0	– c Morley b Barlow	34
J. McC. Blackham b Barnes	5	– b Barlow	6
T. W. Garrett b Bates	10	– c Barnes b Barlow	6
G. E. Palmer b Bates	7	– c G. B. Studd b Bates	4
F. R. Spofforth b Bates	0	– not out	14
B 6, l-b 3, n-b 1	10	B 1	1
	114		153

Australian Bowling

	Overs	Mdns	Runs	Wkts
Palmer	66.3	25	103	5
Spofforth	34	11	57	—
Giffen	49	13	89	4
Garrett	34	16	35	—

English Bowling

	Overs	Mdns	Runs	Wkts	Overs	Mdns	Runs	Wkts
Mr C. T. Studd	4	1	22	—				
Morley	23	16	13	—	2	—	7	—
Barnes	23	7	32	2	3	1	4	—
Barlow	22	18	9	1	31	6	67	4
Bates	26.2	14	28	7	33	14	74	6

SHAW'S TEAM IN AUSTRALIA, 1884-85

William Attewell, William Barnes, Wilfred Flowers, William Henry Scotton, Alfred Shaw and Arthur Shrewsbury of Nottinghamshire; William Bates, John Hunter, Robert Peel and George Ulyett of Yorkshire; John Briggs of Lancashire; James Lillywhite of Sussex; and John Maurice Read of Surrey, formed the Eighth Team of English Cricketers who visited the Australian Colonies, and were the second band of Professionals who went out under the management of Shaw, Shrewsbury and Lillywhite. The Team left Plymouth in the s.s. "Orient" on Friday, September 18, 1884, and reached Suez at eleven o'clock on the morning of Thursday, October 2. In accordance with a previous arrangement a match was played against Twenty-two of the Army, Navy, and Residents of Suez. The scene of the contest was a plain of sand, in the centre of which a piece of cocoanut matting was tightly stretched, and the game resulted as follows:

Shaw's Eleven

G. Ulyett c Hayman b Evans	43
W. H. Scotton b Evans	8
A. Shrewsbury b Bedford	26
W. Barnes c Lane b Bedford	2
W. Bates c Lane b Evans	0
W. Flowers b Stradling	12
J. Briggs run out	2
W. Attewell c Mitchell b Evans	1
R. Peel c Raymond b Bedford	11
J. Hunter not out	9
J. Lillywhite b Bedford	2
B 1	1
	117

The Twenty-two made 40 for eleven wickets.

At 2 p.m. on Tuesday, October 7, the cricketers reached Aden, and at 11.15 on the same day, sailed for Port Adelaide, where they arrived early on the morning of Wednesday, October 29. The voyage had been a very pleasant one, and at Adelaide they were met by the leading members of the South Australian Cricketing Association Committee, who conducted them to the city, where the Mayor accorded them an official reception of a very cordial character, remarking that he was sure their visit would be a very pleasant one. Similar kindly greetings were extended to them wherever they went, but from the moment the members of Murdoch's team landed from the "Mirzapore", prior to the commencement of the third match, it became evident they were animated by a feeling of bitter hostility towards Shaw and his party. As a commencement, the Victoria contingent of the team declined to play for their Colony against the Englishmen, urging as an excuse their want of practice, while it afterwards transpired that Murdoch's Eleven had endeavoured to arrange a match with New South Wales on the same days as those fixed for the contest between Shaw's Team and Victoria. Next, Murdoch and A. Bannerman refused to take part in the match New South Wales v Shaw's Eleven, and after the South Australian Cricket Association had succeeded in bringing about a meeting between Shaw's Team and Murdoch's Eleven at Adelaide, each side receiving £450, the climax of the quarrel was reached when Murdoch's men declined to play for Combined Australia against the Englishmen on New Year's Day. This unpatriotic conduct was severely condemned by the public and press of Australia, as the following extracts will show:

At a luncheon given at Adelaide during a cricket match on New Year's Day the Attorney-General of South Australia (the Hon. C. C. Kingston) said that he could not let that occasion pass, as a lover of the game for itself, without referring to the conduct of the Australian Eleven, who appeared to sink everything for monetary considerations. If the cricketing public of Australia were to allow the game to be sacrificed for money it would be a national calamity from a cricketing point of view. (Applause.) One of the effects of this was that on that day there was a match proceeding in which the full strength of Australia should have been pitted against a worthy representative team of all England, but Australia was not represented in its full strength because of the existence of the Australian Eleven. It did not matter what was the reason why the Australian Eleven refrained from participating in the match – some said it was a difference between their manager and the Englishmen – but the cricketing public of Australia should show their disapproval of this line of conduct when the national cricketing honour was concerned. He hoped that the Australian team would win. (Applause.) He was certain, however, that the combined team who took part in the contest would not be disgraced, but the Australian Eleven would have the reputation of having sacrificed the cricketing honour of their nation to monetary considerations. He would not have referred to this matter, but as an earnest supporter and upholder of manly sports he considered it his duty, in common with others, to protest against cricket being reduced to a mere money-making matter. The fourth Australian Eleven, had received a large share of Australian sympathy, but he trusted a repetition of their conduct would never be witnessed in an Australian team.

Commenting on the above, the *South Australian Register* states: "The pungent criticism of the conduct of the Australian Eleven indulged in by the Attorney-General will be endorsed by most of those who are acquainted with the facts. Very hard things indeed have been said of the team in the other colonies. The spirit they have displayed since their return from their successful and financially profitable trip in the mother country has been most illiberal. Instead of going out of their way to advance the interests of the company of English players now on a visit to Australia they have assumed an attitude of antagonism towards them which can only be attributed to mercenary motives altogether unworthy of them and of Australian cricketers in general. Remembering that they claim to rank as gentlemen players, and not as professionals, and that they met with the most liberal treatment in Great Britain, they owed it to themselves as well as to the visiting players to do all in their power to make the tour of the latter successful. At the same time they owed it to Australia to put their services as cricketers at the disposal of the country in order to maintain its cricketing reputation against the formidable team who have come to gather laurels, as well as gate-money, in these colonies. How little their action has been influenced by a regard for the interests of Australia, and how much by monetary considerations, is illustrated by the nature of the terms they demanded from the South Australian Cricketing Association before agreeing to play on the Adelaide Oval. They insisted upon being placed upon the same footing as the professionals, and thus practically shut out the Association from all chance of realising any profit out of the match. It cannot be doubted that the grasping policy of the Eleven tended to estrange public sympathy here, and caused the victory of the Englishmen to be rather popular than otherwise. The latest grievance against the team is that they have been so tenacious of their financial rights that not one of them has taken part in the match Players v All Australia now proceeding in Melbourne. In one sense it is an advantage that they should be thus excluded, as it has given an opportunity for the bringing together of an independent eleven not ill-qualified to do battle for Australia, but it is, of course, anomalous that from a match against all Australia the redoubtable members of Murdoch's Eleven should all be shut out. It is greatly to be regretted that the Australian team proper should have made such a shabby ending to an otherwise brilliant career."

The Cricket Association of Victoria called upon the Victorian section of the team for an explanation of their refusal to play, and at an adjourned meeting, held on January 13, 1885, the following motion was carried unanimously:

"That the replies received from the Victorian contingent of the Australian Eleven who have been asked for an explanation in refusing to play in the combined match, Australia v England, are unsatisfactory to this Association, and that the selector of teams be instructed not to select any one of them to play in any match played under the auspices of the Association."

This ban was not removed until November 11 of the same year, and one of the results of the antagonism of the Fourth Australian Team, and of the action of the Victorian Association, was that Shaw's men had to play two matches against New South Wales, and one each against Victoria and a combined eleven at Melbourne, without a single member of Murdoch's Team being opposed to them. Peace, however, was partially restored towards the close of the tour, and in the last three matches against representative elevens of Australia, A. C. Bannerman was opposed to the English team on each occasion, Bonnor and Giffen appeared in two matches, and Scott, Palmer, McDonnell and Blackham each played once. Spofforth, it must be stated, was not in accord with the other members of the Australian Team. He did not arrive in Australia until some time after all the others had landed, and was always favourably disposed towards the Englishmen, playing against them whenever circumstances permitted.

Shaw's Team played thirty-three matches in all, eight of which were eleven-a-side contests, and the remainder against twenty-twos, eighteens and fifteens. Of the matches against odds ten were won, fifteen drawn, and not one lost, while of the first-class matches six were won and two lost. The victories were over New South Wales (twice), combined Australia (twice), Victoria, and Murdoch's Australian Eleven; while the defeats in each case were by representative teams of Australia, one match being lost by 6 runs, and the other by eight wickets. In the eight eleven-a-side matches Shaw's Team scored 2,702 runs for the loss of 118 wickets, giving an average of 22.106 runs per wicket, and their opponents lost 151 wickets for 2,450 runs, or an average of 16.34 runs per wicket. The Englishmen gave away 95 extras, and their opponents 118 in those eight matches. In the twenty-five minor matches of the tour Shaw's team scored 5,928 runs for 296 wickets, or an average of 20.8 runs per wicket, their opponents making 4,048 runs for 757 wickets, or an average of only 5.263 runs per wicket.

A perusal of the batting and bowling summaries appended to the last match will show that Barnes was not only at the head of the batsmen both in eleven-a-side matches and those against odds, but that he was also the most successful bowler in the first-class contests of the programme. His average of 43.4 in eleven-a-side matches and 30.14 against odds, coupled with his record of twenty-six wickets at an average cost of 13.5 was a truly grand performance. Shrewsbury with a splendid average of exactly 40 comes next to Barnes in first-class matches, but unlike that batsman, was very far from successful in the minor matches, as his average of 17.7 will testify. Bates showed very fine form all round. His batting in the big matches was the most consistent of any of the team, as with 68 as his largest contribution, he secured the really capital average of 30.3 without the aid of a not out innings. Against odds his average was 23.14, and his excellent bowling figures suggest the idea that he might have had a larger share with advantage to the team. The result of Briggs' dashing play and Scotton's steady defensive cricket fully warranted their inclusion in the team. It will be seen that, in contrast to Barnes, Shrewsbury and Bates, they were more successful in the matches against odds than in the eleven-a-side contests. Ulyett, while he gained the excellent average of 26.24 in the minor matches, was singularly unfortunate in the principal contests, and is actually at the bottom of the list with the very poor average of 11.4. His bowling, though somewhat expensive, was very useful on occasions. Both Read and Flowers were completely out of form with the bat for a long time, but both, on some few occasions proved of the greatest value to their side. Read played up capitally the last month, and Flowers atoned for his ill-success with the bat by bowling in capital form. Long scores were not expected from Attewell, Peel and Hunter, but all are credited with useful averages, and each at times was able to make a stand of considerable value.

Considerably the largest share of the bowling was entrusted to Peel and Attewell, and both acquitted themselves admirably. Peel obtained the enormous number of 321 wickets in the minor matches at an average cost of 4.73 runs per wicket, his performance against Twenty-two of Moss Vale, in which he obtained eighteen wickets for 7 runs, eclipsing all previous feats of English bowlers in Australia. Though taking the largest number of wickets credited to any bowler in the eleven-a-side matches, he was, singularly enough, the most expensive, his thirty-five wickets costing 19.8 runs per wicket. Attewell bowled with great success throughout the tour. In the first-class matches he obtained twenty-eight wickets at an average of 15.8 runs per wicket, and in matches against odds he had an average of 4.148 for 161 wickets.

Hunter kept wicket admirably. He was in brilliant form at times, and always stood up to the fast bowling of Ulyett without a long-stop. In the eleven-a-side matches he stumped six and caught out eleven.

Shaw, who played in eight matches, but did not bowl a ball, left for England towards the end of February, to fulfil an engagement with the Earl of Sheffield, and Lillywhite only took part in two matches.

Shaw's Team left Adelaide, on board the s.s. "Potosi", at 9.30 p.m. on April 6, homeward bound. On arriving at Naples, Attewell, Barnes, Flowers, Scotton, Lillywhite and Ulyett left the ship to travel the remainder of the journey overland, arriving in England on Tuesday, May 12. Shrewsbury, Read, Hunter, Peel, Briggs and Bates landed at Plymouth on the following Friday, after a good passage.

SHAW'S TEAM v TWENTY-TWO OF LITHGOW

Played at Lithgow, December 8, 9, 1887

The English team won a small scoring match by 77 runs, Briggs and Flowers bowling with irresistible effect.

Shaw's Team

M. Read	8 –	0
W. Scotton	4 –	0
W. Barnes	1 –	7
R. G. Barlow	9 –	1
W. Gunn	4 –	0
W. Bates	40 –	2
J. Briggs	2 –	11
W. Flowers	3 –	0
G. Lohmann	6 –	11
J. Clarke	0	
M. Sherwin	3	
Extras		10
	80	42

Twenty-two of Lithgow scored 18 and 27.

English Bowling

	Overs	Mdns	Runs	Wkts	Overs	Mdns	Runs	Wkts
Briggs	16.1	10	7	10	17.3	7	13	17
Flowers	16	9	11	7	18	12	9	3

SHAW'S TEAM v AUSTRALIA

Played at Sydney, January 28, 29, 31, 1887

The great match, and also the most conspicuous triumph of the tour, the Englishmen winning by 13 runs, after being dismissed in their first innings for a total of 45. When stumps were drawn on the Saturday they did not seem to have even a remote chance of success, being only some 20 odd runs to the good with three wickets to fall in their second innings. On the Monday, however, they played up in splendid style, and gained a victory that might fairly be compared to the seven runs win of Australia over England at Kennington Oval in 1882. Briggs, Flowers and Sherwin batted so well that Australia had to go in with 111 to get to win. With the wicket in very fair order this seemed an easy task, and defeat was not thought of, but Barnes bowled so finely, and was so ably supported by Lohmann that the total only reached 97. Barring one mistake the English fielding was magnificent. Except that Giffen was still too ill to appear, the Australian team was almost a representative one, though Palmer and Horan should have been played in preference to Midwinter and McShane.

Shaw's Team

W. Bates c Midwinter b Ferris	8 – b Ferris	24
A. Shrewsbury c McShane b Ferris	2 – b Ferris	29
W. Barnes c Spofforth b Turner	0 – c Moses b Garrett	32
R. G. Barlow b Turner	2 – c Jones b Ferris	4
M. Read c Spofforth b Ferris	5 – b Ferris	0
W. Gunn b Turner	0 – b Turner	4
G. A. Lohmann c Garrett b Ferris	17 – lbw b Ferris	3
J. Briggs c Midwinter b Turner	5 – b Spofforth	33
W. Scotton c Jones b Turner	1 – c Spofforth b Garrett	6
W. Flowers b Turner	2 – c McDonnell b Turner	14
M. Sherwin not out	0 – not out	21
Extras	3 B 7, l-b 7	14
	45	184

Australia

J. McC. Blackham c Sherwin b Lohmann	4	– b Barnes	5
P. McDonnell b Barnes	14	– lbw b Barnes	0
S. P. Jones c Shrewsbury b Bates	31	– c Read b Barnes	18
C. J. B. Turner b Barlow	3	– c and b Barnes	7
H. Moses b Barlow	31	– c Shrewsbury b Barnes	24
P. G. McShane lbw b Briggs	5	– b Briggs	0
W. Midwinter c Shrewsbury b Barlow	0	– lbw b Barnes	10
T. W. Garrett b Lohmann	12	– c Gunn b Lohmann	10
F. R. Spofforth b Lohmann	2	– b Lohmann	5
J. Ferris c Barlow b Barnes	1	– not out	0
A. C. Bannerman not out	15	– b Lohmann	4
B 1	1	B 14	14
	119		97

Australian Bowling

	Overs	Mdns	Runs	Wkts	Overs	Mdns	Runs	Wkts
Turner	18	11	15	6	44.2	22	53	2
Ferris	17.3	7	27	4	61	30	76	5
Spofforth					12	3	17	1
Midwinter					4	1	10	0
Garrett					12	7	8	2
M'Shane					3	0	6	0

English Bowling

	Overs	Mdns	Runs	Wkts	Overs	Mdns	Runs	Wkts
Barlow	35	23	25	3	13	6	20	0
Barnes	22.1	16	19	2	46	29	28	6
Bates	21	9	19	1	17	11	8	0
Lohmann	21	12	30	3	24	11	20	3
Briggs	14	5	25	1	7	5	7	1

SHAW'S TEAM v NEW SOUTH WALES

Played at Sydney, February 18, 19, 21, 1887

The third and concluding match with New South Wales resulted disastrously for the Englishmen, who, on a slow wicket, could do nothing against Turner's bowling, and were beaten by the substantial majority of 122 runs. New South Wales played a splendid game, and had the advantage from start to finish. Next to Turner's wonderful bowling, the feature of the match was a very fine innings of 73 by the left-handed batsman, Moses. Shrewsbury, for the first time in his life, was out twice without getting a run, and in the first innings of the English team Bates made 46 runs before anyone else had scored. The Englishmen, for once, were quite outplayed, the loss of Barnes, both as batsman and bowler, being sadly felt. Lohmann bowled finely.

New South Wales

	First innings		Second innings	
P. McDonnell c Shrewsbury b Lohmann	15	–	c Shrewsbury b Briggs	16
A. Bannerman b Lohmann	3	–	c Shrewsbury b Lohmann	24
R. Allen c Gunn b Bates	41	–	c and b Lohmann	0
S. P. Jones c Shrewsbury b Bates	12	–	c Read b Flowers	1
T. W. Garrett c Sherwin b Barlow	8	–	lbw b Lohmann	4
Cottam b Briggs	20	–	not out	14
C. J. B. Turner c Wood b Lohmann	12	–	c Shrewsbury b Flowers	12
H. Moses b Briggs	9	–	b Lohmann	73
C. Richardson not out	6	–	run out	25
J. Ferris b Lohmann	3	–	c Briggs b Lohmann	0
Wales b Lohmann	2	–	b Lohmann	0
B 2	2		Extras	11
	141			180

Shaw's Team

	First innings		Second innings	
A. Shrewsbury b Turner	0	–	b Turner	0
W. Bates c and b Turner	48	–	c Moses b Ferris	40
R. G. Barlow b Turner	0	–	b Turner	4
W. Scotton b Turner	0	–	c Bannerman b Turner	4
M. Read b Turner	0	–	c Bannerman b Ferris	2
W. Gunn b Ferris	13	–	c Cottam b Ferris	2
G. A. Lohmann b Turner	4	–	b Turner	26
J. Briggs lbw b Garrett	10	–	b Turner	5
W. Flowers b Turner	2	–	c McDonnell b Turner	0
R. Wood not out	10	–	c and b Garrett	9
M. Sherwin b Turner	0	–	not out	0
Extras	12		Extras	8
	99			100

English Bowling

	Overs	Mdns	Runs	Wkts	Overs	Mdns	Runs	Wkts
Briggs	35	14	43	2	30	13	34	1
Lohmann	34	11	56	5	33	13	41	6
Barlow	13	3	24	1	13	4	25	0
Bates	14	7	16	2	15	6	21	0
Flowers					14	4	32	2
Read					10	6	8	0
Wood					8	5	8	0

New South Wales Bowling

	Overs	Mdns	Runs	Wkts	Overs	Mdns	Runs	Wkts
Turner	33.2	14	32	8	29.1	13	27	6
Ferris	30	11	43	1	29	7	62	3
Garrett	5	2	12	1	1	0	3	1

SMOKERS v NON-SMOKERS

Played at Melbourne, March 17, 18, 19, 21, 1887

This game did not count in the averages of the Englishmen, but it was remarkable for producing the highest total ever obtained in a first-class match, the Non-Smokers going in first, and scoring 803. The previous best was 775 by New South Wales against Victoria at

Sydney in 1882. Though the East Melbourne Ground is small, the performance was an extraordinary one, Shrewsbury, Bruce and Gunn batting splendidly. After four days' cricket the result was a draw.

Non-Smokers

A. Shrewsbury	1 3 1 1 1 2 2 4 4 1 4 4 4 4 4 2 2 2 4 4 4 1 2 1 3 4 4 4 4 3 4 2 1 1 1 4 4 2 3 2 4		
	1 1 4 4 1 2 4 1 1 2 4 4 4 2 4 4 1 3 4 4 4 2 1 4 4 1 1 1 4 4 2 4 4 2 4 4 2 2 1 4 1		
	1 1 1 2 4 4	c Duffy b Briggs	236
W. Bruce	1 1 4 4 1 4 2 4 3 6 4 4 4 4 2 1 1 2 3 4 2 3 4 1 3 4 3 2 1 2 4 1 4 3 2 1 1 1 1 4 4		
	4 2 1 1 1 2 1 1 1 1 1 1 4	lbw b Palmer	131
W. Bates	4	b Palmer	4
W. Gunn	3 4 4 1 4 4 2 4 4 4 3 1 1 3 2 4 2 1 1 1 1 4 2 1 4 1 1 4 3 3 4 1 2 2 1 5 2 4 4 2 2		
	1 4 4 3 2 4 4 4 1 4 1 1 3 1 4 1 2	b Boyle	150
R. G. Barlow	2 1 1 1 1 1 1 4 4 1 2 4 1 1 4	b Palmer	29
R. Houston	3 1 2 1 1 4 4 1 1 1 1 4 2 2 1 4 2 1 1 1 1 2 4 1 1 3 1 1 1 1 2 1	c and b Briggs	57
H. Musgrove	3 4 4 1 1 1 2 4 1 2 1 2 1 3 1 4 4 1 1 4 4 1 3 1 1 4 2 1	st Lewis b Briggs	62
J. Worrall	4 2 2 1 4 2 1 1 4 4 1 4 4 4 1 2 1 2 1 2 2 1 1 4 1 1 1 4 4 3 4 2 2 1	b Read	78
W. H. Cooper	4 4 1 4 4 1 1 1 4 1 3 1 1 1 1 4 4 3 1 2	c and b Briggs	46
M. Sherwin	3 1 1	not out	5
W. Barnes		absent	0
		Extras	5
1/196 2/204 3/514 4/524 5/575 6/656 7/686 8/788 9/803			803

Smokers

M. Read st Sherwin b Cooper	30		
G. E. Palmer c Worrall b Bruce	113	c Houston b Worrall	24
J. Briggs c Shrewsbury b Bates	86	st Sherwin b Bates	54
W. Flowers run out	69	b Houston	25
G. Lohmann c Briggs (sub) b Bates	19	lbw b Gunn	2
W. Scotton c Bruce b Bates	11	handled ball	18
H. F. Boyle b Bruce	7	not out	0
G. Browning b Bates	1		
F. Walters st Sherwin b Bates	0		
P. Lewis c Houston b Bates	2		
W. Duffy not out	0		
B 12, l-b 2, w 2, n-b 2	18	B 9, l-b 2, n-b 1	12
	356		135

Smokers' Bowling

	Overs	Mdns	Runs	Wkts		Overs	Mdns	Runs	Wkts
Briggs	55.1	11	141	4	Scotton	26	4	82	0
Palmer	54	10	189	3	Duffy	15	2	52	0
Boyle	31	14	60	1	Read	26	10	43	1
Lohmann	48	18	113	0	Walters	9	4	25	0
Flowers	38	12	93	0					

Non-Smokers' Bowling

	Overs	Mdns	Runs	Wkts	Overs	Mdns	Runs	Wkts
Bates	49	18	73	6	21	8	40	1
Cooper	29	5	85	1	4	0	18	0
Bruce	36.3	10	92	2	14	7	15	0
Worrall	15	7	30	0	12	5	22	1
Gunn	12	4	27	0	6	5	1	1
Houston	9	2	31	0	5	1	13	1
Barnes					8	3	14	0
Shrewsbury					1	1	0	0

SHAW'S TEAM v FIFTEEN OF SOUTH AUSTRALIA

Played at Adelaide, March 24, 25, 26, 1887

The final match of the tour ended in a draw, very much in favour of the Englishmen, who thus maintained their form to the last.

Shaw's Team

A. Shrewsbury c Gooden b Musgrove	15
W. Flowers c Leak b Lyons	17
M. Sherwin c Jarvis b Musgrove	17
W. Gunn b Musgrove	5
W. Bates c Gooden b Musgrove	31
R. G. Barlow lbw b Haldane	53
W. Scotton c Jarvis b Bullough	21
M. Read c Gooden b King	44
G. Lohmann c Waldron b Bullough	1
J. Briggs b Lyons	53
F. Jarvis not out	7
Extras	15
	279

Fifteen of South Australia scored 229 and 132 (for twelve wickets). A. H. Jarvis, with 77 and 42, was top scorer in each innings.

English Bowling

	Overs	Mdns	Runs	Wkts	Overs	Mdns	Runs	Wkts
Lohmann	41	17	72	3	14	6	18	2
Briggs	16	3	25	1	9	4	23	1
Bates	26.2	10	32	3	20	10	23	4
Flowers	39	22	42	0	19	8	50	3
Read	38	21	49	7				
Shrewsbury					5	4	1	1
Sherwin					5	4	1	0

BATTING AVERAGES – ELEVEN-A-SIDE MATCHES

	Innings	Not outs	Runs	Highest Innings	Average
A. Shrewsbury (capt.)	18	4	485	144	34.9
W. Barnes	12	1	319	109	29
W. Bates	17	0	379	86	22.5
W. Gunn	16	1	323	61*	21.8
R. G. Barlow	18	3	310	86	20.10
M. Read	16	0	258	53	16.2
W. Flowers	15	2	192	52	14.10
G. A. Lohmann	15	2	191	40*	14.9
M. Sherwin	16	8	108	25	13.4
J. Briggs	15	0	179	69	11.14
W. Scotton	16	1	163	43*	10.13
R. Wood	5	1	26	10*	6.2

* Signifies not out.

Neither Lillywhite nor Alfred Shaw played in any of the leading fixtures.

BOWLING AVERAGES – ELEVEN-A-SIDE MATCHES

	Innings	Overs	Maidens	Runs	Wickets	Average
W. Barnes	13	374.2	224	337	25	13.12
W. Flowers	16	365.2	204	346	24	14.10
G. A. Lohmann ..	20	763.2	373	915	59	15.30
W. Bates	14	367	162	445	21	21.4
J. Briggs	20	582.3	305	667	30	22.7
R. G. Barlow	19	370	183	439	18	24.7
M. Read	4	28	13	33	1	33

R. Wood (8–5–8–0), bowled in one innings only.

MR VERNON'S TEAM v SOUTH AUSTRALIA

Played at Adelaide, December 24, 26, 27, 28, 1888

In this match – left drawn at a most interesting point – occurred the only unpleasantness of the tour. When the Englishmen seemed to have a one innings victory in prospect, the wicket was watered in the night, and, after looking at first sight to be ruined, it rolled out so hard and true that the South Australian team played a second innings of 493. Naturally such an extraordinary incident gave rise to a great deal of discussion and newspaper comment. A reward was offered, but so far as we know the perpetrators were never discovered. Nor was this the only difficulty that occurred during the game. The South Australian authorities maintained that the Melbourne Club had guaranteed that the match should be played out, and they considered they had a genuine grievance when the Englishmen left for Melbourne on the afternoon of the fourth day to play a game in that city against Combined Australia. It was a pity that so good a match should have given rise to ill-feeling, but we cannot get away from the facts. Some splendid cricket was shown on the wonderfully good Adelaide wicket, Mr W. W. Read for the Englishmen and George Giffen, Godfrey and Jarvis for South Australia bearing off the honours. Giffen's innings was a masterpiece. Mr Read had been suffering from neuralgia, and not doing himself justice, so that his success was all the more welcome.

Mr Vernon's Team

W. W. Read c Musgrove b Giffen	183		
A. E. Stoddart b Giffen	38		
R. Abel c Musgrove b Giffen	4	– not out	23
R. Peel c Godfrey b Lyons	31		
A. E. Newton c and b Giffen	5		
T. C. O'Brien run out	43		
G. F. Vernon b Giffen	27		
M. P. Bowden c and b Lyons	21	– not out	35
J. T. Rawlin c Waldron b Lyons	14		
W. Attewell c Waldron b Lyons	5		
J. Beaumont not out	5		
B 3, l-b 3	6	L-b 1	1
	382		59

South Australia

G. Giffen b Peel	6 – b Attewell	203
A. H. Jarvis c Vernon b Beaumont	75 – c and b Peel	12
J. J. Lyons b Peel	0 – c Abel b Rawlin	33
W. Giffen b Attewell	21 – b Attewell	20
W. Godfrey b Attewell	4 – c Newton b Peel	119
J. Noel b Rawlin	0 – st Bowden b Attewell	10
Blinman c Attewell b Beaumont	12 – c and b Attewell	9
J. E. Craigie not out	12 – c Read b Stoddart	30
G. Waldron b Beaumont	2 – absent	0
Phillips b Attewell	4 – b Rawlin	14
J. Musgrove b Attewell	3 – not out	29
B 2, l-b 1, n-b 1	4 B 6, l-b 2, w 2, n-b 4	14
	143	493

South Australian Bowling

	Overs	Mdns	Runs	Wkts	Overs	Mdns	Runs	Wkts
Musgrove	9	1	37	0	5	2	11	0
Lyons	27.1	6	72	4	6	0	25	0
G. Giffen	78	24	163	5	12	4	22	0
Noel	47	15	94	0				
Phillips	1	0	10	0				

English Bowling

	Overs	Mdns	Runs	Wkts	Overs	Mdns	Runs	Wkts
Peel	26	12	34	2	102	41	138	2
Beaumont	41	21	48	3	38	14	73	0
Attewell	40.3	26	32	4	107	58	103	4
Rawlin	19	9	25	1	122.1	81	87	2
Stoddart					31	12	51	1
Read					5	1	16	0
Abel					6	2	11	0

SHREWSBURY'S TEAM v NEW SOUTH WALES

Played at Sydney, January 13, 14, 16, 17, 1888

A crushing defeat for the Englishmen by 153 runs – the second and last beating sustained by the team during their tour. Turner's marvellous bowling – sixteen wickets for 79 runs – and the splendid batting of Moses were the chief causes of the triumph. In each innings New South Wales had a drier and better wicket to bat on than the Englishmen, but the performances of the two famous cricketers we have named could not be over praised. Lohmann bowled splendidly for the Englishmen, taking fourteen wickets for 81 runs. Shrewsbury and Newham played with masterly skill in the second innings, but the other batsmen could do very little against Turner on a wicket that helped him.

New South Wales

P. S. McDonnell b Lohmann	6 – c Pougher b Lohmann	16
A. C. Bannerman c Newham b Lohmann	16 – c Pougher b Smith	7
H. Moses run out	58 – c Briggs b Lohmann	109
S. P. Jones c Newham b Lohmann	0 – b Lohmann	3
R. C. Allen c and b Lohmann	0 – c Briggs b Lohmann	14
H. W. Hiddlestone c Shrewsbury b Lohmann	2 – c Newham b Lohmann	4
C. T. B. Turner c Newham b Lohmann	19 – c Smith b Lohmann	1
T. W. Garrett c Read b Lohmann	2 – c Pilling b Lohmann	18
F. J. Burton c Lohmann b Preston	30 – b Smith	12
J. J. Ferris b Preston	0 – not out	18
H. Donnan not out	18 – lbw b Smith	5
Extras	2 Extras	9
	153	216

Shrewsbury's Team

M. Read c and b Turner	11 – b Turner	5
W. Newham b Turner	16 – lbw b Garrett	32
A. Shrewsbury c McDonnell b Ferris	9 – c Donnan b Turner	56
L. C. Docker b Turner	4 – b Turner	0
G. A. Lohmann c McDonnell b Ferris	17 – c Bannerman b Turner	5
J. Briggs b Turner	10 – b Turner	0
G. Brann b Turner	0 – c Moses b Turner	3
J. Preston b Turner	3 – c Bannerman b Garrett	6
C. A. Smith c and b Turner	3 – b Turner	0
A. D. Pougher b Turner	6 – c Burton b Turner	17
R. Pilling not out	5 – not out	1
Extras	3 Extras	4
	87	129

English Bowling

	Overs	Mdns	Runs	Wkts	Overs	Mdns	Runs	Wkts
Lohmann	78	47	68	7	70.3	34	97	7
Briggs	55	34	41	0	13	8	11	0
Pougher	17	9	18	0	24	12	95	0
Smith	18	11	9	0	39	18	38	3
Preston	14.2	16	15	2	23	11	26	0

New South Wales Bowling

	Overs	Mdns	Runs	Wkts	Overs	Mdns	Runs	Wkts
Turner	33.3	19	39	8	46	26	40	8
Ferris	33	15	45	2	1	0	12	0
Garrett					25	16	39	2
Jones					5	1	8	0
Donnan					19	6	26	0

SHREWSBURY'S TEAM v SIXTH AUSTRALIAN TEAM

Played at Sydney, March 9, 10, 12, 13, 1888

A remarkable match, played all through on a hard wicket and won by the Englishmen by 158 runs. It will be seen that on the first innings there was only a difference of 22 runs, the scale being turned by Shrewsbury's magnificent score of 206. Rarely has the great Nottingham batsman been seen to better advantage, his display being in every respect most masterly. Almost equally good was Jones' not out innings of 134, when the Australians went in with over 420 wanted to win. Indeed, no match during the tour produced finer cricket than this one. At the close of the first day the Australians had decidedly the best of the game, but their batting broke down completely on the second morning. Turner has seldom bowled better on a hard wicket than in the first innings of the Englishmen, and a word should be said for the batting of Blackham on one side, and C. A. Smith on the other.

Shrewsbury's Team

M. Read b Turner	33	– b Turner	0
J. Briggs b Turner	7	– c Blackham b Turner	54
J. M. Preston c Richardson b Turner	7	– c Blackham b Jones	9
A. Shrewsbury c Jones b Turner	24	– c Trott b Turner	206
W. Newham lbw b Turner	4	– lbw b Ferris	1
G. A. Lohmann c Blackham b Ferris	16	– c and b Trott	39
L. C. Docker st Blackham b Turner	33	– c Richardson b Trott	1
G. Brann b Trott	13	– st Blackham b Turner	3
C. A. Smith c and b Turner	59	– c Blackham b Edwards	40
R. Pilling c Boyle b Ferris	3	– not out	8
A. D. Pougher not out	7	– c Blackham b Jones	24
Extras	6	Extras	17
	212		402

Australians

S. P. Jones b Briggs	35	– not out	134
J. McC. Blackham c Docker b Preston	97	– c Docker b Preston	1
J. D. Edwards c Brann b Preston	8	– c Preston b Briggs	24
C. T. B. Turner c Pilling b Lohmann	7	– c and b Lohmann	17
J. J. Lyons b Preston	1	– lbw b Lohmann	0
P. S. McDonnell c Pilling b Lohmann	15	– c Briggs b Lohmann	29
J. Wood b Preston	2	– b Preston	4
A. D. Richardson b Lohmann	8	– c and b Lohmann	14
H. Trott not out	9	– run out	15
J. J. Ferris run out	2	– b Pougher	13
H. F. Boyle c Briggs b Lohmann	6	– c Docker b Pougher	8
		Extras	7
	190		266

Australian Bowling

	Overs	Mdns	Runs	Wkts	Overs	Mdns	Runs	Wkts
Turner	54	27	72	7	91	43	135	4
Ferris	25.1	8	59	2	66	40	74	1
Trott	14	3	30	1	39	20	77	2
Wood	21	9	32	0	16	10	21	0
Lyons	6	1	13	0	3	0	13	0
Jones					35.3	13	57	2
Boyle					3	1	8	0
Edwards					2	2	0	1

English Bowling

	Overs	Mdns	Runs	Wkts	Overs	Mdns	Runs	Wkts
Lohmann	44.3	20	93	4	53	25	70	4
Briggs	22	10	34	1	39	15	92	1
Preston	30	13	38	4	20	8	48	2
Pougher	3	1	12	0	5.2	1	10	2
Smith	10	4	13	0	12	2	39	0

LORD SHEFFIELD'S TEAM v COMBINED AUSTRALIA

Played at Sydney, January 29, 30, February 1, 2, 3, 1892

The second of the three big matches produced one of the finest performances in the whole history of Australian cricket, a performance, indeed, fully comparable to the seven runs victory at The Oval in 1882, or the great, but unsuccessful, fight on the same ground in 1880. The Englishmen played the same team as at Melbourne, but the Australians made one change in their side, substituting Walter Giffen for Donnan. As events turned out, they would have been wise to have chosen Sidney Gregory instead of Moses, as the latter's injured leg again gave way. The Australians proved victorious by 72 runs, and it can safely be said that the records of first-class cricket furnish few instances of a finer uphill game. Up to the end of the second day everything went in favour of the Englishmen. Thanks to Lohmann's bowling and Abel's batting, they gained indeed so commanding an advantage that the match seemed as good as over. The close of an innings on each side had left them with a lead of 162, and the Australians, on going in for the second time, lost Trott's wicket for a single run. Abel's superb innings of 132 not out lasted five hours and twenty-five minutes, and comprised eleven 4s, ten 3s, sixteen 2s, and twenty-six singles. Only once before had anyone taken his bat right through the innings in an England and Australia match, the previous instance being Dr Barrett's performance at Lord's in 1890. On Monday, February 1, the third day of the match, there came an extraordinary change in the cricket, Lyons, Bannerman, and George Giffen batting with such success that it took the Englishmen all the afternoon to obtain two wickets, the total meanwhile being increased from 1 to 263. Lyons and Bannerman were separated at 175, their partnership having lasted two hours and three-quarters. Lyons certainly gave one chance to Abel at slip when he had made 49, and we believe he offered another to the same fieldsman, but otherwise his 134 – which included sixteen 4s, five 3s, and eight 2s – was a magnificent innings. On the fourth day the weather was unsettled and rain considerably affected the wicket. Everything went wrong with the Englishmen, who made several bad mistakes in the field. The Australians' innings closed for 391, and the Englishmen, wanting 230 to win, had to go in when the ground was in a very treacherous state. Abel, Bean, and Grace were got rid of for 11 runs, and only a downfall of rain prevented further disasters. On the following morning the wicket rolled out much better than anyone could have expected, and the Englishmen still had a chance, Australia's bowling being weakened by the absence of McLeod, who had been called back to Melbourne by the death of his brother. George Giffen and Turner, however, bowled wonderfully well, and despite the very fine batting of Stoddart, the innings was finished off for 156, Australia winning the game by 72 runs, and so gaining the rubber in the test matches. Bannerman's innings of 91 had much to do with the victory. Invaluable as it was, however, it would in a match of less interest have thoroughly tired out the spectators. The New South Wales batsman was actually at the wickets seven hours and twenty-eight minutes. Out of 204 balls bowled at him by Attewell he only scored from five. At the finish of the game there was a scene of almost indescribable enthusiasm.

Combined Australia

A. C. Bannerman c Abel b Lohmann	12	– c Grace b Briggs	91
J. J. Lyons c Grace b Lohmann	41	– c Grace b Lohmann	134
H. Moses c Grace b Lohmann	29	– absent hurt	0
G. Giffen c Abel b Lohmann	6	– lbw b Attewell	49
C. T. B. Turner c MacGregor b Lohmann	15	– not out	14
W. Bruce c Bean b Attewell	15	– c Briggs b Sharpe	72
H. Trott b Lohmann	2	– c Sharpe b Lohmann	1
R. McLeod c Attewell b Lohmann	13	– c Read b Peel	18
W. F. Giffen c and b Lohmann	1	– b Briggs	3
S. T. Callaway run out	1	– c Grace b Briggs	0
J. McC. Blackham not out	3	– lbw b Briggs	0
Extras	7	Extras	9
	145		391

Lord Sheffield's Team

R. Abel not out	132	– c W. Giffen b G. Giffen	1
W. G. Grace b Turner	26	– c Blackham b Turner	5
A. E. Stoddart c Blackham b McLeod	27	– b Turner	69
G. Bean b G. Giffen	19	– c Lyons b Turner	4
M. Read c Turner b G. Giffen	3	– c and b G. Giffen	22
R. Peel c G. Giffen b Turner	10	– st Blackham b G. Goffen	6
G. A. Lohmann b G. Giffen	10	– c Bruce b G. Giffen	15
G. MacGregor lbw b McLeod	3	– c and b G. Giffen	12
J. Briggs lbw b Trott	28	– c Trott b Turner	12
W. Attewell b Trott	0	– c and b G. Giffen	0
J. W. Sharpe c Bannerman b G. Giffen	26	– not out	4
Extras	13	Extras	6
	307		156

English Bowling

	Overs	Mdns	Runs	Wkts	Overs	Mdns	Runs	Wkts
Lohmann	260	18	58	8	306	14	84	2
Attewell	186	20	25	1	276	24	43	1
Briggs	60	1	24	0	196	8	69	4
Sharpe	60	1	31	0	210	7	91	1
Peel					210	13	49	1
Grace					93	2	34	0
Stoddart					24	1	12	0

Australian Bowling

	Overs	Mdns	Runs	Wkts	Overs	Mdns	Runs	Wkts
Turner	222	11	90	2	140	7	46	4
McLeod	108	6	55	2				
G. Giffen	170	5	88	4	168	10	72	6
Trott	84	3	42	2	30	0	11	0
Callaway	102	10	19	0	60	6	21	0

LORD SHEFFIELD'S TEAM v NEW SOUTH WALES

Played at Sydney, February 19, 20, 22, 23, 1892

In this match the Englishmen gave a fine display of cricket, and gained a brilliant victory by seven wickets. Indeed, but for the fact of the order of batting being changed in the second innings they would probably have won even more easily. Moses, owing to his injured leg, was unable to play for New South Wales, and Percy McDonnell's return to the scene of his old triumphs was not at all successful. Having the good fortune to win the toss and go in first on a perfect wicket, the Englishmen ran up a total of 414, in this way securing an advantage which they never lost. Grace and Abel did very well, but the batting honours were carried off by Maurice Read and Lohmann, both of whom got into three figures. Both played finely, though Lohmann had some luck. For New South Wales, Sidney Gregory played better than he had ever done before. His score of 93 not out was obtained in an hour and twenty-five minutes, and, except for one hard chance, was quite free from fault. An unfortunate disagreement marred the pleasure of the match, one of the umpires taking exception to a remark made by W. G. Grace about one of his decisions, and declining to act in the second innings of New South Wales. The matter afterwards gave rise to a good deal of correspondence and discussion.

Lord Sheffield's Team

W. G. Grace b Callaway	45		
R. Abel b Callaway	48	not out	0
A. E. Stoddart b Gould	16	lbw b Turner	17
R. Peel b Callaway	29		
O. G. Radcliffe run out	0	c Gregory b Turner	18
G. A. Lohmann c Gregory b Turner	102		
M. Read c Callaway b Turner	106		
J. Briggs c Wales b Gould	6	c Charlton b Callaway	1
G. MacGregor st Wales b Gould	10		
W. Attewell not out	22	not out	6
J. W. Sharpe b Callaway	16		
Extras	14		
	414		42

New South Wales

P. S. McDonnell c Briggs b Lohmann	5	c Sharpe b Lohmann	2
S. P. Jones b Attewell	5	c Grace b Lohmann	13
A. C. Bannerman c Abel b Grace	29	c Grace b Briggs	49
H. Donnan b Grace	19	b Grace	11
C. T. B. Turner run out	66	b Attewell	7
Clarke c Briggs b Attewell	33	c Attewell b Peel	6
S. E. Gregory c Abel b Lohmann	46	not out	93
Gould lbw b Peel	6	c Lohmann b Briggs	2
S. T. Callaway not out	19	b Attewell	14
P. C. Charlton c Stoddart b Lohmann	0	c MacGregor b Lohman	10
S. Wales lbw b Grace	11	c MacGregor b Grace	0
Extras	5	Extras	3
	244		210

New South Wales Bowling

	Overs	Mdns	Runs	Wkts	Overs	Mdns	Runs	Wkts
Turner	53	19	98	2	8.1	1	23	2
Callaway	62.4	31	92	4	7	2	14	1
Charlton	39	8	77	0	2	0	5	0
Gould	36	5	120	3				
Donnan	4	1	13	0				

English Bowling

	Overs	Mdns	Runs	Wkts	Overs	Mdns	Runs	Wkts
Attewell	54	31	46	2	24	10	38	2
Lohmann	33	18	46	3	40	22	48	3
Briggs	16	9	17	0	17	4	45	2
Sharpe	22	7	36	0	17	7	34	0
Grace	31.1	9	64	3	16	6	29	2
Peel	17	6	30	1	5	0	13	1

ENGLISH TEAM v AUSTRALIA

Played at Sydney, December 14, 15, 17, 18, 19, 20, 1895

This was probably the most sensational match ever played either in Australia or in England. Going in first, the Australians made a poor start, losing three wickets – all bowled down by Richardson – for 21 runs. Iredale and Giffen, however, put on 171 for the fourth wicket, and Giffen and Gregory 139 for the fifth. Giffen's splendidly played 161 lasted a little over four hours and a quarter. At the close of the first day the score stood at 346 for five wickets, and in the end the total reached 586, Gregory and Blackham scoring 154 together for the ninth wicket. In recognition of his wonderful innings of 201 a collection was made for Gregory, the sum subscribed on the ground amounting to a hundred and three pounds. In face of a score of 586 the Englishmen had a dismal prospect, but they set to work with the utmost resolution and kept the Australians in the field from Saturday afternoon till the following Wednesday. Still, though they ran up totals of 325 and 437 – Albert Ward taking the chief honours in each innings – they only set Australia 177 to get. At the close of the fifth day 113 had been scored for two wickets, and the match looked all over. Drenching rain in the night, however, followed by bright sunshine, completely altered the condition of the ground, and Peel – well backed up by Briggs – proved so irresistible that the Englishmen gained an astonishing victory by 10 runs.

Australia

G. H. S. Trott b Richardson	12	– c Gay b Peel	8
J. J. Lyons b Richardson	1	– b Richardson	25
G. Giffen c Ford b Brockwell	161	– lbw b Briggs	41
J. Darling b Richardson	0	– c Brockwell b Peel	53
F. A. Iredale c Stoddart b Ford	81	– c and b Briggs	5
S. E. Gregory c Peel b Stoddart	201	– c Gay b Peel	16
J. Reedman c Ford b Peel	17	– st Gay b Peel	4
C. McLeod b Richardson	15	– not out	2
C. T. B. Turner c Gay b Peel	1	– c Briggs b Peel	2
J. M'C. Blackham b Richardson	74	– c and b Peel	2
E. Jones not out	11	– c MacLaren b Briggs	1
Extras	12	Extras	7
	586		166

England

Mr A. C. MacLaren c Reedman b Turner	4	– b Giffen	20
A. Ward c Iredale b Turner	75	– b Giffen	117
Mr A. E. Stoddart c Jones b Giffen	12	– c Giffen b Turner	36
J. T. Brown run out	22	– c Jones b Giffen	53
R. Peel c Gregory b Giffen	4	– b Giffen	17
Mr F. G. J. Ford st Blackham b Giffen	30	– c and b McLeod	48
W. Brockwell c Blackham b Jones	49	– b Jones	37
W. Lockwood c Giffen b Trott	18	– b Trott	29
J. Briggs b Giffen	57	– b McLeod	42
Mr L. H. Gay c Gregory b Reedman	33	– b Trott	4
T. Richardson not out	0	– not out	12
Extras	21	Extras	21
	325		437

English Bowling

	Overs	Mdns	Runs	Wkts	Overs	Mdns	Runs	Wkts
Richardson	55.3	13	181	5	11	3	27	1
Peel	53	14	140	2	30	9	67	6
Briggs	28	4	96	0	11	2	25	3
Brockwell	22	7	78	1				
Lockwood	3	2	1	0	16	3	40	0
Ford	11	2	47	1				
Stoddart	3	0	31	1				

Australian Bowling

	Overs	Mdns	Runs	Wkts	Overs	Mdns	Runs	Wkts
Turner	44	16	89	2	35	14	78	1
Jones	19	7	44	1	19	0	58	1
Giffen	43	17	75	4	75	25	164	4
McLeod	14	2	25	0	30	7	67	2
Trott	15	4	59	1	12	4	22	2
Reedman	3.3	1	12	1	6	1	12	0
Lyons	2	2	0	0	2	0	12	0
Iredale					2	0	3	0

Umpires: J. Phillips and C. Bannerman.

ENGLISH TEAM v SOUTH AUSTRALIA

Played at Adelaide, March 28, 29, 30, April 1, 2, 1895

The final match of the tour was a sensational one indeed, the Englishmen running up the huge total of 609 and winning by ten wickets. In face of a score of 397 in South Australia's first innings this was a very fine performance. Albert Ward was batting six hours and three-quarters for his 219 – the second highest score obtained for the English team during their trip. Though not entirely free from luck it was a great innings. Equally good was the performance of young Clement Hill, the South Australian colt, who completed his eighteenth year on the first day of the match. The finish of the game was exciting, Brockwell and Ford just hitting off the runs in time to win. South Australia lost A. H. Jarvis's services after the first day, the famous wicket-keeper being thrown out of a trap and so much hurt that he could not play any more. George Giffen's analysis in the first innings of the Englishmen is probably unprecedented in first-class cricket. He was on nearly all through the innings, and had 309 runs hit from him.

South Australia

J. J. Lyons c Peel b Richardson	6	– c Philipson b Peel	32
A. H. Jarvis b Richardson	5	– absent hurt	0
G. Giffen c MacLaren b Briggs	51	– c Brown b Richardson	27
J. Darling b Richardson	15	– b Briggs	36
J. Reedman run out	46	– b Peel	1
H. Dyer b Briggs	0	– not out	40
H. Blinman c Peel b Richardson	3	– c Philipson b Richardson	17
C. Hill not out	150	– c Philipson b Richardson	56
W. F. Giffen b Lockwood	81	– c Philipson b Richardson	4
F. Jarvis b Richardson	31	– b Briggs	27
E. Jones c Ward b Brockwell	1	– b Lockwood	3
L-b 4, n-b 1, w 3	8	B 5, l-b 4, n-b 1, w 2	12
	397		255

England

W. Brockwell lbw b G. Giffen	35	– not out	24
A. Ward lbw b G. Giffen	219		
J. T. Brown b G. Giffen	101		
Mr A. C. MacLaren c and b G. Giffen	18		
Mr F. G. J. Ford run out	106	– not out	18
R. Peel b Lyons	57		
W. Lockwood run out	23		
J. Briggs not out	27		
Mr J. H. Gay c Hill b Lyons	1		
Mr H. Phillipson c Reedman b G. Giffen	2		
T. Richardson c and b Lyons	0		
B 9, l-b 4	13	B 3	3
	609		45

English Bowling

	Overs	Mdns	Runs	Wkts	Overs	Mdns	Runs	Wkts
Richardson	37	8	148	5	44	17	91	4
Peel	26	7	62	0	29	7	62	2
Briggs	32	6	92	2	17	3	54	2
Lockwood	12	1	43	1	11.5	1	36	1
Brockwell	10.4	3	25	1				
Ford	6	1	19	0				

South Australia Bowling

	Overs	Mdns	Runs	Wkts	Overs	Mdns	Runs	Wkts
Jones	37	10	84	0	2	0	19	0
F. Jarvis	21	2	85	0	1.4	0	10	0
G. Giffen	87	12	309	5	4	0	13	0
Lyons	21.1	6	80	3				
Reedman	15	5	38	0				

ENGLISH TEAM v NEW SOUTH WALES

Played at Sydney, November 12, 13, 15, 16, 1898

On no occasion during the tour, except perhaps, in the first test match, were the Englishmen seen to better advantage than in this, their first engagement in Sydney. They gained a brilliant victory by eight wickets, and the match will always be remembered by reason of MacLaren's magnificent batting. He is the only man who, in a match of first-rate importance in Australia, has made two separate hundreds. In both innings he played in his finest form, scoring with special facility from McKibbin's off-break bowling. He and Ranjitsinhji in the second innings put on 180 runs in an hours and fifty-five minutes, and altogether the 237 required were obtained in a shade over two hours and a half. Ranjitsinhji's innings was quite without fault. In the second innings of New South Wales MacKenzie, and the veteran Tom Garrett, added 177 runs together after six wickets had fallen for 131.

New South Wales

First innings		Second innings	
V. Trumper c Ranjitsinhji b Hirst	5	b Richardson	0
S. E. Gregory run out	14	c Storer b Richardson	44
M. A. Noble b Richardson	4	c Storer b Richardson	15
F. A. Iredale lbw b Hayward	89	c Hearne b Richardson	19
H. Donnan run out	104	b Hirst	29
J. J. Kelly c Storer b Richardson	5	not out	2
A. C. Coningham c and b Richardson	0	b Hirst	0
A. C. K. Mackenzie b Richardson	80	c anb b Hirst	59
T. W. Garrett c Ranjitsinhji b Hearne	5	c Storer b Hirst	71
T. R. McKibbin not out	3	b Hearne	7
W. Howell c Druce b Hearne	0	b Richardson	1
Extras	2	Extras	13
	311		260

English Team

Mr A. C. MacLaren c Iredale b Noble	142 – b Noble	100
Mr J. R. Mason b McKibbin	1 – b Noble	4
K. S. Ranjitsinhji c Kelly b Noble	10 – not out	112
T. Hayward c Trumper b Noble	9 – not out	18
Mr N. F. Druce c Donnan b McKibbin	16	
W. Storer c Kelly b Noble	81	
E. Wainwright c Mackenzie b McKibbin	24	
Mr A. E. Stoddart b Noble	32	
G. H. Hirst lbw b McKibbin	16	
J. T. Hearne not out	2	
T. Richardson b McKibbin	0	
Extras	2	Extras 3
	335	237

English Team Bowling

	Overs	Mdns	Runs	Wkts	Overs	Mdns	Runs	Wkts
Richardson	33	9	105	4	38.2	12	80	5
Hirst	22	11	55	1	24	6	66	4
Hearne	27.5	9	55	2	18	5	41	1
Hayward	16	6	48	1	6	0	39	0
Storer	9	1	27	0	4	0	21	0
Wainwright	6	1	19	0				

New South Wales Bowling

	Overs	Mdns	Runs	Wkts	Overs	Mdns	Runs	Wkts
McKibbin	37.1	7	139	5	33	2	64	0
Coningham	11	3	48	0	9.1	2	31	0
Noble	29	4	111	5	21	2	92	2
Howell	13	4	35	0	5	1	22	0
Trumper					3	0	25	0

ENGLISH TEAM v AUSTRALIA

Played at Sydney, December 13, 14, 15, 16, 17, 1898

A very unpleasant incident, which gave rise to almost endless discussion, preceded the first test match, the trustees of the Sydney ground taking it upon themselves to postpone the commencement of the game without consulting the captains of the sides. Heavy rain had fallen, but it was not thought by the players on the Thursday – the match being fixed to start on the following morning – that any postponement would be necessary. As it happened the ground on Saturday, after heavy rain for several hours, was under water, and it thus came about that the anxiously-expected game did not begin till Monday the 13th of December. The delay had one happy result for the Englishmen, Ranjitsinhji, who had been very ill, recovering sufficiently to take his place in the team and playing finer cricket than on any other occasion during the trip. Considering his physical condition – he was quite exhausted after scoring 39, not out, on the first evening – his innings of 175 was a marvellous piece of batting. Before resuming play on the second morning he was in the hands of the doctor. He hit twenty-four 4s, and was batting in all three hours and thirty-five minutes. Scarcely inferior was the cricket shown by MacLaren, who made a third hundred in succession on the Sydney ground. On the second afternoon the Australians in face of a total of 551 lost five wickets for 86, and from these disasters, despite the superb play in the second innings by the two left-handers – Darling and Hill – they never recovered. The Englishmen won the match by nine wickets. With this victory their good fortune in Australia came to an end.

English Team

Mr A. C. MacLaren (capt.) c Kelly b McLeod	109	– not out	50
Mr J. R. Mason b Jones	6	– b McKibbin	32
T. Hayward c Trott b Trumble	72		
W. Storer c and b Trott	43		
Mr N. F. Druce c Gregory b McLeod	20		
G. H. Hirst b Jones	62		
K. S. Ranjitsinhji c Gregory b McKibbin	175	– not out	8
E. Wainwright b Jones	10		
J. T. Hearne c and b McLeod	17		
J. Briggs run out	1		
T. Richardson not out	24		
B 11, w 1	12	B 5, n-b 1	6
	551		96

Australia

J. Darling (SA) c Druce b Richardson	7	– c Druce b Briggs	101
J. J. Lyons (SA) b Richardson	3	– c Hayward b Hearne	25
F. A. Iredale (NSW) c Druce b Hearne	25	– b Briggs	19
C. Hill (SA) b Hearne	19	– b Hearne	86
S. E. Gregory (NSW) c Mason b Hearne	46	– run out	31
G. H. S. Trott (V) (capt.) b Briggs	10	– b Richardson	27
J. J. Kelly (NSW) b Richardson	1	– not out	46
H. Trumble (V) c Storer b Mason	70	– c Druce b Hearne	2
C. McLeod (V) not out	50	– run out	26
T. R. McKibbin (NSW) b Hearne	0	– b Hearne	6
E. Jones (SA) c Richardson b Hearne	0	– lbw b Richardson	3
B 1, l-b 1, n-b 4	6	B 12, l-b 1, w 4, n-b 10	27
	237		408

Australian Bowling

	Overs	Mdns	Runs	Wkts	Overs	Mdns	Runs	Wkts
McKibbin	34	5	113	1	5	1	22	1
Jones	50	8	130	3	9	1	28	0
McLeod	28	12	80	3				
Trumble	40	7	138	1	13	4	40	0
Trott	23	2	78	1				

English Bowling

	Overs	Mdns	Runs	Wkts	Overs	Mdns	Runs	Wkts
Richardson	27	8	71	3	41	9	121	2
Hirst	28	7	57	0	13	3	49	0
Hearne	20.1	7	42	5	38	8	99	4
Briggs	20	7	42	1	22	3	86	2
Hayward	3	1	11	0	5	1	16	0
Mason	2	1	8	1	2	0	10	0

Umpires: J. Phillips and C. Bannerman.

ENGLISH TEAM v AUSTRALIA

Played at Melbourne, January 29, 31, February 1, 2, 1898

Of the five test matches this was perhaps the most eventful. The Englishmen started in wonderful form by getting six wickets down for 57 runs, but after that they were quite outplayed, the Australians gaining a brilliant victory by eight wickets. The turning point of the Australians' first innings was the partnership of Clement Hill and Trumble, 165 runs being put on for the seventh wicket. Never before had Hill given quite so fine a display as his 188. He was batting a little over five hours and all things considered his innings may be described as perhaps the best seen in the Colonies during the season. With only a total of 323 to face on a perfectly sound wicket, the Englishmen seemed to have very good prospects, but they failed miserably, their dismissal for 174 marking the lowest point reached by their batting during the whole trip. They did not do very much better when they followed on, and it is no more than the truth to say that they richly deserved to be beaten. The Australians' played their winning game wonderfully well, the variety and excellence of their bowling calling forth a high compliment from Mr Stoddart when the match was over.

Australia

Batsman	1st inns		2nd inns	
C. McLeod (V) b Hearne	1	–	not out	64
J. Darling (SA) c Hearne b Richardson	12	–	c Druce b Hayward	29
C. Hill (SA) c Stoddart b Hearne	188	–	lbw b Hayward	0
S. E. Gregory (NSW) b Richardson	0	–	not out	21
F. A. Iredale (NSW) c Storer b Hearne	0			
M. A. Noble (NSW) c and b Hearne	4			
G. H. S. Trott (V) (capt.) c Storer b Hearne	7			
H. Trumble (V) c Mason b Storer	46			
J. J. Kelly (NSW) c Storer b Briggs	32			
E. Jones (SA) c Hayward b Hearne	20			
W. Howell (NSW) not out	9			
Extras	4		Extra	1
	323			115

English Team

Batsman	1st inns		2nd inns	
Mr A. C. MacLaren b Howell	8	–	c Iredale b Trumble	45
E. Wainwright c Howell b Trott	6	–	c McLeod b Jones	2
K. S. Ranjitsinhji c Iredale b Trumble	24	–	b Noble	55
T. Hayward c Gregory b Noble	22	–	c and b Trumble	25
W. Storer c and b Trumble	2	–	c Darling b McLeod	26
Mr N. F. Druce lbw b Jones	24	–	c Howell b Trott	16
Mr J. R. Mason b Jones	30	–	b Howell	26
Mr A. E. Stoddart c Darling b Jones	17	–	b Jones	25
J. Briggs not out	21	–	c Darling b Howell	23
J. T. Hearne c Trott b Jones	0	–	not out	4
T. Richardson b Trott	20	–	c Trumble b McLeod	2
			Extras	14
	174			263

English Bowling

	Overs	Mdns	Runs	Wkts	Overs	Mdns	Runs	Wkts
Richardson	26	2	102	2				
Hearne	35.4	13	98	6	7	3	19	0
Hayward	10	4	24	0	10	4	24	2
Briggs	17	4	38	1	6	1	31	0
Stoddart	6	1	22	0				
Storer	4	0	24	1				
Wainwright	3	1	11	0	9	2	21	0
Mason					4	1	10	0
Rajitsinhji					3.4	1	9	0

Australian Bowling

	Overs	Mdns	Runs	Wkts	Overs	Mdns	Runs	Wkts
Howell	16	7	34	1	30	12	58	2
Trott	11.1	1	33	2	12	2	39	1
Noble	7	1	21	1	16	6	31	1
Trumble	15	4	30	2	23	6	40	2
Jones	12	2	56	4	25	7	70	2
McLeod					8.2	4	11	2

Umpires: J. Phillips and C. Bannerman.

ENGLISH TEAM v NEW SOUTH WALES

Played at Sydney, February 5, 7, 8, 9, 10, 11, 1898

Fresh from the loss of the rubber in the test matches, the Englishmen had an extraordinary experience in their return game with New South Wales. The match lasted into the sixth day, and produced the unexampled aggregate of 1739 runs. Richardson could not play and can perhaps congratulate himself upon being out of such a feast of run-getting. The Englishmen required 603 runs in the last innings, but so remarkably was the batting of MacLaren, Wainwright and Ranjitsinhji, that at the close of the fifth day the score stood at 258 for one wicket. However, on the next morning the side went all to pieces before Noble's bowling, New South Wales winning the match by 239 runs. There was a little unpleasantness in this closing stage of the game, it being alleged that Donnan, who was tried as a bowler on the last morning, cut up the pitch. MacKenzie, Gregory and Pye batted finely for the winners, but the most remarkable hitting was that of Howell – not supposed to be much of a batsman – who scored his 95 in sixty-six minutes.

New South Wales

F. A. Iredale c Stoddart b Briggs	2	– b Hearne	7
H. Donnan c Board b Wainwright	41	– c Hirst b Hearne	59
M. A. Noble c MacLaren b Hayward	34	– b Hearne	8
A. C. K. Mackenzie c Hayward b Hearne	130	– c sub. b Mason	52
S. E. Gregory c and b Mason	25	– c Hayward b Briggs	171
V. Trumper b Mason	4	– b Hearne	23
L. W. Pye not out	80	– b Hearne	31
J. J. Kelly b Stoddart	14	– c Hirst b Mason	4
A. L. Newell c Hirst b Stoddart	6	– not out	68
T. R. McKibbin c Druce b Briggs	20	– b Hearne	39
W. Howell b Mason	48	– c Wainwright b Mason	95
B 4, l-b 2, w 3, n-b 2	11	B 10, l-b 2, w 1, n-b 4	17
	415		574

English Team

Mr J. R. Mason c Howell b Noble	11	– c Gregory b Noble	8
E. Wainwright c Howell b Noble	50	– b McKibbin	64
K. S. Ranjitsinhji c Gregory b Noble	37	– c McKibbin b Howell	44
T. Hayward c Howell b Noble	63	– not out	62
G. H. Hirst c Newell b Noble	4	– c Gregory b Noble	5
Mr N. F. Druce c Noble b Trumper	109	– c Kelly b Noble	11
Mr A. E. Stoddart c Iredale b McKibbin	5	– b Noble	6
J. Briggs c Mackenzie b McKibbin	18	– c and b Noble	0
Mr A. C. MacLaren b Noble	61	– b Howell	140
J. H. Board c Mackenzie b McKibbin	14	– b Noble	9
J. T. Hearne not out	6	– b Howell	1
B 4, w 3, n-b 2	9	B 10, l-b 2, n-b 1	13
	387		363

English Bowling

	Overs	Mdns	Runs	Wkts	Overs	Mdns	Runs	Wkts
Hearne	32	13	96	1	54	18	126	6
Briggs	39	13	98	2	38	10	101	1
Hayward	15	3	58	1	34	4	106	0
Wainwright	14	4	32	1	11	2	49	0
Mason	12.2	0	53	3	34	10	120	3
Ranjitsinhji	5	1	17	0	10	2	32	0
Stoddart	13	4	50	2	8	1	22	0
Druce					1	0	1	0

New South Wales Bowling

	Overs	Mdns	Runs	Wkts	Overs	Mdns	Runs	Wkts
Noble	57	15	131	6	37	13	117	6
Howell	12	2	45	0	24.1	4	64	3
McKibbin	27.4	4	108	3	25	5	99	1
Newell	11	1	36	0	4	1	20	0
Pye	11	2	28	0	16	6	37	0
Donnan	3	1	9	0	7	3	9	0
Trumper	7	3	21	1	5	4	4	0

CRICKET IN AUSTRALIA

THE INTER-COLONIAL MATCHES

SOUTH AUSTRALIA v NEW SOUTH WALES

Played at Adelaide, December 19, 20, 22, 23, 1890

In meeting South Australia on the Adelaide ground the New South Wales eleven were seriously handicapped by the absence of Charles Turner, but nevertheless they gained an easy victory by six wickets, this result being chiefly brought about by admirably consistent batting in their first innings and by the capital bowling of Ferris and Charlton. Ferris took in all fourteen wickets for 192 runs, a remarkable average on the Adelaide ground, which is proverbially one of the easiest in the world. It will be noticed that in the first innings of New South Wales eight batsmen reached double figures, the highest individual score, out of a total of 406, being 67, which number was obtained by both Moses and Iredale.

South Australia

J. J. Lyons c Callaway b Ferris	10	– c Bannerman b Ferris	0
A. H. Jarvis b Ferris	13	– c and b Ferris	33
G. Giffen lbw b Charlton	21	– b Charlton	17
J. E. Gooden b Ferris	28	– lbw b Ferris	39
J. Reedman b Ferris	12	– c Wales b Ferris	60
W. A. Magarey b Charlton	0	– c Wales b Callaway	7
H. Blinman not out	73	– c Moses b Ferris	4
W. Giffen c Iredale b Ferris	55	– c Wales b Charlton	2
A. Hill b Ferris	6	– c Wales b Charlton	5
F. Jarvis b Ferris	7	– not out	14
Amos lbw b Ferris	9	– c Wales b Ferris	6
B 3, l-b 4	7	B 3 l-b 1	4
	241		191

New South Wales

A. Bannerman lbw b Lyons	44	– lbw b G. Giffen	17
C. A. Richardson b G. Giffen	56	– not out	2
H. Moses c and b G. Giffen	67	– c A. H. Jarvis b F. Jarvis	3
H. Donnan b G. Giffen	58	– c Blinman b F. Jarvis	0
F. Iredale b G. Giffen	67		
A. P. Marr c W. Giffen b G. Giffen	4	– c A. H. Jarvis b F. Jarvis	0
S. E. Gregory c Blinman b Amos	32	– not out	5
P. C. Charlton st A. H. Jarvis b G. Giffen	34		
J. J. Ferris b F. Jarvis	33		
S. Callaway b F. Jarvis	0		
I. Wales not out	0		
B 2, l-b 9	11		
	406		27

New South Wales Bowling

	Balls	Mdns	Runs	Wkts	Balls	Mdns	Runs	Wkts
Ferris	391	30	84	8	264	13	108	6
Charlton	270	19	74	2	210	13	63	3
Callaway	96	5	44	0	53	3	16	1
Marr	12	0	11	0				
Richardson	30	0	21	0				

South Australia Bowling

	Balls	Mdns	Runs	Wkts	Balls	Mdns	Runs	Wkts
Amos	120	3	87	1				
G. Giffen	501	35	150	6	54	3	10	1
Reedman	144	9	54	0				
Lyons	168	13	59	1				
F. Jarvis	180	9	45	2	59	4	17	3

VICTORIA v SOUTH AUSTRALIA

Played at Melbourne, January 1, 2, 3, 5, 1891

In this match South Australia beat Victoria by an innings and 62 runs. The victory was mainly the work of George Giffen, who has never displayed in a more conspicuous light his pre-eminent qualities as an all-round cricketer. He played an innings of 237, and took in all twelve of the Victorian wickets – five for 89 runs and seven for 103. His magnificent display dwarfed everything else in the game, but several other players showed good batting, notably Trott with a second innings of 81 for Victoria. Phillips again bowled well, taking in an innings of 472 six wickets for 91 runs.

South Australia

J. J. Lyons b McLeod	53
A. H. Jarvis c Houston b Phillips	29
G. Giffen c Blackham b Phillips	237
J. E. Gooden c McLeod b Phillips	1
J. Reedman b Trumble	7
H. Blinman c McLeod b Phillips	50
E. J. Hiscock c Trumble b Phillips	11
J. Noel b Morris	49
L. Evan c Morris b Trott	3
F. Jarvis c Blackham b Phillips	9
E. Serymgour not out	0
B 11, w 12	23
	472

Victoria

R. Houston run out	54	c Evan b Giffen	8
W. Bruce c and b Giffen	58	b Giffen	13
H. Trott c Blinman b Lyons	0	c Gooden b Giffen	81
S. Morris lbw b Giffen	3	b F. Jarvis	0
R. McLeod b Giffen	24	st A. H. Jarvis b Giffen	14
C. Ross not out	29	c Scrymgour b Giffen	6
J. McC. Blackham b F. Jarvis	0	c Hiscock b Giffen	0
J. Worrall c Scrymgour b F. Jarvis	20	run out	1
H. Trumble b Giffen	20	st A. H. Jarvis b Reedman	43
S. Donahoo run out	0	st A. H. Jarvis b Giffen	0
J. Phillips c Scrymgour b Giffen	0	not out	17
B 5, l-b 7	12	W 1, n-b 1	2
	220		190

Victorian Bowling

	Balls	Mdns	Runs	Wkts
Trumble	234	13	104	1
Phillips	334	20	91	6
McLeod	156	7	66	1
Trott	60	2	38	1
Bruce	162	9	58	0
Ross	42	1	18	0
Morris	72	4	39	1
Worrall	144	5	35	0

South Australian Bowling

	Balls	Mdns	Runs	Wkts	Balls	Mdns	Runs	Wkts
Giffen	308	21	89	5	150	5	103	7
F. Jarvis	180	10	74	2	108	2	54	1
Lyons	138	10	42	1	36	1	25	0
Reedman	6	0	3	0	9	0	6	0

NEW SOUTH WALES v VICTORIA

Played at Sydney, January 24, 26, 27, 28, 29, 1891

Charles Turner was fortunately able to play for New South Wales in the return match against Victoria, and thanks to his all-round cricket and the splendid batting of Moses the defeat at Melbourne was handsomely atoned for, New SouthWales winning by an innings and 94 runs. Turner was in his very finest form with the ball, taking at a cost of 174 runs no fewer than fifteen of the twenty Victorian wickets. His innings of 70 was a very brilliant display. Moses, who does all his best performances on the New South Wales ground, scored 147. A feature of the match was the brilliant innings of 106 played for Victoria by Frank Walters, the batsman who failed so conspicuously when he came to England with the Australian team of 1890.

Victoria

First innings		Second innings	
H. Trott c Charlton b Turner	19	c Wales b Turner	4
S. Morris b Turner	0	c Moses b Turner	29
F. H. Walters c Wales b Turner	106	c Charlton b Turner	20
T. Horan c Moses b Turner	20	lbw b Turner	2
R. Houston run out	1	b Charlton	24
H. Trumble b Turner	4	c Garrett b Turner	10
Tarrant b Turner	1	run out	14
J. McC. Blackham c Garrett b Downes	3	c Charlton b Turner	50
J. Phillips lbw b Turner	2	c Bonnor b Charlton	10
J. Worrall not out	22	c Bonnor b Turner	19
J. Carlton c Downes b Turner	1	not out	5
L-b 2	2	B 3	3
	181		190

New South Wales

C. Turner c Carlton b Phillips	70
A. C. Bannerman lbw b Carlton	35
H. Donnan c Houston b Phillips	7
S. E. Gregory c Tarrant b Phillips	1
J. Iredale c Morris b Worrall	46
G. J. Bonnor run out	12
P. C. Charlton b Worrall	28
H. Moses c Tarrant b Phillips	147
T. W. Garrett c Trott b Phillips	76
F. Downes st Blackham b Trott	12
I. Wales not out	12
B 6, l-b 3, w 6, n-b 4	19
	465

New South Wales Bowling

	Balls	Mdns	Runs	Wkts	Balls	Mdns	Runs	Wkts
Turner	191	9	74	8	294	21	100	7
Downes	48	2	30	1	84	7	25	0
Charlton	84	4	38	0	221	15	58	2
Garrett	126	6	42	0	12	1	4	0

Victorian Bowling

	Balls	Mdns	Runs	Wkts
Phillips	336	24	88	5
Trumble	138	7	66	1
Carlton	152	12	113	1
Horan	54	4	24	0
Morris	96	4	33	0
Worrall	264	18	63	2
Trott	90	2	60	1
Walters	12	0	2	0

SOUTH AUSTRALIA v VICTORIA

Played at Adelaide, November 7, 9, 10, 11, 1891

Victoria did not send by any means a representative team to Adelaide, and the result of the match was a single innings victory for South Australia with 164 runs to spare. This decisive issue was clearly due to the two great South Australian cricketers, George Giffen and J. J. Lyons. George Giffen was batting seven hours for his splendid innings of 271, and afterwards followed up his success by taking sixteen wickets for 166 runs. Including this 271, Giffen has during the past five years scored 921 runs against Victoria in seven innings. Lyons's 104 was a fine display, but he gave a couple of chances.

South Australia

J. J. Lyons c Laver b Phillips	104
A. H. Jarvis b McLeod	2
G. Giffen c McLean b Phillips	271
H. Le Haldane c Harry b Phillips	9
H. Blinman c Harry b Phillips	32
W. F. Giffen retired hurt	65
J. Reedman c McLeod b Marshall	11
J. Noel c Harry b Phillips	10
C. W. Hayward lbw b Marshall	27
H. Moore c McLeod b Phillips	0
F. Jarvis not out	19
B 8, l-b 4	12
	562

Victoria

F. H. Walters b G. Giffen	50	– c and b G. Giffen	0
A. N. A. Bowman lbw b G. Giffen	52	– b G. Giffen	0
R. McLeod c Noel b G. Giffen	27	– b G. Giffen	0
J. Harry c and b Lyons	17	– b G. Giffen	19
J. McC. Blackham b G. Giffen	22	– b Lyons	31
H. Stuckey b G. Giffen	7	– st Haldane b G. Giffen	22
H. McLean b G. Giffen	12	– st Haldane b Lyons	33
J. Carlton c Reedman b G. Giffen	16	– c and b G. Giffen	16
F. Laver c Reedman b G. Giffen	5	– c Scrymgour b Moore	1
J. Phillips c Hayward b G. Giffen	13	– not out	39
H. Marshall not out	5	– c Noel b G. Giffen	0
Extras	9	L-b	2
	235		163

Victoria Bowling

	Balls	Mdns	Runs	Wkts
McLeod	240	11	116	1
Laver	168	4	64	0
Marshall	225	6	96	2
Phillips	360	7	156	6
Carlton	132	1	72	0
Blackham	12	1	4	0
Harry	78	5	31	0
McLean	24	0	11	—

South Australian Bowling

	Balls	Mdns	Runs	Wkts	Balls	Mdns	Runs	Wkts
F. Jarvis	132	11	30	0	78	3	29	0
Lyons	198	12	59	1	48	0	51	2
G. Giffen	301	12	96	9	155	4	70	7
Noel	96	4	26	0				
Moore	36	2	13	0	24	1	11	1
Reedman	24	1	2	0				

SOUTH AUSTRALIA v VICTORIA

Played at Adelaide, March 16, 17, 18, 20, 21, 1893

This was the last of the Inter-Colonial matches, and, after some very heavy scoring, Victoria won by five wickets, the victory being mainly due to the fine batting of Laver and McLeod. Distinctly, the feature of the match was the all-round cricket of George Giffen, who scored 43 and 181, and took in all eleven wickets. Seldom can a cricketer have done so much and yet have been on the losing side. His innings of 181 lasted six hours and a quarter, and, except for a very hard chance of being caught and bowled when he had made 20, his batting was without fault. Victoria carried off all the honours of the Australian season, gaining two victories each against New South Wales and South Australia.

South Australia

W. F. Giffen c Lewis b Carlton	21	– c and b Phillips	0
J. J. Lyons c Carlton b Phillips	72	– c Bean b McLeod	62
A. H. Jarvis c Bean b Phillips	6	– c and b Phillips	10
J. Reedman c Harry b Phillips	4	– run out	32
G. Giffen c Trott b Phillips	43	– b Carlton	181
H. Blinman b Harry	41	– b Harry	18
A. Hill c Trott b Harry	13	– b Phillips	19
J. Tardiff b McLeod	25	– c Tarrant b Phillips	2
F. Jarvis c Graham b Phillips	8	– not out	22
W. Amos c Carlton b Phillips	0	– lbw b Carlton	3
E. Jones not out	0	– b McLeod	3
B 4, l-b 1, n-b 4	9	B 2, l-b 6, n-b 2, w 1	11
	242		363

Victoria

P. Lewis b G. Giffen	18	– c and b Reedman	23
H. Stuckey b G. Giffen	37	– c Lyons b Reedman	56
G. H. S. Trott c Lyons b G. Giffen	52	– c Blinman b G. Giffen	20
H. Graham c and b G. Giffen	14	– not out	21
A. Tarrant run out	12		
J. Carlton c Reedman b G. Giffen	2		
J. Phillips b G. Giffen	0		
R. W. McLeod c W. Giffen b G. Giffen	101	– b G. Giffen	15
F. Laver c F. Jarvis b G. Giffen	104	– not out	9
J. Harry not out	14	– c F. Jarvis b Reedman	50
E. Bean c Reedman b G. Giffen	19		
B 6, l-b 18, w 5, n-b 1	30	B 7, l-b 1, n-b 1	9
	403		203

Victoria Bowling

	Overs	Mdns	Runs	Wkts	Overs	Mdns	Runs	Wkts
McLeod	18	5	34	1	34	16	57	2
Carlton	20	2	77	1	23.5	2	68	2
Harry	18	5	47	2	11	0	35	1
Bean	3	0	18	0	9	2	42	0
Laver	12	6	18	0	18	7	28	0
Phillips	23.3	7	39	6	44	15	100	4
Trott					5	0	22	0

South Australia Bowling

	Overs	Mdns	Runs	Wkts	Overs	Mdns	Runs	Wkts
Amos	11	2	35	0	4	1	7	0
Jones	21	9	43	0	4	1	26	0
G. Giffen	64	25	147	9	25	7	88	2
Reedman	17	3	68	0	16	4	46	3
F. Jarvis	30	11	64	0	10	2	27	0
Lyons	3	1	16	0				

NEW SOUTH WALES v SOUTH AUSTRALIA

Played at Sydney, February 22, 23, 25, 26, 1895

Making some amends for previous failures during the season, New South Wales won by 111 runs. Iredale, Gregory, Donnan, Howell, and the veteran Garrett all batted finely, but the chief cause of the victory was the remarkable bowling of McKibbin. Indeed, by taking eight wickets for 66 runs in the second innings of South Australia, the new bowler created quite a sensation, and secured his place in the Australian team in the last of the test matches against Mr Stoddart's eleven.

New South Wales

F. A. Iredale b Jarvis	26	– c Darling b G. Giffen	91
A. C. McKenzie c G. Giffen b Jarvis	14	– c Darling b G. Giffen	7
H. Moses c Jarvis b G. Giffen	1	– b Jones	34
S. E. Gregory b Jones	33	– not out	66
H. Donnan c Lyons b Jarvis	58	– c Hill b Jones	16
L. Moore b Jones	0	– b Jones	5
T. W. Garrett (capt.) c W. F. Giffen b G. Giffen	82	– b G. Giffen	27
S. T. Callaway b G. Giffen	5	– run out	0
T. R. McKibbin b Jarvis	12	– b G. Giffen	8
J. J. Kelly not out	2	– b G. Giffen	4
W. Howell b G. Giffen	1	– c Reedman b G. Giffen	62
Extras	5	Extras	16
	239		336

South Australia

D. Bennett b McKibbin	5	– b McKibbin	0
H. Dyer c Kelly b Donnan	71	– b Howell	3
J. J. Lyons b Howell	22	– b McKibbin	6
G. Giffen (capt.) b McKibbin	15	– st Kelly b McKibbin	65
J. Darling b McKibbin	70	– run out	39
J. Reedman c Iredale c Callaway	30	– lbw b McKibbin	10
F. Jarvis c Callaway b McKibbin	21	– b McKibbin	3
A. Hill run out	30	– not out	15
W. F. Giffen not out	20	– st Kelly b McKibbin	0
J. Noel b McKibbin	0	– b McKibbin	5
E. Jones b McKibbin	2	– c Garrett b McKibbin	10
Extras	18	Extras	4
	304		160

South Australia Bowling

	Overs	Mdns	Runs	Wkts	Overs	Mdns	Runs	Wkts
G. Giffen	37.5	7	114	4	50.2	12	132	6
Jones	12	3	36	2	27	5	95	3
Jarvis	27	4	84	4	18	6	75	0
Noel					5	0	18	0

New South Wales Bowling

	Overs	Mdns	Runs	Wkts	Overs	Mdns	Runs	Wkts
McKibbin	36.4	6	123	6	28.5	7	66	8
Howell	14	2	50	1	19	5	46	1
Callaway	24	10	39	1	4	1	13	0
Garrett	9	5	18	0	6	2	11	0
Iredale	3	0	16	0				
Donnan	10	3	40	1	9	2	20	0

Umpires: G. Bannerman and I. A. Fisher.

NEW SOUTH WALES v SOUTH AUSTRALIA

Played at Sydney, February, 28, 29, March 2, 3, 4, 1896

The game was attended with an extraordinary amount of interest, as New South Wales had to win it to wrest the Sheffield Shield from Victoria. The start greatly favoured South Australia, who, thanks to the admirable batting of Hill and Darling, ran up a total of 400 and looked to have rendered themselves secure against defeat. However, New South Wales were in no way disheartened, and aided by a fine performance on the part of Iredale, headed their opponents' total by 28 runs. The batting of South Australia in the second innings compared most unfavourably with what had gone before, and though Giffen, Lyons, and Darling all did well, and four others ran into double figures, the side were dismissed for 200. South Australia were left with 173 to get to win and the result was seldom in doubt, Donnan and Iredale playing magnificent cricket and winning the match in handsome fashion for New South Wales by nine wickets. In the second innings of South Australia, Turner came back to quite his old form, obtaining six wickets and having only 34 runs hit from him.

South Australia

J. J. Lyons c Coningham b McKibbin	0 – c Donnan b Coningham	46
E. H. Leak b Turner	0 – c Coningham b Turner	17
G. Giffen c Coningham b McKibbin	11 – b Turner	55
J. Darling b Garrett	121 – c Mackenzie b McKibbin	32
C. Hill not out	206 – b Turner	14
J. Reedham b Coningham	17 – b Coningham	3
F. Jarvis b Coningham	0 – run out	11
C. Martin b Coningham	9 – b Turner	13
J. McKenzie b McKibbin	19 – c Garrett b Turner	0
E. Jones run out	5 – b Turner	2
J. Travers c Turner b Garrett	10 – not out	1
L-b 2	2 B 6	6
	400	200

New South Wales

A. C. Mackenzie c Martin b Reedman	45 – run out	20
H. Donnan b Jones	48 – not out	67
F. A. Iredale c McKenzie b Jones	187 – not out	80
S. E. Gregory st McKenzie b Travers	22	
F. H. Walters lbw b Giffen	6	
A. Coningham st McKenzie b Giffen	6	
J. J. Kelly c Darling b Reedman	37	
C. T. B. Turner b Jones	40	
S. T. Callaway b Jones	4	
T. W. Garrett c Jarvis b Giffen	21	
T. R. McKibbin not out	1	
B 9, l-b 1, w 1	11 B 2, l-b 3, w 1	6
	428	173

New South Wales Bowling

	Overs	Mdns	Runs	Wkts	Overs	Mdns	Runs	Wkts
McKibbin	42	9	124	3	27	9	75	1
Turner	42	10	120	1	43.3	25	35	6
Callaway	9	1	33	0	1	1	0	0
Coningham	22	9	65	3	26	6	68	2
Iredale	3	1	15	0				
Walters	1	0	11	0				
Garrett	11	1	30	2	9	4	16	0

South Australia Bowling

	Overs	Mdns	Runs	Wkts	Overs	Mdns	Runs	Wkts
Jones	47	15	110	4	25	10	49	0
Giffen	52.2	9	166	3				
Jarvis	11	0	59	0	23	6	54	0
Reedman	11	4	48	2	9	3	15	0
Travers	11	0	34	1	18.4	4	49	0

SOUTH AUSTRALIA v NEW SOUTH WALES

Played at Adelaide, December 19, 20, 22, 23, 1896

With New South Wales holding the Inter-Colonial Shield presented by Lord Sheffield, their meeting with South Australia aroused a large amount of interest and a wonderfully well contested game ended early on the fourth day in a victory for New South Wales by 51 runs. Up to a certain point the advantage was with South Australia, some fine bowling by Jones and the batting of Lyons and Hill gaining them a lead on the first innings of 25 runs. From this point however, New South Wales gradually obtaining the upper hand. After a bad start Noble, Turner and Garrett played exceedingly well and in the end, South Australia were left with 213 to get to win. Once again the batsmen found McKibbin's bowling too much for them and despite some good cricket by Hill and Bailey, the total only ammounted to 161. McKibbin, by taking in the whole match fifteen wickets for 125 runs, had a big share in the success of his side.

New South Wales

F. A. Iredale b Jones	0	c Darling b Travers	21
A. C. Mackenzie c Reedman b Evans	34	c A. Jarvis b Jones	14
H. Donnan b Jones	35	c and b Evans	6
A. Coningham b Jones	0	c Hill b Jones	1
S. E. Gregory b Evans	0	c Giffen b Evans	3
J. J. Kelly c F. Jarvis b Jones	50	run out	3
M. A. Noble c Darling b Evans	5	c and b Evans	69
C. T. B. Turner c Darling b Evans	9	b Reedman	48
T. W. Garrett run out	13	c Jones b Reedman	49
T. R. McKibbin not out	7	not out	8
W. Howell b Jones	3	b Reedman	0
B 2, l-b 3, n-b 1	6	B 8, l-b 7	15
	162		237

South Australia

J. Darling c Donnan b McKibbin	19	lbw b McKibbin	0
F. Jarvis b McKibbin	7	b McKibbin	0
J. J. Lyons b Howell	78	b McKibbin	1
C. Hill c and b McKibbin	49	c Coningham b McKibbin	51
B. T. R. Bailey c McKibbin b Turner	5	c Kelly b Turner	45
G. Giffen c Kelly b McKibbin	3	c Howell b McKibbin	12
J. Reedman b McKibbin	0	b McKibbin	26
A. E. H. Evans c Kelly b McKibbin	11	c Mackenzie b McKibbin	4
A. H. Jarvis c and b McKibbin	8	b Howell	0
E. Jones b Howell	4	not out	13
J. Travers not out	0	st Kelly b McKibbin	0
L-b 1, w 2	3	B 2, l-b 6, w 1	9
	187		161

South Australia Bowling

	Overs	Mdns	Runs	Wkts	Overs	Mdns	Runs	Wkts
Jones	25.1	6	49	5	24	3	76	2
Jarvis	17	2	54	0	3	2	1	0
Giffen	1	1	0	0	13	1	47	0
Evans	12	2	47	4	20	1	59	3
Travers	5	3	7	0	9	1	24	1
Reedman					4.4	0	15	3

New South Wales Bowling

	Overs	Mdns	Runs	Wkts	Overs	Mdns	Runs	Wkts
Howell	25	6	60	2	23	5	53	1
McKibbin	24.1	6	51	7	23.3	5	74	8
Coningham	4	0	7	0	3	0	15	0
Turner	18	2	68	1	3	1	5	1
Garrett					1	0	5	0

VICTORIA v SOUTH AUSTRALIA

Played at Melbourne, January 1, 2, 4, 5, 1897

In many ways the most remarkable match of the Australian season. The ground was as favourable for one side as the other and after some very heavy scoring Victoria proved successful by 49 runs. Quite a sensation was caused in the first innings of Victoria by the batting of O'Halloran, who signalised his first appearance in an Inter-Colonial match by scoring 128. In conjunction with Roche, he quite altered the aspect of the game and it was largely on the strength of this performance that James Phillips decided to bring the two men over to England. Towards the end of the South Australian innings, it became a question as to whether the side would have to follow on and then occurred a scene which has several times happened in England, but had up to that time never occurred in Australia. Trumble bowled no-balls until the opposing side were within the specified number and though he placed his colony in a much better position his action was, of course, severely criticised. At their second attempt, Victoria began badly, six wickets going down for 63, but thanks to Trott and Trumble, the total reached 230. South Australia were left with 346 to win and though they failed in their endeavour, they made a superb up-hill fight and actually scored 296. Lyons and Darling put on 143 runs for the first wicket, but the brilliant example they set the side was not very well followed up.

Victoria

W. Bruce b Jones	0	– b Jones	8
C. McLeod b Jones	32	– b Jones	0
H. Graham b Jones	0	– run out	9
J. Worrall run out	4	– b Giffen	14
G. H. S. Trott b Jones	42	– b Jones	63
F. Laver c Bailey b Giffen	27	– lbw b Giffen	2
J. Harry c Giffen b Jones	14	– b Jones	8
H. Trumble b Giffen	1	– b Giffen	82
J. O'Halloran not out	128	– c Reedman b Jones	2
W. Roche c Giffen b Jones	29	– b Jones	14
A. E. Johns run out	57	– not out	13
B 17, l-b 5, n-b 1	23	B 15	15
	357		230

South Australia

J. Darling b Roche	25	– c Graham b Trott	65
J. J Lyons c Worrall b Trumble	70	– c Johns b Trumble	110
G. Giffen c Laver b O'Halloran	40	– b Roche	17
C. Hill b Roche	3	– b Roche	4
B. T. R. Bailey c Graham b Trumble	2	– c Johns b Roche	5
J. Reedman b Harry	22	– c Roche b Trott	20
A. E. H. Evans run out	39	– c and b Trumble	18
E. Jones b O'Halloran	5	– c and b McLeod	34
R. Homburg c Harry b Trumble	10	– b Trumble	4
J. Travers not out	10	– not out	2
A. H. Jarvis absent hurt	0	– c Roche b Trumble	0
B 4, l-b 1, n-b 8	13	B 17	17
	239		296

South Australia Bowling

	Overs	Mdns	Runs	Wkts	Overs	Mdns	Runs	Wkts
Jones	51	12	122	6	34	9	84	6
Evans	13	3	63	0	3	0	23	0
Reedman	14.4	4	42	0				
Giffen	22	5	71	2	31.5	3	108	3
Homburg	3	1	8	0				
Travers	6	0	24	0				
Lyons	2	0	5	0				

Victoria Bowling

	Overs	Mdns	Runs	Wkts	Overs	Mdns	Runs	Wkts
Roche	23	7	72	2	30	10	82	3
Trumble	27.4	6	67	3	34.3	13	83	4
Trott	11	23	3	0	15	1	55	2
Harry	6	0	22	1				
O'Halloran	15	7	21	2	9	4	29	0
McLeod					11	3	23	1
Laver					1	1	0	0
Bruce					2	1	7	0

NEW SOUTH WALES v TASMANIA

Played at Sydney, December 9, 10, 12, 1898

Matches against Tasmania do not rank with those in which New South Wales, Victoria and South Australia are opposed to one another, but this particular match was so remarkable in character that the score must be included in *Wisden*. Putting their full strength into the field, New South Wales gained an overwhelming victory by an innings and 487 runs. With a score of 292 not out, Victor Trumper foreshadowed his success in England. Windsor, is though to be one of the most promising slow-bowlers in the Colonies, but on this occasion his wickets cost him 101 runs each. K. E. Burn, who made the top score for Tasmania, will be remembered in connection with the Australian tour in England in 1890.

Tasmania

G. J. Eady c and b McKibbin	10	– c Howell b Noble	10
Gatehouse b McKibbin	1	– b McKibbin	5
Bingham c Duff b McKibbin	19	– b Howell	4
K. E. Burn st Kelly b McKibbin	5	– st Kelly b McKibbin	77
Windsor c Gregory b Noble	43	– c McKenzie b McKibbin	34
Douglas c and b Noble	3	– run out	39
Hammond b Noble	0	– c Duff b McKibbin	22
Butler c Gregory b Noble	0	– c Kelly b Howell	0
Tabart b McKibbin	5	– b McKibbin	0
McAllen not out	23	– b Allen	17
Richardson st Kelly b Noble	11	– not out	2
Extras	10	Extras	12
	130		222

New South Wales

A. C. McKenzie st Gatehouse b Bingham	56	R. A. Duff b Windsor	27
H. Donnan b Bingham	24	J. J. Kelly c McAllen b Eady	60
M. A. Noble b Richardson	38	W. P. Howell c Douglas b Bingham	2
S. E. Gregory c Gatehouse b Eady	43	T. R. McKibbin b Bingham	10
F. A. Iredale c and b Windsor	196	B 23	23
L. W. Pye b Eady	68		
V. Trumper not out	292		839

New South Wales Bowling

	Overs	Mdns	Runs	Wkts	Overs	Mdns	Runs	Wkts
McKibbin	27	8	64	5	41	10	93	5
Noble	12.4	5	25	5	32	15	63	1
Howell	10	4	19	0	35	16	42	3
Pye	4	1	12	0				
Trumper					5	1	12	0

Tasmania Bowling

	Overs	Mdns	Runs	Wkts
Eady	56	7	232	3
Windsor	45	6	202	2
Bingham	39	4	148	4
Richardson	16	0	109	1
Hammond	11	1	53	0
Butler	5	0	23	0
Burn	3	0	28	0
Tabart	3	0	21	0

NEW SOUTH WALES v SOUTH AUSTRALIA

Played at Sydney, January 6, 7, 9, 10, 11, 1899

After some sensational cricket this return match ended on the fifth day in a victory for New South Wales by three wickets. South Australia made a great fight after being more than 200 behind on the first innings, Clement Hill giving further evidence that he was the best bat of the season in the Colonies. New South Wales were in a very critical position during the last innings, but fortunately for them, a fall of rain was not followed by sunshine. Noble and Iredale clearly won the match forcing the hitting in splendid style while the wicket remained easy.

New South Wales

V. Trumper c A. Jarvis b Jones	0	– c Darling b Jones	15
H. Donnan b Jones	5	– b Giffen	1
M. A. Noble c A. Jarvis b Giffen	30	– c Hack b Giffen	101
F. A. Iredale b Jones	20	– c Darling b Reedman	77
S. E. Gregory c Darling b Jones	89	– c Darling b Jones	14
R. A. Duff c Giffen b Jarvis	42	– c Giffen b Reedman	2
J. J. Kelly c Hack b Jones	66	– not out	9
A. Newell c Reedman b Peters	48	– b Jones	19
L. W. Pye b Jones	51	– not out	8
T. R. McKibbin b Giffen	0		
W. Howell not out	18		
Extras	10	B 6, l-b 4	10
	379		256

South Australia

Batsman	1st innings		2nd innings	
J. Darling c McKibbin b Howell	10	–	b Pye	34
F. T. Hack c and b Noble	14	–	b McKibbin	35
C. Hill c Kelly b Howell	12	–	c McKibbin b Pye	159
G. Giffen b McKibbin	8	–	b Pye	68
J. J. Lyons b McKibbin	41	–	b Pye	2
F. Jarvis st Kelly b McKibbin	4	–	b McKibbin	15
J. C. Reedman c Noble b McKibbin	30	–	not out	68
A. Green b McKibbin	0	–	b McKibbin	16
E. Peters not out	17	–	c Kelly b McKibbin	4
E. Jones c Kelly b Newell	24	–	c Trumper b Noble	33
A. H. Jarvis c Kelly b Newell	0	–	b McKibbin	13
B 2, l-b 1, w 1	4		Extras	22
	164			469

South Australia Bowling

	Overs	Mdns	Runs	Wkts	Overs	Mdns	Runs	Wkts
Jones	36.5	4	154	6	30.3	13	69	3
Giffen	33	4	133	2	15	0	79	2
F. Jarvis	12	3	52	1	10	2	40	0
Lyons	3	0	10	0				
Peters	6	1	20	1	2	0	17	0
Reedman					9	0	41	2

New South Wales Bowling

	Overs	Mdns	Runs	Wkts	Overs	Mdns	Runs	Wkts
Howell	11	2	28	2	20	5	66	0
Noble	15	2	51	1	39	11	79	1
McKibbin	17	3	54	5	44.4	10	168	5
Pye	10	4	25	0	38	15	87	4
Newell	2.5	0	2	2	14	5	40	0
Trumper					2	1	6	0
Donnan					1	0	1	0

THE TEAM FOR ENGLAND v THE REST OF AUSTRALIA

Prior to their departure for England, Darling's now famous side played three matches against the Rest of Australia and won them all. At the time the first match was played only nine of the eleven had been definitely picked, but the inclusion of Iredale and Howell in the team pointed clearly to their selection. Subsequently Johns was chosen as second wicket-keeper; a little later Laver earned his place, and finally it was decided to have fourteen men and take Trumper to England.

THE TEAM FOR ENGLAND v REST OF AUSTRALIA

Played at Adelaide, March 17, 18, 20, 21, 1899

After four days of heavy run getting the team for England gained a brilliant victory by seven wickets, Darling and Clement Hill putting on 156 runs together for the second wicket when their side went in to win the game. There were four other partnerships during the match of over a hundred runs, Iredale and Hill scoring 120 runs together, Noble and Kelly 121, Reedman and Trumper 102, Laver and Giffen 149. In the course of the five days 1,553 runs were scored.

Rest of Australia

J. C. Reedman c Kelly b Trumble	51	– c and b Howell	108
J. F. Giller c Gregory b Noble	28	– c Gregory b Noble	43
V. Trumper c Kelly b Noble	6	– run out	46
F. Laver c Trumble b McLeod	30	– c Kelly b Howell	136
H. Donnan b Jones	28	– c Trumble b McLeod	22
H. Graham b Jones	3	– b Howell	21
G. Giffen b Howell	67	– b Howell	59
L. W. Pye b Jones	4	– b McLeod	28
A. Coningham b Howell	21	– b Jones	23
A. E. Johns c Kelly b Trumble	1	– not out	24
T. R. McKibbin not out	0	– b McLeod	1
Extras	9	Extras	16
	248		527

The Team for England

F. A. Iredale run out	85	– c Laver b McKibbin	14
J. Darling c Graham b Coningham	36	– c Pye b Laver	104
C. Hill c Pye b Coningham	76	– not out	101
S. E. Gregory c Jones b Laver	22	– c Johns b Reedman	10
J. Worrall c Trumper b McKibbin	32	– not out	16
C. E. McLeod c Johns b Giffen	17		
M. A. Noble c Graham b Coningham	111		
J. J. Kelly not out	102		
H. Trumble c Graham b McKibbin	24		
E. Jones c Coningham c McKibbin	2		
W. P. Howell c Coningham b McKibbin	5		
Extras	15	Extras	6
	527		251

Team for England Bowling

	Overs	Mdns	Runs	Wkts	Overs	Mdns	Runs	Wkts
Jones	28	5	62	3	31	3	110	1
Noble	29	6	58	2	28	0	99	1
Howell	16.3	7	26	2	49	11	143	4
McLeod	24	7	52	1	40.2	10	94	3
Trumble	20	10	41	2	24	6	65	0

Rest of Australia Bowling

	Overs	Mdns	Runs	Wkts	Overs	Mdns	Runs	Wkts
McKibbin	22.1	0	68	4	14	1	66	1
Pye	23	4	93	0	3	0	11	0
Coningham	26	3	113	3	5	1	7	0
Giller	20	3	65	0	5	1	15	0
Giffen	22	2	83	1	9	0	37	0
Laver	18	2	61	1	13.5	3	63	1
Reedman	6	0	20	0	9	2	23	1
Trumper	2	0	9	0	3	0	23	0

ENGLAND IN SOUTH AFRICA

THE ENGLISH TEAM IN SOUTH AFRICA

It has been stated on the best authority that the cricket tour in South Africa during the winter of 1888-89 – arranged by Major Wharton, and carried out under his direction – did not pay its expenses, but in every other sense than the financial one it was eminently successful. The cricketers were enthusiastically welcomed, and, though some of their early engagements ended unexpectedly in defeat, they repaid the welcome by playing remarkably well. In all, they took part in nineteen matches, winning thirteen, losing four, and leaving two unfinished. All the beatings were sustained in the early part of the trip, and it is no libel to say that for a time generous hospitality had a bad effect upon the cricket. The fact has indeed been acknowledged in print by a member of the team. However, as soon as the men settled down to the serious business of their tour they did even better than might have been expected from the composition of the side, and went on from victory to victory. It was never intended, or considered necessary, to take out a representative English team for a first trip to the Cape, and certain laments which were indulged in at home when the news of the early defeats came to hand were found to be quite uncalled for. The heroes of the trip were undoubtedly Abel and Briggs, the former with the bat and Briggs with the ball literally doing marvels. Three times Abel exceeded the hundred, and his play all through was some of the best ever shown for a travelling side. Mr J. H. Roberts, who went out with the team, was recalled to England by a domestic bereavement, and George Ulyett journeyed to the Cape to take his place. Mr C. A. Smith, the captain of the side, and Mr M. P. Bowden remained behind in South Africa when the tour ended.

ENGLISH TEAM v ELEVEN OF SOUTH AFRICA

Played at Cape Town, March 25, 26, 1889

The last match of the tour and a complete triumph for the Englishmen, who out-played their opponents at every point, and won in an innings with 202 runs to spare. It was the second eleven-a-side fixture, and was more decisively won than any other match during the trip. The South African team, with the exception of Mr Tancred could do absolutely nothing against Briggs, batsmen who had scored well in earlier matches failing dismally. The Lancashire bowler met with wonderful success, taking in all fifteen wickets for 28 runs – a worthy finish up to his brilliant exertions during the trip. Abel too, wound up in splendid form, making his third hundred during the tour. He went in first and was out seventh, scoring 120 out of 287.

English Team

R. Abel b Ashley	120
G. Ulyett b Ashley	22
J. Briggs b Vintcent	6
M. Read c Hutchinson b Ashley	12
F. Hearne b Vintcent	20
H. Wood c Innes b Vintcent	59
Mr M. P. Bowden c Hutchinson b Ashley	25
Mr B. A. F. Grieve c Tancred b Ashley	14
Mr E. J. McMaster c Innes b Ashley	0
Hon. C. J. Coventry not out	1
A. J. Fothergill b Ashley	1
Extras	12
	292

Eleven of South Africa

A. B. Tancred not out	26 – b Briggs	3
A. R. Innes lbw b Fothergill	1 – run out	0
A. E. Ochse run out	1 – b Briggs	3
P. Hutchinson b Briggs	3 – b Briggs	0
O. R. Dunell b Briggs	0 – b Fothergill	5
W. H. Milton b Briggs	7 – b Briggs	4
W. H. Richards c Abel b Fothergill	0 – b Briggs	4
C. H. Vintcent b Briggs	4 – b Briggs	9
F. Smith b Briggs	0 – b Briggs	11
N. Thennissen lbw b Briggs	0 – not out	2
W. H. Ashley b Briggs	1 – b Briggs	0
Extras	4 Extras	2
	47	43

South African Bowling

	Overs	Mdns	Runs	Wkts
Thennissen	20	5	51	0
Innes	12	3	30	0
Ashley	43.1	18	95	7
Vintcent	42	8	88	3
Milton	6	2	16	0

English Bowling

	Overs	Mdns	Runs	Wkts	Overs	Mdns	Runs	Wkts
Fothergill	24	12	26	2	14	4	30	1
Briggs	19.1	11	17	7	14.2	5	11	8
Ulyett	4	4	0	0				

ENGLISH TEAM v EIGHTEEN OF PORT ELIZABETH

Played at Port Elizabeth, February 8, 10, 1896

Thanks to Lohmann's remarkable bowling, the English team, who played twelve men, won by eight wickets.

English Team

Mr C. B. Fry b Bayne	5 – b Mangold	15
Mr A. J. L. Hill c Britton b Mangold	27 – not out	4
T. Hayward c Myburgh b Paterson	44 – not out	1
Lord Hawke b Mangold	0	
Mr H. R. Bromley-Davenport b Mangold	0	
Mr S. M. J. Woods c and b Mangold	2 – c Britton b Gubb	14
G. A. Lohmann run out	0	
Mr C. W. Wright run out	1 – c Bridger b Gubb	5
Sir T. C. O'Brien c Dunell b Gubb	34	
Mr A. M. Miller b Gubb	30	
Mr C. Heseltine b Gubb	0	
E. J. Tyler not out	4	
B 15	15 B 3	3
	162	42

Eighteen of Port Elizabeth scored 93 and 108.

English Bowling

	Overs	Mdns	Runs	Wkts	Overs	Mdns	Runs	Wkts
Woods	6	3	20	0				
Lohmann	19.3	5	38	15	20	3	44	11
Bromley-Davenport	14	3	27	2	8	3	9	3
Fry					12	5	30	3

ENGLISH TEAM v SOUTH AFRICA

Played at Port Elizabeth, February 13, 14, 15, 1896

The South Africans, without A. B. Tancred, Innes, Richards and Rowe, were completely outplayed, the English team winning by 288 runs. The batsmen seemed quite helpless before the skilful bowling of Lohmann, whose analysis in the second innings was extraordinary.

English Team

Sir T. C. O'Brien c Gleeson b Willoughby	17	– b Sinclair	16
G. A. Lohmann c Routledge b Willoughby	0	– b Willoughby	0
T. Hayward c Sinclair b Middleton	30	– c Halliwell b Willoughby	6
Mr C. B. Fry b Middleton	43	– c Halliwell b Middleton	15
Mr A. J. L. Hill run out	25	– b Middleton	37
Mr S. M. J. Woods c Halliwell b Hime	7	– c Poore b Sinclair	53
Mr H. R. Bromley-Davenport c Fichardt b Middleton.	26	– c Poore b Middleton	7
Lord Hawke b Middleton	0	– c Gleeson b Poore	30
Mr C. W. Wright b Sinclair	19	– b Sinclair	33
Mr A. M. Miller not out	4	– not out	20
H. Butt c Halliwell b Middleton	1	– b Middleton	0
B 13	13	B 9	9
	185		226

South Africa

Mr T. Routledge b Davenport	22	– b Lohmann	2
F. Hearne c O'Brien b Davenport	23	– b Lohmann	5
Lieut. R. M. Poore b Lohmann	11	– c O'Brien b Lohmann	10
Mr J. H. Sinclair b Lohmann	4	– b Lohmann	0
Mr C. Hime lbw b Lohmann	0	– b Hayward	8
Mr E. A. Halliwell b Lohmann	13	– c Hayward b Lohmann	3
C. Fichardt lbw b Lohmann	4	– lbw b Davenport	1
Mr R. H. Gleeson c Lohmann b Hayward	3	– not out	1
Mr F. J. Cook b Lohmann	7	– b Lohmann	0
J. Middleton not out	4	– b Lohmann	0
Mr J. Willoughby b Lohmann	0	– c Hayward b Lohmann	0
B 2	2		
	93		30

South African Bowling

	Overs	Mdns	Runs	Wkts	Overs	Mdns	Runs	Wkts
Sinclair	16	5	34	1	20	2	68	3
Willoughby	22	6	54	2	19	4	68	2
Middleton	25.4	6	64	5	36	12	66	4
Hime	7	3	20	1	4	1	11	0
Poore					1.4	0	4	1

English Bowling

	Overs	Mdns	Runs	Wkts	Overs	Mdns	Runs	Wkts
Lohmann	15.4	6	38	7	9.4	5	7	8
Bromley-Davenport	12	2	46	2	3.1	1	23	1
Hayward	3	1	7	1	2	2	0	1

ENGLISH TEAM v ELEVEN OF THE TRANSVAAL

Played at Johannesburg, February 4, 6, 7, 1899

In this match the Englishmen were in great batting form, their 537 with only six wickets down being far and away the biggest score during the tour. Tyldesley at last showed South African cricketers the full extent of his powers, he and Frank Mitchell playing splendidly together. Trott did fine work with bat and ball, and the Englishmen won by an innings and 203 runs.

Transvaal XI

V. Tancred b Trott	27	– b Milligan	8
Sinclair b Haigh	13	– c Mitchell b Milligan	19
Townsend b Haigh	15	– c Board b Cuttell	7
Shepstone c and b Trott	25	– c and b Cuttell	38
Solomon c and b Trott	52	– b Trott	6
A. B. Tancred run out	1	– c and b Trott	13
Dickenson c Milligan b Trott	34	– b Trott	4
Beves b Trott	0	– b Cuttell	12
Hathorn c sub. b Trott	13	– c Trott b Cuttell	0
Johnson not out	5	– b Trott	0
Parkin c Milligan b Trott	14	– not out	11
Extras	12	Extras	5
	211		123

English Team

Mr P. F. Warner c Parkin b A. B. Tancred	0
Mr F. Mitchell c Hawthorn b Parkin	162
J. T. Tyldesley c Parkin b Beves	114
Mr C. E. M. Wilson c Beves b Johnson	29
W. R. Cuttell c Dickinson b Sinclair	43
A. E. Trott not out	101
Mr F. W. Milligan b Sinclair	8
Lord Hawke not out	31
Extras	49
(6 wkts dec.)	537

S. Haigh, J. H. Board and Mr Bromley-Davenport did not bat.

English Team Bowling

	Overs	Mdns	Runs	Wkts	Overs	Mdns	Runs	Wkts
Haigh	22	11	46	2				
Milligan	17	8	44	0	19	7	34	2
Trott	38.3	15	74	7	30	9	66	4
Cuttell	11	3	24	0	10.3	5	18	4
Bromley-Davenport	4	1	11	0				

Transvaal XI Bowling

	Overs	Mdns	Runs	Wkts
A. B. Tancred	8	2	22	1
Sinclair	58	6	186	2
Shepstone	15	4	50	0
Parkin	31	4	108	1
Johnson	19	3	47	1
Hathorn	3	0	12	0
Dickinson	5	0	16	0
Beves	16	3	47	1

ENGLISH TEAM v SOUTH AFRICA

Played at Newlands, Cape Town, April 1, 3, 4, 1899

The tour ended with the return against South Africa and a truly sensational game it proved, Lord Hawke's team winning by 210 runs after having been 85 behind on the first innings. South Africa put a very good team into the field but the side suffered severely through the absence of Llewellyn. On winning the toss the Englishmen naturally expected to make a good score but they collapsed in a deplorable way and after having had 60 on the board for one wicket were all out soon after the luncheon interval for 92. South Africa began by losing five wickets for 61 runs, but Kuys stayed some time with Sinclair and at the drawing of stumps the score was up to 126 for seven wickets. On the following day Sinclair batted in wonderful form scoring 39 out of the first 40 that were added. Standing quite 6 ft. 4 in. he combines driving power with very strong back play. His splendid innings was closed at last by a brilliant catch on the ropes. Going in for a second time against a balance of 85 the Englishmen were for once taxed to the utmost. They did very well and at the call of time had scored 222 for five wickets, Tyldesley being not out 87. On the following day the Lancashire batsman was caught at mid-on for a faultless innings. Only in this match and in the one against the Eleven of the Transvaal was he seen at his best during the tour. When South Africa went in to get 246 it was fully expected that Lord Hawke's eleven would win, but no one was prepared for the collapse that followed. Haigh and Trott bowled in marvellous form and were backed up by fielding that could scarcely have been smarter. Sinclair was out to an extraordinary catch at long-on, Milligan just securing the ball leaning back on the ropes. With the victory in this match the tour of the Englishmen came to an end.

English Team

Mr F. Mitchell c Rowe b Middleton	18	– lbw b Rowe	41
Mr P. F. Warner c Halliwell b Sinclair	31	– b Rowe	23
J. T. Tyldesley b Sinclair	13	– c Shalders b Kuys	112
Mr C. E. M. Wilson not out	10	– b Powell	6
W. R. Cuttell b Sinclair	7	– b Kuys	18
A. E. Trott c Powell b Sinclair	1	– b Rowe	16
S. Haigh c Halliwell b Middleton	0	– c Francis b Sinclair	25
Mr F. W. Milligan b Sinclair	1	– b Sinclair	38
J. H. Board b Sinclair	0	– b Graham	6
Mr A. G. Archer c Powell b Middleton	7	– not out	24
Lord Hawke b Middleton	1	– c and b Sinclair	3
L-b 3	3	B 6, l-b 10, w 1, n-b 1	18
	92		330

South Africa

W. Shalders b Haigh	9 – lbw b Haigh	8
H. H. Francis b Trott	1 – c Haigh b Trott	2
M. Bissett b Haigh	15 – b Trott	1
J. H. Sinclair c Tyldesley b Trott	106 – c Milligan b Haigh	4
B. Powell c Haigh b Trott	5 – b Haigh	11
A. E. Halliwell st Board b Haigh	0 – b Haigh	1
F. Kuys b Cuttell	26 – b Trott	0
C. F. Prince run out	5 – b Haigh	1
R. Graham b Trott	0 – b Trott	2
J. Middleton run out	3 – not out	0
G. Rowe not out	1 – c Mitchell b Haigh	0
B 4, w 1, n-b 1	6 Extras	5
	177	35

South Africa Bowling

	Overs	Mdns	Runs	Wkts	Overs	Mdns	Runs	Wkts
Graham	5	0	26	0	16	4	41	1
Rowe	12	4	19	0	41	8	93	3
Middleton	19	9	18	4	28	7	74	0
Sinclair	12	4	26	6	31.2	8	63	3
Kuys					12	4	31	2
Powell					4	1	10	1

English Team Bowling

	Overs	Mdns	Runs	Wkts	Overs	Mdns	Runs	Wkts
Trott	20.2	5	69	4	1	5	19	4
Haigh	27	4	88	3	11.4	6	11	6
Cuttell	8	3	14	1				
Milligan	2	2	0	0				

BATTING AVERAGES

	Innings	Not outs	Runs	Highest innings	Average
Mr P. F. Warner	27	6	766	132*	36.47
Mr F. Mitchell	26	1	857	162	34.28
J. T. Tyldesley	26	3	742	114	32.26
S. Haigh	21	4	414	74	24.35
W. R. Cuttell	22	0	490	98	22.27
Mr C. E. M. Wilson	18	1	367	69	21.58
A. E. Trott	23	1	472	101*	21.45
Mr F. W. Milligan	23	0	322	46	14.00
J. H. Board	20	5	198	36	13.20
Mr A. G. Archer	16	6	114	24*	11.40
Lord Hawke	24	6	189	31*	10.50
Mr H. R. Bromley-Davenport	18	0	131	32	7.27

Hon. E. Fiennes played in one match and scored 2 and 2.

* *Signifies not out.*

BOWLING AVERAGES

	Overs	Maidens	Runs	Wickets	Average
S. Haigh	489.1	213	876	107	8.18
A. E. Trott	803.1	290	1,626	168	9.67
W. R. Cuttell	338.3	152	521	51	10.21
Mr H. R. Bromley-Davenport	129.4	65	199	17	11.52
Mr F. W. Milligan ..	272.4	107	567	48	11.81
Mr C. E. M. Wilson .	89	38	171	11	15.59

Also bowled: J. T. Tyldesley 6–1–17–2; Mr P. F. Warner 16–6–33–2; Mr A. G. Archer 3–1–6–0; Lord Hawke 6.3–0–18–2; Mr F. Mitchell 15–7–31–1; J. H. Board 4–0–10–0.

THE GENTLEMEN v THE PLAYERS OF ENGLAND

JOHN LILLYWHITE'S MATCH

THE GENTLEMEN v THE PLAYERS OF ENGLAND

Played at Brighton, August 14, 15, 16, 1871

For twenty years had John Lillywhite played – and played well – for his County. For nearly as long a period had "John" been a front rank man as a cricket coach at Public Schools; as a prominent Player in the leading matches of his time; and as a popular pro, all over cricketing England. So when his lengthened career was over, his friends thought that career worthy of public recognition in the form of a "Farewell Benefit Match". The match John's friends selected for this event was the best match possible to select – "The Gentlemen v The Players of England"; equally judicious was the decision to play the match the week immediately following Canterbury, and just as appropriate was the resolve to play the match on the Sussex County Ground, the scene of so many of John's successes. Fortune favoured Lillywhite all round – everything turned up trumps for him. The weather was bright and breezy all three days; the Elevens worthily represented the Amateur and Professional talent of England; and although hundreds were disappointed by that fatal third ball bowled by Shaw, even that turned out "beneficial" to J. L., inasmuch as very many who intended to have been present on the first day only, determined – when the crack cracked at the first ball bowled to him – to have another day in hopes of seeing the great batsman balance that 0 with a triple figure second innings. How largely those hopes were gratified, and what "rare cricket" cropped up during those three days' play under the burning hot sun, be it now our task to briefly tell, first putting on record that the admission charge to the ground was 1s., and that (including admission tickets) £118 10s. on the first day, £171 12s. on the second day, and £88 on the third day, was taken at the gates; and it may as well be recorded here, that on the first day of the match The Sussex County Club Committee presented Lillywhite with a Silver Cup, whereon was engraved the following inscription: – "Presented to John Lillywhite by the County Club in recognition of his great merits as a Cricketer, and of the valuable services which for twenty years he rendered to the County Eleven".

The First Day. – Under a bright hot sun the match was commenced at 12.25, Mr W. G. Grace and Mr Dale starting the batting, and J. C. Shaw and McIntyre the bowling. Shaw began to Mr Dale, who got the second ball away for a single, but the third – a break-back – clean bowled the off stump of Mr Grace's wicket, and, to the manifest astonishment of all present (and subsequent comers that day) the great batsman was out for 0, and the Gentlemen's first wicket down at one run. But this was not all the good fortune that favoured the Players that day, for "Shaw was in form", and quickly had five wickets, as, with the score at 24, Mr Dale "played on"; at 35 the off stump of Mr Green's wicket was bowled; at 62 the leg stump of Mr F. Grace's wicket was upset; and at 64 the middle stump of Mr Lubbock's wicket was put out of shape; all the five wickets then down having been bowled by J. C. Shaw. Then a stand was made by Mr Mitchell and Mr I. D. Walker, whose top-class cricket increased the score from 64 to 129, when Mr Mitchell was run out for 50, a very finely hit innings that included six 4s. Mr Thornton made 14 runs in seventeen minutes; he commenced by sending the ball spinning over a marquee for 4, and the following ball of that over he sent the same road (square-leg) out of the ground for 6; but when the score stood at 154 Mr Thornton, Mr Walker and Mr Turner were all three bowled; and at 4.30 the innings was over for 159 runs, J. C. Shaw having had seven wickets, all bowled. Mr I. D. Walker had "played" in his best form, and "stayed" whilst 90 runs had been made; his 37 included three especially fine drives for 4 each. At a quarter to five Jupp and Smith commenced the Players' innings to the bowling of Mr Appleby and Mr W. G. Grace; the wicket was kept – and well kept – by Mr Turner. With the score at 17 Smith was stumped and McIntyre run out; at 22 Jupp was "lbw" and Daft caught out at wicket; and at 49 Hayward was bowled. Then Carpenter and Charlwood made a stand, and by fine – at times "brilliant" – hitting increased the score by 83 runs, as when "time" was up that evening the Players' innings stood at 132 for five wickets –

Carpenter not out 44. Charlwood not out 46.

The Second Day was a glorious day all round. The sun was bright and hot, the breeze pleasant, the attendance the largest ever seen on the ground, the fielding of the Gentlemen superb, and the two hours and a half hitting of the brothers Grace truly wonderful. At noon the not outs resumed their innings, but so splendid was the fielding that the first thirty balls were bowled for two singles; then Charlwood was bowled for 47 (score 134 for six wickets), thereupon Carpenter had Lillywhite for a mate, but the fielding was so finely effective that it took that generally fast scorer Lillywhite twenty minutes to make 12 runs, when Mr Grace had him, the score at 157 for seven wickets; at 193 Southerton was bowled, Carpenter "lbw", and Phillips stumped; and in this way was the Players' innings summarily ended at 1.30 for the 193 runs scored when the seventh wicket fell. Carpenter's 73 was not only the highest professional score in the match, but it was a thorough skilled display of defence and hit; he commenced at about 5.30 on the Monday, the score at 22 for three wickets; he concluded at 1.30 on the Tuesday, the score at 193 for nine wickets. His 73 included eleven 4s, very fine hits all round; he made two 4s and a single from one over of Mr Strachan's, and three 4s from the first over bowled by Mr G. F. Grace.

The Gentlemen's second innings was commenced at five minutes to three by Mr W. G. Grace and Mr Dale. Mr Grace had rapidly made 21 when he skied one from J. C. Shaw to mid-off where Daft missed the catch, but at 35 J. C. Shaw bowled Mr Dale. Then, at twenty-five minutes past three, Mr G. F. Grace went to the wickets and commenced that memorably brilliant hitting display that was not ended until "the brothers" had – against the Players of England bowling – in two hours and a half put on the extraordinary large number of 240 runs for a wicket. In one hour and five minutes they had hit the score from 35 to 149; at five minutes past five the 200 was up (only one wicket down), and when, at five minutes to six, Hayward bowled Mr G. F. Grace for 98, the score stood at 275 for two wickets. Mr Grace's 98 was a remarkable display of brilliant driving, and included so many as seventeen 4s. A hearty, ringing, deserved cheer greeted the young gentleman's return to the pavilion, and for years to come many a cricketer then present will tell how magnificently young Mr Grace helped his brother to increase by 240 runs the Gentlemen of England's score at Brighton in 1871. Soon after Mr F. Grace left, Hayward bowled Mr Walker (289 for three wickets), but on Mr Mitchell going to the wickets so successful a stand did this gentleman and Mr W. Grace make, that when the day's cricket ceased the Gentlemen's second innings stood at the following phase:

Mr W. Grace not out	200
Mr Dale b Shaw	8
Mr F. Grace b Hayward	98
Mr Walker b Hayward	3
Mr Mitchell not out	37
Extras	7
Only three wickets down	353

The Third Day was another bright hot day, and was productive of some extraordinary hitting by Mr Thornton, and skillful batting by Carpenter and Hayward. On resuming play, Mr Mitchell was out before a run was made that morning; his 37 was a display of very fine leg-hitting. Mr W. Grace and Mr Lubbock then increased the score by 23 runs, when Shaw was shunted for Southerton, in whose first over Mr W. Grace was caught out (at short-leg) by the wicket-keeper, and the great innings was at last ended for 217 runs. Mr W. Grace was first man in at five minutes to three on the Tuesday; when he had made 21 runs he was missed (from J. C. Shaw's bowling) at mid-off by Daft, and when he had made 86 he was missed (from Lillywhite's bowling) at wicket by Phillips. He then hit away in grand form, sent a slow from Daft clear out of the ground for 6, made two 4s and a single from one over of McIntyre's, and when the stumps were drawn at a quarter to seven that day, he had made exactly 200 runs. The next morning he increased his score by 17 runs, and was then out by the wicket-keeper running to short-leg and there cleverly catching the ball. 378 runs were scored whilst Mr Grace was in; his 217 were made by forty-five singles, thirteen 2s, four 3s, thirty-two 4s, and the great on drive over the scorers' box for 6. From 378 Mr Lubbock and Mr Strachan hit the score to 431, when Mr Lubbock was out, and at 454 Mr Green was out. Then Mr Thornton went in, and by gigantic hitting made 34 runs in eight hits; he commenced with a 4 from McIntyre, from whose following over Mr Thornton hit two 4s and a 6, the sixer being a huge on drive clear out of the ground. After luncheon Mr Thornton hit four more 4s, one (a straight drive), the ball pitched on the far wall and bounded inside; had it fallen on t'other side another 6 would have been scored. As it was, 34 runs were made by Mr Thornton in eight hits from the fourteen balls that were bowled to him. The Gentlemen's innings ended at ten minutes past three for 496 runs, the wickets having gone down as under:

1/35 2/275 3/289 4/353 6/431 7/454 8/490 9/496 10/496

At twenty-five minutes to four the second innings of the Players was commenced by Jupp and Smith. With the score at 9 Jupp was bowled; at 32 McIntyre was bowled; at 40 Smith was caught out at mid-off; and at 67 Daft was bowled. Then Hayward and Carpenter, by their fine, finished, skilled batting, increased the score to 135, when Carpenter slipped and was run out for 35, an innings that included six 4s, three of the 4s very fine cuts. At 139 a clever right-hand "c and b" by Mr W. Grace settled Charlwood, and "time" for the last time in this memorable match was called with The Players having made 147 runs for six wickets, Hayward not out 45, played for with all that ease, elegance, and skill that characterised his batting in other days. So ended John Lillywhite's famous match, wherein thirty-six wickets went down, 995 runs were made, and 514 overs bowled, and whereat were assembled the largest gatherings ever seen on the old Brunswick Ground.

The Gentlemen

W. G. Grace Esq. b J. C. Shaw	0	– c Phillips b Southerton	217
J. W. Dale Esq. b J. C. Shaw	9	– b J. C. Shaw	8
C. E. Green Esq. b J. C. Shaw	18	– b McIntyre	11
G. F. Grace Esq. b J. C. Shaw	18	– b Hayward	98
R. A. H. Mitchell Esq. run out	50	– c Phillips b J. C. Shaw	37
A. Lubbock Esq. b J. C. Shaw	0	– c Daft b Lillywhite	41
I. D. Walker Esq. b McIntyre	37	– b Hayward	3
C. I. Thornton Esq. b J. C. Shaw	14	– c and b McIntyre	34
G. Strachan Esq. not out	1	– b McIntyre	34
M. Turner Esq. b J. C. Shaw	0	– run out	0
A. Appleby Esq. lbw b McIntyre	4	– not out	0
B 2, l-b 5, n-b 1	8	B 4, l-b 9	13
	159		496

The Players

H. Jupp lbw b W. G. Grace	6 – b Appleby	2
John Smith (Cambs.) st Turner b W. G. Grace	12 – c Dale b Appleby	27
Martin McIntyre run out	0 – b W. G. Grace	6
Richard Daft c Turner b Appleby	3 – b Appleby	19
R. Carpenter lbw b W. G. Grace	73 – run out	35
Thos. Hayward b W. G. Grace	17 – not out	45
H. Charlwood b Appleby	47 – c and b W. G. Grace	4
James Lillywhite c and b W. G. Grace	12 – not out	2
Southerton b Appleby	16	
Henry Phillips st Turner b Appleby	0	
J. C. Shaw not out	0	
B 6, l-b 1	7 B 2, l-b 5	7
	193	147

The Players' Bowling

	Overs	Mdns	Runs	Wkts	Overs	Mdns	Runs	Wkts
J. C. Shaw	43	20	72	7	50	17	128	2
M. McIntyre	37.2	11	65	2	40.2	10	120	3
Southerton	3	1	14	—	44	20	88	1
Hayward					32	8	79	2
Lillywhite					31	18	50	1
Daft					3	—	18	—

The Gentlemen's Bowling

	Overs	Mdns	Runs	Wkts	Overs	Mdns	Runs	Wkts
Mr Appleby	54	36	53	4	39	21	63	3
Mr W. G. Grace	46	18	72	5	35	16	52	2
Mr Strachan	12	3	38	—				
Mr G. F. Grace	8	4	20	—				
Mr G. F. Grace	8	4	20	—	13	9	7	—
Mr Thornton	4	1	3	—				
Mr Lubbock					10	7	9	—
Mr I. D. Walker					9	3	9	—

Umpires: Alfred Diver and Julius Cæsar.

Mr W. G. Grace's
first match on the Old Sussex Ground
for South Wales Club v Gentlemen
of Sussex,
July 14, 15, 16, 1864.
1st inns, 170 bowled*; 2nd inns, 56 not out
* (bowled off pad)

Mr W. G. Grace's
last match on the Old Sussex Ground
for Gentlemen v Players of
England,
August 14, 15, 16, 1871.
1st inns, 0 bowled*; 2nd inns, 217 caught
* (clean bowled)

THE GENTLEMEN v THE PLAYERS OF ENGLAND

Played at The Oval, June 3, 4, 1873

This was the second of the three Gentlemen v Players of England matches played on London grounds in 1873, and which, like its fellows at Lord's and Prince's, resulted in an emphatic defeat of the Professionals. Mr Tylecote kept wicket for The Gentlemen, and Phillips for The Players, and a look over the two match scores will tell how the sides otherwise differed from those who played in the match at Lord's.

The match at The Oval was favoured with pleasant weather on the first day, good wickets, a crowded pavilion, large and enthusiastic audiences, and one of Mr W. Grace's most successful displays, as 158 runs in the only innings he played, and seven wickets in the only innings he bowled, testify. At 12.22 Mr W. Grace and Mr Longman started the batting; they had made 44 runs from twenty-one overs when McIntyre was put on one side for Emmett, and the second ball Emmett bowled was played hard on to his wicket by Mr W. Grace, but the bails stuck to the stumps as if glued thereto, and, to the uproarious delight of all but the poor Players, "the best and luckiest batsman in England" went on with his hitting in such punishing form that from one over of Emmett's he made two 4s, from the following over of Emmett's he made a 5, and from the over following that of Emmett's he actually made a 6, a 2, and a 4, or 25 runs from three successive overs from one bowler; this big hitting elicited roars of cheering from the on-lookers, and the Players had no luck until the score was hit to 93, when a stump out by Pinder ended Mr Longman's one hour of careful and well-played cricket for an innings of 24 runs. Three good wickets – Mr Hornby's, Mr Yardley's, and Mr Fryer's – were then rapidly wound up, to the evident satisfaction of the Players; but Mr W. Grace and Mr Hadow put on 59 runs, and Mr W. Grace and his brother 39 more; then the crack's time was up, as, after being missed by Jupp at square leg from Alfred Shaw's bowling. Alfred (in his next over) bowled down the middle stump of the great batsman's wicket. Mr W. G. Grace was first man in at 12.22; when one hour had been hit away he had made 63 runs – or more than a run per minute; at two o'clock he had made 81 runs; at 2.30 the score stood at 159 for four wickets, Mr W. G. Grace not out 102; and when at 4.20 he was bowled by Alfred Shaw for 158, the score stood at 245 for six wickets. The hits in this truly great innings were nineteen singles, fifteen 2s, eleven 3s, fifteen 4s, two 5s, and one 6; the 6 was a splendid off-drive from Emmett; one 5 was a drive from Emmett, the other a leg hit from A. Shaw; and the 4s were hits all round – principally leg hits and drives. How fiercely and finely Mr Grace hit after his escape from playing the ball on is told by the eleven successive hits he subsequently made, being: 4-4-5-6-2-4-3-4-4-3 and 5. Mr Grace's successor at the wickets was Mr Tylecote, who stayed and scored so well that he was last man out, and made 49 runs, including three 4s (all drives), a fine drive for 5, and a drive for 6 (the ball being lost for a while.) The Gentlemen's innings concluded at eighteen minutes to six; their wickets fell as follows:

1/93 2/102 3/104 4/147 5/206 6/245 7/256 8/265 9/319 10/330

The Players' first innings calls for no comment beyond the fact of Mr Buchanan's slows having seven of their wickets – five bowled. Their second innings was started by Emmett and Jupp, who gave the spectators enjoyably fine samples of hit and defence, pace and patience, as the Yorkshireman made 33 runs whilst the Surrey man was scoring 6, and they had made the score 74, when a real good catch at mid-off by Mr Strachan settled Emmett for 49, made by three 5s (two of them splendid leg hits), three 4s, etc. Jupp was just ninety minutes scoring his 20 runs, when he was cleverly c and b by Mr W. Grace, who in that same over served Lockwood the same way. Charlwood was out at 114; and both McIntyre and Greenwood were settled at 121; then the two Nottinghamshire men – Alfred Shaw and Oscroft – stayed and played in something like "Players of England" form, and the score was hit by them to 199, when Oscroft was bowled by a slow. Pinder was settled at slip at 203; and when the two Shaw's had added ten more runs, J. C. was had at mid-off; and so at 6.45 on the second day, the Gentlemen had won by an innings and 11 runs, Alfred Shaw not out 36 – a good innings; but the best and biggest innings played by the Players was William Oscroft's 73; he went to the wickets at 4.25 with the score at 74 for two wickets; he left at 6.25, the score at 199 for eight wickets; his hits comprised a 5 to square leg from Mr Buchanan, and seven 4s (four drives, two cuts, and one leg hit – all fine hits.) Mr Buchanan's bowling had ten Players' wickets in the match; and it is a fact worth noting that in the two Gentlemen v Players of England matches played that week in London, Mr Buchanan's bowling had twenty of the Players' wickets – nine bowled.

The Gentlemen

W. G. Grace Esq. b Alfred Shaw 158	C. K. Francis Esq. b J. C. Shaw 0
G. H. Longman Esq. st Pinder b Alfred Shaw . 24	E. F. S. Tylecote Esq. c Humphrey b Emmett . 49
A. N. Hornby Esq. c Jupp b J. C. Shaw 6	G. Strachan Esq. c Humphrey b Emmett .. 21
W. Yardley Esq. b J. C. Shaw 2	D. Buchanan Esq. not out 3
F. E. R. Fryer Esq. c Charlwood b Alfred Shaw . 14	B 5, l-b 4, w 1 10
W. H. Hadow Esq. b Alfred Shaw 29	
G. F. Grace Esq. b Alfred Shaw 14	330

The Players

Ephraim Lockwood c W. Grace b Buchanan	0	– c and b W. Grace	0
H. Jupp c W. Grace b F. Grace	16	– c and b W. Grace	20
Richard Humphrey b F. Grace	4	– c Hadow b W. Grace	0
William Oscroft b Buchanan	6	– b Buchanan	73
Andrew Greenwood c Tylecote b Buchanan	2	– c F. Grace b W. Grace	0
H. Charlwood b Buchanan	24	– c F. Grace b W. Grace	16
Martin McIntyre b Buchanan	7	– st Tylecote b W. Grace	0
Emmett not out	18	– c Strachan b W. Grace	49
Pinder b F. Grace	0	– c Francis b Buchanan	1
Alfred Shaw b Buchanan	14	– not out	36
J. C. Shaw b Buchanan	0	– c F. Grace b Buchanan	5
B 13, l-b 1, w 1	15	B 9, l-b 4	13
	106		213

The Players' Bowling

	Overs	Mdns	Runs	Wkts
J. C. Shaw	53	17	116	3
A. Shaw	50	23	62	5
McIntyre	32	10	76	—
Emmett	17.3	5	66	2

The Gentlemen's Bowling

	Overs	Mdns	Runs	Wkts	Overs	Mdns	Runs	Wkts
Mr Buchanan	36.1	18	53	7	33.2	15	59	3
Mr F. Grace	34	20	38	3	20	10	25	—
Mr Francis	2	2	—	—	27	11	51	—
Mr W. Grace					34	10	65	7

Umpires: Southerton and Thos. Humphrey.

THE THREE GENTLEMEN v PLAYERS OF ENGLAND MATCHES OF 1877

The resolve of the Secretaries in 1875 that in future there should be nine consecutive cricketing days of Gentlemen v Players of England Matches on the London Grounds was duly carried out in 1877, when on the 28th, 29th, and 30th of June (Sunday then intervening), and the 2nd, 3rd, 4th, 5th, 6th, and 7th of July, Gentlemen v Players cricket was in full swing on The Oval, at Lords, and at Prince's.

The weather during these nine days was of extraordinary variety, and those present at the three grounds will not easily forget the glorious sunshine at The Oval, the vivid lightning flash, loud thunder clap, and furious rain-pour at Lord's or that remarkable hail-storm that burst over Prince's, and for twenty minutes gave that ground the appearance of being topped by hoar-frost.

As to the nine days' cricket the batting and fielding will long retain a bright spot in the memories of those who witnessed the play, and when beardless and hearty youngsters of the present day have grown grey and feeble, they will have many a tale to tell the cricketers of the future how, in one of the 1877 matches, Mr W. Grace was bowled out for a one hit (a 3) innings; how perfect was the cricket played by young Arthur Shrewsbury for his 78; how Mr I. D. Walker in one match went twice to the wickets, received but one ball in that match, and that ball bowled him; how unsurpassably splendid Mr J. M. Cotterill hit for his 59 and 92, and what a grand 7, all run out, he made at Lord's; how dashingly Mr A. N. Hornby hit, and how daringly he ran for his 144 (the largest innings hit in the three matches); – with what care, patience, skill, and success Mr W. W. Read played for his 72; how very finely Mr G. F. Grace hit for his 134, and his brother, Mr "W. G." did ditto for his 41; how Ulyett made 53 and 118 in one match; how Mr A. J. Webbe caught out six of them in one innings; how the Hon. A. Lyttelton, as stumper, captured five of them in another innings, and eight in that match; how the Hon. A. and Mr Hornby put on 130 runs whilst they were together; – how the Players were virtually without a wicket-keeper in two of the matches; how finely the Players started the scoring by Lockwood and Shrewsbury hitting 166 runs before a wicket fell, Lockwood making 92; and how very finely the Gentlemen finished off "the glorious match" by Mr G. F. Grace and Mr W. S. Patterson making the requisite 46 runs for the last wicket.

GENTLEMEN v PLAYERS OF ENGLAND

Played at Prince's, July 5, 6, 7, 1877

The 1s. admission charge and adverse weather led to comparatively slack attendances at this match, throughout which there were several indications that the London cricketing public did not take kindly to the nine successive days' doses of Gentlemen v Players matches in one season, especially with six of the nine at the cost of 1s. per day.

The weather during the match was something frightful. A dull, murky, mucky afternoon on the first day culminated at evening in "the storm of the season", when the lightning blazed, the air thundered, and the clouds poured out their waters in grand and awful form; and for one hour and a half London was drenched by the most furious rainstorm that fell over the big city in 1877. And who present at Prince's on the afternoon of the second day will readily forget that fierce outlet of lightning, thunder, rain, and hail that raged o'er the ground from 2.30 until 3, so thickly topping the turf with pea-sized hailstones as to give it the appearance of being coated with hoar-frost. The splendidly-prepared wickets suffered materially from all this; nevertheless, one man played a rare good innings of 72 runs, another hit grandly for 134, a third scored 53 and 118; one side hit an innings of 400 runs, the other one of 234; and when all was over, there had been 831 runs scored for the loss of thirty-one wickets, the Gentlemen having won the match with nine wickets in hand.

On Thursday, at 12.23, the match was commenced by the Gentlemen's batting being started by Mr Read and Mr W. Grace, to the bowling of Southerton and Mycroft, the wicket being kept by Pinder. Mr W. Grace had made a 3 only when Mycroft clean bowled him (middle stump), and the first wicket fell with the score at 10, the Players being greatly elated at settling the great bat so very early. Mr Cotterill was next man in, and by a 4, a 4, a 4, a 3, a 4, and a 4 he characteristically knocked off 23 runs in twenty-seven minutes, when Mycroft c and b him. Then, when the score was 48 for two wickets, and the time one o'clock, Mr F. Grace commenced one of the finest hitting innings he has ever played. He and Mr Read so successfully played the bowling of Southerton, Mycroft, Hill, Ulyett, and Lillywhite, that at luncheon call the score was 123 for two wickets – Mr Read, not out, 59, Mr F. Grace, not out, 28. Rain prevented them resuming play until three o'clock, and shortly after, more rain stayed play for a quarter of an hour; but on going at it again they hit the score to 157, when a clever left-hand catch at point by Hill finished Mr Read's score for 72 – a careful innings played without a chance, and including three 4s (leg-hit and drives) and eight 3s. This was Mr Read's first G. and P. Match; it is to be hoped it will not be his last, for the cricket he played was good enough for any match. Mr F. Grace and Mr Buckland then made it troublous times for the Players, who changed their bowlers frequently, but could not change the batsmen until the score had been rapidly and finely hit from 157 to 236; then Pinder snapped Mr Buckland, and from the following ball that "rare old stumper" settled Mr Gilbert with a surprisingly quick bit of stumping. Mr Buckland's 50 was made in seventy-four minutes. It included four 4s. Mr Monkland hit a couple of 4s, and was then lbw; but Mr E. F. S. Tylecote stayed so well with Mr F. Grace that when he was bowled for 30, the score was at 312. Mr Strachan was bowled first ball, and further on Mr F. Grace was clean bowled (middle stump) by Mycroft, who had then bowled the centre stump of both brothers' wickets. Mr F. Grace was batting whilst the score was increased from 48 to 359. His hitting was very fine – nearly as fine as his 98 in John Lillywhite's G. and P. match at Brighton in 1871, and higher praise than this cannot well be given to Mr F. G.'s 134, which was made by eighteen 4s (72 by fourers!), six 3s, eight 2s, and twenty-eight singles. This truly great innings was deservedly greeted with great applause. Mr H. G. Tylecote and Mr E. H. Butler were last men in; but although the tired Players tried hard, and played until five minutes past time, they could not obtain that last wicket, and the day's cricket closed with the score at 385 for nine wickets – Mr H. G. Tylecote, not out, 30, Mr Butler, not out, 18.

On Friday play was resumed at 12.10; in ten minutes the score was hit to 400, but from the following ball, a well judged catch at long field by Hill brought the innings to a close, the wickets having gone down as follows:

1/10 2/48 3/157 4/236 5/236 6/255 7/312 8/313 9/359 10/400

The Players batting was began at 12.42 by Jupp and Ulyett to the bowling of Mr W. Grace and Mr Gilbert. Thirty overs had been bowled, and 30 runs scored, when Mr Grace gave the ball to Mr Strachan, from whose third over Jupp was had at cover point, and just prior to luncheon Lockwood put one up that the wicket keeper easily caught and so the second wicket fell with the score at 67.

Then, at 2.30, commenced that remarkable storm of all sorts of unpleasant weather, barring snow. For full half-an-hour did the tempest rage, damaging the wickets so much that it was 4.15 ere they could possibly resume play, and even then they played on wickets utterly unfit for cricket. However, Ulyett and Eastwood hit the score to 114, when Mr Buckland bowled Ulyett (middle stump) for 53, the biggest and best played score in that innings. Mr Strachan's cover point fielding then came off so well that at 128 he had Eastwood, and at 146 he captured Charlwood, and when 15 more runs had been made, an amazingly fine one-hand high-up catch, at deep, square leg, by Mr F. Grace, caught out Hill – a good hit, floored by a grand catch that elicited a ringing round of cheers. Then, at 6.10, rain stayed play again, but in half-an-hour they went to work again in most ungenial weather, and by seven o'clock the Players were all out for 181.

On the Saturday the weather was showery, the public interest in the match dead, and the attendance small. The second innings of the Players was commenced at 12.15 by Ulyett and Jupp, but throughout that innings the attention of the (comparatively) few visitors on the ground was wholly centred in the plucky up hill hitting displayed by Ulyett, who, not only saved his side from a one innings defeat, but made 118 of the 225 runs that had been scored when he was ninth man out at five o'clock. Ulyett's 118 included a few chances and fourteen 4s, and although captious "critics" picked holes in his play it must be great batting that causes the page of cricket history to chronicle in one match –

Ulyett b Buckland, 53 – st E. F. S. Tylecote b Gilbert, 118.

If any one fancies this is not a great bit of batting to play against the bowling and fielding of the Gentlemen of England, let him take bat in hand and try to show the cricket world what is great. Mycroft then hit the score to 234 when he was caught out, and so ended the Players batting, their wickets in this, their last innings, in 1877, having fallen thus:

1/31 2/95 3/155 4/178 5/200 6/205 7/214 8/225 9/225 10/234

The Gentleman then scored their required 16 runs for the loss of one man, and at six o'clock they had won by nine wickets.

The Gentlemen

Batsman	1st innings		2nd innings	
W. W. Read Esq. c Hill b Eastwood	72			
W. G. Grace esq. (Captain) b W. Mycroft	3			
J. M. Cotterill Esq. c and b W. Mycroft	23			
G. F. Grace Esq. b W. Mycroft	134			
F. M. Buckland Esq. c Pinder b Emmett	50			
W. Gilbert Esq. st Pinder b Emmett	0	–	c and b W. Mycroft	0
F. G. Monkland Esq. lbw b Southerton	8			
E. F. S. Tylecote Esq. b Ulyett	30			
G. Strachan Esq. b Hill	0	–	not out	8
H. G. Tylecote Esq. not out	37			
E. H. Butler Esq. c Hill b Southerton	26	–	not out	8
B 11, l-b 5, w 1	17			
	400			16

The Players

Batsman	1st innings		2nd innings	
Geo. Ulyett b Buckland	53	–	st E. F. S. Tylecote b Gilbert	118
H. Jupp c W. Grace b Strachan	19	–	b Gilbert	19
Ephraim Lockwood st E. F. S. Tylecote b Strachan	12	–	c Butler b H. G. Tylecote	27
D. Eastwood c Strachan b Buckland	32	–	c Strachan b Buckland	29
H. Charlwood c Strachan b Buckland	21	–	c Buckland b Gilbert	10
Emmett b Buckland	24	–	b Gilbert	6
Allen Hill c F. Grace b W. Grace	2	–	lbw b Gilbert	0
James Lillywhite b W. Grace	0	–	st E. F. S. Tylecote b Gilbert	1
Geo. Pinder c E. F. S. Tylecote b W. Grace	6	–	c and b Buckland	9
W. Mycroft c Cotterill b Buckland	6	–	c H. G. Tylecote b Buckland	9
Southerton not out	0	–	not out	0
B 1, w 4, n-b 1	6		L-b 3, w 3	6
	181			234

The Players' Bowling

	Overs	Mdns	Runs	Wkts	Overs	Mdns	Runs	Wkts
Hill	50	24	78	1				
W. Mycroft	49	20	86	3	6	5	1	1
Southerton	38.3	14	62	2	5.1	—	15	—
Emmett	28	10	49	2				
Eastwood	19	9	33	1				
Ulyett	17	5	42	1				
Lillywhite	5	1	15	—				
Pinder	4	1	18	—				

The Gentlemens' Bowling

	Overs	Mdns	Runs	Wkts	Overs	Mdns	Runs	Wkts
Mr W. Grace	36	12	55	3	1	1	—	—
Mr Gilbert	30	12	38	—	41	12	93	6
Mr Strachan	26	10	30	2	12	3	23	—
Mr Buckland	19.2	6	34	5	32.1	11	52	3
Mr H. G. Tylecote	11	4	18	—	16	3	34	1
Mr Butler					12	6	26	—

Umpires: E. Willsher and E. Henty.

IMPORTANT

The following appeared in *Bell's Life in London* of November 2, 1878:

"QUALIFICATION TO PLAY IN THE MATCH – GENTLEMEN v PLAYERS AT LORD'S

The Committee of the MCC have passed the following resolution:

'That no gentleman ought to make a profit by his services in the Cricket Field, and that for the future, no Cricketer who takes more than his expenses in any match shall be qualified to play for the Gentlemen against the Players at Lord's; but that if any gentleman feels difficulty in joining in the match without pecuniary assistance, he shall not be debarred from playing as a Gentleman by having his actual expenses defrayed'. This rule has been strictly observed by the MCC since the management of the finances of the Club has been in its own hands".

THE GENTLEMEN v THE PLAYERS

Played at The Oval, June 28, 29, 30, 1883

Favoured by exceptionally fine weather during the play, though heavy rain on Friday night made the wicket rather difficult on the third day, this great contest produced some grand cricket and ended in a tie, the only one recorded in the series of matches between the amateurs and professionals of England. The Players had a very strong team both in batting and bowling and were exclusively northerners; whilst the amateurs, for the first time since 1867, lost the services of Dr W. G. Grace. A large and appreciative concourse of spectators watched the play on each of the three days.

Thursday. The Players, having won the toss, commenced their first innings with Barlow and Ulyett to the bowling of Messrs Studd and Rotherham, and the score had reached 92 before Ulyett was caught at the wicket for a hard-hit 63, marred by but one chance, and including seven 4s, three 3s, and seven 2s. At one time he scored 14 in one over from Mr Studd. Shrewsbury assisted to carry the total to 123, when he was bowled for 11, and two runs later Barlow was out for an admirably-played 47, which had taken him about two hours and a quarter to make, and which consisted of four 4s, three 3s, four 2s, and singles. The score advanced to 154, when Mr Rotherham commenced a series of successes by bowling Lockwood. Robinson was out at 171, and Barnes followed him at 173, having made 20. Flowers was c and b at 181; both Emmett and Peate fell at 199; and Sherwin, the last man, was bowled at 203, Mr Rotherham's six wickets having cost only 41 runs. The Gentlemen were first represented by Lord Harris and Mr Lucas, who were opposed by Peate and Barlow. At 42, Mr Lucas, who had played steadily for his 8 runs, was unfortunately run out, and ten runs later Lord Harris was bowled for a freely-hit innings of 38, and just before time Mr Studd was taken at the wicket for a capital 30, the score being 92 for three wickets, Mr C. W. Wright, not out, 11.

Friday. The weather was very hot during this day's play, which was started by Mr Wright (the not out) and Mr Hornby. The latter was run out at 130, having contributed a well hit 20. Mr Steel came in, but lost the partnership of Mr Wright at 135, who had played steadily for 21. Messrs Steel and Forbes were not parted until the total had reached 178, when the Lancashire gentleman was bowled by Barnes for 21, and 11 runs later Mr Forbes also fell a victim to this bowler, having compiled 28 in excellent form. Mr Kemp, having made 6, was out at 195, and Mr Leslie followed at 214. The last wicket gave considerable trouble, and it was not till the score had reached 235 – 32 in excess of the

Players' total – that Mr Frank was bowled. The Players started their second venture with Ulyett and Barlow, Messrs Studd and Rotherham being the bowlers. At 30 Ulyett was caught and bowled, and then Bates and Barlow took the score to 77 before the latter was caught. Shrewsbury and Lockwood did little, and four wickets were down for 89; but Bates and Barnes hit hard and well, and added 63 runs to the total before the former was bowled for a magnificently free and dashing innings of 76, made without a chance, by eleven 4s, two 3s, seven 2s, and twelve singles, his last 30 runs being scored in eight hits. The other five wickets fell for 29 runs, and the total score was only 181, thus leaving the Gentlemen an apparently easy task of getting 150 to win. It will be seen that Mr Steel's bowling was splendidly successful.

Saturday. Messrs Hornby and Lucas began the second innings of the Gentlemen, and were apposed by Peate and Flowers. Mr Hornby left at 18, smartly caught at mid-off. Mr C. T. Studd joined Mr Lucas, and the score was carried to 49 before the former was taken at long-off. During their partnership Mr Lucas, when he had scored 8, cut a ball to Lockwood at point, who held it and appealed for the catch. The umpires, however, were not in a position to give a decision and Mr Lucas resumed his innings. Lord Harris and Mr Wright were speedily dismissed, and four wickets were down for 50 runs. Then Mr Steel, by a freely-hit 31, brought the score to 92. Messrs Forbes, Leslie, and Kemp were all out by the time the telegraph showed 115. With 35 runs to win, Mr Franks joined Mr Lucas, and by careful play the score was taken to 136, when a bailer beat Mr Franks. Fourteen runs were required when Mr Rotherham, the last man, came in. Six were put on, and then the incomer was badly missed by Bates, at long-on, from a lofty drive. With the match at a tie, and the excitement at its highest point, Peate went on, and with his second ball clean bowled Mr Rotherham, leaving Mr Lucas to carry out his bat for 47, a grand display of defence and well-timed hitting, including four 4s, three 3s, and two 2s. Flowers bowled extremely well.

The Players

R. G. Barlow b Steel	47	– c Forbes b Steel	31
G. Ulyett c Kemp b Steel	63	– c and b Rotherham	10
A. Shrewsbury b Studd	11	– b Steel	0
E. Lockwood b Rotherham	18	– b Steel	8
W. Barnes c Steel b Rotherham	20	– st Kemp b Steel	28
W. Robinson c Forbes b Studd	8	– c and b Steel	6
W. Bates not out	19	– b Frank	76
W. Flowers c and b Rotherham	0	– c Lucas b Steel	7
T. Emmett b Rotherham	8	– b Steel	0
E. Peate b Rotherham	0	– c and b Frank	3
M. Sherwin b Rotherham	3	– not out	2
B 1, l-b 5	6	B 4, l-b 6	10
	203		181

The Gentlemen

Lord Harris b Bates	38	– b Barlow	0
A. P. Lucas Esq. run out	8	– not out	47
C. T. Studd Esq. c Sherwin b Emmett	30	– c Robinson Emmett	20
C. W. Wright, Esq. c Bates b Barlow	21	– b Emmett	1
A. N. Hornby Esq. run out	20	– c Shrewsbury b Flowers	11
A. G. Steel Esq. b Barnes	21	– lbw b Flowers	31
W. F. Forbes Esq. c Lockwood b Barnes	28	– c Shrewsbury b Flowers	4
M. C. Kemp Esq. b Barlow	6	– c Barlow b Flowers	2
C. F. H. Leslie Esq. lbw b Barnes	12	– c Shrewsbury b Flowers	5
J. Frank Esq. b Flowers	16	– b Flowers	6
H. Rotherham Esq. not out	13	– b Peate	11
B 19, l-b 2, w 1	22	B 7, l-b 4	11
	235		149

The Gentlemen's Bowling

	Overs	Mdns	Runs	Wkts	Overs	Mdns	Runs	Wkts
Mr Studd	42	16	67	2	18	7	38	—
Mr Rotherham	25.2	8	41	6	18	2	54	1
Mr Steel	40	23	56	2	26	10	43	7
Mr Frank	5	1	15	—	12	8	12	2
Mr Forbes	19	12	18	—	12	4	24	—

The Players' Bowling

	Overs	Mdns	Runs	Wkts	Overs	Mdns	Runs	Wkts
Peate	34	17	39	—	30.2	16	26	1
Barlow	34	13	37	2	23	11	26	1
Barnes	28	13	48	3	18	7	29	—
Bates	22	12	33	1				
Ulyett	14	7	21	—	4	2	7	—
Emmett	8	3	18	1	7	5	10	2
Flowers	11.2	5	17	1	44	24	40	6

Umpires: H. Jupp and J. Street.

RESULTS OF THE TWENTY-SIX GENTLEMEN v PLAYERS OF ENGLAND MATCHES "PLAYED AT THE OVAL"

Year	Winners	How won
1857	Players ...	Ten wickets.
1858	Players ...	Three wickets.
1859	Players ...	Innings and 25 runs.
1860	Players ...	Eight wickets.
1861	Players ...	Innings and 68 runs.
1862	Unfinished	Players had two wkts to fall, and 33 runs to win.
1863	Players ...	Nine wickets.
1864	Players ...	205 runs.
1865	Players ...	118 runs.
1866	Gentlemen	98 runs.
1867	Unfinished	Players 1st innings, 249. Gentlemen, 136 and (7 wickets down) 244.
1868	Gentlemen	Innings and 87 runs.
1869	Gentlemen	17 runs.
1870	Unfinished	Players six wickets to fall, wanting 455 runs to win.
1871	Gentlemen	Five wickets.
1872	Gentlemen	Nine wickets.
1873	Gentlemen	Innings and 11 runs.
1874	Gentlemen	48 runs.
1875	Unfinished	Gentlemen had three wkts to fall, wanting 109 runs to win.
1876	Unfinished	Gentlemen had six wickets to fall, wanting 65 runs to win.
1877	Unfinished	Gentlemen had an innings to play, and 98 runs to score to win.
1878	Gentlemen	55 runs.
1879	Gentlemen	Innings and 126 runs.
1880	Players ...	37 runs.
1881	Gentlemen	Two wickets.
1882	Players ...	87 runs.
1883	A tie.	

Summary: Twenty-seven matches played. The Gentlemen won ten. The Players won ten. Six were unfinished. One was a tie.

GENTLEMEN v PLAYERS

Played at Lord's, July 9, 10, 1888

Like so many great matches during 1888, the annual contest at Lord's between Gentlemen and Players had to be played on a wicket which gave the ball a distinct advantage over the bat. For all that, the game was a thoroughly good one, and the finish proved the most sensational that had been seen in this match on the St John's Wood ground since 1877. There was a curious contrast in the constitution of the two elevens; for, while the Players' team was made up of entirely familiar names, the amateur side only included four men – W. G. Grace, A. G. Steel, W. W. Read and J. Shuter – who had previously represented the Gentlemen at headquarters. Mr Bowden was chosen as wicket-keeper on the strength of the excellent form he had shown for the Gentlemen against the Australians in Derby week, and it was quite a proper compliment to play Messrs Newham, Dixon and Eccles after the brilliant performances they have accomplished of late years for their respective counties. Mr Woods, as the amateur bowler of the year, was of course bound to play and no better change bowler could have been found than Mr C. A. Smith. The first day was very dull, and, though rain fell from time to time, it was never sufficient to stop the cricket. Under the circumstances the attendance was very good, 5,891 people paying for admission at the turnstiles. With the ground in a condition to greatly favour the bowling, the first day's play presented no particularly attractive features, twenty-four wickets going down before seven o'clock for an aggregate of 226 runs. Ulyett, who captained the Players, won the toss and put the Gentlemen in, and though his side ultimately lost the game, we certainly think he did the right thing at the time. The Gentlemen's innings ended rather before a quarter-past three for 84, Peel and Barnes, who were not tried until more than 40 runs had been made, bowling with astonishing success. To show how difficult it was to get runs it is sufficient to say that W. G. Grace was at the wicket thirty-five minutes for 10. The one batsman who seemed able to combine defence with something like facility in run-getting was Newham, who scored 25 out of 36 while he was in, and only fell at last to a fine catch at the wicket. The Players went in at half-past three, and were all out by twenty minutes to six for 107, or 23 runs to the good. Abel, Gunn and Barnes were dismissed for a total of 21, but Ulyett and Maurice Read added 30 for the fourth wicket, Ulyett's 38 being not only the highest but the best innings of the day. Later on Peel played with great resolution, but could get very little assistance. Woods, who was bowling in fine form at this period of the season, took five wickets at a cost of 49 runs; but Smith, with three wickets for 23 runs, had a still better average. On going in for the second time the Gentlemen had rather more than an hour's batting in a very bad light. Grace made 21 out of 24, and then Lohmann shattered his wicket with a terrific break-back. When time was called the score was 35 for four wickets, Shuter being not out 5 – the result of more than an hour's defensive cricket.

On the second day there was a fairly large company, and those who were fortunate enough to be present are not likely to forget the remarkable cricket they witnessed. The Gentlemen's second innings was resumed at five minutes past eleven and ended at a quarter to one, the overnight score being increased to 100. Shuter played by far the best cricket, being at the wickets two hours for his runs. It will be noticed that Attewell and Lohmann took four wickets each, 35 runs being scored from the Surrey man and 20 from Attewell. It was not a little curious that in each innings Lohmann should have clean bowled the two Surrey batsmen. The Players had only 78 runs to get to win, and with the wicket rather firmer and faster than on the previous day there was a general impression that they would make them. Abel and Ulyett commenced the task, and A. G. Steel entrusted the Gentlemen's bowling to Smith and Woods. Abel made 10 runs in the first over, and then, with a very fine ball, Woods clean bowled Ulyett. Abel and Gunn stopped together, and, as the score rose fast, Steel went on himself at 28 in place of Smith. Then came a rapid downfall of the wickets, Gunn leaving at 32, Barnes at 35, Maurice Read at 41, and Briggs at 45. At this point the luncheon interval was taken, the Players with half their wickets down wanted 33 runs to win. After luncheon came the cricket which will cause the match to be remembered. Abel, who had made 27 not out before the interval, added 3 to his score before being clean bowled by Woods, the sixth wicket falling at 53. Attewell then joined Peel, and these two batsmen played so well together than the result became to all appearances a certainty. Seventy runs went on the telegraph board with six wickets down, or only 8 to win with four wickets to fall. As a last resource Steel handed the ball to Smith at 71, and this proved the turning-point of the game. With one added Smith clean bowled Attewell, and as it happened the Players did not get another run, the last three wickets all falling at 72, and the Gentlemen winning an extraordinary game by 5 runs. Peel was bowled by Woods, Lohmann, in trying to score on the on side from Smith, was out lbw, and on Sherwin, the last man, going in Woods dismissed Flowers with a yorker. During the last part of the game the spectators were worked up to a pitch of extreme excitement, and when the end had been reached they crowded in front of the pavilion, and shouted for the men who had had most to do with the victory. Woods and Smith were, of course, the heroes of the moment, and no compliments could have exceeded their deserts. Smith took two wickets for 13 runs, while Woods followed up his good performance of the previous day by taking five wickets for 27 runs; the Cambridge man having the fine record in his first Gentlemen and Players' match of ten wickets for 76 runs. Steel's bowling in this last innings also deserves recognition, and we must not dismiss the match without mentioning Sherwin's wicket-keeping, which was as good as he has ever shown.

Gentlemen

W. G. Grace st Sherwin b Briggs	10	– b Lohmann	21
J. Shuter b Lohmann	1	– b Lohmann	17
W. Newham c Sherwin b Barnes	25	– b Attewell	0
W. W. Read b Lohmann	6	– b Lohmann	4
A. G. Steel b Barnes	7	– c Sherwin b Attewell	1
J. A. Dixon c Abel b Barnes	9	– lbw b Lohmann	9
J. Eccles not out	4	– c and b Attewell	11
Lord George Scott c Sherwin b Peel	4	– b Barnes	8
S. M. J. Woods lbw b Peel	4	– c Lohmann b Barnes	13
M. P. Bowden st Sherwin b Peel	0	– c Lohmann b Attewell	7
C. A. Smith c Sherwin b Peel	9	– not out	4
B 1, l-b 4	5	B 3, l-b 2	5
	84		100

Players

Ulyett b Woods	38	– b Woods	0
Abel b Smith	6	– b Woods	30
Gunn b Smith	0	– c Steel b Woods	5
Barnes c Shuter b Woods	3	– lbw b Steel	1
M. Read b Steel	14	– c Woods b Steel	2
Briggs b Dixon	0	– c and b Steel	4
Peel b Woods	28	– b Woods	9
Attewell b Smith	5	– b Smith	12
Lohmann c Scott b Woods	0	– lbw b Smith	0
Flowers b Woods	5	– b Woods	0
Sherwin not out	3	– not out	0
B 4, l-b 1	5	B 8, l-b 1	9
	107		72

Players' Bowling

	Overs	Mdns	Runs	Wkts	Overs	Mdns	Runs	Wkts
Lohmann	23	10	30	2	46	30	35	4
Briggs	20	11	17	1	22	11	24	0
Peel	23.1	15	17	4				
Barnes	21	13	15	3	7.2	2	16	2
Attewell					31	22	20	4

Gentlemen's Bowling

	Overs	Mdns	Runs	Wkts	Overs	Mdns	Runs	Wkts
Mr Woods	29	11	49	5	26.2	12	27	5
Mr Smith	23	13	23	3	9	6	13	2
Mr Steel	6	1	13	1	18	7	23	3
Mr Dixon	6	2	4	1				
Mr Grace	5	1	13	0				

Umpires: John West and Wheeler.

GENTLEMEN v PLAYERS

Played at Hastings, September 16, 17, 18, 1889

The concluding match of the first-class season, and one that produced a most exciting finish, the interest of the spectators being maintained right up to the last hit. As in the game between North and South in the previous week, the weather kept charmingly fine, and the people of Hastings appeared on the ground in large numbers, fully appreciating the opportunity, so seldom afforded them, of witnessing first-class cricket. Never before had it been attempted to play a Gentlemen and Players' match so late in the season, but the experiment proved so successful that the Hastings committee might very well arrange another fixture of a similar character to conclude the Festival of 1890 if the Australians do not play, as we feel convinced the public take more interest in the meetings of amateurs and professionals than in the somewhat overdone matches between North and South, where the rivalry is not nearly so keen.

Although the teams could in a few instances have been improved upon, they were wonderfully good, and, much to the delight of the inhabitants, two local amateurs, Messrs E. J. McCormick and Herbert Pigg, were included in the Gentlemen's eleven. As will be presently shown, these two gentlemen had a large share in the remarkable victory. Again the wicket afforded the bowlers considerable assistance, and at times the ball got up very awkwardly. The Players had the good luck to win the toss, and this, under the circumstances, was thought to be a great advantage. Owing to a fine piece of fielding on the part of McCormick, Gunn was run out for 7, but there was some admirable batting by Albert Ward, Attewell and Lohmann, and the Players' total ultimately reached 179 – a very creditable score. Ward's 50, which was a fine display of sound and patient batting, occupied just two hours. The Gentlemen made a bad start, Messrs Grace and Radcliffe being each clean bowled by Lohmann, and the score at the end of the first day's play being 36 for the loss of two wickets.

The game, therefore, seemed decidedly in favour of the professionals, and on the Tuesday morning, despite some good batting by Key and Newham, the score was only 134 with seven wickets down when the bell rang for luncheon. On resuming after the interval, however, a great change was experienced. Pigg and McCormick played with pluck and determination, and, though the ninth wicket fell at 184, the total was hit up to 226, thanks mainly to some very fearless and invaluable hitting by Philipson, the Oxford captain. Pigg scored his 35 just at a time when runs were badly wanted, and fully deserved the enthusiastic cheers with which he was received. The Players were left in a minority of 47, and their chances appeared very small indeed when, in the second innings, Lee, Abel and Barnes were got rid of for 17 runs between them. Then it was that Gunn and Albert Ward came to the assistance of their side, and, both playing excellent cricket, remained together until the call of time, the total then standing at 62 for the loss of three good batsmen, or only 15 runs to the good, with seven wickets to fall.

The cricket on the last day was the most interesting of all. When 20 runs had been added Gunn was run out for an excellent innings of 40, and his dismissal was followed by a series of disasters, the score being only 98 when the seventh wicket fell. Lohmann made a plucky effort to put a better appearance on the game for his side, and, as he quickly hit up 17, the Players' total ultimately reached 119. Mr Pigg followed up his successful batting of the previous day by some capital bowling, and it will be seen that he took seven wickets at a cost of only 55 runs. The Gentlemen were left with 73 runs to get to win, but, as the ground had worn a good deal, the task was by no means an easy one against the powerful bowling possessed by the Players. For a time the batsmen appeared helpless against Attewell and Lohmann, both professionals keeping an accurate pitch, and frequently breaking back. Radcliffe was caught at the wicket without scoring, but the greatest blow of all to the Gentlemen was when W. G. Grace was out to a magnificent catch by Gunn in the long field. The hit looked like easily clearing the boundary, but Gunn just got to the ball in time, and, amidst loud cheering, brought off the catch with the left hand. In the fifty minutes' play before luncheon, five of the best wickets on the side went down for 25 runs. After the interval the interest of the spectators was maintained at the highest pitch of excitement, and the chances of the game varied in a remarkable manner. McCormick and W. W. Read played with great pluck at a critical point, but when the ninth wicket fell 8 runs were still required, and the Players seemed to hold the trump card. Fortunately for the Gentlemen, however, McCormick proved equal to the occasion. Lohmann bowled a long hop on the leg side, which the young Sussex amateur promptly despatched to the boundary, and this hit he followed up by sending Attewell to square leg for another 4, the match ending, amid a scene of wild excitement, in a victory for the Gentlemen by one wicket. After the close the spectators assembled in front of the pavilion, and cheered until they were hoarse. Mr Alderman Stubbs, the Mayor of Hastings, publicly presented Mr McCormick with a new bat, and said it was a great thing for the town that, among the many great players they had had in their midst, a local man had been able to carry off the honours. At the meeting of the promoters, held later in the year, it was announced that there was a profit on the Festival of £170 – a most satisfactory result.

Players

W. Gunn run out	7	– run out	40
R. Abel c Page b Stoddart	23	– c Grace b Pigg	5
F. Lee c Newham b Nepean	8	– c McCormick b Pigg	6
W. Barnes c Grace b Pigg	1	– c Grace b Stoddart	6
A. Ward c Stoddart b Pigg	50	– c Read b Pigg	28
R. Peel b Stoddart	19	– c Grace b Pigg	4
G. Ulyett c Newham b Stoddart	3	– b Stoddart	0
W. Attewell c Newham b Pigg	32	– c Philipson b Pigg	5
G. A. Lohmann c Key b Stoddart	23	– b Pigg	17
H. Richardson c Newham b Pigg	0	– b Pigg	0
M. Sherwin not out	0	– not out	4
B 8, l-b 5	13	B 3, n-b 1	4
	179		119

Gentlemen

Mr W. G. Grace b Lohmann	12	– c Gunn b Lohmann	6
Mr O. G. Radcliffe b Lohmann	12	– c Sherwin b Attewell	0
Mr K. J. Key c Lohmann b Richardson	41	– c Ulyett b Attewell	11
Mr A. E. Stoddart c Sherwin b Attewell	5	– c Lohmann b Attewell	0
Mr W. Newham b Richardson	24	– b Lohmann	4
Mr W. W. Read b Attewell	1	– c and b Attewell	12
Mr E. A. Nepean c Peel b Attewell	7	– c and b Attewell	6
Mr E. J. McCormick b Lohmann	20	– not out	25
Mr H. Pigg st Sherwin b Peel	35	– run out	0
Mr H. V. Page b Lohmann	8	– not out	2
Mr H. Philipson not out	25	– c and b Attewell	2
B 31, l-b 5	36	B 7	7
	226		75

Gentlemen's Bowling

	Overs	Mdns	Runs	Wkts	Overs	Mdns	Runs	Wkts
Mr Nepean	21	5	38	1	2	0	2	0
Mr Pigg	33	10	57	4	25.4	7	55	7
Mr Stoddart	18.2	4	51	4	23	3	58	2
Mr Radcliffe	11	6	20	0				
Mr Grace	1	1	0	0				

Players' Bowling

	Overs	Mdns	Runs	Wkts	Overs	Mdns	Runs	Wkts
Attewell	46	28	75	3	29	18	24	6
Lohmann	34	17	52	4	26	9	42	2
Richardson	35	18	39	2				
Peel	9	1	24	1	2	0	2	0

Umpires: R. Thoms and R. Carpenter.

THE LORD'S MATCH

Played at Lord's, July 9, 10, 1894

The MCC in selecting their Gentlemen's Eleven had none of the difficulties that beset the authorities at The Oval, and except that L. C. H. Palairet was on his honeymoon and Ernest Smith could not get away from his duties at Elstree School, they had an absolutely free choice. Naturally, they put into the field a far stronger side than the one beaten at the Surrey ground, the presence of Stoddart, Woods, MacGregor and Hewett making an immense difference. The constitution of the side, however, was nevertheless open to criticism. One of the many batsmen might well have given place to a bowler, and on the form he had been showing in the previous fortnight, W. W. Read had better claims to play than three or four of those who actually appeared. In choosing the professionals the MCC in our judgment made a sad blunder in leaving out Abel, but inasmuch as Mold and David Hunter had played at The Oval they were quite right to give a chance in the representative match to Martin and Storer. The game produced a most surprising result, the Gentlemen winning just before four o'clock on the second afternoon by an innings and 39 runs. It was a brilliant victory thoroughly well earned. Rain on the Sunday evening before the match was followed by a short but very heavy downpour on the Monday morning, and it was not until after one o'clock that the game could be started. Making the most of their opportunity the Gentlemen, on winning the toss, stayed in till a quarter past five, and ran up a total of 254. Having regard to the condition of the ground this was a far larger score than anyone expected when play commenced, but at one time it seemed likely that the Gentlemen would make over 300, 190 being on the board with only four men out. The policy of forcing the hitting while the surface of the ground was still wet proved highly successful, Grace and Stoddart scoring 56 in forty minutes for the first wicket. The 100 was up at the end of an hour and ten minutes, Grace and Jackson being then together. Both these batsmen played very finely, Grace's 56, an innings which lasted just over an hour and a half and included eight 4s, being a worthy companion to his 71 on the previous Thursday at The Oval. Not for a considerable time, indeed, had the great cricketer played a bolder game on a pitch affected by rain. Grace was out at 119, but Jackson stayed till the score reached 195, his share of the 125 runs put on during his stay of an hour and three-quarters being 63. His hitting, more especially on the on side, was brilliant, and so far as could be seen he gave no chance. Though the score was 195 for five wickets, there were eight wickets down for 216, and it looked as though the innings would soon be over. Woods, however, hit away with great vigour, and thanks to him the score was carried to 254 before the last man was got rid of. The Players went in soon after half-past five, and when, owing to the defective light – followed by rain – play ceased for the day, four of the best wickets had fallen to the bowling of Jackson and Woods.

On Tuesday the cricket was of a sensational and altogether unexpected character, Jackson and Woods bowling with such effect that, without a single change being necessary, the Players were got rid of for totals of 108 and 107. This feat of two men bowling unchanged through both innings of a Gentlemen and Players match had only been performed on three previous occasions. The first was in 1853 at Lord's, with Sir Frederick Bathurst and Mathew Kempson; the second was in 1864, also at Lord's, when Willsher and George Tarrant dismissed the Gentlemen for totals of 60 and 59; and the third at The Oval in 1879, when A. G. Steel and A. H. Evans gained the Gentlemen a decisive victory. The performance of Jackson and Woods was the more remarkable from the fact that on the evidence of several of the beaten side, the condition of the ground afforded no sufficient excuse for the failure of the batting. There was nothing in the least astonishing in Woods' analysis, his six wickets costing him in all 124 runs; but Jackson did wonders, taking five wickets for 36 runs in the first innings, and seven for 41 in the second. From lunch time to the end of the game he sent down fourteen overs, five of them maidens, for 24 runs and five wickets. It is safe to say that as a bowler the famous Cambridge and Yorkshire cricketer has never been seen to such advantage. The two bowlers were backed up by admirable fielding, Mordaunt and Stoddart being conspicuously good, and MacGregor at the wicket was in quite his finest form. Of the Players' batting, little that is favourable can be said, but Wainwright did well in both innings, and Gunn, in making his score of 22, maintained a stubborn defence against the bowling for just over an hour. The match proved a great attraction to the public – 7,199 people paying at the gates on the first day, and 6,096 on the second.

Gentlemen

Mr W. G. Grace c Storer b Lockwood	56
Mr A. E. Stoddart c Storer b Briggs	21
Mr H. T. Hewett c Ward b Briggs	12
Mr F. S. Jackson b Flowers	63
Mr G. J. Mordaunt b Brockwell	28
Mr A. C. MacLaren b Brockwell	21
Mr J. Douglas b Flowers	2
Mr J. R. Mason lbw b Briggs	7
Mr H. W. Bainbridge b Flowers	0
Mr S. M. J. Woods not out	27
Mr G. MacGregor c Lockwood b Briggs	5
B 10, l-b 2	12
	254

Players

A. Ward b Woods	2	– b Jackson	13
W. Chatterton c Mason b Jackson	0	– run out	0
W. Brockwell b Jackson	17	– b Woods	12
W. Gunn b Jackson	14	– b Jackson	22
J. Briggs c Hewett b Jackson	12	– c MacGregor b Jackson	13
W. Flowers c and b Woods	16	– c Mason b Jackson	2
W. Lockwood c and b Jackson	0	– b Jackson	3
E. Wainwright run out	34	– b Jackson	27
W. Storer b Woods	1	– c MacGregor b Jackson	0
J. T. Hearne c MacGregor b Woods	1	– b Woods	1
F. Martin not out	0	– not out	11
B 10, l-b 1	11	B 3	3
	108		107

Players' Bowling

	Overs	Mdns	Runs	Wkts
Hearne	12	3	30	0
Martin	12	2	28	0
Wainwright	10	3	28	0
Briggs	22.2	3	49	4
Lockwood	13	4	27	1
Brockwell	13	8	31	2
Flowers	13	2	49	2

Gentlemen's Bowling

	Overs	Mdns	Runs	Wkts	Overs	Mdns	Runs	Wkts
Woods	24.2	8	61	4	21.4	6	63	2
Jackson	24	8	36	5	21	7	41	7

Umpires: W. Hearn and V. A. Titchmarsh.

THE HASTINGS MATCH

Played at Hastings, September 13, 14, 15, 1897

The Hastings authorities had a very similar experience to that of the Scarborough committee in the previous week. They were able to put a capital professional team into the field, but in making up the amateur side had to contend with many disappointments. The Gentlemen made a creditable fight for two days, but on the Wednesday they were quite outplayed, the Professionals – after closing their second innings with only two wickets down – winning the game by 175 runs. In excuse for the Gentlemen, however, it should be said that they had to play the last innings in wretched light. Richardson took thirteen wickets in the match for 141 runs. With this performance he secured the extraordinary record of a thousand wickets in four successive first-class seasons in England.

Players

	First innings		Second innings	
R. Abel c Milligan b Brann	59	–	c Crawford b Stewart	60
A. Ward hit wicket b Grace jun.	25	–	b Milligan	108
J. T. Brown c Wickham b Brann	20	–	not out	50
W. Brockwell c Grace jun. b Mitchell	14			
W. Gunn c Brann b Grace sen.	60			
G. Davidson c Wickham b Milligan	13			
G. R. Baker c and b Milligan	1			
A. A. Lilley c Townsend b Milligan	1	–	not out	2
R. Peel not out	5			
W. Attewell c and b Milligan	3			
T. Richardson b Milligan	4			
B 6, w 2, n-b 1	9		B 9, l-b 9, w 1, n-b 3	22
	214		(2 wkts dec.)	242

Gentlemen

	First innings		Second innings	
Mr V. F. S. Crawford b Richardson	4	–	c Peel b Richardson	5
Mr C. L. Townsend st Lilley b Peel	19	–	b Richardson	4
Mr F. Mitchell c Attewell b Peel	84	–	c and b Attewell	8
Mr W. G. Grace b Richardson	46	–	b Richardson	0
Mr H. C. Stewart b Richardson	13	–	c Davidson b Richardson	22
Mr G. Brann b Richardson	11	–	b Richardson	2
Mr W. L. Murdoch st Lilley b Attewell	1	–	b Attewell	0
Mr C. W. Wright b Richardson	4	–	b Attewell	0
Mr F. W. Milligan lbw b Attewell	0	–	c Davidson b Richardson	16
Mr W. G. Grace jun. b Richardson	16	–	b Richardson	8
Rev. A. P. Wickham not out	8	–	not out	1
B 4, l-b 3, w 1	8		B 1	1
	214			67

Gentlemen's Bowling

	Overs	Mdns	Runs	Wkts	Overs	Mdns	Runs	Wkts
Milligan	29	13	62	5	31	14	76	1
Townsend	11	2	28	0	15	3	37	0
Crawford	6	3	14	0	11	4	21	0
Grace jun.	7	4	13	1	12	5	19	0
Brann	20	8	31	2				
Mitchell	11	2	34	1	10	4	19	0
Grace sen.	7	0	23	1	3	1	6	0
Stewart					5	1	10	1
Murdoch					5	3	7	0
Wright					6	0	25	0

Players' Bowling

	Overs	Mdns	Runs	Wkts	Overs	Mdns	Runs	Wkts
Richardson	44.3	16	98	6	16.4	5	43	7
Attewell	28	17	44	2	16	6	23	3
Davidson	16	6	16	0				
Brockwell	5	1	17	0				
Peel	15	3	31	2				

Umpires: R. Thoms and R. Carpenter.

PRINCE'S CRICKET CLUB

President – The Earl of Cadogan.

The Earl of Cadogan, the Earl of Clarendon, the Earl of Coventry, the Earl of Gosford, the Earl of March, Marquis of Queensberry, Lord Willoughby de Broke, Lord Delamere, Lord Downe, Lord Folkestone, Lord Geo. Hamilton, MP, Lord Metheun, Colonel F. Marshall, Colonel Taylor, MP, Captain W. S. Kenyon Slaney, W. Hart Dyke, Esq., MP, Arthur E. Guest, Esq., MP, and Alfred Lubbock, Esq.

Number of Members – 700. *Size of Ground* – 13 Acres.

Secretary – Geo. Prince. Ground Manager – Thos. Box (of Sussex).

Prince's Cricket Club was formed in 1870; the fact that in its first season Members comprised 700 of the nobility and gentry of England sufficiently indicate its eminent success and the probable important influence of the club on the amateur cricket of the future.

Prince's Cricket Ground is adjacent to, and in connection with, Prince's Racket Court, in Hans Place, Sloane Street. The ground is oblong in shape and 13 acres in extent. It was most carefully made in 1870, it is topped with the very best Down turf obtainable in the country, and "Prince's" has already earned the character of being a quick, and one of the truest playing grounds in England. The whole work of forming and laying out the ground was executed under the supervision of the Messrs Prince. It certainly is a beautiful ground, tastefully laid out regardless of expense, and in "sunny summers" will doubtless be the scene of many a gay, brilliant, and aristocratic gathering. The first match played thereon was:

THE HOUSEHOLD BRIGADE v LORD AND COMMONS (12 a side)

The opening day was Saturday, June 3rd – one of those bittingly cold days that were so prevalent in the early summer (?) of '71. The band of the Scots Fusiliers professionally attended, and despite the nipping wind that blew throughout the afternoon the attendance was a distinguished one, and sufficiently numerous to indicate the new Belgravian Ground would become a favourite fashionable resort during the London cricketing season. The match is noteworthy from the facts that two wickets were bowled in one over; that 14 runs were hit from another over; that Mr Rowley made a drive for 8 (no overthrow and all run out) from the first ball bowled in the second innings of the Brigade, and that when Lord Geo. Hamilton bowled Mr Rowley in that innings and the first H. B. wicket fell for 33, so many as 31 of those 33 runs had been hit by Mr Rowley. The following is the score of the first match played on Prince's Cricket Ground.

The Brigade

C. R. Rowley Esq. c sub b Hamilton	20	– b Hamilton	31
Capt. the Hon. E. Acheson b Lanesborough	14	– b Coventry	16
Capt. Kenyon Slaney b Hamilton	7	– c de Broke b Guest	35
Lieut-Col Parnell b Hamilton	12	– not out	27
Capt. the Hon. E. Baseawen b Coventry	23	– not out	4
Capt. C. H. Hall b Hamilton	3		
Col Beresford lbw b Hamilton	0		
Lieut-Col W. Trefusis b Hamilton	0		
Lord F. Lennox b Hamilton	0		
Capt. Gosling c de Broke b Hamilton	0		
Capt. N. S. Hall not out	10		
Capt. Beauchamp Scott b Coventry	0		
B 5, l-b 1, w 6	12	B 2, l-b 2, w 1	5
	101		118

Lords and Commons

Lord Willoughby de Broke c Rowley b Lennox	26
Earl of Lanesborough c Lennox b Hall	5
H. Brand Esq. run out	10
Hon. W. Strutt b Parnell	4
W. H. Dyke Esq. c and b Parnell	6
Lord Geo. Hamilton run out	19
Earl of Coventry c Slaney b Hall	18
A. Bathurst Esq. b Parnell	0
Lord Garlies b Parnell	0
Marquis of Queensberry c and b Hall	1
Marquis of Bowmont not out	8
Arthur Guest Esq. c Lennox b Hall	5
B 3, w 3	6
	108

Umpires: Walter Price and T. Fennell.

NORTH v SOUTH OF ENGLAND

May 16 – Here we had a match worthy such a club and such a ground as Prince's and "great expectations" had been formed of this, the first great match played there. Thursday, the 16th of May, was the first bright, enjoyable day "after the deluge" that had saturated all England during the preceding days, and Prince's – with its lawn-like turf, its unique grass covered terrace, its many bright striped awnings and "umbrella tents"; with the pleasant, uncrowded, comfortable, easy, lounging form in which somewhere about 2000 visitors were grouped around the cricketers – appeared the prettiest, as it most certainly is the best appointed, and largest cricket ground yet found in London or its surroundings. "It's a magnificent place" exclaimed one old professional, whose name is as familiar as household words in cricketer's mouths, and who has played a prominent part in America, Australia, and on nearly all the grounds in this glorious old cricketing England of ours. "By Jove, it really is splendid." was the enforced exclamation of another famous pro., who, like the old 'un, set foot that morning for the first time on Prince's. A third enthusiastically termed it "a grand ground"; and so rang out its praises from all cricketers and visitors who on that 16th of May put their foot down for the first time on Prince's turf.

THE CRICKETERS' FUND

Result of match for the benefit of the Cricketers' Fund Friendly Society, played between North and South, on Prince's Club Ground, May 15, 16, and 17:

	£	s.	d.
Money taken at gates	276	12	1
Tickets sold	6	10	0
Donations:			
A. H. Walker Esq.	1	1	0
Soames Esq.	1	1	0
C. W. Alcock Esq.	1	1	0
V. E. Walker Esq.	2	2	0
I. D. Walker Esq.	1	1	0
F. H. Boult Esq.	0	10	0
Marks Esq.	0	10	6
Messrs Duke and Son	1	0	0
Messrs Jefferies and Malings	1	1	0
Total	292	9	7

	£	s.	d.
Expenses:			
North	66	0	0
South	40	0	0
Umpires	8	0	0
Money-takers	4	10	0
Gatemen	3	0	0
Scorers	2	0	0
Telegraph Man	0	10	0
Police	3	0	0
Boardmen	2	5	0
Posters	1	17	6
Balls	1	10	0
Stamps, stationery, and postage	0	5	2
Net amount to benefit of fund	159	11	11
Total	292	9	7

Edmond Wilder Esq., kindly gave £5 for tickets and printing.

FINANCIAL STATE OF THE SOCIETY

	£	s.	d.
Invested in Consols	2,304	18	11
At London and County Bank	182	8	8
Total	2,487	7	7

The committee also take this opportunity of acknowledging with thanks a donation of £3 14s. 2d. in April last from the Officers' Cricket Club, late General Depôt Battalion, Chatham, and to thank the Messrs Prince for their kindness in granting the free use of the ground for the above match.

Additional donation received since accounts made by, G. Smith, Esq., 10s.

June 26. John Wisden, Secretary.

(Subsequent to the above, Mr Edmond Wilder sent – through John Lillywhite – a donation of £10 to the Fund.)

PRINCE'S CRICKET CLUB IN 1874
(Formed in 1870 – First Season 1871)

President – Earl Cadogan.

Committee

Arthur Smith Barry, Esq. M.P.	Lord George Hamilton M.P.
Marquis of Bowmont.	Lord Londesborough.
Earl Cadogan.	Alfred Lubbock Esq.
Earl of Clarendon.	Earl of March.
Earl of Coventry.	Colonel Marshall.
Lord Delamere.	Lord Methuen.
Lord Downe.	Marquis of Queensbury.
W. Hart Dyke Esq., M.P.	Captain W. S. Kenyon Slaney.
Lord Folkestone.	Colonel Taylor M.P.
Earl of Gosford.	Colonel Trotter.
Lord Grey de Wilton.	Lord Willoughby de Broke.
Arthur E. Guest Esq., M.P.	

Secretary – Geo. Prince Esq. *Ground Keeper* – T. Box sen.

Ground Bowlers – E. Willsher (Captain); T. Box jun., J. Braddock, A. Burghes, G. Burke, W. Draper, J. Hayward, E. Henty, G. Keeble, A. Luff and J. Newton.

AT PRINCE'S IN 1874

"Under the Elms at Prince's" was one of the most fashionable rendezvous in the London season 1874. Over the whole length and breadth of "the Members' Walk and Ladies' Promenade", so pleasantly shaded by the famous row of elm trees, there had been constructed a Skating Rink, whereon on sunny summer days there congregated numbers of fair devotees, gracefully flitting about in the enjoyment of the invigorating and now fashionable pastime of roller skating. At certain hours this pastime daily attracted large and distinguished assemblages, and throughout the season no meet was more fashionably popular than "under the elms at Prince's".

Cricket at Prince's in 1874 will mainly be remembered for the successful "first's" made by the colt wicket keepers of Yorkshire and Middlesex. For the surprisingly easy victory obtained by the Oxonians over the Middlesex men; for the large enthusiastic gatherings; the splendid batting of Lockwood, Jupp and Oscroft, and the excitingly close fight for victory in the North v South match. For the successful and fine hitting of the captain of the Harrow Eleven, Mr A. J. Webbe, who made 102 of the 142 runs scored by his side against Prince's C. and G.; and, for the great attendances; the curious incidents that cropped up; and the large scores of 110, 104, 99, 93 not out, and 85, that were hit in The Gentlemen v Players' week.

NORTH v SOUTH OF ENGLAND

(*For the benefit of "The Cricketer's Fund"*)

Played at Prince's, June 4, 5, 1874

Those present at Prince's on the 4th of last June saw that now famous ground at its brightest and best. That Thursday was the off-day between the Derby and Oaks, a day of splendid summer weather, and a day in the height of the London season, hence the attendance was a large one, and the takings at the gates (1s. admission) far in excess of any preceding "Fund" day. The scene the ground presented about 6 p.m. that day was indeed splendid. The Ride and the Row in Hyde Park had been then done for the day, and "under the elms at Prince's" there was a crowd of fair and fashionable society flitting o'er the skating rink, promenading, and enjoying the music so pleasantly played by one of the Household Brigade bands. Under the bright coloured umbrella tents on the pretty terrace of turf, and on the terrace itself, were throngs of admirers of cricket; and lolling on the turf, seated on the seats, and standing two – in some parts three – deep there was formed around the ground a compact ring of thousands of spectators who were there for the sole enjoyment of the glorious old game. That neither Mr Ottaway, Mr Buller nor Richard Daft played was a matter of great public disappointment freely outspoken, and it will be advisable for the success of future Fund matches that no cricketer be announced to play who has not pledged his word to do so, and having done so nothing but ill health should excuse him.

It was nearly 12.15 when Mr Hornby and Greenwood commenced the North batting, to the bowling of Lillywhite and Southerton; they had scored but 9 runs when Greenwood was easily had at mid-off, and at 14 Mr Hornby was bowled for seven singles. Lockwood (nearly had at point by Mr W. Grace before he had scored) and Oscroft then made the only stand in the innings. They brought on Mr W. Grace to bowl v Southerton, and the score from 14 to 74, when Oscroft was cleverly caught out at wicket by Pooley for 31, wherein were three good drives for 4 each, and a couple of good cuts for 3 each. Wyld stayed until Lockwood had increased the score to 106, when the Yorkshireman was caught out at long-off by Mr Fryer for 58, made by good all round hitting from Lillywhite, Southerton and Mr W. Grace. Lockwood's hits included four 4s – three drives and a very fine cut – and seven 3s. With four wickets only down and 106 runs scored the innings shaped well for the North, but the next six wickets added only 17 runs, the eighth, ninth and tenth wickets all falling at 123, Lillywhite, after luncheon, finishing off by bowling four overs for three wickets and a hit for 2. But the wickets did not appear to play well. The South commenced batting at 3.40, Mr I. D. Walker and Mr W. Grace opening the innings to the bowling of the two Shaws. From Alfred's few runs were made, but from J.C.'s fifth over Mr Grace made a 3 and Mr Walker two 4s; thereupon Hill bowled v J. C., and when the score was at 55 Mr Grace was had at wicket for 29, a drive for 4 from Hill and four 3s (cuts) being his principal hits. At 57 Jupp was c and b, and at 70 Mr I. D. Walker was out for a steady, well played innings of 26 runs, that included four 4s. At 72 a rare shooter bowled Mr Fryer, and Mr F. Grace was had at cover point; at 87 Pooley and Mr Thornton were both out; at 107 (with successive balls of an over) Hill bowled Humphrey and Lillywhite; and, notwithstanding 55 runs were scored before a wicket fell, the innings was up for 113 runs, or 10 wrong – Hill having eight wickets, twice taking two wickets in an over. Alfred Shaw at one time bowled thirty-six successive balls for a hit for 2. Soon after six o'clock Lockwood and Greenwood commenced the North's second innings. When 3 runs were made Greenwood was out; at 17 Oscroft was out; and when "time" arrived Lockwood had made 17 not out, Wyld 5 not out, and the total was 23 for two wickets.

Friday was another splendid summer day, and the ground was again visited by thousands, who had the pleasure of witnessing one of the closest and most exciting finishes of the season. At 12.15 the not outs resumed their innings, and when they had increased the score to 40 Pooley settled Wyld. At 53 Emmett was bowled, and at 55 Hill rushed out to one from Southerton, and, wholly missing it, had to make way for Mr Hornby, whose battered hand (hurt at Lord's) caused him evident pain and prevented him having complete command over the bat; however, he batted pluckily and luckily, for notwithstanding he was missed at long-on by Mr Thornton and at long-off by Mr Fryer, he made 23 runs before he was well caught out at long-field by Mr Thornton. Lockwood stayed until 105 runs had been made, when he was out for 67, the highest score in the match, and a well played bit of steady cricket, that included four 4s and twenty-six singles. Lockwood's was seventh wicket down. The innings concluded at two o'clock for 128, leaving the South a second innings of 139 runs to play to win.

At 3.15 Mr I. D. Walker and Mr W. Grace commenced the innings to the bowling of Alfred Shaw and Hill, and when 20 runs had been made from twelve overs, cover-point had Mr Walker for 5. Jupp then went in; he had made 8 only when he was missed at slip by Alfred Shaw. After this life the two great batsmen of the South hit away in capital form, brought on various bowling changes and the score to 87, when Alfred Shaw bowled Mr W. Grace for 37, and in his following over he bowled Mr F. Grace, Alfred thus bowling both brothers' wickets with the score at 87. Still the South innings looked a winning one, and when Jupp and Mr Fryer had increased the score to 110 with only three wickets down the match really did appear "safe for the South", but then "the glorious uncertainty, etc.", cropped up in strong form, and a change took place that excitingly revived the hopes of the North, for at 111 Mr Fryer and Mr Thornton both left; at 120 Pooley was done with, and at 121 a rare good ball knocked down the middle stump of Humphrey's wicket. Jupp was then the Northmen's difficulty, for so long as he stayed and a hitter like Charlwood was his mate, with two others to bat, the 18 runs then required to win appeared an easy task; but not so when at 124 Jupp drove one from Alfred Shaw with immense force, and Wyld, fielding deep behind the bowler, put up his right hand and caught and held the ball in fine form, the "smack", as the ball reached the hand, being heard all over the ground. "Hang it, that is hard lines, but it's splendid cricket," exclaimed a well-known Southerner; and so it was, hit and catch being grand, and heartier, lustier, or more deserved cheering never rang out on a cricket ground than greeted Jupp's hit and Wyld's catch at Prince's on the fifth of last June. With 15 to win and two wickets to fall it appeared "anybody's match", but fortune seemed full against the South that day, as at 123 Lillywhite was stumped, and the last man of the South – Southerton – had to go in with 11 runs wanting to win. Charlwood made a single from Hill, and backed that up with a drive for 4 from Alfred Shaw, loud cheers complimenting the big hit. Southerton then played a maiden over from Hill, and Charlwood hit a 2 from Shaw's next over, consequently Hill had another turn at Southerton. The first ball of that over Southerton played, and so he did the second ball, but did not quite stop its travelling power and turning sharply round to push the ball away from the stumps, he had the bad luck to push it against them with just sufficient impetus to shake a bail off, and so, after all Jupp's skilful and gallant fight for the South, the North won this "rare match" by 3 runs.

North

A. N. Hornby Esq. b Lillywhite	7	– c Thornton b Southerton	23
Andrew Greenwood c Jupp b Lillywhite	4	– c and b Southerton	0
Ephraim Lockwood c Fryer b Southerton	58	– c F. Grace b Southerton	67
William Oscroft c Pooley b Lillywhite	31	– c Pooley b Southerton	1
F. Wyld c Pooley b Lillywhite	5	– c Pooley b Lillywhite	10
Emmett c W. Grace b Lillywhite	7	– b Southerton	1
Allen Hill c Jupp b Southerton	4	– b Southerton	1
Alfred Shaw c Lillywhite b Southerton	2	– not out	10
Walter Price b Lillywhite	3	– lbw b Southerton	6
T. Plumb c Southerton b Lillywhite	0	– c Thornton b Lillywhite	0
J. C. Shaw not out	0	– c and b Southerton	5
B 2	2	B 3, l-b 1	4
	123		128

South

	First innings		Second innings	
I. D. Walker Esq. b Hill	26	–	c Greenwood b Hill	5
W. G. Grace Esq. c Plumb b Hill	29	–	b Alfred Shaw	37
H. Jupp c and b Hill	0	–	c Wyld b Alfred Shaw	52
G. F. Grace Esq. c Oscroft b Alfred Shaw	14	–	b Alfred Shaw	0
F. E. R. Fryer Esq. b Hill	1	–	c Greenwood b Alfred Shaw	12
C. I. Thornton Esq. c and b Hill	8	–	b Alfred Shaw	0
Pooley c Wyld b Hill	6	–	c Alfred Shaw b Hill	5
Richard Humphrey b Hill	10	–	b Alfred Shaw	1
H. Charlwood c Hill b Alfred Shaw	11	–	not out	9
James Lillywhite b Hill	0	–	st Plumb b Alfred Shaw	3
Southerton not out	2	–	b Hill	0
B 4, l-b 2	6		B 7, l-b 4	11
	113			135

South Bowling

	Overs	Mdns	Runs	Wkts	Overs	Mdns	Runs	Wkts
Lillywhite	32	11	57	7	34	15	51	2
Southerton	21.1	5	38	3	38	13	70	8
Mr W. Grace	10	2	26	—				
Mr F. Grace					4	3	3	—

North Bowling

	Overs	Mdns	Runs	Wkts	Overs	Mdns	Runs	Wkts
A. Shaw	35	18	42	2	37	16	39	7
Hill	30	14	48	8	27.3	13	36	3
J. C. Shaw	5	1	17	—	22	10	31	—
Emmett					11	4	18	—

Umpires: R. Thoms and Willsher.

HOW THE MATCH BENEFITED "THE FUND"

Receipts	£	s.	d.	Expenditure	£	s.	d.
Received at gates	379	6	6	North Team	51	0	0
Donations:				South Team	40	0	0
Marks Esq.	0	10	6	Umpires, Scorers and Gatekeepers	22	0	0
Messrs Duke and Son	1	0	0	Mr Prince's account	10	0	0
Mr R. Thoms (umpire)	1	0	0	Printing	8	14	6
Messrs Jefferies and Maling	1	1	0	Expenses during Match, Refreshments, Cabs, Messengers, etc.	3	2	6
A. J. W. Biddulph Esq.	2	2	0	Materials	1	16	6
					136	13	6
				Net profit to Fund	248	6	6
	£385	0	0		£385	0	0

(The match played at "Prince's" for the benefit of the Fund in 1873 was a three days' match, the receipts at the gates those three days was £276 12s. 1d., and the net profit to the Fund from that match was £159 11s. 11d.)

PRINCE'S CRICKET CLUB IN 1876

(Formed in 1870 – First Season 1871)

Committee.

Marquis of Bowmont.
Earl of Clarendon.
Earl of Coventry.
Lord Delamere.
Viscount Downe.
Sir W. Hart Dyke, Bart., MP
Viscount Folkestone.
Earl of Gosford.
Lord Grey de Radcliffe.
Arthur E. Guest Esq.
Lord George Hamilton, MP
Lord Londesborough.
Alfred Lubbock Esq.
Earl of March.
Colonel Marshall.
Lord Methuen.
Marquis of Queensberry.
Captain W. S. Kenyon-Slaney.
A. H. Smith-Barry Esq., MP
Colonel Taylor, MP
Colonel Trotter.
Lord Willoughby de Broke.

Secretary – Geo. Prince Esq.

Ground Bowlers – E. Willsher (Captain), T. Box jun., G. Burke, T. Brown, Geo. Hearne jun. (son of George), E. Henty, A. Luff, J. Newland and J. Newton.

CRICKET AT PRINCE'S IN 1876.

The 1876 season at Prince's will be memorable to cricketers for the sudden death of Tom Box; the huge scoring in the Middlesex v Oxford University match; the large number of three figure innings hit by batsmen (so many as eleven scores of 100 or more runs having been hit); and for the cutting off a corner, and consequent – from a cricketer's point of view – disfigurement of the pretty ground, by the formation of a roadway into Sloane Street. Whether this road is to pave the way to "Prince's" being "magnificently mansioned over" is more than this compiler knoweth. Any how the cutting off the NE corner was a sore trouble to poor Tom Box, who complained that it drove him away from his best portion of the ground, and compelled him to pitch wickets on parts where it had not been expected great matches would be played.

HOW THE NORTH v SOUTH MATCH, 1876, BENEFITED 'THE FUND'

Receipts	£	s.	d.
June 1 – Gate money	92	4	0
June 2 – Gate money	85	6	0
June 3 – Gate money	63	18	6
	£241	8	6

Expenditure	£	s.	d.
Paid North XI	53	0	0
Paid South XI	30	0	0
Paid Umpires	10	0	0
Scorers, Money-takers, Telegraph men, Cabs, Refreshments, etc.	12	15	0
Charges for Police, Board-men, etc.	5	9	6
Materials, wrappers and postages	1	13	2
Printing	2	0	0
Extra man at principal entrance	1	0	0
Luncheons for Police, Gate-Keepers and Rolling Ground	2	12	6
Net profit to Fund	122	18	4
	£241	8	6

Subsequently the Fund was increased by a donation of One Guinea from Messrs Jefferies and Co., of Woolwich.

The match played at "Prince's" for the benefit of the Fund in 1873 was a three days' match; the receipts at the gates those three days were £276 12s. 1d., and the net profit to the Fund from that match was £159 11s. 11d. The match in 1874 was over on the second day; £379 6s. 6d. was paid at the gates on those two days as admission money, and the net profit to the Fund from that match was £248 6s. 6d. The match in 1875 lasted three days, and the money taken at the gates on those three days was £254 4s., the net profit to the Fund being £133 17s. 6d.

PRINCE'S CRICKET CLUB IN 1878

(Formed in 1870 – First Season 1871)

Committee.

Marquis of Bowmont; Earl of Clarendon; Earl of Coventry; Lord Delamere; Viscount Downe; Sir W. Hart Dyke, Bart., MP; Viscount Folkestone; Earl of Gosford; Lord Grey de Radcliffe; Arthur E. Guest Esq.; Lord George Hamilton MP; Lord Londesborough; Alfred Lubbock Esq.; Earl of March; Major-General Marshall; Lord Methuen; Marquis of Queensberry; Captain W. S. Kenyon-Slaney; A. H. Smith-Barry Esq., MP; Colonel The Rt. Hon. T. E. Taylor, MP; Colonel Trotter; Lord Willoughby de Broke.

Secretary – Geo. Prince Esq.

Professional Bowlers engaged at Prince's in 1878. – E. Willsher (Captain), T. Box, W. Draper, E. Henty, Newland, Relf and J. Newton (*Ground-keeper*).

Prince's Programme for 1878 was of unusual brevity, comprising as it did but three front rank matches, all of which are duly noticed and fully scored on the following pages. But, numerically weak in matches as that programme was, it included two of the most interesting of the 39 contests played by the Australians in their now memorable cricketing tour throughout the length and breadth of Old England. Those heartless foes to open spaces and Sports and Pastimes – Improvement Mongers and Building Speculators – had still further contracted Prince's since our last issue, and, with a corner cut off at one part, and a large portion sliced off at another, the ground is now of no describable shape whatever; nevertheless, with a bright sun shining, the ring well formed, cricketers hard at it in the centre, and that famous Union Jack flauntingly flapping in the breeze, Prince's is still one of the prettiest grounds in England, and it does seem a pity that, whilst it is a cricket-ground, it should not be more frequently utilised by playing more than three first-class matches on it in one season.

MISCELLANY

INDIVIDUAL INNINGS OF 200 OR MORE RUNS, 1868

By W. H. Knight

"404 runs by one man!" "Of course that is the largest innings yet hit?" – and "Pray, whose is the second highest innings?" – and "Third highest?" – and "Next; and Next?" Such – when Mr E. F. S. Tylecote's great innings became generally known last season – were the oft repeated enquiries respecting the great scores made of those who are supposed to be well posted in these matters. I had my share of such queries, and to the best of my knowledge answered them, but found several of my questioners dubious as to the correctness of my replies on two points; the first was as to Mr Ward's famous 278 having been beaten by Adams. "Who's Adams?" incredulously said they, "Not Tom of Kent surely", and they evidently thought I was cramming them. Then others would not credit that so few professionals had – as one querist said – "done the 200". So when last year's hot, busy, and enormous run-getting season had become part and parcel of cricket history, I thought the said history would be a trifle more complete if these innings of 200 runs were gathered together and published in a form handy for reference. I have collected them, and trust the accompanying list of such innings, with the few "Notes by the way" that precede them, will be found interesting to the readers of "The Cricketer's Almanack".

Mr W. Ward was the first cricketer that played an innings of more than 200 runs. He played his great score for MCC v Norfolk at Lord's in 1820, and in that scientific and elaborate work on the game, *The Cricket Field*, it is stated of this 278 of Mr Ward's that "Mr Morse preserves as a relic the identical ball, and the bat that hit that ball about; a trusty friend (the bat) which served its owner 50 years". (This match is otherwise memorable for being the one wherein one of the greatest batsmen that ever wielded willow – Fuller Pilch (then 17 years old) – made his first appearance on Lord's Ground.) The second of these innings was not hit until 1826, in which season that hard hitting left-hand Yorkshireman, Marsden, hit his 227 at Darnall, an innings that *Scores and Biographies* states Marsden was eight hours playing, and *The Sporting Magazine* of that time records Marsden as having in that innings "struck a ball that alighted a distance of 130 yards from the wicket". After Marsden's innings, as many as eleven years passed without another of these scores being hit, as it was not until 1837 that Adams, of Essex, made his 279, thereby beating Mr Ward's innings by one run; but so generally was Mr Ward's score known, and so comparatively little was Adams's, that for years subsequent many a wager was lost through that extra run of the Walden man's. Full 30 years did Adams's 279 hold its own as the largest innings ever played; indeed, from 1837 to 1859, no innings of 200 or more runs was played; but in '59, that great master of the art of batting, Thomas Hayward, played the highest innings in his brilliant batting career, his 220 for his County against the University, being noticed in the *Bell's Life* of that time thus: – "Hayward remained in, doing as he like, until the stumps were drawn for the day, his score having reached 91 (not out), a splendidly played innings; the following day he increased his score to 220, and the innings closed for 371 runs". It may here be added that Hayward went to the wicket with the score at 20, and that eventually he was stumped out. In that same year (1859), Mr Collins took an Oxford Eleven to Purton, and thereat played the highest innings – 548 runs, only seven wickets down – that up to that time, and for some seasons after, had been played; in that innings Mr Gundry hit his score of 201 runs, and thus two of these scores were for the first time hit in one season. The seasons 1860 and 1861 however were barren of such innings; but in 1862 Mr Brindley went in first man and made his 202 not out, and that bold batsman, dashing hitter, and rapid scorer of runs, Mr E. M. Grace, hit his 208 not out, and also his 241 – an extraordinary batting feat to accomplish in one season; but in that season this extraordinary batsman was in extraordinary hitting form, as in addition to this double 200, Mr E. M. Grace at Lord's hit an innings of 118 runs against MCC, and at Canterbury for MCC, he not only played an innings of 192 not out, but with his bowling had all the ten wickets down (it was a twelve a side match) in the second innings of the Gentlemen of Kent. (In all, Mr E. M. Grace scored 2190 runs in '62, finishing up his hitting that season with 42 and 135 in a match at Bedminster.) In 1863 there appears to have been no innings of 200 runs played; but in 1864 there was a Quidnunc innings played on the Brighton ground, wherein the first wicket went down with the score at 2 only, and the sixth at 109; but the seventh was not done with until the figure 376 were on the board, the principal "reason why" being a very finely played innings of 91 by Mr Bayford, and the very hard hitting of Mr H. Biron, who, by four 5s, twenty-two 4s, eight 3s, twenty-three 2s, and thirty-six singles, hit the great innings of 214 runs. In 1865 there were three innings of more than 200 runs played – one of 229 by Mr Rood, one of 207 by Mr Reade, and one of 216 by Jupp, the Surrey player, who was the last, and is one of the only four professionals that has played an innings of more than 200 runs. Jupp was first man in at 4.15, the stumps were drawn at 6.15; the next day they commenced at eleven o'clock sharp, and at 5.20 Jupp was out for 216, hit together by seven 4s, nineteen 3s, twenty-seven 2s and seventy-seven singles. In 1866 as many as four of these innings of 200 runs were played – one of 220 runs by that exceedingly fine batsman, Mr Alfred Lubbock, one of 269 runs by Mr Scobell, one (in a Marlborough College practice match) of 274 runs by Mr Monnington, and one of 224 not out by Mr W. G. Grace, who was then only eighteen years old, and who a month later on also played an innings of 173 not out; both matches were played on The Oval, and this playing on one ground in about a week two successive innings of 224 and 173 both not outs, the first against Surrey, and the second against the Players of the South, is a batting feat as wonderful as it is unparalleled, and it is the more astonishing for being accomplished by one so young (Mr W. G. Grace was born July 18, 1848). In 1867 there was an innings of 227 played by Mr Worsley (an Oxonian) in a minor match at Lord's; one of 200 by Dr E. M. Grace (who thus has played more of these innings, and hit therein more runs than any other cricketer living or defunct); and one of 219 runs by Mr E. B. Rowley, a splendid hitter, who, in this innings, by a straight drive, "hit the ball a distance of 120 years before it alighted". (Mr Rowley's 219 was one of the "reasons why" that Manchester innings reached the great total of 586 runs, then the largest innings ever played.) But great as had been all these doughty deeds with the bat, vast as had unquestionably been the great scores of Alfred Adams, Mr Ward, Marsden, the two Grace's, Hayward, and others, they were all outdone and put in the shade by the (numerically) greater scores played in 1868, during which very hot and arid season one innings of 404 runs was hit, and five of more than 200 runs – the six innings giving an aggregate of 1543 runs. In fact, "the hitters of the period" in 1868 far away outhit the hitters of any other period, as they played the two largest innings – 689 and 630 – ever played by Elevens or any other sides, and they hit the two largest individual scores – 404 and 289 – hit since the game has been played. Mr Tylecote's 404 was made in a Clifton College practice match, and was hit in six hours, or at the rate of about 67 runs per hour, thus:– Mr Tylecote was first man in of his side, played about half-an-hour, and scored 34 runs on the first day (it was an afternoon's match); on the second afternoon he resumed his innings at 2.45, played up to 5.30, and increased his score to 199; and on the third day he was also at the wickets from 2.45 to 5.30, when he carried his bat out for 404 (out of 630). Mr Tylecote's hits were one 7, five 5s, twenty-one 4s, thirty-nine 3s, forty-two 2s and seventy-seven singles, and barring one 4 (a hit of Mr T.'s out of the field) he ran all the runs made by his side. Mr Batchelor's 289 is by 10 runs the second highest score yet played; it was hit in the highest innings – 689 runs – ever made by a side, and an innings wherein three men hit the astoundingly large number of 555 runs. The others of these innings hit last season were – one of 228 runs by Mr E. P. Ash, one of 211 not out by Mr Pauncefote (Captain of this year's Oxford Eleven), one of 201 runs by Mr A. N. Hornby, and one of 210 by Mr W. G. Grace (who hit this innings the week following his playing his two great innings of 130 and 102 not out, in one match at Canterbury).

INDIVIDUAL INNINGS OF 200 OR MORE RUNS

Total	Player	Title of Match	Venue and Date
404*	Mr E. F. S. Tylecote	Classicals v Moderns	Clifton College, 1868
289	Mr W. J. Batchelor	Long Vacation Club v University Servants	Cambridge, 1868
279	Alfred Adams	Saffron Walden v Bishop Stortford	Saffron Walden, 1837
278	Mr W. Ward	Marylebone Club v Norfolk County	Lord's, 1820
274	Mr T. Monnington	Mr Mullin's House v Rev. J. Bright's House	Marlborough College, 1866
269	Mr J. F. Scobell	Gentlemen of Devon v Gentlemen of Dorset	Torquay, 1866
241	Mr E. M. Grace	Clifton Club v 16 Bristol Grammer School	Clifton, 1862
229	Mr H. Rood	The 4 Brothers Rood v 11 of Finchley Albion	Finchley, 1865
228	Mr E. P. Ash	Moderns v Classics, Haileybury College	Haileybury, 1868
227	Thomas Marsden	Sheffield and Leicester v Nottingham	Darnall, 1826
227	Mr Worsley	Major Thompson's 11 v Middlesex Rifles	Lord's, 1867
224*	Mr W. G. Grace	England v Surrey	The Oval, 1866
220	Thomas Hayward	Cambridge County v Cambridge University	Cambridge, 1959
220	Mr A. Lubbock	West Kent Club v Royal Engineers	Chislehurst, 1866
219	Mr E. B. Rowley	Gentlemen of Lancashire v Gentlemen of Yorkshire	Manchester, 1867
216	H. Jupp	11 Players of South v 14 Gentlemen of South	Southampton, 1865
214	Mr H. Biron	Cambridge Quidnuncs v Gentlemen of Sussex	Brighton, 1864
211*	Mr B. Pauncefote	Brasenose College v Corpus College	Oxford, 1868
210	Mr W. G. Grace	Clifton Club v Civil Service Club	Clifton, 1868
208*	Mr E. M. Grace	Frenchay v Knole Park	Frenchay, 1862
207	Mr H. S. Reade	Staffordshire Rangers v Birkenhead Park Club	Birkenhead, 1865
202*	Mr S. Brindley	Cheltenham v Chepstow	Cheltenham, 1862
201	Mr J. P. Gundry	Mr Collins's Eleven v Purton	Purton, 1859
201	Mr A. N. Hornby	Gentlemen of Cheshire v Gentlemen of Shropshire	Shrewsbury, 1868
200	Mr E. M. Grace	11 of West Gloucestershire v 22 of Wiltshire	Holt, 1868
200	Mr H. Clement	Hillingdon v Houndslow district	———, 1867

* *Signifies not out.*

THE ALL-ENGLAND ELEVEN

Formed in 1846 by William Clarke, the celebrated Nottingham slow-bowler. This Eleven's first match was v Twenty of Sheffield, at Hyde Park Ground, Sheffield, September 1, etc., 1846; Sheffield won by five wickets. Clarke died (August) 1856. The following month (at Leeds) George Parr was appointed Secretary, in which capacity he has since acted.

1870 – Secretary, George Parr, Radcliffe-on-Trent, Nottinghamshire.

UNITED ALL-ENGLAND ELEVEN

Formed in 1852 by James Dean and John Wisden, the celebrated Sussex bowlers. This Eleven's first match was v Twenty-one Gentlemen of Hampshire (with Daniel Day), at East Hants Ground, Portsmouth, August 26, etc., 1852. The United Eleven won the match by nine wickets.

Secretary, Robert Carpenter, Cambridge.

UNITED SOUTH OF ENGLAND ELEVEN

Formed in (November) 1864. John Lillywhite, Treasurer; Edgar Willsher, Secretary. This Eleven's first match was v Twenty-two of Ireland, at Dublin, May 11, etc., 1865. The match was not finished.

1870 – Secretary, Edgar Willsher, Maidstone, Kent.

UNITED NORTH OF ENGLAND ELEVEN

This Eleven was formed in 1869 (back end). President, Lord Londesborough; Vice-Presidents, A. B. Rowley and J. H. Wire Esqs.

Secretaries, Roger Iddison, 6 Rusholme Grove, Rusholme, Manchester; and George Freeman, Malton, Yorkshire.

THREE BROTHERS' THREE-FIGURE INNINGS IN 1869

Or, 2,022 runs in fifteen innings by Messrs W. G., G. F., and E. M. Grace

Mr W. G. Grace hit innings of 180, 172 not out, 138 not out, 127, 122, 121, 117, 111 and 100, or	1,188
Mr G. F. Grace hit innings of 206 not out, 153, 150, 112 not out and 104, or	725
Dr E. M. Grace hit an innings of	109
Total runs in the fifteen innings	2,022

Mr W. G. Grace's 1,188 runs in nine innings (two not outs) is a wonderful batting exploit, especially when it is borne in mind that in five of those innings he played against such bowling as Freeman's, J. C. Shaw's, Willsher's, Emmett's, Wootton's, Alfred Shaw's, Southerton's, Griffith's, R. C. Tinley's, Bennett's, and others. Perhaps it may not be deemed out of place to record here the following incidents in the cricketing career of this great batsman. In 1864 Mr W. G. Grace played his first match at Lord's, i.e., for South Wales Club v I Zingari. In that match he scored an innings of 50 runs, pretty plainly indicating what was "looming in the future" from his bat. His first match at The Oval was also played that season: it was South Wales Club v Surrey Club, wherein he scored 5 and 38 only; but in the following week, at Brighton (for South Wales Club v Gentlemen of Sussex), Mr W. G. Grace scored 170 and 56 not out, and as that match was played July 14, 15, 16, 1864, and Mr W. G. Grace was born July 18, 1848, he was not quite sixteen years old when he played those two innings in one match. The 170 was played without giving a chance, he being out at last by playing the ball on. But of all the many great deeds Mr W. G. Grace has already effected with the bat none surpass the following two successive innings he played on The Oval in 1866:

July 31	For England v Surrey	224 not out	England's Total: 512.
August 27	For Gentlemen v Players of South .	173 not out	Gentlemen's Total: 297.

Mr G. F. Grace's 725 runs in five innings (two not outs) is a cricket item quite in character with the hitting form of the family. It is true these runs were made in country matches, but equally true is it that 725 runs in five innings is a great batting exploit for a lad of eighteen to accomplish. (Mr G. F. Grace was born December 13, 1850.) Mr G. F. Grace's 206 not out must have been a fast bit of scoring indeed; he was No. 1 in, and when the other ten were out the total of the innings was 287, of which number 25 were "extras", so Mr Grace actually hit his 206 whilst the other ten were contributing 56 only. But that he is a fast run-getter was evident on The Oval last autumn, when in the rapidly dying daylight he made 60 runs in the hour. His dashing, vigorous hitting, and the cool, confident way he (at point) put up his hands and – from a very hard cut – made a catch, forcibly recalled to mind the 1863 form of his brother, "The Doctor". (Mr G. F. Grace scored 1,641 runs in thirty-nine innings in 1869.)

Dr E. M. Grace was out of cricket practice in 1869. Had this gentleman been in his 1863 form – a season wherein he hit six innings of three figures, and scored (all told) the enormous total of 3,074 runs – the probability is there would have been a material increase to the Fifteen Three-Figure Innings made by The Three Brothers in 1869.

THE LARGEST INNINGS SCORED IN 1874 – 681 RUNS

ST JOHN'S COLLEGE v CORPUS CHRISTI COLLEGE

Played on Cowley Marsh, Oxford, June 1, 2, 1874

This match was played on the afternoons of June 1, 2, play beginning at 1.45 and ending at 6.30. Corpus went in first and were disposed of for 94 runs, and St John's began to bat at 3.45; Mr Thornton was not out 96, and three wickets down for 210 at the end of the day's play. The next day Mr Thornton added 20, and was then bowled off his pad for an excellent innings of 116, made without a chance. Mr Elwes' 149 was a freely-hit innings, and included three 5s and nineteen 4s. Mr Pulman's 249 not out was composed of two 7s, four 6s, seven 5s, twenty-seven 4s, etc.: his driving and leg-hitting was particularly clean and effective, the ball frequently traversing the lengths of the adjoining grounds. A note-worthy feature of the innings was Mr Nesbitt's long-stopping, 2 byes only being scored in that huge total of 681 runs. The following is the score of the innings hit by the

St John's College Eleven

F. R. Henderson run out	3
R. T. Thornton b Carlyon	116
J. Tanner c Dalton b Thistle	24
R. Briggs c Goldschmidt b Dalton	30
G. P. Elwes st Thistle b Ingleby	149
W. W. Pulman not out	249
F. Champneys b Dalton	6
R. Shetfield c Thistle b Dalton	40
W. Lovell c Seton-Karr b Dalton	0
E. Saye c Ingleby b Dalton	7
E. A. Wells c and b Ingleby	24
B 2, l-b 3, w 26, n-b 2	33
	681

The wickets fell in the following order:

1/11 2/63 3/140 4/232 5/360 6/399 7/557 8/574 9/588 10/681

(Large as the total of this innings is, it is not the largest played, as in 1868, at Cambridge, the CU Long Vacation Club hit an innings of 689 runs.)

THE SMALLEST INNINGS SCORED IN 1874 – A SIDE OUT FOR 2 (Leg-byes)

NETHER STOWEY v BISHOP'S LYDIARD

From *Bell's Life*, of September 19, 1874

Old *Bell* did not state when, or where, this innings was brought off, nor did it state in what part of England "Nether Stowey" or "Bishop's Lydiard" is situated; what *Bell's Life* did state is:

"The smallest score of the season was recently played between Nether Stowey and Bishop's Lydiard. It will be seen that not one of the Nether Stowey batsmen obtained a run in the second innings. As this remarkable score is worthy of record we subjoin it."

Then *Bell* gives the full score of the match, from which is appears Nether Stowey made 33 and 2; and Bishop's Lydiard 106. The following is a transcript from *Bell's Life* of

Nether Stowey's 2nd Innings

C. Routley not out	0	Perrett b Winter	0
W. Rich b Winter	0	Riddle b Winter	0
J. Crang b Winter	0	J. Cogan b Knollys	0
Wade b Winter	0	G. Lock b Knollys	0
G. Bickham b Winter	0	L-b 2	2
W. Routley b Winter	0		—
S. Hayman b Winter	0		2

In another column of *Bell's Life* of September 19, it states that "there were but twenty-eight balls bowled" in the innings.

(Small as the total of this innings is, it is not the smallest on record, as there are others of only 2 runs, and "a few" the total of which are 0.)

THE HIGHEST INDIVIDUAL SCORE RECORDED

W. N. ROE, not out, 415

Played on the University Ground, Cambridge, July 12, 13, 1881

Of the score and the scorer *Bell's Life* thus remarks: "One of the most remarkable games ever played came off on Tuesday and Wednesday on the University Ground, when Caius College L.V.C.C. played Emmanuel L.V.C.C. with two substitutes. Caius went to the wickets first, and put together just a hundred, and then Emmanuel deputed Allcock and one of the substitutes to begin their batting, and on the drawing of stumps on Tuesday, 157 runs had been scored. The play was resumed on Wednesday at 2.40, when Roe soon lost his partner, but he himself continued to score, and was soon into his third century. For two or three minutes Roe played carelessly, but being warned of his so doing, he settled down to careful play. Shortly after this he gave his first chance. He, however, went on hitting very finely, and at 6.30 had made 415 not out; Mr W. N. Roe thereby has beaten E. F. Tylecote's record of 404 not out. Roe was batting four hours fifty-five minutes, and ran no less than 708 runs. His own total included one 6, six fives, sixteen 4s, forty-eight 3s, fifty-two 2s and sixty-seven singles, and had only three "let offs", and not one of those was given till he had made over 200. Previous to Roe coming to Cambridge (in October, 1879), he was at the Clergy Orphan School, Canterbury, where he did great things in 1878, scoring once 226 not out, and on six other occasions he scored over 100, being no less than three times not out. Since his arrival here he has several times scored largely in college matches, but when being tried for his Blue, he has been unsuccessful. Of course the bowling he had in this extraordinary match to contend against was weak in the extreme, but, nevertheless, it was a grand performance."

Caius L.V.C.

G. C. FitzGerald lbw b Roe	29	G. W. Lynch b C. H. Allcock	2
C. E. Broughton b Roe	15	F. M. Clarke not out	5
F. S. Sanders c W. B. Allcock b C. H. Allcock	14	F. E. Nicholl b C. H. Allcock	3
W. C. Davy c Hewetson b Roe	21	G. Lennox-Conyngham b Roe	0
C. S. Bayley c Creak b C. H. Allcock	0	B 6, l-b 1	7
E. L. Burd b C. H. Allcock	0		
R. Threlfall c and b Roe	4		100

Emmanuel L.V.C.

W. N. Roe not out	415	W. B. Allcock not out	8
C. H. Allcock c Broughton b FitzGerald	66		
J. S. Austen c and b Davy	25	B 30, l-b 4, w 4, n-b 3	41
H. S. Cooper b Burd	82		
A. Hewetson c Lynch b Davy	121		708

THE LARGEST INNINGS, 920

THE LONGEST PARTNERSHIP ON RECORD, 605

RICKLING GREEN CRICKET CLUB v ORLEANS CLUB

Played at Rickling Green, August 4, 5, 1882

Rickling Green

Mr R. Spencer	1 2 1 1 1	b Paravicini	6
Mr W. Seabrook	3 2 1 1 3 1	c Spiro b Paravicini	11
Mr H. Taylor	3 1 1 2	c Paravicini b Clarke	7
Mr H. Sworder	2 3 4 1 1 1 3 1 1 2	c Sandeman b Paravicini	19
Mr S. C. Collin	1	c Paravicini b Clarke	1
Frank Silcock	2 3 2 1 2 1 2 1	st Ward b Clarke	14
Mr F. E. Rowe	1 3 2 3 2	c Thornton b Paravicini	11
Mr F. S. H. Judd		b Paravicini	0
Mr B. Spencer	3 2 1 2 4 1 2 1	b Clarke	16
Mr A. B. Taylor	2	b Paravicini	2
Mr A. N. Gilbey		not out	0
		B 6, l-b 1	7
			94

Orleans

Batsman		Runs
Mr C. I. Thornton ..	3 2 3 2 5 c B. Spencer b Sworder	15
Mr G. F. Vernon ...	1 4 2 1 1 1 3 1 1 4 1 1 1 1 2 4 1 1 4 3 4 2 3 1 1 2 1 4 1 1 1 3 1 3 1 1 1 1 1 1 1 4 4 3 2 2 1 1 4 1 1 1 1 1 1 1 1 1 3 1 3 2 2 1 6 4 3 1 6 3 1 1 1 1 1 4 1 2 2 2 4 4 3 1 1 3 1 1 3 1 1 4 1 3 1 1 1 1 3 3 3 1 3 3 2 3 1 1 1 2 2 1 3 1 1 4 2 3 2 3 3 2 1 1 2 2 1 2 1 1 1 1 2 1 1 b Silcock	259
Mr A. H. Trevor ...	3 1 1 1 2 3 2 1 1 2 1 4 5 1 2 3 3 2 1 2 2 3 1 3 1 1 2 1 2 2 1 3 3 3 1 1 1 4 5 1 1 4 1 3 1 2 2 4 4 1 3 3 3 3 5 4 1 3 5 2 1 3 1 3 3 2 1 1 1 1 1 1 4 6 4 1 1 3 1 3 1 1 1 6 1 2 1 3 1 1 3 1 2 1 4 1 1 4 1 1 1 3 6 3 4 4 1 1 1 1 3 1 1 1 4 1 4 5 1 3 2 1 1 4 1 1 2 2 1 2 1 3 2 3 2 2 3 2 1 1 2 3 2 3 3 2 2 6 1 1 2 1 1 4 1 1 1 c Rowe b Sworder	338
Mr P. J. de Paravicini	1 4 1 1 5 1 1 1 1 5 3 1 1 6 1 1 1 4 2 1 2 2 3 1 2 2 1 3 c Gilbey b Judd	58
Mr D. G. Spiro.....	3 2 3 1 2 3 1 1 1 1 3 2 1 4 1 1 1 1 1 1 4 1 2 4 1 4 b Silcock	50
Hon. E. W. H. Ward	1 4 1 2 2 5 2 run out	17
Mr J. C. Partridge...	3 1 1 3 2 1 1 1 1 1 1 2 5 1 2 1 3 1 4 3 4 2 2 4 3 3 1 3 4 1 2 1 4 2 1 4 1 3 1 3 2 1 not out	90
Mr F. Sandeman ...	2 b R. S. Spencer	2
Mr B. Posno	c Silcock b R. S. Spencer	0
Clarke............	1 2 1 1 1 2 2 4 1 2 2 1 3 1 c Sworder b A. B. Taylor	24
Mr W. Sanderson ...	1 1 1 1 4 1 1 1 1 1 2 1 1 3 1 2 b F. Silcock	23
	B 20, l-b 12, w 12	44
		920

Rickling Green Bowling

	Overs	Runs	Wkts		Overs	Runs	Wkts
Silcock	97	291	3	Judd	29	67	1
Sworder	51	145	2	Collins	3	16	—
R. S. Spencer	58	147	2	Seabrook	7	21	—
A. B. Taylor	30	106	1	H. A. Taylor	4	30	—
A. N. Gilbey	14	53	—				

How the Wickets fell

1. Thornton	20	4. Paravicini	727	7. Sandeman	779
2. Vernon	625	5. Ward	771	8. Posno	779
3. Trevor	645	6. Spiro	775	9. Clarke	827

10. Sanderson 920

THE HIGHEST INDIVIDUAL INNINGS ON RECORD

PRIORY PARK, CHICHESTER v WEST OF SCOTLAND

Played at Priory Park, Chichester, July 13, 14, 1885

Previous to the extraordinary performance of Mr J. S. Carrick in this match, Mr W. N. Roe's innings of 415 not out, for Emmanuel L.V.C. v Caius L.V.C., played at Cambridge, July 12, 1881, was the highest credited to any batsman, and the third innings which had reached 400 runs, Mr E. F. S. Tylecote with 404 not out, for Modern v Classical, Clifton College, May 26, 1868, and Mr W. G. Grace, with 400 not out, for the United South of England v Twenty-two of Grimsby, July 12, 13, 14, 1876, being the only other batsmen to achieve this distinction.

At the conclusion of the first day's play the score stood in this form:

West of Scotland

A. Thompson Esq. c Henley b Comber	112
J. S. Carrick Esq. not out	196
C. Craig Esq. not out	2
B 16, l-b 3, w 2	21
	(1 wkt) 331

Nine bowlers were tried, and no fewer than 326 runs were scored before the first wicket fell. Mr A. Thompson gave two chances in his patiently-played innings of 112, the chief hits of which were seven 4s, eight 3s and fourteen 2s.

When the game was resumed on the Tuesday, the score was increased to 398 when the second wicket fell, Mr Craig being caught by the bowler for 31. Mr J. Carrick jun., stayed until the total was 436, when he was bowled for 15. Mr A. Campbell then became Mr J. S. Carrick's partner, and another very long stand was made, 164 runs being added before a separation could be effected. This made the fourth wicket down and the total 600. Then Mr J. Andrews came in, and once more the bowlers were treated mercilessly. No other wicket fell, and when the stumps were drawn and the match abandoned Mr Andrews was not out 49 and Mr J. S. Carrick not out 419. Mr Carrick's off-driving and leg-hitting were quite the best ever seen on the Priory Park Ground. Although the ball more than once fell near a fieldsman it never came to hand, and he only gave two real chances, one at deep mid-on, the other at the wicket. He was batting altogether for eleven hours and a quarter during the two days, and up to the last seemed to be little fatigued. In his remarkable innings he hit one 8 (a magnificent square-leg hit), two 6s, two 5s, thirty 4s and thirty-four 3s. The ten bowlers tried during the match included James Lillywhite, the old Sussex county player, Andrews, Henley, Comber, Heasman, Farr, Austin, Norris, Hooper and Cochrane, and the 695 runs scored from the bat were obtained from 336.2 overs (1,306 balls). At the conclusion of the match Mr Carrick was carried to the dressing-room amid immense cheering, and was afterwards photographed. The total of 745 is the second highest ever made for four wickets, it being exceeded only in the match between Orleans Club and Rickling Green in August, 1882, when the fourth batsman was dismissed with the score 727, the total of the innings being 920, Mr A. H. Trevor making 338 and Mr G. F. Vernon 259, the pair putting on 605 runs for the second wicket.

West of Scotland

A. Thompson Esq. c Henley b Comber	112
J. S. Carrick Esq. not out	419
C. Craig Esq. c and b Heasman	31
J. Carrick jun. Esq. b Henley	15
A. Campbell Esq. c Comber Lillywhite	69
J. Andrews Esq. not out	49
B 38, l-b 6, w 6	50
	(4 wkts) 745

W. Thompson Esq., C. T. Haddes Esq., J. F. Dunlop, Esq., J. Craig Esq. and Butler did not bat.

A RECORD – 470 RUNS FOR NO WICKET

BECKENHAM v BEXLEY

Played at Beckenham, August 1, 1885

Bexley won the toss, and going in first, scored a total of 77, the side batting one short. The team included Mr J. Shuter, captain of the Surrey eleven, who was bowled without scoring, but who, in 1884, in conjunction with T. Ashdown, scored 404 runs for no wicket for Bexley v The Emeriti, and thus established a record.

Beckenham began their innings at half-past two with Mr Leslie Wilson, of the Kent eleven, and Mr W. S. Wyld, who has appeared for Surrey; and when time was called at half-past six the two batsmen were still together, having in four hours put on no fewer than 470 runs. During their long partnership there was scarcely a fluky hit, and only four very difficult chances were given.

L. Wilson not out	246
W. G. Wyld not out	203
B 16, l-b 1, w 4	21
	(no wkt) 470

THE HIGHEST INDIVIDUAL SCORE ON RECORD

CLIFTON COLLEGE – CLARKE'S v NORTH TOWN

A Junior house match at Clifton College, begun on Thursday, June 22, 1899, and completed on the following Wednesday, is noteworthy for having produced the greatest score known to have been made by a single player in a game of any description. The hero of the occasion, A. E. J. Collins, was batting for six hours and fifty minutes, his innings being continued in unequal instalments during five days. His hits included a 6, four 5s, thirty-one 4s, thirty-three 3s and 146 2s. The previous best score was that of A. E. Stoddart, who made 485 for the Hampstead Club against the Stoics in 1886. It is remarkable that it was in a Clifton College game that E. F. S. Tylecote made his score of 404 in 1868.

Clarke's

Collins not out	628
Champion c Monteath b Rendall	27
Gilbert b Crew	9
Sudely c Davis b Sainsbury	8
Sheriff b Crew	6
Galway b Crew	11
Whittey c and b Monteath	42
Spooner b Monteath	0
Leake b Monteath	32
Raine b Monteath	14
Redfern c Fuller-Eberle b Crew	13
Extras	46
	836

North Town

Monteath run out	4	– c and b Gilbert	4
Crew b Collins	10	– c Champion b Gilbert	4
Fedden b Collins	10	– lbw b Collins	1
Sainsbury lbw b Collins	0	– lbw b Collins	13
Barstow b Sheriff	32	– b Collins	0
Fuller-Eberle c Galway b Collins	8	– b Sheriff	15
Rendall b Sudely	9	– b Collins	8
Lindrea b Collins	1	– b Sheriff	11
Ratcliff not out	6	– c Champion b Sheriff	0
Robinson b Collins	0	– c Raine b Sheriff	0
Davies b Collins	4	– not out	0
Extras	3	Extras	5
	87		61

UMPIRES AND WHERE TO FIND THEM

"Their decision should in every case be strictly obeyed, or there will be no pleasure in the game." – Selkirk's "Guide to the Cricket Ground".

F. Bell, Cambridge.
G. Brockwell, Lower Clapton, E.
T. Burlinson, Bradford, Yorkshire.
G. Butler, Trent Bridge Ground, Nottingham.
G. Chatterton, Sheffield, Yorkshire.
S. Dakin, Cambridge.
W. H. Fryer, Coxheath, Linton, Staplehurst, Kent.
Daniel Hayward, Cambridge.
W. Inwood, Tuffnell Park Ground, Holloway, N.
George Lee, Lord's Cricket Ground, St John's Wood Road, NW.
W. Lightowler, Malton, Yorkshire.
W. H. Luck, Tunbridge Wells, Kent.
G. Martin, Leigh, Tunbridge Wells, Kent.
W. Mortlock, Railway Terminus, Waterloo Road, S.
W. Mudie, Surrey Ground, The Oval, Kennington, S.
H. Royston, Lord's Cricket Ground, St John's Wood Road, NW.
Thos Sherman, Mitcham, Surrey.
John Thewlis, Lascelles Hall, near Huddersfield, Yorkshire.
R. Thoms, 31 Princess Terrace, Regent's Park Road, NW.
Henry Wright, Sheffield, Yorkshire.

All the above cricketers are reliable men as to a thorough practical knowledge of the game, and a large majority of them are of extended experience in umpiring; in fact, one of them, Robert Thoms, has in the course of the past eighteen years umpired in more than 1,000 matches, having done duty in Middlesex, Surrey, some MCC, Southgate, Islington Albion (more than 100), Incogniti (over 100), and other matches. In the burning hot season of 1868 Thoms was umpiring every cricketing day of seven successive weeks, and altogether that season he professionally answered the "How's that?" query in no fewer than 83 matches. The experience of such an umpire – the cricket curiosities that must have cropped up in so lengthened a career – his opinions on the working of the laws and of the play of the many eminent cricketers who have taken part in the matches in which he has stood – would, if gathered together, form an interesting cricket book under the title of Recollections of an Umpire who has officiated in more than 1,000 Matches.

ALL THE 20 WICKETS, 1872

Mr C. Absolon – an old and liberal supporter of Metropolitan cricket and cricketers – was the grey-haired hero of this very successful bowling feat, i.e.: – having a hand in the downfall of all the twenty wickets; he bowled ten, two hit wicket, six were caught from his bowling, and he caught out the remaining two. The match made famous by this bowling of Mr Absolon's was Wood Green v United Willesden, played at Wood Green, July 21, 1872. Wood Green won by an innings and 45 runs.

United Willesden

Morley b Absolon	1	– b Absolon	6
Williams b Absolon	0	– c Absolon b Fluker	7
Skipper hit wkt b Absolon	0	– b Absolon	2
Parfitt c Thomas b Absolon	0	– b Absolon	7
Bickwell c Thomas b Absolon	9	– b Absolon	1
Bishop c Absolon b Wheeler	5	– c Chamberlain b Absolon	0
Digby b Absolon	6	– c Ringrose b Absolon	1
Lawrence not out	0	– b Absolon	0
Howard b Absolon	0	– b Absolon	2
Morris hit wkt b Absolon	2	– not out	1
Emerson c Fluker b Absolon	0	– c Wheeler b Absolon	0
Extra	1	Extras	4
	24		31

Mr C. Absolon again: In the United North Eleven v Mr Page's 22 match played at Tuffnell Park last August, Mr C. Absolon bowled W. H. Iddison, John Smith, and Thomas Hayward with three successively delivered balls, and bowled another – Luke Greenwood – with the fifth ball. In that innings of the U. N. E. Mr Absolon's bowling totall'd as follows:

Overs	Mdns	Runs	Wkts	
12.1	5	17	8	(6 bowled)

Summing up Mr Absolon's bowling in 1872, *Bell's Life* of the 2nd of November last states: – "Mr Absolon is entitled to seven hats for taking three wickets in three consecutive balls on seven different occasions. *Bell's Life* also states Mr Absolon scored 1109 runs, and took 519 wickets last season!!!" What makes all this the more remarkable is, Mr Absolon is a welter in weight and a veteran in years.

BITS OF BATTING IN 1873

GOOD FORM

Mr I. D. Walker	13 not out 40 not out	For MCC and Ground v Surrey Club and Ground	In one week of last May.
	64 bowled 42 not out	For Middlesex v Yorkshire	

THREE 6s – ONE 140 YARDS FROM HIT TO PITCH

Mr W. G. Grace. – In an "extra" match between the USEE and eighteen Gentlemen of Edinburgh, last May, Mr W. G. Grace scored 47 runs, making "three splendid hits out of the ground for 6 each – one pitching 140 yards".

AN INNINGS OF 403 RUNS – 170 RUNS IN 65 MINUTES

"A Clean Drive for 10"

The match wherein all this occurred was RE's v RMA, at Woolwich, last August. The 403 runs were made by the RE Eleven. the 170 runs in sixty-five minutes were hit by Mr Renny-Tailyour and Mr H. W. Smith (RE's), and it was Mr H. W. Smith who made "the clean drive for 10". (Mr Tailyour made 137; Mr Smith, 100.)

FOUR BROTHERS, 299 RUNS – 201 RUNS FOR FIRST WICKET

In Mr Penn's annual match played at The Cedars, Lee, Kent, last July, four of the brothers Penn made 299 runs. Mr W. Penn and Mr Frank Penn started the batting; they made 201 runs before the first wicket fell, Mr W. Penn being then out for exactly 100 runs. At 248, Mr Frank Penn was out for 114l a third Mr Penn made 48; and the fourth brother, 37.

80 RUNS IN 40 MINUTES

In the St. John's Wood v Eastbourne match, at Eastbourne, last July, Mr G. W. Creaton made 80 runs in forty minutes for St. John's Wood. Three times did Mr Creaton hit the ball clear out of the ground.

98 AND 90 NOT OUT IN ONE MATCH

Mr G. Podmore made 98 and 90 not out in Residents v Visitors match at Eastbourne, last Autumn.

REMARKABLE FALL OF WICKETS

In a match played at Scarborough, August 6 and 7, 1875, between twelve of Scarborough and Mr Leatham's team, the wickets in Scarborough's second innings fell as follows:

1/11 2/12 3/12 4/12 5/12 6/12 7/12 8/12 9/12 10/12 11/16

Mr Craig's bowling took nine wickets for three runs.

FIRST MAN IN – NOT OUT BOTH INNINGS

Mr J. M. Cotterill. – In the Brighton v Horsham match, played at Horsham, August 30 and 31, Mr J. M. Cotterill was first man in for Brighton, and took his bat out both innings, the published scores chronicling:

Mr J. M. Cotterill not out .... 95 – not out 107

(The totals of the two Brighton innings were 183 and 199.)

INDIVIDUAL INNINGS OF THREE FIGURES HIT IN 1876

The following innings have been compiled from the public papers and private sources. To the papers the compiler feels gratefully indebted, and as gratefully obliged to those gentlemen who so courteously forwarded him requested information.

Over 450 innings of three figures were hit in 1876; to chronicle all that large number in this little book would be absurd; the following have been selected as those possessing most interest to the cricketing public:

OVER 200

Inns	How out	Batsman	Match	Where
400	not out	Mr W. G. Grace	for USEE v 22 of Grimsby	Grimsby
344	caught	Mr W. G. Grace	for MCC v Kent	Canterbury
327	not out	Dr E. M. Grace	for Thornbury v Chewton-Keynsham	Thornbury
318	not out	Mr W. G. Grace	for Gloucestershire v Yorkshire	Cheltenham
307	not out	Mr F. W. Wright	for The Masters v College and Schools	Eastbourne
291	caught	Mr H. Ross	for Shanklin v Ryde	Shanklin
266	caught	Mr G. M. Kenney	for 2nd XI Dublin University v Rathmines School	Ireland
*241		Mr R. B. Stewart	for Lansdown v Chewton-Keynsham	
*226		Wheeler	for Penge v Bromley	
218	not out	Mr W. Jamieson	for Littleburne v Canterbury Citizens	Canterbury
217	not out	Mr F. Townsend	for Clifton Club v Thornbury	Clifton
213	caught	Mr G. F. Grace	for Knole Park v Incogniti	Knole Park
211	bowled	Mr F. Townsend	for Clifton Club v Wells	Durdham Downs
*211		Mr E. O. H. Wilkinson	for 60th Rifles v Swanmore	
206	run out	Mr W. Francis	for Devonshire Park Club v East Sussex	Eastbourne
206	bowled	Mr C. P. Lewis	for Jesus College v Queen's College	Oxford
205	not out	Mr W. Gilbert	for England v Cambridge University	Cambridge

Inns	How out	Batsman	Match	Where
202	not out	Mr D. W. J. Duncan	for Southampton v Swanmore Park	Swanmore
*202	not out	Capt. Welch, RMA	for Officers v The Rest	
201	not out	Mr E. Sainsbury ...	for Corsham v Lansdown	Bath
*200		Mr E. O. H. Wilkinson, (60th Rifles)	for Officers v Rest 3rd Battalion	

* (We are indebted to the *Sportsman* of November 9, for all those innings prefixed *.)

The above twenty-one innings represent 5,212 runs, 2,597 of those runs having been made in ten not out innings. Mr W. G. Grace made 1,062 in three innings, two not outs.

ITEMS IN CONNECTION WITH THE ABOVE

Mr W. G. Grace's 400 not out. – Respecting this wonderful innings a correspondent sent the following particulars to *Bell's Life*: – "Mr W. Grace's score was made as follows: – four 6s, twenty-one 4s, six 3s, fifty-eight 2s, and 158 singles. The bowling was up to the average, the wickets perfection; but Mr Grace's play was acknowledged by all present (including the members of the South team) to be such as they never before witnessed. He gave no chance whatever on the first and second days. On the third day he gave two easy chances – one to short slip, the other to long leg; but he had then scored 350 runs. Altogether, he was at the wickets about thirteen and a half hours, and had no less than fifteen bowlers opposed to him".

It may be added here that on the close of the first day's play the USE score was 215, two wickets down, Mr W. G. Grace not out 140. On the close of the second day's play the score stood at 537, three wickets down! Mr W. G. Grace not out 314; and the innings concluded on the third day at 675, Mr W. G. Grace (first man in) not out 400.

Dr E. M. Grace's 327 not out was chronicled in *The Sportsman* as follows: – "This match was commenced at Thornbury on Wednesday morning, and was signalised by Dr E. M. Grace remaining at the wickets throughout the day, and bringing out his bat for the big contribution of 327 runs to his own account. This not out innings included five 6s, fifty 4s, eleven 3s, seventeen 2s, and thirty singles".

INNINGS OF 500 RUNS AND UPWARDS

The season of 1886, though in respect to big innings it may not be quite up to the record of the previous year, shows many cases of heavy scoring, and the list given below will be found to contain the two highest innings hitherto recorded against the Australians – namely, the 501 by Surrey at The Oval, on July 31, and the innings of Lord Londesborough's Eleven, who at Scarborough, on September 3, made the great total, for a first-class match, of 558. The highest score of the season was the 813 made on August 4 by Hampstead against the Stoics; and there is one performance which, although not reaching the fifth hundred, approaches it so closely that it demands notice, especially as it is the record of the year in inter-county matches, this being the 494 made against Derbyshire at The Oval, on August 6, by Surrey, who, in contrast to this, are also credited with the smallest innings for a first-class county, in the 26 made by them against

Leicestershire on July 8. The following is the list as given by a sporting paper, the club first named being the one making the score:

813	Hampstead v Stoics, August 4.
658	I. Zingari v Bullingdon, June 16.
†643	Eastbourne (Second Eleven) v Nunhead, July 5.
†635	Holloway College Old Boys v Tufnell Park, August 5.
631	Buckhurst Hill v Chelsea United, June 14.
618	Shorncliffe Garrison v Emeriti, June 26.
618	Clifton v Lansdown, June 26.
603	Free Foresters v Shoebury Garrison, June 26.
593	Trinity College, Cambridge v Clare College, June 3.
577	United Services v Parsees, July 17.
558	Lord Londesborough's England Eleven v Australians, September 3.
†544	Brighton Brunswick v Stoics, July 2.
§537	Streatham v Leatherhead, June 26.
530	Cambridge Quidnuncs v Royal Artillery, July 17.
‡524	Perambulators v Etceteras (Oxford), June 18.
*514	The Mote v Royal Marines, June 16.
513	St. John's College LVC v Pembroke College LVC, August 17.
512	Mr H. Lyon's Eleven v Mr J. S. Walter's Eleven, August 5.
†508	South Lancashire Regiment v Worcestershire Regiment, June 17.
506	Incogniti v Rochester, June 16.
501	Surrey v Australians, July 31.

* For four wickets. † Five wickets. ‡ Six wickets. § Seven wickets.

CRICKETERS' FUND FRIENDLY SOCIETY

The above Society, which was founded in 1857 and re-organised in 1864, provides for the relief of professional cricketers who from accident, illness, or old age are incapacitated from following their profession, and also for the temporary relief of the widows and children who have been left destitute by the death of any members. At the beginning of 1886 the funds of the society were in a very impoverished state owing to the very heavy demands made upon it by members for sick pay in the previous year, but thanks to the generosity of the MCC, and to the strenuous efforts of Lord Harris (president) and Mr V. E. Walker, the society has been placed upon a much firmer basis, and saved from drawing upon its small invested capital. At the annual general meeting of the society held at St. John's Tavern, Lord's, on July 12th, 1886, Lord Harris (who took the chair for the first time) proposed a scheme for soliciting support from the individual members of the MCC and other cricket-loving gentlemen, which scheme has been carried into effect with most beneficial results. At this meeting it was decided to lower the sick pay from two pounds to thirty shillings during the cricket season, and from a pound to fifteen shillings during the winter months. The superannuation allowance was also lowered from ten shillings to six shillings a week. The Cricketers' Fund now numbers nearly a hundred members.

Contributions will be thankfully received by Lord Harris, Mr V. E. Walker, or Thomas Hearne, at Lord's Cricket Ground.

EXTRAORDINARY MATCHES

SIXTEEN OF THE COUNTRY ROUND SHEFFIELD v SIXTEEN OF SHEFFIELD

On the Hyde Park Ground at Sheffield, August 13, 1838 (16 a side). Each player was sixty years of age, or upwards. The united ages of the Country side was 1010, and the Town side 1026.

Sixteen of the Country round Sheffield

William Shaw (65) b Buxton	6
William Loukes (63) b Sheldon	12
Joseph Glossop (61) run out	63
William Chapman (63) b Sheldon	7
John Goodison (60) c Archer	16
E. Radcliffe (61) c Archer	4
George Innocent (62) b Hague	0
Timothy Bancroft (62) b Hague	4
Benjamin Oates (64) b Archer	16
Stephen Rose (60) b Hardesty	12
George Handley (64) b Hardesty	4
George Wood (60) b Sheldon	8
John Oates (66) b Bradshaw	9
William Rusby (67) c Archer	1
Joseph Twible (68) run out	0
William Williamson (64) c Slott	0
B 3, w 3	6
	168

Sixteen of Sheffield

William Oxley (67) b Radcliffe	1
John Archer (63) b Radcliffe	10
Samuel Memmott (64) b Radcliffe	3
James Buxton (61) b Chapman	2
William Bradshaw (63), b Radcliffe	11
James Dearman (67) b Radcliffe	2
Joseph Sheldon (60) st Goodison	2
Thomas Dearman (69) c Chapman	0
John Stacey (66) b Radcliffe	22
William Hague (62) b Radcliffe	4
Joseph Wharton (65) b Radcliffe	5
J. Hinchliffe (63) b Chapman	1
George Hardesty (60) b Radcliffe	12
John Castleton (69) not out	6
William Hoyland (67) b Goodison	0
B. Slott (60) b Goodison	5
B 10	10
	96

Unfinished. In the second innings of the Country, Glossop scored 20 (not out), Loukes 10, and six others had an innings, making the score 67.

2nd ROYAL SURREY MILITIA v SHILLINGLEE

The following extraordinary coincidence of getting eleven players out without scoring occurred at Shillinglee Park, Sussex, the seat of the Earl of Winterton, August 13, 1855:

2nd Royal Surrey Militia

Private Dudley b Challen, jun.	0	– c Sadler b Challen jr.	7
Private Plumridge b Heather	0	– b Randall	0
E. Hartnell Esq. b Heather	0	– run out	15
A. Marshall Esq. b Challen jun.	0	– b Randall	23
Private Ayling b Challen jun.	0	– not out	9
Lieut Pontifex b Heather	0	– b Challen jun.	6
Corporal Heyes b Heather	0	– c Challen jun. b Randall	10
Lieut Ball b Heather	0	– b Heather	0
Major Ridley not out	0	– run out	0
Sergeant Ayling run out	0	– c Sadler b Piggott	1
Private Newberry b Heather	0	– b Heather	14
Extra	0	B 5, w 15, n-b 1	21
	0		106

Shillinglee

Earl Winterton b Dudley	5
Mr William Randall b Heyes	17
D. Heather c Hartnell b Heyes	9
Challen jun. c Hartnell b Heyes	8
F. Piggott Esq. b Heyes	0
Challen sen. c Dudley b Heyes	15
J. Sadler Esq. c Ball b Hartnell	7
Lord Turnour b Hartnell	7
T. Sadler Esq. b Hartnell	1
G. Taylor b Hartnell	7
J. Newman not out	7
B4, w 5	9
	92

UNITED ALL ENGLAND ELEVEN v EIGHTEEN OF THE LANDSDOWN CLUB

At Sydenham Field, Bath, June 8, 9, 10, 1865

The United Eleven

G. M. Kelson Esq. b E. M. Grace	11	c and b E. M. Grace	23
J. Thewlis c E. M. Grace b W. G. Grace	26	b H. Grace	1
G. Atkinson c Muttlebury b W. G. Grace	8	b E. M. Grace	1
J. Grundy lbw b E. M. Grace	5	c and b E. M. Grace	4
R. Carpenter b W. G. Grace	9	st Malet b E. M. Grace	22
F. Pryor c Morres b W. G. Grace	0	c Cassan b H. Grace	1
A. Shaw c W. G. Grace b E. M. Grace	13	st Malet b E. M. Grace	6
G. Wootton c E. M. Grace b H. Grace	15	c and b E. M. Grace	12
L. Greenwood b H. Grace	4	not out	13
G. Mason Esq. b H. Grace	3	c Northey b E. M. Grace	0
S. Biddulph not out	0	run out	0
B 3, w 1, n-b 1	5	B 1, l-b 1, w 2	4
	99		87

Eighteen of the Lansdown Club

E. M. Grace Esq. c Kelson b Greenwood	121
A. Pontifex Esq. c Greenwood b Atkinson	10
H. Grace Esq. b Grundy	8
F. Holworthy Esq. (retired unwell)	9
C. G. Wynch Esq. b Atkinson	26
J. Hunter Esq. st Biddulph b Atkinson	6
Capt. Northey b Wootton	18
W. G. Grace Esq. c and b Atkinson	11
W. Style Esq. st Biddulph b Carpenter	20
A. Malet Esq. b Wootton	21
H. W. Barber Esq. b Wootton	4
E. Morres Esq. b Wootton	0
C. H. Fryer Esq. st Biddulph b Carpenter	21
T. Sainsbury Esq. b Carpenter	4
G. Muttlebury Esq. b Wootton	5
E. Cassan Esq. b Carpenter	2
F. Paget Esq. not out	2
W. Attfield Esq. b Wootton	0
B1, l-b 10	11
	299

The Eighteen winning in one innings and 113 runs.

Umpires: J. Dean, sen., and J. Wisden.

ONE LEG v ONE ARM

At Islington, April 22, 23, 1867

One Leg

Randall b Aldridge	1	– b Redfern	3
Murphy run out	0	– b Neal	0
Birchmore c and b Aldridge	46	– b Neal	62
W. Hammond b Aldridge	3	– b Neal	1
Wells b Neale	11	– b Neal	4
W. Brett b Neal	3	– c Worsam b Neal	28
Crabtree c Worsam b Neal	5	– c Worsam b Redfern	0
Barrs c Worsam b Aldridge	8	– c Worsam b Redfern	5
Hackley b Aldridge	5	– b Redfern	4
Butler not out	0	– b Redfern	0
Oliver b Neal	1	– c Worsam b Neal	0
Heath b Aldridge	0	– not out	15
B 1, l-b 5	6	B 5, w 5	10
	89		132

One Arm

R. Smith c Birchmore b Barrs	12	– b Brett	11
W. S. Smith run out	2	– not out	0
B. Neal b Crabtree	12	– b Brett	5
Redfern not out	59	– b Birchmore	9
Aldridge b Crabtree	26	– c and b Crabtree	3
Gurney b Crabtree	4	– b Crabtree	2
Boucher b Wells	5	– c Hackley b Crabtree	7
Hindley b Weels	0		
Worsam b Crabtree	8	– b Crabtree	16
M'Crossen b Wells	5	– b Brett	1
Hines b Butler	1		
Harris b Butler	0	– b Crabtree	2
B 8, w 1	9	B 1, l-b 1, n-b 1	3
	143		59

Drawn.

Umpires: W. Inwood and C. Hall.

NORTH OF THE THAMES v SOUTH OF THE THAMES

At Canterbury, August 3, 4, 5, 1868

North of the Thames

Rev. J. McCormick b E. M. Grace	137	– c Charlwood b W. G. Grace	27
G. Summers c Pooley b Lillywhite	0	– c Willsher b Lillywhite	3
C. Coward c E. M. Grace b Lipscombe	46	– c E. M. Grace b Lillywhite	4
C. F. Buller Esq. b Lipscombe	4	– b Willsher	34
T. Hearne c Jupp b E. M. Grace	29	– st Pooley b W. G. Grace	4
R. A. Mitchell Esq. b Willsher	22	– b Lipscombe	90
T. Plumb c W. G. Grace b E. M. Grace	1	– b W. G. Grace	67
H. N. Tennent Esq. b Willsher	0	– not out	45
J. Grundy c Pooley b E. M. Grace	2	– c Lillywhite b Lipscombe	0
G. Howitt c Pooley b E. M. Grace	1	– c Pooley b Lipscombe	2
G. Wootton not out	1	– thrown out by Lipscombe	0
B 4, l-b 5	9	B 4, l-b 5, w 1	10
	252		286

South of the Thames

W. G. Grace Esq. b Wootton	130	– not out	102
H. Jupp b Wootton	4	– c Plumb b Grundy	9
T. Humphrey st Plumb b Wootton	1	– c Coward b Howitt	35
James Lillywhite b Wootton	0	– b Wootton	5
H. Charlwood b Wootton	14	– c Mitchell b Hearne	27
E. M. Grace Esq. st Plumb b Wootton	13	– b Howitt	0
G. Griffith c Howitt b Wootton	21	– c Mitchell b Hearne	6
E. Pooley b Wootton	3	– b Hearne	0
C. Payne c Plumb b Hearne	31	– c Grundy b Hearne	7
E. Willsher not out	33	– b Howitt	0
R. Lipscomb Esq. st Plumb b M'Cormick	17	– run out	2
B 11, l-b 5, w 1	17	L-b 3, w 1	4
	284		196

The North winning by 58 runs.

Umpires: Mortlock and Fryer.

RIGHT HANDED v LEFT HANDED OF ENGLAND

Played at Lord's, May 9, 10, 1870

This was the opening match of the 84th season of The Marylebone Club. So brilliant an array of the cricketing talent of the country on no prior occasion appeared in an opening match at Lord's, the match being moreover interesting from its not having been played since 1835, and for its being the first match Carpenter, Hayward, and Smith had played in at Lord's since 1866. The weather was bright, but nippingly cold for May. The "Left" were comparatively weak as batsmen, and were without a professed wicket-keeper, so they were defeated by an innings and 8 runs. In less than one hour and a half the first innings of "Left" was played out. For the "Right", John Smith hit very finely for 45; Mr Grace played well for 35; careful and scientific cricket was played by Carpenter; Hayward was bowled off his thigh, and Daft off his pad; Hearne took his bat out for 26, and the innings ended for 185, or 112 on. The second innings of the "Left" is noteworthy for a superb left hand c and b (it came back very hot) by Daft, a well played 21 by Rylott (a right hand hitter), and a remarkably good display of effective defence and free, clean, hard hitting by Killick of Sussex, whose 55 (highest innings in the match) won him the hearty applause of the "Right" Eleven; a higher compliment could not well be paid him. At one o'clock on the second day the "Right" had won in a canter. (Howitt's absence on the second day was caused by a domestic bereavement.)

The Left

James Lillywhite b Grace	26	– b Alfred Shaw	7
H. Killick b Alfred Shaw	0	– c Jupp b Grace	55
Rylott b Alfred Shaw	8	– c and b Daft	21
Griffith c Carpenter b Grace	11	– c Buller b Daft	0
Wootton run out	2	– c Jupp b Grace	10
Emmett b Grace	12	– run out	6
Willsher st Biddulph b Alfred Shaw	0	– b Grace	0
Martin c Jupp b Grace	0	– b Alfred Shaw	2
West b Grace	7	– b Alfred Shaw	0
Howitt not out	0	– absent	0
J. C. Shaw b Grace	0	– not out	0
B 5, l-b 2	7	B 1, l-b 2	3
	73		104

The Right

W. G. Grace Esq. b Wootton	35
Jupp c Killick b J. C. Shaw	8
Richard Daft b Emmett	7
T. Hayward b J. C. Shaw	3
Carpenter c Griffith b Howitt	19
John Smith (Cambridge) b Howitt	45
C. F. Buller Esq. b Wootton	11
T. Hearne not out	26
Alfred Shaw b J. C. Shaw	6
Walter Price hit wkt b Emmett	7
Biddulph b J. C. Shaw	0
B 15, l-b 2, n-b 1	18
	185

Right Hand Bowling

	Overs	Mdns	Runs	Wkts	Overs	Mdns	Runs	Wkts
A. Shaw	21	6	42	3	25.3	12	55	3
Mr W. Grace	20.1	7	24	6	27	11	44	3
Hearne					8	4	7	—
Daft					7	3	15	2

Left Hand Bowling

	Overs	Mdns	Runs	Wkts
J. C. Shaw	36.1	11	49	4
Wootton	29	10	56	2
Emmett	20	8	34	2
Howitt	14	3	28	2

Umpires: Grundy and Royston.

(The First Right v Left match was played at (old) Lord's in 1790.)

AMERICANS v ENGLISHMEN

Played at Germantown, Philadelphia, October 14, 15, 1870

Wilkes' *Spirit of the Times* (from which paper this score, etc., is extracted) stated – "The match was arranged by Mr Rastall, of the Germantown Club, and grew out of a desire on the part of the Young America Club to try the strength of their Eleven against the strongest Eleven of English resident Cricketers which could be gathered to meet them, and not from any boastful or vainglorious spirit of special superiority." The American Eleven were all Amateurs; the Englishmen were the best Amateurs and Professionals selected from the New York and Philadelphia Clubs. The report in *The Spirit* further stated that – "When the last run was scored and the victory was assured, the Englishmen among the crowd of spectators became highly elated, and in their enthusiasm they carried McIntyre off the field." The Englishmen won by nine wickets.

Young America

H. Newhall b Rogerson	45	– c Hargreaves b McIntyre	3
Bussier run out	1	– c Byron b Norley	7
G. Newhall b Rogerson	12	– c Hargreaves b Norley	0
Large c Hargreaves b McIntyre	10	– c Byron b Norley	7
C. Newhall c and b McIntyre	0	– c McIntyre b Norley	5
D. Newhall c Carpenter b McIntyre	24	– b Rogerson	3
Pease c McIntyre b Norley	0	– not out	16
Johns b McIntyre	2	– b Rogerson	0
R. Newhall not out	17	– b Rogerson	5
Stocken b McIntyre	1	– lbw b Norley	17
Baxter c Hargreaves b Rogerson	3	– run out	2
B 2, l-b 3 w 1	6	L-b 4	4
	121		69

Englishmen

Martin McIntyre b C. Newhall	63 – not out	31
Bance c Large b C. Newhall	8 – c and b D. Newhall	2
Eastwood b C. Newhall	26 – not out	8
Hargreaves b C. Newhall	1	
Pearson c Large b D. Newhall	7	
F. Norley b C. Newhall	10	
Rastall c Large b C. Newhall	9	
Byron c G. Newhall b C. Newhall	0	
Rogerson c Bussier b C. Newhall	3	
Keller not out	8	
Carpenter b C. Newhall	7	
L-b 1, w 1, n-b 3	5	L-b 3, w 1 4
	147	45

English Bowling

	Overs	Mdns	Runs	Wkts	Overs	Mdns	Runs	Wkts
F. Norley	26	12	34	1	18	6	20	5
M. McIntyre	24	7	47	5	22	14	15	1
Rogerson	19	6	34	3	13	6	26	3
Pearson					2	—	4	—

American Bowling

	Overs	Mdns	Runs	Wkts	Overs	Mdns	Runs	Wkts
C. Newhall	43.3	18	55	9	11	5	17	—
D. Newhall	39	14	78	1	10.1	1	24	1
Stocken	4	—	9	—				

Umpires: J. Smith and Hunt.

THE GREAT RUN GETTING MATCH

GENTLEMEN OF THE SOUTH v PLAYERS OF THE SOUTH

Played at The Oval, June 29, 30, July 1, 1871

1139 runs were scored in this affair, the largest number by 3 ever made in a match. Moreover, it was the closest contested "thousand runs" match ever played, as after three days' fine and hard hitting (at the rate of 380 runs per day), the match was won by 3 runs only – 3 out of 1139!! The weather and the wickets were in splendid form, and the attendances during the three days great, so many at 7000 visitors being present on that memorable Saturday afternoon. Both sides commenced their scoring in unexpectedly mild form, as the first Players' wicket (Jupp's) went down with their score at 3 only, and the first Gentlemen's (Mr W. Grace's) at 7. In the Players' first innings, Pooley was fifty minutes at wickets for 16 runs, Lillywhite made 11 runs in thirteen minutes, and Charlwood a brilliantly hit 77 in one hour and thirty-five minutes. The Players' innings had been started to the bowling of Mr Absolom and Mr Thornton's old-fashioned fast "18 bounders". The Gentlemen's first innings was started to the bowling of Southerton and fast underhands (innocents) by H. H. Stephenson. In the Gentlemen's first innings Mr

Yardley and Mr Hadow hit the score from 7 for one wicket to 106 for two, when Mr Yardley was stumped for 60. Mr Fryer, Mr Walker and Mr Hadow had severally left when the score was at 151 for five wickets; then it was, at twenty minutes to seven, Mr Thornton went in. He had made a 4 and a single from Southerton when Stephenson's underhands were again tried; the second of these Mr Thornton drove into the country for 6, the third he sent to leg for 4, and when – by one 6, four 4s, four 2s and a single – he had made 31 runs in sixteen minutes, he was superbly caught out by Jupp close by the visitors; thereupon play ceased for that day, the Gentlemen's score at 187 for six wickets – Mr G. F. Grace not out 13.

At noon on Friday, Mr F. Grace and Mr Howell resumed the innings. They increased the score to 265, when Mr Howell hit the ball on; at 287 a splendid catch – so very low down was the ball taken – by Richard Humphrey at mid-on settled Mr Strachan; and at 292 a capital catch at leg by Thomas Humphrey ended Mr G. F. Grace's innings for a remarkably patient and very correctly played 55, so many as 153 runs having been made during young Mr Grace's stay. At twenty minutes past three the innings was over for 323, or 150 on. Then when a couple of the "bounders" had found their way to R. Humphrey's and young Phillips' wickets, and but 29 runs had been scored in the Players' second innings, the match appeared quite a little "Sedan" affair for the Gentlemen; but then Charlwood and Jupp increased the score by 74 runs, when a splendid, a grand right-hand catch at short-leg by Mr Strachan settled Charlwood, and the third wicket fell at 103. Pooley was next man in, and thereabouts Jupp was missed at point by Mr W. Grace, who had the ball but dropped it. From thence Jupp (who had scored 42) and Pooley so rapidly piled up the runs, that by five minutes after six the 200 was up; but a quarter of an hour later on Jupp was "lbw" for 97 – a great innings that included seven 4s and three magnificent hits (two drives and one to leg) for 5 each. Jupp was first man in at twenty-five minutes to four and fourth out at twenty past six with the score at 224. In the succeeding forty minutes Pooley and Lillywhite added 54 runs to the score, as when play ceased at seven o'clock the Players' second innings shaped as follows: –

Four wickets down; 278 runs scored. Pooley not out 93; Lillywhite not out 18. (In Friday's cricket so many as 414 runs were made, but only eight wickets fell.)

On Saturday the pavilion seats were crammed, and the ground thronged by about 7000 of the most excitable visitors that ever congregated on The Oval; and from seven minutes to twelve, when play was renewed, until ten minutes to seven, when this wonderful match was so wonderfully finished by Southerton, an especially strong dose of exciting cricket was played. From 278, the not outs of Friday had hit the score to 303, when Lillywhite lunged out at one from Mr Absolom that clean bowled him; thereupon, with the score at five for 303, Thomas Humphrey went in and stayed the other five men out. At 338 Pooley was run out; at 341 Stephenson was stumped; at 345 Silcock was caught out at wicket; and at 348 Southerton was "bowled by a bounder". Then the last man, Willsher (unwell), with Lillywhite to run his hits, went in, and by steady play he and Humphrey made 50 runs for the last wicket, when Willsher was bowled for 20, and T. Humphrey took his bat out for 40, the innings having finished at five minutes past two for 398, so many as 262 of those runs having been hit by "the Surrey three" – Jupp, Pooley and T. Humphrey. The 125 was Pooley's first three figure innings on The Oval; it included a 5 to leg and nine 4s. Nine of the eleven Gentlemen bowled, and their fielding on Saturday – especially of Mr W. Grace at point and Mr Strachan at leg and cover-point – was simply splendid. With 249 to win, the second innings of the Gentlemen was, at three minutes past three, commenced by Mr W. Grace and Mr Walker to the bowling of Southerton and Lillywhite. (Illness had necessitated Willsher's leaving the ground.) 35 runs had been made from seventeen overs when Lillywhite bowled Mr W. Grace; and when 53 runs had been scored, Mr Hadow's, Mr Yardley's, Mr F. Grace's and Mr Walker's wickets were down. Then, at three minutes past four, and with the score at 53 for five wickets, Mr Thornton batted, and – by one 6, four 5s, six 4s, one 3, three 2s and two singles – made 61 runs in forty-seven minutes; he hit a 5 and a 3 from one over of Lillywhite's, three 4s and a 2 from an over of Southerton's, and a 6 and a 4 from another over of the Mitcham slows; that 4 was a huge drive honestly worth 6; the 6 was a stupendous hit, the ball "pitching" on the racket court. Mr Thornton's last five hits were a 6, a 4, a 5, a 5 and a 5; he left with the score at 138 for six wickets. Then, accompanied bya running fire of eharty cheers from the Gentlemen, Mr Fryer and Mr Howell in one hour increased the score from 138 to 211, when Jupp caught out Mr Howell for 30, whereupon Mr Strachan went in, and from 211 the score was hit to 234, when Southerton, for the first time in the innings, bowled from the gasometer end. This bowling change won the match, as in his third over at that end Southerton bowled Mr Fryer, making eight wickets down for 239 runs; in his following over Southerton bowled Mr Turner (the score still at 239); then, at twenty-five minutes to seven and the score at 10 to win, the last of the Gentlemen, Mr Absolom, was loudly cheered as he walked to the wickets; a louder cheer greeted Mr Strachan making a single from Lillywhite, and still louder applause rang out from the pavilion on Mr Absolom driving one for 4 in the same over. This made the score 5 to win, and piled up the excitement to an indescribable height; excitement that was kept tightly on the stretch by Southerton bowling a maiden over to Mr Strachan, Lillywhite a maiden over to Mr Absolom, and Southerton another maiden to Mr Strachan; then a single by Mr Absolom from Lillywhite brought out a ringing shout from the Gentlemen – a shout, earnest and lusty though it was, that was immediately after drowned by the roar that rang out from the thousands of throats at Southerton bowling Mr Absolom, and thereby, at ten minutes to seven, winning "this match of a thousand" for the Players by 3 runs. No runs were scored from the last twenty balls bowled by Southerton, but those twenty balls included the three wickets. Of Mr Fryer's 76 no praise can possibly be too high; it was a superb display of scientific cricket, commenced at eight minutes to four with the score at 50 for four wickets, and concluded at half-past six with the score at 239 for eight wickets. Of the mass of magnificent batting played in this match, none – for truth, skill, steadiness, and excellence – surpassed the 76 played by Mr Fryer.

The Players

H. Jupp b Absolom	0	– lbw b Absolom	97
Richard Humphrey b Thornton	7	– b Thornton	13
James Phillips b Thornton	5	– b Thornton	7
H. Charlwood c Turner b W. G. Grace	77	– c Strachan b W. G. Grace	37
Pooley st Turner b W. G. Grace	16	– run out	125
James Lillywhite b W. G. Grace	11	– b Absolom	35
Thomas Humphrey b Thornton	20	– not out	40
F. Silcock c Turner b Absolom	13	– c Turner b Hadow	1
H. H. Stephenson not out	15	– st Turner b Hadow	2
Willsher b Absolom	2	– b I. D. Walker	20
Southerton b Thornton	4	– b Thornton	0
B 2, l-b 1	3	B 13, l-b 5, w 2, n-b 1	21
	173		398

The Gentlemen

W. G. Grace Esq. c Lillywhite b Southerton	4	– b Lillywhite	11
W. Yardley Esq. st Pooley b Silcock	60	– c Stephenson b Southerton	3
W. H. Hadow Esq. c Pooley b Southerton	60	– run out	1
F. E. R. Fryer Esq. b Silcock	9	– b Southerton	76
I. D. Walker Esq. c Pooley b Silcock	5	– c T. Humphrey b Southerton	27
G. F. Grace Esq. c T. Humphrey b Silcock	55	– c Pooley b Southerton	0
C. I. Thornton Esq. c Jupp b Southerton	31	– b Lillywhite	61
L. S. Howell Esq. b Lillywhite	47	– c Jupp b Lillywhite	30
G. Strachan Esq. c R. Humphrey b Silcock	15	– not out	19
M. Turner Esq. not out	15	– b Southerton	0
C. Absolom Esq. c and b Southerton	16	– b Southerton	5
B 3, l-b 3	6	B 9, l-b 3	12
	323		245

The Gentlemen's Bowling

	Overs	Mdns	Runs	Wkts	Overs	Mdns	Runs	Wkts
Mr Absolom	31	12	49	3	51	16	116	2
Mr Thornton	29	15	38	4	59	27	83	3
Mr W. Grace	19	3	50	3	24	12	32	1
Mr Strachan	17	6	33	—	15	2	43	—
Mr Hadow					23	8	41	2
Mr Fryer					7	3	21	—
Mr F. Grace					7	1	24	—
Mr Yardley					4	2	16	—
Mr Walker					1.2	—	1	1

The Players' Bowling

	Overs	Mdns	Runs	Wkts	Overs	Mdns	Runs	Wkts
Southerton	62	19	118	4	48.2	15	95	6
Lillywhite	48	24	58	1	56	29	84	3
Silcock	36	17	56	5	18	5	54	—
Willsher	22	12	43	—				
Stephenson	14	2	42	—				

Umpires: W. Mortlock and John Lillywhite.

"WILLSHER'S MATCH."

THE MARRIED v THE SINGLE OF ENGLAND

Played at Lord's, July 10, 12, 1871

"The Committee have granted the use of Lord's ground on July 10, to E. Willsher for his benefit match, and thereby express the high opinion they entertain of his long services and straightforward conduct as a Cricketer." – Marylebone Club Annual Report, 1871.

This great (and rare) compliment paid him by the first Club in England is one that Willsher may well be proud of, for it is a first class testimonial to his merits as a man and a cricketer. Willsher's professional career has indeed been a lengthened one; he first played for Kent in 1847. In 1852 he played his first match at Lord's (Kent v England). In 1854 he became one of the famous All England Eleven. In 1856 he played his first Gentlemen v Players of England match at Lord's. In 1857 he took part (at Lord's) in the first match ever played by the celebrated "Two Elevens". For many years he was the county comrade of such splendid cricketers as Mr Alfred Mynn, Mr Felix, Fuller Pilch, E. Wenman and W. Hillyer; and when these men, by death and time, had "passed away" from the ranks of the Kent contingent, who was it but Edgar Willsher who for many years kept alive the great bowling fame of the once famous old cricketing county? In 1864 Willsher (in conjunction with John Lillywhite) formed the United South Eleven. In 1868 Willsher was Captain of the English Twelve that visited America, and for a period verging on twenty years Willsher has played a prominently successful bowling part in most of the principal matches of each successive season, gaining troops of friends by his excellent conduct, and, with remarkable success, keeping his bowling fame intact to the very last – witness his starting with sixteen successive maiden overs (Mr Dale and Lockwood batting) in the Canterbury Week of 1871.

Married v Single of England, played at Lord's last July for Willsher's benefit, was unfortunate as regards weather. On the first day it was bright and pleasant up to luncheon time; soon after rain fell and frequently stopped play. Throughout that night rain fell heavily and unceasingly, and continued so to fall up to mid day on Tuesday, preventing any play that day. On the Wednesday frequent showers interrupted the cricket, but for all that the match was finished, and the Single won by an innings and 73 runs – a result due to the extraordinary batting of Mr W. G. Grace, who accomplished the rare batting feat of commencing the innings and taking his bat out for 189 (out of a total of 310 – 304 from the bat), and this too against the bowling of J. C. Shaw, Howitt, Alfred Shaw, Southerton, Iddison, and Mr Kelson. The innings did not look promisingly for the Single when Richard Humphrey and Mr Hadow were both out with but 10 runs scored, but then the younger Mr Grace aided his brother; both hit freely, and increased the score from 10 to 118, when the slow bowler "c and b" Mr G. F. Grace for 33. Oscroft was next man in, and at the dinner call at 2.30 the score was 144 for three wickets – Mr W. Grace 96 not out. When Oscroft was stumped for 21, the score was 166 for four wickets – Mr Grace 103. At 201 Mr Pauncefote was had at wicket, and at 216 Charlwood was out, Mr Grace then having made 133. Then the long threatened rain fell, and twice interrupted play before the next wicket fell by Alfred Shaw bowling Lillywhite with the score at 264 for seven wickets (Mr Grace 160). At 289 Henty was bowled by Southerton, who at 310 had the remaining two wickets; and so at 6.25 was the innings finished, Mr Grace taking his bat out for 189 – a truly great innings, the latter part of it being played in a bad light and on wickets beaten out of all form by rain. The hits that made up Mr Grace's 189 not out were:– forty-five singles, seventeen 2s, thirteen 3s, fourteen 4s and three 5s (the 5s being two very fine on drives from Howitt's bowling and a capital cut up the ground from Southerton). On the completion of the Single's innings play ceased for that day. On the Tuesday at noon the water stood in pools on the ground, so the match was not proceeded with until noon the following day; then on wickets wholly unfavourable for batting, the Married men commenced their innings to the bowling of Clayton and Rylott (left hand fast). When Jupp's, Iddison's, and Smith's wickets had fallen for 18 runs, Rylott had bowled fourteen overs (eleven maidens) for 3 runs and two wickets, and with the score at 33 Rylott bowled Daft; indeed, there was no stay made until (at 81 for eight wickets) Southerton faced Alfred Shaw; both hit freely and well, and rapidly increased the score to 159, when the MCC man was bowled for 45 by Clayton, who with the following ball of that over bowled the other Shaw, and thereby, at twenty minutes to four, finished the innings for 159 – Southerton not out 41, an innings that deservedly gained him great applause. At a trifle before four o'clock the Married men commenced their second innings; rain twice interrupted play, but by ten minutes to six half the wickets were down for 56 runs; the sixth fell at 78; the other four wickets were obtained without addition to the score, as Rylott bowled three successive maiden overs, and in the three maiden overs bowled from the other end, Lillywhite had all four wickets, taking three wickets in five balls, – the four wickets in ten balls; and in this left-handed and effective form was the second innings of the Married wound up, the Single winning in a canter.

The Single

W. G. Grace Esq not out	189	James Lillywhite b Alfred Shaw	20
Richard Humphrey b Alfred Shaw	0	Henty b Southerton	5
W. H. Hadow Esq. b Alfred Shaw	6	R. Clayton c J. C. Shaw b Southerton	11
G. F. Grace Esq. c and b Southerton	33	Rylott b Southerton	0
W. Oscroft st Pooley b Alfred Shaw	21	B 2, l-b 4	6
B. Pauncefote Esq. c Pooley b Alfred Shaw	17		
H. Charlwood c Southerton b Kelson	2		310

The Married

John Smith c Humphrey b Rylott	11 – b Clayton	16
H. Jupp b Rylott	1 – c Rylott b Clayton	11
Roger Iddison c W. Grace b Lillywhite	4 – b Lillywhite	12
Richard Daft b Rylott	10 – b Rylott	24
R. Carpenter c Rylott b Lillywhite	12 – c Charlwood b Rylott	2
Pooley c Humphrey b Lillywhite	17 – c Price (for Hadow) b Lillywhite	9
G. M. Kelson Esq. c Henty b Rylott	14 – b Rylott	1
Alfred Shaw b Clayton	45 – not out	0
Howitt b Rylott	0 – b Lillywhite	0
Southerton not out	41 – c Rylott b Lillywhite	0
J. C. Shaw b Clayton	0 – b Lillywhite	0
B 2, l-b 2	4 L-b 3	3
	159	78

The Married Men's Bowling

	Overs	Mdns	Runs	Wkts
A. Shaw	64	28	70	5
Howitt	41	15	93	—
Southerton	29.1	7	56	4
J. C. Shaw	17	6	40	—
Iddison	7	—	30	—
Mr Kelson	3	—	15	1

Bowling of the Single Men

	Overs	Mdns	Runs	Wkts	Overs	Mdns	Runs	Wkts
Rylott	51	30	53	5	23	9	47	3
Lillywhite	41	20	54	3	6	4	5	5
Clayton	10.2	4	13	2	17	9	23	2
Mr W. Grace	8	2	19	—				
Mr G. F. Grace	7	4	16	—				

Umpires: J. Grundy sen. and Biddulph.

Willsher's subscription list in the pavilion at Lord's was generously headed with £20 from the Marylebone Club; the subscriptions on that list totalled £73 9s.

RESULTS OF SINGLE v MARRIED OF ENGLAND MATCHES

At Tunbridge Wells. 1844. The Married won by 9 runs.
At Lord's 1849. The Single won by three wickets.
At The Oval, 1858. The Single won by 16 runs.
At Lord's 1871. The Single won as above.

A TRULY "GREAT" BIT OF BATTING BY MR W. G. GRACE

UNITED SOUTH OF ENGLAND ELEVEN v UNITED NORTH OF ENGLAND ELEVEN

Played at Hull, August 3, 4, 5, 1876

In this match Mr W. G. Grace made 126 and 82. His 126 was part of a total of 159 – 154 from the bat; and when it is considered that Mr Grace made those 126 runs against such bowling as Alfred Shaw's, Hill's, Morley's, Tye's and Oscroft's, and that the other ten good batsmen could only make 28 between them, it becomes a question whether this is not (for merit) the best bit of batting played by Mr W. Grace in 1876. Ephraim Lockwood was also in very fine batting form; he went in with one wicket down, the score at 26, and took his bat out for a splendid, chanceless 108. The match was not finished.

The United South

First innings		Second innings	
W. G. Grace Esq. hit wkt b Alfred Shaw	126	c Greenwood b Lockwood	82
H. Jupp b Alfred Shaw	1	c Lockwood b Alfred Shaw	12
W. Gilbert Esq. run out	0	c and b W. Oscroft	37
G. F. Grace Esq. c Hill b Morley	0	b Alfred Shaw	23
E. Pooley c Alfred Shaw b Tye	14	b W. Oscroft	17
Richard Humphrey b W. Oscroft	3	b Hill	10
George Elliott c Morley b W. Oscroft	4	c Hill b Morley	9
Frank Silcock c Tye b Alfred Shaw	1	b Alfred Shaw	1
W. Jupp c Hill b W. Oscroft	0	c and b Alfred Shaw	2
Henty not out	1	not out	0
Southerton b Hill	4	c Morley b W. Oscroft	1
B 3, l-b 2	5	B 3, l-b 7, w 3	13
	159		207

The United North

First innings		Second innings	
W. Oscroft c W. Grace b Gilbert	51		
Arthur Shrewsbury c E. Pooley b W. Grace	8	not out	8
Ephraim Lockwood not out	108		
Richard Daft st E. Pooley b Gilbert	4		
A. Greenwood c Humphrey b Gilbert	37	not out	4
R. P. Smith Esq. b Southerton	0		
Alfred Shaw b Southerton	0		
R. Butler Esq. b Gilbert	3	b Gilbert	19
Allen Hill st E. Pooley b Gilbert	10		
John Tye c Humphrey b Gilbert	14		
Morley b Gilbert	5		
B 1, l-b 1	2		
	242		31

Umpires: R. Carpenter and G. Griffith.

CRICKET IN THE WINTER OF 1878-79

All England will remember, with a shiver and a shudder, the long, sad, and severe winter of 1878-'79, commencing, as it did in October '78, and continuing – with more or less severity – up to the middle of May '79; and even then the cold, nipping, bronchitis creating winds seemed loth to leave the land they had so sorely stricken with distress, disease, and death. But there is no black cloud without its silver lining, and one bright spot in this dark winter was its severity and length enabled more

CRICKET MATCHES ON THE ICE

to be played than were ever before played in the course of one winter. In chronicling the following matches played on the ice in the winter of 1878-'79, the compiler wishes it to be understood that the summary does not comprise all the matches so played, but only those kindly brought to his notice by correspondents, or extracted from the newspapers; and he regrets that he is unable to give space for the full scores of several of these matches:–

R. GILLOTT'S SIDE v B. CHATTERTON'S SIDE

Played by the Members of the Sheffield Club, December 17, 1878, on the ice that covered the Duke of Devonshire's Swiss Cottage Pond. One condition of the match was that any one obtaining 20 runs should retire. Mr W. Shearstone of Mr Gillott's team was the only man who made the 20, the next highest scorers being Mr R. Gillott with 13, and T. Rowbotham (Mr Chatterton's side) also with 13. They played seven a side, Mr Gillott's team having the best of the match by 11 runs. Totals: – Mr Gillott's Side, 46. Mr Chatterton's Side, 35.

CAMBRIDGE TOWN v CAMBRIDGE UNIVERSITY

Played on the Ice at Grantchester, December 17, 18, 19, 1878

It is to *Bell's Life in London* that the compiler is thankfully indebted to all that follows respecting this match: –

"Mr Coxall of Grantchester having flooded upwards of twenty acres of land in his meadows for the purpose of skating, a cricket match was arranged to be played by the above-named teams under the captaincies of Mr C. Pigg, of Peterhouse, and the ex-All England cricketer, 'Bob' Carpenter. The townsmen were first at the wickets, and after two hours' play on the first day they had lost nine wickets for 193 runs, Newman leading the score with a well played 68, which included a 6, three 5s, three 4s and six 3s. The next day 'Bob' Carpenter (not out 4) was accompanied to the wicket by 'Dan' Hayward, and this pair were not separated until they had been seventy minutes at wickets, and augmented the score by 132 runs, when Hayward was clean bowled for 44; and – in that same over – Carpenter sent the ball into the hands of cover point, having then 89 runs to his credit, mainly made by two 5s (leg hit and cut), one 4, and a dozen 3s. The innings terminated for 326 runs. The ice was very bad when the 'Varsity's innings was commenced by Lilley, and Von-Scott; the former was bowled when only 8 runs had been made. W. Deedes then joined Scott and they succeeded in keeping their wickets intact for nearly another half-hour when the stumps were drawn, the score standing at 61 for one wicket. The match was resumed on the Thursday, several large scores were made, and when time was called the 'Varsity had scored 274 runs for the loss of four wickets. The match was drawn."

Cambridge Town

F. Pryor c Scott b Boucher	13
W. Newman run out	68
J. Fordham b Wawn	42
G. Hoppett b Lilley	3
J. Warrington b Lilley	1
A. Fromant lbw b Lilley	13
W. Thurston run out	37
H. Mason c Wawn b Lilley	9
N. Richardson b Lilley	0
Robert Carpenter c Scott b Boucher	89
Daniel Hayward b Boucher	44
J. Cain not out	0
B 3, l-b 1, w 1, n-b 2	7
	326

Cambridge University

J. Lilley (*Grantchester*) b Newman	6	C. Pigg (*St. Peter's*) not out	34
H. Von E. Scott (*St. Catherine's*) run out	88		
W. Deedes (*Jesus*) b Newman	56	B 13,1-b 1	14
D. A. Wawn (*Jesus*) c and b Carpenter	7		
H. Pigg (*Emmanuel*) not out	69		274

C. E. Boucher (*Trinity Hall*), F. H. Baines (*Christ's*), H. Wood (*Sidney*), A. J. Luckham (*Emmanuel*) and R. E. Leach (*Magdalen*) did not bat.

So 600 runs were made for fifteen wickets. Average, 40 runs per wicket.

T. E. PARR'S ELEVEN v W. S. RICHARDSON'S ELEVEN

This match was played on the ice of Swan's pond, Gateshead, December 21, 1878. – The ice was covered with skaters and spectators, and, no doubt, a satisfactory sum was taken for admission that helped to relieve the distressed and needy of Gateshead.
Totals: – Mr Parr's Side, 30. Mr Richardson's Side, 18.

B. CHATTERTON'S SIDE v M. DODSWORTH'S SIDE

Played on the frozen lake, near to Sandbeck Park, January 6, 1879

By the kind permission of the Earl of Scarborough, this match was played by the Sheffield Skating Club on the lake adjoining his Lordship's Park. To retire when you have made 20 runs was one of the stipulations of the match; the consequence of this prudent regulation being both sides played an innings. Chatterton's side first batted, no fewer than seven of that side having to retire with 20, not out, attached to their names. One man – C. Bridgens – made a hit for which 8 was run; another – T. Gillott – made a 7; another – R. Gillott (a veteran) – hit two 6s; and B. Chatterton also made a 6. Several 5s and 4s were also made for Chatterton's side. When Mr Chatterton "skittled" the wickets down so rapidly that Chatterton's won by a majority of 153 runs.
Totals: – Chatterton's Side, 181. Dodsworth's Side, 28.

CRICKET MATCH ON THE ICE BY MOONLIGHT

About the time Lord Harris's team were playing one of their matches under the bright and burning sun of an Australian summer, an English team were playing their game in the dear old country at home under the bright and brilliant beams of the new year's full moon.

This match by moonlight came about this wise: – The moon was full on the 8th of January, shining with unclouded and truly splendid brightness throughout that evening and night. At the same time a sharp, keen, thoroughly old-fashioned frost was setting the ice in capital form for skating and other icy pastimes. The next day being bright, frosty, and fine, the skating cricketers of the royal borough of Windsor duly announced that

"A Cricket Match would be played by Moonlight on the Ice in Windsor Home Park at seven o'clock that evening."

Consequently several hundred spectators assembled, and the match was played by moonlight. "The game (says the chronicler) causing no end of amusement owing to the difficulties encountered by the players while bowling, batting, and fielding."

Totals: – Mr Bowditch's Side (only nine men batted) 15. Mr Gage's Side (ten men batted) 17.

MR E. W. GLANVILLE'S SIDE v MR G. BROWNING'S SIDE

Played on the Ice at Christ Church College meadow, Oxford, January 10, 1879

The match by moonlight at Windsor was quickly followed by this match on the meadow at Oxford. They played twelve a side, the result being Mr Glanville's side won by four wickets. Mr Browning's side first batted. Mr J. Rogers scored 71, Mr J. Castle 31, and Mr T. Bacon 11, not out. T. Bacon's bowling had six of the Browning wickets, five of the six being bowled down. On Mr Glanville's side batting a great stand was made by the Captain of the Eleven and Mr J. Bacon, Mr Granville scoring 61 runs and Mr J. Bacon 47; and when, in all, seven men were out, it was found Granville's side was two runs in advance of their opponents' total, so the Granville team won by four wickets.

Totals: – Mr Browning's Side, 125. Mr Granville's Side (seven wickets down), 127.

CHESTERFIELD v SHEFFIELD

Played on the Ice on a Dam near Brampton, January 22, 1879

About one thousand people assembled to witness this match, which was played on the understanding that when a man had made 25 runs he was to retire. The Sheffield men had much the best of the battle when "time" was called; but as William Mycroft, H. Charlwood, J. Rowbotham, and other celebrated cricketers played, it will be more satisfactory to give the score; here it is:–

Chesterfield

H. Charlwood (retired) not out	25
J. Clayton b B. Chatterton	23
M. Dury b Brownhill	0
H. Grattan b Brownhill	10
H. Graham run out	2
G. Womersley b Rowbotham	14
C. H. Trown (retired) not out	25
G. R. Hewitt b Rowbotham	0
J. Pearson b Rowbotham	0
W. Mycroft not out	6
L. Gothard b Rowbotham	0
Extras	8
	113

Sheffield

S. Blyde (retired) not out	25
R. Gillott (retired) not out	25
W. Shearstone (retired) not out	25
T. Brownhill b W. Mycroft	5
J. Rowbotham (retired) not out	25
B. Chatterton c sub. b Charlwood	3
J. Gillott st Graham b Charlwood	2
Mr J. Dodsworth not out	4
Extras	1
	125

C. Bridgens, W. Latham and W. Johnson did not bat.

F. THORPE'S SIDE v ROBERT CLAYTON'S SIDE

Played on the Ice at Saundbry Marsh, January 25, 1879

Two Elevens of the Gainsboro' Club, one side captain'd by F. Thorpe, the other by Robert Clayton (of Lord's), played this match on a fine piece of ice. They went to work on the rule that when a batsman had made 20 runs he should leave the sticks; and the result of a most enjoyable day's cricket on the ice was Clayton's side won by 54 runs.

F. Thorpe's Side

H. Rimington b R. Clayton	8	C. Hawkesworth b Box	0
A. Thorpe (retired) not out	20	Howlett run out	1
Fish (retired) not out	20	Scott not out	12
Church b Box	5	W. Brooks b R. Clayton	0
F. Thorpe b Box	0	B 2	2
Lundy b R. Clayton	18		
Brown b R. Clayton	0		86

Robert Clayton's Side

Robert Clayton (retired) not out	20	Watkin (retired) not out	20
Brown (retired) not out	20	J. L. Smith run out	8
H. Scott (retired) not out	20	Box c Fish b Scott	9
Bell run out	0	Drakefield b Fish	10
W. W. Bourne b A. Thorpe	7	B 22, l-b 1	23
Cooper b A. Thorpe	1		
S. Hawkesworth b A. Thorpe	2		140

C. ULLATHORNE'S SIDE v MR L. W. WALLGATE'S SIDE

Played on the Ice at Partington Carrs, January 25, 1879

This match was played by two tens of the Hull Club on the old principle of scoring all the runs you can make. This principle was so effectively carried out on one side that a total of 294 runs was scored, Mr Wallgate making 88, and D. Hearfield 105 (the first 100 made in England in 1879), whereupon he "retired" with all the honours, the papers stating: – "Hearfield ran into three figures, having shown capital cricket". What a pity it is that Hearfield's hits were not reported, they would have been, with great pleasure, inserted here, and would have been perused with much intestet by the readers of "Wisden's". Mr Wallgate's team won by nearly 200 runs, Hearfield alone having made 8 more runs than the whole of Ullathorne's team.

C. Ullathorne's Side

L. Jackson b Wallgate	2	J. Stephenson b Kaye	24
H. Hart b Wallgate	26	S. Coverdale b Wallgate	0
C. Ullathorne run out	16	W. Ellis not out	2
S. Cheavin c Douglas b Wallgate	1		
R. Jenkins run out	2	B 4, l-b 8, w 1	13
Cooper b Wallgate	0		
J. Greenhow run out	11		97

L. W. Wallgate's Side

L. W. Wallgate b Ellis	88
Rev. E. B. Kaye b Hart	25
T. Boddy run out	6
D. Hearfield (retired) not out	105
J. Tattersall b Ellis	0
Richardson run out	2
R. Barrett b Ellis	1
Cuthbert b Ullathorne	39
Douglas run out	6
J. G. Ellis not out	2
B 16, l-b 1, w 3	20
	294

R. C. HALL'S SIDE v R. LINCOLN'S SIDE

Played on the Ice at Grimsby, January 27, 1879

Two thousand people stood out in the cold looking on this match played by sixteen a side, and on the principle of retiring from your wicket when you have made 20 runs. On Hall's side Moss made 20, not out, and made way for others to do likewise if they could, but none could, the two next highest scores being 14 by Coates, and 18, not out, by Quine, both for Lincoln's side. Hall's team included a successful bowler in J. Stevenson, who bowled down nine of the fourteen Lincoln wickets; nevertheless Lincoln's side had the best of the day's cricket by one wicket and seven runs.

Totals: – R. C. Hall's Side, 70. R. Lincoln's Side (fourteen wickets down), 77.

WINGERWORTH v SHEFFIELD

Played on the Ice at Wingerworth, January 20, 1878

This match was played on the "retire when you have made 25 runs" terms. The home team was stated to have been "strengthened by some good players from Chesterfield"; *per contra*, it was alleged "The Sheffield Club was but indifferently represented, fully half their best players being absent". Excellent wickets had been prepared on ice in good condition, and thereon some creditable bowling, batting, and fielding ended in the following score to the credit of Wingerworth by 61 runs.

Wingerworth

Whomerslay (retired) not out	25
M. Clayton (retired) not out	25
C. H. Frown b Shearstone	13
J. Pearson (retired) not out	25
J. Brayshaw run out	1
J. Clayton b Shearstone	7
Graham (retired) not out	25
Gratton not out	22
Holmes b Champion	0
Margenison b Tomlinson	2
Fisher run out	1
Extras	16
	162

Sheffield

R. Gillott c Holmes b J. Clayton	0	W. Booker run out	0
W. Shearstone (retired) not out	25	F. Lawson run out	3
A. Champion (retired) not out	25	W. Fitch not out	9
T. Tomlinson st Graham b M. Clayton	2	Jos. Lee b Frown	0
C. Bridgers (retired) not out	25	Extras	5
J. F. Anderson b M. Clayton	7		
J. Taylor b Whomersley	0		101

LORD HENRY NEVILL'S SIDE v MR WILLIAMS' SIDE

Played on the Ice at Eridge Castle, Kent, February 1, 1879

The Marquis of Abergavenny, with that considerate courtesy characteristic of his race, had the gates of his park thrown open to all who chose to enter and witness the grand Fete on the frozen water of the great lake at his Lordship's seat – Eridge Castle. The Marquis and a distinguished company were present, and some 2000 other visitors assembled, who appeared to heartily enjoy the jolly games of Hockey, played at one end of the lake, and cricket at the other. As to the cricket match both Captains were (as Captains should be) well in front of their men, Lord Henry Neville taking the lead with 70, not out – pronounced by the critics "A remarkably good innings, his lordship having been frequently applauded for the dexterity he displayed, and the command he evinced over skates and bat". But Mr Williams ran a close second to his lordship, both as to skill on skates and run getting, for he scored an innings of 68 in good form; and, if it could have been played out to the pleasant end, the game would doubtless have had a most interesting finish, for when the early darkness stopped play Mr Williams' side had two wickets to fall, with only 53 runs to make to win.

Lord H. Nevill's Side

Ovenden run out	2	Mr Howard st Stafford	26
Stephenson b Williams	49	Mr Forty b Stafford	0
Mr Booty lbw b Simpson	27	Mr Biddlestone st Stafford	12
Pullen b Williams	4	Lord G. Nevill b Wilson	9
Lord Henry Nevill not out	70	B 8, l-b 2, w 6	16
Lord George Pratt run out	4		
Mr W. W. Dickinson run out	9		228

Mr E. S. Williams' Side

Mr E. S. Williams b Booty	68	Mr A. Simpson run out	1
Mr F. W. Stone run out	24	Mr G. Edwards b Booty	13
Mr S. Colran run out	10	W. Knight not out	3
Mr Stafford b Booty	4	Chapman not out	6
Mr Wilson run out	26		
Mr F. W. Ellis run out	21		176

This was the last match played on the ice in that terribly severe and distressful winter, for on the following day (Sunday, February 2) a rapid thaw set in, continuing throughout the Monday; and although winter and rough weather subsequently returned, and discomfortingly continued with us up to the middle of May, there was no further frost sufficiently severe to form and fix ice capable of playing cricket on; and so, with Lord Henry Nevill's match at Eridge Park, was ended the never-to-be-forgotten Cricket on the Ice Season of 1878-79.

ALFRED SHAW'S MATCH AT LORD'S IN 1879

That Alfred Shaw's brilliant bowling services for MCC are to be acknowledged, by the old Club playing a match in compliment to Alfred, at Lord's, on 1879, will be gratifying to all who admire bowling skill of the very highest order and success, civil manly behaviour, and a straight-going, respectful, and deservedly respected man like Shaw, of whom it may not only be truly said that "he never made an enemy, nor lost a friend", but that he has been, and is, a worthy successor at Lord's to Grundy and Wootton, and higher praise than this (as to services and character) cannot be given to any cricketer. Title and date of the match, are expected to be:

NORTH v SOUTH ....Whit Monday, Tuesday, and Wednesday.

We of *Wisden* hope he will have three fine days, a closely contested match, large attendances, and well filled subscription lists.

Alfred Shaw's first match at Lord's was for The Colts of England v MCC and Ground, on May 23, 1864, and so successful was Alfred's bowling debut on the old ground that he took thirteen wickets – eleven bowled – in that match, and thereby faithfully foreshadowed one of the most successful bowling careers ever played at Lord's. In 1865 Shaw was engaged by MCC as a ground bowler at Lord's, and his first match for the old club was v The Knickerbockers, on the 8th of May of that year, when Alfred scored an innings of 30 runs and took thirteen wickets – five bowled. To follow up closely the career that endorsed that start would be a task of unmixed pleasure to the compiler of this book, but want of space forbids that, and he must be content with noting down here the following few, of the very many, great bits of bowling Shaw has delivered in MCC matches:

In 1870, when playing for the old Club against the Cantabs, at Cambridge, Shaw bowled 104 overs (seventy-one maidens) for 75 runs and eight wickets – seven bowled. And it was in that year that he brought off the following great double innings bowling success, for MCC v

Thorndon Hall

A. Baker b Alfred Shaw	52	– b Alfred Shaw	15
A. Nicholas c and b Alfred Shaw	2	– b Alfred Shaw	5
P. Colley hit wkt b Price	6	– st Jardine b Alfred Shaw	0
F. Nicholas b Alfred Shaw	4	– b Alfred Shaw	3
Hon. W. J. Petre, b Alfred Shaw	1	– b Alfred Shaw	2
W. Boardman c Frost b Alfred Shaw	0	– not out	4
P. N. Evans lbw b Alfred Shaw	6	– b Alfred Shaw	3
G. Boardman b Alfred Shaw	0	– b Alfred Shaw	0
J. F. Lescher not out	6	– c Richards b Alfred Shaw	11
A. Crush b Alfred Shaw	0	– b Alfred Shaw	0
E. Boardman b Alfred Shaw	0	– run out	6
L-b 1	1		
	78		49

In 1871, when playing for the first Eleven v Next twenty of MCC and Ground, Shaw's bowling captured eleven (eight bowled) of the "Next twenty's" wickets for 25 runs; and among other good bits that season Alfred's bowling had twelve Oxford wickets (five bowled) for 74 runs, the late Mr Ottaway's, Mr W. H. Hadow's, Hon. G. Harris's (now Lord Harris), and other celebrated batsmen being among the captured twelve.

It was in 1874, as all the cricketing world knows, that Alfred Shaw accomplished his most famous bowling success, by bowling for Nottinghamshire against MCC and Ground:

Overs	Mdns	Runs	Wkts	
41.2	36	7	7	(6 bowled)

The six wickets he bowled down were: – Mr W. G. Grace's, Mr A. W. Ridley's, Mr C. F. Buller's, Lord Harris's, Mr A. W. herbert's and Clayton's. The seventh wicket being Mr I. D. Walker's (stumpted by Biddulph).

In 1875 Shaw bowled in all four of the matches played by MCC against the Universities, his aggregate bowling in those matches being:

Overs	Mdns	Runs	Wkts
372	211	296	31 (21 bowled)

In this way could the compiler continue recording masterpieces of "head bowling" from this cunning right hand sufficient to fill a 32-page book; but he must hold hard, and so (asking the reader to kindly bear in mind Shaw was too unwell to bowl a ball for MCC in 1877) will wind up by chronicling that Alfred Shaw's bowling for MCC in the seasons 1870, 1871, 1872, 1873, 1874, 1875, 1876, and 1878 totals up:

Overs	Mdns	Runs	Wkts
6,035.1	3,314	5,747	688 (371 bowled)

NORTH v SOUTH

Played at Scarborough, September 5, 6, 7, 1889

A truly remarkable match brought the Scarborough Festival to a conclusion. On the last morning the South had to follow their innings against a majority of 163 runs, and so splendidly did Mr W. G. Grace and Abel play, that before they were separated the score had reached 226. This performance takes rank among the best stands ever made for the first wicket in a big match, but it is inferior to the 283 by Mr Grace and Mr B. B. Cooper for the Gentlemen of the South against the Players of the South at The Oval in 1869; the 266 by Shrewsbury and Mr Stoddart for England against the MCC at Lord's in 1887; the 243 by Mr Key and Mr Rashleigh for Oxford against Cambridge at Lord's in 1886; and the 238 by Mr Grace and Mr T. G. Matthews for Gloucestershire against Yorkshire at Sheffield in 1872. The two batsmen were together for three hours and three quarters, and Abel, who left first, was out unluckily, playing a ball on to his wicket. The Surrey batsman was scarcely seen to such complete advantage in any other match during the season. The wicket was one on which the ball always wanted careful watching, and yet his only mistakes were two very sharp chances – one at point and the other to the bowler – when he had made 55 and 76 respectively. He scored 105, and his hits were one 5 (four for an overthrow), eight 4s, five 3s, twelve 2s, and twenty-nine singles. Mr Grace was at the wickets for four hours and thirty-five minutes, scoring at much the same pace nearly all the time, and when a catch at short leg closed his innings, stumps were pulled up and the match left drawn. He gave a difficult chance at cover slip when he had scored 22, and was missed at the wicket when his total was 139, while a ball that he put up between the wickets was just a possible chance to the bowler, but these were very small blemishes in a superb display. His hits were sixteen 4s, five 3s, twenty 2s, and thirty-five singles. So fine was the batting of Hall, Flowers, and Barnes on the first day that the North's score was 228 for two wickets. The wicket-keeping was excellent on both sides.

North

L. Hall b Stoddart	75	G. Ulyett not out	39
W. Flowers c O'Brien b Hadow	75	W. Attewell c Phillipson b Woods	0
W. Barnes c O'Brien b Lohmann	79	F. Shacklock c and b Woods	4
W. Gunn b Wright	17	D. Hunter run out	0
R. Peel b Stoddart	0	B 2, n-b 1	3
W. Chatterton b Wright	29		
Lord Hawke c Lohmann b Woods	39		360

South

Mr W. G. Grace c Barnes b Attewell	3	c Hawke b Chatterton	154
Mr C. I. Thornton c Gunn b Shacklock	7		
Mr A. E. Stoddart b Flowers	77	lbw b Peel	1
Mr T. C. O'Brien b Attewell	5		
Mr E. A. Nepean b Attewell	3	not out	14
R. Abel b Shacklock	35	b Attewell	105
G. A. Lohmann c Chatterton b Shacklock	10		
Mr E. M. Hadow c Attewell b Shacklock	31		
Mr H. Philipson b Shacklock	10		
Mr S. M. J. Woods lbw b Attewell	9		
W. Wright not out	0		
B 4, l-b 2, w 1	7	B 4	4
	197		278

South Bowling

	Overs	Mdns	Runs	Wkts
Lohmann	45	20	104	1
Mr Woods	32.1	12	73	3
Wright	26	10	43	2
Mr Nepean	12	1	47	0
Mr Hadow	7	2	16	1
Mr Stoddart	18	5	50	2
Abel	3	1	7	0
Mr Grace	6	2	17	0

North Bowling

	Overs	Mdns	Runs	Wkts	Overs	Mdns	Runs	Wkts
Attewell	36	18	55	4	44	19	48	1
Shacklock	24	6	79	5	22	5	53	0
Peel	14	7	26	0	38	16	70	1
Flowers	15	12	13	1	16	4	41	0
Ulyett	4	1	17	0	5	1	17	0
Chatterton					6.1	3	10	1
Hall					1	0	7	0
Barnes					7	4	14	0
Gunn					4	1	14	0

NORTH v SOUTH

Played at Scarborough, August 31, September 1, 2, 1891

A match which was full of interest from first to last, and one which produced a close and most exciting finish, arousing the spectators to a very high pitch of enthusiasm. Rain had prevented a ball being bowled in the first match of the Scarborough Festival – that between the MCC and Ground and Yorkshire – and on the opening day of North v South, cricket was only practicable for about two hours. As might have been expected, the ground was very soft and treacherous, and batsmen were placed at a great disadvantage. Two splendid elevens had been selected, but Mr W. G. Grace was away from the South, and Arthur Shrewsbury did not play for the North. On winning the toss, the South fared very badly before the bowling of Briggs and Attewell, and on the first day lost nine wickets for 68 runs. Briggs accomplished the "hat trick", dismissing Murdoch, Hadow, and Ferris with three successive balls. On the second day the weather was far more favourable, and the game was in progress from twenty-five minutes to one until half-past five. Thanks to some brilliant hitting by Lohmann and Mr Woods, the Southern total was increased to 96, but the North exceeded this score by 29 runs, Mr Ernest Smith giving another example of his ability to force the game on a slow wicket. He hit up 56 out of 101 during his stay, and though he gave two chances he deserved great credit for his performance. His chief hits were three 4s, six 3s, and seven 2s. In the last half hour of the day the South lost two wickets for 15 runs, and thus had all the worst of the game, being still 14 runs behind with Mr Stoddart and Abel out. The third day's cricket, however, surpassed all expectations, and kept the interest of the spectators riveted on the game from the first ball to the last. The only batting on the South side worthy of mention was that of Bean and Mr McGregor and the score in the end only reached 81. Attewell and Briggs again bowled wonderfully well. The North had but 53 runs set them to win, and though it was generally thought that they might lose four of five wickets – the ground being extremely difficult – very few persons realised the possibility of the North being beaten. Lord Hawke was bowled with the score at five, but Mr Smith on going in played a forcing game with considerable success. He made a grand drive out of the ground for 6 off Lohmann, and a couple of 4s, and it was almost entirely due to his efforts that 30 went up on the board with only one man out. At this point the game looked as good as over, for with 23 runs to win there were still nine wickets to go down, but then came a rapid and altogether unexpected change in the match, Lohmann and Ferris bowling with extraordinary effect. In quick succession Lohmann dismissed Ulyett, Chatterton and Barnes, and Gunn and Mr Smith leaving soon afterwards, the sixth wicket went down at 40. For all this, however, the game looked in favour of the North, only 13 runs being wanted with four wickets to fall, but the two famous bowlers, encouraged by their success, worked untiringly, and they were finely backed up in the field. Mr Jackson was out lbw to the Australian at 42, and Briggs was dismissed in a similar manner by Lohmann at 45, while Attewell was bowled by the first ball he received. When Hunter, the last man, joined Peel, eight runs were still required. A single was run, and then Mr O'Brien jumped in and caught Peel close to the ground, bringing the innings to a close for 46. This left the South with a sensational but thoroughly well-earned victory by six runs. Lohmann, who took seven wickets for 25 runs, was, of course, the hero of the game, and the great share he had in the triumph of the South will be judged from the fact that in the whole match he took thirteen wickets for 82 runs, and scored 35 for once out.

South

Mr A. E. Stoddart b Attewell	3	– c Chatterton b Attewell	11
Mr T. C. O'Brien c Attewell b Briggs	1	– b Attewell	0
Mr W. L. Murdoch st Hunter b Briggs	17	– c Barnes b Attewell	8
R. Abel b Attewell	1	– c and b Attewell	1
Mr W. W. Read c Ulyett b Briggs	16	– b Attewell	4
G. Bean st Hunter b Briggs	0	– not out	18
G. A. Lohmann not out	30	– c Hawke b Attewell	5
Mr E. M. Hadow lbw b Briggs	0	– lbw b Briggs	2
Mr J. J. Ferris b Briggs	0	– b Briggs	2
Mr G. McGregor lbw b Briggs	9	– b Briggs	20
Mr S. M. J. Woods b Peel	19	– c Ulyett b Briggs	9
		B 1	1
	96		81

North

G. Ulyett c and b Lohmann	3	– b Lohmann	5
Lord Hawke b Ferris	10	– b Lohmann	1
Mr E. Smith c Stoddart b Abel	56	– c Lohmann b Ferris	23
W. Gunn c Woods b Lohmann	6	– b Ferris	3
W. Barnes c McGregor b Lohmann	2	– hit wkt b Lohmann	0
W. Chatterton lbw b Lohmann	11	– b Lohmann	0
R. Peel c Stoddart b Lohmann	3	– c O'Brien b Lohmann	6
Mr F. S. Jackson st McGregor b Ferris	27	– lbw b Ferris	0
J. Briggs b Lohmann	0	– lbw b Lohmann	2
W. Attwell c McGregor b Ferris	5	– b Lohmann	0
D. Hunter not out	1	– not out	0
L-b 1	1	B 6	6
	125		46

North Bowling

	Overs	Mdns	Runs	Wkts	Overs	Mdns	Runs	Wkts
Attewell	32	16	33	2	24	12	32	6
Briggs	31	15	63	7	20	2	39	4
Peel	4	0	0	1	5	1	9	0

South Bowling

	Overs	Mdns	Runs	Wkts	Overs	Mdns	Runs	Wkts
Ferris	19	3	47	3	11	4	15	3
Lohmann	21	4	57	6	11.3	3	25	7
Woods	3	0	19	0				
Abel	1	0	1	1				

Umpires: King and Sherwin.

GENTLEMEN OF ENGLAND v SHERWIN'S NOTTINGHAMSHIRE ELEVEN

Played at Scarborough, September 3, 4, 5, 1891

The concluding match of the Scarborough Festival did not arouse any great amount of interest, and after a fairly good struggle the Gentlemen of England proved successful by 115 runs. The amateurs had a powerful side, but Sherwin's Eleven did not represent the full strength of Nottinghamshire. On the first innings the Gentlemen only gained a lead of nine runs, but afterwards they had all the best of it, and on the concluding day the second innings was declared at an end when eight wickets had fallen for 233. Nottinghamshire were left with 243 to get to win in about three hours, and though Gunn and Bagguley batted well the task proved beyond the capabilities of the team, and the Gentlemen won with an hour to spare. In the first innings of Sherwin's Eleven Mr W. W. Read accomplished the "hat trick", dismissing Barnes, Attewell and Dr Dixon with three successive balls.

Gentlemen

Mr A. E. Stoddart c Bagguley b Shacklock	11	– b Attewell	38
Mr E. M. Hadow c Gunn b Shacklock	0	– st Sherwin b Attewell	53
Mr W. L. Murdoch b Attewell	5	– c Wright b Barnes	22
Mr E. Smith b Shacklock	13	– b Barnes	0
Mr W. W. Read b Shacklock	2	– c Robinson b Attewell	52
Mr C. E. de Trafford b Attewell	33	– c Wright b Flowers	18
Mr T. C. O'Brien not out	25	– not out	23
Lord Hawke lbw b Attewell	1	– st Sherwin b Attewell	3
Mr G. F. Vernon c Robinson b Attewell	2		
Mr S. M. J. Woods c Robinson b Flowers	23	– c Dixon b Redgate	15
Mr J. J. Ferris c Sherwin b Flowers	0		
L-b 1	1	B 7, l-b 2	9
	116	(8 wkts dec.)	233

Sherwin's Nottinghamshire Eleven

Mr C. W. Wright c Read b Ferris	0	– b Woods	2
W. Flowers c Murdoch b Woods	7	– c Smith b Ferris	6
W. Gunn b Read	40	– not out	62
W. Barnes c Stoddart b Read	17	– b Ferris	1
W. Attewell b Read	0	– b Woods	3
Dr Dixon b Read	0	– st Murdoch b Ferris	8
Mr O. Redgate b Stoddart	0	– run out	1
Mr J. S. Robinson lbw b Ferris	10	– b Stoddart	1
R. Bagguley c Smith b Read	12	– b Stoddart	24
M Sherwin c Ferris b Read	3	– b Ferris	0
F. Shacklock not out	6	– b Stoddart	1
B 9, l-b 2, n-b 1	12	B 18	18
	107		127

Sherwin's Nottinghamshire Eleven Bowling

	Overs	Mdns	Runs	Wkts	Overs	Mdns	Runs	Wkts
Shacklock	16	6	36	4				
Attewell	27	12	35	4	41	15	91	4
Bagguley	10	4	27	0	8	1	19	0
Barnes	4	0	17	0	8	4	19	2
Flowers	1.2	1	0	2	13	0	55	1
Dr Dixon					2	0	7	0
Sherwin					6	0	23	0
Mr Redgate					5	2	10	1

Gentlemen's Bowling

	Overs	Mdns	Runs	Wkts	Overs	Mdns	Runs	Wkts
Mr Woods	17	7	36	1	14	2	46	2
Mr Ferris	27	14	26	2	19	9	26	4
Mr Stoddart	5	2	9	1	8.2	5	11	3
Mr Read	15.2	3	24	6	4	1	26	0

Umpires: Henwood and King.

MARRIED v SINGLE

For Clayton's Benefit

Played at Lord's, May 23, 24, 25, 1892

In fitting recognition of long and valuable services on their ground staff, the MCC decided to give the old Yorkshire bowler, Robert Clayton, a benefit during the season, and the above dates, for which a match under the title of Married v Single was arranged, were set apart for that purpose. It was a somewhat curious fact that up to that time no first-class fixture under the same title had been contested at Lord's since 1871, the year in which Clayton made his first appearance in important cricket. Excellent if not thoroughly representative elevens were got together, the Married team, despite the absence of Mr W. G. Grace, being on paper the stronger; but the Single, although they had practically only Lohmann, J. T. Hearne, and Davidson to depend upon for bowling, managed to win a highly interesting match by five wickets – a result largely brought about by the splendid all-round cricket of Lohmann and the batting of Mr Stoddart, Maurice Read, and Henderson. Financially the match was a moderate success, as though 4,047 persons paid on the opening day and 3,457 on Tuesday, only about 1,500 were present on Wednesday, owing to the early finish. The Married won the toss, and after a capital start by Abel and Chatterton, who scored 89 together, and a breakdown in the middle of the innings, A. Hearne, Mr Hornby, Attewell, and Sherwin took the total from 144 for seven wickets to 230 before the end came. Against this the Single obtained 85 for the loss of two wickets by the drawing of stumps. The second day was taken up by the Single completing their innings for 296, and by their opponents making 136 at their second attempt for six wickets, the feature of the play being the batting of the three Surrey men – Read, Lohmann, and Henderson – and Barnes, Alec Hearne, and Briggs. On Wednesday the second innings of the Married closed for 184, and the Single scored the 119 runs required to win for the loss of half their batsmen.

Married

R. Abel c J. T. Hearne b Lohmann	54	– b J. T. Hearne	11
W. Chatterton c J. T. Hearne b Lohmann	45	– c Lohmann b J. T. Hearne	2
W. Gunn st MacGregor b Lohmann	15	– lbw b Lohmann	18
A. Hearne b J. T. Hearne	16	– c Lohmann b Dixon	26
Mr T. C. O'Brien c Stoddart b Lohmann	8	– c MacGregor b Lohmann	9
W. Barnes c Lohmann b J. T. Hearne	2	– b Dixon	35
J. Briggs c and b Lohmann	5	– b Lohmann	37
A. D. Pougher c MacGregor b Lohmann	2	– b J. T. Hearne	20
Mr A. N. Hornby c Dixon b Lohmann	48	– b Lohmann	3
W. Attewell not out	20	– c Stoddart b Lohmann	7
M. Sherwin c MacGregor b J. T. Hearne	13	– not out	9
L-b 2	2	B 6, n-b 1	7
	230		184

Single

Mr A. E. Stoddart c Chatterton b Attewell	42	– c Attewell b A. Hearne	53
A. Shrewsbury b Pougher	6	– b Attewell	1
M. Read c Attewell b Chatterton	61	– b Attewell	0
Mr G. MacGregor b Attewell	4		
Mr G. Kemp b Attewell	5	– b Pougher	0
Mr J. A. Dixon c Sherwin b Attewell	28	– b Briggs	30
Mr O. Redgate c Sherwin b Chatterton	5	– not out	25
G. A. Lohmann c Barnes b Chatterton	58	– not out	4
R. Henderson not out	50		
G. Davidson b Chatterton	2		
J. T. Hearne c sub. b Barnes	24		
B 8, l-b 1, n-b 2	11	L-b 6	6
	296		119

Single Bowling

	Overs	Mdns	Runs	Wkts	Overs	Mdns	Runs	Wkts
Lohmann	56	19	121	7	38	14	58	5
J. T. Hearne	48.4	20	74	3	44	18	73	3
Davidson	18	9	26	0	7	1	13	0
Mr Stoddart	4	1	7	0	5	2	17	0
Mr Dixon					6	2	16	2

Married Bowling

	Overs	Mdns	Runs	Wkts	Overs	Mdns	Runs	Wkts
Attewell	54	19	101	4	21	8	36	2
Briggs	11	1	39	0	6.2	1	16	1
Pougher	12	1	37	1	12	3	19	1
Barnes	25.2	8	56	1	4	0	16	0
A. Hearne	2	0	10	0	7	3	10	1
Chatterton	21	12	42	4	1	0	16	0

Umpires: W. Hearn and V. A. Titchmarsh.

MR C. I. THORNTON'S ENGLAND ELEVEN v SURREY

Played at Scarborough, September 5, 6, 7, 1892

For the third and concluding match of the Scarborough Festival an extremely interesting game had been arranged, Surrey, the champion county for 1892, opposing a very powerful mixed eleven of amateurs and professionals selected by Mr C. I. Thornton and captained by Mr T. C. O'Brien. Except for the absence of Mr Shuter, Surrey were fully represented, and for two days the cricket was varied and interesting, but heavy rain prevented a ball being bowled on the Wednesday, and so what had promised to be a capital match had to be left drawn – certainly in favour of the England Eleven, as Surrey with an innings to play required 280 runs to win. The game presented some very striking features, and perhaps the greatest of them was the wonderful hitting on a slow wicket of Ernest Smith, the Yorkshire amateur. He certainly had a tremendous amount of luck, giving at least six distinct chances, but he made splendid use of the good fortune that attended him, and in the course of two hours actually scored 122 runs out of 174. Among his hits were one 6, eight 4s, four 3s, and twenty-four 2s. On the second day there was some admirable batting by Murdoch and Stoddart, the two men in the course of an hour and forty minutes' adding 124 runs during their partnership.

Mr C. I. Thornton's Eleven

W. Barnes c Wood b Lockwood	3	– b Lockwood	6
Mr W. L. Murdoch b Lohmann	1	– b W. W. Read	83
W. Gunn c and b Lohmann	7	– b Lockwood	2
Mr A. E. Stoddart b Lohmann	25	– c and b Lohmann	73
Mr E. Smith c Abel b Lohmann	122	– b W. W. Read	6
Mr T. C. O'Brien b Richardson	1	– c Abel b W. W. Read	18
E. Wainwright b Richardson	1	– c and b Lohmann	21
R. Peel b Richardson	1	– c Abel b Lohmann	23
Mr J. J. Ferris c and b Abel	0	– c Henderson b Lohmann	2
W. Attewell c W. W. Read b Richardson	14	– not out	1
Mr G. MacGregor not out	1	– st Wood b Lohmann	0
B 8, l-b 1	9	B 11, l-b 1	12
	185		247

Surrey

C. Baldwin b Wainwright	2
M. Read b Wainwright	0
W. Lockwood c Stoddart b Ferris	5
Mr W. W. Read b Attewell	31
R. Abel b Wainwright	42
R. Henderson b Ferris	7
Mr K. J. Key not out	19
G. A. Lohmann c Gunn b Wainwright	6
W. Brockwell c Gunn b Ferris	12
H. Wood b Attewell	8
T. Richardson c MacGregor b Attewell	1
B 15, l-b 5	20
	153

Surrey Bowling

	Overs	Mdns	Runs	Wkts	Overs	Mdns	Runs	Wkts
Lohmann	25.2	2	97	4	39.3	17	69	5
Lockwood	14	3	44	1	25	6	65	2
Richardson	13	5	28	4	5	0	30	0
Abel	2	0	7	1	5	1	12	0
W. W. Read					17	3	59	3

Mr Thornton's Eleven's Bowling

	Overs	Mdns	Runs	Wkts
Wainwright	19	10	35	4
Ferris	21	8	44	3
Peel	7	3	15	0
Attewell	20.1	8	31	3
Smith	2	0	8	0
Barnes	1	1	0	0

Umpires: Butler and King.

EAST OF ENGLAND v WEST OF ENGLAND

Played at Portsmouth, September 5, 6, 7, 1892

Considering the late period of the season at which this contest was arranged, two fairly good sides were got together, Mr Hewett, the Somerset captain, selecting the Western team, and Mr C. W. Wright, the Nottinghamshire amateur, having agreed to captain the East. The game scarcely met with the success it deserved, but it is, we understand, the intention of the United Services Club at Portsmouth to make it an annual fixture. On the opening day the East looked to have a considerable advantage, scoring 122 for three wickets against the West's total of 186, but from that point the game went all in favour of the Western team, the tide being turned by the wonderful bowling of Woods. On the second morning he took six out of the last seven wickets at a cost of 15 runs, and afterwards the West had matters nearly all their own way, winning in the end by 48 runs. Woods in the whole match took thirteen wickets at a cost of 109 runs, and so had a very large share in the victory.

West of England

Mr L. C. H. Palairet b Shilton	33	– b Hornsby	25
Mr H. T. Hewett st Malden b Ford	27	– c Vernon b Hornsby	14
Mr A. E. Gibson lbw b Shilton	12	– b Hornsby	27
Mr W. Morgan c and b Shilton	24	– b Hornsby	8
Mr G. Fowler c Wright b Shilton	20	– c and b Hornsby	0
Mr P. J. T. Henery c Vernon b Hornsby	19	– c Hornsby b Mee	32
Mr S. M. J. Woods b Shilton	7	– st Malden b Hornsby	6
Mr L. H. Gay b Hornsby	20	– b Shilton	15
Mr A. C. M. Croome b Hornsby	0	– c Wright b Hornsby	13
G. B. Nichols c Vernon b Shilton	13	– not out	8
E. J. Tyler not out	7	– b Hornsby	0
B 1, l-b 2, n-b 1	4	B 13, l-b 2	15
	186		163

East of England

Mr C. W. Wright c Tyler b Woods	50	– b Woods	6
Mr H. W. Bainbridge lbw b Tyler	5	– b Woods	4
Mr G. Brann c Fowler b Woods	9	– b Nichols	16
G. Ulyett b Gibson	44	– b Nichols	0
Mr W. Newham b Woods	18	– c sub. b Woods	51
Mr F. G. J. Ford b Woods	6	– b Woods	20
Mr J. H. J. Hornsby b Woods	9	– b Woods	2
Mr G. F. Vernon b Woods	0	– b Nichols	9
Mr E. Malden c Hewett b Palairet	2	– c Hewett b Woods	1
R. J. Mee not out	0	– not out	2
J. E. Shilton b Woods	4	– c Hewett b Morgan	17
B 9, l-b 3	12	B 12, l-b 1, n-b 1	14
	159		142

East of England Bowling

	Overs	Mdns	Runs	Wkts	Overs	Mdns	Runs	Wkts
Mee	13	4	28	0	15	2	20	1
Ford	8	0	32	1	2	0	11	0
Shilton	18.4	2	63	6	25	5	54	1
Hornsby	14	3	59	3	23	5	63	8

West of England Bowling

	Overs	Mdns	Runs	Wkts	Overs	Mdns	Runs	Wkts
Woods	24	7	56	7	27.1	4	53	6
Tyler	20	3	67	1	8	3	24	0
Nichols	8	3	11	0	15	6	28	3
Gibson	6	2	13	1				
Palairet	1	1	0	1	4	2	12	0
Morgan					3	1	11	1

Umpires: R. Thoms and T. Veitch.

NORTH v SOUTH

Played at Hastings, September 11, 12, 13, 1893

The concluding match of a very successful week's cricket at Hastings produced one of the most remarkable instances of rapid scoring ever recorded in first-class cricket. The early stages of the contest pointed to an easy victory for the South, who gained a lead of 93 runs on the first innings, and then got three of the Northern wickets down for eight runs. Later on, Sellers and C. W. Wright played capital cricket, but despite their endeavours the North were 14 runs behind when the fifth wicket went down in the second innings. At this point Ernest Smith and De Trafford became partners and brought about a most wonderful change in the game. Thinking they had the match in hand, the South doubtless took matters a little easily, but before they could realise what was happening Smith and De Trafford obtained a complete mastery over the bowling, and scored at a tremendous pace. Some mistakes were made in the field, and for these blunders the South had to pay a very dear price. The two men got together when the score stood at 79 for five wickets, and in the course of an hour and three-quarters they actually added 254 runs. So far as we know, such a number in so short a space of time is without parallel in a match of importance, and the nearest approach to it that we can recall is the famous stand by I. D. Walker and Alfred Lyttleton for Middlesex against Gloucestershire on the Clifton College ground in 1883. On that occasion Walker and Lyttelton made 324 while together, and at one time scored 226 in an hour and three-quarters. De Trafford's share of the 254 was 110, and though he was a little unsteady at starting and should have been caught by Grace at point when he had made 19, he afterwards settled down and batted as well as he had ever done in his life, making no further mistake until the hit which completed his hundred, when he was let off in the long field by Bean. Among his figures were sixteen 4s, three 3s, and nine 2s. Smith's hitting was even more vigorous than De Trafford's. He went in with the score at 57 for four wickets, and played with the greatest confidence and freedom throughout. He made no mistake until he had scored 94, when he gave a chance to Ferris in the long field, but he grew reckless after completing his hundred and was missed time after time. Smith, who was not got rid of until the third morning scored his 154 in two hours and five minutes, and his remarkable innings was made up by a 6, a 5, twenty-one 4s, five 3s, nine 2s, and twenty-six singles. The South were left with 261 runs to get to win, and though they made a splendid attempt to atone for their previous errors, the North always seemed to have a little the best of the game. Stoddart and Read played extremely well, but the Southern total in the end only reached 235, and thus a most extraordinary match ended in favour of the North by 25 runs. The Hastings week was a complete success from every point of view, and it is satisfactory to know that there was a profit of about £250 of receipts over expenses.

North

Mr C. E. de Trafford b Lockwood	1	– st Wood b Stoddart	110
Mr A. Sellers c Grace b Richardson	47	– b Hearne	48
A. Ward c Wood b Hearne	30	– c Bean b Lockwood	0
F. H. Sugg b Richardson	16	– b Richardson	8
W. Flowers b Hearne	8	– c Wood b Richardson	0
Mr E. Smith b Lockwood	13	– c Stoddart b Richardson	154
Mr C. W. Wright not out	6	– c Read b Richardson	18
R. Peel b Richardson	4	– b Lockwood	2
J. Briggs b Richardson	1	– b Richardson	0
W. Attewell c Ferris b Lockwood	22	– not out	8
M. Sherwin b Lockwood	4	– b Lockwood	0
B 6	6	B 4, w 1	5
	158		353

South

Mr A. E. Stoddart c Smith b Briggs	13 – b Peel	63
Mr W. G. Grace b Smith	0 – c Wright b Smith	8
Mr J. J. Ferris b Briggs	50 – b Peel	36
Mr H. T. Hewett c Attewell b Smith	7 – b Peel	0
G. Bean b Smith	0 – b Smith	6
Mr W. W. Read b Smith	33 – c Attewell b Smith	68
Mr W. L. Murdoch not out	71 – c Smith b Briggs	19
W. Lockwood c Sellers b Smith	4 – b Briggs	16
J. T. Hearne c Sellers b Peel	38 – lbw b Briggs	0
H. Wood st Sherwin b Flowers	10 – c and b Briggs	9
T. Richardson b Flowers	0 – not out	10
B 14, l-b 6, w 4, n-b 1	25	
	251	235

South Bowling

	Overs	Mdns	Runs	Wkts	Overs	Mdns	Runs	Wkts
Richardson	26	7	74	4	23	4	103	5
Lockwood	17	5	47	4	19	5	73	3
Hearne	16	6	24	2	16	2	76	1
Ferris	3	1	7	0	3	0	22	0
Read					2	0	15	0
Grace					5	0	50	0
Stoddart					2	0	9	1

North Bowling

	Overs	Mdns	Runs	Wkts	Overs	Mdns	Runs	Wkts
Smith	25	7	81	5	25.4	6	85	3
Briggs	23	6	63	2	22	6	62	4
Flowers	15.2	8	22	2				
Peel	14	6	43	1	17	3	47	3
Attewell	8	2	17	0	10	1	41	0

Umpires: R. Thoms and R. Carpenter.

MR A. E. STODDART'S ELEVEN v REST OF ENGLAND

Played at Hastings, September 9, 10, 11, 1895

Not even in a year of an Australian visit has a match at Hastings aroused a greater amount of public interest, the single appearance in England of Mr Stoddart's famous combination proving immensely attractive and drawing together vast crowds of spectators on each of the three days. One, of course, could not help regretting that such an important game should have been left absolutely till the end of the season, but the struggle was fully worthy of the occasion, the match being fought out with a keenness and determination that was quite refreshing. The public wanted to know whether we had a better team left behind in England than that which represented us so brilliantly in the Colonies, and this fact seemed to have impressed itself on every member of the two sides. As in the North and South match the weather was all that could be desired, and the game was decided on a capital wicket. Happily the interest was well sustained throughout and Stoddart's team, after having the worst of the position at the drawing of stumps on Tuesday evening, finished up with a display of batting, bowling and fielding that made it easy to understand how harmoniously they had worked together and how they had won so many good matches in Australia. Thanks to some superb batting on the part of W. W. Read and Woods the Rest of England gained a lead of 3 runs on the first innings. Stoddart's team on going in a second time fared badly, only the captain himself being able to offer any serious resistance to the admirable bowling of the England eleven, and at the drawing of stumps on the Tuesday six wickets had fallen for 120 runs. Stoddart's team were thus only 117 ahead with four batsmen to be got rid of. On the last morning, however, an extraordinary chance was brought about by Ford and Lockwood, the two men hitting with merciless severity, and putting on no fewer than 169 runs. With the score at 289 for six wickets Stoddart considered his position perfectly safe and declared the innings closed. Then Richardson and Peel, supported by some of the best fielding seen last season, got rid of the Rest of England for 68, and won the match for Stoddart's team by 218 runs. One could have wished to see F. S. Jackson, L. C. H. Palairet and K. S. Ranjitsinhji in the English eleven, but considering the lateness of the season the Hastings authorities did wonderfully well in getting together so representative a side. It will be seen that the two men standing out of Stoddart's team were L. H. Gay and Walter Humphreys.

Mr Stoddart's Team

A. Ward c Lilley b Mold	29	– c Lilley b Woods	6
W. Brockwell c Pougher b Woods	29	– c Lilley b Pougher	29
Mr A. E. Stoddart c Lilley b Mold	55	– b Mold	59
Mr A. C. MacLaren b Mold	0	– b Woods	7
J. T. Brown c Shrewsbury b Mold	24	– c Grace b Townsend	0
R. Peel c and b Woods	49	– b Pougher	8
Mr F. G. J. Ford b Mold	1	– not out	111
W. Lockwood b Woods	3	– not out	69
J. Briggs b Woods	4		
Mr H. Philipson not out	0		
T. Richardson c Mold b Woods	12		
B 4, l-b 5, n-b 2	11	B 6, l-b 3	9
	217	(6 wkts dec.)	289

Rest of England

Mr W. G. Grace b Richardson	0	– c Stoddart b Richardson	8
R. Abel b Richardson	15	– c Briggs b Peel	7
G. Davidson b Richardson	3	– c Ford b Richardson	5
A. Shrewsbury c Brockwell b Peel	12	– c Philipson b Richardson	1
A. Lilley b Richardson	21	– c Brown b Peel	2
Mr W. W. Read c Philipson b Peel	76	– c Philipson b Peel	18
Mr S. M. J. Woods c Brockwell b Lockwood	67	– c Brown b Peel	6
Mr C. L. Townsend c Peel b Lockwood	1	– c Brown b Peel	7
A. D. Pougher b Richardson	6	– c Brockwell b Richardson	2
F. Martin c Stoddart b Richardson	13	– c Philipson b Richardson	7
A. Mold not out	0	– not out	1
B 3, l-b 1, n-b 2	6	B 4	4
	220		68

Rest of England Bowling

	Overs	Mdns	Runs	Wkts	Overs	Mdns	Runs	Wkts
Mold	31	9	88	5	24	4	78	1
Townsend	9	1	42	0	21	2	71	1
Woods	24.4	3	75	5	15	2	36	2
Davidson	3	2	1	0	6	1	14	0
Pougher					29	13	53	2
Martin					6	0	28	0

Mr Stoddart's Team Bowling

	Overs	Mdns	Runs	Wkts	Overs	Mdns	Runs	Wkts
Richardson	40.1	11	99	6	21	12	21	5
Peel	35	15	69	2	20	4	43	5
Lockwood	9	1	35	2				
Briggs	3	1	10	0				
Brockwell	2	1	1	0				

Umpires: Thoms and Carpenter.

CANADA v THE UNITED STATES

Played at Philadelphia, September 4, 5, 7, 1896

The team which journeyed to Philadelphia was by no means representative of Canada, five of the men originally chosen being unable to play. Nevertheless, Canada, on a wicket greatly affected by rain, won a small scoring match by 40 runs. The victory was clearly due to the bowling of Laing, who had the extraordinary record of fourteen wickets for 54 runs. He is described as a very fast bowler, with a high action, one of the best balls he sends down being a yorker on the leg side. He stands 6 ft 2 ins in height and weighs a little over thirteen stone. Though overshadowed by Laing's greater success, King bowled very finely for the United States. Of the twenty-three matches played between the United States and Canada, the States have won fourteen, Canada seven, and two have been left drawn.

Canada

W. H. Cooper b Patterson	22	c Wood b King	20
J. T. McIntosh b King	0	c Clark b Patterson	13
P. C. Goldingham c Brown b King	10	b King	14
G. S. Lyon c Wood b Patterson	23	b King	1
J. M. Laing c Wood b King	1	b Patterson	23
W. A. Henry b Patterson	3	c Clark b King	6
H. Ackland c Wood b King	3	c Patterson b King	12
E. G. Rykert c and b Patterson	2	not out	12
W. C. Lyttle b Patterson	3	run out	0
W. E. Dean c Clark b Patterson	5	b King	1
H. B. McGiverin not out	3	c Biddle b Patterson	1
B 4, l-b 6, w 2	12	B 8, l-b 6	14
	87		117

United States

G. S. Patterson b McGiverin	3	c Laing	8
J. W. Muir b Laing	3	c Cooper b Laing	10
W. W. Noble b Laing	0	b Laing	1
A. M. Wood c and b McGiverin	5	b Laing	6
F. H. Bohlen b McGiverin	6	b Laing	13
L. A. Biddle b Laing	0	c Cooper b Lyon	23
E. M. Cregar b Laing	0	b Laing	4
J. B. King b Laing	0	c Lyon b Laing	8
H. I. Brown c and b Laing	1	b McGiverin	3
E. W. Clark b McGiverin	9	not out	18
F. W. Ralston not out	14	b Laing	7
B 7, l-b 4	11	B 4, l-b 6, w 1	11
	52		112

United States Bowling

	Overs	Mdns	Runs	Wkts	Overs	Mdns	Runs	Wkts
King	25.2	8	37	4	37	19	41	6
Clark	5	1	8	0	4	1	15	0
Patterson	22	13	22	6	35	16	38	4
Brown	4	0	8	0	3	0	7	0
Cregan					1	0	2	0

Canada Bowling

	Overs	Mdns	Runs	Wkts	Overs	Mdns	Runs	Wkts
Laing	12	4	17	6	27	11	37	8
McGiverin	12	4	24	4	23	6	50	1
Lyon					3	1	3	1
Goldingham					3	1	11	0

HOME COUNTIES v THE REST OF ENGLAND

Played at Hastings, September 7, 8, 9, 1899

The first match of the Hastings Festival was between the Australians and the South of England and the second the fixture under notice. From the time that the Rest of England saved the follow-on there was no prospect of arriving at any definite result, but for all that the closing stages of the match were full of animation, a wonderful display of hitting by Jessop on the Saturday afternoon affording the utmost delight to the crowd. A lot of fine batting was shown during the three days, Stoddart with a capital 44 showing how unnecessary was his retirement from County cricket. Townsend was kept on bowling for an unconscionable time in order that he might secure his hundred wickets in first-class matches and so accomplish the double feat of taking a hundred wickets and scoring 2,000 runs in one season.

Home Counties

Mr A. J. Turner c Rhodes b Townsend	22	– b Jessop	4
R. Abel b Hirst	40	– b Jessop	22
T. Hayward c Tyldesley b Townsend	13	– c MacLaren b Jessop	20
A. Hearne c Jessop b Townsend	15	– not out	51
Mr F. G. J. Ford b Hirst	22	– b Jessop	0
Mr D. L. A. Jephson c Hirst b Townsend	77	– c Rhodes b Townsend	58
K. S. Ranjitsinhji b Hirst	60		
Mr A. E. Stoddart c Board b Hirst	13	– c Mitchell b Rhodes	44
H. Young b Jessop	22		
H. R. Butt c Rhodes b Townsend	25		
Mr W. M. Bradley not out	3		
B 8, l-b 4, n-b 1	13	B 8, l-b 3, n-b 2	13
	331	(6 wkts dec.)	212

Rest of England

Mr A. C. MacLaren c Ford b Bradley	0	– b Young	4
W. G. Quaife b Young	81	– b Bradley	5
J. T. Tyldesley c and b Jephson	0	– c Butt b Bradley	70
Mr F. Mitchell c Butt b Bradley	29	– b Bradley	28
Mr C. L. Townsend b Jephson	6	– c Butt b Bradley	22
Mr G. L. Jessop c A. Hearne b Jephson	26	– not out	100
Mr W. G. Grace b Young	15	– not out	21
G. H. Hirst c A. Hearne b Young	9		
W. R. Cuttell c Hayward b Bradley	38		
J. H. Board not out	17		
W. Rhodes c A. Hearne b Young	0		
B 8, l-b 2, n-b 2	12	B 1	1
	233		251

Rest of England Bowling

	Overs	Mdns	Runs	Wkts	Overs	Mdns	Runs	Wkts
Townsend	54.4	8	163	5	5.2	0	18	1
Rhodes............	17	5	31	0	10	1	35	1
Jessop	14	5	26	1	18	6	67	4
Hirst	31	11	75	4	17	6	44	0
Cuttell	8	2	23	0	13	5	24	0
MacLaren					2	0	11	0

Home Counties' Bowling

	Overs	Mdns	Runs	Wkts	Overs	Mdns	Runs	Wkts
Bradley	21	6	77	3	20	1	85	4
Jephson	22	2	94	3	8	0	38	0
Young	20	4	45	4	16	3	60	1
A. Hearne	10	8	5	0	5	0	31	0
Hayward					6	0	31	0
Ford..............					1	0	5	0

Umpires: R. Thoms and J. Lillywhite.

HINTS FROM THE PRESS BOX, 1892

Many men I have met have said to me. "What a jolly life is yours, watching cricket matches all through the summer!" Yes, the life of a cricket reporter is in many respects a jolly one, seeing that his duty takes him where many thousands of his countrymen assemble for their pleasure. Given fine weather and a good wicket, I know no greater enjoyment than watching the varying fortunes of a game between two well-matched sides, and there are very few phases of journalistic life for which I would care to exchange that of a cricket reporter. One's duties, however, are not confined to looking on at a game at cricket and then sending off an account of what has taken place, as appears to be the idea of the general public. In the first place, looking on at a cricket match as a casual spectator and as a reporter are two very different things. The ordinary onlooker watches the play perhaps quite as keenly as he who has to record the many incidents of the game for the newspapers, but his attention is close or slack according as the play is exciting or not, whereas the man whose duty it is to give a faithful record of what takes place must not let his attention wander for a moment. From the time the first ball is bowled until the drawing of stumps, a matter often of more than seven hours, he has to keep his attention closely fixed upon the game and note every incident. This duty of itself would be a very slight one, but unfortunately for the reporter the exigencies of modern newspaper work necessitate the despatch of telegrams at frequent intervals from within a few minutes of the start of play until the call of time. Now were absolute accuracy not an essential, there would be no great strain in all this, but as that must be the first consideration, with promptitude of despatch next, the cricket writer who aims furthermore to bring out the salient features of the day's cricket (and in this respect the writers on the game to-day have, on Lord Harris's testimony, improved upon their predecessors) has no easy task before him. If he makes a slip in adding up a score, or fails to exercise the utmost promptitude in handing in a message at the telegraph office, he is speedily brought to book; whilst if in writing for morning papers he omits to notice any remarkable incident or prominent feature in the day's play, he is disgusted with himself.

That the cricket reporter does strive his utmost to furnish an accurate and intelligent account of what has taken place I can state as the result of many years' experience; indeed, I know no body of Press men who are keener about their work. Therefore it is that I claim they should be enabled to pursue their avocation under the most advantageous conditions. Three things are absolutely necessary in order that a cricket reporter may follow his calling with advantage to the public and with comfort to himself. First of all a good view of the game is required; next, a convenient place in which to write; and, beyond these necessities, he should be placed in close proximity to the scorers. At many grounds in days gone by, and at some enclosures at the present time, the last consideration was the placing of the Press tent or box in a position whence anything like a fair idea of the game was obtainable. Some corner at long-leg or deep in the slips was apparently the most suitable spot, according to the ideas of a county committee, and if the ground fell off in any direction, there, at the bottom of the slope, were the reporters placed. How, seated as they were, anyone but a committeeman could expect them to obtain an accurate idea of what was taking place passed comprehension, and yet, apart from the players, who, especially the young ones, never care what is said in the papers, there were no people more ready to complain of a real or imagined inaccuracy than the members of a county executive. A tent, usually facing the wind, was considered the most desirable covering for men during eight hours of the day, and even when a Press box was provided, the structure was generally a bare wooden erection in which little protection was afforded from sun, wind or rain. Again, the Press men were placed at one end of the ground, and their very good friends, the official scorers, at the other; whilst when, owing largely to the representations of newspaper men, the telegraph wires were extended to the ground, no effort was made to place the Press box and the telegraph office in proximity.

In many respects matters have, I am glad to think, changed for the better within the last fifteen years, and the managers of cricket grounds are beginning to realise that cricket reporters are not so much necessary evils as men whose efforts do much to popularise the game. While much has been improved of late years, however, only at a few grounds is the necessity of affording immediate and accurate information as to the prospects of play, for instance, adequately recognised. At one ground, too, admission to the pavilion is barred to newspaper men in quest of information concerning a match, but only in a district where it is considered desirable to separate by iron fences the members of a county club from the ordinary visitors to a cricket match. It may not be out of place if I briefly run through the chief cricket grounds of England, and point out where they might easily be improved. In many respects Kennington Oval affords an excellent example to other grounds, for the Press box is lofty and spacious, near the scorers, and in connection by lift with the telegraph office, whilst lavatory accommodation – no slight comfort on a hot August day – is also provided. The desks, however, are ill-adapted for hard work, and better seats – dare I say cushioned seats? – might also be provided.

At Lord's the arrangements for Press men are far from adequate, and, I imagine, it is only the uniform courtesy which one experiences from everyone connected with the headquarters of cricket that has prevented strong representations being made to the MCC. The accommodation is far too rough and limited, and indeed quite unworthy of Lord's Cricket Ground. Up in Yorkshire a good view is, as a rule, obtainable, but the managers of grounds have an abominable habit of placing the scorers about a hundred yards away from the reporters' box, and thus quite fail to realise the necessity for placing reporters, scorers, and telegraph clerks close to one another. At Sheffield, too, the place reserved for reporters is absurdly small, and should at least be doubled in extent. There is a wooden shanty in a bad position which does duty for a Press box at Trent Bridge, Nottingham, but except that it is shared by the telegraph clerks, anything more inadequate as a place for newspaper men to do their work in, it would not be easy to imagine. The view obtainable therefrom is a long-leg one; the box is raised only two or three feet from the ground, and, furthermore, attention is distracted by people passing in front all day long. Nottingham is a delightful town, but Trent Bridge can boast, I think, of the least desirable Press box in England.

After troublous times with the officials at Old Trafford, and journeying from the corner of a covered stand to a wretched box which let in wind, rain, and dust (whichever was the most prominent nuisance of the day), the Manchester Press men have at length obtained a suitable structure in which to do their work. A capital view is obtainable, and the telegraph office is below, but, with that perversity which is the curse of county committees, the scorers are still placed a hundred yards or so distant. Old Trafford, however, is probably the most difficult cricket ground in England at which to obtain information; and whereas everywhere else a Press man can after rain make enquiries in the pavilion whether play is to be continued or the game to be abandoned, I have known the first news of a decision to be conveyed by the sight of the players carrying away their bags to the gates of the Manchester ground. Inasmuch as the executive have built a very good Press box, and thereby shown some consideration for those who, in the pursuit of their calling, have brought heaps of money to the Lancashire County Club, I trust they will take further steps in the path of courtesy, and remove from the Manchester ground the reputation it possesses amongst Press men of being the most disagreeable place in England at which to have to work. Liverpool, owing to the lack of consideration shown by the telegraph authorities, would have no big cricket matches if reporters had their way; but the arrangements at the ground are fairly good, and one may venture into the pavilion without risk of suffering an indignity. At Derby, Press men are fairly well off, except for the distance from the scorers; but at Leicester, of late, the arrangements are far from good, whilst at Birmingham the defect have, I am glad to know, been remedied, with the important exception of a telegraph office on the ground. Down in Kent reporters at cricket matches generally have to sit in tents, and if these were placed with better judgment they would be by no means disagreeable in fine weather; but at the great Canterbury festival I have noticed a gradual tendency to diminish the extent of the Press tent, until it is nowadays by no means large enough to enable those whose duties take them to the St Lawrence ground to conduct their business in comfort. One of the first of Press boxes was that at Brighton, and though it is now a little old-fashioned, the scorers are at hand and the telegraph office is at no great distance. When, however, the Sussex County Club have money to spare, they would do well to erect a structure at one end of the ground, with the telegraph office below and room for both scorers and reporters above.

In the West, again, or rather I should say in Gloucestershire, badly-placed tents are still in vogue, but they are preferable to the small and unsatisfactory box at the Bristol ground, whence only two or three can properly view the game. Down at Taunton everything naturally is on a smaller scale than at the more famous cricket centres, but I take this opportunity of tendering to the Somerset County Club, on behalf of my fellow-Press men, the assurance of our appreciation of the efforts made for the convenience of reporters. With the scorers on our left and the telegraph-office below, the Taunton Press box is one which, with some increase in dimensions, might serve as a pattern all over the country.

Another help to reporters I should like to see extended to all grounds would be the erection of scoring boards, upon which each run is registered as it is made, such as are in use at Lord's, Kennington Oval, and Nottingham, and the practice at Lord's, The Oval, and Brighton of granting newspaper men unlimited printed slips of the score during the day is also a great convenience. A Press box should be placed as nearly as possible in a line with the two wickets, so that an end-on view is obtained therefrom, and it should be raised a considerable height from the ground, with the scorers close at hand, and the telegraph clerks below. These requirements are absolutely necessary for the due fulfilment of a cricket reporter's duties, and considering the importance which is now attached to the game of cricket, and the space which is devoted to it in the newspapers, I think that they are no more than county cricket clubs may be reasonably asked to concede.

C. S. C.

OBITUARIES

CANON CAZENOVE, who died in August, 1893, while playing lawn tennis, performed an extraordinary bowling feat at Oxford on May 5, 6, 1853. Playing for the Undergraduates of Oxford against Oxfordshire, he obtained no fewer than sixteen wickets, securing all the ten in the first innings of the county, and six in the second. Five of the ten wickets were taken in one over, the umpire inadvertently allowing an extra ball. Canon Cazenove was born at Clapton in Middlesex on February 12, 1833, and played for Oxford against Cambridge at Lord's in 1851 and 1852. He was a round-arm bowler of medium pace.

DR HENRY GRACE, the eldest member of the famous cricket family, died on November 13, 1895, from an attack of apoplexy. He was born on January 31, 1833, and was thus in his sixty-third year. Though never coming prominently before the public, like his younger brothers, E. M., W. G. and G. F., Dr Henry was, in his young days, an excellent cricketer, and but for the calls of his profession would probably have played more frequently in important matches. He is described as having been a vigorous bat, a medium-pace round-arm bowler, and an excellent field – mostly at point. He appeared at Lord's for the first time on July 18, 19, 1861, and, with a first innings of 63 not out, materially helped the South Wales Club to beat the MCC by seven wickets. The match is a historical one, inasmuch as it introduced Mr E. M. Grace to Lord's ground. Dr Henry Grace was from the formation of the county club an enthusiastic supporter of Gloucestershire cricket, and was never absent from the county matches played at home.

THE REV. J. H. KIRWAN died on June 13, 1899, at a very advanced age. He played his first match at Lord's for Eton against Harrow in 1834. Mr Kirwan's name will live in cricket history if only by reason of one performance. In the match between the MCC and Eton on July 9, 1835, he bowled down all the ten wickets in the MCC's second innings. After leaving Eton he went up to Cambridge, and in a match between the Town and University on May 24, 1836, he took fifteen of the Town Club's wickets – all being bowled down. He took six wickets in the first innings and nine in the second. He was in the Cambridge eleven, but was unable to play against Oxford at Lord's in 1836. He was a round arm bowler of tremendous pace, with a very low delivery which, Mr Haygarth says, approached a jerk but was allowed.

THOMAS LORD died on April 22, 1899.

CARDINAL MANNING died on January 14, 1892, aged eighty-three. It may seem a little strange to include Cardinal Manning's name in a cricket obituary, but inasmuch as he played for Harrow against Winchester at Lord's in 1825, in the first match that ever took place between the two schools, his claim cannot be disputed.

MR PERCY STANISLAUS McDONNELL, the announcement of whose death at Brisbane at the end of September, 1896, caused a painful shock in English cricket circles, will always be remembered as one of the most brilliant of Australian batsmen. He came to England with the teams of 1880, 1882 and 1884, and paid his fourth and last visit in 1888, when he was captain of the eleven. It seems he had been ill for some little time, and that his death was not so sudden as was at first supposed. A splendid hitter and under all circumstances a dangerous run-getter, McDonnell was in proportion a finer bat on bad wickets than on good ones. Indeed it may be questioned if on a pitch thoroughly ruined by rain he has ever been equalled. Time after time during his visits to England his fearless hitting under almost impossible conditions turned the scale in favour of his side, his greatest achievement being the memorable innings of 82 with which he won the match against the North of England at Old Trafford in 1888. Mr McDonnell was born in London on November 13, 1860, but inasmuch as he was taken out to the Colonies while quite a child, his early cricket associations were entirely Australian. A summary of his doings as a batsman during his four trips to England will no doubt be read with interest.

	Innings	Runs	Highest innings	Average
1880*	19	418	79	23.4
1882	55	900	82	17.16
1884	54	1,225	103	23.29
1888	62	1,323	105	22.51

* Eleven-a-side matches only.

IN MEMORIAM

CHARLES F. PARDON

It would scarcely be fitting to allow the twenty-eighth issue of *Wisden* to appear without some tribute to the memory of the gentleman who for four years filled the post of editor with so much zeal and ability. When Mr Pardon first became associated with it the Almanack had reached a critical stage of its existence, an unfortunate delay in the production of the volume for 1886 – a delay for which we were in no way responsible – having to some extent injured its influence. However, Mr Pardon set to work with characteristic energy to make up the lost ground, and the best proof of his success was found in the largely-increased favour extended to the Almanack by the public during the years of his editorship. His untimely death [in 1890] terminated a friendship to which we shall always look back with keen pleasure.

JOHN WISDEN & CO.

GEORGE PARR (Nottinghamshire) died June 23, 1891. As he was born at Radcliffe-on-Trent on May 22, 1826, he had, at the time of his death, completed his sixty-fifty year. Readers of *Wisden's Almanack* will not need to be told that George Parr for many years occupied an undisputed position as the best bat in England, succeeding Fuller Pilch in that enviable distinction, and holding his own until he, in turn, was supplanted by Hayward and Carpenter. His career as a public player was a very long one, commencing in 1844 and not coming to an end until 1871. He lived all his life in his native village, and the attendance at his funeral there showed the respect in which he was held. With the wreaths on his coffin was placed a branch from the tree at the Trent Bridge ground which has for a generation past been known as "George Parr's Tree". This name it acquired in connection with the great batsman's leg-hitting. Parr was for many years captain of the Nottinghamshire county eleven, a post which, on his retirement, was given to Richard Daft, and he was also for a long period captain of the old All-England Eleven, a position in which he succeeded William Clarke, the first organiser of the team. George Parr went to America with the English team in 1859, and he was also captain of the splendid eleven which journeyed to Australia in the winter of 1863-64. Among the many brilliant innings that he played for his county, the highest, and the one most often referred to, was 130 against Surrey at The Oval in 1859.

RICHARD PILLING, the greatest English wicket-keeper of his day, died on March 28, 1891. He was born on July 5, 1855, and was thus in his thirty-sixth year. Some few details of Pilling's brilliant career were given in *Wisden's Almanack* for 1891, when his portrait appeared, in company with those of Blackham, Sherwin, Wood and McGregor. Pilling made his first appearance for Lancashire in August 1877, and was at once recognised as a wicket-keeper of the highest class. Succeeding Mr Jackson in the county team, he was the regular wicket-keeper for Lancashire from his first match in 1877 down to the end of the season of 1889, and, no doubt, but for the unfortunate failure of his health, would have retained the post for several years longer. Unhappily in the winter of 1889-90 he caught a severe cold while taking part in a football match. An attack of influenza and inflammation of the lungs followed, and from this he never recovered. His constitution, by no means a robust one at the best, broke down completely, consumption developing itself with great rapidity. He was quite unable to play cricket during 1890, and at the end of the season, as a last chance of restoring him to health, the Lancashire County Club sent him on a voyage to Australia. Unfortunately the disease had obtained too strong a hold to be alleviated, and when Pilling came back to England in March, it was seen at once that his case was quite hopeless. Indeed, he had only been in England two or three days before he died. Pilling's career is too fresh in the memory of cricket readers to render any description of it necessary, but we may repeat the opinion we expressed last year that among the wicket-keepers of his day his only superior was Blackham. During his career he paid two professional visits to Australia – as a member of Shaw and Shrewsbury's first combination in 1881-82, and with the fourth in 1887-88.

JOHN PLATTS, the well-known Derbyshire cricketer – one of the best all round players possessed by the county in its early days – died on August 6, 1898. He was in his fiftieth year having been born on December 6, 1848. A tragic interest attached to the start of Platts' career as a cricketer, as it was a ball bowled by him in the MCC and Nottinghamshire match at Lord's in 1870 that caused the death of George Summers. At that time a very fast bowler, Platts afterwards lessened his pace and the catastrophe made such a painful impression upon him, that it is said he never in subsequent years could play, with any pleasure, at Lord's ground. After dropping out of active work in the cricket field he became one of the regular county umpires.

THE REV. JAMES PYCROFT, who died on March 10, 1895, at Brighton, aged eighty-two, will be remembered for all time as the author of *The Cricket Field.* In the course of his long life he wrote much about the game to which he was devoted, but *The Cricket Field* is emphatically the work upon which his fame will rest. A good cricketer himself in his Oxford days, he played at Lord's in 1836 in the second of the long series of matches between the two Universities, among those who took part in the same game being Lord Bessborough – then the Hon. Frederick Ponsonby – Mr R. Broughton and Mr C. G. Taylor. The University match was first played in 1892, and became an annual fixture in 1838. Knowing cricket thoroughly, Mr Pycroft was certainly one of the best writers on the game. He was, if we may judge from some of his works, a little inclined to think that the great men of the Fuller Pilch and Alfred Mynn era were superior to any of their successors, but this perhaps unconscious prejudice in favour of the cricketers of his young days does not make his pages any the less entertaining. He was for about thirty years on the committee of the Sussex County Club, and retained to the last a lively interest in Sussex cricket.

WILLIAM SCOTTON (Nottinghamshire), who died by his own hand on July 9, 1893, was born on January 15, 1856, and was thus in his thirty-eighth year. For some time previous to his tragic end he had been in a very low, depressed condition, the fact that he had lost his place in the Nottinghamshire eleven having, so it was stated at the inquest, preyed very seriously upon his mind. Scotton played his first match at Lord's for Sixteen

Colts of England against the MCC on the May 11, 12, 1874, scoring on that occasion 19 and 0. He was engaged as a groundsman by the MCC in that year and 1875, and after an engagement at Kennington Oval returned to the service of the MCC, of whose ground staff he was a member at the time of his death. His powers were rather slow to ripen, and he had been playing for several years before he obtained anything like a first-rate position. At one period of his career, however, and more particularly during the seasons of 1884 and 1886, he was beyond all question the best professional left-handed batsman in England. In 1884 he scored 567 runs for Nottinghamshire in thirteen matches, with an average of 31.9; in 1885, 442 runs in fourteen engagements, with an average of 22.2; and in 1886, in county fixtures only, 559 runs, with an average of 29.8. Though he several times made higher scores, his finest performance was undoubtedly his innings of 90 for England against Australia at Kennington Oval in August, 1884. The match, as cricket readers will readily remember, resulted in a draw, Australia scoring 551 and England 346 and 85 for two wickets. In England's first innings Scotton went in first, and was the ninth man out, the total when he left being 332. During a stay of five hours and three-quarters he played the bowling of Spofforth, Palmer, Boyle, Midwinter and George Giffen without giving the slightest chance, and but for his impregnable defence it is quite likely that England would have been beaten. Up to a certain time he received very little assistance, but when W. W. Read joined him, 151 runs were put on for the ninth wicket. Against the Australian team of 1886 Scotton played two remarkable innings in company with Mr W. G. Grace, the two batsmen scoring 170 together for the first wicket for England at The Oval, and 156 for Lord Londesborough's Eleven at Scarborough. Scotton's score at The Oval was only 34, but at Scarborough he made 71. Scotton paid three visits to Australia, going out with Shaw and Shrewsbury's teams in 1881, 1884 and 1886. In the three tours he averaged respectively in the eleven-a-side matches, 20.8, 17.3 and 10.13. Few left-handed men have ever played with so straight a bat or possessed such a strong defence, but he carried caution to such extremes that it was often impossible to take any pleasure in seeing him play.

E. M. GRACE IN THE CRICKET FIELD, 1899

During the autumn Mr E. M. Grace was kind enough to send me – to do what I liked with – the statistics of his career in the cricket field from the time when, as a lad of less than ten years old, he played his first match in 1851 down to the end of the past season. Without going into details or separating big matches from small ones, he sent a concise statement of the runs he had scored and the wickets he had taken in forty-nine years, and very wonderful the figures looked. They struck me as so interesting that after seeing to their immediate publication in several newspapers I thought I could not do better than find a place for them in *Wisden's Almanack*. At the time Mr Grace wrote to me I feared he had determined to give up cricket, but in answer to my enquiry he wrote that he had no such intention and should go on playing as long as possible. It is of course unreasonable to expect him at fifty-eight years of age to equal his old feats with either bat or ball but as he is full of vigour and capable of hunting four days a week he will probably be seen in the Thornbury eleven for several seasons to come.

I never look at E. M. Grace's scores in old Almanacks and newspapers without wondering what would have been thought of him if he had not found in his own family a greater than himself. He was the biggest run-getter in the world when he went out to Australia with George Parr's team in 1863, and was a greater force on a side than any other player of that day – V. E. Walker not excepted. When he returned home, however, in the following year W. G. appeared on the scene and it was readily seen that the younger brother would soon be the finer bat of the two. E. M. Grace had by sheer force of genius for the game risen to the top of the tree in defiance of orthodox rules, for with all his great qualities he never played with a straight bat. W. G. also had genius, and played with a bat as straight as Fuller Pilch's. While W. G. went on from strength to strength – at eighteen he was clearly the best bat in England – E. M. dropped to some extent out of public matches, his medical work taking up a good deal of his time. However, with the formation of the Gloucestershire County Club, E. M. started what I may call the second half of his career. He was still quite a young man and, always playing plenty of local cricket, he had kept himself in thorough practice. He helped to lift Gloucestershire in 1876 and 1877 to the very top of the tree and kept his place in the team down to quite recent years. Perhaps he played for a season or two longer than he ought to have done, but one can well understand his reluctance to finally withdraw from an eleven with which he had from its start been so closely associated. During all those long years he did many big things for Gloucestershire but never was his skill as a batsman shown in a brighter light than when he played against the first Australian teams in 1878 and 1880. At Clifton in 1880, though he did not succeed in winning Gloucestershire the match, he astonished Spofforth by hooking to the boundary some of the best balls that greatest of bowlers sent down. His success on that occasion – he scored 65 and 41 – led to what I have always regarded as the crowning triumph of his career. Seventeen years had passed away since he reached his highest point as a batsman, and yet, purely on his merits, he was picked for the first England and Australia match ever played in this country. It was an eventful moment in the history of modern cricket when on that September day in 1880 he and W. G. opened England's innings at The Oval. They scored 92 runs together for the first wicket, and so laid the foundation of England's score of 420. A melancholy interest will always in the Grace family attach to the match as it was the last one – or at any rate the last one of any public interest – in which the three brothers took part together. On September 22, Fred Grace was dead.

It is a thousand pities that E. M. Grace has never been induced to write and publish his recollections of the cricket field. It is not at all right that the endless good stories he tells with such racy humour should all be lost to the world. More than that, he would, I think, be able to give us a fuller and better comparison of the great players of his youth with those of our own day, than has yet appeared. He has enjoyed an almost unique experience, making as he did big scores against Jackson, Tarrant and Willsher, and playing in his later days against Spofforth, Palmer, Turner, Ferris, Lohmann and Richardson. As a batsman, E. M. Grace may fairly be described as the great revolutionist. When he came before the public, batting was a very orthodox science indeed, the "pull" with which we are now almost too familiar being regarded as little less than a sin. E. M. Grace changed all that. Disregarding the protests of the purists he scored where he could and thought nothing of taking the ball from wide of the off stump round to the on-side if by so doing he could score four runs. More than anyone else he enlarged the scope of batting, and those who on the perfectly-prepared wickets of these days pull with such certainty, should modestly remember that E. M. Grace, playing under far less favourable conditions, first showed more than five and thirty years ago how the thing could be done. In regard to his personal characteristics E. M. Grace is very happily hit off in a phrase in the seventh volume of *Scores and Biographies*, Mr Haygarth describing him as "Overflowing with cricket at every pore, full of lusty life, cheerily gay, with energy inexhaustible". The words were written of Mr Grace when he was twenty, and though he is now fifty-eight they still hold good. I am not without hope that the famous cricketer may yet embody his experiences in book form. At one time, at any rate, he was not averse to writing, for he tells me that when returning from Australia in 1864, he wrote a full account of the doings of George Parr's team, intending to publish it when he got back to England. For some reason, however, the project fell through, and the matter, covering ten quires of foolscap, remains in manuscript. The last page, as giving Mr Grace's impressions of Australia five and thirty years ago, will be read with no little interest:

> "I saw what I have told. Australasia was hung with flags and clothed in purple and fine linen. Senators, cheers, complimentary speeches, and brass bands met the Eleven everywhere. But I have no reason to believe that there were hid beneath this glittering surface those festering sores – poverty, ignorance and injustice which are corroding the vitals of so many older states. In all the enjoyment there was nothing forced or unnatural, it was the healthy pleasure-taking of men in at least comfortable circumstances. We did not see the Australians in their business life, but we were sure that when they returned to the ordinary cares of business, though the laugh and frolic might have passed, they would still possess comfort and prosperity. I do not say that suffering never visits the homes of Sydney, Melbourne or Dunedin, nor do I wish to convey the idea that even want is actually unknown – sickness, disappointment, care, anxiety and bereavement cast shadows as dark in the Southern Hemisphere as in the Northern. The widow and the orphan, the victims of disease and accident, the aged and infirm, all these find that even in the golden land there are privations. But the charities of the people are lage and the helpless are few in number. I can say with truth that I have not tried to colour this sketch. For myself it took me nine months from the time I left home to the time I returned. During that time I travelled a little more than thirty thousand miles, saw the three leading Australasian colonies, Ceylon, Aden, the Red Sea, Suez, the Mediterranean, Malta and passed through France and gathered ideas which before had not risen above the horizon of my thoughts. As a cricketer I was not at all successful. I began to play recklessly and could not alter till too late. At Beechworth, when the Eleven had gone home, I played better than I had done all through. Various little sicknesses aided by recklessness, a bad hand, a bad foot, an accident breaking the sheath of one of the muscles of my right elbow so that I could not throw at all, and a continual dimness of sight were sufficient to push me back. If I did not make scores however I made notes – and so, farewell!"

With this quotation I will leave the record of Mr E. M. Grace's career to speak for itself, merely adding that though the figures let us know how many runs he has made and how many wickets he has taken, they cannot tell us that he was, by universal consent, the most brilliant and daring field at point the world of cricket has ever seen.

S. H. P.

Year	Wickets taken	Runs scored	Year	Wickets taken	Runs scored
1851	22	256	1875	369	2,426
1852	26	370	1876	262	2,020
1853	35	431	1877	268	1,351
1854	89	446	1878	260	2,114
1855	73	563	1879	239	2,048
1856	82	579	1880	250	1,384
1857	76	628	1881	253	2,770
1858	69	870	1882	201	2,726
1859	173	1,121	1883	250	3,166
1860	189	1,372	1884	231	2,556
1861	286	1,747	1886	175	1,179
1862	312	2,190	1887	214	1,422
1863	339	3,074	1888	224	2,016
1864	370	2,054	1889	223	1,139
1865	246	1,626	1890	278	1,221
1866	196	1,738	1891	203	1,173
1867	166	1,218	1892	232	1,284
1868	128	1,300	1893	217	1,464
1869	163	1,979	1894	223	1,320
1870	194	1,100	1895	240	973
1871	186	1,538	1896	205	864
1872	239	2,628	1897	227	990
1873	298	2,493	1898	241	831
1874	312	2,052	1899	252	672
				10,006	72,484

E. M. Grace did not play in 1885 owing to an injured knee.

PERSONAL RECOLLECTIONS OF W. G. GRACE, 1895

By LORD HARRIS

The editor of this Annual has asked me to write a short account of Dr W. G. Grace as I have found him during my cricket career. I fear I have but little that is new to add to all that has been already written about W. G., and I also find that five years' absence from first-class cricket, about a quarter of a man's first-class cricketing life, has made sad breaches in my memory.

I well remember the first time I saw the old man – as all cricketers love to call him; it must have been about '67 or '68 that a few of the Eton eleven were taken up to Lord's by Mr Mitchell on a holiday for the express purpose of seeing W. G. bat, and thereby having our own ideas improved. It was a drizzly cold morning, and W. G. in a thick overcoat had a spirited argument with "Mike" as to the weather and the ground being fit for cricket, the former, caring little about standing as a model for us, thinking it was not; and the latter, caring little as to the particular match, thinking it was. I must have seen but little of W. G. between then and '72, except in Canterbury in the week, but in '72 I had a two months' experience of his comradeship during the tour in Canada and the States of Mr R. A. FitzGerald's team, the first amateur eleven that crossed the seas on a cricketing tour, and a right good eleven it was, the best strictly amateur team, I should say, that has ever been made up for that purpose. W. G. and poor Cuthbert Ottaway went in first, and generally put on 100 before the first wicket fell, a pretty good start, with the "Monkey", Alfred Lubbock, and Walter Hadow to follow on; and then what a bowling side it was, Appleby dead on the off stump every ball, and Billy Rose, about the best lob bowler I ever saw, at the other end, and W. G. and C. K. Francis as changes. But the history of the tour, is it not written in *Wickets in the West*, by that prince of cricket reporters, Bob FitzGerald himself? So I will not reproduce the time-honoured allusion to W. G.'s speeches, but content myself with bearing grateful witness to the kindly sympathetic consideration which characterised his comradeship. That tour commenced and cemented a friendship between us which I value at the highest.

From about '76 to '86 I saw a good deal of the old man's play in the big matches, and I shall never see such all-round play again. There may arise a bat as good, and at point and to his own bowling a field as good, and, of course, there have been and will be bowlers as good, but I doubt one generation producing two such all-round cricketers. And remember, my young friends, that this super-excellence was not the result of eminent physical fitness only, it depended a good deal also on the careful life the old man led. He did not play brilliantly despite how he lived, as some, whose all too brief careers I can remember, did, but he regulated his habits of life with such care and moderation that his physical capacity was always at its best, and has lasted in the most marvellous manner. I shall always hold that W. G. was the best and pluckiest field to his own bowling I ever saw. The ground he used to cover to the off – and with the leg break on of course the majority of straight balls went there – made him as good as a twelfth man. He used to have his mid-on nearly straight behind the bowler's arm so as to cover the balls hit straight back. I fancy I've noticed that he has not tried for long leg catches so much since poor dear Fred Grace, the safest catch I ever saw, went home, but it may be only fancy. And then the hot 'uns I've seen him put his hands to, half volleys hit at ten yards distance, low down, with all the momentum of a jump in and a swinging bat, catches that looked like grinding his knuckles against the sole of his boot, but I never saw the old man flinch. And that reminds me of a rather humorous incident when England played the Australians at The Oval late in the year in 1880. We had seen very little of them that year, as, in consequence of the affair at Sydney in '79, they could get no good matches arranged, but late in the year the sore was healed and a match arranged.

Percy MacDonnell was in and Fred Morley bowling, and for some reason, obscure to both of us I should think ever since, W. G. and I agreed that he should go silly mid-off. The wicket was not a slow one, and, under any circumstances, Percy MacDonnell was not the sort of bat to stand close up to on the off side. Well, presently Fred bowled one of his half volleys on the off, MacDonnell gave it the full swing of his powerful shoulders, and the first thing that everyone realised subsequently was that it had hit the old man. He had had no time to stoop, or dodge, or move a finger, but luckily for him, it hit him on the heel of his boot, and he was none the worse. I saw W. G. blink his eyes and look at the batsman in that searching way that others besides myself must have noticed I should think, and he stayed there till the end of the over – after that we thought he might be more useful further back.

I always thought the old man depended rather too much on the umpire for leg before, particularly when I was on the opposite side. He crossed the wicket so far to the off himself that he could not in many instances judge with any accuracy whether the ball pitched straight or not, and I don't think a bowler ought to ask for leg before unless he is pretty sure as to the pitch. I remember one day at Canterbury, the wind was blowing pretty strongly across the ground, and W. G. was lobbing them up in the air to get all the advantage of the wind. I kept on fetching them round to sharp long leg – I never hit him suqare – or trying to, and every time the ball hit my leg he asked, and every time he asked Willsher shook his head, and the old man was getting almost savage, when, at last, I got my left leg too much to the off, and the ball went through my legs and bowled me. Of course, W. G. held that was proof positive that all the others would have hit the wicket too, whilst I held that that was possible, but that none of them had pitched straight.

Another reminiscence connecting him with Canterbury Week is that weary day – or day and a half I might say – when he made his 344. We had got a big score in our first and only innings, and had got MCC out for something small. I thought it rather odd, for the wicket was all right, and our bowling was not very deadly, and my forebodings were well founded. It did not matter what we bowled for that day and a half, most balls went quite impartially to the boundary. Mr Foord Kelcey always declared in after years that about five o'clock on the Friday evening, all our bowling being used up, he and poor old "Bos" (Mr C. A. Absolom) went on permanently!

On the whole, however, I think in those days we used to get rid of W. G. pretty luckily when we met him, but he gave us a severe taste of his quality at Clifton one year, over a century each innings. When he had got 98 second innings I thought perhaps a bad lob might produce results. Henty was no longer a member of the Kent team, or he would have gone on, as he always did when we were in serious difficulties, without taking his pads off, but either Mr Patterson or I could bowl quite as bad a lob as he ever did, so one of us, I forget which, went on, and sure enough something did result. The old man hit a fourer, scored his second century in the same match for the second time in his career, and stumps were drawn. Some people said I did this on purpose to let him get his second century, but that allegation was not founded on absolute knowledge, and a bad lob when a man is well set is sometimes luckier than a good ball.

A lucky selection came off in one Gentlemen v Players' match at The Oval. I was not playing myself, but I saw the ball bowled. The captain of the Players' team had been asked whether there was anybody in particular they wanted to play, and he – either Dicky Daft or Bob Carpenter I think – said they would like to have Emmett, because he might bowl Dr Grace out early, and sure enough Tom bowled him, and first ball I think.

I have referred to poor Fred Grace's fine fielding, and I recall an incident at The Oval in a match we played late in the year for the benefit of the sufferers by the sinking of the "Princess Alice", an excursion boat. Fred was bowling, W. G. was point, and I was mid-off. The batsman skied one so high on the off side that we three had quite a little conversation which of us should have it. It was a horribly cold day, and I had no particular fancy for it, and when Fred said he would have it I was quite ready to resign, knowing he was certain to hold it, which he did.

I do not know whether it is fancy, but I shall always believe that W. G.'s later style of batting is quite different from what it was between '70 and '80. Now he plays the regulation back and forward strokes, but at that time he seemed to me to play every good length straight ball just in front of the popping crease, meeting it with a perfectly straight bat every time, but a kind of half stroke, only possible when great experience of the bowling, a very clear eye, and great confidence are combined. Remembering how many straight balls he used to place on the on side in those days, and the improbability therefore of the full face of the bat being given to the ball at the moment of impact, his extraordinary accuracy of eye can perhaps be realised.

I did not expect when I left England in 1890 ever again to play in a first-class match with my old friend; and – though but for a broken finger I might have done so at Gravesend this year – I fear my expectations will be realised, but I had the opportunity of taking a part in paying him what I know he holds to be as great a compliment as ever was paid him – viz., the decision of the Marylebone Cricket Club to give its support to the National Testimonial which was so enthusiastically started this year. I gave my vote for that decision, not merely because I regard W. G. as the most prominent exponent there has ever been of the finest and purest game that has ever been played, but also because the old man is the kindest and most sympathetic cricketer I have ever played with. As I said in proposing his health some years ago at a banquet the Kent County Club gave in his honour, I never knew a man make a mistake in the field but what W. G. had a kind word to say to, and an excuse to find for him, and I doubt if I could conclude with anything in praise of my old friend which would be truer or more gratifying to his feelings than that.

W. G. GRACE

By A. G. STEEL

Yielding to none in admiration of the "hero" of a hundred centuries, and to none in love for the game in which he is so proficient, I am bound to say I was not altogether pleased with the *Daily Telegraph* testimonial. A national testimonial in honour of the greatest cricketer the world has ever seen, on his completion of a performance which may be a "record" for all time, was indeed fitting. Surely the greatest cricket club in the world – the MCC – was the proper initiator of the testimonial to the greatest cricketer. Day after day, as one read of the flood of shillings pouring in, accompanied by such varied correspondence, one could not but feel a little alarm for the dignity of our great game. But whether the means adopted for raising the testimonial were the right ones or not, the fact remains that it was an enormous success, and showed that the personality of W. G. Grace had taken a deep hold upon all classes of the English people. The enthusiasm was such as has probably never before been kindled concerning the exponent of any modern form of athletics.

The first occasion I ever played against W. G. was at Cambridge in the summer of 1878, and this was also the first time I ever saw him play. I remember being desperately anxious to get him out, but I was disappointed, and on my telling him what pleasure it would give me to get him out, he laughingly replied, "It's only a question of time; if you go on long enough you are bound to get me out". I was not, however, successful on that occasion, but I shall never forget the kindly encouragement I, a young cricketer, received from W. G. the first time I met him. It was not, however, his batting, oddly enough, which struck me as so wonderful, it was his bowling. Never, as far as I know, did any bowler give the same peculiar flight to the ball as W. G. does, and well justified is the remark I have often heard him make of a newly-arrived batsman, "Oh, he's a young one, is he? I think I ought to do for him", and he generally does.

W. G. has, so it goes without saying, a thorough knowledge of the game, and I recollect well in the summer of 1878 an incident which well illustrates the fact. North v South was being played at Lord's. Barlow, the Lancashire professional, was batting, and W. G. was fielding point. Now Barlow had a trick of tapping the ball away after he had played it, and occasionally, in order to excite a laugh from the onlookers, would scamper down the pitch for a yard or two and then back again. On this occasion he just stopped the ball and it lay by his crease; he then tapped it towards point, and perhaps thinking he would hustle that fielder, he went through his performance of dashing down the pitch and back again. He must have been thoroughly upset by the action of point, who, ignoring the ball, quietly asked the umpire, "How's that for hitting the ball twice?" and out Barlow had to go – a lesson which he never forgot. It was, I think, in that very match that W. G. hit two consecutive balls from Alfred Shaw clean out of the Lord's Cricket Ground. It is true the wickets were pitched slightly on the south side of the ground, but they were both glorious knocks; one went clean over the tavern and the other pitched right on the top of it.

One of the finest innings I ever saw W. G. play was his 152 against the Australians in the match England v Australia at The Oval in 1880. Certainly he was batting on a good wicket, but his timing of the ball on this occasion was absolutely perfect, and the crispness of his strokes perfection. W. L. Murdoch made 153 in the second innings of this match; a very fine performance it was, too. I afterwards heard a discussion between some of the Australian team as to whether Murdoch was a finer batsman than Grace. A. Bannerman, the little Stonewaller of his side, clinched it by saying, in his brusque way, "W. G. has forgotten more about batting than Billy (Murdoch) ever knew". And A. Bannerman was a very fine judge of the game.

It is during the annual week at Scarborough that W. G. is, perhaps, seen at his best. The cricket, of course, is good, but there is a sort of holiday aspect about it which is absent from the more serious county and Gentlemen v Players matches that take place earlier in the season. I always used to think that W. G. hit harder and oftener at Scarborough than elsewhere. I recollect one occasion when he was playing for a team called, I think, the Gentlemen of England against the Zingari. The latter had a good batting side, but were very weak in bowling. The wicket was good and the Gentlemen won the toss. As the Zingari went into the field we all thought we were in for a long day's fielding. W. G. and C. I. Thornton came in first; H. W. Forster and I began the bowling. I thought it possible that Thornton's hitting might have an effect on Grace, and it did. In the first over Thornton hit me out of the ground, and not to be denied, W. G. did the same, the very first ball I sent down, but it was too merry to last, and they were both caught in the long field before 30 was up on the telegraph board.

Why has the name of W. G. Grace sunk so deeply into the hearts of all branches of the community? Firstly, because of the national love for the glorious game, and secondly, because of his wonderful skill and the unusual number of years he has maintained the position and name of "champion". It is as a batsman that he has earned this proud title, and it may be of interest to linger for a few moments on the characteristics of his style and play which in their combination have met with such phenomenal success. First of all, W. G. Grace obeys the fundamental rule of batting that is always instilled into young players as the first element of good batting; he keeps his right foot rigid and firm as a rock, and never does he move it during the actual stroke. (Alas! I never could grasp this rule myself or act up to it!) It is an exception, even to slow bowling, for W. G. to move his right foot. Once I remember (I wonder whether he does?) him breaking this rule. During the compilation of one of his hundred centuries, in a match against the Australians at Lord's, he rushed out to hit the slow leg break bowler (Cooper), missed, and after a somewhat undignified skurry back, just got the benefit from the umpire, a man subsequently not loved by the Australians.

The position W. G. takes up at the wicket is one eminently calculated to assist him in the marvellous accuracy of his placing on the leg side. The right foot points slightly in front of the crease, thus enabling him to face the leg and body balls and have the greater command over them. If it had been Grace's practice to stand with his right foot pointing backwards or in the direction of his own wicket (as many good batsmen have done and do) we would never have seen the accurate placing on the leg side which, in my opinion, has done more than any other of his great batting qualities to place him in the position he has so long held. Let anyone try for himself, and he will at once see the commanding power that Grace's position on the left side gives, and how cramped and "hunched" up he feels in the other. Grace's defence, of course, is excellent, and his position at the wickets in this relation is worthy of note. He stands with the right leg as near as possible on the line to the leg stump, without of course, being in front. And every time he plays forward, the left leg and the bat go together, so that should the ball not meet the bat there will be no space between the bat the leg for it to pass through. How often, whilst enjoying that great cricketing luxury of seeing W. G. in his happiest batting vein, one has occasionally shuddered at the sight of that massive leg coming out straight in front to an offstump ball.

This art of playing with the left leg close to the bat is one that must be thoroughly mastered before any man can become a really first class batsman, and W. G. Grace is a master of it. Though using his left leg in this way when playing forward, he is not one of those products of modern days, viz., a batsman who uses his leg on the off side instead of his bat. We should be sorry to think of our great batsman as one of these feeble, faint-hearted players, who, frightened of losing their wickets, dare not use their bats, and who, too timid to try to score, have done so much in many districts to disgust spectators, not with cricket, but with their own wearisome antics. What sort of bowling is W. G. Grace best at? I do not think that any cricketer of experience would hesitate in answering the question. Great, of course, to all styles when at his best, his power of playing fast bowling was the greatest feature of his game. The leg strokes already mentioned, his great height, the quickness of his hand and eye, all combined, gave him at times complete mastery over fast bowling. Bumping balls on the off stump, to a batsman of ordinary height perhaps the most difficult to dispose of, he punishes by hard cuts to the boundary.

What sort of bowling does W. G. Grace like least? I have never asked him this somewhat searching question, nor if I did is it likely that the champion would care to give himself away. His answer, probably, accompanied by a hearty laugh, would be somewhat in this fashion: "Like least, indeed? Why, I love them all." Of course he does; but I have an opinion that on a hard, fast, and true wicket, the slower the bowling the less it is to his liking. His great size prevents him getting quickly to the pitch, and a very slow bowler always has terrors to a fast-footed player that do not present themselves to a quick-footed and active batsman. Whilst discussing W. G. as a batsman, we must not lose sight of another of his great qualities, viz., patience. Never flurried because runs are not coming quite quick enough, never excited because they are coming quicker than usual, he keeps on simply playing the correct game, and even after the hundred goes on the same as before, with his mind fixed upon the two hundred.

It would be impossible, in a short article such as this is, for me to do anything like adequate justice to the merits of the great William Gilbert Grace. There have been some who for a short period have given reason for the belief that his position as champion batsman was being dangerously assailed. I allude to such names as W. L. Murdoch, A. Shrewsbury and A. E. Stoddart. That belief was, however, but fleeting. W. G. Grace has proved his batting powers to be immensely superior to every other cricketer. He is, though nigh on fifty, still the best, and I sincerely hope he will continue for many years to give us all the pleasure of enjoying his magnificent play.

MR W. G. GRACE'S SCORES OF A HUNDRED AND UPWARDS IN FIRST CLASS MATCHES

1866

For England v Surrey 224*
For Gentlemen of South v Players of South 173*

1868

For Gentlemen v Players 134*
For South v North of the Thames .. 130
For South v North of the Thames .. 102*

1869

For Gentlemen v Players of the South 180
For MCC v Surrey 138*
For MCC v Kent 127
For South v North 122
For MCC v Nottinghamshire 121
For MCC v Oxford University 117

1870

For Gentlemen v Players 215
For Gloucestershire v MCC 172
For Gloucestershire v Surrey 143
For MCC v Nottinghamshire 117*
For Gentlemen v Players 109

1871

For South v North 268
For Gentlemen v Players 217
For Single v Married of England ... 189*
For MCC v Surrey 181
For South v North 178
For Gentlemen of England v Cambridge University 162
For MCC v Surrey 146
For Gentlemen of South v Gentlemen of North 118
For MCC v Kent 117
For Gloucestershire v Nottinghamshire 118

1872

For England v Nottinghamshire and Yorkshire 170*
For Gloucestershire v Yorkshire ... 150
For Gentlemen v Players 117
For South v North 114
For Gentlemen v Players 112
For MCC v Yorkshire 101

1873

For South v North 192*
For Gentlemen v Players 163
For Gloucestershire v Surrey 160*
For Gentlemen v Players 158
For Eleven v Fifteen of MCC 152
For Gentlemen of South v Gentlemen of North 145
For Gentlemen v Players of the South 134

1874

For Gloucestershire v Sussex 179
For Gloucestershire v Yorkshire ... 167
For Gentlemen of South v Players of South 150
For Gloucestershire v Yorkshire ... 127
For MCC v Kent 123
For Gloucestershire and Kent v England 121
For Gentlemen v Players 110
For Gentlemen of South v Players of South 104

1875

For Gentlemen v Players 152
For Gloucestershire v Nottinghamshire 119
For Gloucestershire v Yorkshire ... 111

1876

For MCC v Kent 344
For Gloucestershire v Yorkshire ... 318*
For Gloucestershire v Nottinghamshire 177
For Gentlemen v Players 169
For United South v United North .. 126
For South v North 114*
For Gloucestershire v Sussex 104

1877

For South v North 261
For Gloucestershire and Yorkshire v England 110

1878

For Gloucestershire v Nottinghamshire 116

1879

For Gloucestershire v Surrey 123
For Gloucestershire v Nottinghamshire 102
For Gloucestershire v Somerset 113

1880

For England v Australia 152
For Gloucestershire v Lancashire .. 106

1881

For Gloucestershire v Nottinghamshire 182
For Gentlemen v Players 100

1883

For Gloucesteshire v Lancashire ... 112

1884

For Gloucestershire v Australians .. 116*
For Gentlemen of England v Austrians 107
For MCC v Australians 101

1885

For Gloucestershire v Middlesex ... 221*
For Gentlemen v Players 174
For Gloucestershire v Yorkshire ... 132
For Gloucestershire v Surrey 104

* *Signifies not out.*

JOHN WISDEN

BORN AT BRIGHTON, SEPTEMBER 5, 1826,
DIED APRIL 5, 1884

A splendid all-round cricketer in his day; a good bat, a fine field, and as a bowler unsurpassed. A quiet, unassuming, and thoroughly upright man.

A fast friend and a generous employer. Beloved by his intimates and employees, and respected by all with whom he came in contact.

As a given man in the "North" v "South" match of 1850, John Wisden performed the unrivalled feat in a first-class contest of clean bowling the whole of his opponents in their second innings. As an instructor of our national game he was most successful, and during the time he was cricket tutor at Harrow the School were never beaten by Eton.

In 1852, in conjunction with James Dean, he formed the United All England Eleven, and in 1859, with George Parr, took a team of cricketers to Canada and the United States, and thus inaugurated a movement which has had a most important bearing on the prosperity of the game.

In 1855, in partnership with Frederick Lillywhite, he established the cricket outfitting business which for so many years was conducted by him personally, and which is now carried on by those who managed it for many years and enjoyed his fullest confidence. In 1857 he was appointed Secretary to the Cricketers' Fund Friendly Society, and continued to act in that capacity until his death.

In 1864 he issued the first number of the "Cricketers' Almanack", a very primitive production consisting of scores only, but which, thanks to the enthusiasm of subsequent editors, has now been accorded the title of "the most accurate and authentic record of the game" published.

John Wisden was one of the smallest of men who have become famous as cricketers, his height being but 5 ft. 4½ ins, and his weight in his prime being only seven stone. Owing to his diminutive size, and prowess as a cricketer, he earned the soubriquet of "the little wonder".

INDEX

Abel, R., 518, 532, 536, 540, 545, 546, 707-8, 866-7, 935-6.
  carries bat, 402, 842.
  not-out treble century, 542.
  remarkable bowling analysis, 637-8.
Absolom, C. A., scholastic limitations of, 789.
Absolon, C., all twenty wickets in a match, 911-12.
Adelaide, pitch mysteriously tampered with, 837.
Altham, H. S., 654.
The American Cricketer, (periodical), 783.
Andrew, W., 278-9.
Attewell, W., 154-5, 156, 170, 303-4, 440-1, 442.
  curious analysis of, 110.
  deliberately bowls wide, 312.
  bowls 62 maidens in innings, 437.
Australians
  donate match fees to charity, 658.
  bow acknowledgements from Lord's pavilion, 667.
  ill-feeling regarding English tourists, 710.
  record high score, 738-9.
  play at Wembley Park, 741.
  record low score, 742.
  play dazzling cricket, 766.
  accused of sinking everything for money, 829.

Bagguley, R., 446.
Bainbridge, H. W., 278.
Baker, A., 28.
Baker, G. R., 309, 582.
Baker, W. de Chair, receives testimonial, 297.
Baldwin, H., 274.
  benefit match, 279-80.
  fifteen wickets in match, 585-6.
Bannerman, A. C., 738-9.
Bannerman, Charles, 664-5.
  plays on without dislodging bail, 658-9.
Barlow, R. G., 117, 688.
  curious run-out of, 114.
  ingeniously contrives not to score, 323.
Barnes, W., 495-6, 575.
  record stand by, 108-9.
Barratt, E., ten wickets in an innings, 666-7.
Barton, Bombardier, 154.
Baseball, 60-65.
Bates, W., 431, 623, 794, 826-8.
  does hat-trick, 827.
Bats v Broomsticks, 217.
Bean, G., 569, 574-5, 578-9.
  deliberately prolongs innings by bowling no-balls, 512.
Beaumont, J., 503-4.
Bell's Life in London, (periodical), 44, 59, 63, 72, 79, 82, 208, 387, 550, 613, 658, 882, 901, 906, 914.
Bengough, C. W., bowls successively from each end, 140.
Bignall, 288.
Blackman, W., 502-3.
Bland, C., fourteen wickets in match, 802-3.
Bligh, Hon. Ivo., damages himself in tug-o'-war, 825.
Bonnor, G., 123-5, 789.
  smashes Lord's window, 128.
  wins bet with ship's passenger, 653.
  hits ball over Oval pavilion, 685.
  fails to reach Cheltenham, 709.
Bowden, M. P., 269-70, 516.
Bowen, R., 181.
Bowley, T., deliberately tries to get stumped and fails, 512.
Box, T., dies at scoreboard, 388, 899.
Bradford, Capt. E. R., no-balled for throwing by both umpires, 770.
Brain, J. H., 220-1.
  three stumpings in hat-trick, 241-2.
Brann, G., 162-3, 543, 554-5, 568-9, 583, 803.
  century in each innings, 571-2.
Briggs, J., 134-5, 318-19, 337-8, 339, 344, 345-6, 347, 349-50, 352-3, 355-6, 531, 721-2.
  on follow-on law, 170.
  fifteen wickets in match, 731, 867.
  twenty-seven wickets in match, 832.
  amazing analysis of, 867.
Briscoe, 131-2.
Brockwell, W., 232-3, 260, 529, 536, 540, 541.

Brown, J. T., 414, 804, 845.
record opening partnership, 192, 644.
uses foolish backhand, 450.
triple century, 645.
Burghes, A., 386-7.
Bruce, W., 738-9.
Brune, C. J., 18.
Buckland, F. M., 92.
Bull, F. G., 196-7.
Burnup, C. J., 259, 321.
Burton, G., 701-3.
all ten wickets in an innings, 514-15.
sixteen wickets in a match, 628-29.
Bush, R. E., 78-79.
in run-out incident, 209-10.

Calamity on River Thames, charity match in aid of, 668-670.
Cambridge University
record fourth innings of, 98.
record score, 563-4.
pitch measures wrong length, 795.
memories of, 797-801.
Bollinger, consumption of, 801.
Canada v United States, 947-8.
Canadians, miserable display of, 107.
Canterbury Week, 44.
bunting at, 55.
theatricals at, 65.
balls at, 78, 108, 113.
fair maids at, 80.
music's sweet sounds at, 95.
praises for, 99.
best week of all, 111-13.
smoking concert at, 113.
performances by old stagers at, 299, 314.
Cardus, Sir Neville, 5.
Carpenter, R., 196-7, 608.
on follow-on law, 168.
curious appeal against, 276.
Carrick, J. S., hits quadruple century, 909.
Challen, J. B., 462.
Charlwood, H., 474.
Chatterton, W., 191, 371.
Clarke, William, 2.
Clayton, R., benefit match of, 939-41.
Clifton College, 78-9.
Cobden, F., 26, 27.
Collins, A. E. J., hits highest individual score, 910.
Cooper, B. B., 474.
Cotterill, J. M., carries bat twice in match, 913.
County Championship, confusion as to winner, 328-9.
County Champion Cup, 50, 51.
County Cricket Council, 587-91.
Courcy, Arthur, chews umbrella handle, 655.
Cranston, J., 232-3, 634-5.
Crawford, V. F. S., 542.
Cricket on ice, 927-33.
Cricketers' Fund Friendly Society, 123-4, 894-5, 896-900, 915.
Croome, A. C. M., life in danger, 183, 342.
Crossland, J., 329, 333-6, 683.
disapproval of bowling action, 119-20.
breaches residential qualification, 336.
abused by Oval crowd, 497-8.

Daft, Richard, 19, 24, 205, 424.
on follow-on, 167.
Darling, J., 745, 774, 848, 859, 865.
prevented by crowd from making a catch, 743.
one of the best captains, 760.
Davidson, G., 191, 197-8, 371.
Davies, F. C., carried shoulder-high, 48-49.
Day, S. H., 253.
Dean, James, 2.
Dench, C. E., does hat-trick, 258.
Denton, D., 597.
Dickens, Charles, 653.
Diver, E. J., 597-8
Dixon, J. A., 445.
Donnan, H., 846.
causes unpleasantness, 850.
Druce, N. F., 98, 850.
Dudney, W. H., refuses to stump opponent, 512.

Eleven bowlers in innings, 279, 685.
Ellison, M. J., lapse of memory, 590-1.
Emmett, Thomas, 7.
sixteen wickets in a match, 607.
benefit match, 614-16.
takes fourteen wickets during a riot, 820.
England
selectorial blunders of, 767.
S. African tourists defeated by hospitality, 866.
Essex
side greatly incensed, 199.
over-watering pitch, 201.
cricket in mud, 718.

Eton v Harrow, 77-78.
carriages at, 43.
unseemly conduct at, 44.
allocations of seats at, 58-60.
Extras, 120 conceded in one match, 789, 793-4.

Fane, F. L., 202-3, 384-5.
Ferris, J. J., 573-4, 722-3.
amazing analysis of, 157.
takes cottage in Gloucestershire, 800.
fourteen wickets in match, 852.
The Field, 664, 786.
Fishwick, T. S., 600.
FitzGerald, R. A., 43, 44, 58, 61, 76.
writes letter to *Bell's Life*, 59-60.
Flint, J., 184-5, 186-7.
Flowers, Wilfred, 733.
great all-round play of, 120-1.
benefit match, 417-18, 447-8.
Foley, C. P., 563-4.
carries bat, 161-2.
Follow-on (1893), 167-71.
Ford, F. G. J., 234-5, 420, 563-4, 845, 946.
Foster, H. K., 182.
Foster, R. E., 182.
century in each innings, 602.
Foster, W. L., century in each innings, 602.
Fowler, G., 244.
Fox, C. J. M., prefers eating to batting, 569-70.
Francis, C. K., all ten wickets in innings and seventeen in match, 813.
Fry, C. B., 178, 464-5, 470, 577, 585, 769.
first century for Sussex, 243.
carries bat, 417.
no-balled for throwing, 417.
century in each innings, 584.
breaks world long-jump record, 789.

Geeson, F., saves game, 745.
General Election, distractions of, 137.
Gentlemen, qualification to play for, 882.
Giffen, G., 844, 856.
sixteen wickets in match, 699, 700-1.
his bereavement, 709.
brilliant all-round performance, 732-3.
fourteen wickets in match, 745-6.
a batting materpiece, 838.
amazing analysis of, 846.
great all-round performance of, 853-4.
double century and sixteen wickets in match, 855-6.
Gloucestershire
mutinous spirit of, 240.
Bristol crowd damage pitch, 243.
Government v Opposition, 171-2.
Grace, Dr. E. M., 3, 6, 14, 32, 33, 204-5, 472, 904-5, 914, 916, 956-8.
on follow-on law, 167.
as suicidal fielder, 184, 207.
scores century with broomstick, 217.
persuades spectators to reverse umpire's decision, 324.
single-wicket match, 817.
challenges six Australians, 818.
Grace, G. F., 33, 204-5, 206-7, 209-10, 880-1, 904-5.
Grace, H., 33.
Grace, Dr. W. G., 1, 6, 14, 15, 16, 18, 20, 25, 32, 33, 40, 41, 42, 55, 147-8, 173, 181, 199, 206-7, 217-18, 222-3, 234-5, 236-7, 244-5, 250, 305, 393, 425-6, 474, 481-2, 550, 559, 674, 876, 904-5, 912, 914, 926-7, 935-6.
all ten wickets in an innings, 56.
treble centuries, 82, 212-3, 251.
fourteen wickets in match, 86-87, 779-80.
addresses Lord's crowd, 97.
generous offer of, 102.
presentation to of marble clock, 105-6.
sixteen wickets in match, 126-7.
carries bat, 143, 472, 578, 925.
has no opinion, 171.
given police protection, 183, 243.
saves life of team-mate, 183.
intimidates batsman, 208.
testimonial fund, 215-16.
two centuries in match, 226-7, 229-30, 919.
resigns Gloucestershire captaincy, 240.
withdraws resignation, 240.
on field for every ball of match, 315.
match abandoned on mother's death, 333.
offers to change pitch, 368.
last game for Gloucestershire, 419.
Trent Bridge début, 424.
scores eight off one hit, 481.
describes Lohmann's bowling, 604.
century and fifteen wickets in match, 608-10.
kidnaps Midwinter from Lord's, 661.
accused of sharp practice, 678.
carried round ground, 712.
commits error of judgment, 731.
bats at number ten, 733.

Grace, Dr. W. G. – *contd*
involved in financial squabble, 751, 753-4.
a century and twelve wickets, 776.
century and all ten wickets, 807.
insults an umpire, 842.
bails as if glued to stumps of, 877.
personal recollections of, 959, 965.
Grace, W. G. Junior, county début, 239.
Greatorex, T., curious bowling analysis of, 793-4.
Greenwood, L., benefit match, 611-12.
Gregory, S. E., 744, 766, 773, 844, 850.
Grimshaw, I., 623, 794.
Gunn, W., 154-5, 162-3, 410-11, 433, 447, 537, 575, 725.
record partnership, 438.

Hadow, W. H., 35, 36.
Haigh, S., 280.
hat-trick, 647.
Hall, L., 229-30, 796.
carries bat twice in match, 291-2, 294-6.
carries bat, 401.
Halliwell, E. A., 776.
Hampshire, all eleven players bowl, 536.
Harris, Lord, 5, 80-1, 152.
poetic effusions of, 95.
poetic effusions about, 108.
candelabra presented to, 112.
puts politics before cricket, 135.
praises the press, 147.
on residential qualification, 182.
pays tribute to F. Hearne, 304.
cancels a fixture, 333.
offers to extend time limit, 551-2.
indignant epistolary gestures of, 820-2.
memories of W. G. Grace, 959-61.
Hattersley-Smith, Rev. P., 132-3.
Hawke, Lord, 594.
Hayman, H. B., 414.
Hayward, T., 184, 543, 608, 772-3.
returns freakish analysis, 380-1.
not-out treble century, 538.
is fortunate, 544-5.
Hearne, A., 451, 621-2.
carries bat, 311, 315.
Hearne, F., 293, 295-6, 776.
tribute from Lord Harris, 304.
Hearne, G. G., 291-2, 293.
benefit match, 305-307.
Hearne, J. T., 179, 372-3, 403-4, 405-6, 418, 445-6, 742-3, 751-2.
returns amazing analysis, 755-6.
fifteen wickets in match, 810-11.
Hearne, W., 314, 357-8.
Hedley, Capt. W. C., 281, 283, 397-8, 461.
Hewett, H. T.
record opening partnership, 459-61.
leaves field as gesture of disgust, 641.
Hide, Arthur, 554-5.
Hide, J., 156, 552, 556, 559-60.
all ten wickets in match, 113.
emigrates to Australia, 826.
Highbury Park School, dismiss opponents for nothing, 815.
Hill, A. J. L., 278-9, 600.
Hill, C., 749, 766, 768, 849, 859, 863, 865.
celebrates eighteenth birthday, 845.
Hirst, G. H., 544-5, 648.
Hornby, A. N., 134, 324-5.
takes a prisoner, 821.
Horner, C. E., 267.
Howell, W., all ten wickets in a match, 763-4.
Howitt, R. H., 447.
Huish, F. H., breaks collarbone, 367.
Hulme, J., 188-9.
Humphreys, W.
fifteen wickets in a match, 462.
carried off shoulder-high, 573.
Hunter, J., nine catches in match, 223.
Huntsmen v Jockeys, 106.

Iredale, F. A., 747-8, 774, 859.
Islington High School, dismissed without scoring, 815.
I Zingari, 79-80.

Jackson, Hon. F. S., 165-8, 581, 594, 650, 772-3, 804.
curious run-out of, 359.
great bowling of, 890-1.
Jephson, D. L. A., 546.
Jessop, G. L., 6.
treats Richardson casually, 184.
advances reputation, 252.
amazing brilliancy of, 452.
most wonderful display of hitting, 645-6.
syntactical shortcomings of, 789.
astonishing display of, 803.
wonderful display of, 948.
Jones, A. O., 258, 453, 767-9.
Jones, S. P.
questionably run out by W. G. Grace, 678.

Jones, S. P. – *contd*
presented with gold watch & chain, 701.
Jupp, 476-7.

Kelly, J. J., 865.
Kemp, M. C., plays extraordinary innings, 796-7.
Kent
use eleven bowlers in match, 259, 552.
use only eight men in a match, 631-2.
Key, K. J., 136-9, 395-6, 510, 522-3, 808.
Killick, E. H., 470, 769.
King, J. B., wonderful bowling at Brighton, 786-7.
Knight, A. E., 384.
Kortright, C. J., 199-200.

Lacey, F. E., 265, 268.
treble century, 272-3.
Lancashire, highest score, 463.
Largest innings, 79-80, 113-14, 129-31, 463.
Laver, F., 856, 865.
Lee, F., 294-6.
Leicestershire, defeat Australians, 713.
Le Fleming, J., 571-2.
Leveson-Gower, H., his most uncomfortable quarter-hour, 579.
Lilley, A. A., out for hitting ball twice, 184, 596.
Lillywhite, F., 2, 7.
Lillywhite, James, 169, 925.
all ten wickets in an innings, 47-8.
farewell match, 873-6.
Llewellyn, G. C. B., brilliant all-round cricket of, 770-1.
Lockwood, E., 475, 615-16, 617, 927.
Lockwood, W. H., 201-2, 260-1, 522-3, 546.
four wickets in four balls, 528.
Lohmann, G. A., 269-70, 348-9, 499, 513, 516-7, 562, 843.
on follow-on law, 153.
his bowling an intellectual delight, 604.
fourteen wickets in match, 637-8.
twenty-six wickets in match, 867-8.
fifteen wickets in match, 868-9.
amazing analysis of, 869.
all-round cricket of, 937-8.
Lord's
baseball at, 60-5.
crowds at, 65-6.
cads at, 68.
ball hit into printing shop, 87.
police clear field, 91.
state of ground, 97.
semi-darkness at, 110.
tennis court window broken, 128.
tennis court roof hit, 131.
French ambassador at, 146.
Chancellor of the Exchequer at, 146.
hostile demonstration in pavilion of, 175.
light provided in tennis court to find ball, 389.
start delayed by Queen's Jubilee, 394.
Lowry, W. C., fifteen wickets in match, 782-3.
Lucas, A. P., on follow-on law, 168.
Lucas, F. M., 554-5.
Lyons, J. J., 734-5, 841, 855, 861.
Lyttelton, Hon. A., 218-19.
success of lob bowling, 686.
Lyttelton, Hon. E., 662-4.
on follow-on law, 169-70.
Lyttelton, Hon. R. H.
on follow-on law, 170-1.
essay: "The Development of Cricket", 603-6.

McDonnell, P. S., 686-7.
suffers sunstroke, 671.
McGregor, G., 563-4.
county début, 353.
Mackenzie, A. C. K., 850.
Mackinnon, F. A., 266.
MacLaren, A. C., 318-19, 570-1, 848, 850.
scores quadruple century, 182, 463.
refuses to change pitch, 368.
not out though treading on wicket, 370.
century on county début, 565.
sets very dangerous precedent, 582.
exception taken to selection of, 746.
carries bat, 768.
century in each innings, 846-7.
McGahey, C., 374, 384-5.
McIntyre, M., 487-8.
McKibbin.
spectacular analysis of, 755.
victim of Spofforth's accusation, 757.
fourteen wickets in match, 857-8.
fifteen wickets in match, 860.
McLeod, R. W., 856.
Marlow, F. W., 577, 578-9.
Marchant, F., 733-4.
Marlborough College, 65, 92-95, 140-1.
Married v Single, 924-6, 939-41.

Marriott, H. H., 98.
Marten, W., 39, 40.
Martin, F., 303-4.
MCC
 dinner at, 63.
 play v America, 63-4.
 professionals fail to appear, 65.
 annual meeting of, 96-7.
 centenary match, 144-5.
 centenary banquet at, 146-7.
 the 1889 reforms of, 150-3.
Mason, J. R., 451.
Massie, H. H., 672-3.
Mead, W., 195-6, 200-1.
 seventeen wickets in a match, 274, 740.
Mee, P. J., is foolishly run out, 410-11.
Middlesex
 unlikely survival of, 386.
 tie with Somerset, 455-6.
Midwinter, W., 7.
 record stand of, 108-9.
 kidnapped by W. G. Grace, 661.
"The Mitcham Figaro", *see* Southerton
Mitchell, F., 869.
 controversial captaincy of, 176.
Mitchell, R. A. H., on follow-on law, 153, 166.
Moberley, W. O., 212-13.
Mold, A., 237-8, 309-10, 354, 570-1, 633.
 hat-trick, 361.
 16 wickets in match, 367-8.
 15 wickets in match, 447-8, 456-7.
 15 wickets in innings, 576.
Money, W. B., 482.
Moon, L. J., 766.
Mordaunt, G. J., 577.
Morley, F., 187-8, 290, 429-30.
 amazing analysis of, 85-6.
 fatal injury of, 653, 825.
Murdoch, W. W., 687, 730, 803.
 given police protection, 243.
 carries bat, 674.
 omitted from touring side, 732.
 shows hostility to English visitors, 829.
Moses, H., 839, 854.
Mycroft, W., 84-5, 86-8, 126-8, 184-5, 186-7.
 amazing analysis of, 102-3.

Newham, W., 344, 551-2.
 carries bat, 361.
New South Wales
 a riot at Sydney, 818-23.
 its association sends a letter, 822-3.
 Sydney trustees, bad behaviour of, 847.
Nichols, R. W., last wicket partnership, 421.
Nine runs off one ball, 72.
Noble, M., 863, 865.
 the most remarkable defence ever seen, 759.
North v South, 45-8, 65-8, 97-8, 99-102.
Nottinghamshire
 lowest score, 117-18, 157.
 highest score, 574-5.

O'Brien, T. C., 293-4, 331, 398-401.
 kicks off bails, 412-13.
 masquerades as J. E. Johnston, 527.
O'Halloran, J., 861.
One Leg v One Arm, 918.
Oscroft, W., disputed dismissal of, 613.
Ottaway, C. J., 21.
Oval
 disgraceful scenes at, 497.
 a late finish at, 519.
 record score, 542.
 Prince of Wales visits, 692.
 opening of press box, 711.
Oxford v Cambridge
 in 1875: 72-6.
 Jubilee dinner of, 88.
 in 1877: 88-92.
 in 1886: 135-9.
 in 1891: 158-60.
 in 1893: deliberate bowling of wides, 165-6.
 in 1896: deliberate bowling of no-balls, 175-7.
Oxford, smallest total, 85-6.
Over 30 v Under 30, 103-5.

Painter, E. J., 220-1.
Paish, A., 260-1.
Palairet, L. C., 238, 275.
 record opening partnership, 459-61.
 keeps wicket, 460.
 goes on honeymoon, 889.
Pallett, H. J., benefit match, 595.
Palmer, G. E., 690-1.
Pardon, Charles F., 3.
Pardon, Sydney, 3, 4.
Parnham, J., fifteen wickets in a match, 675-6.
Parr, George, 1, 2.
Parris, F., 243.
Parsees, poor performance of, 135.
Patterson, G. S., writes letter to *The Field*, 786.
Patterson, W. H., 298, 299-300, 357.
 surprisingly run out, 510.

Patterson, W. S., wrongly given out, reprieved by spectators, 325.
Paul, A., 367.
Pauncefote, 479-80.
Peate, E., 124-5, 324, 617.
does hat-trick, 618.
remarkable analysis, 621, 696.
Peel, R., 359, 399-401, 581, 594, 719-20, 751-2, 844.
on duration of over, 153.
has to go away, 229.
remarkable analysis, 628.
fifteen wickets in a match, 640-1.
does hat-trick, 937.
Perrin, P., 385.
Philadelphians, over-estimate themselves, 785.
Philipson, H., 397-8.
Phillips, F. A., 470.
Pickett, H., takes all ten wickets, 194.
Pooley, E., 923.
Poore, R. M., 7, 191, 284-5, 286, 602.
two centuries in match, 283.
essay in appreciation of, 286-7.
triple century, 469.
Pougher, A. D., 194-5, 375-6, 377, 378, 381.
hat-trick, 147.
returns amazing analysis, 742-3.
Powell, E. O., 268.
Press, view obscured by umbrellas, 656.
Prince's Ground, 656.
spectators like a quaker meeting, 659.
first match at, 893.
Professionals.
dispute match fee, 665, 750-1, 752-3.

Quaife, W. G., 278, 381, 599, 600.
Quinton, F. W. D., 191.

Richardson, T., 319-20, 377, 380-1, 383-4, 442-3, 465-6, 745.
is treated casually by Jessop, 184, 535.
indisposed through rheumatism, 466.
ten wickets in an innings, 529.
fifteen wickets in a match, 531-2, 532-3, 540, 643-4.
hat-trick, 532, 540.
benefit match, 545-6.
his finest hour, 748-9.
takes thousandth wicket in four seasons, 891.
Ranjitsinhji, K. S., 5, 420, 543, 577, 578-9, 579-80, 778, 847.
brilliant Sussex début, 173.
two centuries in one day, 580-1.
a marvellous test innings, 746-8.
marvellous batting of, 847-8.
Rashleigh, Rev. W., 136-9, 226-7, 317.
Rawlin, J. T., 157, 240-1.
Read, Maurice, 518, 531-2, 707-8, 843.
on follow-on law, 170.
Read, W. W., 220, 340-1, 500, 502, 505, 506-7, 508, 510, 516, 553, 837.
treble century, 513.
century in each innings, 784.
does hat-trick, 938.
Record opening partnership, 192, 536.
Rhodes, W., 200-1.
a wonderful week, 649.
extraordinary success of, 775.
Ridley, A. W., carried shoulder-high, 75-6.
Right-handed v Left-handed of England, 919.
Roberts, F. G., 317-18.
Roberts, J., 227-8.
Roche, W., last wicket partnership, 421.
Roe, W. N., hits quadruple century, 906-7.
Roller, W. E., 340-1, 553.
double century and hat-trick, 506-7.
Rotherham, H., fourteen wickets in match, 806.
Routledge, T., 778.
Rowbotham, 475.
Royal Engineers, 79-80.
Royal Surrey Militia, dismissed by opponents for nought, 916.
Rugby v Marlborough, 140-1.
Russell, T. M., stung by mosquito, 202.
Rylott, A., 117-19, 134-5, 375-6.

Sainsbury, E., run out but continues batting, 780.
Scarborough Festival, 115-17.
Scott, H. J. H., 687.
slaughters Yorkshire bowling, 706.
Scott, S. W., 397-8, 407.
Scott, W., 784.
Sewell, C. O. H., 254.
Sexuagenerians, contest between, 916-17.
Shacklock, F., takes four wickets in four balls, 444.
Sharpe, J. W., 521, 527.
amazing analysis of, 808-9.
Shaw, Alfred, 28, 38, 39, 52, 68-71, 549.
all ten wickets in innings, 57.
his match, 98-101.
fourteen wickets in match, 102.
generous offer from W. G. Grace, 102.
joins Sussex, 360.
seventeen wickets in match, 428-9.

Shaw, Alfred – *contd*
amazing analysis of, 824-5.
shows the flag at Suez, 828.
great performances of, 934-5.
Shaw, J. C., 19, 25, 288, 425-7.
benefit match, 430-2.
Shillinglee, dismiss opponents for nought, 916.
Shrewsbury, A., 7, 144-5, 221-2, 258, 408-9, 495-6, 575.
early promise of, 69.
declines to captain Notts, 184.
arrives late but not too late, 224-5.
carries his bat, 312, 390-2.
record partnership, 438.
rolls into spectator's lap, 669.
Shuter, J., 220, 266-7, 498-9.
on follow-on law, 170.
deliberately sacrifices wickets, 435.
plays on without dislodging bails, 516.
Sinclair, J. H., 871.
Smith, A., 237-8, 570-1.
Smith, C. Aubrey, 559-60.
runs through MCC, 156.
Smith, E., 941, 944.
Smith, G. O., great innings of, 176-7.
Smokers v Non-Smokers, 123-5.
record score, 835.
Somerset
turn up with nine men, 183.
tie with Middlesex, 455-6.
record opening partnership, 459-61.
use all eleven bowlers, 471.
make regrettable decision, 737.
South Africans, shunned by Brightonians, 777.
South Australian Register, 829-30.
Southerton ("The Mitcham Figaro"), 39, 40, 42, 43, 65-8.
Spofforth, F., 653, 678-9, 684, 685, 689-90, 696.
amazing analysis, 680-1.
hat-trick, 690.
fifteen wickets in match, 695.
dislocates finger, 696.
writes a letter on throwing, 757.
The Sportsman, 80, 209, 615, 658, 666, 914.
Steel, A. G., 151, 327-8, 340-1.
all-round cricket as schoolboy, 92-5.
puts love before cricket, 696-7.
memories of W. G. Grace, 962-4.
Steel, D. Q., 493-4.
Stephenson, H. H., on duration of over, 152.
Stoddart, A. E., 144-5, 293-4, 408-9, 412-13, 414.
carries bat, 350-1.
two centuries in match, 410-11.
Storer, W., 189-90, 191, 371.
Streatfeild, astonishing hitting of, 792-30.
Street, A., 380.
Studd, Charles, 7.
Studd, G. B., carries bat, 327.
Studd, H. W., fourteen wickets in a match, 814.
Sugg, F. H., 250, 361-2, 373, 468.
Summers, 23, 24, 25.
Surrey
toasts army, navy and reserve forces, 489.
tie match with Middlesex, 490-2.
tied matches, 492-3.
record score, 506-7, 515-17.
tie match with Lancashire, 530-1.
extraordinary collapse of, 648.
Sussex
new county ground, 547.
unfortunate position, 560-1.
ground obscured by sea mist, 584.
Sydney Morning Herald, refers to conduct of Australians, 819.

Tate, E., 281-2.
Tate, F. W., 300-2, 566-7.
Taylor, T. L., 766.
Thames Calamity Fund, 670.
Thomas, E. L., 578.
Thoms, R.
on batsman deliberately getting out, 168.
tireless energy of, 911.
Thornton, C. I., 923.
on duration of over, 153.
hitting in 1869, 289-90.
hits ball into racket court at Oval, 478.
Thornton, R. T., 905.
Throwing, a symposium, 362-7.
The Times (newspaper), 812.
Townsend, C. L., 202-3, 245-6, 246-7, 254, 255-6, 257, 258, 259, 261, 415-16, 452.
county début, 239.
does hat-trick, 241-2.
sixteen wickets in match, 448-9.
brilliant schoolboy, 792.
de Trafford, C. E., 378, 944.
Trent Bridge
devastating storm at, 427.

Trent Bridge – *contd*
ill-feeling at, 430.
record score at, 446.
Trevor, A. H., 908.
Trott, A., 178-9, 416-17, 418, 420, 422-3, 869.
remarkable analysis of, 651-2.
Trott, G. H. S., 729-30, 744, 749.
Trumble, H., 738-9.
fourteen wickets in match, 735-6.
returns amazing analysis, 754-5.
deliberately bowls no-balls, 861.
Trumper, V., 864.
a brilliant innings, 768.
scores a not-out treble century, 769.
Troup, W., 254, 257, 261.
Tunnicliffe, J., record opening partnership, 192, 644-5.
Turner, A. J., 599.
Turner, C. T. B., 711, 722-3, 723-4, 731.
proves unplayable, 714-15.
seventeen wickets in match, 720-21.
fourteen wickets in a match, 834.
sixteen wickets in a match, 839.
fifteen wickets in a match, 854.
Twelve-a-side bat, 121.
Tyldesley, J. T., 869, 871.
century in each innings, 595.
establishes test claim, 765.
Tyler, E. J., 239, 249, 468.
fifteen wickets in a match, 457-9, 464-5.
all ten wickets in an innings, 465-6.

Ulyett, 223-4, 294-6, 615-16, 617, 881.
carries bat, 122-3.
reference to hinder parts, 659.
Umpires.
inability to give decision, 136.
appointment of, 592-3.
where to find them, 911.

Vernon, G. F., 908.

Wainwright, E., 5, 321, 544-5, 594, 642-3, 645.
ten wickets in an innings, 636.
hat-trick and five wickets in seven balls, 639.
Walker, I. D., 218-19, 386-7.
on duration of over, 151.
unfortunate behaviour of hat, 433.
Walker, R. D., 492.
Walters, F. H., 854.
Ward, A., 284-5, 355-6, 447, 468, 845, 891.
Warner, P. F., carries bat, 415.
Warwickshire, highest score, 600.
Watson, A., 84-5, 349-50.
amazing analysis of, 135.
Webbe, A. J., 293-4, 297-8.
carries bat, 396-7, 625.
Wells, C. M., 453.
deliberately bowls wides, 164.
comments on, 169.
Welford, J. W., 381.
Wickets, size of, 38.
Wilkes' *Spirit of the Times* (periodical), 920.
Willsher, E., benefit match, 924-6.
Wilson, C., 291-2.
Wilson, G. L., 573-4, 577.
Wisden, John, 1, 2, 3, 4, 7, 8-9.
death of, 966.
Wodehouse, P. G., bowls out Tonbridge, 792, 816.
Woodcock, A., 179-80, 194-5, 379, 381-2.
Woods, S. M. J., 470, 525-6, 583.
for Cambridge, 159-61, 239, 248-9.
bowls lobs, 729.
ten wickets in innings and fifteen in match, 801-2.
outstanding bowling of, 942-3.
Woof, W. A., 117-19, 227-8, 236-7.
Wootton, 48-9, 133-4, 511, 556-7.
amazing analysis of, 54-5.
Worrall, J., 769.
Wrathall, H., 646.
Wright, C. W.
wicket-keeping affected by steeple-chasing, 142.
an in-patient at St. Thomas's hospital, 524.
Wright, L. G., 191.
Wynyard, Capt. E. G., 276, 469.

Yardley, W., 25, 26, 27, 77.
Yorkshire
record score, 594.
team walks off field in protest, 613.
Young, H.
fifteen wickets in match, 599.
proves unplayable, 763.